# The Routledge Anthology of Renaissance Drama

Ten non-Shakespearean Renaissance plays and a masque have been brought together for the first time in what is a major text for students of English drama of the late sixteenth and early seventeenth centuries.

The Renaissance saw a dramatic explosion of such force that, four hundred years later, its plays are still amongst the most frequently performed and studied we have. This anthology offers a full introduction to Renaissance theatre in its historical and political context, along with newly edited and comprehensively annotated texts of the following plays:

*The Spanish Tragedy* (Thomas Kyd)
*Arden of Faversham* (Anon.)
*Edward II* (Christopher Marlowe)
*A Woman Killed with Kindness* (Thomas Heywood)
*The Tragedy of Mariam* (Elizabeth Cary)
*The Masque of Blackness* (Ben Jonson)
*The Knight of the Burning Pestle* (Francis Beaumont)
*Epicoene, or the Silent Woman* (Ben Jonson)
*The Roaring Girl* (Thomas Middleton and Thomas Dekker)
*The Changeling* (Thomas Middleton and William Rowley)
*'Tis Pity She's a Whore* (John Ford)

Each play is prefaced by an introductory headnote discussing the thematic focus of the play and its textual history, and is cross-referenced to other plays of the period that relate thematically and generically.

**Simon Barker** is Principal Lecturer in English at the University of Gloucestershire. His research and teaching interests lie in the cultural history of the Tudor and early Stuart periods with an emphasis on drama.

**Hilary Hinds** is Lecturer in English at the University of Lancaster. Her research and teaching focus principally on seventeenth-century literature, and in particular on women's writing from the radical sects.

# The Routledge Anthology of Renaissance Drama

*Edited by Simon Barker and Hilary Hinds*

Routledge
Taylor & Francis Group

LONDON AND NEW YORK

First published 2003
by Routledge
11 New Fetter Lane, London EC4P 4EE

Simultaneously published in the USA and Canada
by Routledge
29 West 35th Street, New York, NY 10001

*Routledge is an imprint of the Taylor & Francis Group*

Typeset in Caslon by The Running Head Limited, Cambridge
Printed and bound in Great Britain by St Edmundsbury Press,
Bury St Edmunds, Suffolk

*British Library Cataloguing in Publication Data*
A catalogue record for this book is available from the British Library

*Library of Congress Cataloging in Publication Data*
The Routledge anthology of Renaissance drama / Simon Barker & Hilary Hinds.
   p. cm.
Includes bibliographical references.
Contents: The Spanish tragedy / Thomas Kyd — Arden of Faversham / Anon. — Edward II /
   Christopher Marlowe — A woman killed with kindness / Thomas Heywood — The tragedy of
   Mariam, the fair queen of Jewry / Elizabeth Cary — The masque of blackness /
   Ben Jonson — The knight of the burning pestle / Francis Beaumont — Epicoene, or, The silent woman /
   Ben Jonson — The roaring girl / Thomas Middleton and Thomas Dekker — The changeling /
   Thomas Middleton and William Rowley — 'Tis pity she's a whore / John Ford.
      1. English drama—Early modern and Elizabethan, 1500–1600. 2. English drama—17th century.
   I. Barker, Simon. II. Hinds, Hilary.

PR1263 .R68 2002
822'.308—dc21

                                                                              2002026872

ISBN 0–415–18733–8 (hbk)
ISBN 0–415–18734–6 (pbk)

# Contents

# Acknowledgements

We should like to thank all those who took part in Routledge's survey of academics who teach early modern drama. The selection of plays in this anthology is based on their responses and we are in debt to them for taking the time to engage, often at length and in detail, with our questionnaire.

We are grateful to our publisher's readers, who read drafts of the volume at various stages of its production. Their painstaking, rigorous and supportive comments have helped us to improve the final text enormously. Thanks, too, to Talia Rodgers and Liz Thompson at Routledge for taking the project on and seeing it through with such enthusiasm and good humour, and to Carole Drummond and David Williams at The Running Head for their meticulous production of the volume.

We should also like to thank the staff of the following libraries for their help: the Bodleian Library, the British Library, and the libraries of the Universities of Birmingham, Lancaster and Gloucestershire.

We should like to acknowledge Cambridge University Press' permission to reproduce the map on p. 6 from Peter Thomson, *Shakespeare's Professional Career*, Cambridge University Press, 1992.

Thanks go to the following people for their various and much appreciated contributions to this book: Peter Barker, Richard Dutton, Alison Findlay, Sonia Massai, Monika Smialkowska, Jackie Stacey, Peter Widdowson, and the *Coille Bheag* focus group. Any errors are, of course, our own.

Simon Barker and Hilary Hinds

# Guide to the Anthology

This collection is intended to make accessible a number of important non-Shakespearean Renaissance plays. Priority has been given to those plays not currently available in affordable editions. To this end, widely republished plays by playwrights such as Marlowe and Jonson (such as *Dr Faustus*, *Volpone* and *The Alchemist*) have been excluded in favour of their less readily available work (*Edward II*, *The Masque of Blackness* and *Epicoene*) and in favour of the work of dramatists such as Heywood, Middleton and Beaumont.

Our hope is that this anthology will stimulate readers' interest in this period of intense cultural and social change. To facilitate further reading and research in the drama of this period and in the critical debates that this drama has generated, a broad range of contextualising materials has been included.

The following plan outlines the nature and scope of these materials, and offers an indication of the composition of the anthology as a whole.

## Introductory material

Introduction | The introduction situates the plays and theatres of the late sixteenth and early seventeenth centuries in their social and cultural context, discussing

- pre-Renaissance theatre
- the different kinds of playhouses
- the plays that were performed in them
- contemporary social, economic and political institutions, and the plays' engagement with these.

Further reading | Comprehensive bibliography of titles relating to topics and issues raised in the introduction.

Chronology | Timeline setting the plays in chronological relation to other significant historical and cultural events.

## The plays

Headnotes | Each play is prefaced with its own introductory headnote, discussing the thematic focus of the play and its textual history.

Further reading | Each headnote is followed by a list of other editions of the play and selected criticism relating to it.

Works of related interest | Each play included in this anthology is cross-referenced to other plays of the period that relate generically and/or thematically.

The plays | The text of each play has been fully edited and footnoted, and the spelling has been modernised.

## Website

For a selection of related Renaissance material that complements and extends this collection, visit *The Routledge Anthology of Renaissance Drama* website at www.routledge.com/textbooks/0415187346

# Introduction

## 'The fashion of play-making': theatre, drama and society in early modern England

Between the 1560s and the 1630s, London witnessed the rise (and sometimes demise) of some fifteen theatres. As well as these purpose-built theatres, a number of pre-existing halls and inns were converted for the public staging of plays and these existed alongside other places of recreation such as bull- and bear-baiting arenas, cock-fighting pits and inns in whose courtyards plays were occasionally performed. That London could sustain this number of places of public entertainment might, at first, seem unremarkable: we are used, after all, to thinking of London as a city of some seven million people with many hundreds of such places. The figures begin to take on a different meaning, however, when we recall that in 1600 the population of London was around 200,000 which, by our standards, is very small. Nonetheless, public or 'amphitheatre' theatres such as the Globe held around 3,000 people and, by 1609, were staging plays every day of the week. These figures illustrate the popularity of the theatre at this time and indicate something of the alacrity with which theatrical entrepreneurs set about meeting the increasing demand for stage plays. By around 1604, there was a playhouse of some kind within two miles of nearly every Londoner, and playgoing enjoyed such popularity that traffic jams often blocked the streets around the theatres. Indeed, a petition of 1619 complained about the problems this caused:

> There is daylie such resort of people, and such multitudes of Coaches (whereof many are Hackney Coaches, bringinge people of all sortes) that sometymes all our streetes cannott containe them . . . And the inhabitantes there cannott come to their howses, nor bringe in their necessary provisions of beere, wood, coale or haye, nor the Tradesmen or shopkeepers utter their wares, nor the passenger goe to the common water staires without danger of their lives and lymmes.
>
> (Bentley 1941–68, vol. 1: 4–5)

The exasperation of the writer on behalf of those living and working in the vicinity of the theatres is clear: the crush of theatre-goers was impeding not only people's access to their houses and to the river (one of the main city thoroughfares) but also interfering with people's livelihoods by hindering trade in the neighbourhood. The account is important too, however, for the way it indicates that playgoing was widespread amongst 'people of all sortes', *all* ranks of society – not only the apprentices who paid a penny to stand in the pit at the public theatres or the law students from the Inns of Court, but also those Londoners wealthy enough to own their own coaches.

Such detailed accounts combine with the statistics about theatre-building to demonstrate the extraordinary popularity of playgoing at the end of the sixteenth century and in the early decades of the seventeenth century. There was indeed a 'fashion of play-making', as Thomas Middleton put it in his preface to *The Roaring Girl* (1611). Although various forms of theatrical entertainment, usually involving religious celebration or instruction, had been important features of the cultural landscape in Europe and beyond for centuries, the rapid expansion of London's purpose-built commercial theatres during the Renaissance was an entirely new phenomenon. The question of how we can account for this expansion continues to fascinate students of this period. We cannot hope fully to account for these changes in a short introduction, but we do wish to point to some of the issues which are debated, often fiercely, to do with the social, economic, political and cultural circumstances which combined to precipitate this expansion in theatrical production, and the ways in which these circumstances are manifested in the plays themselves. Perhaps the best way to begin to address these questions is to return to the location of these theatres: London itself. What changes had taken place in the capital city that enabled it to produce and sustain so many new theatres and new plays over a period of some fifty years?

## City, country, commerce and class

By the end of the sixteenth century, London had become a city in rapid transition, experiencing transformations that were for the most part the outcome of unprecedented and accelerating economic change. Although most people continued to live and work in agricultural communities, towns and cities were nonetheless expanding rapidly and becoming increasingly powerful. This expansion was the result of a number of factors: the development of early forms of manufacturing and trade, an increase in the overall population of the country (doubling from 2.5 million in the 1520s to around 5 million in 1600), and the continuing process of the enclosure of land into larger, privately owned, units of production. Philip Stubbes, writing in *The Anatomie of Abuses* (1583), explained that:

> They take in, and inclose commons, moores, heaths, and other common pastures, wher out the poore commonalitie were wont to have all their forage and feeding for their cattell, & (which is more) corne for them selves to lyve uppon . . . For these inclosures be the causes, why rich men, eat up poore men, as beasts do eat grass.
>
> (Stubbes 1973: n.p.)

Historians debate the extent and effect of this process during the reign of Elizabeth I (1558–1603) but most note the considerable unrest such dispossession caused, especially in times of poor harvest and the accompanying migration to the towns. Early industrial activity, often benefiting from the skills of Protestant immigrants from The Netherlands and France, also drew people from the countryside to the towns in search of wages and the perceived benefits of urban life. The population of London itself was most affected and the city grew to be one of the largest in Europe. The 200,000 people who lived in London in 1600 represented a doubling of the city's population since 1580, and it was to double again, to 400,000, by 1650.

One effect of this increase was to create a large audience for the expanding network of theatres. Many of the people who attended these theatres had a memory of the traditions and cycles of activity in the countryside, as well as a new consciousness of the rigours and, indeed, the dangers of urban life. Many Londoners retained a connection with the countryside through the city's agricultural markets, but London was also rapidly becoming the focus for a new kind of commercial activity which had an increasingly international dimension. For more people than ever before, there emerged an awareness of 'the nation' in relation to the rest of Europe, as well as to the expanding world itself, as news circulated of the settlements made in the territories of the 'new worlds' beyond Europe. The period of history during which the plays in this volume were written was one of increasing exploration and the first tentative 'planting' (of people) overseas. England's only real colony (and most successful plantation of Protestantism) was Ireland. However, whatever the practical successes and failures of these activities, the impulse towards the settlement of overseas territories can be glimpsed surprisingly early in the sixteenth century.

Trade links to the east of Europe (and particularly with Turkey through the Levant Company) opened up possibilities of further links as far as India and China. Some of this business involved the establishment of small groups of traders abroad. The lands across the Atlantic to the west, however, gave rise to the possibility of an entirely different form of activity. The idea arose in the 1560s that a 'stabling place' could be set up in North America through which local raw materials could be exchanged for English cloth. Indeed, in 1582 Humphrey Gilbert declared English sovereignty over Newfoundland but the project failed, as did the idea of a 'New Albion' in what is now California and early plantations in Virginia during 1584 and 1587. It was not until the 1620s that more successful settlements were established, yet this earlier expansion, together with associated tensions in international affairs, particularly with Spain, had made an enlarged concept of the world available for a great number of people. However, there were insecurities about the development of a non-agrarian structure of employment and in the new awareness of the world which it had helped to deliver, and these tensions are revealed in the dramatic writing of the period.

Whilst many of these plays, such as *A Woman Killed with Kindness* (1603), are located in the claustrophobic settings of English (or foreign) country estates, an increasing number, such as *The Knight of the Burning Pestle* (1607), *Epicoene, or The Silent Woman* (1609) and *The Roaring Girl*, established the importance of towns and cities as places recognisable as images of the structure and pattern of everyday life for the theatre audience. Even where town life was represented in European settings (*The Changeling* (1622) is set in Spain, for example, and *'Tis Pity She's a Whore* (1633) in Italy), there would have been a keen sense of identification for London audiences intrigued by the potential for comparison between these imagined overseas locations and their own expanding city. Moreover, a strong element throughout the drama of the seventeenth century is the perceived clash between the ways of the country and the ways of the town. Rural life was idealised for its purity and simplicity, ridiculed and attacked for its lack of sophistication, or both: in *Epicoene*, for instance, Truewit signals the impossibility of finding a chaste wife in the city by suggesting that such a creature existed only in some distant – and undesirable – rural past:

> If you had lived in King Etheldred's time, sir, or Edward the Confessor's, you might, perhaps, have found in some cold country hamlet, then, a dull frosty wench would have been contented with one man; now they will as soon be pleased with one leg or one eye.
>
> (II.ii.39–44)

In *The Roaring Girl*, the countryside figures, on the one hand, as a place for the staging of illicit sexual encounters (at Ware, Hoxton or Brentford, villages outside of, but accessible from, London), or, on the other hand, as a place of impoverishment and dearth (as signalled by the names of Lord Noland and Laxton). In all of these instances the countryside is attributed its meanings only through reference to, and in order to define, its perceived opposite: the city.

The material conditions of city life are a key element in many of these plays. The rich diversity of London's population is represented, together with the opportunities and pitfalls of the new economic order. Although rural life had been, and continued to be, dependent upon the uncertainties of the harvest (and deeply affected over the centuries by disease, high mortality rates and migration), it was also insular and, for the most part, characterised by the stability and continuity of its population. Life in the towns was less predictable, since it depended upon a more complex social and economic structure and a more mobile population. The varying fortunes of trade led to uneven levels of employment, whether in work directly related to enterprise or in the associated positions of servants and those involved in the supply trades. 'Masterless' people, both victims of changing rural economies and ex-soldiers (such as Trapdoor and Tearcat in *The Roaring Girl*), threatened both country and city, and the new concentration of large numbers of people in urban areas helped spread the recurrent bouts of plague, the extent and effect of which can be fairly accurately traced by, amongst other things, the occasions when they forced the closure of the theatres.

Day-to-day life in the city was characterised by high levels of both casual and surprisingly 'organised' crime in a society which lacked anything like a modern police force; indeed, the attention given to 'thieves' cant', the specialist language of criminals and vagrants, in *The Roaring Girl* testifies to the highly developed structures of communication and organisation within this social grouping. Moreover, justice was itself a form of theatre, in the sense that it often resulted in spectacular displays of power by the authorities as a means of deterrence. Whilst the agents of government might initially confine and torture their enemies in the hidden chambers of the Tower of London, it was also common for examples to be made of both political opponents and ordinary criminals in the public areas of the city, with branding, mutilations and hangings being conducted for all to see. In this most unequal of societies, it was not unusual to see women and men publicly abused and chastised through a number of popular rituals and punishments for their lack of conformity to the 'laws' of gender and sexual conduct which governed their lives. This was a society in which the power of the state and the law was demonstrated and enacted precisely through its public 'performance'. Far from the theatre and the law occupying separate spheres of entertainment and social

regulation, then, the plays engaged fundamentally with issues of power and authority, just as the judiciary and the state relied on the power of spectacle.

The plays' engagement with such issues involved a recognition that power and authority were distributed differentially through society, and that the social hierarchies that had previously determined social status and power were undergoing a process of transformation. This evolution of the early modern system of social rank or degree was inextricably bound up with the changing pattern of economic development. The largely rural medieval social formation had for centuries held relatively few opportunities for social advancement, the land-controlling aristocracy presiding over a hierarchy of gentry and peasantry that was firmly linked to their roles within the countryside and mediated through the dual institutions of local feudal justice and the church. However, by the late sixteenth century, this was giving way to a more diverse and rather more fluid system of social hierarchy, where a man's degree depended on a combination of his wealth, power and status, and a woman's usually depended on that of her father or husband. Whilst the social hierarchy was still characterised by the nobility and land-owning gentry at the top, the professions (such as the church, the law, medicine and the army) and major trades (based on wholesaling and retailing) complicated the old structures of rural stratification in that the growing wealth and power of increasingly urban-based groups began to effect a change in their status. These urban elites tended to be drawn from the middling gentry and continued to act in their own interests; however, they also increasingly came to control positions of authority in the towns and cities, on councils and in courts of aldermen, or in guild companies (as demonstrated in *The Knight of the Burning Pestle*). Below them in the hierarchy came the rural yeomen, who acted as the gentry's 'agents' by servicing juries, acting as constables and administering the system of poor relief. In descending order of degree, they were followed by craftsmen, tradesmen and copyholders (tenant farmers), then apprentices and servants (drawn from a number of social groups and therefore most likely to change their position within the social hierarchy) and, finally, husbandmen (who farmed their own smallholdings), cottagers (who supplemented their income with paid labour), labourers and vagrants. These distinctions varied somewhat from locality to locality, but within this general system of social inequality, however, there was constant movement, in that some farm labourers would become yeomen, some urban apprentices would become masters, and so on. The system of fine gradations and stratification operated in as thoroughgoing a way at the lower end of the hierarchy as it did at the higher. However, whilst capable of ranking groups and occupations into a complex and finely tuned system of stratification, contemporaries also increasingly grouped these many positions into three broad clusters: 'gentlemen', 'the middling sort of people' and 'the poor' – a tripartite system closer to the urban-based class system which was to supersede it in the eighteenth century.

The plays' determined preoccupation with matters of social rank is evidence both of the evolution of the social structure, and of the way that this produced a tension between the emerging classes and the old aristocracy which, although it had fought wars within its own ranks, had never conceded its own 'divinely sanctioned' power over the majority of the population. Much of the drama of the period can be seen as fairly even-handedly implying criticism of the beliefs of both the older aristocratic layer of society and the newly-emerging and increasingly influential 'middling sort'. *Epicoene*, for example, is relentless in its excoriation of fashionable and rootless urbanites as represented by Morose, the collegiate ladies, the ersatz Sir John Daw (whose learning is indiscriminate and cavalier, and who 'buys titles'), the Otters, and even the putative 'heroes', the three gallants. Family longevity and continuity, however, is no guarantee of wisdom or good order, as La Foole demonstrates. His family, the La Fooles of London, are the source of all the La Fooles of the land: 'They all come out of our house, the La Fooles o' the north, the La Fooles of the west, the La Fooles of the east and south – we are as ancient a family as any is in Europe' (I.iv.37–40). Even in *The Knight of the Burning Pestle*, which is a much less acerbic comedy than *Epicoene*, a chivalric past is invoked only to be parodied and undercut by a sense of the lack of relevance of such ideals and practices in the new urban context. Perhaps these comedies are exceptional in their unwillingness to identify 'the old order' as more desirable and harmonious than the new. Much of the drama at this time would probably have been viewed as conservatively and nostalgically favouring this system of patronage and stability, seen as increasingly vulnerable and unstable.

## Early modern theatre: origins, locations and dramatic forms

By the 1560s, London, with its rapidly expanding population, its new forms of trade and commerce, and its complex and diverse social composition, was on the brink of a new era of theatre-building and play-performing. The theatres in which the plays were first performed owed their development not only to a remarkable confluence of dramatic tradition, intellectual energy and commercial enterprise, but also to the developments in building skills which allowed structures to be designed specifically for theatrical entertainment. This is not to say, however, that popular dramatic forms and performances were themselves new. On the contrary, the medieval period had been rich in varied forms of drama, much of it closely bound up with the folk traditions of an agrarian society. It is thought, for example, that the popularity of plays dealing with Christian notions of death and resurrection owed something to pre-Christian traditions celebrating the cycle of the changing seasons. Indeed, many of the festivals, particularly Christmas and Easter with their entertainments and rituals, can be seen as having been grafted on to pre-existing pagan celebrations, and the legacy of these combined traditions can be found in the plays of Shakespeare and his contemporaries.

More specifically, it was the church which encouraged the more formal kinds of dramatic tradition from which the early modern theatre descended. The Mystery plays, which were organised in the towns by the guilds of professional artisans, had their origins in dramatic representations of episodes from the Bible which had first been acted in the larger Catholic places of worship as far back as the ninth century. In the years leading up to (and perhaps overlapping with) the establishment of the first public theatres in London, these productions annually retold those key Christian stories which were considered the literal history of human existence. Although central figures (Adam, Noah and Christ) were often played by professional actors, the main cast was drawn from amongst local people, and the form allowed topical references, local customs and even limited social critique to combine with the reinforcement of the truth of Christian teaching.

Medieval Morality plays such as *Mankind* (1464–71) and *Everyman* (c. 1520) had, perhaps, more forceful messages to convey, with their severe warnings against sin and the corruption of the soul. These plays, which toured around towns and villages, dramatised the various temptations to which 'man' was open. Typically a central human figure was visited by emblematic figures representing various sins or moral dilemmas, a tradition handed on to the Renaissance theatre and easily seen in plays such as Christopher Marlowe's *Doctor Faustus* (c. 1589) or Shakespeare's *Macbeth* (1606). In the absence of buildings specifically designed for the theatre, these early plays were staged in market squares, the courtyards of inns and the banqueting halls of the larger mansions (as in the case of the travelling players who act 'The Mousetrap' in *Hamlet* (1600)). Despite the gravity of their spiritual messages, these were also entertainments, and their mixing of comedy with theology is a tradition that perhaps explains the mixing of genres in the plays of the Elizabethan and early Stuart period. Some of the most compelling figures in the plays in this volume happen to be some of the most morally corrupt (Salome in *The Tragedy of Mariam* (1604), De Flores in *The Changeling*, or Giovanni in *'Tis Pity She's a Whore*), and many of the figures of high comedy, such as Moll

Cutpurse in *The Roaring Girl*, are the most philosophically gifted and eloquent.

The poets who turned to the theatre in the period immediately before Shakespeare were well aware of these older traditions and incorporated them into their new work. They were also attuned to the long-standing forms of entertainment at court (where the masque was cultivated) and to such European forms of street entertainment as the *commedia dell'arte* and the earliest forms of Italian opera. The London of the second half of the sixteenth century was fast becoming a cosmopolitan society visited by groups of travelling actors from abroad. In addition, there was an interest in classical forms of theatre, an interest which adds to the sense of the period as the Renaissance, a revaluation of classical culture. A notion of the ideal structure and form of a play was derived from a knowledge of the work of the Greek writer Aristotle (384–322 BC). His early 'criticism' was highly influential in the work of many of the playwrights, his theory of dramatic unity, explained in *The Poetics*, being perhaps most evident in the plays of Ben Jonson. Similarly, the plays of the Roman writer Seneca (4 BC–AD 64) interested contemporary students at Oxford and Cambridge and inspired much early modern tragedy, particularly after the publication of Thomas Newton's *Seneca, His Tenne Tragedies Translated into English* in 1581. Thomas Kyd's *The Spanish Tragedy* (1585) is an early example of such 'Senecan' tragedy, whilst Elizabeth Cary's *The Tragedy of Mariam*, a later play, is 'Senecan' not only in its interest in revenge, but also because it was a 'closet' drama, like Seneca's plays, probably written to be read rather than to be performed on stage.

The evolution of these various influences into the dramatic genres represented in this volume depended, however, upon the practical development of drama into a commercial institution, housed in the new, purpose-built theatres. Until this point, when plays had been performed in halls, market places, inn yards or baiting arenas, payment for the actors had come from diverse sources, either from the host who had invited them to play, or, in cases where performance was in a market place, from passing a hat round after the play. With the new playhouses, the financial relationship between players and audiences changed:

By enclosing the plays inside a special building players made the customers who paid to see what was on offer more selective, and no doubt more demanding. Only those who paid got in. They got in for the exclusive purpose of seeing a play, and they handed their money over to the impresarios and players whose sole interest was in satisfying their demand for entertainment. Moreover a single fixed venue needed a much larger turnover of plays than was needed when the players were on their travels

from one town to another. So the new London playhouses became a massive stimulus to the production of new plays.

(Gurr 1996: 10–11)

The earliest of these new theatres was the Red Lion, built by John Brayne in 1567 in Whitechapel. This was replaced in 1576 when James Burbage (Brayne's brother-in-law and business partner) constructed a building known simply as 'The Theatre' at Shoreditch, then to the north-east of London proper; in the following year, and very near to the Theatre, the Curtain was built. The rapid proliferation of large public theatres is evidence of Londoners' demand for all manner of entertainment. After the building of the Curtain, the favoured location for the erection of public theatres became Southwark, on the south bank of the River Thames, and thus safely outside the jurisdiction of the city authorities who sought, where possible, to suppress the performance of plays. These theatres were located near a similarly expanding array of bear and bull pits, brothels, cockfighting arenas, and other forms of public entertainment which contemporary writers and, in particular, Puritan critics, saw as equally dubious and degrading. Indeed, something like a tradition became established of invective against the theatre, ranging from John Rainold's lectures at Oxford in the reign of Henry VIII to William Prynne's scathing critiques of the 1630s. Stephen Gosson, in his *The School of Abuse*, a pamphlet of 1579, grouped players together with poets and 'pipers' as part of a general moral malaise:

Let us but shut uppe our eares to poets, pipers and players; pull our feete back from resort to theaters, and turne away our eyes from beholding of vanitie, the greatest storme of abuse will bee overblowne, and a faire path troden to amendment of life: were not we so foolish to taste every drugge and buy every trifle, players woulde shut in their shops, and carry their trash to some other country.

(Gosson 1841: 34)

Despite such attacks, theatres and other places of public entertainment proliferated. Southwark's Rose theatre, an archaeological trace of which remains today, was built in 1587, followed by the Swan in 1595 and, most famously, the Globe, which opened in 1599. The Globe was situated a few hundred metres further away from the river than the present replica building, and was said to have been built from the timbers of Burbage's Shoreditch theatre, demolished in 1598. The Globe was itself rebuilt in 1614 after a fire the previous year. Another Southwark theatre was the Hope (1614), also much used for bear-baiting. The Fortune (1600), the Boar's Head (1601) and the Red Bull (1604) were to the north of the Thames, but again outside of the

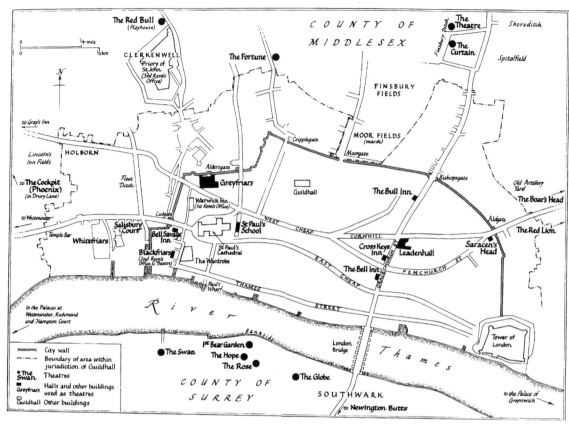

Locations of London's principal theatres, c. 1560–1642

jurisdiction of the London authorities (see map). These theatres attracted large audiences of up to 3,000 people, who were charged a small fee to attend the afternoon performances. Their designation as 'public' theatres results from their capacity, their cheapness and the fact that their clientele was drawn from diverse areas of society. These are also sometimes known as 'amphitheatre' playhouses, however, which indicates something of these buildings' physical properties. Modelled on the inn yard or animal-baiting arena, these theatres were usually polygonal and were partially open to the sky (only the stage and the galleries were covered), and their stages projected into the open central 'pit' or courtyard. Thomas Platter, a German visitor to London in 1599, described the seating arrangements and the atmosphere of the London theatres that he visited:

> Thus daily at two in the afternoon, London has two, sometimes three plays running in different places, competing with each other, and those which play best obtain most spectators. The playhouses are so constructed that they play on a raised platform, so that everyone has a good view. There are different galleries and places, however, where the seating is better and more comfortable and therefore more expensive. For whoever cares to stand below only pays one English penny, but if he wishes to sit he enters by another door, and pays another penny, while if he desires to sit in the most comfortable seats which are cushioned, where he not only sees everything well, but can also be seen, then he pays yet another English penny at another door. And during the performance food and drink are carried round the audience, so that for what one cares to pay one may also have refreshment. The actors are most expensively and elaborately costumed; for it is the English usage for eminent lords or Knights at their decease to bequeath and leave almost the best of their clothes to their serving men, which it is unseemly for the latter to wear, so they offer them then for sale for a small sum to the actors.

> (Platter 1937: 166–7)

Plays written for these public playhouses were shaped by their writers' awareness of the social composition of their audiences as well as the physical characteristics of the buildings in which the plays would be acted. One of the most interesting features of the plays is the way that they frequently draw attention to the fact that they are, indeed, plays. There is none of the aspiration to realism found in many modern forms of drama, although there is an often repeated idea that 'real' life is itself rather like a play, in which we take roles and act out parts. , it is possible to learn much from the lines written for the early modern actor about the emblematic environment in which he worked. The stage itself had a symbolic role. Hell was located below the platform (through a trap door) and heaven was above it, signified by a painted ceiling of stars. Actors would address an audience in full acknowledgement of its presence as part of the 'event'; a few actors could easily be understood to represent a crowd, or even an army; boy actors could be understood to represent women (since there were no professional women actors) and a sense of place or time was indicated in the dialogue at the beginning of a new scene (as there was no scenery or artificial lighting), and a gesture would convey a message understood across the audience to its furthest members. This is not to say that this was a theatre lacking in subtlety; the actors worked their audiences' imaginations to the full. Nor was it a spartan theatre; what the public theatres lacked in the modern sense of 'scenery', they gained not only through the committed involvement of their audiences in the entertainment, but also by the employment of elaborate costume, ingenious props and music.

Theatre clearly demanded then, as now, extremely high levels of organisation. The theatres were profit-making commercial concerns, and the owners, playwrights and companies of actors responded to the demands of their business with rigorous professionalism. Surviving documents from the time, and in particular the diary of the theatre-owner Philip Henslowe, reveal the intricate nature of the finances involved in running a theatre. Money was to be made in the theatres despite the fact that they were constantly under attack from the civic authorities (who thought of actors as little more than vagabonds) and subject to regular closure as a result of recurrent outbreaks of plague. Partly as a result of this precarious existence, acting companies sought patronage from the monarchs and aristocracy of the time, and this is reflected in the titles they assumed, such as the 'King's Men' or 'Queen Anne's Men'. This patronage led the companies to perform at court, which meant that if a play was performed in a public theatre and again before the queen or king, its ultimate audience encompassed the full range of society.

During the seventeenth century the large public theatres began to lose ground to the smaller and more intimate 'private' theatres. The earliest of these had been constructed in the Elizabethan period at the same time as the larger public theatres. Although much

smaller than the Southwark theatres, the Blackfriars, built in 1576 and rebuilt and enlarged by Burbage in 1596, had many of the characteristics of the public theatres: the stage, for example, still featured areas designated as 'heaven' and 'hell', and the audience was still distributed at different levels to watch the plays. But here, as in the Whitefriars (1606) and other private theatres such as the Salisbury Court (1629), the acting space and auditorium were more intimate and the audience more exclusive. These theatres were fully enclosed, and therefore the plays were lit artificially, leaving the audience in darkness. The stage was at one end of a rectangular space, and all members of the audience were seated. The design of these private (or 'hall') theatres meant that their capacity was much smaller than that of the public ones, probably no more than a quarter of the size, and admission prices were much higher.

By the time the Cockpit opened in Drury Lane in 1616 (mostly referred to as the Phoenix after 1617, when it burnt down and was swiftly rebuilt), the private theatres were far more financially secure institutions than the public ones, and playwrights increasingly wrote with these kinds of spaces and audiences in mind. The style of productions changed significantly, and there is a greater uniformity to the social bias in most of the plays from this later part of the historical period. By the end of the first quarter of the seventeenth century, the majority of new plays was being written for these private theatres and for performance by companies with firm connections at court. Older plays, which had been written for the public theatres, were also revived in the various forms of theatre which survived until their closure at the outbreak of civil war in 1642.

During the reigns of the early Stuart monarchs, King James (who had been the king of Scotland since 1567 and became king of England in 1603) and his son, Charles (who succeeded him in 1625), the court became highly preoccupied with the fashionable and politically important dramatic form known as the masque. These courtly entertainments, such as *The Masque of Blackness* (1605), with their combinations of acting, music and dance, usually involved members of the nobility as performers. They relied upon the elaborate Italianate set and costume designs originated by Inigo Jones, and the writing of dramatists such as Ben Jonson, who increasingly turned to the masque form as his career developed. These court productions may account for the particular masque-like quality of some of the 'play-within-a-play' entertainments included in other texts from the period, such as the dumb show in Act IV scene i of *The Changeling*.

These principal places of theatrical entertainment – public theatre, private theatre and court – are the ones which have received most scholarly attention, since they were where the majority of the better known plays and masques of the period were first performed. However, it is important to keep in mind that theatre was also available still from the visiting troupes of players from other parts of Europe and in the form of travelling productions in Britain and Ireland, and there continued to be theatrical activity in the houses of the aristocracy and at the universities of Oxford and Cambridge. Even after the civil war began in 1642, the theatre managed to survive in informal, private arrangements to re-emerge with considerable energy following the restoration of the monarchy in 1660.

## A drama of institutions

Just as the proliferation of purpose-built theatres and the increased public enthusiasm for playgoing can be understood as the outcome of a particular set of social, economic and cultural configurations, so the plays written for these theatres can also be seen to be profoundly shaped by the contemporary circumstances of their production. Although some twentieth-century literary criticism reads this drama as concerned with universal and timeless issues relating to the 'human condition' – love, death, truth, loyalty, justice and morality – more recently, critics have traced the ways in which this drama is precisely *not* 'timeless' but very much 'of its age'. This concept is based upon the drama's close thematic engagement with so many of the key institutions of the time. These institutions, such as the monarchy, the church and the family, structured contemporary society. Such theatrical engagements, moreover, were far from being neutral 'reflections' of the world outside the theatre, but were often astute and passionate contributions to contemporary analyses and debates about the nature and remit of these institutions.

One of the most clear-cut examples of such an engagement concerns the location of the action of these plays: many feature court settings, presided over by figures of authority (kings, dukes or cardinals), which mimic the structures of power established by 'divine right', whereby absolute power, ultimately deriving from God, is invested in the monarch. In these dramatic worlds, we can observe the activities of rival factions, ambitious individuals from further down the social formation and those denied justice by the existing structures and systems. In *The Spanish Tragedy*, for example, following the killing of his son, Hieronimo seeks in vain to obtain justice from the king, the courts and heaven itself, whilst in *Edward II* (1592) we witness a similarly corrupt, divisive and self-interested exercise of political power at *all* levels of governance. In focusing on the imperfect exercise of political power, the plays demonstrate something of the tension which applied to the upper reaches of government in the world beyond the theatre. The considerable alterations in the social composition of the country had a

significant effect upon the way that it was governed. Embedded in the plots of many of the plays, these struggles for power and justice between competing groups or factions can be seen as more or less directly representing and interrogating the vested interests inherent in the wider social formation, and the changes in their capacity to intervene in and influence the political process; and it is to a discussion of these changes that we now turn.

It is impossible to separate political power in early modern England from religious institutions and practices. The conflicts which so indelibly mark the years of Elizabeth I and the two Stuart monarchs who succeeded her (James and Charles) have their origins in the religious turmoil of the middle decades of the sixteenth century. The reign of Elizabeth's father, Henry VIII, had been characterised both by his increasing centralisation of the machinery of government (intended, amongst other things, to put an end to the internal aristocratic disputes which had led to the Wars of the Roses of 1455–85) and by his break with Rome, when the 1534 Act of Supremacy established him as head of the English Church. Apart from a brief respite offered during the reign of Mary (1553–8), Catholics were persecuted throughout the remainder of the sixteenth century, whilst English Protestantism developed in such a way as to represent a powerful new sense of Anglocentric national identity. This is not to claim the successful subjugation of other regional and national identities within the British Isles to an all-powerful English one: whilst Wales had long before been absorbed into England's sphere of influence, Scotland continued to be, until the Act of Union of 1707, a separate country with its own parliament; and Ireland remained only nominally part of the empire declared by Henry in his Act in Restraint of Appeals (1533). Nonetheless, part of the 'Tudor project' under Elizabeth continued to be the development and assertion of an English supremacy, much of which depended on Elizabeth's image as a specifically *Protestant* leader. This was skilfully cultivated and stage-managed throughout her reign, and works of propaganda against Catholicism, together with the 1588 victory over the Armada (a Spanish fleet threatening an invasion of England), helped to seal the association between the monarchy, English nationalism and Protestant theology.

The advent of Protestantism can be closely identified with the increasing influence of a class of gentry which was turning its skills to trade and commerce. Some members of this group had benefited directly from the redistribution of land following Henry's dissolution of Catholic monastic estates between 1536 and 1539. Indeed, Thomas Arden, in *Arden of Faversham* (1592), is an instance of just such a man, his wealth deriving from the sale of the lands belonging to the Abbey of

Faversham. With its ethic of individuality, self-reliance and hard work, Protestantism facilitated the turn to commerce by this segment of English people, as it had done for those abroad in the Reformation stronghold of the Netherlands. Towards the end of Elizabeth's reign, however, and increasingly during the reigns of James and Charles, this rising commercial class identified itself with more rigorous or 'Puritan' forms of Protestantism, seeking to take further the 'purification' of religious practice that they thought had been inadequately implemented by the reformed English church. This group's increasing economic power gave rise to political aspiration, representing itself in the influential trade guilds, the municipal authorities in London and other towns, and increasingly in parliament itself. Encouraged by the Catholic Gunpowder Plot of 1605, and disapproving of the Stuarts' sympathy towards Catholicism, this was the class which consolidated itself with such strength against the monarch's divine right to rule the country that it finally took complete charge in the civil wars of the 1640s. In a piece of theatre decisive enough to draw crowds from across London and beyond, Parliament executed Charles I in January 1649.

Protestantism represented an important break with the past in terms of the way that church services were organised and in the church's theories concerning the relationship between the individual and God. No longer was the priest a necessary intermediary between the believer and God, but each believer was now to take direct responsibility for the state of his or her own spiritual well-being by means of a constant process of prayer, self-scrutiny, and Bible study. The latter was made possible by new translations of the Bible from Latin into English; particularly important here was the 'Geneva' Bible (1560), the most widely used translation until the 1630s, though better known now is the King James (or 'Authorised') version, published in 1611. These translations widened direct access to the 'word of God', which had hitherto been strictly interpreted for church congregations only by priests. The self-reliance and hard work so often associated with Puritanism, then, applied to its adherents' religious beliefs and practices as well as to their business dealings.

Over the years during which the plays in this volume were written, the idea of a hierarchy of priests and bishops controlling the circulation of spiritual ideas was severely challenged, particularly in Puritan circles. The day-to-day conduct of religious life needed to be released from what Puritans saw as the clutter of icons, wealth and elaborate trappings characteristic of Catholicism, many of which had been preserved in the English church established by Henry VIII. The forms of religious worship and organisation which Puritans wanted to introduce were aimed not only at making the individual's relationship with God more direct, but also more democratic. These more Puritan forms of Protestantism were varied, and notoriously difficult to anatomise and characterise, but ranged from a Calvinism which declared that an élite of people were 'predestined' from birth to enter heaven, to those who asserted 'free will' and the ability of any individual to gain salvation through the kind of pure life which was evidence of God's hand in their earthly conduct. Some of the later seventeenth-century religious groups advocated the abolition of church services altogether, stressed the purity of rural life, and drew up egalitarian principles to do with the rights of men and women over property and land. Such beliefs proved much too radical for those Puritans who took the reins of power in the 1640s and 1650s.

The connection between these new forms of religious life and wider aspects of government cannot be overestimated. To a greater or lesser extent, all forms of Protestantism questioned the authority of the older church establishment, but the 'purer' versions increasingly challenged contemporary forms of non-representative national and local government. The ideals of Puritanism were the foundation of many of the new settlements in America of the 1620s onwards and played the biggest part in organised dissent from the authority of the monarchy at home, underpinning the confidence of the new, largely non-aristocratic class which found representation in the parliament which eventually overthrew Charles I.

The plays of the period endlessly rehearse issues to do with the relationship between power, authority, justice and theology (the discussions between Giovanni and the Friar in *'Tis Pity She's a Whore* are a good example of this), and whilst they often mock the extremes of the Puritan lifestyle, they are at the same time almost uniformly committed to reminding their audiences of the 'horrors' of Catholicism. Many plays of the period, and almost all the tragedies of revenge, are set in Catholic countries such as Italy or Spain. These were thought of as places of excess and uncontrolled appetites. Not only were these Mediterranean societies seen as being obsessed with revenge, but all aspects of their culture were thought of as lacking control and regulation. Food, manners, speech, costume and etiquette were much commented on by contemporary travellers as examples of a world of excessive consumption and gratification which lay beyond the English Channel. A particular preoccupation for English writers was with Italian sexual mores, often thought to be perverted, outlandish and undignified. In the realm of politics, Italy was singled out as a loose web of states which rivalled one another in corruption, opportunism and political intrigue. English translations of the Florentine political thinker Machiavelli, which circulated widely amongst the Elizabethan and Stuart intelligentsia, were read as confirming this view. Spain, meanwhile, notably successful in the conquest of territory overseas, had posed an immediate and local threat in the form of the Armada of 1588, and during the period of its threatened return in the 1590s.

In fact, the drama of the time parodied and damned the 'otherness' of all manner of 'foreign' peoples. The distinctive strands of anti-semitism in some plays of the period, such as Marlowe's *The Jew of Malta* (c. 1589) and Shakespeare's *The Merchant of Venice* (1596) had a chilling resonance for twentieth-century readers, and will continue to influence decisions about the re-staging of plays in this century. It is also possible to find casual abuse of the Scots, the Welsh and the Irish. This was the period which saw the development of the ideal of a modern 'Britishness', yet it was clearly based on the assumption that England was culturally superior. Indeed, a series of plays, now known as the 'Elect Nation' plays, were staged by the theatre owner Philip Henslowe in the first few years of the seventeenth century, with the express aim of celebrating and bolstering the superiority of a particular version of Protestant Englishness.

The marked distaste for Mediterranean Catholic culture was accompanied, ironically, by a clear fascination with its perceived excesses. In the drama of the period and in much contemporary prose, Spain and Italy could be made to represent everything that England, officially at least, had abandoned along with the doctrines of the Roman Catholic church, thus strengthening the image of a nation united against the kind of corruption and decay exhibited in these imagined Catholic worlds. Nonetheless, the design of the private theatres was heavily influenced by Italian style, and a vogue developed amongst the aristocracy for southern European music and dance. Given the suspicion that a sympathy for Catholicism lingered at court, these settings might be seen as a way by which the dramatists of the time could invite a critique of the very court which sponsored and witnessed their plays.

The early modern period saw a consolidation of a sense of nation based upon the cultivation of the distinctiveness of English Protestant identity, and a nurturing of history through the chronicles of Holinshed and Stow upon which Shakespeare, Marlowe and others based their historical dramas. However, such a project also raised immediate and unsettling questions, given the layered and fragmented society which witnessed it. For whom did such an identity make most sense, and in whose interests did it work? If a contest was underway over national identity, then the combatants were drawn from a social formation which itself was characterised by considerable instability and change. It was no longer possible, if it ever had been, to recognise a stable aristocracy which had gathered its own wealth and

prestige under conditions dictated and fostered by feudal economic systems, inheritance and an oppressive government machinery. Many new 'entrepreneurs' and beneficiaries of social mobility were able to 'buy into' the nobility, especially in the reign of James Stuart (Sir John Daw in *Epicoene* is mocked by Truewit for just this reason (I.ii.83)). Similarly the new body of politically-minded individuals inspired by a new economic system, which, as they recognised, was fundamentally altering what could be expected from society's political and social institutions, also included modernisers from old and established families.

To a large extent, this contest over a new national identity for the country was fought over the relationship between individuals and the numerous institutions which formed both the structure of the government in particular, and society in general. The existing governmental structure saw the monarch as God's representative on earth. In the body of the king (or queen) reposed the absolute authority (or 'divine right') of the monarch to rule. Royal authority was handed from monarch to monarch through death and succession. The monarch's subjects *circulated* around this absolute authority, against which their own positions in the order of things were defined. The older institutions of government reinforced this hierarchy. Elizabethan Parliaments were summoned in order to ratify and disseminate the power and authority of the queen. During his reign, James Stuart wrote extensively on the laws which governed his divine authority over his subjects, in texts such as *The True Lawe of Free Monarchies* (1603).

A parallel can be made between this model of power and the medieval notion that the earth (the monarch) was the centre of the universe, around which the planets (his or her subjects) simply circulated. Yet just as late medieval science determined, in the face of fierce opposition from the church, that the sun was in fact the centre of the universe, the rising class of politically-minded Protestants sought to de-centre the monarch's authority. They increasingly conceived of power as residing in the institutions through which society was run, and ultimately in the elected chamber of Parliament. The new emphasis was not upon the notion of individuals as *subjects* of the monarch, but as *citizens* in the increasingly complex civil organisation to be found in society in general, particularly the society of the expanding towns and cities. This did not, of course, seamlessly succeed the notion of the individual-as-subject, but operated in tension with it and helped to raise questions about its foundation and reach. In the drama of the period, the city comedies such as *The Roaring Girl* and *The Knight of the Burning Pestle* represent a thoroughly 'civic' world of citizen concerns and values. However, even the history plays, such as Marlowe's *Edward II*, by no means assume an unquestionable legitimacy for the model of individual-as-subject, for if the monarchy itself is represented as a flawed and all-too-human institution, then the subjection of the individual to it can no longer be taken for granted. So, whilst questions about the role of the individual in relation to society's institutions produced a tension at the heart of the political drama which in turn unfolded at the heart of government during the seventeenth century (revolving around such issues as the law, money, divine right, representation and religion), they also created a tension which drives the plots of many of the plays of the period. The fictional worlds of this drama, whether located in contemporary England or in distant Spain and Italy, were inhabited by citizens and subjects whose roles were similarly defined in relation to institutional concerns.

The plays are not, of course, concerned only with the 'politics' of monarchy, government and the church. In a similar way, they also debate the workings of institutions such as the law, commerce and social rank which affected not just those members of society actively involved in early modern politics, but everyone who attended the performances. Evidence that the plays directed their audiences' attentions to the experiences of everyday life can be seen, for example, through their close examination of marriage and the family, the institutions which most directly regulated sexuality. This aspect of Renaissance theatre has caught the interest of recent critics, undoubtedly because of the evolution of these institutions in the second half of the twentieth century. These old plays show how assumptions about sexuality were under intense examination in the early modern period, a time of profound transformation in notions of marriage and the family.

Questions concerning gender, sexuality and the changing structure of the family recur in much early modern drama, and are raised in comedies, tragedies and histories alike; indeed, it is difficult to identify any one play in this anthology that is not concerned to explore the meanings of one or all of these issues. This is perhaps not surprising, given the history of the period leading up to their production, which is notable for the manner in which a variety of governmental and religious institutions sought to regulate and control the sexuality of those subject to their scrutiny. Protestantism inherited a number of religious edicts from the Roman Catholic church that were designed to encourage monogamy, punish sexual irregularities, and formalise the procedures surrounding the marriage ceremony. For example, the practice familiar to modern Christian churchgoers of 'calling the banns', and the procedures for keeping records of marriages, were standardised and consolidated by canon (religious) law with a view to seeking out bigamy, incest and other forbidden practices. Nonetheless, despite the increasing popularity of church marriages throughout the sixteenth century, legal recognition of less formal unions, known as 'clandestine marriages' (no banns, and in a parish away from home), continued, and even canon law recognised as binding any public declaration before witnesses that a man and woman considered themselves married, although a church wedding was necessary to ensure the inheritance of property. Amongst the very poor, evidence suggests that many never contracted any kind of legally recognised marriage, and were thus more free to change their partners at will. Cohabitation could be prosecuted in the church courts, but increasingly this only happened if a child was involved, as there was concern that the child or the mother might become a cost to the parish. Although the Church of England did not recognise divorce, it was the subject of intense scrutiny during the sixteenth and seventeenth centuries, and separations between husbands and wives were not unheard of. Questions about the regulation of marriages were, then, live issues, and can be seen to inform such diverse plays as *The Tragedy of Mariam*, with its interest in the politics of divorce and marital loyalty, *Arden of Faversham*, investigating the terms and meanings of Alice's challenge to the marriage contract, *A Woman Killed with Kindness*, which foregrounds the uneasy combination of economics and sexual desire in marriage partnerships, and *'Tis Pity She's a Whore*, which invites us to examine the foundation of sexual and social taboos in relation to its exposé of the brutal foundations and betrayals of socially sanctioned sexual relationships. The multiplicity of such troubled, and troubling, representations of the family indicates something of the pressures on, challenges to, and uncertainties about the form, foundation and function of this institution during these years.

Alongside, and as a part of, these concerns about marriage went anxieties about changes to the structure of the family itself, and the plays' obsession with conflicts which proceeded from sexual behaviour and the power associated with sexuality and gender offers a commentary on this evolution. The concept of the family had clearly been different in medieval society. Arrangements at the lower end of the social formation could sometimes be more liberal and changeable than they were to become in the early modern period, perhaps more readily following the real and fluctuating circumstances of people's lives and affections. In the upper reaches of society, the 'family' was a grouping which often extended beyond ties of blood to include servants and retainers (and this sense is apparent in *Epicoene*, when Epicoene speaks of 'a family where I govern' (III.iv.56). Marriage was often above all an economic contract, to do with the control of land, the propagation of a dynasty and the strengthening, through amalgamation, of two or more fortunes. The idea of mutual love, leading to the voluntary entering into a partnership for life, was a secondary consideration, if at all. This meant that both men and women could be coerced into marriages against their will which, whilst on one level effective as a means of maintaining the institution of marriage, simultaneously undermined marriage as a secure means of ensuring reproduction within wedlock.

Historians disagree about the extent to which patterns of marriage changed through the sixteenth and seventeenth centuries. Some propose that the coercion of people into loveless marriages based on economic considerations gave way to voluntary consent in the name of love, and an emphasis, particularly amongst Puritans, of the need for *mutual* love and sympathy in marriage; others suggest that the process was much more gradual and partial than this rather optimistic version proposes. All agree, however, on the impossibility of generalising across all social ranks and all localities. What certainly seems to be the case is that this new, more mutual, model of marriage featured as an increasingly important ideal or reference point within the drama of the period; indeed, it is this that is celebrated in the opening scene of *A Woman Killed with Kindness*, when Frankford and Anne have just married:

> You both adorn each other, and your hands
> Methinks are matches. There's equality
> In this fair combination; you are both scholars,
> Both young, both being descended nobly.
> There's music in this sympathy, it carries
> Consort and expectation of much joy,
> Which God bestow on you, from this first day
> Until your dissolution – that's for aye.
>
> (I.i.65–72)

However, this rhetoric of mutuality and equality in fact did little for women's rights in marriage, in many ways making them surrender the power they might have had in earlier generations. Consent secured the economic unit of the modern marriage, which became the building block of the social formation that developed from the early modern period.

Similarly, people were drawn out of a system in which they were coerced into obedience to the queen or king by fear of physical punishment (and dazzled by the splendour of the monarch's power) and into a system in which they consented to the institutions which exercised power on their behalf. None of these new institutional arrangements enhanced the lives of most ordinary people, but they did propagate the *illusion* of progress and participation, and thereby strengthened the systems of organisation which were essential for the emerging new economic order which was to dominate succeeding centuries.

At the same time, there was considerable debate about what constituted desirable or permissible sexual behaviour, as well as about what attributes should be ascribed to masculinity and femininity. Although not categorised in the modern way, homosexuality was an issue at the courts of Elizabeth and James, but probably as part of wider anxieties over gender, power and favouritism. There was certainly concern about the 'effeminate' nature of the contemporary male (as there is with La Foole in *Epicoene*), a concern commonly linked to the perceived unfitness of the contemporary male for military duty. At the same time, some women were seen as overly male in their attire, manner and speech. In the plays, the issue of homosexuality is most evident in *Edward II*, but there were clearly broader anxieties about gender at issue, not least in relation to the issue of the cross-dressing of boy actors for their roles as women. With plays such as *The Roaring Girl* on the stage, with its unambiguous celebration of the values and freedoms enjoyed by its cross-dressing heroine, it is perhaps easier to understand why contemporary commentators continued to rail with such vehemence against what was seen as the pernicious influence of the theatre.

The intimate connection between the institutions of society and the dramatic representations of the tensions which they produced on the contemporary stage was not lost on the authorities. Opposition to the theatre was intense and it is possible to read many accounts, particularly by Puritan commentators such as Philip Stubbes, of the perceived 'excesses' of the theatre. The playhouses and their companies were licensed by government, and individual plays were subject to censorship. These arrangements were particularly enforced by the authorities which controlled London, leading, as was discussed earlier, to the establishment of public theatres beyond their jurisdiction in the suburbs and 'liberties' of London.

What surfaced in Renaissance drama were the anxieties and discontinuities which were inevitably produced in a historical period of unprecedented economic, social and political change. It is hard to think of any issue to do with the uncertain shift of men and women from the strictures of the medieval world into the modern that is not recognised in the theatre of the day. Matters of high state, recent history, the family, the law, economics, sexuality and domestic life were brought before audiences whose changing experiences of these matters must have given the theatre a distinctive resonance and sense of topicality. The theatre was primarily a place of entertainment, and some contemporary commentators praised it for *diverting* people's minds from social unrest or even rebellion. Few accounts exist of audiences' reactions to particular plays, and it is impossible to reproduce the circumstances which would have conditioned their responses. Reading from the perspective of the twenty-first century, however, a perspective shaped by the institutions and values which triumphed in the early modern period, it is possible to see articulated here something of the disquiet and uncertainty which accompanied the transition between two quite distinct periods of history.

Early modern society has been rightly celebrated for the rich diversity of its literature. Yet it is wrong to accompany this celebration with the assertion that these high levels of cultural achievement corresponded to a society of harmony and order. What makes the plays so compelling for modern readers and audiences is the glimpse we get of the *uncertainties* of the world which the plays sought to make sense of; and if we are ourselves products of the world which grew out of these uncertainties (as the use by critics and historians of the phrase 'early modern' to describe this period seeks to imply), then the plays speak to us of the generation of the conditions of our own existence.

Taken together, the plays chosen for this anthology range across issues which, to a greater or lesser degree, have a familiarity for modern readers. The nature of drama is such that these issues are seen as a source of conflict, with either tragic or comic effect, or a mixture of the two. What might disturb us, however, when we compare the worlds of the plays with our own, is the recognition that some of the assumptions we take for granted about 'our' society were open to significant challenge at the time when they were first considered, and that these earlier 'alternatives' sometimes reflect poorly on the sum of human achievement over the centuries since these plays engaged their first audiences.

## References

Bentley, Gerald Eades (1941–68) *The Jacobean and Caroline Stage*, 7 vols, Oxford: Clarendon Press.

Gosson, Stephen (1841) *The School of Abuse, Containing a Pleasant Invective against Poets, Pipers, Players, Jesters, &c.* (first published 1579), London: Shakespeare Society.

Gurr, Andrew (1996) *Playgoing in Shakespeare's London*, 2nd edition, Cambridge: Cambridge University Press.

James I, King of Great Britain (1982) 'The True Lawe of Free Monarchies' (first published 1603), in James Craigie (ed.) *Minor Prose Works of James VI and I*, Edinburgh: Scottish Text Society.

Platter, Thomas (1937) *Thomas Platter's Travels in England 1599*, translated and introduced by Clare Williams, London: Jonathan Cape.

Stubbes, Philip (1973) *The Anatomie of Abuses* (first published 1583), facsimile edition, with a Preface by Arthur Freeman, New York, NY, and London: Garland.

For extracts from these and other relevant background texts, see the website which accompanies this book at: www.routledge.com/textbooks/0415187346

# Further Reading

## Drama criticism

### Drama and society

Belsey, Catherine (1985) *The Subject of Tragedy: Identity and Difference in Renaissance Drama*, London: Methuen.

Bristol, Michael (1985) *Carnival and Theater: Plebeian Culture and the Structure of Authority in Renaissance England*, New York, NY, and London: Routledge.

Burnett, Mark Thornton (1997) *Masters and Servants in English Renaissance Drama and Culture: Authority and Obedience*, Basingstoke: Macmillan.

Clare, Janet (1999) *Art Made Tongue-tied by Authority: Elizabethan and Jacobean Dramatic Censorship*, 2nd edition, Manchester: Manchester University Press.

Dolan, Frances E. (1994) *Dangerous Familiars: Representations of Domestic Crime in England 1550–1700*, Ithaca, NY, and London: Cornell University Press.

Dollimore, Jonathan (1989) *Radical Tragedy: Religion, Ideology and Power in the Drama of Shakespeare and his Contemporaries*, 2nd edition, New York, NY, and London: Harvester Wheatsheaf.

Dutton, Richard (1991) *Mastering the Revels: The Regulation and Censorship of English Renaissance Drama*, Basingstoke: Macmillan.

Findlay, Alison (1994) *Illegitimate Power: Bastards in Renaissance Drama*, Manchester: Manchester University Press.

Grantley, Darryl (2000) *Wit's Pilgrimage: Theatre and the Social Impact of Education in Early Modern England*, Aldershot: Ashgate.

Greenblatt, Stephen (1980) *Renaissance Self-fashioning: From More to Shakespeare*, Chicago, IL, and London: University of Chicago Press.

—— (1988) *Shakespearean Negotiations: The Circulation of Social Energy in Renaissance England*, Oxford: Oxford University Press.

Goldberg, Jonathan (1983) *James I and the Politics of Literature*, Baltimore, MD, and London: Johns Hopkins University Press.

Hall, Joan Lord (1991) *The Dynamics of Role-playing in Jacobean Tragedy*, London: Macmillan.

Heinemann, Margot (1980) *Puritanism and Theatre: Thomas Middleton and Opposition Drama under the Early Stuarts*, Cambridge: Cambridge University Press.

Howard, Jean E. (1994) *The Stage and Social Struggle in Early Modern England*, London: Routledge.

Knights, L. C. (1957) *Drama and Society in the Age of Jonson*, London: Chatto.

McCabe, Richard A. (1993) *Incest, Drama and Nature's Law 1550–1700*, Cambridge: Cambridge University Press.

Mullaney, Steven (1988) *The Place of the Stage: License, Play, and Power in Renaissance England*, Ann Arbor, MI: University of Michigan Press.

Mulryne, J. R. and Shewring, Margaret (eds) (1993) *Theatre and Government under the Early Stuarts*, Cambridge: Cambridge University Press.

Neill, Michael (1997) *Issues of Death: Mortality and Identity in English Renaissance Tragedy*, Oxford: Clarendon Press.

Orgel, Stephen (1975) *The Illusion of Power: Political Theatre in the English Renaissance*, Berkeley, CA: University of California Press.

Orlin, Lena Cowen (ed.) (2000) *Material London, ca. 1600*, Philadelphia, PA: University of Pennsylvania Press.

Scott, Michael (1982) *Renaissance Drama and the Modern Audience*, London: Macmillan.

Shapiro, James (1991) *Rival Playwrights: Marlowe, Jonson and Shakespeare*, New York, NY: Columbia University Press.

Smith, David L., Strier, Richard and Bevington, David (eds) (1995) *The Theatrical City: Culture, Theatre and Politics in London, 1576–1649*, Cambridge: Cambridge University Press.

Smith, Molly (1991) *The Darker World Within*, Madison, WI: Associated University Presses.

—— (1998) *Breaking Boundaries: Politics and Play in the Drama of Shakespeare and His Contemporaries*, Aldershot: Ashgate.

Stallybrass, Peter and White, Allon (1986) *The Politics and Poetics of Transgression*, London: Methuen.

Walker, Greg (1998) *The Politics of Performance in Early Renaissance Drama*, Cambridge: Cambridge University Press.

Whigham, Frank (1996) *Seizures of the Will in Early Modern English Drama*, Cambridge: Cambridge University Press.

### Genre studies

Allman, Eileen Jorge (1999) *Jacobean Revenge Tragedy and the Politics of Virtue*, Newark, DE: University of Delaware Press.

Comensoli, Viviana (1996) *'Household Business': Domestic Plays of Early Modern England*, Toronto: University of Toronto Press.

Gibbons, Brian (1980) *Jacobean City Comedy: A Study of Satiric Plays by Jonson, Marston and Middleton*, 2nd edition, London: Methuen.

Griswold, Wendy (1986) *Renaissance Revivals: City Comedy and Revenge Tragedy in the London Theatre, 1576–1980*, Chicago, IL: University of Chicago Press.

Hope, Jonathan and McMullan, Gordon (eds) (1992) *The Politics of Tragicomedy*, London: Routledge.

Kerrigan, John (1996) *Revenge Tragedy: Aeschylus to Armageddon*, Oxford: Clarendon Press.

Leggatt, Alexander (1999) *An Introduction to English Renaissance Comedy*, Manchester: Manchester University Press.

Lever, J. W. (1971) *The Tragedy of State*, London: Methuen.

Lewalski, Barbara Kiefer (ed.) (1986) *Renaissance Genres: Essays on Theory, History and Interpretation*, Cambridge, MA: Harvard University Press.

Lindley, David (ed.) (1984) *The Court Masque*, Manchester: Manchester University Press.

McMullan, Gordon and Hope, Jonathan (eds) (1992) *The Politics of Tragicomedy*, London: Routledge.

Orgel, Stephen (1965) *The Jonsonian Masque*, Cambridge, MA: Harvard University Press.

Palmer, Daryl W. (1992) *Hospitable Performances: Dramatic Genre and Cultural Practice in Early Modern England*, West Lafayette, IN: Purdue University Press.

Spikes, Judith Doolin (1977) 'The Jacobean History Play and the Myth of the Elect Nation', *Renaissance Drama*, n.s. 8: 117–49.

## Gender, sexuality and the body

Cerasano, S. P. and Wynne-Davies, Marion (eds) (1998) *Readings in Renaissance Women's Drama: Criticism, History and Performance 1594–1998*, London: Routledge.

Comensoli, Viviana and Russell, Anne (eds) (1998) *Enacting Gender on the Renaissance Stage*, Urbana, IL: University of Illinois Press.

Daileader, Celia R. (1998) *Eroticism on the Renaissance Stage*, Cambridge: Cambridge University Press.

Digangi, Mario (1997) *The Homoerotics of Early Modern Drama*, Cambridge: Cambridge University Press.

Ferguson, Margaret, Quilligan, Maureen and Vickers, Nancy J. (eds) (1986) *Rewriting the Renaissance: The Discourses of Sexual Difference in Early Modern Europe*, Chicago, IL, and London: University of Chicago Press.

Findlay, Alison (1999) *A Feminist Perspective on Renaissance Drama*, Oxford: Blackwell.

Findlay, Alison, Hodgson-Wright, Stephanie, with Williams, Gwen (2000) *Women and Dramatic Production, 1550–1700*, London: Longman.

Grantley, Darryl and Taunton, Nina (eds) (2000) *The Body in Late Medieval and Early Modern Culture*, Aldershot: Ashgate.

Howard, Jean (1988) 'Crossdressing, the Theatre and Gender Struggle in Early Modern England', *Shakespeare Quarterly*, 39: 418–40.

Jardine, Lisa (1983) *Still Harping on Daughters*, Brighton: Harvester Wheatsheaf.

Levine, Laura (1994) *Men in Women's Clothing*, Cambridge: Cambridge University Press.

McLuskie, Kathleen (1989) *Renaissance Dramatists*, Hemel Hempstead: Harvester Wheatsheaf.

Orgel, Stephen (1996) *Impersonations: The Performance of Gender in Shakespeare's England*, Cambridge: Cambridge University Press.

Paster, Gail Kern (1993) *The Body Embarrassed: Drama and the Disciplines of Shame in Early Modern England*, Ithaca, NY: Cornell University Press.

Rose, Mary Beth (1988) *The Expense of Spirit: Love and Sexuality in English Renaissance Drama*, Ithaca, NY, and London: Cornell University Press.

Shepherd, Simon (1981) *Amazons and Warrior Women: Varieties of Feminism in Seventeenth-century Drama*, Brighton: Harvester Wheatsheaf.

Traub, Valerie (1992) *Desire and Anxiety: Circulations of Sexuality in Shakespearean Drama*, London and New York, NY: Routledge.

Zimmerman, Susan (ed.) (1992) *Erotic Politics: Desire on the Renaissance Stage*, London and New York, NY: Routledge.

## Drama and the early modern 'other'

Gillies, John (1994) *Shakespeare and the Geography of Difference*, Cambridge: Cambridge University Press.

Hall, Kim (1995) *Things of Darkness: Economies of Race and Gender in Early Modern England*, Ithaca, NY: Cornell University Press.

Hendricks, Margo and Patricia Parker (eds) (1994) *Women, 'Race,' and Writing in the Early Modern Period*, London and New York, NY: Routledge.

Hoenselaars, A. J. (1992) *Images of Englishmen and Foreigners in the Drama of Shakespeare and his Contemporaries: A Study of Stage Characters and National Identity in English Renaissance Drama 1558–1642*, Rutherford, NJ: Fairleigh Dickinson University Press.

Hulme, Peter (1986) *Colonial Encounters: Europe and the Native Caribbean, 1492–1797*, London: Methuen.

Loomba, Ania (1989) *Gender, Race, Renaissance Drama*, Manchester: Manchester University Press.

MacDonald, Joyce Green (ed.) (1997) *Race, Ethnicity and Power in the Renaissance*, Madison, WI, and London: Farleigh Dickinson University Press/Associated University Presses.

Maquerlot, Jean-Pierre and Willems, Michele (eds) (1996) *Travel and Drama in Shakespeare's Time*, London: Longman.

Marrapodi, Michele, Hoenselaars, A. J., Cappuzzo, Marcello and Falzon Santucci, L. (eds) (1993) *Shakespeare's Italy: Functions of Italian Locations in Renaissance Drama*, Manchester: Manchester University Press.

Marrapodi, Michele and Hoenselaars, A. J. (eds) (1998) *The Italian World of English Renaissance Drama: Cultural Exchange and Intertextuality*, Newark, DE: University of Delaware Press.

Parr, Anthony (ed.) (2000) *Three Renaissance Travel Plays*, Manchester: Manchester University Press.

*Renaissance Drama*, 22 (1992): special issue on 'Renaissance Drama in an Age of Colonization'.

Shapiro, James (1996) *Shakespeare and the Jews*, New York, NY: Columbia University Press.

## Surveys and essay collections

Bluestone, Max and Rabkin, Norman (eds) (1970) *Shakespeare's Contemporaries: Modern Studies in English Renaissance Drama*, 2nd edition, Englewood Cliffs, NJ: Prentice-Hall Inc.

Brannigan, John (1998) *New Historicism and Cultural Materialism*, London: Macmillan.

Braunmuller, A. R. and Hattaway, Michael (1990) *The*

*Cambridge Companion to English Renaissance Drama*, Cambridge: Cambridge University Press.

Hadfield, Andrew (2001) *The English Renaissance 1500–1620*, Oxford: Blackwell.

Kastan, David Scott (1999) *A Companion to Shakespeare*, Oxford: Blackwell.

Kastan, David Scott and Stallybrass, Peter (eds) (1991) *Staging the Renaissance: Reinterpretations of Elizabethan and Jacobean Drama*, London: Routledge.

Kinney, Arthur (ed.) (2002) *A Companion to Renaissance Drama*, Oxford: Blackwell.

Leggatt, Alexander (1988) *English Drama: Shakespeare to the Restoration 1590–1660*, London: Longman.

Mousley, Andy (2000) *Renaissance Drama and Contemporary Literary Theory*, Basingstoke: Macmillan.

Rabkin, N. (1969) *Reinterpretations of Elizabethan Drama*, New York, NY: Columbia University Press.

Rynan, Kiernan (ed.) (1996) *New Historicism and Cultural Materialism: A Reader*, London: Arnold.

Wilson, Richard and Dutton, Richard (eds) (1992) *New Historicism and Renaissance Drama*, London: Longman.

## Histories of drama and the theatre

Bentley, Gerald Eades (1941–68) *The Jacobean and Caroline Stage*, 7 vols, Oxford: Clarendon Press.

—— (1984) *The Profession of Player in Shakespeare's Time, 1590–1642*, Princeton, NJ: Princeton University Press.

Berger, Thomas L., Bradford, William C. and Sondergard, Sidney L. (1998) *An Index of Characters in Early Modern Drama*, Cambridge: Cambridge University Press.

Bevington, David M. (1962) *From 'Mankind' to Marlowe*, Cambridge, MA: Harvard University Press.

Cairns, Christopher (ed.) (1999) *The Renaissance Theatre: Texts, Performance and Design*, 2 vols, Aldershot: Ashgate.

Chambers, E. K. (1923) *The Elizabethan Stage*, 4 vols, Oxford: Clarendon Press.

Cox, John D. and Kastan, David Scott (eds) (1997) *A New History of Early English Drama*, New York, NY: Columbia University Press.

Evans, G. Blakemore (ed.) (1989) *Elizabethan–Jacobean Drama*, London: A. & C. Black.

Farnham, Willard (1936) *The Medieval Heritage of Elizabethan Tragedy*, Oxford: Blackwell.

Foakes, R. A. (1985) *Illustrations of the English Stage 1580–1642*, Stanford, CA: Stanford University Press.

Graves, Robert B. (1999) *Lighting the Shakespearean Stage, 1567–1642*, Carbondale, IL: Southern Illinois University Press.

Gurr, Andrew (1996) *Playgoing in Shakespeare's London*, 2nd edition, Cambridge: Cambridge University Press.

Happé, Peter (1999) *English Drama before Shakespeare*, London: Longman.

Harbage, Alfred (1941) *Shakespeare's Audience*, New York, NY: Columbia University Press.

—— (1952) *Shakespeare and the Rival Traditions*, New York, NY: Macmillan.

Ingram, William (1992) *The Business of Playing: The Beginnings of the Adult Professional Theater in Elizabethan London*, Ithaca, NY, and London: Cornell University Press.

Leggatt, Alexander (1998) *English Stage Comedy 1490–1990*, London: Routledge.

Mann, David (1991) *The Elizabethan Player: Contemporary Stage Representation*, London and New York, NY: Routledge.

Murray, John Tucker (1910) *English Dramatic Companies 1558–1642*, 2 vols, London: Constable.

Orrell, John (1988) *The Human Stage: English Theatre Design, 1567–1640*, Cambridge: Cambridge University Press.

Potter, Lois, Craik, T. W. and Leech, Clifford (eds) (1998) *The Revels History of Drama in English*, London: Methuen.

Shepherd, Simon and Womack, Peter (1996) *English Drama: A Cultural History*, Oxford: Blackwell.

Southern, Richard (1973) *The Staging of Plays before Shakespeare*, London: Faber and Faber.

White, Martin (1998) *Renaissance Drama in Action*, London: Routledge.

Wickham, Glynne (1959–99) *Early English Stages 1300–1660*, 5 vols, London and New York, NY: Routledge.

—— (1985) *A History of the Theatre*, Oxford: Phaidon.

Wiseman, Susan (1998) *Drama and Politics in the English Civil War*, Cambridge: Cambridge University Press.

# Histories: social, political and cultural

## Surveys

Abbott, Mary (1996) *Life Cycles in England 1560–1720*, London and New York, NY: Routledge.

Briggs, Julia (1997) *This Stage-play World: Texts and Contexts, 1580–1625*, revised edition, Oxford: Oxford University Press.

Coward, Barry (1988) *Social Change and Continuity in Early Modern England 1550–1750*, London and New York, NY: Longman.

—— (1994) *The Stuart Age 1603–1714*, 2nd edition, London: Longman.

Hill, Christopher (1980) *The Century of Revolution 1603–1714*, 2nd edition, London: Thames and Hudson.

Laslett, Peter (1965) *The World We Have Lost*, London: Methuen.

Mervyn, James (1986) *Society, Politics and Culture: Studies in Early Modern England*, Cambridge: Cambridge University Press.

Rappaport, Steve (1989) *Worlds Within Worlds: Structures of Life in Sixteenth-century London*, Cambridge: Cambridge University Press.

Sharpe, J. A. (1987) *Early Modern England: A Social History 1550–1760*, Part II: *The Social Hierarchy and Social Change*, London: Edward Arnold.

Sinfield, Alan (1983) *Literature in Protestant England, 1560–1660*, London: Croom Helm.

Stone, Lawrence (1965) *Social Change and Revolution in England 1540–1640*, London: Longman.

Stroud, Angus (1999) *Stuart England*, London: Routledge.

Wrightson, Keith (1982) *English Society 1580–1680*, London: Unwin Hyman.

Youings, Joyce (1984) *Sixteenth Century England*, Harmondsworth: Penguin.

## Social status

Beier, A. L. (1985) *Masterless Men: The Vagrancy Problem in England 1560–1640*, London: Methuen.

De Grazia, Margreta, Quilligan, Maureen, and Stallybrass, Peter (eds) (1996) *Subject and Object in Renaissance Culture*, Cambridge: Cambridge University Press.

Heal, Felicity and Holmes, Clive (1994) *The Gentry in England and Wales 1500–1700*, London: Macmillan.

Pound, John (1971) *Poverty and Vagrancy in Tudor England*, London: Longman.

Sharpe, J. A. (1984) *Crime in Early Modern England 1550–1750*, London and New York, NY: Longman.

Stone, Lawrence (1965) *The Crisis of the Aristocracy 1558–1641*, Oxford: Oxford University Press.

Wright, Louis B. (1964) *Middle Class Culture in Elizabethan England*, London: Methuen.

## Family and marriage

Cressy, David (1997) *Birth, Marriage and Death: Ritual, Religion and the Life-cycle in Tudor and Stuart England*, Oxford: Oxford University Press.

Gillis, J. R. (1985) *For Better, For Worse*, Oxford: Oxford University Press.

Houlbrooke, Ralph (1984) *The English Family: 1450–1700*, London: Longman.

Ingram, Martin (1987) *Church Courts, Sex and Marriage in England 1570–1640*, Cambridge: Cambridge University Press.

—— (1989) *English Family Life, 1576–1716*, Oxford: Oxford University Press.

Orlin, Lena Cowen (1994) *Private Matters and Public Culture in Post-Reformation England*, Ithaca, NY, and London: Cornell University Press.

Powell, Chilton (1917) *English Domestic Relations 1487–1653*, New York, NY: Columbia University Press.

Stone, Lawrence (1979) *The Family, Sex and Marriage 1500–1800*, Harmondsworth: Pelican.

—— (1990) *The Road to Divorce: England 1530–1987*, Oxford: Oxford University Press.

Thomas, Keith (1959) 'The Double Standard', *Journal of the History of Ideas*, 20: 195–216.

Todd, Barbara (1985) 'The Remarrying Widow: A Stereotype Reconsidered', in Mary Prior (ed.) *Women in English Society 1500–1800*, London: Methuen.

## Gender relations, sexuality and the body

Bray, Alan (1988) *Homosexuality in Renaissance England*, 2nd edition, London: Gay Men's Press.

Breitenberg, Mark (1996) *Anxious Masculinity in Early Modern England*, Cambridge: Cambridge University Press.

Fletcher, Anthony (1995) *Gender, Sex and Subordination in England 1500–1800*, London and New Haven, CN: Yale University Press.

Goldberg, Jonathan (ed.) (1994) *Queering the Renaissance*, Durham, NC, and London: Duke University Press.

Gowing, Laura (1996) *Domestic Dangers: Women, Words, and Sex in Early Modern England*, Oxford: Clarendon Press.

Hull, Suzanne W. (1982) *Chaste, Silent and Obedient: English Books for Women 1475–1640*, San Marino, CA: Huntington Library Press.

Kelly-Gadol, Joan (1977) 'Did Women Have a Renaissance?', in Renate Bridenthal and Claudia Koonz (eds) *Becoming Visible: Women in European History*, Boston, MA: Houghton Mifflin.

Laurence, Anne (1994) *Women in England 1500–1760: A Social History*, London: Weidenfeld and Nicolson.

Maclean, Ian (1980) *The Renaissance Notion of Woman*, Cambridge: Cambridge University Press.

Matchinske, Megan (1998) *Writing, Gender and State in Early Modern England: Identity Formation and the Female Subject*, Cambridge: Cambridge University Press.

Mendelson, Sara and Crawford, Patricia (1998) *Women in Early Modern England 1550–1720*, Oxford: Oxford University Press.

Prior, Mary (ed.) (1985) *Women in English Society 1500–1800*, London: Methuen.

Sawday, Jonathan (1995) *The Body Emblazoned: Dissection and the Human Body in Renaissance Culture*, London: Routledge.

Smith, Bruce R. (1991) *Homosexual Desire in Shakespeare's England: A Cultural Poetics*, Chicago, IL: University of Chicago Press.

Summers, Claude (ed.) (1992) *Homosexuality in Renaissance and Enlightenment England: Literary Representations in Historical Context*, New York and London: Haworth Press. Also published as a special issue of *Journal of Homosexuality*, 23, 1–2.

Traub, Valerie, Kaplan, Lindsay M. and Callaghan, Dympna (eds) (1996) *Feminist Readings of Early Modern Culture: Emerging Subjects*, Cambridge: Cambridge University Press.

Turner, James Grantham (ed.) (1993) *Sexuality and Gender in Early Modern Europe: Institutions, Texts, Images*, Cambridge: Cambridge University Press.

Wilcox, Helen (ed.) (1996) *Women and Literature in Britain 1500–1700*, Cambridge: Cambridge University Press.

## Travel, colonialism, and the early modern 'other'

Andrew, Kenneth R. (1984) *Trade, Plunder and Settlement: Maritime Enterprise and the Genesis of the British Empire 1480–1630*, Cambridge: Cambridge University Press.

Bradshaw, Brendan, Hadfield, Andrew and Maly, Willy (eds) (1993) *Representing Ireland: Literature and the Origins of Conflict, 1534–1660*, Cambridge: Cambridge University Press.

Brennan, Elizabeth E. (1994) 'The Cheese and the Welsh: Foreigners in Elizabethan Literature', *Renaissance Studies*, 8: 40–64.

Chard, Chloë (1999) *Pleasure and Guilt on the Grand Tour*, Manchester: Manchester University Press.

Fuller, Mary C. (1996) *Voyages in Print: English Travel to America, 1576–1624*, Cambridge: Cambridge University Press.

Greenblatt, Stephen (1991) *Marvelous Possessions: The Wonder of the New World*, Oxford: Clarendon Press.

Hadfield, Andrew (1998) *Literature, Travel and Colonial Writing in the English Renaissance 1545–1625*, Oxford: Clarendon Press.

Hall, Kim F. (1995) *Things of Darkness: Economies of Race and*

*Gender in Early Modern England*, Ithaca, NY: Cornell University Press.

Harris, Jonathan Gil (1998) *Foreign Bodies and the Body Politic: Discourses of Social Pathology in Early Modern England*, Cambridge: Cambridge University Press.

Helgerson, Richard (1992) *Forms of Nationhood: The Elizabethan Writing of England*, Chicago, IL: University of Chicago Press.

Hulme, Peter (1986) *Colonial Encounters: Europe and the Native Caribbean 1492–1797*, London: Routledge.

Knapp, Jeffrey (1992) *An Empire Nowhere: England, America, and Literature from Utopia to The Tempest*, Berkeley, CA: University of California Press.

Kupperman, Karen Ordahl (1980) *Settling with the Indians: The Meeting of English and Indian Cultures in America, 1580–1640*, Totowa, NJ: Rowman and Littlefield.

Linton, Joan Pong (1998) *The Romance of the New World: Gender and the Literary Formations of English Colonialism*, Cambridge: Cambridge University Press.

McEachern, Claire (1996) *The Poetics of English Nationhood, 1590–1612*, Cambridge: Cambridge University Press.

Ralegh, Sir Walter (1997) *The Discoverie of the Large, Rich, and Bewtiful Empyre of Gviana*, Neil L. Whitehead (ed.), Manchester: Manchester University Press.

Sheehan, Bernard W. (1980) *Savagism and Civility: Indians and Englishmen in Colonial Virginia*, Cambridge: Cambridge University Press.

## Religion and the church

Collinson, Patrick (1982) *Godly People: Essays on English Protestantism and Puritanism*, London: Hambledon Press.

—— (1982) *The Religion of Protestants: The Church in English Society 1559–1625*, Oxford: Clarendon Press.

—— (1988) *The Birthpangs of Protestantism: Religion and Cultural Change in the Sixteenth and Seventeenth Centuries*, Basingstoke: Macmillan.

—— (1989) *The Puritan Character: Polemics and Polarities in Early Seventeenth-century English Culture*, Los Angeles, CA: University of California Press.

Crawford, Patricia (1993) *Women and Religion in England 1500–1720*, London and New York, NY: Routledge.

Dickens, A. G. (1989) *The English Reformation*, 2nd edition, London: Batsford.

Fletcher, Anthony and Roberts, Peter (eds) (1994) *Religion, Culture and Society in Early Modern Britain*, Cambridge: Cambridge University Press.

Haigh, Christopher (1993) *English Reformations: Religion, Politics and Society under the Tudors*, Oxford: Clarendon Press.

Hill, Christopher (1964) *Society and Puritanism in Pre-revolutionary England*, London: Secker and Warburg.

Lamont, William (1996) *Puritanism and Historical Controversy*, London: UCL.

Maltby, Judith (1998) *Prayer Book and People in Elizabethan and Early Stuart England*, Cambridge: Cambridge University Press.

McEachern, Claire and Shuger, Debora (eds) (1997) *Religion and Culture in Renaissance England*, Cambridge: Cambridge University Press.

Rosman, Doreen (1996) *From Catholic to Protestant*, London: UCL.

Rowlands, Marie (1985) 'Recusant Women *1560–1640*', in

Mary Prior (ed.) *Women in English Society 1500–1800*, London: Methuen.

Shell, Alison (1999) *Catholicism, Controversy and the English Literary Imagination 1558–1660*, Cambridge: Cambridge University Press.

Thomas, Keith (1974) *Religion and the Decline of Magic*, Harmondsworth: Penguin.

## Politics, monarchy and government

Berry, Philippa (1989) *Of Chastity and Power: Elizabethan Literature and the Unmarried Queen*, London: Routledge.

Elton, G. R. (1974) *Studies in Tudor and Stuart Politics and Government*, Cambridge: Cambridge University Press.

*English Literary Renaissance* (1996), special issue on 'Monarchs', 26, 3.

Guy, John (1990) *Tudor England*, Oxford: Oxford University Press.

—— (ed.) (1995) *The Reign of Elizabeth I: Court and Culture in the Last Decade*, Cambridge: Cambridge University Press.

Hackett, Helen (1995) *Virgin Mother, Maiden Queen: Elizabeth I and the Cult of the Virgin Mary*, Basingstoke: Macmillan.

Haynes, Alan (1992) *Invisible Power: The Elizabethan Secret Services 1570–1603*, Stroud: Alan Sutton Publishing.

Hopkins, Lisa (1990) *Elizabeth I and Her Court*, London and New York, NY: Vision Press and St Martin's Press.

Kishlansky, Mark (1996) *A Monarchy Transformed: Britain 1603–1714*, London: Penguin.

Russell, Conrad (1971) *The Crisis of the Parliaments: English History 1509–1660*, Oxford: Oxford University Press.

Smith, Alan G. (1984) *The Emergence of a Nation State 1529–1660*, London: Longman.

Underdown, David (1992) *Revel, Riot and Rebellion: Popular Politics and Culture in England 1603–1660*, Oxford: Clarendon Press.

Williams, Penry (1979) *The Tudor Regime*, Oxford: Clarendon Press.

## Literacy and education

Barry, Jonathan (1995) 'Literacy and Literature in Popular Culture: Reading and Writing in Historical Perspective', in Tim Harris (ed.) *Popular Culture in England, c. 1500–1850*, London: Macmillan.

Cressy, David (1980) *Literacy and the Social Order*, Cambridge: Cambridge University Press.

Elsky, Martin (1989) *Authorizing Words: Speech, Writing, and Print in the English Renaissance*, Ithaca, NY, and London: Cornell University Press.

Jagodzinski, Cecile M. (1999) *Privacy and Print: Reading and Writing in Seventeenth-Century England*, Charlottesville, VA, University Press of Virginia.

O'Day, Rosemary (1982) *Education and Society 1500–1800: The Social Foundations of Education in Early Modern Britain*, London and New York, NY: Longman.

Patterson, Annabel (1984) *Censorship and Interpretation: The Conditions of Writing and Reading in Early Modern England*, Madison, WI: University of Wisconsin Press.

Raven, James, Small, Helen and Taylor, Naomi (eds) (1996) *The Practice and Representation of Reading in England*, Cambridge: Cambridge University Press.

Simon, Joan (1966) *Education and Society in Tudor England*, Cambridge: Cambridge University Press.

Spufford, Margaret (1981) *Small Books and Pleasant Histories: Popular Fiction and Its Readership in Seventeenth-century England*, London: Methuen.

Watt, Tessa (1991) *Cheap Print and Popular Piety 1550–1640*, Cambridge: Cambridge University Press.

Wheale, Nigel (1999) *Writing and Society: Literacy, Print and Politics in Britain 1590–1660*, London: Routledge.

## Sourcebooks

Aughterson, Kate (ed.) (1995) *Renaissance Woman: Constructions of Femininity in England*, London and New York, NY: Routledge.

Cerasano, S. P. and Wynne-Davies, Marion (eds) (1996) *Renaissance Drama by Women: Texts and Documents*, London and New York, NY: Routledge.

Crawford, Patricia and Gowing, Laura (eds) (2000) *Women's Worlds in Seventeenth-century England: A Sourcebook*, London and New York, NY: Routledge.

Davis, Lloyd (1998) *Gender and Sexuality in the English Renaissance*, London: Garland.

Keeble, N. H. (ed.) (1994) *The Cultural Identity of Seventeenth-Century Woman: A Reader*, London and New York, NY: Routledge.

McCormick, Ian (ed.) (1997) *Secret Sexualities: A Sourcebook of 17th and 18th Century Writing*, London and New York, NY: Routledge.

Rutter, Carol Chillington (ed.) (1999) *Documents of the Rose Playhouse*, Manchester: Manchester University Press.

# Journals

The journals which focus most specifically on early modern drama and literature are:

*Cahiers Elisabéthains*
*English Literary Renaissance*
*Medieval and Renaissance Drama in England*
*Modern Philology*
*Renaissance Drama*
*Renaissance Quarterly*
*Renaissance and Reformation*
*Renaissance Studies*
*The Seventeenth Century*
*Shakespeare Quarterly*
*Shakespeare Survey*
*Studies in English Literature 1500–1900*

Journals with a broader historical focus, but which frequently publish research on early modern culture, include:

*Critical Quarterly*
*English Literary History*
*Gender, Place and Culture*
*Literature and History*
*The Journal of British Studies*
*New Literary History*

*Textual Practice*
*Tulsa Studies in Women's Literature*
*Women's Writing*

Journals publishing work on social and political history include:

*Continuity and Change*
*English Historical Review*
*The Historical Journal*
*History*
*Past and Present*

Recommended, too, is *The Year's Work in English Studies*, an annual publication comprising a series of bibliographical essays offering an overview of new critical work across the field of literary studies. It is invaluable for identifying new titles relating to a given author or topic.

Electronic journals relevant to the field include:

*Comitatus: A Journal of Medieval and Renaissance Studies*
http://www.humnet.ucla.edu/humnet/cmrs/publications/comitatus/comitatu.htm

*Early Modern Literary Studies*
http://www.shu.ac.uk/emls/emlshome.html

*Exemplaria: A Journal of Theory in Medieval and Renaissance Studies*
http://www.english.ufl.edu/exemplaria/

*Explorations in Renaissance Culture*
http://www.smsu.edu/English/eirc/eirc.html

*Renaissance Forum*
http://www.hull.ac.uk/renforum/index.html

# Websites

These link to a wide range of sites relating to early modern writing and history, including on-line, often full-text, editions of early modern writing as well as critical materials. Most sites are freely accessible, but a few are available only through subscription.

*The Early Modern Drama Database*
http://www.columbia.edu/~tdk3/earlymodern.html. See, too, the linked site, *Early Modern Chronology 1453–1715*, at
http://www.columbia.edu/~tdk3/chronology.html

*Literary Resources on the Net*
http://andromeda.rutgers.edu/~jlynch/Lit/ren.html

*Luminarium*
http://www.luminarium.org/lumina.htm

*Renaissance Texts*
http://www.towson.edu/~tinkler/bookmark/rentext.html

*Renaissance Women Online*
http://www.wwp.brown.edu/texts/rwoentry.html

*Renascence Editions*
http://www.uoregon.edu/~rbear/ren.htm

*The Voice of the Shuttle*
http://vos.ucsb.edu/

## *The Routledge Anthology of Renaissance Drama* website

This anthology has its own website. It includes a range of early modern documents selected for their relevance to the plays included in the volume. There are, for example, source texts for some of the plays, accounts of early modern theatres and play-goers, and examples of some of the attacks on and defences of the theatres made at the time. The site also provides links which will help readers undertaking further research into the drama of the English Renaissance.

Visit *The Routledge Anthology of Renaissance Drama* website at www.routledge.com/textbooks/0415187346

# Chronology of English Culture and Society 1558–1642

All the theatres referenced here were in London. The plays are dated by their first known performance or, where there is some doubt about this, the date that critics agree is the most likely. Non-dramatic texts are usually referenced by their publication date. However, where the text circulated earlier in manuscript form, it is included under the earlier date with the date of first publication indicated in brackets.

## Key

- (Pb): Public theatre (also known as amphitheatre or arena theatres) used by adult companies
- (Pt): Private theatre (also known as hall or indoor theatres) initially used by boys', later by adult, companies

| Date | Events | Theatre events | Plays and masques | Non-dramatic texts |
|------|--------|----------------|-------------------|--------------------|
| 1558 | Death of Mary Tudor; accession of Elizabeth I to throne.<br><br>Church of England re-established | | | Knox, *First Blast of the Trumpet against the Monstrous Regiment of Women* |
| 1559 | Act of Supremacy and Act of Uniformity, renouncing Pope's authority in England<br><br>Book of Common Prayer reissued | | | Baldwin, Ferrers *et al.*, *A Mirror for Magistrates* |
| 1560 | | | | 'Geneva' Bible<br><br>Whitehorne's translation of Machiavelli, *The Art of War* |
| 1561 | | | | Hoby's translation of Castiglione, *The Courtier* |
| 1562 | Hawkins begins slaving expeditions to Africa | | Norton and Sackville, *Gorboduc* | |
| 1563 | Convocation of Anglican church approves 39 Articles<br><br>Plague in London; kills thousands<br><br>Poor Law passed: contributions to poor relief made compulsory | | | Foxe, *Acts and Monuments* (in English; first published in Latin in 1559) |
| 1564 | Court of High Commission established in Ireland to enforce conformity<br><br>Riots in Ireland against English plantation | | | |

| Date | Events | Theatre events | Plays and masques | Non-dramatic texts |
|------|--------|----------------|-------------------|--------------------|
| 1565 | Sir Henry Sidney made Lord Deputy of Ireland | | | Golding's translation of Ovid, *Metamorphoses* |
| 1566 | Rebellion against Mary, Queen of Scots | | Gascoigne, *Supposes* | Painter, *Palace of Pleasure* |
| 1567 | Abdication of Mary, Queen of Scots, and accession of James VI to Scottish throne | Red Lion theatre (Pb), Whitechapel, built | | |
| 1568 | Mary, Queen of Scots, flees to England | | | Bishops' Bible |
| 1569 | Pro-Catholic rising in north of England | | | |
| | Munster rebellion in Ireland defeated by Sidney | | | |
| 1570 | Elizabeth I excommunicated by Pope Pius V | | | Ascham, *The Schoolmaster* |
| 1571 | Parliament legislates against recusants | | | |
| | Foxe's *Acts and Monuments* to be placed in all cathedral and collegiate churches | | | |
| 1572 | St Bartholomew's Day massacre of Huguenots in Paris | Actors not under aristocratic patronage declared vagabonds | | |
| | Anti-vagrancy law enacted | | | |
| 1573 | Earl of Essex granted plantation rights in Ireland | | Gascoigne, *Jocasta* | Gascoigne, *Adventures of Master F. J.* |
| 1574 | Statutes of Apparel (sumptuary laws) reissued | | | |
| 1575 | Essex's army massacres inhabitants of Rathlin Island | Paul's playhouse (Pt) opens | | Tasso, *Gerusalemme Liberata* |
| 1576 | First Roman Catholic priest executed at Tyburn | The Theatre (Pb), Shoreditch, built; replaces Red Lion | | Digges's translation of Copernicus |
| | Frobisher resumes search for North-West passage | First Blackfriars theatre (Pt) built | | |
| | Act passed requiring all corporate towns to establish workhouses | Theatre at Newington Butts built | | |
| 1577 | Drake sets out to circumnavigate the world | Curtain theatre (Pb), Shoreditch, built; not used for plays after 1625 | | Holinshed, *Chronicles of England, Scotland and Ireland* |
| | | | | Sidney, 'Old' *Arcadia* |
| 1578 | Drake sails into the Pacific Ocean | | | Lyly, *Euphues; The Anatomy of Wit* |
| 1579 | Drake claims 'New Albion' (now part of California) for England | | Sidney, *The Lady of May* | Gosson, *School of Abuse* |
| | | | | North's translation of Plutarch, *Lives* |
| | Start of Munster rebellion (1579–83) | | | Spenser, *Shepherd's Calendar* |

| Date | Events | Theatre events | Plays and masques | Non-dramatic texts |
|------|--------|----------------|-------------------|--------------------|
| 1580 | Lord Grey made Lord Deputy of Ireland; crushes rebellion; many massacred | Performance of plays on Sunday forbidden | | Montaigne, *Essais* |
| | Drake returns to England, having sailed round the world | | | Sidney, *Apology for Poetry* (published 1595) |
| | Jesuit missionaries arrive in Dover | | | |
| 1581 | Laws against Roman Catholics passed | | Newton, *Seneca, His Ten Tragedies Translated into English* | Hall, *Ten Books of Homer's Iliad* |
| | | | Peele, *The Arraignment of Paris* | Sidney, *Astrophil and Stella* (published 1591) |
| 1582 | Gilbert lands in Newfoundland (now part of Canada) and declares English sovereignty | | | Watson, *Hecatompathia, or The Passionate Century of Love* |
| 1583 | Ralegh sails to Virginia | Queen's Men formed | | Stubbes, *The Anatomy of Abuses* |
| | | Blackfriars theatre closes | | |
| 1584 | Newfoundland established as colony | | Lyly, *Campaspe* | Knox, *History of the Reformation in Scotland* |
| | Ralegh establishes colony at Roanoke, Virginia | | | Hakluyt, 'Discourse of Western Planting' |
| 1585 | Munster plantation in Ireland established | | Kyd, *The Spanish Tragedy* | |
| 1586 | Treaty of Berwick between Scots and English | | Anon., *The Famous Victories of Henry V* | Camden, *Britannia* (in Latin; Holland's English translation published 1610) |
| | Roanoke colony fails; evacuated by Drake | | | Sidney, 'New' *Arcadia* (published 1590) |
| | Death of Sir Philip Sidney | | | Webbe, *Discourse of English Poesy* |
| 1587 | Mary, Queen of Scots executed | Rose theatre (Pb), Bankside, built; demolished c. 1606 | Marlowe, *Tamburlaine the Great, Parts I and II* | Holinshed, *Chronicles of England, Scotland and Ireland*, 2nd edition |
| | Pope begins crusade against England | | | |
| | Second Roanoke colony begun | | | |
| 1588 | Spanish Armada defeated | Death of Richard Tarlton (clown with the Queen's Men) | Lyly, *Endymion* | Harriot, *A Brief and True Report of . . . Virginia* |
| | | | Anon., *Mucedorus* | |
| 1589 | English attacks on coast of Portugal | | Anon., *A Warning for Fair Women* | Hakluyt, *Principal Navigations* |
| | | | Peele, *The Battle of Alcazar* | Nashe, *Anatomy of Absurdity* |
| | | | Greene, *Friar Bacon and Friar Bungay* | Puttenham, *Art of English Poesy* |
| | | | Marlowe, *Dr Faustus; The Jew of Malta* | 'Marprelate' tracts |
| 1590 | Roanoke settlers disappear | Paul's playhouse closes | Anon., *King Leir* | Lodge, *Rosalind* |
| | | | Shakespeare, *Henry VI, Parts II and III; The Two Gentlemen of Verona* | Spenser, *Faerie Queene, Part I* |

| Date | Events | Theatre events | Plays and masques | Non-dramatic texts |
|------|--------|----------------|-------------------|--------------------|
| 1591 | | | Anon., *The True Tragedy of Richard III* | Harrington's translation of Ariosto, *Orlando Furioso* |
| | | | Peele, *Edward I; The Old Wives' Tale* | Ralegh, *A Report about . . . the Isles of Azores* |
| | | | Shakespeare, *Henry VI, Part I; The Taming of the Shrew* | |
| 1592 | Establishment of Presbyterian Church in Scotland | Plague; theatres close for two years | Anon., *Arden of Faversham* | Lyly, *Gallathea* |
| | | First of Lord Mayor's petitions against stage plays | Anon., *Thomas of Woodstock* | |
| | | | Marlowe, *Edward II* | |
| | | | Shakespeare, *The Comedy of Errors* | |
| 1593 | | Death of Marlowe | Marlowe, *The Massacre at Paris* | Donne writing *Songs and Sonnets* |
| | | | Shakespeare, *Titus Andronicus; Richard III* | Marlowe, *Hero and Leander* |
| | | | Mary Sidney, *Antonius* | Shakespeare, *Venus and Adonis* |
| 1594 | First of series of poor harvests, leading to riots | Theatres reopen | Heywood, *The Four Prentices of London* | Drayton, *Piers Gaveston* |
| | Lord Mayor's conference on problem of rogues in London | Death of Kyd | Shakespeare, *Love's Labours Lost* | Nashe, *The Unfortunate Traveller* |
| | Tyrone's Irish rebellion; start of Nine Years' War | | Yarington, *Two Lamentable Tragedies* | Shakespeare, *The Rape of Lucrece* |
| 1595 | Death of Sir Francis Drake | Swan theatre (Pb), Bankside, built; little used after 1597, in disrepair by 1632 | Munday *et al.*, *Sir Thomas More* | Shakespeare, *Sonnets* (published 1609) |
| | Apprentices and masterless men riot in Southwark | | Shakespeare, *Richard II; Romeo and Juliet; A Midsummer Night's Dream* | Spenser, *Amoretti* |
| | Fear of second Armada | | | |
| 1596 | Riots against enclosures and grain prices | Second Blackfriars theatre (Pt) built, but unable to open owing to residents' petition | Jonson, *A Tale of a Tub* | Deloney, *Jack of Newbury* |
| | Essex's attack on Cadiz | | Shakespeare, *King John; The Merchant of Venice* | Ralegh, *Discovery of Guiana* |
| | | | | Spenser, *View of the Present State of Ireland; Faerie Queene, Part II* |
| 1597 | Second Armada fails | | Chapman, *A Humorous Day's Mirth* | Francis Bacon, *Essays* |
| | English campaign in Low Countries | | Jonson, *The Case is Altered* | James Stuart, *Demonology* |
| | Grain riots | | Shakespeare, *Henry IV, Parts I and II; The Merry Wives of Windsor* | |
| | Poor Law enacted; reinforced Act of 1563 | | | |
| 1598 | Anti-vagrancy law passed, making provision for punishment of the masterless | The theatre dismantled; timbers used as frame for the Globe theatre | Chettle and Munday, *Robin Hood, Parts I and II* | Florio, *A World of Words* (Italian–English dictionary) |
| | | | Jonson, *Every Man in His Humour* | Hakluyt, *Principal Navigations*, 2nd edition, 3 vols (1598–1600) |
| | | | Porter, *The Two Angry Women of Abingdon* | Stow, *A Survey of London* |
| | | | Shakespeare, *Much Ado About Nothing* | |

| Date | Events | Theatre events | Plays and masques | Non-dramatic texts |
|------|--------|----------------|-------------------|--------------------|
| 1599 | Earl of Essex's campaign in Ireland<br><br>Death of Spenser | Globe theatre (Pb), Bankside, opens<br><br>Second Blackfriars theatre (Pt) opens<br><br>Paul's playhouse (Pt) reopens | Dekker, *The Shoemaker's Holiday*; *Old Fortunatus*<br><br>Heywood *et al.*; *Edward IV, Parts I and II*<br><br>Jonson, *Every Man Out of His Humour*<br><br>Marston, *Antonio and Mellida*; *Histriomastix*<br><br>Shakespeare, *Henry V*; *As You Like It*; *Julius Caesar* | Daniel, *Poetical Essays*<br><br>James Stuart, *Basilikon Doron* |
| 1600 | East India Company founded<br><br>Essex under house arrest in London | Fortune theatre (Pb), Cripplegate, opens | Chettle, Dekker and Haughton, *Patient Grissel*<br><br>Marston, *Antonio's Revenge*<br><br>Shakespeare, *Hamlet* | Leo Africanus, *History and Description of Africa* |
| 1601 | Essex's revolt and execution<br><br>Further Poor Law enacted<br><br>Defeat of Spanish and Irish forces at Battle of Kinsale | Boar's Head theatre (Pb), Whitechapel, opens (converted inn) | Dekker, *Satiromastix*<br><br>Jonson, *Cynthia's Revels*; *Poetaster*<br><br>Shakespeare, *Twelfth Night* | Dent, *The Plain Man's Pathway to Heaven* |
| 1602 | Re-conquest of Ireland begins<br><br>Bodleian Library founded in Oxford | | Chettle, *The Tragedy of Hoffman*<br><br>Dekker, *The Merry Devil of Edmonton*<br><br>Shakespeare, *Troilus and Cressida* | Lodge's translation of Josephus, *Jewish Antiquities* |
| 1603 | Death of Queen Elizabeth; James VI of Scotland accedes to English throne as James I<br><br>Witchcraft made punishable offence in English law<br><br>Ralegh imprisoned for treason | James I becomes patron of the two boys' theatre companies<br><br>Theatres closed because of plague; 33,500 die in London | Heywood, *A Woman Killed with Kindness*<br><br>Jonson, *Sejanus*<br><br>Marston, *The Malcontent*<br><br>Shakespeare, *Measure for Measure* | Knolles, *General History of the Turks*<br><br>Daniel, *Defence of Rhyme*<br><br>Florio's translation of Montaigne, *Essays* (including 'Of Cannibals')<br><br>James Stuart, *The True Law of Free Monarchies* |
| 1604 | Peace treaty with Spain<br><br>Hampton Court conference: James I rejects Puritan requests for Church of England reform<br><br>James I declared king of 'Great Britain, France and Ireland'<br><br>Anti-vagrancy law of 1597 expanded | Theatres reopen<br><br>Red Bull theatre (Pb), Clerkenwell, opens (converted inn); replaces Boar's Head | Chapman, *Bussy d'Ambois*<br><br>Cary, *The Tragedy of Mariam*<br><br>Daniel, *Philotas*; *The Vision of the Twelve Goddesses*<br><br>Dekker and Webster, *Westward Ho!*<br><br>Heywood, *The Wise Woman of Hogsdon*<br><br>Marston, *The Dutch Courtesan*<br><br>Shakespeare, *Othello*; *All's Well That Ends Well* | Dallington, *The View of France*<br><br>James Stuart, *Counterblast to Tobacco* |

| Date | Events | Theatre events | Plays and masques | Non-dramatic texts |
|---|---|---|---|---|
| 1605 | Gunpowder Plot<br><br>Weymouth explores coast of New England | | Anon., *A Yorkshire Tragedy*<br><br>Chapman, Jonson and Marston, *Eastward Ho!*<br><br>Dekker and Webster, *Northward Ho!*<br><br>Heywood, *If You Know Not Me You Know Nobody*<br><br>Jonson, *The Masque of Blackness*<br><br>Middleton, *Michaelmas Term*; *A Trick to Catch the Old One*<br><br>Shakespeare, *King Lear* | Bacon, *Advancement of Learning* |
| 1606 | Suppression of Roman Catholics by Parliament<br><br>Dutch explore northern coast of 'New Holland' (Australia)<br><br>Virginia Company formed | Whitefriars theatre (Pt) built<br><br>Rose theatre demolished<br><br>Paul's playhouse closes<br><br>'Act to Restrain the Abuses of the Players' passed | Day, *The Isle of Gulls*<br>Jonson, *Volpone*; *Hymenaei*<br>Middleton, *A Mad World, My Masters*<br>Middleton (or Tourneur), *The Revenger's Tragedy*<br>Shakespeare, *Macbeth*; *Antony and Cleopatra* | Drayton, *Poems Lyric and Pastoral* |
| 1607 | English colony founded in Jamestown, Virginia, by John Smith | | Beaumont, *The Knight of the Burning Pestle*<br><br>Chapman, *The Tragedy of Bussy d'Ambois*<br><br>Day, Rowley and Wilkins, *The Travels of the Three English Brothers*<br><br>Middleton, *Your Five Gallants*<br><br>Shakespeare, *Pericles*<br><br>Wilkins, *The Miseries of Enforced Marriage* | |
| 1608 | Quebec founded in 'New France' (now Canada)<br><br>Parliament rejects union with Scotland | King's Men (Shakespeare's company) lease Blackfriars theatre (Pt)<br><br>Theatres close because of plague | Jonson, *Masque of Beauty*<br><br>Shakespeare, *Coriolanus* | Donne writing 'Holy Sonnets' and other religious poems<br><br>Dekker, *The Bellman of London*; *Lanthorn and Candlelight* |
| 1609 | Plantation of Ulster<br><br>Thomas Gates shipwrecked in Bermuda | Theatres reopen in December | Heywood and Rowley, *Fortune by Land and Sea*<br><br>Jonson, *Masque of Queens*; *Epicoene, or The Silent Woman*<br><br>Shakespeare, *The Winter's Tale* | Filmer, *Patriarcha* |

| Date | Events | Theatre events | Plays and masques | Non-dramatic texts |
|---|---|---|---|---|
| 1610 | New anti-vagrancy law passed<br><br>Arbella Stuart, James I's cousin, imprisoned after plot to put her on throne | | Beaumont and Fletcher, *The Maid's Tragedy*<br><br>Chapman, *The Revenge of Bussy D'Ambois*<br><br>Daniel, *Tethys' Festival*<br><br>Jonson, *The Alchemist*<br><br>Shakespeare, *Cymbeline* | Galileo, *Sidereal Messenger* (published in Latin)<br><br>Council of Virginia, *True Declaration of the Colony in Virginia*<br><br>Jourdain, *Discovery of the Bermudas*; Strachey, *True Reportory of the Wrack* (published 1625); both are accounts of Gates' 1609 shipwreck |
| 1611 | | | Beaumont and Fletcher, *A King and No King*<br><br>Dekker, *If It Be Not Good, the Devil Is In It*<br><br>Jonson, *Oberon*; *Cataline His Conspiracy*<br><br>Middleton and Dekker, *The Roaring Girl*<br><br>Shakespeare, *The Tempest*<br><br>Tourneur, *The Atheist's Tragedy* | 'Authorised' (King James) version of the Bible<br><br>Coryat, *Crudities*<br><br>Lanyer, *Salve Deus Rex Judeaorum* |
| 1612 | Lancashire witches hanged<br><br>Prince Henry dies<br><br>Bermuda colonised under Virginia Company charter<br><br>East India Company settles in Gujerat, India | | Fletcher, *The Captain*<br><br>Webster, *The White Devil* | Bacon, *Essays* (2nd edition)<br><br>Drayton, *Poly-Olbion, Part I*<br><br>Heywood, *An Apology for Actors* |
| 1613 | Frances Howard's divorce approved; she marries Somerset; murder of Thomas Overbury | Globe theatre burns down | Campion, *The Somerset Masque*<br><br>Fletcher, *The Scornful Lady*<br><br>Jonson, *The Irish Masque at Court*<br><br>Middleton, *A Chaste Maid in Cheapside*<br><br>Shakespeare and Fletcher, *Henry VIII*; *The Two Noble Kinsmen* | |
| 1614 | Parliament dissolved; not called again until 1621 | Second Globe theatre (Pb) built<br><br>Hope theatre (Pb) built; after 1617 used mainly for bear- and bull-baiting | Fletcher, *Wit Without Money*<br><br>Jonson, *Bartholomew Fair*<br><br>Webster, *The Duchess of Malfi* | Chapman's translation of Homer's *Odyssey*, Books I–XII<br><br>Ralegh, *History of the World* |
| 1615 | John Smith explores coast of New England<br><br>Trial and conviction of Frances Howard for murder of Overbury<br><br>Death of Arbella Stuart in the Tower | | Middleton, *The Witch* | Chapman's translation of the *Odyssey*, Books XIII–XIV<br><br>Crooke, *Microcosmographia: A Description of the Body of Man* |

| Date | Events | Theatre events | Plays and masques | Non-dramatic texts |
|------|--------|----------------|-------------------|--------------------|
| 1616 | King sells peerages to raise money | Deaths of Shakespeare and Beaumont | Jonson, *The Devil is an Ass* | Jonson, *Workes* |
| | Pocohontas arrives in England | Cockpit theatre (Pt) opens | Middleton and Rowley, *A Fair Quarrel* | James Stuart, *Works* |
| | Harvey lectures on circulation of the blood | | | |
| | Ralegh released for final expedition to Guiana | | | |
| 1617 | | Cockpit theatre burns down and is rebuilt; hereafter known as the Phoenix | Jonson, *Christmas His Masque* | Fynes Moryson, *Itinerary Containing His Ten Years Travel* |
| | | | Webster, *The Devil's Law Case* | |
| 1618 | Execution of Ralegh, following his third failed expedition to South America | | Fletcher, *The Loyal Subject* | |
| | Start of Thirty Years' War; fought mostly in Germany, between Catholics and Protestants | | Jonson, *Pleasure Reconciled to Virtue* | |
| | Virginia Charter of Liberties granted | | Middleton, *Hengist, King of Kent* | |
| | Bacon made Lord Chancellor | | | |
| | James I issues 'Declaration concerning Sports' | | | |
| 1619 | First African slaves transported into Jamestown by Dutch | | Ford, *The Laws of Candy* | |
| | Queen Anne dies | | | |
| 1620 | Freedom of worship granted to Roman Catholics in England | | Fletcher, *Women Pleased* | Bacon, *Novum Organum* |
| | Pilgrim Fathers sail from Plymouth to Massachusetts in the *Mayflower* | | Jonson, *News from the New World* | |
| | James I pronounces against women wearing men's apparel | | Middleton and Rowley, *The World Tossed at Tennis* | |
| 1621 | First of three years of bad harvests | Fortune theatre (Pb) burns down; rebuilt | Dekker, Ford and Rowley, *The Witch of Edmonton* | Burton, *Anatomy of Melancholy* |
| | Donne becomes Dean of St Paul's | | Fletcher, *The Wild Goose Chase* | Wroth, *Urania* |
| | Parliament called; Bacon impeached | | | |
| 1622 | Massacre of 300 colonists at Jamestown by Powhatan confederacy | | Fletcher and Massinger, *The Sea Voyage* | Publication in London of *The Courant or Weekly News*, an early newspaper |
| | | | Massinger, *The Duke of Milan* | Drayton, *Poly-Olbion, Part II* |
| | | | Middleton and Rowley, *The Changeling* | |
| 1623 | | | Dekker and Ford, *The Spanish Gypsy* | Shakespeare, 'The First Folio' |
| | | | Fletcher, *The Wandering Lovers* | |

| Date | Events | Theatre events | Plays and masques | Non-dramatic texts |
|---|---|---|---|---|
| 1624 | Collapse of Virginia Company | | Fletcher, *Rule a Wife and Have a Wife* | Smith, *General History of Virginia, New England, and the Summer Isles* |
| | | | Heywood, *The Captives* | |
| | | | Jonson, *Neptune's Triumph for the Return of Albion* | |
| | | | Middleton, *A Game at Chess* | |
| 1625 | Death of James I; accession of his son as Charles I, marriage to Henrietta Maria | Theatres closed for several months, owing to plague | Heywood, *The English Traveller* | Purchas, *Purchas His Pilgrims* |
| | Plague; 35,500 deaths in London | Death of Fletcher | Jonson, *The Fortunate Isles, and Their Union* | |
| | | | Massinger, *A New Way to Pay Old Debts* | |
| | | | Middleton, *Women Beware Women* | |
| | | | Webster and Rowley, *A Cure for a Cuckold* | |
| 1626 | Death of Bacon | | Jonson, *The Staple of News* | Bacon, *New Atlantis* |
| | | | Massinger, *The Roman Actor* | Cary, *The Raign and Death of Edward II* |
| | | | Shirley, *The Maid's Revenge* | Sandys's translation of Ovid, *Metamorphoses* |
| 1627 | Barbados colonised by English | Death of Middleton | Davenant, *The Cruel Brother* | |
| 1628 | | | Ford, *The Lover's Melancholy* | Harvey, *On the Motion of the Heart and Blood* |
| | | | Shirley, *The Witty Fair One* | |
| 1629 | Charles I dissolves Parliament; rules without it for 11 years | Salisbury Court theatre (Pt) opens | Brome, *The Lovesick Maid* | |
| | | | Jonson, *The New Inn* | |
| | Massachusetts Bay Company founded | | Massinger, *The Picture* | |
| 1630 | Peace treaties with Spain and France | Theatres closed for seven months because of plague | Brome, *The City Wit* | |
| | | | Heywood, *The Fair Maid of the West, Part II* | |
| 1631 | Death of Donne | | Brome, *The Queen's Exchange* | |
| | | | Dekker, *The Wonder of a Kingdom* | |
| | | | Ford, *The Broken Heart* | |
| | | | Massinger, *Believe as You List* | |
| | | | Shirley, *Love's Cruelty* | |
| 1632 | | Deaths of Webster and Dekker | Brome, *The Weeding of the Covent Garden* | T. E., *The Law's Resolutions of Women's Rights* |
| | | | Ford, *Love's Sacrifice* | |
| | | | Jonson, *The Magnetic Lady* | Milton, 'L'Allegro' and 'Il Penseroso' |
| | | | Massinger, *The City Madam* | |
| | | | Shirley, *Hyde Park* | |

| Date | Events | Theatre events | Plays and masques | Non-dramatic texts |
|------|--------|----------------|-------------------|--------------------|
| 1633 | Laud appointed Archbishop of Canterbury<br><br>Galileo forced to recant his support for Copernican theory by the Inquisition in Rome<br><br>Charles I reissues 1618 'Declaration Concerning Sports' | | Ford, *'Tis Pity She's a Whore*; *Perkin Warbeck*<br><br>Heywood, *A Maidenhead Well Lost*<br><br>Massinger, *The Guardian*<br><br>Shirley, *The Gamester* | Donne, *Poems*<br><br>Herbert, *The Temple*<br><br>Prynne, *Histriomastix* |
| 1634 | | | Brome and Heywood, *The Late Lancashire Witches*<br><br>Carew, *Coelum Britannicum*<br><br>Davenant, *Love and Honour*<br><br>Milton, *Comus* | |
| 1635 | | | Brome, *The New Academy*<br><br>Heywood, *A Challenge for Beauty*<br><br>Jordan, *Money is an Ass*<br><br>Shirley, *The Coronation* | |
| 1636 | | Theatres closed in May because of plague; 10,500 die in London | Massinger, *The Bashful Lover* | |
| 1637 | Prynne mutilated and jailed for criticising church<br><br>English traders land on the coast of China | Theatres reopen in October<br><br>Deaths of Jonson and Rowley | Brome, *The English Moor*<br>Shirley, *The Royal Master*<br>Suckling, *Aglaura* | Milton, *Lycidas*<br><br>Suckling, 'Session of the Poets' |
| 1638 | | | Brome, *The Antipodes*<br>Davenant, *The Fair Favourite*<br>Ford, *The Lady's Trial*<br>Suckling, *The Goblins* | |
| 1639 | | Death of Cary | Brome, *The Lovesick Court*<br>Davenant, *The Spanish Lovers*<br>Shirley, *The Politician* | |
| 1640 | Short Parliament called in April<br><br>Long Parliament called in November; sits until 1649<br><br>Prynne released<br><br>English trading factory set up in Madras | Death of Ford | Brome, *The Court Beggar*<br>Cavendish and Shirley, *The Country Captain*<br>Davenant, *Salmacida Spolia* | Carew, *Poems*<br><br>Jonson, *Timber*; *Underwoods* |
| 1641 | Star Chamber abolished; Laud impeached | Death of Heywood | Brome, *A Jovial Crew*<br><br>Jordan, *The Walks of Islington and Hogsdon*<br><br>Shirley, *The Cardinal* | Milton, *Of Reformation Touching Church Discipline* |
| 1642 | Civil War begins<br><br>Battle of Edgehill | Parliament closes theatres; reopen 1660 | Shirley, *The Sisters* | Browne, *Religio Medici*<br><br>Denham, 'Cooper's Hill' |

# The Plays

# Editorial Note

The texts of the plays and masque included in this collection have all been newly edited from the earliest published editions with reference to later editions. Further details of editions consulted are included in the headnote to each play. Typographical errors in the first edition have been silently corrected. Textual variants have been footnoted only where significant to the meaning. No typographical distinction has been made between stage directions from the first edition and those added by later editors. The spelling has been modernised throughout. The punctuation has been modernised where necessary to make the text clear to a modern reader, but no attempt has been made to make it conform to current conventions.

In the footnotes, the letters 'SD' indicate stage directions and 'SP' indicate speech prefixes. Where annotations from earlier editions are cited, the name of the editor is given in brackets. Works consulted in the preparation of the footnotes are given below. Any abbreviations used to refer to them are given in brackets.

Blakemore Evans, G. (ed.) (1987) *Elizabethan-Jacobean Drama*, London: A. & C. Black.

Greenblatt, Stephen, Cohen, Walter, Howard, Jean E. and Maus, Katharine Eisaman (eds) (1997) *The Norton Shakespeare*, based on the Oxford edition, New York, NY, London: W. W. Norton and Company.

Harvey, Paul (ed.) (1967) *The Oxford Companion to English Literature*, 4th edition, revised by Dorothy Eagle, Oxford: Clarendon Press.

Linthicum, M. C. (1935) *Costume in the Drama of Shakespeare and his Contemporaries*, Oxford: Clarendon Press.

Partridge, Eric (1947; this edition 1968) *Shakespeare's Bawdy*, London: Routledge.

—— (1973) *The Routledge Dictionary of Historical Slang*, London: Routledge and Kegan Paul.

Ruoff, James E. (1975) *The Macmillan Handbook of Elizabethan and Stuart Literature*, London: Macmillan.

Simpson, J. A. and Weiner, E. S. C. (eds) (1989) *Oxford English Dictionary*, 2nd edition, Oxford: Clarendon Press (OED).

Stephen, Leslie, Smith, George and Lee, Sydney (eds) (1917) *The Dictionary of National Biography*, 22 vols, London: Oxford University Press (DNB).

Stow, John (1971) *A Survey of London*, C. L. Kingsford (ed.), Oxford: Clarendon Press.

Sugden, E. H. (1925) *A Topographical Dictionary to the Works of Shakespeare and his Fellow Dramatists*, Manchester: The University Press (Sugden).

Tilley, M. P. (1950) *A Dictionary of Proverbs in England in the Sixteenth and Seventeenth Centuries*, Ann Arbor, MI: Michigan University Press (Tilley).

Whiting, B. J. (1968) *Proverbs, Sentences, and Proverbial Phrases from English Writings mainly before 1500*, Cambridge, MA, and London: Harvard University Press.

Wynne-Davies, Marion (ed.) (1992) *Bloomsbury Guides to English Literature: The Renaissance*, London: Bloomsbury.

# Thomas Kyd, *The Spanish Tragedy*

First performed 1585
First published 1592

As the earliest play in this collection, *The Spanish Tragedy* can be thought of as establishing a number of significant aspects of style and subject that were to be developed by later playwrights. There is no known source for the play, although some critics believe it may have shared one, now lost, with *Hamlet* (1600) or that an earlier version of *The Spanish Tragedy* may have inspired Shakespeare's work. Whatever the case, Kyd's play was clearly popular in its day and much imitated (and parodied) by other dramatists.

Kyd's play adapts a range of devices and themes from the Roman dramatist Seneca (c. 4 BC–AD 64). The ghost, the use of soliloquy, the play-within-the-play, the madness and suicide (as well as the principal theme of revenge itself) all emerge from the Elizabethan preoccupation with Senecan drama. Kyd's innovations include a topical context for the revenge theme, the 1580 war between Portugal and Spain; and, together with other dramatists of his day, he seems to owe something, in his representation of villainy, to the political philosophy of the Florentine writer Niccolo Machiavelli. In Bel-imperia, Kyd created an eloquent and purposeful female figure, such as had been rare on earlier English stages.

That a play about intrigue, corruption and dishonourable death in Spain was popular in an (officially) Protestant country should not surprise us. Elizabeth had been excommunicated for heresy by Pope Pius V in 1570 and, after an initial period of relative calm, anti-Catholic feeling was running high at the time of *The Spanish Tragedy*. This was exacerbated by increasing anxiety over relations with Spain itself. What may be considered surprising, however, is the manner in which the play invited its audience to consider extremely sensitive aspects of the profound social changes that were occurring in England at the time.

The framing device provided by the presence and commentary of the Ghost of Don Andrea and the figure of Revenge, grounded as it is in a Renaissance vision of a classical underworld, tends to universalise, as well as mirror, the action in the main play. Thus Don Andrea's impatience for revenge (I.v and II.i) is linked to Hieronimo's increasing frustration with the agencies of earthly justice, so that both figures seem situated at

first in the tradition of an 'Everyman'. Hieronimo, however, is able to move forward from this position into one of decisiveness and action. This occurs at the point in the play when, as Andy Mousley has noted, 'the possibility of revenge finding legitimate expression through an official and universally recognised exercise of justice becomes increasingly remote' (Mousley 2000: 68).

Revenge's promise to Don Andrea that he will turn 'their day to night' (I.v.7) never seems in doubt; revenge from beyond the grave seems preordained. The figure of Hieronimo, however, is altogether too human in the uncertainty of his dilemma, his role and the extent of his power. As Catherine Belsey has remarked, Hieronimo is 'uncertain whether he speaks in the name – the discourse – of heaven or hell, or neither' so that when he bites out his tongue (IV.iv.191) he is 'repudiating the right which defines the subject, the right of speech itself' (Belsey 1985: 75).

Hieronimo, as a 'subject', is defined by a range of institutional discourses. His position as Knight Marshal places him at the heart of the Spanish state, yet this guarantees him nothing in a world of such Machiavellian figures as Lorenzo. Indeed, his distracted tearing of the papers of the petitioners (III.xiii.122) signals a despair over the functions of the law which some critics have seen as a parallel with the situation in contemporary England. The empty box of the Pedringano sub-plot is a powerful sign of the manipulation of symbols of justice and redemption in the hands of the cynical: despite his murder of Serberine, the hapless Pedringano is clearly as much a victim of the controlling Lorenzo as Hieronimo has become.

Hieronomo becomes caught between the strictures of Christian teaching, which expressly forbade private acts of revenge (Romans 12.19) and the seductive reasoning of Seneca; on the one hand 'heaven will be revenged of every ill' (III.xiii.2) and on the other 'Strike, and strike home, where wrong is offered thee' (III.xiii.7). Having contemplated suicide, tested the institutions of justice and endured madness, Hieronimo enacts an elaborate private revenge which, paradoxically, sees him operating as an agent of the divine in the justice that Revenge has promised the

Ghost of Don Andrea. As in *Hamlet*, other figures are swept up in the course of vengeance, which careers to a macabre conclusion that begs further questions about justice, the state and the individual.

In *The Spanish Tragedy* and other revenge plays, dramatists were able to explore topical issues from the comparative safety of the stage. Hieronimo's dilemma and consequent actions are a compelling refracted image of the world inhabited by his audience: chivalric values, long-established systems of law and retribution, and implicit faith in divine and human authorities were all giving ground to more secular, pragmatic and 'political' systems of social organisation and cultural expression. Distanced from the action (at once identifying with, but ethically repulsed by, the actions of the figures on the stage) an audience might recognise only too well that such plays as *The Spanish Tragedy* announced the uncertain shift of values and priorities that defined the late sixteenth and early seventeenth centuries. The appeal of these plays to succeeding generations signals that the world that emerged from this uncertainty was the one that shaped their own history.

## Textual note

This edition is based on the octavo-in-fours edition believed to date from 1592, the single copy of which is held by the British Library in London (referred to in the footnotes to the text as Q). A further nine editions were published between 1594 and 1633 (evidence of the popularity of the play), and the corrections and variations in these have influenced modern editions; some of these include the anonymous passages known as the 'Additions' from 1602. This edition retains the unusual four-act structure of the earliest editions but we have introduced scene divisions.

# Further reading

## Editions

Boas, F. S. (ed.) (1901) *Works of Thomas Kyd*, Oxford: Clarendon Press.

Edwards, Philip (ed.) (1959) *The Spanish Tragedy*, The Revels Series, Manchester: Manchester University Press.

Joseph, Bertram (ed.) (1964) *The Spanish Tragedy*, The New Mermaids, London: Ernest Benn.

Kinney, Arthur F. (ed.) (1999) *Renaissance Drama: An Anthology of Plays and Entertainments*, Oxford: Blackwell.

Smith, Emma (ed.) (1998) *The Spanish Tragedie*, Renaissance Dramatists Series, Harmondsworth: Penguin.

McIlwraith, A. K. (ed.) (1938) *Five Elizabethan Tragedies*, The World's Classics Series, Oxford: Oxford University Press.

Mulryne, J. R. (ed.) (1989) *The Spanish Tragedy*, The New Mermaids, London: A. & C. Black.

Wine, M. L. (ed.) (1969) *Drama of the English Renaissance*, Modern Library College Editions, New York, NY: Random House.

## Critical and contextual reading

Adams, Barry B. (1969) 'The Audiences of *The Spanish Tragedy*', *Journal of English and Germanic Philology*, 48, 2: 221–36.

Aggeler, Geoffrey (1987) 'The Eschatological Crux in *The Spanish Tragedy*', *Journal of English and Germanic Philology*, 86, 3: 319–31.

Ardolino, Frank (1995) *Apocalypse and Armada in Kyd's 'Spanish Tragedy'*, Kirksville, MO: Sixteenth Century Essays and Studies.

Baines, Barbara (1980) 'Kyd's Silenus Box and the Limits of Perception', *Journal of Medieval and Renaissance Studies*, 10: 41–51.

Belsey, Catherine (1985) *The Subject of Tragedy: Identity and Difference in Renaissance Drama*, London: Methuen.

Bowers, Fredson (1940) *Elizabethan Revenge Tragedy 1587–1640*, Princeton, NJ: Princeton University Press.

Daalder, Joost (1986) 'The Role of Senex in Kyd's *The Spanish Tragedy*', *Comparative Violence*, 20, 3: 247–60.

Griffin, E. (2001) 'Ethos, Empire and the Valiant Acts of Thomas Kyd's Tragedy of "the Spains"', *English Literary Renaissance*, 31, 2: 192–229.

Hamilton, Donna B. (1974) '*The Spanish Tragedy*: A Speaking Picture', *English Literary Renaissance*, 4, 2: 203–17.

Hattaway, Michael (1982) *Elizabethan Popular Theatre: Plays in Performance*, London: Routledge and Kegan Paul.

Henke, J. T. (1981) 'Politics and Politicians in *The Spanish Tragedy*', *Studies in Philology*, 78, 4: 353–69.

Hill, Eugene D. (1985) 'Senecan and Vergilian Perspectives in *The Spanish Tragedy*', *English Literary Renaissance*, 15, 2: 143–65.

Justice, Steven (1985) 'Spain, Tragedy, and *The Spanish Tragedy*', *Studies in English Literature 1500–1900*, 25: 271–88.

Kerrigan, John (1996) *Revenge Tragedy: Aeschylus to Armageddon*, Oxford: Clarendon Press.

Mazzio, C. (1998) 'Staging the Vernacular: Language and Nation in Thomas Kyd's *The Spanish Tragedy*', *Studies in English Literature 1500–1900*, 38, 2: 207–32.

McAdam, I. (2000) '*The Spanish Tragedy* and the Politico-Religious Unconscious', *Texas Studies in Literature and Language*, 42, 1: 33–60.

McMillan, Scott (1972) 'The Figure of Silence in *The Spanish Tragedy*', *English Literary History*, 39: 27–48.

Mousley, Andy (2000) *Renaissance Drama and Contemporary Literary Theory*, Basingstoke: Macmillan.

Shapiro, James (1991) '"Tragedies Natually Performed": Kyd's Representation of Violence,' in David Scott Kastan and Peter Stallybrass (eds) *Staging the Renaissance: Reinterpretations of Elizabethan and Jacobean Drama*, London and New York, NY: Routledge.

Siemon, James R. (1991) 'Dialogical Formalism: Word, Object and Action in *The Spanish Tragedy*', *Medieval and Renaissance Drama in England*, 7: 87–115.

Smith, Molly (1992) 'The Theater and the Scaffold: Death as Spectacle in *The Spanish Tragedy*', *Studies in English Literature 1500–1900*, 32: 217–32.

Sofer, A. (2000) 'Absorbing Interests: Kyd's Bloody

Handkerchief as Palimpsest', *Comparative Drama*, 34, 2: 127–53.

Stockholder, K. (1990) '"Yet He Can Write": Reading the Silences in *The Spanish Tragedy*', *American Imago*, 47, 2: 93–124.

Whigham, Frank (1996) *Seizures of the Will in Early Modern English Drama*, Cambridge: Cambridge University Press.

## Works of related interest

William Shakespeare, *Titus Andronicus* (1593)
William Shakespeare, *Richard III* (1593)
William Shakespeare, *Hamlet* (1600)
John Marston, *Antonio's Revenge* (1600)
Henry Chettle, *The Tragedy of Hoffman* (1602)
Thomas Middleton or Cyril Tourneur, *The Revenger's Tragedy* (1606)
George Chapman, *The Tragedy of Bussy D'Ambois* (1607)
George Chapman, *The Revenge of Bussy D'Ambois* (1610)
Cyril Tourneur, *The Atheist's Tragedy* (1611)
John Webster, *The White Devil* (1612)
John Webster, *The Duchess of Malfi* (1614)
Thomas Middleton, *The Changeling* (1622)
Thomas Middleton, *Women Beware Women* (1625)
John Ford, *'Tis Pity She's a Whore* (1633)

# The Spanish Tragedy (1585)

## Dramatis personae

GHOST OF ANDREA

REVENGE

KING OF SPAIN

CYPRIAN, DUKE OF CASTILE, *his brother*

LORENZO, *the Duke's son*

BEL-IMPERIA, *Lorenzo's sister*

GENERAL, *of the Spanish Army*

VICEROY OF PORTUGAL

PEDRO, *his brother*

BALTHAZAR, *his son*

ALEXANDRO, *Portuguese nobleman*

VILLUPPO, *Portuguese nobleman*

AMBASSADOR *of Portugal to the Spanish court*

HIERONIMO, *Knight Marshal of Spain*

ISABELLA, *his wife*

HORATIO, *their son*

PEDRINGANO, *servant to Bel-imperia*

SERBERINE, *servant to Balthazar*

CHRISTOPHIL, *servant to Lorenzo*

BAZULTO, *an old man*

*Page to* LORENZO, *Three Watchmen, Messenger, Deputy, Hangman, Maid to* ISABELLA, *Two Portuguese, Servant, Three Citizens, Portuguese Nobles, Soldiers, Officers, Attendants, Halberdiers, Three Knights, Three Kings, a Drummer in the first Dumb-show, Hymen, Two Torch-bearers in the second Dumb-show*

## Act I, scene i

*Enter the* GHOST OF ANDREA, *and with him* REVENGE

ANDREA  When this eternal substance of my soul
  Did live imprisoned in my wanton flesh,
  Each in their function serving other's need,
  I was a courtier in the Spanish court.
  My name was Don Andrea, my descent,
  Though not ignoble, yet inferior far
  To gracious fortunes of my tender youth:
  For there in prime and pride of all my years,
  By duteous service and deserving love,
  In secret I possessed a worthy dame,          10
  Which hight sweet Bel-imperia by name.
  But in the harvest of my summer joys
  Death's winter nipped the blossoms of my bliss,
  Forcing divorce betwixt my love and me.
  For in the late conflict with Portingale
  My valour drew me into danger's mouth,
  Till life to death made passage through my wounds.
  When I was slain, my soul descended straight
  To pass the flowing stream of Acheron:
  But churlish Charon, only boatman there,        20
  Said that my rites of burial not performed,

---

SD  *Enter the* GHOST: a reference in Thomas Dekker's pamphlet *The Seven Deadly Sins of London* (1606) suggests that this entrance was made from the stage trapdoor

1–2  These opening lines can be compared with the parody in *The Knight of the Burning Pestle*, V.316–17: 'When I was mortal, this my costive corpse/Did lap up figs and raisins in the Strand'

8  prime: spring-time

11  hight: was called

18–85  Don Andrea's description of the underworld is developed from Virgil's *Aeneid* (Book VI) with Kyd adapting Virgil to present his own peculiar vision of a classical scene which would have been familar to many in his audience. A parallel is developed between Don Andrea's passage through the underworld and that of Virgil's Aeneas

19  Acheron: associated here with the river Styx, across which the dead were ferried by Charon

I might not sit amongst his passengers.
Ere Sol had slept three nights in Thetis' lap
And slaked his smoking chariot in her flood,
By Don Horatio, our Knight Marshal's son,
My funerals and obsequies were done.
Then was the ferryman of hell content
To pass me over to the slimy strond,
That leads to fell Avernus' ugly waves:
There, pleasing Cerberus with honeyed speech,    30
I passed the perils of the foremost porch.
Not far from hence, amidst ten thousand souls,
Sat Minos, Aeacus, and Rhadamanth,
To whom no sooner gan I make approach,
To crave a passport for my wandering ghost,
But Minos, in graven leaves of lottery,
Drew forth the manner of my life and death.
'This knight', quoth he, 'both lived and died in love,
And for his love tried fortune of the wars,
And by war's fortune lost both love and life.'    40
'Why then,' said Aeacus, 'convey him hence,
To walk with lovers in our fields of love,
And spend the course of everlasting time
Under green myrtle trees and cypress shades.'
'No, no,' said Rhadamanth, 'it were not well
With loving souls to place a martialist:
He died in war, and must to martial fields,
Where wounded Hector lives in lasting pain,
And Achilles' Myrmidons do scour the plain.'
Then Minos, mildest censor of the three,    50
Made this device to end the difference.
'Send him,' quoth he, 'to our infernal king,
To doom him as best seems his majesty.'

To this effect my passport straight was drawn.
In keeping on my way to Pluto's court,
Through dreadful shades of ever-glooming night,
I saw more sights than thousand tongues can tell,
Or pens can write, or mortal hearts can think.
Three ways there were: that on the right-hand side
Was ready way unto the foresaid fields,    60
Where lovers live and bloody martialists,
But either sort contained within his bounds.
The left-hand path, declining fearfully,
Was ready downfall to the deepest hell,
Where bloody Furies shakes their whips of steel,
And poor Ixion turns an endless wheel;
Where usurers are choked with melting gold,
And wantons are embraced with ugly snakes,
And murderers groan with never-killing wounds,
And perjured wights scalded in boiling lead,    70
And all foul sins with torments overwhelmed.
'Twixt these two ways I trod the middle path
Which brought me to the fair Elysian green,
In midst whereof there stands a stately tower,
The walls of brass, the gates of adamant.
Here finding Pluto with his Proserpine,
I showed my passport, humbled on my knee;
Whereat fair Proserpine began to smile,
And begged that only she might give my doom.
Pluto was pleased, and sealed it with a kiss.    80
Forthwith, Revenge, she rounded thee in th'ear,
And bade thee lead me through the gates of horn,
Where dreams have passage in the silent night.
No sooner had she spoke but we were here,
I wot not how, in twinkling of an eye.
REVENGE  Then know, Andrea, that thou art arrived
Where thou shalt see the author of thy death,
Don Balthazar, the prince of Portingale,
Deprived of life by Bel-imperia.
Here sit we down to see the mystery,    90
And serve for Chorus in this tragedy.

---

23 Sol: the Sun
    Thetis: the daughter of Nereus, a sea-god, thus the sea
25 Knight Marshal: an officer in an English royal palace
    with responsibility for upholding the law in the
    household and within 'the verge', an area within a radius
    of twelve miles of the palace
28 strond: strand or shore
29 Avernus: a lake thought of as an entrance to the
    underworld
30 Cerberus: a three-headed dog which guarded the
    entrance
33 Minos, Aeacus, and Rhadamanth: worthy inhabitants of
    the underworld who stood in judgement over those who
    entered
34 gan: began
35 a passport: a safe-conduct
36 Minos: the chief judge, with the casting vote. In Virgil,
    lots are drawn from an urn to determine the fate of the
    dead, but here Minos seems to be reading an account of
    Don Andrea's life in order to judge his worth
46 martialist: a soldier
49 Myrmidons: the killers of Hector
50 censor: judge
53 doom him: make the judgement

55 Pluto's court: Pluto was the king of the underworld
65 Furies: the mythical avengers of wickedness
66 Ixion: a lover condemned to an everlasting treadmill
67 usurers: money-lenders
73 Elysian green: the place of the blessed in the afterlife
76 Proserpine: the queen of the underworld
81 rounded thee: whispered
82 gates of horn: the gates of true dreams in the *Aeneid*
85 wot: know
86–9 The audience is told in advance the substance of the
    drama to come, importantly affecting its response to and
    judgement of the unfolding events. Revenge and Don
    Andrea remain on view throughout the play, often in a
    location somehow 'between' the action and the audience
    (downstage or in a gallery), their presence almost
    mediating the developing action upon which they
    comment as a chorus

# Act I, scene ii

*Enter* SPANISH KING, GENERAL, CASTILE, HIERONIMO

KING  Now say, Lord General, how fares our camp?
GENERAL  All well, my sovereign liege, except some few
　That are deceased by fortune of the war.
KING  But what portends thy cheerful countenance,
　And posting to our presence thus in haste?
　Speak man, hath fortune given us victory?
GENERAL  Victory, my liege, and that with little loss.
KING  Our Portingals will pay us tribute then?
GENERAL  Tribute and wonted homage therewithal.
KING  Then blest be heaven, and guider of the heavens,
　From whose fair influence such justice flows.　　　　11
CASTILE  *O multum dilecte Deo, tibi militat aether,*
　*Et conjuratae curvato poplite gentes*
　*Succumbunt: recti soror est victoria juris.*
KING  Thanks to my loving brother of Castile.
　But General, unfold in brief discourse
　Your form of battle and your war's success,
　That adding all the pleasure of thy news
　Unto the height of former happiness,
　With deeper wage and greater dignity　　　　20
　We may reward thy blissful chivalry.
GENERAL  Where Spain and Portingale do jointly knit
　Their frontiers, leaning on each other's bound,
　There met our armies in their proud array:
　Both furnished well, both full of hope and fear,
　Both menacing alike with daring shows,
　Both vaunting sundry colours of device,
　Both cheerly sounding trumpets, drums and fifes,
　Both raising dreadful clamours to the sky,
　That valleys, hills, and rivers made rebound,　　　　30
　And heaven itself was frighted with the sound.
　Our battles both were pitched in squadron form,
　Each corner strongly fenced with wings of shot:

But ere we joined and came to push of pike
I brought a squadron of our readiest shot
From out our rearward to begin the fight:
They brought another wing to encounter us.
Meanwhile, our ordnance played on either side,
And captains strove to have their valours tried.
Don Pedro, their chief horsemen's colonel,　　　　40
Did with his cornet bravely make attempt
To break the order of our battle ranks:
But Don Rogero, worthy man of war,
Marched forth against him with our musketeers,
And stopped the malice of his fell approach.
While they maintain hot skirmish to and fro,
Both battles join and fall to handy blows,
Their violent shot resembling th'ocean's rage,
When, roaring loud, and with a swelling tide,
It beats upon the rampiers of huge rocks,　　　　50
And gapes to swallow neighbour-bounding lands.
Now while Bellona rageth here and there,
Thick storms of bullets rain like winter's hail,
And shivered lances dark the troubled air.
*Pede pes et cuspide cuspis;*
*Arma sonant armis, vir petiturque viro.*
On every side drop captains to the ground,
And soldiers, some ill-maimed, some slain outright:
Here falls a body scindered from his head,
There legs and arms lie bleeding on the grass,　　　　60
Mingled with weapons and unbowelled steeds,
That scattering overspread the purple plain.
In all this turmoil, three long hours and more,
The victory to neither part inclined,
Till Don Andrea with his brave lanciers,
In their main battle made so great a breach
That, half dismayed, the multitude retired:
But Balthazar, the Portingals' young prince,
Brought rescue, and encouraged them to stay.
Here-hence the fight was eagerly renewed,　　　　70
And in that conflict was Andrea slain—
Brave man at arms, but weak to Balthazar.

---

1　camp: the army in the field
5　posting: speeding
8　Portingals: the Portuguese
　tribute: tribute money
12–14　*O multum dilecte . . . est victoria juris*: 'O one much loved
　of God, for thee the heavens contend, and the united
　peoples fall down on bended knee: victory is sister to just
　right.' Adapted from *De Terio Consulatu Honorii* by the
　Roman poet Claudian (AD 395–404)
20　wage: reward
23　bound: boundary
25　furnished well: well-equipped
27　vaunting sundry colours of device: proudly showing their
　heraldic banners
32　battles both were pitched in squadron form: formations
　of soldiers in squares
33　wings of shot: outer 'wings' of soldiers with guns on the
　outside of the squares

34　push of pike: fighting in close quarters, hand-to-hand
38　ordnance: heavy artillery
41　cornet: cavalry, identified by the cornet banner at their
　head
47　handy: hand-to-hand
50　rampiers: ramparts
52　Bellona: the Roman goddess of war
55–6　*Pede pes . . . petiturque viro*: 'Foot against foot and spear
　against spear, arms ring on arms and man is assailed by
　man'
59　scindered: sundered, or cleaved
61　unbowelled: disembowelled
62　purple: blood-drenched
65　lanciers: lancers
70　Here-hence: as a result of this

Yet while the prince, insulting over him,
Breathed out proud vaunts, sounding to our reproach,
Friendship and hardy valour joined in one
Pricked forth Horatio, our Knight Marshal's son,
To challenge forth that prince in single fight.
Not long between these twain the fight endured,
But straight the prince was beaten from his horse,
And forced to yield him prisoner to his foe:      80
When he was taken, all the rest they fled,
And our carbines pursued them to the death,
Till, Phoebus waning to the western deep,
Our trumpeters were charged to sound retreat.
KING Thanks good Lord General for these good news;
And for some argument of more to come,
Take this and wear it for thy sovereign's sake.
                    *Give him his chain*
But tell me now, hast thou confirmed a peace?
GENERAL No peace, my liege, but peace conditional,
That if with homage tribute be well paid,      90
The fury of your forces will be stayed:
And to this peace their viceroy hath subscribed,
                    *Give the* KING *a paper*
And made a solemn vow that, during life,
His tribute shall be truly paid to Spain.
KING These words, these deeds, become thy person
      well.
But now, Knight Marshal, frolic with thy king,
For 'tis thy son that wins this battle's prize.
HIERONIMO Long may he live to serve my sovereign
      liege,
And soon decay unless he serve my liege.
                    *A tucket afar off*
KING Nor thou, nor he, shall die without reward.      100
What means the warning of the trumpet's sound?
GENERAL This tells me that your grace's men of war,
Such as war's fortune hath reserved from death,
Come marching on towards your royal seat,
To show themselves before your majesty,
For so I gave in charge at my depart.
Whereby by demonstration shall appear,
That all (except three hundred or few more)
Are safe returned and by their foes enriched.

---

73  insulting: proudly exulting
74  sounding to: inferring
76  Pricked forth: spurred on
80  him: himself
83  Phoebus: the sun
      deep: the sea
86  argument: token
89  but: except
91  stayed: stopped
92  subscribed: signed his name
96  frolic: celebrate
99  decay: decline in well-being

*The Army enters;* BALTHAZAR, *between* LORENZO *and*
HORATIO, *captive*

KING A gladsome sight. I long to see them here.      110
                    *They enter and pass by*
Was that the warlike prince of Portingale,
That by our nephew was in triumph led?
GENERAL It was, my liege, the prince of Portingale.
KING But what was he that on the other side
Held him by th'arm as partner of the prize?
HIERONIMO That was my son, my gracious sovereign,
Of whom, though from his tender infancy
My loving thoughts did never hope but well,
He never pleased his father's eyes till now,
Nor filled my heart with overcloying joys.      120
KING Go let them march once more about these walls,
That staying them we may confer and talk
With our brave prisoner and his double guard.
Hieronimo, it greatly pleaseth us,
That in our victory thou have a share,
By virtue of thy worthy son's exploit.

*Enter the Army again*

Bring hither the young prince of Portingale:
The rest march on, but ere they be dismissed,
We will bestow on every soldier
Two ducats, and on every leader ten,      130
That they may know our largess welcomes them.
            *Exeunt all the Army but* BALTHAZAR, LORENZO,
                                      HORATIO
Welcome, Don Balthazar, welcome, nephew,
And thou, Horatio, thou art welcome too.
Young prince, although thy father's hard misdeeds,
In keeping back the tribute that he owes,
Deserve but evil measure at our hands,
Yet shalt thou know that Spain is honourable.
BALTHAZAR The trespass that my father made in peace
Is now controlled by fortune of the wars;
And cards once dealt, it boots not ask why so.      140
His men are slain, a weakening to his realm,
His colours seized, a blot unto his name,
His son distressed, a corsive to his heart:
Those punishments may clear his late offence.
KING Ay, Balthazar, if he observe this truce,
Our peace will grow the stronger for these wars.
Meanwhile live thou, though not in liberty,
Yet free from bearing any servile yoke;
For in our hearing thy deserts were great,

---

120  overcloying: satisfying
122  staying: stopping
131  largess: generosity (in gifts or money)
139  controlled: kept in check
143  corsive: corrosive
144  clear: cancel out
      late: previous, recent

41

And in our sight thyself art gracious.                    150
BALTHAZAR  And I shall study to deserve this grace.
KING  But tell me, for their holding makes me doubt,
    To which of these twain art thou prisoner?
LORENZO  To me, my liege.
HORATIO                    To me, my sovereign.
LORENZO  This hand first took his courser by the reins.
HORATIO  But first my lance did put him from his
    horse.
LORENZO  I seized his weapon, and enjoyed it first.
HORATIO  But first I forced him lay his weapons down.
KING  Let go his arm, upon our privilege.
                                            *They let him go*
    Say, worthy prince, to whether didst thou yield?  160
BALTHAZAR  To him in courtesy, to this perforce:
    He spake me fair, this other gave me strokes;
    He promised life, this other threatened death;
    He wan my love, this other conquered me:
    And truth to say I yield myself to both.
HIERONIMO  But that I know your grace for just and
    wise,
    And might seem partial in this difference,
    Enforced by nature and by law of arms
    My tongue should plead for young Horatio's right.
    He hunted well that was a lion's death,           170
    Not he that in a garment wore his skin:
    So hares may pull dead lions by the beard.
KING  Content thee, Marshal, thou shalt have no
    wrong;
    And for thy sake thy son shall want no right.
    Will both abide the censure of my doom?
LORENZO  I crave no better than your grace awards.
HORATIO  Nor I, although I sit beside my right.
KING  Then by my judgment thus your strife shall end:
    You both deserve and both shall have reward.
    Nephew, thou took'st his weapon and his horse,   180
    His weapons and his horse are thy reward.
    Horatio, thou didst force him first to yield,
    His ransom therefore is thy valour's fee:
    Appoint the sum as you shall both agree.
    But nephew, thou shalt have the prince in guard,
    For thine estate best fitteth such a guest:
    Horatio's house were small for all his train.

Yet in regard thy substance passeth his,
And that just guerdon may befall desert,
To him we yield the armour of the prince.           190
How likes Don Balthazar of this device?
BALTHAZAR  Right well my liege, if this proviso were,
    That Don Horatio bear us company,
    Whom I admire and love for chivalry.
KING  Horatio, leave him not that loves thee so.
    Now let us hence to see our soldiers paid,
    And feast our prisoner as our friendly guest.
                                            *Exeunt*

# Act I, scene iii

*Enter* VICEROY, ALEXANDRO, VILLUPPO, *Attendants*

VICEROY  Is our ambassador despatched for Spain?
ALEXANDRO  Two days, my liege, are passed since his
    depart.
VICEROY  And tribute payment gone along with him?
ALEXANDRO  Ay my good lord.
VICEROY  Then rest we here awhile in our unrest,
    And feed our sorrows with some inward sighs,
    For deepest cares break never into tears.
    But wherefore sit I in a regal throne?
    This better fits a wretch's endless moan.
                                        *Falls to the ground*
    Yet this is higher than my fortunes reach,        10
    And therefore better than my state deserves.
    Ay, ay, this earth, image of melancholy,
    Seeks him whom fates adjudge to misery:
    Here let me lie, now am I at the lowest.
    *Qui jacet in terra, non habet unde cadat.*
    *In me consumpsit vires fortuna nocendo,*
    *Nil superest ut jam possit obesse magis.*
    Yes, Fortune may bereave me of my crown:
    Here, take it now; let Fortune do her worst,
    She will not rob me of this sable weed:           20
    O no, she envies none but pleasant things.
    Such is the folly of despiteful chance!
    Fortune is blind and sees not my deserts,

---

155  courser: horse
159  upon our privilege: upon our absolute authority
160  whether: which of the two
164  wan: won
167  And might seem partial: Hieronimo says that he may not
    be impartial since they are speaking of his son
170-2  Hieronimo says that Horatio should be credited as the
    true victor, referring, as Edwards has done, to the Fourth
    Fable of Avian concerning an ass who dresses in a lion's
    skin
175  censure of my doom: the result of my judgement
177  sit beside: set aside or forgo

188  in regard: with regard to the fact that, or since
189  guerdon: reward
190  him: Horatio
191  device: the judgement (which takes account of the social
    hierarchy as well as the original problem)
15-17  *Qui jacet . . . obesse magis*: 'If one lies on the ground, one
    can fall no further. Towards me fortune has exhausted
    her power to hurt; nothing can harm me more.' The first
    sentence is from Alanus de Insulis, *Lib. Parah*, cap 2, 1.19,
    the second from Seneca's *Agamemnon*, 1.698
20  sable weed: black clothing (expressing his melancholy)
22  despiteful: malicious
23-30  Fortune is blind . . . fickle winds?: Fortune was
    commonly shown as blind and deaf, standing on a rolling
    sphere

So is she deaf and hears not my laments:
And could she hear, yet is she wilful mad,
And therefore will not pity my distress.
Suppose that she could pity me, what then?
What help can be expected at her hands,
Whose foot is standing on a rolling stone,
And mind more mutable than fickle winds?                     30
Why wail I then, where's hope of no redress?
O yes, complaining makes my grief seem less.
My late ambition hath distained my faith,
My breach of faith occasioned bloody wars,
Those bloody wars have spent my treasure,
And with my treasure my people's blood,
And with their blood, my joy and best beloved,
My best beloved, my sweet and only son.
O wherefore went I not to war myself?
The cause was mine, I might have died for both:        40
My years were mellow, his but young and green,
My death were natural, but his was forced.
ALEXANDRO  No doubt, my liege, but still the prince
     survives.
VICEROY  Survives! Ay, where?
ALEXANDRO  In Spain, a prisoner by mischance of war.
VICEROY  Then they have slain him for his father's fault.
ALEXANDRO  That were a breach to common law of arms.
VICEROY  They reck no laws that meditate revenge.
ALEXANDRO  His ransom's worth will stay from foul
     revenge.                                           49
VICEROY  No, if he lived the news would soon be here.
ALEXANDRO  Nay, evil news fly faster still than good.
VICEROY  Tell me no more of news, for he is dead.
VILLUPPO  My sovereign, pardon the author of ill news,
     And I'll bewray the fortune of thy son.
VICEROY  Speak on, I'll guerdon thee whate'er it be:
     Mine ear is ready to receive ill news,
     My heart grown hard 'gainst mischief's battery;
     Stand up I say, and tell thy tale at large.
VILLUPPO  Then hear that truth which these mine eyes
     have seen.
     When both the armies were in battle joined,        60
     Don Balthazar, amidst the thickest troops,
     To win renown did wondrous feats of arms:
     Amongst the rest I saw him hand to hand
     In single fight with their Lord General;
     Till Alexandro, that here counterfeits
     Under the colour of a duteous friend,
     Discharged his pistol at the prince's back,
     As though he would have slain their general.

But therewithal Don Balthazar fell down,
     And when he fell, then we began to fly:            70
     But had he lived, the day had sure been ours.
ALEXANDRO  O wicked forgery! O traitorous miscreant!
VICEROY  Hold thou thy peace! But now, Villuppo, say,
     Where then became the carcase of my son?
VILLUPPO  I saw them drag it to the Spanish tents.
VICEROY  Ay, ay, my nightly dreams have told me this.
     Thou false, unkind, unthankful, traitorous beast,
     Wherein had Balthazar offended thee,
     That thou shouldst thus betray him to our foes?
     Was't Spanish gold that bleared so thine eyes       80
     That thou couldst see no part of our deserts?
     Perchance because thou art Terceira's lord
     Thou hadst some hope to wear this diadem,
     If first my son and then myself were slain:
     But thy ambitious thought shall break thy neck.
     Ay, this was it that made thee spill his blood,
                    *Take the crown and put it on again*
     But I'll now wear it till thy blood be spilt.
ALEXANDRO  Vouchsafe, dread sovereign, to hear me
     speak.
VICEROY  Away with him, his sight is second hell;
     Keep him till we determine of his death.           90
                    *Exeunt Attendants with* ALEXANDRO
     If Balthazar be dead, he shall not live.
     Villuppo, follow us for thy reward.      *Exit* VICEROY
VILLUPPO  Thus have I with an envious, forged tale
     Deceived the king, betrayed mine enemy,
     And hope for guerdon of my villainy.
                                                *Exit*

# Act I, scene iv

*Enter* HORATIO *and* BEL-IMPERIA

BEL-IMPERIA  Signior Horatio, this is the place and hour
     Wherein I must entreat thee to relate
     The circumstance of Don Andrea's death,
     Who, living, was my garland's sweetest flower,
     And in his death hath buried my delights.
HORATIO  For love of him and service to yourself,
     I nill refuse this heavy doleful charge,
     Yet tears and sighs, I fear will hinder me.
     When both our armies were enjoined in fight,
     Your worthy chevalier amidst the thick'st,          10
     For glorious cause still aiming at the fairest,

30 mutable: changeable
42 forced: unnatural
46 fault: crime
48 reck: heed, acknowledge
54 bewray: reveal
55 guerdon: reward
57 mischief: misfortune

72 forgery: malicious fabrication
   miscreant: villain
82 Terceira's lord: as Capitão Donatorio of Terceira, in the
   Azores, Alexandro has tremendous power
93 envious: malicious
7 nill: will not
11 For glorious cause . . . the fairest: aiming to perform in
   the cause of the love inspired by Bel-imperia

Was at the last by young Don Balthazar
Encountered hand to hand: their fight was long,
Their hearts were great, their clamours menacing,
Their strength alike, their strokes both dangerous.
But wrathful Nemesis, that wicked power,
Envying at Andrea's praise and worth,
Cut short his life, to end his praise and worth.
She, she herself, disguised in armour's mask,
(As Pallas was before proud Pergamus)                    20
Brought in a fresh supply of halberdiers,
Which paunched his horse, and dinged him to the
    ground.
Then young Don Balthazar with ruthless rage
Taking advantage of his foe's distress,
Did finish what his halberdiers begun,
And left not till Andrea's life was done.
Then, though too late, incensed with just remorse
I with my band set forth against the prince
And brought him prisoner from his halberdiers.
BEL-IMPERIA  Would thou hadst slain him that so slew
    my love.                                              30
But then was Don Andrea's carcase lost?
HORATIO  No, that was it for which I chiefly strove,
Nor stepped I back till I recovered him:
I took him up, and wound him in mine arms,
And welding him unto my private tent,
There laid him down, and dewed him with my tears
And sighed and sorrowed as became a friend.
But neither friendly sorrow, sighs nor tears
Could win pale Death from his usurpèd right.
Yet this I did, and less I could not do:                 40
I saw him honoured with due funeral.
This scarf I plucked from off his lifeless arm,
And wear it in remembrance of my friend.
BEL-IMPERIA  I know the scarf, would he had kept it
    still,
For had he lived he would have kept it still,
And worn it for his Bel-imperia's sake:
For 'twas my favour at his last depart.
But now wear thou it both for him and me,
For after him thou hast deserved it best.

But, for thy kindness in his life and death,             50
Be sure while Bel-imperia's life endures,
She will be Don Horatio's thankful friend.
HORATIO  And, madam, Don Horatio will not slack
Humbly to serve fair Bel-imperia.
But now, if your good liking stand thereto,
I'll crave your pardon to go seek the prince,
For so the duke your father gave me charge.        *Exit*
BEL-IMPERIA  Ay, go Horatio, leave me here alone,
For solitude best fits my cheerless mood.
Yet what avails to wail Andrea's death,                  60
From whence Horatio proves my second love?
Had he not loved Andrea as he did,
He could not sit in Bel-imperia's thoughts.
But how can love find harbour in my breast,
Till I revenge the death of my beloved?
Yes, second love shall further my revenge.
I'll love Horatio, my Andrea's friend,
The more to spite the prince that wrought his end.
And where Don Balthazar, that slew my love,
Himself now pleads for favour at my hands,               70
He shall in rigour of my just disdain
Reap long repentance for his murderous deed.
For what was't else but murderous cowardice,
So many to oppress one valiant knight,
Without respect of honour in the fight?
And here he comes that murdered my delight.

*Enter* LORENZO *and* BALTHAZAR

LORENZO  Sister, what means this melancholy walk?
BEL-IMPERIA  That for a while I wish no company.
LORENZO  But here the prince is come to visit you.
BEL-IMPERIA  That argues that he lives in liberty.       80
BALTHAZAR  No madam, but in pleasing servitude.
BEL-IMPERIA  Your prison then belike is your conceit.
BALTHAZAR  Ay, by conceit my freedom is enthralled.
BEL-IMPERIA  Then with conceit enlarge yourself again.
BALTHAZAR  What if conceit have laid my heart to gage?
BEL-IMPERIA  Pay that you borrowed and recover it.
BALTHAZAR  I die if it return from whence it lies.
BEL-IMPERIA  A heartless man, and live? A miracle!
BALTHAZAR  Ay lady, love can work such miracles.
LORENZO  Tush, tush, my lord, let go these ambages, 90
And in plain terms acquaint her with your love.

---

16  Nemesis: the goddess of retribution, especially against
    humans
20  Pallas: Athene, one of the divinities associated with the
    Greeks at Troy, or Pergamus. Kyd refers to the *Aeneid*
    where she is mentioned, although it was Juno who was
    'girt with steel'
21  halberdiers: soldiers armed with halberds, a combined
    spear and axe
22  paunched: stabbed in the belly
    dinged: knocked, struck
27  just remorse: sorrow, pity
42  scarf: lady's favour worn by a knight in the field but, now
    worn by Horatio, also representing his loyalty to Don
    Andrea

---

71  disdain: indignation
77–89  Sister, what means . . . such miracles: this line-by-line
    dialogue (stichomythia) is one of the dramatic
    conventions derived from the Roman writer Seneca
82  conceit: imagination
83  enthralled: enslaved
84  enlarge: set free
85  laid my heart to gage: given as a pledge
90  ambages: roundabout ways of speaking

BEL-IMPERIA What boots complaint, when there's no
   remedy?
BALTHAZAR Yes, to your gracious self must I complain,
   In whose fair answer lies my remedy,
   On whose perfection all my thoughts attend,
   On whose aspect mine eyes find beauty's bower,
   In whose translucent breast my heart is lodged.
BEL-IMPERIA Alas, my lord, these are but words of
   course,
   And but device to drive me from this place.
       *She, in going in, lets fall her glove, which Horatio,*
                  *coming out, takes up*
HORATIO Madam, your glove.         **100**
BEL-IMPERIA Thanks good Horatio, take it for thy
   pains.
BALTHAZAR Signior Horatio stooped in happy time.
HORATIO I reaped more grace than I deserved or
   hoped.
LORENZO My lord, be not dismayed for what is past,
   You know that women oft are humorous:
   These clouds will overblow with little wind;
   Let me alone, I'll scatter them myself.
   Meanwhile let us devise to spend the time
   In some delightful sports and revelling.   **109**
HORATIO The king, my lords, is coming hither straight,
   To feast the Portingale ambassador:
   Things were in readiness before I came.
BALTHAZAR Then here it fits us to attend the king,
   To welcome hither our ambassador,
   And learn my father and my country's health.

*Enter the Banquet, Trumpets, the* KING *and*
AMBASSADOR

KING See Lord Ambassador, how Spain entreats
   Their prisoner Balthazar, thy viceroy's son:
   We pleasure more in kindness than in wars.
AMBASSADOR Sad is our king, and Portingale laments,
   Supposing that Don Balthazar is slain.   **120**
BALTHAZAR (*Aside*) So am I slain by beauty's tyranny.
   (*To him*) You see, my lord, how Balthazar is slain:
   I frolic with the Duke of Castile's son,
   Wrapped every hour in pleasures of the court,
   And graced with favours of his majesty.
KING Put off your greetings till our feast be done;
   Now come and sit with us and taste our cheer.
                  *They sit to the banquet*
   Sit down young prince, you are our second guest;
   Brother sit down and nephew take your place;
   Signior Horatio, wait thou upon our cup,   **130**

For well thou hast deserved to be honoured.
Now, Lordings, fall to; Spain is Portugal,
And Portugal is Spain, we both are friends,
Tribute is paid, and we enjoy our right.
But where is old Hieronimo, our marshal?
He promised us, in honour of our guest,
To grace our banquet with some pompous jest.

*Enter* HIERONIMO *with a Drum, three Knights, each with*
*his scutcheon: then he fetches three Kings, the Knights take*
*their crowns and them captive*

Hieronimo, this masque contents mine eye,
Although I sound not well the mystery.
HIERONIMO The first armed knight, that hung his
   scutcheon up,              **140**
       *He takes the scutcheon and gives it to the* KING
   Was English Robert, Earl of Gloucester,
   Who when King Stephen bore sway in Albion,
   Arrived with five and twenty thousand men
   In Portingale, and by success of war
   Enforced the king, then but a Saracen,
   To bear the yoke of the English monarchy.
KING My lord of Portingale, by this you see
   That which may comfort both your king and you,
   And make your late discomfort seem the less.
   But say, Hieronimo, what was the next?   **150**
HIERONIMO The second knight, that hung his
   scutcheon up,        *He doth as he did before*
   Was Edmund, Earl of Kent in Albion,
   When English Richard wore the diadem;
   He came likewise, and razed Lisbon walls,
   And took the King of Portingale in fight:
   For which, and other suchlike service done,
   He after was created Duke of York.
KING This is another special argument,
   That Portingale may deign to bear our yoke,
   When it by little England hath been yoked.   **160**
   But now Hieronimo, what were the last?
HIERONIMO The third and last, not least in our
   account,            *Doing as before*
   Was as the rest a valiant Englishman,
   Brave John of Gaunt, the Duke of Lancaster,
   As by his scutcheon plainly may appear.
   He with a puissant army came to Spain,
   And took our King of Castile prisoner.

---

92  What boots complaint: what point is there in pleading
    your love?
96  aspect: appearance
98  words of course: conventional phrases
105  humorous: temperamental

137  pompous jest: stately entertainment
SD  Although Hieronimo's masque contains errors and is
    difficult to source, it would have appealed to an
    Elizabethan audience's patriotism at a time of constant
    tension between England and Spain. A scutcheon is a
    shield with armorial bearings
139  mystery: hidden meaning
142  Albion: England
158  special argument: appropriate illustration
166  puissant: powerful

AMBASSADOR This is an argument for our viceroy,
  That Spain may not insult for her success,
  Since English warriors likewise conquered Spain, **170**
  And made them bow their knees to Albion.
KING Hieronimo, I drink to thee for this device,
  Which hath pleased both the ambassador and me;
  Pledge me, Hieronimo, if thou love the king.
                         *Takes the cup of* HORATIO
  My lord, I fear we sit but over-long,
  Unless our dainties were more delicate:
  But welcome are you to the best we have.
  Now let us in, that you may be despatched,
  I think our council is already set.
                                *Exeunt omnes*

# Act I, scene v

ANDREA Come we for this from depth of underground,
  To see him feast that gave me my death's wound?
  These pleasant sights are sorrow to my soul,
  Nothing but league, and love, and banqueting!
REVENGE Be still Andrea, ere we go from hence,
  I'll turn their friendship into fell despite,
  Their love to mortal hate, their day to night,
  Their hope into despair, their peace to war,
  Their joys to pain, their bliss to misery.

# Act II, scene i

*Enter* LORENZO *and* BALTHAZAR

LORENZO My lord, though Bel-imperia seem thus coy,
  Let reason hold you in your wonted joy:
  'In time the savage bull sustains the yoke,
  In time all haggard hawks will stoop to lure,
  In time small wedges cleave the hardest oak,
  In time the flint is pierced with softest shower'—
  And she in time will fall from her disdain,

---

  And rue the sufferance of your friendly pain.
BALTHAZAR 'No, she is wilder, and more hard withal,
  Than beast, or bird, or tree, or stony wall.' **10**
  But wherefore blot I Bel-imperia's name?
  It is my fault, not she, that merits blame.
  My feature is not to content her sight,
  My words are rude and work her no delight.
  The lines I send her are but harsh and ill,
  Such as do drop from Pan and Marsyas' quill.
  My presents are not of sufficient cost,
  And being worthless all my labour's lost.
  Yet might she love me for my valiancy;
  Ay, but that's slandered by captivity. **20**
  Yet might she love me to content her sire;
  Ay, but her reason masters his desire.
  Yet might she love me as her brother's friend;
  Ay, but her hopes aim at some other end.
  Yet might she love me to uprear her state;
  Ay, but perhaps she hopes some nobler mate.
  Yet might she love me as her beauty's thrall;
  Ay, but I fear she cannot love at all.
LORENZO My lord, for my sake leave these ecstasies,
  And doubt not but we'll find some remedy. **30**
  Some cause there is that lets you not be loved:
  First that must needs be known, and then removed.
  What if my sister love some other knight?
BALTHAZAR My summer's day will turn to winter's
  night.
LORENZO I have already found a stratagem,
  To sound the bottom of this doubtful theme.
  My lord, for once you shall be ruled by me:
  Hinder me not whate'er you hear or see.
  By force or fair means will I cast about
  To find the truth of all this question out. **40**
  Ho, Pedringano!
PEDRINGANO (*Within*) Signior!
LORENZO                        *Vien qui presto.*

*Enter* PEDRINGANO

PEDRINGANO Hath your lordship any service to
  command me?

---

172 device: entertainment
176 Unless: unless it were that
1–4 Don Andrea complains at being made to witness events
  which necesarily disturb him, a situation which arises for
  ghosts in Senecan tragedy
6 fell despite: cruel hatred
1 coy: unresponsive
2 wonted: accustomed
3–10 'In time . . . stony wall.': these lines echo a popular
  sonnet of the time on the subject of the courting of
  reluctant women by Thomas Watson; see Watson's
  Sonnet XLVII in his *Hecatompathia* (1582)
4 haggard: wild
  stoop to lure: a term derived from the training of hawks
  which swoop to lures of dead birds or bundles of feathers
  shaped to look like birds

8 rue: pity
  sufferance: patient endurance
13 feature: form, bearing, rather than simply the face
16 Pan and Marsyas: two gods who lost flute-playing
  contests with Apollo
  quill: a) reed (as in a flute); b) pen
19 valiancy: valour
20 slandered: brought into disrepute
25 uprear her state: improve her social position
29 ecstasies: unreasoning passions. Lorenzo implies that
  Balthazar is exaggerating
36 sound the bottom: to get to the bottom, as in sounding
  the depth of water beneath a vessel
41 *Vien qui presto*: 'Come here quickly' (Italian)

LORENZO  Ay, Pedringano, service of import.
  And not to spend the time in trifling words,
  Thus stands the case: it is not long thou know'st,
  Since I did shield thee from my father's wrath,
  For thy conveyance in Andrea's love,
  For which thou wert adjudged to punishment.
  I stood betwixt thee and thy punishment;
  And since, thou know'st how I have favoured thee. 50
  Now to these favours will I add reward,
  Not with fair words, but store of golden coin,
  And lands and living joined with dignities,
  If thou but satisfy my just demand.
  Tell truth and have me for thy lasting friend.
PEDRINGANO  Whate'er it be your lordship shall demand,
  My bounden duty bids me tell the truth,
  If case it lie in me to tell the truth.
LORENZO  Then, Pedringano, this is my demand:
  Whom loves my sister Bel-imperia?  60
  For she reposeth all her trust in thee:
  Speak man, and gain both friendship and reward:
  I mean, whom loves she in Andrea's place?
PEDRINGANO  Alas, my lord, since Don Andrea's death,
  I have no credit with her as before,
  And therefore know not if she love or no.
LORENZO  Nay, if thou dally then I am thy foe,
                            *Draws his sword*
  And fear shall force what friendship cannot win.
  Thy death shall bury what thy life conceals.
  Thou diest for more esteeming her than me.  70
PEDRINGANO  O, stay, my lord!
LORENZO  Yet speak the truth and I will guerdon thee,
  And shield thee from whatever can ensue,
  And will conceal whate'er proceeds from thee:
  But if thou dally once again, thou diest.
PEDRINGANO  If Madam Bel-imperia be in love—
LORENZO  What, villain, ifs and ands?
                          *Offers to kill him*
PEDRINGANO  O stay my lord, she loves Horatio.
               BALTHAZAR *starts back*
LORENZO  What, Don Horatio our Knight Marshal's
  son?
PEDRINGANO  Even him my lord.  80
LORENZO  Now say but how know'st thou he is her love;
  And thou shalt find me kind and liberal:
  Stand up, I say, and fearless tell the truth.
PEDRINGANO  She sent him letters which myself
  perused,
  Full-fraught with lines and arguments of love

Preferring him before Prince Balthazar.
LORENZO  Swear on this cross that what thou say'st is
  true,
  And that thou wilt conceal what thou hast told.
PEDRINGANO  I swear to both by him that made us all.
LORENZO  In hope thine oath is true, here's thy reward,
  But if I prove thee perjured and unjust,  91
  This very sword whereon thou took'st thine oath,
  Shall be the worker of thy tragedy.
PEDRINGANO  What I have said is true, and shall for me
  Be still concealed from Bel-imperia.
  Besides, your honour's liberality
  Deserves my duteous service even till death.
LORENZO  Let this be all that thou shalt do for me:
  Be watchful when, and where, these lovers meet,
  And give me notice in some secret sort.  100
PEDRINGANO  I will my lord.
LORENZO  Then shalt thou find that I am liberal.
  Thou know'st that I can more advance thy state
  Than she, be therefore wise and fail me not.
  Go and attend her as thy custom is,
  Lest absence make her think thou dost amiss.
                  *Exit* PEDRINGANO
  Why so: *tam armis quam ingenio*:
  Where words prevail not, violence prevails;
  But gold doth more than either of them both.
  How likes Prince Balthazar this stratagem?  110
BALTHAZAR  Both well, and ill: it makes me glad and
  sad:
  Glad, that I know the hinderer of my love,
  Sad, that I fear she hates me whom I love.
  Glad, that I know on whom to be revenged,
  Sad, that she'll fly me if I take revenge.
  Yet must I take revenge or die myself,
  For love resisted grows impatient.
  I think Horatio be my destined plague:
  First, in his hand he brandished a sword,
  And with that sword he fiercely waged war,  120
  And in that war he gave me dangerous wounds,
  And by those wounds he forced me to yield,
  And by my yielding I became his slave.
  Now in his mouth he carries pleasing words,
  Which pleasing words do harbour sweet conceits,
  Which sweet conceits are limed with sly deceits,
  Which sly deceits smooth Bel-imperia's ears,
  And through her ears dive down into her heart,

---

47  conveyance: secret undertaking
52  store: abundance
58  If case it lie in me: in case I am able
65  credit: particular relationship
71  stay: wait
72  guerdon: reward
85  Full-fraught: loaded

87  this cross: the cross of his sword-hilt
91  unjust: dishonest
100  in some secret sort: by some secret means
103  advance thy state: improve your social and financial status
107  *tam armis quam ingenio*: 'by equal parts of force and skill'
125  sweet conceits: pleasing figures of speech
126  limed: made into traps, as in the use of bird-lime, a sticky
     substance used to trap birds
     smooth: seduce

And in her heart set him where I should stand.
Thus hath he ta'en my body by his force,                    130
And now by sleight would captivate my soul:
But in his fall I'll tempt the destinies,
And either lose my life, or win my love.

LORENZO  Let's go, my lord, your staying stays revenge.
Do you but follow me and gain your love:
Her favour must be won by his remove.

*Exeunt*

# Act II, scene ii

*Enter* HORATIO *and* BEL-IMPERIA

HORATIO  Now, madam, since by favour of your love
Our hidden smoke is turned to open flame,
And that with looks and words we feed our thoughts
(Two chief contents, where more cannot be had),
Thus in the midst of love's fair blandishments,
Why show you sign of inward languishments?

PEDRINGANO *showeth all to the* PRINCE *and* LORENZO,
*placing them in secret above*

BEL-IMPERIA  My heart, sweet friend, is like a ship at sea:
She wisheth port, where riding all at ease,
She may repair what stormy times have worn,
And leaning on the shore, may sing with joy              10
That pleasure follows pain, and bliss annoy.
Possession of thy love is th'only port,
Wherein my heart, with fears and hopes long tossed,
Each hour doth wish and long to make resort;
There to repair the joys that it hath lost,
And sitting safe, to sing in Cupid's choir
That sweetest bliss is crown of love's desire.

BALTHAZAR  O sleep mine eyes, see not my love
profaned;
Be deaf, my ears, hear not my discontent;
Die, heart, another joys what thou deservest.           20

LORENZO  Watch still mine eyes, to see this love
disjoined;
Hear still mine ears, to hear them both lament;
Live, heart, to joy at fond Horatio's fall.

BEL-IMPERIA  Why stands Horatio speechless all this
while?

HORATIO  The less I speak, the more I meditate.

BEL-IMPERIA  But whereon dost thou chiefly meditate?

HORATIO  On dangers past, and pleasures to ensue.

BALTHAZAR  On pleasures past, and dangers to ensue.

BEL-IMPERIA  What dangers and what pleasures dost
thou mean?

HORATIO  Dangers of war and pleasures of our love.   30

LORENZO  Dangers of death, but pleasures none at all.

BEL-IMPERIA  Let dangers go, thy war shall be with me,
But such a war as breaks no bond of peace.
Speak thou fair words, I'll cross them with fair words;
Send thou sweet looks, I'll meet them with sweet
looks;
Write loving lines, I'll answer loving lines;
Give me a kiss, I'll countercheck thy kiss:
Be this our warring peace, or peaceful war.

HORATIO  But gracious madam, then appoint the field
Where trial of this war shall first be made.          40

BALTHAZAR  Ambitious villain, how his boldness
grows!

BEL-IMPERIA  Then be thy father's pleasant bower the
field,
Where first we vowed a mutual amity:
The court were dangerous, that place is safe.
Our hour shall be when Vesper gins to rise,
That summons home distressful travellers.
There none shall hear us but the harmless birds:
Happily the gentle nightingale
Shall carol us asleep ere we be ware,
And singing with the prickle at her breast,           50
Tell our delight and mirthful dalliance.
Till then each hour will seem a year and more.

HORATIO  But, honey sweet, and honourable love,
Return we now into your father's sight:
Dangerous suspicion waits on our delight.

LORENZO  Ay, danger mixed with jealous despite
Shall send thy soul into eternal night.

*Exeunt*

---

131 sleight: trickery
132 in his fall I'll tempt the destinies: in his downfall I'll
tempt the gods of fate
136 his remove: his removal (by death)
2 smoke: emotion
flame: passion
4 contents: sources of contentment
5 blandishments: elaborate speeches
6 languishments: weariness
SD Balthazar and Lorenzo watch the lovers from the balcony
or upper-stage
9 repair: restore
10 sing: celebrate
20 joys: enjoys
23 fond: foolish

34 cross: match, complement
37 countercheck: oppose
42 bower: an arbour, a seat in a garden half-enclosed by
plants and foliage
45 Vesper: Venus, the evening star
gins: begins
46 distressful travellers: weary labourers or 'travaillers'
48 Happily: haply, perhaps
50 prickle at her breast: a thorn at her breast. This is a
reference to the legend of Philomena who revenged
herself on her brother-in-law Tereus after he had raped
her and pricked her breast with a thorn to remember her
suffering
56 jealous: watchful, suspicious. The use of three syllables
maintains the metre

# Act II, scene iii

*Enter* KING OF SPAIN, PORTINGALE, AMBASSADOR, DON
CYPRIAN, *etc.*

KING  Brother of Castile, to the prince's love
    What says your daughter Bel-imperia?
CASTILE  Although she coy it as becomes her kind,
    And yet dissemble that she loves the prince,
    I doubt not, I, but she will stoop in time.
    And were she froward, which she will not be,
    Yet herein shall she follow my advice,
    Which is to love him or forgo my love.
KING  Then, Lord Ambassador of Portingale,
    Advise thy king to make this marriage up,    10
    For strengthening of our late-confirmed league;
    I know no better means to make us friends.
    Her dowry shall be large and liberal:
    Besides that she is daughter and half-heir
    Unto our brother here, Don Cyprian,
    And shall enjoy the moiety of his land,
    I'll grace her marriage with an uncle's gift.
    And this it is: in case the match go forward,
    The tribute which you pay shall be released,
    And if by Balthazar she have a son,    20
    He shall enjoy the kingdom after us.
AMBASSADOR  I'll make the motion to my sovereign
    liege,
    And work it if my counsel may prevail.
KING  Do so, my lord, and if he give consent,
    I hope his presence here will honour us
    In celebration of the nuptial day:
    And let himself determine of the time.
AMBASSADOR  Will't please your grace command me
    aught beside?
KING  Commend me to the king, and so farewell.
    But where's Prince Balthazar to take his leave?    30
AMBASSADOR  That is performed already, my good lord.
KING  Amongst the rest of what you have in charge,
    The prince's ransom must not be forgot;
    That's none of mine, but his that took him prisoner,
    And well his forwardness deserves reward:
    It was Horatio, our Knight Marshal's son.
AMBASSADOR  Between us there's a price already
    pitched,

    And shall be sent with all convenient speed.
KING  Then once again farewell, my lord.    39
AMBASSADOR  Farewell, my Lord of Castile and the
    rest.    *Exit*
KING  Now, brother, you must take some little pains
    To win fair Bel-imperia from her will:
    Young virgins must be ruled by their friends.
    The prince is amiable, and loves her well,
    If she neglect him and forgo his love,
    She both will wrong her own estate and ours.
    Therefore, whiles I do entertain the prince
    With greatest pleasure that our court affords,
    Endeavour you to win your daughter's thought:
    If she give back, all this will come to naught.    50
    *Exeunt*

# Act II, scene iv

*Enter* HORATIO, BEL-IMPERIA, *and* PEDRINGANO

HORATIO  Now that the night begins with sable wings
    To overcloud the brightness of the sun,
    And that in darkness pleasures may be done,
    Come Bel-imperia, let us to the bower,
    And there in safety pass a pleasant hour.
BEL-IMPERIA  I follow thee my love, and will not back,
    Although my fainting heart controls my soul.
HORATIO  Why, make you doubt of Pedringano's faith?
BEL-IMPERIA  No, he is as trusty as my second self.
    Go Pedringano, watch without the gate,    10
    And let us know if any make approach.
PEDRINGANO  (*Aside*) Instead of watching, I'll deserve
    more gold
    By fetching Don Lorenzo to this match.
    *Exit* PEDRINGANO
HORATIO  What means my love?
BEL-IMPERIA      I know not what myself.
    And yet my heart foretells me some mischance.
HORATIO  Sweet say not so, fair fortune is our friend,
    And heavens have shut up day to pleasure us.
    The stars thou see'st hold back their twinkling shine,
    And Luna hides herself to pleasure us.
BEL-IMPERIA  Thou hast prevailed, I'll conquer my
    misdoubt,    20

---

  3  coy it: pretends disinterest
  4  dissemble: pretends
  5  stoop: become obedient
  6  froward: perverse
16  moiety: half-share
19  released: cancelled
22  make the motion: put the proposal
35  forwardness: enterprise
37  pitched: settled, agreed

38  all convenient speed: as quickly as possible
42  will: wilfulness
50  give back: turn her back. Edwards notes that the usual
    meaning of 'retreat' or 'yield' is inappropriate
1–5  A sense of foreboding is invoked in associating night and
    darkness with protection rather than threat
  1  sable: black
  7  controls: oppresses
10  without: outside
13  match: meeting
19  Luna: the moon

And in thy love and counsel drown my fear.
I fear no more, love now is all my thoughts.
Why sit we not? For pleasure asketh ease.
HORATIO The more thou sit'st within these leafy
bowers,
The more will Flora deck it with her flowers.
BEL-IMPERIA Ay, but if Flora spy Horatio here,
Her jealous eye will think I sit too near.
HORATIO Hark, madam, how the birds record by night,
For joy that Bel-imperia sits in sight.
BEL-IMPERIA No, Cupid counterfeits the nightingale, 30
To frame sweet music to Horatio's tale.
HORATIO If Cupid sing, then Venus is not far:
Ay, thou art Venus or some fairer star.
BEL-IMPERIA If I be Venus thou must needs be Mars,
And where Mars reigneth, there must needs be wars.
HORATIO Then thus begin our wars: put forth thy
hand,
That it may combat with my ruder hand.
BEL-IMPERIA Set forth thy foot to try the push of
mine.
HORATIO But first my looks shall combat against thine.
BEL-IMPERIA Then ward thyself: I dart this kiss at thee. 40
HORATIO Thus I retort the dart thou threw'st at me.
BEL-IMPERIA Nay then, to gain the glory of the field,
My twining arms shall yoke and make thee yield.
HORATIO Nay then, my arms are large and strong
withal:
Thus elms by vines are compassed till they fall.
BEL-IMPERIA O let me go, for in my troubled eyes
Now may'st thou read that life in passion dies.
HORATIO O stay a while and I will die with thee,
So shalt thou yield and yet have conquered me.
BEL-IMPERIA Who's there? Pedringano! We are
betrayed!                                          50

*Enter* LORENZO, BALTHAZAR, SERBERINE, PEDRINGANO,
*disguised*

---

23 asketh: requires, demands
25 Flora: the Roman goddess of flowers
28 record: sing
30 counterfeits: imitates
31 frame: compose
34 Venus . . . Mars: Venus (Aphrodite) betrayed her
husband Hephaestus having fallen in love with Mars
(Ares) the god of war
37 ruder: rougher, coarser
40 ward: shield, guard
43 yoke: join
45 Edwards notes that Horatio inverts the traditional notion
that the vine (associated with Venus) held up the elm
even after the elm was dead. Here the vine pulls down
the elm
48 die: an Elizabethan term for orgasm. Mulryne suggests
that this double meaning emphasises the extreme
sensuality of the scene

LORENZO My lord, away with her, take her aside.
O sir, forbear, your valour is already tried.
Quickly despatch, my masters.
                          *They hang him in the arbour*
HORATIO What, will you murder me?
LORENZO Ay, thus, and thus; these are the fruits of
love.                                    *They stab him*
BEL-IMPERIA O save his life and let me die for him!
O save him, brother, save him, Balthazar:
I loved Horatio, but he loved not me.
BALTHAZAR But Balthazar loves Bel-imperia.        59
LORENZO Although his life were still ambitious proud,
Yet is he at the highest now he is dead.
BEL-IMPERIA Murder! Murder! Help, Hieronimo,
help!
LORENZO Come, stop her mouth, away with her.
                    *Exeunt, leaving* HORATIO'*s body*

# Act II, scene v

*Enter* HIERONIMO *in his shirt, etc.*

HIERONIMO What outcries pluck me from my naked
bed,
And chill my throbbing heart with trembling fear,
Which never danger yet could daunt before?
Who calls Hieronimo? Speak, here I am.
I did not slumber, therefore 'twas no dream,
No, no, it was some woman cried for help,
And here within this garden did she cry,
And in this garden must I rescue her.
But stay, what murderous spectacle is this?
A man hanged up and all the murderers gone,  10
And in my bower, to lay the guilt on me.
This place was made for pleasure not for death.
                              *He cuts him down*
Those garments that he wears I oft have seen—
Alas, it is Horatio, my sweet son!
Oh no, but he that whilom was my son.
O was it thou that calledst me from my bed?
O speak, if any spark of life remain:
I am thy father. Who hath slain my son?
What savage monster, not of human kind,
Hath here been glutted with thy harmless blood,  20

---

52 tried: as in 'tried and tested', referring to Horatio's
military reputation
60 ambitious proud: ambitious in seeking to satisfy his pride
61 highest now he is dead: a bleak joke at Horatio's expense
since he is now hanging on a tree (according to
Hieronimo in Act IV). Most editors assume that the tree
is part of the arbour
SD *shirt*: nightshirt
1 naked bed: a proverbial usage. The sleeper is naked, or
not fully dressed
15 whilom: was once

And left thy bloody corpse dishonoured here,
For me, amidst this dark and deathful shades,
To drown thee with an ocean of my tears?
O heavens, why made you night to cover sin?
By day this deed of darkness had not been.
O earth, why didst thou not in time devour
The vild profaner of this sacred bower?
O poor Horatio, what hadst thou misdone,
To leese thy life ere life was new begun?
O wicked butcher, whatsoe'er thou wert,                30
How could thou strangle virtue and desert?
Ay me most wretched, that have lost my joy,
In leesing my Horatio, my sweet boy!

*Enter* ISABELLA

ISABELLA  My husband's absence makes my heart to
        throb—
    Hieronimo!
HIERONIMO  Here, Isabella, help me to lament,
    For sighs are stopped and all my tears are spent.
ISABELLA  What world of grief! My son Horatio!
    O where's the author of this endless woe?
HIERONIMO  To know the author were some ease of
        grief,                                          40
    For in revenge my heart would find relief.
ISABELLA  Then is he gone? And is my son gone too?
    O, gush out, tears, fountains and floods of tears;
    Blow, sighs, and raise an everlasting storm:
    For outrage fits our cursed wretchedness.
HIERONIMO  Sweet lovely rose, ill plucked before thy
        time,
    Fair worthy son, not conquered, but betrayed:
    I'll kiss thee now, for words with tears are stayed.
ISABELLA  And I'll close up the glasses of his sight,
    For once these eyes were only my delight.          50
HIERONIMO  See'st thou this handkercher besmeared
        with blood?
    It shall not from me till I take revenge.
    See'st thou those wounds that yet are bleeding fresh?
    I'll not entomb them till I have revenged.
    Then will I joy amidst my discontent,
    Till then my sorrow never shall be spent.

ISABELLA  The heavens are just, murder cannot be hid:
    Time is the author both of truth and right,
    And time will bring this treachery to light.
HIERONIMO  Meanwhile, good Isabella, cease thy
        plaints,                                        60
    Or at the least dissemble them awhile:
    So shall we sooner find the practice out,
    And learn by whom all this was brought about.
    Come Isabel, now let us take him up,
                        *They take him up*
    And bear him in from out this cursed place.
    I'll say his dirge, singing fits not this case.
    *O aliquis mihi quas pulchrum ver educat herbas*
                HIERONIMO *sets his breast unto his sword*
    *Misceat, et nostro detur medicina dolori;*
    *Aut, si qui faciunt animis oblivia, succos*
    *Praebeat; ipse metam magnum quaecunque per orbem*  70
    *Gramina Sol pulchras effert in luminis oras;*
    *Ipse bibam quicquid meditatur saga veneni,*
    *Quicquid et herbarum vi caeca nenia nectit:*
    *Omnia perpetiar, lethum quoque, dum semel omnis*
    *Noster in extincto moriatur pectore sensus.*
    *Ergo tuos oculos nunquam, mea vita, videbo,*
    *Et tua perpetuus sepelivit lumina somnus?*
    *Emoriar tecum: sic, sic juvat ire sub umbras.*
    *At tamen absistam properato cedere letho,*
    *Ne mortem vindicta tuam tum nulla sequatur.*        80
            *Here he throws it from him and bears the body away*

## Act II, scene vi

ANDREA  Brought'st thou me hither to increase my pain?
    I looked that Balthazar should have been slain;

---

21  dishonoured: Kinney suggests a) disgraced; b) violated
22  this: some editors amend to 'these', but others note that
    this was an acceptable plural form for the time
26  in time: at the appropriate time
27  vild: vile
29  leese: lose
    life was new begun: Horatio should have been entering a
    new life now that the war was over
33  leesing: losing
39  the author of: the one responsible for
45  outrage: passionate behaviour
49  glasses of his sight: his eyes
51  handkercher: handkerchief or small scarf

60  plaints: sorrows
61  dissemble: disguise them or hold them back
62  find the practice out: discover the detail of the plot
66  dirge: funeral song
67–80  *O aliquis . . . nulla sequatur*: 'Let someone mix for me
    the herbs which beautiful spring fosters, and let a salve be
    given for our grief; or let him apply juices, if there are any
    that bring oblivion to men's minds. I myself shall gather
    anywhere in the great world whatever plants the sun
    draws forth into the fair regions of light; I myself shall
    drink whatever drug the wise-woman devises, and
    whatever herbs incantation assembles by its secret power.
    I shall face all things, death even, until the moment our
    every feeling dies in this dead breast. And so shall I never
    again, my life, see those eyes of yours, and has everlasting
    slumber sealed up your light of life? I shall perish with
    you; thus, thus would it please me to go to the shades
    below. But nonetheless I shall keep myself from yielding
    to a hasty death, in case then no revenge should follow
    your death.' Kyd combines his own lines with others
    taken from the classical writers Lucretius, Ovid and
    Virgil
2  looked: expected, hoped

But 'tis my friend Horatio that is slain,
And they abuse fair Bel-imperia,
On whom I doted more than all the world,
Because she loved me more than all the world.

REVENGE Thou talk'st of harvest when the corn is
  green:
  The end is crown of every work well done;
  The sickle comes not till the corn be ripe.
  Be still, and ere I lead thee from this place,     10
  I'll show thee Balthazar in heavy case.

# Act III, scene i

*Enter* VICEROY OF PORTINGALE, *Nobles,* VILLUPPO

VICEROY Infortunate condition of kings,
  Seated amidst so many helpless doubts!
  First we are placed upon extremest height,
  And oft supplanted with exceeding heat,
  But ever subject to the wheel of chance;
  And at our highest never joy we so,
  As we both doubt and dread our overthrow.
  So striveth not the waves with sundry winds
  As Fortune toileth in the affairs of kings,
  That would be feared, yet fear to be beloved,     10
  Sith fear or love to kings is flattery.
  For instance, Lordings, look upon your king,
  By hate deprived of his dearest son,
  The only hope of our successive line.

1 NOBLEMAN I had not thought that Alexandro's heart
  Had been envenomed with such extreme hate:
  But now I see that words have several works,
  And there's no credit in the countenance.

VILLUPPO No, for, my lord, had you beheld the train
  That feigned love had coloured in his looks,     20

When he in camp consorted Balthazar,
Far more inconstant had you thought the sun,
That hourly coasts the centre of the earth,
Than Alexandro's purpose to the prince.

VICEROY No more, Villuppo, thou hast said enough,
  And with thy words thou slay'st our wounded
    thoughts.
  Nor shall I longer dally with the world,
  Procrastinating Alexandro's death:
  Go some of you and fetch the traitor forth,
  That as he is condemned he may die.     30

*Enter* ALEXANDRO *with a Nobleman and Halberts*

2 NOBLEMAN In such extremes will naught but patience
  serve.

ALEXANDRO But in extremes what patience shall I use?
  Nor discontents it me to leave the world
  With whom there nothing can prevail but wrong.

2 NOBLEMAN Yet hope the best.

ALEXANDRO           'Tis Heaven is my hope.
  As for the earth, it is too much infect
  To yield me hope of any of her mould.

VICEROY Why linger ye? Bring forth that daring fiend,
  And let him die for his accursed deed.

ALEXANDRO Not that I fear the extremity of death,     40
  For nobles cannot stoop to servile fear,
  Do I, O king, thus discontented live.
  But this, O this, torments my labouring soul,
  That thus I die suspected of a sin,
  Whereof, as heavens have known my secret thoughts,
  So am I free from this suggestion.

VICEROY No more, I say! To the tortures! When!
  Bind him, and burn his body in those flames,
                *They bind him to the stake*
  That shall prefigure those unquenched fires
  Of Phlegethon prepared for his soul.     50

ALEXANDRO My guiltless death will be avenged on thee,
  On thee, Villuppo, that hath maliced thus,
  Or for thy meed hast falsely me accused.

---

9 sickle: an instrument of harvest but also with a
  connotation of death, as with the scythe
11 heavy case: in a sad state
1 Infortunate: unfortunate
2 Seated: placed
  helpless: beyond help
  doubts: fears
4 heat: fury
5 the wheel of chance: a common image describing rising
  and falling fortune, especially in political terms
7 doubt: suspect
10 That would be feared: that would wish to be feared
11 Sith: since
12 Lordings: Lords
14 successive line: line of succession
17 words . . . works: words do not always represent actual
  deeds
18 credit . . . countenance: a person's outward show (face)
  does not necessarily reflect intention
19 train: treachery
20 coloured: disguised

---

21 consorted: kept company with
23 hourly coasts . . . the earth: refers to the belief that the
  earth was the centre of the universe, thus a symbol of
  constancy
24 purpose: attitude
SD *Halberts*: halberdiers
32–4 Alexandro's distress anticipates Hieronimo's in the next
  scene
34 With whom . . . but wrong: all I ever see is injustice
36 infect: infected
37 any of her mould: anyone born there
46 suggestion: false accusation
47 When!: exclamation of impatience
50 Phlegethon: the river of fire in Hades, the classical Hell
52 maliced: behaved maliciously
53 meed: advantage

VILLUPPO  Nay, Alexandro, if thou menace me,
  I'll lend a hand to send thee to the lake
  Where those thy words shall perish with thy works,
  Injurious traitor, monstrous homicide!

*Enter* AMBASSADOR

AMBASSADOR  Stay, hold a while,
  And here, with pardon of his majesty,
  Lay hands upon Villuppo.
VICEROY                    Ambassador,          60
  What news hath urged this sudden entrance?
AMBASSADOR  Know, sovereign lord, that Balthazar
  doth live.
VICEROY  What say'st thou? Liveth Balthazar our son?
AMBASSADOR  Your highness' son, Lord Balthazar, doth
  live;
  And, well entreated in the court of Spain,
  Humbly commends him to your majesty.
  These eyes beheld, and these my followers;
  With these, the letters of the king's commends,
                              *Gives him letters*
  Are happy witnesses of his highness' health.
          *The* VICEROY *looks on the letters, and proceeds*
VICEROY  (*Reads*) 'Thy son doth live, your tribute is
  received,                                      70
  Thy peace is made, and we are satisfied.
  The rest resolve upon as things proposed
  For both our honours and thy benefit.'
AMBASSADOR  These are his highness' farther articles.
                          *He gives him more letters*
VICEROY  Accursed wretch, to intimate these ills
  Against the life and reputation
  Of noble Alexandro! Come, my lord,
  Let him unbind thee that is bound to death,
  To make a quital for thy discontent.
                              *They unbind him*
ALEXANDRO  Dread lord, in kindness you could do no
  less,                                          80
  Upon report of such a damned fact.
  But thus we see our innocence hath saved
  The hopeless life which thou, Villuppo, sought
  By thy suggestions to have massacred.
VICEROY  Say, false Villuppo, wherefore didst thou thus
  Falsely betray Lord Alexandro's life?
  Him, whom thou knowest that no unkindness else,
  But even the slaughter of our dearest son,

Could once have moved us to have misconceived.
ALEXANDRO  Say, treacherous Villuppo, tell the king, 90
  Wherein hath Alexandro used thee ill?
VILLUPPO  Rent with remembrance of so foul a deed,
  My guilty soul submits me to thy doom:
  For, not for Alexandro's injuries,
  But for reward and hope to be preferred,
  Thus have I shamelessly hazarded his life.
VICEROY  Which, villain, shall be ransomed with thy
  death,
  And not so mean a torment as we here
  Devised for him who thou said'st slew our son,
  But with the bitterest torments and extremes   100
  That may be yet invented for thine end.
                          *Alexandro seems to entreat*
  Entreat me not, go, take the traitor hence.
                          *Exit* VILLUPPO *guarded*
  And, Alexandro, let us honour thee
  With public notice of thy loyalty.
  To end those things articulated here
  By our great lord, the mighty King of Spain,
  We with our Council will deliberate.
  Come, Alexandro, keep us company.
                                          *Exeunt*

# Act III, scene ii

*Enter* HIERONIMO

HIERONIMO  O eyes, no eyes, but fountains fraught
  with tears;
  O life, no life, but lively form of death;
  O world, no world, but mass of public wrongs,
  Confused and filled with murder and misdeeds!
  O sacred heavens! If this unhallowed deed,
  If this inhuman and barbarous attempt,
  If this incomparable murder thus
  Of mine, but now no more my son,
  Shall unrevealed and unrevenged pass,
  How should we term your dealings to be just,    10
  If you unjustly deal with those that in your justice
  trust?
  The night, sad secretary to my moans,
  With direful visions wake my vexed soul,
  And with the wounds of my distressful son

---

55  lake: the lake of Acheron in Hades, into which the
    Phlegethon flows
61  entrance: three syllables
66  commends him: sends greetings
79  quital: recompense
80  in kindness: naturally
81  fact: deed
84  suggestions: false accusations

89  misconceived: suspected
92  Rent: torn
97  ransomed: repaid
105  articulated here: expressed in the letter sent by the King
    of Spain
  1  fraught: filled
  2  lively form of death: death with the appearance of life
  4  Confused: disordered
  12  secretary: confidant
  14  distressful: giving rise to distress

Solicit me for notice of his death.
The ugly fiends do sally forth of hell,
And frame my steps to unfrequented paths,
And fear my heart with fierce inflamed thoughts.
The cloudy day my discontents records,
Early begins to register my dreams                    20
And drive me forth to seek the murderer.
Eyes, life, world, heavens, hell, night, and day,
See, search, show, send some man, some mean, that
    may—                                *A letter falleth*
What's here? A letter? Tush, it is not so!
A letter written to Hieronimo!                   *Red ink*
(*Reads*) 'For want of ink, receive this bloody writ.
Me hath my hapless brother hid from thee:
Revenge thyself on Balthazar and him,
For these were they that murderèd thy son.
Hieronimo, revenge Horatio's death,                   30
And better fare than Bel-imperia doth.'
What means this unexpected miracle?
My son slain by Lorenzo and the prince!
What cause had they Horatio to malign?
Or what might move thee, Bel-imperia,
To accuse thy brother, had he been the mean?
Hieronimo, beware, thou art betrayed,
And to entrap thy life this train is laid.
Advise thee therefore, be not credulous:
This is devised to endanger thee,                     40
That thou by this Lorenzo shouldst accuse,
And he, for thy dishonour done, should draw
Thy life in question, and thy name in hate.
Dear was the life of my beloved son,
And of his death behoves me be revenged:
Then hazard not thine own, Hieronimo,
But live t'effect thy resolution.
I therefore will by circumstances try
What I can gather to confirm this writ,
And, hearkening near the Duke of Castile's house, 50
Close if I can with Bel-imperia,
To listen more, but nothing to bewray.

---

*Enter* PEDRINGANO

Now Pedringano!
PEDRINGANO          Now, Hieronimo!
HIERONIMO Where's thy lady?
PEDRINGANO          I know not; here's my lord.

*Enter* LORENZO

LORENZO How now, who's this? Hieronimo?
HIERONIMO                        My lord.
PEDRINGANO He asketh for my lady Bel-imperia.
LORENZO What to do, Hieronimo? The duke my father
    hath
    Upon some disgrace awhile removed her hence;
    But if it be aught I may inform her of,
    Tell me, Hieronimo, and I'll let her know it.    60
HIERONIMO Nay, nay, my lord, I thank you, it shall not
    need.
    I had a suit unto her, but too late,
    And her disgrace makes me unfortunate.
LORENZO Why so, Hieronimo? Use me.
HIERONIMO O no, my lord, I dare not, it must not be,
    I humbly thank your lordship.
LORENZO                        Why then, farewell.
HIERONIMO My grief no heart, my thoughts no tongue
    can tell.                                  *Exit*
LORENZO Come hither, Pedringano, see'st thou this?
PEDRINGANO My lord, I see it, and suspect it too.
LORENZO This is that damned villain Serberine,       70
    That hath, I fear, revealed Horatio's death.
PEDRINGANO My lord, he could not, 'twas so lately
    done;
    And since, he hath not left my company.
LORENZO Admit he have not, his condition's such,
    As fear or flattering words may make him false.
    I know his humour, and therewith repent
    That e'er I used him in this enterprise.
    But Pedringano, to prevent the worst,
    And 'cause I know thee secret as my soul,
    Here, for thy further satisfaction, take thou this, 80
                            *Gives him more gold*
    And hearken to me. Thus it is devised:
    This night thou must, and prithee so resolve,
    Meet Serberine at Saint Luigi's Park—
    Thou know'st 'tis here hard by behind the house.
    There take thy stand, and see thou strike him sure,
    For die he must, if we do mean to live.
PEDRINGANO But how shall Serberine be there, my lord?
LORENZO Let me alone, I'll send to him to meet

---

18  fear: frighten
23  mean: method
SD  *A letter falleth*: the sudden arrival of the letter indicates
    the way that circumstances, directed by Revenge, move
    towards the working-out of revenge
26  writ: document
27  hapless: luckless
34  malign: hate
36  mean: means
38  train: plot
42–3  should draw/Thy life in question: should endanger your
    life
47  resolution: resolve (to take revenge)
48  by circumstances: by gathering evidence
51  Close: meet or come to an undertanding
52  bewray: disclose

---

62  suit unto her: a request to make to her
74  condition's: disposition's
76  humour: temperament
79  secret: a) secretive; b) reliable
85  strike him sure: kill him
88  Let me alone: leave it to me

The prince and me, where thou must do this deed. **89**
PEDRINGANO It shall be done, my lord, it shall be done,
    And I'll go arm myself to meet him there.
LORENZO When things shall alter, as I hope they will,
    Then shalt thou mount for this: thou know'st my
      mind.                   *Exit* PEDRINGANO
    *Che le Ieron!*

*Enter* PAGE

PAGE         My lord?
LORENZO           Go, sirrah, to Serberine,
    And bid him forthwith meet the prince and me
    At Saint Luigi's Park, behind the house.
    This evening, boy!
PAGE           I go, my lord.
LORENZO But, sirrah, let the hour be eight o'clock.
    Bid him not fail.
PAGE           I fly, my lord.         *Exit*
LORENZO Now to confirm the complot thou hast cast
    Of all these practices, I'll spread the watch,   **101**
    Upon precise commandment from the king,
    Strongly to guard the place where Pedringano
    This night shall murder hapless Serberine.
    Thus must we work that will avoid distrust,
    Thus must we practise to prevent mishap,
    And thus one ill another must expulse.
    This sly enquiry of Hieronimo
    For Bel-imperia breeds suspicion,
    And this suspicion bodes a further ill.   **110**
    As for myself, I know my secret fault;
    And so do they, but I have dealt for them.
    They that for coin their souls endangered,
    To save my life, for coin shall venture theirs:
    And better it's that base companions die,
    Than by their life to hazard our good haps.
    Nor shall they live, for me to fear their faith:
    I'll trust myself, myself shall be my friend,
    For die they shall, slaves are ordained to no other end.
                              *Exit*

---

93 mount: rise socially, but also an ironic joke about
    'mounting' the scaffold
94 *Che le Ieron!*: the meaning is not clear. Possibly equivalent
    to the Italian 'chi là' ('who's there?') with Ieron the name
    of the page
100 complot: plot
    cast: devised
101 practices: deceits
    spread the watch: position the constables
107 expulse: expel
113 for coin: for money (as reward)
115 base companions: low-bred fellow conspirators
116 good haps: good fortune
119 slaves: another contemptuous term for his low-bred
    associates

# Act III, scene iii

*Enter* PEDRINGANO *with a pistol*

PEDRINGANO Now, Pedringano, bid thy pistol hold;
    And hold on, Fortune! Once more favour me;
    Give but success to mine attempting spirit,
    And let me shift for taking of mine aim!
    Here is the gold, this is the gold proposed:
    It is no dream that I adventure for,
    But Pedringano is possessed thereof.
    And he that would not strain his conscience
    For him that thus his liberal purse hath stretched,
    Unworthy such a favour may he fail,   **10**
    And, wishing, want, when such as I prevail.
    As for the fear of apprehension,
    I know, if need should be, my noble lord
    Will stand between me and ensuing harms;
    Besides, this place is free from all suspect.
    Here therefore will I stay and take my stand.

*Enter the* WATCH

1 WATCH I wonder much to what intent it is
    That we are thus expressly charged to watch.
2 WATCH 'Tis by commandment in the king's own
    name.                           **19**
3 WATCH But we were never wont to watch and ward
    So near the duke his brother's house before.
2 WATCH Content yourself, stand close, there's
    somewhat in't.

*Enter* SERBERINE

SERBERINE Here, Serberine, attend and stay thy pace,
    For here did Don Lorenzo's page appoint
    That thou by his command shouldst meet with him.
    How fit a place, if one were so disposed,
    Methinks this corner is, to close with one.
PEDRINGANO Here comes the bird that I must seize
    upon;
    Now, Pedringano, or never, play the man!
SERBERINE I wonder that his lordship stays so long,   **30**
    Or wherefore should he send for me so late?
PEDRINGANO For this, Serberine, and thou shalt ha't.
                         *Shoots the dag*
So, there he lies, my promise is performed.

*The* WATCH *coming forward*

---

1 hold: function properly
4 let me shift: leave it (the taking of aim) to me
10 fail: a) be unsuccessful; b) fall into poverty
15 suspect: suspicion
20 wont to watch and ward: accustomed to keep guard
22 close: a) close; b) concealed
23 stay thy pace: stop walking
27 close: grapple
SD *dag*: a heavy pistol

1 WATCH  Hark gentlemen, this is a pistol shot.
2 WATCH  And here's one slain; stay the murderer.
PEDRINGANO  Now by the sorrows of the souls in hell,
*He strives with the* WATCH
Who first lays hand on me, I'll be his priest.
3 WATCH  Sirrah, confess, and therein play the priest;
Why hast thou thus unkindly killed the man?    **39**
PEDRINGANO  Why? Because he walked abroad so late.
3 WATCH  Come sir, you had been better kept your bed,
Than have committed this misdeed so late.
3 WATCH  Come, to the Marshal's with the murderer!
1 WATCH  On to Hieronimo's! Help me here
To bring the murdered body with us too.
PEDRINGANO  Hieronimo? Carry me before whom you will,
Whate'er he be I'll answer him and you.
And do your worst, for I defy you all.

*Exeunt*

# Act III, scene iv

*Enter* LORENZO *and* BALTHAZAR

BALTHAZAR  How now, my lord, what makes you rise so soon?
LORENZO  Fear of preventing our mishaps too late.
BALTHAZAR  What mischief is it that we not mistrust?
LORENZO  Our greatest ills we least mistrust, my lord,
And inexpected harms do hurt us most.
BALTHAZAR  Why tell me Don Lorenzo, tell me man,
If aught concerns our honour and your own.
LORENZO  Nor you nor me, my lord, but both in one;
For I suspect, and the presumption's great,
That by those base confederates in our fault    **10**
Touching the death of Don Horatio,
We are betrayed to old Hieronimo.
BALTHAZAR  Betrayed, Lorenzo? Tush, it cannot be.
LORENZO  A guilty conscience, urged with the thought
Of former evils, easily cannot err:
I am persuaded, and dissuade me not,
That all's revealed to Hieronimo.
And therefore know that I have cast it thus—

*Enter* PAGE

But here's the page. How now, what news with thee?
PAGE  My lord, Serberine is slain.    **20**
BALTHAZAR  Who? Serberine, my man?

PAGE  Your highness' man, my lord.
LORENZO  Speak page, who murdered him?
PAGE  He that is apprehended for the fact.
LORENZO  Who?
PAGE  Pedringano.
BALTHAZAR  Is Serberine slain, that loved his lord so well?
Injurious villain, murderer of his friend!
LORENZO  Hath Pedringano murdered Serberine?
My lord, let me entreat you to take the pains    **30**
To exasperate and hasten his revenge
With your complaints unto my lord the king.
This their dissension breeds a greater doubt.
BALTHAZAR  Assure thee, Don Lorenzo, he shall die,
Or else his highness hardly shall deny.
Meanwhile I'll haste the Marshal-Sessions,
For die he shall for this his damned deed.

*Exit* BALTHAZAR

LORENZO  Why so, this fits our former policy,
And thus experience bids the wise to deal:
I lay the plot, he prosecutes the point;    **40**
I set the trap, he breaks the worthless twigs,
And sees not that wherewith the bird was limed.
Thus hopeful men, that mean to hold their own,
Must look like fowlers to their dearest friends.
He runs to kill whom I have holp to catch,
And no man knows it was my reaching fatch.
'Tis hard to trust unto a multitude,
Or anyone, in mine opinion,
When men themselves their secrets will reveal.

*Enter a* MESSENGER *with a letter*

Boy!    **50**
PAGE  My lord?
LORENZO  What's he?
MESSENGER  I have a letter to your lordship.
LORENZO  From whence?
MESSENGER  From Pedringano that's imprisoned.
LORENZO  So he is in prison then?
MESSENGER  Ay, my good lord.
LORENZO  What would he with us? He writes us here

---

35  stay: arrest
37  I'll be his priest: I'll attend his death
39  unkindly: unnaturally
40  abroad: out of doors
2   preventing: forestalling
3   not mistrust: anticipate
10  confederates in our fault: partners in our crime
18  cast it thus: laid these plans

24  fact: crime, evil deed
31  exasperate: make harsh
32  complaints: grievances
33  doubt: fear
35  hardly shall deny: Edwards suggests 'shall show harshness in denying me'
36  the Marshal-Sessions: more properly (in England) the Court of Marshalsea
38  policy: immoral strategy (in the Machiavellian sense)
40  prosecutes the point: fulfils the objective for me
42  limed: caught in bird-lime
45  holp: helped
46  my reaching fatch: my far-reaching stratagem

To stand good lord and help him in distress.
Tell him I have his letters, know his mind,
And what we may, let him assure him of.
Fellow, begone: my boy shall follow thee.

*Exit* MESSENGER

This works like wax; yet once more try thy wits. **60**
Boy, go convey this purse to Pedringano,
Thou knowest the prison, closely give it him,
And be advised that none be there about.
Bid him be merry still, but secret;
And though the Marshal-Sessions be today,
Bid him not doubt of his delivery.
Tell him his pardon is already signed,
And thereon bid him boldly be resolved;
For, were he ready to be turned off
(As 'tis my will the uttermost be tried) **70**
Thou with his pardon shalt attend him still.
Show him this box, tell him his pardon's in't,
But open't not, and if thou lov'st thy life,
But let him wisely keep his hopes unknown;
He shall not want while Don Lorenzo lives.
Away!

PAGE    I go my lord, I run.

LORENZO  But sirrah, see that this be cleanly done.

*Exit* PAGE

Now stands our fortune on a tickle point,
And now or never ends Lorenzo's doubts.
One only thing is uneffected yet, **80**
And that's to see the executioner.
But to what end? I list not trust the air
With utterance of our pretence therein,
For fear the privy whispering of the wind
Convey our words amongst unfriendly ears,
That lie too open to advantages.
*E quel che voglio io, nessun lo sa,*
*Intendo io: quel mi basterà.*

*Exit*

## Act III, scene v

*Enter* BOY *with the box*

PAGE  My master hath forbidden me to look in this box,
and by my troth 'tis likely, if he had not warned me, I
should not have had so much idle time; for we men's-
kind in our minority are like women in their
uncertainty: that they are most forbidden, they will
soonest attempt. So I now. By my bare honesty,
here's nothing but the bare empty box. Were it not
sin against secrecy, I would say it were a piece of
gentleman-like knavery. I must go to Pedringano,
and tell him his pardon is in this box; nay, I would
have sworn it, had I not seen the contrary. I cannot
choose but smile to think how the villain will flout
the gallows, scorn the audience, and descant on the
hangman, and all presuming of his pardon from
hence. Will't not be an odd jest, for me to stand and
grace every jest he makes, pointing my finger at this
box, as who would say, 'mock on, here's thy warrant.'
Is't not a scurvy jest, that a man should jest himself to
death? Alas, poor Pedringano, I am in a sort sorry for
thee, but if I should be hanged with thee, I cannot
weep. **21**

*Exit*

## Act III, scene vi

*Enter* HIERONIMO *and the* DEPUTY

HIERONIMO  Thus must we toil in other men's
        extremes,
That know not how to remedy our own;
And do them justice, when unjustly we,
For all our wrongs, can compass no redress.
But shall I never live to see the day
That I may come, by justice of the heavens,
To know the cause that may my cares allay?
This toils my body, this consumeth age,
That only I to all men just must be,

---

56  stand good lord: act as a good lord and his protector
60  works like wax: smoothly goes the way I intended
62  closely: secretly
63  be advised: be careful
64  secret: silent
68  boldly be resolved: feel confident
69  turned off: hanged
77  cleanly: efficiently
78  tickle: precarious
79  doubts: fears
82  list not: have no wish to
83  pretence: intention
84  privy: private
86  advantages: getting the upper hand
87–8  *E quel . . . mi basterà*: 'And what I want, no one knows; I
    understand and that is enough for me' (Italian)

---

SD  *the box* is possibly meant to be associated with Pandora's
    box in which only hope was left when all human
    qualities, both good and ill, had vanished
2  by my troth: by my truth, an oath
4  minority: boyhood
5  uncertainty: fearfulness
13  descant: hold forth about
18  scurvy: bitter
SD  DEPUTY: the assistant to the Knight Marshal
1–10  Hieronimo's concern here is with justice rather than
    simple revenge
1  extremes: difficulties
4  compass: locate
8  toils: burdens
    consumeth age: uses up my life

And neither gods nor men be just to me.                    10

DEPUTY  Worthy Hieronimo, your office asks
A care to punish such as do transgress.

HIERONIMO  So is't my duty to regard his death
Who, when he lived, deserved my dearest blood.
But come, for that we came for, let's begin,
For here lies that which bids me to be gone.

*Enter* OFFICERS, BOY, *and* PEDRINGANO, *with a letter in his hand, bound*

DEPUTY  Bring forth the prisoner, for the court is set.

PEDRINGANO  Gramercy, boy, but it was time to come;
For I had written to my lord anew
A nearer matter that concerneth him,                    20
For fear his lordship had forgotten me.
But sith he hath remembered me so well—
Come, come, come on, when shall we to this gear?

HIERONIMO  Stand forth, thou monster, murderer of
men,
And here, for satisfaction of the world,
Confess thy folly and repent thy fault,
For there's thy place of execution.

PEDRINGANO  This is short work! Well, to your
marshalship
First I confess, nor fear I death therefore,
I am the man, 'twas I slew Serberine.                    30
But sir, then you think this shall be the place
Where we shall satisfy you for this gear?

DEPUTY  Ay, Pedringano.

PEDRINGANO                    Now I think not so.

HIERONIMO  Peace, impudent, for thou shalt find it so:
For blood with blood shall, while I sit as judge,
Be satisfied, and the law discharged.
And though myself cannot receive the like,
Yet will I see that others have their right.
Despatch, the fault's approved and confessed,
And by our law he is condemned to die.                    40

HANGMAN  Come on sir, are you ready?

PEDRINGANO  To do what, my fine officious knave?

HANGMAN  To go to this gear.

PEDRINGANO  O sir, you are too forward; thou wouldst
fain furnish me with a halter, to disfurnish me of my
habit. So I should go out of this gear, my raiment,
into that gear, the rope. But, hangman, now I spy
your knavery, I'll not change without boot, that's flat.

HANGMAN  Come sir.

PEDRINGANO  So then, I must up?                    50

HANGMAN  No remedy.

PEDRINGANO  Yes, but there shall be for my coming
down.

HANGMAN  Indeed, here's a remedy for that.

PEDRINGANO  How? Be turned off?

HANGMAN  Ay, truly; come, are you ready? I pray, sir,
despatch, the day goes away.

PEDRINGANO  What, do you hang by the hour? If you
do, I may chance to break your old custom.

HANGMAN  Faith, you have reason, for I am like to
break your young neck.                    61

PEDRINGANO  Dost thou mock me, hangman? Pray
God I be not preserved to break your knave's pate for
this.

HANGMAN  Alas, sir, you are a foot too low to reach it,
and I hope you will never grow so high while I am in
the office.

PEDRINGANO  Sirrah, dost see yonder boy with the box
in his hand?

HANGMAN  What, he that points to it with his finger?

PEDRINGANO  Ay, that companion.                    71

HANGMAN  I know him not, but what of him?

PEDRINGANO  Dost thou think to live till his old
doublet will make thee a new truss?

HANGMAN  Ay, and many a fair year after, to truss up
many an honester man than either thou or he.

PEDRINGANO  What hath he in his box, as thou
think'st?

HANGMAN  Faith, I cannot tell, nor I care not greatly.
Methinks you should rather hearken to your soul's
health.                    81

PEDRINGANO  Why, sirrah hangman, I take it, that that
is good for the body is likewise good for the soul; and
it may be, in that box is balm for both.

HANGMAN  Well, thou art even the merriest piece of
man's flesh that e'er groaned at my office door.

PEDRINGANO  Is your roguery become an 'office' with a
knave's name?

HANGMAN  Ay, and that shall all they witness that see
you seal it with a thief's name.                    90

---

13  regard: concern myself with
14  dearest blood: utmost loyalty
18  Gramercy: an expression of relief
20  nearer: more serious
23  gear: business
32  gear: deed, behaviour
39  approved: proved
43  this gear: the gallows
44  forward: presumptuous
45  halter: noose
disfurnish . . . habit: referring to the custom which grants
the executioner his victim's clothes or habit

48  boot: compensation
55  turned off: hanged (pushed off the support)
57  despatch: 'let's get to work'
58  by the hour: at set times or at an hourly rate
63  pate: head
71  companion: fellow
74  truss: close-fitting garment
75  truss up: hang
80  hearken: to pay attention to
87  'office': Pedringano mocks the hangman's high notion of
his profession

PEDRINGANO  I prithee, request this good company to
    pray with me.
HANGMAN  Ay marry sir, this is a good motion; my
    masters, you see here's a good fellow.
PEDRINGANO  Nay, nay, now I remember me, let them
    alone till some other time, for now I have no great
    need.
HIERONIMO  I have not seen a wretch so impudent!
    O monstrous times, where murder's set so light;    **99**
    And where the soul that should be shrined in heaven,
    Solely delights in interdicted things,
    Still wandering in the thorny passages
    That intercepts itself of happiness.
    Murder, O bloody monster. God forbid
    A fault so foul should 'scape unpunished.
    Despatch and see this execution done—
    This makes me to remember thee, my son.
                            *Exit* HIERONIMO
PEDRINGANO  Nay soft, no haste.
DEPUTY  Why, wherefore stay you? Have you hope of
    life?    **110**
PEDRINGANO  Why, ay.
HANGMAN  As how?
PEDRINGANO  Why, rascal, by my pardon from the
    king.
HANGMAN  Stand you on that? Then you shall off with
    this.    *He turns him off*
DEPUTY  So, executioner. Convey him hence,
    But let his body be unburied:
    Let not the earth be choked or infect    **119**
    With that which heaven contemns, and men neglect.
                            *Exeunt*

# Act III, scene vii

*Enter* HIERONIMO

HIERONIMO  Where shall I run to breathe abroad my
    woes,
    My woes, whose weight hath wearied the earth?
    Or mine exclaims, that have surcharged the air
    With ceaseless plaints for my deceased son?
    The blustering winds, conspiring with my words,
    At my lament have moved the leafless trees,
    Disrobed the meadows of their flowered green,
    Made mountains marsh with spring-tides of my
    tears,
    And broken through the brazen gates of hell.

Yet still tormented is my tortured soul    **10**
With broken sighs and restless passions,
That winged mount, and hovering in the air,
Beat at the windows of the brightest heavens,
Soliciting for justice and revenge;
But they are placed in those empyreal heights,
Where, counter-mured with walls of diamond,
I find the place impregnable; and they
Resist my woes, and give my words no way.

*Enter* HANGMAN *with a letter*

HANGMAN  O lord sir, God bless you sir, the man sir,
    Petergade sir, he that was so full of merry conceits—
HIERONIMO  Well, what of him?    **21**
HANGMAN  O lord sir, he went the wrong way, the
    fellow had a fair commission to the contrary. Sir,
    here is his passport I pray you sir, we have done him
    wrong.
HIERONIMO  I warrant thee, give it me.
HANGMAN  You will stand between the gallows and me?
HIERONIMO  Ay, ay.
HANGMAN  I thank your Lord Worship.
                            *Exit* HANGMAN
HIERONIMO  And yet, though somewhat nearer me
    concerns,    **30**
    I will, to ease the grief that I sustain,
    Take truce with sorrow while I read on this.
    'My lord, I writ as mine extremes required,
    That you would labour my delivery;
    If you neglect, my life is desperate,
    And in my death I shall reveal the troth.
    You know, my lord, I slew him for your sake;
    And as confederate with the prince and you,
    Won by rewards and hopeful promises,
    I help to murder Don Horatio too.'    **40**
    Holp he to murder mine Horatio?
    And actors in th'accursed tragedy
    Wast thou, Lorenzo, Balthazar and thou,
    Of whom my son, my son deserved so well?
    What have I heard, what have mine eyes beheld?
    O sacred heavens, may it come to pass
    That such a monstrous and detested deed,
    So closely smothered, and so long concealed,

---

93  motion: idea
101  inderdicted: prohibited
102  Still: forever
108  soft: wait a moment
115  Stand: rely
  1  breathe abroad: give expression to
  3  exclaims: cries

11  passions: sufferings
15  empyreal: heavenly
16  counter-mured: doubly-walled as in a castle with
    concentric walls
20  Petergade: this is as near as the hangman can get to
    'Pedringano'
    conceits: jests
23  fair commission: written authority
33  writ: Q has 'write' but editors agree that the past tense is
    correct. Pedringano refers to the earlier letter
    extremes: predicament
48  closely smothered: kept secret

Shall thus by this be vengèd or revealed!
Now see I what I durst not then suspect, 50
That Bel-imperia's letter was not feigned.
Nor feigned she, though falsely they have wronged
Both her, myself, Horatio and themselves.
Now may I make compare, 'twixt hers and this,
Of every accident; I ne'er could find
Till now, and now I feelingly perceive,
They did what heaven unpunished would not leave.
O false Lorenzo, are these thy flattering looks?
Is this the honour that thou didst my son?
And Balthazar, bane to thy soul and me, 60
Was this the ransom he reserved thee for?
Woe to the cause of these constrained wars,
Woe to thy baseness and captivity,
Woe to thy birth, thy body and thy soul,
Thy cursed father, and thy conquered self!
And banned with bitter execrations be
The day and place where he did pity thee!
But wherefore waste I mine unfruitful words,
When naught but blood will satisfy my woes?
I will go plain me to my lord the king, 70
And cry aloud for justice through the court,
Wearing the flints with these my withered feet,
And either purchase justice by entreats
Or tire them all with my revenging threats.

*Exit*

## Act III, scene viii

*Enter* ISABELLA *and her Maid*

ISABELLA So that, you say, this herb will purge the eye,
And this the head?

---

51–2 That Bel-imperia's . . . feigned she: 'He is relieved of two
 doubts, whether or not Bel-imperia really wrote the
 letter, and if so whether or not she was telling the truth'
 (McIlwraith)
54–7 Now may . . . not leave: 'Now I can check on every
 happening, by using the two letters; I could never be sure
 till now – but I see very vividly – that they committed
 this crime which Heaven must and will punish'
 (Mulryne)
55 accident: occurrence, with reference to Horatio's death
 find: understand
62 constrained: forced
66 banned: cursed
70–4 I will . . . revenging threats: Hieronimo determines to
 seek 'official' justice (represented by the king) but this
 speech ominously foreshadows the inadequacy of this and
 the consequent impulse towards private revenge
SD *Enter* ISABELLA *and her Maid*: some editors have begun a
 new act at this point, thus giving *The Spanish Tragedy* the
 five-act format typical of plays of this period. However,
 this revision would mean that Act III would end without
 an exchange between Don Andrea and Revenge
1 purge: cleanse

---

Ah, but none of them will purge the heart:
No there's no medicine left for my disease,
Nor any physic to recure the dead. *She runs lunatic*
Horatio! O, where's Horatio?
MAID Good madam, affright not thus yourself
With outrage for your son Horatio:
He sleeps in quiet in the Elysian fields.
ISABELLA Why, did I not give you gowns and goodly
 things, 10
Bought you a whistle and a whipstalk too,
To be revenged on their villainies?
MAID Madam, these humours do torment my soul.
ISABELLA My soul! Poor soul, thou talks of things
Thou know'st not what—my soul hath silver wings,
That mounts me up unto the highest heavens;
To heaven, ay, there sits my Horatio,
Backed with a troop of fiery cherubins,
Dancing about his newly-healed wounds,
Singing sweet hymns and chanting heavenly notes,
Rare harmony to greet his innocence, 21
That died, ay died a mirror in our days.
But say, where shall I find the men, the murderers,
That slew Horatio? Whither shall I run
To find them out that murdered my son?

*Exeunt*

## Act III, scene ix

BEL-IMPERIA *at a window*

BEL-IMPERIA What means this outrage that is offered
 me?
Why am I thus sequestered from the court?
No notice? Shall I not know the cause
Of this my secret and suspicious ills?
Accursed brother, unkind murderer,
Why bends thou thus thy mind to martyr me?
Hieronimo, why writ I of thy wrongs,
Or why art thou so slack in thy revenge?
Andrea, O Andrea, that thou sawest
Me for thy friend Horatio handled thus, 10
And him for me thus causeless murdered.
Well, force perforce, I must constrain myself

---

5 recure: restore to health
11 whipstalk: whip-handle
13 humours: passions
14–22 Isabella's speech here evokes a Christian afterlife which
 contrasts with the classical descriptions which
 shaped the theology of the play to this point
21 to greet: to honour or celebrate (rather than to welcome)
22 mirror: model of excellence
2 sequestered: kept apart
3 No notice?: kept ignorant?
6 bends: directs
12 force perforce: of necessity

---

To patience, and apply me to the time,
Till heaven, as I have hoped shall set me free.

*Enter* CHRISTOPHIL

CHRISTOPHIL  Come, Madam Bel-imperia, this may
  not be.

                            *Exeunt*

# Act III, scene x

*Enter* LORENZO, BALTHAZAR, *and the* PAGE

LORENZO  Boy, talk no further, thus far things go well.
  Thou art assured that thou sawest him dead?
PAGE  Or else my lord I live not.
LORENZO                That's enough.
  As for his resolution in his end,
  Leave that to him with whom he sojourns now.
  Here, take my ring and give it Christophil,
  And bid him let my sister be enlarged,
  And bring her hither straight.     *Exit* PAGE
  This that I did was for a policy
  To smooth and keep the murder secret,       10
  Which as a nine-days' wonder being o'erblown,
  My gentle sister will I now enlarge.
BALTHAZAR  And time, Lorenzo, for my lord the duke,
  You heard, enquired for her yester-night.
LORENZO  Why, and, my lord, I hope you heard me say
  Sufficient reason why she kept away.
  But that's all one. My lord, you love her?
BALTHAZAR                       Ay.
LORENZO  Then in your love beware, deal cunningly,
  Salve all suspicions; only soothe me up;
  And if she hap to stand on terms with us,       20
  As for her sweetheart, and concealment so,
  Jest with her gently: under feigned jest
  Are things concealed that else would breed unrest.
  But here she comes.

*Enter* BEL-IMPERIA

             Now, sister—
BEL-IMPERIA                  Sister? No!
  Thou art no brother, but an enemy,
  Else wouldst thou not have used thy sister so:
  First, to affright me with thy weapons drawn,

And with extremes abuse my company;
And then to hurry me, like whirlwind's rage,
Amidst a crew of thy confederates,       30
And clap me up where none might come at me,
Nor I at any, to reveal my wrongs.
What madding fury did possess thy wits?
Or wherein is't that I offended thee?
LORENZO  Advise you better, Bel-imperia,
  For I have done you no disparagement;
  Unless, by more discretion than deserved,
  I sought to save your honour and mine own.
BEL-IMPERIA  Mine honour! Why, Lorenzo, wherein
  is't
  That I neglect my reputation so,       40
  As you, or any, need to rescue it?
LORENZO  His highness and my father were resolved
  To come confer with old Hieronimo,
  Concerning certain matters of estate,
  That by the viceroy was determined.
BEL-IMPERIA  And wherein was mine honour touched
  in that?
BALTHAZAR  Have patience, Bel-imperia; hear the rest.
LORENZO  Me next in sight as messenger they sent,
  To give him notice that they were so nigh:
  Now when I came, consorted with the prince       50
  And unexpected, in an arbour there,
  Found Bel-imperia with Horatio—
BEL-IMPERIA  How then?
LORENZO  Why then, remembering that old disgrace,
  Which you for Don Andrea had endured,
  And now were likely longer to sustain,
  By being found so meanly accompanied,
  Thought rather, for I knew no readier mean,
  To thrust Horatio forth my father's way.       59
BALTHAZAR  And carry you obscurely somewhere else,
  Lest that his highness should have found you there.
BEL-IMPERIA  Even so, my lord? And you are witness
  That this is true which he entreateth of?
  You, gentle brother, forged this for my sake,
  And you, my lord, were made his instrument:
  A work of worth, worthy the noting too!

---

13 apply me to the time: accept the situation
4 resolution: courage
7 enlarged: set free
9 policy: strategem
10 smooth: avoid consequences
19 Salve: again, smooth over the situation (as in a healing
  balm)
  soothe me up: agree with me
20 stand on terms with us: be difficult, try to make
  conditions

31 clap me up: lock me up
36 disparagement: dishonour
37 Unless, by . . . than deserved: 'unless it were that,
  showing more concern and foresight than you deserved'
  (Mulryne)
44 Concerning certain matters of estate: 'concerning certain
  matters about possessions which the viceroy had given
  up' (Edwards), although Mulryne notes that 'matters of
  estate' could mean 'matters of importance' or 'state-
  matters'
48 next in sight: standing nearby
57 meanly accompanied: one of a number of references
  throughout the play to Horatio's social inferiority
64 forged this: devised and carried through this action

But what's the cause that you concealed me since?
LORENZO  Your melancholy, sister, since the news
Of your first favourite Don Andrea's death,
My father's old wrath hath exasperate.                    70
BALTHAZAR  And better was't for you, being in
disgrace,
To absent yourself, and give his fury place.
BEL-IMPERIA  But why had I no notice of his ire?
LORENZO  That were to add more fuel to your fire,
Who burnt like Aetna for Andrea's loss.
BEL-IMPERIA  Hath not my father then enquired for
me?
LORENZO  Sister, he hath, and thus excused I thee.
                                *He whispereth in her ear*
But, Bel-imperia, see the gentle prince;
Look on thy love, behold young Balthazar,
Whose passions by thy presence are increased;            80
And in whose melancholy thou may'st see
Thy hate, his love; thy flight, his following thee.
BEL-IMPERIA  Brother, you are become an orator—
I know not, I, by what experience—
Too politic for me, past all compare,
Since last I saw you; but content yourself,
The prince is meditating higher things.
BALTHAZAR  'Tis of thy beauty, then, that conquers
kings;
Of those thy tresses, Ariadne's twines,
Wherewith my liberty thou hast surprised;                90
Of that thine ivory front, my sorrow's map,
Wherein I see no haven to rest my hope.
BEL-IMPERIA  To love and fear, and both at once, my
lord,
In my conceit, are things of more import
Than women's wits are to be busied with.
BALTHAZAR  'Tis I that love.
BEL-IMPERIA                          Whom?
BALTHAZAR                                        Bel-imperia.
BEL-IMPERIA  But I that fear.
BALTHAZAR                          Whom?
BEL-IMPERIA                                        Bel-imperia.
LORENZO  Fear yourself?
BEL-IMPERIA                    Ay, brother.

---

LORENZO                                        How?
BEL-IMPERIA                          As those
That what they love are loath and fear to lose.         99
BALTHAZAR  Then, fair, let Balthazar your keeper be.
BEL-IMPERIA  No, Balthazar doth fear as well as we:
*Et tremulo metui pavidum junxere timorem,*
*Et vanum stolidae proditionis opus.*           *Exit*
LORENZO  Nay and you argue things so cunningly,
We'll go continue this discourse at court.
BALTHAZAR  Led by the lodestar of her heavenly looks,
Wends poor oppressed Balthazar,
As o'er the mountains walks the wanderer,
Incertain to effect his pilgrimage.
                                                *Exeunt*

# Act III, scene xi

*Enter two* PORTINGALES, *and* HIERONIMO *meets them*

1 PORTINGALE  By your leave, sir.
HIERONIMO  Good leave have you: nay, I pray you go,
For I'll leave you; if you can leave me, so.
2 PORTINGALE  Pray you, which is the next way to my
lord the duke's?
HIERONIMO  The next way from me.
PORTINGALE                          To his house, we mean.
HIERONIMO  O, hard by, 'tis yon house that you see.
PORTINGALE  You could not tell us if his son were
there?
HIERONIMO  Who, my lord Lorenzo?
PORTINGALE                          Ay, sir.

*He goeth in at one door and comes out at another*

HIERONIMO                                        O, forbear,
For other talk for us far fitter were.
But if you be importunate to know                        10
The way to him, and where to find him out,
Then list to me, and I'll resolve your doubt.
There is a path upon your left-hand side,
That leadeth from a guilty conscience
Unto a forest of distrust and fear,
A darksome place, and dangerous to pass:
There shall you meet with melancholy thoughts,
Whose baleful humours if you but uphold,
It will conduct you to despair and death;

---

70  exasperate: heightened, made worse
72  give his fury place: let his anger burn itself out
75  Aetna: the volcano in Sicily
89  Ariadne's twines: in classical mythology Ariadne guided
    Theseus through the labyrinth using a thread, but Kyd
    may have confused Ariadne with Arachne, the Lydian
    weaver who was changed into a spider by Athene.
    Whatever the case, Balthazar means that Bel-imperia has
    metaphorically entangled him in the twines of her hair,
    an expression of her beauty
90  surprised: captured
91  front: forehead
94  In my conceit: to my mind

102–3  *Et tremulo . . . proditionis opus*: 'they linked severe dread
       to trembling fear, a futile work of idiotic treason'
       (Mulryne)
106  lodestar: a guiding star
109  Incertain to effect: unlikely to complete
  4  next: nearest
 10  be importunate to know: insist on knowing
 13  a path upon your left-hand side: the path to deepest hell
 18  baleful humours: evil disposition
     uphold: persist in

Whose rocky cliffs when you have once beheld,          20
Within a hugy dale of lasting night,
That, kindled with the world's iniquities,
Doth cast up filthy and detested fumes,
Not far from thence, where murderers have built
A habitation for their cursed souls,
There, in a brazen cauldron, fixed by Jove
In his fell wrath upon a sulphur flame,
Yourselves shall find Lorenzo bathing him
In boiling lead and blood of innocents.
1 PORTINGALE  Ha, ha, ha!                               30
HIERONIMO  Ha, ha, ha!
Why, ha, ha, ha! Farewell, good, ha, ha, ha!    *Exit*
2 PORTINGALE  Doubtless this man is passing lunatic,
Or imperfection of his age doth make him dote.
Come, let's away to seek my lord the duke.
                                                *Exeunt*

# Act III, scene xii

*Enter* HIERONIMO, *with a poniard in one hand, and a rope in the other*

HIERONIMO  Now sir, perhaps I come and see the king,
The king sees me, and fain would hear my suit:
Why, is not this a strange and seld-seen thing,
That standers-by with toys should strike me mute?
Go to, I see their shifts, and say no more.
Hieronimo, 'tis time for thee to trudge:
Down by the dale that flows with purple gore
Standeth a fiery tower; there sits a judge
Upon a seat of steel and molten brass,
And 'twixt his teeth he holds a fire-brand,       10
That leads unto the lake where hell doth stand.
Away, Hieronimo, to him be gone:
He'll do thee justice for Horatio's death.
Turn down this path, thou shalt be with him straight;
Or this, and then thou need'st not take thy breath.
This way or that way? Soft and fair, not so:
For if I hang or kill myself, let's know

---

21  hugy: huge
32  passing: exceedingly
33  imperfection of his age: senility
SD  Hieronimo enters with a dagger and a halter, the 'stock
    "properties" of a would-be suicide' in Elizabethan drama
    (Boas)
3   seld: seldom
4   toys: things (or matters) of no importance
5   shifts: tricks
6   trudge: get moving, but not necessarily slowly, as in the
    modern sense of the word
6–11  Hieronimo, 'tis . . . doth stand: Hieronimo seeks justice
    in a symbolic landscape which recalls that in which Don
    Andrea sought a resting place at the beginning of the
    play
7   purple: blood-red

Who will revenge Horatio's murder then?
No, no! Fie, No! pardon me, I'll none of that:
        *He flings away the dagger and halter*
This way I'll take, and this way comes the king;   20
        *He takes them up again*
And here I'll have a fling at him, that's flat;
And, Balthazar, I'll be with thee to bring,
And thee, Lorenzo! Here's the king; nay, stay,
And here, ay here; there goes the hare away.

*Enter* KING, AMBASSADOR, CASTILE, *and* LORENZO

KING  Now show, Ambassador, what our viceroy saith:
Hath he received the articles we sent?
HIERONIMO  Justice, O, justice to Hieronimo!
LORENZO  Back! See'st thou not the king is busy?
HIERONIMO  O, is he so?
KING  Who is he that interrupts our business?   30
HIERONIMO  Not I. Hieronimo, beware: go by, go by.
AMBASSADOR  Renowned king, he hath received and
    read
Thy kingly proffers, and thy promised league,
And, as a man extremely overjoyed
To hear his son so princely entertained
Whose death he had so solemnly bewailed,
This for thy further satisfaction
And kingly love, he kindly lets thee know:
First, for the marriage of his princely son
With Bel-imperia, thy beloved niece,           40
The news are more delightful to his soul,
Than myrrh or incense to the offended heavens.
In person, therefore, will he come himself,
To see the marriage rites solemnised;
And, in the presence of the court of Spain,
To knit a sure, inexplicable band
Of kingly love, and everlasting league,
Betwixt the crowns of Spain and Portingale,
There will he give his crown to Balthazar,
And make a queen of Bel-imperia.               50
KING  Brother, how like you this our viceroy's love?
CASTILE  No doubt, my lord, it is an argument
Of honourable care to keep his friend,
And wondrous zeal to Balthazar his son;
Nor am I least indebted to his grace
That bends his liking to my daughter thus.
AMBASSADOR  Now last, dread lord, here hath his
    highness sent
(Although he send not that his son return)

---

22  I'll be . . . to bring: I'll get even with you
24  there goes the hare away: Edwards notes that this refers
    to losing something one has tried to achieve or hold
31  go by, go by: be careful, don't get into trouble
46  inexplicable: that which cannot be untied
52  argument: proof
56  bends: directs
58  that: in order that

His ransom due to Don Horatio.

HIERONIMO Horatio! Who calls Horatio?                                    60

KING And well remembered, thank his majesty.
  Here, see it given to Horatio.

HIERONIMO Justice, O justice, justice, gentle king!

KING What is that? Hieronimo?

HIERONIMO Justice, O, justice! O my son, my son,
  My son, whom naught can ransom or redeem!

LORENZO Hieronimo, you are not well advised.

HIERONIMO Away, Lorenzo, hinder me no more,
  For thou hast made me bankrupt of my bliss.
  Give me my son, you shall not ransom him!         70
  Away! I'll rip the bowels of the earth,
                                    *He diggeth with his dagger*
  And ferry over to th' Elysian plains
  And bring my son to show his deadly wounds.
  Stand from about me!
  I'll make a pickaxe of my poniard,
  And here surrender up my marshalship:
  For I'll go marshal up the fiends in hell,
  To be avenged on you all for this.

KING What means this outrage?
  Will none of you restrain his fury?              80

HIERONIMO Nay, soft and fair: you shall not need to
    strive,
  Needs must he go that the devils drive.          *Exit*

KING What accident hath happed Hieronimo?
  I have not seen him to demean him so.

LORENZO My gracious lord, he is with extreme pride,
  Conceived of young Horatio his son,
  And covetous of having to himself
  The ransom of the young prince Balthazar,
  Distract, and in a manner lunatic.

KING Believe me, nephew, we are sorry for't:        90
  This is the love that fathers bear their sons.
  But, gentle brother, go give to him this gold,
  The prince's ransom; let him have his due.
  For what he hath Horatio shall not want:
  Haply Hieronimo hath need thereof.

LORENZO But if he be thus helplessly distract,
  'Tis requisite his office be resigned,
  And given to one of more discretion.

KING We shall increase his melancholy so.
  'Tis best that we see further in it first;         100
  Till when, ourself will exempt the place.
  And brother, now bring in the ambassador,
  That he may be a witness of the match

'Twixt Balthazar and Bel-imperia,
  And that we may prefix a certain time,
  Wherein the marriage shall be solemnised,
  That we may have thy lord the viceroy here.

AMBASSADOR Therein your highness highly shall
    content
  His majesty, that longs to hear from hence.

KING On, then, and hear you, Lord Ambassador.      110
                                                    *Exeunt*

# Act III, scene xiii

*Enter* HIERONIMO *with a book in his hand*

HIERONIMO *Vindicta mihi!*
  Ay, heaven will be revenged of every ill,
  Nor will they suffer murder unrepaid:
  Then stay, Hieronimo, attend their will,
  For mortal men may not appoint their time.
  *'Per scelus semper tutum est sceleribus iter.'*
  Strike, and strike home, where wrong is offered thee;
  For evils unto ills conductors be,
  And death's the worst of resolution.
  For he that thinks with patience to contend         10
  To quiet life, his life shall easily end.
  *'Fata si miseros juvant, habes salutem;*
  *Fata si vitam negant, habes sepulchrum.'*
  If destiny thy miseries do ease,
  Then hast thou health, and happy shalt thou be;
  If destiny deny thee life, Hieronimo,
  Yet shalt thou be assured of a tomb;
  If neither, yet let this thy comfort be,
  Heaven covereth him that hath no burial.
  And to conclude, I will revenge his death!          20
  But how? Not as the vulgar wits of men,
  With open, but inevitable ills,
  As by a secret, yet a certain mean,
  Which under kindship will be cloaked best.
  Wise men will take their opportunity,
  Closely and safely fitting things to time.

---

SD  Hieronimo carries a copy of Seneca

  1  *Vindicta mihi!*: Hieronimo is not quoting Seneca but the
      beginning of a well-known Biblical admonition:
      'vengeance is mine; I will repay, saith the Lord' (Romans
      12.19)

  6  *'Per scelus . . . sceleribus iter'*: 'the safe way for crime is
      through further crimes'; from Seneca's *Agamemnon* (1.115)

12–13  *'Fata si . . . habes sepulchrum'*: from Seneca's *Troades*
      (ll. 511–12). Hieronimo gives a loose translation over the
      next four lines

  21  vulgar: common

22–4  With open . . . cloaked best: Hieronimo seems to
      contrast the crude but effective actions of some revengers
      with the more subtle means he is contemplating

  23  mean: course of action

  24  kindship: kindness

---

  62  see it given to Horatio: the King believes that Horatio is
      still alive

  83  happed: happened to

  84  demean him: behave himself

 101  exempt the place: the meaning is unclear but it possible that
      the King is saying that he will take over Hieronimo's duties
      until the whole situation is clearer, rather than hastily
      removing him from office, as Lorenzo has suggested

But in extremes advantage hath no time;
And therefore all times fit not for revenge.
Thus therefore will I rest me in unrest,
Dissembling quiet in unquietness,     30
Not seeming that I know their villainies;
That my simplicity may make them think
That ignorantly I will let all slip—
For ignorance, I wot, and well they know,
'Remedium malorum iners est.'
Nor aught avails it me to menace them,
Who, as a wintry storm upon a plain,
Will bear me down with their nobility.
No, no, Hieronimo, thou must enjoin
Thine eyes to observation, and thy tongue     40
To milder speeches than thy spirit affords,
Thy heart to patience, and thy hands to rest,
Thy cap to courtesy, and thy knee to bow,
Till to revenge thou know, when, where and how.
     *A noise within*
How now, what noise? What coil is that you keep?

*Enter a* SERVANT

SERVANT  Here are a sort of poor petitioners,
    That are importunate, and it shall please you, sir,
    That you should plead their cases to the king.
HIERONIMO  That I should plead their several actions?
    Why, let them enter, and let me see them.     50

*Enter three* CITIZENS *and an* OLD MAN (SENEX)

1 CITIZEN  So, I tell you this, for learning and for law,
    There's not any advocate in Spain
    That can prevail, or will take half the pain
    That he will, in pursuit of equity.
HIERONIMO  Come near, you men, that thus importune
    me.
    (*Aside*) Now must I bear a face of gravity,
    For thus I used, before my marshalship,
    To plead in causes as corregidor—
    Come on sirs, what's the matter?
2 CITIZEN               Sir, an action.
HIERONIMO  Of battery?
1 CITIZEN         Mine of debt.
HIERONIMO              Give placc.     60
2 CITIZEN  No sir, mine is an action of the case.

3 CITIZEN  Mine an *ejectione firmae* by a lease.
HIERONIMO  Content you sirs, are you determined
    That I should plead your several actions?
1 CITIZEN  Ay sir, and here's my declaration.
2 CITIZEN  And here is my band.
3 CITIZEN               And here is my lease.
     *They give him papers*
HIERONIMO  But wherefore stands yon silly man so mute,
    With mournful eyes and hands to heaven upreared?
    Come hither, father, let me know thy cause.
SENEX  O worthy sir, my cause, but slightly known,     70
    May move the hearts of warlike Myrmidons
    And melt the Corsic rocks with ruthful tears.
HIERONIMO  Say, father, tell me what's thy suit?
SENEX  No sir, could my woes
    Give way unto my most distressful words,
    Then should I not in paper, as you see,
    With ink bewray what blood began in me.
HIERONIMO  What's here? 'The humble supplication
    Of Don Bazulto for his murdered son.'
SENEX  Ay sir.     80
HIERONIMO  No sir, it was my murdered son,
    O my son, my son, O my son Horatio!
    But mine, or thine, Bazulto, be content.
    Here, take my handkercher, and wipe thine eyes,
    Whiles wretched I in thy mishaps may see
    The lively portrait of my dying self.
     *He draweth out a bloody napkin*
    O no, not this: Horatio, this was thine,
    And when I dyed it in thy dearest blood,
    This was a token 'twixt thy soul and me
    That of thy death revenged I should be.
    But here, take this, and this—what, my purse?—     90
    Ay, this, and that, and all of them are thine;
    For all as one are our extremities.
1 CITIZEN  O see the kindness of Hieronimo!
2 CITIZEN  This gentleness shows him a gentleman.
HIERONIMO  See, see, O see thy shame, Hieronimo,
    See here a loving father to his son!
    Behold the sorrows and the sad laments
    That he delivereth for his son's decease!
    If love's effects so strives in lesser things,
    If love enforce such moods in meaner wits,     100
    If love express such power in poor estates—

---

27–8  But in . . . for revenge: Hieronimo notes that only in
    desperate situations ('extremes') would a revenger forgo
    the 'advantage' of considered and subtle revenge. Hence
    his plan, formulated over the next few lines, to delay
35  'Remedium malorum iners est': 'Is an idle remedy for ills';
    from Seneca, *Oedipus*, l. 515
38  nobility: noble rank
46  sort: group
58  corregidor: advocate
61  action of the case: an action which requires a special writ
    to support it

62  *ejectione firmae*: 'a writ to eject a tenant from his holding
    before the expiration of his lease' (Edwards)
66  band: bond
67  silly: pitiable
71  Myrmidons: the fearless followers of Achilles
72  Corsic rocks: the craggy rocks of the island of Corsica to
    which Seneca was exiled
77  blood: passion
100  meaner wits: of lower social rank

Hieronimo, whenas a raging sea
Tossed with the wind and tide, o'erturneth then
The upper billows, course of waves to keep,
Whilst lesser waters labour in the deep,
Then sham'st thou not, Hieronimo, to neglect
The sweet revenge of thy Horatio?
Though on this earth justice will not be found,
I'll down to hell, and in this passion
Knock at the dismal gates of Pluto's court,      110
Getting by force, as once Alcides did,
A troop of Furies and tormenting hags
To torture Don Lorenzo and the rest.
Yet lest the triple-headed porter should
Deny my passage to the slimy strond,
The Thracian poet thou shalt counterfeit:
Come on, old father, be my Orpheus,
And if thou canst no notes upon the harp,
Then sound the burden of thy sore heart's grief,
Till we do gain that Proserpine may grant      120
Revenge on them that murdered my son.
Then will I rent and tear them thus and thus,
Shivering their limbs in pieces with my teeth.

*Tear the papers*

1 CITIZEN  O sir, my declaration!

*Exit Hieronimo and they after*

2 CITIZEN  Save my bond!

*Enter* HIERONIMO

2 CITIZEN  Save my bond!
3 CITIZEN  Alas, my lease! It cost me ten pound,
And you, my lord, have torn the same.
HIERONIMO  That cannot be, I gave it never a wound;
Show me one drop of blood fall from the same:      130
How is it possible I should slay it then?
Tush, no; run after, catch me if you can.

*Exeunt all but the* OLD MAN

BAZULTO *remains till* HIERONIMO *enters again, who,
staring him in the face, speaks*

HIERONIMO  And art thou come, Horatio, from the
depth,

To ask for justice in this upper earth?
To tell thy father thou art unrevenged,
To wring more tears from Isabella's eyes,
Whose lights are dimmed with over-long laments?
Go back my son, complain to Aeacus,
For here's no justice; gentle boy be gone,
For justice is exiled from the earth;      140
Hieronimo will bear thee company.
Thy mother cries on righteous Rhadamanth
For just revenge against the murderers.
SENEX  Alas my lord, whence springs this troubled speech?
HIERONIMO  But let me look on my Horatio.
Sweet boy, how art thou changed in death's black
shade!
Had Proserpine no pity on thy youth,
But suffered thy fair crimson-coloured spring
With withered winter to be blasted thus?
Horatio, thou art older than thy father;      150
Ah ruthless fate, that favour thus transforms!
SENEX  Ah my good lord, I am not your young son.
HIERONIMO  What, not my son? Thou, then, a Fury art,
Sent from the empty kingdom of black night
To summon me to make appearance
Before grim Minos and just Rhadamanth,
To plague Hieronimo that is remiss,
And seeks not vengeance for Horatio's death.
SENEX  I am a grieved man, and not a ghost,
That came for justice for my murdered son.      160
HIERONIMO  Ay, now I know thee, now thou nam'st
thy son;
Thou art the lively image of my grief:
Within thy face my sorrows I may see.
Thy eyes are gummed with tears, thy cheeks are wan,
Thy forehead troubled, and thy muttering lips
Murmur sad words abruptly broken off,
By force of windy sighs thy spirit breathes;
And all this sorrow riseth for thy son:
And selfsame sorrow feel I for my son.
Come in old man, thou shalt to Isabel;      170
Lean on my arm: I thee, thou me shalt stay,
And thou, and I, and she, will sing a song,
Three parts in one, but all of discords framed—
Talk not of cords, but let us now be gone,
For with a cord Horatio was slain.

*Exeunt*

---

102–7  Hieronimo, whenas . . . thy Horatio?: the sea imagery
is not clear, yet the overall impression is that Hieronimo
is moved by the plight of the old man (a meaner wit)
rather as Hamlet is by the First Player's show of grief in
Shakespeare's play
109  passion: suffering
110  Pluto: the god of the underworld
111  Alcides: Hercules
114  triple-headed porter: the monstrous three-headed dog who
guarded the underworld but was defeated by Hercules
116  Thracian poet: Orpheus, who rescued his dead wife from
the underworld by charming Persephone (Proserpine)
with his playing
122  rent: rend

138  Aeacus: a judge in the underworld
142  cries on righteous Rhadamanth: pleads to Rhadamanth, a
judge in the underworld
149  blasted: blighted
151  favour: countenance, looks
153  Fury: avenging spirit
156  Minos: the third judge in the underworld
162  lively: living
171  stay: support
174  cords: pun on 'chord' (musical) and cord meaning rope

# Act III, scene xiv

*Enter* KING OF SPAIN, *the* DUKE, VICEROY, *and* LORENZO,
BALTHAZAR, DON PEDRO *and* BEL-IMPERIA

KING Go brother, it is the Duke of Castile's cause,
  Salute the viceroy in our name.
CASTILE                       I go.
VICEROY Go forth, Don Pedro, for thy nephew's sake,
  And greet the Duke of Castile.
PEDRO                 It shall be so.
KING And now to meet these Portuguese,
  For as we now are, so sometimes were these,
  Kings and commanders of the western Indies.
  Welcome, brave viceroy, to the court of Spain,
  And welcome all his honourable train.
  'Tis not unknown to us, for why you come,     **10**
  Or have so kingly crossed the seas:
  Sufficeth it, in this we note the troth
  And more than common love you lend to us.
  So is it that mine honourable niece,
  (For it beseems us now that it be known)
  Already is betrothed to Balthazar,
  And by appointment and our condescent
  To-morrow are they to be married.
  To this intent we entertain thyself,
  Thy followers, their pleasure and our peace.     **20**
  Speak, men of Portingale, shall it be so?
  If ay, say so; if not, say flatly no.
VICEROY Renowned king, I come not as thou think'st,
  With doubtful followers, unresolved men,
  But such as have upon thine articles
  Confirmed thy motion and contented me.
  Know sovereign, I come to solemnise
  The marriage of thy beloved niece,
  Fair Bel-imperia, with my Balthazar—
  With thee, my son; whom sith I live to see,     **30**
  Here take my crown, I give it her and thee;
  And let me live a solitary life,
  In ceaseless prayers,
  To think how strangely heaven hath thee preserved.
KING See brother, see, how nature strives in him!
  Come, worthy viceroy, and accompany
  Thy friend with thine extremities;
  A place more private fits this princely mood.
VICEROY Or here or where your highness thinks it
  good.

           *Exeunt all but* CASTILE *and* LORENZO

---

9 train: company
12 troth: loyalty
17 condescent: agreement
26 motion: proposal
34 strangely: wonderfully
35 nature strives in him: he weeps
37 extremities: powerful emotions

CASTILE Nay stay, Lorenzo, let me talk with you.     **40**
  See'st thou this entertainment of these kings?
LORENZO I do, my lord, and joy to see the same.
CASTILE And knowest thou why this meeting is?
LORENZO For her, my lord, whom Balthazar doth love,
  And to confirm their promised marriage.
CASTILE She is thy sister?
LORENZO               Who, Bel-imperia?
  Ay, my gracious lord, and this is the day
  That I have longed so happily to see.
CASTILE Thou wouldst be loath that any fault of thine
  Should intercept her in her happiness.     **50**
LORENZO Heavens will not let Lorenzo err so much.
CASTILE Why then, Lorenzo, listen to my words:
  It is suspected and reported too,
  That thou, Lorenzo, wrong'st Hieronimo,
  And in his suits towards his majesty
  Still keep'st him back, and seeks to cross his suit.
LORENZO That I, my lord?
CASTILE I tell thee son, myself have heard it said,
  When, to my sorrow, I have been ashamed
  To answer for thee, though thou art my son.     **60**
  Lorenzo, knowest thou not the common love
  And kindness that Hieronimo hath won
  By his deserts within the court of Spain?
  Or seest thou not the king my brother's care
  In his behalf, and to procure his health?
  Lorenzo, shouldst thou thwart his passions,
  And he exclaim against thee to the king,
  What honour were't in this assembly,
  Or what a scandal were't among the kings
  To hear Hieronimo exclaim on thee?     **70**
  Tell me, and look thou tell me truly too,
  Whence grows the ground of this report in court?
LORENZO My lord, it lies not in Lorenzo's power
  To stop the vulgar, liberal of their tongues:
  A small advantage makes a water-breach,
  And no man lives that long contenteth all.
CASTILE Myself have seen thee busy to keep back
  Him and his supplications from the king.
LORENZO Yourself, my lord, hath seen his passions,
  That ill beseemed the presence of a king;     **80**
  And for I pitied him in his distress,
  I held him thence with kind and courteous words,
  As free from malice to Hieronimo
  As to my soul, my lord.
CASTILE Hieronimo, my son, mistakes thee then.
LORENZO My gracious father, believe me so he doth.

---

50 intercept: interrupt
56 cross: prevent
74 vulgar, liberal: common people, licentious
75 advantage: opportunity
  water-breach: an opening in a wall caused by water
  pressure

But what's a silly man, distract in mind,
To think upon the murder of his son?
Alas, how easy is it for him to err!
But for his satisfaction and the world's,      90
'Twere good, my lord, that Hieronimo and I
Were reconciled, if he misconster me.
CASTILE  Lorenzo, thou hast said; it shall be so;
Go one of you and call Hieronimo.

*Enter* BALTHAZAR *and* BEL-IMPERIA

BALTHAZAR  Come, Bel-imperia, Balthazar's content,
My sorrow's ease and sovereign of my bliss,
Sith heaven hath ordained thee to be mine;
Disperse those clouds and melancholy looks,
And clear them up with those thy sun-bright eyes,
Wherein my hope and heaven's fair beauty lies.      100
BEL-IMPERIA  My looks, my lord, are fitting for my
love,
Which new begun, can show no brighter yet.
BALTHAZAR  New kindled flames should burn as
morning sun.
BEL-IMPERIA  But not too fast, lest heat and all be done.
I see my lord my father.
BALTHAZAR            Truce, my love;
I will go salute him.
CASTILE            Welcome, Balthazar,
Welcome brave prince, the pledge of Castile's peace;
And welcome Bel-imperia. How now, girl?
Why com'st thou sadly to salute us thus?
Content thyself, for I am satisfied;      110
It is not now as when Andrea lived,
We have forgotten and forgiven that,
And thou art graced with a happier love.
But Balthazar, here comes Hieronimo,
I'll have a word with him.

*Enter* HIERONIMO *and a Servant*

HIERONIMO  And where's the duke?
SERVANT            Yonder.
HIERONIMO            Even so:
What new device have they devised, trow?
*Pocas palabras*, mild as the lamb,
Is't I will be revenged? No, I am not the man.
CASTILE  Welcome Hieronimo.      120
LORENZO  Welcome Hieronimo.
BALTHAZAR  Welcome Hieronimo.
HIERONIMO  My lords, I thank you for Horatio.
CASTILE  Hieronimo, the reason that I sent
To speak with you, is this.
HIERONIMO            What, so short?

Then I'll be gone, I thank you for't.
CASTILE  Nay, stay, Hieronimo—go call him, son.
LORENZO  Hieronimo, my father craves a word with
you.
HIERONIMO  With me sir? Why, my lord, I thought you
had done.
LORENZO  (*Aside*) No, would he had.
CASTILE            Hieronimo, I hear
You find yourself aggrieved at my son      131
Because you have not access unto the king,
And say 'tis he that intercepts your suits.
HIERONIMO  Why, is not this a miserable thing, my
lord?
CASTILE  Hieronimo, I hope you have no cause,
And would be loath that one of your deserts
Should once have reason to suspect my son,
Considering how I think of you myself.
HIERONIMO  Your son Lorenzo! Whom, my noble lord?
The hope of Spain, mine honourable friend?      140
Grant me the combat of them, if they dare
*Draws out his sword*
I'll meet him face to face, to tell me so.
These be the scandalous reports of such
As love not me, and hate my lord too much.
Should I suspect Lorenzo would prevent
Or cross my suit, that loved my son so well?
My lord I am ashamed it should be said.
LORENZO  Hieronimo, I never gave you cause.
HIERONIMO  My good lord, I know you did not.
CASTILE            There then pause,
And for the satisfaction of the world,      150
Hieronimo, frequent my homely house,
The Duke of Castile, Cyprian's ancient seat,
And when thou wilt, use me, my son, and it.
But here, before Prince Balthazar and me,
Embrace each other, and be perfect friends.
HIERONIMO  Ay marry, my lord, and shall.
Friends, quoth he? See, I'll be friends with you all:
Specially with you, my lovely lord;
For divers causes it is fit for us
That we be friends, the world is suspicious,      160
And men may think what we imagine not.
BALTHAZAR  Why, this is friendly done, Hieronimo.
LORENZO  And thus I hope old grudges are forgot.
HIERONIMO  What else? It were a shame it should not
be so.
CASTILE  Come on, Hieronimo, at my request;
Let us intreat your company today.
*Exeunt all but* HIERONIMO

---

92   misconster: misconstrue
109  sadly: with a serious demeanour
117  trow?: do you think?
118  *Pocas palabras*: few words (Spanish)

133  intercepts: obstructs
141  the combat of them: the right to meet them in combat
146  cross: obstruct
153  use: make use of

HIERONIMO Your lordship's to command.—Pha! Keep
    your way:
    *Chi mi fa più carezze che non suole,*
    *Tradito mi ha, o tradir vuole.*

                                        *Exit*

## Act III, scene xv

GHOST OF ANDREA *and* REVENGE

ANDREA Awake, Erichtho! Cerberus, awake!
  Solicit Pluto, gentle Proserpine;
  To combat, Acheron and Erebus!
  For ne'er by Styx and Phlegethon in hell
  [. . .]
  Nor ferried Charon to the fiery lakes
  Such fearful sights, as poor Andrea sees!
  Revenge, awake!
REVENGE Awake? For why?
ANDREA Awake, Revenge, for thou art ill advised   **10**
  To sleep away what thou art warned to watch.
REVENGE Content thyself, and do not trouble me.
ANDREA Awake, Revenge, if love, as love hath had,
  Have yet the power or prevalence in hell!
  Hieronimo with Lorenzo is joined in league,
  And intercepts our passage to revenge:
  Awake, Revenge, or we are woe-begone!
REVENGE Thus worldlings ground, what they have
    dreamed, upon.
  Content thyself, Andrea: though I sleep,
  Yet is my mood soliciting their souls;   **20**
  Sufficeth thee that poor Hieronimo
  Cannot forget his son Horatio.
  Nor dies Revenge although he sleep awhile,
  For in unquiet, quietness is feigned,
  And slumbering is a common worldly wile.
  Behold, Andrea, for an instance how
  Revenge hath slept, and then imagine thou
  What 'tis to be subject to destiny.

*Enter a* DUMB SHOW, *they act and exeunt*

ANDREA Awake, Revenge, reveal this mystery.

REVENGE The two first, the nuptial torches bore,   **30**
  As brightly burning as the mid-day's sun;
  But after them doth Hymen hie as fast,
  Clothed in sable, and a saffron robe,
  And blows them out, and quencheth them with
    blood,
  As discontent that things continue so.
ANDREA Sufficeth me; thy meaning's understood;
  And thanks to thee and those infernal powers
  That will not tolerate a lover's woe.
  Rest thee, for I will sit to see the rest.
REVENGE Then argue not, for thou hast thy request.   **40**
                                    *Exeunt*

## Act IV, scene i

*Enter* BEL-IMPERIA *and* HIERONIMO

BEL-IMPERIA Is this the love thou bear'st Horatio?
  Is this the kindness that thou counterfeits?
  Are these the fruits of thine incessant tears?
  Hieronimo, are these thy passions,
  Thy protestations and thy deep laments,
  That thou wert wont to weary men withal?
  O unkind father, O deceitful world!
  With what excuses canst thou show thyself,
  With what [. . .]
  From this dishonour and the hate of men?   **10**
  Thus to neglect the loss and life of him
  Whom both my letters and thine own belief
  Assures thee to be causeless slaughtered.
  Hieronimo, for shame, Hieronimo,
  Be not a history to after times
  Of such ingratitude unto thy son.
  Unhappy mothers of such children then,
  But monstrous fathers, to forget so soon
  The death of those, whom they with care and cost
  Have tendered so, thus careless should be lost.   **20**
  Myself a stranger in respect of thee,
  So loved his life, as still I wish their deaths;
  Nor shall his death be unrevenged by me,
  Although I bear it out for fashion's sake:

---

167 Pha!: an exclamation of contempt
168–9 *Chi mi . . . tradir vuole*: 'He who gives me more caresses
    than usual has betrayed me, or wishes to betray me'
    (Italian)
  1 Erichtho: the Thessalian sorceress
  3 Erebus: spirit of darkness
  4 Styx and Phlegethon: rivers in the underworld
  5 Edwards and others argue that a line is missing here.
    Edwards suggests something like 'Was I distressed with
    outrage sore as this' which gives sense to ll. 4–7
 11 To sleep away: to sleep through
 18 worldlings ground . . . dreamed, upon: mortals base their
    belief on their dreams
 20 mood: anger or attitude

32 Hymen: god of marriage
33 Clothed in . . . saffron robe: Hymen's usual saffron
    (yellow) robe is here covered in sable (black)
 7 unkind: unnatural
 9 With what: the compositor repeats the first two words of
    the previous line and inserts the last six words of the
    succeeding line. A line, therefore, is missing
 15 history: a) example; b) narrative
17–20 Unhappy mothers . . . be lost: a syntactically fractured
    sentence, perhaps reflecting Bel-imperia's state of mind
 20 tendered: nurtured
 21 in respect of: compared to
 24 bear it . . . fashion's sake: 'endure it for the sake of
    appearances' (Kinney)

For here I swear in sight of heaven and earth,
Shouldst thou neglect the love thou shouldst retain
And give it over and devise no more,
Myself should send their hateful souls to hell,
That wrought his downfall with extremest death.

HIERONIMO  But may it be that Bel-imperia          30
Vows such revenge as she hath deigned to say?
Why then, I see that heaven applies our drift
And all the saints do sit soliciting
For vengeance on those cursed murderers.
Madam 'tis true, and now I find it so;
I found a letter, written in your name,
And in that letter, how Horatio died.
Pardon, O pardon, Bel-imperia,
My fear and care in not believing it,
Nor think I thoughtless think upon a mean          40
To let his death be unrevenged at full;
And here I vow (so you but give consent,
And will conceal my resolution)
I will ere long determine of their deaths
That causeless thus have murdered my son.

BEL-IMPERIA  Hieronimo, I will consent, conceal;
And aught that may effect for thine avail
Join with thee to revenge Horatio's death.

HIERONIMO  On then; whatsoever I devise,
Let me entreat you, grace my practices.          50
For why, the plot's already in mine head.
Here they are.

*Enter* BALTHAZAR *and* LORENZO

BALTHAZAR          How now, Hieronimo?
What, courting Bel-imperia?

HIERONIMO                    Ay, my lord,
Such courting as, I promise you,
She hath my heart, but you, my lord, have hers.

LORENZO  But now, Hieronimo, or never,
We are to entreat your help.

HIERONIMO                    My help?
Why, my good lords, assure yourselves of me,
For you have given me cause,
Ay, by my faith have you.

BALTHAZAR          It pleased you          60
At the entertainment of the ambassador
To grace the king so much as with a show:
Now were your study so well furnished,
As, for the passing of the first night's sport,
To entertain my father with the like,

Or any such-like pleasing motion,
Assure yourself it would content them well.

HIERONIMO  Is this all?

BALTHAZAR  Ay, this is all.

HIERONIMO  Why then I'll fit you; say no more.          70
When I was young I gave my mind
And plied myself to fruitless poetry:
Which though it profit the professor naught,
Yet is it passing pleasing to the world.

LORENZO  And how for that?

HIERONIMO                Marry, my good lord, thus—
And yet, methinks, you are too quick with us—
When in Toledo there I studied,
It was my chance to write a tragedy—
See here my lords,          *He shows them a book*
Which long forgot, I found this other day.          80
Now would your lordships favour me so much
As but to grace me with your acting it—
I mean each one of you to play a part—
Assure you it will prove most passing strange
And wondrous plausible to that assembly.

BALTHAZAR  What, would you have us play a tragedy?

HIERONIMO  Why, Nero thought it no disparagement,
And kings and emperors have ta'en delight
To make experience of their wits in plays!

LORENZO  Nay, be not angry good Hieronimo,          90
The prince but asked a question.

BALTHAZAR  In faith, Hieronimo, and you be in earnest,
I'll make one.

LORENZO  And I another.

HIERONIMO  Now my good lord, could you entreat
Your sister Bel-imperia to make one?
For what's a play without a woman in it?

BEL-IMPERIA  Little entreaty shall serve me,
Hieronimo,
For I must needs be employed in your play.

HIERONIMO  Why, this is well; I tell you Lordings,          100
It was determined to have been acted
By gentlemen and scholars too
Such as could tell what to speak.

BALTHAZAR  And now it shall be played by princes and
courtiers,

---

27  devise: plot
32  applies our drift: endorses our plan
39  care: caution
40  thoughtless think: unconcerned
44  determine of: bring about
50  grace: support
51  For why: because
59–60  For you . . . have you: said ironically

66  motion: entertainment
70  Why then I'll fit you: a) furnish you with what you need;
b) give you what you deserve (as punishment)
73  professor: the one who 'professes'
76  too quick: a) too fast or lively in repartee; b) too much
alive
85  plausible: agreeable
87  Nero: the Roman emperor who supported the theatre
and acted in plays. Mulryne notes a possible additional
allusion in the fact that 'he was associated with violence
and deeds of blood'
89  experience: trial
101  determined: intended, arranged

Such as can tell how to speak,
If, as it is our country manner,
You will but let us know the argument.

HIERONIMO  That shall I roundly. The chronicles of
    Spain
Record this written of a knight of Rhodes:
He was betrothed, and wedded at the length    110
To one Perseda, an Italian dame,
Whose beauty ravished all that her beheld,
Especially the soul of Soliman,
Who at the marriage was the chiefest guest.
By sundry means sought Soliman to win
Perseda's love, and could not gain the same.
Then gan he break his passions to a friend,
One of his bashaws whom he held full dear;
Her had this bashaw long solicited,
And saw she was not otherwise to be won    120
But by her husband's death, this knight of Rhodes,
Whom presently by treachery he slew.
She, stirred with an exceeding hate therefore,
As cause of this slew Soliman;
And to escape the bashaw's tyranny
Did stab herself: and this the tragedy.

LORENZO  O excellent!

BEL-IMPERIA        But say, Hieronimo,
What then became of him that was the bashaw?

HIERONIMO  Marry thus: moved with remorse of his
    misdeeds,
Ran to a mountain-top and hung himself.    130

BALTHAZAR  But which of us is to perform that part?

HIERONIMO  O, that will I my lords, make no doubt of
    it:
I'll play the murderer, I warrant you,
For I already have conceited that.

BALTHAZAR  And what shall I?

HIERONIMO  Great Soliman the Turkish emperor.

LORENZO  And I?

HIERONIMO  Erastus the knight of Rhodes.

BEL-IMPERIA  And I?

HIERONIMO  Perseda, chaste and resolute.    140
And here, my lords, are several abstracts drawn,
For each of you to note your parts,

And act it, as occasion's offered you.
You must provide a Turkish cap,
A black mustachio and a fauchion.
    *Gives a paper to* BALTHAZAR
You with a cross like to a knight of Rhodes.
    *Gives another to* LORENZO
And madam, you must attire yourself
    *He giveth* BEL-IMPERIA *another*
Like Phoebe, Flora, or the Huntress,
Which to your discretion shall seem best.
And as for me, my lords, I'll look to one;    150
And, with the ransom that the viceroy sent
So furnish and perform this tragedy,
As all the world shall say Hieronimo
Was liberal in gracing of it so.

BALTHAZAR  Hieronimo, methinks a comedy were
    better.

HIERONIMO  A comedy?
Fie, comedies are fit for common wits:
But to present a kingly troop withal,
Give me a stately-written tragedy,
*Tragedia cothurnata*, fitting kings,    160
Containing matter, and not common things.
My lords, all this must be performed,
As fitting for the first night's revelling.
The Italian tragedians were so sharp of wit
That in one hour's meditation
They would perform anything in action.

LORENZO  And well it may; for I have seen the like
In Paris, 'mongst the French tragedians

HIERONIMO  In Paris? Mass, and well remembered!
There's one thing more that rests for us to do.    170

BALTHAZAR  What's that, Hieronimo? Forget not
    anything.

HIERONIMO  Each one of us must act his part
In unknown languages,
That it may breed the more variety.
As you, my lord, in Latin, I in Greek,
You in Italian; and for because I know
That Bel-imperia hath practised the French,
In courtly French shall all her phrases be.

---

105  how to speak: Balthazar seems to imply that princes and
    courtiers are more eloquent than gentlemen and scholars,
    although the exact meaning of this exchange is uncertain
107  argument: plot, narrative
108  roundly: plainly, immediately
108–40  The drama of Soliman and Perseda, as well as being
    the means by which Hieronimo pursues his revenge,
    rehearses many of the principal relationships in the main
    play
117  break: disclose
118  bashaws: pashas, Turkish courtiers
134  conceited: formed a conception of
141  abstracts drawn: outlines written up

145  fauchion: broad, curved sword
148  Huntress: Diana, goddess of hunting
150  look to: prepare
154  gracing of: adorning
160  *Tragedia cothurnata*: the most serious of Athenian drama,
    performed by an actor wearing buskins (thick-soled
    shoes)
164–6  Reference to the performers of the *Commedia dell'arte*,
    famous for their skills in improvisation
170  rests: remains
173  unknown languages: it is not clear whether or not this
    promise is fulfilled in the subsequent performance,
    although the note in Act IV, scene iv seems to indicate
    that it may have been

BEL-IMPERIA  You mean to try my cunning then,
   Hieronimo.
BALTHAZAR  But this will be a mere confusion,    **180**
   And hardly shall we all be understood.
HIERONIMO  It must be so, for the conclusion
   Shall prove the invention and all was good.
   And I myself in an oration,
   And with a strange and wondrous show besides,
   That I will have there behind a curtain,
   Assure yourself, shall make the matter known.
   And all shall be concluded in one scene,
   For there's no pleasure ta'en in tediousness.
BALTHAZAR  (*Aside to* LORENZO) How like you this? **190**
LORENZO  Why, thus my lord,
   We must resolve to soothe his humours up.
BALTHAZAR  On then Hieronimo, farewell till soon.
HIERONIMO  You'll ply this gear?
LORENZO               I warrant you.
                   *Exeunt all but* HIERONIMO
HIERONIMO                Why so.
   Now shall I see the fall of Babylon,
   Wrought by the heavens in this confusion.
   And if the world like not this tragedy,
   Hard is the hap of old Hieronimo.
                           *Exit*

# Act IV, scene ii

*Enter* ISABELLA *with a weapon*

ISABELLA  Tell me no more! O monstrous homicides!
   Since neither piety nor pity moves
   The king to justice or compassion,
   I will revenge myself upon this place
   Where thus they murdered my beloved son.
                 *She cuts down the arbour*
   Down with these branches and these loathsome
     boughs
   Of this unfortunate and fatal pine:
   Down with them, Isabella, rent them up
   And burn the roots from whence the rest is sprung.
   I will not leave a root, a stalk, a tree,     **10**
   A bough, a branch, a blossom, nor a leaf,
   No, not an herb within this garden-plot.

---

179  cunning: skill
181  hardly: with difficulty
183  invention: basic idea
185  strange and wonderous show: this refers to the body of
     Horatio
192  soothe his humours up: indulge his whims
194  ply this gear: carry out this business
195  fall of Babylon: this could refer to both the wicked city of
     Babylon (see Revelation 18) and the Tower of Babel with
     its many tongues. Babylon was also a term used by
     Elizabethans to signify Rome to which Spain paid
     allegiance

Accursed complot of my misery,
Fruitless for ever may this garden be!
Barren the earth, and blissless whosoever
Imagines not to keep it unmanured!
An eastern wind commixed with noisome airs
Shall blast the plants and the young saplings;
The earth with serpents shall be pestered,
And passengers, for fear to be infect,    **20**
Shall stand aloof, and, looking at it, tell,
'There, murdered, died the son of Isabel.'
Ay, here he died, and here I him embrace:
See where his ghost solicits with his wounds
Revenge on her that should revenge his death.
Hieronimo, make haste to see thy son,
For sorrow and despair hath cited me
To hear Horatio plead with Rhadamanth:
Make haste, Hieronimo, to hold excused
Thy negligence in pursuit of their deaths,    **30**
Whose hateful wrath bereaved him of his breath.
Ah nay, thou dost delay their deaths,
Forgives the murderers of thy noble son,
And none but I bestir me—to no end.
And as I curse this tree from further fruit,
So shall my womb be cursed for his sake;
And with this weapon will I wound the breast,
                     *She stabs herself*
The hapless breast that gave Horatio suck.
                           *Exit*

# Act IV, scene iii

*Enter* HIERONIMO; *he knocks up the curtain. Enter the*
DUKE OF CASTILE

CASTILE  How now Hieronimo, where's your fellows,
   That you take all this pain?
HIERONIMO  O sir, it is for the author's credit
   To look that all things may go well.
   But, good my lord, let me entreat your grace
   To give the king the copy of the play:
   This is the argument of what we show.
CASTILE  I will, Hieronimo.
HIERONIMO  One thing more, my good lord.
CASTILE  What's that?    **10**

---

13  complot: plot
16  unmanured: barren, uncultivated
17  noisome: pestilent
20  passengers: passers-by
32–4  Ah nay . . . no end: 'Even Isabella is deceived by
     Hieronimo's plan of stealthy and circumspect revenge'
     (Mulryne)
SD  *he knocks up the curtain*: somehow Hieronimo has to erect
     a curtain (possibly over one of the doors at the rear of an
     Elizabethan stage) in order to conceal Horatio's body
1  fellows: fellow actors

HIERONIMO  Let me entreat your grace
  That, when the train are passed into the gallery,
  You would vouchsafe to throw me down the key.
CASTILE  I will, Hieronimo.                    *Exit* CASTILE
HIERONIMO  What are you ready, Balthazar?
  Bring a chair and a cushion for the king.

*Enter* BALTHAZAR *with a chair*

  Well done, Balthazar; hang up the title.
  Our scene is Rhodes—what, is your beard on?
BALTHAZAR  Half on, the other is in my hand.
HIERONIMO  Despatch for shame, are you so long?    20
                              *Exit* BALTHAZAR
  Bethink thyself, Hieronimo,
  Recall thy wits, recompt thy former wrongs
  Thou has received by murder of thy son;
  And lastly, not least, how Isabel,
  Once his mother and thy dearest wife,
  All woe-begone for him, hath slain herself.
  Behoves thee then, Hieronimo, to be revenged.
  The plot is laid of dire revenge:
  On then, Hieronimo, pursue revenge,
  For nothing wants but acting of revenge.    30
                              *Exit* HIERONIMO

# Act IV, scene iv

*Enter* SPANISH KING, VICEROY, *the* DUKE OF CASTILE,
*and their train*

KING  Now, Viceroy, shall we see the tragedy
  Of Soliman the Turkish emperor,
  Performed of pleasure by your son the prince,
  My nephew Don Lorenzo, and my niece.
VICEROY  Who, Bel-imperia?
KING  Ay, and Hieronimo, our marshal,
  At whose request they deign to do't themselves:
  These be our pastimes in the court of Spain.
  Here, brother, you shall be the book-keeper:
  This is the argument of that they show.    10
                              *He giveth him a book*

---

12  gallery: probably meaning the hall of an Elizabethan
    house rather than the upper gallery of the theatre
13  throw me down the key: throw the key to the ground
17  the title: reference to the practice of using a title-board to
    introduce the play to the audience
20  Despatch: hurry
22  recompt: recall to mind
3  of pleasure: at their pleasure
9  book-keeper: the person who had the one copy of the
    complete play in an Elizabethan theatre (who could also
    prompt the actors). The audience would already know
    'the argument of that they show' but whether or not the
    note below, addressing *the reader* of *The Spanish Tragedy*,
    means that the play-within-a-play was then performed
    'in sundry languages' is unknown

*Gentlemen, this play of Hieronimo, in sundry languages,
was thought good to be set down in English more largely,
for the easier understanding to every public reader.*

*Enter* BALTHAZAR, BEL-IMPERIA *and* HIERONIMO

BALTHAZAR  *Bashaw, that Rhodes is ours, yield heavens
    the honour,
  And holy Mahomet, our sacred prophet;
  And be thou graced with every excellence
  That Soliman can give, or thou desire.
  But thy desert in conquering Rhodes is less
  Than in reserving this fair Christian nymph,
  Perseda, blissful lamp of excellence,
  Whose eyes compel, like powerful adamant,
  The warlike heart of Soliman to wait.*
KING  See, Viceroy, that is Balthazar, your son,    20
  That represents the emperor Soliman:
  How well he acts his amorous passion.
VICEROY  Ay, Bel-imperia hath taught him that.
CASTILE  That's because his mind runs all on
    Bel-imperia.
HIERONIMO  *Whatever joy earth yields betide your majesty.*
BALTHAZAR  *Earth yields no joy without Perseda's love.*
HIERONIMO  *Let then Perseda on your grace attend.*
BALTHAZAR  *She shall not wait on me, but I on her:
  Drawn by the influence of her lights, I yield.
  But let my friend, the Rhodian knight, come forth,    30
  Erasto, dearer than my life to me,
  That he may see Perseda, my beloved.*

*Enter* LORENZO *as Erasto*

KING  Here comes Lorenzo; look upon the plot,
  And tell me, brother, what part plays he?
BEL-IMPERIA  *Ah, my Erasto, welcome to Perseda.*
LORENZO  *Thrice happy is Erasto that thou liv'st—
  Rhodes' loss is nothing to Erasto's joy;
  Sith his Perseda lives, his life survives.*
BALTHAZAR  *Ah, Bashaw, here is love between Erasto
  And fair Perseda, sovereign of my soul.*    40
HIERONIMO  *Remove Erasto, mighty Soliman,
  And then Perseda will be quickly won.*
BALTHAZAR  *Erasto is my frend, and while he lives
  Perseda never will remove her love.*
HIERONIMO  *Let not Erasto live to grieve great Soliman.*
BALTHAZAR  *Dear is Erasto in our princely eye.*
HIERONIMO  *But if he be your rival, let him die.*

---

16  *reserving*: protecting, preserving
18  *adamant*: magnetic loadstone
19  *wait*: attend on her
20-4  See, Viceroy . . . on Bel-imperia: Kyd reinforces the
    parallels between the actors and the parts they have been
    given
29  *lights*: eyes
33  plot: the argument (and the cast-list) found in the book
37  *to*: compared to

BALTHAZAR *Why, let him die: so love commandeth me.*
  *Yet grieve I that Erasto should so die.*
HIERONIMO *Erasto, Soliman saluteth thee,*          50
  *And lets thee wit by me his highness' will*
  *Which is, thou shouldst be thus employed.*          Stab him
BEL-IMPERIA                                  *Ay me,*
  *Erasto! See, Soliman, Erasto's slain!*
BALTHAZAR *Yet liveth Soliman to comfort thee.*
  *Fair queen of beauty, let not favour die,*
  *But with a gracious eye behold his grief,*
  *That with Perseda's beauty is increased,*
  *If by Perseda his grief be not released.*
BEL-IMPERIA *Tyrant, desist soliciting vain suits;*
  *Relentless are mine ears to thy laments,*          60
  *As thy butcher is pitiless and base,*
  *Which seized on my Erasto, harmless knight,*
  *Yet thy power thou thinkest to command,*
  *And to thy power Perseda doth obey;*
  *But were she able, thus she would revenge*
  *Thy treacheries on thee, ignoble prince:*          Stab him
  *And on herself she would be thus revenged.*          Stab herself
KING Well said, old Marshal, this was bravely done!
HIERONIMO But Bel-imperia plays Perseda well.
VICEROY Were this in earnest, Bel-imperia,          70
  You would be better to my son than so.
KING But now what follows for Hieronimo?
HIERONIMO Marry, this follows for Hieronimo:
  Here break we off our sundry languages
  And thus conclude I in our vulgar tongue.
  Haply you think, but bootless are your thoughts,
  That this is fabulously counterfeit
  And that we do as all tragedians do:
  To die today, for fashioning our scene,
  The death of Ajax, or some Roman peer,          80
  And in a minute starting up again,
  Revive to please tomorrow's audience.
  No, princes; know I am Hieronimo,
  The hopeless father of a hapless son,
  Whose tongue is tuned to tell his latest tale,
  Not to excuse gross errors in the play.
  I see your looks urge instance of these words;
  Behold the reason urging me to this:
                              *Shows his dead son*
  See here my show, look on this spectacle.
  Here lay my hope, and here my hope hath end;          90
  Here lay my heart, and here my heart was slain;
  Here lay my treasure, here my treasure lost;

Here lay my bliss, and here my bliss bereft;
But hope, heart, treasure, joy, and bliss,
All fled, failed, died, yea, all decayed with this.
From forth these wounds came breath that gave me
    life;
They murdered me that made these fatal marks.
The cause was love, whence grew this mortal hate,
The hate, Lorenzo and young Balthazar,
The love, my son to Bel-imperia.          100
But night, the coverer of accursed crimes,
With pitchy silence hushed these traitors' harms
And lent them leave, for they had sorted leisure
To take advantage in my garden-plot
Upon my son, my dear Horatio:
There merciless they butchered up my boy,
In black dark night, to pale dim cruel death.
He shrieks, I heard, and yet methinks I hear,
His dismal outcry echo in the air.
With soonest speed I hasted to the noise,          110
Where hanging on a tree I found my son,
Through-girt with wounds, and slaughtered as you see.
And grieved I, think you, at this spectacle?
Speak, Portuguese, whose loss resembles mine:
If thou canst weep upon thy Balthazar,
'Tis like I wailed for my Horatio.
And you, my lord, whose reconciled son
Marched in a net, and thought himself unseen
And rated me for brainsick lunacy,
With 'God amend that mad Hieronimo!'—          120
How can you brook our play's catastrophe?
And here behold this bloody handkercher,
Which at Horatio's death I weeping dipped
Within the river of his bleeding wounds:
It as propitious, see I have reserved,
And never hath it left my bloody heart,
Soliciting remembrance of my vow
With these, O these accursed murderers:
Which now performed, my heart is satisfied.
And to this end the bashaw I became          130
That might revenge me on Lorenzo's life,
Who therefore was appointed to the part,
And was to represent the knight of Rhodes,
That I might kill him more conveniently.
So, Viceroy, was this Balthazar, thy son—
That Soliman which Bel-imperia
In person of Perseda murdered—

---

55 *favour*: your love
68 Well said: the king compliments Hieronimo on his play
75 vulgar: everyday
76 Haply: perhaps
   bootless: unavailing
77 fabulously counterfeit: a complete fiction
85 latest: last
87 instance: explanation

96 From forth . . . me life: a) Horatio's death took away
   Hieromino's life-breath; b) the discovery of his murdered
   body inspired Hieronimo's new 'life' as a revenger
103 sorted: sought out
112 Through-girt: pierced through
118 Marched in a net: a proverbial term for concealment,
   deception
119 rated: berated
125 propitious: of good omen

Solely appointed to that tragic part
That she might slay him that offended her.
Poor Bel-imperia missed her part in this:    **140**
For though the story saith she should have died,
Yet I of kindness, and of care to her,
Did otherwise determine of her end;
But love of him whom they did hate too much
Did urge her resolution to be such.
And princes, now behold Hieronimo,
Author and actor in this tragedy,
Bearing his latest fortune in his fist:
And will as resolute conclude his part
As any of the actors gone before.    **150**
And, gentles, thus I end my play:
Urge no more words: I have no more to say.
                  *He runs to hang himself*

KING  O hearken, Viceroy! Hold, Hieronimo!
Brother, my nephew and thy son are slain!

VICEROY  We are betrayed! My Balthazar is slain!
Break ope the doors, run, save Hieronimo.
          *They break in, and hold* HIERONIMO
Hieronimo, do but inform the king of these events;
Upon mine honour thou shalt have no harm.

HIERONIMO  Viceroy, I will not trust thee with my life,
Which I this day have offered to my son.    **160**
Accursed wretch,
Why stayest thou him that was resolved to die?

KING  Speak, traitor; damned, bloody murderer, speak!
For now I have thee I will make thee speak—
Why hast thou done this undeserving deed?

VICEROY  Why hast thou murdered my Balthazar?

CASTILE  Why hast thou butchered both my children
thus?

HIERONIMO  O, good words!
As dear to me was my Horatio
As yours, or yours, or yours, my lord, to you.    **170**
My guiltless son was by Lorenzo slain,
And by Lorenzo and that Balthazar
Am I at last revenged thoroughly,
Upon whose souls may heavens be yet avenged
With greater far than these afflictions.

CASTILE  But who were thy confederates in this?

VICEROY  That was thy daughter Bel-imperia;
For by her hand my Balthazar was slain:
I saw her stab him.

KING            Why speak'st thou not?

HIERONIMO  What lesser liberty can kings afford    **180**
Than harmless silence? Then afford it me:
Sufficeth I may not, nor I will not tell thee.

KING  Fetch forth the tortures.
Traitor as thou art, I'll make thee tell.

HIERONIMO                 Indeed,
Thou may'st torment me, as his wretched son
Hath done in murdering my Horatio,
But never shalt thou force me to reveal
The thing which I have vowed inviolate.
And therefore in despite of all thy threats,
Pleased with their deaths, and eased with their
revenge,    **190**
First take my tongue, and afterwards my heart.
                 *He bites out his tongue*

KING  O monstrous resolution of a wretch!
See, Viceroy, he hath bitten forth his tongue
Rather than to reveal what we required.

CASTILE  Yet can he write.

KING  And if in this he satisfy us not,
We will devise th'extremest kind of death
That ever was invented for a wretch.
      *Then he makes signs for a knife to mend his pen*

CASTILE  O, he would have a knife to mend his pen.

VICEROY  Here; and advise thee that thou write the
troth.    **200**

KING  Look to my brother! Save Hieronimo!
      *He with a knife stabs the* DUKE *and himself*
What age hath ever heard such monstrous deeds?
My brother, and the whole succeeding hope
That Spain expected after my decease!
Go bear his body hence, that we may mourn
The loss of our beloved brother's death;
That he may be entombed, whate'er befall:
I am the next, the nearest, last of all.

VICEROY  And thou, Don Pedro, do the like for us;
Take up our hapless son, untimely slain:    **210**
Set me with him, and he with woeful me,
Upon the main-mast of a ship unmanned,
And let the wind and tide haul me along
To Scylla's barking and untamed gulf,
Or to the loathsome pool of Acheron,
To weep my want for my sweet Balthazar:
Spain hath no refuge for a Portingale.
    *The trumpets sound a dead march, the* KING OF SPAIN
    *mourning after his brother's body, and the* VICEROY OF
        PORTINGALE *bearing the body of his son*

---

153  Hold, Hieronimo: there is a debate over whether the
instruction is addressed to Hieronimo (to hold back from
hanging himself) or to the others (to arrest him); we
prefer the former

171–5  My guiltless . . . these afflictions: Hieronimo repeats his
explanation (which some critics have found tedious) yet
more detail is provided and the sense of 'justice' is
enhanced. The dramatic contrast between Hieronimo's
urgent explanation and his later silence is complete

---

200  troth: truth
213  haul: drive
214  Scylla's barking and untamed gulf: Scylla and Charybdis
were rocks between Italy and Sicily. Homer refers to
Scylla as 'barking'
215  Acheron: one of the rivers of the underworld
216  my want for: my loss of

GHOST OF ANDREA *and* REVENGE

ANDREA  Ay, now my hopes have end in their effects,
  When blood and sorrow finish my desires:
  Horatio murdered in his father's bower,
  Vild Serberine by Pedringano slain,
  False Pedringano hanged by quaint device,
  Fair Isabella by herself misdone,
  Prince Balthazar by Bel-imperia stabbed,
  The Duke of Castile and his wicked son
  Both done to death by old Hieronimo,
  My Bel-imperia fallen as Dido fell,                    10
  And good Hieronimo slain by himself:
  Ay, these were spectacles to please my soul.
  Now will I beg at lovely Proserpine,
  That, by the virtue of her princely doom,
  I may consort my friends in pleasing sort,
  And on my foes work just and sharp revenge.
  I'll lead my friend Horatio through those fields
  Where never-dying wars are still inured:
  I'll lead fair Isabella to that train
  Where pity weeps but never feeleth pain:               20
  I'll lead my Bel-imperia to those joys
  That vestal virgins and fair queens possess;
  I'll lead Hieronimo where Orpheus plays,
  Adding sweet pleasure to eternal days.
  But say, Revenge, for thou must help, or none,
  Against the rest how shall my hate be shown?
REVENGE  This hand shall hale them down to deepest
    hell,
  Where none but Furies, bugs and tortures dwell.
ANDREA  Then, sweet Revenge, do this at my request;
  Let me be judge, and doom them to unrest:              30
  Let loose poor Tityus from the vulture's gripe,
  And let Don Cyprian supply his room;
  Place Don Lorenzo on Ixion's wheel,
  And let the lover's endless pains surcease—
  (Juno forgets old wrath, and grants him ease):
  Hang Balthazar about Chimaera's neck,
  And let him there bewail his bloody love,
  Repining at our joys that are above;
  Let Serberine go roll the fatal stone,
  And take from Sisyphus his endless moan;               40
  False Pedringano for his treachery,
  Let him be dragged through boiling Acheron,
  And there live, dying still in endless flames,
  Blaspheming gods and all their holy names.
REVENGE  Then haste we down to meet thy friends and
    foes:
  To place thy friends in ease, the rest in woes.
  For here, though death hath end their misery,
  I'll there begin their endless tragedy.

                                              *Exeunt*

---

4  Vild: vile
5  quaint: cunning
6  misdone: slain
10  as Dido fell: Dido killed herself after losing Aeneas
    (*Aeneid*, Book IV)
14  doom: justice
15  consort: accompany
18  inured: carried on
19  train: company
22  vestal virgins: virgins dedicated to the Roman goddess
    Vesta who vowed themselves to chastity

28  bugs: bugbears, horrors of the imagination
31  Tityus: a giant, punished by having his liver devoured by
    vultures
32  Don Cyprian: Duke of Castile, who had disapproved of
    Don Andrea's relationship with Bel-imperia
    supply his room: take his place
34  the lover: Ixion, who had tried to seduce Juno
36  Chimaera's neck: Chimaera was a monster of Greek
    mythology with the head of a lion, body of a goat and tail
    of a dragon
40  Sisyphus: in Greek legend, the king of Crete, punished
    in the underworld by having, eternally, to roll a stone up
    a hill
43  still: continually
47  end: ended

# Anon., *Arden of Faversham*

First performed 1592
First published 1592

In the epilogue to *Arden of Faversham*, the murder of Arden, a wealthy landowner from Faversham in Kent, by his wife, Alice, her lover, Mosby, and their accomplices is called a 'naked tragedy'. This description accurately suggests a plot characterised by its simplicity and brutality, and driven by naked (and generally unattractive) emotion and appetite. There are no convoluted twists and turns, no counter-plots or double bluffs; instead, we see one failed attempt on Arden's life after another until, inexorably, we arrive at the moment of its successful enactment. The murder itself is, even after the protracted build-up, shocking in its ruthlessness: Mosby, Shakebag (one of the hired killers) and Alice take it in turns to stab him as he sits at home playing backgammon. The motive for the murder is Alice Arden's love for Mosby, a love represented (with a few important exceptions, as in i.98–104) as lustful, importunate, deceitful and unsympathetic.

Thus far, the co-ordinates are familiar ones: the wronged husband, the adulterous and duplicitous wife, the heinous murder, followed by judicial retribution to reinstate the moral order. As the title-page of the first edition tells us, the play shows 'the great malice and dissimulation of a wicked woman, the unsatiable desire of filthy lust and the shameful end of all murderers'. However, as recent critics have noted, this well-worn didactic trajectory is complicated by a number of factors. First, Arden himself is wrongdoer as well as wronged: he is a grasping landowner, a beneficiary of the recent transfer of land from church to private ownership following the dissolution of the monasteries by Henry VIII in the 1530s. Arden is shown to be content to take land, legally but immorally, from its rightful holders, and this in turn speeds his own downfall, for one of those he has dispossessed, Greene, joins forces with Alice in plotting his murder. The interweaving of these two strands points to the parallels between the behaviours of Alice and of Arden himself: both refuse to be constrained by the social bonds (conferred by marriage and by property) which ought to guarantee loyalty and 'honesty' (with its connotations of honour and chastity as well as moral rectitude). Indeed, the unrestrained appetites of both – his for property, hers for Mosby – impel the plot. The meshing of the 'private' wrongdoing of Alice and Mosby with the 'public' immorality of Arden within this single narrative complicates the categories of 'heroes' and 'villains', of 'cause' and 'effect', and, indeed, of 'public' and 'private' (see Belsey 1985, Orlin 1985 and 1994, and Comensoli 1996). The blurred boundaries between these categories result in a play in which it becomes increasingly difficult to locate a secure point of attachment for audience sympathies in any single character. The 'nakedly' brutal murder is perhaps the only element of the play about which an unequivocal judgement can be reached; the complexity of motivation which drives the plot towards this act refuses any other such straightforward verdicts.

Equally disturbing are some of the notes struck in the resolution of the play: the execution of the wholly innocent Bradshaw and the only marginally involved Susan, for example, and the escape of the guilty Clarke. Also unsettling is the realization that the honest Franklin, seen throughout as the only real voice of loyalty and integrity, had been fully cognizant of his friend Arden's rapaciousness (he tells us that Arden lay murdered 'in that plot of ground/Which he by force and violence held from Reede' (Epilogue 10–11)), yet had never challenged it. The apparently straightforward tale of wrongdoing revealed and justly brought to book becomes altogether bleaker and more troubling as the plot unfolds and concludes.

The play is a domestic tragedy: that is, rather than dealing with the downfalls of kings and nobility, as tragedy typically does, it is concerned with the misfortunes and misdeeds of the middle ranks of society. But the generic classification of 'tragedy' tells only half the story, for *Arden of Faversham* has as much in common with 'history' plays as it does with tragedy. Like them, it is based in fact: Thomas Arden was murdered in Faversham by his wife, Alice, in 1551. Its principal source, like theirs, is the record of British history so well used by other dramatists: Raphael Holinshed's *Chronicles of England, Scotland and Ireland* (1577; second edition, 1587), which contains a 5,000-word account of the murder, an event which had figured large in the popular imagination since the time it had taken place. Reading the play as 'history' instead of (or as well as) 'tragedy' draws attention away from the characters and their individual and flawed acts and desires, and focuses it instead on the social, economic and political forces that shape and constrain them. From this perspective, *Arden of Faversham* becomes a play profoundly concerned with the deleterious impact of the Reformation, and the consequent transfers of land ownership, on social and kinship bonds and responsibilities. Arden's rise in the social hierarchy is matched by Mosby's aspirations in this regard; Black Will and Shakebag are part of the landless, rootless vagabond stratum that proliferated as a result of these transfers of land; Michael is torn between the irreconcilable positions of loyal servant and self-interested individualist. Reading *Arden* as 'history' suggests a thoroughness of social analysis within the play that would otherwise remain occluded.

Whilst the sources of *Arden of Faversham* in contemporary chronicles are beyond doubt, the question of the play's authorship remains unresolved. Despite attempts to attribute it to Shakespeare, Marlowe and Kyd, critics now agree that we have no choice but to retain the attribution to 'Anonymous' for the foreseeable future.

## Textual note

The first edition of *Arden of Faversham* was published in 1592, the second in 1599 and the third in 1633; these quarto editions are referred to as Q1, Q2 and Q3 respectively in the footnotes. This edition is based on Q1. Significant differences between the three quartos have been footnoted. The main source for the play, the account of the murder in Holinshed's *Chronicles*, is reproduced in the editions of the play edited by Sturgess, Wine and White. Wine also includes the account from The Wardmote Book of Faversham. Kinney includes John Stow's account in his collection.

# Further reading

## Editions

Baskervill, Charles Read, Heltzel, Virgil B., and Nethercot, Arthur H. (eds) (1934) *Elizabethan and Stuart Plays*, New York, NY: Henry Holt and Co.

Bayne, Ronald (ed.) (1897) *Arden of Faversham*, London: J. M. Dent and Co.

Bullen, A. H. (ed.) (1887) *Arden of Faversham: A Tragedy*, reprinted from the edition of 1592, London: J. W. Jarvis and Son.

Farmer, J. S. (ed.) (1911) *Arden of Faversham*, facsimile edition of 1592 quarto, Tudor Facsimile Series.

Gassner, John (ed.) (1967) *Elizabethan Drama*, New York, NY: Bantam.

Kinney, Arthur F. (ed.) (1999) *Renaissance Drama: An Anthology of Plays and Entertainments*, Oxford: Blackwell.

Macdonald, Hugh, and Smith, D. Nichol (eds) (1947) *Arden of Faversham 1592*, Oxford: The Malone Society Reprints, for Oxford University Press.

Sturgess, Keith (ed.) (1969) *Three Elizabethan Domestic Tragedies: Arden of Faversham; A Yorkshire Tragedy; A Woman Killed with Kindness*, Harmondsworth: Penguin.

Thorndike, Ashley (ed.) (1958) *Minor Elizabethan Drama: Volume One: Pre-Shakespearean Tragedies*, London: J. M. Dent and Sons.

Tucker Brooke, C. F. (ed.) (1908) *The Shakespeare Apocrypha: Being a Collection of Fourteen Plays which Have Been Ascribed to Shakespeare*, Oxford: Clarendon Press.

Warnnke, Karl and Proescholdt, Ludwig (eds) (1888) *Pseudo-Shakespearian Plays, V: Arden of Faversham*, Halle: Max Niemeyer.

White, Martin (ed.) (1982) *Arden of Faversham*, The New Mermaids, London: Ernest Benn Ltd.

Wine, M. L. (ed.) (1973) *The Tragedy of Master Arden of Faversham*, The Revels Series, London: Methuen.

## Critical and contextual commentaries

Attwell, David (1991) 'Property, Status, and the Subject in a Middle-Class Tragedy: *Arden of Faversham*', *English Literary Renaissance*, 21, 3: 328–48.

Belsey, Catherine (1985) 'Alice Arden's Crime', in *The Subject of Tragedy: Identity and Difference in Renaissance Drama*, London: Methuen.

Bluestone, Max (1970) 'The Imagery of Tragic Melodrama in *Arden of Faversham*', in Max Bluestone and Norman Rabkin (eds) *Shakespeare's Contemporaries: Modern Studies in English Renaissance Drama*, 2nd edition, Englewood Cliffs, NJ: Prentice-Hall Inc.

Breen, John M. (1994) 'The So-called Carnival Body in *Arden of Faversham*', *Cahiers Elisabéthains*, 45: 13–20.

Comensoli, Viviana (1996) '*Household Business*': Domestic Plays of Early Modern England*, Toronto, Buffalo, and London: University of Toronto Press.

Dolan, Frances E. (1992) 'The Subject('s) Role: Petty Treason and the Forms of Domestic Rebellion', *Shakespeare Quarterly*, 43: 317–40.

Helgerson, Richard (1997) 'Murder in Faversham: Holinshed's Impertinent History', in Donald R. Kelley and David Harris Sacks (eds) *The Historical Imagination in Early Modern Britain: History, Rhetoric and Fiction 1500–1800*, Cambridge: Cambridge University Press.

Hyde, Patricia (1996) *Thomas Arden in Faversham: The Man Behind the Myth*, Faversham: The Faversham Society.

Leggatt, Alexander (1983) '*Arden of Faversham*', *Shakespeare Survey*, 36: 121–33.

Lieblein, Leonore (1983) 'The Context of Murder in English Domestic Plays, 1590–1610', *Studies in English Literature 1500–1900*, 23, 2: 181–96.

Orlin, Lena Cowen (1985) 'Man's House as his Castle in *Arden of Faversham*', *Medieval and Renaissance Drama in England*, 2: 57–89.

—— (1994) *Private Matters and Public Culture in Post-Reformation England*, Ithaca, NY, and London: Cornell University Press.

Schutzman, Julie R. (1996) 'Alice Arden's Freedom and the Suspended Moment of *Arden of Faversham*', *Studies in English Literature 1500–1900*, 36, 2: 289–314.

Sullivan Jr, Garrett A. (1994) "'Arden Lay Murdered in that Plot of Ground": Surveying, Land and *Arden of Faversham*', *English Literary History*, 61, 2: 231–52.

Whigham, Frank (1996) 'Hunger and Pain in *Arden of Faversham*', in *Seizures of the Will in Early Modern English Drama*, Cambridge: Cambridge University Press.

## Works of related interest

Anon., *A Warning for Fair Women* (1589)

Robert Yarington, *Two Lamentable Tragedies* (1594)

Thomas Heywood, *A Woman Killed with Kindness* (1603)

Elizabeth Cary, *The Tragedy of Mariam, the Fair Queen of Jewry* (1604)

Anon., *A Yorkshire Tragedy* (1605)

George Wilkins, *The Miseries of Enforced Marriage* (1607)

# *Arden of Faversham* (1592)

## Dramatis personae

ARDEN, *a landowner*

FRANKLIN, *his friend*

ALICE, *Arden's wife*

ADAM FOWLE, *landlord of the Flower-de-Luce*

MICHAEL, *Arden's servant*

MOSBY, *Alice Arden's lover*

CLARKE, *a painter*

GREENE, *a tenant*

SUSAN, *Mosby's sister and Alice's servingmaid*

BRADSHAW, *a goldsmith*

BLACK WILL⎱
⎰ *hired murderers*
SHAKEBAG⎰

A PRENTICE

LORD CHEINY, *and his* MEN

A FERRYMAN

DICK REEDE, *sailor and inhabitant of Faversham*

A SAILOR, *his friend*

MAYOR OF FAVERSHAM, *and the* WATCH

## Scene i

*Enter* ARDEN *and* FRANKLIN

FRANKLIN  Arden, cheer up thy spirits and droop no
more.

Scene i: there are no act or scene divisions in the quartos.
We follow recent editions in dividing the play into
eighteen scenes

My gracious Lord the Duke of Somerset
Hath freely given to thee and to thy heirs,
By letters patents from his majesty,
All the lands of the Abbey of Faversham.
Here are the deeds,
Sealed and subscribed with his name and the
king's.
Read them, and leave this melancholy mood.
ARDEN  Franklin, thy love prolongs my weary life;     10
And, but for thee, how odious were this life,
That shows me nothing but torments my soul,
And those foul objects that offend mine eyes;
Which makes me wish that for this veil of
heaven
The earth hung over my head and covered me.
Love letters passed 'twixt Mosby and my wife,
And they have privy meetings in the town.
Nay, on his finger did I spy the ring
Which at our marriage day the priest put on.
Can any grief be half so great as this?
FRANKLIN  Comfort thyself, sweet friend; it is not
strange     20
That women will be false and wavering.
ARDEN  Ay, but to dote on such a one as he
Is monstrous, Franklin, and intolerable.
FRANKLIN  Why, what is he?
ARDEN  A botcher, and no better at the first,
Who, by base brokage getting some small stock,
Crept into service of a nobleman,
And by his servile flattery and fawning

2  Duke of Somerset: Edward Seymour, the Duke of
Somerset, was appointed Lord Protector (see l. 34 below)
to King Edward VI on his accession (aged 13) in 1547.
DNB notes Somerset's 'rapacity in profiting by the
dissolution of the monasteries'
4  letters patents: open letters or documents, usually from a
sovereign, conferring 'some right, privilege, title,
property, or office' (OED)
13  for this veil of heaven: instead of the sky
25  botcher: 'a tailor who does repairs' (OED)
at the first: since he was born (Wine); in his origins
(Sturgess)
26  base brokage: pimping; shady deals (White)

Is now become the steward of his house,
And bravely jets it in his silken gown.          30
FRANKLIN  No nobleman will count'nance such a
    peasant.
ARDEN  Yes, the Lord Clifford, he that loves not me.
    But through his favour let not him grow proud,
    For were he by the Lord Protector backed,
    He should not make me to be pointed at.
    I am by birth a gentleman of blood,
    And that injurious ribald that attempts
    To violate my dear wife's chastity
    (For dear I hold her love, as dear as heaven)
    Shall on the bed which he thinks to defile     40
    See his disseuered joints and sinews torn,
    Whilst on the planchers pants his weary body,
    Smeared in the channels of his lustful blood.
FRANKLIN  Be patient, gentle friend, and learn of me
    To ease thy grief and save her chastity.
    Entreat her fair; sweet words are fittest engines
    To raze the flint walls of a woman's breast.
    In any case be not too jealous,
    Nor make no question of her love to thee;
    But, as securely, presently take horse,          50
    And lie with me at London all this term;
    For women when they may will not,
    But being kept back, straight grow outrageous.
ARDEN  Though this abhors from reason, yet I'll try it,
    And call her forth, and presently take leave.
    How, Alice!

*Here enters* ALICE

ALICE  Husband, what mean you to get up so early?

---

29  steward: official in charge of the domestic arrangements
    and expenditure of a large household (as is Malvolio in
    *Twelfth Night*, and Antonio Bologna in *The Duchess of
    Malfi*)
30  bravely jets it: swaggers about
32  Lord Clifford: according to the sources, Mosby was
    servant to Sir Edward (later Lord) North, Alice's
    stepfather and Arden's former master. These facts are
    omitted here, and Lord Clifford is introduced as a
    fictional substitute
33  his: i.e. Lord Clifford's
    him: i.e. Mosby
36  a gentleman of blood: well born
37  ribald: base fellow (Q3; riball Q1)
43  planchers: floorboards
43  channels: streams
46  Entreat: treat
    engines: contrivances of war, and hence also of plots
47  raze: eds (race Qs)
50  as securely: confidently
    presently: immediately
51  lie: lodge
    term: one of the yearly sessions of the law courts
54  abhors from: goes against

Summer nights are short, and yet you rise ere day.
Had I been wake you had not rise so soon.
ARDEN  Sweet love, thou know'st that we two, Ovid-
    like,                                              60
    Have often chid the morning when it 'gan to peep,
    And often wished that dark Night's purblind steeds
    Would pull her by the purple mantle back
    And cast her in the ocean to her love.
    But this night, sweet Alice, thou hast killed my heart;
    I heard thee call on Mosby in thy sleep.
ALICE  'Tis like I was asleep when I named him,
    For being awake he comes not in my thoughts.
ARDEN  Ay, but you started up and suddenly,
    Instead of him, caught me about the neck.          70
ALICE  Instead of him? Why, who was there but you?
    And where but one is, how can I mistake?
FRANKLIN  Arden, leave to urge her over-far.
ARDEN  Nay, love, there is no credit in a dream.
    Let it suffice I know thou lovest me well.
ALICE  Now I remember whereupon it came:
    Had we no talk of Mosby yesternight?
FRANKLIN  Mistress Alice, I heard you name him once
    or twice.
ALICE  And thereof came it, and therefore blame not me.
ARDEN  I know it did, and therefore let it pass.      80
    I must to London, sweet Alice, presently.
ALICE  But tell me, do you mean to stay there long?
ARDEN  No longer than till my affairs be done.
FRANKLIN  He will not stay above a month at most.
ALICE  A month? Ay me! Sweet Arden, come again
    Within a day or two or else I die.
ARDEN  I cannot long be from thee, gentle Alice.
    Whilst Michael fetch our horses from the field,
    Franklin and I will down unto the quay,
    For I have certain goods there to unload.          90
    Meanwhile prepare our breakfast, gentle Alice,
    For yet ere noon we'll take horse and away.
                                *Exeunt* ARDEN *and* FRANKLIN
ALICE  Ere noon he means to take horse and away!
    Sweet news is this. Oh, that some airy spirit
    Would, in the shape and likeness of a horse,
    Gallop with Arden 'cross the ocean
    And throw him from his back into the waves!
    Sweet Mosby is the man that hath my heart,
    And he usurps it, having nought but this,

---

59  rise: pronounced 'riz'; obsolete alternative to 'risen'
    (Wine)
60  Ovid-like: Ovid (43 BC–AD 18) was a Roman poet famed
    for (amongst other things) his love poetry. Lines 60–4
    here have been compared with his Elegy XIII in Book I
    of the *Amores*, translated by Christopher Marlowe
62  purblind: totally blind
73  leave: cease
83  than: eds (there Qs)
99  he: i.e. Arden

That I am tied to him by marriage.  100
Love is a god, and marriage is but words,
And therefore Mosby's title is the best.
Tush! Whether it be or no, he shall be mine
In spite of him, of Hymen, and of rites.

*Here enters* ADAM *of the Flower-de-Luce*

And here comes Adam of the Flower-de-Luce.
I hope he brings me tidings of my love.
How now, Adam, what is the news with you?
Be not afraid, my husband is now from home.
ADAM  He whom you wot of, Mosby, Mistress Alice,
Is come to town, and sends you word by me  110
In any case you may not visit him.
ALICE  Not visit him?
ADAM  No, nor take no knowledge of his being here.
ALICE  But tell me, is he angry or displeased?
ADAM  Should seem so, for he is wondrous sad.
ALICE  Were he as mad as raving Hercules
I'll see him. Ay, and were thy house of force,
These hands of mine should raze it to the ground
Unless that thou wouldst bring me to my love.
ADAM  Nay, and you be so impatient, I'll be gone.  120
ALICE  Stay, Adam, stay; thou wert wont to be my
friend.
Ask Mosby how I have incurred his wrath;
Bear him from me these pair of silver dice
With which we played for kisses many a time,
And when I lost I won, and so did he—
Such winning and such losing Jove send me!
And bid him, if his love do not decline,
To come this morning but along my door,
And as a stranger but salute me there.
This may he do without suspect or fear.  130
ADAM  I'll tell him what you say, and so farewell.
                                        *Exit* ADAM
ALICE  Do, and one day I'll make amends for all.
I know he loves me well but dares not come
Because my husband is so jealous,

And these my narrow-prying neighbours blab,
Hinder our meetings when we would confer.
But, if I live, that block shall be removed,
And Mosby, thou that comes to me by stealth,
Shalt neither fear the biting speech of men
Nor Arden's looks. As surely shall he die  140
As I abhor him and love only thee.

*Here enters* MICHAEL

How now, Michael, whither are you going?
MICHAEL  To fetch my master's nag. I hope you'll think
on me.
ALICE  Ay; but Michael, see you keep your oath,
And be as secret as you are resolute.
MICHAEL  I'll see he shall not live above a week.
ALICE  On that condition, Michael, here is my hand:
None shall have Mosby's sister but thyself.
MICHAEL  I understand the painter here hard by
Hath made report that he and Sue is sure.  150
ALICE  There's no such matter, Michael; believe it not.
MICHAEL  But he hath sent a dagger sticking in a heart,
With a verse or two stolen from a painted cloth,
The which I hear the wench keeps in her chest.
Well, let her keep it! I shall find a fellow
That can both write and read and make rhyme too,
And if I do—well, I say no more.
I'll send from London such a taunting letter
As she shall eat the heart he sent with salt,
And fling the dagger at the painter's head.  160
ALICE  What needs all this? I say that Susan's thine.
MICHAEL  Why, then, I say that I will kill my master
Or anything that you will have me do.
ALICE  But, Michael, see you do it cunningly.
MICHAEL  Why, say I should be took, I'll ne'er confess
That you know anything; and Susan, being a maid,
May beg me from the gallows of the shrieve.
ALICE  Trust not to that, Michael.
MICHAEL  You cannot tell me, I have seen it, I.
But, mistress, tell her whether I live or die  170
I'll make her more worth than twenty painters can,

---

104  Hymen: the god of marriage
SD  *Flower-de-Luce*: an inn situated near Arden's house.
OED notes that the current form ('fleur de lis') 'is
scarcely found in Eng. before the 19th c.'
109  wot: know
111  In any case: under any circumstances
116  raving Hercules: Hercules went mad and committed
suicide after putting on a shirt soaked in the poisoned
blood of Nessus, the centaur killed by Hercules. The
shirt was sent to him by his wife, Deianira, in the belief
that it would act as a charm to restore her unfaithful
husband's love for her
117  of force: fortified
120  and: if

135  narrow-prying Q2–3 (marrow-prying Q1). Eds follow
Q2–3, but do not reject the possibility that Q1 may be the
correct reading
149  hard by: near by
150  sure: betrothed
153  painted cloth: 'as opposed to woven cloth, and therefore a
cheap substitute for tapestry. The design frequently
incorporated verses and mottoes' (White)
159  As: that
she: eds (not in Qs)
166–7  Susan . . . gallows: 'It was a common belief that a virgin
could save a man from being hanged by offering to marry
him' (White)
167  shrieve: sheriff
171  worth: wealthy

For I will rid mine elder brother away,
And then the farm of Bolton is mine own.
Who would not venture upon house and land,
When he may have it for a right-down blow?

*Here enters* MOSBY

ALICE Yonder comes Mosby. Michael, get thee gone,
And let not him nor any know thy drifts.
                                   *Exit* MICHAEL
  Mosby, my love!
MOSBY Away, I say, and talk not to me now.
ALICE A word or two, sweetheart, and then I will. 180
  'Tis yet but early days; thou needest not fear.
MOSBY Where is your husband?
ALICE 'Tis now high water, and he is at the quay.
MOSBY There let him be; henceforward know us not.
ALICE Is this the end of all thy solemn oaths?
  Is this the fruit thy reconcilement buds?
  Have I for this given thee so many favours,
  Incurred my husband's hate, and—out, alas!—
  Made shipwreck of mine honour for thy sake?
  And dost thou say 'henceforward know me not'? 190
  Remember when I locked thee in my closet,
  What were thy words and mine? Did we not both
  Decree to murder Arden in the night?
  The heavens can witness, and the world can tell,
  Before I saw that falsehood look of thine,
  'Fore I was tangled with thy 'ticing speech,
  Arden to me was dearer than my soul—
  And shall be still. Base peasant, get thee gone,
  And boast not of thy conquest over me,
  Gotten by witchcraft and mere sorcery. 200
  For what hast thou to countenance my love,
  Being descended of a noble house,
  And matched already with a gentleman
  Whose servant thou may'st be? And so farewell.
MOSBY Ungentle and unkind Alice; now I see
  That which I ever feared and find too true:
  A woman's love is as the lightning flame
  Which even in bursting forth consumes itself.
  To try thy constancy have I been strange.
  Would I had never tried, but lived in hope. 210
ALICE What needs thou try me whom thou never
  found false?

MOSBY Yet pardon me, for love is jealous.
ALICE So lists the sailor to the mermaid's song;
  So looks the traveller to the basilisk.
  I am content for to be reconciled,
  And that I know will be mine overthrow.
MOSBY Thine overthrow? First let the world dissolve!
ALICE Nay, Mosby, let me still enjoy thy love,
  And happen what will, I am resolute.
  My saving husband hoards up bags of gold 220
  To make our children rich, and now is he
  Gone to unload the goods that shall be thine,
  And he and Franklin will to London straight.
MOSBY To London, Alice? If thou'lt be ruled by me,
  We'll make him sure enough for coming there.
ALICE Ah, would we could!
MOSBY I happened on a painter yesternight,
  The only cunning man of Christendom,
  For he can temper poison with his oil
  That whoso looks upon the work he draws 230
  Shall, with the beams that issue from his sight,
  Suck venom to his breast and slay himself.
  Sweet Alice, he shall draw thy counterfeit,
  That Arden may by gazing on it perish.
ALICE Ay, but Mosby, that is dangerous,
  For thou or I or any other else,
  Coming into the chamber where it hangs, may die.
MOSBY Ay, but we'll have it covered with a cloth
  And hung up in the study for himself.
ALICE It may not be, for when the picture's drawn, 240
  Arden, I know, will come and show it me.
MOSBY Fear not; we'll have that shall serve the turn.
  This is the painter's house; I'll call him forth.
ALICE But, Mosby, I'll have no such picture, I.
MOSBY I pray thee leave it to my discretion.
  How, Clarke!

*Here enters* CLARKE

  Oh, you are an honest man of your word; you served
  me well.

---

172 rid . . . away: i.e. kill
173 Bolton: eds agree this is probably Boughton-under-
    Blean, a village a few miles from Canterbury
175 right-down: downright
177 drifts: schemes
181 early days: early in the day
186 reconcilement: agreement (between Mosby and Alice)
191 closet: private room
200 mere: downright
201 countenance: 'be in keeping with' (eds)
209 strange: distant, cold

213 mermaid's song: lured sailors to their deaths with their
    singing
214 basilisk: fabulous reptile, whose glance could kill
218 still: always
221 our children: no Arden children are mentioned in the
    play, though they are in Holinshed. White speculates
    that here Alice is anticipating the children she will have
    with Mosby being made rich by Arden's wealth
223 straight: straightaway
225 for: to prevent (him) from (OED)
228 only: most
231-2 whoso looks . . . sight: a contemporary theory held that
    the eyes saw by sending out beams to the objects in view
233 counterfeit: portrait
243 the painter's house: probably indicating a door at the rear
    of the stage
246 Clarke: the name is the playwright's invention

CLARKE Why sir, I'll do it for you at any time,
  Provided, as you have given your word,
  I may have Susan Mosby to my wife. **250**
  For as sharp-witted poets, whose sweet verse
  Make heavenly gods break off their nectar draughts
  And lay their ears down to the lowly earth,
  Use humble promise to their sacred Muse,
  So we that are the poets' favourites
  Must have a love. Ay, love is the painter's Muse,
  That makes him frame a speaking countenance,
  A weeping eye that witnesses heart's grief.
  Then tell me, Master Mosby, shall I have her?
ALICE 'Tis pity but he should; he'll use her well. **260**
MOSBY Clarke, here's my hand; my sister shall be thine.
CLARKE Then, brother, to requite this courtesy,
  You shall command my life, my skill, and all.
ALICE Ah, that thou couldst be secret!
MOSBY Fear him not. Leave; I have talked sufficient.
CLARKE You know not me that ask such questions.
  Let it suffice I know you love him well,
  And fain would have your husband made away;
  Wherein, trust me, you show a noble mind,
  That rather than you'll live with him you hate, **270**
  You'll venture life and die with him you love.
  The like will I do for my Susan's sake.
ALICE Yet nothing could enforce me to the deed
  But Mosby's love. Might I without control
  Enjoy thee still, then Arden should not die;
  But seeing I cannot, therefore let him die.
MOSBY Enough, sweet Alice; thy kind words makes me
  melt.
  (*To* CLARKE) Your trick of poisoned pictures we
  dislike;
  Some other poison would do better far.
ALICE Ay, such as might be put into his broth, **280**
  And yet in taste not to be found at all.
CLARKE I know your mind, and here I have it for you.
  Put but a dram of this into his drink,
  Or any kind of broth that he shall eat,
  And he shall die within an hour after.
ALICE As I am a gentlewoman, Clarke, next day
  Thou and Susan shall be married.
MOSBY And I'll make her dowry more than I'll talk of,
  Clarke.
CLARKE Yonder's your husband. Mosby, I'll be gone.
                  *Exit* CLARKE

*Here enters* ARDEN *and* FRANKLIN

ALICE In good time. See where my husband comes. **290**
  Master Mosby, ask him the question yourself.
MOSBY Master Arden, being at London yesternight,
  The Abbey lands whereof you are now possessed
  Were offered me on some occasion
  By Greene, one of Sir Antony Ager's men.
  I pray you, sir, tell me, are not the lands yours?
  Hath any other interest herein?
ARDEN Mosby, that question we'll decide anon.
  Alice, make ready my breakfast; I must hence.
                  *Exit* ALICE
  As for the lands, Mosby, they are mine **300**
  By letters patents from his majesty.
  But I must have a mandate for my wife;
  They say you seek to rob me of her love.
  Villain, what makes thou in her company?
  She's no companion for so base a groom.
MOSBY Arden, I thought not on her, I came to thee;
  But rather than I pocket up this wrong—
FRANKLIN What will you do, sir?
MOSBY Revenge it on the proudest of you both.
      *Then* ARDEN *draws forth* MOSBY's *sword*
ARDEN So, sirrah, you may not wear a sword! **310**
  The statute makes against artificers.
  I warrant that I do. Now use your bodkin,
  Your Spanish needle, and your pressing iron,
  For this shall go with me. And mark my words,
  You goodman botcher, 'tis to you I speak:
  The next time that I take thee near my house,
  Instead of legs I'll make thee crawl on stumps.
MOSBY Ah, Master Arden, you have injured me;
  I do appeal to God and to the world. **319**
FRANKLIN Why, canst thou deny wert a botcher once?
MOSBY Measure me what I am, not what I was.
ARDEN Why, what art thou now but a velvet drudge,

---

290–1 See . . .yourself: 'Alice speaks these lines for Arden to
  hear, in order to allay his suspicions at finding her with
  Mosby. Mosby understands immediately, and responds
  accordingly' (White)
294 occasion: pretext
295 Sir Antony Ager: in reality, Sir Anthony Aucher
302 mandate: deed of ownership
304 makes thou: are you doing
305 groom: fellow; also a serving man (eds)
307 pocket up: submit to
310 sirrah: 'A term of address . . . expressing contempt,
  reprimand, or assumption of authority on the part of the
  speaker' (OED)
311 statute: passed under Edward III and forbidding anyone
  under the rank of gentleman from carrying a sword (eds)
  makes against: decrees against
312 I . . . do: I have a warrant for what I do
315 goodman: 'prefixed (sometimes with ironical intention)
  to the names of those beneath the rank of gentleman'
  (White)
322 velvet drudge: 'menial in velvet livery' (Sturgess)

---

251–6 For as . . . love: i.e. 'just as poets need a muse to inspire
  their art, so painters need love to inspire theirs'
260 but: unless
  use: treat
268 fain: willingly, gladly
274 control: restraint

A cheating steward, and base-minded peasant?

MOSBY Arden, now thou hast belched and vomited
The rancorous venom of thy mis-swoll'n heart,
Hear me but speak. As I intend to live
With God and His elected saints in heaven,
I never meant more to solicit her;
And that she knows, and all the world shall see.
I loved her once—sweet Arden, pardon me.          330
I could not choose, her beauty fired my heart.
But time hath quenched these over-raging coals,
And, Arden, though I now frequent thy house,
'Tis for my sister's sake, her waiting-maid,
And not for hers. Mayest thou enjoy her long;
Hell-fire and wrathful vengeance light on me
If I dishonour her or injure thee.

ARDEN Mosby, with these thy protestations
The deadly hatred of my heart is appeased,
And thou and I'll be friends if this prove true.          340
As for the base terms I gave thee late,
Forget them, Mosby; I had cause to speak
When all the knights and gentlemen of Kent
Make common table-talk of her and thee.

MOSBY Who lives that is not touched with slanderous
tongues?

FRANKLIN Then, Mosby, to eschew the speech of men,
Upon whose general bruit all honour hangs,
Forbear his house.

ARDEN Forbear it! Nay, rather frequent it more.
The world shall see that I distrust her not.          350
To warn him on the sudden from my house
Were to confirm the rumour that is grown.

MOSBY By my faith, sir, you say true,
And therefore will I sojourn here awhile
Until our enemies have talked their fill;
And then, I hope, they'll cease and at last confess
How causeless they have injured her and me.

ARDEN And I will lie at London all this term
To let them see how light I weigh their words.

*Here enters* ALICE *and* MICHAEL

ALICE Husband, sit down; your breakfast will be cold.
ARDEN Come, Master Mosby, will you sit with us?          361
MOSBY I cannot eat, but I'll sit for company.
ARDEN Sirrah Michael, see our horse be ready.
          *Exit* MICHAEL, *returning soon after*
ALICE Husband, why pause ye? Why eat you not?
ARDEN I am not well; there's something in this broth
That is not wholesome. Didst thou make it, Alice?
ALICE I did, and that's the cause it likes not you.
          *Then she throws down the broth on the ground*

There's nothing that I do can please your taste.
You were best to say I would have poisoned you.
I cannot speak or cast aside my eye,          370
But he imagines I have stepped awry.
Here's he that you cast in my teeth so oft;
Now will I be convinced or purge myself.
I charge thee speak to this mistrustful man,
Thou that wouldst see me hang, thou, Mosby, thou.
What favour hast thou had more than a kiss
At coming or departing from the town?

MOSBY You wrong yourself and me to cast these doubts;
Your loving husband is not jealous.

ARDEN Why, gentle Mistress Alice, cannot I be ill          380
But you'll accuse yourself?
Franklin, thou hast a box of mithridate;
I'll take a little to prevent the worst.

FRANKLIN Do so, and let us presently take horse.
My life for yours, ye shall do well enough.

ALICE Give me a spoon; I'll eat of it myself.
Would it were full of poison to the brim!
Then should my cares and troubles have an end.
Was ever silly woman so tormented?

ARDEN Be patient, sweet love; I mistrust not thee.          390
ALICE God will revenge it, Arden, if thou dost,
For never woman loved her husband better
Than I do thee.

ARDEN I know it, sweet Alice; cease to complain,
Lest that in tears I answer thee again.

FRANKLIN Come, leave this dallying, and let us away.
ALICE Forbear to wound me with that bitter word;
Arden shall go to London in my arms.

ARDEN Loth am I to depart, yet I must go.
ALICE Wilt thou to London then, and leave me here?
Ah, if thou love me, gentle Arden, stay.          401
Yet if thy business be of great import,
Go if thou wilt; I'll bear it as I may.
But write from London to me every week,
Nay, every day, and stay no longer there
Than thou must needs, lest that I die for sorrow.

ARDEN I'll write unto thee every other tide,
And so farewell, sweet Alice, till we meet next.

ALICE Farewell, husband, seeing you'll have it so.
And, Master Franklin, seeing you take him hence,
In hope you'll hasten him home I'll give you this.          411
          *And then she kisseth him*

FRANKLIN And if he stay the fault shall not be mine.
Mosby, farewell, and see you keep your oath.

MOSBY I hope he is not jealous of me now.
ARDEN No, Mosby, no; hereafter think of me
As of your dearest friend. And so farewell.
          *Exeunt* ARDEN, FRANKLIN *and* MICHAEL

---

341 late: lately
347 bruit: report
353 my faith: eds (faith my Qs)
367 likes not you: displeases you

---

373 convinced: proved guilty
382 mithridate: a universal antidote
389 silly: helpless, defenceless

ALICE I am glad he is gone; he was about to stay,
But did you mark me then how I brake off?
MOSBY Ay, Alice, and it was cunningly performed.
But what a villain is this painter Clarke!            420
ALICE Was it not a goodly poison that he gave!
Why, he's as well now as he was before.
It should have been some fine confection
That might have given the broth some dainty taste.
This powder was too gross and populous.
MOSBY But had he eaten but three spoonfuls more,
Then had he died and our love continued.
ALICE Why, so it shall, Mosby, albeit he live.
MOSBY It is unpossible, for I have sworn
Never hereafter to solicit thee                      430
Or, whilst he lives, once more importune thee.
ALICE Thou shalt not need; I will importune thee.
What, shall an oath make thee forsake my love?
As if I have not sworn as much myself,
And given my hand unto him in the church!
Tush, Mosby. Oaths are words, and words is wind,
And wind is mutable. Then I conclude
'Tis childishness to stand upon an oath.
MOSBY Well proved, Mistress Alice; yet, by your leave,
I'll keep mine unbroken whilst he lives.             440
ALICE Ay, do, and spare not. His time is but short,
For if thou beest as resolute as I,
We'll have him murdered as he walks the streets.
In London many alehouse ruffians keep,
Which, as I hear, will murder men for gold.
They shall be soundly fee'd to pay him home.

*Here enters* GREENE

MOSBY Alice, what's he that comes yonder? Knowest
thou him?
ALICE Mosby, be gone. I hope 'tis one that comes
To put in practice our intended drifts.   *Exit* MOSBY
GREENE Mistress Arden, you are well met.           450
I am sorry that your husband is from home
Whenas my purposed journey was to him.
Yet all my labour is not spent in vain,
For I suppose that you can full discourse
And flat resolve me of the thing I seek.
ALICE What is it, Master Greene? If that I may
Or can with safety, I will answer you.
GREENE I heard your husband hath the grant of late,
Confirmed by letters patents from the king,
Of all of the lands of the Abbey of Faversham,      460
Generally intitled, so that all former grants

Are cut off, whereof I myself had one;
But now my interest by that is void.
This is all, Mistress Arden; is it true nor no?
ALICE True, Master Greene; the lands are his in state,
And whatsoever leases were before
Are void for term of Master Arden's life.
He hath the grant under the Chancery seal.
GREENE Pardon me, Mistress Arden; I must speak,
For I am touched. Your husband doth me wrong   470
To wring me from the little land I have.
My living is my life; only that
Resteth remainder of my portion.
Desire of wealth is endless in his mind,
And he is greedy-gaping still for gain;
Nor cares he though young gentlemen do beg,
So he may scrape and hoard up in his pouch.
But seeing he hath taken my lands, I'll value life
As careless as he is careful for to get;
And tell him this from me: I'll be revenged,        480
And so as he shall wish the Abbey lands
Had rested still within their former state.
ALICE Alas, poor gentleman, I pity you,
And woe is me that any man should want.
God knows, 'tis not my fault. But wonder not
Though he be hard to others when to me—
Ah, Master Greene, God knows how I am used!
GREENE Why, Mistress Arden, can the crabbed churl
Use you unkindly? Respects he not your birth,
Your honourable friends, nor what you brought?  490
Why, all Kent knows your parentage and what you
are.
ALICE Ah, Master Greene, be it spoken in secret here,
I never live good day with him alone.
When he is at home, then have I froward looks,
Hard words, and blows to mend the match withal.
And though I might content as good a man,
Yet doth he keep in every corner trulls;
And weary with his trugs at home,
Then rides he straight to London; there, forsooth,
He revels it among such filthy ones                 500
As counsels him to make away his wife.
Thus live I daily in continual fear,

---

425 gross and populous: indelicate or indigestible, and
perceptible (Wine)
444 keep: live, lodge
446 to pay him home: i.e. to murder him
454 full discourse: fully explain
455 flat resolve: make completely clear to
461 Generally intitled: deeded without any exceptions

465 in state: by law
468 Chancery seal: 'the Court of the Lord Chancellor was the
highest in the land, next to the House of Lords' (White)
470 touched: affected
472 living: land
472–3 only . . . portion: only my land remains from my
inheritance
475 still: always
477 so: so long as
479 careful for to get: eager to acquire possessions
490 what you brought: i.e. as your dowry
494 froward: bad-tempered
497, 498 trulls, trugs: prostitutes

In sorrow, so despairing of redress
As every day I wish with hearty prayer
That he or I were taken forth the world.
GREENE Now trust me, Mistress Alice, it grieveth me
So fair a creature should be so abused.
Why, who would have thought the civil sir so sullen?
He looks so smoothly. Now, fie upon him, churl!
And if he live a day he lives too long. 510
But frolic, woman; I shall be the man
Shall set you free from all this discontent.
And if the churl deny my interest,
And will not yield my lease into my hand,
I'll pay him home, whatever hap to me.
ALICE But speak you as you think?
GREENE Ay, God's my witness, I mean plain dealing,
For I had rather die than lose my land.
ALICE Then, Master Greene, be counselled by me:
Endanger not yourself for such a churl, 520
But hire some cutter for to cut him short;
And here's ten pound to wager them withal.
When he is dead you shall have twenty more;
And the lands whereof my husband is possessed
Shall be intitled as they were before.
GREENE Will you keep promise with me?
ALICE Or count me false and perjured whilst I live.
GREENE Then here's my hand, I'll have him so
    dispatched.
I'll up to London straight; I'll thither post,
And never rest till I have compassed it. 530
Till then farewell.
ALICE Good fortune follow all your forward thoughts.
                                    *Exit* GREENE
And whosoever doth attempt the deed
A happy hand I wish, and so farewell.
All this goes well. Mosby, I long for thee
To let thee know all that I have contrived.

*Here enters* MOSBY *and* CLARKE

MOSBY How now, Alice, what's the news?
ALICE Such as will content thee well, sweetheart.
MOSBY Well, let them pass awhile, and tell me, Alice,
How have you dealt and tempered with my sister? 540
What, will she have my neighbour Clarke or no?
ALICE What, Master Mosby! Let him woo himself.
Think you that maids look not for fair words?
Go to her, Clarke, she's all alone within.

---

511 frolic: cheer up
513 interest: legal right to property
521 cutter: cut-throat
522 wager: pay
529 post: ride with haste
530 compassed: achieved
532 forward: eager
539 them: i.e. the news
540 tempered with: persuaded

Michael, my man, is clean out of her books.
CLARKE I thank you, Mistress Arden, I will in,
And if fair Susan and I can make a gree,
You shall command me to the uttermost,
As far as either goods or life may stretch.
                                    *Exit* CLARKE
MOSBY Now, Alice, let's hear thy news. 550
ALICE They be so good that I must laugh for joy
Before I can begin to tell my tale.
MOSBY Let's hear them, that I may laugh for company.
ALICE This morning, Master Greene—Dick Greene, I
    mean,
From whom my husband had the Abbey land—
Came hither railing for to know the truth,
Whether my husband had the lands by grant.
I told him all, whereat he stormed amain
And swore he would cry quittance with the churl
And, if he did deny his interest, 560
Stab him, whatsoever did befall himself.
Whenas I saw his choler thus to rise,
I whetted on the gentleman with words,
And, to conclude, Mosby, at last we grew
To composition for my husband's death.
I gave him ten pound to hire knaves,
By some device to make away the churl.
When he is dead he should have twenty more
And repossess his former lands again.
On this we 'greed, and he is ridden straight 570
To London to bring his death about.
MOSBY But call you this good news?
ALICE Ay, sweetheart, be they not?
MOSBY 'Twere cheerful news to hear the churl were
    dead,
But trust me, Alice, I take it passing ill
You would be so forgetful of our state
To make recount of it to every groom.
What! To acquaint each stranger with our drifts,
Chiefly in case of murder—why, 'tis the way
To make it open unto Arden's self, 580
And bring thyself and me to ruin both.
Forewarned, forearmed; who threats his enemy
Lends him a sword to guard himself withal.
ALICE I did it for the best.
MOSBY Well, seeing 'tis done, cheerly let it pass.
You know this Greene; is he not religious?
A man, I guess, of great devotion?
ALICE He is.

---

545 out of her books: out of favour with her
547 make a gree: come to terms
558 amain: with all his strength
559 cry quittance with: be even with
563 whetted on: incited
565 composition: agreement (for payment)
575 passing: extremely
585 cheerly: cheerfully

MOSBY Then, sweet Alice, let it pass. I have a drift
    Will quiet all, whatever is amiss.         590

*Here enters* CLARKE *and* SUSAN

ALICE How now, Clarke, have you found me false?
    Did I not plead the matter hard for you?
CLARKE You did.
MOSBY And what? Will't be a match?
CLARKE A match, i'faith, sir. Ay, the day is mine.
    The painter lays his colours to the life,
    His pencil draws no shadows in his love;
    Susan is mine.
ALICE You make her blush.
MOSBY What, sister, is it Clarke must be the man?   600
SUSAN It resteth in your grant. Some words are passed,
    And haply we be grown unto a match
    If you be willing that it shall be so.
MOSBY Ah, Master Clarke, it resteth at my grant;
    You see my sister's yet at my dispose.
    But, so you'll grant me one thing I shall ask,
    I am content my sister shall be yours.
CLARKE What is it, Master Mosby?
MOSBY I do remember once in secret talk
    You told me how you could compound by art   610
    A crucifix impoisoned,
    That whoso look upon it should wax blind,
    And with the scent be stifled, that ere long
    He should die poisoned that did view it well.
    I would have you make me such a crucifix,
    And then I'll grant my sister shall be yours.
CLARKE Though I am loth, because it toucheth life,
    Yet rather or I'll leave sweet Susan's love,
    I'll do it, and with all the haste I may.
    But for whom is it?         620
ALICE Leave that to us. Why, Clarke, is it possible
    That you should paint and draw it out yourself,
    The colours being baleful and impoisoned,
    And no ways prejudice yourself withal?
MOSBY Well questioned, Alice. Clarke, how answer
    you that?
CLARKE Very easily. I'll tell you straight
    How I do work of these impoisoned drugs:
    I fasten on my spectacles so close
    As nothing can any way offend my sight;
    Then, as I put a leaf within my nose,   630

    So put I rhubarb to avoid the smell,
    And softly as another work I paint.
MOSBY 'Tis very well, but against when shall I have it?
CLARKE Within this ten days.
MOSBY 'Twill serve the turn.
    Now, Alice, let's in and see what cheer you keep.
                    *Exit* CLARKE
    I hope now Master Arden is from home,
    You'll give me leave to play your husband's part.
ALICE Mosby, you know who's master of my heart;
    He well may be the master of the house.     640
                         *Exeunt*

# Scene ii

*Here enters* GREENE *and* BRADSHAW

BRADSHAW See you them that comes yonder, Master
    Greene?
GREENE Ay, very well. Do you know them?

*Here enters* BLACK WILL *and* SHAKEBAG

BRADSHAW The one I know not, but he seems a knave,
    Chiefly for bearing the other company;
    For such a slave, so vile a rogue as he,
    Lives not again upon the earth.
    Black Will is his name. I tell you, Master Greene,
    At Boulogne he and I were fellow soldiers,
    Where he played such pranks
    As all the camp feared him for his villainy.   10
    I warrant you he bears so bad a mind
    That for a crown he'll murder any man.
GREENE (*Aside*) The fitter is he for my purpose, marry!
BLACK WILL How now, fellow Bradshaw! Whither
    away so early?
BRADSHAW Oh, Will, times are changed; no fellows
    now,
    Though we were once together in the field;
    Yet thy friend to do thee any good I can.   18
BLACK WILL Why, Bradshaw, was not thou and I
    fellow soldiers at Boulogne, where I was a corporal
    and thou but a base mercenary groom? 'No fellows
    now' because you are a goldsmith and have a little
    plate in your shop? You were glad to call me 'fellow
    Will' and, with a cursy to the earth, 'one snatch, good

---

596–7 The painter . . . love: White suggests as a possible
    meaning for these lines: 'The painter reproduces life
    faithfully, and, in this case, his pencil need draw no
    shadows in his love'
602 haply: perhaps
606 so: if
618 or: than
623 baleful: noxious
624 prejudice: endanger
629 offend: harm

631 rhubarb: believed to have medicinal properties
632 softly as another: 'as easily as with any other' (White)
SD Only White of the eds suggests including this stage
    direction, but its insertion makes sense in the light of the
    lines that follow
11 warrant: assure
13 marry!: an oath derived from the name of the Virgin
    Mary
23 cursy: obsolete form of curtsey
    snatch: morsel

corporal', when I stole the half ox from John the victualler, and domineered with it amongst good fellows in one night. 26

BRADSHAW Ay, Will, those days are past with me.

BLACK WILL Ay, but they be not past with me, for I keep that same honourable mind still. Good neighbour Bradshaw, you are too proud to be my fellow, but were it not that I see more company coming down the hill, I would be fellows with you once more, and share crowns with you too. But let that pass, and tell me whither you go. 34

BRADSHAW To London, Will, about a piece of service Wherein haply thou may'st pleasure me.

BLACK WILL What is it?

BRADSHAW Of late, Lord Cheiny lost some plate,
Which one did bring and sold it at my shop,
Saying he served Sir Antony Cooke. 40
A search was made, the plate was found with me,
And I am bound to answer at the 'size.
Now Lord Cheiny solemnly vows,
If law will serve him, he'll hang me for his plate.
Now I am going to London upon hope
To find the fellow. Now, Will, I know
Thou art acquainted with such companions.

BLACK WILL What manner of man was he?

BRADSHAW A lean-faced, writhen knave,
Hawk-nosed and very hollow-eyed, 50
With mighty furrows in his stormy brows,
Long hair down his shoulders curled;
His chin was bare, but on his upper lip
A mutchado, which he wound about his ear.

BLACK WILL What apparel had he?

BRADSHAW A watchet satin doublet all to-torn
(The inner side did bear the greater show),
A pair of threadbare velvet hose, seam rent,
A worsted stocking rent above the shoe,
A livery cloak, but all the lace was off; 60
'Twas bad, but yet it served to hide the plate.

BLACK WILL Sirrah Shakebag, canst thou remember since we trolled the bowl at Sittingburgh, where I broke the tapster's head of the Lion with a cudgel-stick?

SHAKEBAG Ay, very well, Will.

BLACK WILL Why, it was with the money that the plate was sold for. Sirrah Bradshaw, what wilt thou give him that can tell thee who sold thy plate?

BRADSHAW Who, I pray thee, good Will?

BLACK WILL Why, 'twas one Jack Fitten. He's now in Newgate for stealing a horse, and shall be arraigned the next 'size. 72

BRADSHAW Why then, let Lord Cheiny seek Jack Fitten forth,
For I'll back and tell him who robbed him of his plate.
This cheers my heart. Master Greene, I'll leave you,
For I must to the Isle of Sheppey with speed.

GREENE Before you go, let me entreat you
To carry this letter to Mistress Arden of Faversham
And humbly recommend me to herself.

BRADSHAW That will I, Master Greene, and so farewell.
Here, Will, there's a crown for thy good news. 81

*Exit* BRADSHAW

BLACK WILL Farewell, Bradshaw; I'll drink no water for thy sake whilst this lasts. Now, gentleman, shall we have your company to London?

GREENE Nay, stay, sirs,
A little more: I needs must use your help,
And in a matter of great consequence,
Wherein if you'll be secret and profound,
I'll give you twenty angels for your pains.

BLACK WILL How? Twenty angels? Give my fellow George Shakebag and me twenty angels, and if thou'lt have thy own father slain that thou mayest inherit his land, we'll kill him. 93

SHAKEBAG Ay, thy mother, thy sister, thy brother, or all thy kin.

GREENE Well, this it is: Arden of Faversham
Hath highly wronged me about the Abbey land,
That no revenge but death will serve the turn.
Will you two kill him? Here's the angels down,
And I will lay the platform of his death. 100

BLACK WILL Plat me no platforms! Give me the money and I'll stab him as he stands pissing against a wall, but I'll kill him.

SHAKEBAG Where is he?

GREENE He is now at London, in Aldersgate Street.

---

25 domineered: revelled
33 and share crowns with you: i.e. rob you (eds)
40 Sir Antony Cooke: tutor to Edward VI
42 'size: assize
49 writhen: contorted
54 mutchado: moustache
56 watchet: pale blue
   all to-torn: completely torn
57 The . . . show: 'more of the lining than the outside was visible' (White)
59 worsted: wool fabric (eds); (wosted $Q_I$, $Q_3$; wosten $Q_2$)
63 trolled the bowl: handed round the drinking cup
   Sittingburgh: Sittingbourne, a town in Kent about 9 miles from Faversham

64 tapster's . . . Lion: the head of the tapster at the Lion Inn
71 Newgate: a London prison
   arraigned: charged
88 profound: cunning
89 angels: gold coins, worth about ten shillings (50 pence), so named because they were imprinted with the device of the Archangel Michael
100 platform: plan
105 Aldersgate Street; a fashionable street, running south from Aldersgate to St Martin's-le-Grand

SHAKEBAG He's dead as if he had been condemned by
an Act of Parliament if once Black Will and I swear
his death.

GREENE Here is ten pound, and when he is dead
Ye shall have twenty more. 110

BLACK WILL My fingers itches to be at the peasant. Ah,
that I might be set a work thus through the year and
that murder would grow to an occupation that a man
might without danger of law. Zounds! I warrant I
should be warden of the company. Come, let us be
going, and we'll bait at Rochester, where I'll give thee
a gallon of sack to handsel the match withal.

*Exeunt*

# Scene iii

*Here enters* MICHAEL

MICHAEL I have gotten such a letter as will touch the
painter, and thus it is: 2

*Here enters* ARDEN *and* FRANKLIN *and hears* MICHAEL
*read this letter*

'My duty remembered, Mistress Susan, hoping in
God you be in good health, as I, Michael, was at the
making hereof. This is to certify you that, as the
turtle true, when she hath lost her mate, sitteth alone,
so I, mourning for your absence, do walk up and
down Paul's till one day I fell asleep and lost my
master's pantofles. Ah, Mistress Susan, abolish that
paltry painter, cut him off by the shins with a
frowning look of your crabbed countenance, and
think upon Michael, who, drunk with the dregs of
your favour, will cleave as fast to your love as a plaster

of pitch to a galled horseback. Thus hoping you will
let my passions penetrate, or rather impetrate, mercy
of your meek hands, I end. 16
Yours, Michael, or else not Michael.'

ARDEN Why, you paltry knave!
Stand you here loitering, knowing my affairs,
What haste my business craves to send to Kent? 20

FRANKLIN 'Faith, friend Michael, this is very ill,
Knowing your master hath no more but you,
And do ye slack his business for your own?

ARDEN Where is the letter, sirrah? Let me see it.
*Then he* (MICHAEL) *gives him the letter*
See, Master Franklin, here's proper stuff:
Susan my maid, the painter, and my man,
A crew of harlots, all in love, forsooth.
Sirrah, let me hear no more of this,
Now, for thy life, once write to her a word!

*Here enters* GREENE, BLACK WILL, *and* SHAKEBAG

Wilt thou be married to so base a trull? 30
'Tis Mosby's sister. Come I once at home,
I'll rouse her from remaining in my house.
Now, Master Franklin, let us go walk in Paul's.
Come, but a turn or two and then away.
*Exeunt* ARDEN, FRANKLIN *and* MICHAEL

GREENE The first is Arden, and that's his man;
The other is Franklin, Arden's dearest friend.

BLACK WILL Zounds, I'll kill them all three.

GREENE Nay, sirs, touch not his man in any case;
But stand close, and take you fittest standing,
And at his coming forth speed him. 40
To the Nag's Head, there is this coward's haunt.
But now I'll leave you till the deed be done.
*Exit* GREENE

SHAKEBAG If he be not paid his own, ne'er trust
Shakebag.

BLACK WILL Sirrah Shakebag, at his coming forth I'll
run him through, and then to the Blackfriars and
there take water and away.

---

114 might: i.e. might follow his occupation (murder)
Zounds!: oath derived from 'By God's wounds'
115 warden of the company: Black Will imagines a guild
('company') of murderers, resembling the official livery
companies of the City of London, of which he would be
governor or member ('warden')
116 bait: stop for food and rest
117 sack: white wine from Spain
handsel: 'confirm or inaugurate with an omen of success'
(Wine)
3–17 Michael's letter is a parody of the euphuistic style
(named after John Lyly's *Euphues: The Anatomy of Wit*
(1578) and *Euphues and His England* (1580)) in vogue in
the 1580s. It is characterised by an elaborate and
sententious formality derived from its exploitation of
rhetorical devices
5 certify: assure
6 turtle: turtle dove
8 Paul's: the central aisle of St Paul's Cathedral in London,
known as Paul's Walk (or Duke Humphrey's Walk), was
a popular meeting-place for merchants and businessmen,
as well as the haunt of prostitutes and pickpockets
9 pantofles: galoshes

13–14 plaster . . . horseback: part of a remedy for diseases in
horses (Wine)
14 galled: sore
15 impetrate: obtain by entreaty
20 to send: i.e. to be sent
27 harlots: lewd persons of either sex
29 Now: Qs. Some eds emend to 'Nor', but, as Wine notes,
'Now' makes good sense as part of an exclamation
39 stand close: hide yourselves
fittest standing: best position; one specific sense of this is
associated with hunting
43 paid his own: i.e. killed
45 Blackfriars: a fashionable residential district, which, even
after the dissolution of the Dominican monastery there
in 1538, retained its right of sanctuary; see xv.12n
46 take water: cross the Thames by boat

SHAKEBAG  Why, that's the best; but see thou miss him
  not.

BLACK WILL  How can I miss him, when I think on the
  forty angels I must have more?

*Here enters a* PRENTICE

PRENTICE  'Tis very late; I were best shut up my stall,
  for here will be old filching when the press comes
  forth of Paul's.                                                     52

*Then lets he down his window, and it breaks* BLACK WILL's
                              *head*

BLACK WILL  Zounds! Draw, Shakebag, draw! I am
  almost killed.

PRENTICE  We'll tame you, I warrant.

BLACK WILL  Zounds, I am tame enough already.

*Here enters* ARDEN, FRANKLIN, *and* MICHAEL

ARDEN  What troublesome fray or mutiny is this?

FRANKLIN  'Tis nothing but some brabbling, paltry fray,
  Devised to pick men's pockets in the throng.

ARDEN  Is't nothing else? Come, Franklin, let us away.
              *Exeunt* ARDEN, FRANKLIN, *and* MICHAEL

BLACK WILL  What 'mends shall I have for my broken
  head?                                                                  60

PRENTICE  Marry, this 'mends, that if you get you not
  away all the sooner, you shall be well beaten and sent
  to the Counter.                                            *Exit* PRENTICE

BLACK WILL  Well, I'll be gone; but look to your signs,
  for I'll pull them down all. Shakebag, my broken
  head grieves me not so much as by this means Arden
  hath escaped. (*Here enters* GREENE) I had a glimpse of
  him and his companion.

GREENE  Why, sirs, Arden's as well as I; I met him and
  Franklin going merrily to the ordinary. What, dare
  you not do it?                                                         71

BLACK WILL  Yes, sir, we dare do it; but were my
  consent to give again we would not do it under ten
  pound more. I value every drop of my blood at a
  French crown. I have had ten pound to steal a dog,
  and we have no more here to kill a man. But that a
  bargain is a bargain and so forth, you should do it
  yourself.

---

50  stall: book stall, of which there were many in St Paul's
  churchyard
51  old filching: much stealing
  press: crowd
SD  *breaks*: grazes, bruises
54  tame: hurt (White)
57  brabbling: noisy
60  'mends: amends
63  Counter: a London prison
66  as: as the fact that
70  ordinary: tavern dining room
73  to give: to be given
75  French crown: worth about five shillings at this time

GREENE  I pray thee, how came thy head broke?        79

BLACK WILL  Why, thou seest it is broke, dost thou not?

SHAKEBAG  Standing against a stall, watching Arden's
  coming, a boy let down his shop window and broke
  his head; whereupon arose a brawl, and in the tumult
  Arden escaped us and passed by unthought on. But
  forbearance is no acquittance; another time we'll do
  it, I warrant thee.

GREENE  I pray thee, Will, make clean thy bloody brow,
  And let us bethink us on some other place
  Where Arden may be met with handsomely.
  Remember how devoutly thou hast sworn                90
  To kill the villain; think upon thine oath.

BLACK WILL  Tush, I have broken five hundred oaths!
  But wouldst thou charm me to effect this deed,
  Tell me of gold, my resolution's fee;
  Say thou seest Mosby kneeling at my knees,
  Off'ring me service for my high attempt;
  And sweet Alice Arden, with a lap of crowns,
  Comes with a lowly cursy to the earth,
  Saying 'Take this but for thy quarterage;
  Such yearly tribute will I answer thee.'             100
  Why, this would steel soft-mettled cowardice,
  With which Black Will was never tainted with.
  I tell thee, Greene, the forlorn traveller,
  Whose lips are glued with summer's parching heat,
  Ne'er longed so much to see a running brook
  As I to finish Arden's tragedy.
  Seest thou this gore that cleaveth to my face?
  From hence ne'er will I wash this bloody stain
  Till Arden's heart be panting in my hand.

GREENE  Why, that's well said; but what saith
  Shakebag?                                                             110

SHAKEBAG  I cannot paint my valour out with words;
  But give me place and opportunity,
  Such mercy as the starven lioness,
  When she is dry-sucked of her eager young,
  Shows to the prey that next encounters her,
  On Arden so much pity would I take.

GREENE  So should it fare with men of firm resolve.
  And now, sirs, seeing this accident
  Of meeting him in Paul's hath no success,
  Let us bethink us on some other place                 120
  Whose earth may swallow up this Arden's blood.

*Here enters* MICHAEL

  See, yonder comes his man. And wot you what?
  The foolish knave is in love with Mosby's sister,

---

89  handsomely: readily
95–7  Mosby . . . Alice Arden: since Greene did not mention
  Mosby or Alice Arden when hiring Black Will and
  Shakebag to kill Arden, Wine suggests that this reference
  may indicate authorial or textual confusion
99  quarterage: quarterly payment
100  answer: guarantee

And for her sake, whose love he cannot get
Unless Mosby solicit his suit,
The villain hath sworn the slaughter of his master.
We'll question him, for he may stead us much.
How now, Michael, whither are you going?

MICHAEL  My master hath new supped,
And I am going to prepare his chamber.          130

GREENE  Where supped Master Arden?

MICHAEL  At the Nag's Head, at the eighteen pence
ordinary. How now, Master Shakebag! What, Black
Will! God's dear lady, how chance your face is so
bloody?

BLACK WILL  Go to, sirrah; there is a chance in it. This
sauciness in you will make you be knocked.

MICHAEL  Nay, and you be offended, I'll be gone.

GREENE  Stay, Michael, you may not 'scape us so.
Michael, I know you love your master well.          140

MICHAEL  Why, so I do; but wherefore urge you that?

GREENE  Because I think you love your mistress better.

MICHAEL  So think not I. But say, i'faith, what if I
should?

SHAKEBAG  Come to the purpose. Michael, we hear
You have a pretty love in Faversham.

MICHAEL  Why, have I two or three, what's that to
thee?

BLACK WILL  You deal too mildly with the peasant.
Thus it is:
'Tis known to us you love Mosby's sister;
We know besides that you have ta'en your oath
To further Mosby to your mistress' bed          150
And kill your master for his sister's sake.
Now, sir, a poorer coward than yourself
Was never fostered in the coast of Kent.
How comes it then that such a knave as you
Dare swear a matter of such consequence?

GREENE  Ah, Will—

BLACK WILL  Tush, give me leave, there's no more but
this:
Sith thou hast sworn, we dare discover all,
And hadst thou or shouldst thou utter it,
We have devised a complot under hand,          160
Whatever shall betide to any of us,
To send thee roundly to the devil of hell.

And therefore thus: I am the very man,
Marked in my birth-hour by the Destinies,
To give an end to Arden's life on earth;
Thou but a member but to whet the knife
Whose edge must search the closet of his breast.
Thy office is but to appoint the place,
And train thy master to his tragedy;
Mine to perform it when occasion serves.          170
Then be not nice, but here devise with us
How and what way we may conclude his death.

SHAKEBAG  So shalt thou purchase Mosby for thy
friend,
And by his friendship gain his sister's love.

GREENE  So shall thy mistress be thy favourer,
And thou disburdened of the oath thou made.

MICHAEL  Well, gentlemen, I cannot but confess,
Sith you have urged me so apparently,
That I have vowed my master Arden's death;
And he whose kindly love and liberal hand          180
Doth challenge nought but good deserts of me
I will deliver over to your hands.
This night come to his house at Aldersgate;
The doors I'll leave unlocked against you come.
No sooner shall ye enter through the latch,
Over the threshold to the inner court,
But on your left hand shall you see the stairs
That leads directly to my master's chamber.
There take him and dispose him as ye please.
Now it were good we parted company.          190
What I have promised I will perform.

BLACK WILL  Should you deceive us, 'twould go wrong
with you.

MICHAEL  I will accomplish all I have revealed.

BLACK WILL  Come, let's go drink. Choler makes me as
dry as a dog.

*Exeunt* BLACK WILL, GREENE *and* SHAKEBAG.
*Manet* MICHAEL

MICHAEL  Thus feeds the lamb securely on the down
Whilst through the thicket of an arbour brake
The hunger-bitten wolf o'erpries his haunt
And takes advantage to eat him up.
Ah, harmless Arden, how, how hast thou misdone
That thus thy gentle life is levelled at?          200

---

127  stead us much: 'give us useful information' (White)
132  eighteen pence ordinary: fixed price of the meal in the
ordinary
136  Go to: exclamation of protest
138  and: if
141  urge: bring to attention
148  known Q2, Q3 (kowne Q1)
158  Sith: since
discover: reveal
160  complot: plot
under hand: in secret
162  roundly: promptly

164  Destinies: i.e. the three Fates, goddesses who presided
over people's births, lives and deaths
166  member: helper
169  train: lure
171  nice: squeamish, coy
178  apparently: plainly
181  challenge: deserve, claim
deserts of: deeds from
184  against you come: in anticipation of your coming
SD  *Manet*: remains
199  harmless: innocent
200  levelled: aimed

The many good turns that thou hast done to me
Now must I quittance with betraying thee.
I, that should take the weapon in my hand
And buckler thee from ill-intending foes,
Do lead thee with a wicked, fraudful smile,
As unsuspected to the slaughterhouse.
So have I sworn to Mosby and my mistress,
So have I promised to the slaughtermen;
And should I not deal currently with them,
Their lawless rage would take revenge on me.          210
Tush, I will spurn at mercy for this once.
Let pity lodge where feeble women lie;
I am resolved, and Arden needs must die.

*Exit* MICHAEL

## Scene iv

*Here enters* ARDEN *and* FRANKLIN

ARDEN  No, Franklin, no. If fear or stormy threats,
If love of me or care of womanhood,
If fear of God or common speech of men,
Who mangle credit with their wounding words
And couch dishonour as dishonour buds,
Might 'join repentance in her wanton thoughts,
No question then but she would turn the leaf
And sorrow for her dissolution.
But she is rooted in her wickedness,
Perverse and stubborn, not to be reclaimed.          10
Good counsel is to her as rain to weeds,
And reprehension makes her vice to grow
As Hydra's head that plenished by decay.
Her faults, methink, are painted in my face
For every searching eye to overread;
And Mosby's name, a scandal unto mine,
Is deeply trenched in my blushing brow.

Ah, Franklin, Franklin, when I think on this,
My heart's grief rends my other powers
Worse than the conflict at the hour of death.          20
FRANKLIN  Gentle Arden, leave this sad lament.
She will amend, and so your griefs will cease;
Or else she'll die, and so your sorrows end.
If neither of these two do haply fall,
Yet let your comfort be that others bear
Your woes twice doubled all with patience.
ARDEN  My house is irksome; there I cannot rest.
FRANKLIN  Then stay with me in London; go not
home.
ARDEN  Then that base Mosby doth usurp my room
And makes his triumph of my being thence.          30
At home or not at home, where'er I be,
Here, here it lies (*points to his heart*), ah, Franklin,
here it lies
That will not out till wretched Arden dies.

*Here enters* MICHAEL

FRANKLIN  Forget your griefs awhile; here comes your
man.
ARDEN  What o'clock is't, sirrah?
MICHAEL                                            Almost ten.
ARDEN  See, see how runs away the weary time.
Come, Master Franklin, shall we go to bed?

*Exeunt* ARDEN *and* MICHAEL. *Manet* FRANKLIN

FRANKLIN  I pray you, go before; I'll follow you.
Ah, what a hell is fretful jealousy!
What pity-moving words, what deep-fetched sighs, 40
What grievous groans and overlading woes
Accompanies this gentle gentleman.
Now will he shake his care-oppressed head,
Then fix his sad eyes on the sullen earth,
Ashamed to gaze upon the open world;
Now will he cast his eyes up towards the heavens,
Looking that ways for redress of wrong.
Sometimes he seeketh to beguile his grief,
And tells a story with his careful tongue;
Then comes his wife's dishonour in his thoughts     50
And in the middle cutteth off his tale,
Pouring fresh sorrow on his weary limbs.
So woe-begone, so inly charged with woe,
Was never any lived and bare it so.

*Here enters* MICHAEL

MICHAEL  My master would desire you come to bed.
FRANKLIN  Is he himself already in his bed?

*Exit* FRANKLIN. *Manet* MICHAEL

---

202 quittance: repay
204 buckler: shield
209 currently: honestly, faithfully
  4 credit: honour, reputation
  5 couch: eds disagree on the exact meaning of this word in
    the context of this line, pointing to such relevant variant
    meanings as 'spread', 'cause to germinate', 'embroider',
    'plant out in the earth' and 'give expression to'. All these
    definitions, however, indicate that the general sense of
    the line concerns the deliberate cultivation or
    encouragement of dishonourable acts
  6 'join: enjoin
  8 dissolution: dissolute living
 13 Hydra's head . . . decay: 'the second labour of Hercules
    was to kill the Lernaean Hydra, an enormous serpent
    with nine heads, each of which was *replenished* with two
    more when cut off' (White). Wine suggests 'by decay'
    might mean 'by decapitation'
    plenished: eds (perisht Qs)
 17 trenched: cut

24 fall: befall
40 moving Q2, Q3 (moning Q1)
48 beguile: divert attention from
49 careful: full of care
54 Was: i.e. there was

MICHAEL He is and fain would have the light away.
Conflicting thoughts encamped in my breast
Awake me with the echo of their strokes;
And I, a judge to censure either side, 60
Can give to neither wished victory.
My master's kindness pleads to me for life
With just demand, and I must grant it him;
My mistress she hath forced me with an oath,
For Susan's sake the which I may not break,
For that is nearer than a master's love;
That grim-faced fellow, pitiless Black Will,
And Shakebag, stern in bloody stratagem—
Two rougher ruffians never lived in Kent—
Have sworn my death if I infringe my vow, 70
A dreadful thing to be considered of.
Methinks I see them with their boltered hair,
Staring and grinning in thy gentle face,
And in their ruthless hands their daggers drawn,
Insulting o'er thee with a peck of oaths
Whilst thou, submissive, pleading for relief,
Art mangled by their ireful instruments.
Methinks I hear them ask where Michael is,
And pitiless Black Will cries 'Stab the slave!
The peasant will detect the tragedy.' 80
The wrinkles in his foul, death-threat'ning face
Gapes open wide, like graves to swallow men.
My death to him is but a merriment,
And he will murder me to make him sport.
He comes, he comes! Ah, Master Franklin, help!
Call up the neighbours or we are but dead.

*Here enters* FRANKLIN *and* ARDEN

FRANKLIN What dismal outcry calls me from my rest?
ARDEN What hath occasioned such a fearful cry?
Speak, Michael! Hath any injured thee?
MICHAEL Nothing, sir; but as I fell asleep 90
Upon the threshold, leaning to the stairs,
I had a fearful dream that troubled me,
And in my slumber thought I was beset
With murderer thieves that came to rifle me.
My trembling joints witness my inward fear.
I crave your pardons for disturbing you.
ARDEN So great a cry for nothing I ne'er heard.
What, are the doors fast locked and all things safe?
MICHAEL I cannot tell; I think I locked the doors.

ARDEN I like not this, but I'll go see myself. 100
*He tries the doors*
Ne'er trust me but the doors were all unlocked.
This negligence not half contenteth me.
Get you to bed, and if you love my favour
Let me have no more such pranks as these.
Come, Master Franklin, let us go to bed.
FRANKLIN Ay, by my faith; the air is very cold.
Michael, farewell; I pray thee dream no more.

*Exeunt*

# Scene v

*Here enters* BLACK WILL, GREENE, *and* SHAKEBAG

SHAKEBAG Black night hath hid the pleasures of the day,
And sheeting darkness overhangs the earth
And with the black fold of her cloudy robe
Obscures us from the eyesight of the world,
In which sweet silence such as we triumph.
The lazy minutes linger on their time,
Loth to give due audit to the hour,
Till in the watch our purpose be complete,
And Arden sent to everlasting night.
Greene, get you gone and linger here about, 10
And at some hour hence come to us again,
Where we will give you instance of his death.
GREENE Speed to my wish whose will so'er says no;
And so I'll leave you for an hour or two. *Exit* GREENE
BLACK WILL I tell thee, Shakebag, would this thing
were done;
I am so heavy that I can scarce go.
This drowsiness in me bodes little good.
SHAKEBAG How now, Will, become a precisian?
Nay, then, let's go sleep when bugs and fears
Shall kill our courages with their fancy's work. 20
BLACK WILL Why, Shakebag, thou mistakes me much
And wrongs me too in telling me of fear.
Wert not a serious thing we go about,
It should be slipped till I had fought with thee
To let thee know I am no coward, I.
I tell thee, Shakebag, thou abusest me.
SHAKEBAG Why, thy speech bewrayed an inly kind of
fear,

---

72 boltered: in tangled knots, matted (as in 'blood-boltered
Banquo', *Macbeth*, IV.i.123). However, Qs' spelling
(bolstred) may be correct, suggesting 'stiff, rigid, bristly'
(Wine)
75 Insulting: exulting
peck: heap
80 detect: disclose, reveal
91 leaning to: leaning against
94 rifle: rob

2 sheeting: enfolding
8 watch: one of the periods into which the night was divided
12 instance: evidence
13 Speed: success
whose will . . . no: 'no matter who wills the contrary'
(eds)
18 precisian: puritan
19 bugs: bugbears, terrors
20 fancy's work: effect on our imaginations
22 telling: accusing (White)
24 slipped: deferred
27 bewrayed: revealed

And savoured of a weak, relenting spirit.
Go forward now in that we have begun,
And afterwards attempt me when thou darest.    30

BLACK WILL  And if I do not, heaven cut me off!
But let that pass, and show me to this house,
Where thou shalt see I'll do as much as Shakebag.

SHAKEBAG  This is the door (*He tries it*) —but soft,
methinks 'tis shut.
The villain Michael hath deceived us.

BLACK WILL  Soft, let me see. Shakebag, 'tis shut
indeed.
Knock with thy sword; perhaps the slave will hear.

SHAKEBAG  It will not be; the white-livered peasant
Is gone to bed and laughs us both to scorn.

BLACK WILL  And he shall buy his merriment as dear    40
As ever coistrel bought so little sport.
Ne'er let this sword assist me when I need,
But rust and canker after I have sworn,
If I, the next time that I meet the hind,
Lop not away his leg, his arm, or both.

SHAKEBAG  And let me never draw a sword again,
Nor prosper in the twilight, cockshut light,
When I would fleece the wealthy passenger,
But lie and languish in a loathsome den,
Hated and spit at by the goers-by,    50
And in that death may die unpitied
If I, the next time that I meet the slave,
Cut not the nose from off the coward's face
And trample on it for this villainy.

BLACK WILL  Come, let's go seek out Greene; I know
he'll swear.

SHAKEBAG  He were a villain and he would not swear.
'Twould make a peasant swear amongst his boys,
That ne'er durst say before but 'yea' and 'no',
To be thus flouted of a coisterel.

BLACK WILL  Shakebag, let's seek out Greene, and in
the morning,    60
At the alehouse 'butting Arden's house,
Watch the out-coming of that prick-eared cur,
And then let me alone to handle him.

*Exeunt*

# Scene vi

*Here enters* ARDEN, FRANKLIN, *and* MICHAEL

ARDEN  Sirrah, get you back to Billingsgate
And learn what time the tide will serve our turn.
Come to us in Paul's. First go make the bed,
And afterwards go hearken for the flood.

*Exit* MICHAEL

Come, Master Franklin, you shall go with me.
This night I dreamed that being in a park,
A toil was pitched to overthrow the deer,
And I upon a little rising hill
Stood whistly watching for the herd's approach.
Even there, methoughts, a gentle slumber took me,    10
And summoned all my parts to sweet repose.
But in the pleasure of this golden rest
An ill-thewed foster had removed the toil,
And rounded me with that beguiling home
Which late, methought, was pitched to cast the deer.
With that he blew an evil-sounding horn,
And at the noise another herdman came
With falchion drawn, and bent it at my breast,
Crying aloud, 'Thou art the game we seek.'
With this I waked and trembled every joint,    20
Like one obscured in a little bush
That sees a lion foraging about,
And when the dreadful forest king is gone,
He pries about with timorous suspect
Throughout the thorny casements of the brake,
And will not think his person dangerless,
But quakes and shivers though the cause be gone.
So trust me, Franklin, when I did awake
I stood in doubt whether I waked or no,
Such great impression took this fond surprise.    30
God grant this vision bedeem me any good.

FRANKLIN  This fantasy doth rise from Michael's fear,
Who being awaked with the noise he made,
His troubled senses yet could take no rest;
And this, I warrant you, procured your dream.

ARDEN  It may be so; God frame it to the best!

---

30  attempt: attack, engage with
38  white-livered: cowardly
41  coistrel: knave; see l. 59 for variant spelling
44  hind: fellow
47  cockshut light: 'evening time when (a) poultry are shut
up for the night or, more appropriately, (b) woodcocks
(i.e. gulls) "shoot" or fly through the woods and are
caught in nets' (Wine)
48  passenger: passer-by
56  and: if
62  prick-eared: with pointed ears

---

1  Billingsgate: landing place used by travellers from abroad
or from the lower reaches of the Thames
7  toil: net
pitched: fixed in place
9  whistly: silently
13  ill-thewed foster: ill-natured forester
14  rounded: surrounded
beguiling home: i.e. the net
15  cast: overthrow
18  falchion: a curved broadsword
24  suspect: suspicion, apprehension
25  brake: thicket
30  took . . . surprise: 'this foolish terror gave me' (eds)
31  bedeem . . . good: 'foretells no danger for me' (White)
36  frame: bring about

But oftentimes my dreams presage too true.
FRANKLIN  To such as note their nightly fantasies,
　Some one in twenty may incur belief.
　But use it not; 'tis but a mockery.　　　　　　40
ARDEN  Come, Master Franklin, we'll now walk in
　Paul's,
　And dine together at the ordinary,
　And by my man's direction draw to the quay,
　And with the tide go down to Faversham.
　Say, Master Franklin, shall it not be so?
FRANKLIN  At your good pleasure, sir; I'll bear you
　company
　　　　　　　　　　　　　　　　　　　*Exeunt*

## Scene vii

*Here enters* MICHAEL *at one door. Here enters* GREENE,
BLACK WILL *and* SHAKEBAG *at another door*

BLACK WILL  Draw, Shakebag, for here's that villain
　Michael.
GREENE  First, Will, let's hear what he can say.
BLACK WILL  Speak, milksop slave, and never after
　speak!
MICHAEL  For God's sake, sirs, let me excuse myself,
　For here I swear by heaven and earth and all,
　I did perform the outmost of my task,
　And left the doors unbolted and unlocked.
　But see the chance: Franklin and my master
　Were very late conferring in the porch,
　And Franklin left his napkin where he sat,　　10
　With certain gold knit in it, as he said.
　Being in bed he did bethink himself,
　And coming down he found the doors unshut.
　He locked the gates and brought away the keys,
　For which offence my master rated me.
　But now I am going to see what flood it is,
　For with the tide my master will away,
　Where you may front him well on Rainham Down,
　A place well-fitting such a stratagem.
BLACK WILL  Your excuse hath somewhat mollified my
　choler.　　　　　　　　　　　　　　　　20
　Why now, Greene, 'tis better now nor e'er it was.

GREENE  But, Michael, is this true?
MICHAEL  As true as I report it to be true.
SHAKEBAG  Then, Michael, this shall be your penance:
　To feast us all at the Salutation,
　Where we will plot our purpose thoroughly.
GREENE  And, Michael, you shall bear no news of this
　tide
　Because they two may be in Rainham Down
　Before your master.
MICHAEL  Why, I'll agree to anything you'll have me,　30
　So you will except of my company.
　　　　　　　　　　　　　　　　　　　*Exeunt*

## Scene viii

*Here enters* MOSBY

MOSBY  Disturbed thoughts drives me from company
　And dries my marrow with their watchfulness.
　Continual trouble of my moody brain
　Feebles my body by excess of drink
　And nips me as the bitter north-east wind
　Doth check the tender blossoms in the spring.
　Well fares the man, howe'er his cates do taste,
　That tables not with foul suspicion;
　And he but pines amongst his delicates
　Whose troubled mind is stuffed with discontent.　10
　My golden time was when I had no gold;
　Though then I wanted, yet I slept secure;
　My daily toil begat me night's repose,
　My night's repose made daylight fresh to me.
　But since I climbed the top bough of the tree
　And sought to build my nest among the clouds,
　Each gentle starry gale doth shake my bed
　And makes me dread my downfall to the earth.
　But whither doth contemplation carry me?
　The way I seek to find, where pleasure dwells,　20
　Is hedged behind me that I cannot back
　But needs must on, although to danger's gate.
　Then, Arden, perish thou by that decree,
　For Greene doth ear the land and weed thee up
　To make my harvest nothing but pure corn.

---

40  use it not: 'do not engage in such a practice' (White)
43  quay: i.e. at Billingsgate
　3  milksop: cowardly
　6  outmost: utmost
　8  chance: mischance
　10  napkin: handkerchief
　11  knit: tied up
　15  rated: berated
　18  front: confront
　　Rainham Down: open countryside around Rainham, a
　　Kent village about 5 miles from Rochester, notorious for
　　its ruffians and highwaymen
　21  nor: than

25  Salutation: a tavern in Newgate Street (White)
31  except Q1, Q2 (accept Q3). Either reading is possible, but
　　most eds agree on 'except' on the grounds of Michael's
　　desire (iii.190) not to be seen in the cut-throats' company
　7  cates: choice food
　8  tables: dines
　9  delicates: delicacies
　17  Each gentle starry gale: Qs read 'stary'; we follow Wine
　　in emending to 'starry'. Some eds propose 'Each gentlest
　　airy gale' instead, but the sense of Wine's version does
　　not seem problematic enough to warrant such a change,
　　even though it offers a greater clarity of meaning
　24  ear: plough

And for his pains I'll heave him up awhile
And, after, smother him to have his wax;
Such bees as Greene must never live to sting.
Then is there Michael and the painter too,
Chief actors to Arden's overthrow, 30
Who, when they shall see me sit in Arden's seat,
They will insult upon me for my meed,
Or fright me by detecting of his end.
I'll none of that, for I can cast a bone
To make these curs pluck out each other's throat,
And then am I sole ruler of mine own.
Yet Mistress Arden lives; but she's myself,
And holy church rites makes us two but one.
But what for that I may not trust you, Alice?
You have supplanted Arden for my sake, 40
And will extirpen me to plant another.
'Tis fearful sleeping in a serpent's bed,
And I will cleanly rid my hands of her.

*Here enters* ALICE *with a prayerbook*

But here she comes, and I must flatter her.
How now, Alice! What, sad and passionate?
Make me partaker of thy pensiveness;
Fire divided burns with lesser force.
ALICE  But I will dam that fire in my breast
Till by the force thereof my part consume.
Ah, Mosby! 50
MOSBY  Such deep pathaires, like to a cannon's burst
Discharged against a ruinated wall,
Breaks my relenting heart in thousand pieces.
Ungentle Alice, thy sorrow is my sore;
Thou know'st it well, and 'tis thy policy
To forge distressful looks to wound a breast
Where lies a heart that dies when thou art sad.
It is not love that loves to anger love.
ALICE  It is not love that loves to murder love.
MOSBY  How mean you that? 60
ALICE  Thou knowest how dearly Arden loved me.
MOSBY  And then?
ALICE  And then—conceal the rest, for 'tis too bad,
Lest that my words be carried with the wind
And published in the world to both our shames.
I pray thee, Mosby, let our springtime wither;

Our harvest else will yield but loathsome weeds.
Forget, I pray thee, what hath passed betwixt us,
For now I blush and tremble at the thoughts.
MOSBY  What, are you changed? 70
ALICE  Ay, to my former happy life again,
From title of an odious strumpet's name
To honest Arden's wife, not Arden's honest wife.
Ha, Mosby, 'tis thou hast rifled me of that,
And made me sland'rous to all my kin.
Even in my forehead is thy name engraven,
A mean artificer, that low-born name.
I was bewitched; woe worth the hapless hour
And all the causes that enchanted me!
MOSBY  Nay, if thou ban, let me breathe curses forth, 80
And, if you stand so nicely at your fame,
Let me repent the credit I have lost.
I have neglected matters of import
That would have stated me above thy state,
Forslowed advantages, and spurned at time.
Ay, Fortune's right hand Mosby hath forsook
To take a wanton giglot by the left.
I left the marriage of an honest maid
Whose dowry would have weighed down all thy
     wealth,
Whose beauty and demeanour far exceeded thee. 90
This certain good I lost for changing bad,
And wrapped my credit in thy company.
I was bewitched—that is no theme of thine!—
And thou unhallowed hast enchanted me.
But I will break thy spells and exorcisms,
And put another sight upon these eyes
That showed my heart a raven for a dove.
Thou art not fair, I viewed thee not till now;
Thou art not kind, till now I knew thee not.
And now the rain hath beaten off thy gilt 100
Thy worthless copper shows thee counterfeit.
It grieves me not to see how foul thou art,
But mads me that ever I thought thee fair.
Go, get thee gone, a copesmate for thy hinds!
I am too good to be thy favourite.
ALICE  Ay, now I see, and too soon find it true,
Which often hath been told me by my friends,
That Mosby loves me not but for my wealth,

---

26  heave him up: extol
27  smother: smoke. The line refers to the practice of
     smoking out bees to reach their wax and honey
32  meed: reward
34  a bone: i.e. Susan
39  what for that: what about the fact that
41  extirpen: root out
45  passionate: sorrowful
48–9  But I . . . consume: 'I will suppress the passion that I
     have for you . . . until by the force of its own violence it
     consumes itself and disappears' (Wine)
51  pathaires: sad and passionate outbursts

73  honest [2nd instance]: chaste (as in l. 88)
78  woe worth: a curse upon
80  ban: curse
81  stand . . . fame: scruple so fastidiously at your reputation
     (eds)
84  stated: placed, raised
85  Forslowed: wasted
87  giglot: lewd, wanton woman
94  unhallowed: wicked
95  exorcisms: spells
104  copesmate: companion (in contemptuous sense)
     hinds: servants

Which too incredulous I ne'er believed.
Nay, hear me speak, Mosby, a word or two;                    110
I'll bite my tongue if it speak bitterly.
Look on me, Mosby, or I'll kill myself;
Nothing shall hide me from thy stormy look.
If thou cry war there is no peace for me;
I will do penance for offending thee
And burn this prayerbook, where I here use
The holy word that had converted me.
See, Mosby, I will tear away the leaves,
And all the leaves, and in this golden cover
Shall thy sweet phrases and thy letters dwell,               120
And thereon will I chiefly meditate
And hold no other sect but such devotion.
Wilt thou not look? Is all thy love overwhelmed?
Wilt thou not hear? What malice stops thine ears?
Why speaks thou not? What silence ties thy tongue?
Thou hast been sighted as the eagle is,
And heard as quickly as the fearful hare,
And spoke as smoothly as an orator,
When I have bid thee hear, or see, or speak.
And art thou sensible in none of these?                      130
Weigh all thy good turns with this little fault
And I deserve not Mosby's muddy looks.
A fount once troubled is not thickened still;
Be clear again, I'll ne'er more trouble thee.
MOSBY  Oh, no, I am a base artificer,
My wings are feathered for a lowly flight.
Mosby? Fie, no! Not for a thousand pound.
Make love to you? Why, 'tis unpardonable;
We beggars must not breathe where gentles are.
ALICE  Sweet Mosby is as gentle as a king,                   140
And I too blind to judge him otherwise.
Flowers do sometimes spring in fallow lands,
Weeds in gardens, roses grow on thorns;
So whatso'er my Mosby's father was,
Himself is valued gentle by his worth.
MOSBY  Ah, how you women can insinuate,
And clear a trespass with your sweet-set tongue.
I will forget this quarrel, gentle Alice,
Provided I'll be tempted so no more.

*Here enters* BRADSHAW

ALICE  Then with thy lips seal up this new-made
match.                                                       150
MOSBY  Soft, Alice, for here comes somebody.
ALICE  How now, Bradshaw, what's the news with you?

BRADSHAW  I have little news, but here's a letter
That Master Greene importuned me to give you.
ALICE  Go in, Bradshaw; call for a cup of beer.
'Tis almost suppertime; thou shalt stay with us.
                    *Exit* BRADSHAW. *Then she reads the letter*
'We have missed of our purpose at London, but shall
perform it by the way. We thank our neighbour
Bradshaw.
                              Yours, Richard Greene.'
How likes my love the tenor of this letter?                  160
MOSBY  Well, were his date complete and expired.
ALICE  Ah, would it were! Then comes my happy hour.
Till then my bliss is mixed with bitter gall.
Come, let us in to shun suspicion.
MOSBY  Ay, to the gates of death to follow thee.
                                                  *Exeunt*

# Scene ix

*Here enters* GREENE, BLACK WILL, *and* SHAKEBAG

SHAKEBAG  Come, Will, see thy tools be in a readiness.
Is not thy powder dank, or will thy flint strike fire?
BLACK WILL  Then ask me if my nose be on my face,
Or whether my tongue be frozen in my mouth.
Zounds, here's a coil!
You were best swear me on the intergatories
How many pistols I have took in hand,
Or whether I love the smell of gunpowder,
Or dare abide the noise the dag will make,
Or will not wink at flashing of the fire.                    10
I pray thee, Shakebag, let this answer thee,
That I have took more purses in this Down
Than e'er thou handlest pistols in thy life.
SHAKEBAG  Ay, haply thou hast picked more in a
throng;
But should I brag what booties I have took,
I think the overplus that's more than thine
Would mount to a greater sum of money
Than either thou or all thy kin are worth.
Zounds, I hate them as I hate a toad
That carry a muscado in their tongue                          20
And scarce a hurting weapon in their hand.
BLACK WILL  Oh Greene, intolerable!
It is not for mine honour to bear this.

---

122  hold . . . sect: keep no other religious faith (eds)
127  quickly: sharply
130  sensible: capable of feeling
131  thy good turns: good turns done to you
133  A fount once troubled: eds (A fence of trouble Qs)
     still: for ever
139  gentles: people of gentle birth
147  clear a trespass: acquit yourselves

SD  *the letter*: this was, in fact, written in scene ii, before the
     failed attempts on Arden's life in London
161  his date: his (i.e. Arden's) term of life
5    coil: fuss
6    intergatories: interrogatories: i.e. questions put to
     someone under oath
9    dag: pistol
10   wink: blink
16   overplus: surplus
20   muscado: musket

Why, Shakebag, I did serve the king at Boulogne,
And thou canst brag of nothing that thou has done.
SHAKEBAG Why, so can Jack of Faversham,
That sounded for a fillip on the nose,
When he that gave it him holloed in his ear,
And he supposed a cannon-bullet hit him.
                                                        *Then they fight*
GREENE I pray you, sirs, list to Aesop's talk:            30
Whilst two stout dogs were striving for a bone,
There comes a cur and stole it from them both;
So, while you stand striving on these terms of
    manhood,
Arden escapes us and deceives us all.
SHAKEBAG Why, he begun.
BLACK WILL                      And thou shalt find I'll end.
I do but slip it until better time.
But if I do forget—
    *Then he kneels down and holds up his hands to heaven*
GREENE Well, take your fittest standings, and once
    more
Lime your twigs to catch this weary bird.
I'll leave you, and at your dag's discharge         40
Make towards, like the longing water-dog
That coucheth till the fowling-piece be off,
Then seizeth on the prey with eager mood.
Ah, might I see him stretching forth his limbs
As I have seen them beat their wings ere now.
SHAKEBAG Why, that thou shalt see if he come this way.
GREENE Yes, that he doth, Shakebag, I warrant thee.
But brawl not when I am gone in any case,
But, sirs, be sure to speed him when he comes;
And in that hope I'll leave you for an hour.         50
                                                        *Exit* GREENE
BLACK WILL *and* SHAKEBAG *take up their positions*

*Here enters* ARDEN, FRANKLIN, *and* MICHAEL

MICHAEL 'Twere best that I went back to Rochester.
The horse halts downright; it were not good
He travelled in such pain to Faversham.
Removing of a shoe may haply help it.
ARDEN Well, get you back to Rochester; but, sirrah,
    see ye

Overtake us ere we come to Rainham Down,
For it will be very late ere we get home.
MICHAEL (*Aside*) Ay, God he knows, and so doth Will
    and Shakebag,
That thou shalt never go further than that Down;
And therefore have I pricked the horse on purpose, 60
Because I would not view the massacre.
                                                        *Exit* MICHAEL
ARDEN Come, Master Franklin, onwards with your tale.
FRANKLIN I assure you, sir, you task me much.
A heavy blood is gathered at my heart,
And on the sudden is my wind so short
As hindereth the passage of my speech.
So fierce a qualm yet ne'er assailed me.
ARDEN Come, Master Franklin, let us go on softly.
The annoyance of the dust or else some meat
You ate at dinner cannot brook with you.          70
I have been often so and soon amended.
FRANKLIN Do you remember where my tale did leave?
ARDEN Ay, where the gentleman did check his wife.
FRANKLIN She being reprehended for the fact,
Witness produced that took her with the deed,
Her glove brought in which there she left behind,
And many other assured arguments,
Her husband asked her whether it were not so.
ARDEN Her answer then? I wonder how she looked,
Having forsworn it with such vehement oaths,       80
And at the instant so approved upon her.
FRANKLIN First did she cast her eyes down to the earth,
Watching the drops that fell amain from thence;
Then softly draws she forth her handkerchief,
And modestly she wipes her tear-stained face;
Then hemmed she out, to clear her voice should
    seem,
And with a majesty addressed herself
To encounter all their accusations.
Pardon me, Master Arden, I can no more;
This fighting at my heart makes short my wind.     90
ARDEN Come, we are almost now at Rainham Down.
Your pretty tale beguiles the weary way;
I would you were in state to tell it out.
SHAKEBAG (*Aside*) Stand close, Will, I hear them
    coming.

*Here enters* LORD CHEINY *with his* MEN

---

27 sounded: swooned
   fillip: punch
28 holloed: shouted
31 stout: valiant
36 slip: postpone
38 fittest standings: see iii.39n
39 Lime your twigs: birdlime was a sticky substance spread
   on twigs to catch birds
   weary: wearisome
41 water-dog: dog trained to retrieve water-fowl
42 coucheth: lies down
   fowling-piece: gun
52 halts downright: limps badly

---

60 pricked the horse: pierced the foot of the horse to cause
   lameness
68 softly: slowly
70 brook with: agree with
72 leave: leave off
73 check: reprove
75 took . . . deed: caught her in the act
81 approved upon: proved against
86 hemmed she out: she cleared her throat
88 encounter: counter

BLACK WILL (*Aside*) Stand to it, Shakebag, and be
  resolute.
LORD CHEINY Is it so near night as it seems,
  Or will this black-faced evening have a shower?
  (*Seeing* ARDEN) What, Master Arden? You are well
  met.
  I have longed this fortnight's day to speak with you.
  You are a stranger, man, in the Isle of Sheppey.  **100**
ARDEN Your honour's always! Bound to do you service.
LORD CHEINY Come you from London and ne'er a man
  with you?
ARDEN My man's coming after,
  But here's my honest friend that came along with me.
LORD CHEINY (*To* FRANKLIN) My Lord Protector's man
  I take you to be.
FRANKLIN Ay, my good lord, and highly bound to you.
LORD CHEINY You and your friend come home and sup
  with me.
ARDEN I beseech your honour pardon me;
  I have made a promise to a gentleman,
  My honest friend, to meet him at my house.  **110**
  The occasion is great, or else would I wait on you.
LORD CHEINY Will you come tomorrow and dine with
  me,
  And bring your honest friend along with you?
  I have divers matters to talk with you about.
ARDEN Tomorrow we'll wait upon your honour.
LORD CHEINY One of you stay my horse at the top of
  the hill.  *Seeing* BLACK WILL
  What, Black Will! For whose purse wait you?
  Thou wilt be hanged in Kent when all is done.
BLACK WILL Not hanged, God save your honour.
  I am your beadsman, bound to pray for you.  **120**
LORD CHEINY I think thou ne'er saidest prayer in all thy
  life.
  One of you give him a crown.
  And, sirrah, leave this kind of life.
  If thou beest 'tainted for a penny matter
  And come in question, surely thou wilt truss.
  Come, Master Arden, let us be going;
  Your way and mine lies four mile together.
        *Exeunt. Manet* BLACK WILL *and* SHAKEBAG
BLACK WILL The devil break all your necks at four
  miles' end!
  Zounds, I could kill myself for very anger!
  His lordship chops me in even when  **130**
  My dag was levelled at his heart.
  I would his crown were molten down his throat.
SHAKEBAG Arden, thou hast wondrous holy luck.

  Did ever man escape as thou hast done?
  Well, I'll discharge my pistol at the sky,
  For by this bullet Arden might not die.

*Here enters* GREENE

GREENE What, is he down? Is he dispatched?
SHAKEBAG Ay, in health towards Faversham to shame
  us all.
GREENE The devil he is! Why, sirs, how escaped he?
SHAKEBAG When we were ready to shoot  **140**
  Comes my Lord Cheiny to prevent his death.
GREENE The Lord of Heaven hath preserved him.
BLACK WILL The Lord of Heaven a fig! The Lord
  Cheiny hath preserved him,
  And bids him to a feast, to his house at Shorlow.
  But by the way once more I'll meet with him,
  And if all the Cheinies in the world say no,
  I'll have a bullet in his breast tomorrow.
  Therefore come, Greene, and let us to Faversham.
GREENE Ay, and excuse ourselves to Mistress Arden.
  Oh, how she'll chafe when she hears of this!  **150**
SHAKEBAG Why, I'll warrant you she'll think we dare
  not do it.
BLACK WILL Why then let us go and tell her all the
  matter,
  And plot the news to cut him off tomorrow.
        *Exeunt*

# Scene x

*Here enters* ARDEN *and his wife* ALICE, FRANKLIN *and*
MICHAEL

ARDEN See how the Hours, the guardant of heaven's
  gate,
  Have by their toil removed the darksome clouds,
  That Sol may well discern the trampled pace
  Wherein he wont to guide his golden car.
  The season fits; come, Franklin, let's away.
ALICE I thought you did pretend some special hunt
  That made you thus cut short the time of rest.
ARDEN It was no chase that made me rise so early,
  But, as I told thee yesternight, to go

---

143  The Lord . . . fig!: eds (Preserved, a fig! Q$_s$)
144  Shorlow: Shurland, on the Isle of Sheppey, Lord
    Cheiny's residence
153  plot the news: devise a new plan (White)
  1  the Hours: allusion to the daughters of Zeus and
    Themis, who were the guardians of the gates of
    Olympus, and presided over the changes of the seasons
    and of the weather
    guardant: guardian
  3  Sol: the sun personified
    discern Q3 (deserve Q1, Q2)
    pace: path, passage
  6  pretend: intend

---

120  beadsman: one paid to pray for others
124-5  If . . . truss: i.e. 'If you are caught and accused of even
    the most trivial offence and come to trial, you will surely
    hang' (Wine)
130  chops me in: suddenly interrupts

To the Isle of Sheppey, there to dine with my Lord
    Cheiny,            10
For so his honour late commanded me.
ALICE Ay, such kind husbands seldom want excuses.
  Home is a wild cat to a wand'ring wit.
  The time hath been—would God it were not past—
  That honour's title nor a lord's command
  Could once have drawn you from these arms of mine.
  But my deserts or your desires decay,
  Or both; yet if true love may seem desert,
  I merit still to have thy company.
FRANKLIN Why, I pray you, sir, let her go along with us;
  I am sure his honour will welcome her,    21
  And us the more for bringing her along.
ARDEN Content. (*To* MICHAEL) Sirrah, saddle your
    mistress' nag.
ALICE No. Begged favour merits little thanks.
  If I should go our house would run away
  Or else be stol'n; therefore I'll stay behind.
ARDEN Nay, see how mistaking you are. I pray thee, go.
ALICE No, no, not now.
ARDEN Then let me leave thee satisfied in this,
  That time nor place nor persons alter me,    30
  But that I hold thee dearer than my life.
ALICE That will be seen by your quick return.
ARDEN And that shall be ere night and if I live.
  Farewell, sweet Alice; we mind to sup with thee.
                          *Exit* ALICE
FRANKLIN Come, Michael, are our horses ready?
MICHAEL Ay, your horses are ready, but I am not
  ready, for I have lost my purse with six-and-thirty
  shillings in it, with taking up of my master's nag.
FRANKLIN Why, I pray you, let us go before,
  Whilst he stays behind to seek his purse.    40
ARDEN Go to, sirrah! See you follow us to the Isle of
    Sheppey,
  To my Lord Cheiny's, where we mean to dine.
      *Exeunt* ARDEN *and* FRANKLIN. *Manet* MICHAEL
MICHAEL So, fair weather after you, for before you lies
  Black Will and Shakebag in the broom close, too
  close for you. They'll be your ferrymen to long home.

*Here enters the Painter* CLARKE

But who is this? The painter, my corrival, that would
  needs win Mistress Susan.
CLARKE How now, Michael? How doth my mistress
  and all at home?    51
MICHAEL Who? Susan Mosby? She is your mistress,
  too?
CLARKE Ay. How doth she and all the rest?
MICHAEL All's well but Susan; she is sick.
CLARKE Sick? Of what disease?
MICHAEL Of a great fear.
CLARKE A fear of what?
MICHAEL A great fever.
CLARKE A fever! God forbid!
MICHAEL Yes, faith, and of a lurdan, too, as big as
  yourself.    60
CLARKE Oh, Michael, the spleen prickles you. Go to;
  you carry an eye over Mistress Susan.
MICHAEL Ay, faith, to keep her from the painter.
CLARKE Why more from a painter than from a serving-
  creature like yourself?
MICHAEL Because you painters make but a painting-
  table of a pretty wench and spoil her beauty with
  blotting.
CLARKE What mean you by that?
MICHAEL Why, that you painters paint lambs in the
  lining of wenches' petticoats, and we servingmen put
  horns to them to make them become sheep.    72
CLARKE Such another word will cost you a cuff or a
  knock.
MICHAEL What, with a dagger made of a pencil? Faith,
  'tis too weak, and therefore thou too weak to win
  Susan.
CLARKE Would Susan's love lay upon this stroke!
                *Then he breaks* MICHAEL'*s head*

*Here enters* MOSBY, GREENE *and* ALICE

ALICE I'll lay my life this is for Susan's love.
  (*To* MICHAEL) Stayed you behind your master to this
    end?    80
  Have you no other time to brabble in

---

12  want: lack
17  deserts: merits
    desires: eds (deserues Q1; desernes Q2; deserves Q3)
18  desert: deserving
25-6  house . . . stol'n: i.e. household matters would get out of
    hand, and the house might be robbed
33  and if: if
34  mind: intend
38  taking up: 'to bring (a horse, ox etc.) from pasture into
    the stable' (OED)
44  broom close: enclosed field of shrubs
45  ferrymen: i.e. Charon, who ferried the dead across the
    River Styx to Hades
    long home: i.e. the grave

46  corrival: rival in love (OED)
59  lurdan: loafer, rascal (with a play on 'fever-lurden', the
    disease of laziness)
61  spleen: irritability
    prickles: goads
62  carry . . . over: have your eye on
66-7  painting-table: 'a board or flat surface on which a
    picture is painted; hence, the picture itself' (OED)
70-2  Why . . . sheep: meaning obscure, but eds agree that the
    jibe concerns the sexual rivalry between Michael and
    Clarke; 'horns' refers either to a cuckold's horns or to an
    erect penis
81  brabble: brawl

But now, when serious matters are in hand?
Say, Clarke, hast thou done the thing thou promised?
CLARKE Ay, here it is; the very touch is death.
ALICE Then this, I hope, if all the rest do fail,
Will catch Master Arden
And make him wise in death that lived a fool.
Why should he thrust his sickle in our corn,
Or what hath he to do with thee, my love,
Or govern me that am to rule myself?                    90
Forsooth, for credit sake I must leave thee!
Nay, he must leave to live that we may love,
May live, may love; for what is life but love?
And love shall last as long as life remains,
And life shall end before my love depart.
MOSBY Why, what's love without true constancy?
Like to a pillar built of many stones,
Yet neither with good mortar well compact,
Nor cement to fasten it in the joints,
But that it shakes with every blast of wind,            100
And being touched, straight falls unto the earth
And buries all his haughty pride in dust.
No, let our love be rocks of adamant
Which time nor place nor tempest can asunder.
GREENE Mosby, leave protestations now,
And let us bethink us what we have to do.
Black Will and Shakebag I have placed
In the broom close, watching Arden's coming.
Let's to them and see what they have done.

*Exeunt*

# Scene xi

*Here enters* ARDEN *and* FRANKLIN

ARDEN Oh ferryman, where art thou?

*Here enters the* FERRYMAN

FERRYMAN Here, here! Go before to the boat, and I
will follow you.
ARDEN We have great haste; I pray thee come away.
FERRYMAN Fie, what a mist is here!
ARDEN This mist, my friend, is mystical,
Like to a good companion's smoky brain
That was half-drowned with new ale overnight.
FERRYMAN 'Twere pity but his skull were opened to
make more chimney room.                                 10
FRANKLIN Friend, what's thy opinion of this mist?
FERRYMAN I think 'tis like to a curst wife in a little
house, that never leaves her husband till she have
driven him out at doors with a wet pair of eyes. Then

looks he as if his house were afire, or some of his
friends dead.
ARDEN Speaks thou this of thine own experience?
FERRYMAN Perhaps ay, perhaps no; for my wife is as
other women are, that is to say, governed by the
moon.                                                   20
FRANKLIN By the moon? How, I pray thee?
FERRYMAN Nay, thereby lies a bargain, and you shall
not have it fresh and fasting.
ARDEN Yes, I pray thee, good ferryman.
FERRYMAN Then for this once let it be midsummer
moon; but yet my wife has another moon.
FRANKLIN Another moon?
FERRYMAN Ay, and it hath influences and eclipses.
ARDEN Why then, by this reckoning you sometimes
play the man in the moon.                               30
FERRYMAN Ay, but you had not best to meddle with
that moon lest I scratch you by the face with my
bramble-bush.
ARDEN I am almost stifled with this fog; come, let's
away.
FRANKLIN And sirrah, as we go, let us have some more
of your bold yeomanry.
FERRYMAN Nay, by my troth, sir, but flat knavery.

*Exeunt*

# Scene xii

*Here enters* BLACK WILL *at one door and* SHAKEBAG *at
another*

SHAKEBAG Oh Will, where art thou?
BLACK WILL Here, Shakebag, almost in hell's mouth,
where I cannot see my way for smoke.
SHAKEBAG I pray thee speak still that we may meet by
the sound, for I shall fall into some ditch or other
unless my feet see better than my eyes.
BLACK WILL Didst thou ever see better weather to run
away with another man's wife or play with a wench at
potfinger?                                               9
SHAKEBAG No; this were a fine world for chandlers if
this weather would last, for then a man should never
dine nor sup without candle-light. But, sirrah Will,
what horses are those that passed?

---

84 it: i.e. the poisoned crucifix (see i.609–16)
92 leave: cease
9 but: unless
12 curst: shrewish
14 at: of

---

19–20 governed . . . moon: i.e. inconstant
23 fresh and fasting: 'having an appetite or inclination'
   (OED); the sense seems to be 'even though you have an
   inclination to know'
25 midsummer: sometimes alluded to as a time when lunacy
   is supposed to be prevalent
33 bramble-bush: the Man in the Moon was traditionally
   said to have a lantern, a dog and a thorn bush; see
   *A Midsummer Night's Dream*, V.i.247–51
37 yeomanry: yeoman's talk: honest, homely speech
9 at potfinger: sexual allusion

BLACK WILL  Why, didst thou hear any?

SHAKEBAG  Ay, that I did.

BLACK WILL  My life for thine, 'twas Arden and his
companion, and then all our labour's lost.

SHAKEBAG  Nay, say not so; for if it be they, they may
haply lose their way as we have done, and then we
may chance meet with them.                          20

BLACK WILL  Come, let us go on like a couple of blind
pilgrims.              *Then* SHAKEBAG *falls into a ditch*

SHAKEBAG  Help, Will, help! I am almost drowned.

*Here enters the* FERRYMAN

FERRYMAN  Who's that that calls for help?

BLACK WILL  'Twas none here; 'twas thou thyself.

FERRYMAN  I came to help him that called for help.
Why, how now? Who is this that's in the ditch? You
are well enough served to go without a guide such
weather as this!

BLACK WILL  Sirrah, what companies hath passed your
ferry this morning?                                 31

FERRYMAN  None but a couple of gentlemen that went
to dine at my Lord Cheiny's.

BLACK WILL  Shakebag, did not I tell thee as much?

FERRYMAN  Why, sir, will you have any letters carried
to them?

BLACK WILL  No, sir; get you gone.

FERRYMAN  Did you ever see such a mist as this?

BLACK WILL  No, nor such a fool as will rather be
hocked than get his way.                            40

FERRYMAN  Why, sir, this is no Hock Monday; you are
deceived. What's his name, I pray you, sir?

SHAKEBAG  His name is Black Will.

FERRYMAN  I hope to see him one day hanged upon a
hill.                                *Exit* FERRYMAN

SHAKEBAG  See how the sun hath cleared the foggy
mist,
Now we have missed the mark of our intent.

*Here enters* GREENE, MOSBY, *and* ALICE

MOSBY  Black Will and Shakebag, what make you here?
What, is the deed done? Is Arden dead?

BLACK WILL  What could a blinded man perform in
arms?                                               50
Saw you not how till now the sky was dark,
That neither horse nor man could be discerned?
Yet did we hear their horses as they passed.

GREENE  Have they escaped you then and passed the
ferry?

SHAKEBAG  Ay, for a while; but here we two will stay,
And at their coming back meet with them once
more.
Zounds, I was ne'er so toiled in all my life
In following so slight a task as this.

MOSBY  How cam'st thou so berayed?

BLACK WILL  With making false footing in the dark;   60
He needs would follow them without a guide.

ALICE  Here's to pay for a fire and good cheer.
Get you to Faversham, to the Flower-de-Luce,
And rest yourselves until some other time.

GREENE  Let me alone; it most concerns my state.

BLACK WILL  Ay, Mistress Arden, this will serve the
turn
In case we fall into a second fog.
          *Exeunt* GREENE, BLACK WILL *and* SHAKEBAG

MOSBY  These knaves will never do it; let us give it over.

ALICE  First tell me how you like my new device:
Soon, when my husband is returning back,           70
You and I both marching arm in arm,
Like loving friends, we'll meet him on the way,
And boldly beard and brave him to his teeth.
When words grow hot and blows begin to rise,
I'll call those cutters forth your tenement,
Who, in a manner to take up the fray,
Shall wound my husband Hornsby to the death.

MOSBY  Ah, fine device! Why, this deserves a kiss.
                                            *Exeunt*

# Scene xiii

*Here enters* DICK REEDE *and a* SAILOR

SAILOR  Faith, Dick Reede, it is to little end.
His conscience is too liberal and he too niggardly
To part from anything may do thee good.

REEDE  He is coming from Shorlow as I understand.
Here I'll intercept him, for at his house
He never will vouchsafe to speak with me.
If prayers and fair entreaties will not serve
Or make no batt'ry in his flinty breast,

*Here enters* FRANKLIN, ARDEN, *and* MICHAEL

I'll curse the carl and see what that will do.

---

28  to go: for going
30  companies: groups of people
40  hocked: hamstrung
     get: i.e. get on
41  Hock Monday: second Monday after Easter, a popular
     festival

57  toiled: fatigued
59  berayed: covered with mud
65  Let me alone: 'either "Leave me alone to deal with
     them", or "Let me be the one to take care of things"'
     (White); see xiv.325
69  device: scheme
73  beard: defy
75  tenement: dwelling place
77  Hornsby: i.e. the cuckold
2  liberal: unrestrained
9  carl: churlish fellow

See where he comes to further my intent.—    10
Master Arden, I am now bound to the sea.
My coming to you was about the plot of ground
Which wrongfully you detain from me.
Although the rent of it be very small,
Yet will it help my wife and children,
Which here I leave in Faversham, God knows,
Needy and bare. For Christ's sake, let them have it!

ARDEN Franklin, hearest thou this fellow speak?
That which he craves I dearly bought of him
Although the rent of it was ever mine.    20
Sirrah, you that ask these questions,
If with thy clamorous impeaching tongue
Thou rail on me as I have heard thou dost,
I'll lay thee up so close a twelve month's day
As thou shalt neither see the sun nor moon.
Look to it; for, as surely as I live,
I'll banish pity if thou use me thus.

REEDE What, wilt thou do me wrong and threat me
   too?
Nay then, I'll tempt thee, Arden; do thy worst.
God, I beseech thee, show some miracle    30
On thee or thine in plaguing thee for this.
That plot of ground which thou detains from me—
I speak it in an agony of spirit—
Be ruinous and fatal unto thee!
Either there be butchered by thy dearest friends,
Or else be brought for men to wonder at,
Or thou or thine miscarry in that place,
Or there run mad and end thy cursed days.

FRANKLIN Fie, bitter knave, bridle thine envious
   tongue;
For curses are like arrows shot upright,    40
Which, falling down, light on the shooter's head.

REEDE Light where they will! Were I upon the sea,
As oft I have in many a bitter storm,
And saw a dreadful southern flaw at hand,
The pilot quaking at the doubtful storm,
And all the sailors praying on their knees,
Even in that fearful time would I fall down
And ask of God, whate'er betide of me,
Vengeance on Arden, or some misevent,
To show the world what wrong the carl hath done.  50
This charge I'll leave with my distressful wife;
My children shall be taught such prayers as these.
And thus I go, but leave my curse with thee.

    *Exeunt* REEDE *and* SAILOR

ARDEN It is the railingest knave in Christendom,

---

24 lay . . . so close: imprison you
29 tempt: provoke
37 miscarry: come to harm, die
39 envious: malicious
44 flaw: squall
45 doubtful: dreaded
49 misevent: mischance

And oftentimes the villain will be mad.
It greatly matters not what he says,
But I assure you I ne'er did him wrong.

FRANKLIN I think so, Master Arden.

ARDEN Now that our horses are gone home before,
My wife may haply meet me on the way;    60
For God knows she is grown passing kind of late
And greatly changed from the old humour
Of her wonted frowardness,
And seeks by fair means to redeem old faults.

FRANKLIN Happy the change that alters for the best.
But see in any case you make no speech
Of the cheer we had at my Lord Cheiny's,
Although most bounteous and liberal,
For that will make her think herself more wronged
In that we did not carry her along;    70
For sure she grieved that she was left behind.

ARDEN Come, Franklin, let us strain to mend our pace
And take her unawares, playing the cook,

*Here enters* ALICE *and* MOSBY *arm in arm*

For I believe she'll strive to mend our cheer.

FRANKLIN Why, there's no better creatures in the
   world
Than women are when they are in good humours.

ARDEN Who is that? Mosby? What, so familiar?
Injurious strumpet and thou ribald knave,
Untwine those arms.

ALICE Ay, with a sugared kiss let them untwine.   80

ARDEN Ah, Mosby! Perjured beast! Bear this and all!

MOSBY And yet no horned beast; the horns are thine.

FRANKLIN Oh monstrous! Nay then, 'tis time to draw!

ALICE Help! Help! They murder my husband!

*Here enters* BLACK WILL *and* SHAKEBAG

SHAKEBAG Zounds, who injures Master Mosby?
   *They fight.* SHAKEBAG *and* MOSBY *are wounded*
Help, Will, I am hurt.

MOSBY I may thank you, Mistress Arden, for this
   wound.
    *Exeunt* MOSBY, BLACK WILL, *and* SHAKEBAG

ALICE Ah, Arden, what folly blinded thee?
Ah, jealous harebrain man what hast thou done?
When we, to welcome thee, intended sport,   90
Came lovingly to meet thee on thy way,
Thou drew'st thy sword, enraged with jealousy,
And hurt thy friend whose thoughts were free from
   harm;
All for a worthless kiss and joining arms,

---

62 humour: disposition
63 frowardness: ill humour
67 cheer: hospitality
72 mend: increase
82 horned beast: i.e. cuckold

Both done but merrily to try thy patience.
And me unhappy that devised the jest,
Which, though begun in sport, yet ends in blood!
FRANKLIN Marry, God defend me from such a jest!
ALICE Couldst thou not see us friendly smile on thee
When we joined arms and when I kissed his cheek?
Hast thou not lately found me over-kind?                101
Didst thou not hear me cry they murder thee?
Called I not help to set my husband free?
No, ears and all were 'witched. Ah me accursed,
To link in liking with a frantic man!
Henceforth I'll be thy slave, no more thy wife;
For with that name I never shall content thee.
If I be merry, thou straightways thinks me light;
If sad, thou sayest the sullens trouble me;
If well attired, thou thinks I will be gadding;         110
If homely, I seem sluttish in thine eye.
Thus am I still, and shall be while I die,
Poor wench abused by thy misgovernment.
ARDEN But is it for truth that neither thou nor he
Intendedst malice in your misdemeanour?
ALICE The heavens can witness of our harmless
thoughts.
ARDEN Then pardon me, sweet Alice, and forgive this
fault.
Forget but this, and never see the like.
Impose me penance, and I will perform it;
For in thy discontent I find a death,                   120
A death tormenting more than death itself.
ALICE Nay, hadst thou loved me as thou dost pretend,
Thou wouldst have marked the speeches of thy
friend,
Who going wounded from the place, he said
His skin was pierced only through my device.
And if sad sorrow taint thee for this fault
Thou wouldst have followed him and seen him
dressed,
And cried him mercy whom thou hast misdone;
Ne'er shall my heart be eased till this be done.
ARDEN Content thee, sweet Alice, thou shalt have thy
will,                                                    130
Whate'er it be. For that I injured thee
And wronged my friend, shame scourgeth my
offence.
Come thou thyself and go along with me,
And be a mediator 'twixt us two.
FRANKLIN Why, Master Arden, know you what you
do?

Will you follow him that hath dishonoured you?
ALICE Why, canst thou prove I have been disloyal?
FRANKLIN Why, Mosby taunts your husband with the
horn.
ALICE Ay, after he had reviled him
By the injurious name of perjured beast.               140
He knew no wrong could spite a jealous man
More than the hateful naming of the horn.
FRANKLIN Suppose 'tis true, yet is it dangerous
To follow him whom he hath lately hurt.
ALICE A fault confessed is more than half amends,
But men of such ill spirit as yourself
Work crosses and debates 'twixt man and wife.
ARDEN I pray thee, gentle Franklin, hold thy peace;
I know my wife counsels me for the best.
I'll seek out Mosby where his wound is dressed         150
And salve his hapless quarrel if I may.
                                    *Exeunt* ARDEN *and* ALICE
FRANKLIN He whom the devil drives must go perforce.
Poor gentleman, how soon he is bewitched.
And yet, because his wife is the instrument,
His friends must not be lavish in their speech.
                                              *Exit* FRANKLIN

# Scene xiv

*Here enters* BLACK WILL, SHAKEBAG, *and* GREENE

BLACK WILL Sirrah Greene, when was I so long in
killing a man?
GREENE I think we shall never do it; let us give it over.
SHAKEBAG Nay! Zounds, we'll kill him though we be
hanged at his door for our labour.
BLACK WILL Thou knowest, Greene, that I have lived
in London this twelve years, where I have made some
go upon wooden legs for taking the wall on me;
divers with silver noses for saying, 'There goes Black
Will.' I have cracked as many blades as thou hast
done nuts.                                               11
GREENE Oh, monstrous lie!
BLACK WILL Faith, in a manner I have. The bawdy-
houses have paid me tribute; there durst not a whore
set up unless she have agreed with me first for
opening her shop windows. For a cross word of a
tapster I have pierced one barrel after another with
my dagger and held him by the ears till all his beer
hath run out. In Thames Street a brewer's cart was
like to have run over me; I made no more ado but

---

109 sullens: sulks
112 still: always
    while: until
127 him: i.e. his wounds
128 misdone: wronged
131 For that: because

147 crosses and debates: troubles and quarrels
151 hapless: unfortunate
  8 taking the wall: i.e. walking next to the wall (the cleaner
    and safer position), thereby forcing Black Will into the
    street
  9 silver noses: i.e. false noses

went to the clerk and cut all the notches off his tallies
and beat them about his head. I and my company
have taken the constable from his watch and carried
him about the fields on a coltstaff. I have broken a
sergeant's head with his own mace, and bailed whom
I list with my sword and buckler. All the tenpenny
alehouses would stand every morning with a quart
pot in their hand, saying, 'Will it please your worship
drink?' He that had not done so had been sure to
have had his sign pulled down and his lattice borne
away the next night. To conclude, what have I not
done? Yet cannot do this; doubtless he is preserved
by miracle.                                                    **33**

*Here enters* ALICE *and* MICHAEL

GREENE  Hence, Will; here comes Mistress Arden.
ALICE  Ah, gentle Michael, art thou sure they're
    friends?
MICHAEL  Why, I saw them when they both shook
    hands;
    When Mosby bled he even wept for sorrow,
    And railed on Franklin that was cause of all.
    No sooner came the surgeon in at doors,
    But my master took to his purse and gave him money,
    And, to conclude, sent me to bring you word     **41**
    That Mosby, Franklin, Bradshaw, Adam Fowle,
    With divers of his neighbours and his friends,
    Will come and sup with you at our house this night.
ALICE  Ah, gentle Michael, run thou back again,
    And when my husband walks into the fair,
    Bid Mosby steal from him and come to me;
    And this night shall thou and Susan be made sure.
MICHAEL  I'll go tell him.
ALICE  And as thou goest, tell John cook of our guests,
    And bid him lay it on; spare for no cost.          **51**
                         *Exit* MICHAEL
BLACK WILL  Nay, and there be such cheer, we will bid
    ourselves. Mistress Arden, Dick Greene and I do
    mean to sup with you.

ALICE  And welcome shall you be. Ah, gentlemen,
    How missed you of your purpose yesternight?
GREENE  'Twas long of Shakebag, that unlucky villain. **57**
SHAKEBAG  Thou dost me wrong; I did as much as any.
BLACK WILL  Nay then, Mistress Alice, I'll tell you how
    it was. When he should have locked with both his
    hilts, he in a bravery flourished over his head. With
    that comes Franklin at him lustily and hurts the
    slave; with that he slinks away. Now his way had
    been to have come in hand and feet, one and two
    round at his costard. He like a fool bears his sword-
    point half a yard out of danger. I lie here for my life.
    (*He takes up a position of defence*) If the devil come and
    he have no more strength than fence, he shall never
    beat me from this ward; I'll stand to it. A buckler in a
    skilful hand is as good as a castle; nay, 'tis better than
    a sconce, for I have tried it. Mosby, perceiving this,
    began to faint. With that comes Arden with his
    arming-sword and thrust him through the shoulder
    in a trice.                                                  **74**
ALICE  Ay, but I wonder why you both stood still.
BLACK WILL  Faith, I was so amazed I could not strike.
ALICE  Ah, sirs, had he yesternight been slain,
    For every drop of his detested blood
    I would have crammed in angels in thy fist,
    And kissed thee, too, and hugged thee in my arms. **80**
BLACK WILL  Patient yourself; we cannot help it now.
    Greene and we two will dog him through the fair,
    And stab him in the crowd, and steal away.

*Here enters* MOSBY, *his arm bandaged*

ALICE  It is unpossible. But here comes he
    That will, I hope, invent some surer means.
    Sweet Mosby, hide thy arm; it kills my heart.
MOSBY  Ay, Mistress Arden, this is your favour.

---

21 tallies: sticks on which notches were made to record
    accounts
24 coltstaff: pole used for carrying a tub or 'cowl'
25 sergeant: responsible for arresting offenders and
    summoning them to court
    mace: staff of office
26 list: wished
26–7 tenpenny alehouses: i.e. keepers of alehouses selling ale
    at tenpence a quart
30 lattice: red- or green-painted lattices were alehouse signs
46 the fair: St Valentine's fair, held annually in Faversham.
    This fair figures significantly in Holinshed's account of
    Arden's murder
50 John cook: i.e. John the cook
51 lay it on: spare no expense
52 and: if
    bid: invite

56 missed you: did you fail
57 long of: because of
60 locked: attacked
61 hilts: swords
    in a bravery: with bravado
64 in: eds (not in Qs)
65 round: directly
    costard: head
68 fence: fencing skill
69 ward: defensive posture
    I'll stand to it: i.e. 'I'll fight fiercely'. However, Qs'
    punctuation here is ambiguous, so that the phrase might
    instead be read as beginning the next sentence, meaning
    'I'll maintain that . . .'
71 sconce: a small fort
    this: i.e. Shakebag's injury
72 faint: lose heart
73 arming-sword: sword with which he was armed
79 angels: coins
81 Patient yourself: be patient
87 favour: gift or token from a lover

ALICE Ah, say not so; for when I saw thee hurt
  I could have took the weapon thou let'st fall
  And run at Arden, for I have sworn       90
  That these mine eyes, offended with his sight,
  Shall never close till Arden's be shut up.
  This night I rose and walked about the chamber,
  And twice or thrice I thought to have murdered him.
MOSBY What, in the night? Then had we been undone!
ALICE Why, how long shall he live?
MOSBY Faith, Alice, no longer than this night.
  Black Will and Shakebag, will you two
  Perform the complot that I have laid?
BLACK WILL Ay, or else think me as a villain.     100
GREENE And rather than you shall want, I'll help
  myself.
MOSBY You, Master Greene, shall single Franklin forth
  And hold him with a long tale of strange news,
  That he may not come home till suppertime.
  I'll fetch Master Arden home, and we, like friends,
  Will play a game or two at tables here.
ALICE But what of all this? How shall he be slain?
MOSBY Why, Black Will and Shakebag, locked within
  the countinghouse,
  Shall, at a certain watchword given, rush forth.
BLACK WILL What shall the watchword be?     110
MOSBY 'Now I take you'—that shall be the word.
  But come not forth before in any case.
BLACK WILL I warrant you; but who shall lock me in?
ALICE That will I do; thou'st keep the key thyself.
MOSBY Come, Master Greene go you along with me.
  See all things ready, Alice, against we come.
ALICE Take no care for that; send you him home.
                *Exeunt* MOSBY *and* GREENE
  And if he e'er go forth again blame me.
  Come, Black Will, that in mine eyes art fair;
  Next unto Mosby do I honour thee.     120
  Instead of fair words and large promises
  My hands shall play you golden harmony.
  How like you this? Say, will you do it, sirs?
BLACK WILL Ay, and that bravely, too. Mark my device:
  Place Mosby, being a stranger, in a chair,
  And let your husband sit upon a stool,
  That I may come behind him cunningly
  And with a towel pull him to the ground,

Then stab him till his flesh be as a sieve.
  That done, bear him behind the Abbey,     130
  That those that find him murdered may suppose
  Some slave or other killed him for his gold.
ALICE A fine device! You shall have twenty pound,
  And when he is dead you shall have forty more.
  And lest you might be suspected staying here,
  Michael shall saddle you two lusty geldings.
  Ride whither you will, to Scotland or to Wales;
  I'll see you shall not lack where'er you be.
BLACK WILL Such words would make one kill a
  thousand men!
  Give me the key; which is the countinghouse?     140
ALICE Here would I stay and still encourage you,
  But that I know how resolute you are.
SHAKEBAG Tush! You are too faint-hearted; we must
  do it.
ALICE But Mosby will be there, whose very looks
  Will add unwonted courage to my thought,
  And make me the first that shall adventure on him.
BLACK WILL Tush, get you gone; 'tis we must do the
  deed.
  When this door opens next, look for his death.
            *Exeunt* BLACK WILL *and* SHAKEBAG
ALICE Ah, would he now were here, that it might
  open.
  I shall no more be closed in Arden's arms,     150
  That like the snakes of black Tisiphone
  Sting me with their embracings. Mosby's arms
  Shall compass me, and, were I made a star,
  I would have none other spheres but those.
  There is no nectar but in Mosby's lips!
  Had chaste Diana kissed him, she like me
  Would grow love-sick, and from her wat'ry bower
  Fling down Endymion and snatch him up.
  Then blame not me that slay a silly man
  Not half so lovely as Endymion.     160

*Here enters* MICHAEL

MICHAEL Mistress, my master is coming hard by.
ALICE Who comes with him?
MICHAEL Nobody but Mosby.
ALICE That's well, Michael. Fetch in the tables; and,
  when thou hast done, stand before the countinghouse
  door.
MICHAEL Why so?
ALICE Black Will is locked within to do the deed.

---

93  This night: i.e. last night
101  want: fail
106  tables: backgammon
108  countinghouse: private room used as an office
116  against: by the time that
117  Take . . . that: don't worry about that
122  play . . . harmony: i.e. give you money
124  bravely: splendidly
125–6  chair . . . stool: chairs were still relatively scarce,
    outnumbered by stools and forms

129  sieve Q2, Q3 (sine Q1). Sturgess suggests that 'seine' (a
    fishing net) is 'marginally possible'
146  adventure: venture
151  Tisiphone: one of the Furies, avengers of crimes,
    especially crimes against kin; represented with snakes
    encircling her arms and in her hair
156–60  Diana . . . Endymion: the moon goddess Diana fell in
    love with Endymion, a beautiful mortal

MICHAEL What, shall he die tonight?

ALICE Ay, Michael.                                                        170

MICHAEL But shall not Susan know it?

ALICE Yes, for she'll be as secret as ourselves.

MICHAEL That's brave! I'll go fetch the tables.

ALICE But Michael, hark to me a word or two:
When my husband is come in, lock the street door;
He shall be murdered ere the guests come in.

*Exit* MICHAEL *and re-enters shortly with the tables*

*Here enters* ARDEN *and* MOSBY

Husband, what mean you to bring Mosby home?
Although I wished you to be reconciled,
'Twas more for fear of you than love of him.
Black Will and Greene are his companions,        180
And they are cutters and may cut you short;
Therefore, I thought it good to make you friends.
But wherefore do you bring him hither now?
You have given me my supper with his sight.

MOSBY Master Arden, methinks your wife would have
me gone.

ARDEN No, good Master Mosby, women will be
prating.
Alice, bid him welcome; he and I are friends.

ALICE You may enforce me to it if you will,
But I had rather die than bid him welcome.
His company hath purchased me ill friends,       190
And therefore will I ne'er frequent it more.

MOSBY (*Aside*) Oh, how cunningly she can dissemble!

ARDEN Now he is here, you will not serve me so.

ALICE I pray you be not angry or displeased;
I'll bid him welcome, seeing you'll have it so.
You are welcome, Master Mosby. Will you sit down?

MOSBY I know I am welcome to your loving husband,
But for yourself you speak not from your heart.

ALICE And if I do not, sir, think I have cause.

MOSBY Pardon me, Master Arden, I'll away.       200

ARDEN No, good Master Mosby.

ALICE We shall have guests enough though you go
hence.

MOSBY I pray you, Master Arden, let me go.

ARDEN I pray thee, Mosby, let her prate her fill.

ALICE The doors are open, sir; you may be gone.

MICHAEL (*Aside*) Nay, that's a lie, for I have locked the
doors.

---

ARDEN Sirrah, fetch me a cup of wine; I'll make them
friends.        *Exit* MICHAEL, *and re-enters with wine*
And, gentle Mistress Alice, seeing you are so stout,
You shall begin. Frown not; I'll have it so.

ALICE I pray you meddle with that you have to do.   210

ARDEN Why, Alice, how can I do too much for him
Whose life I have endangered without cause?

ALICE 'Tis true; and seeing 'twas partly through my
means,
I am content to drink to him for this once.
Here, Master Mosby! And, I pray you, henceforth
Be you as strange to me as I to you.
Your company hath purchased me ill friends,
And I for you, God knows, have undeserved
Been ill spoken of in every place;               219
Therefore, henceforth frequent my house no more.

MOSBY I'll see your husband in despite of you.
Yet, Arden, I protest to thee by heaven,
Thou ne'er shalt see me more after this night.
I'll go to Rome rather than be forsworn.

ARDEN Tush, I'll have no such vows made in my house.

ALICE Yes, I pray you, husband, let him swear;
And on that condition, Mosby, pledge me here.

MOSBY Ay, as willingly as I mean to live.

ARDEN Come, Alice, is our supper ready yet?       229

ALICE It will by then you have played a game at tables.

ARDEN Come, Master Mosby, what shall we play for?

MOSBY Three games for a French crown, sir, and please
you.

ARDEN Content.                    *Then they play at the tables*

*Enter* BLACK WILL *and* SHAKEBAG

BLACK WILL (*Aside*) Can he not take him yet? What a
spite is that!

ALICE (*Aside*) Not yet, Will. Take heed he see thee not.

BLACK WILL (*Aside*) I fear he will spy me as I am
coming.

MICHAEL (*Aside*) To prevent that, creep betwixt my legs.

MOSBY One ace, or else I lose the game.
                                        *He throws the dice*

ARDEN Marry, sir, there's two for failing.

MOSBY Ah, Master Arden, 'Now I can take you.'       240
                *Then* BLACK WILL *pulls him down with a towel*

ARDEN Mosby! Michael! Alice! What will you do?

BLACK WILL Nothing but take you up, sir, nothing
else.

---

173  brave: splendid
179  of you: for you
180  Greene: Sturgess notes that we might expect Shakebag,
     not Greene, to be mentioned here, since Greene (unlike
     Shakebag) is not a 'cutter', and was not involved in the
     fight in scene xiii. 'Greene', he suggests, better suits the
     rhythm of the line, but White suggests 'it might well be a
     dangerous slip on Alice's part that momentarily chills the
     hearts of her accomplices'
184  given me my supper: i.e. taken away my appetite

208  stout: stubborn
209  begin: i.e. offer the first toast
227  pledge: drink to
232  French crown: see iii.75n
     and: if it
238  ace: i.e. on the dice
239  for failing: i.e. in case one is not enough
242  take you up: deal with you (playing on the watchword)

MOSBY There's for the pressing iron you told me of.
*He stabs him*
SHAKEBAG And there's for the ten pound in my sleeve.
*Stabs him*
ALICE What, groans thou? Nay then, give me the
    weapon.
    Take this for hind'ring Mosby's love and mine.
*Stabs him*
MICHAEL Oh, Mistress!         ARDEN *dies*
BLACK WILL Ah, that villain will betray us all.
MOSBY Tush, fear him not; he will be secret.    **249**
MICHAEL Why, dost thou think I will betray myself?
SHAKEBAG In Southwark dwells a bonny northern lass,
    The widow Chambley; I'll to her house now,
    And if she will not give me harborough,
    I'll make booty of the quean, even to her smock.
BLACK WILL Shift for yourselves; we two will leave you
    now.
ALICE First lay the body in the countinghouse.
*Then they lay the body in the countinghouse*
BLACK WILL We have our gold. Mistress Alice, adieu;
    Mosby, farewell, and Michael, farewell too.
*Exeunt* BLACK WILL *and* SHAKEBAG

*Enter* SUSAN

SUSAN Mistress, the guests are at the doors.
    Hearken, they knock. What, shall I let them in?   **260**
ALICE Mosby, go thou and bear them company.
*Exit* MOSBY
    And, Susan, fetch water and wash away this blood.
*Exit* SUSAN, *returns with water, and washes the floor*
SUSAN The blood cleaveth to the ground and will not
    out.
ALICE But with my nails I'll scrape away the blood.—
    The more I strive the more the blood appears.
SUSAN What's the reason, Mistress, can you tell?
ALICE Because I blush not at my husband's death.

*Here enters* MOSBY

MOSBY How now, what's the matter? Is all well?
ALICE Ay, well, if Arden were alive again!
    In vain we strive, for here his blood remains.   **270**

MOSBY Why, strew rushes on it, can you not?
    This wench doth nothing; fall unto the work.
ALICE 'Twas thou that made me murder him.
MOSBY                   What of that?
ALICE Nay, nothing, Mosby, so it be not known.
MOSBY Keep thou it close, and 'tis unpossible.
ALICE Ah, but I cannot. Was he not slain by me?
    My husband's death torments me at the heart.
MOSBY It shall not long torment thee, gentle Alice.
    I am thy husband; think no more of him.

*Here enters* ADAM FOWLE *and* BRADSHAW

BRADSHAW How now, Mistress Arden, what ail you
    weep?                             **280**
MOSBY Because her husband is abroad so late.
    A couple of ruffians threat'ned him yesternight,
    And she, poor soul, is afraid he should be hurt.
ADAM Is't nothing else? Tush, he'll be here anon.

*Here enters* GREENE

GREENE Now, Mistress Arden, lack you any guests?
ALICE Ah, Master Greene, did you see my husband
    lately?
GREENE I saw him walking behind the Abbey even now.

*Here enters* FRANKLIN

ALICE I do not like this being out so late.
    Master Franklin, where did you leave my husband?
FRANKLIN Believe me, I saw him not since morning.
    Fear you not, he'll come anon. Meantime,   **291**
    You may do well to bid his guests sit down.
ALICE Ay, so they shall. Master Bradshaw, sit you
    there;
    I pray you be content, I'll have my will.
    Master Mosby, sit you in my husband's seat.
MICHAEL (*Aside*) Susan, shall thou and I wait on them?
    Or, and thou say'st the word, let us sit down too.
SUSAN (*Aside*) Peace, we have other matters now in
    hand.
    I fear me, Michael, all will be bewrayed.   **299**
MICHAEL (*Aside*) Tush, so it be known that I shall
    marry thee in the morning I care not though I be
    hanged ere night. But to prevent the worst I'll buy
    some ratsbane.
SUSAN (*Aside*) Why, Michael, wilt thou poison thyself?
MICHAEL (*Aside*) No, but my mistress, for I fear she'll
    tell.
SUSAN (*Aside*) Tush, Michael, fear not her; she's wise
    enough.

---

243 pressing iron: see i.313
SD The sources suggest that Mosby attacked Arden with his
    pressing iron. White is the only ed to include this in his
    stage direction; all other eds have concluded that, in the
    play, he stabs him. There is no stage direction in Qs
251 Southwark: London borough south of the Thames,
    known for its crime and brothels as well as its playhouses
253 harborough: harbour, shelter
254 make . . . quean: take the harlot by force
263–5 The blood cleaveth . . . appears: compare *Macbeth*
    II.ii.58–9: 'Will all great Neptune's ocean wash this
    blood/Clean from my hand?'

271 rushes: a common floor covering
275 close: secret
280 what . . . weep?: i.e. what ails you that you weep?
299 bewrayed: betrayed, revealed
303 ratsbane: rat poison

MOSBY  Sirrah Michael, give's a cup of beer.
　Mistress Arden, here's to your husband.
ALICE  My husband!　　　　　　　　　　　309
FRANKLIN  What ails you, woman, to cry so suddenly?
ALICE  Ah, neighbours, a sudden qualm came over my
　　heart;
　My husband's being forth torments my mind.
　I know something's amiss; he is not well,
　Or else I should have heard of him ere now.
MOSBY  (*Aside*) She will undo us through her
　　foolishness.
GREENE  Fear not, Mistress Arden, he's well enough.
ALICE  Tell not me; I know he is not well.
　He was not wont for to stay thus late.
　Good Master Franklin, go and seek him forth,
　And if you find him send him home to me,　　320
　And tell him what a fear he hath put me in.
FRANKLIN  (*Aside*) I like not this; I pray God all be well.—
　I'll seek him out and find him if I can.
　　　　　　*Exeunt* FRANKLIN, MOSBY, *and* GREENE
ALICE  (*Aside*) Michael, how shall I do to rid the rest
　　away?
MICHAEL  (*Aside*) Leave that to my charge; let me
　　alone.—
　'Tis very late, Master Bradshaw,
　And there are many false knaves abroad,
　And you have many narrow lanes to pass.
BRADSHAW  Faith, friend Michael, and thou sayest true.
　Therefore I pray thee light's forth and lend's a link.
　　　　　　*Exeunt* BRADSHAW, ADAM FOWLE, *and* MICHAEL
ALICE  Michael, bring them to the doors, but do not
　　stay;　　　　　　　　　　　　　　　331
　You know I do not love to be alone.
　Go, Susan, and bid thy brother come.
　But wherefore should he come? Here is nought but
　　fear.
　Stay, Susan, stay, and help to counsel me.
SUSAN  Alas, I counsel! Fear frights away my wits.
*Then they open the countinghouse door and look upon* ARDEN
ALICE  See, Susan, where thy quondam master lies;
　Sweet Arden, smeared in blood and filthy gore.
SUSAN  My brother, you, and I shall rue this deed.
ALICE  Come, Susan, help to lift his body forth,
　And let our salt tears be his obsequies.　　341
　　　　　*They bring his body out of the countinghouse*

*Here enters* MOSBY *and* GREENE

MOSBY  How now, Alice, whither will you bear him?
ALICE  Sweet Mosby, art thou come? Then weep that
　　will;
　I have my wish in that I joy thy sight.

GREENE  Well, it 'hoves us to be circumspect.
MOSBY  Ay, for Franklin thinks that we have murdered
　　him.
ALICE  Ay, but he cannot prove it for his life.
　We'll spend this night in dalliance and in sport.

*Here enters* MICHAEL

MICHAEL  Oh mistress, the mayor and all the watch　349
　Are coming towards our house with glaives and bills.
ALICE  Make the door fast; let them not come in.
MOSBY  Tell me, sweet Alice, how shall I escape?
ALICE  Out at the back door, over the pile of wood
　And for one night lie at the Flower-de-Luce.
MOSBY  That is the next way to betray myself.
GREENE  Alas, Mistress Arden, the watch will take me
　　here,
　And cause suspicion where else would be none.
ALICE  Why, take that way that Master Mosby doth;
　But first convey the body to the fields.
*Then* MOSBY, GREENE, MICHAEL *and* SUSAN *bear the body*
　　　　　　　　　　　　*into the fields and then return*
MOSBY  Until tomorrow, sweet Alice; now farewell,　360
　And see you confess nothing in any case.
GREENE  Be resolute, Mistress Alice; betray us not,
　But cleave to us as we will stick to you.
　　　　　　　　　　*Exeunt* MOSBY *and* GREENE
ALICE  Now let the judge and juries do their worst;
　My house is clear and now I fear them not.
SUSAN  As we went it snowed all the way,
　Which makes me fear our footsteps will be spied.
ALICE  Peace, fool! The snow will cover them again.
SUSAN  But it had done before we came back again.　369
ALICE  Hark, hark, they knock! Go, Michael, let them
　　in.　　　　　　　　　　　　MICHAEL *opens the door*

*Here enters the* MAYOR *and the* WATCH

　How now, Master Mayor, have you brought my
　　husband home?
MAYOR  I saw him come into your house an hour ago.
ALICE  You are deceived; it was a Londoner.
MAYOR  Mistress Arden, know you not one that is
　　called Black Will?
ALICE  I know none such. What mean these questions?
MAYOR  I have the Council's warrant to apprehend him.
ALICE  (*Aside*) I am glad it is no worse.—
　Why, Master Mayor, think you I harbour any such?
MAYOR  We are informed that here he is,

---

325  let me alone: see xii.65n
330  link: torch
337  quondam: former

---

345  'hoves: behoves
349  watch: street patrol which acted as police
350  glaives and bills: swords and halberds
355  next: quickest
369  done: i.e. stopped snowing
373  a Londoner: i.e. a stranger to the mayor. Holinshed
　　reports that, after the murder, Alice sent for two
　　Londoners to come to supper

And therefore pardon us, for we must search.          380
ALICE  Ay, search, and spare you not, through every room.
  Were my husband at home you would not offer this.

*Here enters* FRANKLIN

  Master Franklin, what mean you come so sad?
FRANKLIN  Arden, thy husband and my friend, is slain.
ALICE  Ah, by whom? Master Franklin, can you tell?
FRANKLIN  I know not; but behind the Abbey
  There he lies murdered in most piteous case.
MAYOR  But Master Franklin, are you sure 'tis he?
FRANKLIN  I am too sure; would God I were deceived.
ALICE  Find out the murderers; let them be known.  390
FRANKLIN  Ay, so they shall. Come you along with us.
ALICE  Wherefore?
FRANKLIN            Know you this hand-towel and this
  knife?
SUSAN  (*Aside*) Ah, Michael, through this thy
  negligence
  Thou hast betrayed and undone us all.
MICHAEL  (*Aside*) I was so afraid I knew not what I did.
  I thought I had thrown them both into the well.
ALICE  It is the pig's blood we had to supper.
  But wherefore stay you? Find out the murderers.
MAYOR  I fear me you'll prove one of them yourself.
ALICE  I one of them? What mean such questions?  400
FRANKLIN  I fear me he was murdered in this house
  And carried to the fields, for from that place
  Backwards and forwards may you see
  The print of many feet within the snow.
  And look about this chamber where we are,
  And you shall find part of his guiltless blood;
  For in his slipshoe did I find some rushes,
  Which argueth he was murdered in this room.
MAYOR  Look in the place where he was wont to sit.
  See, see! His blood! It is too manifest.          410
ALICE  It is a cup of wine that Michael shed.
MICHAEL  Ay, truly.
FRANKLIN  It is his blood which, strumpet, thou hast
  shed.
  But if I live, thou and thy complices
  Which have conspired and wrought his death shall
  rue it.
ALICE  Ah, Master Franklin, God and heaven can tell
  I loved him more than all the world beside.
  But bring me to him; let me see his body.
FRANKLIN  Bring that villain and Mosby's sister too;
  And one of you go to the Flower-de-Luce          420
  And seek for Mosby, and apprehend him too.
                                        *Exeunt*

---

387  piteous case: pitiful state
397  to: for
407  slipshoe: slipper
419  that villain: i.e. Michael

# Scene xv

*Here enters* SHAKEBAG *solus*

SHAKEBAG  The widow Chambley in her husband's days
    I kept;
  And now he's dead she is grown so stout
  She will not know her old companions.
  I came thither, thinking to have had
  Harbour as I was wont,
  And she was ready to thrust me out at doors.
  But whether she would or no I got me up,
  And as she followed me I spurned her down the
    stairs
  And broke her neck, and cut her tapster's throat;
  And now I am going to fling them in the Thames.  10
  I have the gold; what care I though it be known?
  I'll cross the water and take sanctuary.
                                *Exit* SHAKEBAG

# Scene xvi

*Here enters the* MAYOR, MOSBY, ALICE, FRANKLIN,
MICHAEL, *and* SUSAN *guarded by the* WATCH

MAYOR  See, Mistress Arden, where your husband lies.
  Confess this foul fault and be penitent.
ALICE  Arden, sweet husband, what shall I say?
  The more I sound his name the more he bleeds.
  This blood condemns me, and in gushing forth
  Speaks as it falls and asks me why I did it.
  Forgive me, Arden; I repent me now;
  And would my death save thine thou shouldst not
    die.
  Rise up, sweet Arden, and enjoy thy love,
  And frown not on me when we meet in heaven;   10
  In heaven I love thee though on earth I did not.
MAYOR  Say, Mosby, what made thee murder him?
FRANKLIN  Study not for an answer, look not down.
  His purse and girdle found at thy bed's head
  Witness sufficiently thou didst the deed.
  It bootless is to swear thou didst it not.

---

SD  *solus*: alone
1  kept: i.e. as a mistress
2  stout: proud
8  spurned: kicked
12  take sanctuary: take refuge, in one of the areas of a church
    or royal palace where criminals were safe from arrest
4–6  The more . . . did it: 'It was popularly believed that the
    corpse of a murdered man bled in the presence of his
    killer' (White); see *Richard III* I.ii.55–61, where the corpse
    of the murdered Henry VI bleeds anew in the presence of
    his killer, Richard, Duke of York
13  Study not: do not try to invent
14  girdle: belt (to carry purse)
16  bootless: pointless

MOSBY I hired Black Will and Shakebag, ruffians both,
　And they and I have done this murd'rous deed.
　But wherefore stay we? Come and bear me hence.
FRANKLIN Those ruffians shall not escape. I will up to
　London　　　　　　　　　　　　　　　　　　　20
　And get the Council's warrant to apprehend them.
　　　　　　　　　　　　　　　　　　　　*Exeunt*

# Scene xvii

*Here enters* BLACK WILL

BLACK WILL Shakebag, I hear, hath taken sanctuary;
　But I am so pursued with hues and cries
　For petty robberies that I have done
　That I can come unto no sanctuary.
　Therefore must I in some oyster-boat
　At last be fain to go aboard some hoy,
　And so to Flushing. There is no staying here.
　At Sittingburgh the watch was like to take me,
　And, had I not with my buckler covered my head
　And run full blank at all adventures,　　　　10
　I am sure I had ne'er gone further than that place,
　For the constable had twenty warrants to apprehend
　me;
　Besides that, I robbed him and his man once at
　Gadshill.
　Farewell, England; I'll to Flushing now.
　　　　　　　　　　　　　　　*Exit* BLACK WILL

# Scene xviii

*Here enters the* MAYOR, MOSBY, ALICE, MICHAEL, SUSAN,
*and* BRADSHAW *and the* WATCH

MAYOR Come, make haste, and bring away the
　prisoners.
BRADSHAW Mistress Arden, you are now going to God,
　And I am by the law condemned to die
　About a letter I brought from Master Greene.
　I pray you, Mistress Arden, speak the truth:
　Was I ever privy to your intent or no?

ALICE What should I say? You brought me such a
　letter,
　But I dare swear thou knewest not the contents.
　Leave now to trouble me with worldly things,
　And let me meditate upon my Saviour Christ,　　10
　Whose blood must save me for the blood I shed.
MOSBY How long shall I live in this hell of grief?
　Convey me from the presence of that strumpet.
ALICE Ah, but for thee I had never been strumpet.
　What cannot oaths and protestations do
　When men have opportunity to woo?
　I was too young to sound thy villainies,
　But now I find it, and repent too late.
SUSAN Ah, gentle brother, wherefore should I die?
　I knew not of it till the deed was done.　　　20
MOSBY For thee I mourn more than for myself,
　But let it suffice I cannot save thee now.
MICHAEL And if your brother and my mistress
　Had not promised me you in marriage,
　I had ne'er given consent to this foul deed.
MAYOR Leave to accuse each other now,
　And listen to the sentence I shall give:
　Bear Mosby and his sister to London straight,
　Where they in Smithfield must be executed;
　Bear Mistress Arden unto Canterbury,　　　30
　Where her sentence is she must be burnt;
　Michael and Bradshaw in Faversham must suffer
　death.
ALICE Let my death make amends for all my sins.
MOSBY Fie upon women!—this shall be my song.
　But bear me hence, for I have lived too long.
SUSAN Seeing no hope on earth, in heaven is my hope.
MICHAEL Faith, I care not, seeing I die with Susan.
BRADSHAW My blood be on his head that gave the
　sentence!
MAYOR To speedy execution with them all!
　　　　　　　　　　　　　　　　　　*Exeunt*

# Epilogue

*Here enters* FRANKLIN

FRANKLIN Thus have you seen the truth of Arden's
　death.
　As for the ruffians, Shakebag and Black Will,
　The one took sanctuary, and being sent for out,
　Was murdered in Southwark as he passed
　To Greenwich where the Lord Protector lay.
　Black Will was burnt in Flushing on a stage;

---

17 I hired . . . Shakebag: actually hired by Greene; but, as
　eds agree, this confession testifies to Mosby's awareness
　that the game is up and to his desire to have the affair
　concluded quickly
6 hoy: small boat
8 like: likely
10 full . . . adventures: 'headlong whatever the outcome'
　(White)
13 Gadshill: a hill on the road between London and
　Rochester, famous for its robberies. In *1 Henry IV*, the
　place where Prince Harry and Poins pretend to rob
　Falstaff (II.iv)
4 About: on account of
6 privy to: aware of

---

9 Leave: cease
17 sound: sound out
29 Smithfield: an open space east of the Tower of London,
　often used for executions
6 stage: scaffold

Greene was hanged at Osbridge in Kent;
The painter fled, and how he died we know not.
But this above the rest is to be noted:
Arden lay murdered in that plot of ground          10
Which he by force and violence held from Reede;
And in the grass his body's print was seen
Two years and more after the deed was done.

Gentlemen, we hope you'll pardon this naked
    tragedy,
Wherein no filed points are foisted in
To make it gracious to the ear or eye;
For simple truth is gracious enough,
And needs no other points of glozing stuff.

*Exit*

---

14  naked: plain
15  filed points: rhetorical figures. 'Points' were also the laces
    attaching hose to doublet, 'hence the probable play on
    the idea that the author was not adding adornments to
    his simple style' (Wine)
18  glozing: specious

---

7  Osbridge: i.e. Ospringe, in Kent

# Christopher Marlowe, *Edward II*

First performed 1592
First published 1594

Edward II offers compelling evidence of the way that the Elizabethan theatres provided a forum for the representation and analysis of political and social circumstances that had an immediate resonance for their audiences. It may at first seem strange that a history play should perform this function, dealing, as *Edward II* does, with the events of two and a half centuries before; yet Tudor 'history' was conspicuously concerned (as perhaps the discipline of history always is) with the fashioning and interpretation of events, rather than the provision of a mere record, or still less, an objective account. Tudor intellectuals were obsessively interested in stories of the past and employed a variety of cultural forms in order to shape them, ranging from the chronicles of Ralph Holinshed (d. 1580) and John Stowe (c. 1525–1605), to the extended homage to the genealogy of Elizabeth I that is *The Faerie Queene* (1590–96), the epic poem by Edmund Spenser (1552–99). By the time *Edward II* was first staged, Shakespeare had completed the three parts of *Henry VI*, and his *Richard III*, celebrating the Tudors' overthrowing of a demonised Richard, appeared at roughly the same time as Marlowe's play.

As a medium for 'history', the theatre was an unstable and highly suggestive cultural institution. One of the many reservations that Elizabethan critics had about the theatre was that it allowed men to dress and behave like kings, implicitly demystifying (and in a public arena to boot) the aura of divinity that successful monarchs had so carefully cultivated. Moreover, the theatre condensed or extracted themes that were pertinent to its audiences, so that a play like *Edward II* spoke to them of issues that were extremely topical and sensitive in an intimate and unsettling way. It is no wonder, for example, that Elizabeth considered that Shakespeare's *Richard II*, a play often compared to *Edward II* for its portrayal of the undermining power of favourites, suggested something of the circle of influence in her own court.

Marlowe's depiction of Edward as a weak king unable to mediate between his personal desires and his public duty sets up a number of conflicts that might have seemed entirely relevant in late Tudor England. The figure of Gaveston embodies a number of 'alien' values and characteristics in the dramatic world of the play that were also a cause of anxiety in the Elizabethan court; as such, he is a kind of catalyst, provoking reaction and conflict which show the deep fault-lines within sovereignty itself. First, there is Gaveston's foreignness: Marlowe is at pains to emphasise his French origins and Italian clothes and manners, in a framework of references that serves to distinguish him from the English court. This might have endorsed the contemporary post-Armada suspicion of foreign influence that dominated Tudor domestic and foreign policy. In fact the play is also laced with anti-Catholic sentiment that positions it ideologically in the realm of late sixteenth-century Reformation thinking rather than in its historical medieval setting. Edward's tirade against Rome's interference in English affairs (I.iv.97–105) may, when the play was first performed, have served to reinforce popular Tudor feeling against residual Catholic support and the increasing intolerance of established church structures.

Second is the question of Gaveston's social rank. Few plays of the period are quite as centred on questions of title and family; the barons' response (III.ii.65–7) to Edward's casual bestowal of titles on the lowly Gaveston (I.i.154–6) disrupts the feudal certainties of the historical world of the play, but begged questions too about the distribution of power and favour that also dominated the court of Elizabeth. Edward's indulgence of his favourite threatened the institutions that monarchy was supposed to endorse and perpetuate, showing how susceptible these were to personal whim and political expedience, but it also raised the historical spectre of the divided kingdom, a spectre that haunted Tudor administrations from a more recent past.

For modern audiences the play's forthright presentation of homosexuality is perhaps the most striking element of the play. Sodomy was a capital offence in Marlowe's time, but not, surprisingly perhaps, the taboo subject of later centuries. Although the nobles are quick to describe Edward's desires as unnatural, it is not his passion itself that offends so much as the transgression of social hierarchies. Indeed, Mortimer Senior cites Alexander, Hercules, Achilles, Tully and Socrates as great men who had their 'minions', and hopes that, as far as Edward is concerned, 'riper years will wean him from such toys'

(I.iv.402). The play contains scenes of verbal and physical homosexual exchange that would have offended the censors of the twentieth-century theatre; in the twenty-first century the play asks us to examine Tudor codes of friendship (and the classical models the Tudors admired) for evidence of a discontinuity in the treatment of homosexuality across the centuries.

*Edward II* emerges as a radical play that would have disturbed and challenged its Elizabethan audiences. Its dramatic enactment of the deposition and murder of a king, its investigation of the cycle and circles of sovereignty, and its examination of the power of rhetoric to shape social and political realities, all lead to a question that was constantly debated in Marlowe's time, especially as Elizabeth aged and the problem of the succession loomed: if a monarch's power is derived from God, what rights have their subjects? At the end of *Edward II*, as a new and unpromising cycle begins with Edward III, the talk is of retribution, fates, tragedy and lost innocence; there is little scope for analysis or reform. It is as if the shockingly graphic death of Edward, and his scream, which (according to Holinshed) 'did move many within the castle and town of Berkeley to compassion', has reduced language itself to a formulaic dullness, leaving the audience to open debate about the issues that the play itself closes down.

## Textual note

This edition is based on the octavo edition of 1594, the single copy of which is held by the Zentralbibliothek in Zurich in Switzerland (referred to in the footnotes to the text as Q). Some improvements to punctuation and spelling were made in subsequent editions in 1598, 1612 and 1622. We have followed other editors in introducing act and scene divisions, and in addressing the many inconsistencies in stage directions, speech prefixes and place names that appear in the early editions. Extracts from the principal source for the play, Ralph Holinshed's *Chronicles* (1577), and other related documents are usefully reproduced in the edition of the play by Charles Forker.

# Further reading

## Editions

Bevington, David and Rasmussen, Eric (eds) (1995) *Doctor Faustus and Other Plays*, Oxford: Oxford University Press.

Dyce, Alexander (ed.) (1850, revised 1858) *The Works of Christopher Marlowe*, London: William Pickering.

Forker, Charles R. (ed.) (1994) *Edward II*, The Revels Series, Manchester and New York, NY: Manchester University Press.

Gill, Roma (ed.) (1967) *Edward II*, London: Oxford University Press.

Kinney, Arthur F. (ed.) (1999) *Renaissance Drama: An Anthology of Plays and Entertainments*, Oxford: Blackwell.

Merchant, Moelwyn (ed.) (1967) *Edward II*, The New Mermaids, London: Ernest Benn.

Steane, J. B. (ed.) (1986) *Christopher Marlowe: The Complete Plays*, Penguin Classics, Harmondsworth: Penguin.

Wiggins, Martin and Lindsey, Robert (eds) (1997) *Edward II*, The New Mermaids, London: A. & C. Black.

Wine, M. L. (ed.) (1969) *Drama of the English Renaissance*, Modern Library College Editions, New York, NY: Random House.

## Critical and contextual commentaries

Belsey, Catherine (1992) 'Desire's Excess and the English Renaissance Theatre: *Edward II, Troilus and Cressida, Othello*', in Susan Zimmerman (ed.), *Erotic Politics: Desire on the Renaissance Stage*, New York, NY, and London: Routledge.

Belt, Debra (1991) 'Anti-Theatricalism and Rhetoric in Marlowe's *Edward II*', *English Literary Renaissance*, 21, 2: 134–60.

Bredbeck, Gregory W. (1991) *Sodomy and Interpretation: Marlowe to Milton*, Ithaca, NY: Cornell University Press.

Cole, Douglas (1962) *Suffering and Evil in the Plays of Christopher Marlowe*, Princeton, NJ: Princeton University Press.

Comensoli, Viviana (1993) 'Homophobia and the Regulation of Desire: A Psychoanalytic Reading of Marlowe's *Edward II*', *Journal of the History of Sexuality*, 4, 2: 175–200.

Friedenreich, Kenneth, Gill, Roma and Kuriyama, Constance B. (eds) (1988) *'A Poet and a Filthy Play-Maker': New Essays on Christopher Marlowe*, New York, NY: AMS Press.

Grantley, Darryl and Roberts, Peter (eds) (1996) *Christopher Marlowe and English Renaissance Culture*, Aldershot: Scholar Press.

Greenblatt, Stephen (1980) *Renaissance Self-fashioning: From More to Shakespeare*, Chicago, IL, and London: Chicago University Press.

Guybray, S. (1991) 'Homophobia and the Depoliticizing of Edward II', *English Studies in Canada*, 17, 2: 125–49.

Leech, Clifford (1986) *Christopher Marlowe: Poet for the Stage*, New York, NY: AMS Press.

Levin, Harry (1954) *The Overreacher: A Study of Christopher Marlowe*, London: Faber & Faber.

McCloskey, Susan (1985) 'The Worlds of Edward II', *Renaissance Drama*, 16: 35–48.

McElroy, John F. (1984) 'Repetition, Contrariety, and Individualism in *Edward II*', *Studies in English Literature 1500–1900*, 24, 2: 205–24.

Parks, J. (1999) 'History, Tragedy and Truth in Christopher Marlowe's Edward II', *Studies in English Literature 1500–1900*, 39, 2: 275–90.

Purkiss, Diane (1994) *Renaissance Women: The Plays of Elizabeth Cary, The Poems of Aemilia Canter*, London: William Pickering.

Ryan, P. (1998) 'Marlowe's *Edward II* and the Medieval Passion Play', *Comparative Drama*, 32, 4: 465–95.

Sanders, Wilbur (1968) *The Dramatist and the Received Idea: Studies in the Plays of Marlowe and Shakespeare*, London: Cambridge University Press.

Simkin, Stevie (2000) *A Preface to Marlowe*, Harlow: Longman.

Smith, Bruce R. (1991) *Homosexual Desire in Shakespeare's England*, Chicago, IL, and London: Chicago University Press.

Thurn, David H. (1990) 'Sovereignty, Disorder, and Fetishism in Marlowe's *Edward II*', *Renaissance Drama*, new series 21: 115–41.

Voss, James (1982) '*Edward II*: Marlowe's Historical Tragedy', *English Studies*, 63, 6: 517–30.

Weil, Judith (1977) *Christopher Marlowe: Merlin's Prophet*, Cambridge: Cambridge University Press.

Wilson, Richard (ed.) (1999) *Christopher Marlowe*, Harlow: Longman.

## Works of related interest

Anon., *The Famous Victories of Henry V* (1586)

William Shakespeare, *Henry VI, Parts I, II and III* (1590–1)

George Peele, *Edward I* (1591)

Anon., *Jack Straw* (1591)

Anon., *Arden of Faversham* (1592)

Anon., *Thomas of Woodstock* (1592)

William Shakespeare, *Richard III* (1593)

William Shakespeare, *Richard II* (1595)

Anthony Munday *et al.*, *Sir Thomas More* (1595)

William Shakespeare, *King John* (1596)

William Shakespeare, *Henry IV, Parts I and II* (1597)

William Shakespeare, *Henry V* (1599)

Thomas Heywood *et al.*, *Edward IV, Parts I and II* (1599)

Ben Jonson, *The Masque of Blackness* (1605)

John Fletcher and William Shakespeare, *Henry VIII* (1613)

Elizabeth Cary, *The Raign and Death of Edward II* (1626) [extracted in Purkiss 1994]

John Ford, *Perkin Warbeck* (1633)

# *Edward II* (1592)

## Dramatis personae

EDWARD II, *King of England*

ISABELLA, *Queen of England, the King of France's sister*

PRINCE EDWARD, *their son, later King Edward III*

EDMUND, EARL OF KENT, *brother of Edward II*

PIERS GAVESTON, *later Earl of Cornwall*

LADY MARGARET DE CLARE, *daughter of the Earl of Gloucester, niece of Edward II, engaged to Piers Gaveston*

GUY, EARL OF WARWICK

EARL OF ARUNDEL *(Edmund Fitzalan)*

EARL OF PEMBROKE *(Aymer de Valence)*

SIR JOHN MALTRAVERS

SIR THOMAS GOURNEY

THOMAS, EARL OF LANCASTER

HENRY, EARL OF LEICESTER

SIR THOMAS BERKELEY

MORTIMER SENIOR *(Roger Mortimer of Chirke)*

MORTIMER JUNIOR *(Roger Mortimer of Wigmore), his nephew*

SPENCER SENIOR *(Hugh le Despenser),* EARL OF WINCHESTER

SPENCER JUNIOR *(Hugh le Despenser),* EARL OF WILTSHIRE, *later Earl of Gloucester, his son*

THE ARCHBISHOP OF CANTERBURY *(Walter Reynolds)*

THE BISHOP OF COVENTRY *(Walter Langton)*

THE BISHOP OF WINCHESTER *(John Stratford)*

THE ABBOT OF NEATH

HENRY DE BEAUMONT, *a supporter of the King*

SIR WILLIAM TRUSSEL, *a representative of the Parliament*

SIR JOHN OF HAINAULT, *a supporter of the Queen*

BALDOCK, *a scholar, tutor to Lady Margaret*

LIGHTBORNE, *an assassin*

LEVUNE, *a Frenchman*

RHYS AP HOWELL

JAMES, *Pembroke's servant*

A HORSE-BOY, *Pembroke's servant*

THREE POOR MEN

THE CLERK OF THE CROWN

PEMBROKE'S MEN

A CHAPLAIN

A HERALD

A POST FROM SCOTLAND

A POST FROM FRANCE

THE MAYOR OF BRISTOL

A MOWER

THE KING'S CHAMPION

*Lords, Ladies-in-Waiting, Soldiers, Monks, Guards, Attendants, Servants*

### *The scene*

ENGLAND AND FRANCE

## Act I, scene i

*Enter* GAVESTON *reading on a letter that was brought him from the King*

GAVESTON 'My father is deceased; come, Gaveston,
And share the kingdom with thy dearest friend.'
Ah, words that make me surfeit with delight!

---

3 surfeit: oveflow

What greater bliss can hap to Gaveston,
Than live and be the favourite of a king?
Sweet prince, I come; these, these thy amorous lines
Might have enforced me to have swum from France,
And, like Leander, gasped upon the sand,
So thou wouldst smile and take me in thy arms.
The sight of London to my exiled eyes       10
Is as Elysium to a new-come soul;
Not that I love the city or the men,
But that it harbours him I hold so dear,
The King, upon whose bosom let me die,
And with the world be still at enmity.
What need the arctic people love starlight,
To whom the sun shines both by day and night?
Farewell, base stooping to the lordly peers;
My knee shall bow to none but to the King.
As for the multitude, that are but sparks       20
Raked up in embers of their poverty,
*Tanti!* I'll fan first on the wind
That glanceth at my lips and flieth away.

*Enter* THREE POOR MEN

But how now, what are these?
POOR MEN  Such as desire your worship's service.
GAVESTON  What canst thou do?
1 POOR MAN  I can ride.
GAVESTON  But I have no horses. What art thou?
2 POOR MAN  A traveller.       29
GAVESTON  Let me see, thou wouldst do well to wait at
  my trencher and tell me lies at dinner-time; and, as I
  like your discoursing, I'll have you. And what art
  thou?
3 POOR MAN  A soldier, that hath served against the Scot.
GAVESTON  Why, there are hospitals for such as you;
  I have no war, and therefore, sir, be gone.
3 POOR MAN  Farewell, and perish by a soldier's hand,
  That wouldst reward them with an hospital.

GAVESTON  (*Aside*) Ay, ay. These words of his move me
  as much
As if a goose should play the porcupine,       40
And dart her plumes, thinking to pierce my breast.
But yet it is no pain to speak men fair;
I'll flatter these, and make them live in hope.
(*To them*) You know that I came lately out of France,
And yet I have not viewed my lord the King;
If I speed well, I'll entertain you all.
POOR MEN  We thank your worship.
GAVESTON  I have some business; leave me to myself.
POOR MEN  We will wait here about the court.       *Exeunt*
GAVESTON  Do. These are not men for me;       50
I must have wanton poets, pleasant wits,
Musicians, that with touching of a string
May draw the pliant King which way I please.
Music and poetry is his delight;
Therefore I'll have Italian masques by night,
Sweet speeches, comedies, and pleasing shows;
And in the day when he shall walk abroad,
Like sylvan nymphs my pages shall be clad,
My men like satyrs grazing on the lawns
Shall with their goat-feet dance an antic hay;       60
Sometime a lovely boy in Dian's shape,
With hair that gilds the water as it glides,
Crownets of pearl about his naked arms,
And in his sportful hands an olive tree
To hide those parts which men delight to see,
Shall bathe him in a spring; and there hard by,
One like Actaeon peeping through the grove,

---

4  hap: happen to
7  France: Edward I had exiled Gaveston to his home in
   Ponthieu, Gascony
8  Leander: Marlowe's *Hero and Leander* (c. 1593, published
   in 1598 with additional lines by George Chapman) retold
   the classical story of Leander who swam the Hellespont
   each night to be with his lover, Hero
11  Elysium: the classical Greek name for heaven
14  die: a) swoon; b) enjoy sexual orgasm
20-1  multitude, that . . . their poverty: the multitude are mere
   embers by comparison with Edward, who burns like the
   sun
22  *Tanti!*: 'So much for that' (corruption of *tant' è*) (Italian)
31  trencher: plate, or place at a table
   lies: travellers' tales
34  the Scot: Edward I's wars against the Scots (led by
   Robert the Bruce)
35  hospitals: often squalid 'spital houses' for the poor,
   including ex-soldiers

41  And dart . . . my breast: it was thought that porcupines
   could shoot their quills, if under threat
46  speed well: prosper (by rising in social rank)
   entertain: take into service
51  wanton: lascivious
   pleasant wits: pleasing, witty companions
53  pliant: easily influenced, manipulated
55  masques: elaborate courtly entertainments originating in
   Italy, they became popular in the courts of Elizabeth I
   and the early Stuarts. Gaveston's allusion is, therefore,
   anachronistic
57  abroad: outdoors
58  sylvan nymphs: female spirits of the woods
59  satyrs: part-human and part-goat, satyrs are associated
   with Bacchus, the classical god of wine and revelry
60  antic: grotesque
   hay: country dance involving snake-like movement
61  Dian's shape: Diana was the classical goddess of the
   moon
63  Crownets: bracelets
64  sportful: playful
66  hard: near
67  Actaeon: in classical mythology Actaeon spied on the
   goddess Diana as she bathed; as punishment she turned
   him into a stag and he was then killed by his own
   hunting dogs

Shall by the angry goddess be transformed,
And running in the likeness of an hart,
By yelping hounds pulled down, and seem to die. 70
Such things as these best please his majesty.
My lord! Here comes the King and the nobles
From the parliament; I'll stand aside.

*Enter* EDWARD THE KING, LANCASTER, MORTIMER
SENIOR, MORTIMER JUNIOR, EDMUND, EARL OF KENT,
GUY, EARL OF WARWICK, *and attendants*

EDWARD  Lancaster.
LANCASTER  My lord?
GAVESTON  (*Aside*) That Earl of Lancaster do I abhor.
EDWARD  Will you not grant me this? (*Aside*) In spite of
   them
  I'll have my will, and these two Mortimers
  That cross me thus shall know I am displeased.
MORTIMER SENIOR  If you love us, my lord, hate
   Gaveston. 80
GAVESTON  (*Aside*) That villain Mortimer, I'll be his
   death.
MORTIMER JUNIOR  Mine uncle here, this earl, and I
   myself
  Were sworn to your father at his death,
  That he should ne'er return into the realm;
  And know, my lord, ere I will break my oath,
  This sword of mine that should offend your foes,
  Shall sleep within the scabbard at thy need,
  And underneath thy banners march who will,
  For Mortimer will hang his armour up.
GAVESTON  (*Aside*) *Mort Dieu!* 90
EDWARD  Well Mortimer, I'll make thee rue these
   words.
  Beseems it thee to contradict thy king?
  Frownst thou thereat, aspiring Lancaster?
  The sword shall plane the furrows of thy brows
  And hew these knees that now are grown so stiff.
  I will have Gaveston; and you shall know
  What danger 'tis to stand against your king.
GAVESTON  (*Aside*) Well done, Ned.
LANCASTER  My lord, why do you thus incense your
   peers
  That naturally would love and honour you, 100
  But for that base and obscure Gaveston?
  Four earldoms have I besides Lancaster:

Derby, Salisbury, Lincoln, Leicester.
These will I sell to give my soldiers pay,
Ere Gaveston shall stay within the realm.
Therefore if he be come, expel him straight.
KENT  Barons and earls, your pride hath made me mute.
  But now I'll speak, and to the proof I hope:
  I do remember in my father's days,
  Lord Percy of the North, being highly moved, 110
  Braved Mowbery in presence of the King.
  For which, had not his highness loved him well,
  He should have lost his head, but with his look
  The undaunted spirit of Percy was appeased,
  And Mowbery and he were reconciled.
  Yet dare you brave the King unto his face?
  Brother, revenge it; and let these their heads
  Preach upon poles for trespass of their tongues.
WARWICK  O, our heads!
EDWARD  Ay, yours; and therefore I would wish you
   grant. 120
WARWICK  Bridle thy anger, gentle Mortimer.
MORTIMER JUNIOR  I cannot, nor I will not; I must
   speak.
  Cousin, our hands I hope shall fence our heads,
  And strike off his that makes you threaten us.
  Come uncle, let us leave the brainsick King,
  And henceforth parley with our naked swords.
MORTIMER SENIOR  Welshry hath men enough to save
   our heads.
WARWICK  All Warwickshire will love him for my sake.
LANCASTER  And northward Gaveston hath many
   friends.
  Adieu my lord; and either change your mind, 130
  Or look to see the throne where you should sit
  To float in blood, and at thy wanton head
  The glozing head of thy base minion thrown.

               *Exeunt* NOBLES *except* KENT
EDWARD  I cannot brook these haughty menaces:
  Am I a king and must be overruled?

---

73  stand aside: Gaveston retreats to the side or back of the
   stage until l. 139
79  cross: oppose
90  *Mort Dieu!*: 'by God's death', reminding us of Gaveston's
   French origins. Later in the play 'Latin is used to
   characterise English nobility' (Kinney)
91  rue: regret
92  Beseems it thee: 'is it fitting for you'
98  Ned: familiar name for Edward
100  naturally: by reason of social rank

108  to the proof: irrefutably
110  moved: angry
111  Braved: challenged
118  Preach upon poles: the heads of executed traitors were
   displayed as a warning to others: see *The Knight of the
   Burning Pestle*, II.469–70
120  grant: assent
123  Cousin: Mortimer Junior's use of this familiar term to his
   king is presumptuous
   fence: shield
126  parley: negotiate
127  Welshry: the people of Wales
129  And northward . . . many friends: meant ironically.
   Lancaster implies exactly the opposite
133  glozing: flattering
   minion: a) servant; b) homosexual lover, derived from
   *mignon* (sweet) (French)
134  brook: endure

Brother, display my ensigns in the field.
I'll bandy with the barons and the earls,
And either die or live with Gaveston.

GAVESTON  I can no longer keep me from my lord.  **139**

*He steps forward*

EDWARD  What, Gaveston! Welcome! Kiss not my hand;
Embrace me, Gaveston, as I do thee!
Why shouldst thou kneel; knowest thou not who I
am?
Thy friend, thy self, another Gaveston!
Not Hylas was more mourned of Hercules
Than thou hast been of me since thy exile.

GAVESTON  And since I went from hence, no soul in
hell
Hath felt more torment than poor Gaveston.

EDWARD  I know it. (*To* KENT) Brother, welcome home
my friend.
(*To* GAVESTON) Now let the treacherous Mortimers
conspire,
And that high-minded Earl of Lancaster.  **150**
I have my wish, in that I joy thy sight,
And sooner shall the sea o'erwhelm my land
Than bear the ship that shall transport thee hence.
I here create thee Lord High Chamberlain,
Chief Secretary to the state and me,
Earl of Cornwall, King and Lord of Man.

GAVESTON  My lord, these titles far exceed my worth.

KENT  Brother, the least of these may well suffice
For one of greater birth than Gaveston.  **159**

EDWARD  Cease brother for I cannot brook these words.
(*To* GAVESTON) Thy worth, sweet friend, is far above
my gifts,
Therefore to equal it, receive my heart.
If for these dignities thou be envied,
I'll give thee more, for but to honour thee
Is Edward pleased with kingly regiment.
Fear'st thou thy person? Thou shalt have a guard.
Wants thou gold? Go to my treasury.
Wouldst thou be loved and feared? Receive my seal,
Save or condemn, and in our name command
What so thy mind affects or fancy likes.  **170**

GAVESTON  It shall suffice me to enjoy your love,
Which whiles I have, I think myself as great
As Caesar riding in the Roman street,
With captive kings at his triumphant car.

*Enter the* BISHOP OF COVENTRY

EDWARD  Whither goes my lord of Coventry so fast?

BISHOP OF COVENTRY  To celebrate your father's
exequies.
But is that wicked Gaveston returned?

EDWARD  Ay, priest, and lives to be revenged on thee
That wert the only cause of his exile.

GAVESTON  'Tis true, and but for reverence of these
robes  **180**
Thou shouldst not plod one foot beyond this place.

BISHOP OF COVENTRY  I did no more than I was bound
to do;
And Gaveston, unless thou be reclaimed,
As then I did incense the parliament,
So will I now, and thou shalt back to France.

GAVESTON  Saving your reverence, you must pardon me.

EDWARD  Throw off his golden mitre, rend his stole,
And in the channel christen him anew.

*Attacks* COVENTRY

KENT  Ah brother, lay not violent hands on him,
For he'll complain unto the See of Rome.  **190**

GAVESTON  Let him complain unto the See of Hell;
I'll be revenged on him for my exile.

EDWARD  No, spare his life, but seize upon his goods.
Be thou lord bishop, and receive his rents,
And make him serve thee as thy chaplain.
I give him thee; here, use him as thou wilt.

GAVESTON  He shall to prison, and there die in bolts.

EDWARD  Ay, to the Tower, the Fleet, or where thou wilt.

BISHOP OF COVENTRY  For this offence be thou accursed
of God.

EDWARD  Who's there?

*Enter* GUARDS

Convey this priest to the Tower.

---

136  ensigns: military banners
137  bandy: take and return blows (a metaphor from tennis)
144  Hylas: Hercules was grief-stricken when his beloved
youth Hylas was killed by water nymphs during the
voyage of the Argonauts in search of the Golden Fleece
150  high-minded: arrogant
151  joy: enjoy
156  King and Lord of Man: the Isle of Man enjoyed a certain
autonomy and, according to Gill, their rulers were known
as kings until 1829. The idea of Gaveston being a 'Lord
of Man' may also have a homoerotic overtone
165  regiment: royal authority
168  seal: a material token of royal authority (usually a ring)
170  affects: desires

174  car: chariot
176  exequies: funeral rites
183  reclaimed: subdued
184  incense: incite
186  Saving your reverence: a polite term here used
sarcastically
187  Throw off . . . rend his stole: seize his ecclesiastical head-
dress (mitre) and tear his vestment (stole)
188  channel: open sewer
190  See of Rome: the Pope
194  rents: a) rents from church properties; b) ecclesiastical taxes
197  bolts: leg irons
198  the Tower, the Fleet: the Tower of London (used for
political prisoners), the Fleet prison (used for common
prisoners and debtors)

BISHOP OF COVENTRY                                 True, true!

*Exit* BISHOP *under guard*

EDWARD  But in the meantime Gaveston, away,          201
And take possession of his house and goods.
Come, follow me, and thou shalt have my guard
To see it done and bring thee safe again.

GAVESTON  What should a priest do with so fair a
house?
A prison may beseem his holiness.

*Exeunt*

# Act I, scene ii

*Enter both the* MORTIMERS *on one side,* WARWICK, *and*
LANCASTER *on the other*

WARWICK  'Tis true, the Bishop is in the Tower,
And goods and body given to Gaveston.

LANCASTER  What, will they tyrannize upon the
Church?
Ah, wicked King! Accursèd Gaveston!
This ground which is corrupted with their steps
Shall be their timeless sepulchre, or mine.

MORTIMER JUNIOR  Well, let that peevish Frenchman
guard him sure;
Unless his breast be sword-proof he shall die.

MORTIMER SENIOR  How now, why droops the Earl of
Lancaster?

MORTIMER JUNIOR  Wherefore is Guy of Warwick
discontent?                                         10

LANCASTER  That villain Gaveston is made an earl.

MORTIMER SENIOR  An earl!

WARWICK  Ay, and besides, Lord Chamberlain of the
realm,
And Secretary too, and Lord of Man.

MORTIMER SENIOR  We may not, nor we will not suffer
this.

MORTIMER JUNIOR  Why post we not from hence to
levy men?

LANCASTER  'My Lord of Cornwall' now at every word;
And happy is the man whom he vouchsafes
For vailing of his bonnet one good look.

---

200  True, true: Coventry reacts to the fact that 'convey', as
      well as meaning 'conduct', commonly meant 'steal'
206  may beseem: may (ironically) be appropriate for a priest
      seeking ascetic conditions for holy meditation
  2  goods and body: see I.i.193–4
  3  tyrannize upon the church: Edward is seen as having
      usurped the authority of the Church by imprisoning a
      bishop
  7  peevish: foolish
      him: himself
 11  villain: a) rascal; b) a person of low birth
 16  post: travel at speed
      levy men: raise an army
 19  vailing: doffing

Thus, arm in arm, the King and he doth march—    20
Nay more, the guard upon his lordship waits,
And all the court begins to flatter him.

WARWICK  Thus leaning on the shoulder of the King,
He nods, and scorns, and smiles at those that pass.

MORTIMER SENIOR  Doth no man take exceptions at the
slave?

LANCASTER  All stomach him, but none dare speak a
word.

MORTIMER JUNIOR  Ah, that bewrays their baseness,
Lancaster.
Were all the earls and barons of my mind,
We'll hale him from the bosom of the King,
And at the court gate hang the peasant up,        30
Who, swoll'n with venom of ambitious pride,
Will be the ruin of the realm and us.

*Enter the* ARCHBISHOP OF CANTERBURY, *talking to a*
CHAPLAIN

WARWICK  Here comes my Lord of Canterbury's grace.

LANCASTER  His countenance bewrays he is displeased.

ARCHBISHOP OF CANTERBURY  (*To* CHAPLAIN) First
were his sacred garments rent and torn,
Then laid they violent hands upon him next,
Himself imprisoned and his goods asseized;
This certify the Pope. Away, take horse!

*Exit* CHAPLAIN

LANCASTER  My lord, will you take arms against the
King?

ARCHBISHOP OF CANTERBURY  What need I? God
himself is up in arms                              40
When violence is offered to the Church.

MORTIMER JUNIOR  Then will you join with us that be
his peers
To banish or behead that Gaveston?

ARCHBISHOP OF CANTERBURY  What else, my lords?
For it concerns me near;
The bishopric of Coventry is his.

*Enter* ISABELLA *the Queen*

MORTIMER JUNIOR  Madam, whither walks your
majesty so fast?

ISABELLA  Unto the forest, gentle Mortimer,
To live in grief and baleful discontent;
For now my lord the King regards me not,
But dotes upon the love of Gaveston.              50

---

26  stomach: resent
27  bewrays: reveals
29  hale: drag
38  certify: inform
44  near: a) deeply; b) personally (as ecclesiastical business)
47  forest: wilderness, figuratively representing her sense of
      alienation from her husband
48  baleful: wretched

He claps his cheeks and hangs about his neck,
Smiles in his face and whispers in his ears;
And when I come he frowns, as who should say,
'Go whither thou wilt, seeing I have Gaveston.'
MORTIMER SENIOR  Is it not strange that he is thus
  bewitched?
MORTIMER JUNIOR  Madam, return unto the court
  again.
That sly inveigling Frenchman we'll exile,
Or lose our lives; and yet, ere that day come,
The King shall lose his crown, for we have power
And courage too, to be revenged at full.      **60**
ARCHBISHOP OF CANTERBURY  But yet lift not your
  swords against the King.
LANCASTER  No, but we'll lift Gaveston from hence.
WARWICK  And war must be the means, or he'll stay
  still.
ISABELLA  Then let him stay; for rather than my lord
Shall be oppressed by civil mutinies,
I will endure a melancholy life,
And let him frolic with his minion.
ARCHBISHOP OF CANTERBURY  My lords, to ease all this
  but hear me speak.
We and the rest that are his councillors
Will meet and with a general consent      **70**
Confirm his banishment with our hands and seals.
LANCASTER  What we confirm the King will frustrate.
MORTIMER JUNIOR  Then may we lawfully revolt from
  him.
WARWICK  But say, my lord, where shall this meeting
  be?
ARCHBISHOP OF CANTERBURY  At the New Temple.
MORTIMER JUNIOR  Content.
ARCHBISHOP OF CANTERBURY  And in the meantime I'll
  entreat you all
To cross to Lambeth, and there stay with me.
LANCASTER  Come then, let's away.
MORTIMER JUNIOR      Madam, farewell.
ISABELLA  Farewell, sweet Mortimer; and for my sake,
Forbear to levy arms against the King.      **81**
MORTIMER JUNIOR  Ay, if words will serve; if not, I
  must.
          *Exeunt*

---

51  claps: pats
57  inveigling: a) deceiving; b) seducing
62  lift: a) steal; b) hang
63  still: forever
72  frustrate: defeat
75  New Temple: 'A building established and used by the
    Knights Templar until their suppression in 1308'
    (Wiggins and Lindsey) and 'in Edward II's time, the site
    of frequent disputes between the crown and wealthy
    subjects' (Kinney)
78  Lambeth: Lambeth Palace, the London residence of the
    Archbishop of Canterbury since 1197

# Act I, scene iii

*Enter* GAVESTON *and the* EARL OF KENT

GAVESTON  Edmund, the mighty prince of Lancaster,
That hath more earldoms than an ass can bear,
And both the Mortimers, two goodly men,
With Guy of Warwick, that redoubted knight,
Are gone towards Lambeth; there let them remain.
          *Exeunt*

# Act I, scene iv

*Enter* NOBLES LANCASTER, WARWICK, PEMBROKE,
MORTIMER SENIOR, MORTIMER JUNIOR, *and the*
ARCHBISHOP OF CANTERBURY, *with attendants*

LANCASTER  Here is the form of Gaveston's exile;
May it please your lordship to subscribe your name.
ARCHBISHOP OF CANTERBURY  Give me the paper.
LANCASTER  Quick, quick, my lord; I long to write my
  name.
WARWICK  But I long more to see him banished hence.
MORTIMER JUNIOR  The name of Mortimer shall fright
  the King,
Unless he be declined from that base peasant.

*Enter* EDWARD THE KING *and* GAVESTON *and* KENT.
EDWARD *takes the throne, seating* GAVESTON *at his side*

EDWARD  What, are you moved that Gaveston sits
  here?
It is our pleasure; we will have it so.
LANCASTER  Your grace doth well to place him by your
  side,      **10**
For nowhere else the new earl is so safe.
MORTIMER SENIOR  What man of noble birth can brook
  this sight?
*Quam male conveniunt!*
See what a scornful look the peasant casts.
PEMBROKE  Can kingly lions fawn on creeping ants?
WARWICK  Ignoble vassal, that like Phaëthon
Aspir'st unto the guidance of the sun.

---

1  Edmund: Gaveston addresses Kent in an informal way
4  redoubted: feared
1  form: document
7  declined: separated
8  sits here: Gaveston takes the place normally reserved for
    Queen Isabella
13  *Quam male conveniunt!*: 'How badly they suit one
    another!'
16  Ignoble vassal: slave of low birth
    Phaëthon: 'the son of Phoebus Apollo, the sun-god, who
    presumptuously asked his father to let him drive the
    chariot of the sun, lost control of the horses, was struck
    by a bolt of lightning, and plummeted disastrously to
    earth' (Forker)

MORTIMER JUNIOR  Their downfall is at hand, their
  forces down;
  We will not thus be faced and over-peered.
EDWARD  Lay hands on that traitor Mortimer!     **20**
MORTIMER SENIOR  Lay hands on that traitor
  Gaveston!     *The* NOBLES *draw their swords*
KENT  Is this the duty that you owe your king?
WARWICK  We know our duties; let him know his peers.
     *The* NOBLES *seize* GAVESTON
EDWARD  Whither will you bear him? Stay, or ye shall
  die.
MORTIMER SENIOR  We are no traitors, therefore
  threaten not.
GAVESTON  No, threaten not, my lord, but pay them
  home.
  Were I a king—
MORTIMER JUNIOR  Thou villain, wherefore talks thou
  of a king,
  That hardly art a gentleman by birth?
EDWARD  Were he a peasant, being my minion,     **30**
  I'll make the proudest of you stoop to him.
LANCASTER  My lord, you may not thus disparage us.
  Away, I say, with hateful Gaveston.
MORTIMER SENIOR  And with the Earl of Kent that
  favours him.
     *Exeunt* GAVESTON *and* KENT *under guard*
EDWARD  Nay, then lay violent hands upon your king.
  Here, Mortimer, sit thou in Edward's throne;
  Warwick and Lancaster, wear you my crown.
  Was ever king thus overruled as I?
LANCASTER  Learn then to rule us better and the realm.
MORTIMER JUNIOR  What we have done, our heart-
  blood shall maintain.     **40**
WARWICK  Think you that we can brook this upstart
  pride?
EDWARD  Anger and wrathful fury stops my speech.
ARCHBISHOP OF CANTERBURY  Why are you moved? Be
  patient, my lord,
  And see what we your councillors have done.
     *He gives the document of Gaveston's exile to* EDWARD
MORTIMER JUNIOR  My lords, now let us all be resolute,
  And either have our wills or lose our lives.
EDWARD  Meet you for this, proud overdaring peers?
  Ere my sweet Gaveston shall part from me,
  This isle shall fleet upon the ocean
  And wander to the unfrequented Inde.     **50**

ARCHBISHOP OF CANTERBURY  You know that I am
  legate to the Pope;
  On your allegiance to the See of Rome,
  Subscribe as we have done to his exile.
MORTIMER JUNIOR  Curse him if he refuse, and then
  may we
  Depose him and elect another king.
EDWARD  Ay, there it goes, but yet I will not yield.
  Curse me. Depose me. Do the worst you can.
LANCASTER  Then linger not, my lord, but do it
  straight.
ARCHBISHOP OF CANTERBURY  Remember how the
  Bishop was abused;
  Either banish him that was the cause thereof,     **60**
  Or I will presently discharge these lords
  Of duty and allegiance due to thee.
EDWARD  It boots me not to threat; I must speak fair,
  The legate of the Pope will be obeyed.
  (*To* CANTERBURY) My lord, you shall be Chancellor
  of the realm;
  Thou Lancaster, High Admiral of our fleet.
  Young Mortimer and his uncle shall be earls,
  And you, Lord Warwick, President of the North,
  (*To* PEMBROKE) And thou of Wales. If this content
  you not,
  Make several kingdoms of this monarchy,     **70**
  And share it equally amongst you all,
  So I may have some nook or corner left
  To frolic with my dearest Gaveston.
ARCHBISHOP OF CANTERBURY  Nothing shall alter us;
  we are resolved.
LANCASTER  Come, come, subscribe.
MORTIMER JUNIOR  Why should you love him whom
  the world hates so?
EDWARD  Because he loves me more than all the world.
  Ah, none but rude and savage-minded men
  Would seek the ruin of my Gaveston;
  You that be noble born should pity him.     **80**
WARWICK  You that are princely born should shake him
  off.
  For shame subscribe, and let the lown depart.
MORTIMER SENIOR  Urge him, my lord.
ARCHBISHOP OF CANTERBURY  Are you content to
  banish him the realm?
EDWARD  I see I must, and therefore am content;
  Instead of ink, I'll write it with my tears.
     *He signs the document*

---

19  faced: bullied
    over-peered: looked down upon, with a pun on 'peer'
    (lord)
26  pay them home: chastise them
32  disparage: vilify
49  fleet: drift
50  Inde: a) India; b) East Indies. Edward's image implies 'to
    the ends of the earth' (Kinney)

51  legate: representative
54  Curse: excommunicate
61–2  Or I . . . to thee: when rulers were excommunicated,
    their subjects were absolved of all allegiance to them, as
    was the case with the excommunication of Elizabeth I in
    1570
78  rude: uncivilised
82  lown: peasant

MORTIMER JUNIOR  The King is love-sick for his
   minion.
EDWARD  'Tis done, and now accursèd hand fall off.
LANCASTER  Give it me; I'll have it published in the
   streets.
MORTIMER JUNIOR  I'll see him presently dispatched
   away.                                   90
ARCHBISHOP OF CANTERBURY  Now is my heart at ease.
WARWICK                   And so is mine.
PEMBROKE  This will be good news to the common
   sort.
MORTIMER SENIOR  Be it or no, he shall not linger here.
                   *Exeunt all, except* EDWARD
EDWARD  How fast they run to banish him I love;
   They would not stir, were it to do me good.
   Why should a king be subject to a priest?
   Proud Rome, that hatchest such imperial grooms,
   For these thy superstitious taper-lights,
   Wherewith thy antichristian churches blaze,
   I'll fire thy crazèd buildings and enforce      100
   The papal towers to kiss the lowly ground,
   With slaughtered priests make Tiber's channel swell,
   And banks raised higher with their sepulchres.
   As for the peers that back the clergy thus,
   If I be king, not one of them shall live.

*Enter* GAVESTON

GAVESTON  My lord, I hear it whispered everywhere
   That I am banished and must fly the land.
EDWARD  'Tis true, sweet Gaveston. O were it false!
   The legate of the Pope will have it so,
   And thou must hence, or I shall be deposed.     110
   But I will reign to be revenged of them,
   And therefore, sweet friend, take it patiently.
   Live where thou wilt—I'll send thee gold enough.
   And long thou shalt not stay, or if thou dost,
   I'll come to thee; my love shall ne'er decline.
GAVESTON  Is all my hope turned to this hell of grief?
EDWARD  Rend not my heart with thy too-piercing
   words.
   Thou from this land, I from my self am banished.
GAVESTON  To go from hence grieves not poor
   Gaveston,
   But to forsake you, in whose gracious looks     120
   The blessedness of Gaveston remains,
   For nowhere else seeks he felicity.
EDWARD  And only this torments my wretched soul,
   That whether I will or no, thou must depart.

   Be Governor of Ireland in my stead,
   And there abide till fortune call thee home.
   Here, take my picture, and let me wear thine.
                 *They exchange miniature portraits*
   O might I keep thee here, as I do this,
   Happy were I, but now most miserable.
GAVESTON  'Tis something to be pitied of a king.     130
EDWARD  Thou shalt not hence; I'll hide thee,
   Gaveston.
GAVESTON  I shall be found, and then 'twill grieve me
   more.
EDWARD  Kind words and mutual talk makes our grief
   greater.
   Therefore, with dumb embracement, let us part—
   Stay, Gaveston, I cannot leave thee thus.
GAVESTON  For every look my lord drops down a tear;
   Seeing I must go, do not renew my sorrow.
EDWARD  The time is little that thou hast to stay,
   And therefore give me leave to look my fill.
   But come, sweet friend, I'll bear thee on thy way.   140
GAVESTON  The peers will frown.
EDWARD  I pass not for their anger; come, let's go.
   O that we might as well return as go.

*Enter* EDMUND EARL OF KENT *and* QUEEN
ISABELLA

ISABELLA  Whither goes my lord?
EDWARD  Fawn not on me, French strumpet; get thee
   gone.
ISABELLA  On whom but on my husband should I
   fawn?
GAVESTON  On Mortimer, with whom, ungentle
   Queen—
   I say no more; judge you the rest, my lord.
ISABELLA  In saying this, thou wrongst me, Gaveston.
   Is't not enough that thou corrupts my lord,     150
   And art a bawd to his affections,
   But thou must call mine honour thus in question?
GAVESTON  I mean not so; your grace must pardon me.
EDWARD  Thou art too familiar with that Mortimer,
   And by thy means is Gaveston exiled;
   But I would wish thee reconcile the lords,
   Or thou shalt ne'er be reconciled to me.
ISABELLA  Your highness knows it lies not in my power.

---

89  published: proclaimed
97  imperial grooms: imperious servants
98  taper-lights: candles for devotional use
100  crazèd: a) cracked; b) unsound
102  Tiber's channel: the River Tiber in Rome
121  blessedness: exceptional happiness

131  hence: go
134  dumb: silent
140  bear: accompany
142  pass: care
SD  *Enter* EDMUND: Kent has no lines but his quiet
    witnessing of the exchange between Edward, Isabella and
    Gaveston is important in explaining his later actions
147  Gaveston is the first to accuse Isabella of adultery
151  bawd to his affections: procurer, pander to his (sexual)
    desires

EDWARD Away then, touch me not; come Gaveston.

ISABELLA Villain, 'tis thou that robb'st me of my lord.

GAVESTON Madam, 'tis you that rob me of my lord. **161**

EDWARD Speak not unto her; let her droop and pine.

ISABELLA Wherein, my lord, have I deserved these
words?
Witness the tears that Isabella sheds,
Witness this heart, that sighing for thee breaks,
How dear my lord is to poor Isabel.

EDWARD And witness heaven how dear thou art to me.
There weep; for till my Gaveston be repealed,
Assure thyself thou com'st not in my sight.

*Exeunt* EDWARD *and* GAVESTON *and* KENT

ISABELLA O miserable and distressèd Queen! **170**
Would when I left sweet France and was embarked,
That charming Circe, walking on the waves,
Had changed my shape, or at the marriage-day
The cup of Hymen had been full of poison,
Or with those arms that twined about my neck
I had been stifled, and not lived to see
The King my lord thus to abandon me.
Like frantic Juno will I fill the earth
With ghastly murmur of my sighs and cries,
For never doted Jove on Ganymede **180**
So much as he on cursèd Gaveston.
But that will more exasperate his wrath;
I must entreat him, I must speak him fair,
And be a means to call home Gaveston.
And yet he'll ever dote on Gaveston,
And so am I forever miserable.

*Enter the* NOBLES LANCASTER, WARWICK, PEMBROKE,
MORTIMER SENIOR, *and* MORTIMER JUNIOR *to* ISABELLA
THE QUEEN

---

159 touch me not: a) keep away from me; b) do not meddle
in my business
167 And witness . . . to me: Wiggins and Lindsey note that
as this line is spoken 'many productions have Edward
and Gaveston embrace or kiss as lovers'
168 repealed: recalled from exile
172 Circe: enchantress who turned Odysseus's men into pigs.
Marlowe's source is Ovid's *Metamorphoses*, XIV
174 Hymen: god of marriage
175 those arms: Edward's arms
178–80 Like frantic . . . on Ganymede: Juno fell into a frenzy
of jealousy when her husband Jupiter chose the youth
Ganymede to be his cup-bearer. Marlowe's source is
*Metamorphoses*, X. The comparison of Ganymede to
Gaveston in this scene 'underscores the homosexuality of
the king's passion, for a "Ganymede" was the standard
term in Marlowe's age for the younger partner in a love
affair between males' (Forker)
179 murmur: a) rumour; b) report
182 exasperate: aggravate
183 entreat: a) negotiate with; b) beg
fair: courteously
185 ever: always

LANCASTER Look where the sister of the King of
France
Sits wringing of her hands and beats her breast.

WARWICK The King, I fear, hath ill entreated her.

PEMBROKE Hard is the heart that injures such a saint.

MORTIMER JUNIOR I know 'tis 'long of Gaveston she
weeps. **191**

MORTIMER SENIOR Why? He is gone.

MORTIMER JUNIOR      Madam, how fares your grace?

ISABELLA Ah, Mortimer! Now breaks the King's hate
forth,
And he confesseth that he loves me not.

MORTIMER JUNIOR Cry quittance, madam, then; and
love not him.

ISABELLA No, rather will I die a thousand deaths.
And yet I love in vain; he'll ne'er love me.

LANCASTER Fear ye not, madam; now his minion's
gone,
His wanton humour will be quickly left.

ISABELLA O never, Lancaster! I am enjoined **200**
To sue unto you all for his repeal.
This wills my lord, and this must I perform
Or else be banished from his highness' presence.

LANCASTER For his repeal! Madam, he comes not back
Unless the sea cast up his shipwrack body.

WARWICK And to behold so sweet a sight as that
There's none here but would run his horse to death.

MORTIMER JUNIOR But madam, would you have us call
him home?

ISABELLA Ay, Mortimer, for till he be restored,
The angry King hath banished me the court; **210**
And therefore, as thou lovest and tend'rest me,
Be thou my advocate unto these peers.

MORTIMER JUNIOR What, would ye have me plead for
Gaveston?

MORTIMER SENIOR Plead for him he that will, I am
resolved.

LANCASTER And so am I; my lord, dissuade the Queen.

ISABELLA O Lancaster, let him dissuade the King,
For 'tis against my will he should return.

WARWICK Then speak not for him; let the peasant go.

ISABELLA 'Tis for myself I speak, and not for him.

PEMBROKE No speaking will prevail, and therefore
cease. **220**

MORTIMER JUNIOR Fair Queen, forbear to angle for the
fish
Which, being caught, strikes him that takes it dead—

---

189 entreated: treated
191 'long of: on account of (London dialect form)
195 Cry quittance: a) retaliate; b) renounce the marriage
199 wanton humour: amorous disposition (as in the
Elizabethan belief that bodily fluids (humours) were
responsible for the individual's state of mind)
200 enjoined: obliged
211 tend'rest: cares for

I mean that vile torpedo, Gaveston,
That now, I hope, floats on the Irish seas.
ISABELLA Sweet Mortimer, sit down by me a while,
And I will tell thee reasons of such weight
As thou wilt soon subscribe to his repeal.
MORTIMER JUNIOR It is impossible; but speak your
   mind.
ISABELLA Then thus—but none shall hear it but
   ourselves.

              ISABELLA *and* MORTIMER JUNIOR *talk apart*
LANCASTER My lords, albeit the Queen win Mortimer,
Will you be resolute and hold with me?     **231**
MORTIMER SENIOR Not I, against my nephew.
PEMBROKE Fear not, the Queen's words cannot alter
   him.
WARWICK No? Do but mark how earnestly she pleads.
LANCASTER And see how coldly his looks make denial.
WARWICK She smiles! Now, for my life, his mind is
   changed.
LANCASTER I'll rather lose his friendship, I, than grant.
MORTIMER JUNIOR (*Returning*) Well, of necessity, it
   must be so.
My lords, that I abhor base Gaveston
I hope your honours make no question;     **240**
And therefore, though I plead for his repeal,
'Tis not for his sake, but for our avail—
Nay, for the realm's behoof and for the King's.
LANCASTER Fie Mortimer, dishonour not thyself!
Can this be true, 'twas good to banish him?
And is this true, to call him home again?
Such reasons make white black and dark night day.
MORTIMER JUNIOR My lord of Lancaster, mark the
   respect.
LANCASTER In no respect can contraries be true.   **249**
ISABELLA Yet, good my lord, hear what he can allege.
WARWICK All that he speaks is nothing; we are resolved.
MORTIMER JUNIOR Do you not wish that Gaveston
   were dead?
PEMBROKE I would he were.
MORTIMER JUNIOR Why then, my lord, give me but
   leave to speak.
MORTIMER SENIOR But nephew, do not play the
   sophister.
MORTIMER JUNIOR This which I urge is of a burning
   zeal

To mend the King and do our country good.
Know you not Gaveston hath store of gold,
Which may in Ireland purchase him such friends
As he will front the mightiest of us all?     **260**
And whereas he shall live and be beloved,
'Tis hard for us to work his overthrow.
WARWICK Mark you but that, my lord of Lancaster.
MORTIMER JUNIOR But were he here, detested as he is,
How easily might some base slave be suborned
To greet his lordship with a poniard,
And none so much as blame the murderer,
But rather praise him for that brave attempt,
And in the chronicle, enrol his name
For purging of the realm of such a plague.     **270**
PEMBROKE He saith true.
LANCASTER Ay, but how chance this was not done
   before?
MORTIMER JUNIOR Because, my lords, it was not
   thought upon.
Nay more, when he shall know it lies in us
To banish him, and then to call him home,
'Twill make him vail the topflag of his pride
And fear to offend the meanest nobleman.
MORTIMER SENIOR But how if he do not, nephew?
MORTIMER JUNIOR Then may we with some colour rise
   in arms,
For howsoever we have borne it out,     **280**
'Tis treason to be up against the King.
So shall we have the people of our side,
Which, for his father's sake, lean to the King
But cannot brook a night-grown mushroom—
Such a one as my lord of Cornwall is—
Should bear us down of the nobility.
And when the commons and the nobles join,
'Tis not the King can buckler Gaveston;
We'll pull him from the strongest hold he hath.
My lords, if to perform this I be slack,     **290**
Think me as base a groom as Gaveston.
LANCASTER On that condition Lancaster will grant.

---

223  torpedo: cramp-fish or sting-ray
224  floats: sails
226  weight: importance
234  mark: observe
237  grant: assent
242  avail: advantage
243  behoof: benefit
248  respect: special circumstances
250  allege: offer as a reason
255  sophister: philosopher who employs specious arguments

257  mend: reform
260  front: confront
261  whereas: while
265  suborned: bribed
266  poniard: dagger
268  brave attempt: justified attack
269  the chronicle: history
276  vail the topflag: lower a flag (colour) in submission
     (naval)
279  colour: pretext
282  of: on
284  night-grown mushroom: a metaphor for a political or
     social upstart (since mushrooms can spring up overnight)
286  Should bear us down: overwhelm us
288  buckler: shield
289  hold: stronghold, castle
291  groom: servant

PEMBROKE  And so will Pembroke.
WARWICK  And I.
MORTIMER SENIOR  And I.
MORTIMER JUNIOR  In this I count me highly gratified,
    And Mortimer will rest at your command.
ISABELLA  And when this favour Isabel forgets,
    Then let her live abandoned and forlorn.

*Enter* KING EDWARD *mourning, with* BEAUMONT *and the*
CLERK OF THE CROWN, *with attendants*

    But see, in happy time, my lord the King,    **300**
    Having brought the Earl of Cornwall on his way,
    Is new returned. This news will glad him much,
    Yet not so much as me; I love him more
    Than he can Gaveston. Would he loved me
    But half so much, then were I treble blessed.
EDWARD  He's gone, and for his absence thus I mourn.
    Did never sorrow go so near my heart
    As doth the want of my sweet Gaveston;
    And could my crown's revenue bring him back,
    I would freely give it to his enemies    **310**
    And think I gained, having bought so dear a friend.
ISABELLA  Hark how he harps upon his minion.
EDWARD  My heart is as an anvil unto sorrow,
    Which beats upon it like the Cyclops' hammers,
    And with the noise turns up my giddy brain
    And makes me frantic for my Gaveston.
    Ah, had some bloodless Fury rose from hell,
    And with kingly sceptre struck me dead,
    When I was forced to leave my Gaveston.
LANCASTER  *Diablo!* What passions call you these?    **320**
ISABELLA  My gracious lord, I come to bring you news.
EDWARD  That you have parlied with your Mortimer.
ISABELLA  That Gaveston, my lord, shall be repealed.
EDWARD  Repealed? The news is too sweet to be true.
ISABELLA  But will you love me if you find it so?
EDWARD  If it be so, what will not Edward do?
ISABELLA  For Gaveston, but not for Isabel.
EDWARD  For thee, fair Queen, if thou lov'st Gaveston;
    I'll hang a golden tongue about thy neck,
    Seeing thou hast pleaded with so good success.    **330**
                *He embraces her*
ISABELLA  No other jewels hang about my neck
    Than these, my lord; nor let me have more wealth
    Than I may fetch from this rich treasury.
    O how a kiss revives poor Isabel.
EDWARD  Once more receive my hand, and let this be
    A second marriage 'twixt thyself and me.

---

314  Cyclops' hammers: in classical mythology Cyclops forged
      thunderbolts for the gods
317  Fury: the Furies tormented wrongdoers in the
      underworld
320  *Diablo!*: the devil! (Spanish)
329  golden tongue: an item of jewellery
332  Than these: i.e. Edward's arms

ISABELLA  And may it prove more happy than the first.
    My gentle lord, bespeak these nobles fair
    That wait attendance for a gracious look,
    And on their knees salute your majesty.    **340**
                *The* NOBLES *kneel*
EDWARD  Courageous Lancaster, embrace thy king,
    And as gross vapours perish by the sun,
    Even so let hatred with thy sovereign's smile;
    Live thou with me as my companion.
LANCASTER  This salutation overjoys my heart.
EDWARD  Warwick shall be my chiefest counsellor:
    These silver hairs will more adorn my court
    Than gaudy silks or rich embroidery.
    Chide me, sweet Warwick, if I go astray.
WARWICK  Slay me, my lord, when I offend your grace.
EDWARD  In solemn triumphs and in public shows    **351**
    Pembroke shall bear the sword before the King.
PEMBROKE  And with this sword Pembroke will fight
    for you.
EDWARD  But wherefore walks young Mortimer aside?
    Be thou commander of our royal fleet,
    Or if that lofty office like thee not,
    I make thee here Lord Marshal of the realm.
MORTIMER JUNIOR  My lord, I'll marshal so your
    enemies
    As England shall be quiet and you safe.
EDWARD  And as for you, Lord Mortimer of Chirke,
    Whose great achievements in our foreign war    **361**
    Deserves no common place nor mean reward,
    Be you the general of the levied troops
    That now are ready to assail the Scots.
MORTIMER SENIOR  In this your grace hath highly
    honoured me,
    For with my nature war doth best agree.
ISABELLA  Now is the King of England rich and strong,
    Having the love of his renownèd peers.
EDWARD  Ay, Isabel, ne'er was my heart so light.
    Clerk of the Crown, direct our warrant forth    **370**
    For Gaveston to Ireland; Beaumont, fly
    As fast as Iris or Jove's Mercury.

---

338  bespeak: speak to
342  gross vapours: thick mists, fog
348  gaudy: ornate
352  the sword: the sword of state
356  like: please
360  Mortimer of Chirke: Mortimer Senior, whose estate was
      in the border (Marches) area of Shropshire (England)
      and Wales. Mortimer Junior (of Wigmore) held lands
      further south on the border between the English county
      of Herefordshire and Wales
370  Clerk of the Crown: an officer of the court responsible
      for drawing up writs
372  Iris or Jove's Mercury: in classical mythology Iris and
      Mercury were messengers for Juno and Jupiter
      respectively

BEAUMONT It shall be done, my gracious lord.

*Exit* BEAUMONT, *with the clerk of the crown*

EDWARD Lord Mortimer, we leave you to your charge.
Now let us in and feast it royally
Against our friend the Earl of Cornwall comes.
We'll have a general tilt and tournament,
And then his marriage shall be solemnized;
For wot you not that I have made him sure
Unto our cousin, the Earl of Gloucester's heir?    380

LANCASTER Such news we hear, my lord.

EDWARD That day, if not for him, yet for my sake,
Who in the triumph will be challenger,
Spare for no cost; we will requite your love.

WARWICK In this, or aught, your highness shall
command us.

EDWARD Thanks, gentle Warwick; come, let's in and
revel.    *Exeunt all, except the* MORTIMERS

MORTIMER SENIOR Nephew, I must to Scotland; thou
stayest here.
Leave now to oppose thyself against the King;
Thou seest by nature he is mild and calm,
And seeing his mind so dotes on Gaveston,    390
Let him without controlment have his will.
The mightiest kings have had their minions:
Great Alexander loved Hephaestion;
The conquering Hercules for Hylas wept;
And for Patroclus stern Achilles drooped.
And not kings only, but the wisest men:
The Roman Tully loved Octavius,
Grave Socrates, wild Alcibiades.
Then let his grace, whose youth is flexible
And promiseth as much as we can wish,    400
Freely enjoy that vain light-headed Earl,
For riper years will wean him from such toys.

MORTIMER JUNIOR Uncle, his wanton humour grieves
not me,
But this I scorn, that one so basely born
Should by his sovereign's favour grow so pert,
And riot it with the treasure of the realm
While soldiers mutiny for want of pay.
He wears a lord's revenue on his back,
And Midas-like he jets it in the court
With base outlandish cullions at his heels,    410
Whose proud fantastic liveries make such show
As if that Proteus, god of shapes, appeared.
I have not seen a dapper jack so brisk;
He wears a short Italian hooded cloak,
Larded with pearl; and in his Tuscan cap
A jewel of more value than the crown.
Whiles other walk below, the King and he
From out a window laugh at such as we,
And flout our train and jest at our attire.
Uncle, 'tis this that makes me impatient.    420

MORTIMER SENIOR But nephew, now you see the King
is changed.

MORTIMER JUNIOR Then so am I, and live to do him
service;
But whiles I have a sword, a hand, a heart,
I will not yield to any such upstart.
You know my mind. Come, uncle, let's away.

*Exeunt*

# Act II, scene i

*Enter* SPENCER JUNIOR *and* BALDOCK

BALDOCK Spencer,
Seeing that our lord th' Earl of Gloucester's dead,
Which of the nobles dost thou mean to serve?

SPENCER JUNIOR Not Mortimer, nor any of his side,
Because the King and he are enemies.
Baldock, learn this of me: a factious lord
Shall hardly do himself good, much less us;
But he that hath the favour of a king
May with one word advance us while we live.
The liberal Earl of Cornwall is the man    10

---

376 Against: until
379 sure: betrothed
380 the Earl of Gloucester's heir: i.e. Lady Margaret de Clare
391 controlment: restraint
393–5 Alexander loved . . . stern Achilles: 'famous male
companions and couples sometimes portrayed as
homosexual unions' (Kinney)
397 Tully loved Octavius: Marcus Tullius Cicero (106–43 BC),
a Roman statesman, and Octavius Caesar (63 BC–AD 14).
There is no recorded evidence of a homosexual
relationship between these two men although Cicero
expressed great loyalty to Octavius
398 Socrates, wild Alcibiades: Socrates, the Greek
philosopher (c. 450–404 BC) argued for the purity of
homosexual love. Alcibiades was his pupil
402 toys: trifles

409 Midas-like: King Midas of Phrygia was given the power
of turning anything he touched into gold by the Greek
god Dionysus
jets: struts
410 outlandish cullions: foreign low fellows
412 Proteus: a sea god who could change shape
413 dapper jack: fashionable gentleman (see the character
Jack Dapper in *The Roaring Girl*)
brisk: smartly dressed
414–15 Italian hooded cloak: Gaveston's Italian clothes may
signify both his politics and his homosexuality since Italy
was thought of by the Elizabethans as a place of both
political (Machiavellian) intrigue and sexual 'deviance'
(see Introduction)
415 Larded: encrusted
417 other: others
419 flout our train: mock our attendants
6 factious: seditious
10 liberal: a) gentle (as in a gentleman); b) licentious

On whose good fortune Spencer's hope depends.
BALDOCK  What, mean you then to be his follower?
SPENCER JUNIOR  No, his companion; for he loves me well
And would have once preferred me to the King.
BALDOCK  But he is banished; there's small hope of him.
SPENCER JUNIOR  Ay, for a while; but, Baldock, mark the end:
A friend of mine told me in secrecy
That he's repealed and sent for back again;
And even now, a post came from the court
With letters to our lady from the King,　　20
And as she read, she smiled, which makes me think
It is about her lover, Gaveston.
BALDOCK  'Tis like enough, for since he was exiled,
She neither walks abroad nor comes in sight.
But I had thought the match had been broke off
And that his banishment had changed her mind.
SPENCER JUNIOR  Our lady's first love is not wavering;
My life for thine, she will have Gaveston.
BALDOCK  Then hope I by her means to be preferred,
Having read unto her since she was a child.　　30
SPENCER JUNIOR  Then, Baldock, you must cast the scholar off
And learn to court it like a gentleman.
'Tis not a black coat and a little band,
A velvet-caped cloak, faced before with serge,
And smelling to a nosegay all the day,
Or holding of a napkin in your hand,
Or saying a long grace at a table's end,
Or making low legs to a nobleman,
Or looking downward, with your eyelids close,
And saying, 'Truly, an't may please your honour',　　40
Can get you any favour with great men.
You must be proud, bold, pleasant, resolute,
And now and then, stab, as occasion serves.
BALDOCK  Spencer, thou knowest I hate such formal toys,
And use them but of mere hypocrisy.
Mine old lord, whiles he lived, was so precise

That he would take exceptions at my buttons,
And, being like pins' heads, blame me for the bigness,
Which made me curate-like in mine attire,
Though inwardly licentious enough　　50
And apt for any kind of villainy.
I am none of these common pedants, I,
That cannot speak without 'propterea quod'.
SPENCER JUNIOR  But one of those that saith 'quandoquidem'
And hath a special gift to form a verb.
BALDOCK  Leave off this jesting—here my lady comes.
*They draw aside*

*Enter the* LADY MARGARET DE CLARE

LADY MARGARET  The grief for his exile was not so much
As is the joy of his returning home.
This letter came from my sweet Gaveston.
*She reads a letter*
What needst thou, love, thus to excuse thyself?　　60
I know thou couldst not come and visit me.
'I will not long be from thee, though I die':
This argues the entire love of my lord;
'When I forsake thee, death seize on my heart.'
But rest thee here where Gaveston shall sleep.
Now to the letter of my lord the King.
*She reads another letter*
He wills me to repair unto the court
And meet my Gaveston. Why do I stay,
Seeing that he talks thus of my marriage-day?
Who's there? Baldock?　　70

BALDOCK *and* SPENCER JUNIOR *come forward*

See that my coach be ready; I must hence.
BALDOCK  It shall be done, madam.
LADY MARGARET  And meet me at the park pale presently.　　*Exit* BALDOCK
Spencer, stay you and bear me company,
For I have joyful news to tell thee of.
My lord of Cornwall is a-coming over
And will be at the court as soon as we.
SPENCER JUNIOR  I knew the King would have him home again.
LADY MARGARET  If all things sort out, as I hope they will,
Thy service, Spencer, shall be thought upon.　　80

---

16　end: conclusion
20　our lady: Margaret de Clare, daughter of the Earl of Gloucester
30　Having read . . . a child: Baldock is Margaret's tutor
32　court it: behave like a courtier (rather than a scholar)
33–40　Spencer Junior describes the typical dress of a (sixteenth-century) poor scholar
35　nosegay: posy of flowers
36　napkin: handkerchief
37　at a table's end: i.e. at the socially inferior end of a formal meal
38　making low legs: bowing
43　stab: a) betray; b) make quick repartee (with pun on sexual intercourse)

53–4　'propterea quod' and 'quandoquidem': both mean 'because', 'but presumably one was regarded as ponderous, the other elegant. Baldock means he is no mere pedant, using old-fashioned constructions' (J. B. Steane)
55　to form: to conjugate
67　repair: come
71　coach: an anachronistic reference
73　park pale: the fence of an estate
　　presently: directly

SPENCER JUNIOR  I humbly thank your ladyship.
LADY MARGARET  Come, lead the way; I long till I am
    there.

                                        *Exeunt*

# Act II, scene ii

*Enter* EDWARD, ISABELLA THE QUEEN, LANCASTER,
MORTIMER JUNIOR, WARWICK, PEMBROKE, KENT,
*attendants*

EDWARD  The wind is good, I wonder why he stays.
    I fear me he is wrecked upon the sea.
ISABELLA  Look, Lancaster, how passionate he is,
    And still his mind runs on his minion.
LANCASTER  My lord—
EDWARD  How now, what news? Is Gaveston arrived?
MORTIMER JUNIOR  Nothing but Gaveston! What
        means your grace?
    You have matters of more weight to think upon;
    The King of France sets foot in Normandy.
EDWARD  A trifle! We'll expel him when we please.    10
    But tell me, Mortimer, what's thy device
    Against the stately triumph we decreed?
MORTIMER JUNIOR  A homely one, my lord, not worth
        the telling.
EDWARD  Prithee let me know it.
MORTIMER JUNIOR  But seeing you are so desirous, thus
        it is:
    A lofty cedar tree fair flourishing,
    On whose top branches kingly eagles perch,
    And by the bark a canker creeps me up
    And gets unto the highest bough of all;
    The motto: *Æque tandem.*                       20
EDWARD  And what is yours, my lord of Lancaster?
LANCASTER  My lord, mine's more obscure than
        Mortimer's:

---

82  long: am restless
2   upon the sea: Edward is waiting for Gaveston near
    Tynemouth Castle in the north-east of England as
    though Gaveston is sailing there from Ireland. The
    geography is anomalous, but Marlowe conflates
    Gaveston's two banishments, the first to Flanders and
    the second to Ireland. There is evidence that the two
    met actually met at Chester in the north-west of
    England
4   runs on: is preoccupied by
9   Normandy: then part of English crown territory
11  device: heraldic emblem
12  Against the stately triumph: prepared for the public
    entertainment
13  homely: plain
16  lofty cedar tree: symbol of social order
18  canker: worm (i.e. Gaveston)
    creeps me up: creeps up
20  *Æque tandem*: equal in height

Pliny reports there is a flying fish
Which all the other fishes deadly hate,
And therefore, being pursued, it takes the air;
No sooner is it up, but there's a fowl
That seizeth it. This fish, my lord, I bear;
The motto this: *Undique mors est.*
EDWARD  Proud Mortimer! Ungentle Lancaster!
    Is this the love you bear your sovereign?       30
    Is this the fruit your reconcilement bears?
    Can you in words make show of amity,
    And in your shields display your rancorous minds?
    What call you this but private libelling
    Against the Earl of Cornwall and my brother?
ISABELLA  Sweet husband, be content; they all love you.
EDWARD  They love me not that hate my Gaveston.
    I am that cedar; shake me not too much.
    And you the eagles; soar ye ne'er so high,
    I have the jesses that will pull you down,       40
    And '*Æque tandem*' shall that canker cry
    Unto the proudest peer of Britainy.
    Though thou compar'st him to a flying fish,
    And threatenest death whether he rise or fall,
    'Tis not the hugest monster of the sea
    Nor foulest harpy that shall swallow him.
MORTIMER JUNIOR  (*To the* NOBLES) If in his absence
        thus he favours him,
    What will he do whenas he shall be present?

*Enter* GAVESTON

LANCASTER  That shall we see: look where his lordship
        comes.
EDWARD  My Gaveston!                                 50
    Welcome to Tynemouth, welcome to thy friend.
    Thy absence made me droop and pine away;
    For as the lovers of fair Danaë,
    When she was locked up in a brazen tower,
    Desired her more and waxed outrageous,
    So did it sure with me; and now thy sight
    Is sweeter far than was thy parting hence
    Bitter and irksome to my sobbing heart.
GAVESTON  Sweet lord and King, your speech
        preventeth mine,

---

23  Pliny: Roman scholar (AD 23–79)
28  *Undique mors est*: death is on all sides
35  my brother: i.e. Gaveston
40  jesses: straps fastened to the legs of hunting birds
42  Britainy: Britain
46  harpy: classical bird-like creatures with female faces and
    breasts
53  Danaë: in classical mythology she was imprisoned in a
    tower by her father after an oracle prophesied that her
    child would kill him. She became pregnant by the god
    Jupiter who entered the tower as a shower of gold
55  waxed outrageous: grew unrestrained
59  preventeth: anticipates

Yet have I words left to express my joy: 60
The shepherd nipped with biting winter's rage
Frolics not more to see the painted spring
Than I do to behold your majesty.
EDWARD Will none of you salute my Gaveston?
LANCASTER Salute him? Yes! Welcome, Lord
Chamberlain.
MORTIMER JUNIOR Welcome is the good Earl of
Cornwall.
WARWICK Welcome, Lord Governor of the Isle of Man.
PEMBROKE Welcome, Master Secretary.
KENT Brother, do you hear them? 69
EDWARD Still will these earls and barons use me thus!
GAVESTON My lord, I cannot brook these injuries.
ISABELLA (*Aside*) Ay me, poor soul, when these begin
to jar.
EDWARD Return it to their throats; I'll be thy warrant.
GAVESTON Base leaden earls that glory in your birth,
Go sit at home and eat your tenants' beef,
And come not here to scoff at Gaveston,
Whose mounting thoughts did never creep so low
As to bestow a look on such as you.
LANCASTER Yet I disdain not to do this for you.
*Draws his sword*
EDWARD Treason, treason! Where's the traitor? 79
PEMBROKE (*pointing to* GAVESTON) Here, here!
EDWARD Convey hence Gaveston; they'll murder him.
GAVESTON The life of thee shall salve this foul disgrace.
MORTIMER JUNIOR Villain, thy life, unless I miss mine
aim. *He wounds* GAVESTON
ISABELLA Ah, furious Mortimer, what hast thou done?
MORTIMER JUNIOR No more than I would answer were
he slain. *Exit* GAVESTON *with attendants*
EDWARD Yes, more than thou canst answer, though he
live;
Dear shall you both aby this riotous deed.
Out of my presence! Come not near the court.
MORTIMER JUNIOR I'll not be barred the court for
Gaveston. 89
LANCASTER We'll hale him by the ears unto the block.
EDWARD Look to your own heads; his is sure enough.

---

62 painted: colourful
72 jar: quarrel
73 Return it to their throats: 'reject their abuse'
warrant: protection
74 leaden: as in cheap coinage (as opposed to gold coins
known as 'nobles')
75 eat your tenants' beef: a peculiarly French insult as the
French considered the English great eaters of beef; 'beef-
witted' also meant 'stupid'
82 salve: atone for
85 answer: answer for
87 both: i.e. Mortimer Junior and Lancaster
aby: pay for
91 sure: safe

WARWICK Look to your own crown, if you back him
thus.
KENT Warwick, these words do ill beseem thy years.
EDWARD Nay, all of them conspire to cross me thus;
But if I live, I'll tread upon their heads
That think with high looks thus to tread me down.
Come, Edmund, let's away and levy men;
'Tis war that must abate these barons' pride.
*Exit* EDWARD THE KING, *with* ISABELLA *and* KENT
WARWICK Let's to our castles, for the King is moved.
MORTIMER JUNIOR Moved may he be and perish in his
wrath. 100
LANCASTER Cousin, it is no dealing with him now.
He means to make us stoop by force of arms,
And therefore let us jointly here protest
To prosecute that Gaveston to the death.
MORTIMER JUNIOR By heaven, the abject villain shall
not live.
WARWICK I'll have his blood or die in seeking it.
PEMBROKE The like oath Pembroke takes.
LANCASTER And so doth Lancaster.
Now send our heralds to defy the King
And make the people swear to put him down.

*Enter a* POST

MORTIMER JUNIOR Letters? From whence? 110
POST From Scotland, my lord.
LANCASTER Why how now, cousin, how fares all our
friends?
MORTIMER JUNIOR (*Reading a letter*) My uncle's taken
prisoner by the Scots.
LANCASTER We'll have him ransomed, man; be of good
cheer.
MORTIMER JUNIOR They rate his ransom at five
thousand pound.
Who should defray the money but the King,
Seeing he is taken prisoner in his wars?
I'll to the King.
LANCASTER Do cousin, and I'll bear thee company. 119
WARWICK Meantime, my lord of Pembroke and myself
Will to Newcastle here and gather head.
MORTIMER JUNIOR About it then, and we will follow
you.
LANCASTER Be resolute and full of secrecy.
WARWICK I warrant you.
*Exeunt all but* MORTIMER JUNIOR *and* LANCASTER
MORTIMER JUNIOR Cousin, an if he will not ransom
him,

---

93 these words . . . thy years: Warwick was a senior peer and
Kent implies that he should have more wisdom
101 Cousin: a broad term for a relative or friend
103 protest: determine
104 prosecute: pursue
116 defray: pay
121 gather head: raise an army

I'll thunder such a peal into his ears
As never subject did unto his king.
LANCASTER Content; I'll bear my part. Holla! Who's
there?

*Enter a* GUARD

MORTIMER JUNIOR Ay, marry, such a guard as this
doth well.
LANCASTER Lead on the way.
GUARD                        Whither will your lordships?
MORTIMER JUNIOR Whither else but to the King?  **131**
GUARD His highness is disposed to be alone.
LANCASTER Why, so he may, but we will speak to him.
GUARD You may not in, my lord.
MORTIMER JUNIOR May we not?

*Enter* EDWARD *and* KENT

EDWARD How now, what noise is this?
    Who have we there? Is't you?    *He starts to exit,*
                *ignoring* MORTIMER JUNIOR *and* LANCASTER
MORTIMER JUNIOR Nay, stay, my lord; I come to bring
    you news:
    Mine uncle's taken prisoner by the Scots.
EDWARD Then ransom him.                        **140**
LANCASTER 'Twas in your wars: you should ransom
    him.
MORTIMER JUNIOR And you shall ransom him, or
    else—
KENT What, Mortimer, you will not threaten him?
EDWARD Quiet yourself; you shall have the broad seal
    To gather for him thoroughout the realm.
LANCASTER Your minion Gaveston hath taught you
    this.
MORTIMER JUNIOR My lord, the family of the
    Mortimers
    Are not so poor but, would they sell their land,
    Would levy men enough to anger you.
    We never beg, but use such prayers as these.  **150**
                        *He grasps his sword*
EDWARD Shall I still be haunted thus?
MORTIMER JUNIOR Nay, now you are here alone, I'll
    speak my mind.
LANCASTER And so will I; and then, my lord, farewell.
MORTIMER JUNIOR The idle triumphs, masques,
    lascivious shows,
    And prodigal gifts bestowed on Gaveston
    Have drawn thy treasure dry and made thee weak;

The murmuring commons overstretchèd hath.
LANCASTER Look for rebellion, look to be deposed:
    Thy garrisons are beaten out of France,
    And, lame and poor, lie groaning at the gates;  **160**
    The wild O'Neill, with swarms of Irish kerns,
    Lives uncontrolled within the English pale;
    Unto the walls of York the Scots made road
    And, unresisted, drave away rich spoils.
MORTIMER JUNIOR The haughty Dane commands the
    narrow seas,
    While in the harbour ride thy ships unrigged.
LANCASTER What foreign prince sends thee
    ambassadors?
MORTIMER JUNIOR Who loves thee but a sort of
    flatterers?
LANCASTER Thy gentle Queen, sole sister to Valois,
    Complains that thou hast left her all forlorn.  **170**
MORTIMER JUNIOR Thy court is naked, being bereft of
    those
    That makes a king seem glorious to the world—
    I mean the peers whom thou shouldst dearly love.
    Libels are cast again thee in the street,
    Ballads and rhymes made of thy overthrow.
LANCASTER The northern borderers, seeing their
    houses burnt,
    Their wives and children slain, run up and down
    Cursing the name of thee and Gaveston.
MORTIMER JUNIOR When wert thou in the field with
    banner spread?
    But once! And then thy soldiers marched like players,
    With garish robes, not armour; and thyself,  **181**
    Bedaubed with gold, rode laughing at the rest,
    Nodding and shaking of thy spangled crest
    Where women's favours hung like labels down.
LANCASTER And thereof came it that the fleering
    Scots,
    To England's high disgrace, have made this jig:
    'Maids of England, sore may you mourn,

---

128  Content: agreed
129  marry: to be sure (contracted from the oath 'By Mary')
134  in: enter
144  broad seal: the authority that would allow Mortimer
    Junior to beg for money (implying that he has none)
145  thoroughout: throughout
151  haunted: pursued, tormented
155  prodigal: lavish

---

157  murmuring commons overstretchèd hath: the
    discontented common people complain, presumably at
    the high levels of taxation
161  O'Neill: possibly a reference to Hugh O'Neill, an Ulster
    chieftain during the reign of Elizabeth I
    kerns: footsoldiers
162  English pale: the area of land around Dublin in Ireland
    preserved for English settlers, hence the expression
    'beyond the pale'
164  drave: drove
    spoils: loot, plunder
165  the narrow seas: the English Channel
169  Valois: i.e. King Philip of France
174  Libels: subversive leaflets or 'broadsides'
180  players: actors
184  favours: tokens of affection (such as gloves or scarves)
    labels: parchment strips for attaching seals to documents
185  fleering: sneering

For your lemans you have lost at Bannocks bourne.
With a heave and a ho.
What weeneth the King of England,                        190
So soon to have won Scotland?
With a rombelow.'
MORTIMER JUNIOR  Wigmore shall fly, to set my uncle
    free.
LANCASTER  And when 'tis gone, our swords shall
    purchase more.
  If ye be moved, revenge it as you can;
  Look next to see us with our ensigns spread.
            *Exeunt* NOBLES LANCASTER *and* MORTIMER JUNIOR
EDWARD  My swelling heart for very anger breaks!
  How oft have I been baited by these peers
  And dare not be revenged, for their power is great?
  Yet, shall the crowing of these cockerels              200
  Affright a lion? Edward, unfold thy paws
  And let their lives' blood slake thy fury's hunger.
  If I be cruel and grow tyrannous,
  Now let them thank themselves and rue too late.
KENT  My lord, I see your love to Gaveston
  Will be the ruin of the realm and you,
  For now the wrathful nobles threaten wars;
  And therefore, brother, banish him forever.
EDWARD  Art thou an enemy to my Gaveston?
KENT  Ay, and it grieves me that I favoured him.        210
EDWARD  Traitor, be gone; whine thou with Mortimer.
KENT  So will I, rather than with Gaveston.
EDWARD  Out of my sight, and trouble me no more.
KENT  No marvel though thou scorn thy noble peers,
  When I thy brother am rejected thus.
EDWARD  Away!                                *Exit* KENT
  Poor Gaveston, that hast no friend but me.
  Do what they can, we'll live in Tynemouth here,
  And, so I walk with him about the walls,
  What care I though the earls begirt us round?         220

*Enter* ISABELLA THE QUEEN, THREE LADIES (MARGARET
DE CLARE *with two* LADIES IN WAITING), GAVESTON,
BALDOCK, *and* SPENCER JUNIOR

  Here comes she that's cause of all these jars.

ISABELLA  My lord, 'tis thought the earls are up in arms.
EDWARD  Ay, and 'tis likewise thought you favour him.
ISABELLA  Thus do you still suspect me without cause.
LADY MARGARET  Sweet uncle, speak more kindly to
    the Queen.
GAVESTON  (*Aside to* EDWARD)  My lord, dissemble with
    her, speak her fair.
EDWARD  Pardon me, sweet, I forgot myself.
ISABELLA  Your pardon is quickly got of Isabel.
EDWARD  The younger Mortimer is grown so brave
  That to my face he threatens civil wars.              230
GAVESTON  Why do you not commit him to the Tower?
EDWARD  I dare not, for the people love him well.
GAVESTON  Why then, we'll have him privily made
    away.
EDWARD  Would Lancaster and he had both caroused
  A bowl of poison to each other's health.
  But let them go, and tell me what are these?
                  *Indicates* BALDOCK *and* SPENCER JUNIOR
LADY MARGARET  Two of my father's servants whilst he
    lived;
  May't please your grace to entertain them now.
EDWARD  Tell me, where wast thou born? What is
    thine arms?
BALDOCK  My name is Baldock, and my gentry            240
  I fetched from Oxford, not from heraldry.
EDWARD  The fitter art thou, Baldock, for my turn;
  Wait on me, and I'll see thou shalt not want.
BALDOCK  I humbly thank your majesty.
EDWARD  Knowest thou him, Gaveston?
GAVESTON                              Ay, my lord.
  His name is Spencer; he is well allied.
  For my sake let him wait upon your grace;
  Scarce shall you find a man of more desert.
EDWARD  Then, Spencer, wait upon me; for his sake
  I'll grace thee with a higher style ere long.         250
SPENCER JUNIOR  No greater titles happen unto me
  Than to be favoured of your majesty.
EDWARD  (*To* LADY MARGARET)
  Cousin, this day shall be your marriage feast.
  And, Gaveston, think that I love thee well
  To wed thee to our niece, the only heir

---

188  lemans: sweethearts
     Bannocks bourne: Edward was defeated at Bannockburn
     in 1314 having failed to secure nearby Stirling Castle from
     the Scots. Historically, Gaveston was dead by the time of
     this defeat
190  weeneth: hopes
192  rombelow: meaningless refrain rhyming with 'a heave
     and a ho' which derived from sea shanties
193  Wigmore shall fly: Wigmore Castle (in Herefordshire)
     shall be quickly sold
196  ensigns: banners raised in battle
200–1  cockerels/Affright a lion: lions (also symbols of royalty)
     were proverbially afraid of the crowing of the cock
220  begirt: surround, enclose

223  him: i.e. Mortimer Junior
226  speak her fair: address her courteously
229  brave: defiant
233  privily made away: murdered
234  caroused: quaffed:
238  entertain: employ
241  Oxford, not from heraldry: Baldock claims his status
     through his Oxford education rather than through
     birth
246  well allied: of good birth
250  style: title
253  Cousin: niece (Edward's sister, Joan of Arc, had married
     the Earl of Gloucester)

Unto the Earl of Gloucester late deceased.
GAVESTON I know, my lord, many will stomach me,
But I respect neither their love nor hate.
EDWARD The headstrong barons shall not limit me;
He that I list to favour shall be great.          260
Come, let's away; and when the marriage ends,
Have at the rebels and their complices.

*Exeunt*

## Act II, scene iii

*Enter* LANCASTER, MORTIMER JUNIOR, WARWICK,
PEMBROKE, KENT

KENT My lords, of love to this our native land
I come to join with you and leave the King;
And in your quarrel and the realm's behoof
Will be the first that shall adventure life.
LANCASTER I fear me you are sent of policy
To undermine us with a show of love.
WARWICK He is your brother; therefore have we cause
To cast the worst and doubt of your revolt.
KENT Mine honour shall be hostage of my truth;
If that will not suffice, farewell, my lords.          10
MORTIMER JUNIOR Stay, Edmund; never was
    Plantagenet
False of his word, and therefore trust we thee.
PEMBROKE But what's the reason you should leave him
    now?
KENT I have informed the Earl of Lancaster.
LANCASTER And it sufficeth. Now, my lords, know
    this,
That Gaveston is secretly arrived,
And here in Tynemouth frolics with the King.
Let us with these our followers scale the walls,
And suddenly surprise them unawares.
MORTIMER JUNIOR I'll give the onset.
WARWICK                         And I'll follow thee.
MORTIMER JUNIOR This tattered ensign of my
    ancestors,          21
Which swept the desert shore of that dead sea
Whereof we got the name of Mortimer,
Will I advance upon these castle walls.
Drums strike alarum. Raise them from their sport,
And ring aloud the knell of Gaveston.          *Alarums*

---

257 stomach: resent
260 list: choose
  4 adventure: risk
  5 policy: as a trick
  8 cast: consider
 23 Mortimer: Mortimer Junior suggests that the family
    name derives from the Latin for the Dead Sea (*Mortum
    Mare*) because of having fought in the Crusades. In fact
    the name derived from Mortemer in Normandy
 25 alarum: call to arms

LANCASTER None be so hardy as to touch the King
But neither spare you Gaveston nor his friends.

*Exeunt*

## Act II, scene iv

*Enter* EDWARD THE KING *and* SPENCER JUNIOR; *from
separate doors to them* GAVESTON, *unseen by* EDWARD *and*
SPENCER JUNIOR, *with* ISABELLA, LADY MARGARET DE
CLARE, *and attendants*

EDWARD O tell me, Spencer, where is Gaveston?
SPENCER JUNIOR I fear me he is slain, my gracious lord.
EDWARD No, here he comes! Now let them spoil and
    kill.
Fly, fly, my lords; the earls have got the hold.
Take shipping and away to Scarborough;
Spencer and I will post away by land.
GAVESTON O stay, my lord; they will not injure you.
EDWARD I will not trust them, Gaveston. Away!
GAVESTON Farewell, my lord.
EDWARD (*To* LADY MARGARET) Lady, farewell.          10
LADY MARGARET Farewell, sweet uncle, till we meet
    again.
EDWARD Farewell, sweet Gaveston, and farewell, niece.
ISABELLA No farewell to poor Isabel, thy Queen?
EDWARD Yes, yes—for Mortimer, your lover's sake.

*Exeunt all, except* ISABELLA

ISABELLA Heavens can witness, I love none but you.
From my embracements thus he breaks away;
O that mine arms could close this isle about,
That I might pull him to me where I would,
Or that these tears that drizzle from mine eyes
Had power to mollify his stony heart          20
That when I had him we might never part.

*Enter the* BARONS (LANCASTER, WARWICK, MORTIMER
JUNIOR). *Alarums*

LANCASTER I wonder how he 'scaped?
MORTIMER JUNIOR Who's this, the Queen?
ISABELLA Ay, Mortimer, the miserable Queen,
Whose pining heart, her inward sighs have blasted,
And body with continual mourning wasted.
These hands are tired with haling of my lord
From Gaveston, from wicked Gaveston,
And all in vain; for when I speak him fair,
He turns away and smiles upon his minion.          30
MORTIMER JUNIOR Cease to lament, and tell us where's
    the King?
ISABELLA What would you with the King? Is't him you
    seek?

---

27 hardy: reckless
 3 spoil: plunder
 4 hold: fortress
 6 post: go quickly (by horse)

LANCASTER  No, madam, but that cursèd Gaveston.
  Far be it from the thought of Lancaster
  To offer violence to his sovereign.
  We would but rid the realm of Gaveston;
  Tell us where he remains, and he shall die.
ISABELLA  He's gone by water unto Scarborough.
  Pursue him quickly and he cannot 'scape;
  The King hath left him, and his train is small.         40
WARWICK  Forslow no time, sweet Lancaster; let's
  march.
MORTIMER JUNIOR  How comes it that the King and he
  is parted?
ISABELLA  That this your army, going several ways,
  Might be of lesser force, and with the power
  That he intendeth presently to raise
  Be easily suppressed; and therefore be gone.
MORTIMER JUNIOR  Here in the river rides a Flemish
  hoy;
  Let's all aboard and follow him amain.
LANCASTER  The wind that bears him hence will fill our
  sails.
  Come, come aboard—'tis but an hour's sailing.         50
MORTIMER JUNIOR  Madam, stay you within this castle
  here.
ISABELLA  No, Mortimer, I'll to my lord the King.
MORTIMER JUNIOR  Nay, rather sail with us to
  Scarborough.
ISABELLA  You know the King is so suspicious,
  As if he hear I have but talked with you,
  Mine honour will be called in question;
  And therefore, gentle Mortimer, be gone.
MORTIMER JUNIOR  Madam, I cannot stay to answer
  you;
  But think of Mortimer as he deserves.

*Exeunt* LANCASTER, WARWICK, AND MORTIMER
  JUNIOR
ISABELLA  So well hast thou deserved, sweet Mortimer,
  As Isabel could live with thee forever.                61
  In vain I look for love at Edward's hand,
  Whose eyes are fixed on none but Gaveston.
  Yet once more I'll importune him with prayers;
  If he be strange and not regard my words,
  My son and I will over into France,
  And to the King, my brother, there complain
  How Gaveston hath robbed me of his love.
  But yet I hope my sorrows will have end
  And Gaveston this blessèd day be slain.                70
                                            *Exit*

---

41  Forslow: waste
47  Flemish hoy: small Flemish fishing boat
48  amain: with all speed
60–1  So well . . . thee forever: 'Marlowe obviously prepares
      the ground here for Isabella's adultery' (Forker)
65  strange: a) estranged: b) unresponsive

## Act II, scene v

*Enter* GAVESTON, *pursued*

GAVESTON  Yet, lusty lords, I have escaped your hands,
  Your threats, your 'larums, and your hot pursuits;
  And though divorced from King Edward's eyes,
  Yet liveth Piers of Gaveston unsurprised,
  Breathing, in hope (*malgrado* all your beards
  That muster rebels thus against your king)
  To see his royal sovereign once again.

*Enter the* NOBLES (LANCASTER, WARWICK, PEMBROKE,
MORTIMER JUNIOR), SOLDIERS, JAMES, HORSE-BOY, AND
PEMBROKE'S MEN

WARWICK  Upon him, soldiers! Take away his
  weapons.
MORTIMER JUNIOR  Thou proud disturber of thy
  country's peace,
  Corrupter of thy king, cause of these broils,          10
  Base flatterer, yield! And were it not for shame—
  Shame and dishonour to a soldier's name—
  Upon my weapon's point here shouldst thou fall,
  And welter in thy gore.
LANCASTER                Monster of men,
  That, like the Greekish strumpet, trained to arms
  And bloody wars so many valiant knights,
  Look for no other fortune, wretch, than death;
  King Edward is not here to buckler thee.
WARWICK  Lancaster, why talk'st thou to the slave?
  Go, soldiers, take him hence; for by my sword,         20
  His head shall off. Gaveston, short warning
  Shall serve thy turn; it is our country's cause
  That here severely we will execute
  Upon thy person: hang him at a bough!
GAVESTON  My lord—
WARWICK  Soldiers, have him away.
  But for thou wert the favourite of a king,
  Thou shalt have so much honour at our hands.
                *He gestures to indicate beheading*
GAVESTON  I thank you all, my lords; then I perceive

---

1  lusty: insolent
5  *malgrado* all your beards: *malgrado* means 'in spite of'
   (Italian); Gaveston may here be alluding to the long
   beards of his English pursuers (as opposed to the clean-
   shaven French)
10  broils: disturbances
15  Greekish strumpet: Helen of Troy, abducted by Paris
    and thus the cause of the Trojan War
    trained: lured
18  buckler: shield (i.e. protect)
21  warning: notice. Warwick considers Gaveston so
    irredeemable that he should not be allowed to prepare
    himself spiritually for death
27  But for: even though
28  so much honour: the nobility were exempt from hanging

That heading is one, and hanging is the other,   30
And death is all.

*Enter the* EARL OF ARUNDEL

LANCASTER  How now, my lord of Arundel?
ARUNDEL  My lords, King Edward greets you all by me.
WARWICK  Arundel, say your message.
ARUNDEL             His majesty,
  Hearing that you had taken Gaveston,
  Entreateth you by me, that but he may
  See him before he dies; for why, he says,
  And sends you word, he knows that die he shall;
  And if you gratify his grace so far,
  He will be mindful of the courtesy.   40
WARWICK  How now?
GAVESTON         Renownèd Edward, how thy name
  Revives poor Gaveston.
WARWICK          No, it needeth not.
  Arundel, we will gratify the King
  In other matters; he must pardon us in this.
  Soldiers, away with him.
GAVESTON  Why, my lord of Warwick,
  Will not these delays beget my hopes?
  I know it, lords, it is this life you aim at;
  Yet grant King Edward this.
MORTIMER JUNIOR       Shalt thou appoint
  What we shall grant? Soldiers, away with him!  50
  (*To* ARUNDEL) Thus we'll gratify the King:
  We'll send his head by thee; let him bestow
  His tears on that, for that is all he gets
  Of Gaveston, or else his senseless trunk.
LANCASTER  Not so, my lord, lest he bestow more cost
  In burying him than he hath ever earned.
ARUNDEL  My lords, it is his majesty's request,
  And in the honour of a king he swears
  He will but talk with him and send him back.
WARWICK  When, can you tell? Arundel, no; we wot  60
  He that the care of realm remits,
  And drives his nobles to these exigents
  For Gaveston, will, if he seize him once,
  Violate any promise to possess him.
ARUNDEL  Then if you will not trust his grace in keep,
  My lords, I will be pledge for his return.
MORTIMER JUNIOR  It is honourable in thee to offer
  this,
  But for we know thou art a noble gentleman,

---

30  heading: beheading
37  for why: because
40  be mindful of: take into consideration
60  wot: know
61  remits: abandons
62  exigents: exigencies, severe measures
      seize: take possession of
      in keep: in custody
66  be pledge: stake my own life (as security)

We will not wrong thee so,
  To make away a true man for a thief.   70
GAVESTON  How meanst thou, Mortimer? That is over-
  base!
MORTIMER JUNIOR  Away, base groom, robber of kings'
  renown;
  Question with thy companions and thy mates.
PEMBROKE  My lord Mortimer, and you my lords each
  one,
  To gratify the King's request therein,
  Touching the sending of this Gaveston,
  Because his majesty so earnestly
  Desires to see the man before his death,
  I will upon mine honour undertake
  To carry him and bring him back again,  80
  Provided this, that you, my lord of Arundel
  Will join with me.
WARWICK         Pembroke, what wilt thou do?
  Cause yet more bloodshed? Is it not enough
  That we have taken him, but must we now
  Leave him on 'had I wist' and let him go?
PEMBROKE  My lords, I will not over-woo your
  honours,
  But if you dare trust Pembroke with the prisoner,
  Upon mine oath I will return him back.
ARUNDEL  My lord of Lancaster, what say you in this?
LANCASTER  Why, I say, let him go on Pembroke's word.
PEMBROKE  And you, lord Mortimer?  91
MORTIMER JUNIOR  How say you, my lord of Warwick?
WARWICK  Nay, do your pleasures; I know how 'twill
  prove.
PEMBROKE  Then give him me.
GAVESTON         Sweet sovereign, yet I come
  To see thee ere I die.
WARWICK  (*Aside*)      Yet not perhaps,
  If Warwick's wit and policy prevail.
MORTIMER JUNIOR  My lord of Pembroke, we deliver
  him you;
  Return him on your honour. Sound away!
    *Trumpets sound. Exeunt all but* PEMBROKE, ARUNDEL,
  GAVESTON *and* PEMBROKE'S MEN, FOUR SOLDIERS, *with*
                JAMES, *and* HORSE-BOY
PEMBROKE  (*To* ARUNDEL) My lord, you shall go with
  me;
  My house is not far hence—out of the way  100
  A little—but our men shall go along.
  We that have pretty wenches to our wives,
  Sir, must not come so near and balk their lips.

---

70  make away: murder
73  Question: argue
85  'had I wist': 'had I known' (proverbial)
93  do your pleasures: do as you will
96  wit and policy: cunning and strategy
103  balk: neglect

ARUNDEL 'Tis very kindly spoke, my lord of Pembroke;
Your honour hath an adamant of power
To draw a prince.
PEMBROKE So my lord. Come hither, James.
I do commit this Gaveston to thee;
Be thou this night his keeper. In the morning
We will discharge thee of thy charge; be gone. **109**
GAVESTON Unhappy Gaveston, whither goest thou now?

*Exit* GAVESTON, *with* PEMBROKE'S MEN *and* JAMES

HORSE-BOY My lord, we'll quickly be at Cobham.

*Exeunt* PEMBROKE *and* ARUNDEL, *with the*
HORSE-BOY *and* SOLDIERS

# Act II, scene vi

*Enter* GAVESTON *mourning, with* JAMES *and the* EARL OF
PEMBROKE'S MEN

GAVESTON O treacherous Warwick, thus to wrong thy
friend!
JAMES I see it is your life these arms pursue.
GAVESTON Weaponless must I fall and die in bands.
O, must this day be period of my life,
Centre of all my bliss? An ye be men,
Speed to the King.

*Enter* WARWICK *and his company*

WARWICK My lord of Pembroke's men,
Strive you no longer; I will have that Gaveston.
JAMES Your lordship doth dishonour to yourself
And wrong our lord, your honourable friend.
WARWICK No, James, it is my country's cause I follow. **10**
Go, take the villain; soldiers, come away,
We'll make quick work. Commend me to your
master,
My friend, and tell him that I watched it well.
(*To* GAVESTON) Come, let thy shadow parley with
King Edward.
GAVESTON Treacherous Earl, shall I not see the King?
WARWICK The King of Heaven perhaps, no other king.
Away!

*Exeunt* WARWICK *and his men, with* GAVESTON. JAMES
*remains with the others*

JAMES Come fellows, it booted not for us to strive.
We will in haste go certify our lord.

*Exeunt*

# Act III, scene i

*Enter* KING EDWARD *and Spencer* JUNIOR, *AND* BALDOCK,
*with drums and fifes*

EDWARD I long to hear an answer from the barons
Touching my friend, my dearest Gaveston.
Ah, Spencer, not the riches of my realm
Can ransom him; ah, he is marked to die.
I know the malice of the younger Mortimer;
Warwick, I know, is rough, and Lancaster
Inexorable; and I shall never see
My lovely Piers, my Gaveston, again.
The barons overbear me with their pride.
SPENCER JUNIOR Were I King Edward, England's
sovereign, **10**
Son to the lovely Eleanor of Spain,
Great Edward Longshanks' issue, would I bear
These braves, this rage, and suffer uncontrolled
These barons thus to beard me in my land,
In mine own realm? My lord, pardon my speech.
Did you retain your father's magnanimity,
Did you regard the honour of your name,
You would not suffer thus your majesty
Be counterbuffed of your nobility.
Strike off their heads, and let them preach on poles;
No doubt such lessons they will teach the rest, **21**
As by their preachments they will profit much
And learn obedience to their lawful king.
EDWARD Yea, gentle Spencer, we have been too mild,
Too kind to them, but now have drawn our sword,
And if they send me not my Gaveston,
We'll steel it on their crest and poll their tops.
BALDOCK This haught resolve becomes your majesty,

---

105 adamant: magnet, loadstone
109 discharge: relieve
111 Cobham: there is a Cobham in Kent and another in
Surrey. Neither makes sense since Pembroke's house was
at Deddington in Oxfordshire
1 thy friend: i.e. Pembroke
2 arms: i.e. soldiers
3 bands: bonds
4 period: the end
5 Centre of all my bliss: a) nadir, the low point; b) the day
of reunion with Edward
An: if
7 Strive you: struggle
13 watched it: guarded (Gaveston)
14 shadow: ghost

18 booted not: was useless
19 certify: inform
11 Eleanor of Spain: Eleanor of Castile, Edward I's first wife
12 Longshanks: Edward I acquired this name because of his
long legs
13 braves: insults
14 beard: defy (as in 'pluck by the beard')
16 magnanimity: courage (associated with nobility)
19 counterbuffed of: opposed by
20 preach on poles: see I.i.118n
22 preachments: exhortations
27 steel it: sharpen (his sword)
poll their tops: cut off their heads (referring to the
pollarding of tree-tops and punning on Spencer Junior's
'poles')
28 haught: lofty

Not to be tied to their affection
As though your highness were a schoolboy still,       30
And must be awed and governed like a child.

*Enter* HUGH SPENCER SENIOR, *an old man, father to the
young* SPENCER JUNIOR, *with his truncheon, and soldiers*

SPENCER SENIOR  Long live my sovereign, the noble
       Edward,
In peace triumphant, fortunate in wars.
EDWARD  Welcome, old man. Com'st thou in Edward's
       aid?
Then tell thy prince of whence and what thou art.
SPENCER SENIOR  Lo, with a band of bowmen and of
       pikes,
Brown bills and targeteers, four hundred strong,
Sworn to defend King Edward's royal right,
I come in person to your majesty:
Spencer, the father of Hugh Spencer there,       40
Bound to your highness everlastingly
For favours done in him unto us all.
EDWARD  Thy father, Spencer?
SPENCER JUNIOR                  True, an it like your grace,
That pours in lieu of all your goodness shown,
His life, my lord, before your princely feet.
EDWARD  Welcome ten thousand times, old man,
       again.
Spencer, this love, this kindness to thy king
Argues thy noble mind and disposition.
Spencer, I here create thee Earl of Wiltshire,
And daily will enrich thee with our favour       50
That, as the sunshine, shall reflect o'er thee.
Beside, the more to manifest our love,
Because we hear Lord Bruce doth sell his land
And that the Mortimers are in hand withal,
Thou shalt have crowns of us, t'outbid the barons;
And Spencer, spare them not, but lay it on.
Soldiers, a largess, and thrice welcome all.

---

29  affection: support, desires
31  awed: frightened
SD  *truncheon*: staff, symbol of authority (and of war)
35  of whence and what thou art: 'where you come from and
     what is your name'
36  bowmen and of pikes: lines of bowmen (archers) were
     protected in the field by lines of sharpened lances (pikes)
     driven by their bearers into the ground ahead
36  Brown bills: footsoldiers with bronzed halberds
     (metonymic)
     targeteers: shield-carrying footsoldiers
43  an it like: if it please
48  Argues: proves; 'Ironically, this statement emphasises the
     fact that Spencer Senior is not, by birth, a nobleman'
     (Wiggins and Lindsey)
54  in hand withal: i.e. engaged with this transaction
56  spare them . . . it on: do not be frugal (with the crowns)
     but be extravagant (in your counter-offer)
57  largess: bounty

*Enter* ISABELLA THE QUEEN *and* PRINCE EDWARD *her
son, and* LEVUNE, *a Frenchman*

SPENCER JUNIOR  My lord, here comes the Queen.
EDWARD                           Madam, what news?
ISABELLA  News of dishonour, lord, and discontent:
Our friend Levune, faithful and full of trust,       60
Informeth us by letters and by words
That Lord Valois our brother, King of France,
Because your highness hath been slack in homage,
Hath seizèd Normandy into his hands.
These be the letters, this the messenger.
EDWARD  Welcome Levune. (*To* ISABELLA) Tush, Sib,
       if this be all,
Valois and I will soon be friends again.
But to my Gaveston—shall I never see,
Never behold thee now? Madam, in this matter
We will employ you and your little son;       70
You shall go parley with the King of France.
Boy, see you bear you bravely to the King
And do your message with a majesty.
PRINCE EDWARD  Commit not to my youth things of
       more weight
Than fits a prince so young as I to bear.
And fear not, lord and father; heaven's great beams
On Atlas' shoulder shall not lie more safe
Than shall your charge committed to my trust.
ISABELLA  Ah, boy, this towardness makes thy mother
       fear
Thou art not marked to many days on earth.       80
EDWARD  Madam, we will that you with speed be
       shipped,
And this our son. Levune shall follow you
With all the haste we can dispatch him hence.
Choose of our lords to bear you company,
And go in peace; leave us in wars at home.
ISABELLA  Unnatural wars, where subjects brave their
       king:
God end them once. My lord, I take my leave
To make my preparation for France.
                    *Exeunt* ISABELLA *and* PRINCE EDWARD

*Enter* LORD ARUNDEL

EDWARD  What, Lord Arundel, dost thou come alone?
ARUNDEL  Yea, my good lord, for Gaveston is dead.  90
EDWARD  Ah, traitors, have they put my friend to
       death?

---

66  Sib: sibling, or an 'affectionate diminutive of Isabella'
     (Gill)
77  Atlas' shoulder: in classical mythology Atlas supported
     the sky on his shoulder
79  towardness: boldness
80  many days on earth: for Marlowe's audience this would
     be ironic, since Edward III actually reigned from 1327–77
87  once: once and for all

Tell me, Arundel, died he ere thou cam'st,
Or didst thou see my friend to take his death?
ARUNDEL Neither, my lord, for as he was surprised,
Begirt with weapons and with enemies round,
I did your highness' message to them all,
Demanding him of them—entreating rather—
And said, upon the honour of my name,
That I would undertake to carry him
Unto your highness, and to bring him back.          100
EDWARD And tell me, would the rebels deny me that?
SPENCER JUNIOR Proud recreants!
EDWARD                    Yea, Spencer, traitors all.
ARUNDEL I found them at the first inexorable;
The Earl of Warwick would not bide the hearing,
Mortimer hardly; Pembroke and Lancaster
Spake least. And when they flatly had denied,
Refusing to receive me pledge for him,
The Earl of Pembroke mildly thus bespake:
'My lords, because our sovereign sends for him
And promiseth he shall be safe returned,          110
I will this undertake: to have him hence
And see him re-delivered to your hands.'
EDWARD Well, and how fortunes that he came not?
SPENCER JUNIOR Some treason or some villainy was
cause.
ARUNDEL The Earl of Warwick seized him on his way,
For, being delivered unto Pembroke's men,
Their lord rode home, thinking his prisoner safe;
But ere he came, Warwick in ambush lay,
And bare him to his death, and in a trench
Struck off his head, and marched unto the camp.          120
SPENCER JUNIOR A bloody part, flatly against law of
arms.
EDWARD O, shall I speak, or shall I sigh and die?
SPENCER JUNIOR My lord, refer your vengeance to the
sword
Upon these barons; hearten up your men.
Let them not unrevenged murder your friends.
Advance your standard, Edward, in the field,
And march to fire them from their starting holes.
EDWARD (Kneeling) By earth, the common mother of
us all,
By heaven and all the moving orbs thereof,
By this right hand and by my father's sword,          130
And all the honours 'longing to my crown,
I will have heads and lives for him as many

As I have manors, castles, towns, and towers.     Rises
Treacherous Warwick! Traitorous Mortimer!
If I be England's king, in lakes of gore
Your headless trunks, your bodies will I trail,
That you may drink your fill and quaff in blood,
And stain my royal standard with the same,
That so my bloody colours may suggest
Remembrance of revenge immortally          140
On your accursed traitorous progeny—
You villains that have slain my Gaveston.
And in this place of honour and of trust,
Spencer, sweet Spencer, I adopt thee here;
And merely of our love we do create thee
Earl of Gloucester and Lord Chamberlain,
Despite of times, despite of enemies.
SPENCER JUNIOR My lord, here is a messenger from the
barons
Desires access unto your majesty.
EDWARD Admit him near.          150

*Enter the* HERALD *from the* BARONS, *with his coat of
arms*

HERALD Long live King Edward, England's lawful lord.
EDWARD So wish not they, iwis, that sent thee hither.
Thou com'st from Mortimer and his complices—
A ranker rout of rebels never was.
Well, say thy message.
HERALD The barons up in arms, by me salute
Your highness with long life and happiness,
And bid me say as plainer to your grace,
That if without effusion of blood
You will this grief have ease and remedy,          160
That from your princely person you remove
(*Indicating* SPENCER JUNIOR) This Spencer, as a
putrefying branch
That deads the royal vine whose golden leaves
Impale your princely head, your diadem,
Whose brightness such pernicious upstarts dim,
Say they; and lovingly advise your grace
To cherish virtue and nobility,
And have old servitors in high esteem,

---

145  merely: by command rather than by succession. 'The
word suggests that Edward's motive for honouring
Spencer Junior is personal attraction, not an aspect of his
vengeance upon the murderers of Gaveston' (Forker)
152  iwis: assuredly (from the Middle English *ywis*)
154  rout: band
158  plainer: complainant
163  deads: deadens, kills
the royal vine: anachronistic, since it was the crowns of
later monarchs that were decorated with vines (Edward's
had strawberry leaves)
164  Impale: encircle
diadem: crown
168  old servitors: long-standing supporters

---

94  surprised: ambushed
102  recreants: breakers of loyalty
104  bide: abide
113  fortunes: does it happen
121  part: act
123  refer: assign
127  fire them from their starting holes: smoke them from
their hiding places (metaphor from hunting)
129  moving orbs: heavenly bodies thought to circle the earth

And shake off smooth dissembling flatterers.
This granted, they, their honours, and their lives   **170**
Are to your highness vowed and consecrate.
SPENCER JUNIOR  Ah, traitors, will they still display
    their pride?
EDWARD  Away! Tarry no answer, but be gone.
Rebels! Will they appoint their sovereign
His sports, his pleasures, and his company?
Yet ere thou go, see how I do divorce
Spencer from me.          *Embraces* SPENCER JUNIOR
              Now get thee to thy lords,
And tell them I will come to chastise them
For murdering Gaveston. Hie thee, get thee gone;
Edward with fire and sword follows at thy heels.   **180**
                    *Exit* HERALD
My lords, perceive you how these rebels swell?
Soldiers, good hearts, defend your sovereign's right,
For now, even now, we march to make them stoop.
Away!
                    *Exeunt*

# Act III, scene ii

*Alarums, excursions, a great fight, and a retreat. Enter*
EDWARD THE KING, SPENCER SENIOR, SPENCER JUNIOR,
*and the* NOBLEMEN *of the King's side*

EDWARD  Why do we sound retreat? Upon them, lords!
This day I shall pour vengeance with my sword
On those proud rebels that are up in arms,
And do confront and countermand their king.
SPENCER JUNIOR  I doubt it not, my lord; right will
    prevail.
SPENCER SENIOR  'Tis not amiss, my liege, for either part
To breathe a while; our men with sweat and dust
All choked well near, begin to faint for heat,
And this retire refresheth horse and man.
SPENCER JUNIOR  Here come the rebels.          **10**

*Enter the* BARONS, MORTIMER JUNIOR, LANCASTER,
KENT, WARWICK, PEMBROKE *with the others*

MORTIMER JUNIOR  Look, Lancaster,
Yonder is Edward among his flatterers.
LANCASTER  And there let him be,
Till he pay dearly for their company.
WARWICK  And shall, or Warwick's sword shall smite in
    vain.
EDWARD  What, rebels, do you shrink and sound retreat?

MORTIMER JUNIOR  No, Edward, no; thy flatterers faint
    and fly.
LANCASTER  Thou'd best betimes forsake thee and their
    trains,
For they'll betray thee, traitors as they are.
SPENCER JUNIOR  Traitor on thy face, rebellious
    Lancaster.          **20**
PEMBROKE  Away, base upstart; brav'st thou nobles thus?
SPENCER SENIOR  A noble attempt and honourable deed
Is it not, trow ye, to assemble aid
And levy arms against your lawful king?
EDWARD  For which ere long their heads shall satisfy
T'appease the wrath of their offended king.
MORTIMER JUNIOR  Then, Edward, thou wilt fight it to
    the last,
And rather bathe thy sword in subjects' blood
Than banish that pernicious company?
EDWARD  Ay, traitors all! Rather than thus be braved,
Make England's civil towns huge heaps of stones   **31**
And ploughs to go about our palace gates.
WARWICK  A desperate and unnatural resolution.
Alarum to the fight!
Saint George for England and the barons' right!
EDWARD  Saint George for England and King Edward's
    right!
                *Exeunt severally. Alarums*

*Enter* EDWARD, SPENCER SENIOR, SPENCER JUNIOR,
BALDOCK, LEVUNE, *and* SOLDIERS *with the* BARONS
KENT, WARWICK, LANCASTER, *and* MORTIMER JUNIOR
*captives*

EDWARD  Now, lusty lords, now not by chance of war
But justice of the quarrel and the cause,
Vailed is your pride. Methinks you hang the heads,
But we'll advance them, traitors! Now 'tis time   **40**
To be avenged on you for all your braves
And for the murder of my dearest friend,
To whom right well you knew our soul was knit:
Good Piers of Gaveston, my sweet favourite—
Ah rebels, recreants, you made him away!
KENT  Brother, in regard of thee and of thy land,
Did they remove that flatterer from thy throne.
EDWARD  So, sir, you have spoke; away, avoid our
    presence.          *Exit* KENT
Accursèd wretches, was't in regard of us,
When we had sent our messenger to request   **50**
He might be spared to come to speak with us,
And Pembroke undertook for his return,

---

171  consecrate: made sacred
173  Tarry: await
174  appoint: grant, allow
183  make them stoop: humiliate them
SD  *excursions*: groups of soldiers rush across the stage as in
    battle
9  retire: pause, temporary retreat

18  Thou'd: thou had
23  trow ye: think you
35  Saint George: Patron Saint of England (in fact not
    adopted as such until the reign of Edward III)
39  Vailed: lowered
40  advance: raise the victims' heads on pikes (like standards)
48  avoid: depart

That thou, proud Warwick, watched the prisoner,
Poor Piers, and headed him against law of arms?
For which thy head shall overlook the rest
As much as thou in rage outwent'st the rest.

WARWICK Tyrant, I scorn thy threats and menaces;
  'Tis but temporal that thou canst inflict.

LANCASTER The worst is death, and better die to live,
  Than live in infamy under such a king.     60

EDWARD Away with them, my lord of Winchester,
  These lusty leaders, Warwick and Lancaster.
  I charge you roundly off with both their heads.
  Away!

WARWICK Farewell, vain world.

LANCASTER              Sweet Mortimer, farewell.

      *Exeunt* WARWICK *and* LANCASTER, *guarded with*
                            SPENCER SENIOR

MORTIMER JUNIOR England, unkind to thy nobility,
  Groan for this grief; behold how thou art maimed.

EDWARD Go take that haughty Mortimer to the Tower;
  There see him safe bestowed. And for the rest,
  Do speedy execution on them all.
  Begone!     70

MORTIMER JUNIOR What, Mortimer! Can ragged stony
  walls
  Immure thy virtue that aspires to heaven?
  No, Edward, England's scourge, it may not be;
  Mortimer's hope surmounts his fortune far.

              *Exit* MORTIMER JUNIOR *under guard*

EDWARD Sound drums and trumpets! March with me
  my friends
  Edward this day hath crowned him king anew.

       *Exit, attended.* SPENCER JUNIOR, LEVUNE *and*
                         BALDOCK *remain*

SPENCER JUNIOR Levune, the trust that we repose in thee
  Begets the quiet of King Edward's land.
  Therefore be gone in haste, and with advice
  Bestow that treasure on the lords of France;     80
  That therewithal enchanted, like the guard
  That suffered Jove to pass in showers of gold
  To Danaë, all aid may be denied
  To Isabel the Queen, that now in France
  Makes friends, to cross the seas with her young son,
  And step into his father's regiment.

LEVUNE That's it these barons and the subtle Queen
  Long levelled at.

BALDOCK          Yea, but Levune, thou seest

These barons lay their heads on blocks together;
What they intend, the hangman frustrates clean.   90

LEVUNE Have you no doubts, my lords; I'll clap 's close
  Among the lords of France with England's gold
  That Isabel shall make her plaints in vain,
  And France shall be obdurate with her tears.

SPENCER JUNIOR Then make for France amain;
  Levune, away!
  Proclaim King Edward's wars and victories.

                        *Exeunt*

# Act IV, scene i

*Enter* EDMUND *the* EARL OF KENT

EDMUND Fair blows the wind for France; blow, gentle
  gale,
  Till Edmund be arrived for England's good.
  Nature, yield to my country's cause in this:
  A brother—no, a butcher of thy friends—
  Proud Edward, dost thou banish me thy presence?
  But I'll to France, and cheer the wrongèd Queen,
  And certify what Edward's looseness is.
  Unnatural king, to slaughter noblemen
  And cherish flatterers. Mortimer, I stay
  Thy sweet escape; stand gracious, gloomy night   10
  To his device.

*Enter* MORTIMER JUNIOR *disguised*

MORTIMER JUNIOR Holla! Who walketh there? Is't you
  my lord?

KENT Mortimer, 'tis I;
  But hath thy potion wrought so happily?

MORTIMER JUNIOR It hath, my lord; the warders all
  asleep,
  I thank them, gave me leave to pass in peace.
  But hath your grace got shipping unto France?

KENT Fear it not.

                        *Exeunt*

# Act IV, scene ii

*Enter* ISABELLA THE QUEEN *and her son* PRINCE
EDWARD

ISABELLA Ah boy, our friends do fail us all in France;
  The lords are cruel and the King unkind.

---

54  headed: beheaded
55  overlook: 'be mounted on a higher pole than'
58  temporal: earthly suffering (rather than spiritual)
61  my lord of Winchester: i.e. Spencer Senior
71  ragged: rugged
72  Immure: enclose (within walls)
83  To Danaë: see II.ii.53n
86  regiment: authority
88  levelled: aimed (as in shooting)

90  clean: absolutely
91  clap 's: clap us; seal a bargain (as with a clap of the hands)
    close: secretly
7  looseness: a) incompetence; b) sexual misconduct
9  stay: await
10  gracious: in grace. Kent calls upon the darkness of night
    to aid Mortimer Junior's escape
11  device: plan, intent
14  thy potion . . . so happily?: 'has your drug worked so well?'

What shall we do?

PRINCE EDWARD     Madam, return to England
And please my father well, and then a fig
For all my uncle's friendship here in France.
I warrant you, I'll win his highness quickly;
'A loves me better than a thousand Spencers.

ISABELLA  Ah boy, thou art deceived at least in this,
To think that we can yet be tuned together.
No, no, we jar too far. Unkind Valois!     10
Unhappy Isabel! When France rejects,
Whither, O whither dost thou bend thy steps?

*Enter* SIR JOHN OF HAINAULT

SIR JOHN  Madam, what cheer?

ISABELLA                     Ah, good Sir John of Hainault,
Never so cheerless, nor so far distressed.

SIR JOHN  I hear, sweet lady, of the King's unkindness.
But droop not, madam; noble minds contemn
Despair. Will your grace with me to Hainault
And there stay time's advantage with your son?
How say you, my lord, will you go with your friends,
And shake off all our fortunes equally?     20

PRINCE EDWARD  So pleaseth the Queen, my mother,
me it likes.
The King of England nor the court of France
Shall have me from my gracious mother's side,
Till I be strong enough to break a staff,
And then have at the proudest Spencer's head.

SIR JOHN  Well said, my lord.

ISABELLA  Oh, my sweet heart, how do I moan thy
wrongs,
Yet triumph in the hope of thee, my joy.
Ah, sweet Sir John, even to the utmost verge
Of Europe, or the shore of Tanais,     30
Will we with thee to Hainault, so we will.

The Marquis is a noble gentleman;
His grace, I dare presume, will welcome me.

*Enter* EDMUND *the* EARL OF KENT *and* MORTIMER
JUNIOR

But who are these?

KENT                     Madam, long may you live
Much happier than your friends in England do.

ISABELLA  Lord Edmund and Lord Mortimer alive!
Welcome to France. The news was here, my lord,
That you were dead, or very near your death.

MORTIMER JUNIOR  Lady, the last was truest of the
twain;
But Mortimer, reserved for better hap,     40
Hath shaken off the thraldom of the Tower,
(*To* PRINCE EDWARD) And lives t'advance your
standard, good my lord.

PRINCE EDWARD  How mean you, an the King my
father lives?
No, my lord Mortimer, not I, I trow.

ISABELLA  Not, son? Why not? I would it were no
worse;
But gentle lords, friendless we are in France.

MORTIMER JUNIOR  Monsieur le Grand, a noble friend
of yours,
Told us at our arrival all the news:
How hard the nobles, how unkind the King
Hath showed himself. But madam, right makes room
Where weapons want; and though a many friends     51
Are made away—as Warwick, Lancaster,
And others of our party and faction—
Yet have we friends, assure your grace, in England
Would cast up caps and clap their hands for joy,
To see us there appointed for our foes.

KENT  Would all were well and Edward well reclaimed,
For England's honour, peace, and quietness.

MORTIMER JUNIOR  But by the sword, my lord, it must
be deserved.
The King will ne'er forsake his flatterers.     60

SIR JOHN  My lords of England, sith the ungentle King

---

4  a fig: obscene expression of contempt (where a thumb is
thrust through two fingers)
6  warrant: assure
7  'A: he
10  jar: become discordant (as in music)
12  Whither does . . . thy steps?: i.e. 'what is my next course
of action?'
16  contemn: despise
17  Hainault: Flemish county in the Low Countries,
bordering France
20  shake off: cast off (our shared hopes of French support)
23  have me: move me
24  a staff: lance (to be broken in battle)
25  have at: attack
27  moan: lament
29  utmost verge: the furthest limit
30  Tanais: the Latin name for the River Don which
Elizabethans thought of as the border between Europe
and Asia

32  Marquis: i.e. Sir John's brother, William, Count of
Hainault
41  thraldom: bondage
44  trow: reckon, think
47  Monsieur le Grand: an invented figure with no historical
origin
49  hard: obdurate:
the King: i.e. of France
50  makes room: makes way
51  want: are lacking
a many: many (for emphasis)
52  made away: killed
56  appointed: armed
57  reclaimed: a) subdued; b) taken back
61  sith: since

Of France refuseth to give aid of arms
To this distressèd queen his sister here,
Go you with her to Hainault. Doubt ye not,
We will find comfort, money, men, and friends
Ere long, to bid the English King a base.
How say, young prince, what think you of the match?

PRINCE EDWARD  I think King Edward will outrun us
   all.

ISABELLA  Nay son, not so; and you must not
   discourage
   Your friends that are so forward in your aid.     **70**

KENT  Sir John of Hainault, pardon us, I pray;
   These comforts that you give our woeful Queen
   Bind us in kindness all at your command.

ISABELLA  Yea, gentle brother; and the God of heaven
   Prosper your happy motion, good Sir John.

MORTIMER JUNIOR  This noble gentleman, forward in
   arms,
   Was born, I see, to be our anchor-hold.
   Sir John of Hainault, be it thy renown
   That England's Queen and nobles in distress
   Have been by thee restored and comforted.     **80**

SIR JOHN  Madam, along, and you, my lord, with me,
   That England's peers may Hainault's welcome see.

*Exeunt*

# Act IV, scene iii

*Enter* EDWARD THE KING, ARUNDEL, *the two* SPENCERS,
SENIOR *and* JUNIOR, *with others*

EDWARD  Thus after many threats of wrathful war,
   Triumpheth England's Edward with his friends;
   And triumph Edward with his friends uncontrolled.
   (*To* SPENCER JUNIOR) My lord of Gloucester, do you
   hear the news?

SPENCER JUNIOR  What news, my lord?

EDWARD  Why man, they say there is great execution
   Done through the realm. My lord of Arundel,
   You have the note, have you not?

ARUNDEL  From the Lieutenant of the Tower, my lord.

EDWARD  I pray let us see it. What have we there?     **10**
   Read it Spencer.

SPENCER JUNIOR  (*Reads their names*) [The Lord
   William Tuchet, the Lord William Fitzwilliam, the
   Lord Warren de Lisle, the Lord Henry Bradborne,
   and the Lord William Chenie barons, with John
   Page, an esquire, were drawn and hanged at Pomfret
   [. . .] and then shortly after, Roger Lord Clifford,
   John Lord Mowbray, and Sir Gosein D'Eivill,
   barons, were drawn and hanged at York. At Bristol in
   like manner were executed Sir Henry de Willington
   and Sir Henry Montfort, baronets; and at Gloucester,
   the Lord John Gifford and Sir William Elmebridge,
   knights; and at London, the Lord Henry Tyes,
   baron; at Winchelsea, Sir Thomas Culpepper,
   knight: at Windsor, the Lord Francis de Aldham,
   baron; and at Canterbury, the Lord Bartholomew de
   Badlesmere and the Lord Bartholomew de
   Ashburnham, barons. Also, at Cardiff in Wales, Sir
   William Fleming, knight, was executed. Divers were
   executed in their counties, as Sir Thomas Mandit
   and others.]

EDWARD  Why so, they 'barked apace a month ago;
   Now, on my life, they'll neither bark nor bite.
   Now, sirs, the news from France; Gloucester, I trow
   The lords of France love England's gold so well
   As Isabella gets no aid from thence.
   What now remains? Have you proclaimed, my lord,
   Reward for them can bring in Mortimer?

SPENCER JUNIOR  My lord, we have; and if he be in
   England,
   A will be had ere long, I doubt it not.     **20**

EDWARD  If, dost thou say? Spencer, as true as death,
   He is in England's ground; our port masters
   Are not so careless of their king's command.

*Enter a* POST *with letters*

   How now, what news with thee? From whence come
   these?

POST  Letters, my lord, and tidings forth of France
   To you, my lord of Gloucester, from Levune.

EDWARD  Read.     **27**

SPENCER JUNIOR  (*Reads the letter*) 'My duty to your
   honour premised, *etcetera*, I have according to
   instructions in that behalf, dealt with the King of
   France's lords, and effected that the Queen, all
   discontented and discomforted, is gone. Whither? If
   you ask, with Sir John of Hainault, brother to the
   Marquis, into Flanders. With them are gone Lord
   Edmund and the Lord Mortimer, having in their

---

66 bid the . . . a base: a challenge to an opponent to risk
   becoming a prisoner (from a children's game)
67 match: game
74 brother: i.e. brother-in-law
75 motion: proposal
76 forward: ardent
3 uncontrolled: without censure
8 note: official notification of the dead
11 Read it Spencer: Marlowe's text does not include the list
   of names. We follow other editors by inserting the list
   from *Holinshed's Chronicles of England, Scotland and
   Ireland*, 2nd edition (1587)

12 'barked: embarked (on their treason)
   apace: swiftly
15 love England's gold: Edward's bribe has worked
20 A will be had: he will be captured
28–9 'My duty . . . honour premised': formal opening for a
   report
31 effected: brought about

company divers of your nation, and others; and, as
constant report goeth, they intend to give King
Edward battle in England sooner than he can look
for them. This is all the news of import.
> Your honour's in all service, Levune.'

EDWARD Ah, villains, hath that Mortimer escaped? **41**
With him is Edmund gone associate?
And will Sir John of Hainault lead the round?
Welcome, i' God's name, madam, and your son;
England shall welcome you and all your rout.
Gallop apace bright Phoebus through the sky,
And dusky night, in rusty iron car,
Between you both shorten the time, I pray,
That I may see that most desirèd day
When we may meet these traitors in the field. **50**
Ah, nothing grieves me but my little boy
Is thus misled to countenance their ills,
Come, friends, to Bristol, there to make us strong;
And, winds, as equal be to bring them in
As you injurious were to bear them forth.
> *Exeunt*

## Act IV, scene iv

*Enter* ISABELLA THE QUEEN, *her son* PRINCE EDWARD,
EDMUND *the* EARL OF KENT, MORTIMER JUNIOR, *and* SIR
JOHN OF HAINAULT, *with soldiers*

ISABELLA Now lords, our loving friends and
countrymen,
Welcome to England all. With prosperous winds
Our kindest friends in Belgia have we left,
To cope with friends at home. A heavy case,
When force to force is knit, and sword and glaive
In civil broils makes kin and countrymen
Slaughter themselves in others, and their sides
With their own weapons gored. But what's the help?
Misgoverned kings are cause of all this wrack;
And Edward, thou art one among them all, **10**
Whose looseness hath betrayed thy land to spoil
And made the channels overflow with blood.

---

37 constant: consistent, reliable
43 lead the round: lead the dance (the next stage)
46 Phoebus: Apollo, the classical god of the sun, who drove
  the sun across the sky in a chariot
52 countenance their ills: support their crimes
2 prosperous: favourable
3 Belgia: the Low Countries
4 cope: engage in battle
  friends: kinsfolk, relatives
  heavy case: sad state of affairs
5 glaive: 'lance, but in the sixteenth century the word came
  also to mean "bill" and "sword"' (Forker)
8 help: remedy
9 Misgoverned: unruly
  wrack: destruction

Of thine own people patron shouldst thou be,
But thou—
MORTIMER JUNIOR Nay madam, if you be a warrior,
Ye must not grow so passionate in speeches.
Lords, sith that we are by sufferance of heaven
Arrived and armèd in this prince's right,
Here for our country's cause swear we to him
All homage, fealty, and forwardness.
And for the open wrongs and injuries **20**
Edward hath done to us, his Queen, and land,
We come in arms to wreak it with the sword,
That England's Queen in peace may repossess
Her dignities and honours, and withal
We may remove these flatterers from the King,
That havocs England's wealth and treasury.
SIR JOHN Sound trumpets, my lord, and forward let us
march;
Edward will think we come to flatter him.
KENT I would he never had been flattered more.
> *Trumpets sound. Exeunt*

## Act IV, scene v

*Enter* EDWARD THE KING, BALDOCK, *and* SPENCER
JUNIOR, *flying about the stage*

SPENCER JUNIOR Fly, fly, my lord! The Queen is over-
strong;
Her friends do multiply and yours do fail.
Shape we our course to Ireland, there to breathe.
EDWARD What, was I born to fly and run away,
And leave the Mortimers conquerors behind?
Give me my horse, and let's r'enforce our troops,
And in this bed of honour die with fame.
BALDOCK O no, my lord; this princely resolution
Fits not the time. Away! We are pursued.
> *Exeunt*

## Act IV, scene vi

*Enter* EDMUND *the* EARL OF KENT *alone with a sword and
target*

KENT This way he fled, but I am come too late.

---

13 patron: a) exemplary; b) benefactor; c) father-figure
16 sufferance: permission
17 this prince's: i.e. young Prince Edward's
19 homage, fealty, and forwardness: respect, loyalty and
  eagerness
22 wreak: avenge (wreak vengeance)
26 havocs: misuses (literally 'lays waste')
2 fail: a) decline in number; b) die; c) are exhausted
5 the Mortimers: historically inaccurate since Mortimer
  Senior was dead by this time, not having survived his
  imprisonment in the Tower of London
7 bed of honour: i.e. England

Edward, alas, my heart relents for thee.
Proud traitor Mortimer, why dost thou chase
Thy lawful king, thy sovereign, with thy sword?
(*Addressing himself*) Vile wretch, and why hast thou,
    of all unkind,
Borne arms against thy brother and thy king?
Rain showers of vengeance on my cursèd head,
Thou God, to whom in justice it belongs
To punish this unnatural revolt.
Edward, this Mortimer aims at thy life;    10
O fly him then! But Edmund, calm this rage;
Dissemble or thou diest, for Mortimer
And Isabel do kiss while they conspire;
And yet she bears a face of love, forsooth.
Fie on that love that hatcheth death and hate!
Edmund, away; Bristol to Longshanks' blood
Is false. Be not found single for suspect;
Proud Mortimer pries near into thy walks.

*Enter* ISABELLA THE QUEEN, MORTIMER JUNIOR, *the*
*young* PRINCE EDWARD, *and* SIR JOHN OF HAINAULT
*with soldiers*

ISABELLA  Successful battles gives the God of kings
    To them that fight in right and fear his wrath.    20
    Since then successfully we have prevailed,
    Thanks be heaven's great architect and you.
    Ere farther we proceed, my noble lords,
    We here create our well-belovèd son,
    Of love and care unto his royal person,
    Lord Warden of the realm; and sith the fates
    Have made his father so infortunate,
    Deal you, my lords, in this, my loving lords,
    As to your wisdoms fittest seems in all.
KENT  Madam, without offence, if I may ask,    30
    How will you deal with Edward in his fall?
PRINCE EDWARD  Tell me, good uncle, what Edward do
    you mean?
KENT  Nephew, your father; I dare not call him king.
MORTIMER JUNIOR  My lord of Kent, what needs these
    questions?
    'Tis not in her controlment, nor in ours,
    But as the realm and Parliament shall please,
    So shall your brother be disposed of.

---

5  unkind: unnatural (as he is acting against his own
    brother)
12  Dissemble: be deceptive
14  forsooth: in truth
16–17  Bristol: the Mayor of Bristol has joined the rebellion
17  single: alone
18  walks: movement
22  architect: God
    you: Isabella's supporters
26  Lord Warden: viceroy (appointed during a king's
    minority)
28  Deal: proceed

(*Aside to* ISABELLA) I like not this relenting mood in
    Edmund;
    Madam, 'tis good to look to him betimes.
ISABELLA  (*Aside to* MORTIMER JUNIOR) My lord, the
    Mayor of Bristol knows our mind?    40
MORTIMER JUNIOR  (*Aside*) Yea, madam, and they
    'scape not easily
    That fled the field.
ISABELLA             Baldock is with the King;
    A goodly chancellor, is he not, my lord?
SIR JOHN  So are the Spencers, the father and the son.
KENT  (*To himself*) This Edward is the ruin of the
    realm.

*Enter* RHYS AP HOWELL, *and the* MAYOR OF BRISTOL,
*with* SPENCER SENIOR, *guarded by soldiers*

RHYS AP HOWELL  God save Queen Isabel and her
    princely son.
    Madam, the Mayor and citizens of Bristol,
    In sign of love and duty to this presence,
    Present by me this traitor to the state—
    Spencer, the father to that wanton Spencer,    50
    That, like the lawless Catiline of Rome,
    Revelled in England's wealth and treasury.
ISABELLA  We thank you all.
MORTIMER JUNIOR          Your loving care in this
    Deserveth princely favours and rewards.
    But where's the King and the other Spencer fled?
RHYS AP HOWELL  Spencer the son, created Earl of
    Gloucester,
    Is with that smooth-tongued scholar Baldock gone,
    And shipped but late for Ireland with the King.
MORTIMER JUNIOR  Some whirlwind fetch them back,
    or sink them all!
    They shall be started thence, I doubt it not.    60
PRINCE EDWARD  Shall I not see the King my father
    yet?
KENT  (*Aside*) Unhappy Edward, chased from England's
    bounds.
SIR JOHN  Madam, what resteth? Why stand ye in a
    muse?
ISABELLA  I rue my lord's ill fortune, but, alas,
    Care of my country called me to this war.
MORTIMER JUNIOR  Madam, have done with care and
    sad complaint;
    Your king hath wronged your country and himself,

---

38  relenting: pitying
48  presence: i.e. royal presence
51  Catiline of Rome: the corrupt Lucius Sergius Catalina
    (d. 62 BC) whose name was a byword for treason in
    Elizabethan England
58  but late: just lately
60  started: forced out from a hiding place (hunting term)
63  resteth: remains to be done
    in a muse: in thought, in a trance

And we must seek to right it as we may.
Meanwhile, have hence this rebel to the block;
Your lordship cannot privilege your head.                    70
SPENCER SENIOR  Rebel is he that fights against his
    prince;
  So fought not they that fought in Edward's right.
MORTIMER JUNIOR  Take him away; he prates.
                               *Exit* SPENCER SENIOR, *guarded*
                 You, Rhys ap Howell,
  Shall do good service to her majesty,
  Being of countenance in your country here,
  To follow these rebellious runagates.
  We in meanwhile, madam, must take advice
  How Baldock, Spencer, and their complices
  May in their fall be followed to their end.
                                             *Exeunt*

# Act IV, scene vii

*Enter the* ABBOT, MONKS, KING EDWARD, SPENCER
JUNIOR, *and* BALDOCK, *the latter three disguised as monks*

ABBOT  Have you no doubt, my lord, have you no fear;
  As silent and as careful will we be
  To keep your royal person safe with us,
  Free from suspect and fell invasion
  Of such as have your majesty in chase—
  Yourself, and those your chosen company—
  As danger of this stormy time requires.
EDWARD  Father, thy face should harbour no deceit;
  O hadst thou ever been a king, thy heart,
  Pierced deeply with sense of my distress,                  10
  Could not but take compassion of my state.
  Stately and proud, in riches and in train,
  Whilom I was powerful and full of pomp;
  But what is he, whom rule and empery
  Have not in life or death made miserable?
  Come Spencer, come Baldock, come sit down by me;
  Make trial now of that philosophy
  That in our famous nurseries of arts
  Thou sucked'st from Plato and from Aristotle.
  Father, this life contemplative is heaven—                 20

O that I might this life in quiet lead!
  But we, alas, are chased; and you, my friends,
  Your lives and my dishonour they pursue.
  Yet, gentle monks, for treasure, gold nor fee,
  Do you betray us and our company.
MONKS  Your grace may sit secure, if none but we
  Do wot of your abode.
SPENCER JUNIOR  Not one alive; but shrewdly I suspect
  A gloomy fellow in a mead below;
  A gave a long look after us, my lord,                      30
  And all the land, I know, is up in arms—
  Arms that pursue our lives with deadly hate.
BALDOCK  We were embarked for Ireland, wretched we,
  With awkward winds and sore tempests driven
  To fall on shore and here to pine in fear
  Of Mortimer and his confederates.
EDWARD  Mortimer! Who talks of Mortimer?
  Who wounds me with the name of Mortimer,
  That bloody man? (*Kneeling*) Good father, on thy lap
  Lay I this head, laden with mickle care.                   40
  O might I never open these eyes again,
  Never again lift up this drooping head,
  O never more lift up this dying heart!
SPENCER JUNIOR  Look up, my lord. Baldock, this
    drowsiness
  Betides no good. Here even we are betrayed.

*Enter, with Welsh hooks,* RHYS AP HOWELL, *a* MOWER,
*and the* EARL OF LEICESTER, *with* SOLDIERS

MOWER  Upon my life, those be the men ye seek.
RHYS AP HOWELL  Fellow, enough. (*To* LEICESTER) My
    lord, I pray be short;
  A fair commission warrants what we do.
LEICESTER  (*Aside*) The Queen's commission, urged by
    Mortimer.
  What cannot gallant Mortimer with the Queen?              50

---

70  Your lordship . . . your head: 'your new rank will not
      prevent beheading' (Kinney)
75  countenance: authority
76  runagates: renegades, traitors
77  take advice: consider
 4  fell: cruel
 5  chase: pursuit (as in hunting)
13  Whilom: formerly
      pomp: splendour
14  empery: empire
18  nurseries of arts: the universities at Oxford and
      Cambridge
20  this life contemplative: the reflective, devotional life as
      opposed to the active life (a standard medieval contrast)

27  wot: know
28  shrewdly: intuitively
29  gloomy fellow: the Mower, whom Spencer Junior supposes
      to be the Grim Reaper, the personification of death
      mead: meadow
      below: beyond the walls of the Abbey
34  sore: harsh
39  bloody: bloodthirsty
40  mickle: much (northern English and still used in Scotland)
44  drowsiness: an ill omen (see *Arden of Faversham*, v.16–17)
SD  *Welsh hooks*: either military weapons or, as many critics
      think, agricultural tools. Forker convincingly argues for
      the latter since 'if they are scythelike tools [they] would
      give visual point to the symbolism of the "gloomy fellow"
      mentioned earlier and add effectively to our sense of the
      king's vulnerability by introducing a note of roughness –
      even of rustic savagery – to the moment of his capture'
48  fair commission: legal authority
      warrants: authorises
50  gallant: a) bold; b) her lover

Alas, see where he sits and hopes unseen
T'escape their hands that seek to reave his life.
Too true it is: *quem dies vidit veniens superbum,*
*Hunc dies vidit fugiens iacentem.*
But Leicester, leave to grow so passionate.
(*Aloud*) Spencer and Baldock, by no other names,
I arrest you of high treason here.
Stand not on titles, but obey th'arrest;
'Tis in the name of Isabel the Queen.
My lord, why droop you thus?                        60
EDWARD  O day! The last of all my bliss on earth,
    Centre of all misfortune. O my stars!
    Why do you lour unkindly on a king?
    Comes Leicester, then, in Isabella's name
    To take my life, my company, from me?
    Here, man, rip up this panting breast of mine
    And take my heart in rescue of my friends.
RHYS AP HOWELL  Away with them.
SPENCER JUNIOR                    It may become thee yet
    To let us take our farewell of his grace.
ABBOT  My heart with pity earns to see this sight;    70
    A king to bear these words and proud commands!
EDWARD  Spencer, ah sweet Spencer, thus then must
    we part?
SPENCER JUNIOR  We must, my lord; so will the angry
    heavens.
EDWARD  Nay, so will hell and cruel Mortimer;
    The gentle heavens have not to do in this.
BALDOCK  My lord, it is in vain to grieve or storm.
    Here humbly of your grace we take our leaves;
    Our lots are cast. I fear me, so is thine.
EDWARD  In heaven we may, in earth never shall we
    meet.
    And Leicester, say, what shall become of us?    80
LEICESTER  Your majesty must go to Kenilworth.
EDWARD  'Must'! 'Tis somewhat hard when kings must
    go.
LEICESTER  Here is a litter ready for your grace
    That waits your pleasure; and the day grows old.

RHYS AP HOWELL  As good be gone, as stay and be
    benighted.
EDWARD  A litter hast thou? Lay me in a hearse,
    And to the gates of hell convey me hence;
    Let Pluto's bells ring out my fatal knell,
    And hags howl for my death at Charon's shore,
    For friends hath Edward none but these, and these,
    And these must die under a tyrant's sword.    91
RHYS AP HOWELL  My lord, be going; care not for these,
    For we shall see them shorter by the heads.
EDWARD  Well, that shall be shall be; part we must:
    Sweet Spencer, gentle Baldock, part we must.
    Hence feignèd weeds, unfeignèd are my woes.
    Father, farewell. Leicester, thou stay'st for me,
    And go I must. Life, farewell with my friends.
                *Exeunt* EDWARD *and* LEICESTER
SPENCER JUNIOR  O, is he gone? Is noble Edward gone,
    Parted from hence, never to see us more?    100
    Rend, sphere of heaven, and fire forsake thy orb!
    Earth melt to air! Gone is my sovereign,
    Gone, gone, alas, never to make return.
BALDOCK  Spencer, I see our souls are fleeted hence;
    We are deprived the sunshine of our life.
    Make for a new life, man; throw up thy eyes,
    And heart and hand to heaven's immortal throne,
    Pay nature's debt with cheerful countenance.
    Reduce we all our lessons unto this:
    To die, sweet Spencer, therefore live we all;    110
    Spencer, all live to die, and rise to fall.
RHYS AP HOWELL  Come, come, keep these
    preachments till you come to the place appointed.
    You, and such as you are, have made wise work in

---

52  reave: take away by force
53–4  *quem dies . . . fugiens iacentem*: from Seneca's *Thyestes*,
    ll. 613–14. Jasper Heywood translated it in 1560 as:
    'Whom dawn of the day hath seen in pryde to
    reign,/Him overthrown hath seen the evening late'
55  leave to grow so passionate: 'Leicester's sympathy for
    Edward here prepares us for his later replacement by
    Berkeley' (Forker)
56  no other names: Spencer and Baldock have been stripped
    of their recently acquired titles
63  lour: frown
67  rescue: a) ransom; b) release
70  earns: grieves
81  Kenilworth: castle and town in Warwickshire. Q has
    Killingworth which many editors and directors preserve
    for its ominous overtones
83  litter: coach carried by men

88  Pluto's bells: Pluto was the keeper of the underworld and
    ruler of the dead
89  Charon's shore: the ferryman of the classical world who
    took the dead across the river Styx (see *The Spanish
    Tragedy*, I.i.20–2)
93  shorter by the heads: i.e. they will be beheaded
96  feignèd weeds: false clothes (he removes his monkish
    disguise)
101  Rend: be torn apart
    sphere of . . . thy orb: some Elizabethan astronomers
    thought (not uncontroversially) that the sun was a sphere
    or orb of fire (*coelum igneum*)
104  fleeted hence: left our bodies
105  the sunshine of our life: i.e. Edward
108  Pay nature's debt: die
109  Reduce: summarise
110–11  To die . . . to fall: Baldock's meditation on death (and
    tragedy) reminds us of his scholarly background,
    although the sentiment itself may have seemed a little
    commonplace to an Elizabethan audience
113  preachments: sermons
    place appointed: place of execution (where the
    condemned could make a speech to spectators). Rhys ap
    Howell is in characteristically sarcastic mood

England. Will your lordships away?

MOWER Your worship, I trust, will remember me?

RHYS AP HOWELL Remember thee, fellow? What else?
Follow me to the town.

*Exeunt*

# Act V, scene i

*Enter* EDWARD THE KING, LEICESTER, *with the* BISHOP
OF WINCHESTER, *and* TRUSSEL *for the crown, and
attendants*

LEICESTER Be patient, good my lord, cease to lament.
Imagine Kenilworth Castle were your court,
And that you lay for pleasure here a space,
Not of compulsion or necessity.

EDWARD Leicester, if gentle words might comfort me,
Thy speeches long ago had eased my sorrows,
For kind and loving hast thou always been.
The griefs of private men are soon allayed,
But not of kings: the forest deer, being struck,
Runs to an herb that closeth up the wounds;          10
But when the imperial lion's flesh is gored,
He rends and tears it with his wrathful paw,
And, highly scorning that the lowly earth
Should drink his blood, mounts up into the air.
And so it fares with me, whose dauntless mind
The ambitious Mortimer would seek to curb,
And that unnatural Queen, false Isabel,
That thus hath pent and mewed me in a prison.
For such outrageous passions cloy my soul,
As with the wings of rancour and disdain          20
Full often am I soaring up to heaven
To plain me to the gods against them both.
But when I call to mind I am a king,
Methinks I should revenge me of the wrongs
That Mortimer and Isabel have done.
But what are kings, when regiment is gone,
But perfect shadows in a sunshine day?
My nobles rule; I bear the name of king;
I wear the crown, but am controlled by them—

By Mortimer and my unconstant Queen          30
Who spots my nuptial bed with infamy,
Whilst I am lodged within this cave of care,
Where sorrow at my elbow still attends
To company my heart with sad laments,
That bleeds within me for this strange exchange.
But tell me, must I now resign my crown
To make usurping Mortimer a king?

BISHOP OF WINCHESTER Your grace mistakes; it is for
England's good
And princely Edward's right we crave the crown.

EDWARD No, 'tis for Mortimer, not Edward's head,   40
For he's a lamb encompassed by wolves
Which in a moment will abridge his life.
But if proud Mortimer do wear this crown,
Heavens turn it to a blaze of quenchless fire,
Or, like the snaky wreath of Tisiphon,
Engirt the temples of his hateful head;
So shall not England's vine be perished,
But Edward's name survives, though Edward dies.

LEICESTER My lord, why waste you thus the time away?
They stay your answer: will you yield your crown?  50

EDWARD Ah Leicester, weigh how hardly I can brook
To lose my crown and kingdom without cause,
To give ambitious Mortimer my right,
That like a mountain overwhelms my bliss;
In which extreme my mind here murdered is.
But what the heavens appoint, I must obey.

*He removes his crown*

Here, take my crown—the life of Edward too.
Two kings in England cannot reign at once.
But stay awhile; let me be king till night,
That I may gaze upon this glittering crown;        60
So shall my eyes receive their last content,
My head, the latest honour due to it,
And jointly both yield up their wished right.
Continue ever, thou celestial sun;
Let never silent night possess this clime.
Stand still, you watches of the element;
All times and seasons rest you at a stay,

---

116 remember me: a) with remuneration; b) if the Mower is a
symbol of death, the last lines of the act take on a more
surreal and haunting aspect

3 lay: resided
space: period of time, an interval

8 allayed: abated

9–10 forest deer . . . the wounds: reference to the belief that a
deer, wounded by an arrow, would seek out the healing
herb dittany

18 pent: shut up
mewed: caged (a 'mew' was a cage for birds and animals)

19 outrageous: excessive

22 plain me: complain

27 perfect: mere, simple

---

30 unconstant: unfaithful

35 strange exchange: change of circumstances unnatural to a
king

43–4 this crown . . . quenchless fire: in classical mythology
Jason deserted Medea for Creusa. Medea gave her a
golden crown which burst into flames on her head (see
Euripides, *Medea*, ll. 1,186–94)

45 Tisiphon: Tisiphone, one of the Furies who had snakes
as hair (see *Arden of Faversham* xiv.151)

47 vine: symbol of royal lineage

50 stay: await

51 weigh: consider

66 watches of the element: the planets and stars. The night
was divided in four parts or 'watches'

67 rest you at a stay: i.e. remain fixed

That Edward may be still fair England's king.
But day's bright beams doth vanish fast away,
And needs I must resign my wishèd crown.    **70**
Inhuman creatures, nursed with tiger's milk,
Why gape you for your sovereign's overthrow?
My diadem, I mean, and guiltless life.
See, monsters, see, I'll wear my crown again.
                  *He puts on the crown*
What, fear you not the fury of your king?
But hapless Edward, thou art fondly led.
They pass not for thy frowns as late they did,
But seek to make a new-elected king,
Which fills my mind with strange despairing
   thoughts,
Which thoughts are martyred with endless torments;
And in this torment, comfort find I none    **81**
But that I feel the crown upon my head.
And therefore let me wear it yet a while.
TRUSSEL  My lord, the parliament must have present
   news,
And therefore say, will you resign or no?
                  *The King rageth*
EDWARD  I'll not resign, but whilst I live—
Traitors, be gone, and join you with Mortimer.
Elect, conspire, install, do what you will;
Their blood and yours shall seal these treacheries.
BISHOP OF WINCHESTER  This answer we'll return, and
   so farewell.    **90**
       *The* BISHOP OF WINCHESTER *and* TRUSSEL *begin*
                   *to leave*
LEICESTER  Call them again, my lord, and speak them
   fair,
For if they go, the Prince shall lose his right.
EDWARD  Call thou them back; I have no power to
   speak.
LEICESTER  My lord, the King is willing to resign.
BISHOP OF WINCHESTER  If he be not, let him choose—
EDWARD  O would I might! But heavens and earth
   conspire
To make me miserable.        *He removes the crown*
            Here, receive my crown.
Receive it? No, these innocent hands of mine
Shall not be guilty of so foul a crime.
He of you all that most desires my blood    **100**
And will be called the murderer of a king,
Take it. What, are you moved? Pity you me?

---

71  tiger's milk: tigers were a symbol of cruelty
76  fondly: foolishly
77  pass: care
    late: recently
84  present news: a prompt report
86  I'll not . . . I live: the line is metrically short and some
    editors supply another foot (such as 'be king'), yet the
    shortened line well reflects Edward's despair
92  right: inheritance

Then send for unrelenting Mortimer
And Isabel, whose eyes, being turned to steel,
Will sooner sparkle fire than shed a tear.
Yet stay, for rather than I will look on them,
Here, here!      *He gives the crown to the* BISHOP
           Now, sweet God of heaven,
Make me despise this transitory pomp,
And sit for aye enthronizèd in heaven.
Come death, and with thy fingers close my eyes,   **110**
Or if I live, let me forget myself.
BISHOP OF WINCHESTER  My lord.
EDWARD  Call me not lord! Away, out of my sight!
Ah, pardon me; grief makes me lunatic.
Let not that Mortimer protect my son;
More safety is there in a tiger's jaws
Than his embracements.    *He gives a handkerchief*
           Bear this to the Queen,
Wet with my tears and dried again with sighs.
If with the sight thereof she be not moved,
Return it back and dip it in my blood.    **120**
Commend me to my son, and bid him rule
Better than I. Yet how have I transgressed,
Unless it be with too much clemency?
TRUSSEL  And thus, most humbly, do we take our leave.
EDWARD  Farewell. I know the next news that they
   bring
Will be my death, and welcome shall it be;
To wretched men death is felicity.

*Enter* BERKELEY *with a letter*

LEICESTER  Another post. What news brings he?
EDWARD  Such news as I expect. Come, Berkeley, come,
And tell thy message to my naked breast.    **130**
BERKELEY  My lord, think not a thought so villainous
Can harbour in a man of noble birth.
To do your highness service and devoir,
And save you from your foes, Berkeley would die.
LEICESTER  (*Reading the letter*) My lord, the council of
   the Queen commands
That I resign my charge.
EDWARD  And who must keep me now? Must you, my
   lord?
BERKELEY  Ay, my most gracious lord, so 'tis decreed.
EDWARD  (*Taking the letter*) By Mortimer, whose name
   is written here.      *He tears up the letter*
Well may I rend his name that rends my heart!   **140**
This poor revenge hath something eased my mind.
So may his limbs be torn, as is this paper!
Hear me, immortal Jove, and grant it too.

---

109  for aye enthronizèd: for ever enthroned
115  protect: be Lord Protector (during Prince Edward's
     minority)
133  devoir: duty
143  Jove: Jupiter, the supreme god of Roman mythology

BERKELEY  Your grace must hence with me to Berkeley
    straight.
EDWARD  Whither you will; all places are alike,
    And every earth is fit for burial.
LEICESTER  (*To* BERKELEY) Favour him, my lord, as
    much as lieth in you.
BERKELEY  Even so betide my soul as I use him.
EDWARD  Mine enemy hath pitied my estate,
    And that's the cause that I am now removed.    **150**
BERKELEY  And thinks your grace that Berkeley will be
    cruel?
EDWARD  I know not; but of this am I assured,
    That death ends all, and I can die but once.
    Leicester, farewell.
LEICESTER  Not yet, my lord; I'll bear you on your way.
                                 *Exeunt*

# Act V, scene ii

*Enter* MORTIMER JUNIOR, *and* QUEEN ISABELLA

MORTIMER JUNIOR  Fair Isabel, now have we our desire.
    The proud corrupters of the light-brained King
    Have done their homage to the lofty gallows,
    And he himself lies in captivity.
    Be ruled by me, and we will rule the realm.
    In any case, take heed of childish fear,
    For now we hold an old wolf by the ears,
    That if he slip will seize upon us both,
    And grip the sorer, being gripped himself.
    Think therefore, madam, that imports us much    **10**
    To erect your son with all the speed we may,
    And that I be Protector over him,
    For our behoof will bear the greater sway
    Whenas a king's name shall be underwrit.
ISABELLA  Sweet Mortimer, the life of Isabel,
    Be thou persuaded that I love thee well,
    And therefore, so the Prince my son be safe,
    Whom I esteem as dear as these mine eyes,
    Conclude against his father what thou wilt,
    And I myself will willingly subscribe.    **20**
MORTIMER JUNIOR  First would I hear news that he
    were deposed,
    And then let me alone to handle him.

---

148  so betide my soul: 'let my soul be so treated'
149  estate: condition
  2  light-brained: wanton, frivolous
  7  old wolf by the ears: proverbial
  9  grip the sorer: tighten his grip
 10  imports us much: it is most important for us
 11  erect: establish (on the throne)
13–14  For our . . . be underwrit: i.e. Mortimer and the Queen
      will have more authority once he can act in the King's
      name as Protector
 19  Conclude: decide

*Enter* MESSENGER

MORTIMER JUNIOR  Letters, from whence?
MESSENGER             From Kenilworth, my lord.
ISABELLA  How fares my lord the King?
MESSENGER  In health, madam, but full of pensiveness.
ISABELLA  Alas, poor soul, would I could ease his grief

*Enter the* BISHOP OF WINCHESTER *with the crown*

    Thanks, gentle Winchester.
    (*To the* MESSENGER)      Sirrah, be gone.
                            *Exit* MESSENGER
BISHOP OF WINCHESTER  The King hath willingly
    resigned his crown.
ISABELLA  O happy news! Send for the Prince, my son.
BISHOP OF WINCHESTER  Further, ere this letter was
    sealed, Lord Berkeley came,    **30**
    So that he now is gone from Kenilworth.
    And we have heard that Edmund laid a plot
    To set his brother free; no more but so.
    The lord of Berkeley is so pitiful
    As Leicester that had charge of him before.
ISABELLA  Then let some other be his guardian.
               *Exit* BISHOP OF WINCHESTER
MORTIMER JUNIOR  Let me alone—here is the privy
    seal.
    (*Calls offstage*) Who's there? Call hither Gourney and
    Maltravers.
    To dash the heavy-headed Edmund's drift,
    Berkeley shall be discharged, the King removed,    **40**
    And none but we shall know where he lieth.
ISABELLA  But Mortimer, as long as he survives
    What safety rests for us, or for my son?
MORTIMER JUNIOR  Speak, shall he presently be
    dispatched and die?
ISABELLA  I would he were, so it were not by my means.

*Enter* MALTRAVERS *and* GOURNEY

MORTIMER JUNIOR  Enough. Maltravers, write a letter
    presently
    Unto the Lord of Berkeley from ourself,
    That he resign the King to thee and Gourney;
    And when 'tis done, we will subscribe our name.

---

25  pensiveness: melancholy
34  so pitiful: as sympathetic (to Edward)
37  privy seal: the official symbol of royal authority
38  Gourney and Maltravers: according to Holinshed these
    men were 'Sir Thomas Gourney' and 'the lord
    Maltreuers' ('Gurney' and 'Matrevis' in Q) but 'Marlowe
    deprives them of titles and treats them as hired thugs'
    (Forker)
39  To dash . . . Edmund's drift: 'to frustrate the stupid
    Edward's plan'
43  rests: remains
44  dispatched: killed
48  resign: surrender, turn over

MALTRAVERS  It shall be done, my lord.
MORTIMER JUNIOR                Gourney.
GOURNEY                        My lord? **50**
MORTIMER JUNIOR  As thou intendest to rise by
    Mortimer,
  Who now makes Fortune's wheel turn as he please,
  Seek all the means thou canst to make him droop,
  And neither give him kind word nor good look.
GOURNEY  I warrant you, my lord.
MORTIMER JUNIOR  And this above the rest, because we
    hear
  That Edmund casts to work his liberty,
  Remove him still from place to place by night,
  And at the last he come to Kenilworth,
  And then from thence to Berkeley back again.   **60**
  And by the way to make him fret the more,
  Speak curstly to him; and in any case
  Let no man comfort him if he chance to weep,
  But amplify his grief with bitter words.
MALTRAVERS  Fear not, my lord, we'll do as you
    command.
MORTIMER JUNIOR  So now away; post thitherwards
    amain.
ISABELLA  Whither goes this letter? To my lord the
    King?
  Commend me humbly to his majesty,
  And tell him that I labour all in vain
  To ease his grief and work his liberty.   **70**
  And bear him this, as witness of my love.
            *She gives* MALTRAVERS *a jewel*
MALTRAVERS  I will, madam.
     *Exeunt* MALTRAVERS *and* GOURNEY. ISABELLA *and*
            MORTIMER JUNIOR REMAIN

*Enter the young* PRINCE EDWARD *and the* EARL OF KENT
*talking with him*

MORTIMER JUNIOR  (*Aside to* ISABELLA) Finely
    dissembled; do so still, sweet Queen.
  Here comes the young Prince with the Earl of Kent.
ISABELLA  (*Aside to* MORTIMER JUNIOR)
  Something he whispers in his childish ears.
MORTIMER JUNIOR  (*Aside*) If he have such access unto
    the Prince,

Our plots and stratagems will soon be dashed.
ISABELLA  (*Aside*) Use Edmund friendly, as if all were
    well.
MORTIMER JUNIOR  How fares my honourable lord of
    Kent?
KENT  In health, sweet Mortimer. How fares your
    grace?   **80**
ISABELLA  Well—if my lord your brother were
    enlarged.
KENT  I hear of late he hath deposed himself.
ISABELLA  The more my grief.
MORTIMER JUNIOR  And mine.
KENT  (*Aside*) Ah, they do dissemble.
ISABELLA  Sweet son, come hither; I must talk with
    thee.
MORTIMER JUNIOR  (*To* KENT) Thou, being his uncle
    and the next of blood,
  Do look to be Protector over the Prince.
KENT  Not I, my lord; who should protect the son
  But she that gave him life—I mean, the Queen?   **90**
PRINCE EDWARD  Mother, persuade me not to wear the
    crown;
  Let him be king. I am too young to reign.
ISABELLA  But be content, seeing it his highness'
    pleasure.
PRINCE EDWARD  Let me but see him first, and then I
    will.
KENT  Ay, do, sweet nephew.
ISABELLA  Brother, you know it is impossible.
PRINCE EDWARD  Why, is he dead?
ISABELLA  No, God forbid.
KENT  I would those words proceeded from your heart.
MORTIMER JUNIOR  Inconstant Edmund, dost thou
    favour him   **100**
  That wast a cause of his imprisonment?
KENT  The more cause have I now to make amends.
MORTIMER JUNIOR  I tell thee 'tis not meet that one so
    false
  Should come about the person of a prince.
  (*To* PRINCE EDWARD) My lord, he hath betrayed the
    King, his brother,
  And therefore trust him not.
PRINCE EDWARD  But he repents and sorrows for it now.
ISABELLA  Come son, and go with this gentle lord and
    me.
PRINCE EDWARD  With you I will, but not with
    Mortimer.
MORTIMER JUNIOR  Why, youngling, 'sdain'st thou so
    of Mortimer?   **110**
  Then I will carry thee by force away.

---

52  Fortune's wheel: an Elizabethan personification saw
    Fortune with a wheel which turned to determine human
    fate, thus the arrogance of those (such as Mortimer
    Junior) who consider themselves able to control its spin.
    Marlowe uses the image most effectively in *Tamburlaine*:
    'I hold the Fates bound fast in iron chains/And with my
    hand turn Fortune's wheel about' (I.ii.174–5)
57  casts: plans
62  curstly: meanly, cruelly
66  post thitherwards amain: go there with speed
73  dissembled: feigned
    still: continually

81  enlarged: released
82  deposed himself: abdicated
92  him: i.e. Edward II
110  'sdain'st: contracted form of 'distainest'

PRINCE EDWARD  Help, uncle Kent, Mortimer will
    wrong me.
           *Exit* MORTIMER JUNIOR *with* PRINCE EDWARD
ISABELLA  Brother Edmund, strive not; we are his
    friends.
    Isabel is nearer than the Earl of Kent.
KENT  Sister, Edward is my charge; redeem him.
ISABELLA  Edward is my son, and I will keep him.
                                        *Exit*
KENT  Mortimer shall know that he hath wrongèd me.
    Hence will I haste to Kenilworth Castle
    And rescue agèd Edward from his foes,
    To be revenged on Mortimer and thee.       120
                                          *Exit*

# Act V, scene iii

*Enter* MALTRAVERS *and* GOURNEY *with torches, with*
EDWARD THE KING, *and soldiers*

MALTRAVERS  My lord, be not pensive; we are your
    friends.
    Men are ordained to live in misery;
    Therefore come, dalliance dangereth our lives.
EDWARD  Friends, whither must unhappy Edward go?
    Will hateful Mortimer appoint no rest?
    Must I be vexèd like the nightly bird
    Whose sight is loathsome to all winged fowls?
    When will the fury of his mind assuage?
    When will his heart be satisfied with blood?
    If mine will serve, unbowel straight this breast,   10
    And give my heart to Isabel and him;
    It is the chiefest mark they level at.
GOURNEY  Not so, my liege; the Queen hath given this
    charge
    To keep your grace in safety.
    Your passions make your dolours to increase.
EDWARD  This usage makes my misery increase.
    But can my air of life continue long
    When all my senses are annoyed with stench?
    Within a dungeon England's king is kept,

Where I am starved for want of sustenance.    20
    My daily diet is heart-breaking sobs,
    That almost rends the closet of my heart.
    Thus lives old Edward, not relieved by any,
    And so must die, though pitied by many.
    O water, gentle friends, to cool my thirst
    And clear my body from foul excrements.
MALTRAVERS  Here's channel water, as our charge is
    given;
    Sit down, for we'll be barbers to your grace.
EDWARD  Traitors, away! What, will you murder me,
    Or choke your sovereign with puddle water?   30
GOURNEY  No, but wash your face and shave away your
    beard,
    Lest you be known and so be rescuèd.
MALTRAVERS  Why strive you thus? Your labour is in
    vain.
EDWARD  The wren may strive against the lion's
    strength,
    But all in vain; so vainly do I strive
    To seek for mercy at a tyrant's hand.    *They wash him*
                  *with puddle water, and shave his beard away*
    Immortal powers, that knows the painful cares
    That waits upon my poor distressed soul,
    O level all your looks upon these daring men,
    That wrongs their liege and sovereign, England's king.
    O Gaveston, it is for thee that I am wronged;   41
    For me, both thou and both the Spencers died,
    And for your sakes a thousand wrongs I'll take.
    The Spencers' ghosts, wherever they remain,
    Wish well to mine; then tush, for them I'll die.
MALTRAVERS  'Twixt theirs and yours shall be no
    enmity.
    Come, come away. Now put the torches out;
    We'll enter in by darkness to Kenilworth.

*Enter* EDMUND *the* EARL OF KENT

GOURNEY  How now, who comes there?
MALTRAVERS  Guard the King sure; it is the Earl of
    Kent.    50
EDWARD  O gentle brother, help to rescue me.
MALTRAVERS  Keep them asunder; thrust in the King.
KENT  Soldiers, let me but talk to him one word.
GOURNEY  Lay hands upon the Earl for this assault.
KENT  Lay down your weapons; traitors, yield the King!
MALTRAVERS  Edmund, yield thou thyself, or thou shalt
    die.    *Soldiers seize* KENT
KENT  Base villains, wherefore do you grip me thus?

---

114  nearer: i.e. nearer in blood (as a mother compared to an
     uncle)
115  charge: responsibility
     redeem: release
119  agèd: used to distinguish Edward II from his son.
     Historically Edward was 43 years old at this point
  3  dalliance: delay
6–7  vexèd like . . . winged fowls: the owl (an omen of death)
     was commonly thought to have been persecuted by birds
     of the day
 10  unbowel: cut open
     straight: at once
 12  mark: target
 15  dolours: sadness
 17  air of life: breath

22  closet: private chamber
26  excrements: faeces (but with an older sense of 'hair' that
     Maltravers and Gourney take to be Edward's meaning)
27  channel: drain, sewer
     charge: command
44  remain: dwell

GOURNEY  Bind him, and so convey him to the court.
KENT  Where is the court but here? Here is the King,
  And I will visit him. Why stay you me?    **60**
MALTRAVERS  The court is where Lord Mortimer
  remains.
  Thither shall your honour go; and so, farewell.
               *Exeunt* MALTRAVERS *and* GOURNEY, *with*
                          EDWARD THE KING.
      EDMUND *the* EARL OF KENT *and the* SOLDIERS *remain*
KENT  O, miserable is that commonweal, where lords
  Keep courts and kings are locked in prison!
SOLDIER  Wherefore stay we? On, sirs, to the court.
KENT  Ay, lead me whither you will, even to my death,
  Seeing that my brother cannot be released.
                               *Exeunt*

# Act V, scene iv

*Enter* MORTIMER JUNIOR *alone*

MORTIMER JUNIOR  The King must die, or Mortimer
  goes down;
  The commons now begin to pity him.
  Yet he that is the cause of Edward's death
  Is sure to pay for it when his son is of age,
  And therefore will I do it cunningly.
  This letter, written by a friend of ours,
  Contains his death, yet bids them save his life:
  (*He reads*) '*Edwardum occidere nolite timere, bonum est*;
  Fear not to kill the King, 'tis good he die.'
  But read it thus, and that's another sense:    **10**
  '*Edwardum occidere nolite, timere bonum est*;
  Kill not the King, 'tis good to fear the worst.'
  Unpointed as it is, thus shall it go,
  That, being dead, if it chance to be found,
  Maltravers and the rest may bear the blame,
  And we be quit that caused it to be done.
  Within this room is locked the messenger
  That shall convey it and perform the rest.
  And by a secret token that he bears,
  Shall he be murdered when the deed is done.    **20**
  Lightborne, come forth.

*Enter* LIGHTBORNE

  Art thou as resolute as thou wast?
LIGHTBORNE  What else, my lord? And far more
  resolute.
MORTIMER JUNIOR  And hast thou cast how to
  accomplish it?
LIGHTBORNE  Ay, ay, and none shall know which way
  he died.
MORTIMER JUNIOR  But at his looks, Lightborne, thou
  wilt relent.
LIGHTBORNE  Relent? Ha, ha! I use much to relent.
MORTIMER JUNIOR  Well, do it bravely, and be secret.
LIGHTBORNE  You shall not need to give instructions;
  'Tis not the first time I have killed a man.
  I learned in Naples how to poison flowers,    **30**
  To strangle with a lawn thrust through the throat,
  To pierce the windpipe with a needle's point,
  Or, whilst one is asleep, to take a quill
  And blow a little powder in his ears,
  Or open his mouth and pour quicksilver down.
  But yet I have a braver way than these.
MORTIMER JUNIOR  What's that?
LIGHTBORNE  Nay, you shall pardon me; none shall
  know my tricks.
MORTIMER JUNIOR  I care not how it is, so it be not
  spied.
  Deliver this to Gourney and Maltravers.    **40**
               *He gives the letter to* LIGHTBORNE
  At every ten miles' end thou hast a horse.
  (*Giving a token*) Take this. Away, and never see me
  more.
LIGHTBORNE  No?
MORTIMER JUNIOR  No, unless thou bring me news of
  Edward's death.
LIGHTBORNE  That will I quickly do. Farewell, my lord.
                              *Exit*
MORTIMER JUNIOR  The Prince I rule, the Queen do I
  command,
  And with a lowly congé to the ground
  The proudest lords salute me as I pass;
  I seal, I cancel, I do what I will.

---

59  Where is . . . but here: the court was considered to be
  wherever the monarch was present, rather than a fixed
  place
63  commonweal: state
2  commons: common people
13  Unpointed: unpunctuated
14  being dead: i.e once Edward is dead
16  quit: acquitted, exculpated
21  Lightborne: the assassin's name derives from 'Lucifer'; a
  figure with this name had appeared in the popular
  Chester cycle of Mystery plays (see Introduction)

26  use much: i.e. am accustomed to (facetiously)
27  bravely: a) fearlessly; b) skilfully
30–6  I learned . . . these: Lightborne's 'training' in Naples
  plays upon the popular conception of Italy as a place of
  political (Machiavellian) intrigue and elaborate murder
  (see Introduction)
31  lawn: linen
34  powder: usually arsenic (a similar fate to that of Hamlet's
  father in Shakespeare's play (I.v.59–70)
35  quicksilver: mercury
36  braver: more cunning
SD  the secret token already referred to in ll. 19–20
47  congé: bow
49  seal: authorise documents

Feared am I more than loved; let me be feared,   **50**
And when I frown, make all the court look pale.
I view the Prince with Aristarchus' eyes,
Whose looks were as a breeching to a boy.
They thrust upon me the protectorship
And sue to me for that that I desire.
While at the council table, grave enough,
And not unlike a bashful Puritan,
First I complain of imbecility,
Saying it is *onus quam gravissimum*,
Till being interrupted by my friends,   **60**
*Suscepi* that *provinciam*, as they term it,
And to conclude, I am Protector now.
Now is all sure: the Queen and Mortimer
Shall rule the realm, the King, and none rule us.
Mine enemies will I plague, my friends advance,
And what I list command, who dare control?
*Maior sum quam cui possit fortuna nocere.*
And that this be the coronation day,
It pleaseth me, and Isabel the Queen.
     *Trumpets sound within*
The trumpets sound; I must go take my place.   **70**

*Enter the young* KING EDWARD III, *the* ARCHBISHOP
OF CANTERBURY, CHAMPION, NOBLES, *and* QUEEN
ISABELLA

ARCHBISHOP OF CANTERBURY  Long live King Edward,
   by the grace of God,
  King of England and Lord of Ireland.
CHAMPION  If any Christian, Heathen, Turk, or Jew
  Dares but affirm that Edward's not true king,
  And will avouch his saying with the sword,
  I am the Champion that will combat him.
MORTIMER JUNIOR  None comes. Sound trumpets.
     *Trumpets sound*

---

50  Feared am . . . be feared: Mortimer Junior alludes to a
    well-known piece from Machiavelli's *The Prince*, which
    circulated surreptitiously in Marlowe's time either in
    manuscript or as *Il Principe*, with a fictitious imprint
    'Parlermo' (1584). Edward Dacres translated the book
    into English for publication in 1640
52  Aristarchus: proverbially harsh schoolmaster who lived at
    Alexandria in the second century BC
53  breeching: whipping
55  sue: petition
57  bashful Puritan: clearly anachronistic; Puritan strictures
    are here associated with extreme hypocrisy
58  imbecility: weakness
59  *onus quam gravissimum*: 'a very heavy burden'
61  *Suscepi* that *provinciam*: 'I have undertaken that office'
66  list: desire to
67  *Maior sum . . . fortuna nocere*: 'I am so great that Fortune
    cannot harm me'
68  coronation day: historically Edward III was crowned on
    Candlemas Day 1327 by the Archbishop of Canterbury
    (Walter Reynolds)

KING EDWARD III          Champion, here's to thee.
     *He raises his goblet*
ISABELLA  Lord Mortimer, now take him to your
  charge.

*Enter* SOLDIERS *with* EDMUND *the* EARL OF KENT
*prisoner*

MORTIMER JUNIOR  What traitor have we there with
  blades and bills?
SOLDIER  Edmund, the Earl of Kent.
KING EDWARD III         What hath he done? **80**
SOLDIER  A would have taken the King away perforce,
  As we were bringing him to Kenilworth.
MORTIMER JUNIOR  Did you attempt his rescue,
  Edmund? Speak.
KENT  Mortimer, I did; he is our king,
  And thou compell'st this prince to wear the crown.
MORTIMER JUNIOR  Strike off his head! He shall have
  martial law.
KENT  Strike off my head? Base traitor, I defy thee.
KING EDWARD III  My lord, he is my uncle and shall
  live.
MORTIMER JUNIOR  My lord, he is your enemy and shall
  die.
KENT  Stay, villains.   **90**
KING EDWARD III  Sweet mother, if I cannot pardon
  him,
  Entreat my Lord Protector for his life.
ISABELLA  Son, be content; I dare not speak a word.
KING EDWARD III  Nor I, and yet methinks I should
  command;
  But seeing I cannot, I'll entreat for him.
  (*To* MORTIMER JUNIOR) My lord, if you will let my
    uncle live,
  I will requite it when I come to age.
MORTIMER JUNIOR  'Tis for your highness' good, and
  for the realm's.
  (*To* SOLDIERS) How often shall I bid you bear him
    hence?
KENT  Art thou king? Must I die at thy command? **100**
MORTIMER JUNIOR  At our command. Once more, away
  with him.
KENT  Let me but stay and speak; I will not go.
  Either my brother or his son is king,
  And none of both them thirst for Edmund's blood.
  And therefore, soldiers, whither will you hale me?
     *They hale* EDMUND *the* EARL OF KENT *away and carry*
          *him to be beheaded*

---

79  blades and bills: swords and halberds
81  perforce: by force, violently
86  martial law: summary execution without trial
101  At our command: Mortimer Junior refers on one level to
    himself (as Protector) and Isabella, yet 'our' also suggests
    the royal plural, indicating his own ambition
104  none of both them: neither of them

KING EDWARD III  What safety may I look for at his hands,
  If that my uncle shall be murdered thus?
ISABELLA  Fear not, sweet boy, I'll guard thee from thy foes.
  Had Edmund lived, he would have sought thy death.
  Come son, we'll ride a-hunting in the park.  110
KING EDWARD III  And shall my uncle Edmund ride with us?
ISABELLA  He is a traitor; think not on him. Come.
  *Exeunt*

## Act V, scene v

*Enter* MALTRAVERS *and* GOURNEY

MALTRAVERS  Gourney, I wonder the King dies not,
  Being in a vault up to the knees in water,
  To which the channels of the castle run,
  From whence a damp continually ariseth
  That were enough to poison any man,
  Much more a king, brought up so tenderly.
GOURNEY  And so do I, Maltravers. Yesternight
  I opened but the door to throw him meat,
  And I was almost stifled with the savour.
MALTRAVERS  He hath a body able to endure  10
  More than we can inflict; and therefore now
  Let us assail his mind another while.
GOURNEY  Send for him out thence, and I will anger him.

*Enter* LIGHTBORNE

MALTRAVERS  But stay, who's this?
LIGHTBORNE            My Lord Protector greets you.  *He gives them the letter*
GOURNEY  What's here? I know not how to construe it.
MALTRAVERS  Gourney, it was left unpointed for the nonce:
  (*Reading*) 'Edwardum occidere nolite timere'—
  That's his meaning.
LIGHTBORNE  (*Showing the token*) Know you this token?
  I must have the King.
MALTRAVERS  Ay, stay a while; thou shalt have answer straight.  20
  (*Aside to* GOURNEY) This villain's sent to make away the King.
GOURNEY  (*Aside to* MALTRAVERS) I thought as much.
MALTRAVERS  (*Aside to* GOURNEY)        And when the murder's done,
  See how he must be handled for his labour.

---

8  meat: food
9  savour: stench
16  unpointed for the nonce: 'unpunctuated on purpose'
21  make away: murder

*Pereat iste!* Let him have the King. What else?
  (*To* LIGHTBORNE) Here is the keys; this is the lake.
  Do as you are commanded by my lord.
LIGHTBORNE  I know what I must do; get you away—
  Yet be not far off; I shall need your help.
  See that in the next room I have a fire,
  And get me a spit, and let it be red hot.  30
MALTRAVERS  Very well.
GOURNEY  Need you anything besides?
LIGHTBORNE  What else? A table and a featherbed.
GOURNEY  That's all?
LIGHTBORNE  Ay, ay; so when I call you, bring it in.
MALTRAVERS  Fear not you that.
GOURNEY  Here's a light to go into the dungeon.
          *Exit* MALTRAVERS *and* GOURNEY
LIGHTBORNE  So now must I about this gear; ne'er was there any
  So finely handled as this king shall be.
  Foh! Here's a place indeed with all my heart.  40

*Enter* EDWARD

EDWARD  Who's there? What light is that? Wherefore comes thou?
LIGHTBORNE  To comfort you and bring you joyful news.
EDWARD  Small comfort finds poor Edward in thy looks.
  Villain, I know thou com'st to murder me.
LIGHTBORNE  To murder you, my most gracious lord?
  Far is it from my heart to do you harm.
  The Queen sent me to see how you were used,
  For she relents at this your misery.
  And what eyes can refrain from shedding tears
  To see a king in this most piteous state?  50
EDWARD  Weep'st thou already? List awhile to me,
  And then thy heart, were it as Gourney's is,
  Or as Maltravers', hewn from the Caucasus,
  Yet will it melt ere I have done my tale.
  This dungeon where they keep me is the sink
  Wherein the filth of all the castle falls.
LIGHTBORNE  O villains!
EDWARD  And there in mire and puddle have I stood
  This ten days' space; and lest that I should sleep,
  One plays continually upon a drum.  60

---

24  *Pereat iste!*: 'Let him die'
25  lake: a) dungeon; b) lake of hell
33  featherbed: stuffed palliasse
38  about this gear: 'get on with this business'
40  Foh!: Lightborne reacts to the dungeon's stench
47  used: being treated
51  List: listen
53  Caucasus: the mountain range between the Black and Caspian Seas known for its harsh landscape and bitterly cold winters
55  sink: cesspool

They give me bread and water, being a king,
So that for want of sleep and sustenance
My mind's distempered and my body's numbed,
And whether I have limbs or no, I know not.
O, would my blood dropped out from every vein,
As doth this water from my tattered robes.
Tell Isabel the Queen I looked not thus
When for her sake I ran at tilt in France
And there unhorsed the Duke of Cleremont.

LIGHTBORNE  O speak no more, my lord; this breaks
     my heart.                                                70
     Lie on this bed and rest yourself awhile.

EDWARD  These looks of thine can harbour nought but
     death.
     I see my tragedy written in thy brows.
     Yet stay awhile; forbear thy bloody hand,
     And let me see the stroke before it comes,
     That even then when I shall lose my life,
     My mind may be more steadfast on my God.

LIGHTBORNE  What means your highness to mistrust
     me thus?

EDWARD  What means thou to dissemble with me thus?

LIGHTBORNE  These hands were never stained with
     innocent blood,                                          80
     Nor shall they now be tainted with a king's.

EDWARD  Forgive my thought, for having such a
     thought.
     One jewel have I left; receive thou this.
     Still fear I, and I know not what's the cause,
     But every joint shakes as I give it thee.
     O if thou harbour'st murder in thy heart,
     Let this gift change thy mind and save thy soul.
     Know that I am a king—O, at that name,
     I feel a hell of grief. Where is my crown?
     Gone, gone. And do I remain alive?                       90

LIGHTBORNE  You're overwatched, my lord; lie down
     and rest.

EDWARD  But that grief keeps me waking, I should sleep;
     For not these ten days have these eyes' lids closed.
     Now as I speak they fall, and yet with fear
     Open again. O wherefore sits thou here?

LIGHTBORNE  If you mistrust me, I'll be gone, my lord.

EDWARD  No, no, for if thou mean'st to murder me,
     Thou wilt return again, and therefore stay.
                                        *He falls asleep*

LIGHTBORNE  He sleeps.

EDWARD  (*Starting*) O let me not die! Yet stay, O stay
     awhile.                                                 100

LIGHTBORNE  How now, my lord?

EDWARD  Something still buzzeth in mine ears
     And tells me, if I sleep I never wake.
     This fear is that which makes me tremble thus;
     And therefore tell me, wherefore art thou come?

LIGHTBORNE  To rid thee of thy life. Maltravers, come!

*Enter* MALTRAVERS

EDWARD  I am too weak and feeble to resist;
     Assist me, sweet God, and receive my soul.

LIGHTBORNE  Run for the table.          *Exit* MALTRAVERS

*Enter* MALTRAVERS *with* GOURNEY, *carrying a table and
hot spit*

EDWARD  O spare me, or dispatch me in a trice!          110

LIGHTBORNE  So, lay the table down and stamp on it;
     But not too hard, lest that you bruise his body.
          *They seize* EDWARD *and hold him down with the table.*
     LIGHTBORNE *murders him with the spit. He screams as he
                              is penetrated and dies*

MALTRAVERS  I fear me that this cry will raise the town,
     And therefore let us take horse and away.

LIGHTBORNE  Tell me, sirs, was it not bravely done?

GOURNEY  Excellent well. Take this for thy reward.
          *Then* GOURNEY *stabs* LIGHTBORNE
     Come, let us cast the body in the moat,
     And bear the King's to Mortimer, our lord.
     Away!
                         *Exeunt, dragging the bodies*

# Act V, scene vi

*Enter* MORTIMER JUNIOR *and* MALTRAVERS

MORTIMER JUNIOR  Is't done, Maltravers, and the
     murderer dead?

MALTRAVERS  Ay, my good lord; I would it were
     undone.

MORTIMER JUNIOR  Maltravers, if thou now growest
     penitent
     I'll be thy ghostly father; therefore choose
     Whether thou wilt be secret in this,
     Or else die by the hand of Mortimer.

MALTRAVERS  Gourney, my lord, is fled, and will, I fear,
     Betray us both; therefore let me fly.

MORTIMER JUNIOR  Fly to the savages!

MALTRAVERS  I humbly thank your honour.          *Exit*

MORTIMER JUNIOR  As for myself, I stand as Jove's huge
     tree,                                                   11
     And others are but shrubs compared to me.

---

63  distempered: deranged
68  ran at tilt: jousted
83  jewel: possibly that sent by Isabella at V.ii.71
89–90  Where is . . . remain alive?: Edward means that a king
     without a crown is usually dead
91  overwatched: lacking sleep
92  grief: distress, anxiety

102  buzzeth: whispers
115  bravely: skilfully
9  to the savages: i.e. beyond 'civilisation'
11  Jove's huge tree: the oak (like Jove because of its size and
     strength)

All tremble at my name, and I fear none;
Let's see who dare impeach me for his death.

*Enter* ISABELLA THE QUEEN

ISABELLA  Ah, Mortimer, the King my son hath news
His father's dead, and we have murdered him.
MORTIMER JUNIOR  What if he have? The King is yet a
child.
ISABELLA  Ay, ay, but he tears his hair and wrings his
hands,
And vows to be revenged upon us both.
Into the council chamber he is gone                       20
To crave the aid and succour of his peers.

*Enter* KING EDWARD III, *with the* LORDS *and attendants*

Ay me, see where he comes, and they with him.
Now, Mortimer, begins our tragedy.
FIRST LORD  Fear not, my lord; know that you are a king.
KING EDWARD III  Villain!
MORTIMER JUNIOR  How now, my lord?
KING EDWARD III  Think not that I am frighted with
thy words.
My father's murdered through thy treachery,
And thou shalt die; and on his mournful hearse
Thy hateful and accursèd head shall lie                   30
To witness to the world that by thy means
His kingly body was too soon interred.
ISABELLA  Weep not, sweet son.
KING EDWARD III  Forbid not me to weep; he was my
father.
And had you loved him half so well as I,
You could not bear his death thus patiently.
But you, I fear, conspired with Mortimer.
FIRST LORD  (*To* MORTIMER JUNIOR) Why speak you
not unto my lord the King?
MORTIMER JUNIOR  Because I think it scorn to be
accused.
Who is the man dare say I murdered him?                   40
KING EDWARD III  Traitor, in me my loving father
speaks
And plainly saith, 'twas thou that murd'redst him.
MORTIMER JUNIOR  But hath your grace no other proof
than this?
KING EDWARD III  Yes, if this be the hand of Mortimer.
                              *He presents a letter*
MORTIMER JUNIOR  (*Aside to* ISABELLA) False Gourney
hath betrayed me and himself.
ISABELLA  (*Aside to* MORTIMER JUNIOR) I feared as
much; murder cannot be hid.

MORTIMER JUNIOR  'Tis my hand; what gather you by
this?
KING EDWARD III  That thither thou didst send a
murderer.
MORTIMER JUNIOR  What murderer? Bring forth the
man I sent.
KING EDWARD III  Ah, Mortimer, thou knowest that he
is slain;                                                50
And so shalt thou be too. Why stays he here?
Bring him unto a hurdle, drag him forth;
Hang him, I say, and set his quarters up!
But bring his head back presently to me.
ISABELLA  For my sake, sweet son, pity Mortimer.
MORTIMER JUNIOR  Madam, entreat not; I will rather
die
Than sue for life unto a paltry boy.
KING EDWARD III  Hence with the traitor, with the
murderer.
MORTIMER JUNIOR  Base Fortune, now I see that in thy
wheel
There is a point to which, when men aspire,              60
They tumble headlong down; that point I touched,
And seeing there was no place to mount up higher,
Why should I grieve at my declining fall?
Farewell, fair Queen. Weep not for Mortimer,
That scorns the world, and as a traveller
Goes to discover countries yet unknown.
KING EDWARD III  What! Suffer you the traitor to
delay?
                  *Exit* MORTIMER JUNIOR *under guard, with the*
                                          FIRST LORD
ISABELLA  As thou received'st thy life from me,
Spill not the blood of gentle Mortimer.
KING EDWARD III  This argues that you spilt my father's
blood,                                                   70
Else would you not entreat for Mortimer.
ISABELLA  I spill his blood? No!
KING EDWARD III  Ay, madam, you; for so the rumour
runs.
ISABELLA  That rumour is untrue; for loving thee
Is this report raised on poor Isabel.
KING EDWARD III  I do not think her so unnatural.
SECOND LORD  My lord, I fear me it will prove too true.

---

17  yet: still
21  succour: support
36  patiently: calmly
46  murder cannot be hid: proverbial; see *The Spanish Tragedy*:
    'The heavens are just, murder cannot be hid' (II.v.57)

---

52  hurdle: a frame or sledge on which condemned prisoners
    were transported
53  Hang him . . . quarters up: 'Mortimer Junior is to be
    hanged, drawn and quartered rather than merely
    beheaded, the normal privilege of aristocratic traitors
    granted even to Gaveston, Baldock and the Spencers'
    (Wiggins and Lindsey)
66  countries yet unknown: i.e. the lands beyond death
75  Is this . . . poor Isabel: she tries to imply that the rumours
    are only the result of her attempts (with Mortimer) to
    safeguard the throne

KING EDWARD III  Mother, you are suspected for his
    death,
  And therefore we commit you to the Tower
  Till further trial may be made thereof;      **80**
  If you be guilty, though I be your son,
  Think not to find me slack or pitiful.

ISABELLA  Nay, to my death, for too long have I lived
  Whenas my son thinks to abridge my days.

KING EDWARD III  Away with her. Her words enforce
    these tears,
  And I shall pity her if she speak again.

ISABELLA  Shall I not mourn for my belovèd lord,
  And with the rest accompany him to his grave?

SECOND LORD  Thus, madam, 'tis the King's will you
    shall hence.

ISABELLA  He hath forgotten me; stay, I am his mother.

SECOND LORD  That boots not; therefore, gentle
  madam, go.      **91**

ISABELLA  Then come, sweet death, and rid me of this
  grief.      *Exit under guard*

*Enter* FIRST LORD *with the head of* MORTIMER JUNIOR

FIRST LORD  My lord, here is the head of Mortimer.

KING EDWARD III  Go fetch my father's hearse, where it
    shall lie,
  And bring my funeral robes.    *Exeunt attendants*
               Accursèd head!
  Could I have ruled thee then, as I do now,
  Thou hadst not hatched this monstrous treachery.

*Enter attendants with the hearse of* KING EDWARD II *and
funeral robes*

  Here comes the hearse; help me to mourn, my lords.
  Sweet father, here unto thy murdered ghost
  I offer up this wicked traitor's head.    **100**
  And let these tears, distilling from mine eyes,
  Be witness of my grief and innocency.
          *Exeunt, with a funeral march*

FINIS

---

79  to the Tower: historically Isabel was placed under house
    arrest at Castle Rising in Norfolk
80  trial: investigation
84  abridge: shorten
85  enforce: produce
91  boots: matters

---

101  distilling: falling from (in droplets)

# Thomas Heywood, *A Woman Killed with Kindness*

First performed 1603
First published 1607

'What can sooner print modesty in the souls of the wanton than by discovering unto them the monstrousness of their sin?' So wrote Thomas Heywood in his defence of the contemporary stage, *An Apology for Actors* (1612), in which he argued that drama worked by example to extol virtue and reform vice. *A Woman Killed with Kindness*, explicitly concerned as it is with feminine modesty and wantonness, in many ways could be said to be the dramatic exemplification of Heywood's rhetoric: in this play, the familiar iconic figures of the unchaste and the chaste woman are manifested in the contrasting forms of an adulterous wife, Anne Frankford, and a dutiful sister, Susan Mountford. In accordance with Heywood's claim for the admonitory moral power of drama, the former is rewarded with ostracism, self-loathing and death, the latter with marriage and an elevated social position.

If we accept Heywood's claims for the didacticism of drama, this begs the question of what precisely this play is teaching. Some critics, such as Adams and Ure, have read it as a moral homily, or at least as working within an explicitly Christian framework. Such readings see the play as, on the one hand, exhorting women to virtue (Anne herself explicitly urges the married women in the audience to '[m]ake me your instance' (xiii.141)), and, on the other hand, recommending men to respond to such transgressions with Christian forgiveness (Anne's husband does not punish her adultery with death, as he might have done, but with banishment). However, such conclusions serve to gloss over some of the play's ambiguities. One dimension of these ambiguities is signalled by the play's paradoxical title: in what sense might it be 'kind' to kill a woman? The closing line of the play suggests that the 'kindness' of the title is Frankford's, in foregoing revenge and merely banishing Anne, thereby allowing her the opportunity to repent and obtain forgiveness. Some might ask, though, whether this is a case of Frankford having revenge by the back door, and with a clear conscience. He might exhibit Christian mercy in not killing Anne and her lover, Wendoll, when he first discovers them, but he nonetheless sees his wife die as a direct result of her adultery and, to boot, is able to transfer the responsibility for her death on to Anne herself. This reading is given some weight by Frankford's vow to

'torment thy soul/ And kill thee even with kindness' (xiii.153–4).

Frankford's kindness extends not only to his wife, however, but also to Wendoll, whom he welcomes into his household with such unexpected enthusiasm and warmth as to trouble even Wendoll himself, who remarks that 'This kindness grows of no alliance 'twixt us' (vi.33). is integration into Frankford's 'family' (a term which at this time still denoted all members of the extended household) shifts the emotional centre of gravity away from the husband and wife so recently celebrated in idealised terms for their mutual adoration, sympathy and equality (i.55–72), and towards the friendship between Frankford and Wendoll, the latter characterising this new-found intimacy in striking terms: 'I am to his body/As necessary as his digestion' (vi.41–2). We might, then, reread the title to take account of this initial, destabilising act of 'kindness' on the part of Frankford towards Wendoll, and its part in the ensuing events.

There are other instances of 'kindness' in the play which further complicate the word's meanings. Turning to the sub-plot, for example, Acton's 'kindness' to his enemy Mountford in discharging his debts suggests the way that generosity can serve as an act of manipulation on the part of the giver, and as a torment to the receiver by conferring painful obligations; as Mountford says, 'His kindness like a burden hath surcharged me' (xiv.63). Furthermore, instances of 'unkindness' in the play serve to remind us that the etymological relationship between the words 'kind' and 'kin' does not necessarily translate into a 'kindness' in familial relationships. Mountford's plight is met with uniform unkindness from his family (see scene ix), an unkindness matched or surpassed by his own attempt to prostitute his sister Susan to Acton in order to preserve his own honour. This etymological link might, in turn, suggest yet another inflection within the play's title: Anne Frankford can be seen as a woman killed by 'kindness' in the sense of 'kinship'. She is defined and constrained by a series of social and legal prescriptions concerning her familial position and duties, and it is these, ultimately, that result in her death. 'Kindness' in this play never denotes simple acts of generosity, nor confirms straightforwardly the ties of kinship, but is always riven by competing impulses and implications.

Heywood's plot, drawn in part from the English translation of an Italian novella by Illicini which had appeared in translation in William Painter's *Palace of Pleasure* (1566), is an unusual example of the dramatic sub-genre of 'domestic tragedy'. Unlike *Arden of Faversham*, for example, a play with which this otherwise has much in common, *A Woman Killed with Kindness* does not revolve around a murder, and neither is it based on recent historical events. In other respects, however, this play epitomises the distinctive 'domestic' character of this group of plays. Like *Arden of Faversham*, this play works with the structures, dynamics and ideologies informing a middle-rank household and marriage, and troubles these by showing the pressures and contradictions manifest within and upon them. Whilst this might have been a 'barren subject' (Prologue, line 5) in comparison with the excesses of plot, rhetoric and situation of other contemporary tragedies, it is perhaps this very domesticity—still familiar, still exercising us, yet made strange by the framing of the central 'domestic' relationships—that constitutes the interest of these plays for modern readers and audiences.

## Textual note

The copytext for this edition is the first edition of 1607 (referred to in the footnotes to the text as Q1). The second edition of the play is lost, but major differences between Q1 and the third edition (Q3) of 1617 are footnoted.

# Further reading

## Editions

Baskervill, Charles Read, Heltzel, Virgil B. and Nethercot, Arthur H. (eds) (1934) *Elizabethan and Stuart Plays*, New York, NY: Henry Holt and Co.

Gassner, John (ed.) (1967) *Elizabethan Drama*, New York, NY: Bantam.

Heywood, Thomas (1971) *A Woman Killed with Kindness*, facsimile edition, Menston, Yorkshire: Scolar Press.

Kinney, Arthur F. (ed.) (1999) *Renaissance Drama: An Anthology of Plays and Entertainments*, Oxford: Blackwell.

Neilson, William Allen (ed.) (1939) *The Chief Elizabethan Dramatists Excluding Shakespeare: Selected Plays*, Cambridge, MA: Houghton Mifflin Company.

Scobie, Brian (ed.) (1985) *A Woman Killed with Kindness*, The New Mermaids, London: A. & C. Black.

Shepherd, R. H. (ed.) (1874) *The Dramatic Works of Thomas Heywood*, vol. II, London: John Pearson.

Spencer, Hazelton (ed.) (1933) *Elizabethan Plays*, Boston, MA: D. C. Heath and Company.

Sturgess, Keith (ed.) (1969) *Three Elizabethan Domestic Tragedies: Arden of Faversham; A Yorkshire Tragedy; A Woman Killed with Kindness*, Harmondsworth: Penguin.

Van Fossen, R. W. (ed.) (1961) *A Woman Killed with Kindness: Thomas Heywood*, The Revels Plays, London: Methuen.

Verity, A. Wilson (ed.) (1888) *Thomas Heywood*, The Mermaid Series, London: Vizetelly & Co.

## Critical and contextual commentaries

Adams, Henry Hitch (1943) *English Domestic or Homiletic Tragedy 1575–1642*, New York, NY: Columbia University Press.

Atkinson, David (1989) 'An Approach to the Main Plot of Thomas Heywood's *A Woman Killed with Kindness*', *English Studies*, 70, 1: 15–27.

Bach, Rebecca Ann (1998) 'The Homosocial Imaginary of *A Woman Killed with Kindness*', *Textual Practice*, 12, 3: 503–24.

Baines, Barbara J. (1984) *Thomas Heywood*, Boston, MA: Twayne.

Belsey, Catherine (1985) *The Subject of Tragedy: Identity and Difference in Renaissance Drama*, London: Methuen.

Bowers, Rick (1984) '*A Woman Killed with Kindness*: Plausibility on a Smaller Scale', *Studies in English Literature 1500–1900*, 24, 2: 293–306.

Bromley, Laura G. (1986) 'Domestic Conduct in *A Woman Killed with Kindness*', *Studies in English Literature 1500–1900*, 26, 2: 259–76.

Cary, Cecile Williamson (1974) '"Go Break This Lute": Music in Heywood's *A Woman Killed with Kindness*', *Huntington Library Quarterly*, 37, 2: 111–22.

Comensoli, Viviana (1996) *'Household Business': Domestic Plays of Early Modern England*, Toronto, Buffalo, and London: University of Toronto Press.

Cook, David (1964) '*A Woman Killed with Kindness*: An UnShakespearian Tragedy', *English Studies*, 45, 5: 353–72.

Dolan, Frances E. (1994) *Dangerous Familiars: Representations of Domestic Crime in England 1550–1700*, Ithaca, NY: Cornell University Press.

Findlay, Alison (1999) *A Feminist Perspective on Renaissance Drama*, Oxford: Blackwell.

Gutierrez, Nancy A. (1989) 'The Irresolution of Melodrama: The Meaning of Adultery in *A Woman Killed with Kindness*', *Exemplaria: A Journal of Theory in Medieval and Renaissance Studies*, 1: 265–91.

Henderson, Diana E. (1986) 'Many Mansions: Reconstructing *A Woman Killed with Kindness*', *Studies in English Literature 1500–1900*, 26, 2: 277–94.

Kiefer, Frederick (1986) 'Heywood as Moralist in *A Woman Killed with Kindness*', *Medieval and Renaissance Drama in England*, 3: 83–98.

McQuade, Paula (2000) '"A Labyrinth of Sin": Marriage and Moral Capacity in Thomas Heywood's *A Woman Killed with Kindness*', *Modern Philology*, 98, 2: 231–50.

Orlin, Lena Cowan (1994) *Private Matters and Public Culture in Post-Reformation England*, Ithaca, NY: Cornell University Press.

Panek, Jennifer (1994) 'Punishing Adultery in *A Woman Killed with Kindness*', *Studies in English Literature 1500–1900*, 34, 2: 357–78.

Rudnytsky, P. L. (1983) '*A Woman Killed with Kindness* as Subtext for *Othello*', *Renaissance Drama*, 14: 103–24.

Spacks, Patricia M. (1959) 'Honor and Perception in *A Woman*

*Killed with Kindness*', *Modern Language Quarterly*, 20: 321–32.

Ure, Peter (1970) 'Marriage and the Domestic Drama in *A Woman Killed with Kindness*', in Max Bluestone and Norman Rabkin (eds) *Shakespeare's Contemporaries: Modern Studies in English Renaissance Drama*, 2nd edition, Englewood Cliffs, NJ: Prentice-Hall Inc.

Wentworth, Michael (1990) 'Thomas Heywood's *A Woman Killed with Kindness* as Domestic Morality', in David G. Allen and Robert A. White (eds) *Traditions and Innovations: Essays on British Literature of the Middle Ages and Renaissance*, Newark, DE: University of Delaware Press.

## Works of related interest

William Shakespeare, *The Taming of the Shrew* (1591)
William Shakespeare, *The Merry Wives of Windsor* (1597)
Henry Chettle, Thomas Dekker and William Haughton, *Patient Grissel* (1600)
Elizabeth Cary, *The Tragedy of Mariam* (1604)
William Shakespeare, *Othello* (1604)
George Wilkins, *The Miseries of Enforced Marriage* (1607)
Thomas Middleton, *Women Beware Women* (1625)

# *A Woman Killed with Kindness** (1603)

## Dramatis personae

JOHN FRANKFORD

ANNE FRANKFORD, *his wife, sister of Sir Francis Acton*

WENDOLL, *friend of Frankford*

SIR CHARLES MOUNTFORD

SUSAN MOUNTFORD, *his sister*

SIR FRANCIS ACTON

CRANWELL, *friend of Frankford*

MALBY, *friend of Sir Francis*

OLD MOUNTFORD, *uncle of Sir Charles*

TYDY, *cousin of Sir Charles*

SANDY, *former friend of Sir Charles*

RODER, *former tenant of Sir Charles*

SHAFTON, *false friend of Sir Charles*

NICK, *servant of Frankford*

JENKIN, *servant of Frankford*

SPIGGOT, *Frankford's butler*

SISLY MILK-PAIL, *servingwoman to Frankford*

ROGER BRICKBAT ⎫
JACK SLIME ⎭ *country men, Frankford's farm servants*

JOAN MINIVER ⎫
JANE TRUBKIN ⎬ *country women, Frankford's farm servants*
ISBEL MOTLEY ⎭

SHERIFF

KEEPER OF THE PRISON

SERGEANT

MUSICIANS, HUNTSMEN, FALCONERS, SERVINGMEN,
SERVINGWOMEN, CARTERS, COACHMAN, FRANKFORD'S
CHILDREN, OFFICERS

## The Prologue

I come but like a harbinger, being sent
To tell you what these preparations mean:
Look for no glorious state, our muse is bent
Upon a barren subject, a bare scene.
We could afford this twig a timber tree,
Whose strength might boldly on your favours build;
Our russet, tissue; drone, a honey bee;
Our barren plot, a large and spacious field;
Our coarse fare, banquets; our thin water, wine;
Our brook, a sea; our bat's eyes, eagle's sight;     10
Our poet's dull and earthy muse, divine:
Our ravens, doves; our crow's black feathers, white.
  But gentle thoughts, when they may give the foil,
  Save them that yield, and spare where they may spoil.

## Scene i

*Enter* MASTER JOHN FRANKFORD, MISTRESS ANNE,
SIR FRANCIS ACTON, SIR CHARLES MOUNTFORD,
MASTER MALBY, MASTER WENDOLL, *and* MASTER
CRANWELL

SIR FRANCIS  Some music there! None lead the bride a
  dance?

---

* The title is proverbial. Van Fossen notes other
   Renaissance examples of its use, the most famous being
   in *The Taming of the Shrew* (1591), when Petruchio
   promises to torment Kate, pretending 'That all is done in
   reverent care of her': 'This is a way to kill a wife with
   kindness,/And thus I'll curb her mad and headstrong
   humour' (IV.1.185, 189–90)

3 glorious state: ostentatious splendour
5 afford . . . tree: wish this twig were a tree
7 russet: coarse cloth
   tissue: fine cloth
11 Our poet's . . . divine: Sturgess punctuates thus: 'Our
   poets dull and earthy, Muse divine'. We follow here the
   punctuation of Van Fossen and Scobie
13 gentle thoughts: i.e. those of the audience
   give the foil: overthrow (term from wrestling)
   Scene i: there are no Act or scene divisions in Qs. We
   follow recent eds in dividing the play into seventeen scenes

SIR CHARLES  Yes, would she dance 'The Shaking of the
    Sheets'.
  But that's the dance her husband means to lead her.
WENDOLL  That's not the dance that every man must
    dance
  According to the ballad.
SIR FRANCIS               Music ho!
  By your leave, sister—by your husband's leave
  I should have said—the hand that but this day
  Was given you in the church I'll borrow. Sound!
  This marriage music hoists me from the ground.    **9**
FRANKFORD  Aye, you may caper, you are light and free.
  Marriage hath yoked my heels, pray then pardon me.
SIR FRANCIS  I'll have you dance too, brother.
SIR CHARLES            Master Frankford,
  You are a happy man, sir, and much joy
  Succeed your marriage mirth; you have a wife
  So qualified and with such ornaments
  Both of the mind and body. First, her birth
  Is noble, and her education such
  As might become the daughter of a prince;
  Her own tongue speaks all tongues, and her own
    hand
  Can teach all strings to speak in their best grace,   **20**
  From the shrill treble, to the hoarsest bass.
  To end her many praises in one word,
  She's beauty and perfection's eldest daughter,
  Only found by yours, though many a heart hath
    sought her.
FRANKFORD  But that I know your virtues and chaste
    thoughts,
  I should be jealous of your praise, Sir Charles.
CRANWELL  He speaks no more than you approve.
MALBY  Nor flatters he that gives to her her due.
ANNE  I would your praise could find a fitter theme
  Than my imperfect beauty to speak on.        **30**
  Such as they be, if they my husband please,
  They suffice me now I am married.
  His sweet content is like a flattering glass,
  To make my face seem fairer to mine eye,
  But the least wrinkle from his stormy brow,
  Will blast the roses in my cheeks that grow.
SIR FRANCIS  A perfect wife already, meek and patient.
  How strangely the word 'husband' fits your mouth,
  Not married three hours since, sister. 'Tis good;
  You that begin betimes thus, must needs prove   **40**
  Pliant and duteous in your husband's love.
  Godamercies, brother, wrought her to it already?

'Sweet husband,' and a curtsy the first day.
  Mark this, mark this, you that are bachelors,
  And never took the grace of honest man,
  Mark this against you marry, this one phrase:
  'In a good time that man both wins and woos
  That takes his wife down in her wedding shoes.'
FRANKFORD  Your sister takes not after you, Sir Francis.
  All his wild blood your father spent on you;     **50**
  He got her in his age when he grew civil.
  All his mad tricks were to his land entailed,
  And you are heir to all. Your sister, she
  Hath to her dower her mother's modesty.
SIR CHARLES  Lord, sir, in what a happy state live you;
  This morning, which to many seems a burden
  Too heavy to bear, is unto you a pleasure.
  This lady is no clog, as many are.
  She doth become you like a well-made suit
  In which the tailor hath used all his art,       **60**
  Not like a thick coat of unseasoned frieze,
  Forced on your back in summer; she's no chain
  To tie your neck, and curb you to the yoke,
  But she's a chain of gold to adorn your neck.
  You both adorn each other, and your hands
  Methinks are matches. There's equality
  In this fair combination; you are both scholars,
  Both young, both being descended nobly.
  There's music in this sympathy, it carries
  Consort and expectation of much joy,        **70**
  Which God bestow on you, from this first day
  Until your dissolution—that's for aye.
SIR FRANCIS  We keep you here too long, good brother
    Frankford.
  Into the hall! Away, go cheer your guests!
  What, bride, and bridegroom both withdrawn at
    once?
  If you be missed, the guests will doubt their welcome,
  And charge you with unkindness!
FRANKFORD                 To prevent it,
  I'll leave you here, to see the dance within.

---

2  'The . . . Sheets': popular tune and ballad, with sexual
    allusion (in the ballad, the dance is of death; see ll. 4–5)
15  qualified: with such qualities
21  shrill Q1 (shrill'st Q3)
27  approve: confirm
42  Godamercies Q1 (Gramercies Q3). An exclamation of
    approval

45  took . . . man: i.e. married
46  against: in anticipation of the time when
47  In . . . time: at the right moment
48  takes . . . shoes: 'that tames his wife at once' (Van
    Fossen)
50  spent: expended
51  got: begot
    civil: more responsible or respectable
52  to . . . entailed: 'bestowed inseparable with the land'
    (Scobie)
54  to her dower: as her dowry
58  clog: impediment
61  unseasoned: unseasonable
    frieze: coarse woollen cloth
65–6  your . . . matches: you are well matched
69  sympathy: harmony
70  Consort: a) harmony; b) companionship

ANNE  And so will I. *Exeunt* FRANKFORD *and* ANNE
SIR FRANCIS  To part you it were sin.
  Now gallants, while the town musicians        80
  Finger their frets within, and the mad lads
  And country lasses, every mother's child
  With nosegays and bride-laces in their hats,
  Dance all their country measures, rounds and jigs,
  What shall we do? Hark, they are all on the hoigh;
  They toil like mill horses, and turn as round—
  Marry, not on the toe. Ay, and they caper,
  But without cutting. You shall see tomorrow
  The hall floor pecked and dinted like a millstone,
  Made with their high shoes; though their skill be
    small,                        90
  Yet they tread heavy where their hobnails fall.
SIR CHARLES  Well, leave them to their sports. Sir
  Francis Acton,
  I'll make a match with you: meet me tomorrow
  At Chevy Chase, I'll fly my hawk with yours.
SIR FRANCIS  For what? For what?
SIR CHARLES           Why, for a hundred pound.
SIR FRANCIS  Pawn me some gold of that.
SIR CHARLES              Here are ten angels;
  I'll make them good a hundred pound tomorrow
  Upon my hawk's wing.
SIR FRANCIS        'Tis a match, 'tis done.
  Another hundred pound upon your dogs,
  Dare you Sir Charles?
SIR CHARLES        I dare. Were I sure to lose   100
  I durst do more than that. Here's my hand,
  The first course for a hundred pound.
SIR FRANCIS            A match.
WENDOLL  Ten angels on Sir Francis Acton's hawk;
  As much upon his dogs.
CRANWELL  I am for Sir Charles Mountford; I have
  seen
  His hawk and dog both tried. What, clap you hands?
  Or is't no bargain?
WENDOLL        Yes, and stake them down;
  Were they five hundred they were all my own.
SIR FRANCIS  Be stirring early with the lark tomorrow.
  I'll rise into my saddle ere the sun       110
  Rise from his bed.

SIR CHARLES       If there you miss me, say
  I am no gentleman; I'll hold my day.
SIR FRANCIS  It holds on all sides. Come, tonight let's
  dance.
  Early tomorow let's prepare to ride;
  We had need be three hours up before the bride.
                           *Exeunt*

# Scene ii

*Enter* NICK *and* JENKIN, JACK SLIME, ROGER BRICKBAT
*with* COUNTRY WENCHES *including* SISLY MILK-PAIL, *and*
TWO *or* THREE MUSICIANS

JENKIN  Come Nick, take you Joan Miniver to trace
  withall; Jack Slime, traverse you with Sisly Milk-pail.
  I will take Jane Trubkin, and Roger Brickbat shall
  have Isbel Motley; and now that they are busy in the
  parlour, come, strike up, we'll have a crash here in the
  yard.
NICK  My humour is not compendious: dancing I
  possess not, though I can foot it; yet since I am fallen
  into the hands of Sisly Milk-pail, I assent.       9
JACK SLIME  Truly Nick, though we were never brought
  up like serving courtiers, yet we have been brought up
  with serving creatures, ay and God's creatures too, for
  we have been brought up to serve sheep, oxen, horses
  and hogs, and such like; and though we be but
  country fellows, it may be in the way of dancing we
  can do the horse-trick as well as servingmen.
ROGER BRICKBAT  Ay, and the cross-point too.
JENKIN  O Slime, O Brickbat! Do not you know that
  comparisons are odious? Now we are odious ourselves
  too, therefore there are no comparisons to be made
  betwixt us.                             21
NICK  I am sudden, and not superfluous;
  I am quarrelsome, and not seditious;
  I am peaceable, and not contentious;
  I am brief, and not compendious.
  Slime, foot it quickly. If the music overcome not my
  melancholy I shall quarrel, and if they suddenly do
  not strike up, I shall presently strike thee down.

---

81  frets: divisions on fingerboard of lute
83  bride-laces: 'pieces of lace used to bind up pieces of
    rosemary worn at weddings' (Sturgess)
85  on the hoigh: excited
86  as round: as easily, as briskly (OED)
87  not . . . toe: 'i.e. flat-footed' (Van Fossen)
88  cutting: twirling the feet
96  Pawn: pledge
    angels: gold coins
102  course: race or competition between two dogs
106  clap: shake (to confirm the agreement)
107  stake them down: 'put down stake-money' (Sturgess)

112  hold my day: keep my appointment
1  trace: dance
2  traverse: dance
5  crash: frolic
7  humour: disposition
    compendious: Nick's error for 'comprehensive' (eds)
9  assent Q1 (consent Q3)
11  like . . . courtiers: 'i.e. like gentlemen' (Scobie)
16, 17  horse-trick, cross-point: 'dances, with sexual
    implication' (Sturgess)
22  sudden . . . superfluous: prompt, but without doing more
    than is necessary
25  compendious: succinct, concise, economical. Unclear
    how this is in opposition to 'brief'; see l. 7

JENKIN  No quarelling, for God's sake! Truly, if you do,
  I shall set a knave between you.      **30**

JACK SLIME  I come to dance, not to quarrel. Come,
  what shall it be? 'Rogero'?

JENKIN  'Rogero'? No, we will dance 'The Beginning of
  the World'.

SISLY  I love no dance so well as 'John, Come Kiss Me
  Now'.

NICK  Ay, that have ere now deserved a cushion, call for
  'The Cushion Dance'.

ROGER BRICKBAT  For my part, I like nothing so well as
  'Tom Tyler'.      **40**

JENKIN  No, we'll have 'The Hunting of the Fox'.

JACK SLIME  'The Hay', 'The Hay', there's nothing like
  'The Hay'.

NICK  I have said, I do say, and I will say again—

JENKIN  Every man agree to have it as Nick says.

ALL  Content.

NICK  It hath been, it now is, and it shall be—

SISLY  What Master Nich'las, what?

NICK  'Put on Your Smock a Monday'.      **49**

JENKIN  So the dance will come cleanly off. Come, for
  God's sake agree of something! If you like not that,
  put it to the musicians or let me speak for all, and
  we'll have 'Sellenger's Round'.

ALL  That! That! That!

NICK  No, I am resolved thus it shall be:
  First take hands, then take you to your heels.

JENKIN  Why, would you have us run away?

NICK  No, but I would have you shake your heels.
  Music, strike up!

*They dance.* NICK *dancing speaks stately and scurvily, the*
*rest after the country fashion.*

JENKIN  Hey, lively my lasses, here's a turn for thee.  **60**
                        *Exeunt*

# Scene iii

*Wind horns. Enter* SIR CHARLES, SIR FRANCIS, MALBY,
CRANWELL, WENDOLL, FALCONERS, *and* HUNTSMEN

SIR CHARLES  So! Well cast off. Aloft, aloft! Well
  flown!
  O now she takes her at the souse, and strikes her

Down to the earth, like a swift thunderclap.

WENDOLL  She hath struck ten angels out of my way.

SIR FRANCIS  A hundred pound from me.

SIR CHARLES              What, falconer!

FALCONER  At hand, sir.

SIR CHARLES  Now she hath seized the fowl, and 'gins
  to plume her,
  Rebeck her not; rather stand still and check her.
  So! Seize her gets, her jesses, and her bells.
  Away!      **10**

SIR FRANCIS  My hawk killed too.

SIR CHARLES        Ay, but 'twas at the querre,
  Not at the mount, like mine.

SIR FRANCIS          Judgement, my masters!

CRANWELL  Yours missed her at the ferre.

WENDOLL  Ay, but our merlin first hath plumed the
  fowl,
  And twice renewed her from the river too.
  Her bells, Sir Francis, had not both one weight,
  Nor was one semitune above the other;
  Methinks these Milan bells do sound too full,
  And spoil the mounting of your hawk.

SIR CHARLES           'Tis lost.

SIR FRANCIS  I grant it not. Mine likewise seized a fowl
  Within her talents, and you saw her paws  **21**
  Full of the feathers; both her petty singles
  And her long singles gripped her more than other.
  The terrials of her legs were stained with blood;
  Not of the fowl only she did discomfit
  Some of her feathers, but she brake away.
  Come, come, your hawk is but a rifler.

---

30  knave: i.e. himself
32  'Rogero': the name of a popular dance tune, as are the
  other names that follow
37  deserved a cushion: 'earned the right to some luxury'
  (Van Fossen)
49  Smock: a woman's undergarment
SD  *speaks*: reveals, shows himself
  scurvily: sourly, rudely
SD  *Wind*: blow
  FALCONERS: eds (falconer Qs)
  The scene opens in the middle of the hawking match
2  at the souse: as the prey rises from the ground

2–3  O . . . thunderclap: punctuated as prose in Qs
8  rebeck: recall
9  gets . . . bells: 'jesses' (leather straps) and bells were
  attached to the hawk's legs; 'gets' are probably the same
  as jesses
11  at the querre: i.e. before the prey rose from the ground
13  ferre: a falconry term indicating one or other side of the
  river
14  merlin: type of hawk
15  renewed: driven back
16–17  Her bells . . . other: i.e. the bells were not pitched and
  weighted as they ought to be
21  talents: talons
22–3  petty . . . long singles: outer and middle claws
24  terrials: eds agree this is an error, probably for 'terrets'
  (part of hawk's harness)
24–6  with blood . . . away: 'i.e. our hawk drew blood, not just
  feathers, but the prey escaped' (Scobie)
25  discomfit: tear out
27–31  Come . . . perch: Sturgess attributes l. 27 to Sir Charles,
  allowing him then to follow Q1's speech ascriptions. We
  follow Van Fossen and Scobie in adopting Q3's
  ascriptions
27  rifler: 'hawk which seizes feathers without capturing its
  prey' (Sturgess)

SIR CHARLES How?

SIR FRANCIS Ay, and your dogs are trindle-tails and curs.

SIR CHARLES You stir my blood!
You keep not a good hound in all your kennel, 30
Nor one good hawk upon your perch.

SIR FRANCIS How, knight?

SIR CHARLES So, knight? You will not swagger, sir?

SIR FRANCIS Why, say I did?

SIR CHARLES Why sir, I say you would gain as much by swaggering
As you have got by wagers on your dogs.
You will come short in all things.

SIR FRANCIS Not in this!
Now I'll strike home.

SIR CHARLES Thou shalt to thy long home,
Or I will want my will.

SIR FRANCIS All they that love Sir Francis, follow me.

SIR CHARLES All that affect Sir Charles draw on my part. 40

CRANWELL On this side heaves my hand.

WENDOLL Here goes my heart.

*They divide themselves.* SIR CHARLES, CRANWELL, FALCONER, *and* HUNTSMAN *fight against* SIR FRANCIS, WENDOLL, *his* FALCONER, *and* HUNTSMAN, *and* SIR CHARLES *hath the better, and beats them away, killing both of Sir Francis his men. Exeunt all except* SIR CHARLES

SIR CHARLES My God! What have I done? What have I done?
My rage hath plunged into a sea of blood
In which my soul lies drowned, poor innocent
For whom we are to answer. Well, 'tis done,
And I remain the victor. A great conquest,
When I would give this right hand, nay this head,
To breathe in them new life whom I have slain.
Forgive me God, 'twas in the heat of blood,
And anger quite removes me from myself: 50
It was not I, but rage, did this vile murder;
Yet I, and not my rage, must answer it.
Sir Francis Acton, he is fled the field,
With him, all those that did partake his quarrel,
And I am left alone, with sorrow dumb,
And in my height of conquest, overcome.

*Enter* SUSAN

SUSAN Oh God, my brother wounded among the dead;
Unhappy jest that in such earnest ends.

The rumour of this fear stretched to my ears,
And I am come to know if you be wounded. 60

SIR CHARLES Oh sister, sister, wounded at the heart.

SUSAN My God forbid!

SIR CHARLES In doing that thing which he forbade,
I am wounded, sister.

SUSAN I hope not at the heart.

SIR CHARLES Yes, at the heart.

SUSAN Oh God! A surgeon there!

SIR CHARLES Call me a surgeon, sister, for my soul;
The sin of murder it hath pierced my heart,
And made a wide wound there; but for these scratches,
They are nothing, nothing.

SUSAN Charles, what have you done?
Sir Francis hath great friends, and will pursue you 70
Unto the utmost danger of the law.

SIR CHARLES My conscience is become my enemy,
And will pursue me more than Acton can.

SUSAN Oh fly, sweet brother.

SIR CHARLES Shall I fly from thee?
What, Sue, art weary of my company?

SUSAN Fly from your foe.

SIR CHARLES You, sister, are my friend,
And flying you, I shall pursue my end.

SUSAN Your company is as my eyeball dear;
Being far from you, no comfort can be near.
Yet fly to save your life. What would I care 80
To spend my future age in black despair,
So you were safe? And yet to live one week
Without my brother Charles, through every cheek
My streaming tears would downwards run so rank
Till they could set on either side a bank,
And in the midst a channel; so my face
For two salt water brooks shall still find place.

SIR CHARLES Thou shalt not weep so much, for I will stay
In spite of danger's teeth. I'll live with thee,
Or I'll not live at all. I will not sell 90
My country, and my father's patrimony,
No, thy sweet sight, for a vain hope of life.

*Enter* SHERIFF *with* OFFICERS

SHERIFF Sir Charles, I am made the unwilling instrument
Of your attach and apprehension.
I am sorry that the blood of innocent men
Should be of you exacted. It was told me

---

28 trindle-tails: curly-tailed (and hence low-bred) dogs
32 swagger: bluster
37 long home: grave
SD *killing both* Q3 (killing one Q1)
44 innocent Q1; i.e. the soul. Some editors follow Q3's 'innocents', i.e. the slain men

59 fear: event to be feared
71 danger: jurisdiction, penalty
75 What, Sue: eds (What *Iane* Q1; Why *Sue* Q3)
83 every: either
84 rank: profusely
87 still: always
94 attach: arrest

That you were guarded with a troop of friends,
And therefore I come armed.

SIR CHARLES                    O Master Sheriff,
I came into the field with many friends,
But see, they all have left me; only one          100
Clings to my sad misfortune, my dear sister.
I know you for an honest gentleman;
I yield my weapons and submit to you.
Convey me where you please.

SHERIFF                    To prison then,
To answer for the lives of these dead men.

SUSAN  O God! O God!

SIR CHARLES                    Sweet sister, every strain
Of sorrow from your heart augments my pain;
Your grief abounds and hits against my breast.

SHERIFF  Sir, will you go?

SIR CHARLES                    Even where it likes you best.
*Exeunt*

# Scene iv

*Enter* MASTER FRANKFORD *in a study*

FRANKFORD  How happy am I amongst other men
That in my mean estate embrace content.
I am a gentleman, and by my birth
Companion with a king; a king's no more.
I am possessed of many fair revenues,
Sufficient to maintain a gentleman.
Touching my mind, I am studied in all arts,
The riches of my thoughts, and of my time
Have been a good proficient. But the chief
Of all the sweet felicities on earth,          10
I have a fair, a chaste, and loving wife,
Perfection all, all truth, all ornament.
If man on earth may truly happy be,
Of these at once possessed, sure I am he.

*Enter* NICK

NICK  Sir, there's a gentleman attends without to speak
with you.

FRANKFORD  On horseback?

NICK  Ay, on horseback.

FRANKFORD  Entreat him to alight; I will attend him.
Knowest thou him, Nick?

NICK                    I know him; his name's
Wendoll.          20
It seems he comes in haste. His horse is booted
Up to the flank in mire, himself all spotted

And stained with plashing. Sure he rid in fear
Or for a wager; horse and man both sweat.
I ne'er saw two in such a smoking heat.

FRANKFORD  Intreat him in. About it instantly.

*Exit* NICK

This Wendoll I have noted, and his carriage
Hath pleased me much. By observation
I have noted many good deserts in him:
He's affable and seen in many things,          30
Discourses well, a good companion,
And though of small means, yet a gentleman
Of a good house, somewhat pressed by want.
I have preferred him to a second place
In my opinion, and my best regard.

*Enter* WENDOLL, ANNE, *and* NICK

ANNE  O Master Frankford, Master Wendoll here
Brings you the strangest news that ere you heard.

FRANKFORD  What news, sweet wife? What news good
Master Wendoll?

WENDOLL  You knew the match made 'twixt Sir Francis
Acton
And Sir Charles Mountford?

FRANKFORD                    True, with their hounds
and hawks.          40

WENDOLL  The matches were both played.

FRANKFORD                    Ha! And which won?

WENDOLL  Sir Francis, your wife's brother, had the worst,
And lost the wager.

FRANKFORD                    Why, the worse his chance.
Perhaps the fortune of some other day
Will change his luck.

ANNE                    Oh, but you hear not all.
Sir Francis lost, and yet was loth to yield.
In brief, the two knights grew to difference,
From words to blows, and so to banding sides,
Where valorous Sir Charles slew in his spleen
Two of your brother's men: his falconer,          50
And his good huntsman, whom he loved so well.
More men were wounded, no more slain outright.

FRANKFORD  Now, trust me, I am sorry for the knight.
But is my brother safe?

WENDOLL                    All whole and sound,
His body not being blemished with one wound.
But poor Sir Charles is to the prison led,
To answer at th'assize for them that's dead.

FRANKFORD  I thank your pains, sir. Had the news been
better

---

108  abounds: overflows
109  likes: pleases
SD  *in a study*: in deep contemplation
  2  mean: moderate
  9  Have . . . proficient: have made profitable use
  14  at once: at the same time

23  plashing: splashing
27  carriage: conduct
29  deserts: qualities
30  seen: accomplished
34  preferred: promoted
      second place: i.e. after that held by Anne
48  banding sides: 'forming factions' (Sturgess)

Your will was to have brought it, Master Wendoll.
Sir Charles will find hard friends; his case is heinous,
And will be most severely censured on.                    61
I am sorry for him. Sir, a word with you.
I know you, sir, to be a gentleman
In all things, your possibilities but mean.
Please you to use my table and my purse;
They are yours.

WENDOLL            O Lord, sir, I shall never deserve it!

FRANKFORD   O sir, disparage not your worth too much;
You are full of quality and fair desert.
Choose of my men which shall attend on you,
And he is yours. I will allow you, sir,                   70
Your man, your gelding, and your table,
All at my own charge. Be my companion.

WENDOLL   Master Frankford, I have oft been bound to
   you
By many favours; this exceeds them all
That I shall never merit your least favour.
But when your last remembrance I forget,
Heaven at my soul exact that weighty debt.

FRANKFORD   There needs no protestation, for I know
   you
Virtuous, and therefore grateful. Prithee Nan,
Use him with all thy loving'st courtesy.                  80

ANNE   As far as modesty may well extend,
It is my duty to receive your friend.

FRANKFORD   To dinner; come sir. From this present
   day,
Welcome to me forever. Come away!
                    *Exeunt* FRANKFORD, ANNE *and* WENDOLL

NICK   I do not like this fellow by no means;
I never see him but my heart still earns.
Zounds, I could fight with him, yet know not why;
The devil and he are all one in my eye.

*Enter* JENKIN

JENKIN   O Nick, what gentleman is that comes to lie at
   our house? My master allows him one to wait on
   him, and I believe it will fall to thy lot.            91

NICK   I love my master, by these hilts I do,
But rather than I'll ever come to serve him,
I'll turn away my master.

*Enter* SISLY

SISLY   Nich'las, where are you Nich'las? You must come
   in, Nich'las, and help the young gentleman off with
   his boots.

NICK   If I pluck off his boots, I'll eat the spurs,
And they shall stick fast in my throat like burrs.
                                        *Exit* NICK

SISLY   Then Jenkin, come you?                           100

JENKIN   'Tis no boot for me to deny it. My master hath
   given me a coat here, but he takes pains himself to
   brush it once or twice a day with a holly wand.

SISLY   Come, come, make haste, that you may wash
   your hands again, and help to serve in dinner.   *Exit*

JENKIN   (*To audience*) You may see, my masters, though
   it be afternoon with you, 'tis but early days with us,
   for we have not dined yet. Stay but a little, I'll but go
   in and help to bear up the first course and come to
   you again presently.                                  110
                                                *Exit*

# Scene v

*Enter* MALBY *and* CRANWELL

MALBY   This is the sessions day; pray, can you tell me
How young Sir Charles hath sped? Is he acquit,
Or must he try the law's strict penalty?

CRANWELL   He's cleared of all, spite of his enemies,
Whose earnest labours was to take his life.
But in this suit of pardon he hath spent
All the revenues that his father left him,
And he is now turned a plain countryman,
Reformed in all things. See, sir, here he comes.

*Enter* SIR CHARLES *and his* KEEPER

KEEPER   Discharge your fees and you are then at
   freedom.                                               10

SIR CHARLES   Here, Master Keeper, take the poor
   remainder
Of all the wealth I have. My heavy foes
Have made my purse light, but, alas, to me
'Tis wealth enough that you have set me free.

MALBY   God give you joy of your delivery;

---

58–9   Had the news . . . it: 'i.e. You would have brought us
        more pleasing news had you any choice in the matter'
        (Scobie)
60   find hard friends: find friends with difficulty
64   possibilities: resources
75   That: so that
76   your last remembrance: 'i.e. this latest kindness' (Scobie)
86   earns: grieves; Scobie also notes a variant meaning of
        'curdles'
87   Zounds: exclamation, from 'God's wounds'
92   hilts: i.e. of dagger

101   boot: avail (with pun)
102   coat: i.e. servant's livery
103   brush . . . holly wand: 'i.e. to give me a beating' (Scobie)
107–8   afternoon . . . dined yet: performances of plays began at
        about 2.00 p.m.; the usual time for dinner was midday
3   try: undergo
6   of: for
8   a plain countryman: 'i.e. he is no longer a landlord'
        (Scobie)
9   Reformed: changed
SD   SIR CHARLES Q3 (SIR FRANCIS Q1)

I am glad to see you abroad, Sir Charles.

SIR CHARLES  The poorest knight in England, Master
   Malby;
   My life hath cost me all the patrimony
   My father left his son. Well, God forgive them
   That are the authors of my penury.      **20**

*Enter* SHAFTON

SHAFTON  Sir Charles, a hand, a hand—at liberty!
   Now by the faith I owe, I am glad to see it.
   What want you? Wherein may I pleasure you?
SIR CHARLES  O me! O most unhappy gentleman!
   I am not worthy to have friends stirred up
   Whose hands may help me in this plunge of want.
   I would I were in heaven to inherit there
   Th'immortal birthright which my Saviour keeps,
   And by no unthrift can be bought and sold;
   For here on earth, what pleasures should we trust?  **30**
SHAFTON  To rid you from these contemplations
   Three hundred pounds you shall receive of me—
   Nay, five for fail. Come sir, the sight of gold
   Is the most sweet receipt for melancholy,
   And will revive your spirits. You shall hold law
   With your proud adversaries. Tush, let Frank Acton
   Wage with knighthoodlike expense with me,
   And he will sink, he will. Nay, good Sir Charles
   Applaud your fortune, and your fair escape
   From all these perils.
SIR CHARLES          Oh sir, they have undone me.  **40**
   Two thousand and five hundred pound a year
   My father at his death possessed me of,
   All which the envious Acton made me spend.
   And notwithstanding all this large expense,
   I had much ado to gain my liberty;
   And I have now only a house of pleasure
   With some five hundred pounds, reserved
   Both to maintain me and my loving sister.
SHAFTON  (*Aside*) That must I have; it lies convenient
   for me.
   If I can fasten but one finger on him,     **50**
   With my full hand I'll gripe him to the heart.
   'Tis not for love I proffered him this coin,

---

16  abroad: at liberty
22  owe: own
23  want: lack
26  plunge: crisis
33  for fail: to be on the safe side
34  receipt: recipe
35  hold law: engage in litigation
37  Wage: contend
46  house of pleasure: summer house
48  Both to maintain: to maintain both
51  gripe: to grip, clutch or seize; to seek to get hold of; also
    'to oppress by miserly or penurious treatment; to "pinch",
    "squeeze"' (OED)

But for my gain and pleasure. (*To* SIR CHARLES)
   Come, Sir Charles,
   I know you have need of money; take my offer.
SIR CHARLES  Sir, I accept it, and remain indebted
   Even to the best of my unable power.
   Come, gentlemen, and see it tendered down.

                              *Exeunt*

# Scene vi

*Enter* WENDOLL, *melancholy*

WENDOLL  I am a villain if I apprehend
   But such a thought; then, to attempt the deed—
   Slave, thou art damned without redemption.
   I'll drive away this passion with a song.
   A song! Ha, ha! A song, as if, fond man,
   Thy eyes could swim in laughter when thy soul
   Lies drenched and drowned in red tears of blood.
   I'll pray, and see if God within my heart
   Plant better thoughts. Why, prayers are meditations,
   And when I meditate—O God forgive me—  **10**
   It is on her divine perfections.
   I will forget her; I will arm myself
   Not to entertain a thought of love to her;
   And when I come by chance into her presence
   I'll hale these balls until my eye-strings crack
   From being pulled and drawn to look that way.

*Enter over the stage* FRANKFORD, ANNE, *and* NICK

   O God! O God! With what a violence
   I am hurried to my own destruction.
   There goest thou, the most perfect'st man
   That ever England bred a gentleman;  **20**
   And shall I wrong his bed? Thou God of thunder,
   Stay, in thy thoughts of vengeance and of wrath,
   Thy great, almighty, and all-judging hand
   From speedy execution on a villain,
   A villain, and a traitor to his friend.

*Enter* JENKIN

JENKIN  Did your worship call?
WENDOLL  (*Not noticing* JENKIN) He doth maintain me,
   he allows me largely
   Money to spend—
JENKIN  (*Aside*) By my faith, so do not you me, I cannot
   get a cross of you.        **30**
WENDOLL         My gelding and my man.

---

56  unable: feeble
57  tendered down: paid
1  apprehend: conceive
5  fond: foolish
15  balls: eyeballs
27  largely: generously
30  cross: a coin

JENKIN (*Aside*) That's Sorrel and I.

WENDOLL This kindness grows of no alliance 'twixt us.

JENKIN (*Aside*) Nor is my service of any great
acquaintance.

WENDOLL I never bound him to me by desert;
Of a mere stranger, a poor gentleman,
A man by whom in no kind he could gain,
He hath placed me in the height of all his thoughts,
Made me companion with the best and chiefest
In Yorkshire. He cannot eat without me,    **40**
Nor laugh without me; I am to his body
As necessary as his digestion,
And equally do make him whole or sick.
And shall I wrong this man? Base man! Ingrate!
Hast thou the power straight with thy gory hands
To rip thy image from his bleeding heart?
To scratch thy name from out the holy book
Of his remembrance, and to wound his name,
That holds thy name so dear, or rend his heart
To whom thy heart was joined and knit together?   **50**
And yet I must. Then, Wendoll, be content.
Thus villains, when they would, cannot repent.

JENKIN (*Aside*) What a strange humour is my new
master in. Pray God he be not mad. If he should be
so, I should never have any mind to serve him in
Bedlam. It may be he is mad for missing of me.

WENDOLL (*Seeing* JENKIN) What, Jenkin? Where's your
mistress?

JENKIN Is your worship married?

WENDOLL Why dost thou ask?    **59**

JENKIN Because you are my master, and if I have a
mistress, I would be glad like a good servant to do my
duty to her.

WENDOLL I mean where's Mistress Frankford?

JENKIN Marry, sir, her husband is riding out of town,
and she went very lovingly to bring him on his way to
horse. Do you see, sir, here she comes, and here I go.

WENDOLL Vanish.    *Exit* JENKIN

*Enter* ANNE

ANNE You are well met, sir. Now in troth my husband
Before he took horse had a great desire
To speak with you. We sought about the house,   **70**
Hallowed into the fields, sent every way
But could not meet you. Therefore he enjoined me
To do unto you his most kind commends.

Nay, more, he wills you as you prize his love,
Or hold in estimation his kind friendship,
To make bold in his absence and command
Even as himself were present in the house,
For you must keep his table, use his servants,
And be a present Frankford in his absence.

WENDOLL I thank him for his love.    **80**
(*Aside*) Give me a name, you whose infectious
tongues
Are tipped with gall and poison; as you would
Think on a man that had your father slain,
Murdered thy children, made your wives base
strumpets,
So call me, call me so! Print in my face
The most stigmatic title of a villain
For hatching treason to so true a friend.

ANNE Sir, you are much beholding to my husband.
You are a man most dear in his regard.    **89**

WENDOLL I am bound unto your husband and you too.
(*Aside*) I will not speak to wrong a gentleman
Of that good estimation, my kind friend.
I will not! Zounds, I will not! I may choose,
And I will choose. Shall I be so misled?
Or shall I purchase to my father's crest
The motto of a villain? If I say
I will not do it, what thing can enforce me?
Who can compel me? What sad destiny
Hath such command upon my yielding thoughts?
I will not. Ha! Some fury pricks me on;   **100**
The swift fates drag me at their chariot wheel,
And hurry me to mischief. Speak I must—
Injure myself, wrong her, deceive his trust.

ANNE Are you not well, sir, that you seem thus troubled?
There is sedition in your countenance.

WENDOLL And in my heart, fair angel, chaste and wise.
I love you. Start not, speak not, answer not.
I love you—nay, let me speak the rest.
Bid me to swear, and I will call to record
The host of heaven.

ANNE           The host of heaven forbid   **110**
Wendoll should hatch such a disloyal thought.

WENDOLL Such is my fate; to this suit I was born:
To wear rich pleasure's crown, or fortune's scorn.

ANNE My husband loves you.

WENDOLL           I know it.

ANNE                   He esteems you
Even as his brain, his eye-ball, or his heart.

WENDOLL I have tried it.

---

33 alliance: kinship
34 of . . . acquaintance: because of any close relationship
36 mere: complete
37 kind: way
45 straight: directly, immediately
47 name: reputation
56 Bedlam: famous London asylum for the insane
65–6 bring . . . horse: accompany him to his horse
73 do . . . commends: give you his kindest regards

78 keep: maintain
86 stigmatic: infamous
98 sad: distressing
105 sedition: tumult, discord (not in OED in this figurative
sense)
116 tried it: put it to the test

ANNE His purse is your exchequer, and his table
  Doth freely serve you.
WENDOLL           So I have found it.
ANNE O with what face of brass, what brow of steel,
  Can you unblushing speak this to the face      120
  Of the espoused wife of so dear a friend?
  It is my husband that maintains your state;
  Will you dishonour him? I am his wife
  That in your power hath left his whole affairs;
  It is to me you speak?
WENDOLL          O speak no more,
  For more than this I know and have recorded
  Within the red-leaved table of my heart.
  Fair, and of all beloved, I was not fearful
  Bluntly to give my life into your hand,
  And at one hazard all my earthly means.      130
  Go, tell your husband; he will turn me off,
  And I am then undone. I care not, I—
  'Twas for your sake. Perchance in rage he'll kill me.
  I care not—'twas for you. Say I incur
  The general name of villain through the world,
  Of traitor to my friend—I care not, I.
  Beggary, shame, death, scandal, and reproach:
  For you I'll hazard all—what care I?
  For you I'll live, and in your love I'll die.
ANNE You move me, sir, to passion and to pity.   140
  The love I bear my husband is as precious
  As my soul's health.
WENDOLL        I love your husband too,
  And for his love I will engage my life.
  Mistake me not, the augmentation
  Of my sincere affection borne to you
  Doth no whit lessen my regard of him.
  I will be secret, lady, close as night,
  And not the light of one small glorious star
  Shall shine here in my forehead to bewray
  That act of night.
ANNE         What shall I say?      150
  My soul is wandering, and hath lost her way.
  O Master Wendoll, O.
WENDOLL        Sigh not, sweet saint,
  For every sigh you breathe draws from my heart
  A drop of blood.
ANNE         I ne'er offended yet.
  My fault, I fear, will in my brow be writ.
  Women that fall not quite bereft of grace
  Have their offences noted in their face.

  I blush and am ashamed. O Master Wendoll,
  Pray God I be not born to curse your tongue
  That hath enchanted me. This maze I am in    160
  I fear will prove the labyrinth of sin.

*Enter* NICK *unobserved*

WENDOLL The path of pleasure, and the gate to bliss,
  Which on your lips I knock at with a kiss.
NICK (*Aside*) I'll kill the rogue.
WENDOLL Your husband is from home, your bed's no
  blab—
  Nay, look not down and blush.
           *Exeunt* ANNE *and* WENDOLL
NICK          Zounds, I'll stab.
  Ay, Nick, was it thy chance to come just in the nick?
  I love my master, and I hate that slave;
  I love my mistress, but these tricks I like not.
  My master shall not pocket up this wrong;    170
  I'll eat my fingers first. What sayest thou, metal?
            *Drawing his dagger*
  Does not the rascal Wendoll go on legs
  That thou must cut off? Hath he not hamstrings
  That thou must hough? Nay metal, thou shalt stand
  To all I say. I'll henceforth turn a spy,
  And watch them in their close conveyances.
  I never looked for better of that rascal
  Since he came miching first into our house.
  It is that Satan hath corrupted her,
  For she was fair and chaste. I'll have an eye    180
  In all their gestures. Thus I think of them:
  If they proceed as they have done before,
  Wendoll's a knave, my mistress is a etcetera.
                *Exit*

## Scene vii

*Enter* CHARLES *and* SUSAN

SIR CHARLES Sister, you see we are driven to hard shift
  To keep this poor house we have left unsold.
  I am now enforced to follow husbandry,
  And you to milk; and do we not live well?
  Well, I thank God.
SUSAN        O brother, here's a change
  Since old Sir Charles died in our father's house.

---

127  table: notebook
130  at one hazard: 'at once put at risk' (Scobie)
140  passion: sorrow (Sturgess)
147  close: secret
148  glorious: boastful
149  bewray: divulge, betray
153–4  every sigh . . . blood: reference to the popular belief that
     a sigh cost one's heart a drop of blood

160  maze: a) state of bewilderment; b) labyrinth
165  blab: tell-tale
170  pocket up: submit to
174  hough: cut (to disable)
176  close conveyances: secret dealings
178  miching: sneaking
181  gestures: actions
183  etcetera Q1 (— Q3); i.e. 'whore'
  1  hard shift: a difficult way of earning a living
  3  husbandry: i.e. farming

SIR CHARLES  All things on earth thus change, some up,
   some down;
   Content's a kingdom, and I wear that crown.

*Enter* SHAFTON *with a* SERGEANT

SHAFTON  Good morrow, good morrow, Sir Charles.
   What, with your sister
   Plying your husbandry? Sergeant, stand off.    10
   You have a pretty house here, and a garden,
   And goodly ground about it. Since it lies
   So near a lordship that I lately bought,
   I would fain buy it of you. I will give you—
SIR CHARLES  O pardon me; this house successively
   Hath 'longed to me and my progenitors
   Three hundred year. My great-great-grandfather,
   He in whom first our gentle style began,
   Dwelt here, and in this ground increased this molehill
   Unto that mountain which my father left me.    20
   Where he the first of all our house begun,
   I now the last will end and keep this house,
   This virgin title never yet deflowered
   By any unthrift of the Mountford's line.
   In brief I will not sell it for more gold
   Than you could hide or pave the ground withal.
SHAFTON  Ha, ha! A proud mind and a beggar's purse.
   Where's my three hundred pounds, beside the use?
   I have brought it to an execution
   By course of law. What? Is my money ready?    30
SIR CHARLES  An execution sir, and never tell me
   You put my bond in suit? You deal extremely.
SHAFTON  Sell me the land and I'll acquit you straight.
SIR CHARLES  Alas, alas! 'Tis all trouble hath left me
   To cherish me and my poor sister's life.
   If this were sold our names should then be quite
   Razed from the bead-roll of gentility.
   You see what hard shift we have made to keep it
   Allied still to our own name. This palm you see
   Labour hath glowed within; her silver brow,    40
   That never tasted a rough winter's blast
   Without a mask or fan, doth with a grace
   Defy cold winter and his storms outface.
SUSAN  Sir, we feed sparing and we labour hard,
   We lie uneasy, to reserve to us
   And our succession this small plot of ground.
SIR CHARLES  I have so bent my thoughts to husbandry,
   That I protest I scarcely can remember
   What a new fashion is, how silk or satin
   Feels in my hand. Why, pride is grown to us    50
   A mere, mere stranger. I have quite forgot
   The names of all that ever waited on me;
   I cannot name ye any of my hounds,
   Once from whose echoing mouths I heard all the
     music
   That e'er my heart desired. What should I say?
   To keep this place I have changed myself away.
SHAFTON  Arrest him at my suit. Actions and actions
   Shall keep thee in perpetual bondage fast.
   Nay, more, I'll sue thee by a late appeal,
   And call thy former life in question.    60
   The keeper is my friend; thou shalt have irons
   And usage such as I'll deny to dogs. Away with him!
SIR CHARLES  You are too timorous; but trouble is my
    master
   And I will serve him truly. My kind sister,
   Thy tears are of no force to mollify
   This flinty man. Go to my father's brother,
   My kinsmen and allies; entreat them from me
   To ransom me from this injurious man
   That seeks my ruin.
SHAFTON             Come, irons, irons away!
   I'll see thee lodged far from the sight of day.    70
                        *Exeunt except* SUSAN

*Enter* SIR FRANCIS *and* MALBY

SUSAN  My heart's so hardened with the frost of grief
   Death cannot pierce it through. Tyrant too fell!
   So lead the fiends condemned souls to hell.
SIR FRANCIS  Again to prison! Malby, hast thou seen
   A poor slave better tortured? Shall we hear
   The music of his voice cry from the grate
   'Meat for the Lord's sake'? No, no, yet I am not
   Throughly revenged. They say he hath a pretty wench
   Unto his sister: shall I, in mercy sake
   To him and to his kindred, bribe the fool    80
   To shame herself by lewd, dishonest lust?

---

SD  SERGEANT: officer charged with arresting offenders and
    summoning them to court
13  lordship: estate
18  gentle style: title to gentility
28  use: interest
29  have . . . execution: 'have had prepared a warrant of
    seizure' (Sturgess)
32  put . . . suit: 'set the law in motion concerning my bond'
    (Scobie)
    extremely: severely
36  names: eds (means Qs)
37  bead-roll: list
40  her: i.e. Susan's

46  succession: descendants
51  mere: absolute
56  changed . . . away: 'transformed my way of life'
    (Sturgess)
57  actions: i.e. legal actions
60  former life: 'i.e. judgement which had granted him his
    life' (Sturgess)
63  timorous: terrible, dreadful
67  allies: relatives
72  fell: cruel
76  grate: prison bars
81  dishonest: dishonourable

I'll proffer largely, but the deed being done
I'll smile to see her base confusion.

MALBY Methinks, Sir Francis, you are full revenged
For greater wrongs than he can proffer you.
See where the poor sad gentlewoman stands.

SIR FRANCIS Ha, ha! Now I will flout her poverty,
Deride her fortunes, scoff her base estate.
My very soul the name of Mountford hates.
But stay, my heart! O what a look did fly           90
To strike my soul through with thy piercing eye.
I am enchanted, all my spirits are fled,
And with one glance my envious spleen struck dead.

SUSAN (*Seeing them*) Acton, that seeks our blood!
*Runs away*

SIR FRANCIS                     O chaste and fair!

MALBY Sir Francis, why Sir Francis? Zounds, in a trance!
Sir Francis, what cheer, man? Come, come, how is't?

SIR FRANCIS Was she not fair? Or else this judging eye
Cannot distinguish beauty.

MALBY                     She was fair.

SIR FRANCIS She was an angel in a mortal's shape,
And ne'er descended from old Mountford's line.    100
But soft, soft, let me call my wits together.
A poor, poor wench, to my great adversary
Sister, whose very souls denounce stern war
One against other. How now, Frank, turned fool
Or madman, whether? But no! Master of
My perfect senses and directest wits.
Then why should I be in this violent humour
Of passion and of love, and with a person
So different every way, and so opposed
In all contractions and still warring actions?    110
Fie, fie, how I dispute against my soul.
Come, come, I'll gain her, or in her fair quest
Purchase my soul free and immortal rest.
*Exeunt*

# Scene viii

*Enter* THREE *or* FOUR SERVINGMEN *including* NICK *and*
SPIGGOT *the Butler, one with a voider and a wooden knife
to take away all, another the salt and bread; another the*
table-cloth *and napkins, another the* carpet. JENKIN *with
two lights after them*

JENKIN So, march in order and retire in battle 'ray. My
master and the guests have supped already; all's taken
away. Here, now spread for the servingmen in the
hall. Butler, it belongs to your office.

SPIGGOT I know it, Jenkin. What do you call the
gentleman that supped there tonight?

JENKIN Who, my master?

SPIGGOT No, no, Master Wendoll, he is a daily guest. I
mean the gentleman that came but this afternoon.    9

JENKIN His name is Master Cranwell. God's light!
Hark within there, my master calls to lay more billets
on the fire. Come, come! Lord, how we that are in
office here in the house are troubled. One spread the
carpet in the parlour and stand ready to snuff the
lights; the rest be ready to prepare their stomachs.
More lights in the hall there! Come Nich'las.
*Exeunt all but* NICK

NICK I cannot eat, but had I Wendoll's heart
I would eat that; the rogue grows impudent.
Oh I have seen such vild, notorious tricks,
Ready to make my eyes dart from my head.           20
I'll tell my master, by this air I will;
Fall what may fall, I'll tell him. Here he comes.

*Enter* FRANKFORD, *as it were brushing the crumbs from his
clothes with a napkin, and newly risen from supper*

FRANKFORD Nich'las, what make you here? Why are
you not
At supper in the hall there with your fellows?

NICK Master, I stayed your rising from the board
To speak with you.

FRANKFORD              Be brief then, gentle Nich'las,
My wife and guests attend me in the parlour.
Why dost thou pause? Now Nich'las, you want
money,
And unthrift-like would eat into your wages
Ere you have earned it. Here's, sir, half-a-crown.  30
Play the good husband and away to supper.

NICK (*Aside*) By this hand, an honourable gentleman. I
will not see him wronged. (*To* FRANKFORD) Sir, I
have served you long. You entertained me seven years
before your beard. You knew me, sir, before you
knew my mistress.

---

82 largely: generously
83 base confusion: degrading ruin
90 O: eds (or Qs)
92 spirits: source of hostile feelings
93 envious spleen: malicious anger
103 whose very souls: i.e. Mountford's and mine
    denounce: announce
105 whether?: which?
110 contractions: dealings
112 her fair quest: 'quest of fair her' (Van Fossen). Sturgess
    suggests 'fair quest of her'

---

SD *voider*: tray or basket for clearing the table
   *carpet*: table cover
11 billets: thick pieces of wood
13 office: service
19 vild: vile
25 stayed: awaited
28 want: lack
31 Play the good husband: i.e. be thrifty
34 entertained: employed

FRANKFORD  What of this, good Nich'las?

NICK  I never was a makebate or a knave.
  I have no fault but one—I am given to quarrel,
  But not with women. I will tell you, master,     40
  That which will make your heart leap from your
    breast,
  Your hair to startle from your head, your ears to
    tingle.

FRANKFORD  What preparation's this to dismal news?

NICK  'Sblood sir, I love you better than your wife.
  I'll make it good.

FRANKFORD  Thou art a knave, and I have much ado
  With wonted patience to contain my rage
  And not to break thy pate. Thou art a knave;
  I'll turn you with your base comparisons
  Out of my doors.     50

NICK  Do, do.
  There's not room for Wendoll and me too
  Both in one house. O master, master,
  That Wendoll is a villain.

FRANKFORD  Ay, saucy!     FRANKFORD *strikes him*

NICK  Strike, strike, do strike, yet hear me. I am no fool,
  I know a villain when I see him act
  Deeds of a villain. Master, master, that base slave
  Enjoys my mistress, and dishonours you.

FRANKFORD  Thou hast killed me with a weapon whose
  sharpened point     60
  Hath pricked quite through and through my
    shivering heart.
  Drops of cold sweat sit dangling on my hairs
  Like morning's dew upon the golden flowers,
  And I am plunged into a strange agony.
  What didst thou say? If any word that touched
  His credit or her reputation,
  It is as hard to enter my belief
  As Dives into heaven.

NICK      I can gain nothing.
  They are two that never wronged me. I knew before
  'Twas but a thankless office, and perhaps     70
  As much as my service or my life is worth.
  All this I know, but this and more,
  More by a thousand dangers could not hire me
  To smother such a heinous wrong from you.
  I saw, and I have said.

FRANKFORD  (*Aside*) 'Tis probable. Though blunt, yet
  he is honest.
  Though I durst pawn my life, and on their faith
  Hazard the dear salvation of my soul,

Yet in my trust I may be too secure.
May this be true? O may it? Can it be?     80
Is it by any wonder possible?
Man, woman, what thing mortal may we trust,
When friends and bosom wives prove so unjust?
(*To* NICK) What instance hast thou of this strange
  report?

NICK  Eyes, eyes.

FRANKFORD  Thy eyes may be deceived I tell thee,
  For should an angel from the heavens drop down
  And preach this to me that thyself hast told,
  He should have much ado to win belief,
  In both their loves I am so confident.     90

NICK  Shall I discourse the same by circumstance?

FRANKFORD  No more; to supper, and command your
  fellows
  To attend us and the strangers. Not a word;
  I charge thee on thy life, be secret then,
  For I know nothing.

NICK  I am dumb. And now that I have eased my
  stomach,
  I will go fill my stomach.     *Exit*

FRANKFORD  Away, be gone.
  She is well born, descended nobly,
  Virtuous her education; her repute     100
  Is in the general voice of all the country
  Honest and fair; her carriage, her demeanour
  In all her actions that concern the love
  To me, her husband, modest, chaste, and godly.
  Is all this seeming gold plain copper?
  But he, that Judas that hath borne my purse,
  And sold me for a sin—O God, O God,
  Shall I put up these wrongs? No, shall I trust
  The bare report of this suspicious groom
  Before the double gilt, the well-hatched ore     110
  Of their two hearts? No, I will loose these thoughts.
  Distraction I will banish from my brow,
  And from my looks exile sad discontent,
  Their wonted favours in my tongue shall flow.
  Till I know all, I'll nothing seem to know.
  Lights and a table there! Wife, Master Wendoll
  And gentle Master Cranwell—

*Enter* ANNE, MASTER WENDOLL, MASTER CRANWELL,
NICK *and* JENKIN *with cards, carpet, stools and other
necessaries*

FRANKFORD  O you are a stranger, Master Cranwell,
  you,

---

38  makebate: trouble-maker
45  I'll make it good: i.e. I'll justify my words. Van Fossen
    suggests that Frankford is threatening Nicholas at this
    point
59  enjoys: i.e. sexually
66  credit: reputation
68  Dives: the rich man sent to hell in the parable in Luke 16

84  instance: evidence
91  discourse . . . circumstance: relate this story in detail
93  strangers: visitors
96  eased my stomach: i.e. 'got it off my chest'
108  put up: put up with
110  double gilt: a) refined gold; b) double guilt
    well-hatched: richly inlaid

And often balk my house; faith, you are a churl.
Now we have supped, a table and to cards.          120
JENKIN A pair of cards, Nich'las, and a carpet to cover
the table. Where's Sisly with her counters and her
box? Candles and candlesticks there!

*Enter* SISLY *and a* SERVINGMAN, *with counters and
candles*

Fie, we have such a household of serving creatures!
Unless it be Nick and I, there's not one amongst
them all can say boo to a goose. Well said, Nick.
                *They spread a carpet, set down lights and cards*
ANNE Come Master Frankford, who shall take my
part?
FRANKFORD Marry, that will I, sweet wife.
WENDOLL No, by my faith, sir, when you are together I
sit out; it must be Mistress Frankford and I, or else it
is no match.                                      131
FRANKFORD I do not like that match.
NICK (*Aside*) You have no reason, marry, knowing all.
FRANKFORD 'Tis no great matter neither. Come,
Master Cranwell, shall you and I take them up?
CRANWELL At your pleasure, sir.
FRANKFORD I must look to you, Master Wendoll, for
you will be playing false—nay, so will my wife too.
NICK (*Aside*) Ay, I will be sworn she will.
ANNE Let them that are taken playing false forfeit the
set.                                              140
FRANKFORD Content. It shall go hard but I'll take you.
CRANWELL Gentlemen, what shall our game be?
WENDOLL Master Frankford, you play best at Noddy.
FRANKFORD You shall not find it so; indeed you shall
not.
ANNE I can play at nothing so well as Double Ruff.
FRANKFORD If Master Wendoll and my wife be
together, there's no playing against them at double
hand.
NICK I can tell you, sir, the game that Master Wendoll
is best at.                                       150
WENDOLL What game is that, Nick?
NICK Marry sir, Knave Out of Doors.
WENDOLL She and I will take you at Lodam.

ANNE Husband, shall we play at Saint?
FRANKFORD (*Aside*) My saint's turned devil. (*To them*)
No, we'll none of Saint. You're best at New Cut,
wife; you'll play at that.
WENDOLL If you play at New Cut, I am soonest hitter
of any here, for a wager.
FRANKFORD (*Aside*) 'Tis me they play on; well, you may
draw out,                                         160
For all your cunning; 'twill be to your shame.
I'll teach you at your New Cut a new game.
(*To them*) Come, come.
CRANWELL If you cannot agree upon the game, to Post
and Pair.
WENDOLL We shall be soonest pairs, and my good
host,
When he comes late home, he must kiss the post.
FRANKFORD Whoever wins, it shall be to thy cost.
CRANWELL Faith, let it be Vide-ruff, and let's make
honours.
FRANKFORD If you make honours, one thing let me
crave,
Honour the King, and Queen; except the knave.   170
WENDOLL Well, as you please for that. Lift who shall
deal.
ANNE The least in sight. What are you, Master
Wendoll?
WENDOLL (*Cutting the cards*) I am a knave.
NICK (*Aside*)                          I'll swear it.
ANNE                                    I a queen.
FRANKFORD (*Aside*) A quean thou should'st say. (*To
them*) Well, the cards are mine.
They are the grossest pair that e'er I felt.
ANNE Shuffle, I'll cut. (*Aside*) Would I had never dealt.
                                  FRANKFORD *deals the cards*
FRANKFORD I have lost my dealing.
WENDOLL                       Sir, the fault's in me.
This queen I have more than my own, you see.
Give me the stock.              WENDOLL *deals*

---

153, 154 Lodam, Saint: card games
156 New Cut: card game (with sexual implication; 'cut' was
    an opprobrious term used for a man or woman)
158 hitter: obscure; probably 'point-scorer'
160 draw out: 'i.e. so pick your cards as to lose the game'
    (Van Fossen)
164 Post and Pair: a betting game, played with three cards
    each
166 kiss the post: be disappointed, excluded
168 Vide-ruff: another variant of Ruff
    make honours: probably 'name the highest cards' (eds)
171 Lift . . . deal: cut for the deal (with *double entendre* on
    'deal': see l. 176 below)
172 least: lowest
174 quean: harlot
175 grossest pair: 'a) thickest pack; b) most immoral couple'
    (Van Fossen)
179 stock: cards not yet dealt

---

119 balk: avoid
121 pair: pack
127 take my part: be my partner
138 playing false: cheating a) at cards, and b) with my wife.
    These kinds of double meanings are to be found in
    practically all the exchanges that follow
140 set: game
143 Noddy: a) card game; b) fool
145 Double Ruff: a) card game, like whist; b) *double* also
    meant deceitful, and *ruff* meant excitement, passion
149–9 double hand: 'i.e. a) when they are partners in a card
    game, b) at duplicity' (Scobie)
152 Knave Out of Doors: card game (with innuendo)

FRANKFORD          My mind's not on my game.
  (*Aside*) Many a deal I have lost, the more's your
    shame.                                                    180
  (*To him*) You have served me a bad trick, Master
    Wendoll.
WENDOLL  Sir, you must take your lot. To end this
    strife,
  I know I have dealt better with your wife.
FRANKFORD  (*Aside*) Thou hast dealt falsely then.
ANNE  What's trumps?
WENDOLL  Hearts. Partner, I rub.
FRANKFORD  (*Aside*) Thou robb'st me of my soul, of her
    chaste love;
  In thy false dealing, thou hast robbed my heart.
  Booty you play; I like a loser stand,
  Having no heart, or here, or in my hand.                   190
  (*To them*) I will give o'er the set; I am not well.
  Come, who will hold my cards?
ANNE  Not well, sweet Master Frankford?
  Alas, what ail you? 'Tis some sudden qualm.
WENDOLL  How long have you been so, Master
    Frankford?
FRANKFORD  Sir, I was lusty, and I had my health,
  But I grew ill when you began to deal.
  Take hence this table.

*Enter* SERVANTS *to remove the table, cards, etc.*

                      Gentle Master Cranwell,
  You are welcome; see your chamber at your pleasure.
  I am sorry that this megrim takes me so,                   200
  I cannot sit and bear you company.
  Jenkin, some lights, and show him to his chamber.
ANNE  A night gown for my husband quickly there.

*Enter* SERVANT *with nightgown, and exit*

  It is some rheum or cold.
WENDOLL                     Now, in good faith,
  This illness you have got by sitting late
  Without your gown.
FRANKFORD            I know it, Master Wendoll.
  Go, go, to bed, lest you complain like me.
  Wife, prithee wife, into my bed-chamber.
  The night is raw and cold and rheumatic.                   209
  Leave me my gown and light; I'll walk away my fit.
WENDOLL  Sweet sir, good night.          *Exit* WENDOLL

---

181  trick: a) hand of cards; b) piece of roguery
186  rub: take all the cards of one suit
189  Booty you play: i.e. you play falsely. 'To play booty' is to
       play badly with the intention of losing, in order to
       victimise another player
190  or . . . or: either . . . or
196  lusty: healthy
200  megrim: migraine
204  rheum: cold, catarrh
209  rheumatic: rheum-inducing

FRANKFORD  Myself, good night.
ANNE                      Shall I attend you, husband?
FRANKFORD  No, gentle wife, thou'lt catch cold in thy
    head.
  Prithee begone, sweet; I'll make haste to bed.
ANNE  No sleep will fasten on mine eyes, you know,
  Until you come.
FRANKFORD         Sweet Nan, I prithee go.    *Exit* ANNE
  (*To* NICK) I have bethought me. Get me by degrees
  The keys of all my doors, which I will mould
  In wax, and take their fair impression,                    219
  To have by them new keys. This being compassed,
  At a set hour a letter shall be brought me,
  And when they think they may securely play,
  They are nearest to danger. Nick, I must rely
  Upon thy trust and faithful secrecy.
NICK  Build on my faith.
FRANKFORD                To bed then, not to rest.
  Care lodges in my brain, grief in my breast.
                                              *Exeunt*

# Scene ix

*Enter* SUSAN, OLD MOUNTFORD, SANDY, RODER *and*
TYDY

OLD MOUNTFORD  You say my nephew is in great
    distress;
  Who brought it to him but his own lewd life?
  I cannot spare a cross. I must confess
  He was my brother's son; why, niece, what then?
  This is no world in which to pity men.
SUSAN  I was not born a begger, though his extremes
  Enforce this language from me; I protest
  No fortune of mine own could lead my tongue
  To this base key. I do beseech you, uncle,
  For the name's sake, for Christianity,                      10
  Nay, for God's sake, to pity his distress.
  He is denied the freedom of the prison,
  And in the hole is laid with men condemned.
  Plenty he hath of nothing but of irons,
  And it remains in you to free him thence.
OLD MOUNTFORD  Money I cannot spare. Men should
    take heed.
  He lost my kindred when he fell to need.          *Exit*
SUSAN  Gold is but earth; thou earth enough shalt have
  When thou hast once took measure of thy grave.
  You know me, Master Sandy, and my suit.             20

---

212  Myself: 'i.e. my intimate friend' (Scobie)
217  by degrees: gradually
220  compassed: achieved
2    lewd: wicked
3    cross: coin
10   the name's sake: the sake of the family reputation
13   hole: dungeon

SANDY  I knew you, lady, when the old man lived;
  I knew you ere your brother sold his land.
  Then you were Mistress Sue, tricked up in jewels;
  Then you sung well, played sweetly on the flute;
  But now I neither know you nor your suit.          *Exit*
SUSAN  You, Master Roder, was my brother's tenant.
  Rent-free he placed you in that wealthy farm
  Of which you are possessed.
RODER                    True he did,
  And have I not there dwelt still for his sake?
  I have some business now, but without doubt     30
  They that have hurled him in will help him out.   *Exit*
SUSAN  Cold comfort still. What say you, cousin Tydy?
TYDY  I say this comes of roisting, swaggering.
  Call me not cousin; each man for himself.
  Some men are born to mirth and some to sorrow.
  I am no cousin unto them that borrow.          *Exit*
SUSAN  O Charity, why art thou fled to heaven,
  And left all things on this earth uneven?
  Their scoffing answers I will ne'er return,
  But to myself his grief in silence mourn.       40

*Enter* SIR FRANCIS *and* MALBY

SIR FRANCIS  She is poor; I'll therefore tempt her with
    this gold.
  Go, Malby, in my name deliver it,
  And I will stay thy answer.
MALBY  Fair Mistress, as I understand, your grief
  Doth grow from want, so I have here in store
  A means to furnish you, a bag of gold
  Which to your hands I freely tender you.
SUSAN  I thank you, heavens, I thank you, gentle sir.
  God make me able to requite this favour.
MALBY  This gold Sir Francis Acton sends by me,    50
  And prays you—                          *whispering*
SUSAN  Acton! O God, that name I am born to curse.
  Hence, bawd! Hence, broker! See, I spurn his gold;
  My honour never shall for gain be sold.
SIR FRANCIS  Stay, lady, stay.
SUSAN                    From you I'll posting hie,
  Even as the doves from feathered eagles fly.   *Exit*
SIR FRANCIS  She hates my name, my face; how should
    I woo?
  I am disgraced in everything I do.
  The more she hates me and disdains my love,
  The more I am wrapped in admiration          60

Of her divine and chaste perfections.
Woo her with gifts I cannot, for all gifts
Sent in my name she spurns. With looks I cannot,
For she abhors my sight. Nor yet with letters,
For none she will receive. How then, how then?
Well, I will fasten such a kindness on her
As shall o'ercome her hate and conquer it.
Sir Charles, her brother, lies in execution
For a great sum of money, and besides,
The appeal is sued still for my huntsmen's death,   70
Which only I have power to reverse.
In her I'll bury all my hate of him.
Go seek the keeper, Malby, bring me to him.
To save his body, I his debts will pay;
To save his life, I his appeal will stay.
                              *Exeunt*

# Scene x

*Enter* SIR CHARLES *in prison, with irons, his feet bare, his garments all ragged and torn*

SIR CHARLES  Of all on the earth's face most miserable,
  Breathe in the hellish dungeon thy laments.
  Thus like a slave ragged, like a felon gyved,
  That hurls thee headlong to this base estate.
  O unkind uncle! O my friends ingrate!
  Unthankful kinsmen! Mountfords all too base,
  To let thy name lie fettered in disgrace.
  A thousand deaths here in this grave I die;
  Fear, hunger, sorrow, cold—all threat my death,
  And join together to deprive my breath.       10
  But that which most torments me, my dear sister
  Hath left to visit me, and from my friends
  Hath brought no hopeful answer; therefore I
  Divine they will not help my misery.
  If it be so, shame, scandal, and contempt
  Attend their covetous thoughts, need make their
    graves.
  Usurers they live, and may they die like slaves.

*Enter* KEEPER

KEEPER  Knight, be of comfort for I bring thee freedom
  From all thy troubles.
SIR CHARLES              Then I am doomed to die;
  Death is the end of all calamity.              20

---

33  roisting: revelling
38  uneven: unjust
39  return: 'either a) report (to Charles) or b) reply to,
    respond to' (Scobie)
43  stay: await
45  in store: in abundance
SD  *whispering*: eds (&c. Qs)
53  broker: procurer
55  posting: hurriedly

68  in execution: imprisoned following his failure to pay his
    debt
70  appeal is sued: 'prosecution is in hand' (Sturgess)
3   gyved: shackled
4   That: Qs. Verity and Sturgess suggest 'what' in its place,
    changing the line to a question
5   ingrate: ungrateful
10  deprive: deprive me of
12  left: ceased

KEEPER  Live! Your appeal is stayed, the execution
  Of all your debts discharged, your creditors
  Even to the utmost penny satisfied,
  In sign whereof your shackles I knock off.
  You are not left so much indebted to us
  As for your fees; all is dischargd, all paid.
  Go freely to your house, or where you please.
  After long miseries, embrace your ease.
SIR CHARLES  Thou grumblest out the sweetest music to me
  That ever organ played. Is this a dream?                     30
  Or do my waking senses apprehend
  The pleasing taste of these applausive news?
  Slave that I was to wrong such honest friends,
  My loving kinsmen and my near allies.
  Tongue I will bite thee for the scandal breath
  Against such faithful kinsmen. They are all
  Composed of pity and compassion,
  Of melting charity, and of moving ruth.
  That which I spake before was in my rage;
  They are my friends, the mirrors of this age,        40
  Bounteous and free. The noble Mountfords' race,
  Ne'er bred a covetous thought or humour base.

*Enter* SUSAN

SUSAN  I can no longer stay from visiting
  My woeful brother. While I could I kept
  My hapless tidings from his hopeful ear.
SIR CHARLES  Sister, how much am I indebted to thee
  And to thy travail.
SUSAN                What, at liberty?
SIR CHARLES  Thou seest I am, thanks to thy industry.
  O unto which of all my courteous friends
  Am I thus bound? My uncle Mountford, he            50
  Even of an infant loved me; was it he?
  So did my cousin Tydy; was it he?
  So Master Roder, Master Sandy too;
  Which of all these did this high kindness do?
SUSAN  Charles, can you mock me in your poverty,
  Knowing your friends deride your misery?
  Now I protest I stand so much amazed
  To see your bonds free and your irons knocked off
  That I am rapt into a maze of wonder,
  The rather for I know not by what means            60
  This happiness hath chanced.
SIR CHARLES                   Why, by my uncle,
  My cousins, and my friends; who else, I pray,
  Would take upon them all my debts to pay?

SUSAN  O brother, they are men all of flint,
  Pictures of marble, and as void of pity
  As chased bears. I begged, I sued, I kneeled,
  Laid open all your griefs and miseries,
  Which they derided. More than that, denied us
  A part in their alliance, but in pride,
  Said that our kindred with our plenty died.          70
SIR CHARLES  Drudges too much! What, did they? O known evil:
  Rich fly the poor, as good men shun the devil.
  Whence should my freedom come? Of whom alive,
  Saving of those, have I deserved so well?
  Guess, sister, call to mind, remember me.
  These I have raised, these follow the world's guise,
  Whom, rich in honour, they in woe despise.
SUSAN  My wits have lost themselves. Let's ask the keeper.
SIR CHARLES  Gaoler!
KEEPER  At hand, sir.                                   80
SIR CHARLES  Of courtesy resolve me one demand:
  What was he took the burden of my debts
  From off my back, stayed my appeal to death,
  Discharged my fees, and brought me liberty?
KEEPER  A courteous knight, one called Sir Francis Acton,
SUSAN  Acton!
SIR CHARLES  Ha! Acton! O me, more distressed in this
  Than all my troubles. Hale me back,
  Double my irons, and my sparing meals
  Put into halves, and lodge me in a dungeon          90
  More deep, more dark, more cold, more comfortless.
  By Acton freed! Not all thy manacles
  Could fetter so my heels, as this one word
  Hath thralled my heart, and it must now lie bound
  In more strict prison than thy stony gaol.
  I am not free; I go but under bail.
KEEPER  My charge is done, sir, now I have my fees.
  As we get little, we will nothing leese.      *Exit*
SIR CHARLES  By Acton freed, my dangerous opposite.
  Why? To what end? Or what occasion? Ha!          100
  Let me forget the name of enemy,
  And with indifference balance this high favour. Ha!
SUSAN  (*Aside*) His love to me, upon my soul 'tis so;

---

21  Your appeal is stayed: 'the charge has been withdrawn' (Sturgess)
32  applausive: agreeable
38  ruth: pity
40  mirrors: exemplars
42  humour: disposition
47  travail: exertion, trouble

65  Pictures: statues
66  chased: tormented (as in bear-baiting)
69  alliance: kinship
71  Drudges too much: slaves too base
75  remember: remind
76  raised: mentioned, named
    guise: fashion
98  leese: lose
99  opposite: adversary
102  indifference: impartiality
    balance: weigh

That is the root from whence these strange things
  grow.
SIR CHARLES  Had this proceeded from my father, he
That by the law of nature is most bound
In offices of love, it had deserved
My best employment to requite that grace.
Had it proceeded from my friends, or him,
From them this action had deserved my life;      110
And from a stranger more, because from such
There is less execution of good deeds.
But he, nor father, nor ally, nor friend,
More than a stranger, both remote in blood
And in his heart opposed my enemy,
That this high bounty should proceed from him!
O there I lose myself. What should I say?
What think, what do, his bounty to repay?
SUSAN  You wonder, I am sure, whence this strange
  kindness
Proceeds in Acton. I will tell you, brother.      120
He dotes on me, and oft hath sent me gifts,
Letters and tokens; I refused them all.
SIR CHARLES  I have enough. Though poor, my heart is
  set
In one rich gift to pay back all my debt.

                                   *Exeunt*

# Scene xi

*Enter* FRANKFORD *and* NICK, *with keys, and a letter in his
hand*

FRANKFORD  This is the night, and I must play the
  touch
To try two seeming angels. Where's my keys?
NICK  They are made according to your mould in wax.
I bade the smith be secret, gave him money,
And there they are. The letter, sir.
FRANKFORD  True, take it; there it is.
And when thou seest me in my pleasant'st vein
Ready to sit to supper, bring it me.
NICK  I'll do't; make no more question but I'll do't.  *Exit*

*Enter* ANNE, CRANWELL, WENDOLL, *and* JENKIN

ANNE  Sirrah, 'tis six o'clock already struck.        10
Go bid them spread the cloth and serve in supper.
JENKIN  It shall be done forsooth, mistress. Where is
Spiggot the butler, to give us out salt and trenchers?

WENDOLL  We that have been a-hunting all the day
Come with prepared stomachs, Master Frankford.
We wished you at our sport.
FRANKFORD  My heart was with you, and my mind was
  on you.
Fie, Master Cranwell, you are still thus sad.
A stool, a stool! Where's Jenkin, and where's Nick?
'Tis supper time at least an hour ago.              20
What's the best news abroad?
WENDOLL                          I know none good.
FRANKFORD  (*Aside*) But I know too much bad.

*Enter* SPIGGOT, *the butler, and* JENKIN *with a tablecloth,
bread, trenchers, and salt, then exeunt*

CRANWELL  Methinks, sir, you might have that interest
In your wife's brother to be more remiss
In this hard dealing against poor Sir Charles,
Who, as I hear, lies in York Castle, needy
And in great want.
FRANKFORD  Did not more weighty business of my own
Hold me away, I would have laboured peace
Betwixt them with all care; indeed I would sir.      30
ANNE  I'll write unto my brother earnestly
In that behalf.
WENDOLL              A charitable deed,
And will beget the good opinion
Of all your friends that love you, Mistress Frankford.
FRANKFORD  That's you for one; I know you love Sir
  Charles
(*Aside*) And my wife too well.
WENDOLL                          He deserves the love
Of all true gentlemen. Be yourselves judge.
FRANKFORD  But supper, ho! Now as thou lovest me,
  Wendoll,
Which I am sure thou dost, be merry, pleasant,
And frolic it tonight. Sweet Master Cranwell,      40
Do you the like. Wife, I protest my heart
Was ne'er more bent on sweet alacrity.
Where be those lazy knaves to serve in supper?

*Enter* NICK

NICK  Sir, here's a letter.
FRANKFORD  Whence comes it? And who brought it?
NICK  A stripling that below attends your answer,
And as he tells me it is sent from York.
FRANKFORD  Have him into the cellar; let him taste a cup
Of our March beer. Go, make him drink.      *Reads*

---

119–22 set as prose in Qs
  SD *letter . . . hand*: it is not entirely clear, either in the SD or
    the text, who has the letter; it is probably, though not
    necessarily, Frankford (see ll. 5–6)
  1 play the touch: make a test (from alchemy: use a
    touchstone to test gold)
  2 angels: coins (with pun)
  13 trenchers: plates

23–4 interest/In: influence with
24 remiss: lenient
  SD *Aside*: we follow most recent eds in making this an aside.
    Sturgess, however, suggests that if 'too' is taken to mean
    'very', this could be spoken directly to Wendoll as a
    veiled warning
42 alacrity: enjoyment
49 March beer: strong beer brewed in March

NICK I'll make him drunk, if he be a Trojan. *Exit*

FRANKFORD My boots and spurs! Where's Jenkin? God
    forgive me,         **51**
    How I neglect my business. Wife, look here,
    I have a matter to be tried tomorrow
    By eight o'clock, and my attorney writes me
    I must be there betimes with evidence,
    Or it will go against me. Where's my boots?

*Enter* JENKIN *with boots and spurs*

ANNE I hope your business craves no such dispatch
    That you must ride tonight.
WENDOLL (*Aside*)         I hope it doth.
FRANKFORD God's me! No such dispatch?
    Jenkin, my boots. Where's Nick? Saddle my roan,  **60**
    And the gray dapple for himself.    *Exit* JENKIN
                     Content ye,
    It much concerns me. Gentle Master Cranwell
    And Master Wendoll, in my absence use
    The very ripest pleasure of my house.
WENDOLL Lord, Master Frankford, will you ride
    tonight?
    The ways are dangerous.
FRANKFORD           Therefore will I ride
    Appointed well, and so shall Nick, my man.
ANNE I'll call you up by five o'clock tomorrow.
FRANKFORD No, by my faith, wife, I'll not trust to that.
    'Tis not such easy rising in a morning    **70**
    From one I love so dearly. No, by my faith,
    I shall not leave so sweet a bedfellow,
    But with much pain. You have made me a sluggard
    Since I first knew you.
ANNE           Then if you needs will go
    This dangerous evening, Master Wendoll,
    Let me entreat you bear him company.
WENDOLL With all my heart, sweet mistress. My boots
    there!
FRANKFORD Fie, fie, that for my private business
    I should disease my friend, and be a trouble
    To the whole house. Nick!           **80**
NICK (*Off-stage*) Anon sir.
FRANKFORD Bring forth my gelding. As you love me, sir,
    Use no more words. A hand, good Master Cranwell.
CRANWELL Sir, God be your good speed.
FRANKFORD Goodnight, sweet Nan. Nay, nay, a kiss
    and part.
    (*Aside*) Dissembling lips, you suit not with my heart.
                        *Exit* FRANKFORD

WENDOLL (*Aside*) How business, time and hours all
    gracious proves
    And are the furtherers to my newborn love.
    I am husband now in Master Frankford's place,
    And must command the house. (*To* ANNE) My
    pleasure is           **90**
    We will not sup abroad so publicly,
    But in your private chamber, Mistress Frankford.
ANNE (*To* WENDOLL) O sir, you are too public in your
    love,
    And Master Frankford's wife—
CRANWELL           Might I crave favour,
    I would entreat you I might see my chamber.
    I am on the sudden grown exceeding ill,
    And would be spared from supper.
WENDOLL           Light there, ho!
    See you want nothing, sir, for if you do
    You injury that good man, and wrong me too.
CRANWELL I will make bold. Goodnight.    *Exit*
WENDOLL           How all conspire
    To make our bosom sweet and full entire.   **101**
    Come, Nan, I prithee let us sup within.
ANNE O what a clog unto the soul is sin.
    We pale offenders are still full of fear;
    Every suspicious eye brings danger near,
    When they whose clear heart from offence are free,
    Despise report, base scandals to outface,
    And stand at mere defiance with disgrace.
WENDOLL Fie, fie, you talk too like a Puritant.
ANNE You have tempted me to mischief, Master
    Wendoll.           **110**
    I have done I know not what. Well, you plead
    custom;
    That which for want of wit I granted erst
    I now must yield through fear. Come, come, let's in.
    Once o'er shoes, we are straight o'er head in sin.
WENDOLL My jocund soul is joyful above measure;
    I'll be profuse in Frankford's richest treasure.

                           *Exeunt*

---

50 Trojan: good fellow; drunkard
59 God's me: i.e. 'God save me'
61 Content ye: be assured
66 ways are dangerous: i.e. because of highwaymen
67 Appointed: equipped
79 disease: inconvenience
86 suit not: do not match

SD  *Aside*: eds are divided as to whether Wendoll's first four
    lines are an aside, and the final two and a half only
    addressed to Anne. We follow Van Fossen and Scobie in
    taking them to be so, particularly in the light of ll. 93–4
    and Cranwell's continued presence
99  injury: synonymous with 'injure' at this date
101 bosom: desires
103 clog: impediment
104 pale: i.e. fearful
106 When: whereas
107 report: rumour
108 mere: complete
109 Puritan: Puritan, i.e. prude
110 mischief: wickedness
111 plead custom: 'i.e. that sin has acquired the force of right
    by habitual practice' (Scobie)
112 erst: first

# Scene xii

*Enter* SISLY, JENKIN, SPIGGOT *the butler, and other*
SERVINGMEN

JENKIN  My mistress and Master Wendoll, my master, sup
in her chamber tonight. Sisly, you are preferred from
being the cook to be chambermaid. Of all the loves
betwixt thee and me, tell me what thou thinkest of this.

SISLY  Mum; there's an old proverb, 'When the cat's
away, the mouse may play.'

JENKIN  Now you talk of a cat, Sisly, I smell a rat.

SISLY  Good words, Jenkin, lest you be called to answer
them.                                                             9

JENKIN  Why, God make my mistress an honest
woman—are not these good words? Pray God my
new master play not the knave with my old master—
is there any hurt in this? God send no villainy
intended, and if they do sup together, pray God they
do not lie together. God keep my mistress chaste,
and make us all His servants—what harm is there in
all this? Nay, more: here is my hand; thou shalt never
have my heart unless thou say 'Amen'.

SISLY  Amen, I pray God, I say.                                   19

*Enter* SERVINGMEN

SERVINGMAN  My mistress sends that you should make
less noise, to lock up the doors, and see the houshold
all got to bed. You, Jenkin, for this night are made
the porter, to see the gates shut in.

JENKIN  Thus by little and little I creep into office.
Come to kennel, my masters, to kennel; 'tis eleven
o'clock already.

SERVINGMAN  When you have locked the gates in, you
must send up the keys to my mistress.

SISLY  Quickly, for God's sake, Jenkin, for I must carry
them. I am neither pillow nor bolster, but I know
more than both.                                                  31

JENKIN  To bed, good Spiggot; to bed, good honest
serving creatures, and let us sleep as snug as pigs in
pease-straw.

*Exeunt*

# Scene xiii

*Enter* FRANKFORD *and* NICK

FRANKFORD  Soft, soft. We have tied our geldings to a tree

---

2  preferred: promoted
5  Mum: be silent
8  answer: answer for
24  creep into office: slyly get promotion (Sturgess). Van
Fossen glosses 'office' as 'office of a bawd or pander'
33–4  snug . . . pease-straw: proverbial. Pease-straw was straw
from the pea plant
1–3  set as prose in Qs

---

Two flight-shoot off, lest by their thundering hooves
They blab our coming back. Hearest thou no noise?

NICK  Hear? I hear nothing but the owl and you.

FRANKFORD  So; now my watch's hand points upon
twelve,
And it is dead midnight. Where are my keys?

NICK  Here, sir.

FRANKFORD  This is the key that opes my outward gate,
This is the hall door, this my withdrawing chamber.
But this, that door that's bawd unto my shame,         10
Fountain and spring of all my bleeding thoughts,
Where the most hallowed order and true knot
Of nuptial sanctity hath been profaned.
It leads to my polluted bedchamber,
Once my terrestrial heaven, now my earth's hell,
The place where sins in all their ripeness dwell.
But I forget myself; now to my gate.

NICK  It must ope with far less noise than Cripplegate,
or your plot's dashed.                                         19

FRANKFORD  So, reach me my dark-lantern to the rest.
Tread softly, softly.

NICK                     I will walk on eggs this pace.

FRANKFORD  A general silence hath surprised the house,
And this is the last door. Astonishment,
Fear and amazement play against my heart,
Even as a madman beats upon a drum.
O keep my eyes, you heavens, before I enter,
From any sight that may transfix my soul;
Or if there be so black a spectacle,
O strike mine eyes stark blind; or if not so,
Lend me such patience to digest my grief                   30
That I may keep this white and virgin hand
From any violent outrage or red murder.
And with that prayer I enter.                         *Exit*

NICK  Here's a circumstance!
A man may be made cuckold in the time
That he's about it. And the case were mine,
As 'tis my master's,—'sblood, that he makes me
swear—

---

2  Two flight-shoot: two bow-shots. 'Flight-shoot': arrows
feathered for long range
3  blab: betray
9  withdrawing chamber: private room
18  Cripplegate: one of the gates to the city of London,
situated near the Red Bull theatre, where this play is
likely to have been staged
20  dark-lantern: a lantern with a shutter for concealing the
light
to the rest: i.e of the gates (eds)
21  walk . . . pace: i.e. I could walk on eggs at this pace
(proverbial)
22  surprised: overtaken
34  circumstance: roundabout behaviour (eds)
36  And: if

I would have placed his action, entered there.
I would, I would.

*Enter* FRANKFORD

FRANKFORD O, O!                                                    40
NICK Master, 'sblood, master, master!
FRANKFORD O me unhappy, I have found them lying
  Close in each other's arms, and fast asleep.
  But that I would not damn two precious souls
  Bought with my Saviour's blood, and send them
    laden
  With all their scarlet sins upon their backs
  Unto a fearful judgement, their two lives
  Had met upon my rapier.
NICK 'Sblood, master, have you left them sleeping still?
  Let me go wake them.
FRANKFORD                 Stay; let me pause a while.    50
  O God, O God, that it were possible
  To undo things done, to call back yesterday;
  That Time could turn up his swift sandy glass,
  To untell the days, and to redeem these hours.
  Or that the sun
  Could, rising from the west, draw his coach
    backward,
  Take from the account of time so many minutes,
  Till he had all these seasons called again,
  Those minutes and those actions done in them,
  Even from her first offence, that I might take her    60
  As spotless as an angel in my arms.
  But O! I talk of things impossible,
  And cast beyond the moon. God give me patience,
  For I will in to wake them.                      *Exit*
NICK                          Here's patience perforce!
  He needs must trot afoot that tires his horse.

*Enter* WENDOLL *running over the stage in a nightgown,*
FRANKFORD *after him with his sword drawn; the maid in*
*her smock stays his hand and clasps hold on him. He pauses*
*a while*

FRANKFORD I thank thee, maid; thou like the angel's
    hand
  Hast stayed me from a bloody sacrifice.
  Go, villain, and my wrongs sit on thy soul
  As heavy as this grief doth upon mine.
  When thou recordest my many courtesies          70
  And shalt compare them with thy treacherous heart,

Lay them together, weigh them equally,
'Twill be revenge enough. Go, to thy friend
A Judas; pray, pray, lest I live to see
Thee Judas-like hanged on an elder tree.

*Enter* ANNE *in her smock, nightgown and night attire*

ANNE O by what word, what title, or what name
  Shall I entreat your pardon? Pardon! O
  I am as far from hoping such sweet grace
  As Lucifer from heaven. To call you husband!
  O me most wretched, I have lost that name;         80
  I am no more your wife.
NICK                     'Sblood, sir, she sounds.
FRANKFORD Spare thou thy tears, for I will weep for
    thee;
  And keep thy countenance, for I'll blush for thee.
  Now I protest, I think 'tis I am tainted,
  For I am most ashamed, and 'tis more hard
  For me to look upon thy guilty face
  Then on the sun's clear brow. What wouldst thou
    speak?
ANNE I would I had no tongue, no ears, no eyes,
  No apprehension, no capacity.
  When do you spurn me like a dog? When tread me
  Under your feet? When drag me by the hair?        91
  Though I deserve a thousand thousandfold
  More than you can inflict, yet, once my husband,
  For womanhood—to which I am a shame
  Though once an ornament—even for His sake
  That hath redeemed our souls, mark not my face
  Nor hack me with your sword, but let me go
  Perfect and undeformed to my tomb.
  I am not worthy that I should prevail
  In the least suit, no, not to speak to you,       100
  Nor look on you, nor to be in your presence.
  Yet, as an abject, this one suit I crave;
  This granted, I am ready for my grave.
FRANKFORD My God with patience arm me! Rise, nay,
    rise,
  And I'll debate with thee. Was it for want
  Thou playedst the strumpet? Wast thou not supplied
  With every pleasure, fashion, and new toy,
  Nay, even beyond my calling?
ANNE                          I was.
FRANKFORD Was it then disability in me,
  Or in thine eye seemed he a properer man?         110

---

38  placed his action: established his case (eds)
47  fearful judgement: i.e. if they have no opportunity to
     repent (Sturgess)
49–50 lineation as in Q3; set as prose in Q1
53  sandy glass: i.e. hourglass filled with sand
54  untell: count backwards
63  cast . . . moon: conjecture wildly (Van Fossen)
66–7 angel's . . . sacrifice: allusion to Abraham's proposed
     sacrifice of Isaac; Genesis 22.11–12

75  elder tree: believed to be the tree on which Judas hanged
     himself
81  sounds: swoons
89  apprehension . . . capacity: i.e. the active and passive
     powers of the mind
102 abject: outcast
107 toy: trinket
108 calling: rank. Scobie also notes a variant meaning of 'duty'
110 properer: more attractive

ANNE  Oh no.

FRANKFORD  Did I not lodge thee in my bosom?
  Wear thee here in my heart?

ANNE  You did.

FRANKFORD  I did indeed; witness my tears I did.
  Go bring my infants hither.

*Exit* MAID *and returns with* TWO CHILDREN
                  O Nan, O Nan,
  If either fear of shame, regard of honour,
  The blemish of my house, nor my dear love,
  Could have withheld thee from so lewd a fact,
  Yet for these infants, these young harmless souls,
  On whose white brows thy shame is charactered,
  And grows in greatness as they wax in years—    120
  Look but on them, and melt away in tears.
  Away with them, lest as her spotted body
  Hath stained their names with stripe of bastardy,
  So her adulterous breath may blast their spirits,
  With her infectious thoughts. Away with them!

ANNE  In this one life I die ten thousand deaths.

FRANKFORD  Stand up, stand up. I will do nothing
    rashly.
  I will retire a while into my study,
  And thou shalt hear thy sentence presently.    *Exit*

ANNE  'Tis welcome, be it death. O me, base strumpet,
  That having such a husband, such sweet children,  131
  Must enjoy neither. O to redeem my honour
  I would have this hand cut off, these my breasts
    seared,
  Be racked, strappadoed, put to any torment;
  Nay, to whip but this scandal out, I would hazard
  The rich and dear redemption of my soul.
  He cannot be so base, as to forgive me,
  Nor I so shameless to accept his pardon.
  O women, women, you that have yet kept
  Your holy matrimonial vow unstained,    140
  Make me your instance: when you tread awry,
  Your sins like mine will on your conscience lie.

*Enter* SISLY, SPIGGOT, *all the* SERVINGMEN, *and* JENKIN,
*as newly come out of bed*

ALL  Oh mistress, mistress, what have you done,
    mistress?

NICK  'Sblood, what a caterwauling keep you here.

JENKIN  O Lord, mistress, how comes this to pass? My

master is run away in his shirt, and never so much as
called me to bring his clothes after him.

ANNE  See what guilt is; here stand I in this place,
  Ashamed to look my servants in the face.

*Enter* MASTER FRANKFORD *and* CRANWELL, *whom seeing
she falls on her knees*

FRANKFORD  My words are registered in heaven already;
  With patience hear me. I'll not martyr thee,    151
  Nor mark thee for a strumpet, but with usage
  Of more humility torment thy soul,
  And kill thee, even with kindness.

CRANWELL                      Master Frankford—

FRANKFORD  Good Master Cranwell—woman, hear thy
    judgment:
  Go make thee ready in thy best attire,
  Take with thee all thy gowns, all thy apparel;
  Leave nothing that did ever call thee mistress,
  Or by whose sight being left here in the house
  I may remember such a woman by.    160
  Choose thee a bed and hangings for a chamber,
  Take with thee everything that hath thy mark,
  And get thee to my manor seven mile off,
  Where live. 'Tis thine; I freely give it thee.
  My tenants by shall furnish thee with wains
  To carry all thy stuff within two hours;
  No longer will I limit thee my sight.
  Choose which of all my servants thou likest best,
  And they are thine to attend thee.

ANNE                            A mild sentence.

FRANKFORD  But as thou hopest for heaven, as thou
    believest    170
  Thy name's recorded in the book of life,
  I charge thee never after this sad day
  To see me, or to meet me, or to send
  By word, or writing, gift, or otherwise
  To move me, by thyself, or by thy friends,
  Nor challenge any part in my two children.
  So farewell, Nan, for we will henceforth be
  As we had never seen, ne'er more shall see.

ANNE  How full my heart is in my eyes appears.
  What wants in words, I will supply in tears.    180

FRANKFORD  Come, take your coach, your stuff; all
    must along.
  Servants and all make ready, all be gone.
  It was thy hand cut two hearts out of one.

                                *Exeunt*

---

117  fact: action
119  charactered: written
122  spotted: morally stained
123  stripe of bastardy: i.e. badge of shame
124  blast: blight
134  strappadoed: the strappado was a torture in which the
     arms were fastened behind the back and the prisoner
     hoisted by them into the air and then allowed to fall part
     way back

146  shirt: nightshirt
165  by: nearby
     wains: carts
167  limit: allow
171  book of life: the Bible, the book in which are written the
     names of those who will inherit eternal life
176  challenge: claim

# Scene xiv

*Enter* SIR CHARLES, *gentlemanlike, and* SUSAN *his sister, gentlewomanlike*

SUSAN  Brother, why have you tricked me like a bride?
  Bought me this gay attire, these ornaments?
  Forget you our estate, our poverty?
SIR CHARLES  Call me not brother, but imagine me
  Some barbarous outlaw, or uncivil kerne,
  For if thou shutt'st thy eye, and only hearest
  The words that I shall utter, thou shalt judge me
  Some staring ruffian, not thy brother Charles.
  O Susan!
SUSAN  O brother, what doth this strange language
  mean?                                      10
SIR CHARLES  Dost love me, sister? Wouldst thou see
  me live
  A bankrupt beggar in the world's disgrace
  And die indebted to my enemies?
  Wouldst thou behold me stand like a huge beam
  In the world's eye, a byword and a scorn?
  It lies in thee of these to acquit me free,
  And all my debt I may outstrip by thee.
SUSAN  By me? Why I have nothing, nothing, left;
  I owe even for the clothes upon my back.
  I am not worth—
SIR CHARLES         O sister, say not so.     20
  It lies in you my downcast state to raise,
  To make me stand on even points with the world.
  Come, sister, you are rich! Indeed you are.
  And in your power you have, without delay,
  Acton's five hundred pound back to repay.
SUSAN  Till now I had thought you loved me. By mine
  honour,
  Which I had kept as spotless as the moon,
  I ne'er was mistress of that single doit
  Which I reserved not to supply your wants.
  And do you think that I would hoard from you?  30
  Now, by my hopes in heaven, knew I the means
  To buy you from the slavery of your debts,
  Especially from Acton, whom I hate,
  I would redeem it with my life or blood.
SIR CHARLES  I challenge it, and, kindred set apart,

  Thus ruffianlike I lay siege to your heart.
  What do I owe to Acton?
SUSAN  Why, some five hundred pounds, toward which
  I swear
  In all the world I have not one denier.
SIR CHARLES  It will not prove so. Sister, now resolve
  me:                                     40
  What do you think—and speak your conscience—
  Would Acton give might he enjoy your bed?
SUSAN  He would not shrink to spend a thousand
  pound
  To give the Mountfords' name so deep a wound.
SIR CHARLES  A thousand pound! I but five hundred
  owe;
  Grant him your bed, he's paid with interest so.
SUSAN  Oh brother!
SIR CHARLES         O sister! Only this one way,
  With that rich jewel you my debts may pay.
  In speaking this my cold heart shakes with shame,
  Nor do I woo you in a brother's name,     50
  But in a stranger's. Shall I die in debt
  To Acton, my grand foe, and you still wear
  The precious jewel that he holds so dear?
SUSAN  My honour I esteem as dear and precious
  As my redemption.
SIR CHARLES        I esteem you, sister,
  As dear for so dear prizing it.
SUSAN              Will Charles
  Have me cut off my hands, and send them Acton?
  Rip up my breast, and with my bleeding heart
  Present him as a token?
SIR CHARLES          Neither, sister,
  But hear me in my strange assertion:    60
  Thy honour and my soul are equal in my regard,
  Nor will thy brother Charles survive thy shame.
  His kindness like a burden hath surcharged me,
  And under his good deeds I stooping go,
  Not with an upright soul. Had I remained
  In prison still, there doubtless I had died.
  Then unto him that freed me from that prison
  Still do I owe that life. What moved my foe
  To enfranchise me? 'Twas, sister, for your love.
  With full five hundred pounds he bought your love,
  And shall he not enjoy it? Shall the weight    71
  Of all this heavy burden lean on me,
  And will not you bear part? You did partake
  The joy of my release; will you not stand
  In joint bond bound to satisfy the debt?

---

1 tricked: decked
5 uncivil kerne: uncivilised peasant
8 staring: wild
14–15 a huge beam . . . eye: allusion to the passage in Christ's
  Sermon on the Mount concerning the mote and the
  beam (Matthew 7.3)
15 byword: an object of scorn or contempt
22 points: terms
28 doit: a Dutch coin worth half a farthing, used to signify a
  trifling sum. A denier (l. 39) was the name of another
  coin used in this way

36 ruffianlike: Q3 and all subsequent eds except Sturgess.
  Q1's 'Russian-like', Sturgess suggests, may be correct, as
  Russians were synonymous with uncivil roughness
40 resolve: tell, inform
63 His: i.e. Acton's
69 enfranchise: free
75 joint bond bound: bound with me jointly

Shall I be only charged?
SUSAN                 But that I know
  These arguments come from an honoured mind,
  As in your most extremity of need,
  Scorning to stand in debt to one you hate,
  Nay, rather would engage your unstained honour   **80**
  Then to be held ingrate, I should condemn you.
  I see your resolution, and assent;
  So Charles will have me, and I am content.
SIR CHARLES  For this I tricked you up.
SUSAN                 But here's a knife,
  To save mine honour, shall slice out my life.
SIR CHARLES  I know thou pleasest me a thousand times
  More in that resolution than thy grant.
  (*Aside*) Observe her love: to soothe them in my suit
  Her honour she will hazard, though not lose.
  To bring me out of debt, her rigorous hand   **90**
  Will pierce her heart. O wonder, that will choose,
  Rather than stain her blood, her life to lose.
  (*To her*) Come, you sad sister to a woeful brother,
  This is the gate. I'll bear him such a present,
  Such an acquittance for the knight to seal,
  As will amaze his senses, and surprise
  With admiration all his fantasies.

*Enter* ACTON *and* MALBY

SUSAN  Before his unchaste thoughts shall seize on me
  'Tis here shall my imprisoned soul set free.
SIR FRANCIS  How! Mountford with his sister hand in
    hand!   **100**
  What miracle's afoot?
MALBY               It is a sight
  Begets in me much admiration.
SIR CHARLES  Stand not amazed to see me thus
    attended.
  Acton, I owe thee money, and being unable
  To bring thee the full sum in ready coin,
  Lo! For thy more assurance, here's a pawn,
  My sister, my dear sister, whose chaste honour
  I prize above a million. Here—nay, take her;
  She's worth your money, man; do not forsake her.
SIR FRANCIS  (*Aside*) I would he were in earnest.   **110**
SUSAN  Impute it not to my immodesty.
  My brother being rich in nothing else
  But in his interest that he hath in me,
  According to his poverty hath brought you

Me, all his store, whom howso'er you prize
  As forfeit to your hand, he values highly,
  And would not sell, but to acquit your debt
  For any emperor's ransom.
SIR FRANCIS  (*Aside*)          Stern heart, relent;
  Thy former cruelty at length repent.
  Was ever known in any former age   **120**
  Such honourable wrested courtesy?
  Lands, honours, lives, and all the world forgo
  Rather than stand engaged to such a foe.
SIR CHARLES  Acton, she is too poor to be thy bride,
  And I too much opposed to be thy brother.
  There, take her to thee, if thou hast the heart
  To seize her as a rape or lustful prey,
  To blur our house that never yet was stained,
  To murder her that never meant thee harm,
  To kill me now whom once thou savedst from death,
  Do them at once on her; all these rely   **131**
  And perish with her spotted chastity.
SIR FRANCIS  You overcome me in your love, Sir
    Charles.
  I cannot be so cruel to a lady
  I love so dearly. Since you have not spared
  To engage your reputation to the world,
  Your sister's honour which you prize so dear,
  Nay, all the comforts which you hold on earth,
  To grow out of my debt, being your foe,
  Your honoured thoughts, lo, thus I recompense:   **140**
  Your metamorphised foe receives your gift
  In satisfaction of all former wrongs.
  This jewel I will wear here in my heart,
  And where before I thought her for her wants
  Too base to be my bride, to end all strife
  I seal you my dear brother, her my wife.
SUSAN  You still exceed us. I will yield to fate
  And learn to love where I till now did hate.
SIR CHARLES  With that enchantment you have
    charmed my soul,
  And made me rich even in those very words.   **150**
  I pay no debt but am indebted more;
  Rich in your love, I never can be poor.
SIR FRANCIS  All's mine is yours; we are alike in state.
  Let's knit in love what was opposed in hate:
  Come, for our nuptials we will straight provide,
  Blest only in our brother and fair bride.

                              *Exeunt*

---

80  engage: compromise
88  to soothe . . . suit: 'to appease those who are pursuing me'
    (Scobie)
95  acquittance: document of release
97  admiration: wonder
99  'Tis here: i.e. the knife
106  pawn: pledge
SD  *Aside*: eds; but Acton may instead be speaking to Malby

121  wrested: 'achieved by struggle' (Sturgess)
127  lustful prey: prey to your lust
131  rely: rely upon
139  To grow out of: 'i.e. in order to grow out of, to disburden
    yourself' (Scobie)
144  wants: circumstances of want (eds)
155  straight: immediately
156  Blest only . . . bride: i.e. with no dowry

# Scene xv

*Enter* CRANWELL, FRANKFORD, *and* NICK

CRANWELL  Why do you search each room about your
    house,
  Now that you have dispatched your wife away?
FRANKFORD  O sir, to see that nothing may be left
  That ever was my wife's. I loved her dearly,
  And when I do but think of her unkindness,
  My thoughts are all in hell, to avoid which torment
  I would not have a bodkin or a cuff,
  A bracelet, necklace, or rebato wire,
  Nor anything that ever was hers
  Left me, by which I might remember her.      10
  Seek round about.
NICK  'Sblood, master, here's her lute flung in a corner.
FRANKFORD  Her lute! O God, upon this instrument
  Her fingers have run quick division,
  Sweeter than that which now divides our hearts.
  These frets have made me pleasant, that have now
  Frets of my heartstrings made. O Master Cranwell,
  Oft hath she made this melancholy wood,
  Now mute and dumb for her disastrous chance,
  Speak sweetly many a note, sound many a strain   20
  To her own ravishing voice, which being well strung,
  What pleasant strange airs have they jointly sung.
  Post with it after her. Now nothing's left;
  Of her and hers I am at once bereft.
NICK  I'll ride and overtake her, do my message,
  And come back again.                  *Exit*
CRANWELL          Meantime, sir, if you please,
  I'll to Sir Francis Acton and inform him
  Of what hath past betwixt you and his sister.
FRANKFORD  Do as you please. How ill am I bestead
  To be a widower ere my wife be dead.      30
                             *Exeunt*

# Scene xvi

*Enter* ANNE, *with* JENKIN, *her maid* SISLY, *her*
COACHMAN, *and* THREE CARTERS.

ANNE  Bid my coach stay. Why should I ride in state,
  Being hurled so low down by the hand of fate?
  A seat like to my fortunes let me have,
  Earth for my chair, and for my bed a grave.

---

7  bodkin: pin for fastening hair
8  rebato wire: wire used to support ruff or collar
14  run quick division: executed a rapid melodic passage (eds)
16  frets: divisions on fingerboard (with pun in l. 17)
     pleasant: merry
19  for her disastrous chance: because of her misfortune
22  strange: exceptional
23  Post: hurry
29  bestead: situated

JENKIN  Comfort good mistress; you have watered your
  coach with tears already. You have but two mile now
  to go to your manor. A man cannot say by my old
  Master Frankford as he may say by me, that he wants
  manors, for he hath three or four, of which this is one
  that we are going to.                   10
SISLY  Good mistress, be of good cheer. Sorrow you see
  hurts you, but helps you not. We all mourn to see
  you so sad.
CARTER  Mistress, I spy one of my landlord's men
  Come riding post. 'Tis like he brings some news.
ANNE  Comes he from Master Frankford, he is welcome;
  So are his news, because they come from him.

*Enter* NICK

NICK  There.                        *Gives her the lute*
ANNE  I know the lute. Oft have I sung to thee;
  We both are out of tune, both out of time.    20
NICK  Would that had been the worst instrument that
  e'er you played on. My master commends him to ye;
  there's all he can find that was ever yours. He hath
  nothing left that ever you could lay claim to but his
  own heart, and he could afford you that. All that I
  have to deliver you is this. He prays you to forget
  him, and so he bids you farewell.
ANNE  I thank him. He is kind and ever was.
  All you that have true feeling of my grief,
  That know my loss, and have relenting hearts,   30
  Gird me about, and help me with your tears
  To wash my spotted sins. My lute shall groan;
  It cannot weep, but shall lament my moan.   *She plays*

*Enter* WENDOLL *unobserved*

WENDOLL  Pursued with horror of a guilty soul,
  And with the sharp scourge of repentance lashed,
  I fly from my own shadow. O my stars!
  What have my parents in their lives deserved
  That you should lay this penance on their son?
  When I but think of Master Frankford's love,
  And lay it to my treason, or compare      40
  My murdering him for his relieving me,
  It strikes a terror like a lightning's flash
  To scorch my blood up. Thus I, like the owl
  Ashamed of day, live in these shadowy woods
  Afraid of every leaf or murmuring blast,
  Yet longing to receive some perfect knowledge
  How he hath dealt with her. (*Sees* ANNE) O my sad
  fate!

---

9  manors: an obvious pun on 'manners'
15  post: with speed
21  instrument: sexual pun
31  Gird me about: gather round me
40  lay: compare
46  perfect: correct

Here, and so far from home, and thus attended.
O God, I have divorced the truest turtles
That ever lived together, and being divided          50
In several places, make their several moan;
She in the fields laments, and he at home.
So poets write that Orpheus made the trees
And stones to dance to his melodious harp,
Meaning the rustic and the barbarous hinds,
That had no understanding part in them;
So she from these rude carters tears extracts,
Making their flinty hearts with grief to rise
And draw down rivers from their rocky eyes.

ANNE  (*To* NICK) If you return unto your master say—
Though not from me, for I am all unworthy          61
To blast his name so with a strumpet's tongue—
That you have seen me weep, wish myself dead.
Nay, you may say too, for my vow is passed,
Last night you saw me eat and drink my last.
This to your master you may say and swear,
For it is writ in heaven and decreed here.

NICK  I'll say you wept; I'll swear you made me sad.
Why, how now, eyes? What now? What's here to do?
I am gone, or I shall straight turn baby too.          70

WENDOLL  (*Aside*) I cannot weep; my heart is all on fire.
Cursed be the fruits of my unchaste desire.

ANNE  Go break this lute upon my coach's wheel,
As the last music that I e'er shall make—
Not as my husband's gift, but my farewell
To all earth's joy; and so your master tell.

NICK  If I can for crying.

WENDOLL  (*Aside*)          Grief, have done,
Or like a madman I shall frantic run.

ANNE  You have beheld the woefullest wretch on earth,
A woman made of tears. Would you had words          80
To express but what you see; my inward grief
No tongue can utter, yet unto your power
You may describe my sorrow, and disclose
To thy sad master my abundant woes.

NICK  I'll do your commendations.

ANNE          O no,
I dare not so presume, nor to my children.
I am disclaimed in both; alas, I am.
O never teach them when they come to speak
To name the name of mother. Chide their tongue
If they by chance light on that hated word;          90

Tell them 'tis naught, for when that word they name,
Poor pretty souls, they harp on their own shame.

WENDOLL  (*Aside*) To recompense her wrongs, what
canst thou do?
Thou hast made her husbandless and childless too.

ANNE  I have no more to say. Speak not for me,
Yet you may tell your master what you see.

NICK  I'll do it.          *Exit*

WENDOLL  (*Aside*) I'll speak to her, and comfort her in
grief.
O, but her wound cannot be cur'd with words.
No matter though, I'll do my best good will,          100
To work a cure on her whom I did kill.

ANNE  So, now unto my coach, then to my home,
So to my deathbed, for from this sad hour,
I never will nor eat, nor drink, nor taste
Of any cates that may preserve my life.
I never will nor smile, nor sleep, nor rest,
But when my tears have washed my black soul white,
Sweet Saviour, to thy hands I yield my sprite.

WENDOLL  (*To her*) O Mistress Frankford!

ANNE          O for God's sake fly!
The devil doth come to tempt me ere I die.          110
My coach! This sin that with an angel's face
Courted mine honour till he sought my wrack,
In my repentant eyes seems ugly black.

*Exeunt all except* WENDOLL *and* JENKIN, *the*
CARTERS *whistling*

JENKIN  What, my young master that fled in his shirt?
How come you by your clothes again? You have
made our house in a sweet pickle, have you not, think
you? What, shall I serve you still, or cleave to the old
house?

WENDOLL  Hence, slave! Away with thy unseasoned
mirth.
Unless thou canst shed tears, and sigh, and howl,          120
Curse thy sad fortunes, and exclaim on fate,
Thou art not for my turn.

JENKIN  Marry, and you will not, another will. Farewell
and be hanged. Would you had never come to have
kept this coil within our doors. We shall ha' you run
away like a sprite again.          *Exit*

WENDOLL  She's gone to death; I live to want and woe,
Her life, her sins, and all upon my head.

---

49  turtles: turtle doves, proverbially faithful
51  several: separate
53  Orpheus: legendary Greek poet so skilled that wild beasts
    were spellbound by his music. Wendoll's version of the
    tale was a common Renaissance one
55  hinds: rustics
64  passed: made
82  unto your power: as far as you are able
85  do your commendations: present your remembrances

91  naught: eds. Qs read 'nought'. Presumably a pun was
    intended on the two meanings ('wicked' and 'nothing')
105  cates: food
108  sprite: spirit
112  wrack: ruin
119  unseasoned: unseasonable
121  exclaim on: blame, rail at
122  for my turn: suitable for my purposes
123  and: if
125  kept this coil: made this trouble

And I must now go wander like a Cain
In foreign countries and remoted climes, 130
Where the report of my ingratitude
Cannot be heard. I'll over first to France,
And so to Germany, and Italy,
Where, when I have recovered, and by travel
Gotten those perfect tongues, and that these rumours
May in their height abate, I will return.
And I divine, however now dejected,
My worth and parts being by some great man
praised,
At my return I may in court be raised.

*Exit*

# Scene xvii

*Enter* SIR FRANCIS, SIR CHARLES, CRANWELL, MALBY
*and* SUSAN

SIR FRANCIS Brother, and now my wife, I think these
troubles
Fall on my head by justice of the heavens,
For being so strict to you in your extremities,
But we are now atoned. I would my sister
Could with like happiness o'ercome her griefs
As we have ours.
SUSAN You tell us, Master Cranwell, wondrous things
Touching the patience of that gentleman,
With what strange virtue he demeans his grief.
CRANWELL I told you what I was witness of. 10
It was my fortune to lodge there that night.
SIR FRANCIS O that same villain Wendoll! 'Twas his
tongue
That did corrupt her; she was of herself
Chaste and devoted well. Is this the house?
CRANWELL Yes, sir, I take it here your sister lies.
SIR FRANCIS My brother Frankford showed too mild a
spirit
In the revenge of such a loathed crime;
Less than he did, no man of spirit could do.
I am so far from blaming his revenge
That I commend it. Had it been my case 20
Their souls at once had from their breasts been freed;
Death to such deeds of shame is the due meed.

*Enter* JENKIN *and* SISLY

JENKIN O my mistress, my mistress, my poor mistress!
SISLY Alas that ever I was born! What shall I do for my
poor mistress?
SIR CHARLES Why, what of her?
JENKIN O Lord, sir, she no sooner heard that her
brother and his friends were come to see how she did,
but she for very shame of her guilty conscience, fell
into a swoon, and we had much ado to get life into
her. 31
SUSAN Alas that she should bear so hard a fate;
Pity it is repentance comes too late.
SIR FRANCIS Is she so weak in body?
JENKIN O sir I can assure you there's no help of life in
her, for she will take no sustenance. She hath plainly
starved herself, that now she is as lean as a lath. She
ever looks for the good hour. Many gentlemen and
gentlewomen of the country are come to comfort her.

*Enter* ANNE *in her bed*

MALBY How fare you, Mistress Frankford? 40
ANNE Sick, sick, O sick! Give me some air, I pray you.
Tell me, O tell me, where's Master Frankford?
Will not he deign to see me ere I die?
MALBY Yes, Mistress Frankford; divers gentlemen,
Your loving neighbours, with that just request
Have moved and told him of your weak estate,
Who, though with much ado to get belief,
Examining of the general circumstance,
Seeing your sorrow and your penitence,
And hearing therewithal the great desire 50
You have to see him ere you left the world,
He gave to us his faith to follow us,
And sure he will be here immediately.
ANNE You half revived me with those pleasing news.
Raise me a little higher in my bed.
Blush I not, brother Acton? Blush I not, Sir Charles?
Can you not read my fault writ in my cheek?
Is not my crime there? Tell me, gentlemen.
SIR CHARLES Alas, good mistress, sickness hath not left
you
Blood in your face enough to make you blush. 60
ANNE Then sickness like a friend my fault would hide.
Is my husband come? My soul but tarries
His arrive and I am fit for heaven.
SIR FRANCIS I came to chide you, but my words of hate
Are turned to pity and compassionate grief.
I came to rate you, but my brawls, you see,
Melt into tears, and I must weep by thee.

---

129 Cain: condemned by God to wander the earth as a
punishment for the murder of his brother Abel; see
Genesis 4.8–14
135 Gotten . . . tongues: learnt those languages perfectly
137 divine: predict
4 atoned: reconciled
9 demeans: expresses
14 devoted well: faithful
22 meed: recompense

27–31, 35–9 set as verse Q1, as prose Q3
38 the good hour: i.e. the hour of death
46 moved: taken action
52 faith: promise
66 rate: berate
brawls: reproaches

*Enter* FRANKFORD

Here's Master Frankford now.

FRANKFORD  Good morrow, brother; good morrow
    gentlemen.
  God, that hath laid this cross upon our heads,     70
  Might, had He pleased, have made our cause of
    meeting
  On a more fair and a more contented ground.
  But he that made us, made us to this woe.

ANNE  And is he come? Methinks that voice I know.

FRANKFORD  How do you, woman?

ANNE  Well, Master Frankford, well; but shall be better,
  I hope, within this hour. Will you vouchsafe,
  Out of your grace and your humanity,
  To take a spotted strumpet by the hand?

FRANKFORD  That hand once held my heart in faster
    bonds                                            80
  Than now 'tis gripped by me. God pardon them
  That made us first break hold.

ANNE                             Amen, amen.
  Out of my zeal to heaven, whither I am now bound,
  I was so impudent to wish you here,
  And once more beg your pardon. O good man,
  And father to my children, pardon me.
  Pardon, O pardon me! My fault so heinous is
  That if you in this world forgive it not,
  Heaven will not clear it in the world to come.
  Faintness hath so usurped upon my knees          90
  That kneel I cannot; but on my heart's knees
  My prostrate soul lies thrown down at your feet
  To beg your gracious pardon. Pardon, O pardon me!

FRANKFORD  As freely from the low depth of my soul
  As my Redeemer hath forgiven his death,
  I pardon thee. I will shed tears for thee,
  Pray with thee, and in mere pity
  Of thy weak state, I'll wish to die with thee.

ALL  So do we all.

NICK  (*Aside*) So will not I!                      100
  I'll sigh and sob, but, by my faith, not die.

SIR FRANCIS  O Master Frankford, all the near alliance
  I lose by her shall be supplied in thee.
  You are my brother by the nearest way;
  Her kindred hath fallen off, but yours doth stay.

FRANKFORD  Even as I hope for pardon at that day
  When the great Judge of Heaven in scarlet sits,
  So be thou pardoned. Though thy rash offence
  Divorced our bodies, thy repentant tears
  Unite our souls.

SIR CHARLES          Then comfort, Mistress Frankford;
  You see your husband hath forgiven your fall;    111
  Then rouse your spirits and cheer your fainting soul.

SUSAN  How is it with you?

SIR FRANCIS                 How do you feel yourself?

ANNE  Not of this world.

FRANKFORD  I see you are not, and I weep to see it.
  My wife, the mother to my pretty babes,
  Both those lost names I do restore thee back.
  And with this kiss I wed thee once again.
  Though thou art wounded in thy honoured name,
  And with that grief upon thy deathbed liest,     120
  Honest in heart, upon my soul, thou diest.

ANNE  Pardoned on earth, soul, thou in heaven art free.
  Once more thy wife, dies thus embracing thee.    *Dies*

FRANKFORD  New married, and new widowed; O she's
    dead,
  And a cold grave must be our nuptial bed.

SIR CHARLES  Sir, be of good comfort, and your heavy
    sorrow
  Part equally amongst us; storms divided
  Abate their force, and with less rage are guided.

CRANWELL  Do, Master Frankford; he that hath least part
  Will find enough to drown one troubled heart.    130

SIR FRANCIS  Peace with thee, Nan. Brothers and
    gentlemen,
  All we that can plead interest in her grief,
  Bestow upon her body funeral tears.
  Brother, had you with threats and usage bad
  Punished her sin, the grief of her offence
  Had not with such true sorrow touched her heart.

FRANKFORD  I see it had not; therefore on her grave
  I will bestow this funeral epitaph,
  Which on her marble tomb shall be engraved.
  In golden letters shall these words be filled:   140
  Here lies she whom her husband's kindness killed.

# The Epilogue

An honest crew, disposed to be merry,
Came to a tavern by and called for wine.
The drawer brought it, smiling like a cherry,
And told them it was pleasant, neat, and fine.
  'Taste it,' quoth one. He did so. 'Fie!' quoth he,
  'This wine was good; now't runs too near the lee.'

----

76  better: i.e. in heaven
90  usurped upon: taken possession of
97  mere: absolute
102 alliance: kinship
105 Her . . . stay: 'Although she, being about to die, will cease
    to be my sister, you are still of my kin' (Van Fossen)

----

119 honoured name: reputation
121 Honest: chaste
123 Once more thy wife: 'i.e. having once more been restored
    to being your wife, (she dies)' (Scobie)
140 filled: most eds take this to mean that the letters would
    be filled in with gold. Sturgess, however, suggests that
    Q1's 'fild' might mean 'filed': 'arranged in order'
  2  by: nearby
  4  neat: pure
  6  lee: lees, sediment

Another sipped, to give the wine his due,
And said unto the rest it drunk too flat.
The third said it was old, the fourth too new.
'Nay,' quoth the fifth, 'the sharpness likes me not.'   10
    Thus, gentlemen, you see how in one hour
    The wine was new, old, flat, sharp, sweet, and sour.

Unto this wine we do allude our play,
Which some will judge too trivial, some too grave.
You as our guests we entertain this day
And bid you welcome to the best we have.
    Excuse us, then; good wine may be disgraced
    When every several mouth hath sundry taste.

---

13   allude: compare

# Elizabeth Cary, *The Tragedy of Mariam, The Fair Queen of Jewry*

Written 1604–6
First published 1613

As with so many of the plays in this collection, the terms, meanings and limits of femininity can be seen to lie at the heart of *The Tragedy of Mariam*. Like *The Roaring Girl*, it examines the constituents of the often fragile balance of power between women and men within marriage; like *A Woman Killed with Kindness*, it investigates the terms of, pressures on, and limits to marital duty and loyalty; like *Epicoene*, the issue of women's speech versus women's silence is fundamental to the progression of the plot.

What is striking about *The Tragedy of Mariam*, however, is the complexity and the ambiguity of its representation of gendered power relations. For example, the apparently simple polar opposites, such as the good and the bad woman, around which the play is structured turn out to be rather more complicated than they at first seem. Of course, Mariam is clearly the heroine, her tragic death precipitated by her 'virtues' of honesty, conscience and integrity, and Salome is her evil foil, duplicitous, scheming and ruthless. Yet Salome has an energy and a wit, reminiscent of Edmund in *King Lear* or of Richard III, which are not unattractive, and her analysis of the injustice of women's unequal access to divorce, together with her rousing resolution to 'be the custom-breaker, and begin/To show my sex the way to freedom's door' (I.iv.309–10) have proved particularly compelling for modern readers. In the light of this, it is, moreover, striking that Salome's murderous duplicity remains unpunished at the end of the play. Even the figure of Mariam herself shares some of these ambiguities. Whilst her death (read by some critics, such as Beilin, as prefigurative of Christ's) is without doubt the tragic climax of the play, it is significant that the last we see of Mariam, in IV.viii, is with Doris (Herod's first wife, whom he divorced to marry Mariam) voicing her complaint against Mariam for having usurped her place and for ignoring the pain she caused. Her complaint is not wholly unjust, and this scene thereby constitutes an ambiguous and unsettling final glimpse of the tragic heroine, and one which serves only to highlight the idealising 'constructedness' of the retrospective reports of Mariam in Act V. Far from positioning the women characters on a linear axis somewhere between 'good' and 'bad', the play instead figures them within a network of multiple and mutually informing, but ultimately indeterminate, relationships with each other.

Equally ambiguous are the representations of women's relationships to speech and silence. Reproducing conventional early modern ideological wisdom that women's honour depended in large part on their docility and obedience, characterised by a deferential silence, Sohemus suggests that Mariam's refusal to constrain her 'public voice' (I.i.1) will be her downfall (III.iii.183–4). This is a view with which the Chorus, albeit in an opaque and complicated way, concurs (see the third Chorus) and which Herod himself confirms, linking her speech with her supposed infidelity: 'She's unchaste;/Her mouth will ope to every stranger's ear' (IV.vii.432–3). Yet Pheroras reads the silence of Graphina, an idealised model of deferential femininity, as 'a sign of discontent', and urges her to 'move [her] tongue' (II.i.41). If the characters themselves cannot be consigned to polar positions, neither can the stance taken in the play on the meanings of women's speech, whether 'public' or 'private'.

*The Tragedy of Mariam* occupies an important position in the histories both of English women's writing and of Renaissance drama. It is the first original tragedy written by an Englishwoman (although women had published translations of classical and French plays before). It is also one of only a dozen extant English closet dramas: plays in the tradition of Senecan revenge tragedy, and taken by most critics to have been written not for performance on the public stage, but to be read, either privately or aloud in groups– though it is worth noting that, contrary to this assumption, Wright argues strongly for the dramatic, as well as rhetorical and intellectual, achievement of *Mariam* and, in demonstration of this, has directed a production of it (see Wright 1996: 20–3). These elements have contributed to its status as a key 'recovered' text—one that had been allowed to disappear from view for over three centuries but which, thanks to the work of (in this case) contemporary feminist scholarship, has been substantially re-evaluated.

Nor is the case closed regarding the significance of this text. Whilst its passage back into print was the outcome of feminist critical intervention, and a feminist critical perspective has informed readings of the play in relation both to Cary's own biography and to the position of women writing for publication in Jacobean England more generally (see, for example, Ferguson 1991; Gutierrez 1991), this approach does not exhaust the possible readings of the play. Callaghan (1994), for example, has asked why a play that is set in Palestine among the Jews has been read as so 'obviously' about gender rather than 'race', and goes on to show how, throughout the text, the meanings of gender are persistently and variously inflected through ideas about 'race'. Fischer (1985), Lewalski (1993) and Shannon (1994) begin from the pre-existing generic association of the closet drama with issues of public morality and government, and read the play as an intervention into debates about tyranny, both domestic and state, and civil order and disorder. Findlay (1999), in turn, offers new perspectives on the play by reading it within the context of other generic affiliations: namely, the revenge play and the domestic tragedy. Having initially been reclaimed as an 'exceptional', even anomalous, text, *The Tragedy of Mariam* has now been shown to be central to the debates that characterise contemporary critical interest in Renaissance drama as a whole.

## Textual note

This edition is based on the first edition of 1613 printed in London by Thomas Creede. This quarto edition is referred to in the footnotes as Q. We number the lines of each act continuously rather than scene by scene, since scene breaks frequently denote the entry of a new character rather than a break in the action.

# Further reading

## Editions

Cerasano, S. P. and Wynne-Davies, Marion (eds) (1996) *Renaissance Drama by Women: Texts and Documents*, London: Routledge.

Fitzmaurice, James, Roberts, Josephine A., Barash, Carol L., Cunnar, Eugene R. and Gutierrez, Nancy A. (eds) (1997) *Major Women Writers of Seventeenth-century England*, Ann Arbor, MI: University of Michigan Press.

Purkiss, Diane (ed.) (1994) *Renaissance Women: The Plays of Elizabeth Cary, The Poems of Aemilia Lanyer*, London: William Pickering.

Travitsky, Betty S. and Cullen, Patrick (eds) (1996) *The Early Modern Englishwoman: A Facsimile Library of Essential Works*; Part 1: *Printed Writings, 1500–1640*. Volume 2: *Works by and Attributed to Elizabeth Cary*, introduced by Margaret W. Ferguson, Aldershot: Scolar Press.

Weller, Barry and Ferguson, Margaret W. (eds) (1994) *Elizabeth Cary, Lady Falkland: The Tragedy of Mariam, The Fair Queen of Jewry, with The Lady Falkland: Her Life*, Berkeley, CA: University of California Press.

Wright, Stephanie J. (ed.) (1996) *Elizabeth Cary: The Tragedy of Mariam, The Fair Queen of Jewry*, Staffordshire: Keele University Press.

## Critical and contextual commentaries

Beilin, Elaine V. (1987) *Redeeming Eve: Women Writers of the English Renaissance*, Princeton, NJ: Princeton University Press.

Belsey, Catherine (1985) *The Subject of Tragedy: Identity and Difference in Renaissance Drama*, London: Methuen.

Bennett, Alexandra G. (2000) 'Female Performativity in *The Tragedy of Mariam*', *Studies in English Literature 1500–1900*, 40, 2: 293–309.

Callaghan, Dympna (1994) 'Re-Reading Elizabeth Cary's *The Tragedie of Mariam, The Faire Queene of Jewry*', in Margo Hendricks and Patricia Parker (eds) *Women, 'Race', and Writing in the Early Modern Period*, London and New York, NY: Routledge.

Ferguson, Margaret W. (1991) 'The Spectre of Resistance: *The Tragedy of Mariam*', in David Scott Kastan and Peter Stallybrass (eds) *Staging the Renaissance: Reinterpretations of Elizabethan and Jacobean Drama*, London: Routledge.

Findlay, Alison (1999) *A Feminist Perspective on Renaissance Drama*, Oxford: Blackwell.

Fischer, Sandra K. (1985) 'Elizabeth Cary and Tyranny, Religious and Domestic', in Margaret P. Hannay (ed.) *Silent But for the Word: Tudor Women as Patrons, Translators and Writers of Religious Works*, Kent, OH: Kent State University Press.

Gutierrez, Nancy A. (1991) 'Valuing *Mariam*: Genre Study and Feminist Analysis', *Tulsa Studies in Women's Literature*, 10, 2: 233–51.

Hiscock, Andrew (1997) 'The Hateful Cuckoo: Elizabeth Cary's *Tragedie of Mariam*, A Renaissance Drama of Dispossession', *Forum for Modern Language Studies*, 33, 2: 97–114.

Kegl, Rosemary (1999) 'Theaters, Households, and a "Kind of History" in Elizabeth Cary's *The Tragedy of Mariam*', in Viviana Comensoli and Anne Russell (eds) *Enacting Gender on the English Renaissance Stage*, Urbana and Chicago, IL: University of Illinois Press.

Krontiris, Tina (1992) *Oppositional Voices: Women as Writers and Translators in the English Renaissance*, London: Routledge.

Lewalski, Barbara Kiefer (1993) *Writing Women in Jacobean England*, Cambridge, MA, and London: Harvard University Press.

Miller, Naomi J. (1997) 'Domestic Politics in Elizabeth Cary's *The Tragedy of Mariam*', *Studies in English Literature 1500–1900*, 37, 2: 353–69.

Quilligan, Maureen (1993) 'Staging Gender: William Shakespeare and Elizabeth Cary', in James Grantham Turner (ed.) *Sexuality and Gender in Early Modern Europe: Institutions, Texts, Images*, Cambridge: Cambridge University Press.

Shannon, Laurie J. (1994) '*The Tragedie of Mariam*: Cary's Critique of the Terms of Founding Social Discourses', *English Literary Renaissance*, 24, 1: 135–53.

Skura, Meredith (1997) 'The Reproduction of Mothering in *Mariam, Queen of Jewry*: A Defense of "Biographical Criticism"', *Tulsa Studies in Women's Literature*, 16, 1: 27–56.

Straznicky, Marta (1994) '"Profane Stoical Paradoxes": *The Tragedie of Mariam* and Sidnean Closet Drama', *English Literary Renaissance*, 24, 1: 104–34.

## Works of related interest

Thomas Kyd, *The Spanish Tragedy* (1585)
Anon., *Arden of Faversham* (1592)
Mary Sidney, *Antonius* (1592)
Henry Chettle, Thomas Dekker and William Haughton, *Patient Grissel* (1600)
Thomas Heywood, *A Woman Killed with Kindness* (1603)
Ben Jonson, *The Masque of Blackness* (1605)

# The Tragedy of Mariam, The Fair Queen of Jewry (1604)

## To Diana's Earthly Deputess, and My Worthy Sister, Mistress Elizabeth Cary

When cheerful Phoebus his full course hath run,
His sister's fainter beams our hearts doth cheer:
So your fair brother is to me the sun,
And you his sister as my moon appear.

You are my next belov'd, my second friend,
For when my Phoebus' absence makes it night,
Whilst to th'Antipodes his beams do bend,
From you my Phoebe, shines my second light.

He like to Sol, clear-sighted, constant, free,
You Luna-like, unspotted, chaste, divine:        10
He shone on Sicily, you destined be
T'illumine the now obscured Palestine.
My first was consecrated to Apollo,
My second to Diana now shall follow.

E. C.

---

Dedication: probably to the playwright's sister-in-law, also called Elizabeth, who married Philip Cary, brother of Cary's husband Henry, in 1609. It has also been suggested that the dedication might be to Henry Cary's own sister Elizabeth. This sonnet is found in only two of the extant copies of *Mariam*

1  Phoebus: the Greek god of the sun
3  brother: i.e. Henry Cary
7  Antipodes: the other side of the earth
8  Phoebe: the moon; this and Luna (l. 10) are alternative names for Diana
9  Sol: the sun; this and Phoebus are alternative names for Apollo
11  Sicily: Cary seems to have written an earlier play, now lost, set in Sicily and dedicated to her husband (hence the reference to 'my first' in l. 13)

## The names of the speakers

HEROD, *King of Judea*

DORIS, *his first wife*

MARIAM, *his second wife*

SALOME, *Herod's sister*

ANTIPATER, *his son by Doris*

ALEXANDRA, *Mariam's mother*

SILLEUS, *Prince of Arabia*

CONSTABARUS, *husband to Salome*

PHERORAS, *Herod's brother*

GRAPHINA, *his love*

BABAS' FIRST SON

BABAS' SECOND SON

ANANELL, *the high priest*

SOHEMUS, *a counsellor to Herod*

NUNTIO *a messenger*

BUTLER, *another messenger*

SILLEUS'S MAN

SOLDIER

CHORUS, *a company of Jews*

## The Argument

Herod, the son of Antipater (an Idumean), having crept by the favour of the Romans into the Jewish monarchy, married Mariam, the granddaughter of Hircanus, the rightful king and priest, and for her (besides her high

---

1  Idumean: another name for the Edomites, not considered true Jews, and therefore a pejorative term in this context
3  granddaughter: eds (daughter Q); see next paragraph, where the error is corrected with regard to Mariam's brother

blood, being of singular beauty) he repudiated Doris, his former wife, by whom he had children.                                6

This Mariam had a brother called Aristobolus, and next him and Hircanus his grandfather, Herod in his wife's right had the best title. Therefore to remove them, he charged the first with treason and put him to death, and drowned the second under colour of sport. Alexandra, daughter to the one, and mother to the other, accused him for their deaths before Antony.    13

So when he was forced to go answer this accusation at Rome, he left the custody of his wife to Josephus his uncle, that had married his sister Salome, and out of a violent affection (unwilling any should enjoy her after him) he gave strict and private commandment, that if he were slain, she should be put to death. But he returned with much honour, yet found his wife extremely discontented, to whom Josephus had (meaning it for the best, to prove Herod loved her) revealed his charge.                                       23

So by Salome's accusation he put Josephus to death, but was reconciled to Mariam, who still bore the death of her friends exceeding hardly.

In this meantime Herod was again necessarily to revisit Rome, for Caesar having overthrown Antony, his great friend, was likely to make an alteration of his fortune.                                                       30

In his absence, news came to Jerusalem that Caesar had put him to death; their willingness it should be so, together with the likelihood, gave this rumour so good credit, as Sohemus that had suceeded Josephus' charge succeeded him likewise in revealing it. So at Herod's return, which was speedy and unexpected, he found Mariam so far from joy, that she showed apparant signs of sorrow. He still desiring to win her to a better humour, she being very unable to conceal her passion, fell to upbraiding him with her brother's death. As they were thus debating, came in a fellow with a cup of wine, who, hired by Salome, said first it was a love potion, which Mariam desired to deliver to the king; but afterwards he affirmed that it was a poison, and that Sohemus had told her somewhat which procured the vehement hate in her.                                  46

The king hearing this, more moved with jealousy of Sohemus than with this intent of poison, sent her away, and presently after by the instigation of Salome, she was beheaded. Which rashness was afterward punished in him, with an intolerable and almost frantic passion for her death.

---

10–11   first . . . second: in fact these should be reversed, as
        Herod arranged for Aristobolus to be drowned and had
        Hircanus accused of treason
13   Antony: Mark Antony (c. 83–30 BC)
28   Caesar: Octavius Caesar defeated Antony at the battle of
     Actium (31 BC)
45   somewhat: something

# Act I, scene i

MARIAM *sola*

MARIAM  How oft have I with public voice run on
    To censure Rome's last hero for deceit,
    Because he wept when Pompey's life was gone,
    Yet when he lived, he thought his name too great.
    But now I do recant, and, Roman lord,
    Excuse too rash a judgement in a woman:
    My sex pleads pardon, pardon then afford,
    Mistaking is with us but too too common.
    Now do I find, by self-experience taught,
    One object yields both grief and joy:                          10
    You wept indeed, when on his worth you thought,
    But joyed that slaughter did your foe destroy.
    So at his death your eyes true drops did rain,
    Whom dead, you did not wish alive again.
    When Herod lived, that now is done to death,
    Oft have I wished that I from him were free:
    Oft have I wished that he might lose his breath,
    Oft have I wished his carcass dead to see.
    Then rage and scorn had put my love to flight,
    That love which once on him was firmly set;                    20
    Hate hid his true affection from my sight,
    And kept my heart from paying him his debt.
    And blame me not, for Herod's jealousy
    Had power even constancy itself to change:
    For he by barring me from liberty,
    To shun my ranging, taught me first to range.
    But yet too chaste a scholar was my heart,
    To learn to love another than my lord:
    To leave his love, my lesson's former part,
    I quickly learned, the other I abhorred.                       30
    But now his death to memory doth call
    The tender love that he to Mariam bare:
    And mine to him; this makes those rivers fall,
    Which by another thought unmoistened are.
    For Aristobolus, the loveliest youth
    That ever did in angel's shape appear,
    The cruel Herod was not moved to ruth;
    Then why grieves Mariam Herod's death to hear?
    Why joy I not the tongue no more shall speak,

---

SD   *sola*: alone
 3   he: Weller and Ferguson suggest this refers to Julius
     Caesar's reaction to the severed head of his dead
     adversary, Pompey
 4   Yet: although
10   the line is two syllables short
26   shun: prevent
29–30  To leave . . . abhorred: i.e. although I learned to reject
     Herod, I could not commit adultery
32   bare: bore
34   unmoistened: i.e. dried up
35   loveliest: eds (lowlyest Q)

That yielded forth my brother's latest doom?          40
Both youth and beauty might thy fury break,
And both in him did ill befit a tomb.
And worthy grandsire ill did he requite,
His high ascent alone by thee procured,
Except he murdered thee to free the sprite
Which still he thought on earth too long immured.
How happy was it that Sohemus' mind
Was moved to pity my distressed estate!
Might Herod's life a trusty servant find,
My death to his had been unseparate.          50
These thoughts have power his death to make me bear,
Nay more, to wish the news may firmly hold:
Yet cannot this repulse some falling tear,
That will against my will some grief unfold.
And more I owe him for his love to me,
The deepest love that ever yet was seen:
Yet had I rather much a milkmaid be,
Than be the monarch of Judea's queen.
It was for nought but love he wished his end
Might to my death but the vaunt-courier prove:          60
But I had rather still be foe than friend,
To him that saves for hate, and kills for love.
Hard-hearted Mariam, at thy discontent
What floods of tears have drenched his manly face?
How canst thou then so faintly now lament
Thy truest lover's death, a death's disgrace:
Ay, now mine eyes you do begin to right
The wrongs of your admirer and my lord;
Long since you should have put your smiles to flight,
Ill doth a widowed eye with joy accord.          70
Why now methinks the love I bore him then,
When virgin freedom left me unrestrained,
Doth to my heart begin to creep again,
My passion now is far from being feigned.
But tears fly back, and hide you in your banks,
You must not be to Alexandra seen:
For if my moan be spied, but little thanks
Shall Mariam have, from that incensed queen.

# Act I, scene ii

MARIAM, ALEXANDRA

ALEXANDRA  What means these tears? My Mariam
    doth mistake,
The news we heard did tell the tyrant's end:          80

What weepst thou for thy brother's murd'rer's sake,
Will ever wight a tear for Herod spend?
My curse pursue his breathless trunk and spirit,
Base Edomite, the damnèd Esau's heir:
Must he ere Jacob's child the crown inherit?
Must he, vile wretch, be set in David's chair?
No, David's soul, within the bosom placed
Of our forefather Abram, was ashamed:
To see his seat with such a toad disgraced,
That seat that hath by Judah's race been famed.          90
Thou fatal enemy to royal blood,
Did not the murder of my boy suffice
To stop thy cruel mouth that gaping stood?
But must thou dim the mild Hircanus' eyes,
My gracious father, whose too ready hand
Did lift this Idumean from the dust;
And he, ungrateful caitiff, did withstand
The man that did in him most friendly trust.
What kingdom's right could cruel Herod claim,
Was he not Esau's issue, heir of hell?          100
Then what succession can he have but shame?
Did not his ancestor his birthright sell?
O yes, he doth from Edom's name derive
His cruel nature which with blood is fed:
That made him me of sire and son deprive,
He ever thirsts for blood, and blood is red.
Weepst thou because his love to thee was bent?
And readst thou love in crimson characters?
Slew he thy friends to work thy heart's content?
No: hate may justly call that action hers.          110
He gave the sacred priesthood for thy sake
To Aristobolus; yet doomed him dead
Before his back the ephod warm could make,
And ere the mitre settled on his head.
Oh had he given my boy no less than right,
The double oil should to his forehead bring
A double honour, shining doubly bright:
His birth anointed him both priest and king.
And say my father and my son he slew,
To royalize by right your prince-born breath:          120
Was love the cause, can Mariam deem it true,
That Herod gave commandment for her death?

---

40 latest: final
41 thy: i.e. Herod's
45 Except: unless
45 sprite: spirit
47 mind: eds (maide Q)
60 vaunt-courier: forerunner
66 death's disgrace: i.e. his death is disgraced by the
    faintness of her lamentation

82 wight: person
84 Edomite: see note to l. 1 of 'The Argument'
85 Jacob's child: a descendant of Jacob (such as Hircanus or
    Aristobolus)
86 chair: throne (of Judea)
90 famed: eds (fain'd Q)
97 caitiff: wretch
102 ancestor . . . sell: Esau sold his birthright to his brother
    Jacob
103–6 Edom's name . . . blood is red: Edom, meaning 'the red',
    was an alternative name given to Esau; see Genesis 25.29–34
113 ephod: garment worn by Jewish priests
122 Herod: eds (Mariam Q)

I know by fits he showed some signs of love,
And yet not love, but raging lunacy:
And this his hate to thee may justly prove,
That sure he hates Hircanus' family.
Who knows if he, unconstant wavering lord,
His love to Doris had renewed again?
And that he might his bed to her afford,
Perchance he wished that Mariam might be slain. **130**

MARIAM
Doris? Alas, her time of love was past,
Those coals were raked in embers long ago,
If Mariam's love, and she, was now disgraced,
Nor did I glory in her overthrow.
He not a whit his first-born son esteemed,
Because as well as his he was not mine:
My children only for his own he deemed,
These boys that did descend from royal line.
These did he style his heirs to David's throne;
My Alexander, if he live, shall sit **140**
In the majestic seat of Solomon;
To will it so, did Herod think it fit.

ALEXANDRA Why? Who can claim from Alexander's brood
That gold-adornèd lion-guarded chair?
Was Alexander not of David's blood?
And was not Mariam Alexander's heir?
What more than right could Herod then bestow,
And who will think except for more than right
He did not raise them, for they were not low,
But born to wear the crown in his despite. **150**
Then send those tears away that are not sent
To thee by reason, but by passion's power:
Thine eyes to cheer, thy cheeks to smiles be bent,
And entertain with joy this happy hour.
Felicity, if when she comes, she finds
A mourning habit, and a cheerless look,
Will think she is not welcome to thy mind,
And so perchance her lodging will not brook.
Oh, keep her whilst thou hast her; if she go
She will not easily return again: **160**
Full many a year have I endured in woe,
Yet still have sued her presence to obtain;

And did not I to her as presents send
A table, that best art did beautify,
Of two, to whom heaven did best feature lend,
To woo her love by winning Antony?
For when a prince's favour we do crave,
We first their minions' loves do seek to win:
So I, that sought felicity to have,
Did with her minion Antony begin. **170**
With double sleight I sought to captivate
The warlike lover, but I did not right:
For if my gift had borne but half the rate,
The Roman had been overtaken quite.
But now he farèd like a hungry guest,
That to some plenteous festival is gone;
Now this, now that, he deems to eat were best,
Such choice doth make him let them all alone.
The boy's large forehead first did fairest seem,
Then glanced his eye upon my Mariam's cheek: **180**
And that without comparison did deem,
What was in either but he most did seek.
And thus distracted, either's beauties' might
Within the other's excellence was drowned:
Too much delight did bear him from delight,
For either's love, the other's did confound.
Where if thy portraiture had only gone,
His life from Herod, Antony had taken:
He would have loved thee, and thee alone,
And left the brown Egyptian clean forsaken. **190**
And Cleopatra then to seek had been
So firm a lover of her wanèd face;
Then great Antonius' fall we had not seen,
By her that fled to have him hold the chase.
Then Mariam in a Roman's chariot set,
In place of Cleopatra might have shown:
A mart of beauties in her visage met,
And part in this, that they were all her own.

MARIAM Not to be empress of aspiring Rome
Would Mariam like to Cleopatra live: **200**
With purest body will I press my tomb,
And wish no favours Antony could give.

---

164 table: portrait. Alexandra sent a picture of her two children, Aristobolus and Mariam, to Antony, to try to win his favour. According to Cary's source, Josephus, Antony sent only for Aristobolus (a request that Herod denied); here, however, Cary suggests that he was equally attracted to the two
173 rate: value
185 bear: eds (bare Q). Some eds emend to 'bar'; Weller and Ferguson retain 'bare' to condense these two meanings as well as a third ('bare' meaning 'strip')
191 to seek had been: i.e. would have had to seek
194 her . . . chase: in the Battle of Actium (31 BC), Antony followed Cleopatra's fleeing ship, thereby losing the battle and the war to Octavius
197 mart: market

---

SP MARIAM: eds (NUN: Q)
133 If: some eds suggest emending to 'of', running this line on from the one before, and removing the comma after 'she'
141 Solomon: king of Israel, renowned for his wisdom
146 Alexander's heir: although Mariam has been talking of her son Alexander, Alexandra is here referring to her husband, Mariam's father, also called Alexander
146–50 What more . . . his despite: meaning obscure; Wright suggests 'everyone will be of the opinion that Mariam's son is the rightful heir (Mariam being a direct descendant of David) rather than the fact that he was named as heir by Herod'
155 Felicity: the personification of good fortune

ALEXANDRA Let us retire us, that we may resolve
  How now to deal in this reversèd state:
  Great are th'affairs that we must now revolve,
  And great affairs must not be taken late.

# Act I, scene iii

MARIAM, ALEXANDRA, SALOME

SALOME More plotting yet? Why, now you have the
    thing
  For which so oft you spent your suppliant breath,
  And Mariam hopes to have another king,
  Her eyes do sparkle joy for Herod's death.     210
ALEXANDRA If she desired another king to have,
  She might before she came in Herod's bed
  Have had her wish. More kings than one did crave
  For leave to set a crown upon her head.
  I think with more than reason she laments,
  That she is freed from such a sad annoy:
  Who is't will weep to part from discontent,
  And if she joy, she did not causeless joy.
SALOME You durst not thus have given your tongue the
    rein
  If noble Herod still remained in life:     220
  Your daughter's betters far, I dare maintain,
  Might have rejoiced to be my brother's wife.
MARIAM My betters far! Base woman, 'tis untrue:
  You scarce have ever my superiors seen,
  For Mariam's servants were as good as you,
  Before she came to be Judea's queen.
SALOME Now stirs the tongue that is so quickly moved,
  But more than once your choler have I borne:
  Your fumish words are sooner said than proved,
  And Salome's reply is only scorn.     230
MARIAM Scorn those that are for thy companions held.
  Though I thy brother's face had never seen,
  My birth thy baser birth so far excelled,
  I had to both of you the princess been.
  Thou parti-Jew, and parti-Edomite,
  Thou mongrel, issued from rejected race,
  Thy ancestors against the heavens did fight,
  And thou like them wilt heavenly birth disgrace.
SALOME Still twit you me with nothing but my birth,
  What odds betwixt your ancestors and mine?     240
  Both born of Adam, both were made of earth,
  And both did come from holy Abraham's line.

MARIAM I favour thee when nothing else I say;
  With thy black acts I'll not pollute my breath,
  Else to thy charge I might full justly lay
  A shameful life, besides a husband's death.
SALOME 'Tis true indeed, I did the plots reveal,
  That passed betwixt your favourites and you:
  I meant not, I, a traitor to conceal.
  Thus Salome your minion Joseph slew.     250
MARIAM Heaven, dost thou mean this infamy to
    smother?
  Let slandered Mariam ope thy closèd ear:
  Self-guilt hath ever been suspicion's mother,
  And therefore I this speech with patience bear.
  No, had not Salome's unsteadfast heart
  In Josephus' stead her Constabarus placed,
  To free herself she had not used the art
  To slander hapless Mariam for unchaste.
ALEXANDRA Come Mariam, let us go: it is no boot
  To let the head contend against the foot.     260
        *Exeunt* MARIAM *and* ALEXANDRA

# Act I, scene iv

SALOME, *sola*

SALOME Lives Salome to get so base a style
  As foot to the proud Mariam? Herod's spirit
  In happy time for her endured exile,
  For did he live she should not miss her merit.
  But he is dead, and though he were my brother,
  His death such store of cinders cannot cast
  My coals of love to quench: for though they smother
  The flames a while, yet will they out at last.
  Oh blest Arabia, in best climate placed,
  I by the fruit will censure of the tree:     270
  'Tis not in vain thy happy name thou hast,
  If all Arabians like Silleus be:
  Had not my fate been too too contrary,
  When I on Constabarus first did gaze,
  Silleus had been object to mine eye:
  Whose looks and personage must all eyes amaze.
  But now, ill-fated Salome, thy tongue
  To Constabarus by itself is tied:
  And now, except I do the Hebrew wrong,

---

205 revolve: consider
228 choler: anger
229 fumish: irascible
237 ancestors . . . fight: the Old Testament prophets
    considered Edom's conflict with Israel to be in defiance
    of divine will; see Ezekiel 25.13; Jeremiah 49.7–22; Amos
    1.11–12; Obadiah 1.18
239 twit: taunt

250 Joseph slew: Josephus was the uncle of Herod and
    Salome, and Salome's first husband; see above, 'The
    Argument', paras 3–4
253 suspicion's: eds (suspitious Q)
259 boot: use
261 style: name, title
262–3 Herod's spirit . . . exile: i.e. 'luckily for Mariam, Herod
    is dead' (Wright)
264 she should . . . merit: she would get what she deserved
270 fruit . . . tree: allusion to Matthew 7.20: 'Wherefore by
    their fruits ye shall know them'; see too Matthew 7.17–19
272 Silleus: chief minister to King Obodas of Arabia

I cannot be the fair Arabian bride.    280
What childish lets are these? Why stand I now
On honourable points? 'Tis long ago
Since shame was written on my tainted brow,
And certain 'tis that shame is honour's foe.
Had I upon my reputation stood,
Had I affected an unspotted life,
Josephus' veins had still been stuffed with blood,
And I to him had lived a sober wife.
Then had I never cast an eye of love
On Constabarus' now detested face,    290
Then had I kept my thoughts without remove,
And blushed at motion of the least disgrace.
But shame is gone, and honour wiped away,
And impudency on my forehead sits:
She bids me work my will without delay,
And for my will I will employ my wits.
He loves, I love; what then can be the cause
Keeps me from being the Arabian's wife?
It is the principles of Moses' laws,
For Constabarus still remains in life.    300
If he to me did bear as earnest hate
As I to him, for him there were an ease:
A separating bill might free his fate
From such a yoke that did so much displease.
Why should such privilege to man be given?
Or given to them, why barred from women then?
Are men than we in greater grace with heaven?
Or cannot women hate as well as men?
I'll be the custom-breaker, and begin
To show my sex the way to freedom's door,    310
And with an offering will I purge my sin;
The law was made for none but who are poor.
If Herod had lived, I might to him accuse
My present lord. But for the future's sake,
Then would I tell the king he did refuse
The sons of Babas in his power to take.
But now I must divorce him from my bed,
That my Silleus may possess his room.
Had I not begged his life he had been dead;

I curse my tongue, the hind'rer of his doom;    320
But then my wand'ring heart to him was fast,
Nor did I dream of change. Silleus said,
He would be here, and see, he comes at last:
Had I not named him, longer had he stayed.

# Act I, scene v

SALOME, SILLEUS

SILLEUS Well found, fair Salome, Judea's pride.
   Hath thy innated wisdom found the way
   To make Silleus deem him deified,
   By gaining thee, a more than precious prey?
SALOME I have devised the best I can devise;
   A more imperfect means was never found,    330
   But what cares Salome? It doth suffice
   If our endeavours with their end be crowned.
   In this our land we have an ancient use,
   Permitted first by our law-giver's head:
   Who hates his wife, though for no just abuse,
   May with a bill divorce her from his bed.
   But in this custom women are not free,
   Yet I for once will wrest it; blame not thou
   The ill I do, since what I do's for thee,
   Though others blame, Silleus should allow.    340
SILLEUS Thinks Salome, Silleus hath a tongue
   To censure her fair actions? Let my blood
   Bedash my proper brow, for such a wrong,
   The being yours, can make even vices good:
   Arabia joy, prepare thy earth with green,
   Thou never happy wert indeed till now:
   Now shall thy ground be trod by beauty's queen,
   Her foot is destined to depress thy brow.
   Thou shalt, fair Salome, command as much
   As if the royal ornament were thine:    350
   The weakness of Arabia's king is such,
   The kingdom is not his so much as mine:
   My mouth is our Obodas' oracle,
   Who thinks not aught but what Silleus will.
   And thou rare creature, Asia's miracle,
   Shalt be to me as it: Obodas still.
SALOME 'Tis not for glory I thy love accept,
   Judea yields me honour's worthy store;
   Had not affection in my bosom crept,
   My native country should my life deplore.    360
   Were not Silleus he with whom I go,
   I would not change my Palestine for Rome;
   Much less would I, a glorious state to show,
   Go far to purchase an Arabian tomb.
SILLEUS Far be it from Silleus so to think;

---

281 lets: obstacles
281–2 stand . . . points?: why do I now insist on a strict code
   of honourable behaviour?
283 shame . . . brow: i.e. by a blush
292 motion: emotion
303 separating bill: i.e. a bill of divorcement; see
   Deuteronomy 24.1, which describes this as a male
   prerogative
315–16 he did refuse . . . take: rather than killing them, as
   Herod had ordered him to, Constabarus had hidden
   Babas' sons; see II.ii
319 Had I . . . dead: when Herod learnt of Constabarus'
   attempt to establish independence for Idumea, of which
   he was governor, he threatened to execute him. It was
   only Salome's pleading that saved him

326 innated: innate
334 law-giver's head: i.e. Moses
343 proper: own
360 deplore: grieve over

I know it is thy gratitude requites
The love that is in me, and shall not shrink
Till death do sever me from earth's delights.

SALOME  But whist: methinks the wolf is in our talk.
Be gone, Silleus. Who doth here arrive?                   370
'Tis Constabarus that doth hither walk;
I'll find a quarrel, him from me to drive.

SILLEUS  Farewell; but were it not for thy command,
In his despite Silleus here would stand.

*Exit*

# Act I, scene vi

SALOME, CONSTABARUS

CONSTABARUS  Oh Salome, how much you wrong your
      name,
Your race, your country, and your husband most!
A stranger's private conference is shame;
I blush for you, that have your blushing lost.
Oft have I found, and found you to my grief,
Consorted with this base Arabian here;                    380
Heaven knows that you have been my comfort chief,
Then do not now my greater plague appear.
Now by the stately carvèd edifice
That on Mount Sion makes so fair a show,
And by the altar fit for sacrifice,
I love thee more than thou thyself dost know.
Oft with a silent sorrow have I heard
How ill Judea's mouth doth censure thee,
And did I not thine honour much regard,
Thou shouldst not be exhorted thus for me.               390
Didst thou but know the worth of honest fame,
How much a virtuous woman is esteemed,
Thou wouldst like hell eschew deservèd shame,
And seek to be both chaste and chastely deemed.
Our wisest prince did say, and true he said,
A virtuous woman crowns her husband's head.

SALOME  Did I for this uprear thy low estate?
Did I for this requital beg thy life,
That thou hadst forfeited to hapless fate,
To be to such a thankless wretch the wife?               400
This hand of mine hath lifted up thy head,
Which many a day ago had fallen full low,
Because the sons of Babas are not dead;
To me thou dost both life and fortune owe.

CONSTABARUS  You have my patience often exercised;

Use make my choler keep within the banks.
Yet boast no more, but be by me advised:
A benefit upbraided, forfeits thanks.
I prithee Salome, dismiss this mood,
Thou dost not know how ill it fits thy place:           410
My words were all intended for thy good,
To raise thine honour and to stop disgrace.

SALOME  To stop disgrace? Take thou no care for me,
Nay do thy worst, thy worst I set not by.
No shame of mine is like to light on thee,
Thy love and admonitions I defy.
Thou shalt no hour longer call me wife;
Thy jealousy procures my hate so deep
That I from thee do mean to free my life,
By a divorcing bill before I sleep.                      420

CONSTABARUS  Are Hebrew women now transformed
      to men?
Why do you not as well our battles fight,
And wear our armour? Suffer this, and then
Let all the world be topsy-turvèd quite.
Let fishes graze, beasts swim, and birds descend,
Let fire burn downwards whilst the earth aspires,
Let winter's heat and summer's cold offend,
Let thistles grow on vines, and grapes on briars,
Set us to spin or sow, or at the best
Make us wood-hewers, water-bearing wights:              430
For sacred service let us take no rest,
Use us as Joshua did the Gibonites.

SALOME  Hold on your talk, till it be time to end,
For me I am resolved it shall be so:
Though I be first that to this course do bend,
I shall not be the last, full well I know.

CONSTABARUS  Why then be witness heav'n, the judge
      of sins,
Be witness spirits that eschew the dark,
Be witness angels, witness cherubins,
Whose semblance sits upon the holy Ark;                 440
Be witness earth, be witness Palestine,
Be witness David's City, if my heart
Did ever merit such an act of thine,
Or if the fault be mine that makes us part.
Since mildest Moses, friend unto the Lord,
Did work his wonders in the land of Ham,
And slew the first-born babes without a sword,
In sign whereof we eat the holy lamb,
Till now that fourteen hundred years are past,

---

369  whist: hush
377  conference: conversation
383–4  stately . . . show: the temple of Jerusalem
395  wisest prince: Solomon; see Proverbs 12.4
399  to: eds (omitted Q); its inclusion renders the line
      metrically regular. Other eds punctuate thus: ' . . .
      forfeited? Hapless fate/To be . . . the wife!'

406  make: Q. Some eds emend to 'makes' or 'made', but it
      makes sense thus if read as 'May use [i.e. habit] . . .'
414  set not by: care not for
432  Joshua . . . Gibonites: Joshua condemned the Gibonites
      to perpetual servitude for their attempt to deceive him;
      see Joshua 9
440  Ark: the Ark of the Covenant which held the tablets on
      which were written the Ten Commandments
446  land of Ham: i.e. Egypt

Since first the law with us hath been in force:                           450
You are the first, and will, I hope, be last,
That ever sought her husband to divorce.
SALOME  I mean not to be led by precedent;
  My will shall be to me instead of law.
CONSTABARUS  I fear me much you will too late repent,
  That you have ever lived so void of awe.
  This is Silleus' love that makes you thus
  Reverse all order; you must next be his.
  But if my thoughts aright the cause discuss,
  In winning you, he gains no lasting bliss;                              460
  I was Silleus, and not long ago
  Josephus then was Constabarus now:
  When you became my friend you proved his foe,
  As now for him you break to me your vow.
SALOME  If once I loved you, greater is your debt,
  For certain 'tis that you deserved it not.
  And undeservèd love we soon forget,
  And therefore that to me can be no blot.
  But now fare ill my once belovèd lord,                                  469
  Yet never more beloved than now abhorred.                          *Exit*
CONSTABARUS  Yet Constabarus biddeth thee farewell.
  Farewell light creature. Heaven forgive thy sin.
  My prophesying spirit doth foretell
  Thy wavering thoughts do yet but new begin.
  Yet I have better 'scaped than Joseph did,
  But if our Herod's death had been delayed,
  The valiant youths that I so long have hid,
  Had been by her, and I for them, betrayed.
  Therefore in happy hour did Caesar give
  The fatal blow to wanton Antony:                                        480
  For had he lived, our Herod then should live,
  But great Antonius' death made Herod die.
  Had he enjoyed his breath, not I alone
  Had been in danger of a deadly fall,
  But Mariam had the way of peril gone,
  Though by the tyrant most beloved of all:
  The sweet-faced Mariam, as free from guilt
  As heaven from spots; yet had her lord come back
  Her purest blood had been unjustly spilt,
  And Salome it was would work her wrack.                           490
  Though all Judea yield her innocent,
  She often hath been near to punishment.                             *Exit*

CHORUS
Those minds that wholly dote upon delight,
Except they only joy in inward good,
Still hope at last to hop upon the right,
And so from sand they leap in loathsome mud.
  Fond wretches, seeking what they cannot find,
  For no content attends a wavering mind.

If wealth they do desire, and wealth attain,
Then wondrous fain would they to honour leap;                   500
If mean degree they do in honour gain,
They would but wish a little higher step.
  Thus step to step and wealth to wealth they add,
  Yet cannot all their plenty make them glad.

Yet oft we see that some in humble state,
Are cheerful, pleasant, happy, and content,
When those indeed that are of higher state,
With vain additions do their thoughts torment.
  Th'one would to his mind his fortune bind,
  Th'other to his fortune frames his mind.                             510

To wish variety is sign of grief,
For if you like your state as now it is,
Why should an alteration bring relief?
Nay, change would then be feared as loss of bliss.
  That man is only happy in his fate
  That is delighted in a settled state.

Still Mariam wished she from her lord were free,
For expectation of variety;
Yet now she sees her wishes prosperous be,
She grieves, because her lord so soon did die.                      520
  Who can those vast imaginations feed,
  Where in a property contempt doth breed?

Were Herod now perchance to live again,
She would again as much be grieved at that;
All that she may, she ever doth disdain,
Her wishes guide her to she knows not what.
  And sad must be their looks, their honour sour,
  That care for nothing being in their power.

# Act II, scene i

PHERORAS *and* GRAPHINA

PHERORAS  'Tis true Graphina, now the time draws nigh
  Wherein the holy priest with hallowed right,
  The happy long-desirèd knot shall tie,
  Pheroras and Graphina to unite.
  How oft have I with lifted hands implored
  This blessèd hour, till now implored in vain,
  Which hath my wishèd liberty restored,

450  law: i.e. the law of Moses
494  Except: unless
497  Fond: foolish

500  fain: eagerly
501  If: eds (Of Q)
522  in a property: regarding something already possessed
528  being: that is
SD  PHERORAS *and* GRAPHINA: the sub-plot concerning
    Pheroras (Herod's younger brother) and the slave girl is
    mentioned only briefly in Cary's source, the Jewish
    historian Josephus's *The Antiquities*, translated by
    Thomas Lodge in 1602; the name Graphina is Cary's
    invention. In 'Graphina' she invents a name that seems to
    allude to the Greek for writing, *graphesis*; for a discussion
    of the name see Ferguson 1991: 237–8

And made my subject self my own again.
Thy love, fair maid, upon mine eye doth sit,
Whose nature hot doth dry the moisture all,　　　10
Which were in nature and in reason fit
For my monarchal brother's death to fall.
Had Herod lived, he would have plucked my hand
From fair Graphina's palm perforce, and tied
The same in hateful and despisèd band,
For I had had a baby to my bride:
Scarce can her infant tongue with easy voice
Her name distinguish to another's ear;
Yet had he lived, his power, and not my choice,
Had made me solemnly the contract swear.　　　20
Have I not cause in such a change to joy?
What though she be my niece, a princess born?
Near blood's without respect, high birth a toy,
Since love can teach us blood and kindred's scorn.
What booted it that he did raise my head,
To be his realm's co-partner, kingdom's mate?
Withal, he kept Graphina from my bed,
More wished by me than thrice Judea's state.
Oh, could not he be skilful judge in love,
That doted so upon his Mariam's face?　　　30
He, for his passion, Doris did remove;
I needed not a lawful wife displace.
It could not be but he had power to judge,
But he that never grudged a kingdom's share,
This well-known happiness to me did grudge,
And meant to be therein without compare.
Else had I been his equal in love's host,
For though the diadem on Mariam's head
Corrupt the vulgar judgements, I will boast
Graphina's brow's as white, her cheeks as red.　　　40
Why speaks thou not, fair creature? Move thy tongue,
For silence is a sign of discontent:
It were to both our loves too great a wrong
If now this hour do find thee sadly bent.

GRAPHINA　Mistake me not my lord; too oft have I
Desired this time to come with wingèd feet,
To be enwrapped with grief when 'tis too nigh.
You know my wishes ever yours did meet:
If I be silent, 'tis no more but fear
That I should say too little when I speak.　　　50
But since you will my imperfections bear,
In spite of doubt I will my silence break;
Yet might amazement tie my moving tongue,
But that I know before Pheroras' mind.
I have admirèd your affection long,

And cannot yet therein a reason find.
Your hand hath lifted me from lowest state
To highest eminency, wondrous grace,
And me, your handmaid, have you made your mate,
Though all but you alone do count me base.　　　60
You have preserved me pure at my request,
Though you so weak a vassal might constrain
To yield to your high will; then last not best
In my respect a princess you disdain;
Then need not all these favours study crave,
To be requited by a simple maid?
And study still you know must silence have,
Then be my cause for silence justly weighed,
But study cannot boot, nor I requite,
Except your lowly handmaid's steadfast love　　　70
And fast obedience may your mind delight;
I will not promise more than I can prove.

PHERORAS　That study needs not let Graphina smile,
And I desire no greater recompense.
I cannot vaunt me in a glorious style,
Nor show my love in far-fetched eloquence:
But this believe me, never Herod's heart
Hath held his prince-born beauty-famèd wife
In nearer place than thou, fair virgin, art,
To him that holds the glory of his life.　　　80
Should Herod's body leave the sepulchre,
And entertain the severed ghost again,
He should not be my nuptial hinderer,
Except he hindered it with dying pain.
Come fair Graphina, let us go in state,
This wish-endearèd time to celebrate.

　　　　　　　　　　　　　　　　　　　*Exeunt*

# Act II, scene ii

CONSTABARUS *and* BABAS' SONS

BABAS' FIRST SON　Now, valiant friend, you have our
　　　lives redeemed,
Which lives, as saved by you, to you are due:
Command and you shall see yourself esteemed,
Our lives and liberties belong to you.　　　90
This twice six years, with hazard of your life,
You have concealed us from the tyrant's sword;
Though cruel Herod's sister were your wife,
You durst in scorn of fear this grace afford.
In recompense we know not what to say,
A poor reward were thanks for such a merit;
Our truest friendship at your feet we lay,
The best requital to a noble spirit.

---

16　baby to my bride: Pheroras was engaged to one of
　　Herod's young daughters
24　us: absent in Q; editorial addition to regularise metre
44　bent: inclined
54　But: except
55　admirèd: wondered at

71　fast: firm
73　let . . . smile: i.e. prevent Graphina's smile
81–2　Should Herod's . . . again: i.e. if Herod's body and soul
　　were reunited

CONSTABARUS Oh how you wrong our friendship,
    valiant youth:
  With friends there is not such a word as debt;    **100**
  Where amity is tied with bond of truth,
  All benefits are there in common set.
  Then is the golden age with them renewed:
  All names of properties are banished quite,
  Division, and distinction, are eschewed,
  Each hath to what belongs to others right.
  And 'tis not sure so full a benefit,
  Freely to give, as freely to require:
  A bounteous act hath glory following it,
  They cause the glory that the act desire.    **110**
  All friendship should the pattern imitate
  Of Jesse's son and valiant Jonathan,
  For neither sovereign's nor father's hate
  A friendship fixed on virtue sever can.
  Too much of this; 'tis written in the heart,
  And needs no amplifying with the tongue:
  Now may you from your living tomb depart,
  Where Herod's life hath kept you over long.
  Too great an injury to a noble mind,
  To be quick buried; you had purchased fame    **120**
  Some years ago, but that you were confined,
  While thousand meaner did advance their name.
  Your best of life, the prime of all your years,
  Your time of action is from you bereft.
  Twelve winters have you overpassed in fears:
  Yet if you use it well, enough is left.
  And who can doubt but you will use it well?
  The sons of Babas have it by descent,
  In all their thoughts each action to excel,
  Boldly to act, and wisely to invent.    **130**
BABAS' SECOND SON Had it not like the hateful cuckoo
    been,
  Whose riper age his infant nurse doth kill,
  So long we had not kept ourselves unseen,
  But Constabarus safely crossed our will:
  For had the tyrant fixed his cruel eye
  On our concealèd faces, wrath had swayed
  His justice so, that he had forced us die.
  And dearer price than life we should have paid,
  For you our truest friend had fall'n with us,
  And we, much like a house on pillars set,    **140**
  Had clean depressed our prop, and therefore thus

  Our ready will with our concealment met.
  But now that you, fair lord, are dangerless,
  The sons of Babas shall their rigour show,
  And prove it was not baseness did oppress
  Our hearts so long, but honour kept them low.
BABAS' FIRST SON Yet do I fear this tale of Herod's death
  At last will prove a very tale indeed;
  It gives me strongly in my mind, his breath
  Will be preserved to make a number bleed.    **150**
  I wish not therefore to be set at large,
  Yet peril to myself I do not fear:
  Let us for some days longer be your charge,
  Till we of Herod's state the truth do hear.
CONSTABARUS What, art thou turned a coward, noble
    youth,
  That thou beginst to doubt undoubted truth?
BABAS' FIRST SON Were it my brother's tongue that
    cast this doubt,
  I from his heart would have the question out
  With this keen falchion, but 'tis you, my lord,
  Against whose head I must not lift a sword:    **160**
  I am so tied in gratitude.
CONSTABARUS           Believe
  You have no cause to take it ill;
  If any word of mine your heart did grieve
  The word dissented from the speaker's will.
  I know it was not fear the doubt begun,
  But rather valour and your care of me:
  A coward could not be your father's son.
  Yet know I doubts unnecessary be:
  For who can think that in Antonius' fall,
  Herod his bosom friend should 'scape unbruised?    **170**
  Then, Caesar, we might thee an idiot call,
  If thou by him shouldst be so far abused.
BABAS' SECOND SON Lord Constabarus, let me tell you
    this,
  Upon submission Caesar will forgive:
  And therefore though the tyrant did amiss,
  It may fall out that he will let him live.
  Not many years agone it is since I,
  Directed thither by my father's care,
  In famous Rome for twice twelve months did lie,
  My life from Hebrews' cruelty to spare.    **180**
  There, though I were but yet of boyish age,
  I bent mine eye to mark, mine ears to hear,
  Where I did see Octavius, then a page,
  When first he did to Julius' sight appear:

---

112  Jesse's son . . . Jonathan: i.e. David and Jonathan, types
    of male friendship; see 1 Samuel 18 to 2 Samuel 1
120  quick buried: buried alive
128  descent: heredity
131  hateful cuckoo: the cuckoo lays its eggs in other birds'
    nests, the young cuckoo then displaces the young of the
    resident birds
134  safely: some eds emend to 'safety'; the sense, however, is
    clear as it stands if 'safely' is taken as 'in the interests of
    safety'

149  It gives . . . mind: i.e. I have a presentiment
152  fear: eds (leare Q); Purkiss emends to 'leer' (i.e. 'look
    askance at')
159  falchion: curved broadsword
179  lie: eds (live Q)
183  Octavius: Octavius (later Caesar Augustus), great-
    nephew of Julius Caesar
184  Julius: Julius Caesar

Methought I saw such mildness in his face,
And such a sweetness in his looks did grow
Withal, commixed with so majestic grace,
His phys'nomy his fortune did foreshow.
For this I am indebted to mine eye,
But then mine ear received more evidence,                     190
By that I knew his love to clemency,
How he with hottest choler could dispense.

CONSTABARUS  But we have more than barely heard the
   news,
It hath been twice confirmed. And though some tongue
Might be so false with false report t'abuse,
A false report hath never lasted long.
But be it so that Herod have his life,
Concealment would not then a whit avail:
For certain 'tis, that she that was my wife
Would not to set her accusation fail.                        200
And therefore now as good the venture give
And free ourselves from blot of cowardice,
As show a pitiful desire to live,
For, who can pity but they must despise?

BABAS' FIRST SON  I yield, but to necessity I yield;
I dare upon this doubt engage mine arm,
That Herod shall again this kingdom wield,
And prove his death to be a false alarm.

BABAS' SECOND SON  I doubt it too; God grant it be an
   error.
'Tis best without a cause to be in terror:                   210
And rather had I, though my soul be mine,
My soul should lie, than prove a true divine.

CONSTABARUS  Come, come, let fear go seek a dastard's
   nest,
Undaunted courage lies in a noble breast.

*Exeunt*

# Act II, scene iii

DORIS *and* ANTIPATER

DORIS  You royal buildings bow your lofty side,
And stoop to her that is by right your queen;
Let your humility upbraid the pride
Of those in whom no due respect is seen.
Nine times have we with trumpets' haughty sound,
And banishing sour leaven from our taste,                    220
Observed the feast that takes the fruit from ground,

---

188  phys'nomy: physiognomy; i.e. facial features, especially
    when taken to reveal character
206  doubt: suspicion, fear
209  doubt: fear, suspect
212  divine: prophet
213  dastard's: ignoble coward's
215  You: eds (Your Q)
220–1  banishing sour leaven . . . ground: references to the
    Jewish feast of Passover

Since I, fair city, did behold thee last;
So long it is since Mariam's purer cheek
Did rob from mine the glory; and so long
Since I returned my native town to seek,
And with me nothing but the sense of wrong.
And thee my boy, whose birth though great it were,
Yet have thy after fortunes proved but poor.
When thou wert born, how little did I fear
Thou shouldst be thrust from forth thy father's door.
Art thou not Herod's right begotten son?                     231
Was not the hapless Doris Herod's wife?
Yes: ere he had the Hebrew kingdom won,
I was companion to his private life.
Was I not fair enough to be a queen?
Why, ere thou wert to me, false monarch, tied,
My lake of beauty might as well be seen,
As after I had lived five years thy bride.
Yet then thine oaths came pouring like the rain,
Which all affirmed my face without compare:                  240
And that if thou mightst Doris' love obtain,
For all the world besides thou didst not care.
Then was I young, and rich, and nobly born,
And therefore worthy to be Herod's mate;
Yet thou ungrateful cast me off with scorn,
When Heaven's purpose raised your meaner fate.
Oft have I begged for vengeance for this fact,
And with dejected knees, aspiring hands,
Have prayed the highest power to enact
The fall of her that on my trophy stands.                    250
Revenge I have according to my will,
Yet where I wished this vengeance did not light:
I wished it should high-hearted Mariam kill,
But it against my whilom lord did fight.
With thee sweet boy I came, and came to try
If thou before his bastards might be placed
In Herod's royal seat and dignity.
But Mariam's infants here are only graced,
And now for us there doth no hope remain.
Yet we will not return till Herod's end                      260
Be more confirmed; perchance he is not slain.
So glorious fortunes may my boy attend,
For if he live, he'll think it doth suffice
That he to Doris shows such cruelty:
For as he did my wretched life despise,
So do I know I shall despisèd die.
Let him but prove as natural to thee
As cruel to thy miserable mother;
His cruelty shall not upbraided be
But in thy fortunes. I his faults will smother.              270

---

237  lake: Q; some eds emend to 'lack'
250  trophy: a structure erected as a memorial of a victory in
    war; here used figuratively in relation to Mariam's
    triumph over Doris for Herod
254  whilom: former

ANTIPATER  Each mouth within the city loudly cries
    That Herod's death is certain; therefore we
    Had best some subtle hidden plot devise,
    That Mariam's children might subverted be,
    By poison's drink, or else by murderous knife,
    So we may be advanced, it skills not how:
    They are but bastards, you were Herod's wife,
    And foul adultery blotteth Mariam's brow.
DORIS  They are too strong to be by us removed,
    Or else revenge's foulest spotted face          280
    By our detested wrongs might be approved,
    But weakness must to greater power give place.
    But let us now retire to grieve alone,
    For solitariness best fitteth moan.
                                                    *Exeunt*

# Act II, scene iv

SILLEUS *and* CONSTABARUS

SILLEUS  Well met Judean lord, the only wight
    Silleus wished to see. I am to call
    Thy tongue to strict account.
CONSTABARUS                      For what despite
    I ready am to hear, and answer all.
    But if directly at the cause I guess
    That breeds this challenge, you must pardon me,  290
    And now some other ground of fight profess,
    For I have vowed, vows must unbroken be.
SILLEUS  What may be your exception? Let me know.
CONSTABARUS  Why, aught concerning Salome; my
        sword
    Shall not be wielded for a cause so low,
    A blow for her my arm will scorn t'afford.
SILLEUS  It is for slandering her unspotted name;
    And I will make thee, in thy vow's despite,
    Suck up the breath that did my mistress blame,
    And swallow it again to do her right.           300
CONSTABARUS  I prithee give some other quarrel ground
    To find beginning: rail against my name,
    Or strike me first, or let some scarlet wound
    Inflame my courage, give me words of shame;
    Do thou our Moses' sacred laws disgrace,
    Deprave our nation, do me some despite:
    I'm apt enough to fight in any case,
    But yet for Salome I will not fight.
SILLEUS  Nor I for aught but Salome: my sword
    That owes his service to her sacred name        310
    Will not an edge for other cause afford;
    In other fight I am not sure of fame.
CONSTABARUS  For her, I pity thee enough already,
    For her, I therefore will not mangle thee:
    A woman with a heart so most unsteady,

Will of herself sufficient torture be.
    I cannot envy for so light a gain,
    Her mind with such unconstancy doth run:
    As with a word thou didst her love obtain,
    So with a word she will from thee be won.       320
    So light as her possessions for most day
    Is her affections lost, to me 'tis known:
    As good go hold the wind as make her stay,
    She never loves, but till she call her own.
    She merely is a painted sepulchre,
    That is both fair, and vilely foul at once:
    Though on her outside graces garnish her,
    Her mind is filled with worse then rotten bones.
    And ever ready lifted is her hand,
    To aim destruction at a husband's throat:       330
    For proofs, Josephus and myself do stand,
    Though once on both of us she seemed to dote.
    Her mouth, though serpent-like it never hisses,
    Yet like a serpent, poisons where it kisses.
SILLEUS  Well, Hebrew, well, thou bark'st, but wilt not
        bite.
CONSTABARUS  I tell thee still for her I will not fight.
SILLEUS  Why then, I call thee coward.
CONSTABARUS                          From my heart
    I give thee thanks. A coward's hateful name
    Cannot to valiant minds a blot impart,
    And therefore I with joy receive the same.      340
    Thou know'st I am no coward: thou wert by
    At the Arabian battle th'other day,
    And saw'st my sword with daring valiancy
    Amongst the faint Arabians cut my way.
    The blood of foes no more could let it shine,
    And 'twas enamellèd with some of thine.
    But now have at thee: not for Salome
    I fight, but to discharge a coward's style.
    Here 'gins the fight that shall not parted be,
    Before a soul or two endure exile.     *They fight*
SILLEUS  Thy sword hath made some windows for my
        blood,                                      351
    To show a horrid crimson phys'nomy.
    To breathe for both of us methinks 'twere good;
    The day will give us time enough to die.

---

276  skills: matters
293  exception: eds (expectation Q)

321–2  So light as . . . 'tis known: the syntax of these lines is
        slightly obscure, but the general sense is 'her affections
        are inconstant, and change daily, as I know'
325  painted sepulchre: i.e. one professedly righteous but
        inwardly wicked; a hypocrite; see Matthew 23.27: 'Woe
        unto you, scribes and Pharisees, hypocrites! for ye are like
        unto whited sepulchres, which indeed appear beautiful
        outward, but are within full of dead men's bones, and of
        all uncleanness'
341  by: nearby
348  style: name
352  phys'nomy: see II.ii.188n

CONSTABARUS With all my heart take breath; thou
    shalt have time,
And if thou list, a twelvemonth; let us end.
Into thy cheeks there doth a paleness climb,
Thou canst not from my sword thyself defend.
What needest thou for Salome to fight?
Thou hast her, and mayst keep her; none strives for
    her:    360
I willingly to thee resign my right,
For in my very soul I do abhor her.
Thou seest that I am fresh, unwounded yet,
Then not for fear I do this offer make:
Thou art with loss of blood to fight unfit,
For here is one, and there another take.
SILLEUS I will not leave, as long as breath remains
Within my wounded body: spare your words.
My heart in blood's stead courage entertains;
Salome's love no place for fear affords.    370
CONSTABARUS Oh could thy soul but prophesy like
    mine,
I would not wonder thou shouldst long to die:
For Salome, if I aright divine,
Will be than death a greater misery.
SILLEUS Then list, I'll breathe no longer.
CONSTABARUS                Do thy will;
I hateless fight, and charitably kill.    *They fight*
Pity thyself, Silleus, let not death
Intrude before his time into thy heart.
Alas it is too late to fear: his breath
Is from his body now about to part.    380
How far'st thou, brave Arabian?
SILLEUS                Very well.
My leg is hurt, I can no longer fight.
It only grieves me that so soon I fell,
Before fair Salom's wrongs I came to right.
CONSTABARUS Thy wounds are less than mortal. Never
    fear,
Thou shalt a safe and quick recovery find.
Come, I will thee unto my lodging bear;
I hate thy body, but I love thy mind.
SILLEUS Thanks, noble Jew, I see a courteous foe;
Stern enmity to friendship can no art.    390
Had not my heart and tongue engaged me so,
I would from thee no foe, but friend depart.
My heart to Salome is tied too fast
To leave her love for friendship, yet my skill
Shall be employed to make your favour last,
And I will honour Constabarus still.
CONSTABARUS I ope my bosom to thee, and will take

Thee in, as friend, and grieve for thy complaint;
But if we do not expedition make,
Thy loss of blood I fear will make thee faint.    400
    *Exeunt*

CHORUS
To hear a tale with ears prejudicate,
It spoils the judgement, and corrupts the sense;
That human error given to every state,
Is greater enemy to innocence.
    It makes us foolish, heady, rash, unjust;
    It makes us never try before we trust.

It will confound the meaning, change the words,
For it our sense of hearing much deceives;
Besides no time to judgement it affords,
To weigh the circumstance our ear receives.    410
    The ground of accidents it never tries,
    But makes us take for truth ten thousand lies.

Our ears and hearts are apt to hold for good
That we ourselves do most desire to be:
And then we drown objections in the flood
Of partiality; 'tis that we see
    That makes false rumours long with credit past,
    Though they like rumours must conclude as last.

The greatest part of us prejudicate,
With wishing Herod's death do hold it true;    420
The being once deluded doth not bate
The credit to a better likelihood due.
    Those few that wish it not, the multitude
    Do carry headlong, so they doubts conclude.

They not object the weak uncertain ground,
Whereon they built this tale of Herod's end,
Whereof the author scarcely can be found,
And all because their wishes that way bend.
    They think not of the peril that ensu'th,
    If this should prove the contrary to truth.    430

On this same doubt, on this so light a breath,
They pawn their lives, and fortunes. For they all
Behave them as the news of Herod's death
They did of most undoubted credit call.
    But if their actions now do rightly hit,
    Let them commend their fortune, not their wit.

---

SD  *They fight*: this appears as part of Constabarus's speech in
    Q: 'I, I, they fight'
390  Stern enmity . . . art: i.e. no art can turn stern enmity to
    friendship
393  too: eds (so Q)

399  expedition: haste
414  That: that which
421  bate: abate
425  They: i.e. the minority who doubted the rumour
426  they: i.e. the majority who circulated the rumour
435  hit: prove to be right, succeed

# Act III, scene i

PHERORAS, SALOME

PHERORAS Urge me no more Graphina to forsake,
    Not twelve hours since I married her for love;
    And do you think a sister's power can make
    A resolute decree so soon remove?
SALOME Poor minds they are that honour not affects.
PHERORAS Who hunts for honour, happiness neglects.
SALOME You might have been both of felicity
    And honour too in equal measure seized.
PHERORAS It is not you can tell so well as I,
    What 'tis can make me happy, or displeased.     10
SALOME To match for neither beauty nor respects
    One mean of birth, but yet of meaner mind,
    A woman full of natural defects,
    I wonder what your eye in her could find.
PHERORAS Mine eye found loveliness, mine ear found
    wit,
    To please the one, and to enchant the other;
    Grace on her eye, mirth on her tongue doth sit,
    In looks a child, in wisdom's house a mother.
SALOME But say you thought her fair, as none thinks
    else,
    Knows not Pheroras, beauty is a blast,     20
    Much like this flower which to day excels,
    But longer than a day it will not last.
PHERORAS Her wit exceeds her beauty.
SALOME     Wit may show
    The way to ill as well as good, you know.
PHERORAS But wisdom is the porter of her head,
    And bars all wicked words from issuing thence.
SALOME But of a porter, better were you sped,
    If she against their entrance made defence.
PHERORAS But wherefore comes the sacred Ananell,
    That hitherward his hasty steps doth bend?     30
    Great sacrificer, y'are arrivèd well,
    Ill news from holy mouth I not attend.

# Act III, scene ii

PHERORAS, SALOME, ANANELL

ANANELL My lips, my son, with peaceful tidings
    blessed,
    Shall utter honey to your list'ning ear:
    A word of death comes not from priestly breast,
    I speak of life: in life there is no fear.
    And for the news I did the heavens salute,

    And filled the temple with my thankful voice:
    For though that mourning may not me pollute,
    At pleasing accidents I may rejoice.     40
PHERORORAS Is Herod then revived from certain
    death?
SALOME What? Can your news restore my brother's
    breath?
ANANELL Both so, and so: the king is safe and sound,
    And did such grace in royal Caesar meet,
    That he with larger style than ever crowned,
    Within this hour Jerusalem will greet.
    I did but come to tell you, and must back
    To make preparatives for sacrifice:
    I knew his death your hearts like mine did rack,
    Though to conceal it proved you wise.     *Exit*
SALOME How can my joy sufficiently appear?     51
PHERORAS A heavier tale did never pierce mine ear.
SALOME Now Salome of happiness may boast.
PHERORAS But now Pheroras is in danger most.
SALOME I shall enjoy the comfort of my life.
PHERORAS And I shall lose it, losing of my wife.
SALOME Joy heart, for Constabarus shall be slain.
PHERORAS Grieve soul, Graphina shall from me be
    ta'en.
SALOME Smile cheeks, the fair Silleus shall be mine.
PHERORAS Weep eyes, for I must with a child combine.
SALOME Well brother, cease your moans; on one
    condition     61
    I'll undertake to win the king's consent:
    Graphina still shall be in your tuition,
    And her with you be ne'er the less content.
PHERORAS What's the condition? Let me quickly
    know,
    That I as quickly your command may act:
    Were it to see what herbs in Ophir grow,
    Or that the lofty Tyrus might be sacked.
SALOME 'Tis not so hard a task. It is no more
    But tell the king that Constabarus hid     70
    The sons of Babas, done to death before;
    And 'tis no more than Constabarus did.
    And tell him more that I for Herod's sake,
    Not able to endure our brother's foe,
    Did with a bill our separation make,

---

5  honour not affects: i.e. that does not aspire to honour
20  blast: i.e. transient, like a puff of wind
25  porter: gatekeeper
27  were you sped: would you fare
32  attend: expect

60  combine: marry; see II.i.16n
63  tuition: protection
67  Ophir: a region noted in the Old Testament as a source of gold
68  Tyrus: the city of Tyre, a wealthy Phoenician trading port celebrated for its beauty and power
71  done: some eds suggest emending to 'doomed'
73  I: eds (he Q)
74  our: eds (his Q). Editors differ in the emendments they make in this and with regard to the previous line, though they all agree that the sense demands some change. We follow Wright's changes

Though loth from Constabarus else to go.
PHERORAS  Believe this tale for told: I'll go from hence,
    In Herod's ear the Hebrew to deface;
    And I that never studied eloquence,
    Do mean with eloquence this tale to grace.     *Exit*
SALOME  This will be Constabarus' quick dispatch,   81
    Which from my mouth would lesser credit find:
    Yet shall he not decease without a match,
    For Mariam shall not linger long behind.
    First jealousy; if that avail not, fear
    Shall be my minister to work her end:
    A common error moves not Herod's ear,
    Which doth so firmly to his Mariam bend.
    She shall be chargèd with so horrid crime,
    As Herod's fear shall turn his love to hate:   90
    I'll make some swear that she desires to climb,
    And seeks to poison him for his estate.
    I scorn that she should live my birth t'upbraid,
    To call me base and hungry Edomite;
    With patient show her choler I betrayed,
    And watched the time to be revenged by sleight.
    Now tongue of mine with scandal load her name,
    Turn hers to fountains, Herod's eyes to flame.
    Yet first I will begin Pheroras' suit,
    That he my earnest business may effect;   100
    And I of Mariam will keep me mute,
    Till first some other doth her name detect.

*Enter* SILLEUS' MAN

    Who's there? Silleus' man? How fares your lord,
    That your aspects do bear the badge of sorrow?
SILLEUS' MAN  He hath the marks of Constabarus' sword,
    And for a while desires your sight to borrow.
SALOME  My heavy curse the hateful sword pursue,
    My heavier curse on the more hateful arm
    That wounded my Silleus. But renew
    Your tale again. Hath he no mortal harm?   110
SILLEUS' MAN  No sign of danger doth in him appear,
    Nor are his wounds in place of peril seen:
    He bids you be assured you need not fear,
    He hopes to make you yet Arabia's queen.
SALOME  Commend my heart to be Silleus' charge;
    Tell him my brother's sudden coming now
    Will give my foot no room to walk at large,
    But I will see him yet ere night, I vow.
                                   *Exeunt*

# Act III, scene iii

MARIAM *and* SOHEMUS

MARIAM  Sohemus, tell me what the news may be
    That makes your eyes so full, your cheeks so blue?   120

SOHEMUS  I know not how to call them. Ill for me
    'Tis sure they are: not so I hope for you.
    Herod—
MARIAM    Oh, what of Herod?
SOHEMUS                      Herod lives.
MARIAM  How! Lives? What, in some cave or forest
    hid?
SOHEMUS  Nay, back returned with honour. Caesar
    gives
    Him greater grace then e'er Antonius did.
MARIAM  Foretell the ruin of my family,
    Tell me that I shall see our city burned,
    Tell me I shall a death disgraceful die,
    But tell me not that Herod is returned.   130
SOHEMUS  Be not impatient madam, be but mild,
    His love to you again will soon be bred.
MARIAM  I will not to his love be reconciled,
    With solemn vows I have forsworn his bed.
SOHEMUS  But you must break those vows.
MARIAM                    I'll rather break
    The heart of Mariam. Cursed is my fate.
    But speak no more to me, in vain ye speak
    To live with him I so profoundly hate.
SOHEMUS  Great queen, you must to me your pardon
    give,
    Sohemus cannot now your will obey:   140
    If your command should me to silence drive,
    It were not to obey, but to betray.
    Reject and slight my speeches, mock my faith,
    Scorn my observance, call my counsel nought:
    Though you regard not what Sohemus saith,
    Yet will I ever freely speak my thought.
    I fear ere long I shall fair Mariam see
    In woeful state, and by herself undone:
    Yet for your issue's sake more temp'rate be,
    The heart by affability is won.   150
MARIAM  And must I to my prison turn again?
    Oh, now I see I was an hypocrite:
    I did this morning for his death complain,
    And yet do mourn, because he lives, ere night.
    When I his death believed, compassion wrought,
    And was the stickler 'twixt my heart and him;
    But now that curtain's drawn from off my thought,
    Hate doth appear again with visage grim,
    And paints the face of Herod in my heart,
    In horrid colours with detested look;   160
    Then fear would come, but scorn doth play her part,
    And saith that scorn with fear can never brook.
    I know I could enchain him with a smile,
    And lead him captive with a gentle word.
    I scorn my look should ever man beguile,
    Or other speech than meaning to afford.

---

102  detect: expose to scandal

137  speak: i.e. urge me
166  other . . . afford: or say anything other than what I mean

Else Salome in vain might spend her wind,
In vain might Herod's mother whet her tongue:
In vain had they complotted and combined,
For I could overthrow them all ere long.                 170
Oh what a shelter is mine innocence,
To shield me from the pangs of inward grief:
'Gainst all mishaps it is my fair defence,
And to my sorrows yields a large relief.
To be commandress of the triple earth,
And sit in safety, from a fall secure,
To have all nations celebrate my birth,
I would not that my spirit were impure.
Let my distressèd state unpitied be,
Mine innocence is hope enough for me.              *Exit*
SOHEMUS  Poor guiltless queen. Oh that my wish might
        place                                         181
A little temper now about thy heart:
Unbridled speech is Mariam's worst disgrace,
And will endanger her without desert.
I am in greater hazard. O'er my head,
The fatal axe doth hang unsteadily;
My disobedience once discovered,
Will shake it down: Sohemus so shall die.
For when the king shall find we thought his death
Had been as certain as we see his life,              190
And marks withal I slighted so his breath
As to preserve alive his matchless wife—
Nay more, to give to Alexander's hand
The regal dignity, the sovereign power,
How I had yielded up at her command
The strength of all the city, David's tower—
What more than common death may I expect,
Since I too well do know his cruelty?
'Twere death a word of Herod's to neglect,

What then to do directly contrary?                   200
Yet life I quit thee with a willing spirit,
And think thou could'st not better be employed:
I forfeit thee for her that more doth merit,
Ten such were better dead than she destroyed.
But fare thee well, chaste queen, well may I see
The darkness palpable, and rivers part;
The sun stand still, nay more, retorted be,
But never woman with so pure a heart.
Thine eyes' grave majesty keeps all in awe,
And cuts the wings of every loose desire;            210
Thy brow is table to the modest law,
Yet though we dare not love, we may admire.
And if I die, it shall my soul content,
My breath in Mariam's service shall be spent.       *Exit*

CHORUS
'Tis not enough for one that is a wife
To keep her spotless from an act of ill,
But from suspicion she should free her life,
And bare her self of power as well as will.
    'Tis not so glorious for her to be free,
    As by her proper self restrained to be.         220

When she hath spacious ground to walk upon,
Why on the ridge should she desire to go?
It is no glory to forbear alone
Those things that may her honour overthrow.
    But 'tis thankworthy, if she will not take
    All lawful liberties for honour's sake.

That wife her hand against her fame doth rear,
That more than to her lord alone will give
A private word to any second ear,
And though she may with reputation live,             230
    Yet though most chaste, she doth her glory blot,
    And wounds her honour, though she kills it not.

When to their husbands they themselves do bind,
Do they not wholly give themselves away?
Or give they but their body, not their mind,
Reserving that, though best, for others' prey?
    No sure, their thoughts no more can be their own,
    And therefore should to none but one be known.

---

175  triple earth: eds offer various glosses: the heavens, seas
     and underworld (Cerasano and Wynne-Davies); the
     known world, consisting of Europe, Asia and Africa
     (Fitzmaurice *et al.*); a reference to Antony's interest in
     her, Antony being one of the triumvirate who ruled
     Rome (Purkiss); and an allusive repetition of Mariam's
     comparison of herself with Cleopatra, as in I.ii.199–202
     (Weller and Ferguson). Purkiss and Weller and Ferguson
     note a parallel with *Antony and Cleopatra* I.i.12, which it
     almost certainly predates. Compare with the reference to
     'the triple world' in Jonson's *The Masque of Blackness*,
     l. 240 and note
182  temper: moderation
186  fatal axe . . . unsteadily: reference to the sword of
     Damocles. Dionysius hung a sword by a single hair above
     Damocles' head to illustrate to him the instability of regal
     fortune
191  breath: command
193  Alexander's: some eds emend to 'Alexandra', but this
     seems unnecessary, given that Alexander is the name of
     Mariam's son; see the discussion between Mariam and
     Alexandra in I.ii

206  darkness . . . part: reference to the one of the plagues of
     Egypt and to the parting of the Red Sea; see Exodus
     10.21 and 14.21–2
207  retorted be: be turned back in its course; see Joshua
     10.12–14
210  cuts the wings: allusion to Cupid, the winged god of
     love
211  table: i.e. tablet
218  bare: condenses sense of 'bar' as well as 'bare'
223  alone: only
236  prey: eds (pray Q). It would also be possible to read the
     line thus: '. . . for others, pray?'

Then she usurps upon another's right,
That seeks to be by public language graced, 240
And though her thoughts reflect with purest light,
Her mind, if not peculiar, is not chaste.
　For in a wife it is no worse to find
　A common body, than a common mind.

And every mind though free from thought of ill,
That out of glory seeks a worth to show,
When any's ears but one therewith they fill,
Doth in a sort her pureness overthrow.
　Now Mariam had, but that to this she bent,
　Been free from fear, as well as innocent. 250

# Act IV, scene i

*Enter* HEROD *and his* ATTENDANTS

HEROD　Hail happy city, happy in thy store,
　And happy that thy buildings such we see;
　More happy in the temple where w'adore,
　But most of all that Mariam lives in thee.

*Enter* NUNTIO

　Art thou returned? How fares my Mariam?
NUNTIO　She's well my lord, and will anon be here
　As you commanded.
HEROD　　　　　　Muffle up thy brow,
　Thou day's dark taper. Mariam will appear,
　And where she shines, we need not thy dim light.
　Oh haste thy steps, rare creature, speed thy pace, 10
　And let thy presence make the day more bright,
　And cheer the heart of Herod with thy face.
　It is an age since I from Mariam went,
　Methinks our parting was in David's days:
　The hours are so increased by discontent,
　Deep sorrow, Joshua-like, the season stays.
　But when I am with Mariam, time runs on:
　Her sight can make months minutes, days of weeks,
　An hour is then no sooner come than gone,
　When in her face mine eye for wonders seeks. 20
　You world-commanding city, Europe's grace,
　Twice hath my curious eye your streets surveyed,
　And I have seen the statue-fillèd place,
　That once if not for grief had been betrayed.
　I all your Roman beauties have beheld,

And seen the shows your aediles did prepare,
I saw the sum of what in you excelled,
Yet saw no miracle like Mariam rare.
The fair and famous Livia, Caesar's love,
The world's commanding mistress did I see, 30
Whose beauties both the world and Rome approve;
Yet Mariam, Livia is not like to thee.
Be patient but a little while, mine eyes
Within your compassed limits be contained:
That object straight shall your desires suffice,
From which you were so long a while restrained.
How wisely Mariam doth the time delay,
Lest sudden joy my sense should suffocate;
I am prepared, thou needst no longer stay.
Who's there? My Mariam, more than happy fate? 40
Oh no, it is Pheroras; welcome brother.
Now for a while, I must my passion smother.

# Act IV, scene ii

HEROD, PHERORAS

PHERORAS　All health and safety wait upon my lord,
　And may you long in prosperous fortunes live
　With Rome-commanding Caesar at accord,
　And have all honours that the world can give.
HEROD　Oh brother, now thou speak'st not from thy
　　heart.
　No, thou hast struck a blow at Herod's love,
　That cannot quickly from my memory part,
　Though Salome did me to pardon move. 50
　Valiant Phasaelus, now to thee farewell,
　Thou wert my kind and honourable brother;
　Oh hapless hour, when you self-stricken fell,
　Thou father's image, glory of thy mother.
　Had I desired a greater suit of thee,
　Than to withhold thee from a harlot's bed,
　Thou wouldst have granted it; but now I see
　All are not like that in a womb are bred.
　Thou wouldst not, hadst thou heard of Herod's
　　death,
　Have made his burial time thy bridal hour; 60
　Thou wouldst with clamours, not with joyful breath,
　Have showed the news to be not sweet but sour.
PHERORAS　Phasaelus' great worth I know did stain
　Pheroras' petty valour; but they lie
　(Excepting you yourself) that dare maintain
　That he did honour Herod more than I.
　For what I showed, love's power constrained me
　　show,

---

242　peculiar: private, exclusive to one person
249　but . . . bent: if not for her inclination to speak
　1　store: plenty
　5　Art . . . Mariam?: this line appears before the SD in Q
　8　taper: candle, i.e. the sun
　14　David's days: i.e. some thousand years ago
　16　Joshua-like: see Joshua 10.12–13, where he makes the sun
　　and moon stand still
　21　city: i.e. Rome

26　aediles: officials in charge of supervising (amongst other
　things) the city's public games
29　Livia: Livia Drusilla, wife of Caesar Augustus
51　Phasaelus: Herod's brother, who committed suicide
　when taken prisoner of war

And pardon loving faults for Mariam's sake.
HEROD  Mariam, where is she?
PHEROAS                           Nay, I do not know,
But absent use of her fair name I make;                    70
You have forgiven greater faults than this,
For Constabarus, that against your will
Preserved the sons of Babas, lives in bliss,
Though you commanded him the youths to kill.
HEROD  Go, take a present order for his death,
And let those traitors feel the worst of fears.
Now Salome will whine to beg his breath,
But I'll be deaf to prayers, and blind to tears.
PHEROAS  He is, my lord, from Salome divorced,
Though her affection did to leave him grieve;            80
Yet was she by her love to you enforced
To leave the man that would your foes relieve.
HEROD  Then haste them to their death. (*Exit*
  PHEROAS) I will requite
Thee gentle Mariam—Salome, I mean;
The thought of Mariam doth so steal my spirit,
My mouth from speech of her I cannot wean.

# Act IV, scene iii

HEROD, MARIAM

HEROD  And here she comes indeed; happily met
My best and dearest half. What ails my dear?
Thou dost the difference certainly forget
'Twixt dusky habits and a time so clear.                   90
MARIAM  My lord, I suit my garment to my mind,
And there no cheerful colours can I find.
HEROD  Is this my welcome? Have I longed so much
To see my dearest Mariam discontent?
What is't that is the cause thy heart to touch?
Oh speak, that I thy sorrow may prevent.
Art thou not Jewry's queen, and Herod's too?
Be my commandress, be my sovereign guide;
To be by thee directed I will woo,
For in thy pleasure lies my highest pride.              100
Or if thou think Judea's narrow bound
Too strict a limit for thy great command,
Thou shalt be empress of Arabia crowned,
For thou shalt rule, and I will win the land.
I'll rob the holy David's sepulchre
To give thee wealth, if thou for wealth do care:
Thou shalt have all they did with him inter,
And I for thee will make the temple bare.
MARIAM  I neither have of power nor riches want,
I have enough, nor do I wish for more;                   110

Your offers to my heart no ease can grant,
Except they could my brother's life restore.
No, had you wished the wretched Mariam glad,
Or had your love to her been truly tied,
Nay, had you not desired to make her sad,
My brother nor my grandsire had not died.
HEROD  Wilt thou believe no oaths to clear thy lord?
How oft have I with execration sworn?
Thou art by me belov'd, by me adored,
Yet are my protestations heard with scorn.              120
Hircanus plotted to deprive my head
Of this long settled honour that I wear:
And therefore I did justly doom him dead,
To rid the realm from peril, me from fear.
Yet I for Mariam's sake do so repent
The death of one whose blood she did inherit:
I wish I had a kingdom's treasure spent,
So I had ne'er expelled Hircanus' spirit.
As I affected that same noble youth,
In lasting infamy my name enrol,                        130
If I not mourned his death with hearty truth.
Did I not show to him my earnest love,
When I to him the priesthood did restore?
And did for him a living priest remove,
Which never had been done but once before.
MARIAM  I know that moved by importunity,
You made him priest, and shortly after die.
HEROD  I will not speak, unless to be believed,
This froward humour will not do you good;
It hath too much already Herod grieved,                 140
To think that you on terms of hate have stood.
Yet smile my dearest Mariam, do but smile,
And I will all unkind conceits exile.
MARIAM  I cannot frame disguise, nor never taught
My face a look dissenting from my thought.
HEROD  By heav'n you vex me; build not on my love.
MARIAM  I will not build on so unstable ground.
HEROD  Nought is so fixed, but peevishness may move.
MARIAM  'Tis better slightest cause than none were
  found.
HEROD  Be judge yourself, if ever Herod sought          150
Or would be moved a cause of change to find;
Yet let your look declare a milder thought,
My heart again you shall to Mariam bind.
How oft did I for you my mother chide,
Revile my sister, and my brother rate,
And tell them all my Mariam they belied;
Distrust me still, if these be signs of hate.

---

75  present: immediate
90  habits: clothing
105  I'll rob . . . sepulchre: Josephus gives an account of
  Herod's raid on the tomb of Solomon and David after
  Mariam's death

---

128  Disruption to both the rhyme scheme and the sense at
  this point suggests that a line following this one may be
  missing
129  noble youth: i.e. Aristobolus
139  froward: peevish, rebellious
143  conceits: judgements, opinions; imaginings
155  rate: berate

# Act IV, scene iv

*Enter* BUTLER

HEROD What hast thou here?
BUTLER                     A drink procuring love;
    The queen desired me to deliver it.
MARIAM  Did I? Some hateful practice this will prove,
    Yet can it be no worse than heavens permit.          **161**
HEROD  Confess the truth, thou wicked instrument
    To her outrageous will; 'tis poison sure;
    Tell true, and thou shalt 'scape the punishment
    Which if thou do conceal thou shalt endure.
BUTLER  I know not, but I doubt it be no less,
    Long since the hate of you her heart did cease.
HEROD  Know'st thou the cause thereof?
BUTLER                     My lord, I guess
    Sohemus told the tale that did displease.
HEROD  Oh heaven! Sohemus false! Go, let him die, **170**
    Stay not to suffer him to speak a word:  *Exit* BUTLER
    Oh damnèd villain, did he falsify
    The oath he swore ev'n of his own accord?
    Now do I know thy falsehood, painted devil,
    Thou white enchantress. Oh thou art so foul,
    That hyssop cannot cleanse thee, worst of evil.
    A beauteous body hides a loathsome soul.
    Your love, Sohemus, moved by his affection,
    Though he have ever heretofore been true,
    Did blab forsooth, that I did give direction,          **180**
    If we were put to death, to slaughter you.
    And you in black revenge attended now
    To add a murder to your breach of vow.
MARIAM  Is this a dream?
HEROD                     Oh heaven, that t'were no
        more;
    I'll give my realm to who can prove it so.
    I would I were like any begger poor,
    So I for false my Mariam did not know.
    Foul pith contained in the fairest rind
    That ever graced a cedar. Oh thine eye
    Is pure as heaven, but impure thy mind,                 **190**
    And for impurity shall Mariam die.
    Why didst thou love Sohemus?
MARIAM                     They can tell
    That say I loved him; Mariam says not so.
HEROD  Oh, cannot impudence the coals expel
    That for thy love in Herod's bosom glow;
    It is as plain as water, and denial
    Makes of thy falsehood but a greater trial.

Hast thou beheld thyself, and couldst thou stain
So rare perfection? Even for love of thee
I do profoundly hate thee. Wert thou plain,          **200**
Thou shouldst the wonder of Judea be.
But oh, thou art not. Hell itself lies hid
Beneath thy heavenly show. Yet wert thou chaste,
Thou mightst exalt, pull down, command, forbid,
And be above the wheel of fortune placed.
Hadst thou complotted Herod's massacre,
That so thy son a monarch might be styled,
Not half so grievous such an action were,
As once to think, that Mariam is defiled.
Bright workmanship of nature sullied o'er          **210**
With pitchèd darkness now thine end shall be:
Thou shalt not live, fair fiend, to cozen more,
With heav'nly semblance, as thou coz'nedst me.
Yet must I love thee in despite of death,
And thou shalt die in the despite of love:
For neither shall my love prolong thy breath,
Nor shall thy loss of breath my love remove.
I might have seen thy falsehood in thy face:
Where couldst thou get thy stars that served for eyes
Except by theft, and theft is foul disgrace?          **220**
This had appeared before, were Herod wise,
But I'm a sot, a very sot, no better;
My wisdom long ago a-wand'ring fell;
Thy face encount'ring it, my wit did fetter,
And made me for delight my freedom sell.
Give me my heart, false creature; 'tis a wrong
My guiltless heart should now with thine be slain;
Thou hadst no right to lock it up so long,
And with usurper's name, I Mariam stain.

*Enter* BUTLER

HEROD  Have you designed Sohemus to his end?          **230**
BUTLER  I have, my lord.
HEROD                     Then call our royal guard
    To do as much for Mariam. (*Exit* BUTLER) They
        offend
    Leave ill unblamed, or good without reward.

*Enter* SOLDIERS

    Here, take her to her death. Come back, come back;
    What, meant I to deprive the world of light,
    To muffle Jewry in the foulest black,
    That ever was an opposite to white?
    Why, whither would you carry her?
SOLDIER                     You bade
    We should conduct her to her death, my lord.

---

160  practice: plot
163  poison: eds (passion Q). The emendation is made on the
     grounds of both sense and the account given in Josephus;
     some eds retain 'passion'
176  hyssop: herb used in Jewish ceremonial purification
182  attended: waited

---

203  Yet wert: eds (Yet never wert Q); on the grounds of
     sense and metre we follow Purkiss and Cerasano and
     Wynne-Davies in this emendation
213  heav'nly: eds (heavy Q)
232–3  They offend/Leave: i.e. they offend who leave

HEROD  Why, sure I did not, Herod was not mad;    240
 Why should she feel the fury of the sword?
 Oh, now the grief returns into my heart,
 And pulls me piecemeal: love and hate do fight;
 And now hath love acquired the greater part,
 Yet now hath hate, affection conquered quite.
 And therefore bear her hence; and Hebrew, why
 Seize you with lion's paws the fairest lamb
 Of all the flock? She must not, shall not, die;
 Without her I most miserable am.
 And with her more than most; away, away,    250
 But bear her but to prison, not to death.
 And is she gone indeed? Stay, villains, stay;
 Her looks alone preserved your sovereign's breath.
 Well, let her go; but yet she shall not die;
 I cannot think she meant to poison me.
 But certain 'tis she lived too wantonly,
 And therefore shall she never more be free.

          *Exeunt*

## Act IV, scene v

BUTLER

BUTLER  Foul villain, can thy pitchy-coloured soul
 Permit thine ear to hear her causeless doom,
 And not enforce thy tongue that tale control,    260
 That must unjustly bring her to her tomb?
 Oh Salome, thou hast thyself repaid
 For all the benefits that thou hast done;
 Thou art the cause I have the queen betrayed,
 Thou hast my heart to darkest falsehood won.
 I am condemned, heav'n gave me not my tongue
 To slander innocents, to lie, deceive,
 To be the hateful instrument to wrong,
 The earth of greatest glory to bereave.
 My sin ascends and doth to heaven cry,    270
 It is the blackest deed that ever was;
 And there doth sit an angel notary
 That doth record it down, in leaves of brass.
 Oh how my heart doth quake. Achitophel,
 Thou foundst a means thyself from shame to free;
 And sure my soul approves thou didst not well;
 All follow some, and I will follow thee.

          *Exit*

## Act IV, scene vi

CONSTABARUS, BABAS' SONS, *and their* GUARD

CONSTABARUS  Now here we step our last, the way to
  death,
 We must not tread this way a second time;
 Yet let us resolutely yield our breath,    280
 Death is the only ladder, heav'n to climb.
BABAS' FIRST SON  With willing mind I could myself
  resign,
 But yet it grieves me with a grief untold,
 Our death should be accompanied with thine,
 Our friendship we to thee have dearly sold.
CONSTABARUS  Still wilt thou wrong the sacred name of
  friend?
 Then shouldst thou never style it friendship more,
 But base mechanic traffic that doth lend,
 Yet will be sure they shall the debt restore.
 I could with needless compliment return,    290
 'Tis for thy ceremony, I could say,
 'Tis I that made the fire your house to burn,
 For but for me she would not you betray.
 Had not the damnèd woman sought mine end,
 You had not been the subject of her hate;
 You never did her hateful mind offend,
 Nor could your deaths have freed her nuptial fate.
 Therefore fair friends, though you were still unborn,
 Some other subtlety devised should be,
 Whereby my life, though guiltless, should be torn; 300
 Thus have I proved, 'tis you that die for me.
 And therefore should I weakly now lament,
 You have but done your duties; friends should die
 Alone, their friends' disaster to prevent,
 Though not compelled by strong necessity.
 But now farewell fair city, never more
 Shall I behold your beauty shining bright;
 Farewell, of Jewish men the worthy store,
 But no farewell to any female wight.
 You wavering crew: my curse to you I leave,    310
 You had but one to give you any grace,
 And you yourselves will Mariam's life bereave;
 Your commonwealth doth innocency chase.
 You creatures made to be the human curse,
 You tigers, lionesses, hungry bears,
 Tear-massacring hyenas; nay, far worse,
 For they for prey do shed their feignèd tears,

---

259 causeless: eds (caules Q)
275 Thou foundst . . . free: Achitophel was a counsellor to
 David and plotted his overthrow with Absalom, David's
 son. Achitophel hanged himself when Absalom
 disregarded his advice; see 2 Samuel 17.23

287 style: call
288 base . . . traffic: low commercial transaction
289 they: i.e. those who borrow
297 her: Weller and Ferguson (your Q). We follow Weller
 and Ferguson's emendation
310 wavering crew: i.e. women
316 Tear-massacring hyenas: hyenas were said to produce
 tears as they devoured their prey

But you will weep (you creatures cross to good)
For your unquenchèd thirst of human blood.
You were the angels cast from heav'n for pride, 320
And still do keep your angels' outward show,
But none of you are inly beautified,
For still your heav'n-depriving pride doth grow.
Did not the sins of man require a scourge,
Your place on earth had been by this withstood;
But since a flood no more the world must purge,
You stayed in office of a second flood.
You giddy creatures, sowers of debate,
You'll love today, and for no other cause
But for you yesterday did deeply hate; 330
You are the wreck of order, breach of laws.
Your best are foolish, froward, wanton, vain,
Your worst, adulterous, murderous, cunning, proud,
And Salome attends the latter train,
Or rather she their leader is allowed.
I do the sottishness of men bewail,
That do with following you enhance your pride:
'Twere better that the human race should fail,
Than be by such a mischief multiplied.
Cham's servile curse to all your sex was given, 340
Because in Paradise you did offend;
Then do we not resist the will of heaven,
When on your wills like servants we attend?
You are to nothing constant but to ill,
You are with nought but wickedness indued;
Your loves are set on nothing but your will,
And thus my censure I of you conclude.
You are the least of goods, the worst of evils,
Your best are worse then men, your worst than devils.

BABAS' SECOND SON Come, let us to our death; are we
not blest? 350
Our death will freedom from these creatures give,
Those trouble-quiet sowers of unrest;
And this I vow, that had I leave to live,
I would for ever lead a single life,
And never venture on a devilish wife.

*Exeunt*

---

318 cross to: opposed to
324 man: eds (many Q)
325 by this: by now
326 a flood . . . purge: see Genesis 9.11
327 in office of: in place of
332 froward: see IV.iii.139n
340–1 Cham's . . . offend: these lines conflate two Old
Testament curses: 1) Cham or (Ham), the son of Noah,
was condemned to servitude when he brought his
brothers to see their father drunk and naked, instead of
covering him; see Genesis 9.22, 25; 2) the curse of Eve for
her transgression in Eden; see Genesis 3.16

# Act IV, scene vii

HEROD *and* SALOME

HEROD Nay, she shall die. Die, quoth you; that she
shall;
But for the means. The means! Methinks 'tis hard
To find a means to murder her withal,
Therefore I am resolved she shall be spared.
SALOME Why, let her be beheaded.
HEROD That were well;
Think you that swords are miracles like you? 361
Her skin will every curtlax-edge refel,
And then your enterprise you well may rue.
What if the fierce Arabian notice take,
Of this your wretched weaponless estate:
They answer, when we bid resistance make,
That Mariam's skin their falchions did rebate.
Beware of this; you make a goodly hand,
If you of weapons do deprive our land.
SALOME Why, drown her then.
HEROD Indeed a sweet device;
Why, would not every river turn her course 371
Rather than do her beauty prejudice,
And be reverted to the proper source?
So not a drop of water should be found
In all Judea's quondam fertile ground.
SALOME Then let the fire devour her.
HEROD 'Twill not be;
Flame is from her derived into my heart:
Thou nursest flame, flame will not murder thee,
My fairest Mariam, fullest of desert.
SALOME Then let her live for me.
HEROD Nay, she shall die;
But can you live without her?
SALOME Doubt you that? 381
HEROD I'm sure I cannot; I beseech you try.
I have experience but I know not what.
SALOME How should I try?
HEROD Why, let my love be slain;
But if we cannot live without her sight
You'll find the means to make her breathe again,
Or else you will bereave my comfort quite.
SALOME Oh aye, I warrant you. *Exit*
HEROD What, is she gone,
And gone to bid the world be overthrown?
What, is her heart's composure hardest stone? 390
To what a pass are cruel women grown?

---

362 curtlax: variant of curtal-ax (cutlass): a short, broad sword
refel: repulse
367 falchions: see II.ii.159n
rebate: blunt
375 quondam: once
377 derived: conducted
380 for me: as far as I am concerned

*Enter* SALOME

She is returned already; have you done?
Is't possible you can command so soon
A creature's heart to quench the flaming sun,
Or from the sky to wipe away the moon?
SALOME If Mariam be the sun and moon, it is,
For I already have commanded this.
HEROD But have you seen her cheek?
SALOME                                    A thousand times.
HEROD But did you mark it too?
SALOME                                    Aye, very well.
HEROD What is't?
SALOME                    A crimson bush, that ever limes    400
The soul whose foresight doth not much excel.
HEROD Send word she shall not die. Her cheek a
    bush—
Nay, then I see indeed you marked it not.
SALOME 'Tis very fair, but yet will never blush,
Though foul dishonours do her forehead blot.
HEROD Then let her die, 'tis very true indeed,
And for this fault alone shall Mariam bleed.
SALOME What fault, my lord?
HEROD                                    What fault is't? You that
    ask,
If you be ignorant, I know of none,
To call her back from death shall be your task;    410
I'm glad that she for innocent is known.
For on the brow of Mariam hangs a fleece
Whose slenderest twine is strong enough to bind
The hearts of kings; the pride and shame of Greece,
Troy-flaming Helen's, not so fairly shined.
SALOME 'Tis true indeed, she lays them out for nets,
To catch the hearts that do not shun a bait;
'Tis time to speak, for Herod sure forgets
That Mariam's very tresses hide deceit.
HEROD Oh, do they so? Nay, then you do but well;    420
In sooth I thought it had been hair.
Nets call you them? Lord, how they do excel;
I never saw a net that showed so fair.
But have you heard her speak?
SALOME                                    You know I have.
HEROD And were you not amazed?
SALOME                                    No, not a whit.
HEROD Then 'twas not her you heard; her life I'll save,
For Mariam hath a world-amazing wit.

SALOME She speaks a beauteous language, but within
Her heart is false as powder; and her tongue
Doth but allure the auditors to sin,                    430
And is the instrument to do you wrong.
HEROD It may be so; nay, 'tis so: she's unchaste;
Her mouth will ope to every stranger's ear.
Then let the executioner make haste,
Lest she enchant him, if her words he hear.
Let him be deaf, lest she do him surprise
That shall to free her spirit be assigned.
Yet what boots deafness if he have his eyes?
Her murderer must be both deaf and blind.
For if he see, he needs must see the stars            440
That shine on either side of Mariam's face,
Whose sweet aspect will terminate the wars,
Wherewith he should a soul so precious chase.
Her eyes can speak, and in their speaking move;
Oft did my heart with reverence receive
The world's mandates. Pretty tales of love
They utter, which can human bondage weave.
But shall I let this heaven's model die,
Which for a small self-portraiture she drew?
Her eyes like stars, her forehead like the sky,       450
She is like heaven, and must be heavenly true.
SALOME Your thoughts do rave with doting on the
    queen:
Her eyes are ebon-hued, and you'll confess
A sable star hath been but seldom seen;
Then speak of reason more, of Mariam less.
HEROD Yourself are held a goodly creature here,
Yet so unlike my Mariam in your shape,
That when to her you have approachèd near,
Myself hath often ta'en you for an ape.
And yet you prate of beauty; go your ways,            460
You are to her a sunburnt blackamoor;
Your paintings cannot equal Mariam's praise,
Her nature is so rich, you are so poor.
Let her be stayed from death, for if she die,
We do we know not what to stop her breath;
A world cannot another Mariam buy.
Why stay you lingering? Countermand her death.
SALOME Then you'll no more remember what hath
    passed;
Sohemus' love and hers shall be forgot.
'Tis well in truth: that fault may be her last,       470
And she may mend, though yet she love you not.
HEROD Oh God, 'tis true: Sohemus. Earth and heav'n,
Why did you both conspire to make me cursed,

---

399 mark: note
400 limes: ensnares, as with birdlime (a sticky substance used
    to trap birds)
412 fleece: hair; probably also alludes to the highly prized
    Golden Fleece of Colchis
415 Troy . . . Helen: the recovery of Helen, who had eloped
    with (or was abducted by) Paris, prince of Troy, was the
    ostensible object of the Trojan War. Troy was eventually
    burnt down by the Greeks in revenge

---

429 powder: either a) gunpowder, noted for its volatility; or
    b) cosmetic powder
449 she: i.e. heaven
454 sable: heraldic term for 'black'
462 paintings: effects achieved with cosmetics
465 to stop her breath: in stopping her breath

In coz'ning me with shows, and proofs unev'n?
She showed the best, and yet did prove the worst.
Her show was such, as had our singing king,
The holy David, Mariam's beauty seen,
The Hittite had then felt no deadly sting,
Nor Bethsabe had never been a queen.
Or had his son, the wisest man of men,             480
Whose fond delight did most consist in change,
Beheld her face, he had been stayed again;
No creature having her can wish to range.
Had Asuerus seen my Mariam's brow,
The humble Jew, she might have walked alone:
Her beauteous virtue should have stayed below,
Whiles Mariam mounted to the Persian throne.
But what avails it all? For in the weight
She is deceitful, light as vanity;
Oh, she was made for nothing but a bait,            490
To train some hapless man to misery.
I am the hapless man that have been trained
To endless bondage. I will see her yet.
Methinks I should discern her if she feigned;
Can human eyes be dazed by woman's wit?
Once more these eyes of mine with hers shall meet,
Before the headsman do her life bereave.
Shall I for ever part from thee, my sweet,
Without the taking of my latest leave?
SALOME  You had as good resolve to save her now;   500
I'll stay her death, 'tis well determinèd:
For sure she never more will break her vow,
Sohemus and Josephus both are dead.
HEROD  She shall not live, nor will I see her face;
A long-healed wound a second time doth bleed.
With Joseph I remember her disgrace;
A shameful end ensues a shameful deed.
Oh, that I had not called to mind anew
The discontent of Mariam's wavering heart;
'Twas you, you foul-mouthed Ate, none but you,     510
That did the thought hereof to me impart.

---

474  unev'n: unjust
476  singing king: David, author of the Psalms
478–9  The Hittite . . . queen: David had an adulterous
      relationship with Bathsheba ('Bethsabe'). When she
      became pregnant, he arranged for her husband, Uriah the
      Hittite, to be killed in battle so that he could marry her;
      see 2 Samuel 11
480–1  his son . . . change: Solomon was noted both for his
      wisdom and for his numerous wives and concubines; see 1
      Kings 11.1–8
485  The humble Jew: Esther, noted for her beauty, became the
      second wife of Ahasuerus, the Persian king; see Esther 2
488  weight: scales
491  train: lure
501  determinèd: resolved
507  ensues: follows
510  Ate: daughter of Zeus, goddess of evil, who incites men
      to wickedness and strife

Hence from my sight, my black tormenter, hence;
For hadst not thou made Herod unsecure,
I had not doubted Mariam's innocence,
But still had held her in my heart for pure.
SALOME  I'll leave you to your passion; 'tis no time
To purge me now, though of a guiltless crime.    *Exit*
HEROD  Destruction take thee; thou hast made my heart
As heavy as revenge. I am so dull,
Methinks I am not sensible of smart,              520
Though hideous horrors at my bosom pull.
My head weighs downwards; therefore will I go
To try if I can sleep away my woe.

                                                   *Exit*

# Act IV, scene viii

MARIAM

MARIAM  Am I the Mariam that presumed so much,
And deemed my face must needs preserve my breath?
Aye, I it was that thought my beauty such,
As it alone could countermand my death.
Now death will teach me: he can pale as well
A cheek of roses as a cheek less bright,
And dim an eye whose shine doth most excel,       530
As soon as one that casts a meaner light.
Had not myself against myself conspired,
No plot, no adversary from without,
Could Herod's love from Mariam have retired,
Or from his heart have thrust my semblance out.
The wanton queen that never loved for love,
False Cleopatra, wholly set on gain,
With all her sleights did prove, yet vainly prove,
For her the love of Herod to obtain.
Yet her allurements, all her courtly guile,       540
Her smiles, her favours, and her smooth deceit,
Could not my face from Herod's mind exile,
But were with him of less than little weight.
That face and person that in Asia late
For beauty's goddess, Paphos' queen, was ta'en:
That face that did captive great Julius' fate,
That very face that was Antonius' bane.
That face that to be Egypt's pride was born,
That face that all the world esteemed so rare,
Did Herod hate, despise, neglect, and scorn,      550
When with the same, he Mariam's did compare.
This made that I improvidently wrought,
And on the wager even my life did pawn;
Because I thought, and yet but truly thought,
That Herod's love could not from me be drawn.
But now, though out of time, I plainly see
It could be drawn, though never drawn from me;

---

538  prove: try
545  Paphos' queen: Venus, goddess of love and beauty, who,
      according to legend, rose from the sea near Paphos

Had I but with humility been graced,
As well as fair I might have proved me wise;
But I did think because I knew me chaste,          560
One virtue for a woman might suffice.
That mind for glory of our sex might stand,
Wherein humility and chastity
Doth march with equal paces hand in hand;
But one, if single seen, who setteth by?
And I had singly one, but 'tis my joy,
That I was ever innocent, though sour;
And therefore can they but my life destroy,
My soul is free from adversary's power.

*Enter* DORIS

You princes great in power, and high in birth,    570
Be great and high, I envy not your hap;
Your birth must be from dust, your power on earth;
In heav'n shall Mariam sit in Sara's lap.
DORIS  In heav'n! Your beauty cannot bring you thither;
Your soul is black and spotted, full of sin:
You in adult'ry lived nine year together,
And heav'n will never let adult'ry in.
MARIAM  What art thou that dost poor Mariam pursue?
Some spirit sent to drive me to despair,
Who sees for truth that Mariam is untrue?        580
If fair she be, she is as chaste as fair.
DORIS  I am that Doris that was once beloved,
Beloved by Herod, Herod's lawful wife;
'Twas you that Doris from his side removed,
And robbed from me the glory of my life.
MARIAM  Was that adult'ry? Did not Moses say
That he that being matched did deadly hate,
Might by permission put his wife away,
And take a more beloved to be his mate?
DORIS  What did he hate me for? For simple truth?   590
For bringing beauteous babes for love to him?
For riches? Noble birth, or tender youth?
Or for no stain did Doris' honour dim?
Oh, tell me Mariam, tell me if you know,
Which fault of these made Herod Doris' foe.
These thrice three years have I with hands held up,
And bowèd knees fast nailèd to the ground,
Besought for thee the dregs of that same cup,
That cup of wrath that is for sinners found.
And now thou art to drink it: Doris' curse       600
Upon thyself did all this while attend,
But now it shall pursue thy children worse.
MARIAM  Oh Doris, now to thee my knees I bend,

That heart that never bowed to thee doth bow.
Curse not mine infants, let it thee suffice
That heav'n doth punishment to me allow.
Thy curse is cause that guiltless Mariam dies.
DORIS  Had I ten thousand tongues, and every tongue
Inflamed with poison's power and steeped in gall,
My curses would not answer for my wrong,         610
Though I in cursing thee employed them all.
Hear thou that didst Mount Gerarim command,
To be a place whereon with cause to curse:
Stretch thy revenging arm, thrust forth thy hand,
And plague the mother much, the children worse.
Throw flaming fire upon the baseborn heads
That were begotten in unlawful beds.
But let them live till they have sense to know
What 'tis to be in miserable state;
Then be their nearest friends their overthrow,    620
Attended be they by suspicious hate.
And Mariam, I do hope this boy of mine
Shall one day come to be the death of thine.   *Exit*
MARIAM  Oh, heaven forbid! I hope the world shall see
This curse of thine shall be returned on thee.
Now earth, farewell, though I be yet but young,
Yet I, methinks, have known thee too too long.  *Exit*

CHORUS
The fairest action of our human life
Is scorning to revenge an injury:
For who forgives without a further strife,       630
His adversary's heart to him doth tie.
    And 'tis a firmer conquest truly said,
    To win the heart than overthrow the head.

If we a worthy enemy do find,
To yield to worth, it must be nobly done;
But if of baser metal be his mind,
In base revenge there is no honour won.
    Who would a worthy courage overthrow,
    And who would wrestle with a worthless foe?

We say our hearts are great and cannot yield;    640
Because they cannot yield it proves them poor.
Great hearts are tasked beyond their power but seld.
The weakest lion will the loudest roar.
    Truth's school for certain doth this same allow,
    High-heartedness doth sometimes teach to bow.

---

565  setteth by: takes account of
566  I . . . one: i.e. I had only one of the two virtues
573  Sara's: Sarah was the wife of Abraham and 'mother' of
     the Jewish people; 'Sara's lap' is a feminine equivalent to
     'the bosom of Abraham' (i.e. 'heaven')
599  cup of wrath: see Isaiah 51.17 and Revelation 16.19

612  Mount Gerarim: probably refers to Mount Gerizim,
     paired with Mount Ebal. Moses told the Israelites that
     blessings should be pronounced from the former and
     curses from the latter; see Deuteronomy 27.12–13. Cary
     seems to have confused the two. Cerasano and Wynne-
     Davies note that Mount Gerizim was the peak on which
     Abraham was to sacrifice his son Isaac
642  seld: seldom. Q is punctuated thus: ' . . . power, but
     seld/The weakest . . . '; we follow most eds in
     repunctuating in order that the sense fits the context

A noble heart doth teach a virtuous scorn:
To scorn to owe a duty over-long,
To scorn to be for benefits forborne,
To scorn to lie, to scorn to do a wrong,
    To scorn to bear an injury in mind,     650
    To scorn a free-born heart slave-like to bind.

But if for wrongs we needs revenge must have,
Then be our vengeance of the noblest kind.
Do we his body from our fury save,
And let our hate prevail against our mind?
    What can 'gainst him a greater vengeance be,
    Than make his foe more worthy far then he?

Had Mariam scorned to leave a due unpaid,
She would to Herod then have paid her love,
And not have been by sullen passion swayed.     660
To fix her thoughts all injury above
    Is virtuous pride. Had Mariam thus been proved,
    Long famous life to her had been allowed.

# Act V, scene i

NUNTIO

NUNTIO When, sweetest friend, did I so far offend
    Your heavenly self, that you, my fault to quit,
    Have made me now relator of her end,
    The end of beauty, chastity and wit?
    Was none so hapless in the fatal place
    But I, most wretched, for the queen t'choose?
    'Tis certain I have some ill-boding face
    That made me culled to tell this luckless news.
    And yet no news to Herod. Were it new
    To him, unhappy't had not been at all.     10
    Yet do I long to come within his vew,
    That he may know his wife did guiltless fall;
    And here he comes. Your Mariam greets you well.

*Enter* HEROD

HEROD What? Lives my Mariam? Joy, exceeding joy!
    She shall not die.
NUNTIO            Heav'n doth your will repel.
HEROD Oh do not with thy words my life destroy,
    I prithee tell no dying tale: thine eye
    Without thy tongue doth tell but too too much.
    Yet let thy tongue's addition make me die;
    Death welcome comes to him whose grief is such.     20
NUNTIO I went amongst the curious gazing troop,
    To see the last of her that was the best,

To see if death had heart to make her stoop,
To see the sun-admiring phoenix' nest.
When there I came, upon the way I saw
The stately Mariam not debased by fear;
Her look did seem to keep the world in awe,
Yet mildly did her face this fortune bear.
HEROD Thou dost usurp my right, my tongue was framed
    To be the instrument of Mariam's praise.     30
    Yet speak: she cannot be too often famed:
    All tongues suffice not her sweet name to raise.
NUNTIO But as she came she Alexandra met,
    Who did her death (sweet queen) no whit bewail,
    But as if nature she did quite forget,
    She did upon her daughter loudly rail.
HEROD Why stopped you not her mouth? Where had she words
    To darken that, that heaven made so bright?
    Our sacred tongue no epithet affords
    To call her other than the world's delight.     40
NUNTIO She told her that her death was too too good,
    And that already she had lived too long;
    She said, she shamed to have a part in blood
    Of her that did the princely Herod wrong.
HEROD Base pick-thank devil. Shame, 'twas all her glory,
    That she to noble Mariam was the mother.
    But never shall it live in any story:
    Her name, except to infamy, I'll smother.
    What answer did her princely daughter make?
NUNTIO She made no answer, but she looked the while,
    As if thereof she scarce did notice take,     51
    Yet smiled a dutiful, though scornful, smile.
HEROD Sweet creature, I that look to mind do call;
    Full oft hath Herod been amazed withal.
    Go on.
NUNTIO She came unmoved, with pleasant grace,
    As if to triumph her arrival were,
    In stately habit, and with cheerful face,
    Yet every eye was moist but Mariam's there.
    When justly opposite to me she came,
    She picked me out from all the crew;     60
    She beckoned to me, called me by my name,
    For she my name, my birth, and fortune knew.
HEROD What did she name thee? Happy, happy man,
    Wilt thou not ever love that name the better?
    But what sweet tune did this fair dying swan

---

648 forborne: treated leniently
653 noblest kind: Weller and Ferguson note that,
    proverbially, forgiveness is the noblest form of revenge
658 a due: probably a reference to the mutual obligations
    (often taken to be specifically sexual) of marriage: the
    'marriage debt'; see 1 Corinthians 7.3–5

24 sun-admiring . . . nest: in Egyptian mythology, the
    phoenix built itself a nest every five hundred years, on
    which it consumed itself by fire and then rose, renewed,
    from the ashes; hence, a symbol of Christ's resurrection
45 pick-thank: flattering
55 Go on: in Q, these words begin Nuntio's next speech
59 justly: precisely
65 swan: traditionally, swans were supposed to sing before
    they died

Afford thine ear? Tell all, omit no letter.
NUNTIO 'Tell thou my lord,' said she—
HEROD       Me, meant she me?
 Is't true, the more my shame: I was her lord;
 Were I not made her lord, I still should be;
 But now her name must be by me adored.  70
 Oh say, what said she more? Each word she said
 Shall be the food whereon my heart is fed.
NUNTIO 'Tell thou my lord thou saw'st me lose my
 breath.'
HEROD Oh, that I could that sentence now control.
NUNTIO 'If guiltily eternal be my death—'
HEROD I hold her chaste ev'n in my inmost soul.
NUNTIO 'By three days hence, if wishes could revive,
 I know himself would make me oft alive.'
HEROD Three days; three hours, three minutes, not so
 much,
 A minute in a thousand parts divide;  80
 My penitency for her death is such
 As in the first I wished she had not died.
 But forward in thy tale.
NUNTIO      Why, on she went,
 And after she some silent prayer had said,
 She did as if to die she were content,
 And thus to heav'n her heav'nly soul is fled.
HEROD But art thou sure there doth no life remain?
 Is't possible my Mariam should be dead?
 Is there no trick to make her breathe again?
NUNTIO Her body is divided from her head.  90
HEROD Why, yet methinks there might be found by art
 Strange ways of cure; 'tis sure rare things are done
 By an inventive head, and willing heart.
NUNTIO Let not, my lord, your fancies idly run.
 It is as possible it should be seen
 That we should make the holy Abraham live,
 Though he entombed two thousand years had been,
 As breath again to slaughtered Mariam give.
 But now for more assaults prepare your ears.
HEROD There cannot be a further cause of moan;  100
 This accident shall shelter me from fears.
 What can I fear? Already Mariam's gone.
 Yet tell ev'n what you will.
NUNTIO      As I came by
 From Mariam's death, I saw upon a tree
 A man that to his neck a cord did tie,
 Which cord he had designed his end to be.
 When me he once discerned, he downwards bowed,
 And thus with fearful voice he cried aloud,

'Go tell the king he trusted ere he tried;
 I am the cause that Mariam causeless died.'  110
HEROD Damnation take him, for it was the slave
 That said she meant with poison's deadly force
 To end my life, that she the crown might have,
 Which tale did Mariam from herself divorce.
 Oh, pardon me, thou pure unspotted ghost,
 My punishment must needs sufficient be,
 In missing that content I valued most,
 Which was thy admirable face to see.
 I had but one inestimable jewel,
 Yet one I had, no monarch had the like,  120
 And therefore may I curse myself as cruel:
 'Twas broken by a blow myself did strike.
 I gazed thereon and never thought me blessed,
 But when on it my dazzled eye might rest,
 A precious mirror made by wondrous art,
 I prized it ten times dearer than my crown,
 And laid it up fast folded in my heart.
 Yet I in sudden choler cast it down,
 And pashed it all to pieces: 'twas no foe
 That robbed me of it; no Arabian host,  130
 Nor no Armenian guide, hath used me so,
 But Herod's wretched self hath Herod crossed.
 She was my graceful moiety; me accursed,
 To slay my better half and save my worst.
 But sure she is not dead, you did but jest
 To put me in perplexity a while;
 'Twere well indeed if I could so be dressed;
 I see she is alive; methinks you smile.
NUNTIO If sainted Abel yet deceasèd be,
 'Tis certain Mariam is as dead as he.  140
HEROD Why then go call her to me, bid her now
 Put on fair habit, stately ornament,
 And let no frown o'ershade her smoothest brow,
 In her doth Herod place his whole content.
NUNTIO She'll come in stately weeds to please your
 sense,
 If now she come attired in robe of heaven;
 Remember you yourself did send her hence,
 And now to you she can no more be given.
HEROD She's dead, hell take her murderers; she was
 fair,
 Oh what a hand she had, it was so white,  150
 It did the whiteness of the snow impair:
 I never more shall see so sweet a sight.

---

69 Were . . . should be: punctuated as in Q. Some eds
  emend to 'Were I not mad, her lord I still should be'
74 sentence: 'both utterance and death sentence' (Weller
  and Ferguson)
82 first: i.e. the first thousandth of a minute
105 A man . . . tie: like Judas, following Christ's death; see
  Matthew 27.3–5

109 he trusted . . . tried: i.e. he trusted others before he
  attempted to find the truth; see Chorus 2, stanzas 1, 3
119 inestimable jewel: see Proverbs 31.10
129 pashed: smashed
133 moiety: half
137 dressed: chided
139 Abel: Adam's second son, murdered by Cain; thus a
  figure of innocence slain, and a type of Christ
145 weeds: dress

NUNTIO 'Tis true, her hand was rare.

HEROD                                Her hand? Her hands:
She had not singly one of beauty rare,
But such a pair as here where Herod stands,
He dares the world to make to both compare.
Accursèd Salome, hadst thou been still,
My Mariam had been breathing by my side:
Oh never had I, had I had my will,
Sent forth command, that Mariam should have died.
But Salome, thou didst with envy vex,                161
To see thyself outmatchèd in thy sex:
Upon your sex's forehead Mariam sat,
To grace you all like an imperial crown,
But you fond fool have rudely pushed thereat,
And proudly pulled your proper glory down.
One smile of hers, nay, not so much, a look
Was worth a hundred thousand such as you.
Judea, how canst thou the wretches brook
That robbed from thee the fairest of the crew?     170
You dwellers in the now deprivèd land,
Wherein the matchless Mariam was bred,
Why grasp not each of you a sword in hand,
To aim at me your cruel sovereign's head?
Oh, when you think of Herod as your king,
And owner of the pride of Palestine,
This act to your remembrance likewise bring,
'Tis I have overthrown your royal line.
Within her purer veins the blood did run,
That from her grandam Sara she derived,            180
Whose beldame age the love of kings hath won;
Oh, that her issue had as long been lived.
But can her eye be made by death obscure?
I cannot think but it must sparkle still;
Foul sacrilege to rob those lights so pure,
From out a temple made by heav'nly skill.
I am the villain that have done the deed,
The cruel deed, though by another's hand:
My word, though not my sword, made Mariam bleed,
Hircanus' grandchild died at my command,           190
That Mariam that I once did love so dear,
The partner of my now detested bed.
Why shine you, sun, with an aspect so clear?
I tell you once again my Mariam's dead.
You could but shine, if some Egyptian blowse,
Or Ethiopian dowdy lose her life:
This was—then wherefore bend you not your
    brows?—

The king of Jewry's fair and spotless wife.
Deny thy beams, and moon, refuse thy light,
Let all the stars be dark, let Jewry's eye          200
No more distinguish which is day and night,
Since her best birth did in her bosom die.
Those fond idolaters, the men of Greece,
Maintain these orbs are safely governèd,
That each within themselves have gods apiece,
By whom their steadfast course is justly led.
But were it so, as so it cannot be,
They all would put their mourning garments on:
Not one of them would yield a light to me,
To me that is the cause that Mariam's gone.         210
For though they feign their Saturn melancholy,
Of sour behaviours, and of angry mood,
They feign him likewise to be just and holy,
And justice needs must seek revenge for blood.
Their Jove, if Jove he were, would sure desire
To punish him that slew so fair a lass:
For Leda's beauty set his heart on fire,
Yet she not half so fair as Mariam was.
And Mars would deem his Venus had been slain,
Sol to recover her would never stick,               220
For if he want the power her life to gain,
Then physic's god is but an empiric.
The queen of love would storm for beauty's sake,
And Hermes too, since he bestowed her wit;
The night's pale light for angry grief would shake,
To see chaste Mariam die in age unfit.
But oh, I am deceived, she passed them all
In every gift, in every property;

---

161 vex: fret
169 brook: endure
180 grandam: female ancestor
181 beldame: a 'beldame' was a remote female ancestor;
    hence, here, 'grandmotherly'
195–6 blowse . . . dowdy: a 'blowse' was a ruddy, fat-faced
    wench, a slattern; a 'dowdy' was a shabby, vulgar woman;
    the references are to Cleopatra

---

204–6 these orbs . . . justly led: i.e. each planet is controlled
    by a single god. Herod refers to the planets by a mixture
    of Greek and Roman names
211 feign: Weller and Ferguson note that the extant copies of
    Q are divided equally here and two lines below between
    'faine' (meaning feign) and 'fame'. Whilst both make
    sense, we follow Weller and Ferguson in adopting 'feign',
    since the emphasis of Herod's speech is on the fictional
    nature of these beliefs
    Saturn: Roman equivalent to Greek Kronos; the ruler of
    the gods until usurped by his son Zeus; the planet was
    associated with melancholy and a harsh wisdom
215 Jove: ruler of the gods; also known as Zeus (Greek) or
    Jupiter (Roman)
217 Leda: seduced by Jove in the shape of a swan
219 Mars: Roman god of war (Ares in Greek mythology)
    Venus: Roman goddess of love (Aphrodite in Greek
    mythology)
220 Sol: the sun; Apollo
222 physic's god: Apollo, god of the sun and medicine
    empiric: quack, fraud
223 queen of love: Venus
224 Hermes: messenger of the gods, famed for his wit
    (Mercury in Roman mythology)
225 night's pale light: the moon

Her excellencies wrought her timeless fall,
And they rejoiced, not grieved, to see her die.    **230**
The Paphian goddess did repent her waste,
When she to one such beauty did allow;
Mercurius thought her wit his wit surpassed,
And Cynthia envied Mariam's brighter brow.
But these are fictions, they are void of sense,
The Greeks but dream, and dreaming falsehoods tell;
They neither can offend nor give defence,
And not by them it was my Mariam fell.
If she had been like an Egyptian black,
And not so fair, she had been longer lived;    **240**
Her overflow of beauty turnèd back,
And drowned the spring from whence it was derived.
Her heav'nly beauty 'twas that made me think
That it with chastity could never dwell;
But now I see that heav'n in her did link
A spirit and a person to excel.
I'll muffle up myself in endless night,
And never let mine eyes behold the light.
Retire thyself, vile monster, worse than he
That stained the virgin earth with brother's blood.    **250**
Still in some vault or den enclosèd be,
Where with thy tears thou mayest beget a flood,
Which flood in time may drown thee; happy day
When thou at once shalt die and find a grave.
A stone upon the vault someone shall lay,
Which monument shall an inscription have.
And these shall be the words it shall contain:
'Here Herod lies, that hath his Mariam slain.'
*Exeunt*

CHORUS
Whoever hath beheld with steadfast eye
The strange events of this one only day,    **260**
How many were deceived? How many die,
That once today did grounds of safety lay?
    It will from them all certainty bereave,
    Since twice six hours so many can deceive.

This morning Herod held for surely dead,
And all the Jews on Mariam did attend;
And Constabarus rise from Salom's bed,
And neither dreamed of a divorce or end.
    Pheroras joyed that he might have his wife,
    And Babas' sons for safety of their life.    **270**

Tonight our Herod doth alive remain,
The guiltless Mariam is deprived of breath;
Stout Constabarus both divorced and slain,
The valiant sons of Babas have their death.
    Pheroras sure his love to be bereft,
    If Salome her suit unmade had left.

Herod this morning did expect with joy,
To see his Mariam's much belovèd face;
And yet ere night he did her life destroy,
And surely thought she did her name disgrace.    **280**
    Yet now again, so short do humours last,
    He both repents her death and knows her chaste.

Had he with wisdom now her death delayed,
He at his pleasure might command her death;
But now he hath his power so much betrayed,
As all his woes cannot restore her breath.
    Now doth he strangely, lunatically rave,
    Because his Mariam's life he cannot save.

This day's events were certainly ordained
To be the warning to posterity:    **290**
So many changes are therein contained,
So admirably strange variety.
    This day alone, our sagest Hebrews shall
    In after times the school of wisdom call.

FINIS

---

231  Paphian goddess: Venus
234  Cynthia: goddess of the moon (Diana in Roman
      mythology)
246  person: body
249–50  he/That . . . blood: i.e. Cain, who killed his brother
      Abel; see Genesis 4.8–16
258  'Here . . . slain': compare the final lines of *A Woman
      Killed with Kindness*
260  one only day: reference to the classical dramatic unity of
      time, which stated that a play's action should take place
      within a single day. The other unities were of action
      (there should be nothing extraneous to the main plot),
      and of place (the action should be limited to a single
      location). These principles derived from Aristotle's
      *Poetics*, and were expanded by Italian and French critics
      of the sixteenth and seventeenth centuries

---

281  humours: moods

# Ben Jonson, *The Masque of Blackness*

First performed 1605
First published 1608

*The Masque of Blackness* was performed before the court of King James on Twelfth Night, 1605, the culmination of the Christmas festivities. It is difficult to gain a sense of the occasion simply from the sparse dialogue, stage directions and commentary that are all that now remain of this ephemeral entertainment. Fortunately, however, there are many contemporary accounts of this and other masques which give a clearer idea of, particularly, their visual impact – for these were, in all senses, spectacular events. As was usual with masques, the performance of *The Masque of Blackness* was characterised by elaborate stage design, apparatus and costumes, the result of Jonson's first collaboration with the architect Inigo Jones, and cost in the region of £3,000 (an enormous sum for the time – John Chamberlain records, for example, that Lady Cope rented a house in Drury Lane, London, for £30 a year; see Thomson 1965).

Also typical was the masque's highly symbolic mythological narrative framework which closed in a choreographed dance in which the masquers and audience came together, symbolically dissolving the distinction between them and ensuring that the piece was resolved in a magnificent demonstration of courtly harmony and unity – though, as David Lindley reminds us, this was invariably followed by the less dignified feasting and dancing that was the real high point of the evening (Lindley 1995: x).

Characteristically, too, the chief masquers were drawn from the court itself, and, whilst they did not have speaking parts (these being reserved for professional actors), they nonetheless constituted the focal point of the performance. In this case, Queen Anne and eleven of her closest female companions from the court occupied this position, taking the roles of the daughters of Niger, their faces and forearms blackened to represent twelve Ethiopian beauties in search of the land (subsequently revealed to be England) where the beams of the never-setting sun (King James) would be sufficiently powerful to 'blanch an Ethiop' (line 254).

These details not only suggest something of the lavish character of the masque, but also serve as an apposite footnote to the historical commonplace that women did not act on the public stage until after the Restoration. Whilst masques were not 'public' entertainments in the same way that plays staged at the Globe or the Blackfriars theatres were, they were nonetheless performed before large, if selected, numbers of people: the assembled court, foreign ambassadors, invited dignitaries and other observers, including servants. It is thus misleading to construe them as 'private' events; indeed, the very point of the spectacle was precisely to 'publicise' the court, to encourage the wide circulation of accounts of its learning, wealth, generosity and power. Women not only took part in these very public entertainments, but also were often, as here, the visual, narrative and ideological centre of the event. Whether, however, this phenomenon is to be read as an instance of women appropriating the field and terms of the spectacle for themselves (Queen Anne was, after all, the instigator of this masque), or whether it serves merely to testify further to the commodification and circulation of women in culture as objects of exchange and as indicators of men's status and munificence (since the whole spectacle was constructed in the service of the glorification of James's court) remains a subject for critical debate.

The masque, then, was an ostentatious and self-regarding spectacle, in which the court basked in a refraction of its own magnificence and opulence. It was a form generally intended to provoke awe and wonder in its audience but, whilst the Venetian ambassador records just such an approving response, not all spectators were so uncritical. Dudley Carleton watched *The Masque of Blackness* and his accounts of it suggest something of the anxiety such performances were able to occasion. Carleton wrote that the costumes of the Queen and the other ladies were 'rich, but too light and Curtizan-like for such great ones' (Herford and Simpson 1941 vol. x: 448). His disapproval turns on a perceived incompatibility between noble femininity and public self-exhibition; their combination, as here, conjured for him the 'curtizan', an examplar of sexualised public female display. This association was perhaps heightened by the Queen's visible pregnancy at the time of the performance. This fact was explicitly on show, integrated into the masque's iconography as a sign of the court's fruitfulness (see lines 110 and 275).

Clearly, the meanings of the masque's opulence were not, for Carleton, gender-neutral: the extravagance of the ladies' costumes resonated uncomfortably with other kinds of feminine excess. Such hostility was, moreover, intensified by the ladies' disguises as 'blackamores'; of these, Carleton wrote that they were 'lothsome'; he could not 'imagine a more ugly Sight, than a Troop of lean-cheek'd Moors' (Herford and Simpson 1941 vol. x: 449, 448). Here, he seems to balk at the masque's insistence that the ladies combine beauty with blackness, taking blackness instead as an unambiguous marker of ugliness. Whilst the ladies' 'beauty' might be read as precisely contingent upon, even confirmed by, their *dissatisfaction* with their blackness, and the dynamic of the plot to be towards the resolution of this paradox, there is nonetheless, for Carleton, something profoundly disturbing about a spectacle that asks him to applaud a feminine beauty racially marked by blackness.

Carleton's comments suggest why critics have become increasingly interested in *The Masque of Blackness*, and its sequel of 1608, *The Masque of Beauty*, when the ladies, now 'blanched', return. Lynda Boose summarises the interest thus: 'Jonson's two masques could together constitute a metanarrative of race and gender representation in English literature: the female blackmoors that made a symbolic foray on England's literary shores and attempted to enter early seventeenth-century representation were sent packing and welcomed back only when they had washed off their color' (Boose 1994: 53). Critics read these court entertainments as laying bare some of the faultlines along which early modern discourses of gender and 'race' are constructed. Moreover, these are exposed as an integral part of one of the key processes whereby political power itself was produced and maintained: namely, through spectacle. The early modern court was a site in which 'the power of sovereignty work[ed] primarily by making itself *visible*; it promulgate[d] and extend[ed] itself through public progresses, entertainments and propaganda' (Halpern 1991: 3). In few places was this process as starkly visible as in the spectacle of the court masque, a display in which conspicuous consumption was so manifestly in the service of conspicuous self-production.

## Textual note

*The Masque of Blackness* was first published in Quarto in 1608, and then in the Folio *Workes* of 1616. There is one manuscript edition which is in the British Library. These are referred to in the footnotes as (respectively) Q, F and MS. This edition follows the 1616 *Workes*.

# Further reading
## Editions

Herford, C. H. and Simpson, P. and E. (eds) (1941) *Ben Jonson*, vols VII and x, Oxford: Clarendon Press.
Jonson, Ben (1976) *The Workes of Benjamin Jonson, 1616*, D. Hayward Brock (ed.), London: Scolar Press.
Kinney, Arthur F. (ed.) (1999) *Renaissance Drama: An Anthology of Plays and Entertainments*, Oxford: Blackwell.
Lindley, David (ed.) (1995) *Court Masques: Jacobean and Caroline Entertainments 1605–1640*, Oxford: Oxford University Press.
Orgel, Stephen (ed.) (1969) *Ben Jonson: The Complete Masques*, New Haven, CT, and London: Yale University Press.

## Critical and contextual commentaries

Aasand, Hardin (1992) '"To Blanch an Ethiop and Revive a Corse": Queen Anne and *The Masque of Blackness*', *Studies in English Literature 1500–1900*, 32, 2: 271–85.
Bevington, David, and Holbrook, Peter (eds) (1998) *The Politics of the Stuart Court Masque*, Cambridge: Cambridge University Press.
Boose, Lynda E. (1994) '"The Getting of a Lawful Race": Racial Discourse in Early Modern England and the Unrepresentable Black Woman', in Margo Hendricks and Patricia Parker (eds) *Women, 'Race', and Writing in the Early Modern Period*, London: Routledge.
Floyd-Wilson, Mary (1998) 'Temperature, Temperance, and Racial Difference in Ben Jonson's *The Masque of Blackness*', *English Literary Renaissance*, 28, 2: 183–209.
Gordon, D. J. (1975) *The Renaissance Imagination*, Stephen Orgel (ed.), Berkeley, CA: University of California Press.
Gossett, Suzanne (1988) '"Man-maid, begone": Women in Masques', *English Literary Renaissance*, 18: 96–113.
Hall, Kim F. (1991) 'Sexual Politics and Cultural Identity in *The Masque of Blackness*', in Sue-Ellen Case and Janelle Reinelt (eds) *The Performance of Power: Theatrical Discourse and Politics*, Iowa City, IA: University of Iowa Press; revised version also in Kim Hall (1995) *Things of Darkness: Economies of Race and Gender in Early Modern England*, Ithaca, NY: Cornell University Press.
Halpern, Richard (1991) *The Poetics of Primitive Accumulation: English Renaissance Culture and the Genealogy of Capital*, Ithaca, NY, and London: Cornell University Press.
Kelly, Ann Cline (1977) 'The Challenge of the Impossible: Ben Jonson's *Masque of Blackness*', *College Language Association Journal*, 20, 3: 341–55.
Lindley, David (ed.) (1984) *The Court Masque*, Manchester: Manchester University Press.
McManus, Clare (1998) '"Defacing the Carcass": Anne of Denmark and Jonson's *The Masque of Blackness*', in Julie Sanders, Kate Chedgzoy and Susan Wiseman (eds) *Refashioning Ben Jonson: Gender, Politics and the Jonsonian Canon*, Basingstoke: Macmillan.
Meagher, John C. (1966) *Method and Meaning in Jonson's Masques*, Notre Dame, ID: Notre Dame University Press.
Mickel, Lesley (1999) *Ben Jonson's Antimasques: A History of Growth and Decline*, Aldershot: Ashgate.

Orgel, Stephen (1965) *The Jonsonian Masque*, Cambridge, MA: Harvard University Press.

—— (1975) *The Illusion of Power: Political Theater in the English Renaissance*, Berkeley, CA: University of California Press.

Parry, Graham (1981) *The Golden Age Restor'd: The Culture of the Stuart Court*, Manchester: Manchester University Press.

Siddiqi, Yumna (1992) 'Dark Incontinents: The Discourses of Race and Gender in Three Renaissance Masques', *Renaissance Drama*, new series 23: 139–63.

Thomson, Elizabeth McClure (1965) *The Chamberlain Letters: A Selection of the Letters of John Chamberlain Concerning Life in England from 1597 to 1626*, London: John Murray.

Wynne-Davies, Marion (1992) 'The Queen's Masque: Renaissance Women and the Seventeenth-century Court Masque', in S. P. Cerasano and Marion Wynne-Davies (eds) *Gloriana's Face: Women, Public and Private, in the English Renaissance*, Hemel Hempstead: Harvester Wheatsheaf.

## Works of related interest

Elizabeth Cary, *The Tragedy of Mariam* (1604)
Samuel Daniel, *The Vision of the Twelve Goddesses* (1604)
Ben Jonson, *The Masque of Beauty* (1608)
Ben Jonson, *The Masque of Queens* (1609)
Ben Jonson, *Epicoene, or The Silent Woman* (1609)
Samuel Daniel, *Tethys' Festival* (1610)
Ben Jonson, *The Irish Masque at Court* (1613)
Ben Jonson, *Neptune's Triumph for the Return of Albion* (1624)
Ben Jonson, *The Fortunate Isles, and Their Union* (1625)
Thomas Carew, *Coelum Britannicum* (1634)

# The Masque of Blackness (1605)

The honour and splendour of these spectacles was such in the performance as, could those hours have lasted, this of mine now had been a most unprofitable work. But, when it is the fate even of the greatest and most absolute births to need and borrow a life of posterity, little had been done to the study of magnificence in these if presently with the rage of the people, who, as a part of greatness, are privileged by custom to deface their carcases, the spirits had also perished. In duty, therefore, to that majesty who gave them their authority and grace, and, no less than the most royal of predecessors, deserves eminent celebration for these solemnities, I add this later hand to redeem them as well from ignorance as envy, two common evils, the one of censure, the other of oblivion.                                   16

Pliny, Solinus, Ptolemy, and of late Leo the African, remember unto us a river in Ethiopia famous by the name of Niger, of which the people were called *Nigritae*, now Negroes, and are the blackest nation of the world. This river taketh spring out of a certain lake, eastward, and after a long race falleth into the western ocean. Hence, because it was her majesty's will to have them blackamores at first, the invention was derived by me, and presented thus.                                   26

*First, for the scene, was drawn a Landtschap, consisting of small woods, and here and there a void place filled with huntings; which falling, an artificial sea was seen to shoot forth, as if it flowed to the land, raised with waves which seemed to move, and in some places the billow to break, as imitating that orderly disorder which is common in nature. In front of this sea were placed six tritons in moving and sprightly actions, their upper parts human, save that their hairs were blue, as partaking of the sea colour, their desinent parts fish, mounted above their heads, and all varied in disposition. From their backs were borne out certain light pieces of taffeta, as if carried by the wind, and their music made out of wreathed shells. Behind these, a pair of sea-maids, for song, were as conspicuously seated; between which, two great sea-horses, as big as the life, put forth themselves, the one mounting aloft and writhing his head from the other, which seemed to sink forwards; so intended for variation, and that the figure behind might come off better; upon their backs, Oceanus and Niger were advanced.*                                   47

*Oceanus presented in a human form, the colour of*

---

5 absolute: perfect; here, noble
7 these: i.e. these masques
8–9 rage . . . carcases: traditionally, the audience was permitted to tear down the scenery and plunder the decorations at the end of a masque
14 them: i.e. the spirits (see l. 10)
17 Pliny *Natural History* V.viii.[43–4]; Solinus [Julius Solinus] *Polyhistor* [or *Collectanea Rerum Memorabilium* xxvii.5 and xxx.1]; Ptolemy [Ptolemy of Alexandria, *Geography*] IV.vi.[4–5]; Leo the African [Joannes Leo Africanus] *Description of Africa* [I, 'Division of Africa']. [Jonson's note]
21 river: some take it to be the same with Nilus, which is by Lucan called *Melas*, signifying *niger* [black]. Howsoever, Pliny, in the place above noted, hath this: 'The river Niger has the same nature as the Nile; it produces reeds, papyrus and the same animals.' See Solinus above-mentioned. [Jonson's note; here and throughout Jonson's own notes, passages in inverted commas or italics appeared in Latin or Greek in the original]
22 lake: Lake Chad

24 them: the masquers
27 *Landtschap*: landscape, painted on a curtain. (The Dutch spelling of the word indicates its novelty)
29 *huntings*: i.e. by animals of their prey
   *falling*: the landscape-curtain fell in front of the stage, rather than being drawn across it
29–32 *artificial sea . . . break*: a machine turned, raising and lowering coloured cloths
34 *tritons*: the form of these tritons, with their trumpets, you may read lively described in Ovid, *Metamorphoses* I.[330ff.]: 'He calls the sea-coloured triton,' etc., and in Virgil, *Aeneid* X.[209ff.]: 'He sails upon the huge triton,' *et seq.* [Jonson's note]. Tritons were sea-gods
36 *desinent*: lower
46 *upon their backs*: Lucian in *Rhetoron Didaskalos* [*The Professor of Public Speaking*, 6] presents Nilus so, 'sitting on a hippopotamus.' And Statius Neptune, in the *Thebaid* [II.45]. [Jonson's note]

*his flesh blue, and shadowed with a robe of sea-green;*
*his head grey and horned, as he is described by the*
*ancients; his beard of the like mixed colour. He was*
*garlanded with algae, or sea-grass, and in his hand a*
*trident.* **53**

*Niger in form and colour of an Ethiop, his hair and*
*rare beard curled, shadowed with a blue and bright*
*mantle; his front, neck and wrists adorned with pearl;*
*and crowned with an artificial wreath of cane and*
*paper-rush.*

*These induced the masquers, which were twelve*
*nymphs, Negroes, and daughters of Niger, attended by*
*so many of the Oceaniae, which were their light-*
*bearers.* **63**

*The masquers were placed in a great concave shell,*
*like mother of pearl, curiously made to move on those*
*waters, and rise with the billow; the top thereof was*
*stuck with a chevron of lights, which, indented to the*
*proportion of the shell, struck a glorious beam upon them*
*as they were seated one above another; so that they were*
*all seen, but in an extravagant order.*

*On sides of the shell did swim six huge sea-monsters,*
*varied in their shape and dispositions, bearing on their*
*backs the twelve torch-bearers, who were planted there*
*in several greces, so as the backs of some were seen, some*
*in purfle, or side, others in face; and all having their*
*lights burning out of whelks or murex shells.* **75**

*The attire of the masquers was alike in all, without*
*difference: the colours, azure and silver; their hair thick*

*and curled upright in tresses, like pyramids, but returned*
*on the top with a scroll and antique dressing of feathers*
*and jewels interlaced with ropes of pearl. And for the*
*front, ear, neck and wrists, the ornament was of the*
*most choice and orient pearl, best setting off from the*
*black.*

*For the light-bearers, sea-green, waved about the*
*skirts with gold and silver; their hair loose and flowing,*
*garlanded with sea-grass, and that stuck with branches*
*of coral.* **87**

*These thus presented, the scene behind seemed a vast*
*sea, and united with this that flowed forth, from the*
*termination or horizon of which (being the level of the*
*state, which was placed in the upper end of the hall) was*
*drawn, by the lines of perspective, the whole work*
*shooting downwards from the eye; which decorum made*
*it more conspicuous, and caught the eye afar off with a*
*wandering beauty. To which was added an obscure and*
*cloudy night-piece, that made the whole set off. So much*
*for the bodily part, which was of Master Inigo Jones his*
*design and act.* **98**

*By this, one of the tritons, with the two sea-maids,*
*began to sing to the others' loud music, their voices being*
*a tenor and two trebles.*

Song

Sound, sound aloud
The welcome of the orient flood
Into the west;
Fair Niger, son to great Oceanus,
Now honoured thus,
With all his beauteous race,
Who, though but black in face,

---

49 *shadowed*: covered
50 *horned*: the Ancients induced Oceanus always with a
   bull's head, *on account of the violence of the winds by*
   *which he is stirred up and driven, or because he is borne*
   *against the shore raging like a bull.* Euripides in the
   *Orestes* [1376–9]: 'The land, which bull-headed
   Ocean rolls round and circles with his arms.' And
   rivers sometimes were so called. Look Virgil on the
   Tiber and the Eridanus, *Georgics* IV.[369–72];
   *Aeneid* VIII.[77]; Horace, *Odes* IV.xiv.[25]; and
   Euripides in *Ion* [untraced; not in *Ion*]. [Jonson's
   note]
55 *rare*: thin
56 *front*: forehead
58 *paper-rush*: papyrus
59 *induced*: brought in
61 *Oceaniae*: the daughters of Oceanus and Tethys; see
   Hesiod in the *Theogeny* [346–70], Orpheus in the
   *Hymns* [*Homeric Hymns* ii.(*To Demeter*)5], and Virgil
   in the *Georgics* [IV.382]. [Jonson's note]. The
   Oceaniae were sea-nymphs
64 *curiously*: ingeniously
69 *extravagant*: a) unusual; b) moving about
71 *dispositions*: positions
73 *greces*: steps
74 *purfle*: profile

77–8 *their hair . . . pyramids*: words not in Q or F; added
   from MS
88–9 *scene . . . flowed forth*: the effect of a single sea was
   produced by the backdrop and the wave
   machine
90–1 *level of the state*: height of the throne; thus the king
   alone had the perfect viewing position
96 *night-piece*: upper part of the scenery, through which
   the moon later descends
97 *Inigo Jones*: architect and stage designer (1573–1652);
   throughout his career as writer of court
   entertainments, Jonson collaborated with him
99 *this*: i.e. this time
101 *trebles*: sopranos
105 son: all rivers are said to be the sons of the Ocean for,
   as the ancients thought, out of the vapours exhaled by
   the heat of the sun, rivers and fountains were
   begotten. And both by Orpheus in the *Hymns*
   [*Orphica* LXXXIII] and Homer, *Iliad* XIV.[201, 246,
   302], Oceanus is celebrated *as father and source of gods*
   *and things, because nothing is born or decays without*
   *moisture.* [Jonson's note]

Yet are they bright,
And full of life and light,　　　　110
To prove that beauty best
Which not the colour but the feature
Assures unto the creature.

OCEANUS　Be silent, now the ceremony's done,
　And Niger, say, how comes it, lovely son,
　That thou, the Ethiop's river, so far east,
　Art seen to fall into th'extremest west
　Of me, the king of floods, Oceanus,
　And in mine empire's heart salute me thus?
　My ceaseless current now amazèd stands,　120
　To see thy labour through so many lands
　Mix thy fresh billow with my brackish stream;
　And in thy sweetness stretch thy diadem
　To these far distant and unequalled skies,
　This squarèd circle of celestial bodies.

NIGER　Divine Oceanus, 'tis not strange at all
　That, since the immortal souls of creatures mortal
　Mix with their bodies, yet reserve forever
　A power of separation, I should sever
　My fresh streams from thy brackish, like things
　　　fixed,　　　　130
　Though with thy powerful saltness thus far mixed.
　'Virtue, though chained to earth, will still live free,
　And hell itself must yield to industry.'

OCEANUS　But what's the end of thy herculean labours
　Extended to these calm and blessèd shores?

NIGER　To do a kind and careful father's part,
　In satisfying every pensive heart
　Of these my daughters, my most lovèd birth:
　Who, though they were the first formed dames of
　　earth,

And in whose sparkling and refulgent eyes　　140
The glorious sun did still delight to rise;
Though he (the best judge and most formal cause
Of all dames' beauties) in their firm hues draws
Signs of his fervent'st love, and thereby shows
That in their black the perfect'st beauty grows,
Since the fixed colour of their curlèd hair,
Which is the highest grace of dames most fair,
No cares, no age can change, or there display
The fearful tincture of abhorrèd grey,
Since Death herself (herself being pale and blue)
Can never alter their most faithful hue;　　151
All which are arguments to prove how far
Their beauties conquer in great beauty's war,
And more, how near divinity they be
That stand from passion or decay so free.
Yet since the fabulous voices of some few
Poor brainsick men, styled poets here with you,
Have with such envy of their graces sung
The painted beauties other empires sprung;
Letting their loose and wingèd fictions fly　　160
To infect all climates, yea, our purity;
As of one Phaëton, that fired the world,
And that before his heedless flames were hurled
About the globe, the Ethiops were as fair
As other dames, now black with black despair;
And in respect of their complexions changed,
Are eachwhere since for luckless creatures ranged.
Which when my daughters heard, as women are
Most jealous of their beauties, fear and care
Possessed them whole; yea, and believing them,
They wept such ceaseless tears into my stream　171
That it hath thus far overflowed his shore
To seek them patience; who have since e'ermore
As the sun riseth charged his burning throne
With volleys of revilings, 'cause he shone
On their scorched cheeks with such intemperate
　fires,
And other dames made queens of all desires.
To frustrate which strange error oft I sought,

---

110　full of life: perhaps a reference to Queen Anne, who was
　　six months pregnant at the time of the performance
112　feature: form
122　Mix: there wants not enough in nature to authorise
　　this part of our fiction in separating Niger from the
　　Ocean (beside the fable of Alpheus, and that to
　　which Virgil alludes of Arethusa in his tenth eclogue
　　[4–5]: 'When you glide beneath Sicilian waves, may
　　the briny sea not mix her stream with yours'),
　　examples of Nilus, Jordan and others, whereof see
　　Nicanor, book I *De Fluminibus* [a lost work; see
　　Herford and Simpson X.452, l. 118n.], and Plutarch in
　　the *Life of Sulla* [xx.4], even of this our river (as some
　　think) by the name of Melas. [Jonson's note]
125　squarèd . . . bodies: 'i.e. heavenly bodies perfectly
　　transformed into an earthly realm' (Orgel)
133　hell . . . industry': reference to Horace, *Odes* I.iii.36:
　　'herculean effort overcame hell'
139　first formed: read Diodorous Siculus, [*The Library of
　　History*] III.[ii.1]. It is a conjecture of the old ethnics
　　that they which dwell under the south were the first
　　begotten of the earth. [Jonson's note]

142　formal cause: Aristotelian term, meaning 'creator of
　　the form or essence'
145　black: usually signified ugliness at this time
162　Phaëton: *the famous story*; Ovid, *Metamorphoses* II.[1ff].
　　[Jonson's note]. Phaëton was the son of Apollo, the sun
　　god. He could not control the horses of the sun god,
　　and drove them too close to the earth, so that Zeus
　　destroyed him to prevent the world from catching fire
167　luckless: alluding to that of Juvenal, *Satire* v.[54], 'and
　　whom you would rather not meet at midnight'.
　　[Jonson's note]
170　them: the poets [Jonson's note]
174　charged: a custom of the Ethiops, notable in
　　Herodotus [II.22] and Diodorus Siculus [III.ix.2]; see
　　Pliny, *Natural History* V.viii.[45]. [Jonson's note]

Though most in vain, against a settled thought
As women's are, till they confirmed at length        **180**
By miracle what I with so much strength
Of argument resisted; else they feigned:
For in the lake where their first spring they gained,
As they sat cooling their soft limbs one night,
Appeared a face all circumfused with light
(And sure they saw't, for Ethiops never dream)
Wherein they might decipher through the stream
These words:
    That they a land must forthwith seek
    Whose termination, of the Greek,        **190**
    Sounds *–tania*; where bright Sol, that heat
    Their bloods, doth never rise or set,
    But in his journey passeth by,
    And leaves that climate of the sky
    To comfort of a greater light,
    Who forms all beauty with his sight.
In search of this have we three princedoms passed
That speak out *–tania* in their accents last;
Black Mauritania first, and secondly
Swarth Lusitania; next we did descry        **200**
Rich Aquitania, and yet cannot find
The place unto these longing nymphs designed.
Instruct and aid me, great Oceanus:
What land is this that now appears to us?

OCEANUS This land that lifts into the temperate air
His snowy cliff is Albion the fair,
So called of Neptune's son, who ruleth here;
For whose dear guard, myself four thousand year,
Since old Deucalion's days, have walked the round

About his empire, proud to see him crowned        **210**
Above my waves.

*At this, the moon was discovered in the upper part of the
house, triumphant in a silver throne, made in figure of a
pyramis. Her garments white and silver, the dressing of
her head antique, and crowned with a luminary or
sphere of light, which striking of the clouds, and
heightened with silver, reflected as natural clouds do by
the splendour of the moon. The heaven about her was
vaulted with blue silk, and set with stars of silver,
which had in them their several lights burning. The
sudden sight of which made Niger to interrupt Oceanus,
with this present passion.*        **222**

NIGER           O see, our silver star!
Whose pure, auspicious light greets us thus far!
Great Aethiopia, goddess of our shore,
Since with particular worship we adore
Thy general brightness, let particular grace
Shine on my zealous daughters: show the place
Which long their longings urged their eyes to see.
Beautify them, which long have deified thee.        **230**

AETHIOPIA Niger, be glad; resume thy native cheer.
Thy daughters' labours have their period here,
And so thy errors. I was that bright face
Reflected by the lake, in which thy race
Read mystic lines; which skill Pythagoras
First taught to men by a reverberate glass.
This blessèd isle doth with that *–tania* end,
Which there they saw inscribed, and shall extend
Wished satisfaction to their best desires.
Britannia, which the triple world admires,        **240**
This isle hath now recovered for her name,
Where reign those beauties that with so much fame
The sacred muses' sons have honourèd,

---

186  never dream: Pliny, ibid. [Jonson's note]
191  Sol: the sun
192  rise or set: consult with Tacitus in the *Life of Agricola*
    [12], and the *Panegyric to Constantine* [anonymous; in
    XII *Panegyrici Latini*, ed. E. Baehrens (Leipzig, 1911),
    VI, 9 (p. 207)]. [Jonson's note]
195  greater light: i.e. King James
199  Mauritania: the land of the Moors, in northern
    Africa, now Morocco and part of Algeria
200  Swarth: swarthy, dark
    Lusitania: Portugal and western Spain
201  Aquitania: southwestern France
202  designed: designated, indicated
206  Albion: Orpheus in his *Argonautica* calls it 'white
    land' [untraced; not in *Argonautica*. The reference is
    from Camden's *Britannia* (London, 1586), p. 20.
    [Jonson's note]. Albion was a traditional poetic name
    for England
207  Neptune's son: alluding to the rite of styling princes
    after the name of their princedoms; so is he still
    Albion and Neptune's son that governs. As also his
    being dear to Neptune in being so embraced by him
    [Jonson's note]. The reference is again to King James
209  Deucalion: survivor of a great flood; a Greek
    equivalent to Noah

214  pyramis: pyramid
222  *present*: immediate
225  Aethiopia: the Ethiopians worshipped the moon by
    that surname; see Stephanus [of Byzantium], *De
    Urbibus*, under the word *Aithiopian*, and his reasons.
    [Jonson's note]
232  period: end
235  Pythagoras . . . glass: Pythagoras was supposed to be
    able to reflect messages on to the moon by writing in
    blood on a mirror
    reverberate: reflecting
240  triple world: heaven, earth and the underworld.
    Together these admire James's 'triple world': his three
    kingdoms of Scotland, England and Wales. Compare
    the reference to the 'triple earth' in *The Tragedy of
    Mariam*, III.ii.175
241  recovered for her name: James tried to introduce the
    name 'Great Britain' when he became king of
    England and Wales as well as of Scotland in 1604.
    Despite the claim made in l. 250, the name was not
    popular

And from bright Hesperus to Eos spread.
With that great name Britannia, this blest isle
Hath won her ancient dignity and style,
*A world divided from the world*, and tried
The abstract of it in his general pride.
For were the world with all his wealth a ring,
Britannia, whose new name makes all tongues sing,
Might be a diamond worthy to enchase it,                           251
Ruled by a sun that to this height doth grace it,
Whose beams shine day and night, and are of force
To blanch an Ethiop, and revive a corse.
His light sciential is, and, past mere nature,
Can salve the rude defects of every creature.
 Call forth thy honoured daughters, then,
 And let them, 'fore the Britain men,
 Indent the land with those pure traces
 They flow with in their native graces.                        260
 Invite them boldly to the shore;
 Their beauties shall be scorched no more;
 This sun is temperate, and refines
 All things on which his radiance shines.

*Here the tritons sounded, and they danced on shore,
every couple as they advanced severally presenting their
fans, in one of which were inscribed their mixed names,
in the other a mute hieroglyphic expressing their mixed
qualities. Which manner of symbol I rather chose than
imprese, as well for strangeness as relishing of
antiquity, and more applying to that original doctrine of
sculpture which the Egyptians are said first to have
brought from the Ethiopians.*                                      273

|  |  | The names | The symbols |
|---|---|---|---|
| *The Queen* | 1 | EUPHORIS | A golden tree |
| *Countess of Bedford* | | AGLAIA | laden with fruit |
| *Lady Herbert* | 2 | DIAPHANE | The figure |
| *Countess of Derby* | | EUCAMPSE | *icosahedron* of crystal |
| *Lady Rich* | 3 | OCYTE | A pair of |
| *Countess of Suffolk* | | KATHARE | naked feet in a river |
| *Lady Bevill* | 4 | NOTIS | The |
| *Lady Effingham* | | PSYCHROTE | salamander simple |
| *Lady Elizabeth Howard* | 5 | GLYCYTE | A cloud full |
| *Lady Susan de Vere* | | MALACIA | of rain, dropping |
| *Lady Wroth* | 6 | BARYTE | An urn, |
| *Lady Walsingham* | | PERIPHERE | sphered with wine |

The names of the Oceaniae were                                     293

| DORIS | CYDIPPE | BEROE | IANTHE |
|---|---|---|---|
| PETRAEA | GLAUCE | ACASTE | LYCORIS |
| OCYRHOE | TYCHE | CLYTIA | PLEXAURE |

*Their own single dance ended, as they were about to
make choice of their men, one from the sea was heard to
call 'em with this charm, sung by a tenor voice.*

 SONG

Come away, come away,                                              300
We grow jealous of your stay;
If you do not stop your ear,
We shall have more cause to fear

---

244 Hesperus to Eos: evening, the west, and dawn, the
 east, respectively
246 style: characterisation
247 *A world . . . world*: referring to the popular notion that
 Britain was a separate and especially fortunate world
247–8 tried . . . pride: 'experienced the ideal of it through
 England's own pride in herself' (Orgel)
251 enchase: set in
254 blanch . . . corse: proverbial impossibilities; 'corse':
 corpse
255 sciential: which has the power of science
259 Indent: leave footprints on
 traces: footsteps
266–7 *every couple . . . fans*: 'the ladies advanced in pairs,
 displaying fans to the audience, on one of which was
 the pair of names, on the other a picture which
 represented their allegorical nature. The names are
 largely Jonson's coinage; the emblems are drawn from
 Renaissance sources such as Valeriano's *Hieroglyphica*.
 The names of the Oceaniae come from Hesiod's
 *Theogeny*' (Lindley)
270 imprese: emblems
273 *from the Ethiopians*: Diodorus Siculus, [*The Library of
 History* III.iii.4]; Herodotus [*History* II.110]. [Jonson's
 note]

---

274 *The names*: the meanings of the names are: *Euphoris*:
 abundance; *Aglaia*: splendour; *Diaphane*: transparent;
 *Eucampse*: flexibility; *Ocyte*: swiftness; *Kathare*:
 spotless; *Notis*: moisture; *Psychrote*: coldness; *Glycyte*:
 sweetness; *Malacia*: delicacy; *Baryte*: weight;
 *Periphere*: revolving, circular
 *The symbols*: the significance of these is as follows:
 *golden tree*: fertility; *icosahedron*: twenty-sided figure,
 symbolising water; *naked feet in a river*: purity;
 *salamander*: a reptile which cannot be harmed by fire,
 and can extinguish it; *cloud . . . dropping*: education;
 *urn . . . wine*: the earth
293 Oceaniae: Hesiod in the *Theogeny* [346ff]. [Jonson's
 note]; see l. 61n above

Sirens of the land, than they
To doubt the sirens of the sea.

*Here they danced with their men several measures and*
*corantos. All which ended, they were again accited to sea*
*with a song of two trebles, whose cadences were iterated*
*by a double echo from several parts of the land.*

SONG

Daughters of the subtle flood,                             310
   Do not let earth longer entertain you;
1ST ECHO  Let earth longer entertain you.
2ND ECHO      Longer entertain you.

'Tis to them enough of good
   That you give this little hope to gain you.
1ST ECHO  Give this little hope to gain you.
2ND ECHO      Little hope to gain you.

If they love,
   You shall quickly see;
      For when to flight you move,                  320
         They'll follow you, the more you flee.
1ST ECHO  Follow you, the more you flee.
2ND ECHO      The more you flee.

If not, impute it each to other's matter;
   They are but earth—
1ST ECHO  But earth,
2ND ECHO      Earth—
         And what you vowed was water.
1ST ECHO  You vowed was water.

AETHIOPIA  Enough, bright nymphs, the night
  grows old,                                         330
And we are grieved we cannot hold
You longer light; but comfort take.
Your father only to the lake
Shall make return; yourselves, with feasts,
Must here remain the Ocean's guests.

Nor shall this veil the sun hath cast
Above your blood more summers last;
For which, you shall observe these rites:
Thirteen times thrice, on thirteen nights
(So often as I fill my sphere                               340
With glorious light throughout the year),
You shall, when all things else do sleep
Save your chaste thoughts, with reverence steep
Your bodies in that purer brine
And wholesome dew called rosmarine;
Then with that soft and gentler foam,
Of which the ocean yet yields some,
Whereof bright Venus, beauty's queen,
Is said to have begotten been,
You shall your gentler limbs o'er-lave,                    350
And for your pains perfection have;
So that, this night, the year gone round,
You do again salute the ground,
And in the beams of yond' bright sun
Your faces dry, and all is done.

*At which, in a dance they returned to the sea, where they*
*took their shell; and with this full song went out.*

SONG

Now Dian with her burning face
  Declines apace,
By which our waters know                                    360
  To ebb, that late did flow.
Back seas, back nymphs, but with a forward grace
  Keep, still, your reverence to the place;
And shout with joy of favour you have won
  In sight of Albion, Neptune's son.

*So ended the first masque, which, beside the singular*
*grace of the music and dances, had that success in the*
*nobility of performance as nothing needs to the*
*illustration but the memory by whom it was*
*personated.*

---

306–7 *measures and corantos*: slow, stately dances and
   dances with a running or gliding step
307 *accited*: summoned

345 rosmarine: sea dew
352 year gone round: the sequel to this masque, *The*
   *Masque of Beauty* (in which, as promised, the ladies
   reappear having been 'blanched' by the sun-king's
   beams) was, however, not produced until three years
   later, in 1608
358 Dian: Diana, goddess of the moon

# Francis Beaumont, *The Knight of the Burning Pestle*

First performed 1607–8
First published 1613

*The Knight of the Burning Pestle* was written for the private Blackfriars Theatre, built by Richard Burbage in 1596, and was performed by a company of boy actors. The play is significant for the information it offers in the Induction and elsewhere about contemporary acting companies and the public taste in theatre, as well as other popular cultural forms, such as the chivalric romance. This, together with its representation of social class, and its very specific sense of the geography of London and its environs, gives *The Knight of the Burning Pestle* a particular authority for students of early seventeenth-century theatre. Beaumont's play is a network of overlapping dramatic narratives. The Induction and the Interludes supply a commentary on (and intervene in) the two 'inner' narratives, that of Venturewell and his family (the story of 'The London Merchant') and the enactment of 'The Knight of the Burning Pestle' itself. That the one story parodies London's aspiring merchant class, and the other satirises that class's taste for chivalric romance, gives the play a special sense of topicality. The Citizen's 'Down with your title, boy, down with your title!' (Induction, 29), in response to what he predicts will be yet another Blackfriars play poking fun at his class, is humorous but also emphatic; it is a cry from the heart of a class that was sensitive about its own emerging, but as yet ill-defined, position at the centre of London's economic and social transformation.

The sensitivity to social rank and identity is confirmed as it is exposed in Venturewell's attempts at manipulation in the business of his daughter Luce's marriage: he is entirely willing to enhance his social position at the expense of his daughter's genuine desire for the 'unsuitable' Jasper. In turn, Jasper, similarly dismissed by his own mother, can rely on neither professional bonds (his indentures as an apprentice) or family loyalty. As for his love for Luce, and her love for him, these become tellingly confused by the play's continual recourse to the enactment of chivalric codes, such as in the scene in Waltham Forest in Act III where Jasper 'tests' Luce. Humorous and bizarre as they are, such episodes suggest that in this dramatic world, as much as in any tragedy, the 'experience' of the social is dictated by 'codes' of representation that are shaped by value judgements which confine rather than liberate.

The enactment of 'The Knight of the Burning Pestle' superficially suggests an innocent preoccupation by the citizens with the old stories of chivalric adventure and nobility. They celebrate, and Beaumont parodies, the tales of Guy of Warwick and Bevis of Hampton, meshing these with narratives derived from popular Spanish prose romances. However, such evocations of the past also had a clear place in the official and semi-official discourse of the Tudor and early Stuart state. Edmund Spenser (1552–99) had written his chivalric romance, *The Faerie Queene* (1590–6), with a seriousness that borders on the melancholic, framing a mythologised national history that underpinned Elizabethan Protestant identity. *The Faerie Queene* is referred to in *The Knight of the Burning Pestle* (II.180), but the contrast between Spenser's stately epic and Beaumont's parody is complete, undermining a project that, in more widely accessible forms than Spenser's, was represented in ballads, pageants and other popular forms of entertainments.

Some of these entertainments were presented at Mile End and it is not surprising that, towards the end of *The Knight of the Burning Pestle*, the action shifts to this location. Here, beyond the city walls of London, was where the serious business of training soldiers had traditionally taken place, an activity that the play parodies in a subversive way. Yet it was also the scene of the kind of 'misrule' and carnival espoused by Rafe and Merrythought, but severely condemned by the Puritans who were emerging as the more powerful and politically motivated representatives of the social class from which Beaumont drew his characters.

*The Knight of the Burning Pestle* is a compelling and often hilarious account of the workings of early seventeenth-century theatre, a parody of contemporary concerns over an evolving system of social class, and a critique of an earlier genre of plays that celebrated an ideal of 'Merry England', such as Thomas Dekker's *The Shoemaker's Holiday* (1599). Yet many critics agree that the framing device of the Induction and Interludes tempts us to share the considerable and, finally, unattractive, prejudices of the Citizen and his Wife. Indeed, the play may put us in the position of endorsing easy solutions to the problematic social distinctions that shape the world of the play, favouring a sense of order above the chaos that is achieved through the intersection of social class with chivalric romance and festive release. Merrythought, with his constant recourse to song in the face of adversity, makes us laugh until, perhaps, we consider the terms, and price, of his good humour. As Arthur Kinney has remarked, 'Merrythought, after all, is forever genial, yet that very geniality depends on the willingness of others to support him – he survives on the legacy of others. He can also carry his one-dimensional philosophy to an excess we would consider inhuman: "If both my sons were on the gallows, I would sing"' (Kinney 1999: 389). As with much of the comedy of the period, *The Knight of the Burning Pestle* suggests that, beyond the laughter, there was a very real uncertainty in the shift from a late-medieval world into a recognisably modern one.

## Textual note

*The Knight of the Burning Pestle* was once thought to have been written jointly by Francis Beaumont and his long-term collaborator, John Fletcher (1579–1625), but we follow recent editors, and the evidence of careful analysis of the play's stylistic cohesion, in attributing it to Beaumont alone. This edition is based on the quarto of 1613 (referred to in the footnotes as Q1) and the two further quartos dated 1635 (Q2 and Q3). The play was reprinted from Q3 (which may, in fact, have been later than 1635) for the second Beaumont and Fletcher folio of 1679. Copies of these early editions are held in the British Library in London. This edition reproduces the seventeenth-century division of the play into Acts and Interludes; further subdivision (into scenes), although favoured by some modern editors, suggests an undermining of the unusual sense of pace and cohesion achieved by the continued presence on the stage of the Citizen and the Citizen's Wife.

# Further reading

## Editions

Dyce, Alexander (ed.) (1843–6) *The Works of Beaumont and Fletcher*, London: Edward Moxon.
Hattaway, Michael (ed.) (1970) *The Knight of the Burning Pestle*, The New Mermaids, London: A. & C. Black.
Kinney, Arthur F. (ed.) (1999) *Renaissance Drama: An Anthology of Plays and Entertainments*, Oxford: Blackwell.
Murch, H. S. (1908) *The Knight of the Burning Pestle*, Yale Studies in English, XXXIII, New York, NY.
Wine, M. L. (ed.) (1969) *Drama of the English Renaissance*, Modern Library College Editions, New York, NY: Random House.

## Critical and contextual commentaries

Aspinall, D. (1997) 'The Role of Folk Humor in 17th-century Receptions of Beaumont's *The Knight of the Burning Pestle*', *Philological Quarterley*, 76, 2: 169–91.
Bliss, Lee (1987) '"Don Quixote in England": The Case for *The Knight of the Burning Pestle*', *Viator: Medieval and Renaissance Studies*, 18: 361–80.
Bliss, Lee (1987) *Francis Beaumont*, Boston, MA: Twayne Publishers.
Bristol, Michael D. (1985) *Carnival and Theater*, London: Methuen.
Cook, Ann J. (1981) *The Privileged Playgoers of Shakespeare's London 1576–1642*, Princeton, NJ: Princeton University Press.
Finkelpearl, Philip J. (1990) *Court and Country Politics in the Plays of Beaumont and Fletcher*, Princeton, NJ: Princeton University Press.
Hattaway, Michael (1982) *Elizabethan Popular Theatre*, London: Routledge and Kegan Paul.
Iselin, Pierre (ed.) (1996) *Francis Beaumont and John Fletcher: The Knight of the Burning Pestle*, Paris, France: Didier Erudition.
Kirsch, Arthur C. (1972) *Jacobean Dramatic Perspectives*, Charlottesville, VA: University of Virginia Press.
Leech, Clifford (1962) *The John Fletcher Plays*, London: Chatto & Windus.
Lesser, Z. (1999) 'Walter Burre's *The Knight of the Burning Pestle*', *English Literary Renaissance*, 29, 1: 22–43.
Lindsay, E. S. (1924) 'The Music of the Songs in Fletcher's Plays,' *Studies in Philology*, XXI.
Miller, Ronald F. (1978) 'Dramatic Form and Dramatic Imagination in Beaumont's *The Knight of the Burning Pestle*', *English Literary Renaissance*, 8, 1: 67–84.
Osborne, Laurie E. (1991) 'Female Audiences and Female Authority in *The Knight of the Burning Pestle*', *Exemplaria*, 3, 2: 491–517.
Samuelson, David A. (1979) 'The Order in Beaumont's *Knight of the Burning Pestle*', *English Literary Renaissance*, 9, 2: 302–18.
Steinberg, Glenn A. (1991) '"You Know the Plot/We Both Agreed On?": Plot, Self-consciousness, and *The London Merchant* in Beaumont's *The Knight of the Burning Pestle*', *Medieval and Renaissance Drama in England*, 5: 211–24.
Weimann, Robert (1978) *Shakespeare and the Popular Tradition in the Theatre*, London, Baltimore, MD: Johns Hopkins University Press.

## Works of related interest

Thomas Kyd, *The Spanish Tragedy* (1585)
Anon., *Mucedorus* (1588)
George Peele, *The Old Wives' Tale* (1591)
George Peele, *Edward I* (1591)
Thomas Heywood, *The Four Prentices of London* (1594)
Thomas Dekker, *The Shoemaker's Holiday* (1599)
Thomas Dekker, *Old Fortunatus* (1599)
George Chapman, Ben Jonson and John Marston, *Eastward Ho!* (1605)
Thomas Heywood, *If You Know Not Me You Know Nobody* (1605)
John Day, William Rowley and George Wilkins, *The Travels of the Three English Brothers* (1607)

# The Knight of the Burning Pestle (1607)

## To His Many Ways Endeared Friend Master Robert Keysar

Sir, this unfortunate child who in eight days (as lately I have learned) was begot and born, soon after was by his parents (perhaps because he was so unlike his brethren) exposed to the wide world, who for want of judgement, or not understanding the privy mark of irony about it (which showed it was no offspring of any vulgar brain) utterly rejected it; so that for want of acceptance it was even ready to give up the ghost, and was in danger to have been smothered in perpetual oblivion, if you (out of your direct antipathy to ingratitude) had not been moved both to relieve and cherish it. Wherein I must needs commend both your judgement, understanding, and singular love to good wits. You afterwards sent it to me, yet being an infant and somewhat ragged; I have fostered it privately in my bosom these two years, and now to show my love return it to you, clad in good lasting clothes, which scarce memory will wear out, and able to speak for itself; and, withal, as it telleth me, desirous to try his fortune in the world, where if yet it be welcome, father, foster-father, nurse, and child, all have their desired end. If it be slighted or traduced, it hopes his father will beget him a younger brother who shall revenge his quarrel, and challenge the world either of fond and merely literal interpretation, or illiterate misprision. Perhaps it will be thought to be of the race

of *Don Quixote*: we both may confidently swear it is his elder above a year; and therefore may (by virtue of his birthright) challenge the wall of him. I doubt not but they will meet in their adventures, and I hope the breaking of one staff will make them friends; and perhaps they will combine themselves, and travel through the world to seek their adventures. So I commit him to his good fortune, and myself to your love. **34**

Your assured friend

W.B.

## To the Readers of this Comedy

Gentlemen, the world is so nice in these our times, that for apparel, there is no fashion; for music, which is a rare art (though now slighted), no instrument; for diet, none but the French kickshaws that are delicate; and for plays, no invention but that which now runneth an invective way, touching some particular person, or else it is contemned before it is throughly understood. This is all that I have to say, that the author had no intent to wrong anyone in this comedy, but as a merry passage, here and there interlaced it with delight, which he hopes will please all, and be hurtful to none. **12**

---

Robert Keysar: London goldsmith who, from about 1606, had financed The Children of the Revels at the Blackfriars Theatre

1 eight days: the period of composition (taken literally by many scholars)

2–3 his parents: one piece of evidence for the idea of joint authorship, i.e. with John Fletcher

3 brethren: other plays

6 no offspring . . . vulgar brain: not an ordinary citizen comedy

7 utterly rejected: either it was not performed or it was not appreciated

14 ragged: the author's foul papers (manuscript)

20 father, foster-father, nurse, and child: i.e. author, dedicatee, publisher, and play

---

26 *Don Quixote*: the first part of Cervantes' novel was printed in Spain in 1605 and an English translation (by Shelton) appeared in 1612, but both the original and the translation are known to have circulated in some form before this

28 challenge the wall: claim the safer part of a footpath (close to the wall) and thus take precedence

30 breaking of one staff: an incident from Cervantes

36 W.B.: Walter Burre, the publisher

1 nice: fastidious

4 kickshaws: from *quelque chose* (French), dainties

7 throughly: thoroughly

# The Prologue

Where the bee can suck no honey, she leaves her sting behind; and where the bear cannot find origanum to heal his grief, he blasteth all other leaves with his breath. We fear it is like to fare so with us, that seeing you cannot draw from our labours sweet content, you leave behind you a sour mislike and with open reproach blame our good meaning because you cannot reap the wonted mirth. Our intent was at this time to move inward delight, not outward lightness; and to breed (if it might be) soft smiling, not loud laughing, knowing it to the wise to be as great pleasure to hear counsel mixed with wit, as to the foolish to have sport mingled with rudeness. They were banished the theatre of Athens, and from Rome hissed, that brought parasites on the stage with apish actions, or fools with uncivil habits, or courtezans with immodest words. We have endeavoured to be as far from unseemly speeches to make your ears glow, as we hope you will be free from unkind reports, or, mistaking the author's intention (who never aimed at any one particular in this play), to make our cheeks blush. And thus I leave it and thee to thine own censure, to like, or dislike. *Vale.*                    22

# The Speakers' Names

THE PROLOGUE

*Then a* CITIZEN, GEORGE

*The* CITIZEN'S WIFE, NELL, *and*

RAFE, *her man, sitting below amidst the spectators*

VENTUREWELL, *a rich* MERCHANT

JASPER, *his apprentice*

MASTER HUMPHREY, *a friend to the merchant*

LUCE, *the merchant's daughter*

MISTRESS MERRYTHOUGHT, *Jasper's mother*

MICHAEL, *a second son of Mistress Merrythought*

OLD MASTER MERRYTHOUGHT

TIM, *a* SQUIRE ⎫
                      ⎬ *Apprentices*
GEORGE, *a* DWARF ⎭

A TAPSTER

A BOY *that danceth and singeth*

AN HOST

A BARBER

*Three* KNIGHTS *supposed captives*

A WOMAN, *supposed captive*

A SERGEANT

SOLDIERS

WILLIAM HAMERTON, *a pewterer*

GEORGE GREENGOOSE, *a poulterer*

POMPIONA, *a daughter to the King of Moldavia*

*Boys, Gentlemen, Attendants, Servants*

# Induction

GENTLEMEN *seated upon the stage. The* CITIZEN, *his* WIFE, *and* RAFE *below among the audience*

*Enter* PROLOGUE

PROLOGUE  From all that's near the court, from all that's great
      Within the compass of the city-walls,
      We now have brought our scene—

*Enter* CITIZEN *on to the stage from the audience below*

CITIZEN  Hold your peace, goodman boy.
PROLOGUE  What do you mean, sir?
CITIZEN  That you have no good meaning. This seven years there hath been plays at this house, I have observed it, you have still girds at citizens; and now you call your play *The London Merchant*. Down with your title, boy, down with your title!      10
PROLOGUE  Are you a member of the noble city?
CITIZEN  I am.

---

The Prologue: from Q2, reprinted *Sapho and Phao* (1584) by John Lyly (c. 1554–1606)
2  origanum: a herb of the marjoram family
14  parasites: low-born (sometimes grotesque) attendants upon the rich
22  *Vale*: farewell
The Speakers' Names: from Q2

*Three* KNIGHTS: eds (Two KNIGHTS Q2)
SD  GENTLEMEN: tobacco-smoking gallants who paid for seats on the stage
1  court: at Westminster
2  city-walls: the walls that enclosed London north of the Thames
4  Hold your peace, goodman boy: parody of John Day's *Isle of Gulls* (1606) in which the Prologue is interrupted by playgoers telling him what they want to see
6–7  This seven . . . this house: The Children of the Revels played at Blackfriars from 1600 to 1608
8  still: always
      girds: sneers
9  *The London Merchant*: probably the play about Venturewell and his family
10  title: a placard bearing the title of the play
11  member: citizen

PROLOGUE And a freeman?

CITIZEN Yea, and a grocer.

PROLOGUE So, grocer, then by your sweet favour, we intend no abuse to the city.

CITIZEN No, sir? Yes, sir! If you were not resolved to play the jacks, what need you study for new subjects, purposely to abuse your betters? Why could not you be contented, as well as others, with *The Legend of Whittington*, or *The Life and Death of Sir Thomas Gresham, with the Building of the Royal Exchange*, or *The Story of Queen Elenor, with the Rearing of London Bridge upon Wool-sacks*? **24**

PROLOGUE You seem to be an understanding man. What would you have us do, sir?

CITIZEN Why, present something notably in honour of the commons of the city.

PROLOGUE Why, what do you say to *The Life and Death of Fat Drake, or The Repairing of Fleet-privies*? **30**

CITIZEN I do not like that; but I will have a citizen, and he shall be of my own trade.

PROLOGUE Oh, you should have told us your mind a month since. Our play is ready to begin now.

CITIZEN 'Tis all one for that; I will have a grocer, and he shall do admirable things.

PROLOGUE What will you have him do?

CITIZEN Marry, I will have him—

WIFE *below*

WIFE Husband, husband.

RAFE *below*

RAFE Peace, mistress. **40**

WIFE Hold thy peace, Rafe; I know what I do, I warrant'ee.—Husband, husband.

CITIZEN What say'st thou, cony?

WIFE Let him kill a lion with a pestle, husband; let him kill a lion with a pestle.

CITIZEN So he shall.—I'll have him kill a lion with a pestle.

WIFE Husband, shall I come up, husband?

CITIZEN Ay, cony.—Rafe, help your mistress this way.—Pray, gentlemen, make her a little room.—I pray you, sir, lend me your hand to help up my wife; I thank you, sir.—So. **52**

WIFE *comes up on to the stage*

WIFE By your leave, gentlemen all, I'm something troublesome; I'm a stranger here; I was ne'er at one of these plays, as they say, before; but I should have seen *Jane Shore* once, and my husband hath promised me any time this twelvemonth to carry me to *The Bold Beauchamps*; but in truth he did not. I pray you bear with me.

CITIZEN Boy, let my wife and I have a couple of stools, and then begin, and let the grocer do rare things. **61**

PROLOGUE But sir, we have never a boy to play him; everyone hath a part already.

WIFE Husband, husband, for God's sake let Rafe play him; beshrew me if I do not think he will go beyond them all.

CITIZEN Well remembered, wife.—Come up, Rafe.—I'll tell you, gentlemen, let them but lend him a suit of reparel and necessaries, and, by gad, if any of them all blow wind in the tail on him, I'll be hanged. **70**

RAFE *comes up on to the stage*

WIFE I pray you, youth, let him have a suit of reparel.—I'll be sworn, gentlemen, my husband tells you true: he will act you sometimes at our house, that all the neighbours cry out on him. He will fetch you up a couraging part so in the garret, that we are all as feared, I warrant you, that we quake again. We'll fear

---

13 freeman: one enjoying the privileges of the City following a successful apprenticeship

14 grocer: one of London's twelve great livery companies (which also included the Mercers, Drapers, Fishmongers, Goldsmiths, Skinners, Merchant Taylors, Haberdashers, Salters, Ironmongers, Vintners and Clothworkers)

15 favour: play on 'face'

18 play the jacks: play tricks (i.e. 'play the knave')

19 betters: adult companies

20-4 all plays that glorified London. Dick Whittington was the legendary Lord Mayor who rose to his position from low estate; a play about him was entered in the Stationers' Register in 1605. Thomas Gresham appears in *If You Know Not Me, You Know Nobody*, (1605) by Thomas Heywood; he built the Royal Exchange, a place of resort opened by Elizabeth I. Queen Eleanor appears in *Edward I* (1591) by George Peele; 'The Building of London Bridge upon Woolsacks' was a contemporary dance inspired by the raising of taxes on wool to finance the bridge

25 understanding: a joke referring to the fact that the spectators were below the stage

28 commons: the body of freemen

29-30 *The Life . . . Fleet-privies*: probably an invention (Fleet Ditch was used as a sewer)

36 admirable: wonderful

43 cony: rabbit (and term of endearment)

44 kill a . . . a pestle: the kind of romance satirised in *The Knight of the Burning Pestle* often included battles with wild animals. An apprentice in Thomas Heywood's *The Four Prentices of London* (c. 1594) claims he killed a lion

48 shall I come up?: women rarely sat on the stage

65 *Jane Shore*: mistress of Edward IV who appears in Heywood's *Edward IV* (1599)

57-8 *The Bold Beauchamps*: a lost play attributed to Heywood

65 beshrew me: 'the devil take me'

69 reparel: apparel (archaic)

70 blow wind in the tail: come near (from horse-racing)

74 cry out: complain of

75 couraging: spirited

our children with him: if they be never so unruly, do but cry, 'Rafe comes, Rafe comes', to them, and they'll be as quiet as lambs.—Hold up thy head, Rafe; show the gentlemen what thou canst do; speak a huffing part; I warrant you the gentlemen will accept of it.                                                                               82

CITIZEN  Do, Rafe, do.

RAFE  By heaven, methinks it were an easy leap
To pluck bright honour from the pale-faced moon,
Or dive into the bottom of the sea
Where never fathom-line touched any ground
And pluck up drowned honour from the lake of hell.

CITIZEN  How say you, gentlemen, is it not as I told you?                                                                               90

WIFE  Nay, gentlemen, he hath played before, my husband says, Mucedorus before the wardens of our company.

CITIZEN  Ay, and he should have played Jeronimo with a shoemaker for a wager.

PROLOGUE  He shall have a suit of apparel if he will go in.

CITIZEN  In, Rafe; in, Rafe; and set out the grocery in their kind, if thou lov'st me.                               *Exit* RAFE

WIFE  I warrant our Rafe will look finely when he's dressed.                                                                               100

PROLOGUE  But what will you have it called?

CITIZEN  *The Grocers' Honour.*

PROLOGUE  Methinks *The Knight of the Burning Pestle* were better.

WIFE  I'll be sworn, husband, that's as good a name as can be.

CITIZEN  Let it be so. Begin, begin; my wife and I will sit down.

PROLOGUE  I pray you, do.

CITIZEN  What stately music have you? You have shawms?                                                                               111

PROLOGUE  Shawms? No.

CITIZEN  No? I'm a thief if my mind did not give me so. Rafe plays a stately part, and he must needs have shawms; I'll be at the charge of them myself, rather than we'll be without them.

PROLOGUE  So you are like to be.

CITIZEN  Why, and so I will be. There's two shillings; let's have the waits of Southwark. They are as rare fellows as any are in England; and that will fetch them all o'er the water with a vengeance, as if they were mad.                                                                               122

PROLOGUE  You shall have them. Will you sit down then?

CITIZEN  Ay. Come, wife.

WIFE  Sit you merry all, gentlemen. I'm bold to sit amongst you for my ease.

PROLOGUE  From all that's near the court, from all that's great
Within the compass of the city-walls,
We now have brought our scene. Fly far from hence
All private taxes, immodest phrases,                                       130
Whate'er may but show like vicious:
For wicked mirth never true pleasure brings,
But honest minds are pleased with honest things.
—Thus much for that we do; but for Rafe's part you must answer for yourself.                               *Exit*

CITIZEN  Take you no care for Rafe; he'll discharge himself, I warrant you.

WIFE  I' faith, gentlemen, I'll give my word for Rafe.

# Act I

*Enter* MERCHANT VENTUREWELL *and* JASPER, *his prentice*

MERCHANT  Sirrah, I'll make you know you are my prentice,
And whom my charitable love redeemed
Even from the fall of fortune; gave thee heat
And growth to be what now thou art, new cast thee;
Adding the trust of all I have at home,
In foreign staples, or upon the sea,
To thy direction; tied the good opinions
Both of myself and friends to thy endeavours:
So fair were thy beginnings. But with these,

---

81  huffing: bombastic

84–8  By heaven . . . of hell: a version of Hotspur's speech in *1 Henry IV*, I.iii.199–3; Shakespeare's fourth line reads: 'And pluck up drownèd honour by the locks' (Rafe substitutes a contemporary commonplace)

92  Mucedorus: reference to a popular anonymous play of the late sixteenth century that mixed high romance with buffoonery
before the wardens: livery companies played at the Guildhall and at court; the companies were directed by wardens

94  Jeronimo: i.e. Hieronimo, the protagonist of *The Spanish Tragedy*

96  go in: to the tiring-house (behind the stage) where costumes were kept

97–8  in their kind: each company had its distinctive livery

103  *The Knight of the Burning Pestle*: a pestle would be used by grocers as a tool in the preparation of their wares, but it also had a phallic connotation. 'Burning' means 'gilded' but also refers to the effects of syphilis

111  shawms: early oboes

119  waits: musicians employed by the City

121  o'er the water: over the Thames (from Southwark)

130  private taxes: attacks on individuals
immodest phrases: obscenities

136  discharge: a) acquit; b) ejaculate

1  Sirrah: common form of address (to an inferior)

3  fall of fortune: poverty

3–4  heat/And growth: room and board

4  new cast: reformed

5  trust: use

6  staples: a) storehouses; b) centres of trade

9  fair: promising

As I remember, you had never charge 10
To love your master's daughter, and even then
When I had found a wealthy husband for her.
I take it, sir, you had not; but, however,
I'll break the neck of that commission
And make you know you are but a merchant's factor.
JASPER Sir, I do liberally confess I am yours,
Bound both by love and duty to your service,
In which my labour hath been all my profit.
I have not lost in bargain, nor delighted
To wear your honest gains upon my back, 20
Nor have I given a pension to my blood,
Or lavishly in play consumed your stock.
These, and the miseries that do attend them,
I dare with innocence proclaim are strangers
To all my temperate actions. For your daughter,
If there be any love to my deservings
Borne by her virtuous self, I cannot stop it;
Nor am I able to refrain her wishes.
She's private to herself and best of knowledge
Whom she'll make so happy as to sigh for. 30
Besides, I cannot think you mean to match her
Unto a fellow of so lame a presence,
One that hath little left of nature in him.
MERCHANT 'Tis very well, sir. I can tell your wisdom
How all this shall be cured.
JASPER                         Your care becomes you.
MERCHANT And thus it must be, sir: I here discharge you
My house and service. Take your liberty,
And when I want a son I'll send for you.        Exit
JASPER These be the fair rewards of them that love.
Oh you that live in freedom, never prove 40
The travail of a mind led by desire!

*Enter* LUCE

LUCE Why, how now, friend? Struck with my father's
thunder?
JASPER Struck, and struck dead, unless the remedy
Be full of speed and virtue. I am now

What I expected long, no more your father's.
LUCE But mine.
JASPER                 But yours, and only yours, I am;
That's all I have to keep me from the statute.
You dare be constant still?
LUCE                         Oh, fear me not.
In this I dare be better than a woman:
Nor shall his anger nor his offers move me, 50
Were they both equal to a prince's power.
JASPER You know my rival?
LUCE                     Yes, and love him dearly,
Even as I love an ague or foul weather;
I prithee, Jasper, fear him not.
JASPER                         Oh, no,
I do not mean to do him so much kindness.
But to our own desires: you know the plot
We both agreed on?
LUCE                 Yes, and will perform
My part exactly.
JASPER             I desire no more.
Farewell, and keep my heart; 'tis yours.
LUCE                                 I take it; 59
He must do miracles makes me forsake it.    *Exeunt*
CITIZEN Fie upon 'em, little infidels: what a matter's
here now! Well, I'll be hanged for a halfpenny, if
there be not some abomination knavery in this play.
Well, let 'em look to't. Rafe must come, and if there
be any tricks a-brewing—
WIFE Let 'em brew and bake too, husband, a God's
name. Rafe will find all out, I warrant you, and they
were older than they are.—

*Enter* BOY

I pray, my pretty youth, is Rafe ready?
BOY He will be presently. 70
WIFE Now, I pray you, make my commendations unto
him, and withal carry him this stick of liquorice. Tell
him his mistress sent it him, and bid him bite a piece;
'twill open his pipes the better, say.    *Exit* BOY

*Enter* MERCHANT *and* MASTER HUMPHREY

---

13 you had not: i.e. given up your love for someone superior
(in social rank)
however: notwithstanding
14 commission: a) act of courtship; b) professional remit
15 factor: agent, deputy
16 liberally: willingly
21 pension: market value
22 play: gambling
28 refrain: curb
29 private to . . . of knowledge: free to decide and knows
best of all
32 presence: personality
33 little left of nature: 'little life-force'
38 son: i.e. son-in-law
40 prove: experience
44 speed and virtue: determination and goodness

47 the statute: a) that against rogues, vagabonds and
masterless men; b) that of 1562 which meant that
apprentices could not leave their masters' parishes. Both
statutes were enforced by provision for imprisonment
49 better than a woman: women were thought to be
irredeemably 'inconstant'
53 ague: fever (often the result of damp weather)
54 I prithee: 'I pray you'
61 infidels: 'George's natural and class loyalty is to the
merchant' (Kinney)
67 and: if
69 pretty: clever
72–4 stick of . . . better, say: liquorice was used to loosen
phlegm and clear the throat; the Wife has a supply of
such remedies which are mocked throughout the play

MERCHANT  Come, sir, she's yours; upon my faith, she's
    yours;
  You have my hand. For other idle lets
  Between your hopes and her, thus with a wind
  They are scattered and no more. My wanton prentice,
  That like a bladder blew himself with love,
  I have let out, and sent him to discover        80
  New masters yet unknown.
HUMPHREY               I thank you, sir,
  Indeed, I thank you, sir; and ere I stir
  It shall be known, however you do deem,
  I am of gentle blood and gentle seem.
MERCHANT  Oh, sir, I know it certain.
HUMPHREY               Sir, my friend,
  Although, as writers say, all things have end,
  And that we call a pudding hath his two,
  Oh, let it not seem strange, I pray, to you,
  If in this bloody simile I put
  My love, more endless than frail things or gut.    90
WIFE  Husband, I prithee, sweet lamb, tell me one
  thing, but tell me truly:—Stay youths, I beseech you,
  till I question my husband.
CITIZEN  What is it, mouse?
WIFE  Sirrah, didst thou ever see a prettier child? How
  it behaves itself, I warrant ye, and speaks, and looks,
  and perts up the head?—I pray you, brother, with
  your favour, were you never none of Master
  Monkester's scholars?                  99
CITIZEN  Chicken, I prithee heartily, contain thyself;
  the childer are pretty childer; but when Rafe comes,
  lamb—
WIFE  Ay, when Rafe comes, cony.—Well, my youth,
  you may proceed.
MERCHANT  Well, sir, you know my love, and rest, I
  hope,
  Assured of my consent. Get but my daughter's,
  And wed her when you please. You must be bold,
  And clap in close unto her. Come, I know
  You have language good enough to win a wench.

---

76  lets: obstacles
78  wanton: promiscuous,
79  bladder: inflatable animal's bladder (with obscene
    connotation)
84  gentle blood: some status
87  pudding: blood sausage
92  youths: the boy actors
94  mouse: term of endearment (as is 'chicken' and others)
95  prettier: more clever
97  perts: perks
98–9  Master Monkester: Richard Mulcaster was Master of
    St Paul's School from 1596 to 1608 and its boys' troupe
    played at the Whitefriar's Theatre
101  childer: children (dialect)
108  clap in close unto her: embrace
109  wench: a) young girl; b) prostitute

WIFE  A whoreson tyrant! H'as been an old stringer in's
  days, I warrant him.                    III
HUMPHREY  I take your gentle offer, and withal
  Yield love again for love reciprocal.
MERCHANT  What, Luce! Within there!

*Enter* LUCE

LUCE                    Called you, sir?
MERCHANT                   I did.
  Give entertainment to this gentleman
  And see you be not froward.—To her, sir;
  My presence will but be an eye-sore to you.    *Exit*
HUMPHREY  Fair Mistress Luce, how do you do? Are
  you well?
  Give me your hand, and then I pray you tell
  How doth your little sister and your brother,    120
  And whether you love me or any other.
LUCE  Sir, these are quickly answered.
HUMPHREY              So they are,
  Where women are not cruel. But how far
  Is it now distant from this place we are in,
  Unto that blessed place, your father's warren?
LUCE  What makes you think of that, sir?
HUMPHREY             Even that face;
  For, stealing rabbits whilom in that place,
  God Cupid, or the keeper, I know not whether,
  Unto my cost and charges brought you thither,
  And there began—
LUCE            Your game, sir.
HUMPHREY              Let no game  130
  Or any thing that tendeth to the same,
  Be evermore remembered, thou fair killer,
  For whom I sat me down and brake my tiller.
WIFE  There's a kind gentleman, I warrant you. When
  will you do as much for me, George?
LUCE  Beshrew me, sir, I am sorry for your losses;
  But as the proverb says, I cannot cry.
  I would you had not seen me.
HUMPHREY           So would I,
  Unless you had more maw to do me good.
LUCE  Why, cannot this strange passion be withstood?
  Send for a constable and raise the town.    141
HUMPHREY  Oh no, my valiant love will batter down
  Millions of constables, and put to flight

---

110  stringer: fornicator
112  withal: also, as well
116  froward: perverse
125  warren: land preserved for the breeding of rabbits
127  whilom: while (archaic)
128  whether: which
133  tiller: a) beam of a crossbow; b) sexual quibble
137  proverb: 'I am sorry for you but I cannot cry'
139  maw: craving

Even that great watch of Midsummer day at night.
LUCE Beshrew me, sir, 'twere good I yielded then;
Weak women cannot hope, where valiant men
Have no resistance.
HUMPHREY            Yield then, I am full
Of pity, though I say it, and can pull
Out of my pocket, thus, a pair of gloves.
Look, Lucy, look: the dog's tooth nor the dove's  150
Are not so white as these, and sweet they be,
And whipped about with silk, as you may see.
If you desire the price, shoot from your eye
A beam to this place, and you shall espy
F. S., which is to say, my sweetest honey,
They cost me three and two pence, or no money.
LUCE Well, sir, I take them kindly, and I thank you.
What would you more?
HUMPHREY            Nothing.
LUCE                      Why then, farewell.
HUMPHREY Nor so, nor so; for, lady, I must tell,
Before we part, for what we met together;  160
God grant me time, and patience, and fair weather.
LUCE Speak, and declare your mind in terms so brief.
HUMPHREY I shall. Then, first and foremost, for relief
I call to you, if that you can afford it;
I care not at what price for, on my word, it
Shall be repaid again, although it cost me
More than I'll speak of now. For love hath tossed me
In furious blanket like a tennis-ball,
And now I rise aloft, and now I fall.
LUCE Alas, good gentleman, alas the day.  170
HUMPHREY I thank you heartily, and, as I say,
Thus do I still continue without rest,
I'th' morning like a man, at night a beast,
Roaring and bellowing mine own disquiet,
That much I fear, forsaking of my diet
Will bring me presently to that quandàry,
I shall bid all adieu.
LUCE            Now, by Saint Mary,
That were great pity.
HUMPHREY            So it were, beshrew me.

Then ease me, lusty Luce, and pity show me.
LUCE Why, sir, you know my will is nothing worth  180
Without my father's grant; get his consent,
And then you may with assurance try me.
HUMPHREY The worshipful your sire will not deny me;
For I have asked him, and he hath replied,
'Sweet Master Humphrey, Luce shall be thy bride'.
LUCE Sweet Master Humphrey, then I am content.
HUMPHREY And so am I, in truth.
LUCE                      Yet take me with you;
There is another clause must be annexed,
And this it is: I swore and will perform it,
No man shall ever joy me as his wife  190
But he that stole me hence. If you dare venture,
I am yours—you need not fear, my father loves you—
If not, farewell for ever.
HUMPHREY            Stay, nymph, stay;
I have a double gelding, coloured bay,
Sprung by his father from Barbarian kind;
Another for myself, though somewhat blind,
Yet true as trusty tree.
LUCE            I am satisfied;
And so I give my hand. Our course must lie
Through Waltham Forest, where I have a friend
Will entertain us. So, farewell, Sir Humphrey,  200
And think upon your business.            *Exit* LUCE
HUMPHREY            Though I die,
I am resolved to venture life and limb
For one so young, so fair, so kind, so trim.
                              *Exit* HUMPHREY
WIFE By my faith and troth, George, and, as I am
virtuous, it is e'en the kindest young man that ever
trod on shoe leather. Well, go thy ways; if thou hast
her not, 'tis not thy fault.
CITIZEN I prithee, mouse, be patient; 'a shall have her,
or I'll make some of 'em smoke for't.  209
WIFE That's my good lamb, George. Fie, this stinking
tobacco kills me, would there were none in
England.—Now I pray, gentlemen, what good does
this stinking tobacco do you? Nothing, I warrant you;
make chimneys o'your faces.—Oh, husband,
husband, now, now, there's Rafe, there's Rafe.

---

144  that great watch: the annual pageant (held on 24 June) at which the City and livery companies mustered the militia and constabulary to serve for the following year
149  a pair of gloves: gloves were traditional love-tokens given at betrothals and weddings
152  whipped: embroidered
153–4  shoot from . . . this place: it was thought that a beam of light 'shot' from the eye returned with the image of what it struck
155  F.S.: a) Humphrey bought them for someone else; b) a merchant's mark; c) they were inherited
156  three and two pence: the gloves were expensive
167–8  For love . . . furious blanket: Don Quixote was humiliated in this way
175  diet: a common treatment for venereal disease

179  lusty: intended as 'pretty'
187  take me with you: let this be clear
190  joy: enjoy
194  double gelding: horse for two riders
195  Barbarian: Barbary, a famous breed of horses from the Saracen area of Africa
199  Waltham Forest: north of London in Hertfordshire
204  troth: truth
208  'a: he
209  smoke: suffer
211  tobacco: smoking was identified with 'gallants' and condemned in many circles. King James discussed the habit in *A Counterblast to Tobacco* (1604)

*Enter* RAFE *like a grocer in's shop, with two prentices* TIM *and* GEORGE *reading Palmerin of England*

CITIZEN  Peace, fool, let Rafe alone. Hark you Rafe; do not strain yourself too much at the first.—Peace!— Begin, Rafe.                                                        **218**

RAFE  (*reads*) 'Then Palmerin and Trineus, snatching their lances from their dwarfs, and clasping their helmets, galloped amain after the giant; and Palmerin, having gotten a sight of him, came posting amain, saying: "Stay, traitorous thief, for thou mayst not so carry away her that is worth the greatest lord in the world", and with these words gave him a blow on the shoulder, that he struck him besides his elephant; and Trineus, coming to the knight that had Agricola behind him, set him soon besides his horse, with his neck broken in the fall, so that the princess, getting out of the throng, between joy and grief said: "All happy knight, the mirror of all such as follow arms, now may I be well assured of the love thou bearest me".' I wonder why the kings do not raise an army of fourteen or fifteen hundred thousand men, as big as the army that the Prince of Portigo brought against Rosicleer, and destroy these giants; they do much hurt to wandering damsels that go in quest of their knights.                                                  **238**

WIFE  Faith, husband, and Rafe says true; for they say the King of Portugal cannot sit at his meat, but the giants and the ettins will come and snatch it from him.                                                        **242**

CITIZEN  Hold thy tongue.—On, Rafe.

RAFE  And certainly those knights are much to be commended, who neglecting their possessions, wander with a squire and a dwarf through the deserts to relieve poor ladies.

WIFE  Ay, by my faith, are they, Rafe; let 'em say what they will, they are indeed. Our knights neglect their

possessions well enough, but they do not the rest.  **250**

RAFE  There are no such courteous and fair well-spoken knights in this age: they will call one 'the son of a whore', that Palmerin of England would have called 'fair sir', and one that Rosicleer would have called 'right beauteous damsel', they will call 'damned bitch'.                                                          **256**

WIFE  I'll be sworn will they, Rafe; they have called me so an hundred times about a scurvy pipe of tobacco.

RAFE  But what brave spirit could be content to sit in his shop with a flappet of wood and a blue apron before him, selling mithridatum and dragon's water to visited houses, that might pursue feats of arms, and through his noble achievements procure such a famous history to be written of his heroic prowess?

CITIZEN  Well said, Rafe, some more of those words, Rafe.

WIFE  They go finely, by my troth.                          **267**

RAFE  Why should not I then pursue this course, both for the credit of myself and our company? For amongst all the worthy books of achievements I do not call to mind that I yet read of a grocer errant. I will be the said knight. Have you heard of any that hath wandered unfurnished of his squire and dwarf? My elder prentice Tim shall be my trusty squire, and little George my dwarf. Hence my blue apron! Yet in remembrance of my former trade, upon my shield shall be portrayed a burning pestle, and I will be called the Knight o'th' Burning Pestle.

WIFE  Nay, I dare swear thou wilt not forget thy old trade; thou wert ever meek.                                  **280**

RAFE  Tim.

TIM  Anon.

RAFE  My beloved squire, and George my dwarf, I charge you that from henceforth you never call me by any other name but the 'Right Courteous and Valiant Knight of the Burning Pestle', and that you never call any female by the name of a woman or wench, but 'Fair Lady', if she have her desires, if not, 'Distressed Damsel'; that you call all forests and heaths 'deserts', and all horses 'palfreys'.                                            **290**

WIFE  This is very fine, faith. Do the gentlemen like

---

SD  *like a grocer in's shop*: Rafe wears the blue livery of an apprentice
   *Palmerin of England*: Rafe actually reads from *Palmerin d'Olivia* translated from the Spanish by Anthony Munday. *Palmerin of England* was the sequel

227  elephant: 'horse' in the original but the effect is to parody the book

228  Agricola: the princess 'Agriola' in the Spanish text and Munday's translation
   set him . . . his horse: unhorsed him

231  mirror: model, paragon

235  Portigo: Portugal

236  Rosicleer: hero of Ortuñez de Calahorra's *Espejo de Principes y Caualleros*, one of the romances owned by Don Quixote (translated into English as *The Mirror of Knighthood* by Margaret Tyler (1578–1601))

237–8  wandering damsels . . . their knights: a reversal of romantic convention

241  ettins: giants (from German)

249–50  Our knights . . . the rest: possibly a reference to the sale of knighthoods by King James

251–6  There are . . . 'damned bitch': a parody of Gertrude's speech in *Eastward Ho!* (1605) by George Chapman, Ben Jonson and John Marston

260  flappet: shop's counter

261  mithridatum and dragon's water: a herbal medicine (named after King Mithridates and used against poisons) and another, stronger, preparation believed to cure fever.
   visited: i.e. by the plague

271  grocer errant: Kinney notes that there was, in fact, a precedent in the figure of Eustace in Thomas Heywood's *Four Prentices of London*

Rafe, think you, husband?

CITIZEN  Ay, I warrant thee, the players would give all the shoes in their shop for him.

RAFE  My beloved squire Tim, stand out. Admit this were a desert, and over it a knight errant pricking, and I should bid you inquire of his intents, what would you say?

TIM  Sir, my master sent me to know whither you are riding?  300

RAFE  No, thus: 'Fair sir, the Right Courteous and Valiant Knight of the Burning Pestle commanded me to inquire upon what adventure you are bound, whether to relieve some distressed damsels, or otherwise'.

CITIZEN  Whoreson blockhead cannot remember!

WIFE  I'faith, and Rafe told him on't before—all the gentlemen heard him.—Did he not, gentlemen? Did not Rafe tell him on't?  309

GEORGE  Right Courteous and Valiant Knight of the Burning Pestle here is a distressed damsel, to have a halfpenny-worth of pepper.

WIFE  That's a good boy. See, the little boy can hit it; by my troth, it's a fine child.

RAFE  Relieve her with all courteous language. Now shut up shop; no more my prentice, but my trusty squire and dwarf. I must bespeak my shield and arming pestle.  *Exeunt* TIM *and* GEORGE

CITIZEN  Go thy ways, Rafe. As I'm a true man, thou art the best on 'em all.  320

WIFE  Rafe, Rafe.

RAFE  What say you, mistress?

WIFE  I prithee come again quickly, sweet Rafe.

RAFE  By and by.  *Exit* RAFE

*Enter* JASPER *and his mother,* MISTRESS MERRYTHOUGHT

MISTRESS MERRYTHOUGHT  Give thee my blessing? No, I'll ne'er give thee my blessing, I'll see thee hanged first; it shall ne'er be said I gave thee my blessing. Th'art thy father's own son, of the right blood of the Merrythoughts. I may curse the time that e'er I knew thy father; he hath spent all his own, and mine too, and when I tell him of it, he laughs and dances, and sings, and cries, 'A merry heart lives long-a'. And thou art a wastethrift, and art run away from thy

master that loved thee well, and art come to me; and I have laid up a little for my younger son Michael, and thou think'st to bezzle that, but thou shalt never be able to do it.

*Enter* MICHAEL

—Come hither Michael, come, Michael, down on thy knees; thou shalt have my blessing.  339

MICHAEL  I pray you, mother, pray to God to bless me.

MISTRESS MERRYTHOUGHT  God bless thee; but Jasper shall never have my blessing. He shall be hanged first, shall he not, Michael? How say'st thou?

MICHAEL  Yes, forsooth, mother, and grace of God.

MISTRESS MERRYTHOUGHT  That's a good boy.

WIFE  I'faith, it's a fine spoken child.

JASPER  Mother, though you forget a parent's love, I must preserve the duty of a child. I ran not from my master, nor return To have your stock maintain my idleness.  350

WIFE  Ungracious child, I warrant him; hark how he chops logic with his mother!—Thou hadst best tell her she lies; do, tell her she lies.

CITIZEN  If he were my son, I would hang him up by the heels, and flay him, and salt him, whoreson halter-sack!

JASPER  My coming only is to beg your love, Which I must ever, though I never gain it. And howsoever you esteem of me There is no drop of blood hid in these veins  360 But I remember well belongs to you That brought me forth, and would be glad for you To rip them all again, and let it out.

MISTRESS MERRYTHOUGHT  I'faith, I had sorrow enough for thee, God knows; but I'll hamper thee well enough. Get thee in, thou vagabond, get thee in, and learn of thy brother Michael.  *Exeunt* JASPER *and* MICHAEL

OLD MERRYTHOUGHT  (*within*)
(*Sings*)    *Nose, nose, jolly red nose,*
                *And who gave thee this jolly red nose?*  369

MISTRESS MERRYTHOUGHT  Hark, my husband; he's singing and hoiting, and I'm fain to cark and care,

---

294  shoes in their shop: boys' costumes were elaborate and costly
296  pricking: spurring on his horse
308  gentlemen: the other playgoers on the stage
318  arming: armorial
328  right: legitimate
332  'A merry heart lives long-a': adapted from the song sung by Autolycus in Shakespeare's *The Winter's Tale* (1609), IV.iii.1113–16; a similar line is sung by Silence in his *2 Henry IV* (1597), V.iii.47
333  wastethrift: spendthrift

336  bezzle: squander (from embezzle)
344  forsooth: truly
350  stock: a) provisions; b) money
352  chops logic: formulates specious but cleverly conceived arguments
356  halter-sack: gallows bird
364–5  sorrow enough: in childbirth
365  hamper: a) basket for infants: b) prison fetters (as Jasper is a 'masterless man')
368–9  Nose, nose . . . red nose?: refrain from *Deuteromelia* (1609) by Thomas Ravenscroft
371  hoiting: revelling, roistering
         cark: carp, fret

and all little enough.—Husband, Charles, Charles Merrythought.

*Enter* OLD MERRYTHOUGHT

OLD MERRYTHOUGHT
　(*Sings*)　*Nutmegs and ginger, cinnamon and cloves,*
　　　　　*And they gave me this jolly red nose.*
MISTRESS MERRYTHOUGHT If you would consider your state, you would have little list to sing, iwis.
OLD MERRYTHOUGHT It should never be considered while it were an estate, if I thought it would spoil my singing.　　　　　380
MISTRESS MERRYTHOUGHT But how wilt thou do, Charles? Thou art an old man, and thou canst not work, and thou hast not forty shillings left, and thou eatest good meat, and drinkest good drink, and laughest?
OLD MERRYTHOUGHT And will do.
MISTRESS MERRYTHOUGHT But how wilt thou come by it, Charles?　　　　　388
OLD MERRYTHOUGHT How? Why, how have I done hitherto this forty years? I never came into my dining room, but at eleven and six o'clock I found excellent meat and drink o'th'table; my clothes were never worn out, but next morning a tailor brought me a new suit; and without question it will be so ever. Use makes perfectness. If all should fail, it is but a little straining myself extraordinary, and laugh myself to death.
WIFE It's a foolish old man this: is not he, George?
CITIZEN Yes, cony.　　　　　399
WIFE Give me a penny i'th'purse while I live, George.
CITIZEN Ay, by lady, cony, hold thee there.
MISTRESS MERRYTHOUGHT Well, Charles, you promised to provide for Jasper, and I have laid up for Michael. I pray you, pay Jasper his portion; he's come home, and he shall not consume Michael's stock. He says his master turned him away, but I promise you truly, I think he ran away.
WIFE No indeed, Mistress Merrythought, though he be a notable gallows, yet I'll assure you his master did turn him away, even in this place; 'twas, i'faith, within this half hour, about his daughter; my husband was by.　　　　　412

CITIZEN Hang him, rogue. He served him well enough: love his master's daughter! By my troth, cony, if there were a thousand boys, thou wouldst spoil them all with taking their parts. Let his mother alone with him.
WIFE Ay, George, but yet truth is truth.
OLD MERRYTHOUGHT Where is Jasper? He's welcome how ever. Call him in; he shall have his portion. Is he merry?　　　　　421
MISTRESS MERRYTHOUGHT Ay, foul chive him, he is too merry.—Jasper! Michael!

*Enter* JASPER *and* MICHAEL

OLD MERRYTHOUGHT Welcome, Jasper, though thou run'st away, welcome; God bless thee. 'Tis thy mother's mind thou shouldst receive thy portion. Thou hast been abroad, and I hope hast learned experience enough to govern it; thou art of sufficient years. Hold thy hand: one, two, three, four, five, six, seven, eight, nine, there's ten shillings for thee. Thrust thyself into the world with that, and take some settled course. If fortune cross thee, thou hast a retiring place; come home to me; I have twenty shillings left. Be a good husband, that is, wear ordinary clothes, eat the best meat, and drink the best drink; be merry, and give to the poor, and believe me, thou hast no end of thy goods.
JASPER Long may you live free from all thought of ill, And long have cause to be thus merry still. But, father—　　　　　440
OLD MERRYTHOUGHT No more words, Jasper, get thee gone; thou hast my blessing; thy father's spirit upon thee. Farewell, Jasper.
　(*Sings*)　*But yet, or ere you part, oh cruel,*
　　　　　*Kiss me, kiss me, sweeting, mine own dear*
　　　　　*jewel.*
So, now begone; no words.　　　　　*Exit* JASPER
MISTRESS MERRYTHOUGHT So, Michael, now get thee gone too.
MICHAEL Yes forsooth, mother; but I'll have my father's blessing first.　　　　　450
MISTRESS MERRYTHOUGHT No, Michael, 'tis no matter for his blessing; thou hast my blessing; begone. I'll fetch my money and jewels and follow thee; I'll stay

---

377　state: estate, dignity
　　list: desire
　　iwis: for certain
391　eleven and six o'clock: the hours of the day's main meals
394–5　Use makes perfectness: 'practice makes perfect' (proverbial)
400　Give me . . . I live: i.e. never leave me destitute
401　hold thee there: stick to that
404　portion: inheritance
405　stock: inheritance
409　notable gallows: deserving of hanging

416　taking their parts: a) supporting them; b) pun on sexual organs
420　how ever: in any case
422　foul chive: ill betide
427–37　Thou has . . . thy goods: parody of *Old Fortunatus* (1599) by Thomas Dekker
432　cross: oppose
434　Be a good husband: prudent (as in 'husbanding' his goods)
444–5　*But yet . . . dear jewel*: from Song XV in *First Book of Songs or Airs* (1597) by John Dowland

no longer with him, I warrant thee. (*Exit* MICHAEL)
Truly, Charles, I'll begone too.

OLD MERRYTHOUGHT  What! You will not?

MISTRESS MERRYTHOUGHT  Yes, indeed will I.

OLD MERRYTHOUGHT

(*Sings*)    *Hey-ho, farewell, Nan,*
       *I'll never trust wench more again, if I can.* **459**

MISTRESS MERRYTHOUGHT  You shall not think, when
all your own is gone, to spend that I have been
scraping up for Michael.

OLD MERRYTHOUGHT  Farewell, good wife, I expect it
not; all I have to do in this world is to be merry,
which I shall, if the ground be not taken from me;
and if it be,

(*Sings*)    *When earth and seas from me are reft,*
       *The skies aloft for me are left.*

                             *Exeunt*

FINIS ACTUS PRIMI

# Interlude I

BOY *danceth. Music*

WIFE  I'll be sworn he's a merry old gentleman for all
that. Hark, hark, husband, hark! Fiddles, fiddles! Now
surely they go finely. They say 'tis present death for
these fiddlers to tune their rebecks before the great
Turk's grace, is't not, George? But look, look, here's a
youth dances.—Now, good youth, do a turn o'th'
toe.—Sweetheart, i'faith, I'll have Rafe come and do
some of his gambols.—He'll ride the wild mare,
gentlemen, 'twould do your hearts good to see him.—
I thank you, kind youth; pray, bid Rafe come. **10**

CITIZEN  Peace, cony.—Sirrah, you scurvy boy, bid the
players send Rafe, or by God's [. . .] and they do not,
I'll tear some of their periwigs beside their heads: this
is all riff-raff.

                                    *Exit* BOY

---

460  think: i.e. stop to think, but
467  *reft*: taken away
  3  present: instant
  4  rebecks: early fiddles
  5  Turk's grace: some seventeenth-century travellers
      reported that Sultans were feared for their impatience
  8  gambols: leaping
8–9  wild mare: she means see-saw (proverbial for sexual
      intercourse)
 12  God's [. . .]: the omitted word is probably 'body' (Christ's
      body on the cross). Some eds note the Act to Restrain
      the Abuses of the Players (1606) as an explanation for
      this omission; compare Act II, l. 245
 13  periwigs: wigs were frequently worn by actors in
      performance

# Act II

*Enter* MERCHANT *and* HUMPHREY

MERCHANT  And how, faith, how goes it now, son
    Humphrey?

HUMPHREY  Right worshipful, and my beloved friend
    And father dear, this matter's at an end.

MERCHANT  'Tis well—it should be so, I'm glad the girl
    Is found so tractable.

HUMPHREY             Nay, she must whirl
    From hence (and you must wink; for so, I say,
    The story tells) tomorrow before day.

WIFE  George, dost thou think in thy conscience now
'twill be a match? Tell me but what thou think'st,
sweet rogue. Thou seest the poor gentleman, dear
heart, how it labours and throbs, I warrant you, to be
at rest. I'll go move the father for't. **12**

CITIZEN  No, no, I prithee sit still, honeysuckle; thou't
spoil all. If he deny him, I'll bring half a dozen good
fellows myself, and in the shutting of an evening
knock't up, and there's an end.

WIFE  I'll buss thee for that, i'faith, boy. Well, George,
well, you have been a wag in your days, I warrant
you; but God forgive you, and I do with all my heart.

MERCHANT  How was it, son? You told me that
    tomorrow                           **20**
    Before day break you must convey her hence?

HUMPHREY  I must, I must, and thus it is agreed:
    Your daughter rides upon a brown-bay steed,
    I on a sorrel, which I bought of Brian,
    The honest host of the Red Roaring Lion,
    In Waltham situate. Then, if you may,
    Consent in seemly sort, lest by delay
    The fatal sisters come and do the office,
    And then you'll sing another song.

MERCHANT                Alas,
    Why should you be thus full of grief to me,    **30**
    That do willing as yourself agree
    To anything, so it be good and fair?
    Then steal her when you will, if such a pleasure
    Content you both; I'll sleep and never see it,
    To make your joys more full. But tell me why
    You may not here perform your marriage?

WIFE  God's blessing o'thy soul, old man! I'faith, thou

---

  6  wink: turn a blind eye
 15  shutting of an evening: dusk
 16  knock't up: put an end to this
 17  buss: kiss
 18  wag: mischievous youth
 24  sorrel: chestnut-coloured horse
 25  host: publican
 26  situate: located
 28  fatal sisters: the Three Furies who control a man's life
 30  full of grief to me: 'complain about me'

art loath to part true hearts, I see.—'A has her,
George, and I'm as glad on't.—Well, go thy ways,
Humphrey, for a fair-spoken man; I believe thou hast
not thy fellow within the walls of London; and I
should say the suburbs too I should not lie.—Why
dost not rejoice with me, George?                                    43

CITIZEN  If I could but see Rafe again, I were as merry
as mine host, i'faith.

HUMPHREY  The cause you seem to ask, I thus declare
(Help me, oh Muses nine): your daughter sware
A foolish oath, the more it was the pity;
Yet none but myself within this city
Shall dare to say so, but a bold defiance                            50
Shall meet him, were he of the noble science.
And yet she sware, and yet why did she swear?
Truly, I cannot tell, unless it were
For her own ease, for sure sometimes an oath,
Being sworn, thereafter is like cordial broth.
And this it was she swore: never to marry
But such a one whose mighty arm could carry
(As meaning me, for I am such a one)
Her bodily away through stick and stone,
Till both of us arrive, at her request,                              60
Some ten miles off, in the wild Waltham Forest.

MERCHANT  If this be all, you shall not need to fear
Any denial in your love. Proceed;
I'll neither follow nor repent the deed.

HUMPHREY  Good night, twenty good nights, and
twenty more.
And twenty more good nights—that makes
threescore.                                                  *Exeunt*

*Enter* MISTRESS MERRYTHOUGHT *with jewel casket and
purse of money, and her son* MICHAEL

MISTRESS MERRYTHOUGHT  Come Michael, art thou
not weary, boy?

MICHAEL  No, forsooth, mother, not I.

MISTRESS MERRYTHOUGHT  Where be we now, child?    70

MICHAEL  Indeed, forsooth, mother, I cannot tell,
unless we be at Mile End. Is not all the world Mile
End, mother?

MISTRESS MERRYTHOUGHT  No, Michael, not all the
world, boy; but I can assure thee, Michael, Mile End

is a goodly matter; there has been a pitch-field, my
child, between the naughty Spaniels and the English
men; and the Spaniels ran away, Michael, and the
English men followed. My neighbour Coxstone was
there, boy, and killed them all with a birding piece.

MICHAEL  Mother, forsooth—                                           81

MISTRESS MERRYTHOUGHT  What says my white boy?

MICHAEL  Shall not my father go with us too?

MISTRESS MERRYTHOUGHT  No, Michael, let thy father
go snick up; he shall never come between a pair of
sheets with me again while he lives. Let him stay at
home and sing for his supper, boy. Come, child, sit
down, and I'll show my boy fine knacks indeed. Look
here, Michael, here's a ring, and here's a brooch, and
here's a bracelet, and here's two rings more, and
here's money and gold by th'eye, my boy.                             91

MICHAEL  Shall I have all this, mother?

MISTRESS MERRYTHOUGHT  Ay, Michael, thou shalt
have all, Michael.

CITIZEN  How lik'st thou this, wench?

WIFE  I cannot tell; I would have Rafe, George; I'll see
no more else, indeed la, and I pray you let the youths
understand so much by word of mouth; for I tell you
truly, I'm afraid o' my boy. Come, come, George,
let's be merry and wise. The child's a fatherless child;
and say they should put him into a strait pair of
gaskins, 'twere worse than knot-grass: he would never
grow after it.                                                       103

*Enter* RAFE, TIM *as* SQUIRE, *and* GEORGE *as* DWARF

CITIZEN  Here's Rafe, here's Rafe.

WIFE  How do you, Rafe? You are welcome Rafe, as I
may say; it's a good boy, hold up thy head, and be not
afraid; we are thy friends, Rafe; the gentlemen will
praise thee, Rafe, if thou play'st thy part with
audacity. Begin, Rafe, o'God's name.                                 109

RAFE  My trusty squire, unlace my helm; give me my
hat. Where are we, or what desert may this be?

----

42  suburbs: ironic, since these were the unsavoury areas
    beyond the jurisdiction of the city authorities
47  Muses nine: ironic, since the Muses inspire anything but
    pledges
51  noble science: fencing or boxing
55  cordial: restorative
65–6  Good night . . . makes threescore: a parody of many
    speeches from plays, including the balcony scene from
    Shakespeare's *Romeo and Juliet* (c. 1595)
72  Mile End: a hamlet one mile beyond the old walls of the
    city (on the road beyond Aldgate) used as a training
    ground for the militia of citizen soldiers

76  pitch-field: mock battle, one of the many kinds of
    entertainment staged at Mile End in addition to the
    musters of the militia which were themselves often seen
    as a source of entertainment
77  naughty: wicked
78  Spaniels: Spanish
80  birding piece: amateurish gun
82  white: darling (white boy could mean favourite son)
85  snick up: hang himself
88  knacks: trinkets (as in 'knick-knacks')
91  by th'eye: unlimited in quantity
97  youths: boy actors
101 strait: tight
102 gaskins: breeches
    knot-grass: a weed supposed to stunt growth (and hinder
    sexuality); see Lysander's comment in Shakespeare's
    *A Midsummer Night's Dream* (c. 1595), III.ii.329–31

GEORGE  Mirror of knighthood, this is, as I take it, the
  perilous Waltham Down, in whose bottom stands
  the enchanted valley.
MISTRESS MERRYTHOUGHT  Oh Michael, we are
  betrayed, we are betrayed! Here be giants! Fly, boy;
  fly, boy; fly!
  *Exeunt* MOTHER *and* MICHAEL *dropping purse and casket*
RAFE  Lace on my helm again. What noise is this?
  A gentle lady flying the embrace
  Of some uncourteous knight? I will relieve her.    120
  Go, squire, and say, the knight that wears this pestle
  In honour of all ladies, swears revenge
  Upon that recreant coward that pursues her.
  Go comfort her, and that same gentle squire
  That bears her company.
TIM                    I go brave knight.    *Exit*
RAFE  My trusty dwarf and friend, reach me my shield,
  And hold it while I swear. First by my knighthood;
  Then by the soul of Amadis de Gaul,
  My famous ancestor; then by my sword
  The beautious Brionella girt about me;    130
  By this bright burning pestle, of mine honour
  The living trophy; and by all respect
  Due to distressed damsels: here I vow
  Never to end the quest of this fair lady
  And that forsaken squire, till by my valour
  I gain their liberty.
GEORGE            Heaven bless the knight    136
  That thus relieves poor errant gentlewomen.  *Exeunt*
WIFE  Ay, marry, Rafe, this has some savour in't.—
  I would see the proudest of them all offer to carry his
  books after him. But, George, I will not have him go
  away so soon—I shall be sick if he go away, that I
  shall. Call Rafe again, George, call Rafe again; I
  prithee, sweetheart, let him come fight before me,
  and let's ha' some drums and some trumpets, and let
  him kill all that comes near him, and thou lov'st me,
  George.                                      146
CITIZEN  Peace a little, bird; he shall kill them all, and
  they were twenty more on 'em than there are.

*Enter* JASPER

JASPER  Now, Fortune, if thou be'st not only ill,

Show me thy better face, and bring about    150
Thy desperate wheel, that I may climb at length
And stand. This is our place of meeting
If love have any constancy. Oh age,
Where only wealthy men are counted happy!
How shall I please thee, how deserve thy smiles,
When I am only rich in misery?
My father's blessing, and this little coin
Is my inheritance, a strong revènue
From earth thou art, and to earth I give thee.
                          *Casts the money away*
There grow and multiply, whilst fresher air    160
Breeds me a fresher fortune.—How, illusion?
                          *Spies the casket*
What, hath the devil coined himself before me?
'Tis metal good, it rings well; I am walking,
And taking too, I hope. Now God's dear blessing
Upon his heart that left it here. 'Tis mine;
These pearls, I take it, were not left for swine.    *Exit*
WIFE  I do not like that this unthrifty youth should
  embezzle away the money; the poor gentlewoman his
  mother will have a heavy heart for it, God knows.
CITIZEN  And reason good, sweetheart.    170
WIFE  But let him go. I'll tell Rafe a tale in's ear shall
  fetch him again with a wanion, I warrant him, if he
  be above ground; and besides, George, here are a
  number of sufficient gentlemen can witness, and
  myself, and yourself, and the musicians, if we be
  called in question. But here comes Rafe, George;
  thou shalt hear him speak, an he were an emperal.

*Enter* RAFE *and* GEORGE *as* DWARF

RAFE  Comes not Sir Squire again?
GEORGE                    Right courteous knight,
  Your squire doth come and with him comes the lady,

*Enter* MISTRESS MERRYTHOUGHT *and* MICHAEL *and* TIM
*as* SQUIRE

For and the Squire of Damsels, as I take it.    180

---

112  GEORGE: from this point Q1 substitutes the speech prefix
    DWARFE for GEORGE
123  recreant: a) dishonourable; b) traitorous
128  Amadis de Gaul: a Spanish knight, hero of a romance
    named after him (translated by Anthony Munday in
    parts from 1590 to 1618)
130  Brionella: mistress of Palmerin's friend, Ptolome
    girt: fastened
139–40  carry his books: 'follow like a lowly pedant' (Hattaway)
149–52  Fortune, if . . . And stand: Jasper wants the wheel of
    Fortune (governing his fate) to raise rather than lower
    him (thus showing its happier face)

159  From earth . . . give thee: i.e. from dust to dust (in the
    sense of the cycle of Fortune)
160  grow and multiply: parody of Christ's parable of the
    talents (Matthew 25.14–30)
162  coined: formed
166  These pearls . . . for swine: see Matthew 7.6
168  embezzle: squander
172  wanion: vengeance
174  sufficient: able
177  an: as if
    emperal: emperor
180  For and: as well as
    the Squire of Damsels: 'In Spenser's *The Faerie Queene*
    [1590–6], III.vii.51ff, appears the Squire of Dames whose
    task it is to find three hundred ladies who would "abide
    for ever chaste and sound". When Satyrane meets him he
    has found three' (Hattaway)

RAFE  Madam, if any service or devoir
    Of a poor errant knight may right your wrongs,
    Command it; I am prest to give you succour,
    For to the holy end I bear my armour.
MISTRESS MERRYTHOUGHT  Alas sir, I am a poor
    gentlewoman, and I have lost my money in this
    forest.
RAFE  Desert, you would say, lady, and not lost
    Whilst I have sword and lance. Dry up your tears
    Which ill befit the beauty of that face,                 190
    And tell the story, if I may request it,
    Of your disastrous fortune.
MISTRESS MERRYTHOUGHT  Out, alas! I left a thousand
    pound, a thousand pound, e'en all the money I had
    laid up for this youth, upon the sight of your
    mastership; you looked so grim, and, as I may say it,
    saving your presence, more like a giant than a mortal
    man.
RAFE  I am as you are, lady; so are they
    All mortal. But why weeps this gentle squire?          200
MISTRESS MERRYTHOUGHT  Has he not cause to weep,
    do you think, when he hath lost his inheritance?
RAFE  Young hope of valour, weep not; I am here
    That will confound thy foe and pay it dear
    Upon his coward head, that dares deny
    Distressed squires and ladies equity.
    I have but one horse, on which shall ride
    This lady fair behind me, and before
    This courteous squire; fortune will give us more
    Upon our next adventure. Fairly speed              210
    Beside us, squire and dwarf, to do us need.     *Exeunt*
CITIZEN  Did not I tell you, Nell, what your man would
    do? By the faith of my body, wench, for clean action
    and good delivery they may all cast their caps at him.
WIFE  And so they may, i'faith, for I dare speak it
    boldly, the twelve companies of London cannot
    match him, timber for timber. Well, George, and he
    be not inveigled by some of these paltry players, I ha'
    much marvel; but, George, we ha' done our parts if
    the boy have any grace to be thankful.                 220
CITIZEN  Yes, I warrant thee, duckling.

*Enter* HUMPHREY *and* LUCE

HUMPHREY  Good Mistress Luce, however I in fault am
    For your lame horse, you're welcome unto Waltham.
    But which way now to go or what to say
    I know not truly till it be broad day.
LUCE  Oh fear not, Master Humphrey, I am guide
    For this place good enough.
HUMPHREY                              Then up and ride,
    Or, if it please you, walk for your repose,
    Or sit, or if you will, go pluck a rose;
    Either of which shall be indifferent              230
    To your good friend and Humphrey, whose consent
    Is so entangled ever to your will,
    As the poor harmless horse is to the mill.
LUCE  Faith, and you say the word, we'll e'en sit down
    And take a nap.
HUMPHREY              'Tis better in the town,
    Where we may nap together; for, believe me,
    To sleep without a snatch would mickle grieve me.
LUCE  You're merry, Master Humphrey.
HUMPHREY                                     So I am,
    And have been ever merry from my dam.
LUCE  Your nurse had the less labour.
HUMPHREY                                   Faith, it may be,
    Unless it were by chance I did beray me.          241

*Enter* JASPER

JASPER  Luce, dear friend Luce!
LUCE                          Here, Jasper.
JASPER                                       You are mine.
HUMPHREY  If it be so, my friend, you use me fine;
    What do you think I am?
JASPER                       An arrant noddy.
HUMPHREY  A word of obloquy! Now, by God's body,
    I'll tell thy master, for I know thee well.
JASPER  Nay, and you be so forward for to tell,
    Take that, and that, and tell him, sir, I gave it,
                                            *Beats him*
    And say I paid you well.
HUMPHREY                     Oh, sir, I have it,
    And do confess the payment. Pray be quiet.      250
JASPER  Go, get to your night-cap and the diet

---

181  devoir: duty (in chivalric terms)
183  prest: prepared, from *prêt* (French)
185–7  I am . . . this forest: see *Palmerin d'Olivia*: 'Palmerin
    and Ptoleme met with a Damsel, who made great moan
    for a casket which two knights had forcibly taken from
    her' (I.21)
200  All: wholly
206  equity: justice
213  clean: adroit
214  cast their caps at: give up trying to imitate
216  twelve companies: see Induction, l. 14n
217  timber for timber: like for like
218  inveigled: boys were sometime kidnapped as possible actors

229  pluck a rose: a) urinate (most eds); b) euphemism for
    defecate (Wine)
235  nap: a) sleep; b) drink
237  snatch: snack
    mickle: much (northern English and still used in
    Scotland)
239  dam: mother
241  beray: befoul myself
244  arrant noddy: itinerant fool (or simpleton)
245  God's body: see Interlude I, l. 12n
250  confess: acknowledge
    quiet: at peace
251  night-cap: nightcaps were especially worn during ill
    health

To cure your beaten bones.

LUCE                    Alas, poor Humphrey,
Get thee some wholesome broth with sage and
    comfrey;
A little oil of roses and a feather
To 'noint thy back withal.

HUMPHREY                    When I came hither,
Would I had gone to Paris with John Dory.

LUCE  Farewell, my pretty Nump; I am very sorry
I cannot bear thee company.

HUMPHREY                    Farewell;
The devil's dam was ne'er so banged in hell.    259

        *Exeunt* LUCE *and* JASPER. *Manet* HUMPHREY

WIFE  This young Jasper will prove me another thing,
o'my conscience, and he may be suffered. George,
dost not see, George, how 'a swaggers, and flies at the
very heads o'folks as he were a dragon? Well, if I do
not do his lesson for wronging the poor gentleman, I
am no true woman. His friends that brought him up
might have been better occupied, iwis, than ha'
taught him these fegaries; he's e'en in the highway to
the gallows, God bless him.

CITIZEN  You're too bitter, cony; the young man may
do well enough for all this.    270

WIFE  Come hither, Master Humphrey; has he hurt you?
Now beshrew his fingers for't. Here, sweetheart, here's
some green ginger for thee. Now beshrew my heart,
but 'a has peppernel in's head as big as a pullet's egg.
Alas, sweet lamb, how thy temples beat! Take the
peace on him, sweetheart, take the peace on him.

*Enter a* BOY

CITIZEN  No, no, you talk like a foolish woman. I'll ha'
Rafe fight with him, and swinge him up well-
favouredly. Sirrah boy, come hither; let Rafe come in
and fight with Jasper.    280

WIFE  Ay, and beat him well; he's an unhappy boy.

BOY  Sir, you must pardon us; the plot of our play lies

contrary, and 'twill hazard the spoiling of our play.

CITIZEN  Plot me no plots. I'll ha' Rafe come out; I'll
make your house too hot for you else.

BOY  Why, sir, he shall; but if anything fall out of order,
the gentlemen must pardon us.

CITIZEN  Go your ways, goodman boy. (*Exit* BOY)—I'll
hold him a penny he shall have his bellyful of fighting
now. Ho, here comes Rafe; no more.    290

*Enter* RAFE, MISTRESS MERRYTHOUGHT, MICHAEL, TIM
*as* SQUIRE, *and* GEORGE *as* DWARF

RAFE  What knight is that, squire? Ask him if he keep
The passage, bound by love of lady fair,
Or else but prickant.

HUMPHREY                    Sir, I am no knight,
But a poor gentleman, that this same night
Had stolen from me on yonder green
My lovely wife, and suffered (to be seen
Yet extant on my shoulders) such a greeting
That whilst I live I shall think of that meeting.

WIFE  Ay, Rafe, he beat him unmercifully, Rafe; and
thou spar'st him, Rafe, I would thou wert hanged. 300

CITIZEN  No more, wife, no more.

RAFE  Where is the caitiff wretch hath done this deed?
Lady, your pardon, that I may proceed
Upon the quest of this injurious knight.
And thou, fair squire, repute me not the worse,
In leaving the great venture of the purse
And the rich casket till some better leisure.

*Enter* JASPER *and* LUCE

Here comes the broker hath purloined my treasure.

RAFE  Go, squire, and tell him I am here,
An errant knight at arms, to crave delivery    310
Of that fair lady to her own knight's arms.
If he deny, bid him take choice of ground,
And so defy him.

TIM                    From the knight that bears
The golden pestle, I defy thee, knight,
Unless thou make fair restitution
Of that bright lady.

JASPER                    Tell the knight that sent thee
He is an ass, and I will keep the wench
And knock his head-piece.

RAFE                    Knight, thou art but dead,

253  comfrey: medicinal plant (*symphytum officinale*) with
    pink-purple or cream flowers found near ditches and
    streams; common in the south of England
256  John Dory: hero of a song (music by Thomas
    Ravenscroft, 1609) who is captured by highwaymen on
    his way to visit the King of France
257  Nump: a) a fool; b) nickname for Humphrey
259  The devil's . . . in hell: reference to Morality plays in
    which the devil and his kin were belaboured by vices
267  fegaries: vagaries, pranks
273  green ginger: medicine to relieve aches and pains
274  peppernel: lump, swelling
275–6  Take the peace on him: obtain sureties for his good
    conduct
278  with: for, on his behalf
    swinge: thrash
278–9  well-favouredly: thoroughly
281  unhappy: good-for-nothing

283  spoiling: 'George and Nell have attempted to redo the
    play by adding Rafe: now they attempt to rewrite it;
    eventually they will want to displace it' (Kinney)
289  hold: bet
291–2  keep/The passage: guard the entrance to the castle
293  prickant: riding fast (but with sexual connotation)
296  wife: i.e. betrothed
302  caitiff: wicked
304  injurious: malicious
308  broker: pimp

If thou recall not thy uncourteous terms.

WIFE  Break's pate, Rafe; break's pate, Rafe, soundly. 320

JASPER  Come, knight, I am ready for you. Now your
    pestle                *Snatches away his pestle*
Shall try what temper, sir, your mortar's of.
(*Recites*) 'With that he stood upright in his stirrups,
and gave the Knight of the Calf-skin such a knock
(*Knocks* RAFE *down*) that he forsook his horse and
down he fell; and then he leaped upon him, and
plucking off his helmet—'

HUMPHREY  Nay, and my noble knight be down so
    soon,
Though I can scarcely go, I needs must run.
                     *Exeunt* HUMPHREY *and* RAFE

WIFE  Run, Rafe; run, Rafe; run for thy life, boy; Jasper
comes, Jasper comes.            331

JASPER  Come, Luce, we must have other arms for you;
Humphrey and Golden Pestle, both adieu.    *Exeunt*

WIFE  Sure the devil, God bless us, is in this springald.
Why, George, didst ever see such a fire-drake? I am
afraid my boy's miscarried; if he be, though he were
Master Merrythought's son a thousand times, if there
be any law in England, I'll make some of them smart
for't.            339

CITIZEN  No, no, I have found out the matter,
sweetheart: Jasper is enchanted; as sure as we are here,
he is enchanted. He could no more have stood in
Rafe's hands than I can stand in my Lord Mayor's. I'll
have a ring to discover all enchantments, and Rafe
shall beat him yet. Be no more vexed, for it shall be so.

*Enter* RAFE, TIM *as* SQUIRE, GEORGE *as* DWARF,
MISTRESS MERRYTHOUGHT *and* MICHAEL

WIFE  Oh, husband, here's Rafe again.—Stay, Rafe, let
me speak with thee. How dost thou, Rafe? Art thou
not shroadly hurt? The foul great lungies laid
unmercifully on thee; there's some sugar-candy for
thee. Proceed, thou shalt have another bout with him.

CITIZEN  If Rafe had him at the fencing-school, if he did
not make a puppy of him, and drive him up and down
the school, he should ne'er come in my shop more.

MISTRESS MERRYTHOUGHT  Truly, Master Knight of
the Burning Pestle, I am weary.    355

MICHAEL  Indeed la, mother, and I am very hungry.

RAFE  Take comfort, gentle dame, and you, fair squire,
For in this desert there must needs be placed
Many strong castles held by courteous knights;
And till I bring you safe to one of those,    360
I swear by this my order ne'er to leave you.

WIFE  Well said, Rafe.—George, Rafe was ever
comfortable, was he not?

CITIZEN  Yes, duck.

WIFE  I shall ne'er forget him, when we had lost our
child (you know it was strayed almost, alone, to
Puddle Wharf, and the criers were abroad for it, and
there it had drowned itself but for a sculler), Rafe was
the most comfortablest to me: 'Peace, mistress', says
he, 'let it go; I'll get you another as good'. Did he not,
George, did he not say so?    371

CITIZEN  Yes indeed did he, mouse.

GEORGE  I would we had a mess of pottage and a pot of
drink, squire, and were going to bed.

TIM  Why, we are at Waltham town's end, and that's
the Bell Inn.

GEORGE  Take courage, valiant knight, damsel, and
    squire;
I have discovered, not a stone's cast off,
An ancient castle held by the old knight
Of the most holy order of the Bell,    380
Who gives to all knights errant entertain.
There plenty is of food, and all prepared
By the white hands of his own lady dear.
He hath three squires that welcome all his guests:
The first hight Chamberlino, who will see
Our beds prepared, and bring us snowy sheets,
Where never footman stretched his buttered hams;
The second hight Tapstero, who will see
Our pots full filled and no froth therein;
The third, a gentle squire, Ostlero hight    390
Who will our palfreys slick with wisps of straw,
And in the manger put them oats enough,

---

320  pate: head
324  Calf-skin: refers to the calf-skin vellum on which old
    romances were written
329  go: walk
334  springald: stripling
335  fire-drake: dragon
336  miscarried: come to harm
342  have stood in: withstood
348  shroadly: severely (archaic form of 'shrewdly')
    lungies: louts (from Longinus, the soldier who thrust a
    spear into the body of Christ)
352  puppy: coward

361  my order: i.e. of knighthood
363  comfortable: helpful
367  Puddle Wharf: Thames landing place at the foot of
    St Andrew's Hill (now Puddle Dock, near Blackfriars
    Bridge)
    criers were abroad for it: one responsibility of town criers
    was to help find lost children
368  sculler: either an oarsman or a light river boat
370  get: play on 'beget'
373  mess of pottage: stew of boiled vegetables (and
    sometimes meat)
378  I have discovered: the episode that begins here, where an
    inn is mistaken for a castle, is taken from Book I of *Don
    Quixote*
385  hight: called (archaic)
387  Where never . . . buttered hams: footmen ran with their
    masters' carriages and greased their calves to prevent cramp
391  slick: make sleek

And never grease their teeth with candle-snuff.

WIFE That same dwarf's a pretty boy, but the squire's a
groutnoll.

RAFE Knock at the gates, my squire, with stately lance.

*Enter* TAPSTER

TAPSTER Who's there?—You're welcome, gentlemen;
will you see a room?

GEORGE Right courteous and valiant Knight of the
Burning Pestle, this is the Squire Tapstero.                    400

RAFE Fair Squire Tapstero, I, a wandering knight
Hight of the Burning Pestle, in the quest
Of this fair lady's casket and wrought purse
Losing myself in this vast wilderness,
Am to this castle well by fortune brought;
Where, hearing of the goodly entertain
Your knight of holy order of the Bell
Gives to all damsels and all errant knights,
I thought to knock, and now am bold to enter.    409

TAPSTER An't please you see a chamber, you are very
welcome.                                              *Exeunt*

WIFE George, I would have something done, and I
cannot tell what it is.

CITIZEN What is it, Nell?

WIFE Why, George, shall Rafe beat nobody again?
Prithee, sweetheart, let him.

CITIZEN So he shall, Nell; and if I join with him, we'll
knock them all.

*Enter* HUMPHREY *and* MERCHANT

WIFE Oh, George, here's Master Humphrey again
now, that lost Mistress Luce, and Mistress Luce's
father. Master Humphrey will do somebody's errand,
I warrant him.                                         422

HUMPHREY Father, it's true in arms I ne'er shall clasp
her,
For she is stol'n away by your man Jasper.

WIFE I thought he would tell him.

MERCHANT Unhappy that I am to lose my child!
Now I begin to think on Jasper's words,
Who oft hath urged to me thy foolishness.
Why didst thou let her go? Thou lov'st her not,
That wouldst bring home thy life, and not bring her.

HUMPHREY Father, forgive me. Shall I tell you true?  431
Look on my shoulders, they are black and blue.
Whilst to and fro fair Luce and I were winding,
He came and basted me with a hedge-binding.

MERCHANT Get men and horses straight; we will be
there
Within this hour. You know the place again?

HUMPHREY I know the place where he my loins did
swaddle.
I'll get six horses, and to each a saddle.

MERCHANT Meantime I'll go talk with Jasper's father.
                                                    *Exeunt*

WIFE George, what wilt thou lay with me now, that
Master Humphrey has not Mistress Luce yet? Speak,
George, what wilt thou lay with me?                   442

CITIZEN No; Nell, I warrant thee Jasper is at
Puckeridge with her by this.

WIFE Nay, George, you must consider Mistress Luce's
feet are tender, and, besides, 'tis dark; and I promise
you truly, I do not see how he should get out of
Waltham Forest with her yet.

CITIZEN Nay, cony, what wilt thou lay with me that
Rafe has her not yet?                                 450

WIFE I will not lay against Rafe, honey, because I have
not spoken with him. But look, George, peace; here
comes the merry old gentleman again.

*Enter* OLD MERRYTHOUGHT

OLD MERRYTHOUGHT

(*Sings*)     *When it was grown to dark midnight,*
             *And all were fast asleep,*
             *In came Margaret's grimly ghost,*
             *And stood at William's feet.*         457
I have money and meat and drink beforehand till
tomorrow at noon; why should I be sad? Methinks I
have half a dozen jovial spirits within me (*sings*) *I am*
*three merry men, and three merry men.* To what end
should any man be sad in this world? Give me a man
that when he goes to hanging cries (*sings*) *Troll the*
*black bowl to me!* and a woman that will sing a catch in
her travail. I have seen a man come by my door with a

---

393  grease their . . . with candle-snuff: a common trick which
     prevented horses from eating
395  groutnoll: blockhead
403  wrought: embroidered
421  errand: worthy deed (errant Q1)
434  basted: beat

435  straight: at once
437  swaddle: beat soundly (from 'swathe')
440  lay: wager (with sexual connotation)
444  Puckeridge: a Hertfordshire village twenty-three miles
     north of London (and sixteen miles beyond Waltham
     Forest)
454-7  *When it . . . William's feet*: a version of a verse from 'Fair
     Margaret and Sweet William' (traditional)
456  *grimly*: grim-looking
460-1  *I am . . . merry men*: from a song that appears in *Old*
     *Wives' Tale* (1591) by George Peele
463-4  *Troll the . . . to me*: from a song that appears in *Summer's*
     *Last Will and Testament* (1592) by Thomas Nashe (1567–
     1601); see also 'The Second Three-Man's Song' from
     Thomas Dekker's *The Shoemaker's Holiday* (1599)
463  *Troll*: pass
464  *black bowl*: drinking vessel
     catch: short, often bawdy song
465  travail: labour

serious face, in a black cloak, without a hat-band,
carrying his head as if he looked for pins in the street;
I have looked out of my window half a year after, and
have spied that man's head upon London Bridge. 'Tis
vile. Never trust a tailor that does not sing at his work:
his mind is of nothing but filching.                               471

WIFE  Mark this, George, 'tis worth noting; Godfrey
my tailor, you know, never sings, and he had fourteen
yards to make this gown; and I'll be sworn Mistress
Pennistone the draper's wife had one made with
twelve.

OLD MERRYTHOUGHT
(Sings)    'Tis mirth that fills the veins with blood,
           More than wine, or sleep, or food;
           Let each man keep his heart at ease,
           No man dies of that disease.                            480
           He that would his body keep
           From diseases, must not weep;
           But whoever laughs and sings,
           Never he his body brings
           Into fevers, gouts or rheums,
           Or lingeringly his lungs consumes,
           Or meets with achès in the bone,
           Or catarrhs, or griping stone,
           But contented lives for aye;
           The more he laughs, the more he may.                   490

WIFE  Look, George, how say'st thou by this, George?
Is't not a fine old man?—Now God's blessing o'thy
sweet lips.—When wilt thou be so merry, Geoge?
Faith, thou art the frowning'st little thing, when thou
art angry, in a country.

*Enter* MERCHANT

CITIZEN  Peace, cony, thou shalt see him taken down
too, I warrant thee. Here's Luce's father come now.

OLD MERRYTHOUGHT
(Sings)    As you came from Walsingham
           From that holy land,
           There met you not with my true love                    500
           By the way as you came?

MERCHANT  Oh, Master Merrythought, my daughter's
gone!

This mirth becomes you not, my daughter's gone.

OLD MERRYTHOUGHT
(Sings)    Why, an if she be, what care I?
           Or let her come, or go, or tarry.

MERCHANT  Mock not my misery; it is your son
Whom I have made my own, when all forsook him,
Has stol'n my only joy, my child, away.

OLD MERRYTHOUGHT
(Sings)    He set her on a milk-white steed,
           And himself upon a grey,                               510
           He never turned his face again,
           But he bore her quite away.

MERCHANT  Unworthy of the kindness I have shown
To thee and thine! Too late I well perceive
Thou art consenting to my daughter's loss.

OLD MERRYTHOUGHT  Your daughter! What a stir's
here wi' yer daughter? Let her go, think no more on
her, but sing loud. If both my sons were on the
gallows, I would sing,
(Sings)    Down, down, down they fall,                           520
           Down, and arise they never shall.

MERCHANT  Oh, might I behold her once again,
And she once more embrace her aged sire.

OLD MERRYTHOUGHT  Fie, how scurvily this goes. 'And
she once more embrace her aged sire'? You'll make a
dog on her will ye? She cares much for her aged sire,
I warrant you.
(Sings)    She cares not for her daddy, nor
           She cares not for her mammy;
           For she is, she is, she is, she is                     530
           My Lord of Lowgave's lassy.

MERCHANT  For this thy scorn, I will pursue that son
Of thine to death.

OLD MERRYTHOUGHT  Do, and when you ha' killed
him,
(Sings)    Give him flowers enow, palmer, give him
               flowers enow,
           Give him red, and white, and blue, green,
               and yellow.

MERCHANT  I'll fetch my daughter.

OLD MERRYTHOUGHT  I'll hear no more o' your
daughter; it spoils my mirth.                                     540

MERCHANT  I say, I'll fetch my daughter.

---

466–7 *without a hat-band*: sign of a Puritan
469–70 *head upon London Bridge*: after execution the heads
       of traitors were displayed on London Bridge as a warning
       to others; see *Edward II*, I.i.118
471 *filching*: stealing
473 *my tailor*: tailors were believed to be dishonest
       *fourteen yards*: see *The Roaring Girl*, II.ii.90n
487 *achès*: pronounced 'aitches'
488 *catarrhs*: inflammation of the nose and throat
       *griping stone*: painful gallstone
498–501 *As you . . . you came?*: a popular ballad about a village
       in Norfolk that was, until 1538, a major Roman Catholic
       shrine to the Virgin Mary

504–5 *Why, an . . . or tarry*: from 'Farewell, Dear Love', a
       popular song that appears in Shakespeare's *Twelfth Night*
       (1601–2), II.iii.91
509–12 *He set . . . milk-white steed*: corresponds to a verse in
       'The Ballad of the Knight and the Shepherd's Daughter'
520–1 *Down, down . . . never shall*: from 'Sorrow's Story' in
       John Dowland's *Second Book of Songs and Airs* (1600)
525–6 *make a dog on her*: Venturewell has called himself
       Luce's 'sire'
536 *enow*: enough
       *palmer*: pilgrim

OLD MERRYTHOUGHT
(*Sings*)   *Was never man for lady's sake,*
          *Down, down,*
          *Tormented as I, poor Sir Guy,*
          *De derry down,*
          *For Lucy's sake, that lady bright,*
          *Down, down,*
          *As ever men beheld with eye,*
          *De derry down.*
MERCHANT   I'll be revenged, by heaven.            **550**
                                          *Exeunt*

FINIS ACTUS SECUNDI

# Interlude II

*Music*

WIFE   How dost thou like this, George?
CITIZEN   Why, this is well, cony; but if Rafe were hot
   once, thou shouldst see more.
WIFE   The fiddlers go again, husband.
CITIZEN   Ay, Nell, but this is scurvy music. I gave the
   whoreson gallows money, and I think he has not got
   me the waits of Southwark. If I hear 'em not anon,
   I'll twinge him by the ears.—You musicians, play
   'Baloo'.
WIFE   No, good George, lets ha' 'Lachrimae'.         **10**
CITIZEN   Why, this is it, cony.
WIFE   It's all the better, George. Now, sweet lamb,
   what story is that painted upon the cloth? The
   Confutation of Saint Paul?
CITIZEN   No, lamb, that's Rafe and Lucrece.
WIFE   Rafe and Lucrece? Which Rafe? Our Rafe?
CITIZEN   No, mouse, that was a Tartarian.
WIFE   A Tartarian! Well, I would the fiddlers had done,
   that we might see our Rafe again.

---

542–9   *Was never . . . derry down*: from the medieval legend of
        Guy of Warwick, a popular hero of romance and ballads
   2   hot: aroused
   8   twinge: tweak
   9   'Baloo': a common word in the refrains of lullabies;
        possibly referring here to 'Lady Bothwell's Lamentation'
   10  'Lachrimae': a set of pavans (courtly dances) by John
        Dowland (1605)
   13  story is . . . the cloth?: a painted cloth (arras) or tapestry
        hung behind the stage
   13–14  The Confutation of Saint Paul?: a bawdy malapropism
        for 'The Conversion of Saint Paul'
   15  Rafe and Lucrece: bawdy pun on *The Rape of Lucrece*, a
        poem by Shakespeare (1594) and a play by Thomas
        Heywood (1608)
   17  Tartarian: a) another mispronunciation, of (Sextus)
        Tarquinius who raped Lucrece: b) cant term for thief; c)
        reference to the proverbial cruelty toward women of the
        inhabitants of Tartary, north of the Himalayas

# Act III

*Enter* JASPER *and* LUCE

JASPER   Come, my dear deer, though we have lost our way,
   We have not lost ourselves. Are you not weary
   With this night's wandering, broken from your rest,
   And frighted with the terror that attends
   The darkness of this wild unpeopled place?
LUCE   No, my best friend, I cannot either fear
   Or entertain a weary thought, whilst you
   (The end of all my full desires) stand by me.
   Let them that lose their hopes, and live to languish
   Amongst the number of forsaken lovers,         **10**
   Tell the long weary steps, and number time,
   Start at a shadow, and shrink up their blood,
   Whilst I (possessed with all content and quiet)
   Thus take my pretty love, and thus embrace him.
JASPER   You have caught me, Luce, so fast, that whilst I
      live
   I shall become your faithful prisoner,
   And wear these chains for ever. Come, sit down
   And rest your body, too, too delicate
   For these disturbances. So, will you sleep?
   Come, do not be more able than you are;         **20**
   I know you are not skilful in these watches,
   For women are no soldiers; be not nice,
   But take it; sleep, I say.
LUCE                          I cannot sleep,
   Indeed I cannot, friend.
JASPER                       Why, then we'll sing,
   And try how that will work upon our senses.
LUCE   I'll sing, or say, or anything but sleep.
JASPER   Come, little mermaid, rob me of my heart
   With that enchanting voice.
LUCE                          You mock me, Jasper.

          SONG
JASPER   *Tell me, dearest, what is love?*
LUCE     *'Tis a lightning from above,*         **30**
         *'Tis an arrow, 'tis a fire,*
         *'Tis a boy they call Desire,*
            *'Tis a smile*
            *Doth beguile*

---

   3   broken: roused
   11  Tell: count
   12  shrink up their blood: fear was thought to dry up the
        elements of the body
   20  able: capable of endurance
   21  watches: vigils
   22  nice: reluctant, fastidious
   23  take it: yield
   29–42  *Tell me . . . love anew*: the music for this song has
        survived (see E. S. Lindsay in the further reading section
        for this play)

| JASPER | *The poor hearts of men that prove.* |
| | *Tell me more, are women true?* |
| LUCE | *Some love change, and so do you.* |
| JASPER | *Are they fair, and never kind?* |
| LUCE | *Yes, when men turn with the wind.* |
| JASPER | *Are they froward* 40 |
| LUCE | *Ever toward* |
| | *Those that love to love anew.* |

JASPER Dissemble it no more; I see the god
  Of heavy sleep lay on his heavy mace
  Upon your eyelids.
LUCE                    I am very heavy.    *She falls asleep*
JASPER Sleep, sleep, and quiet rest crown thy sweet
    thoughts.
  Keep from her fair blood distempers; startings,
  Horrors, and fearful shapes; let all her dreams
  Be joys, and chaste delights, embraces, wishes,
  And such new pleasures as the ravished soul    50
  Gives to the senses. So, my charms have took.
  Keep her, you powers divine, whilst I contemplate
  Upon the wealth and beauty of her mind.
  She is only fair and constant, only kind,
  And only to thee, Jasper. Oh my joys,
  Whither will you transport me? Let not fullness
  Of my poor buried hopes come up together
  And overcharge my spirits. I am weak.
  Some say (however ill) the sea and women
  Are governed by the moon: both ebb and flow,    60
  Both full of changes. Yet to them that know
  And truly judge, these but opinions are,
  And heresies to bring on pleasing war
  Between our tempers, that without these were
  Both void of after-love, and present fear,
  Which are the best of Cupid. Oh thou child
  Bred from despair, I dare not entertain thee,
  Having a love without the faults of women,
  And greater in her perfect goods than men;
  Which to make good, and please myself the stronger,
  Though certainly I am certain of her love,    71
  I'll try her, that the world and memory

---

35 *prove*: strive
44 heavy mace: a mace was the emblem of Morpheus, the
   classical god of sleep
45 heavy: drowsy
47 distempers: mental or physical disorders
50 ravished: 'transported from the body' (Kinney)
54 is only: alone is
62–6 these but . . . of Cupid: 'empty and false notions that
   pleasantly disturb the balance of our emotions; for
   without these we should not experience either love in
   retrospect or the pangs of anxiety which are love's chief
   joys' (Hattaway)
70 make good: demonstrate
72 try: put to the test

May sing to aftertimes her constancy.
                              *He draws his sword*
  Luce, Luce, awake.
LUCE                    Why do you fright me, friend,
  With those distempered looks? What makes your
    sword
  Drawn in your hand? Who hath offended you?
  I prithee, Jasper, sleep; thou art wild with watching.
JASPER Come, make your way to heaven, and bid the
    world
  (With all the villainies that stick upon it)
  Farewell; you're for another life.
LUCE                              Oh Jasper,    80
  How have my tender years committed evil
  (Especially against the man I love)
  Thus to be cropped untimely?
JASPER                      Foolish girl,
  Canst thou imagine I could love his daughter,
  That flung me from my fortune into nothing,
  Discharged me his service, shut the doors
  Upon my poverty, and scorned my prayers,
  Sending me, like a boat without a mast,
  To sink or swim? Come, by this hand you die;
  I must have life and blood to satisfy    90
  Your father's wrongs.
WIFE Away, George, away; raise the watch at Ludgate,
  and bring a mittimus from the justice for this
  desperate villain.—Now I charge you, gentlemen, see
  the king's peace kept.—Oh, my heart, what a varlet's
  this to offer manslaughter upon the harmless
  gentlewoman!
CITIZEN I warrant thee, sweetheart, we'll have him
  hampered.
LUCE Oh, Jasper, be not cruel;    100
  If thou wilt kill me, smile and do it quickly,
  And let not many deaths appear before me.
  I am a woman made of fear and love,
  A weak, weak woman; kill not with thy eyes,
  They shoot me through and through. Strike, I am
    ready;
  And, dying, still I love thee.

*Enter MERCHANT, HUMPHREY, and his men*

MERCHANT                    Whereabouts?
JASPER (*Aside*) No more of this, now to myself again.
HUMPHREY There, there he stands with sword, like
    martial knight,
  Drawn in his hand; therefore beware the fight,

---

77 wild with watching: mad with anxiety
83 cropped untimely: 'cut off from life before my time'
92 Ludgate: a station for the watch (and used as a prison)
93 mittimus: a warrant, from its opening word 'we send'
99 hampered: confined

You that be wise; for, were I good Sir Bevis,           110
  I would not stay his coming, by your leaves.
MERCHANT Sirrah, restore my daughter.
JASPER                                    Sirrah, no.
MERCHANT Upon him, then.
WIFE So, down with him, down with him, down with
  him! Cut him i'th' leg, boys, cut him i'th' leg!
MERCHANT Come your ways, minion. I'll provide a
  cage
  For you, you're grown so tame.—Horse her away.
HUMPHREY Truly I'm glad your forces have the day.
                              *Exeunt, manet* JASPER
JASPER They are gone, and I am hurt; my love is lost,
  Never to get again. Oh, me unhappy,           120
  Bleed, bleed, and die! I cannot. Oh my folly,
  Thou hast betrayed me! Hope, where art thou fled?
  Tell me if thou be'st anywhere remaining.
  Shall I but see my love again? Oh, no!
  She will not deign to look upon her butcher,
  Nor is it fit she should; yet I must venture.
  Oh, chance, or fortune, or whate'er thou art
  That men adore for powerful, hear my cry,
  And let me loving live, or losing die.
WIFE Is'a gone, George?                        130
CITIZEN Ay, cony.
WIFE Marry, and let him go, sweetheart. By the faith o'
  my body, 'a has put me into such a fright that I
  tremble, as they say, as 'twere an aspen leaf. Look o'
  my little finger, George, how it shakes. Now, i'truth,
  every member of my body is the worse for't.
CITIZEN Come, hug in mine arms, sweet mouse; he
  shall not fright thee any more. Alas, mine own dear
  heart, how it quivers.

*Enter* MISTRESS MERRYTHOUGHT, RAFE, MICHAEL, TIM
*as* SQUIRE, GEORGE *as* DWARF, HOST *and a* TAPSTER

WIFE Oh, Rafe, how dost thou, Rafe? How hast thou
  slept tonight? Has the knight used thee well?  141
CITIZEN Peace, Nell; let Rafe alone.
TAPSTER Master, the reckoning is not paid.
RAFE Right courteous knight, who, for the order's sake
  Which thou hast ta'en, hang'st out the holy bell,
  As I this flaming pestle bear about,
  We render thanks to your puissant self,
  Your beauteous lady, and your gentle squires,

For thus refreshing of our wearied limbs,
  Stiffened with hard achievements in wild desert.  150
TAPSTER Sir, there is twelve shillings to pay.
RAFE Thou merry squire Tapstero, thanks to thee
  For comforting our souls with double jug;
  And if advent'rous fortune prick thee forth,
  Thou jovial squire, to follow feats of arms,
  Take heed thou tender every lady's cause,
  Every true knight, and every damsel fair;
  But spill the blood of treacherous Saracens
  And false enchanters that with magic spells
  Have done to death full many a noble knight.  160
HOST Thou valiant Knight of the Burning Pestle, give
  ear to me: there is twelve shillings to pay, and as I am
  a true knight, I will not bate a penny.
WIFE George, I pray thee tell me, must Rafe pay twelve
  shillings now?
CITIZEN No, Nell, no; nothing but the old knight is
  merry with Rafe.
WIFE Oh, is't nothing else? Rafe will be as merry as he.
RAFE Sir knight, this mirth of yours becomes you well;
  But to requite this liberal courtesy,           170
  If any of your squires will follow arms,
  He shall receive from my heroic hand
  A knighthood, by the virtue of this pestle.
HOST Fair knight, I thank you for your noble offer;
  Therefore, gentle knight,
  Twelve shillings you must pay, or I must cap you.
WIFE Look, George, did not I tell thee as much; the
  Knight of the Bell is in earnest. Rafe shall not be
  beholding to him—give him his money, George, and
  let him go snick up.                            180
CITIZEN Cap Rafe? No.—Hold your hand, Sir Knight
  of the Bell; there's your money. Have you anything to
  say to Rafe now? Cap Rafe!
WIFE I would you should know it, Rafe has friends that
  will not suffer him to be capped for ten times so
  much, and ten times to the end of that.—Now take
  thy course, Rafe.
MISTRESS MERRYTHOUGHT Come, Michael, thou and I
  will go home to thy father; he hath enough left to

---

110 Sir Bevis: the hero of the famous medieval romance of
    Sir Bevis of Hampton
111 stay: wait for
116 minion: 'hussy'
117 you're: until you are
125 deign: condescend
141 tonight: i.e. last night
143 the reckoning: the bill for food, drink and
    accommodation at an inn
147 puissant: powerful, noble

---

151 twelve shillings: a modest amount for the services
    received
153 double jug: strong ale
154 advent'rous: hazardous
    prick thee forth: spur you on
156 tender: care for
158 Saracens: a loosely applied term; the 'enemies of the
    Crusaders, Moors who are the enemy of Don Quixote
    and, by extension, villains in the romances' (Kinney)
159 false enchanters: those whom Don Quixote believed
    could turn inns into castles
163 bate: deduct
176 cap: seize, arrest
179 beholding: indebted

keep us a day or two, and we'll set fellows abroad to
cry our purse and our casket. Shall we, Michael? **191**

MICHAEL Ay, I pray, mother. In truth my feet are full
of chilblains with travelling.

WIFE Faith, and those chilblains are a foul trouble.
Mistress Merrythought, when your youth comes
home, let him rub all the soles of his feet and the
heels and his ankles with a mouse skin—or, if none
of your people can catch a mouse, when he goes to
bed let him roll his feet in the warm embers, and I
warrant you he shall be well; and you may make him
put his fingers between his toes and smell to them;
it's very sovereign for his head if he be costive. **202**

MISTRESS MERRYTHOUGHT Master Knight of the
Burning Pestle, my son Michael and I bid you
farewell; I thank your worship heartily for your
kindness.

RAFE Farewell, fair lady, and your tender squire.
If, pricking through these deserts, I do hear
Of any traitorous knight who through his guile
Hath light upon your casket and your purse, **210**
I will despoil him of them and restore them.

MISTRESS MERRYTHOUGHT I thank your worship.

*Exit with* MICHAEL

RAFE Dwarf, bear my shield; squire, elevate my lance;
And now farewell, you Knight of holy Bell.

CITIZEN Ay, ay, Rafe, all is paid.

RAFE But yet before I go, speak, worthy knight,
If aught you do of sad adventures know,
Where errant knight may through his prowess win
Eternal fame, and free some gentle souls
From endless bonds of steel and ling'ring pain. **220**

HOST (*to* TAPSTER) Sirrah, go to Nick the barber, and
bid him prepare himself as I told you before, quickly.

TAPSTER I am gone, sir. *Exit* TAPSTER

HOST Sir knight, this wilderness affordeth none
But the great venture where full many a knight
Hath tried his prowess and come off with shame,
And where I would not have you lose your life
Against no man, but furious fiend of hell.

RAFE Speak on, sir knight, tell what he is and where;
For here I vow upon my blazing badge, **230**
Never to blaze a day in quietness;
But bread and water will I only eat,
And the green herb and rock shall be my couch,
Till I have quelled that man or beast or fiend
That works such damage to all errant knights.

HOST Not far from hence, near to a craggy cliff,
At the north end of this distressed town,
There doth stand a lowly house
Ruggedly builded, and in it a cave
In which an ugly giant now doth won, **240**
Ycleped Barbaroso. In his hand
He shakes a naked lance of purest steel,
With sleeves turned up, and him before he wears
A motley garment to preserve his clothes
From blood of those knights which he massacres,
And ladies gent. Without his door doth hang
A copper basin on a prickant spear,
At which no sooner gentle knights can knock
But the shrill sound fierce Barbaroso hears,
And rushing forth, brings in the errant knight, **250**
And sets him down in an enchanted chair.
Then with an engine which he hath prepared,
With forty teeth, he claws his courtly crown;
Next makes him wink, and underneath his chin
He plants a brazen pece of mighty bord,
And knocks his bullets round about his cheeks,
Whilst with his fingers, and an instrument
With which he snaps his hair off, he doth fill
The wretch's ears with a most hideous noise.
Thus every knight adventurer he doth trim, **260**
And now no creature dares encounter him.

RAFE In God's name, I will fight with him. Kind sir,
Go but before me to this dismal cave
There this huge giant Barbaroso dwells,
And, by that virtue that brave Rosicleer
That damned brood of ugly giants slew,

---

191 to cry: proclaim the loss of
202 sovereign: beneficial
    costive: constipated
211 despoil: deprive by force
217 sad: grave
221 Nick: a) Don Quixote's barber was called Master
    Nicholas; b) play on the barber's profession
234 quelled: slain

240 ugly: fearsome
241 Ycleped: called, named (archaic)
    Barbaroso: a) barbarian; b) barber
242 lance: i.e. razor
245 which he massacres: i.e. whose hair he cuts
246 gent: fair
247 A copper . . . prickant spear: the traditional sign of a
    barber-surgeon: an upright ('prickant') pole of red and
    white that, together with the basin, signified that a
    barber could also draw teeth and let blood
248 can: do
252 engine: comb
253 crown: head
254 wink: cleanse his eyes (see III.i.394)
255 pece: cup
    bord: rim
256 bullets: small balls of soap
258–9 snaps his . . . hideous noise: refers to the much-
    satirised long hair of gallants: see, for example Francis
    Beaumont's *The Woman Hater, or The Hungry Courtier*
    (1606)
260 trim: can also mean thrash or trounce
266 That damned brood of ugly giants slew: reference to
    Rosicleer's adventure with the giant Brandagedeon and
    his thirty knights in *The Mirror of Knighthood*, I.xxxvi

And Palmerin Frannarco overthrew,
I doubt not but to curb this traitor foul
And to the devil send his guilty soul.
HOST  Brave sprighted knight, thus far I will perform
This your request: I'll bring you within sight       271
Of this most loathsome place, inhabited
By a more loathsome man; but dare not stay,
For his main force swoops all he sees away.
RAFE  Saint George, set on before! March, squire and
page.                                        *Exeunt*
WIFE  George, dost think Rafe will confound the giant?
CITIZEN  I hold my cap to a farthing he does. Why,
Nell, I saw him wrestle with the great Dutchman and
hurl him.                                         280
WIFE  Faith, and that Dutchman was a goodly man, if
all things were answerable to his bigness; and yet they
say there was a Scotchman higher than he, and that
they two and a knight met and saw one another for
nothing; but of all the sights that ever were in
London since I was married, methinks the little child
that was so fair grown about the members was the
prettiest, that and the hermaphrodite.
CITIZEN  Nay, by your leave, Nell, Ninivie was better.
WIFE  Ninivie? Oh, that was the story of Joan and the
wall, was it not, George?                         291
CITIZEN  Yes, lamb.

*Enter* MISTRESS MERRYTHOUGHT

WIFE  Look, George, here comes Mistress
Merrythought again, and I would have Rafe come
and fight with the giant. I tell you true, I long to
see't.
CITIZEN  Good Mistress Merrythought, begone, I pray
you, for my sake. I pray you, forbear a little; you shall
have audience presently; I have a little business.   299
WIFE  Mistress Merrythought, if it please you to refrain
your passion a little till Rafe have dispatched the
giant out of the way, we shall think ourselves much
bound to you. I thank you, good Mistress
Merrythought.           *Exit* MISTRESS MERRYTHOUGHT

*Enter a* BOY

CITIZEN  Boy, come hither; send away Rafe and this
whoreson giant quickly.
BOY  In good faith, sir, we cannot. You'll utterly spoil
our play, and make it to be hissed, and it cost money;
you will not suffer us to go on with our plot.—I pray,
gentlemen, rule him.                              310
CITIZEN  Let him come now and dispatch this, and I'll
trouble you no more.
BOY  Will you give me your hand of that?
WIFE  Give him thy hand, George, do, and I'll kiss him.
I warrant thee the youth means plainly.
BOY  I'll send him to you presently.          *Exit* BOY
WIFE  I thank you, little youth.—Faith, the child hath a
sweet breath, George, but I think it be troubled with
the worms. *Carduus benedictus* and mare's milk were
the only thing in the world for't. Oh, Rafe's here,
George.—God send thee good luck, Rafe.           321

*Enter* RAFE, HOST, TIM *as* SQUIRE, *and* GEORGE *as*
DWARF

HOST  Puissant knight, yonder his mansion is;
Lo, where the spear and copper basin are;
Behold that string on which hangs many a tooth
Drawn from the gentle jaw of wandering knights.
I dare not stay to sound; he will appear.   *Exit* HOST
RAFE  Oh, faint not, heart. Susan, my lady dear,
The cobbler's maid in Milk Street, for whose sake
I take these arms, oh let the thought of thee
Carry thy knight through all adventurous deeds,   330
And in the honour of thy beauteous self
May I destroy this monster Barbaroso.—
Knock, squire, upon the basin till it break
With the shrill strokes, or till the giant speak.

*Enter* BARBER

WIFE  Oh, George, the giant, the giant!—Now, Rafe,
for thy life.
BARBER  What fond unknowing wight is this that dares
So rudely knock at Barbaroso's cell,
Where no man comes but leaves his fleece behind?
RAFE  I, traitorous caitiff, who am sent by fate       340
To punish all the sad enormities

___

267  Frannarco: the giant slain by Palmerin in *Palmerin d'Olivia*, I.li
274  main: full
275  Saint George, set on before!: battle cry invoking the patron saint of England
278  hold: pledge
279  the great Dutchman: possibly a reference to a famous German fencer who lived in early seventeenth-century London; 'Dutchman' was a term for speakers of both Dutch and German
288  hermaphrodite: the citizens' taste for 'freaks' is referred to in *Epicoene* and was satirised in a number of plays, for example, Jonson's *The Alchemist* (1610), V.i.21ff
289  Ninivie: a contemporary puppet play about Jonah and the whale

315  plainly: honestly
319  *Carduus benedictus*: the blessed thistle (used as a medicinal cure-all)
mare's milk: considered a good purgative
326  sound: blow a horn
328  Milk Street: between Cheapside and Gresham Street, originally London's milk market
337  fond: foolish
wight: man (archaic)
339  fleece: a) beard; b) money (as in to 'fleece' someone)
340  caitiff: wretch

Thou hast committed against ladies gent
And errant knights. Traitor to God and men,
Prepare thyself; this is the dismal hour
Appointed for thee to give strict account
Of all thy beastly treacherous villainies.
BARBER  Foolhardy knight, full soon thou shalt aby
                    *He takes down his pole*
This fond reproach: thy body will I bang,
And, lo, upon that string thy teeth shall hang.
Prepare thyself, for dead soon shalt thou be.      350
RAFE  Saint George for me!
BARBER  Gargantua for me!                    *They fight*
WIFE  To him, Rafe, to him! Hold up the giant; set out
    thy leg before, Rafe.
CITIZEN  Falsify a blow, Rafe; falsify a blow; the giant
    lies open on the left side.
WIFE  Bear't off; bear't off still. There, boy.—Oh,
    Rafe's almost down, Rafe's almost down.
RAFE  Susan, inspire me.—Now have up again.
WIFE  Up, up, up, up, up! So, Rafe, down with him,
    down with him, Rafe.                            361
CITIZEN  Fetch him o'er the hip, boy.
WIFE  There, boy; kill, kill, kill, kill, kill, Rafe.
CITIZEN  No, Rafe, get all out of him first.
                    *RAFE knocks the BARBER down*
RAFE  Presumptuous man, see to what desperate end
    Thy treachery hath brought thee. The just gods,
    Who never prosper those that do despise them,
    For all the villainies which thou hast done
    To knights and ladies, now have paid thee home
    By my stiff arm, a knight adventurous.          370
    But say, vile wretch, before I send thy soul
    To sad Avernus, whither it must go,
    What captives hold'st thou in thy sable cave?
BARBER  Go in and free them all; thou hast the day.
RAFE  Go, squire and dwarf, search in this dreadful
    cave,
    And free the wretched prisoners from their bonds.
            *Exeunt TIM as SQUIRE and GEORGE as DWARF*
BARBER  I crave for mercy, as thou art a knight,
    And scorn'st to spill the blood of those that beg.
RAFE  Thou show'd'st no mercy, nor shalt thou have any;
    Prepare thyself, for thou shalt surely die.      380

----

*Enter* TIM *as* SQUIRE *leading one winking, with a basin
under his chin*

TIM  Behold, brave knight, here is one prisoner
    Whom this wild man hath usèd as you see.
WIFE  This is the first wise word I heard the squire
    speak.
RAFE  Speak what thou art, and how thou hast been
    used,
    That I may give him condign punishment.
I KNIGHT  I am a knight that took my journey post
    Northward from London, and in courteous wise
    This giant trained me to his loathsome den
    Under pretence of killing of the itch;          390
    And all my body with a powder strewed,
    That smarts and stings, and cut away my beard
    And my curled locks wherein were ribbons tied,
    And with a water washed my tender eyes
    (Whilst up and down about me still he skipped),
    Whose virtue is, that till mine eyes be wiped
    With a dry cloth, for this my foul disgrace
    I shall not dare to look a dog i'th' face.
WIFE  Alas, poor knight.—Relieve him, Rafe; relieve
    poor knights whilst you live.                    400
RAFE  My trusty squire, convey him to the town,
    Where he may find relief.—Adieu, fair knight.
        *Exit* KNIGHT *with* TIM, *who presently re-enters*

*Enter* GEORGE *as* DWARF *leading one with a patch o'er his
nose*

GEORGE  Puissant Knight of the Burning Pestle hight,
    See here another wretch, whom this foul beast
    Hath scorched and scored in this inhuman wise.
RAFE  Speak me thy name and eke thy place of birth,
    And what hath been thy usage in this cave.
2 KNIGHT  I am a knight, Sir Pockhole is my name,
    And by my birth I am a Londoner,
    Free by my copy; but my ancestors          410
    Were Frenchmen all; and riding hard this way
    Upon a trotting horse, my bones did ache;
    And I, faint knight, to ease my weary limbs,

----

347  aby: pay for
349  string thy teeth shall hang: barbers hung strings of
    extracted teeth outside their premises
352  Gargantua: folktale hero (rather than the giant from
    Rabelais whose work had not been translated at this
    time)
355  falsify: feign
369  paid thee home: fully punished
372  Avernus: a deep lake near Naples believed to be an
    entrance to the underworld
373  sable: black
374  day: victory

SD  *winking*: with his eyes shut
386  condign: suitable
387  post: in haste
389  trained: lured
390  itch: a symptom of venereal disease
393  ribbons: fashionable adornment for foppish knights
SD  *patch o'er his nose*: sign of suffering from an advanced case
    of syphilis
405  scorched: slashed (with a knife)
    scored: cut
406  eke: also (archaic)
410  copy: certificate of admission to the freedom of the City
411  Frenchman: therefore associated with syphilis, 'the
    French disease'
412  my bones did ache: symptom of advanced syphilis

Light at this cave, when straight this furious fiend,
With sharpest instrument of purest steel
Did cut the gristle of my nose away,
And in the place this velvet plaster stands.
Relieve me, gentle knight, out of his hands.

WIFE Good Rafe, relieve Sir Pockhole and send him
away, for, in truth, his breath stinks.          420

RAFE Convey him straight after the other knight.—
Sir Pockhole fare you well.

2 KNIGHT                    Kind sir, goodnight.

*Exeunt* KNIGHT *with* GEORGE, *who then re-enters.*
*Cries within*

3 KNIGHT (*within*) Deliver us.

WOMAN (*within*) Deliver us.

WIFE Hark, George, what a woeful cry there is. I think
some woman lies in there.

3 KNIGHT (*within*) Deliver us.

WOMAN (*within*) Deliver us.

RAFE What ghastly noise is this? Speak, Barbaroso,
Or by this blazing steel thy head goes off.       430

BARBER Prisoners of mine, whom I in diet keep.
Send lower down into the cave,
And in a tub that's heated smoking hot,
There may they find them and deliver them.

RAFE Run, squire and dwarf, deliver them with speed.

*Exeunt* TIM *as* SQUIRE *and* GEORGE *as* DWARF

WIFE But will not Rafe kill this giant? Surely I am
afeared if he let him go he will do as much hurt as
ever he did.

CITIZEN Not so, mouse, neither, if he could convert
him.                                              440

WIFE Ay, George, if he could convert him; but a giant
is not so soon converted as one of us ordinary people.
There's a pretty tale of a witch that had the devil's
mark about her, God bless us, that had a giant to her
son, that was called Lob-lie-by-the-fire; didst never
hear it, George?

*Enter* TIM *as* SQUIRE *leading a man with a glass of lotion
in his hand, and* GEORGE *as the* DWARF *leading a woman
with diet-bread and drink*

CITIZEN Peace, Nell, here comes the prisoners.

GEORGE Here be these pinèd wretches, manful knight,
That for these six weeks have not seen a wight.

RAFE Deliver what you are, and how you came      450
To this sad cave, and what your usage was.

3 KNIGHT I am an errant knight that followed arms
With spear and shield, and in my tender years
I stricken was with Cupid's fiery shaft,
And fell in love with this my lady dear,
And stole her from her friends in Turnbull Street,
And bore her up and down from town to town
Where we did eat and drink and music hear,
Till at the length, at this unhappy town
We did arrive, and coming to this cave,          460
This beast us caught and put us in a tub
Where we this two months sweat, and should have
    done
Another month if you had not relieved us.

WOMAN This bread and water hath our diet been,
Together with a rib cut from a neck
Of burnèd mutton; hard hath been our fare.
Release us from this ugly giant's snare.

3 KNIGHT This hath been all the food we have received
But only twice a day, for novelty,
He gave a spoonful of this hearty broth          470

*Pulls out a syringe*

To each of us, through this same slender quill.

RAFE From this infernal monster you shall go,
That useth knights and gentle ladies so.—
Convey them hence.

*Exeunt* 3 KNIGHT *and* WOMAN *with* TIM *and* GEORGE
*who presently re-enter*

CITIZEN Cony, I can tell thee the gentlemen like Rafe.

WIFE Ay, George, I see it well enough.—Gentlemen, I
thank you all heartily for gracing my man Rafe, and I
promise you you shall see him oft'ner.

BARBER Mercy, great knight, I do recant my ill,
And henceforth never gentle blood will spill.     480

RAFE I give thee mercy; but yet shalt thou swear
Upon my burning pestle to perform
Thy promise uttered.

BARBER I swear and kiss.          *Kisses pestle*

RAFE                    Depart then, and amend.—

*Exit* BARBER

Come, squire and dwarf, the sun grows towards his
    set,
And we have many more adventures yet.     *Exeunt*

---

417 velvet plaster: covering for both the scars of war and
     those produced by the incisions made as a treatment for
     syphilis
420 breath stinks: as a result of taking mercury, used in the
     treatment of syphilis
423 Deliver us: parody of the Litany for General Supplication
     in *The Book of Common Prayer* (1549, revised 1552 and 1559)
433 tub: sweating tubs were believed to cure venereal disease
439 convert: converting 'heathens' was a common element in
     chivalric romance
443–4 devil's mark: the marks (spots or tooth marks) believed
     to identify witches
 SD *diet-bread*: special bread used in the treatment of
     syphilis

448 pinèd: wasted, starved
450 Deliver: state
456 Turnbull Street: originally Turnmill Street, running
     south from Clerkenwell Green and known for its
     prostitutes
465 rib cut from a neck: extremely poor quality meat
466 mutton: prostitute (slang)
470 hearty: nourishing

CITIZEN Now Rafe is in this humour, I know he would ha' beaten all the boys in the house if they had been set on him.                                                    489

WIFE Ay, George, but it is well as it is; I warrant you the gentlemen do consider what it is to overthrow a giant. But look, George, here comes Mistress Merrythought and her son Michael.—Now you are welcome, Mistress Merrythought, now Rafe has done, you may go on.

*Enter* MISTRESS MERRYTHOUGHT *and* MICHAEL

MISTRESS MERRYTHOUGHT Mick, my boy.

MICHAEL Ay, forsooth, mother.                             497

MISTRESS MERRYTHOUGHT Be merry, Mick; we are at home now, where, I warrant you, you shall find the house flung out at the windows. (*Music within*) Hark, hey dogs, hey; this is the old world, i'faith, with my husband. If I get in among 'em, I'll play 'em such a lesson that they shall have little list to come scraping hither again.—Why, Master Merrythought, husband, Charles Merrythought.

OLD MERRYTHOUGHT (*within*)

(*Sings*)    *If you will sing and dance and laugh,*
             *And hollo and laugh again,*
             *And then cry, 'There, boys, there', why then*
             *One, two, three, and four,*
             *We shall be merry within this hour.*      510

MISTRESS MERRYTHOUGHT Why, Charles, do you not know your own natural wife? I say, open the door, and turn me out those mangy companions; 'tis more than time that they were fellow and fellow-like with you. You are a gentleman, Charles, and an old man, and father of two children; and I myself (though I say it) by my mother's side niece to a worshipful gentleman, and a conductor; he has been three times in his majesty's service at Chester, and is now the fourth time, God bless him and his charge, upon his journey.                                                       521

OLD MERRYTHOUGHT (*within*)

(*Sings*)    *Go from my window, love, go;*

*Go from my window, my dear;*
*The wind and the rain*
*Will drive you back again;*
*You cannot be lodged here.*                            526

Hark you, Mistress Merrythought, you that walk upon adventures and forsake your husband because he sings with never a penny in his purse; what, shall I think myself the worse? Faith, no, I'll be merry. You come out here—here's none but lads of mettle, lives of a hundred years and upwards; care never drunk their bloods, nor want made 'em warble, (*Sings*) *Heigh-ho, my heart is heavy.*                          534

MISTRESS MERRYTHOUGHT Why, Master Merrythought, what am I that you should laugh me to scorn thus abruptly? Am I not your fellow-feeler, as we may say, in all our miseries, your comforter in health and sickness? Have I not brought you children? Are they not like you, Charles? Look upon thine own image, hard-hearted man. And yet for all this—                                                      542

OLD MERRYTHOUGHT (*within*)

(*Sings*)    *Begone, begone, my Juggy, my puggy,*
             *Begone, my love, my dear.*
             *The weather is warm*
             *'Twill do thee no harm*
             *Thou canst not be lodged here.*

—Be merry, boys; some light music, and more wine.

WIFE He's not in earnest, I hope, George, is he?

CITIZEN What if he be, sweetheart?                       550

WIFE Marry, if he be, George, I'll make bold to tell him he's an ingrant old man to use his bed-fellow so scurvily.

CITIZEN What, how does he use her, honey?

WIFE Marry come up, Sir Saucebox, I think you'll take his part, will you not? Lord, how hot you are grown. You are a fine man, an' you had a fine dog; it becomes you sweetly.

CITIZEN Nay, prithee, Nell, chide not. For as I am an honest man and a true Christian grocer, I do not like his doings.                                               561

WIFE I cry you mercy then, George. You know we are all frail and full of infirmities.—D'ee hear, Master Merrythought, may I crave a word with you?

OLD MERRYTHOUGHT (*within*)
Strike up lively, lads.

WIFE I had not thought, in truth, Master

---

487   humour: mood
500   house flung . . . the windows: signs of riotous living (proverbial)
501   world: behaviour, habit
503   list: desire
       scraping: playing (the fiddle)
507   *hollo*: shout
517   worshipful: honourable
518   conductor: captain
519   Chester: Cheshire port of embarkation for Ireland with a reputation for military corruption
522–6 and 543–7: *Go from . . . lodged here*: popular song that appears in a number of contemporary plays, including John Fletcher's *Monsieur Thomas* (1610–16), III.iii and *The Woman's Prize* (c. 1604), I.iii

531   mettle: courage
531–2 lives of . . . and upwards: their merry lives have kept them young
543   *Juggy*: diminutive of Joan
       *puggy*: term of endearment
551   Marry: indeed
552   ingrant: ignorant
555   Marry come up: 'now, now' (a taunt)
562   cry you mercy: beg your pardon

Merrythought, that a man of your age and discretion, as I may say, being a gentleman, and therefore known by your gentle conditions, could have used so little respect to the weakness of his wife. For your wife is your own flesh, the staff of your age, your yoke-fellow, with whose help you draw through the mire of this transitory world. Nay, she's your own rib. And again—                                          **574**

OLD MERRYTHOUGHT (*within*)

(*Sings*)      *I come not hither for thee to teach,*
              *I have no pulpit for thee to preach,*
              *I would thou hadst kissed me under the breech,*
              *As thou art a lady gay.*

WIFE  Marry, with a vengeance! I am heartily sorry for the poor gentlewoman.—But if I were thy wife, i'faith, grey-beard, i'faith—                        **581**

CITIZEN  I prithee, sweet honeysuckle, be content.

WIFE  Give me such words that am a gentlewoman born! Hang him, hoary rascal! Get me some drink, George, I am almost molten with fretting: now beshrew his knave's heart for it.           *Exit Citizen*

OLD MERRYTHOUGHT (*within*) Play me a light lavolta. Come, be frolic. Fill the good fellows' wine.

MISTRESS MERRYTHOUGHT  Why, Master Merrythought, are you disposed to make me wait here? You'll open, I hope; I'll fetch them that shall open else.                                            **592**

OLD MERRYTHOUGHT (*at window*) Good woman, if you will sing I'll give you something; if not—

      SONG
      *You are no love for me, Marg'ret,*
      *I am no love for you.*           *Leaves window*

(*within*) Come aloft, boys, aloft.                  **597**

MISTRESS MERRYTHOUGHT  Now a churl's fart in your teeth, sir.—Come, Mick, we'll not trouble him; 'a shall not ding us i'th'teeth with his bread and his broth, that he shall not. Come, boy; I'll provide for thee, I warrant thee. We'll go to Master Venturewell's, the merchant; I'll get his letter to mine host of the Bell in Waltham; there I'll place thee with the tapster. Will not that do well for thee, Mick? And let me alone for that old cuckoldly knave your

father; I'll use him in his kind, I warrant ye.
                                          *Exeunt*

FINIS ACTUS TERTII

# Interlude III

*Music. Enter* BOY *and* CITIZEN

WIFE  Come, George, where's the beer?

CITIZEN  Here, love.

WIFE  This old fornicating fellow will not out of my mind yet.—Gentlemen, I'll begin to you all, and I desire more of your acquaintance, with all my heart. (*Drinks*) Fill the gentlemen some beer, George. (BOY *danceth*) Look, George, the little boy's come again; methinks he looks something like the Prince of Orange in his long stocking, if he had a little harness about his neck. George, I will have him dance 'Fading'.—'Fading' is a fine jig, I'll assure you, gentlemen.—Begin, brother.—Now 'a capers, sweetheart.—Now a turn o'th'toe, and then tumble. Cannot you tumble, youth?                         **14**

BOY  No, indeed, forsooth.

WIFE  Nor eat fire?

BOY  Neither.

WIFE  Why then, I thank you heartily. There's twopence to buy you points withal.
                                          *Exit* BOY

# Act IV

*Enter* JASPER *and* BOY

JASPER (*gives a letter*) There, boy, deliver this, but do it well.
      Hast thou provided me four lusty fellows
      Able to carry me? And art thou perfect
      In all thy business?

BOY                  Sir, you need not fear:
      I have my lesson here and cannot miss it.
      The men are ready for you, and what else
      Pertains to this employment.

JASPER (*gives him money*)      There, my boy;

---

569  conditions: qualities
571–2  yoke-fellow: companion (from ploughing)
587  lavolta: lively dance for couples
588  frolic: merry
595–6  *You are . . . for you*: possibly from a ballad about Fair Margaret and Sweet William (see II.427–30). Printed as part of the song in Q1–3
597  Come aloft: 'the expression is generally found applied to apes that were taught to vault: here it is used merely as an incitement to mirth' (Dyce)
600  ding: strike, i.e. taunt
606  cuckoldly: adulterous

607  in his kind: according to his nature
4  begin to: toast
8–9  Prince of Orange: Prince Maurice of Nassau, whose picture (in his 'long stocking') was widely known
9  harness: armour
11  Fading: a) an Irish dance; b) sexual orgasm
12  capers: lively dancing
13  tumble: somersault (with sexual connotation)
19  points: laces for tying hose to doublet
2  lusty: vigorous
3  perfect: instructed (as in 'perfected')

Take it, but buy no land.

BOY                              Faith, sir, 'twere rare
To see so young a purchaser. I fly,
And on my wings carry your destiny.                    *Exit*

JASPER  Go, and be happy.—Now, my latest hope,      **11**
Forsake me not, but fling thy anchor out
And let it hold. Stand fixed, thou rolling stone,
Till I enjoy my dearest. Hear me, all
You powers that rule in men celestial.                 *Exit*

WIFE  Go thy ways; thou art as crooked a sprig as ever
grew in London. I warrant him, he'll come to some
naughty end or other, for his looks say no less.
Besides, his father (you know, George) is none of the
best; you heard him take me up like a flirt-gill, and
sing bawdy songs upon me; but, i'faith, if I live,
George—                                                **22**

CITIZEN  Let me alone, sweetheart—I have a trick in
my head shall lodge him in the Arches for one year,
and make him sing *peccavi* ere I leave him, and yet he
shall never know who hurt him neither.

WIFE  Do, my good George, do.

*Enter* BOY

CITIZEN  What shall we have Rafe do now, boy?

BOY  You shall have what you will, sir.

CITIZEN  Why, so, sir; go and fetch me him then, and
let the Sophy of Persia come and christen him a
child.                                                  **32**

BOY  Believe me, sir, that will not do so well. 'Tis stale;
it has been had before at the Red Bull.

WIFE  George, let Rafe travel over great hills, and let
him be very weary, and come to the King of

Cracovia's house, covered with black velvet, and there
let the king's daughter stand in her window all in
beaten gold, combing her golden locks with a comb
of ivory, and let her spy Rafe, and fall in love with
him, and come down to him, and carry him into her
father's house, and then let Rafe talk with her.       **42**

CITIZEN  Well said, Nell, it shall be so.—Boy, let's ha't
done quickly.

BOY  Sir, if you will imagine all this to be done already,
you shall hear them talk together. But we cannot
present a house covered with black velvet, and a lady
in beaten gold.

CITIZEN  Sir boy, let's ha't as you can, then.

BOY  Besides, it will show ill-favouredly to have a
grocer's prentice to court a king's daughter.          **51**

CITIZEN  Will it so, sir? You are well read in histories! I
pray you, what was Sir Dagonet? Was not he prentice
to a grocer in London? Read the play of *The Four
Prentices of London*, where they toss their pikes so. I
pray you, fetch him in, sir, fetch him in.

BOY  It shall be done.—It is not our fault, gentlemen.
                                                       *Exit*

WIFE  Now we shall see fine doings, I warrant'ee,
George. Oh, here they come; how prettily the King
of Cracovia's daughter is dressed.                     **60**

*Enter* RAFE *and the* LADY POMPIONA, TIM *as* SQUIRE *and*
GEORGE *as* DWARF

CITIZEN  Ay, Nell, it is the fashion of that country, I
warrant'ee.

LADY  Welcome, sir knight, unto my father's court,
King of Moldavia; unto me, Pompiona,
His daughter dear. But sure you do not like
Your entertainment, that will stay with us
No longer but a night.

RAFE                          Damsel right fair,
I am on many sad adventures bound,
That call me forth into the wilderness;
Besides, my horse's back is something galled,          **70**

---

8  buy no land: from 'he that buys land buys many stones'
    (proverbial)

11–12  my latest . . . anchor out: anchors often appeared in
    emblems associated with hope

13  rolling stone: a) the earth; b) metaphor for uncertain
    fortune

15  powers that . . . men celestial: reference to the Neo-
    Platonic figure Venus Coelestis (Heavenly Love) who
    possesses the minds of those whose intellects pass beyond
    the sensible to the heavenly

16  sprig: youth

18  naughty: mischievous

20  flirt-gill: promiscuous woman (slang)

24  Arches: St Mary de Arcubus, a church in Cheapside
    where the Ecclesiastical Court of Appeal for the Province
    of Canterbury sat to hear cases of abuse of church law

25  *peccavi*: 'I have sinned'

31–2  Sophy of . . . a child: reference to the Sophy of Persia,
    godfather to Robert Sherley's child in *The Travels of the
    Three English Brothers* (c. 1607) by John Day, William
    Rowley and George Wilkins

34  the Red Bull: a popular theatre in Clerkenwell, but also
    known for presenting bombastic ('stale') plays of little
    consequence

---

37  Cracovia: Cracow, capital of Poland (until 1609)
    black: eds (omitted from Q1)

39  beaten gold: an example of the elaborate costumes used
    for entertainments presented at court, such as Ben
    Jonson's *The Masque of Blackness* (1605)

53  Sir Dagonet: King Arthur's fool but possibly known to
    early seventeenth-century audiences from 'Arthur's
    Show', an exhibition of archery held at Mile End; see
    *2 Henry IV*, III.ii.257

54–5  *The Four Prentices of London*: in Heywood's play Eustace
    and Guy toss and catch their pikes to show their
    readiness for war

64  Moldavia: a Danubian province (now in Romania); the
    Prince of Moldavia was with a Turkish delegation to the
    English court in November 1607

70  galled: sore

Which will enforce me ride a sober pace.
But many thanks, fair lady, be to you,
For using errant knight with courtesy.

LADY But say, brave knight, what is your name and
 birth?

RAFE My name is Rafe; I am an Englishman,
As true as steel, a hearty Englishman,
And prentice to a grocer in the Strand
By deed indent, of which I have one part.
But Fortune calling me to follow arms,
On me this holy order I did take          80
Of Burning Pestle, which in all men's eyes
I bear, confounding ladies' enemies.

LADY Oft have I heard of your brave countrymen,
And fertile soil and store of wholesome food;
My father oft will tell me of a drink
In England found, and 'nipitato' called,
Which driveth all the sorrow from your hearts.

RAFE Lady, 'tis true, you need not lay your lips
To better nipitato than there is.

LADY And of a wild fowl he will often speak          90
Which 'powdered beef and mustard' callèd is.
For there have been great wars 'twixt us and you;
But truly, Rafe, it was not long of me.
Tell me then, Rafe, could you contented be
To wear a lady's favour in your shield?

RAFE I am a knight of religious order,
And will not wear a favour of a lady's
That trusts in Antichrist and false traditions.

CITIZEN Well said, Rafe, convert her if thou canst.

RAFE Besides, I have a lady of my own          100
In merry England, for whose virtuous sake
I took these arms, and Susan is her name,
A cobbler's maid in Milk Street, whom I vow
Ne'er to forsake whilst life and pestle last.

LADY Happy that cobbling dame, whoe'er she be,
That for her own, dear Rafe, hath gotten thee;
Unhappy I, that ne'er shall see the day
To see thee more, that bear'st my heart away.

RAFE Lady, farewell; I needs must take my leave.

LADY Hard-hearted Rafe, that ladies dost deceive.          110

CITIZEN Hark thee, Rafe, there's money for thee; give
 something in the King of Cracovia's house; be not
 beholding to him.

RAFE Lady, before I go, I must remember

Your father's officers, who, truth to tell,
Have been about me very diligent.
Hold up thy snowy hand, thou princely maid:
There's twelve pence for your father's chamberlain;
And another shilling for his cook,
For, by my troth, the goose was roasted well;          120
And twelve pence for your father's horse-keeper,
For 'nointing my horse back—and for his butter,
There is another shilling—to the maid
That washed my boot-hose, there's an English groat:
And twopence to the boy that wiped my boots;
And last, fair lady, there is for yourself
Threepence, to buy you pins at Bumbo Fair.

LADY Full many thanks; and I will keep them safe
Till all the heads be off, for thy sake, Rafe.

RAFE Advance, my squire and dwarf; I cannot stay.          130

LADY Thou kill'st my heart in parting thus away.
 *Exeunt*

WIFE I commend Rafe yet that he will not stoop to a
 Cracovian. There's properer women in London than
 any are there, iwis. But here comes Master
 Humphrey and his love again now, George.

CITIZEN Ay, cony, peace.

*Enter* MERCHANT, HUMPHREY, LUCE, *and* BOY. LUCE
*kneels*

MERCHANT Go, get you up; I will not be entreated.
And, gossip mine, I'll keep you sure hereafter
From gadding out again with boys and unthrifts.
Come, they are women's tears; I know your
 fashion.—          140
Go, sirrah, lock her in, and keep the key
Safe as you love your life.          *Exeunt* LUCE *and* BOY
     Now, my son Humphrey,
You may both rest assured of my love
In this, and reap your own desire.

HUMPHREY I see this love you speak of, through your
 daughter,
Although the hole be little; and hereafter
Will yield the like in all I may, or can,
Fitting a Christian, and a gentleman.

MERCHANT I do believe you, my good son, and thank
 you:

---

77  Strand Q2 (strond Q1)
78  deed indent: duplicate agreement of indenture between
    apprentice and master; the deed was torn irregularly
    ('indented') so that it could be proved genuine if the two
    parts matched
82  confounding: a) confusing, bewildering; b) defeating
86  'nipitato': prime ale
91  powdered: salted
93  long: on account
105 cobbling: could also mean 'bungling'

124  boot-hose: elaborately embroidered footless stockings
     which covered the calf
125  boots: the footwear of gallants and would-be gentlemen
127  pins: elaborate pins were a fashionable gift
     Bumbo Fair: probably from a drink sold at fairs (made
     from rum, water, sugar and nutmeg)
132  stoop: submit
133  properer: handsomer
137  up: either from kneeling or to her chamber
138  gossip: female friend
139  unthrifts: prodigals
140  women's tears: i.e. not to be taken seriously

For 'twere an impudence to think you flattered.     **150**
HUMPHREY  It were indeed; but shall I tell you why?
  I have been beaten twice about the lie.
MERCHANT  Well, son, no more of compliment. My
    daughter
  Is yours again; appoint the time, and take her;
  We'll have no stealing for it. I myself
  And some few of our friends will see you married.
HUMPHREY  I would you would, i'faith, for, be it
    known,
  I ever was afraid to lie alone.
MERCHANT  Some three days hence, then.
HUMPHREY                              Three days? Let me see:
  'Tis somewhat of the most; yet I agree     **160**
  Because I mean against the appointed day
  To visit all my friends in new array.

*Enter* SERVANT

SERVANT  Sir, there's a gentlewoman without would
  speak with your worship.
MERCHANT  What is she?
SERVANT  Sir, I asked her not.
MERCHANT  Bid her come in.                    *Exit* SERVANT

*Enter* MISTRESS MERRYTHOUGHT *and* MICHAEL

MISTRESS MERRYTHOUGHT  Peace be to your worship. I
  come as a poor suitor to you, sir, in the behalf of this
  child.                                     **170**
MERCHANT  Are you not wife to Merrythought?
MISTRESS MERRYTHOUGHT  Yes, truly; would I had
  ne'er seen his eyes! He has undone me and himself
  and his children, and there he lives at home, and
  sings and hoits and revels among his drunken
  companions; but, I warrant you, where to get a penny
  to put bread in his mouth he knows not; and
  therefore, if it like your worship, I would entreat your
  letter to the honest host of the Bell in Waltham, that
  I may place my child under the protection of his
  tapster, in some settled course of life.     **181**
MERCHANT  I'm glad the heavens have heard my
    prayers. Thy husband,
  When I was ripe in sorrows, laughed at me;
  Thy son, like an unthankful wretch, I having
  Redeemed him from his fall and made him mine,
  To show his love again, first stole my daughter,
  Then wronged this gentleman, and, last of all,
  Gave me that grief had almost brought me down
  Unto my grave, had not a stronger hand
  Relieved my sorrows. Go, and weep as I did,     **190**
  And be unpitied; for I here profess

An everlasting hate to all thy name.
MISTESS MERRYTHOUGHT  Will you so, sir? How say
  you by that?—Come, Mick, let him keep his wind to
  cool his porridge. We'll go to thy nurse's, Mick; she
  knits silk stockings, boy, and we'll knit too, boy, and
  be beholding to none of them all.
              *Exeunt* MICHAEL *and his* MOTHER

*Enter a* BOY *with a letter*

BOY  Sir, I take it you are the master of this house.
MERCHANT  How then, boy?
BOY  Then to yourself, sir, comes this letter.     **200**
MERCHANT  From whom, my pretty boy?
BOY  From him that was your servant; but no more
  Shall that name ever be, for he is dead:
  Grief of your purchased anger broke his heart.
  I saw him die, and from his hand received
  This paper, with a charge to bring it hither;
  Read it, and satisfy yourself in all.     **207**
MERCHANT  (*reads letter*) 'Sir, that I have wronged your
  love, I must confess; in which I have purchased to
  myself, besides mine own undoing, the ill opinion of
  my friends. Let not your anger, good sir, outlive me,
  but suffer me to rest in peace with your forgiveness;
  let my body (if a dying man may so much prevail
  with you) be brought to your daughter, that she may
  truly know my hot flames are now buried, and,
  withal, receive a testimony of the zeal I bore her
  virtue. Farewell for ever, and be ever happy. Jasper.'
  God's hand is great in this. I do forgive him;
  Yet I am glad he's quiet, where I hope
  He will not bite again.—Boy, bring the body,     **220**
  And let him have his will, if that be all.
BOY  'Tis here without, sir.
MERCHANT                  So, sir, if you please,
  You may conduct it in; I do not fear it.
HUMPHREY  I'll be your usher, boy, for though I say it,
  He owed me something once, and well did pay it.
                                          *Exeunt*

*Enter* LUCE *alone*

LUCE  If there be any punishment inflicted
  Upon the miserable, more than yet I feel,
  Let it together seize me, and at once
  Press down my soul. I cannot bear the pain
  Of these delaying tortures. Thou that art     **230**
  The end of all, and the sweet rest of all,
  Come, come, oh Death, bring me to thy peace,
  And blot out all the memory I nourish
  Both of my father and my cruel friend.
  Oh wretched maid, still living to be wretched,

---

155  We'll have . . . for it: 'we'll not have another elopement'
160  of the most: overlong
161  against: in expectation of
175  hoits: laughs

204  purchased: incurred by his conduct
218  great: evident
224  usher: either a doorkeeper or an assistant

To be a say to Fortune in her changes,
And grow to number times and woes together!
How happy had I been, if, being born,
My grave had been my cradle.

*Enter* SERVANT

SERVANT                              By your leave,
  Young mistress, here's a boy hath brought a coffin. **240**
  What 'a would say, I know not, but your father
  Charged me to give you notice. Here they come.
                                        *Exit*

*Enter two* (CARRIER *and* BOY) *bearing a coffin,*
JASPER *in it*

LUCE  For me I hope 'tis come, and 'tis most welcome.
BOY  Fair mistress, let me not add greater grief
  To that great store you have already. Jasper,
  That whilst he lived was yours, now dead
  And here enclosed, commanded me to bring
  His body hither, and to crave a tear
  From those fair eyes, though he deserved not pity
  To deck his funeral; for so he bid me        **250**
  Tell her for whom he died.
    LUCE                          He shall have many.—
  Good friends, depart a little, whilst I take
  My leave of this dead man that once I lov'd:
                      *Exeunt* COFFIN CARRIER *and* BOY
  Hold yet a little, life, and then I give thee
  To thy first heavenly being. Oh, my friend!
  Hast thou deceived me thus, and got before me?
  I shall not long be after. But, believe me,
  Thou wert too cruel, Jasper, 'gainst thyself
  In punishing the fault I could have pardoned,
  With so untimely death. Thou didst not wrong me,
  But ever wert most kind, most true, most loving;  **261**
  And I the most unkind, most false, most cruel.
  Didst thou but ask a tear? I'll give thee all,
  Even all my eyes can pour down, all my sighs,
  And all myself, before thou goest from me.
  These are but sparing rites; but if thy soul
  Be yet about this place, and can behold
  And see what I prepare to deck thee with,
  It shall go up, borne on the wings of peace,
  And satisfied. First will I sing thy dirge,        **270**
  Then kiss thy pale lips, and then die myself,
  And fill one coffin and one grave together.
            SONG
            *Come you whose loves are dead,*
            *And whiles I sing*
            *Weep and wring*
            *Every hand, and every head*

*Bind with cypress and sad yew;*
*Ribands black and candles blue*
*For him that was of men most true.*

  *Come with heavy moaning,*                         **280**
  *And on his grave*
  *Let him have*
  *Sacrifice of sighs and groaning;*
  *Let him have fair flowers enow,*
  *White and purple, green and yellow,*
  *For him that was of men most true.*
  Thou sable cloth, sad cover of my joys,
  I lift thee up, and thus I meet with death.
JASPER  (*rising out of the coffin*) And thus you meet the
  living.
LUCE          Save me, heaven!
JASPER  Nay, do not fly me, fair; I am no spirit;    **290**
  Look better on me; do you know me yet?
LUCE  Oh, thou dear shadow of my friend.
JASPER                              Dear substance;
  I swear I am no shadow; feel my hand,
  It is the same it was. I am your Jasper.
  Your Jasper that's yet living, and yet loving.
  Pardon my rash attempt, my foolish proof
  I put in practice of your constancy;
  For sooner should my sword have drunk my blood
  And set my soul at liberty, than drawn
  The least drop from that body; for which boldness
  Doom me to anything: if death, I take it,         **301**
  And willingly.
LUCE          This death I'll give you for it.   *Kisses him*
  So, now I am satisfied; you are no spirit,
  But my own truest, truest, truest friend.
  Why do you come thus to me?
JASPER                              First to see you,
  Then to convey you hence.
LUCE                              It cannot be,
  For I am locked up here and watched at all hours,
  That 'tis impossible for me to 'scape.
JASPER  Nothing more possible. Within this coffin
  Do you convey yourself; let me alone,             **310**
  I have the wits of twenty men about me.
  Only I crave the shelter of your closet
  A little, and then fear me not. Creep in,
  That they may presently convey you hence.
  Fear nothing, dearest love, I'll be your second.

---

236  say: test, touchstone (from 'assay')
266  sparing: meagre
270  dirge: hymn for a funeral

277  *cypress and sad yew*: traditional emblems of mourning; see
     *Twelfth Night*, II.iv.50–65
278  *blue*: the colour of constancy
285  *White and . . . and yellow*: symbols of purity, sorrow, the
     soul, and divinity respectively
292  shadow: shade, departed spirit
312  closet: private room
313  fear me not: 'do not have fear for me'
315  second: support

LUCE *lies down in the coffin, and* JASPER *covers her*
*with the cloth*

Lie close, so; all goes well yet.—Boy.

*Enter* BOY *and* COFFIN CARRIER

BOY                                        At hand, sir.
JASPER  Convey away the coffin, and be wary.
BOY  'Tis done already.
JASPER                            Now must I go conjure.      *Exit*

*Enter* MERCHANT

MERCHANT  Boy, boy!
BOY  Your servant, sir.                                    320
MERCHANT  Do me this kindness, boy (hold, here's a
    crown): before thou bury the body of this fellow,
    carry it to his old merry father, and salute him from
    me, and bid him sing; he hath cause.
BOY  I will, sir.
MERCHANT  And then bring me word what tune he is
    in, and have another crown; but do it truly. I have
    fitted him a bargain now will vex him.
BOY  God bless your worship's health, sir.                329
MERCHANT  Farewell, boy.                             *Exeunt*

*Enter* MASTER MERRYTHOUGHT

WIFE  Ah, old Merrythought, art thou there again?
    Let's hear some of thy songs.
OLD MERRYTHOUGHT
    (*Sings*)    *Who can sing a merrier note*
                *Than he that cannot change a groat?*
    Not a denier left, and yet my heart leaps. I do wonder
    yet, as old as I am, that any man will follow a trade,
    or serve, that may sing and laugh, and walk the
    streets. My wife and both my sons are I know not
    where; I have nothing left, nor know I how to come
    by meat to supper, yet am I merry still, for I know I
    shall find it upon the table at six o'clock. Therefore,
    hang thought.                                         342
    (*Sings*)    *I would not be a serving man*
                *To carry the cloak-bag still,*
                *Nor would I be a falconer*
                *The greedy hawks to fill;*
                *But I would be in a good house,*
                *And have a good master too,*
                *But I would eat and drink of the best,*
                *And no work would I do.*              350

This is it that keeps life and soul together: mirth.
This is the philosopher's stone that they write so
much on, that keeps a man ever young.

*Enter a* BOY

BOY  Sir, they say they know all your money is gone,
    and they will trust you for no more drink.
OLD MERRYTHOUGHT  Will they not? Let 'em choose.
    The best is, I have mirth at home, and need not send
    abroad for that; let them keep their drink to
    themselves.
    (*Sings*)    *For Jillian of Bury she dwells on a hill,*      360
                *And she hath good beer and ale to sell,*
                *And of good fellows she thinks no ill;*
                *And thither will we go now, now, now,*
                *And thither will we go now.*
                *And when you have made a little stay,*
                *You need not ask what is to pay,*
                *But kiss your hostess and go your way;*
                *And thither, etc.*

*Enter another* BOY

2 BOY  Sir, I can get no bread for supper.                369
OLD MERRYTHOUGHT  Hang bread and supper! Let's
    preserve our mirth, and we shall never feel hunger,
    I'll warrant you. Let's have a catch; boy, follow me;
    come, sing this catch:
    (*They sing*)  *Ho, ho, nobody at home!*
                *Meat, nor drink, nor money ha' we none.*
                *Fill the pot, Eedy,*
                *Never more need I.*
    So, boys, enough; follow me; let's change our place
    and we shall laugh afresh.

                                                    *Exeunt*

FINIS ACT IV

# Interlude IV

WIFE  Let him go, George; 'a shall not have any
    countenance from us, nor a good word from any i'th'
    company, if I may strike stroke in't.
CITIZEN  No more 'a sha'not, love; but, Nell, I will have
    Rafe do a very notable matter now, to the eternal
    honour and glory of all grocers.—Sirrah, you there,
    boy! Can none of you hear?

---

316  close: hidden
318  conjure: perform the trick
326  tune: mood
328  fitted: furnished
333–4  *Who can . . . a groat?*: a catch from Ravenscroft's
    *Pammelia* (1606)
335  denier: French coin of very small value
342  hang: dismiss all
344  *cloak-bag*: portmanteau

---

352  philosopher's stone: the stone which, in alchemy, heals
    wounds, turns base metals into gold, and prolongs life
372  catch: song sung as a round
373  sing this catch: these words are slightly separated from
    the preceding 'come' in Q1–2 and some eds present them
    as a stage direction
374–7  *Ho, ho . . . need I*: a catch from *Pammelia*
2  countenance: favour
3  strike stroke: have my say

*Enter* BOY

BOY  Sir, your pleasure?

CITIZEN  Let Rafe come out on May Day in the morning, and speak upon a conduit with all his scarfs about him, and his feathers and his rings and his knacks.                                                    12

BOY  Why, sir, you do not think of our plot. What will become of that, then?

CITIZEN  Why sir, I care not what become on't. I'll have him come out, or I'll fetch him out myself. I'll have something done in honour of the city. Besides, he hath been long enough upon adventures. Bring him out quickly, or, if I come in amongst you—

BOY  Well, sir, he shall come out. But if our play miscarry, sir, you are like to pay for't.          *Exit* BOY

CITIZEN  Bring him away, then.                        22

WIFE  This will be brave, i'faith; George, shall not he dance the morris too for the credit of the Strand?

CITIZEN  No, sweetheart, it will be too much for the boy.

*Enter* RAFE

Oh, there he is, Nell; he's reasonable well in reparel, but he has not rings enough.

RAFE  London, to thee I do present the merry month of May;
Let each true subject be content to hear me what I say:
For from the top of conduit head, as plainly may appear,                                                30
I will both tell my name to you and wherefore I came here.
My name is Rafe, by due descent though not ignoble I,
Yet far inferior to the flock of gracious grocery;
And by the common counsel of my fellows in the Strand,
With gilded staff and crossed scarf, the May Lord here I stand.
Rejoice, oh English hearts, rejoice; rejoice, oh lovers dear;
Rejoice, oh city, town, and country; rejoice eke every shire.

For now the fragrant flowers do spring and sprout in seemly sort,
The little birds do sit and sing, the lambs do make fine sport.
And now the birchen tree doth bud, that makes the schoolboy cry;                                          40
The morris rings while hobby-horse doth foot it feateously.
The lords and ladies now abroad for their disport and play,
Do kiss sometimes upon the grass, and sometimes in the hay.
Now butter with a leaf of sage is good to purge the blood;
Fly Venus and phlebotomy, for they are neither good.
Now little fish on tender stone begin to cast their bellies,
And sluggish snails, that erst were mute, do creep out of their shellies.
The rumbling rivers now do warm for little boys to paddle,
The sturdy steed now goes to grass, and up they hang his saddle.
The heavy hart, the bellowing buck, the rascal, and the pricket,                                         50
Are now among the yeoman's peas, and leave the fearful thicket.
And be like them, oh you, I say, of this same noble town,
And lift aloft your velvet heads, and, slipping off your gown,
With bells on legs and napkins clean unto your shoulders tied,

9  May Day: the festival of spring with festivities, speeches, dancing and song. A good account can be found in Philip Stubbes's *The Anatomy of Abuses* (1583), Ch. xiii

10  conduit: fountain, cistern

10–12  scarfs about . . . his knacks: the accoutrements of Morris dancing

28–63  London, to . . . I cease: written in lines of fourteen syllables as a parody of May Day speeches and, possibly, hymn books

32  My name . . . ignoble I: parodies the speech by the Ghost of Don Andrea in *The Spanish Tragedy*, I.i.5–7, by Thomas Kyd

35  gilded staff and crossed scarf: symbols of the May Lord's authority

40  birchen tree: the branches of the birch were used for corporal punishment

41  hobby-horse: a wooden frame that allowed dancers to pretend to be horses. It became a principal focus of Puritan attacks on May Day celebrations because of the sexual symbolism of its rocking motion
feateously: nimbly

44  butter: thought to take on medicinal properties during the spring

45  Venus and phlebotomy: sexual intercourse (here represented by the classical goddess of love) and blood-letting (phlebotomy) were both believed to weaken the body

46  cast their bellies: spawn

47  snails: believed to trace the lover's name in the ashes of a hearth
erst: formerly

50  rascal: young or inferior deer in a herd
pricket: two-year-old buck

53  velvet heads: a) the new antlers of deer; b) the antlers of a new cuckold

54–5  bells on . . . and garters: more Morris dancer's accoutrements

With scarfs and garters as you please, and 'Hey for
  our town' cried,
March out, and show your willing minds, by twenty
  and by twenty,
To Hogsdon or to Newington, where ale and cakes
  are plenty.
And let it ne'er be said for shame, that we the youths
  of London
Lay thrumming of our caps at home, and left our
  custom undone.
Up then, I say, both young and old, both man and
  maid a-maying,               **60**
With drums and guns that bounce aloud, and merry
  tabor playing!
Which to prolong, God save our king, and send his
  country peace,
And root out treason from the Land! And so, my
  friends, I cease.

*Exit*

# Act V

*Enter* MERCHANT, *solus*

MERCHANT  I will have no great store of company at the
wedding: a couple of neighbours and their wives; and
we will have a capon in stewed broth, with marrow,
and a good piece of beef, stuck with rosemary.

*Enter* JASPER, *his face mealed*

JASPER  Forbear thy pains, fond man; it is too late.
MERCHANT  Heaven bless me! Jasper?
JASPER                  Ay, I am his ghost,
  Whom thou hast injured for his constant love,
  Fond worldly wretch, who dost not understand
  In death that true hearts cannot parted be.
  First, know thy daughter is quite borne away     **10**
  On wings of angels, through the liquid air,
  To far out of thy reach, and never more
  Shalt thou behold her face. But she and I
  Will in another world enjoy our loves,
  Where neither father's anger, poverty,
  Nor any cross that troubles earthly men
  Shall make us sever our united hearts.

And never shalt thou sit, or be alone
In any place, but I will visit thee
With ghastly looks, and put into thy mind     **20**
The great offences which thou didst to me.
When thou art at thy table with thy friends,
Merry in heart, and filled with swelling wine,
I'll come in midst of all thy pride and mirth,
Invisible to all men but thyself,
And whisper such a sad tale in thine ear
Shall make thee let the cup fall from thy hand,
And stand as mute and pale as Death itself.
MERCHANT  Forgive me, Jasper. Oh, what might I do,
  Tell me, to satisfy thy troubled ghost?     **30**
JASPER  There is no means; too late thou think'st of
  this.
MERCHANT  But tell me what were best for me to do?
JASPER  Repent thy deed, and satisfy my father,
  And beat fond Humphrey out of thy doors.

*Exit* JASPER

*Enter* HUMPHREY

WIFE  Look, George, his very ghost would have folks
  beaten.
HUMPHREY  Father, my bride is gone, fair Mistress Luce;
  My soul's the fount of vengeance, mischief's sluice.
MERCHANT  Hence, fool, out of my sight with thy fond
  passion!
  Thou hast undone me.          *Beats him*
HUMPHREY          Hold, my father dear,    **40**
  For Luce thy daughter's sake, that had no peer.
MERCHANT  Thy father, fool? There's some blows
  more, begone!
  Jasper, I hope thy ghost be well appeased
  To see thy will performed. Now will I go
  To satisfy thy father for thy wrongs.
HUMPHREY  What shall I do? I have been beaten twice
  And Mistress Luce is gone. Help me, device!
  Since my true love is gone, I never more
  Whilst I do live, upon the sky will pore,
  But in the dark will wear out my shoe soles    **50**
  In passion in Saint Faith's Church under Paul's.  *Exit*
WIFE  George, call Rafe hither; if you love me, call Rafe
  hither. I have the bravest thing for him to do,
  George; prithee call him quickly.
CITIZEN  Rafe, why Rafe, boy!

*Enter* RAFE

---

57  Hogsdon or to Newington: places of resort and
    recreation
59  thrumming of our caps: decorating caps with tassels (a
    sign of wasting time)
    custom: 'wenching'
61  tabor: small drum
3–4  capon . . . with rosemary: traditional seventeenth-century
    wedding fare
SD  *mealed*: whitened with flour
  5  pains: labours (in preparation)
16  cross: impediment

---

19–28  a parody of Shakespeare's *Macbeth* (1606), III.iv.48–143
  38  fount: source
  39  passion: grief
  47  device: contrivance
  51  Saint Faith's . . . under Paul's: St Faith's was a parish church
      located in the crypt of St Paul's underneath the choir;
      gallants would parade in the aisle of the cathedral above
  53  bravest: most splendid

RAFE Here, sir. **56**

CITIZEN Come hither, Rafe; come to thy mistress, boy.

WIFE Rafe, I would have thee call all the youths together in battle-ray, with drums, and guns, and flags, and march to Mile End in pompous fashion, and there exhort your soldiers to be merry and wise, and to keep their beards from burning, Rafe; and then skirmish, and let your flags fly, and cry, 'Kill, kill, kill'. My husband shall lend you his jerkin, Rafe, and there's a scarf, for the rest, the house shall furnish you, and we'll pay for't. Do it bravely, Rafe, and think before whom you perform, and what person you represent. **68**

RAFE I warrant you, mistress, if I do it not for the honour of the city and the credit of my master, let me never hope for freedom.

WIFE 'Tis well spoken, i'faith. Go thy ways; thou art a spark indeed.

CITIZEN Rafe, Rafe, double your files bravely, Rafe.

RAFE I warrant you, sir. *Exit* RAFE

CITIZEN Let him look narrowly to his service, I shall take him else. I was there myself a pikeman once in the hottest of the day, wench; had my feather shot sheer away, the fringe of my pike burnt off with powder, my pate broken with a scouring-stick, and yet I thank God I am here. *Drum within*

WIFE Hark, George, the drums. **82**

CITIZEN Ran, tan, tan, tan; ran, tan. Oh, wench, an thou hadst but seen little Ned of Aldgate, Drum-Ned, how he made it roar again, and laid on like a tyrant, and then struck softly till the ward came up, and then thundered again, and together we go. 'Sa, sa, sa, bounce', quoth the guns; 'Courage, my hearts', quoth the captains, 'Saint George', quoth the pikemen; and withal here they lay, and there they lay. And yet for all this I am here, wench. **91**

WIFE Be thankful for it, George, for indeed 'tis wonderful.

*Enter* RAFE *and his company, with drums and colours*

RAFE March fair, my hearts! Lieutenant, beat the rear up.—Ancient, let your colours fly; but have a great

care of the butchers' hooks at Whitechapel; they have been the death of many a fair ancient.—Open your files that I may take a view both of your persons and munition.—Sergeant, call a muster.

SERGEANT A stand!—William Hamerton, pewterer!

HAMERTON Here, captain. **101**

RAFE A corslet and a Spanish pike; 'tis well. Can you shake it with a terror?

HAMERTON I hope so, captain.

RAFE Charge upon me. (HAMERTON *charges upon* RAFE) 'Tis with the weakest. Put more strength, William Hamerton, more strength. As you were again.—Proceed, Sergeant.

SERGEANT George Greengoose, poulterer!

GREENGOOSE Here. **111**

RAFE Let me see your piece, neighbour Greengoose; when was she shot in?

GREENGOOSE An't like you, master captain, I made a shot even now, partly to scour her, and partly for audacity.

RAFE It should seem so certainly, for her breath is yet inflamed; besides, there is a main fault in the touch-hole, it runs and stinketh; and I tell you moreover, and believe it, ten such touch-holes would breed the pox in the army. Get you a feather, neighbour, get you a feather, sweet oil, and paper, and your piece may do well enough yet. Where's your powder? **122**

GREENGOOSE Here.

RAFE What, in a paper? As I am a soldier and a gentleman, it craves a martial court. You ought to die for't. Where's your horn? Answer me to that.

GREENGOOSE An't like you, sir, I was oblivious.

RAFE It likes me not you should be so; 'tis a shame for you, and a scandal to all our neighbours, being a man of worth and estimation, to leave your horn behind you: I am afraid 'twill breed example. But let me tell you no more on't.—Stand, till I view you all.—What's become o'th nose of your flask? **133**

1 SOLDIER Indeed la, captain, 'twas blown away with powder.

RAFE Put on a new one at the city's charge.—Where's

---

59 battle-ray: battle formation
60 pompous: ceremonial
64 jerkin: jacket or short coat
65 house: theatre
71 freedom: rank of freeman in the Grocers' Company
74 double your files: combine your two ranks
76 narrowly: closely
 service: manœuvres
77 take: reprehend
80 scouring-stick: cane used for clearing the barrel of a gun
86 ward: detachment of the militia
94–5 beat the rear up: round up with a roll of the drums
95 Ancient: ensign-bearer

96 Whitechapel: a parish to the east of Aldgate known for its butchers' shops
99 muster: roll
102 corslet: armour covering the body
 Spanish pike: 'probably superior to the English' (Kinney)
103 shake it: with sexual connotation
111 piece: gun (but with sexual connotation)
117–18 touch-hole: the ignition hole in the breech of a gun but, as with most of the technical language in this scene, with a sexual connotation
120 pox: syphilis
121 feather, sweet oil, and paper: materials for cleaning a gun
126 horn: a) powder horn; b) cuckold's horn
127 oblivious: forgetful

the stone of this piece?                                    **137**

2 SOLDIER  The drummer took it out to light tobacco.

RAFE  'Tis a fault, my friend; put it in again.—You want
a nose—and you a stone.—Sergeant, take a note on't,
for I mean to stop it in the pay.—Remove, and
march! Soft and fair, gentlemen, soft and fair!
Double your files! As you were! Faces about! Now,
you with the sodden face, keep in there! Look to your
match, sirrah, it will be in your fellow's flask anon.
So, make a crescent now; advance your pikes; stand,
and give ear! Gentlemen, countrymen, friends, and
my fellow-soldiers, I have brought you this day from
the shops of security and the counters of content, to
measure out in these furious fields honour by the ell,
and prowess by the pound. Let it not, oh, let it not, I
say, be told hereafter the noble issue of this city
fainted, but bear yourselves in this fair action like
men, valiant men, and freemen. Fear not the face of
the enemy, nor the noise of the guns, for believe me,
brethren, the rude rumbling of a brewer's car is far
more terrible, of which you have a daily experience,
neither let the stink of powder offend you, since a
more valiant stink is nightly with you. To a resolved
mind his home is everywhere. I speak not this to take
away the hope of your return; for you shall see, I do
not doubt it, and that very shortly, your loving wives
again, and your sweet children, whose care doth bear
you company in baskets. Remember, then, whose
cause you have in hand, and like a sort of true-born
scavengers, scour me this famous realm of enemies. I
have no more to say but this: stand to your tacklings,
lads, and show to the world you can as well brandish
a sword as shake an apron. Saint George, and on, my
hearts!                                                     **170**

OMNES  Saint George! Saint George!

WIFE  'Twas well done, Rafe. I'll send thee a cold capon
a-field, and a bottle of March beer; and it may be,
come myself to see thee.

---

137  stone: a) flint; b) testicle
139  want: lack (also implying the effects of syphilis)
144  sodden face: a) drunken; b) suffering the effects of the
       sweating-tub treatment for syphilis
145  match: fuse for igniting musket
146–70  stand, and . . . my hearts!: Rafe's exhortation to his
       soldiers parodies that of Richard to his troops in
       Shakespeare's *Richard III* (1593), V.vi.44–81, echoes a
       number of other pre-battle speeches in the history plays,
       and contains some of the rhetorical features of Antony's
       speech in *Julius Caesar* (1599–1600) III.ii.70–104
150  ell: a measure of forty-five inches
159  valiant stink: another reference with sexual
       connotations
164  baskets: i.e. of provisions
165  sort: company
167  tacklings: a) weapons; b) genitals
173  March beer: strong beer (brewed early in the season)

---

CITIZEN  Nell, the boy has deceived me much; I did not
think it had been in him. He has performed such a
matter, wench, that if I live, next year I'll have him
captain of the galley-foist, or I'll want my will.     **178**

*Enter* OLD MERRYTHOUGHT

OLD MERRYTHOUGHT  Yet, I thank God, I break not a
wrinkle more than I had. Not a stoup, boys? Care live
with cats, I defy thee! My heart is as sound as an oak,
and though I want drink to wet my whistle, I can
sing:
(*Sings*)      *Come no more there, boys, come no more*
                    *there;*
                *For we shall never whilst we live, come any*
                    *more there.*

*Enter a* BOY *and* COFFIN CARRIERS *with a coffin*

BOY  God save you, sir.

OLD MERRYTHOUGHT  It's a brave boy. Canst thou sing?

BOY  Yes, sir, I can sing, but 'tis not so necessary at this
time.

OLD MERRYTHOUGHT
(*Sings*)      *Sing we, and chant it,*                    **190**
                *Whilst love doth grant it.*

BOY  Sir, sir, if you knew what I have brought you, you
would have little list to sing.

OLD MERRYTHOUGHT
(*Sings*)      *Oh, the minion round,*
                *Full long I have thee sought,*
                *And now I have thee found,*
                *And what hast thou here brought?*

BOY  A coffin, sir, and your dead son Jasper in it.

OLD MERRYTHOUGHT  Dead?
(*Sings*)      *Why, farewell he.*                         **200**
                *Thou wast a bonny boy,*
                *And I did love thee.*

*Enter* JASPER

JASPER  Then, I pray you, sir, do so still.

OLD MERRYTHOUGHT  Jasper's ghost?
(*Sings*)      *Thou art welcome from Stygian lake so soon;*
                *Declare to me what wondrous things in*
                    *Pluto's court are done.*

JASPER  By my troth, sir, I ne'er came there; 'tis too hot
for me, sir.

---

178  galley-foist: the Lord Mayor's state barge
179  break: show
180  stoup: measure of drink (two quarts)
180–1  Care live with cats: 'Care will kill a cat'
       (proverbial)
184–5  Come no . . . more there: from *Ballets to Five Voices* by
       Thomas Morley (1595 and 1600)
205  *Stygian lake*: the river Styx in the classical underworld
       (Hades)
207  *Pluto's court*: Pluto was the king of Hades

OLD MERRYTHOUGHT  A merry ghost, a very merry
   ghost!                                  **211**
   (*Sings*)     *And where is your true love. Oh, where is*
                    *yours?*
JASPER  Marry, look you, sir.
            *Heaves up the Coffin, and* LUCE *climbs out*
OLD MERRYTHOUGHT  Ah, ha! Art thou good at that,
   i'faith?
   (*Sings*)     *With hey, trixy, terlery-whiskin,*
                  *The world it runs on wheels,*
                  *When the young man's —,*
                  *Up goes the maiden's heels.*     **219**

MISTRESS MERRYTHOUGHT *and* MICHAEL *within*

MISTRESS MERRYTHOUGHT  (*within*) What, Master
   Merrythought, will you not let's in? What do you
   think shall become of us?
OLD MERRYTHOUGHT  What voice is that that calleth at
   our door?
MISTRESS MERRYTHOUGHT  (*within*) You know me well
   enough; I am sure I have not been such a stranger to
   you.
OLD MERRYTHOUGHT
   (*Sings*)     *And some they whistled, and some they sung,*
                  *Hey, down, down!*
                  *And some did loudly say,*     **230**
                  *Ever as the Lord Barnet's horn blew,*
                  *Away, Musgrave, away.*
MISTRESS MERRYTHOUGHT  (*within*) You will not have
   us starve here, will you, Master Merrythought?
JASPER  Nay, good sir, be persuaded, she is my mother.
   If her offences have been great against you, let your
   own love remember she is yours, and so forgive
   her.
LUCE  Good Master Merrythought, let me entreat you;
   I will not be denied.                    **240**
MISTRESS MERRYTHOUGHT  (*within*) Why, Master
   Merrythought, will you be a vexed thing still?
OLD MERRYTHOUGHT  Woman, I take you to my love
   again; but you shall sing before you enter; therefore
   dispatch your song and so come in.
MISTRESS MERRYTHOUGHT  (*within*) Well, you must
   have your will when all's done.—Mick, what song
   canst thou sing, boy?
MICHAEL  (*within*) I can sing none, forsooth, but
   'A Lady's Daughter of Paris' properly.     **250**

MISTRESS MERRYTHOUGHT *with* MICHAEL (*within*)
   SONG
          *It was a lady's daughter, etc.*

OLD MERRYTHOUGHT *admits* MISTRESS
MERRYTHOUGHT *and* MICHAEL

OLD MERRYTHOUGHT  Come, you're welcome home
   again.
   (*Sings*)     *If such danger be in playing,*
                  *And jest must to earnest turn,*
                  *You shall go no more a-maying.*    **256**
MERCHANT  (*within*) Are you within, sir? Master
   Merrythought?
JASPER  It is my master's voice. Good sir, go hold him
   in talk, whilst we convey ourselves into some inward
   room.                       *Exit with* LUCE
OLD MERRYTHOUGHT  What are you? Are you merry?
   You must be very merry if you enter.
MERCHANT  (*within*) I am, sir.
OLD MERRYTHOUGHT  Sing then.
MERCHANT  (*within*) Nay, good sir, open to me.
OLD MERRYTHOUGHT  Sing, I say, or, by the merry
   heart, you come not in.
MERCHANT  (*within*) Well, sir, I'll sing:
   (*Sings*)     *Fortune my foe, etc.*          **270**

OLD MERRYTHOUGHT *admits* MERCHANT

OLD MERRYTHOUGHT  You are welcome, sir, you are
   welcome. You see your entertainment; pray you, be
   merry.
MERCHANT  Oh, Master Merrythought, I am come to
   ask you
   Forgiveness for the wrongs I offered you
   And your most virtuous son; they're infinite;
   Yet my contrition shall be more than they.
   I do confess my hardness broke his heart,
   For which just heaven hath given me punishment
   More than my age can carry. His wandering spirit, **280**

---

215  *The world it runs on wheels*: proverbial
216  *When the young man's . . .*: the omitted word is possibly
     'frisking'. Some editors note the Act to Restrain the
     Abuses of the Players (1606) as an explanation for this
     omission (as in Interlude I.11)
228–32  *And some . . . Musgrave, away*: from the ballad of Little
     Margaret and Lady Barnard
237  *own love*: self-love
242  *vexed*: cantankerous

251  *It was a lady's daughter, etc.*: from a broadside ballad that
     begins:
     It was a lady's daughter,
     Of Paris properly,
     Her mother her commanded
     To mass that she should hie:
     O pardon me, dear mother,
     Her daughter dear did say,
     Unto that filthy idol
     I never can obey
254–6  *If such . . . more a-maying*: from 'My Love Hath Vowed'
     in Philip Rosseter's *Book of Airs* (1601)
     *playing*: flirting
270  *Fortune my foe, etc.*: from a very popular song that begins:
     Fortune my foe, why dost thou frown on me?
     And will thy favours never better be?
     Wilt thou, I say, for ever breed my pain?
     And wilt thou not restore my joys again?

Not yet at rest, pursues me everywhere,
Crying, 'I'll haunt thee for thy cruelty'.
My daughter, she is gone, I know not how,
Taken invisible, and whether living
Or in grave, 'tis yet uncertain to me.
Oh Master Merrythought, these are the weights
Will sink me to my grave. Forgive me, sir.

OLD MERRYTHOUGHT  Why, sir, I do forgive you, and
    be merry;
And if the wag in's lifetime played the knave,
Can you forgive him too?

MERCHANT                        With all my heart, sir.  290

OLD MERRYTHOUGHT  Speak it again, and heartily.

MERCHANT                                I do, sir,
    Now, by my soul, I do.

OLD MERRYTHOUGHT
(Sings)      *With that came out his paramour;*
             *She was as white as the lily flower,*
             *Hey, trolly, trolly, lolly.*

*Enter* LUCE *and* JASPER

             *With that came out her own dear knight,*
             *He was as true as ever did fight. etc.*
Sir, if you will forgive 'em, clap their hands together;
there's no more to be said i'th' matter.

MERCHANT  I do, I do.                        300

CITIZEN  I do not like this.—Peace, boys, hear me one
of you. Everybody's part is come to an end but Rafe's,
and he's left out.

BOY  'Tis long of yourself, sir; we have nothing to do
with his part.

CITIZEN  Rafe, come away.—Make an end on him as
you have done of the rest, boys; come.

WIFE  Now, good husband, let him come out and die.

CITIZEN  He shall Nell.—Rafe, come away quickly and
die, boy.                                    310

BOY  'Twill be very unfit he should die, sir, upon no
occasion, and in a comedy too.

CITIZEN  Take you no care of that, sir boy, is not his
part at an end, think you, when he's dead?—Come
away, Rafe.

*Enter* RAFE, *with a forked arrow through his head*

RAFE  When I was mortal, this my costive corpse
Did lap up figs and raisins in the Strand,

Where sitting, I espied a lovely dame,
Whose master wrought with lingel and with awl,
And under ground he vamped many a boot.  320
Straight did her love prick forth me, tender sprig,
To follow feats of arms in warlike wise
Through Waltham Desert, where I did perform
Many achievements, and did lay on ground
Huge Barbaroso, that insulting giant,
And all his captives soon set at liberty.
Then honour pricked me from my native soil
Into Moldavia, where I gained the love
Of Pompiona, his beloved daughter,
But yet proved constant to the black-thumbed maid
Susan, and scorned Pompiona's love.         331
Yet liberal I was, and gave her pins,
And money for her father's officers.
I then returned home, and thrust myself
In action, and by all men chosen was
Lord of the May, where I did flourish it,
With scarfs and rings, and posy in my hand.
After this action, I preferrèd was,
And chosen city captain at Mile End,
With hat and feather and with leading-staff,  340
And trained my men and brought them all off clear
(Save one man that berayed him with the noise).
But all these things I Rafe did undertake
Only for my beloved Susan's sake.
Then coming home, and sitting in my shop
With apron blue, Death came unto my stall
To cheapen *aqua vitae*—but ere I
Could take the bottle down, and fill a taste,
Death caught a pound of pepper in his hand,
And sprinkled all my face and body o'er,     350
And in an instant vanished away.

CITIZEN  'Tis a pretty fiction i'faith.

RAFE  Then took I up my bow and shaft in hand,
And walked into Moorfields to cool myself;
But there grim cruel Death met me again,
And shot this forked arrow through my head,
And now I faint. Therefore be warned by me,
My fellows every one, of forked heads.
Farewell, all you good boys in merry London;
Ne'er shall we more upon Shrove Tuesday meet  360

---

289  wag: mischievous boy
298  clap their hands together: i.e. as a sign of betrothal
304  long: on account
  SD  *forked*: barbed. Parody of the entrance of Clifford in *The
      True Tragedy of Richard Duke of York* (1595)
316–51  parody of ghost scenes in *Eastward Ho!* (1605) by
      George Chapman, Ben Jonson and John Marston, *The
      Spanish Tragedy*, and *Richard III*
316  costive: reluctant (plays on 'constipated')
317  figs and raisins: fruits used as laxatives

319  lingel: waxed thread used by shoemakers
320  vamped: renewed the uppers of
321  prick: spur (with sexual connotation)
325  insulting: bragging
329  his: i.e. the King of Moldavia's
337  posy: bouquet
340  leading-staff: officer's baton
342  berayed him: befouled himself
347  cheapen: bargain for
354  Moorfields: a popular summer resort north of the city
      walls beyond Moorgate
358  forked heads: i.e. of cuckolds

And pluck down houses of iniquity.
My pain increaseth.—I shall never more
Hold open, whilst another pumps both legs,
Nor daub a satin gown with rotten eggs;
Set up a stake, oh, never more I shall.
I die; fly, fly, my soul, to Grocers' Hall.
Oh, oh, oh, etc.

WIFE  Well said, Rafe. Do your obeisance to the
gentlemen and go your ways. Well said, Rafe.      **369**

*Exit* RAFE

OLD MERRYTHOUGHT  Methinks all we, thus kindly and
unexpectedly reconciled, should not depart without a
song.

MERCHANT  A good motion.

OLD MERRYTHOUGHT  Strike up, then.

> SONG
> *Better music ne'er was known*
> *Than a choir of hearts in one.*
> *Let each other that hath been*
> *Troubled with the gall or spleen,*
> *Learn of us to keep his brow*
> *Smooth and plain as ours are now.*      **380**
> *Sing, though before the hour of dying;*
> *He shall rise, and then be crying,*
> *'Hey, ho, 'tis nought but mirth,*
> *That keeps the body from the earth'.*

*Exeunt* OMNES

# Epilogus

CITIZEN  Come Nell, shall we go? The play's done.

WIFE  Nay, by my faith, George, I have more manners
than so; I'll speak to these gentlemen first.—I thank
you all, gentlemen, for your patience and
countenance to Rafe, a poor fatherless child; and if I
might see you at my house, it should go hard but I
would have a pottle of wine and a pipe of tobacco for
you; for, truly, I hope you do like the youth, but I
would be glad to know the truth. I refer it to your
own discretions, whether you will applaud him or no;
for I will wink, and whilst you shall do what you will.
I thank you with all my heart. God give you good
night.—Come, George.

*Exeunt*

FINIS

---

360–1 Shrove Tuesday . . . of iniquity: the last day before Lent
was a time of revelry and riot for apprentices who
sometimes attacked theatres and brothels

364  satin gown: the dress of gallants as dandies

365  Set up a stake: reference to the use of staked cockerels as
targets

371  depart: i.e. take leave of one another

---

7  pottle: measure of two quarts
tobacco: Nell's sense of hospitality (and social climbing)
outweighs her antipathy to tobacco at I.210–14

11  will wink: close my eyes
whilst: meanwhile

# Ben Jonson, *Epicoene, or The Silent Woman*

First performed 1609
First published 1616

In many ways, *Epicoene, or The Silent Woman* works
with the most familiar of comic raw materials. In
Dauphine Eugenie's plot against his uncle, Morose, we
see the struggle of youth versus age; in the manoeuvres
of Sir John Daw and Sir Amorous La Foole, Tom
Otter and his wife, and the collegiate ladies, the play
offers the customary comic battle of women versus
men; and in the play's setting, in Jacobean London, we
have a sense of the contest between a new kind of urban
social order and an older, less commercialised one.
Throughout, too, the recourse to dissembling and
disguise, in particular to cross-dressing, and the
dependence on characters' foibles, distortions or
excesses as a source of humour and a trigger of the
comic action indicate that we are in recognisable
Renaissance comic territory. These staples, however, do
not bring with them the usual reassurances or
affirmations offered by such comedy. The end of the
play, for example, is neither reintegrative nor restitutive.
Although the young gallant, Dauphine, outwits Morose
and secures his inheritance, thereby ensuring the
triumph of youth over age (as comedy suggests it must),
this is no natural succession and it is marked by no
honouring of the generation on the wane. Instead,
Dauphine revels in his success with a gratuitous and
chilling cruelty, telling Morose that 'I'll not trouble you
till you trouble me with your funeral, which I care not
how soon it come' (V.iv.232–3).

Such relentlessness and remorselessness are
fundamental to the play as a whole. There is no relief
from, and no alternative to, the parade of buffoons,
dandies and viragos that rolls across the stage, no one
whose values offer a secure point of anchorage to the
spectator/reader tossed between one set of follies,
perversions or vices and another. The confusion or
blurring of gender roles, for example, is all but total: the
women are masculine and emasculating; the men are
effeminate, ineffectual, or both. The misogyny of the
characters is similarly unremitting, varied and vigorous
(see, for example Truewit's attempt to dissuade Morose
from marriage in II.ii), and is unalleviated by the more
general but less acid misanthropy that also,
undoubtedly, informs the play. Likewise, disguise and
dissembling proliferate: Truewit pretends to be a
messenger, Daw to be scholarly, La Foole to be a

servant, Morose to be impotent, Otter and Cutbeard to
be lawyer and parson, and Epicoene to be a woman. No
counterweight of 'reality' underlies these pretences.
Beneath is either absence: Truewit says of Daw, 'A
fellow so utterly nothing, as he knows not what he
would be' (II.iv.164–5), or more pretence: the boy who
has played Epicoene, Truewit assures us, will continue
to dissemble in the post-play world (V.iv.269–70). In
this 'comedy of affliction' (II.vi.38), all are afflicted;
none is immune.

If anything mitigates the harshness of this diagnosis,
it is the sense that these ills are not the timeless and
universal results of a fallen human nature, but are
socially produced. This is a city comedy, a play rooted
in its urban setting and the lives and mores of its
citizens (see Gibbons 1980). Characteristically for plays
of this kind, the excesses of the characters are
represented, as Tom Otter's tirade against his wife
suggests, as those of the city itself:

> All her teeth were made i' the Blackfriars, both her
> eyebrows i' the Strand, and her hair in Silver Street.
> Every part o' the town owns a piece of her . . . She
> takes herself asunder still when she goes to bed, into
> some twenty boxes.
>
> (IV.ii.84–9)

Mistress Otter is, quite literally, the product (and
indeed the property) of the newly burgeoning consumer
markets of Jacobean London, with their energy,
clamour and glamour. Whilst the play invites criticism
of the superficiality and triviality of this consumerist
playground, we also need to beware of assuming our
own immunity to its appeal, for it is this very energy,
with its noise, inventiveness and exuberance, that drives
the plot, generates the wit, and thereby constitutes the
pleasure, of this play.

The topicality of *Epicoene* is, paradoxically, as much a
result of its classicism as of its devotion to
contemporary detail. As the notes to the text make
clear, Jonson, as was his custom, drew on and adapted
the work of a wide range of classical authors – here, in
particular the Greek rhetorician Libanius (AD 314–393),
the Roman poet Ovid (43 BC–AD 18) and the satirist
Juvenal (c. AD 60–c. 130). These models, however, far

from rendering Jonson's work archaic or obscure, give the playwright much of his caustic rhetorical arsenal. Indeed, those passages that offer a real sense of the texture of life in, and social mores of, Jacobean London (such as Truewit's diatribe against women (II.ii), or Morose's railing against noise (III.vi, IV.iv) are, more likely than not, those that are drawn most directly from their sources.

*Epicoene* was first staged in December 1609 or January 1610, by one of the boys' acting companies, at the Whitefriars, a private theatre. It was Jonson's first play for the public stage since *Volpone*, four years before, as he had concentrated on writing court masques in the intervening years. The new play was a success but was nonetheless closed in February 1610, owing to a complaint made by the king's cousin, Arbella Stuart, who detected in it a scurrilous reference to herself (see V.i.26n, the Dedication, and Jonson's defence in the second Prologue). The play was later revived at court in 1636 and, significantly, was the first play to be staged on the reopening of the theatres in 1660, after the accession of Charles II to the throne. It was much admired, by critics as diverse as Samuel Pepys and John Dryden, and proved to be the model for Restoration comic dramatists such as Etherage, Wycherley and Congreve. Its popularity declined after the mid-eighteenth century, however, and it was only in the late twentieth century, with its concern with questions of the cultural construction of gender and sexuality, that the critical gaze fell on the play again. It shows, as yet, no sign of being diverted.

## Textual note

The copytext for this edition is Jonson's 1616 folio, *The Workes of Benjamin Jonson*.

# Further reading

## Editions

Adams, Robert M. (ed.) (1979) *Ben Jonson's Plays and Masques: Texts of the Plays and Masques, Jonson on his Work, Contemporary Readers on Jonson Criticism*, New York, NY: W. W. Norton and Company.
Beaurline, L. A. (ed.) (1966) *Ben Jonson: Epicoene, or The Silent Woman*, Regents Renaissance Drama Series, London: Edward Arnold.
Dutton, Richard (ed.) (2003) *Epicoene, or The Silent Woman*, The Revels Plays, Manchester: Manchester University Press.
Gifford, W. (ed.) (1875) *The Works of Ben Jonson*, vol. III, notes by Francis Cunningham, London: Bickers and Son, Henry Sotheran and Co.
Herford, C. H. and Simpson, Percy (eds) (1954) *Ben Jonson*, vol. V (corrected version of 1937 edition), Oxford: Clarendon Press.
Heyward Brock, D. (ed.) (1976) *The Workes of Benjamin Jonson*, facsimile edition, London: Scolar Press.

Holdsworth, R. V. (ed.) (1979) *Epicoene, or The Silent Woman*, The New Mermaids, London: A. & C. Black.
Ostovich, Helen (ed.) (1997) *Ben Jonson: Four Comedies*, London and New York, NY: Longman.
Partridge, Edward (ed.) (1971) *Ben Jonson: Epicoene*, The Yale Ben Jonson, New Haven, CT, and London: Yale University Press.
Procter, Johanna (ed.) (1989) *The Selected Plays of Ben Jonson*, vol. I, Cambridge: Cambridge University Press.
Schelling, Felix (ed.) (1910) *The Complete Plays of Ben Jonson*, vol. I, Everyman's Library, London: J. M. Dent and Sons.
Wilkes, G. A. (ed.) (1982) *The Complete Plays of Ben Jonson*, vol. III, Oxford: Clarendon Press (based on Herford and Simpson's edition).

## Critical and contextual commentaries

Ayers, P. K. (1987) 'Dreams of the City: The Urban and the Urbane in Jonson's *Epicoene*', *Philological Quarterly*, 66, 1: 73–86.
Barish, Jonas A. (1960) *Ben Jonson and the Language of Prose Comedy*, Cambridge, MA: Harvard University Press.
Barton, Anne (1984) *Ben Jonson, Dramatist*, Cambridge: Cambridge University Press.
Boehrer, Bruce T. (1994) '*Epicoene*, Charivari, Skimmington', *English Studies*, 75, 1: 17–33.
Donaldson, Ian (1970) *The World Upside Down: Comedy from Jonson to Fielding*, Oxford: Clarendon Press.
—— (ed.) (1985) *Ben Jonson*, Oxford: Oxford University Press.
Dutton, Richard (1984) *Ben Jonson: To the First Folio*, Cambridge: Cambridge University Press.
Gibbons, Brian (1980) *Jacobean City Comedy*, 2nd edition, London: Methuen.
Jones, Emrys (1982) 'The First West End Comedy', *Proceedings of the British Academy*, 48: 215–58.
Knapp, Peggy (1991) 'Ben Jonson and the Publicke Riot: Ben Jonson's Comedies', in David Scott Kastan and Peter Stallybrass (eds) *Staging the Renaissance: Reinterpretations of Elizabethan and Jacobean Drama*, London: Routledge.
Knights, L. C. (1937) *Drama and Society in the Age of Jonson*, London: Chatto and Windus.
Lanier, Douglas (1994) 'Masculine Silence: *Epicoene* and Jonsonian Stylistics', *College Literature*, 21, 2: 1–18.
Levine, Laura (1994) *Men in Women's Clothing: Anti-Theatricality and Effeminization, 1579–1642*, Cambridge: Cambridge University Press.
Millard, Barbara C. (1984) '"An Acceptable Violence": Sexual Contest in Jonson's *Epicoene*', *Medieval and Renaissance Drama in England*, 1: 143–58.
Mirabelli, Philip (1989) 'Silence, Wit, and Wisdom in *The Silent Woman*', *Studies in English Literature 1500–1900*, 29, 2: 309–36.
Newman, Karen (1991) 'City Talk: Woman and Commodification: *Epicoene* (1609)', in David Scott Kastan and Peter Stallybrass (eds) *Staging the Renaissance: Reinterpretations of Elizabethan and Jacobean Drama*, London: Routledge.
Partridge, Edward (1958, reprinted 1976) *The Broken Compass: A Study of the Major Comedies of Ben Jonson*, Westport, CT: Greenwood Press.
Pelling, Margaret (1986) 'Appearance and Reality: Barber-surgeons, the Body and Disease', in A. L. Beier and Roger

Finlay (eds) *London 1500–1700: The Making of the Metropolis*, London: Longman.

Salingar, Leo (1986) 'Farce and Fashion in *The Silent Woman*', in *Dramatic Form in Shakespeare and the Jacobeans*, Cambridge: Cambridge University Press.

Swann, Marjorie (1998) 'Refashioning Society in Ben Jonson's *Epicoene*', *Studies in English Literature 1500–1900*, 38, 2: 297–315.

Womack, Peter (1986) *Ben Jonson*, Oxford: Blackwell.

## Works of related interest

Ben Jonson, *Every Man in His Humour* (1598)
Henry Porter, *The Two Angry Women of Abington* (1598)
Thomas Dekker, *Satiromastix* (1601)
John Marston, *The Dutch Courtesan* (1604)
Thomas Middleton, *A Trick to Catch the Old One* (1605)
Ben Jonson, *Volpone* (1606)
Ben Jonson, *The Alchemist* (1610)
Thomas Middleton and Thomas Dekker, *The Roaring Girl* (1611)
Thomas Middleton, *A Chaste Maid in Cheapside* (1613)
Ben Jonson, *Bartholomew Fair* (1614)
Philip Massinger, *The City Madam* (1632)

# *Epicoene, or The Silent Woman* (1609)

## To the Truly Noble, by All Titles, Sir Francis Stuart:

Sir,
My hope is not so nourished by example, as it will
conclude this dumb piece should please you by cause it
hath pleased others before, but by trust, that when you
have read it, you will find it worthy to have displeased
none. This makes that I now number you not only in
the names of favour, but the names of justice, to what I
write; and do, presently, call you to the exercise of that
noblest and manliest virtue: as coveting rather to be
freed in my fame by the authority of a judge than the
credit of an undertaker. Read therefore, I pray you, and
censure. There is not a line or syllable in it changed
from the simplicity of the first copy. And when you
shall consider, through the certain hatred of some, how
much a man's innocency may be endangered by an
uncertain accusation, you will, I doubt not, so begin to
hate the iniquity of such natures as I shall love the
contumely done me, whose end was so honourable as to
be wiped off by your sentence.

Your unprofitable but true lover,     20
BEN. JONSON

## The Persons of the Play

MOROSE, *a gentleman that loves no noise*

DAUPHINE EUGENIE, *a knight, his nephew*

CLERIMONT, *a gentleman, his friend*

TRUEWIT, *another friend*

EPICOENE, *a young gentleman, supposed the silent woman*

JOHN DAW, *a knight, her servant*

AMOROUS LA FOOLE, *a knight also*

THOMAS OTTER, *a land and sea captain*

CUTBEARD, *a barber*

MUTE, *one of Morose his servants*     10

MADAME HAUGHTY ⎫
MADAME CENTAURE ⎬ *ladies collegiates*
MISTRESS MAVIS ⎭

---

Sir Francis Stuart: 'a learned gentleman', one of the
fashionable 'heroes and wits' (John Aubrey, *Brief Lives*
(1898) II.239) who met at the Mermaid tavern; he was
grandson of Mary, Queen of Scots's half-brother, James

2 example: i.e. comparative instances from the past
3 dumb piece: a) silent play (because its performance had
  been suppressed by the authorities); b) silent woman
  (depreciatory: 'piece' suggests a woman as a sexual object).
  by cause: because
6 makes: means
8 presently: now
10 fame: reputation
11 undertaker: guarantor; also, political 'fixer'
12 censure: judge
13 simplicity: straightforwardness
16 accusation: i.e. that *Epicoene* contained an allusion to the
   engagement that the bogus Prince of Moldavia claimed
   he had entered into with Lady Arbella Stuart, James I's
   cousin; see second prologue, below, and V.i.26n

1 MOROSE: peevish, stubborn, fretful (from Latin *morosus*)
2 DAUPHINE EUGENIE: 'well-born heir', from Greek (ευγενιος:
  well-born), and dauphin (title of king of France's eldest
  son). The feminising of 'dauphin' by the addition of the
  final 'e' is indicative of the 'epicene' nature of this character;
  the same can be said of both La Foole's and Madame
  Centaure's names. 'Eugenie' also suggests French *génie*
  (wit). The connection with the French is significant, as this
  indicates both fashion and sexual unnaturalness in the play
3 CLERIMONT: echoes French *clairement* (clearly, plainly)
5 EPICOENE: having the characteristics of both sexes
6 JOHN DAW: i.e. jackdaw, a bird known for its 'loquacity
  and thievish propensities' (OED); 'daw' also meant a
  simpleton or fool
  servant: lover devoted to his mistress
7 LA FOOLE: the feminine form of the name; see note to l. 2
  above
8 OTTER: amphibious animal (see I.iv.26), creature of two
  elements; thus suggestive of indeterminacy
12 CENTAURE: mythical creature, half man, half horse;
   suggestive of wildness and animal lustfulness
   *collegiates*: belonging to a college, i.e. a club or society
13 MAVIS: a song thrush; eds also cite sense from John
   Florio's *A World of Words* (1598): 'an ill face'

MISTRESS TRUSTY, *the Lady Haughty's woman* ⎫
MISTRESS OTTER, *the Captain's wife* ⎬ *pretenders*
⎭

*Parson, Pages, Servants, Musicians*

**The scene**

LONDON

# Prologue

Truth says, of old, the art of making plays
   Was to content the people, and their praise
   Was to the poet money, wine, and bays.
But in this age a sect of writers are,
   That only for particular likings care,
   And will taste nothing that is popular.
With such we mingle neither brains nor breasts;
   Our wishes, like to those make public feasts
   Are not to please the cooks' tastes, but the guests'.
Yet if those cunning palates hither come,      10
   They shall find guests' entreaty and good room;
   And though all relish not, sure, there will be some
That, when they leave their seats, shall make 'em say,
   Who wrote that piece could so have wrote a play,
   But that he knew this was the better way.
For to present all custard or all tart
   And have no other meats to bear a part,
   Or to want bread and salt, were but coarse art.
The poet prays you, then, with better thought
   To sit, and when his cates are all in brought,    20
   Though there be none far-fet, there will dear-bought
Be fit for ladies; some for lords, knights, squires,

Some for your waiting-wench and city-wires,
   Some for your men and daughters of Whitefriars.
Nor is it only while you keep your seat
   Here that his feast will last, but you shall eat
   A week at ord'naries on his broken meat:
       If his muse be true,
       Who commends her to you.

# Another, occasioned by some person's impertinent exception

The ends of all who for the scene do write
   Are, or should be, to profit and delight.
And still 't hath been the praise of all best times,
   So persons were not touched, to tax the crimes.
Then, in this play, which we present tonight,
   And make the object of your ear and sight,
On forfeit of yourselves, think nothing true,
   Lest so you make the maker to judge you.
For he knows, poet never credit gained
   By writing truths, but things (like truths) well
     feigned.            10
If any yet will (with particular sleight
   Of application) wrest what he doth write,
And that he meant or him or her will say,
   They make a libel which he made a play.

---

14–15 *pretenders*: claimants, aspirants (to membership of the ladies' college)
1–2 the art . . . people: echoing the opening lines of the prologue to *Andria* by the Roman comic poet Terence
3 bays: fame (from wreath of bay laurel given to poets)
4–5 sect . . . particular likings: perhaps an allusion to playwrights (such as Marston and Chapman) who wrote only for the 'particular likings' (special tastes) of the private theatre audiences; Jonson himself wrote for both private and public playhouses; see Introduction
8 those make: those who make
10 cunning: learned, expert
11 entreaty: entertainment
12 all relish not: not everything is to their taste
16 custard: open pie of fruit or meat, covered with a spiced and sweetened mixture of broth or milk and eggs
17 meats: dishes
20 cates: food, especially delicacies
21–2 none . . . ladies: proverbial: 'dear bought and far fetched are dainties for ladies' (Tilley 1950: 138; D12)

23 city-wires: fashionable city women; wires were used to support their ruffs and hair
24 Whitefriars: a reference to the theatre in which *Epicoene* was performed; also the area in which the theatre was located, notorious as a refuge for thieves and prostitutes since it was outside the jurisdiction of the city authorities
27 ord'naries: eating houses
   broken meat: fragments of food left after a meal
29 her: i.e. herself
   *occasioned . . . exception*: see Dedication, l. 16n
1 scene: stage
1–2 The ends . . . delight: famous Horatian maxim (*Ars Poetica*, 343–4)
3 still: always
4 So: as long as
   touched: accused
   So . . . crimes: maxim from Martial, *Epigrams*, X.xxxiii
7 true: real, relating to an actual event
8 maker: poet (literal meaning of Greek ποιητης)
9–10 poet . . . feigned: from Horace, *Ars Poetica*, 338
12 application: interpreting play or literary text as referring to real contemporary events and people; a popular pastime of London audiences
13 or . . . or: either . . . or

# Act I, scene i

*Enter* CLERIMONT. *He comes out making himself ready, followed by* BOY

CLERIMONT  Ha' you got the song yet perfect I ga' you, boy?

BOY  Yes, sir.

CLERIMONT  Let me hear it.

BOY  You shall, sir, but i' faith let nobody else.

CLERIMONT  Why, I pray?

BOY  It will get you the dangerous name of a poet in town, sir, besides me a perfect deal of ill will at the mansion you wot of, whose lady is the argument of it, where now I am the welcom'st thing under a man that comes there.                                                11

CLERIMONT  I think, and above a man too, if the truth were racked out of you.

BOY  No, faith, I'll confess before, sir. The gentlewomen play with me and throw me o' the bed, and carry me in to my lady; and she kisses me with her oiled face, and puts a peruke o' my head, and asks me an' I will wear her gown, and I say no; and then she hits me a blow o' the ear and calls me innocent, and lets me go.        19

CLERIMONT  No marvel if the door be kept shut against your master, when the entrance is so easy to you— well, sir, you shall go there no more, lest I be fain to seek your voice in my lady's rushes a fortnight hence. Sing, sir.                                                    BOY *sings*

*Enter* TRUEWIT

TRUEWIT  Why, here's the man that can melt away his time, and never feels it! What, between his mistress abroad and his ingle at home, high fare, soft lodging, fine clothes, and his fiddle, he thinks the hours ha' no wings or the day no post-horse. Well, sir gallant, were you struck with the plague this minute, or condemned to any capital punishment tomorrow, you would begin then to think, and value every article o' your time, esteem it at the true rate, and give all for't.                                              34

CLERIMONT  Why, what should a man do?

TRUEWIT  Why, nothing, or that which, when 'tis done, is as idle. Hearken after the next horse-race, or hunting-match; lay wagers, praise Puppy, or Peppercorn, Whitefoot, Franklin; swear upon Whitemane's party; spend aloud that my lords may hear you; visit my ladies at night, and be able to give 'em the character of every bowler or bettor o' the green. These be the things wherein your fashionable men exercise themselves, and I for company.        44

CLERIMONT  Nay, if I have thy authority, I'll not leave yet. Come, the other are considerations when we come to have grey heads and weak hams, moist eyes and shrunk members. We'll think on 'em then; then we'll pray and fast.

TRUEWIT  Ay, and destine only that time of age to goodness which our want of ability will not let us employ in evil?                                              52

CLERIMONT  Why then 'tis time enough.

TRUEWIT  Yes: as if a man should sleep all the term and think to effect his business the last day. Oh, Clerimont, this time, because it is an incorporeal thing, and not subject to sense, we mock ourselves the fineliest out of it, with vanity and misery indeed; not seeking an end of wretchedness, but only changing the matter still.                              60

CLERIMONT  Nay, thou'lt not leave now—

TRUEWIT  See but our common disease! With what justice can we complain that great men will not look upon us nor be at leisure to give our affairs such dispatch as we expect, when we will never do it to ourselves, nor hear nor regard ourselves.

CLERIMONT  Foh, thou hast read Plutarch's *Morals*

---

SD  *making . . . ready*: dressing
1  perfect: i.e. perfectly memorised
7  dangerous . . . poet: because poets (including playwrights) satirised their follies, they were regarded with scorn: 'He is upbraidingly called a poet, as if it were a most contemptible nickname' (Jonson, *Discoveries*, ll. 284–5, p. 529, in Donaldson 1985)
9  wot: know
   argument: subject
10  under: less than (with sexual pun; see 'ingle', l. 27)
17  an': if
19  innocent: simpleton; also, child
22  fain: obliged
22–3  lest I . . . rushes: i.e. in case you gain sexual maturity too early. Clerimont suggests this by referring to the breaking (and thus lowering) of the boy's voice, when it would be found 'in my lady's rushes', i.e. at floor level (rushes were used as a floor covering). His voice is significant because he sings, and Clerimont does not wish him to lose his treble. The phrase also has obvious sexual connotations.
27  abroad: away from home
   ingle: boy kept for homosexual purposes, catamite

33  article o' your time: moment
37  idle: vain, useless
   Hearken: inquire
38–40  Puppy . . . Whitemane: 'horses o' the time' (Jonson's marginal note)
40  spend aloud: talk noisily; Holdsworth suggests 'spend ostentatiously'
45  leave: leave off
54  term: when the law courts were in session
58  fineliest: most perfectly or ingeniously
60  still: continually
62  disease: i.e. discontent, caused by lack of patronage
67  Plutarch's *Morals*: the *Moralia*, widely read in the Renaissance

now, or some such tedious fellow; and it shows so vilely with thee, 'fore God, 'twill spoil thy wit utterly. Talk me of pins, and feathers, and ladies, and rushes, and such things, and leave this stoicity alone till thou mak'st sermons.                                                    72

TRUEWIT  Well, sir. If it will not take, I have learned to lose as little of my kindness as I can. I'll do good to no man against his will, certainly. When were you at the college?

CLERIMONT  What college?

TRUEWIT  As if you knew not!

CLERIMONT  No, faith, I came but from court yesterday.                                                          80

TRUEWIT  Why, is it not arrived there yet, the news? A new foundation, sir, here i' the town, of ladies that call themselves the Collegiates, an order between courtiers and country madams, that live from their husbands, and give entertainment to all the Wits and Braveries o' the time, as they call 'em; cry down, or up, what they like or dislike in a brain or a fashion with most masculine, or rather hermaphroditical authority; and every day gain to their college some new probationer.                                                 90

CLERIMONT  Who is the president?

TRUEWIT  The grave and youthful matron, the Lady Haughty.

CLERIMONT  A pox of her autumnal face, her pieced beauty: there's no man can be admitted till she be ready, nowadays, till she has painted, and perfumed, and washed, and scoured, but the boy here; and him she wipes her oiled lips upon like a sponge. I have made a song, I pray thee hear it, o' the subject.

BOY *sings*

SONG

Still to be neat, still to be dressed,                      100
As you were going to a feast;
Still to be powdered, still perfumed:
Lady, it is to be presumed,
Though art's hid causes are not found,
All is not sweet, all is not sound.

Give me a look, give me a face,
That makes simplicity a grace;
Robes loosely flowing, hair as free:
Such sweet neglect more taketh me
Than all th' adulteries of art.                            110
They strike mine eyes, but not my heart.

TRUEWIT  And I am, clearly, o' the other side: I love a good dressing before any beauty o' the world. Oh, a woman is, then, like a delicate garden; nor is there one kind of it: she may vary every hour; take often counsel of her glass, and choose the best. If she have good ears, show 'em; good hair, lay it out; good legs, wear short clothes; a good hand, discover it often; practise any art to mend breath, cleanse teeth, repair eyebrows, paint, and profess it.                       120

CLERIMONT  How? Publicly?

TRUEWIT  The doing of it, not the manner: that must be private. Many things that seem foul i' the doing, do please, done. A lady should indeed study her face, when we think she sleeps; nor, when the doors are shut, should men be inquiring; all is sacred within, then. Is it for us to see their perukes put on, their false teeth, their complexion, their eyebrows, their nails? You see gilders will not work but enclosed. They must not discover how little serves, with the help of art, to adorn a great deal. How long did the canvas hang afore Aldgate? Were the people suffered to see the city's *Love* and *Charity* while they were rude stone, before they were painted and burnished? No. No more should servants approach their mistresses but when they are complete, and finished.              136

CLERIMONT  Well said, my Truewit.

TRUEWIT  And a wise lady will keep a guard always upon the place, that she may do things securely. I once followed a rude fellow into a chamber, where the poor madam, for haste, and troubled, snatched at her peruke to cover her baldness and put it on the wrong way.

CLERIMONT  Oh prodigy!                                     144

TRUEWIT  And the unconscionable knave held her in compliment an hour, with that reversed face, when I

---

68  some . . . fellow: Seneca, the Roman stoic philosopher, to whose *De Brevitate Vitae* Truewit has been alluding

70  pins . . . feathers . . . rushes: trivialities; 'ladies' are also included in this category

71  stoicity: stoicism (Clerimont's coinage)

73  take: succeed

85–6  Wits and Braveries: gallants, noted respectively for witty talk and fashionable dress

86–7  cry down, or up: decry or applaud

94  pieced: a) patched; b) pieced together

100–11  Still . . . heart: translation of anonymous lyric, *Semper munditias, semper, Basilissa, decores*, in the *Anthologia Latina*, first published 1572

100  Still: always

107  simplicity: lack of adornment

109  taketh: captivates

110  adulteries: adulterations

113  dressing: adornment

118  discover: reveal, as also in I.i.130

120  profess: declare

122–48  derived from Ovid, *Ars Amatoria*, III, ll. 209–47

131–4  How . . . burnished: Aldgate, the main eastern gate to the city of London, was rebuilt in 1609. The new gate had a statue on each side, one representing Peace, the other Charity

135  servants: lovers

144  prodigy: monstrous thing

still looked when she should talk from the tother side.

CLERIMONT Why thou shouldst ha' relieved her.

TRUEWIT No, faith, I let her alone, as we'll let this argument, if you please, and pass to another. When saw you Dauphine Eugenie? **152**

CLERIMONT Not these three days. Shall we go to him this morning? He is very melancholic, I hear.

TRUEWIT Sick o' the uncle, is he? I met that stiff piece of formality, his uncle, yesterday, with a huge turban of nightcaps on his head, buckled over his ears.

CLERIMONT Oh, that's his custom when he walks abroad. He can endure no noise, man. **160**

TRUEWIT So I have heard. But is the disease so ridiculous in him as it is made? They say he has been upon divers treaties with the fishwives and orange-women, and articles propounded between them. Marry, the chimney-sweepers will not be drawn in.

CLERIMONT No, nor the broom-men: they stand out stiffly. He cannot endure a costardmonger, he swoons if he hears one.

TRUEWIT Methinks a smith should be ominous. **168**

CLERIMONT Or any hammerman. A brazier is not suffered to dwell in the parish, nor an armourer. He would have hanged a pewterer's 'prentice once upon a Shrove Tuesday's riot for being o' that trade, when the rest were quit.

TRUEWIT A trumpet should fright him terribly, or the hautboys?

CLERIMONT Out of his senses. The waits of the city have a pension of him, not to come near that ward. This youth practised on him, one night, like the bellman, and never left till he had brought him down to the door with a long sword, and there left him flourishing with the air. **181**

BOY Why, sir! He hath chosen a street to lie in, so narrow at both ends, that it will receive no coaches, nor carts, nor any of these common noises; and therefore we that love him devise to bring him in such as we may, now and then, for his exercise, to breathe him. He would grow resty else in his ease. His virtue would rust without action. I entreated a bearward, one day, to come down with the dogs of some four parishes that way, and I thank him he did, and cried his games under Master Morose's window, till he was sent crying away, with his head made a most bleeding spectacle to the multitude. And, another time, a fencer, marching to his prize, had his drum most tragically run through, for taking that street in his way, at my request. **196**

TRUEWIT A good wag. How does he for the bells?

CLERIMONT Oh, i' the queen's time he was wont to go out of town every Saturday at ten o'clock, or on holiday eves. But now, by reason of the sickness, the perpetuity of ringing has made him devise a room with double walls, and treble ceilings, the windows close shut, and caulked; and there he lives by candlelight. He turned away a man last week for having a pair of new shoes that creaked. And this fellow waits on him now in tennis-court socks, or slippers soled with wool; and they talk each to other in a trunk. See, who comes here. **208**

# Act I, scene ii

*Enter* DAUPHINE

DAUPHINE How now! What ail you, sirs? Dumb?

TRUEWIT Struck into stone, almost, I am here, with tales o' thine uncle! There was never such a prodigy heard of.

---

155 Sick o' the uncle: pun on 'sick of the mother' (hysteria)
161 made: made out to be
been: entered
161–73 derived from Libanius, *Declamation* XXVI, sections 8 and 36
162–3 fishwives and orangewomen: notoriously noisy street-vendors
articles: terms and conditions
165 broom-men: either street-sweepers or broom-sellers
166 stiffly: resolutely
costardmonger: fruit-seller
169 hammerman: metal-worker
brazier: worker in brass
172 Shrove Tuesday's riot: traditionally the time that apprentices went on the rampage, wrecking theatres and brothels
173 quit: acquitted
175 hautboys: oboes (French *hautbois*)
176 waits: bands of street musicians, maintained at the public charge
177 ward: district of the city
178 This youth: i.e. Clerimont's boy
practised: played a trick

179 bellman: night-watchman, who called the hours, ringing a bell
182 lie: live
187 breathe: exercise briskly (usually used of horses)
resty: sluggish (used of horses)
188 virtue: special quality (i.e. obsession with noise); also 'vigour'
189 bearward: keeper of bears for baiting
191 cried his games: announced the bear-baiting
194 prize: fencing-match
197 wag: mischievous boy
200 sickness: plague, particularly virulent in 1609 (the year *Epicoene* was written)
201 perpetuity of ringing: a reference to the tolling of bells for those dead of the plague
204 turned . . . man: dismissed a servant
208 trunk: speaking-tube
3 prodigy: monster

DAUPHINE I would you would once lose this subject, my masters, for my sake. They are such as you are that have brought me into that predicament I am with him.

TRUEWIT How is that?

DAUPHINE Marry, that he will disinherit me, no more. He thinks I and my company are authors of all the ridiculous acts and monuments are told of him.    11

TRUEWIT 'Slid, I would be the author of more, to vex him; that purpose deserves it: it gives thee law of plaguing him. I'll tell thee what I would do. I would make a false almanac; get it printed; and then ha' him drawn out on a coronation day to the Tower Wharf, and kill him with the noise of the ordnance. Disinherit thee! He cannot, man. Art not thou next of blood, and his sister's son?

DAUPHINE Ay, but he will thrust me out of it, he vows, and marry.    21

TRUEWIT How! That's a more portent. Can he endure no noise, and will venture on a wife?

CLERIMONT Yes. Why, thou art a stranger, it seems, to his best trick yet. He has employed a fellow this half year, all over England, to hearken him out a dumb woman, be she of any form, or any quality, so she be able to bear children: her silence is dowry enough, he says.

TRUEWIT But I trust to God he has found none.    30

CLERIMONT No, but he has heard of one that's lodged i' the next street to him, who is exceedingly soft-spoken; thrifty of her speech; that spends but six words a day. And her he's about now, and shall have her.

TRUEWIT Is't possible! Who is his agent i' the business?

CLERIMONT Marry, a barber, one Cutbeard, an honest fellow, one that tells Dauphine all here.

TRUEWIT Why, you oppress me with wonder! A woman, and a barber, and love no noise!    39

CLERIMONT Yes, faith. The fellow trims him silently and has not the knack with his shears or his fingers; and that continence in a barber he thinks so eminent a virtue, as it has made him chief of his counsel.    43

TRUEWIT Is the barber to be seen? Or the wench?

CLERIMONT Yes, that they are.

TRUEWIT I pray thee, Dauphine, let's go thither.

DAUPHINE I have some business now; I cannot i' faith.

TRUEWIT You shall have no business shall make you neglect this, sir. We'll make her talk, believe it; or if she will not, we can give out at least so much as shall interrupt the treaty. We will break it. Thou art bound in conscience, when he suspects thee without cause, to torment him.    53

DAUPHINE Not I, by any means. I'll give no suffrage to't. He shall never ha' that plea against me, that I opposed the least fant'sy of his. Let it lie upon my stars to be guilty, I'll be innocent.

TRUEWIT Yes, and be poor, and beg; do, innocent, when some groom of his has got him an heir, or this barber, if he himself cannot. Innocent! I pray thee, Ned, where lies she? Let him be innocent still.    61

CLERIMONT Why, right over against the barber's, in the house where Sir John Daw lies.

TRUEWIT You do not mean to confound me!

CLERIMONT Why?

TRUEWIT Does he that would marry her know so much?

CLERIMONT I cannot tell.

TRUEWIT 'Twere enough of imputation to her, with him.    70

CLERIMONT Why?

TRUEWIT The only talking sir i'th'town! Jack Daw! And he teach her not to speak—God b'w'you. I have some business too.

CLERIMONT Will you not go thither then?

TRUEWIT Not with the danger to meet Daw, for mine ears.

CLERIMONT Why? I thought you two had been upon very good terms.

TRUEWIT Yes, of keeping distance.    80

---

4  once: once and for all

11  acts and monuments: the first edition (1563) of John Foxe's *Book of Martyrs* was entitled *Acts and Monuments*. This anti-Catholic history of the Christian church made special reference to the Protestant martyrs of Mary Tudor's reign (1553–8), and proved very popular, going into four editions during the author's lifetime (1516–87) alone

12  'Slid: God's (eye)lid; a common oath

13  that purpose: i.e. Morose's plan to disinherit Dauphine. gives thee law: authorises you

16  Tower Wharf: where guns fired a salute on the anniversary of James VI of Scotland's coronation as James I of England

22  more: greater

26  hearken him out: search out

27  quality: rank

38  oppress: overwhelm

39  woman . . . barber: both traditionally noted for being talkative

41  knack: snapping or clicking noise

43  chief of his counsel: his main confidant

50  give out: put about

51  treaty: negotiation

54  suffrage: consent

56  fant'sy: 'fancy, imagination; also, fantasy – whim, desire, delusion' (Procter)
    lie upon: be ordained by

58  innocent: fool, simpleton

59  groom: servant
    got: begot

64  confound: dumbfound, amaze

69  to her: against her

72  only: pre-eminent

CLERIMONT  They say he is a very good scholar.

TRUEWIT  Ay, and he says it first. A pox on him, a fellow that pretends only to learning, buys titles, and nothing else of books in him.

CLERIMONT  The world reports him to be very learned.

TRUEWIT  I am sorry the world should so conspire to belie him.

CLERIMONT  Good faith, I have heard very good things come from him.                                              **89**

TRUEWIT  You may. There's none so desperately ignorant to deny that: would they were his own. God b'w'you, gentlemen.                                    *Exit*

CLERIMONT  This is very abrupt!

# Act I, scene iii

DAUPHINE  Come, you are a strange open man to tell everything thus.

CLERIMONT  Why, believe it, Dauphine, Truewit's a very honest fellow.

DAUPHINE  I think no other, but this frank nature of his is not for secrets.

CLERIMONT  Nay, then, you are mistaken, Dauphine; I know where he has been well trusted, and discharged the trust very truly and heartily.          **9**

DAUPHINE  I contend not, Ned, but with the fewer a business is carried, it is ever the safer. Now we are alone, if you'll go thither, I am for you.

CLERIMONT  When were you there?

DAUPHINE  Last night: and such a Decameron of sport fallen out. Boccace never thought of the like. Daw does nothing but court her; and the wrong way. He would lie with her, and praises her modesty; desires that she would talk, and be free, and commends her silence in verses, which he reads and swears are the best that ever man made. Then rails at his fortunes, stamps, and mutines why he is not made a councillor and called to affairs of state.                        **22**

CLERIMONT  I pray thee, let's go. I would fain partake

this. Some water, boy.                              *Exit* BOY

DAUPHINE  We are invited to dinner together, he and I, by one that came thither to him, Sir La Foole.

CLERIMONT  Oh, that's a precious manikin!

DAUPHINE  Do you know him?                          **28**

CLERIMONT  Ay, and he will know you too, if e'er he saw you but once, though you should meet him at church in the midst of prayers. He is one of the Braveries, though he be none o' the Wits. He will salute a judge upon the bench, and a bishop in the pulpit, a lawyer when he is pleading at the bar, and a lady when she is dancing in a masque, and put her out. He does give plays, and suppers, and invites his guests to 'em aloud, out of his window, as they ride by in coaches. He has a lodging in the Strand for the purpose, or to watch when ladies are gone to the china-houses, or the Exchange, that he may meet 'em by chance and give 'em presents, some two or three hundred pounds' worth of toys, to be laughed at. He is never without a spare banquet, or sweetmeats in his chamber, for their women to alight at and come up to, for a bait.    **44**

DAUPHINE  Excellent! He was a fine youth last night, but now he is much finer! What is his christen name? I ha' forgot.

*Enter* BOY

CLERIMONT  Sir Amorous La Foole.

BOY  The gentleman is here below that owns that name.

CLERIMONT  'Heart, he's come to invite me to dinner, I hold my life.                                           **51**

DAUPHINE  Like enough. Pray thee, let's ha' him up.

CLERIMONT  Boy, marshal him.

BOY  With a truncheon, sir?

---

83  pretends only to: makes a claim to

9  heartily: sincerely

10  contend: dispute

12  thither: i.e. to visit Epicoene

14  Decameron of sport: 'masterpiece of fun' (Herford and Simpson). *The Decameron* (1349–51), a collection of one hundred tales written by Giovanni Boccaccio (1313–75), is much concerned with the intrigues and follies of romantic love. *The Decameron* had great influence on English authors, and translations of many of the tales had appeared in William Painter's *Palace of Pleasure* (1566–7), a volume on which many contemporary dramatists drew
   fallen out: happened

18  free: uninhibited in her speech, and sexually

21  mutines why: rebels because

24  Some water: some eds gloss this as a call for a boat to carry them on the river (a common form of travel); however, since Clerimont entered in I.i 'making himself ready', the call for water could also relate to these doubtless elaborate rituals of washing and dressing

27  manikin: little man, puppet

35–6  give plays: pays for private performances by professional theatre companies (eds)

38  Strand: street in central London where many of the gentry lived

39  china-houses: shops selling goods from China and other eastern countries; fashionable meeting places at this time

40  Exchange: the New Exchange, with its many fashionable milliners' and jewellers' shops, was situated in the Strand and opened in 1609

42  toys: trifles, trumpery
   banquet: course of sweetmeats, fruit and wine

43–4  their women: serving-women of the ladies

44  bait: a) refreshment, snack; b) food as a lure (using the women to catch the ladies) (Holdsworth)

46  christen: Christian

53  marshal: usher

54  truncheon: a) marshal's baton; b) cudgel

CLERIMONT Away, I beseech you. (*Exit* BOY) I'll make him tell us his pedigree now; and what meat he has to dinner; and who are his guests; and the whole course of his fortunes, with a breath.

## Act I, scene iv

*Enter* LA FOOLE

LA FOOLE 'Save, dear Sir Dauphine, honoured Master Clerimont.

CLERIMONT Sir Amorous! You have very much honested my lodging with your presence.

LA FOOLE Good faith, it is a fine lodging! Almost as delicate a lodging as mine.

CLERIMONT Not so, sir.

LA FOOLE Excuse me, sir, if it were i' the Strand, I assure you. I am come, Master Clerimont, to entreat you wait upon two or three ladies to dinner today. 10

CLERIMONT How, sir! Wait upon 'em? Did you ever see me carry dishes?

LA FOOLE No, sir, dispense with me; I meant to bear 'em company.

CLERIMONT Oh, that I will, sir. The doubtfulness o' your phrase, believe it, sir, would breed you a quarrel once an hour with the terrible boys, if you should but keep 'em fellowship a day.

LA FOOLE It should be extremely against my will, sir, if I contested with any man. 20

CLERIMONT I believe it, sir. Where hold you your feast?

LA FOOLE At Tom Otter's, sir.

DAUPHINE Tom Otter? What's he?

LA FOOLE Captain Otter, sir; he is a kind of gamester, but he has had command, both by sea and by land.

DAUPHINE Oh, then he is *animal amphibium*?

LA FOOLE Ay, sir. His wife was the rich china-woman that the courtiers visited so often, that gave the rare entertainment. She commands all at home.

CLERIMONT Then she is Captain Otter? 30

LA FOOLE You say very well, sir. She is my kinswoman, a La Foole by the mother side, and will invite any great ladies for my sake.

DAUPHINE Not of the La Fooles of Essex?

LA FOOLE No, sir, the La Fooles of London.

CLERIMONT (*Aside to* DAUPHINE) Now h'is in. **36**

LA FOOLE They all come out of our house, the La Fooles o' the north, the La Fooles of the west, the La Fooles of the east and south—we are as ancient a family as any is in Europe—but I myself am descended lineally of the French La Fooles—and we do bear for our coat yellow, or *or*, checkered *azure*, and *gules*, and some three or four colours more, which is a very noted coat, and has, sometimes, been solemnly worn by divers nobility of our house—but let that go, antiquity is not respected now—I had a brace of fat does sent me, gentlemen, and half a dozen of pheasants, a dozen or two of godwits, and some other fowl, which I would have eaten while they are good, and in good company—there will be a great lady or two, my Lady Haughty, my Lady Centaure, Mistress Dol Mavis—and they come a' purpose to see the silent gentlewoman, Mistress Epicoene, that honest Sir John Daw has promised to bring thither—and then Mistress Trusty, my Lady's woman, will be there too, and this honourable knight, Sir Dauphine, with yourself, Master Clerimont—and we'll be very merry, and have fiddlers, and dance—I have been a mad wag, in my time, and have spent some crowns since I was a page in court to my Lord Lofty, and after my Lady's gentleman-usher, who got me knighted in Ireland, since it pleased my elder brother to die—I had as fair a gold jerkin on that day as any was worn in the Island Voyage, or at Caliz, none dispraised, and I came over in it hither, showed myself to my friends in court, and after went down to my tenants, in the

---

56 meat: food
58 with a breath: all in one breath
 1 'Save: God save you
 4 honested: honoured
13 dispense with me: excuse me (affectedly), though Clerimont's reponse plays with the sense of 'do without me'
17 terrible boys: 'roaring boys' were gangs of swaggering young men ready to fight at the least provocation
24 gamester: player of a game; in this case, bear-baiting
27 china-woman: owner of a china-house
28 rare: pun on a) excellent and b) infrequent

---

36 in: 'underway' (Holdsworth)
42 coat: coat of arms (though also suggests the motley coat of a jester)
42–3 *or . . . azure . . . gules*: heraldic terms for gold, blue and red
44 noted: celebrated
   sometimes: in former times (as well as the usual meaning)
48 godwits: marsh birds, seen as a delicacy
61 after: i.e. after that, I was
62 gentleman-usher: gentleman who serves a person of higher rank
   Ireland: Robert Devereux, Earl of Essex (1566–1601), had created so many knights in his 1599 campaign to subjugate Ireland that he was accused of cheapening the title. A group of these newly created knights formed Essex's escort on his unauthorised return to England in September 1599, after which Elizabeth held him in detention
65 Island Voyage: Essex's expedition to the Azores in 1597, which aimed to defeat Spain's Irish Armada, ended in failure and recrimination
   Caliz: Cadiz, captured from the Spanish by Essex and the English fleet in 1596

country, and surveyed my lands, let new leases, took
their money, spent it in the eye o' the land here, upon
ladies—and now I can take up at my pleasure.      **70**

DAUPHINE  Can you take up ladies, sir?

CLERIMONT  Oh, let him breathe, he has not recovered.

DAUPHINE  Would I were your half, in that
commodity—

LA FOOLE  No, sir, excuse me: I meant money, which
can take up anything. I have another guest or two to
invite and say as much to, gentlemen. I'll take my
leave abruptly, in hope you will not fail—Your
servant.                                       *Exit*

DAUPHINE  We will not fail you, sir precious La Foole;
but she shall that your ladies come to see, if I have
credit afore Sir Daw.                          **82**

CLERIMONT  Did you ever hear such a wind-fucker as
this?

DAUPHINE  Or such a rook as the other, that will betray
his mistress to be seen! Come, 'tis time we prevented
it.

CLERIMONT  Go.

                                              *Exeunt*

# Act II, scene i

*Enter* MOROSE, MUTE

MOROSE  Cannot I yet find out a more compendious
method than by this trunk to save my servants the
labour of speech, and mine ears the discord of
sounds? Let me see. All discourses but mine own
afflict me, they seem harsh, impertinent, and
irksome. Is it not possible that thou shouldst answer
me by signs, and I apprehend thee, fellow? Speak
not, though I question you. You have taken the ring
off from the street door, as I bade you? Answer me
not by speech, but by silence, unless it be otherwise.
(*At the breaches, still the fellow makes legs, or signs*) Very

good. And you have fastened on a thick quilt, or
flock-bed, on the outside of the door; that if they
knock with their daggers, or with brickbats, they can
make no noise? But with your leg, your answer,
unless it be otherwise.—Very good. This is not only
fit modesty in a servant, but good state and discretion
in a master. And you have been with Cutbeard, the
barber, to have him come to me?—Good. And he
will come presently? Answer me not but with your
leg, unless it be otherwise; if it be otherwise, shake
your head or shrug.—(MUTE *makes a leg*) So. Your
Italian and Spaniard are wise in these! And it is a
frugal and comely gravity. How long will it be, ere
Cutbeard come? Stay, if an hour, hold up your whole
hand; if half an hour, two fingers; if a quarter, one.—
(MUTE *holds up one finger bent*) Good; half a quarter?
'Tis well. And have you given him a key, to come in
without knocking?—Good. And is the lock oiled,
and the hinges, today?—Good. And the quilting of
the stairs nowhere worn out, and bare?—Very good. I
see by much doctrine and impulsion, it may be
effected. Stand by. The Turk in this divine discipline
is admirable, exceeding all the potentates of the
earth; still waited on by mutes, and all his commands
so executed; yea, even in the war (as I have heard)
and in his marches, most of his charges and
directions given by signs, and with silence: an
exquisite art! And I am heartily ashamed and angry
oftentimes that the princes of Christendom should
suffer a barbarian to transcend 'em in so high a point
of felicity. I will practise it hereafter. (*One winds a
horn without*) How now? Oh! Oh! What villain, what
prodigy of mankind is that? Look. (*Exit* MUTE. *Horn
sounds again*)—Oh! cut his throat, cut his throat!
What murderer, hell-hound, devil can this be?      **46**

*Enter* MUTE

MUTE  It is a post from the court—

MOROSE  Out, rogue! And must thou blow thy horn
too?

MUTE  Alas, it is a post from the court, sir, that says he
must speak with you, pain of death—

MOROSE  Pain of thy life, be silent!

---

69  eye o' the land: i.e. London
70  take up: borrow money (with interest on the loan)
73  half: partner
74  commodity: 'the practice by which borrowers had to
    receive part of a loan in worthless goods, which were
    bought back by the moneylender at a much lower price'
    (Procter)
76  take up: buy
81–2  have credit afore: take precedence to
83  wind-fucker: kestrel; used as a term of opprobrium
85  rook: simpleton
 1  compendious: expeditious, direct
 2  trunk: speaking-tube
 5  impertinent: irrelevant
 8  ring: door-knocker
SD  *breaches*: breaks in the text
    *still*: always
    *makes legs*: bows

14  brickbats: pieces of brick
15  But: only
17  state: dignified behaviour
    discretion: judgement
20  presently: immediately
32  doctrine: teaching
    impulsion: instigation, prompting
33  stand by: stand aside
35  still: always
SD  *winds*: blows
44  prodigy: monster
50  post: express messenger

# Act II, scene ii

*Enter* TRUEWIT *with a post-horn and halter*

TRUEWIT  By your leave, sir (I am a stranger here), is your name Master Morose? Is your name Master Morose? Fishes! Pythagoreans all! This is strange! What say you, sir, nothing? Has Harpocrates been here, with his club, among you? Well sir, I will believe you to be the man, at this time; I will venture upon you, sir. Your friends at court commend 'em to you, sir—

MOROSE  (*Aside*) Oh men! Oh manners! Was there ever such an impudence?                                                           10

TRUEWIT  And are extremely solicitous for you, sir.

MOROSE  Whose knave are you?

TRUEWIT  Mine own knave, and your compeer, sir.

MOROSE  Fetch me my sword—

TRUEWIT  You shall taste the one half of my dagger if you do, groom, and you the other if you stir, sir; be patient, I charge you, in the king's name, and hear me without insurrection. They say you are to marry? To marry! Do you mark, sir?

MOROSE  How then, rude companion!                                             20

TRUEWIT  Marry, your friends do wonder, sir, the Thames being so near, wherein you may drown so handsomely; or London Bridge, at a low fall, with a fine leap, to hurry you down the stream; or such a delicate steeple i' the town, as Bow, to vault from; or a braver height, as Paul's; or if you affected to do it nearer home, and a shorter way, an excellent garret window into the street; or a beam in the said garret, with this halter (*he shows him a halter*), which they have sent, and desire that you would sooner commit

your grave head to this knot, than to the wedlock noose; or take a little sublimate, and go out of the world like a rat, or a fly (as one said) with a straw i' your arse: any way, rather than to follow this goblin matrimony. Alas, sir, do you ever think to find a chaste wife, in these times? Now? When there are so many masques, plays, puritan preachings, mad folks, and other strange sights to be seen daily, private and public? If you had lived in King Etheldred's time, sir, or Edward the Confessor's, you might, perhaps, have found in some cold country hamlet, then, a dull frosty wench would have been contented with one man; now, they will as soon be pleased with one leg, or one eye. I'll tell you, sir, the monstrous hazards you shall run with a wife.

MOROSE  Good sir! Have I ever cozened any friends of yours of their land? Bought their possessions? Taken forfeit of their mortgage? Begged a reversion from 'em? Bastarded their issue? What have I done, that may deserve this?                                                        50

TRUEWIT  Nothing, sir, that I know, but your itch of marriage.

MOROSE  Why, if I had made an assassinate upon your father, vitiated your mother, ravished your sisters—

TRUEWIT  I would kill you, sir, I would kill you, if you had.

MOROSE  Why, you do more in this, sir: it were a vengeance centuple for all facinorous acts that could be named, to do that you do—                                           59

TRUEWIT  Alas, sir, I am but a messenger: I but tell you what you must hear. It seems your friends are careful after your soul's health, sir, and would have you know the danger (but you may do your pleasure for all them, I persuade not, sir). If, after you are married, your wife do run away with a vaulter, or the Frenchman that walks upon ropes, or him that dances the jig, or a fencer for his skill at his weapon, why, it is not their fault; they have discharged their consciences when you know what may happen. Nay,

---

3  Fishes: i.e. as dumb as fishes
   Pythagoreans: an ascetic brotherhood, following the philosophy of the 6th-century BC Greek philospher, Pythagoras. On joining the sect, a vow of silence was taken (to last for five years) for the purpose of self-examination
4  Harpocrates: god of silence; the club was, through a confusion, acquired from Hercules
6–7  venture upon: hazard an approach to
9  Oh men! Oh manners!: echo of Cicero's exclamation in *In Catilinam*, I.2, '*O tempora, O mores*' (O times! O manners!)
10  impudence: shamelessness
13  compeer: equal
18–45, 119–51  much of Truewit's diatribe against women and marriage is adapted from Juvenal's *Satires*, VI
20  companion: fellow (contemptuous)
23  fall: ebb-tide
25  Bow: St Mary-le-Bow, in Cheapside
26  braver: more splendid
   Paul's: the old St Paul's Cathedral, later destroyed by fire in 1666

32  sublimate: mercuric chloride, used as rat poison
33–4  fly . . . arse: in spider and fly fights, a popular pastime, a straw was thrust into the fly's tail
37  mad folks: Bedlam (derivative of Bethlehem) hospital for the insane was visited for entertainment
39  Etheldred: Ethelred the Unready (978–1016), the father of Edward the Confessor (1042–66)
46  cozened: cheated
48  reversion from: right of succession to an estate or office away from
49  Bastarded: rendered illegitimate
51  itch of: hankering after
53  made . . . upon: murdered
54  vitiated: corrupted
58  facinorous: wicked, criminal
65–7  vaulter . . . jig . . . weapon: with sexual innuendoes

suffer valiantly, sir, for I must tell you all the perils that you are obnoxious to. If she be fair, young, and vegetous, no sweetmeats ever drew more flies; all the yellow doublets and great roses i' the town will be there. If foul, and crooked, she'll be with them and buy those doublets and roses, sir. If rich and that you marry her dowry, not her, she'll reign in your house as imperious as a widow. If noble, all her kindred will be your tyrants. If fruitful, as proud as May, and humorous as April; she must have her doctors, her midwives, her nurses, her longings every hour, though it be for the dearest morsel of man. If learned, there was never such a parrot; all your patrimony will be too little for the guests that must be invited to hear her speak Latin and Greek; and you must lie with her in those languages too, if you will please her. If precise, you must feast all the silenced brethren, once in three days; salute the sisters; entertain the whole family or wood of 'em; and hear long-winded exercises, singings, and catechizings, which you are not given to, and yet must give for, to please the zealous matron your wife, who, for the holy cause, will cozen you over and above. You begin to sweat, sir? But this is not half, i' faith; you may do your pleasure notwithstanding, as I said before, I come not to persuade you. (*The* MUTE *is stealing away*) Upon my faith, master servingman, if you do stir, I will beat you.                    **97**

MOROSE  Oh, what is my sin, what is my sin?

TRUEWIT  Then, if you love your wife, or rather dote on her, sir, oh, how she'll torture you, and take pleasure i' your torments! You shall lie with her but when she lists; she will not hurt her beauty, her complexion; or it must be for that jewel, or that pearl, when she does; every half hour's pleasure must be bought anew, and with the same pain and charge you wooed her at first. Then, you must keep what servants she please;

what company she will; that friend must not visit you without her licence; and him she loves most she will seem to hate eagerliest, to decline your jealousy; or feign to be jealous of you first, and for that cause go live with her she-friend, or cousin at the college, that can instruct her in all the mysteries of writing letters, corrupting servants, taming spies; where she must have that rich gown for such a great day; a new one for the next; a richer for the third; be served in silver; have the chamber filled with a succession of grooms, footmen, ushers, and other messengers, besides embroiderers, jewellers, tire-women, sempsters, feathermen, perfumers; while she feels not how the land drops away, nor the acres melt, nor foresees the change, when the mercer has your woods for her velvets; never weighs what her pride costs, sir, so she may kiss a page or a smooth chin that has the despair of a beard; be a stateswoman, know all the news, what was done at Salisbury, what at the Bath, what at court, what in progress; or so she may censure poets, and authors, and styles, and compare 'em, Daniel with Spenser, Jonson with the tother youth, and so forth; or be thought cunning in controversies, or the very knots of divinity; and have often in her mouth the state of the question, and then skip to the mathematics and demonstration, and answer in religion to one, in state to another, in bawdry to a third.                    **134**

---

71  obnoxious: liable
72  vegetous: lively
73  roses: rosettes decorating the shoe
74–5  be . . . buy: 'seek their company and pay for' (Holdsworth)
78  proud: a) arrogant; b) spirited; c) lascivious
   humorous: capricious
82  parrot: see, for example, the learned Lady Wouldbe, wife of Sir Pol, in Jonson's *Volpone* (1606)
86  precise: puritanical
87  silenced brethren: Puritan clergy who lost their licences to preach in 1604, after the Hampton Court conference, which was convened to try to settle points of dispute between the Church party and the Puritans; see Jonson's *The Alchemist* (1610) III.i.38
88  wood: crowd (from Latin *silva*, crowd or collection); punning on 'wood' meaning 'mad'
89  exercises: religious devotions
105  charge: expense

109  eagerliest: most fiercely
    decline: avert
111  she-friend, or cousin: 'both terms could mean "mistress" or "strumpet", and cousin was also a euphemism for lover' (Holdsworth)
118  tire-women: dressmakers
    sempsters: tailors (male or female)
119  feathermen: sellers of feathers (such as Tiltyard in *The Roaring Girl*)
121  mercer: dealer in costly fabrics
122  so: as long as
124  stateswoman: 'pretender to knowledge of affairs of state' (Procter)
125  Salisbury: where fashionable race-meetings were held
    Bath: fashionable for its medicinal baths
    progress: monarch's state visit to different regions of the kingdom
126  censure: judge
127–8  Daniel with Spenser: Samuel Daniel was an Elizabethan poet sometimes compared with Edmund Spenser by his contemporaries; Jonson himself did so, to the detriment of Daniel; see Herford and Simpson I.132
    tother youth: most eds take this to be Shakespeare, though other suggestions have been Samuel Daniel, Thomas Dekker, or John Marston
129  cunning: skilful
130  knots: intricate problems
131  state: main issue
133  state: politics

MOROSE  Oh, oh!

TRUEWIT  All this is very true, sir. And then her going in disguise to that conjuror, and this cunning woman: where the first question is, how soon you shall die? Next, if her present servant love her? Next that, if she shall have a new servant? And how many? Which of her family would make the best bawd, male or female? What precedence she shall have by her next match? And sets down the answers, and believes 'em above the scriptures. Nay, perhaps she'll study the art.                                    **145**

MOROSE  Gentle sir, ha' you done? Ha' you had your pleasure o' me? I'll think of these things.

TRUEWIT  Yes, sir; and then comes reeking home of vapour and sweat with going afoot, and lies in a month of a new face, all oil and birdlime; and rises in asses' milk, and is cleansed with a new fucus. God b'w'you, sir. One thing more (which I had almost forgot). This too, with whom you are to marry, may have made a conveyance of her virginity aforehand, as your wise widows do of their states, before they marry, in trust to some friend, sir: who can tell? Or if she have not done it yet, she may do, upon the wedding day, or the night before, and antedate you cuckold. The like has been heard of, in nature. 'Tis no devised, impossible thing, sir. God b'w'you. I'll be bold to leave this rope with you, sir, for a remembrance. Farewell, Mute.                    *Exit*

MOROSE  Come, ha' me to my chamber; but first shut the door. (*The horn again*) Oh, shut the door, shut the door. Is he come again?                              **165**

*Enter* CUTBEARD

CUTBEARD  'Tis I, sir, your barber.

MOROSE  Oh, Cutbeard, Cutbeard, Cutbeard! Here has

---

137  conjuror: astrologer
      cunning woman: wise woman, fortune-teller
139  servant: lover
142  precedence: 'right of preceding others at formal social occasions' (Holdsworth)
145  art: i.e. fortune-telling
148  reeking: steaming (from exertion)
149  lies in: is in labour (as in childbirth)
150  birdlime: sticky substance used to snare birds; here, used of cosmetic ingredient
      rises: some eds emend to 'rinses', on the basis that this is closer to the sense in Juvenal; most, however, agree that 'rises' is as suggestive, and has the advantage of introducing an ironic parallel with 'lies in'
151  fucus: cosmetic face-wash
154  conveyance: legal transfer of property from one person to another (in this example, to prevent it becoming the property of the new husband)
155  states: estates
156  friend: lover
160  devised: contrived

---

been a cut-throat with me: help me in to my bed, and give me physic with thy counsel.

                                            *Exeunt*

# Act II, scene iii

*Enter* DAW, CLERIMONT, DAUPHINE, EPICOENE

DAW  Nay, and she will, let her refuse at her own charges; 'tis nothing to me, gentlemen. But she will not be invited to the like feasts or guests every day.

CLERIMONT  Oh, by no means, she may not refuse— (*they dissuade her privately*) to stay at home if you love your reputation. 'Slight, you are invited thither o' purpose to be seen, and laughed at by the lady of the college, and her shadows. This trumpeter hath proclaimed you.                                          **9**

DAUPHINE  You shall not go; let him be laughed at in your stead, for not bringing you; and put him to his extemporal faculty of fooling, and talking loud to satisfy the company.

CLERIMONT  He will suspect us, talk aloud.—Pray, Mistress Epicoene, let's see your verse; we have Sir John Daw's leave: do not conceal your servant's merit and your own glories.

EPICOENE  They'll prove my servant's glories, if you have his leave so soon.                                  **19**

DAUPHINE  (*Aside to* EPICOENE) His vainglories, lady!

DAW  Show 'em, show 'em, mistress, I dare own 'em.

EPICOENE  Judge you what glories!

DAW  Nay, I'll read 'em myself too: an author must recite his own works. It is a madrigal of modesty.
      'Modest and fair, for fair and good are near
            Neighbours, howe'er –'

DAUPHINE  Very good.

CLERIMONT  Ay, is't not?

DAW       'No noble virtue ever was alone
                But two in one.'                              **30**

DAUPHINE  Excellent!

CLERIMONT  That again, I pray, Sir John.

DAUPHINE  It has something in't like rare wit, and sense.

CLERIMONT  Peace.

DAW       'No noble virtue ever was alone

---

169  give me physic: many barbers were also surgeons and medical practitioners
1    and: if
2    charges: cost
8    shadows: parasites, toadies
      This trumpeter: i.e. Daw
12   fooling: acting foolishly
17   glories: a) triumphs; b) boasts (Holdsworth)
24   madrigal: love lyric
25–40  Daw's lyric comprises Renaissance platitudes; compare Pierre Charron's *Of Wisdom*, trans. S. Lennard (1612) and Anon., *England's Parnassus* (1600) (eds)
33   rare: pun on a) fine, and b) infrequent; see I.iv.28n

---

But two in one.
    Then, when I praise sweet modesty, I praise
    Bright beauty's rays:
    And having praised both beauty' and modesty,
    I have praised thee.'                                          40
DAUPHINE  Admirable!
CLERIMONT  How it chimes, and cries tink i' the close,
    divinely!
DAUPHINE  Ay, 'tis Seneca.
CLERIMONT  No, I think 'tis Plutarch.
DAW  The dor on Plutarch, and Seneca, I hate it: they
    are mine own imaginations, by that light. I wonder
    those fellows have such credit with gentlemen!
CLERIMONT  They are very grave authors.                            49
DAW  Grave asses! Mere essayists! A few loose
    sentences, and that's all. A man would talk so his
    whole age; I do utter as good things every hour, if
    they were collected and observed, as either of 'em.
DAUPHINE  Indeed, Sir John!
CLERIMONT  He must needs, living among the Wits
    and Braveries too.
DAUPHINE  Ay, and being president of 'em as he is.
DAW  There's Aristotle, a mere commonplace fellow;
    Plato, a discourser; Thucydides and Livy, tedious and
    dry; Tacitus, an entire knot, sometimes worth the
    untying, very seldom.                                          61
CLERIMONT  What do you think of the poets, Sir John?
DAW  Not worthy to be named for authors. Homer, an
    old tedious prolix ass, talks of curriers, and chines of
beef; Virgil, of dunging of land, and bees; Horace, of
    I know not what.
CLERIMONT  I think so.
DAW  And so Pindarus, Lycophron, Anacreon,
    Catullus, Seneca the tragedian, Lucan, Propertius,
    Tibullus, Martial, Juvenal, Ausonius, Statius,
    Politian, Valerius Flaccus, and the rest—                     71
CLERIMONT  What a sackful of their names he has got!
DAUPHINE  And how he pours 'em out! Politian with
    Valerius Flaccus!
CLERIMONT  Was not the character right of him?
DAUPHINE  As could be made, i' faith.
DAW  And Persius, a crabbed coxcomb, not to be
    endured.
DAUPHINE  Why, whom do you account for authors, Sir
    John Daw?                                                      80
DAW  *Syntagma juris civilis, Corpus juris civilis, Corpus
    juris canonici,* the King of Spain's Bible.
DAUPHINE  Is the King of Spain's Bible an author?
CLERIMONT  Yes, and *Syntagma.*
DAUPHINE  What was that *Syntagma,* sir?
DAW  A civil lawyer, a Spaniard.
DAUPHINE  Sure, *Corpus* was a Dutchman.
CLERIMONT  Ay, both the Corpuses, I knew 'em: they
    were very corpulent authors.
DAW  And then there's Vatablus, Pomponatius,
    Symancha; the other are not to be received within the
    thought of a scholar.                                         92
DAUPHINE  'Fore God, you have a simple learned
    servant, lady, in titles.
CLERIMONT  I wonder that he is not called to the helm,
    and made a councillor!
DAUPHINE  He is one extraordinary.
CLERIMONT  Nay, but in ordinary! To say truth, the
    state wants such.
DAUPHINE  Why, that will follow.                                  100

---

39  beauty': the apostrophe indicates the elision of the second
    syllable
42  chimes: jingles
    cries tink: tinkles
    close: conclusion of a musical phrase
46  The dor on: a scoff: i.e 'a fig for' (with a pun on his own
    name)
    Plutarch, and Seneca: see I.i.67–8n
50  essayists: Jonson himself had a low opinion of essayists;
    see his *Timber, or Discoveries* (1640) 719ff
    sentences: maxims
58–61  Aristotle . . . seldom: Partridge notes that, ironically,
    Daw's comments are true in ways of which he himself is
    unaware; see pp. 181–2 of his edition
58  commonplace: trivial; but also, through Latin *locus
    communis,* a universal truth
59  discourser: talker (pejoratively); but also a writer, like
    Plato, of discourses
    Thucydides: c. 460–c. 400 BC; greatest Greek historian
    Livy: 59 BC–AD 17; Roman historian. His name suggests
    'livid' (Latin *liveo*), blue or black, the colour of
    melancholy, the dry humour (Partridge)
60  Tacitus: c. AD 55–c. 117; Roman historian. His name
    means 'secret, hidden'
64  curriers: groomers of horses
    chines: backbones. In *The Iliad,* VII.321, Ajax is given the
    whole chine of an ox by Agamemnon

65  dunging . . . bees: reference to Virgil's poem on
    agriculture and animal husbandry, *The Georgics,* I.79–81
    and IV
68–71  Pindarus . . . the rest: a random jumble of major and
    more obscure Greek and Latin poets, together with an
    Italian humanist (Politian)
75  character: character sketch (at I.ii.72–91)
81–2  *Syntagma* . . . Bible: titles of books that Daw takes to be
    authors' names. The first two titles are the same book,
    collections of Roman law; the third is the collection of
    canon law; the fourth the polyglot Bible sponsored by
    Philip II of Spain
87  Dutchman: the English thought of the Dutch as fat,
    owing to their liking of butter and alcohol
90–1  Vatablus, Pomponatius, Symancha: minor sixteenth-
    century scholars
93  simple: absolutely (with pun)
97  extraordinary: outside the regular staff (with pun)
98  in ordinary: full-time (with pun on 'undistinguished')
99  wants: requires (with pun on 'lacks')

CLERIMONT  I muse a mistress can be so silent to the dotes of such a servant.

DAW  'Tis her virtue, sir. I have written somewhat of her silence too.

DAUPHINE  In verse, Sir John?

CLERIMONT  What else?

DAUPHINE  Why, how can you justify your own being of a poet, that so slight all the old poets?

DAW  Why, every man that writes in verse is not a poet; you have of the Wits that write verses, and yet are no poets: they are poets that live by it, the poor fellows that live by it.                                                     112

DAUPHINE  Why, would not you live by your verses, Sir John?

CLERIMONT  No, 'twere pity he should. A knight live by his verses? He did not make 'em to that end, I hope.

DAUPHINE  And yet the noble Sidney lives by his, and the noble family not ashamed.

CLERIMONT  Ay, he professed himself; but Sir John Daw has more caution: he'll not hinder his own rising i' the state so much! Do you think he will? Your verses, good Sir John, and no poems.    122

DAW        'Silence in woman is like speech in man,
                Deny't who can.'

DAUPHINE  Not I, believe it; your reason, sir.

DAW            'Nor is't a tale
          That female vice should be a virtue male,
          Or masculine vice, a female virtue be:
                You shall it see
                Proved with increase,          130
          I know to speak, and she to hold her peace.'
Do you conceive me, gentlemen?

DAUPHINE  No, faith; how mean you 'with increase', Sir John?

DAW  Why, 'with increase' is when I court her for the common cause of mankind; and she says nothing, but *consentire videtur*: and in time is *gravida*.

DAUPHINE  Then this is a ballad of procreation?

CLERIMONT  A madrigal of procreation; you mistake.

EPICOENE  Pray give me my verses again, servant.    140

DAW  If you'll ask 'em aloud, you shall.

---

102  dotes: natural endowments; also, follies
113  live by: earn their living by; not considered appropriate behaviour for a gentleman. Dauphine then alludes to the other meaning: 'gain immortality by'
117  Sidney: Sir Philip Sidney (1554–86), soldier and scholar. Author of *Arcadia* (1590), *Astrophil and Stella* (1591) and *An Apology for Poetry* (1595). His works (published posthumously by his sister, the Countess of Pembroke) were highly influential
119  professed: declared
132  conceive: understand (with pun on procreation)
136  common cause of mankind: 'procreation' (Procter)
137  *consentire videtur*: she seems to consent
        *gravida*: pregnant

*Walks apart with* EPICOENE

CLERIMONT  See, here's Truewit again!

# Act II, scene iv

*Enter* TRUEWIT *with his post-horn*

CLERIMONT  Where hast thou been, in the name of madness, thus accoutred with thy horn?

TRUEWIT  Where the sound of it might have pierced your senses with gladness had you been in ear-reach of it. Dauphine, fall down and worship me: I have forbid the banns, lad. I have been with thy virtuous uncle and have broke the match.

DAUPHINE  You ha' not, I hope.                          8

TRUEWIT  Yes, faith; and thou shouldst hope otherwise, I should repent me; this horn got me entrance, kiss it. I had no other way to get in, but by feigning to be a post; but when I got in once, I proved none, but rather the contrary, turned him into a post, or a stone, or what is stiffer, with thund'ring into him the incommodities of a wife, and the miseries of marriage. If ever Gorgon were seen in the shape of a woman, he hath seen her in my description. I have put him off o' that scent forever. Why do you not applaud, and adore me, sirs? Why stand you mute? Are you stupid? You are not worthy o' the benefit.  20

DAUPHINE  Did not I tell you? Mischief!—

CLERIMONT  I would you had placed this benefit somewhere else.

TRUEWIT  Why so?

CLERIMONT  'Slight, you have done the most inconsiderate, rash, weak thing that ever man did to his friend.

DAUPHINE  Friend! If the most malicious enemy I have had studied to inflict an injury upon me, it could not be a greater.                                          30

TRUEWIT  Wherein, for God's sake? Gentlemen, come to yourselves again.

DAUPHINE  But I presaged thus much afore to you.

CLERIMONT  Would my lips had been soldered, when I spake on't. 'Slight, what moved you to be thus impertinent?

TRUEWIT  My masters, do not put on this strange face to pay my courtesy: off with this visor. Have good turns done you and thank 'em this way?            39

---

6  forbid the banns: formally objected to the proposed marriage
12  post: messenger
       none: i.e. not a post (or block of wood, and thus silent)
15  incommodities: disadvantages
16  Gorgon: one of three female monsters of Greek myth whose gaze turned people to stone
20  stupid: stupefied; also, slow-witted
33  presaged: gave warning of (see I.iii.1–11)

DAUPHINE 'Fore heav'n, you have undone me. That which I have plotted for, and been maturing now these four months, you have blasted in a minute; now I am lost, I may speak. This gentlewoman was lodged here by me o' purpose, and, to be put upon my uncle, hath professed this obstinate silence for my sake, being my entire friend; and one that for the requital of such a fortune as to marry him, would have made me very ample conditions; where now all my hopes are utterly miscarried by this unlucky accident.  **49**

CLERIMONT Thus 'tis when a man will be ignorantly officious; do services and not know his why; I wonder what courteous itch possessed you! You never did absurder part i' your life, nor a greater trespass to friendship, to humanity.

DAUPHINE Faith, you may forgive it best: 'twas your cause principally.

CLERIMONT I know it; would it had not.

*Enter* CUTBEARD

DAUPHINE How now, Cutbeard, what news?  **58**

CUTBEARD The best, the happiest that ever was, sir. There has been a mad gentleman with your uncle this morning—(*seeing* TRUEWIT) I think this be the gentleman—that has almost talked him out of his wits, with threat'ning him from marriage—

DAUPHINE On, I pray thee.

CUTBEARD And your uncle, sir, he thinks 'twas done by your procurement; therefore he will see the party you wot of, presently; and if he like her, he says, and that she be so inclining to dumb as I have told him, he swears he will marry her today, instantly, and not defer it a minute longer.  **70**

DAUPHINE Excellent! Beyond our expectation!

TRUEWIT Beyond your expectation? By this light, I knew it would be thus.

DAUPHINE Nay, sweet Truewit, forgive me.

TRUEWIT No, I was 'ignorantly officious, impertinent'; this was the 'absurd, weak part'.

CLERIMONT Wilt thou ascribe that to merit now, was mere fortune?

TRUEWIT Fortune? Mere providence. Fortune had not a finger in't. I saw it must necessarily in nature fall out so: my genius is never false to me in these things. Show me how it could be otherwise.  **82**

DAUPHINE Nay, gentlemen, contend not; 'tis well now.

TRUEWIT Alas, I let him go on with 'inconsiderate', and 'rash', and what he pleased.

CLERIMONT Away, thou strange justifier of thyself, to be wiser than thou wert by the event.

TRUEWIT Event! By this light, thou shalt never persuade me but I foresaw it as well as the stars themselves.  **90**

DAUPHINE Nay, gentlemen, 'tis well now; do you two entertain Sir John Daw with discourse while I send her away with instructions.

TRUEWIT I'll be acquainted with her first, by your favour.  *They approach* EPICOENE *and* DAW

CLERIMONT Master Truewit, lady, a friend of ours.

TRUEWIT I am sorry I have not known you sooner, lady, to celebrate this rare virtue of your silence.

CLERIMONT Faith, an' you had come sooner, you should ha' seen and heard her well celebrated in Sir John Daw's madrigals.  **101**

*Exeunt* DAUPHINE, EPICOENE, *and* CUTBEARD

TRUEWIT Jack Daw, God save you; when saw you La Foole?

DAW Not since last night, Master Truewit.

TRUEWIT That's miracle! I thought you two had been inseparable.

DAW He's gone to invite his guests.

TRUEWIT Gods so, 'tis true! What a false memory have I towards that man! I am one: I met him e'en now, upon that he calls his delicate fine black horse, rid into a foam with posting from place to place, and person to person, to give 'em the cue—  **112**

CLERIMONT Lest they should forget?

TRUEWIT Yes; there was never poor captain took more pains at a muster to show men, than he at this meal to show friends.

DAW It is his quarter-feast, sir.

CLERIMONT What! Do you say so, Sir John?

TRUEWIT Nay, Jack Daw will not be out, at the best friends he has, to the talent of his wit. Where's his mistress, to hear and applaud him? Is she gone?  **121**

DAW Is Mistress Epicoene gone?

CLERIMONT Gone afore with Sir Dauphine, I warrant, to the place.

---

42–3 now . . . speak: proverbial
44 put upon: a) imposed on; b) trick
46–7 for the requital of: in return for
48 conditions: provision
52 did: played
56 cause: fault
67 wot: know
    presently: immediately
77 was: which was
79 Mere: sheer
    providence: foresight

---

81 genius: attendant spirit
87 event: outcome
110 delicate: exquisite
117 quarter-feast: 'feast given every quarter-day when La Foole's rents have been paid in; or feast given every quarter sessions, during the town's social season' (Procter)
119–20 out . . . wit: 'lose his jest which reveals the natural capacity of his wit to the full, even at the expense of his best friends' (Procter)

TRUEWIT  Gone afore! That were a manifest injury, a disgrace and a half, to refuse him at such a festival time as this, being a Bravery, and a Wit too.

CLERIMONT  Tut, he'll swallow it like cream: he's better read in *jure civili* than to esteem anything a disgrace is offered him from a mistress.                          130

DAW  Nay, let her e'en go; she shall sit alone, and be dumb in her chamber a week together, for Sir John Daw, I warrant her. Does she refuse me?

CLERIMONT  No, sir, do not take it so to heart: she does not refuse you, but a little neglect you. Good faith, Truewit, you were to blame to put it into his head that she does refuse him.

TRUEWIT  She does refuse him, sir, palpably, however you mince it. An' I were as he, I would swear to speak ne'er a word to her today for't.          140

DAW  By this light, no more I will not.

TRUEWIT  Nor to anybody else, sir.

DAW  Nay, I will not say so, gentlemen.

CLERIMONT  (*Aside to* TRUEWIT) It had been an excellent happy condition for the company, if you could have drawn him to it.

DAW  I'll be very melancholic, i' faith.

CLERIMONT  As a dog, if I were as you, Sir John.

TRUEWIT  Or a snail, or a hog-louse: I would roll myself up for this day, in troth, they should not unwind me.                                         150

DAW  By this picktooth, so I will.

CLERIMONT  (*Aside to* TRUEWIT) 'Tis well done: he begins already to be angry with his teeth.

DAW  Will you go, gentlemen?

CLERIMONT  Nay, you must walk alone if you be right melancholic, Sir John.

TRUEWIT  Yes, sir, we'll dog you, we'll follow you afar off.                                               *Exit* DAW

CLERIMONT  Was there ever such a two yards of knighthood, measured out by time, to be sold to laughter?                                            162

TRUEWIT  A mere talking mole! Hang him, no mushroom was ever so fresh. A fellow so utterly nothing, as he knows not what he would be.

CLERIMONT  Let's follow him; but first let's go to Dauphine; he's hovering about the house to hear what news.

TRUEWIT  Content.

*Exeunt*

---

129  *jure civili*: civil law (see II.iii.81)
132–3  for Sir John Daw: for all Sir John Daw cares
139  mince: minimise
148  dog: proverbially melancholy; also, a term of abuse
149  hog-louse: wood-louse
152  picktooth: toothpick; a fashionable accessory
163  mere: absolute
      mole: proverbially blind
164  mushroom: upstart

# Act II, scene v

*Enter* MOROSE, EPICOENE, CUTBEARD, MUTE

MOROSE  Welcome, Cutbeard; draw near with your fair charge; and in her ear softly entreat her to unmask. (EPICOENE *unmasks*) So. Is the door shut? (MUTE *makes a leg*) Enough. Now, Cutbeard, with the same discipline I use to my family, I will question you. As I conceive, Cutbeard, this gentlewoman is she you have provided, and brought, in hope she will fit me in the place and person of a wife? Answer me not but with your leg, unless it be otherwise.—Very well done, Cutbeard. I conceive besides, Cutbeard, you have been pre-acquainted with her birth, education, and qualities, or else you would not prefer her to my acceptance, in the weighty consequence of marriage.—This I conceive, Cutbeard. Answer me not but with your leg, unless it be otherwise.—Very well done, Cutbeard. Give aside now a little, and leave me to examine her condition and aptitude to my affection. (*He goes about her and views her*) She is exceeding fair, and of a special good favour; a sweet composition or harmony of limbs; her temper of beauty has the true height of my blood. The knave hath exceedingly well fitted me without: I will now try her within.—Come near, fair gentlewoman; let not my behaviour seem rude, though unto you, being rare, it may haply appear strange. (*She curtsies*) Nay, lady, you may speak, though Cutbeard, and my man, might not: for of all sounds, only the sweet voice of a fair lady has the just length of mine ears. I beseech you, say, lady, out of the first fire of meeting eyes (they say) love is stricken: do you feel any such motion, suddenly shot into you, from any part you see in me? Ha, lady? (*Curtsy*) Alas, lady, these answers by silent curtsies from you are too courtless and simple. I have ever had my breeding in court; and she that shall be my wife must be accomplished with courtly and audacious ornaments. Can you speak, lady?

EPICOENE  (*She speaks softly*) Judge you, forsooth.       36

MOROSE  What say you, lady? Speak out, I beseech you.

EPICOENE  Judge you, forsooth.

MOROSE  O' my judgement, a divine softness! But can

---

5  family: household
12  prefer: recommend
17  condition: disposition
19  favour: beauty
20  her temper . . . blood: i.e. her kind of beauty suits my passions exactly
21  without: in external appearance
22  try her within: test her character (with sexual innuendo)
24  rare: of uncommon excellence
27  just length of: 'exact attunement to' (Procter)
30  motion: emotion (with innuendo)
32  courtless: uncourtly
35  audacious: spirited; but also suggesting 'shameless'

you naturally, lady, as I enjoin these by doctrine and industry, refer yourself to the search of my judgement, and (not taking pleasure in your tongue, which is a woman's chiefest pleasure) think it plausible to answer me by silent gestures, so long as my speeches jump right with what you conceive? (*Curtsy*) Excellent! Divine! If it were possible she should hold out thus! Peace, Cutbeard, thou art made forever, as thou hast made me, if this felicity have lasting; but I will try her further. Dear lady, I am courtly, I tell you, and I must have mine ears banqueted with pleasant and witty conferences, pretty girds, scoffs, and dalliance in her that I mean to choose for my bed-fere. The ladies in court think it a most desperate impair to their quickness of wit and good carriage, if they cannot give occasion for a man to court 'em, and when an amorous discourse is set on foot, minister as good matter to continue it as himself; and do you alone so much differ from all them, that what they (with so much circumstance) affect, and toil for, to seem learned, to seem judicious, to seem sharp, and conceited, you can bury in yourself, with silence, and rather trust your graces to the fair conscience of virtue, than to the world's or your own proclamation? **64**

EPICOENE I should be sorry else.

MOROSE What say you, lady? Good lady, speak out.

EPICOENE I should be sorry, else.

MOROSE That sorrow doth fill me with gladness! Oh, Morose! Thou art happy above mankind! Pray that thou mayst contain thyself. I will only put her to it once more, and it shall be with the utmost touch and test of their sex.—But hear me, fair lady, I do also love to see her whom I shall choose for my heifer to be the first and principal in all fashions; precede all the dames at court, by a fortnight; have her council of tailors, lineners, lace-women, embroiderers, and sit with 'em sometimes twice a day, upon French

intelligences; and then come forth varied like Nature, or oft'ner than she, and better, by the help of Art, her emulous servant. This do I affect. And how will you be able, lady, with this frugality of speech, to give the manifold (but necessary) instructions for that bodice, these sleeves, those skirts, this cut, that stitch, this embroidery, that lace, this wire, those knots, that ruff, those roses, this girdle, that fan, the tother scarf, these gloves? Ha? What say you, lady? **86**

EPICOENE I'll leave it to you, sir.

MOROSE How, lady? Pray you, rise a note.

EPICOENE I leave it to wisdom, and you, sir.

MOROSE Admirable creature! I will trouble you no more; I will not sin against so sweet a simplicity. Let me now be bold to print, on those divine lips, the seal of being mine. (*Kisses her*) Cutbeard, I give thee the lease of thy house free; thank me not, but with thy leg.—I know what thou wouldst say, she's poor, and her friends deceased: she has brought a wealthy dowry in her silence, Cutbeard; and in respect of her poverty, Cutbeard, I shall have her more loving, and obedient, Cutbeard. Go thy ways, and get me a minister presently, with a soft, low voice, to marry us, and pray him he will not be impertinent, but brief as he can; away; softly, Cutbeard. (*Exit* CUTBEARD) Sirrah, conduct your mistress into the dining room, your now-mistress. (*Exeunt* MUTE *and* EPICOENE) Oh my felicity! How I shall be revenged on mine insolent kinsman, and his plots to fright me from marrying! This night I will get an heir, and thrust him out of my blood like a stranger. He would be knighted, forsooth, and thought by that means to reign over me, his title must do it: no, kinsman, I will now make you bring me the tenth lord's and the sixteenth lady's letter, kinsman; and it shall do you no good, kinsman. Your knighthood itself shall come on its knees, and it shall be rejected; it shall be sued for its fees to execution, and not be redeemed; it shall cheat at the twelvepenny ordinary, it knighthood, for its diet all the term time, and tell tales

---

40 these: i.e. Cutbeard and Mute
   doctrine: instruction
44 plausible: agreeable
45 jump right: tally
52 girds: gibes
53 bed-fere: bedfellow
54 impair: injury
55 carriage: behaviour
59 circumstance: ado
60 affect: aim at
61 conceited: witty
63 conscience: inward knowledge
69 happy: fortunate
71 touch: trial
73 heifer: bride (literally, a cow that has not yet calfed); see Judges 14.18: 'And he said unto them, If ye had not ploughed with my heifer, ye had not found out my riddle'
76 lineners: drapers

77–8 French intelligences: news from France (of the latest fashions)
80 affect: like
83 cut: decorative slash in sleeve to reveal lining beneath
84 wire: to support hair or ruff
   knots: bows
85 roses: see II.ii.73n
100 presently: immediately
101 impertinent: irrelevant
111 letter: i.e. of commendation
114 to execution: 'as far as seizure by writ of possession (for debt)' (Procter)
115 twelvepenny ordinary: one of the more expensive eating-houses
   it: archaic form of its or his, used in baby talk; in this passage, used contemptuously

for it in the vacation, to the hostess; or it knighthood shall do worse, take sanctuary in Coleharbour, and fast. It shall fright all it friends with borrowing letters; and when one of the fourscore hath brought it knighthood ten shillings, it knighthood shall go to the Cranes, or the Bear at the Bridgefoot, and be drunk in fear; it shall not have money to discharge one tavern reckoning, to invite the old creditors to forbear it knighthood, or the new that should be, to trust it knighthood. It shall be the tenth name in the bond, to take up the commodity of pipkins and stone jugs; and the part thereof shall not furnish it knighthood forth for the attempting of a baker's widow, a brown baker's widow. It shall give it knighthood's name for a stallion to all gamesome citizens' wives, and be refused, when the master of a dancing school or (how do you call him?) the worst reveller in the town is taken; it shall want clothes, and by reason of that, wit, to fool to lawyers. It shall not have hope to repair itself by Constantinople, Ireland, or Virginia; but the best and last fortune to it knighthood shall be to make Dol Tearsheet, or Kate Common, a lady, and so it knighthood may eat.                                     **139**

*Exit*

# Act II, scene vi

*Enter* TRUEWIT, DAUPHINE, CLERIMONT

TRUEWIT  Are you sure he is not gone by?

DAUPHINE  No, I stayed in the shop ever since.

CLERIMONT  But he may take the other end of the lane.

DAUPHINE  No, I told him I would be here at this end;

---

118  Coleharbour: or Coldharborough, a seedy area that had become a sanctuary for debtors and vagrants

119  borrowing: begging

122  Cranes . . . Bear: the Three Cranes on Upper Thames Street, and the Bear at the southern end of London Bridge: popular taverns

125  forbear: to abstain from enforcing the payment of money after it has become due

126  tenth name: 'tenth man to be paid off (who therefore gets very little)' (Procter)

127  commodity: worthless goods borrowers obliged to take as part of loan; see I.iv.74n
pipkins: small earthenware jugs

129  brown: a) coarse bread; b) dark-complexioned; both seen as inferior options

132  how: pun on name of Edmund Howe, the public chronicler

134  fool to: trick; Holdsworth suggests 'play the fool in front of'

136  Constantinople, Ireland, or Virginia: places in which people tried to recoup lost fortunes or escape the law

137–8  Dol Tearsheet, or Kate Common: prostitutes. Dol Tearsheet is in *2 Henry IV*; compare Dol Common in *The Alchemist*

---

I appointed him hither.

TRUEWIT  What a barbarian it is to stay then!

*Enter* CUTBEARD

DAUPHINE  Yonder he comes.

CLERIMONT  And his charge left behind him, which is a very good sign, Dauphine.

DAUPHINE  How now, Cutbeard, succeeds it, or no?  **10**

CUTBEARD  Past imagination, sir, *omnia secunda*; you could not have prayed to have had it so well: *saltat senex*, as it is i' the proverb, he does triumph in his felicity; admires the party! He has given me the lease of my house too! And I am now going for a silent minister to marry 'em, and away.

TRUEWIT  'Slight, get one o' the silenced ministers, a zealous brother would torment him purely.

CUTBEARD  *Cum privilegio*, sir.

DAUPHINE  Oh, by no means; let's do nothing to hinder it now; when 'tis done and finished, I am for you, for any device of vexation.  **22**

CUTBEARD  And that shall be within this half hour, upon my dexterity, gentlemen. Contrive what you can in the meantime, *bonis avibus*.  *Exit*

CLERIMONT  How the slave doth Latin it!

TRUEWIT  It would be made a jest to posterity, sirs, this day's mirth, if ye will.

CLERIMONT  Beshrew his heart that will not, I pronounce.  **30**

DAUPHINE  And for my part. What is't?

TRUEWIT  To translate all La Foole's company and his feast hither today to celebrate this bride-ale.

DAUPHINE  Ay, marry, but how will't be done?

TRUEWIT  I'll undertake the directing of all the lady guests thither, and then the meat must follow.

CLERIMONT  For God's sake, let's effect it; it will be an excellent comedy of affliction, so many several noises.

DAUPHINE  But are they not at the other place already, think you?  **40**

TRUEWIT  I'll warrant you for the college-honours: one

---

5  appointed him hither: arranged to meet him here

6  it: i.e. he

11–13  *omnia secunda . . . saltat senex*: Latin proverb: 'All's well; the old boy is cutting capers' (Herford and Simpson)

15–16  silenced ministers: see II.ii.87n

18  purely: perfectly; also, 'in the Puritan manner'

19  *Cum privilegio*: with authority

25  *bonis avibus*: the omens being favourable

26  Latin: since many barbers were also surgeons, such an affectation was not unlikely

32  translate: transfer

33  bride-ale: wedding feast

36  meat: food

38  several: different

39  the other place: i.e. Otter's house

41  I'll . . . for: I can guarantee you about college-honours: i.e. the collegiates (see III.iii.77)

o' their faces has not the priming colour laid on yet,
nor the other her smock sleeked.

CLERIMONT  Oh, but they'll rise earlier than ordinary to
a feast.

TRUEWIT  Best go see, and assure ourselves.

CLERIMONT  Who knows the house?

TRUEWIT  I'll lead you; were you never there yet?

DAUPHINE  Not I.

CLERIMONT  Nor I.                                                    50

TRUEWIT  Where ha' you lived then? Not know Tom
Otter!

CLERIMONT  No. For God's sake, what is he?

TRUEWIT  An excellent animal, equal with your Daw or
La Foole, if not transcendent; and does Latin it as
much as your barber. He is his wife's subject, he calls
her princess, and at such times as these, follows her
up and down the house like a page, with his hat off,
partly for heat, partly for reverence. At this instant,
he is marshalling of his bull, bear, and horse.       60

DAUPHINE  What be those, in the name of Sphinx?

TRUEWIT  Why, sir, he has been a great man at the
Bear Garden in his time; and from that subtle sport,
has ta'en the witty denomination of his chief
carousing cups. One he calls his bull, another his
bear, another his horse. And then he has his lesser
glasses, that he calls his deer, and his ape, and several
degrees of 'em too; and never is well, nor thinks any
entertainment perfect, till these be brought out, and
set o' the cupboard.                                    70

CLERIMONT  For God's love! We should miss this if we
should not go.

TRUEWIT  Nay, he has a thousand things as good, that
will speak him all day. He will rail on his wife, with
certain commonplaces, behind her back; and to her
face—

DAUPHINE  No more of him. Let's go see him, I
petition you.

*Exeunt*

# Act III, scene i

*Enter* OTTER, MISTRESS OTTER. TRUEWIT, CLERIMONT,
DAUPHINE *presently follow, unobserved*

OTTER  Nay, good princess, hear me *pauca verba*.

MISTRESS OTTER  By that light, I'll ha' you chained up
with your bull-dogs and bear-dogs, if you be not civil
the sooner. I'll send you to kennel, i' faith. You were
best bait me with your bull, bear, and horse! Never a
time that the courtiers or collegiates come to the
house, but you make it a Shrove Tuesday! I would
have you get your Whitsuntide velvet cap, and your
staff i' your hand, to entertain 'em; yes, in troth, do.

OTTER  Not so, princess, neither, but under correction,
sweet princess, gi' me leave—these things I am
known to the courtiers by. It is reported to them for
my humour, and they receive it so, and do expect it.
Tom Otter's bull, bear, and horse is known all over
England, in *rerum natura*.                              15

MISTRESS OTTER  'Fore me, I will 'na-ture' 'em over to
Paris Garden and 'na-ture' you thither too, if you
pronounce 'em again. Is a bear a fit beast, or a bull, to
mix in society with great ladies? Think i' your
discretion, in any good polity?                         20

OTTER  The horse then, good princess.

MISTRESS OTTER  Well, I am contented for the horse:
they love to be well horsed, I know. I love it myself.

OTTER  And it is a delicate fine horse this. *Poetarum
Pegasus*. Under correction, princess, Jupiter did turn
himself into a—*taurus*, or bull, under correction,
good princess.                                          27

MISTRESS OTTER  By my integrity, I'll send you over to
the Bankside, I'll commit you to the master of the
Garden, if I hear but a syllable more. Must my house,
or my roof, be polluted with the scent of bears, and
bulls, when it is perfumed for great ladies? Is this
according to the instrument, when I married you?
That I would be princess, and reign in mine own
house; and you would be my subject, and obey me?
What did you bring me, should make you thus
peremptory? Do I allow you your half-crown a day,

---

43  sleeked: ironed, smoothed
61  Sphinx: asker of riddles
63  Bear Garden: bear- and bull-baiting arena on Bankside,
     next to Paris Garden; see Introduction
65  cups: their lids were shaped like these animals' heads
68  degrees: sizes
74  speak: reveal things about
1  *pauca verba*: few words

4–5  were best: had best
5  with: along with
7  Shrove Tuesday: see I.i.172n
8  velvet cap: worn for a holiday, such as Whitsun
10  under correction: subject to correction; used to suggest
     deference
13  humour: characteristic oddity; here an affectation of a
     humour, according to Jonson's own criteria (see Jonson,
     *Every Man Out of His Humour* (1599), Induction, ll. 88–
     117)
15  *rerum natura*: here, 'the natural order of things'; more
     usually (as at III.ii.6) 'the world'
16  'Fore me: before me (a common asseveration)
20  discretion: judgement
     good polity: well-ordered society
23  horsed: with sexual innuendo ('mount', 'ride')
24–5  *Poetarum Pegasus*: the poets' Pegasus
25–6  Jupiter . . . bull: Jupiter assumed the shape of a bull
     when he carried off Europa, with whom he was
     enamoured
33  instrument: formal legal agreement
37  peremptory: self-willed

to spend where you will among your gamesters, to vex and torment me at such times as these? Who gives you your maintenance, I pray you? Who allows you your horse-meat and man's meat? Your three suits of apparel a year? Your four pair of stockings, one silk, three worsted? Your clean linen, your bands, and cuffs when I can get you to wear 'em? 'Tis mar'l you ha' 'em on now. Who graces you with courtiers, or great personages, to speak to you out of their coaches, and come home to your house? Were you ever so much as looked upon by a lord, or a lady, before I married you, but on the Easter or Whitsun holidays, and then out at the Banqueting House window, when Ned Whiting, or George Stone, were at the stake? 52

TRUEWIT (*Aside*) For God's sake, let's go stave her off him.

MISTRESS OTTER Answer me to that. And did not I take you up from thence, in an old greasy buff-doublet, with points; and green velvet sleeves, out at the elbows? You forget this.

TRUEWIT (*Aside*) She'll worry him, if we help not in time.                                              *They come forward*

MISTRESS OTTER Oh, here are some o' the gallants! Go to, behave yourself distinctly, and with good morality; or I protest, I'll take away your exhibition.

## Act III, scene ii

TRUEWIT By your leave, fair Mistress Otter, I'll be bold to enter these gentlemen in your acquaintance.

MISTRESS OTTER It shall not be obnoxious, or diffícil, sir.

TRUEWIT How does my noble captain? Is the bull, bear, and horse in *rerum natura* still?

OTTER Sir, *sic visum superis*.

---

41 horse-meat: horse fodder
41–2 three suits: a servant's allowance; see *King Lear* II.ii.14–15; III.iv.124–5
43 bands: collars
44 mar'l: marvel
50 Banqueting House: at Whitehall, where bull- and bear-baits were sometimes held
51 Ned Whiting, or George Stone: champion bears
53, 59 stave her off . . . worry: terms from bear-baiting
56–7 buff-doublet: leather jacket, as worn by ordinary soldiers
57 points: laces
62 distinctly, and with good morality: affected ways of saying 'well', 'properly'
63 exhibition: allowance
3 obnoxious, or diffícil: offensive or troublesome (affectedly)
6 *rerum natura*: see III.i.15n
7 *sic visum superis*: as those above decree

MISTRESS OTTER I would you would but intimate 'em, do. Go your ways in, and get toasts and butter made for the woodcocks. That's a fit province for you.    10
                                                          *Exit* OTTER

CLERIMONT (*Aside to* TRUEWIT *and* DAUPHINE) Alas, what a tyranny is this poor fellow married to!

TRUEWIT Oh, but the sport will be anon, when we get him loose.

DAUPHINE Dares he ever speak?

TRUEWIT No Anabaptist ever railed with the like licence: but mark her language in the meantime I beseech you.

MISTRESS OTTER Gentlemen, you are very aptly come. My cousin, Sir Amorous, will be here briefly.    20

TRUEWIT In good time, lady. Was not Sir John Daw here, to ask for him and the company?

MISTRESS OTTER I cannot assure you, Master Truewit. Here was a very melancholy knight in a ruff, that demanded my subject for somebody, a gentleman, I think.

CLERIMONT Ay, that was he, lady.

MISTRESS OTTER But he departed straight, I can resolve you.

DAUPHINE What an excellent choice phrase this lady expresses in!    31

TRUEWIT Oh, sir, she is the only authentical courtier, that is not naturally bred one, in the city.

MISTRESS OTTER You have taken that report upon trust, gentlemen.

TRUEWIT No, I assure you, the court governs it so, lady, in your behalf.

MISTRESS OTTER I am the servant of the court, and courtiers, sir.

TRUEWIT They are rather your idolaters.    40

MISTRESS OTTER Not so, sir.

*Enter* CUTBEARD. DAUPHINE, TRUEWIT *and* CLERIMONT *talk with him apart*

DAUPHINE How now, Cutbeard? Any cross?

CUTBEARD Oh, no, sir, *omnia bene*. 'Twas never better

---

8 intimate: 'either "get intimate with", an affected way of saying "go and join (your animals)"; or, threateningly, "start that topic again . . . " ("*Intimare*, to intimate . . . to proclaim, set abroach", Florio, 1611)' (Procter)
9 toasts and butter: the correct food to serve with woodcock; but also meant milksop
10 woodcocks: the birds, but 'woodcock' also meant fool
16 Anabaptist: here, loosely, 'puritan'; more strictly, a Puritan sect which rejected infant baptism, in favour of voluntary adult baptism
20 briefly: shortly
25 my subject: i.e. Otter
29 resolve: assure (affectedly)
36 governs: determines
42 cross: hindrance

o' the hinges, all's sure. I have so pleased him with a curate that he's gone to't almost with the delight he hopes for soon.

DAUPHINE What is he, for a vicar? 47

CUTBEARD One that has catched a cold, sir, and can scarce be heard six inches off; as if he spoke out of a bulrush that were not picked, or his throat were full of pith; a fine quick fellow and an excellent barber of prayers. I came to tell you, sir, that you might *omnem movere lapidem* (as they say), be ready with your vexation.

DAUPHINE Gramercy, honest Cutbeard; be thereabouts with thy key to let us in.

CUTBEARD I will not fail you, sir: *ad manum.* *Exit*

TRUEWIT Well, I'll go watch my coaches.

CLERIMONT Do, and we'll send Daw to you, if you meet him not. *Exit* TRUEWIT

MISTRESS OTTER Is Master Truewit gone? 61

DAUPHINE Yes, lady, there is some unfortunate business fallen out.

MISTRESS OTTER So I judged by the physiognomy of the fellow that came in; and I had a dream last night too of the new pageant, and my Lady Mayoress, which is always very ominous to me. I told it my Lady Haughty t'other day, when her honour came hither to see some China stuffs; and she expounded it out of Artemidorus, and I have found it since very true. It has done me many affronts. 71

CLERIMONT Your dream, lady?

MISTRESS OTTER Yes, sir, anything I do but dream o' the city. It stained me a damask table-cloth, cost me eighteen pound at one time; and burnt me a black satin gown, as I stood by the fire at my Lady Centaure's chamber in the college, another time. A third time, at the lord's masque, it dropped all my wire and my ruff with wax candle, that I could not go up to the banquet. A fourth time, as I was taking coach to go to Ware to meet a friend, it dashed me a new suit all over (a crimson satin doublet, and black velvet skirts) with a brewer's horse, that I was fain to go in and shift me, and kept my chamber a leash of days for the anguish of it. 85

DAUPHINE These were dire mischances, lady.

CLERIMONT I would not dwell in the city, and 'twere so fatal to me.

MISTRESS OTTER Yes, sir, but I do take advice of my doctor, to dream of it as little as I can. 90

DAUPHINE You do well, Mistress Otter.

*Enter* DAW; CLERIMONT *takes him aside*

MISTRESS OTTER Will it please you to enter the house farther, gentlemen?

DAUPHINE And your favour, lady; but we stay to speak with a knight, Sir John Daw, who is here come. We shall follow you, lady.

MISTRESS OTTER At your own time, sir. It is my cousin Sir Amorous his feast—

DAUPHINE I know it, lady. 99

MISTRESS OTTER And mine together. But it is for his honour; and therefore I take no name of it, more than of the place.

DAUPHINE You are a bounteous kinswoman.

MISTRESS OTTER Your servant, sir. *Exit*

# Act III, scene iii

CLERIMONT *comes forward with* DAW

CLERIMONT Why, do not you know it, Sir John Daw?

DAW No, I am a rook if I do.

CLERIMONT I'll tell you then: she's married by this time! And whereas you were put i' the head that she was gone with Sir Dauphine, I assure you Sir Dauphine has been the noblest, honestest friend to you, that ever gentleman of your quality could boast of. He has discovered the whole plot, and made your mistress so acknowledging, and indeed so ashamed of her injury to you, that she desires you to forgive her, and but grace her wedding with your presence today—she is to be married to a very good fortune, she says, his uncle, old Morose; and she willed me in private to tell you, that she shall be able to do you more favours, and with more security now, than before. 15

DAW Did she say so, i' faith?

CLERIMONT Why, what do you think of me, Sir John! Ask Sir Dauphine.

---

43 *omnia bene*: all's well
43–4 'Twas . . . hinges: things have never run more smoothly
47 What . . . vicar?: what sort of vicar is he?
49–50 as . . . picked: 'i.e. huskily; *picked* = cleaned out, cleared' (Procter)
52–3 *omnem . . . lapidem*: leave no stone unturned
55 Gramercy: thanks
57 *ad manum*: at hand
66 pageant: procession at the installation of the new Lord Mayor
70 Artemidorus: second-century Greek author of a treatise on the meaning of dreams
81 Ware: 20 miles north of London; notorious for amorous assignations
82–3 crimson satin . . . velvet: fashionable and expensive fabrics, usually associated with the nobility
doublet: normally a man's garment
84 shift me: change my clothes
leash: three (hunting term)
87 and: if
88 fatal: ominous
101 name: credit
of the place: for providing the place
4 put i' the head: made to think

DAW Nay, I believe you. Good Sir Dauphine, did she desire me to forgive her? 20

DAUPHINE I assure you, Sir John, she did.

DAW Nay, then, I do with all my heart, and I'll be jovial.

CLERIMONT Yes, for look you, sir, this was the injury to you. La Foole intended this feast to honour her bridal day, and made you the property to invite the college ladies, and promise to bring her; and then at the time she should have appeared (as his friend) to have given you the dor. Whereas now, Sir Dauphine has brought her to a feeling of it, with this kind of satisfaction, that you shall bring all the ladies to the place where she is, and be very jovial; and there she will have a dinner which shall be in your name, and so disappoint La Foole, to make you good again and, as it were, a saver i' the man. 34

DAW As I am a knight, I honour her, and forgive her heartily.

CLERIMONT About it then presently. Truewit is gone before to confront the coaches, and to acquaint you with so much if he meet you. Join with him, and 'tis well. (*Enter* LA FOOLE) See, here comes your antagonist, but take you no notice, but be very jovial.

LA FOOLE Are the ladies come, Sir John Daw, and your mistress? (*Exit* DAW) Sir Dauphine! You are exceeding welcome, and honest Master Clerimont. Where's my cousin? Did you see no collegiates, gentlemen? 45

DAUPHINE Collegiates! Do you not hear, Sir Amorous, how you are abused?

LA FOOLE How, sir!

CLERIMONT Will you speak so kindly to Sir John Daw, that has done you such an affront? 50

LA FOOLE Wherein, gentlemen? Let me be a suitor to you to know, I beseech you!

CLERIMONT Why, sir, his mistress is married today to Sir Dauphine's uncle, your cousin's neighbour, and he has diverted all the ladies and all your company thither, to frustrate your provision, and stick a disgrace upon you. He was here now to have enticed us away from you too; but we told him his own, I think.

LA FOOLE Has Sir John Daw wronged me so inhumanly?

DAUPHINE He has done it, Sir Amorous, most maliciously, and treacherously; but if you'll be ruled by us, you shall quit him, i' faith. 62

LA FOOLE Good gentlemen, I'll make one, believe it! How, I pray?

DAUPHINE Marry, sir, get me your pheasants, and your godwits, and your best meat, and dish it in silver dishes of your cousin's presently, and say nothing, but clap me a clean towel about you, like a sewer; and bare-headed, march afore it with a good confidence ('tis but over the way, hard by) and we'll second you, where you shall set it o' the board, and bid 'em welcome to't, which shall show 'tis yours, and disgrace his preparation utterly; and for your cousin, whereas she should be troubled here at home with care of making and giving welcome, she shall transfer all that labour thither, and be a principal guest herself, sit ranked with the college-honours, and be honoured, and have her health drunk as often, as bare, and as loud as the best of 'em. 79

LA FOOLE I'll go tell her presently. It shall be done, that's resolved. *Exit*

CLERIMONT I thought he would not hear it out, but 'twould take him.

DAUPHINE Well, there be guests and meat now; how shall we do for music?

CLERIMONT The smell of the venison going through the street will invite one noise of fiddlers or other.

DAUPHINE I would it would call the trumpeters thither.

CLERIMONT Faith, there is hope; they have intelligence of all feasts. There's good correspondence betwixt them and the London cooks. 'Tis twenty to one but we have 'em. 92

DAUPHINE 'Twill be a most solemn day for my uncle, and an excellent fit of mirth for us.

CLERIMONT Ay, if we can hold up the emulation betwixt Foole and Daw, and never bring them to expostulate.

DAUPHINE Tut, flatter 'em both (as Truewit says) and you may take their understandings in a purse-net.

---

22 jovial: cheerful
25 property: tool, means
28 the dor: a snub; see II.iii.46n
29 feeling of: sensitivity to
33 make . . . again: 'recoup your losses (as in gambling)' (Procter)
34 saver: 'a gambling term, "one who escapes loss, though without gain" (Dr Johnson)' (Procter)
   i' the man: of your manhood; with pun on 'main', meaning 'main point, turning the tables on La Foole; also, fixed score in the dice game, hazard, which if thrown by the caster enabled the other players to regain their stake money' (Procter)
56 provision: preparations
58 his own: his true character

62 quit: repay
63 make one: join in
68 sewer: chief attendant at a meal who supervised the setting of the table, the seating of the guests and the serving of the dishes
69 bare-headed: i.e. like a servant
70 second: follow
79 bare: bare-headed
87 noise: band
93 solemn: a) ceremonious; b) gloomy
95 emulation: contention, rivalry
97 expostulate: declare their grievances
99 purse-net: bag-shaped net with draw-string opening, used for catching rabbits

They'll believe themselves to be just such men as we make 'em, neither more nor less. They have nothing, not the use of their senses, but by tradition.    102

LA FOOLE *enters like a sewer*

CLERIMONT  See! Sir Amorous has his towel on already. Have you persuaded your cousin?

LA FOOLE  Yes, 'tis very feasible: she'll do anything, she says, rather than the La Fooles shall be disgraced.

DAUPHINE  She is a noble kinswoman. It will be such a pestling device, Sir Amorous! It will pound all your enemy's practices to powder, and blow him up with his own mine, his own train.    110

LA FOOLE  Nay, we'll give fire, I warrant you.

CLERIMONT  But you must carry it privately, without any noise, and take no notice by any means—

*Enter* OTTER

OTTER  Gentlemen, my princess says you shall have all her silver dishes, *festinate*; and she's gone to alter her tire a little and go with you—

CLERIMONT  And yourself too, Captain Otter.

DAUPHINE  By any means, sir.

OTTER  Yes, sir, I do mean it; but I would entreat my cousin Sir Amorous, and you gentlemen, to be suitors to my princess, that I may carry my bull, and my bear, as well as my horse.    122

CLERIMONT  That you shall do, Captain Otter.

LA FOOLE  My cousin will never consent, gentlemen.

DAUPHINE  She must consent, Sir Amorous, to reason.

LA FOOLE  Why, she says they are no decorum among ladies.

OTTER  But they are *decora*, and that's better, sir.

CLERIMONT  Ay, she must hear argument. Did not Pasiphae, who was a queen, love a bull? And was not Callisto, the mother of Arcas, turned into a bear, and made a star, Mistress Ursula, i' the heavens?    132

OTTER  Oh God! That I could ha' said as much! I will

have these stories painted i' the Bear Garden, *ex Ovidii Metamorphosi*.

DAUPHINE  Where is your princess, captain? Pray be our leader.

OTTER  That I shall, sir.

CLERIMONT  Make haste, good Sir Amorous.

*Exeunt*

# Act III, scene iv

*Enter* MOROSE, EPICOENE, PARSON, CUTBEARD

MOROSE  Sir, there's an angel for yourself, and a brace of angels for your cold. Muse not at this manage of my bounty. It is fit we should thank fortune double to nature, for any benefit she confers upon us; besides, it is your imperfection, but my solace.

PARSON  I thank your worship, so is it mine now.

*The* PARSON *speaks as having a cold*

MOROSE  What says he, Cutbeard?

CUTBEARD  He says *praesto*, sir: whensoever your worship needs him, he can be ready with the like. He got this cold with sitting up late, and singing catches with cloth-workers.    11

MOROSE  No more. I thank him.

PARSON  God keep your worship and give you much joy with your fair spouse. Umh, umh.    *He coughs*

MOROSE  Oh, oh! Stay, Cutbeard! Let him give me five shillings of my money back. As it is bounty to reward benefits, so is it equity to mulct injuries. I will have it. What says he?

CUTBEARD  He cannot change it, sir.

MOROSE  It must be changed.    20

CUTBEARD  (*Aside to* PARSON) Cough again.

MOROSE  What says he?

CUTBEARD  He will cough out the rest, sir.

PARSON  Umh, umh, umh.    *Coughs again*

MOROSE  Away, away with him, stop his mouth, away, I forgive it—    *Exit* CUTBEARD *with* PARSON

EPICOENE  Fie, Master Morose, that you will use this violence to a man of the church.

MOROSE  How!    29

EPICOENE  It does not become your gravity or breeding (as you pretend in court) to have offered this outrage

---

102  tradition: i.e. handing over
108  pestling: crushing (as with pestle)
109  practices: plots
110  train: line of gunpowder, laid to detonate a mine; also, a snare or trick
112  carry: manage
115  *festinate*: quickly
116  tire: headdress
126  no decorum: unseemly
128  *decora*: beautiful
130  Pasiphae . . . bull: Pasiphae was married to Minos, king of Crete. When he refused to sacrifice a bull to Neptune, the god punished him by making Pasiphae fall in love with the bull. Their offspring was the Minotaur
131  Callisto: loved by Jupiter (by whom she had a son, Arcas); changed by Juno into a bear, and after her death into a constellation (the Great Bear) by Jupiter. The story is recounted in Ovid's *Metamorphoses*, II.401–507

134–5  *ex . . . Metamorphosi*: out of Ovid's *Metamorphoses*; the story of Pasiphae in fact comes from Ovid's *Ars Amatoria*, I.295–326
1  angel: gold coin, worth about ten shillings
2  manage: management
3–4  double to: twice as much as
8  *praesto*: at your service
10  catches: part-songs, rounds
11  cloth-workers: who customarily sang whilst working
17  mulct: fine
30  gravity: dignity
31  pretend: claim

on a waterman, or any more boisterous creature, much less on a man of his civil coat.

MOROSE  You can speak then!

EPICOENE  Yes, sir.

MOROSE  Speak out, I mean.

EPICOENE  Ay, sir. Why, did you think you had married a statue? Or a motion only? One of the French puppets, with the eyes turned with a wire? Or some innocent out of the hospital, that would stand with her hands thus, and a plaice mouth, and look upon you?                                                        42

MOROSE  Oh immodesty! A manifest woman! What, Cutbeard!

EPICOENE  Nay, never quarrel with Cutbeard, sir, it is too late now. I confess it doth bate somewhat of the modesty I had, when I writ simply maid; but I hope I shall make it a stock still competent to the estate and dignity of your wife.

MOROSE  She can talk!                                               50

EPICOENE  Yes, indeed, sir.

MOROSE  What sirrah! None of my knaves there? (*Enter* MUTE) Where is this impostor, Cutbeard?

MUTE *makes signs*

EPICOENE  Speak to him, fellow, speak to him. I'll have none of this coacted, unnatural dumbness in my house, in a family where I govern.          *Exit* MUTE

MOROSE  She is my regent already! I have married a Penthesilea, a Semiramis, sold my liberty to a distaff!

# Act III, scene v

*Enter* TRUEWIT

TRUEWIT  Where's Master Morose?

---

33  civil coat: sober profession
38  motion: puppet
40  innocent: half-wit
    hospital: i.e. Bedlam; see II.ii.37n
41  hands thus: probably loosely crossed in front, indicating
    obedience or idiocy (eds)
    plaice mouth: small, puckered mouth, like a fish's
43  A manifest woman: i.e. manifestly a woman
46  bate: lessen
47  writ: designated myself
48  stock: fund, or capital sum; also, dowry
    competent: appropriate, sufficient
    estate: status
52  knaves: servants
55  coacted: compulsory
56  family: household
58  Penthesilea: queen of the Amazons, who fought against
    the Greeks at Troy; see III.v.43
    Semiramis: Assyrian warrior-queen. After her husband's
    death, she dressed in men's clothes to govern
    distaff: staff on which thread is made; this was
    traditionally women's work, and hence the word came to
    stand metonymically for 'woman'

MOROSE  Is he come again? Lord have mercy upon me.

TRUEWIT  I wish you all joy, Mistress Epicoene, with your grave and honourable match.

EPICOENE  I return you the thanks, Master Truewit, so friendly a wish deserves.

MOROSE  She has acquaintance, too!                           7

TRUEWIT  God save you, sir, and give you all contentment in your fair choice here. Before I was the bird of night to you, the owl, but now I am the messenger of peace, a dove, and bring you the glad wishes of many friends, to the celebration of this good hour.

MOROSE  What hour, sir?

TRUEWIT  Your marriage hour, sir. I commend your resolution, that (notwithstanding all the dangers I laid afore you, in the voice of a night-crow) would yet go on, and be yourself. It shows you are a man constant to your own ends, and upright to your purposes, that would not be put off with left-handed cries.                                                        21

MOROSE  How should you arrive at the knowledge of so much?

TRUEWIT  Why, did you ever hope, sir, committing the secrecy of it to a barber, that less than the whole town should know it? You might as well ha' told it the conduit, or the bakehouse, or the infantry that follow the court, and with more security. Could your gravity forget so old and noted a remnant as *lippis et tonsoribus notum*? Well, sir, forgive it yourself now, the fault, and be communicable with your friends. Here will be three or four fashionable ladies, from the college, to visit you presently, and their train of minions and followers.                                     34

MOROSE  Bar my doors! Bar my doors! Where are all my eaters, my mouths now? (*Enter* SERVANTS) Bar up my doors, you varlets!

EPICOENE  He is a varlet that stirs to such an office. Let 'em stand open. I would see him that dares move his eyes toward it. Shall I have a barricado made against my friends, to be barred of any pleasure they can bring in to me with honourable visitation?          42

*Exit* SERVANTS

---

10, 17  owl . . . night-crow: bearers of evil omen, the latter not
        denoting a specific bird
20  left-handed: sinister, ill-omened (Latin *sinister* means
    'left')
27  conduit: place from which fresh water was collected; a
    place where gossip was exchanged, as was the bakehouse.
    infantry . . . court: the 'blackguard' or most menial
    servants employed by the court; they brought up the rear
    on royal progresses
29  remnant: scrap of quotation
29–30  *lippis et tonsoribus notum*: 'known to the bleary-eyed
       and to barbers' (Horace, *Satires*, I.vii.3)
31  communicable: affable

MOROSE  Oh, Amazonian impudence!

TRUEWIT  Nay, faith, in this, sir, she speaks but reason, and methinks is more continent than you. Would you go to bed so presently, sir, afore noon? A man of your head and hair should owe more to that reverend ceremony, and not mount the marriage-bed like a town bull, or a mountain goat, but stay the due season; and ascend it then with religion, and fear. Those delights are to be steeped in the humour and silence of the night; and give the day to other open pleasures, and jollities of feast, of music, of revels, of discourse: we'll have all, sir, that may make your hymen high and happy.                                      55

MOROSE  Oh, my torment, my torment!

TRUEWIT  Nay, if you endure the first half hour, sir, so tediously, and with this irksomeness, what comfort, or hope, can this fair gentlewoman make to herself hereafter, in the consideration of so many years as are to come—                                                     61

MOROSE  Of my affliction. Good sir, depart, and let her do it alone.

TRUEWIT  I have done, sir.

MOROSE  That cursed barber!

TRUEWIT  (Yes, faith, a cursed wretch indeed, sir.)

MOROSE  I have married his cittern, that's common to all men. Some plague above the plague—

TRUEWIT  (All Egypt's ten plagues—)

MOROSE  Revenge me on him.                                   70

TRUEWIT  'Tis very well, sir. If you laid on a curse or two more, I'll assure you he'll bear 'em. As, that he may get the pox with seeking to cure it, sir? Or, that while he is curling another man's hair, his own may drop off? Or, for burning some male bawd's lock, he may have his brain beat out with the curling-iron?

MOROSE  No, let the wretch live wretched. May he get the itch, and his shop so lousy as no man dare come at him, nor he come at no man.

TRUEWIT  (Ay, and if he would swallow all his balls for pills, let not them purge him.)                             81

MOROSE  Let his warming-pan be ever cold.

TRUEWIT  (A perpetual frost underneath it, sir.)

MOROSE  Let him never hope to see fire again.

TRUEWIT  (But in hell, sir.)

MOROSE  His chairs be always empty, his scissors rust, and his combs mould in their cases.

TRUEWIT  Very dreadful that! (And may he lose the invention, sir, of carving lanterns in paper.)

MOROSE  Let there be no bawd carted that year to employ a basin of his; but let him be glad to eat his sponge for bread.                                              92

TRUEWIT  And drink lotium to it, and much good do him.

MOROSE  Or, for want of bread—

TRUEWIT  Eat ear-wax, sir. I'll help you. Or, draw his own teeth and add them to the lute-string.

MOROSE  No, beat the old ones to powder, and make bread of them.

TRUEWIT  (Yes, make meal o' the millstones.)              100

MOROSE  May all the botches, and burns, that he has cured on others break out upon him.

TRUEWIT  And he now forget the cure of 'em in himself, sir; or, if he do remember it, let him ha' scraped all his linen into lint for't, and have not a rag left him to set up with.

MOROSE  Let him never set up again, but have the gout in his hands forever. Now no more, sir.

TRUEWIT  Oh, that last was too high set! You might go less with him, i' faith, and be revenged enough; as, that he be never able to new-paint his pole—      III

MOROSE  Good sir, no more. I forgot myself.

TRUEWIT  Or, want credit to take up with a comb-maker—

---

47  head and hair: judgement and character (with ironic allusion to Morose's appearance)

49  stay: wait

50  religion, and fear: awe and dread (of the solemnity of marriage)

51  humour: a) moisture (see 'steeped'); b) inclination, fancy (Holdsworth)

55  hymen: wedding
    high: dignified

58  tediously: a) irritatedly; b) tiresomely (Holdsworth)

66  (Yes . . . sir.): eds vary in how they interpret the enclosing of Truewit's words in parentheses. Procter takes them to indicate his 'choric role', building on and then taking over Morose's curses, whilst Beaurline takes them to show that the words are spoken *sotto voce*

67  cittern: a lute-like instrument kept in barber's shops for customers to play on to pass the time

69  ten plagues: sent by God to persuade Pharaoh to release the Israelites (Exodus 7–12)

73  pox: syphilis. Barbers, also surgeons/medical practitioners at this time, would have treated this

75  lock: love-lock

78  the itch: contagious skin disease, scabies

80  balls: of soap

89  lanterns in paper: barbers cut out lanterns from oiled paper, and sold them

91  basin: barbers hired out metal basins for people in the crowd to beat when bawds (procuresses or pimps) were carted through the streets as a punishment

93  lotium: stale urine, used by barbers to dress hair

96  ear-wax . . . teeth: barbers also cleaned ears and pulled teeth, which were then hung on strings in the shops

100  millstones: '"grinders", teeth' (Procter)

101  botches: boils

105  scraped . . . lint: lint, a soft material used to dress wounds, was made by scaping linen cloth

106–7  set up with . . . set up: set up in business with . . . set hair

109  too high set: went too far (gambling term)
     go less: go for lower stakes (from gambling)

113  want credit . . . with: be unable to get goods on credit from

MOROSE  No more, sir.

TRUEWIT  Or, having broken his glass in a former despair, fall now into a much greater, of ever getting another—

MOROSE  I beseech you, no more.

TRUEWIT  Or, that he never be trusted with trimming of any but chimney-sweepers—                                    121

MOROSE  Sir—

TRUEWIT  Or, may he cut a collier's throat with his razor by chance-medley, and yet hang for't.

MOROSE  I will forgive him, rather than hear any more. I beseech you, sir.

## Act III, scene vi

*Enter* DAW, HAUGHTY, CENTAURE, MAVIS, TRUSTY

DAW  This way, madam.

MOROSE  Oh, the sea breaks in upon me! Another flood! An inundation! I shall be o'erwhelmed with noise. It beats already at my shores. I feel an earthquake in myself for't.

DAW  Give you joy, mistress.

MOROSE  Has she servants too!

DAW  I have brought some ladies here to see and know you. (*She kisses them severally as he presents them*) My Lady Haughty, this my Lady Centaure, Mistress Dol Mavis, Mistress Trusty, my Lady Haughty's woman. Where's your husband? Let's see him: can he endure no noise? Let me come to him.                                    13

MOROSE  What nomenclator is this!

TRUEWIT  Sir John Daw, sir, your wife's servant, this.

MOROSE  A Daw, and her servant! Oh, 'tis decreed, 'tis decreed of me, and she have such servants.

*Attempts to leave*

TRUEWIT  Nay, sir, you must kiss the ladies, you must not go away now; they come toward you to seek you out.                                    20

HAUGHTY  I' faith, Master Morose, would you steal a marriage thus, in the midst of so many friends, and not acquaint us? Well, I'll kiss you, notwithstanding the justice of my quarrel. You shall give me leave, mistress, to use a becoming familiarity with your husband.

EPICOENE  Your ladyship does me an honour in it, to let me know he is so worthy your favour; as you have done both him and me grace to visit so unprepared a pair to entertain you.                                    30

MOROSE  Compliment! Compliment!

EPICOENE  But I must lay the burden of that upon my servant here.

HAUGHTY  It shall not need, Mistress Morose; we will all bear, rather than one shall be oppressed.

MOROSE  I know it; and you will teach her the faculty, if she be to learn it.

*The collegiates talk apart with* TRUEWIT

HAUGHTY  Is this the silent woman?

CENTAURE  Nay! She has found her tongue since she was married, Master Truewit says.                                    40

HAUGHTY  Oh, Master Truewit! Save you. What kind of creature is your bride here? She speaks, methinks!

TRUEWIT  Yes, madam, believe it, she is a gentlewoman of very absolute behaviour, and of a good race.

HAUGHTY  And Jack Daw told us she could not speak.

TRUEWIT  So it was carried in plot, madam, to put her upon this old fellow, by Sir Dauphine, his nephew, and one or two more of us; but she is a woman of an excellent assurance, and an extraordinary happy wit and tongue. You shall see her make rare sport with Daw ere night.                                    51

HAUGHTY  And he brought us to laugh at her!

TRUEWIT  That falls out often, madam, that he that thinks himself the master-wit is the master-fool. I assure your ladyship, ye cannot laugh at her.

HAUGHTY  No, we'll have her to the college: and she have wit, she shall be one of us! Shall she not, Centaure? We'll make her a collegiate.

CENTAURE  Yes, faith, madam, and Mavis and she will set up a side.                                    60

TRUEWIT  Believe it, madam, and Mistress Mavis, she will sustain her part.

MAVIS  I'll tell you that when I have talked with her, and tried her.

HAUGHTY  Use her very civilly, Mavis.

MAVIS  So I will, madam.

MAVIS *walks apart with* EPICOENE

MOROSE  Blessed minute, that they would whisper thus ever.

TRUEWIT  In the meantime, madam, would but your ladyship help to vex him a little: you know his disease, talk to him about the wedding-ceremonies, or call for your gloves, or—                                    72

---

121, 123  chimney-sweepers . . . colliers: the least desirable customers, because probably the dirtiest

124  chance-medley: manslaughter, homicide by misadventure

2–3  Another flood: '*another* may mean "second", the first being the flood of Genesis, vii' (Holdsworth)

SD  *severally*: in turn

14  nomenclator: announcer of guests' names (with pun on 'clatter')

16–17  'tis decreed of me: judgement is passed on me and: if

21–2  steal a marriage: get married secretly

36–7  faculty . . . it: 'ability (to bear [sexual] burdens) if she has not learnt it already; taking up the sexual sense of *oppressed*, "ravished" (Latin *opprimere*)' (Holdsworth)

44  absolute: perfect
race: family

60  a side: a partnership in cards

HAUGHTY  Let me alone. Centaure, help me. Master
bridegroom, where are you?

MOROSE  Oh, it was too miraculously good to last!

HAUGHTY  We see no ensigns of a wedding here, no
character of a bride-ale: where be our scarfs, and our
gloves? I pray you give 'em us. Let's know your
bride's colours, and yours, at least.

CENTAURE  Alas, madam, he has provided none.      80

MOROSE  Had I known your ladyship's painter, I would.

HAUGHTY  He has given it you, Centaure, i' faith. But
do you hear, Master Morose, a jest will not absolve
you in this manner. You that have sucked the milk of
the court, and from thence have been brought up to
the very strong meats and wine of it; been a courtier
from the biggen to the night-cap (as we may say);
and you to offend in such a high point of ceremony
as this, and let your nuptials want all marks of
solemnity! How much plate have you lost today (if
you had but regarded your profit), what gifts, what
friends, through your mere rusticity?      92

MOROSE  Madam—

HAUGHTY  Pardon me, sir, I must insinuate your errors
to you. No gloves? No garters? No scarfs? No
epithalamium? No masque?

DAW  Yes, madam, I'll make an epithalamium, I
promised my mistress, I have begun it already: will
your ladyship hear it?

HAUGHTY  Ay, good Jack Daw.      100

MOROSE  Will it please your ladyship command a
chamber and be private with your friend? You shall
have your choice of rooms to retire to after: my whole
house is yours. I know it hath been your ladyship's
errand into the city at other times, however now you
have been unhappily diverted upon me; but I shall be
loth to break any honourable custom of your
ladyship's. And therefore, good madam—

EPICOENE  Come, you are a rude bridegroom, to
entertain ladies of honour in this fashion.      110

CENTAURE  He is a rude groom indeed.

---

73  Let me alone: i.e. leave it to me
76  ensigns: signs
77–8  scarfs . . . gloves: given to guests at weddings
79  colours: of the bride and groom, worn by their respective
friends (eds)
81  painter: cosmetician
82  given it you: i.e scored a point over you
86  strong meats: solid food
87  biggen: baby's bonnet
90  solemnity: ceremoniousness
92  mere rusticity: sheer uncouthness
95  garters: the bride's garters were competed for by the
young men and bridesmaids
96  epithalamium: wedding song in honour of bride and
groom
104  it: i.e. such an assignation
111  groom: a) bridegroom; b) servant

TRUEWIT  By that light, you deserve to be grafted, and
have your horns reach from one side of the island to
the other.—(*Aside to* MOROSE) Do not mistake me,
sir; I but speak this to give the ladies some heart
again, not for any malice to you.

MOROSE  Is this your bravo, ladies?

TRUEWIT  As God help me, if you utter such another
word, I'll take mistress bride in and begin to you in a
very sad cup, do you see? Go to, know your friends
and such as love you.      121

# Act III, scene vii

*Enter* CLERIMONT *with* MUSICIANS

CLERIMONT  By your leave, ladies. Do you want any
music? I have brought you variety of noises. Play, sirs,
all of you.      *Music of all sorts*

MOROSE  Oh, a plot, a plot, a plot, a plot upon me! This
day I shall be their anvil to work on, they will grate
me asunder. 'Tis worse than the noise of a saw.

CLERIMONT  No, they are hair, rosin, and guts. I can
give you the receipt.

TRUEWIT  Peace, boys.

CLERIMONT  Play, I say.      10

TRUEWIT  Peace, rascals. (*To* MOROSE) You see who's
your friend now, sir? Take courage, put on a martyr's
resolution. Mock down all their attemptings with
patience. 'Tis but a day, and I would suffer heroically.
Should an ass exceed me in fortitude? No. You betray
your infirmity with your hanging dull ears, and make
them insult: bear up bravely, and constantly.
(LA FOOLE *with* SERVANTS *passes over sewing the meat,
followed by* MISTESS OTTER) Look you here, sir, what
honour is done you unexpected by your nephew; a
wedding-dinner come, and a knight-sewer before it,
for the more reputation, and fine Mistress Otter,
your neighbour, in the rump, or tail of it.      22

MOROSE  Is that Gorgon, that Medusa come? Hide me,
hide me!

---

112  grafted: i.e. to have cuckold's horns grafted on to your head
117  bravo: hired bully
119–20  begin . . . cup: 'drink your health in a way most
unpleasant to you (cuckold you)' (Procter)
2  noises: bands of musicians (with suggestion of usual
sense); see II.vi.38
5  grate: grind; also, harass, irritate
7  hair . . . guts: to produce the sound from a violin:
horsehair for the bow, rosin to rub on it, and gut for the
strings
8  receipt: formula
15  ass: proverbial beast of endurance; also of stupidity
16  infirmity: weakness
17  insult: exult
SD  *sewing the meat*: directing the serving of the dishes
23  Medusa: the most fearsome of the Gorgons

TRUEWIT I warrant you, sir, she will not transform you. Look upon her with a good courage. Pray you entertain her and conduct your guests in. No? Mistress bride, will you entreat in the ladies? Your bridegroom is so shamefaced here—

EPICOENE Will it please your ladyship, madam? 30

HAUGHTY With the benefit of your company, mistress.

EPICOENE Servant, pray you perform your duties.

DAW And glad to be commanded, mistress.

CENTAURE How like you her wit, Mavis?

MAVIS Very prettily, absolutely well.

MISTRESS OTTER (*Trying to take precedence*) 'Tis my place.

MAVIS You shall pardon me, Mistress Otter.

MISTRESS OTTER Why, I am a collegiate.

MAVIS But not in ordinary. 40

MISTRESS OTTER But I am.

MAVIS We'll dispute that within. *Exit ladies with* DAW

CLERIMONT Would this had lasted a little longer.

TRUEWIT And that they had sent for the heralds. (*Enter* OTTER) Captain Otter, what news?

OTTER I have brought my bull, bear, and horse, in private, and yonder are the trumpeters without, and the drum, gentlemen. *The drum and trumpets sound*

MOROSE Oh, oh, oh! 49

OTTER And we will have a rouse in each of 'em, anon, for bold Britons, i' faith. *They sound again*

MOROSE Oh, oh, oh! *Exit* MOROSE

ALL Follow, follow, follow!

*Exeunt*

# Act IV, scene i

*Enter* TRUEWIT, CLERIMONT

TRUEWIT Was there ever poor bridegroom so tormented? Or man, indeed?

CLERIMONT I have not read of the like in the chronicles of the land.

TRUEWIT Sure, he cannot but go to a place of rest, after all this purgatory.

CLERIMONT He may presume it, I think.

TRUEWIT The spitting, the coughing, the laughter, the neezing, the farting, dancing, noise of the music, and her masculine and loud commanding, and urging the whole family, makes him think he has married a Fury.

CLERIMONT And she carries it up bravely.

TRUEWIT Ay, she takes any occasion to speak: that's the height on't.

CLERIMONT And how soberly Dauphine labours to satisfy him that it was none of his plot! 16

TRUEWIT And has almost brought him to the faith i' the article. (*Enter* DAUPHINE) Here he comes.— Where is he now? What's become of him, Dauphine?

DAUPHINE Oh, hold me up a little, I shall go away i' the jest else. He has got on his whole nest of night-caps, and locked himself up i' the top o' the house, as high as ever he can climb from the noise. I peeped in at a cranny, and saw him sitting over a cross-beam o' the roof, like him o' the saddler's horse in Fleet Street, upright; and he will sleep there. 26

CLERIMONT But where are your collegiates?

DAUPHINE Withdrawn with the bride in private.

TRUEWIT Oh, they are instructing her i' the college grammar. If she have grace with them, she knows all their secrets instantly.

CLERIMONT Methinks the Lady Haughty looks well today, for all my dispraise of her i' the morning. I think I shall come about to thee again, Truewit. 34

TRUEWIT Believe it, I told you right. Women ought to repair the losses time and years have made i' their features with dressings. And an intelligent woman, if she know by herself the least defect, will be most curious to hide it; and it becomes her. If she be short, let her sit much, lest when she stands, she be thought to sit. If she have an ill foot, let her wear her gown the longer, and her shoe the thinner. If a fat hand, and scald nails, let her carve the less, and act in gloves. If a sour breath, let her never discourse fasting, and always talk at her distance. If she have black and rugged teeth, let her offer the less at laughter, especially if she laugh wide, and open. 47

CLERIMONT Oh, you shall have some women, when they laugh, you would think they brayed, it is so rude, and—

TRUEWIT Ay, and others that will stalk i' their gait like

---

25 transform: i.e. to stone (see II.iv.16n)
29 shamefaced: bashful
40 in ordinary: see II.iii.98n
44 heralds: who decided questions of precedence
56 rouse: deep drink
9 neezing: sneezing
11 Fury: avenging female deity
12 carries . . . bravely: 'keeps it up splendidly' (Holdsworth)

14 height on't: best of it
17–18 faith . . . article: reference to Articles of Faith, the statements to which ministers of the Church of England have to subscribe
20–1 go . . . jest: die laughing
21 nest: set, in which the smaller fit inside the larger
25 saddler's horse: model horse and rider, outside a saddler's shop
30 have . . . them: in favour with them
34 come . . . thee: come round to your opinion
35–139 Truewit's comments on women derive from Ovid's *Ars Amatoria*, I, II and III
38 by: about
39 curious: careful
43 scald: scaly, scabbed
carve . . . act: both words meant 'gesture'
46 offer: attempt

an estrich, and take huge strides. I cannot endure such a sight. I love measure i' the feet and number i' the voice: they are gentlenesses that oft-times draw no less than the face. **55**

DAUPHINE How cam'st thou to study these creatures so exactly? I would thou wouldst make me a proficient.

TRUEWIT Yes, but you must leave to live i' your chamber then a month together upon *Amadis de Gaule*, or *Don Quixote*, as you are wont; and come abroad where the matter is frequent, to court, to tiltings, public shows, and feasts, to plays, and church sometimes: thither they come to show their new tires too, to see, and to be seen. In these places a man shall find whom to love, whom to play with, whom to touch once, whom to hold ever. The variety arrests his judgement. A wench to please a man comes not down dropping from the ceiling, as he lies on his back droning a tobacco-pipe. He must go where she is. **70**

DAUPHINE Yes, and be never the near.

TRUEWIT Out, heretic! That diffidence makes thee worthy it should be so.

CLERIMONT He says true to you, Dauphine.

DAUPHINE Why?

TRUEWIT A man should not doubt to overcome any woman. Think he can vanquish 'em, and he shall; for though they deny, their desire is to be tempted. Penelope herself cannot hold out long. Ostend, you saw, was taken at last. You must persever, and hold to your purpose. They would solicit us, but that they are afraid. Howsoever, they wish in their hearts we should solicit them. Praise 'em, flatter 'em, you shall never want eloquence, or trust; even the chastest

delight to feel themselves that way rubbed. With praises you must mix kisses too. If they take them, they'll take more. Though they strive, they would be overcome. **88**

CLERIMONT Oh, but a man must beware of force.

TRUEWIT It is to them an acceptable violence, and has oft-times the place of the greatest courtesy. She that might have been forced, and you let her go free without touching, though she then seem to thank you, will ever hate you after; and glad i' the face, is assuredly sad at the heart.

CLERIMONT But all women are not to be taken all ways. **97**

TRUEWIT 'Tis true. No more than all birds, or all fishes. If you appear learned to an ignorant wench, or jocund to a sad, or witty to a foolish, why, she presently begins to mistrust herself. You must approach them i' their own height, their own line: for the contrary makes many that fear to commit themselves to noble and worthy fellows, run into the embraces of a rascal. If she love wit, give verses, though you borrow 'em of a friend, or buy 'em, to have good. If valour, talk of your sword, and be frequent in the mention of quarrels, though you be staunch in fighting. If activity, be seen o' your barbary often, or leaping over stools, for the credit of your back. If she love good clothes or dressing, have your learned council about you every morning, your French tailor, barber, linener, *et cetera*. Let your powder, your glass, and your comb be your dearest acquaintance. Take more care for the ornament of your head, than the safety; and wish the commonwealth rather troubled, than a hair about you. That will take her. Then if she be covetous and craving, do you promise anything, and perform sparingly; so shall you keep her in appetite still. Seem as you would give, but be like a barren field that yields little, or unlucky dice to foolish and hoping gamesters. Let your gifts be slight, and dainty, rather than precious. Let cunning be above cost. Give

---

52 estrich: ostrich
53 measure: grace (in dancing)
   number: rhythm
54 gentlenesses: elegancies
   draw: attract
57 proficient: learner
58 leave: cease
59–60 *Amadis . . . Quixote*: chivalric romances despised as frivolous by Jonson
61 matter is frequent: material is plentiful
62 tiltings: jousts (by now, mock-combats staged for courtly entertainment)
69 droning: sucking (as on a bagpipe)
71 near: nearer
78 deny: refuse
79 Penelope: wife of Odysseus, who resisted her suitors for twenty years until her husband returned
   Ostend: captured by the Spanish in 1604 after a three-year siege
80 persever: persevere
84 want . . . trust: i.e. lack eloquence, or lack trust from your audience

---

85 rubbed: annoyed
87 strive: struggle
   would be: wish to be
92 and: if
101 presently: immediately
102 height . . . line: high and low parries (in fencing)
109 staunch: cautious
    activity: exercise
    barbary: horse
111 back: 'a "good back" implies sexual prowess' (Holdsworth)
116 safety: i.e. of your head
123–4 Let . . . cost: let your ingenuity be greater than your expense

cherries at time of year, or apricots; and say they were sent you out o' the country, though you bought 'em in Cheapside. Admire her tires; like her in all fashions; compare her in every habit to some deity; invent excellent dreams to flatter her, and riddles; or, if she be a great one, perform always the second parts to her: like what she likes, praise whom she praises; and fail not to make the household and servants yours, yea, the whole family, and salute 'em by their names ('tis but light cost if you can purchase 'em so) and make her physician your pensioner, and her chief woman. Nor will it be out of your gain to make love to her too, so she follow, not usher, her lady's pleasure. All blabbing is taken away when she comes to be a part of the crime. **139**

DAUPHINE On what courtly lap hast thou late slept, to come forth so sudden and absolute a courtling?

TRUEWIT Good faith, I should rather question you, that are so hearkening after these mysteries. I begin to suspect your diligence, Dauphine. Speak, art thou in love in earnest?

DAUPHINE Yes, by my troth, am I; 'twere ill dissembling before thee.

TRUEWIT With which of 'em, I pray thee?

DAUPHINE With all the collegiates.

CLERIMONT Out on thee! We'll keep you at home, believe it, i' the stable, and you be such a stallion. **151**

TRUEWIT No. I like him well. Men should love wisely, and all women: some one for the face, and let her please the eye; another for the skin, and let her please the touch; a third for the voice, and let her please the ear; and where the objects mix, let the senses so too. Thou wouldst think it strange, if I should make 'em all in love with thee afore night!

DAUPHINE I would say thou hadst the best philtre i' the world, and couldst do more than Madam Medea, or Doctor Forman. **161**

TRUEWIT If I do not, let me play the mountebank for my meat while I live, and the bawd for my drink.

DAUPHINE So be it, I say.

---

125 at time of year: in season
128 habit: outfit
130 a great one: of high rank
    second parts: supporting roles
135 physician your pensioner: 'i.e. buy his support' (Holdsworth)
136 woman: maidservant
    out of your gain: outside your interests
141 courtling: courtier
143 hearkening: enquiring
159 philtre: love potion
160 Medea: magician, who helped Jason win the Golden Fleece, and restored youth to his father, Aeson
161 Doctor Forman: Simon Forman (1552–1611) was a noted London astrologer, quack and supplier of love potions

# Act IV, scene ii

*Enter* OTTER, DAW, LA FOOLE

OTTER Oh lord, gentlemen, how my knights and I have missed you here!

CLERIMONT Why, captain, what service, what service?

OTTER To see me bring up my bull, bear, and horse to fight.

DAW Yes, faith, the captain says we shall be his dogs to bait 'em.

DAUPHINE A good employment.

TRUEWIT Come on, let's see a course then.

LA FOOLE I am afraid my cousin will be offended if she come. **11**

OTTER Be afraid of nothing. Gentlemen, I have placed the drum and the trumpets, and one to give 'em the sign when you are ready. (*Brings out the cups*) Here's my bull for myself, and my bear for Sir John Daw, and my horse for Sir Amorous. Now, set your foot to mine, and yours to his, and—

LA FOOLE Pray God my cousin come not.

OTTER Saint George and Saint Andrew, fear no cousins. Come, sound, sound! *Et rauco strepuerunt cornua cantu.* **21**

*Drum and trumpets sound. They drink*

TRUEWIT Well said, captain, i' faith; well fought at the bull.

CLERIMONT Well held at the bear.

TRUEWIT 'Low, 'low, captain!

DAUPHINE Oh, the horse has kicked off his dog already.

LA FOOLE I cannot drink it, as I am a knight.

TRUEWIT Gods so! Off with his spurs, somebody.

LA FOOLE It goes again my conscience. My cousin will be angry with it. **31**

DAW I ha' done mine.

TRUEWIT You fought high and fair, Sir John.

CLERIMONT At the head.

DAUPHINE Like an excellent bear-dog.

CLERIMONT (*Aside to* DAW) You take no notice of the business, I hope.

DAW (*Aside to* CLERIMONT) Not a word, sir, you see we are jovial.

---

3 service: 'in the military sense: operation' (Holdsworth)
4–84 the metaphors here are drawn from bull- and bear-baiting
9 course: a) drinking round; b) bout between dogs and baited animals
16–17 set . . . mine: stance taken in drinking bouts
19–20 fear no cousins: adapting the proverb 'Fear no colours'
20–1 *Et . . . cantu*: 'And the trumpets sounded with hoarse note' (Virgil, *Aeneid*, VIII, 2)
22 Well said: well done
25 'Low: a cry to urge on dogs
19 Off . . . spurs: i.e. strip him of his knighthood

OTTER  Sir Amorous, you must not equivocate. It must be pulled down, for all my cousin. 41

CLERIMONT  (*Aside to* LA FOOLE) 'Sfoot, if you take not your drink, they'll think you are discontented with something; you'll betray all, if you take the least notice.

LA FOOLE  (*Aside to* CLERIMONT) Not I, I'll both drink and talk then.

OTTER  You must pull the horse on his knees, Sir Amorous. Fear no cousins. *Jacta est alea.*

TRUEWIT  (*Aside to* DAUPHINE *and* CLERIMONT) Oh, now he's in his vein, and bold. The least hint given him of his wife now will make him rail desperately. 52

CLERIMONT  Speak to him of her.

TRUEWIT  Do you, and I'll fetch her to the hearing of it.
*Exit*

DAUPHINE  Captain he-Otter, your she-Otter is coming, your wife.

OTTER  Wife! Buz. *Titivilitium.* There's no such thing in nature. I confess, gentlemen, I have a cook, a laundress, a house-drudge, that serves my necessary turns, and goes under that title; but he's an ass that will be so uxorious to tie his affections to one circle. Come, the name dulls appetite. Here, replenish again: another bout. Wives are nasty, sluttish animals. *Fills the cups*

DAUPHINE  Oh, captain! 65

OTTER  As ever the earth bare, *tribus verbis.* Where's Master Truewit?

DAW  He's slipped aside, sir.

CLERIMONT  But you must drink and be jovial.

DAW  Yes, give it me. 70

LA FOOLE  And me too.

DAW  Let's be jovial.

LA FOOLE  As jovial as you will.

OTTER  Agreed. Now you shall ha' the bear, cousin, and Sir John Daw the horse, and I'll ha' the bull still. Sound, Tritons o' the Thames. *Nunc est bibendum, nunc pede libero—*

MOROSE *speaks from above, the trumpets sounding*

MOROSE  Villains, murderers, sons of the earth, and traitors, what do you there?

CLERIMONT  Oh, now the trumpets have waked him, we shall have his company. 81

OTTER  A wife is a scurvy clogdogdo; an unlucky thing, a very foresaid bear-whelp, without any good fashion or breeding: *mala bestia.*

*His wife is brought out to hear him by* TRUEWIT

DAUPHINE  Why did you marry one then, captain?

OTTER  A pox—I married with six thousand pound, I. I was in love with that. I ha' not kissed my Fury these forty weeks.

CLERIMONT  The more to blame you, captain.

TRUEWIT  Nay, Mistress Otter, hear him a little first. 90

OTTER  She has a breath worse than my grandmother's, *profecto.*

MISTRESS OTTER  Oh treacherous liar! Kiss me, sweet Master Truewit, and prove him a slandering knave.

TRUEWIT  I'll rather believe you, lady.

OTTER  And she has a peruke that's like a pound of hemp made up in shoe-threads.

MISTRESS OTTER  Oh viper, mandrake!

OTTER  A most vile face! And yet she spends me forty pound a year in mercury and hogs' bones. All her teeth were made i' the Blackfriars, both her eyebrows i' the Strand, and her hair in Silver Street. Every part o' the town owns a piece of her. 103

MISTRESS OTTER  I cannot hold.

OTTER  She takes herself asunder still when she goes to bed, into some twenty boxes; and about next day noon is put together again, like a great German clock; and so comes forth and rings a tedious larum to the whole house, and then is quiet again for an hour, but for her quarters. Ha' you done me right, gentlemen? 111

MISTRESS OTTER  No, sir, I'll do you right with my quarters, with my quarters.

*She falls upon him and beats him*

OTTER  Oh hold, good princess!

TRUEWIT  Sound, sound. *Drum and trumpets sound*

CLERIMONT  A battle, a battle.

---

49  *Jacta est alea*: 'The die is cast': Caesar's words on crossing the Rubicon

57  Buz: exclamation of impatience
*Titivilitium*: a vile thing of no value (from Plautus, *Casina*, 347)

60–1  ass . . . circle: 'like a donkey driving a rotary mill' (Holdsworth); with pun on 'circle' meaning female genitalia

66  *tribus verbis*: in three words; i.e. briefly

76  Tritons: classical sea gods who blew shell-trumpets

76–7  *Nunc . . . libero*: 'Now is the time for drinking, now with free foot . . .' (Horace, *Odes*, I.xxxvii.1)

78  sons of earth: bastards (Latin *terrae filii*); base-born

82  clogdogdo: obscure; some eds suggest 'clog fit for a dog' ('clog' meaning weight placed around dog's neck when training it)

83  very foresaid: truly predictable (eds)

84  *mala bestia*: evil beast

92  *profecto*: truly

98  mandrake: poisonous plant whose root was said to resemble a human form; a common term of abuse

100  mercury and hogs' bones: used in cosmetics

100–8  derived from Martial, *Epigrams*, IX.xxxvii.1–6

107–8  German clock: i.e. always in need of repair; the comparison is made frequently in Jacobean drama

108  larum: alarm

110  quarters: a) quarter hours, b) living quarters
done me right: 'matched me drink for drink (a set phrase)' (Holdsworth)

113  quarters: blows (in fencing)

BEN JONSON

MISTRESS OTTER You notorious stinkardly bearward, does my breath smell?

OTTER Under correction, dear princess. Look to my bear, and my horse, gentlemen.                           120

MISTRESS OTTER Do I want teeth, and eyebrows, thou bull-dog?

TRUEWIT Sound, sound still.               *They sound again*

OTTER No, I protest, under correction—

MISTRESS OTTER Ay, now you are under correction, you protest; but you did not protest before correction, sir. Thou Judas, to offer to betray thy princess! I'll make thee an example—

MOROSE *descends with a long sword*

MOROSE I will have no such examples in my house, Lady Otter.                                                    130

MISTRESS OTTER Ah—

MOROSE Mistress Mary Ambree, your examples are dangerous. (*She runs off, followed by* DAW *and* LA FOOLE) Rogues, hell-hounds, Stentors, out of my doors, you sons of noise and tumult, begot on an ill May Day, or when the galley-foist is afloat to Westminster! (*Drives out the* MUSICIANS) A trumpeter could not be conceived but then!

DAUPHINE What ails you, sir?                                 139

MOROSE They have rent my roof, walls, and all my windows asunder, with their brazen throats.     *Exit*

TRUEWIT Best follow him, Dauphine.

DAUPHINE So I will.                                          *Exit*

CLERIMONT Where's Daw and La Foole?

OTTER They are both run away, sir. Good gentlemen, help to pacify my princess, and speak to the great ladies for me. Now must I go lie with the bears this fortnight, and keep out o' the way, till my peace be made, for this scandal she has taken. Did you not see my bull-head, gentlemen?                                    150

CLERIMONT Is't not on, captain?

TRUEWIT No:—(*Aside to* CLERIMONT) but he may make a new one, by that is on.

OTTER Oh, here 'tis. And you come over, gentlemen,

and ask for Tom Otter, we'll go down to Ratcliffe, and have a course i' faith, for all these disasters. There's *bona spes* left.

TRUEWIT Away, captain, get off while you are well.

*Exit* OTTER

CLERIMONT I am glad we are rid of him.                       159

TRUEWIT You had never been, unless we had put his wife upon him. His humour is as tedious at last, as it was ridiculous at first.

# Act IV, scene iii

*Enter* HAUGHTY, MISTRESS OTTER, MAVIS, DAW, LA FOOLE, CENTAURE, EPICOENE. TRUEWIT *and* CLERIMONT *move aside and observe*

HAUGHTY We wondered why you shrieked so, Mistress Otter.

MISTRESS OTTER Oh God, madam, he came down with a huge long naked weapon in both his hands, and looked so dreadfully! Sure he's beside himself.

MAVIS Why, what made you there, Mistress Otter?

MISTRESS OTTER Alas, Mistress Mavis, I was chastising my subject, and thought nothing of him.

DAW (*To* EPICOENE) Faith, mistress, you must do so too. Learn to chastise. Mistress Otter corrects her husband so, he dares not speak but under correction.

LA FOOLE And with his hat off to her: 'twould do you good to see.                                               13

HAUGHTY In sadness, 'tis good and mature counsel: practise it, Morose. I'll call you Morose still now, as I call Centaure and Mavis: we four will be all one.

CENTAURE And you'll come to the college and live with us?

HAUGHTY Make him give milk and honey.

MAVIS Look how you manage him at first, you shall have him ever after.                                       21

CENTAURE Let him allow you your coach and four horses, your woman, your chambermaid, your page, your gentleman-usher, your French cook, and four grooms.

HAUGHTY And go with us to Bedlam, to the china-houses, and to the Exchange.

CENTAURE It will open the gate to your fame.

---

119 Under correction: see III.i.10n
124 protest: avow
132 Mary Ambree: according to a ballad, she disguised herself as a soldier and took part in the siege of Ghent in 1584
134 Stentors: Stentor was a Greek warrior in the Trojan War, whose voice was as powerful as those of fifty men
135–6 ill May Day: reference to the May Day riot of 1517, though any May Day, with its noisy festivities, would have been a torment to Morose
136 galley-foist: state barge which annually took the Lord Mayor to Westminster to be sworn in; again accompanied by noisy celebrations
149 scandal: offence
150 bull-head: cover for the cup
153 by that: by copying the one that is on: i.e. Otter's own head, with its cuckold's horns, would provide an apt model for a replacement

155 Ratcliffe: suburb of London outside the jurisdiction of the city authorities; hence, a refuge for rogues
156 course: see IV.ii.9n
157 *bona spes*: good hope
6 made you: were you doing
14 In sadness: seriously
15 Morose: i.e. the masculine form of address
19 milk and honey: as found in the Promised Land; i.e. everything you could want
20 manage: handle (as of horses)
26–7 china-houses . . . Exchange: see I.iii.35n, 40n

HAUGHTY Here's Centaure has immortalized herself, with taming of her wild male. 30

MAVIS Ay, she has done the miracle of the kingdom.

EPICOENE But ladies, do you count it lawful to have such plurality of servants, and do 'em all graces?

HAUGHTY Why not? Why should women deny their favours to men? Are they the poorer, or the worse?

DAW Is the Thames the less for the dyer's water, mistress?

LA FOOLE Or a torch, for lighting many torches?

TRUEWIT (*Aside*) Well said, La Foole; what a new one he has got! 40

CENTAURE They are empty losses women fear in this kind.

HAUGHTY Besides, ladies should be mindful of the approach of age, and let no time want his due use. The best of our days pass first.

MAVIS We are rivers that cannot be called back, madam: she that now excludes her lovers may live to lie a forsaken beldame, in a frozen bed.

CENTAURE 'Tis true, Mavis; and who will wait on us to coach then? Or write, or tell us the news then? Make anagrams of our names, and invite us to the cockpit, and kiss our hands all the play-time, and draw their weapons for our honours? 53

HAUGHTY Not one.

DAW Nay, my mistress is not altogether unintelligent of these things; here be in presence have tasted of her favours.

CLERIMONT (*Aside*) What a neighing hobby-horse is this!

EPICOENE But not with intent to boast 'em again, servant. And have you those excellent receipts, madam, to keep yourselves from bearing of children?

HAUGHTY Oh yes, Morose. How should we maintain our youth and beauty else? Many births of a woman make her old, as many crops make the earth barren.

## Act IV, scene iv

*Enter* MOROSE, DAUPHINE; *they speak apart*

MOROSE Oh my cursed angel, that instructed me to this fate!

DAUPHINE Why, sir?

MOROSE That I should be seduced by so foolish a devil as a barber will make!

DAUPHINE I would I had been worthy, sir, to have partaken your counsel; you should never have trusted it to such a minister.

MOROSE Would I could redeem it with the loss of an eye, nephew, a hand, or any other member. 10

DAUPHINE Marry, God forbid, sir, that you should geld yourself, to anger your wife.

MOROSE So it would rid me of her! And that I did supererogatory penance, in a belfry, at Westminster Hall, i' the cockpit, at the fall of a stag, the Tower Wharf (what place is there else?), London Bridge, Paris Garden, Billingsgate, when the noises are at their height and loudest. Nay, I would sit out a play that were nothing but fights at sea, drum, trumpet, and target! 20

DAUPHINE I hope there shall be no such need, sir. Take patience, good uncle. This is but a day, and 'tis well worn too now.

MOROSE Oh, 'twill be so forever, nephew, I foresee it, forever. Strife and tumult are the dowry that comes with a wife.

TRUEWIT I told you so, sir, and you would not believe me.

MOROSE Alas, do not rub those wounds, Master Truewit, to blood again; 'twas my negligence. Add not affliction to affliction. I have perceived the effect of it, too late, in Madam Otter. 32

EPICOENE (*Coming forward*) How do you, sir?

MOROSE Did you ever hear a more unnecessary question? As if she did not see! Why, I do as you see, empress, empress.

EPICOENE You are not well, sir! You look very ill! Something has distempered you.

MOROSE Oh horrible, monstrous impertinencies! Would not one of these have served? Do you think, sir? Would not one of these have served? 41

---

32–64 derived from Ovid, *Ars Amatoria*, III

36–8 Is the . . . torches: clichés, here with sexual connotations ('in sexual slang *water* meant semen, *torch* penis, and *burn* infect with venereal disease' (Holdsworth))

39 new one: i.e. original turn of phrase

48 beldame: hag

51 cockpit: probably the Cockpit, a small private theatre in Whitehall, where cock-fights as well as plays were staged (see Introduction); with a sexual innuendo

58 hobby-horse: buffoon

60 receipts: formulas, prescriptions

1 instructed: directed

14 supererogatory: beyond the call of duty

14–15 Westminster Hall: had shops and law courts, and therefore crowds

15 cockpit: see IV.iii.51n
  fall of a stag: accompanied by barking of hounds and sounding of horns

15–16 Tower Wharf: see I.ii.16n

17 Paris Garden: a baiting house
  Billingsgate: food market; its fishwives made it a byword for raucousness

18–19 play . . . sea: e.g. Heywood and Rowley's *Fortune by Land and Sea* (1609), a romance drama of the kind despised by Jonson

20 target: shield

38 distempered: upset; also, 'unbalanced' (with regard to the humours, or fluids, of which the body was taken to be composed)

39 impertinencies: irrelevances

TRUEWIT Yes, sir, but these are but notes of female
kindness, sir; certain tokens that she has a voice, sir.

MOROSE Oh, is't so? Come, and't be no otherwise—
what say you?

EPICOENE How do you feel yourself, sir?

MOROSE Again that!

TRUEWIT Nay, look you, sir: you would be friends with
your wife upon unconscionable terms, her silence—

EPICOENE They say you are run mad, sir.                    50

MOROSE Not for love, I assure you, of you; do you see?

EPICOENE Oh lord, gentlemen! Lay hold on him for
God's sake. What shall I do? Who's his physician
(can you tell?) that knows the state of his body best,
that I might send for him? Good sir, speak. I'll send
for one of my doctors else.

MOROSE What, to poison me, that I might die intestate
and leave you possessed of all?

EPICOENE Lord, how idly he talks, and how his eyes
sparkle! He looks green about the temples! Do you
see what blue spots he has?                               61

CLERIMONT Ay, it's melancholy.

EPICOENE Gentlemen, for heaven's sake counsel me.
Ladies! Servant, you have read Pliny and Paracelsus:
ne'er a word now to comfort a poor gentlewoman? Ay
me! What fortune had I to marry a distracted man?

DAW I'll tell you, mistress—

TRUEWIT (Aside) How rarely she holds it up!

MOROSE What mean you, gentlemen?

EPICOENE What will you tell me, servant?                  70

DAW The disease in Greek is called μανία, in Latin
insania, furor, vel ecstasis melancholica, that is, egressio,
when a man ex melancholico evadit fanaticus.

MOROSE Shall I have a lecture read upon me alive?

DAW But he may be but phreneticus yet, mistress, and
phrenetis is only delirium, or so—

EPICOENE Ay, that is for the disease, servant; but what
is this to the cure? We are sure enough of the disease.

MOROSE Let me go!                                         79

TRUEWIT Why, we'll entreat her to hold her peace, sir.

MOROSE Oh no. Labour not to stop her. She is like a
conduit-pipe, that will gush out with more force
when she opens again.

HAUGHTY I'll tell you, Morose, you must talk divinity
to him altogether, or moral philosophy.

LA FOOLE Ay, and there's an excellent book of moral
philosophy, madam, of Reynard the Fox, and all the
beasts, called Doni's Philosophy.

CENTAURE There is, indeed, Sir Amorous La Foole.

MOROSE Oh misery!                                         90

LA FOOLE I have read it, my Lady Centaure, all over to
my cousin here.

MISTRESS OTTER Ay, and 'tis a very good book as any
is, of the moderns.

DAW Tut, he must have Seneca read to him, and
Plutarch and the ancients; the moderns are not for
this disease.

CLERIMONT Why, you discommended them too today,
Sir John.

DAW Ay, in some cases; but in these they are best, and
Aristotle's Ethics.                                      101

MAVIS Say you so, Sir John? I think you are deceived:
you took it upon trust.

HAUGHTY Where's Trusty, my woman? I'll end this
difference. I prithee, Otter, call her. Her father and
mother were both mad when they put her to me.

                                          Exit MISTRESS OTTER

MOROSE I think so.—Nay, gentlemen, I am tame. This
is but an exercise, I know, a marriage ceremony,
which I must endure.

HAUGHTY And one of 'em (I know not which) was
cured with The Sick Man's Salve; and the other with
Greene's Groatsworth of Wit.                             112

TRUEWIT A very cheap cure, madam.

HAUGHTY Ay, it's very feasible.

---

42  notes: signs
43  kindness: a) concern b) behaviour natural to her kind (i.e.
    women)
49  unconscionable: unreasonable, unjust
59–61  how idly . . . he has: 'symptoms of madness comically
    ascribed to Menaechmus of Epidamnus in Plautus's
    Menaechmi, 829–30' (Procter)
62  melancholy: irritability; also, in original Greek sense,
    frenzy, madness (eds)
64  Pliny: AD 23–79; a Roman, author of Historia Naturalis
    Paracelsus: 1493–154; Swiss scientist and authority on
    medicine
71  μανία: mania, madness
72–3  insania . . . fanaticus: 'madness . . . insanity, frenzy, or
    melancholic ecstasy . . . . a going out of one's mind . . .
    from a state of melancholy becomes mad'
74  Shall I . . . alive?: i.e. shall I be treated like a cadaver in
    an anatomy class whilst I'm still alive?
75  phreneticus: suffering from phrenitis: inflammation of the
    brain
76  delirium: temporary mental disturbance

85  altogether: uninterruptedly
88  Doni's Philosophy: collection of oriental beast fables,
    translated from Antonio Francesco Doni's Italian version
    into English by Sir Thomas North as The Moral
    Philosophy of Doni (1570); the fable of Reynard the Fox is
    not included
106  put her to me: put her in my charge
108  exercise: a) test, trial, as of saint or martyr; b)
    performance of a ceremony; c) training, as of an animal
111  The Sick Man's Salve: popular religious tract by Thomas
    Becon, urging patience and humility in times of illness;
    seventeen editions appeared between 1561 and 1632
112  Greene's . . . Wit: dramatist Robert Greene's popular
    confessional and admonitory pamphlet of 1592, written
    on his death-bed
113  cheap: 'a groat (the cost of the pamphlet) = fourpence'
    (Procter)

*Enter* MISTRESS OTTER *with* TRUSTY

MISTRESS OTTER  My lady called for you, Mistress
  Trusty; you must decide a controversy.
HAUGHTY  Oh, Trusty, which was it you said, your
  father or your mother, that was cured with *The Sick
  Man's Salve*?
TRUSTY  My mother, madam, with the *Salve*.          120
TRUEWIT  Then it was The Sick Woman's Salve.
TRUSTY  And my father with the *Groatsworth of Wit*.
  But there was other means used: we had a preacher
  that would preach folk asleep still; and so they were
  prescribed to go to church, by an old woman that was
  their physician, thrice a week—
EPICOENE  To sleep?
TRUSTY  Yes, forsooth; and every night they read
  themselves asleep on those books.
EPICOENE  Good faith, it stands with great reason.
  I would I knew where to procure those books.       131
MOROSE  Oh.
LA FOOLE  I can help you with one of 'em, Mistress
  Morose, the *Groatsworth of Wit*.
EPICOENE  But I shall disfurnish you, Sir Amorous; can
  you spare it?
LA FOOLE  Oh, yes, for a week or so; I'll read it myself
  to him.
EPICOENE  No, I must do that, sir; that must be my
  office.                                            140
MOROSE  Oh, oh!
EPICOENE  Sure, he would do well enough, if he could
  sleep.
MOROSE  No, I should do well enough if you could
  sleep. Have I no friend that will make her drunk? Or
  give her a little laudanum, or opium?
TRUEWIT  Why, sir, she talks ten times worse in her sleep.
MOROSE  How!
CLERIMONT  Do you not know that, sir? Never ceases
  all night.                                         150
TRUEWIT  And snores like a porcpisce.
MOROSE  Oh, redeem me, fate, redeem me, fate! For
  how many causes may a man be divorced, nephew?
DAUPHINE  I know not truly, sir.
TRUEWIT  Some divine must resolve you in that, sir, or
  canon lawyer.
MOROSE  I will not rest, I will not think of any other
  hope or comfort, till I know.
                    *Exeunt* MOROSE *and* DAUPHINE
CLERIMONT  Alas, poor man.
TRUEWIT  You'll make him mad indeed, ladies, if you
  pursue this.                                       161
HAUGHTY  No, we'll let him breathe, now, a quarter of

an hour or so.
CLERIMONT  By my faith, a large truce.
HAUGHTY  Is that his keeper, that is gone with him?
DAW  It is his nephew, madam.
LA FOOLE  Sir Dauphine Eugenie.
CENTAURE  He looks like a very pitiful knight—
DAW  As can be. This marriage has put him out of all.
LA FOOLE  He has not a penny in his purse, madam—
DAW  He is ready to cry all this day.                171
LA FOOLE  A very shark, he set me i' the nick t'other
  night at primero.
TRUEWIT  (*Aside*) How these swabbers talk!
CLERIMONT  (*Aside*) Ay, Otter's wine has swelled their
  humours above a spring-tide.
HAUGHTY  Good Morose, let's go in again. I like your
  couches exceeding well: we'll go lie, and talk there.
EPICOENE  I wait on you, madam.                      179
      *Exeunt all but* EPICOENE, TRUEWIT, CLERIMONT
TRUEWIT  'Slight, I will have 'em as silent as signs, and
  their posts too, ere I ha' done. Do you hear, lady
  bride? I pray thee now, as thou art a noble wench,
  continue this discourse of Dauphine within; but
  praise him exceedingly. Magnify him with all the
  height of affection thou canst (I have some purpose
  in't) and but beat off these two rooks, Jack Daw and
  his fellow, with any discontentment hither, and I'll
  honour thee forever.
EPICOENE  I was about it, here. It angered me to the
  soul to hear 'em begin to talk so malapert.        190
TRUEWIT  Pray thee perform it, and thou winn'st me an
  idolater to thee everlasting.
EPICOENE  Will you go in, and hear me do it?
TRUEWIT  No, I'll stay here. Drive 'em out of your
  company, 'tis all I ask; which cannot be any way
  better done than by extolling Dauphine, whom they
  have so slighted.
EPICOENE  I warrant you: you shall expect one of 'em
  presently.                                  *Exit*
CLERIMONT  What a cast of kastrils are these, to hawk
  after ladies thus?                               201
TRUEWIT  Ay, and strike at such an eagle as Dauphine.
CLERIMONT  He will be mad when we tell him. Here he
  comes.

---

124  still: always
135  disfurnish: deprive
151  porcpisce: porpoise (Latin *porcus piscis*, pig fish)
156  canon lawyer: specialises in ecclesiastical law

165  keeper: as if he were a lunatic
172  shark: cheat
     set . . . nick: unclear; Holdsworth suggests it means
     'cleaned me out', with La Foole muddling terms from
     Primero (a card game) with hazard (a dice game): with
     'set' meaning bet against, and 'nick' being the winning
     score in hazard
174  swabbers: low fellows
187  discontentment: annoyance
190  malapert: impudently
200  cast of kastrils: pair of kestrels. 'Kastril' was a term of
     contempt; see I.iv.83n

# Act IV, scene v

*Enter* DAUPHINE

CLERIMONT  Oh sir, you are welcome.

TRUEWIT  Where's thine uncle?

DAUPHINE  Run out o' doors in's night-caps, to talk
with a casuist about his divorce. It works admirably.

TRUEWIT  Thou wouldst ha' said so, and thou hadst
been here! The ladies have laughed at thee, most
comically, since thou went'st, Dauphine.

CLERIMONT  And asked if thou wert thine uncle's
keeper?                                                      9

TRUEWIT  And the brace of baboons answered yes, and
said thou wert a pitiful poor fellow, and didst live
upon posts; and hadst nothing but three suits of
apparel, and some few benevolences that lords ga'
thee to fool to 'em, and swagger.

DAUPHINE  Let me not live, I'll beat 'em. I'll bind 'em
both to grand madam's bed-posts and have 'em
baited with monkeys.

TRUEWIT  Thou shalt not need, they shall be beaten to
thy hand, Dauphine. I have an execution to serve
upon 'em, I warrant thee, shall serve; trust my plot. 20

DAUPHINE  Ay, you have many plots! So you had one,
to make all the wenches in love with me.

TRUEWIT  Why, if I do not yet afore night, as near as
'tis; and that they do not every one invite thee, and be
ready to scratch for thee, take the mortgage of my
wit.

CLERIMONT  'Fore God, I'll be his witness; thou shalt
have it, Dauphine; thou shalt be his fool forever if
thou dost not.                                              29

TRUEWIT  Agreed. Perhaps 'twill be the better estate.
Do you observe this gallery, or rather lobby, indeed?
Here are a couple of studies, at each end one: here
will I act such a tragicomedy between the Guelphs
and the Ghibellines, Daw and La Foole—which of
'em comes out first will I seize on (you two shall be
the chorus behind the arras, and whip out between

---

the acts and speak). If I do not make 'em keep the
peace for this remnant of the day, if not of the year, I
have failed once—I hear Daw coming: hide, and do
not laugh, for God's sake.                                 40

DAUPHINE *and* CLERIMONT *hide*

*Enter* DAW

DAW  Which is the way into the garden, trow?

TRUEWIT  Oh, Jack Daw! I am glad I have met with
you. In good faith, I must have this matter go no
further between you. I must ha' it taken up.

DAW  What matter, sir? Between whom?

TRUEWIT  Come, you disguise it—Sir Amorous and
you. If you love me, Jack, you shall make use of your
philosophy now, for this once, and deliver me your
sword. This is not the wedding the centaurs were at,
though there be a she-one here. The bride has
entreated me I will see no blood shed at her bridal;
you saw her whisper me erewhile.          *Takes his sword*

DAW  As I hope to finish Tacitus, I intend no murder. 53

TRUEWIT  Do you not wait for Sir Amorous?

DAW  Not I, by my knighthood.

TRUEWIT  And your scholarship too?

DAW  And my scholarship too.

TRUEWIT  Go to, then I return you your sword, and ask
you mercy; but put it not up, for you will be
assaulted. I understood that you had apprehended it,
and walked here to brave him; and that you had held
your life contemptible, in regard of your honour.     62

DAW  No, no, no such thing, I assure you. He and I
parted now as good friends as could be.

TRUEWIT  Trust not you to that visor. I saw him since
dinner with another face: I have known many men in
my time vexed with losses, with deaths, and with
abuses, but so offended a wight as Sir Amorous did I
never see, or read of. For taking away his guests, sir,
today, that's the cause; and he declares it behind your
back, with such threat'nings and contempts—he said
to Dauphine you were the arrant'st ass—          72

DAW  Ay, he may say his pleasure.

---

4  casuist: theologian who resolves cases of conscience

7  comically: derisively; also, in a comical manner

12  upon posts: by running errands
three suits: see III.i.41–2n

18–19  to thy hand: for you

19  execution: legal writ

25  scratch: fight

33  tragicomedy: Holdsworth notes that this was a new form
of drama, introduced by Beaumont and Fletcher at
around this time; the suggestion is that such a hybrid,
unclassical form deserves principal actors like Daw and
La Foole

33–4  Guelphs . . . Ghibellines: rival political factions in
medieval Italy

36  arras: thick tapestry, hanging across a recess at the back
of the stage

41  trow: do you think

42–3  compare the ensuing trick on Daw and La Foole with
the duel engineered by Sir Toby Belch between the
reluctant antagonists Viola and Sir Andrew Aguecheek
in *Twelfth Night* (1601), III.ii and III.iv

44  taken up: made up

49  This . . . at: at the marriage of Peirithous and
Hippodamia, a drunken centaur's attempt to rape the
bride resulted in a bloody battle

50  she-one: there were no female centaurs in classical myth

53  Tacitus: prolific Roman historian

59  put it not up: do not sheathe it

65  visor: mask

68  wight: man (archaic)

70  cause: subject of the dispute

TRUEWIT And swears you are so protested a coward
that he knows you will never do him any manly or
single right, and therefore he will take his course.

DAW I'll give him any satisfaction, sir—but fighting.

TRUEWIT Ay, sir, but who knows what satisfaction he'll
take? Blood he thirsts for, and blood he will have;
and whereabouts on you he will have it, who knows,
but himself?                                                  81

DAW I pray you, Master Truewit, be you a mediator.

TRUEWIT Well, sir, conceal yourself then in this study
till I return. (*He puts him up behind a door*) Nay, you
must be content to be locked in; for, for mine own
reputation, I would not have you seen to receive a
public disgrace, while I have the matter in managing.
Gods so, here he comes: keep your breath close, that
he do not hear you sigh.—In good faith, Sir
Amorous, he is not this way; I pray you be merciful,
do not murder him; he is a Christian as good as you;
you are armed as if you sought a revenge on all his
race. Good Dauphine, get him away from this place.
I never knew a man's choler so high but he would
speak to his friends, he would hear reason.—Jack
Daw. Jack Daw! Asleep?                                        96

DAW Is he gone, Master Truewit?

TRUEWIT Ay, did you hear him?

DAW Oh God, yes.

TRUEWIT (*Aside*) What a quick ear fear has!               100

DAW (*Coming out*) But is he so armed, as you say?

TRUEWIT Armed? Did you ever see a fellow set out to
take possession?

DAW Ay, sir.

TRUEWIT That may give you some light to conceive of
him; but 'tis nothing to the principal. Some false
brother i' the house has furnished him strangely. Or,
if it were out o' the house, it was Tom Otter.

DAW Indeed, he's a captain, and his wife is his
kinswoman.                                                   110

TRUEWIT He has got somebody's old two-hand sword,
to mow you off at the knees. And that sword hath
spawned such a dagger!—But then he is so hung with
pikes, halberds, petronels, calivers, and muskets, that
he looks like a justice of peace's hall; a man of two
thousand a year is not sessed at so many weapons as

he has on. There was never fencer challenged at so
many several foils. You would think he meant to
murder all Saint Pulchre's parish. If he could but
victual himself for half a year in his breeches, he is
sufficiently armed to overrun a country.                    121

DAW Good lord, what means he, sir! I pray you,
Master Truewit, be you a mediator.

TRUEWIT Well, I'll try if he will be appeased with a leg
or an arm; if not, you must die once.

DAW I would be loth to lose my right arm, for writing
madrigals.

TRUEWIT Why, if he will be satisfied with a thumb, or
a little finger, all's one to me. You must think I'll do
my best.                                                     130

DAW Good sir, do.

*He puts him up again, and then* DAUPHINE *and*
CLERIMONT *come forth*

CLERIMONT What hast thou done?

TRUEWIT He will let me do nothing, man, he does all
afore me; he offers his left arm.

CLERIMONT His left wing, for a Jack Daw.

DAUPHINE Take it, by all means.

TRUEWIT How! Maim a man forever, for a jest? What
a conscience hast thou?

DAUPHINE 'Tis no loss to him: he has no employment
for his arms but to eat spoon-meat. Beside, as good
maim his body as his reputation.                             141

TRUEWIT He is a scholar, and a wit, and yet he does
not think so. But he loses no reputation with us, for
we all resolved him an ass before. To your places
again.

CLERIMONT I pray thee, let me be in at the other a
little.

TRUEWIT Look, you'll spoil all: these be ever your
tricks.

CLERIMONT No, but I could hit of some things that
thou wilt miss, and thou wilt say are good ones.           151

TRUEWIT I warrant you. I pray forbear, I'll leave it off
else.

DAUPHINE Come away, Clerimont.            *They hide*

*Enter* LA FOOLE

TRUEWIT Sir Amorous!

---

74 protested: declared
75–6 do . . . right: 'grant him the right to meet you man-to-
man in an honourable duel' (Holdsworth)
103 take possession: of his property, when ownership was in
dispute; this often required force, or the threat of it
106 principal: original
107 brother: associate
114 halberds: spears-cum-battle-axes
petronels: large pistols
calivers: light muskets
116 sessed: assessed (for provision of weapons to the
monarch)

117–18 at . . . foils: to fight with so many different kinds of
sword
119 Saint Pulchre's: St Sepulchre's was a large and crowded
London parish
120 breeches: known as 'slops', it was the fashion at the time
for these to be voluminous
125 once: once for all
140 spoon-meat: baby food
143 so: i.e. 'that his body might as well be maimed'
(Holdsworth)
144 resolved him: decided he was

LA FOOLE  Master Truewit.

TRUEWIT  Whither were you going?

LA FOOLE  Down into the court, to make water.

TRUEWIT  By no means, sir; you shall rather tempt your
breeches.                                                160

LA FOOLE  Why, sir?

TRUEWIT  (*Opening the other door*) Enter here, if you
love your life.

LA FOOLE  Why? Why?

TRUEWIT  Question till your throat be cut, do; dally till
the enraged soul find you.

LA FOOLE  Who's that?

TRUEWIT  Daw it is; will you in?

LA FOOLE  Ay, ay, I'll in; what's the matter?

TRUEWIT  Nay, if he had been cool enough to tell us
that, there had been some hope to atone you, but he
seems so implacably enraged.                                172

LA FOOLE  'Slight, let him rage. I'll hide myself.

TRUEWIT  Do, good sir. But what have you done to him
within, that should provoke him thus? You have
broke some jest upon him afore the ladies—

LA FOOLE  Not I, never in my life broke jest upon any
man. The bride was praising Sir Dauphine, and he
went away in snuff, and I followed him, unless he
took offence at me in his drink erewhile, that I would
not pledge all the horse-full.                              181

TRUEWIT  By my faith, and that may be, you remember
well; but he walks the round up and down, through
every room o' the house, with a towel in his hand,
crying, 'Where's La Foole? Who saw La Foole?' and
when Dauphine and I demanded the cause, we can
force no answer from him but 'Oh revenge, how
sweet art thou! I will strangle him in this towel'—
which leads us to conjecture that the main cause of
his fury is for bringing your meat today, with a towel
about you, to his discredit.                                191

LA FOOLE  Like enough. Why, and he be angry for that,
I'll stay here, till his anger be blown over.

TRUEWIT  A good becoming resolution, sir. If you can
put it on o' the sudden.

LA FOOLE  Yes, I can put it on. Or I'll away into the
country presently.

TRUEWIT  How will you get out o' the house, sir? He
knows you are i' the house, and he'll watch you this

se'en-night but he'll have you. He'll outwait a
sergeant for you.                                           201

LA FOOLE  Why, then I'll stay here.

TRUEWIT  You must think how to victual yourself in
time, then.

LA FOOLE  Why, sweet Master Truewit, will you entreat
my cousin Otter to send me a cold venison pasty, a
bottle or two of wine, and a chamber-pot?

TRUEWIT  A stool were better, sir, of Sir A-jax his
invention.

LA FOOLE  Ay, that will be better indeed; and a pallet to
lie on.                                                     211

TRUEWIT  Oh, I would not advise you to sleep by any
means.

LA FOOLE  Would you not, sir? Why, then I will not.

TRUEWIT  Yet there's another fear—

LA FOOLE  Is there, sir? What is't?

TRUEWIT  No, he cannot break open this door with his
foot, sure.

LA FOOLE  I'll set my back against it, sir. I have a good
back.                                                       220

TRUEWIT  But then if he should batter.

LA FOOLE  Batter! If he dare, I'll have an action of
battery against him.

TRUEWIT  Cast you the worst. He has sent for powder
already, and what he will do with it, no man knows:
perhaps blow up the corner o' the house where he
suspects you are. Here he comes! In, quickly. (*He
feigns as if one were present, to fright the other, who is
run in to hide himself*) I protest, Sir John Daw, he is
not this way. What will you do? Before God, you
shall hang no petard here. I'll die rather. Will you not
take my word? I never knew one but would be
satisfied.—Sir Amorous, there's no standing out. He
has made a petard of an old brass pot, to force your
door. Think upon some satisfaction, or terms, to
offer him.                                                  236

LA FOOLE  (*Within*) Sir, I'll give him any satisfaction. I
dare give any terms.

TRUEWIT  You'll leave it to me then?

LA FOOLE  Ay, sir. I'll stand to any conditions.

TRUEWIT *calls forth* CLERIMONT *and* DAUPHINE

TRUEWIT  How now, what think you, sirs? Were't not a
difficult thing to determine which of these two feared
most?

CLERIMONT  Yes, but this fears the bravest; the other a

---

159–60  tempt your breeches: 'test (the capacity of) your
  breeches' (Procter)

171  atone: reconcile

176  broke . . . him: made some joke about him

179  in snuff: indignantly

181  pledge: take my turn and drink: see IV.ii.28

183  walks the round: a military metaphor from the patrol
  which goes round a camp or fortress to check that the
  sentries are vigilant (eds)

195  put it on: a) adopt; b) feign, assume

199  watch: watch out for

201  sergeant: officer with power of arrest

208  A-jax: reference to Sir John Harington's treatise on the
  flushing toilet, *The Metamorphosis of Ajax* (1596), with its
  pun on 'a jakes' (a privy)

210  pallet: straw mattress

224  Cast: forecast, anticipate

231  petard: small bomb, mine

233  standing out: resisting, withstanding

whiniling dastard, Jack Daw! But La Foole, a brave
heroic coward! And is afraid in a great look and a
stout accent. I like him rarely.

TRUEWIT Had it not been pity these two should ha'
been concealed?

CLERIMONT Shall I make a motion? 250

TRUEWIT Briefly. For I must strike while 'tis hot.

CLERIMONT Shall I go fetch the ladies to the
catastrophe?

TRUEWIT Umh? Ay, by my troth.

DAUPHINE By no mortal means. Let them continue in
the state of ignorance, and err still: think 'em wits
and fine fellows, as they have done. 'Twere sin to
reform them.

TRUEWIT Well, I will have 'em fetched, now I think
on't, for a private purpose of mine; do, Clerimont,
fetch 'em, and discourse to 'em all that's past and
bring 'em into the gallery here. 262

DAUPHINE This is thy extreme vanity now, thou
think'st thou wert undone, if every jest thou mak'st
were not published.

TRUEWIT Thou shalt see how unjust thou art presently.
Clerimont, say it was Dauphine's plot. (*Exit*
CLERIMONT) Trust me not if the whole drift be not
for thy good. There's a carpet i' the next room; put it
on, with this scarf over thy face and a cushion o' thy
head, and be ready when I call Amorous. Away—
(*Exit* DAUPHINE) John Daw! 272

*Brings* DAW *out of study*

DAW What good news, sir?

TRUEWIT Faith, I have followed, and argued with him
hard for you. I told him you were a knight, and a
scholar; and that you knew fortitude did consist *magis
patiendo quam faciendo, magis ferendo quam feriendo.*

DAW It doth so indeed, sir.

TRUEWIT And that you would suffer, I told him: so at
first he demanded, by my troth, in my conceit too
much. 281

DAW What was it, sir?

TRUEWIT Your upper lip, and six o' your fore-teeth.

DAW 'Twas unreasonable.

TRUEWIT Nay, I told him plainly, you could not spare
'em all. So after long argument (*pro et con*, as you
know) I brought him down to your two butter-teeth,
and them he would have.

DAW Oh, did you so? Why, he shall have 'em.

---

245  whiniling: whimpering, whining
250  motion: proposal
253  catastrophe: dénouement (of a play)
265  published: made widely known
269  carpet: tablecloth of tapestry or thick wool
276-7  *magis . . . feriendo*: 'more in suffering than in doing,
       more in enduring than in striking'
280  conceit: opinion
287  butter-teeth: front teeth

---

*Enter above* HAUGHTY, CENTAURE, MAVIS, MISTRESS
OTTER, EPICOENE, TRUSTY, *and* CLERIMONT

TRUEWIT But he shall not, sir, by your leave. The
conclusion is this, sir, because you shall be very good
friends hereafter, and this never to be remembered,
or upbraided; besides, that he may not boast he has
done any such thing to you in his own person, he is
to come here in disguise, give you five kicks in
private, sir, take your sword from you, and lock you
up in that study, during pleasure. Which will be but a
little while, we'll get it released presently. 298

DAW Five kicks? He shall have six, sir, to be friends.

TRUEWIT Believe me, you shall not overshoot yourself
to send him that word by me.

DAW Deliver it, sir. He shall have it with all my heart,
to be friends.

TRUEWIT Friends? Nay, and he should not be so, and
heartily too, upon these terms, he shall have me to
enemy while I live. Come, sir, bear it bravely.

DAW Oh God, sir, 'tis nothing.

TRUEWIT True. What's six kicks to a man that reads
Seneca?

DAW I have had a hundred, sir. 310

TRUEWIT Sir Amorous! No speaking one to another, or
rehearsing old matters.

DAUPHINE *comes forth and kicks him*

DAW One, two, three, four, five. I protest, Sir
Amorous, you shall have six.

TRUEWIT Nay, I told you you should not talk. Come,
give him six, and he will needs. (DAUPHINE *kicks him
again*) Your sword. (DAW *gives* TRUEWIT *his sword*)
Now return to your safe custody: you shall presently
meet afore the ladies, and be the dearest friends one
to another—(DAW *goes into his study*). Give me the
scarf, now, thou shalt beat the other barefaced. Stand
by—(*Exit* DAUPHINE). Sir Amorous! 321

*Brings out* LA FOOLE

LA FOOLE What's here? A sword!

TRUEWIT I cannot help it, without I should take the
quarrel upon myself; here he has sent you his
sword—

LA FOOLE I'll receive none on't.

TRUEWIT And he wills you to fasten it against a wall,
and break your head in some few several places
against the hilts.

LA FOOLE I will not: tell him roundly. I cannot endure
to shed my own blood. 330

TRUEWIT Will you not?

---

297  during pleasure: for as long as he pleases
300  overshoot: overreach
321  by: to one side
323  without: unless
328  several: different
330  roundly: plainly

LA FOOLE No. I'll beat it against a fair flat wall, if that will satisfy him; if not, he shall beat it himself, for Amorous.

TRUEWIT Why, this is strange starting off, when a man undertakes for you! I offered him another condition: will you stand to that?

LA FOOLE Ay, what is't?

TRUEWIT That you will be beaten in private.            340

LA FOOLE Yes. I am content, at the blunt.

TRUEWIT Then you must submit yourself to be hoodwinked in this scarf, and be led to him, where he will take your sword from you, and make you bear a blow over the mouth, *gules*, and tweaks by the nose, *sans nombre*.

LA FOOLE I am content. But why must I be blinded?

TRUEWIT That's for your good, sir: because if he should grow insolent upon this and publish it hereafter to your disgrace (which I hope he will not do) you might swear safely and protest he never beat you, to your knowledge.            352

LA FOOLE Oh, I conceive.

TRUEWIT I do not doubt but you'll be perfect good friends upon't, and not dare to utter an ill thought one of another, in future.

LA FOOLE Not I, as God help me, of him.

TRUEWIT Nor he of you, sir. If he should—Come, sir. (*Blindfolds him*) All hid, Sir John.

*DAUPHINE enters to tweak him*

LA FOOLE Oh, Sir John, Sir John! Oh, o-o-o-o-o-Oh—            361

TRUEWIT Good Sir John, leave tweaking, you'll blow his nose off. 'Tis Sir John's pleasure you should retire into the study. Why, now you are friends. All bitterness between you, I hope, is buried; you shall come forth by and by, Damon and Pythias upon't; and embrace with all the rankness of friendship that can be. (*Exit* LA FOOLE) I trust we shall have 'em tamer i' their language hereafter. Dauphine, I worship thee. God's will, the ladies have surprised us!

---

336  starting off: swerving (said of horses)
337  undertakes: stands surety
341  at the blunt: with the flat of the sword
343  hoodwinked: a) blindfolded; b) fooled
345  *gules*: red; i.e. a bloody mouth; an ironic reference to I.iv.43
346  *sans nombre*: numberless
359  All hid: the cry in hide-and-seek
366  Damon and Pythias: a type of loyal friendship, each offering to die in the place of the other. They were the subject of an eponymous play, by Richard Edwards, published in 1571
367  rankness: a) abundance; b) foulness (Holdsworth)

# Act IV, scene vi

*Enter from above* HAUGHTY, CENTAURE, MAVIS, MISTRESS OTTER, EPICOENE, TRUSTY, *and* CLERIMONT, *having discovered part of the past scene above*

HAUGHTY Centaure, how our judgements were imposed on by these adulterate knights!

CENTAURE Nay, madam, Mavis was more deceived than we, 'twas her commendation uttered 'em in the college.

MAVIS I commended but their wits, madam, and their braveries. I never looked toward their valours.

HAUGHTY Sir Dauphine is valiant, and a Wit too, it seems?

MAVIS And a Bravery too.            10

HAUGHTY Was this his project?

MISTRESS OTTER So Master Clerimont intimates, madam.

HAUGHTY Good Morose, when you come to the college, will you bring him with you? He seems a very perfect gentleman.

EPICOENE He is so, madam, believe it.

CENTAURE But when will you come, Morose?

EPICOENE Three or four days hence, madam, when I have got me a coach, and horses.            20

HAUGHTY No, tomorrow, good Morose, Centaure shall send you her coach.

MAVIS Yes, faith, do, and bring Sir Dauphine with you.

HAUGHTY She has promised that, Mavis.

MAVIS He is a very worthy gentleman in his exteriors, madam.

HAUGHTY Ay, he shows he is judicial in his clothes.

CENTAURE And yet not so superlatively neat as some, madam, that have their faces set in a brake!

HAUGHTY Ay, and have every hair in form!            30

MAVIS That wear purer linen than ourselves, and profess more neatness than the French hermaphrodite!

EPICOENE Ay, ladies, they, what they tell one of us, have told a thousand, and are the only thieves of our fame; that think to take us with that perfume, or with

---

2  adulterate: counterfeit
4  uttered: made known; also, put into circulation (as is false currency)
7  braveries: fine clothes
10  Bravery: see I.i.85–6n
29  set in a brake: assume a fixed expression. A brake was a frame in which a horse's hoof was secured whilst being shod
32–3  French hermaphrodite: perhaps indicative only of an assumed general French effeminacy; or perhaps a reference to a current side-show attraction (see *The Knight of the Burning Pestle* III.288), or to Henri III of France (d. 1589), a notorious transvestite
36  fame: reputation

that lace, and laugh at us unconscionably when they have done.

HAUGHTY But Sir Dauphine's carelessness becomes him. 40

CENTAURE I could love a man for such a nose!

MAVIS Or such a leg!

CENTAURE He has an exceeding good eye, madam!

MAVIS And a very good lock!

CENTAURE Good Morose, bring him to my chamber first.

MISTRESS OTTER Please your honours to meet at my house, madam?

TRUEWIT (*Aside* to DAUPHINE) See how they eye thee, man! They are taken, I warrant thee. 50

HAUGHTY You have unbraced our brace of knights here, Master Truewit.

TRUEWIT Not I, madam, it was Sir Dauphine's engine; who, if he have disfurnished your ladyship of any guard or service by it, is able to make the place good again, in himself.

HAUGHTY There's no suspicion of that, sir.

CENTAURE God so, Mavis, Haughty is kissing.

MAVIS Let us go too and take part. 59

HAUGHTY But I am glad of the fortune (beside the discovery of two such empty caskets) to gain the knowledge of so rich a mine of virtue as Sir Dauphine.

CENTAURE We would be all glad to style him of our friendship, and see him at the college.

MAVIS He cannot mix with a sweeter society, I'll prophesy, and I hope he himself will think so. 67

DAUPHINE I should be rude to imagine otherwise, lady.

TRUEWIT (*Aside* to DAUPHINE) Did not I tell thee, Dauphine? Why, all their actions are governed by crude opinion, without reason or cause; they know not why they do anything; but as they are informed, believe, judge, praise, condemn, love, hate, and in emulation one of another, do all these things alike. Only, they have a natural inclination sways 'em generally to the worst, when they are left to themselves. But pursue it, now thou hast 'em. 77

HAUGHTY Shall we go in again, Morose?

EPICOENE Yes, madam.

CENTAURE We'll entreat Sir Dauphine's company.

TRUEWIT Stay, good madam, the interview of the two friends, Pylades and Orestes: I'll fetch 'em out to you straight.

HAUGHTY Will you, Master Truewit?

DAUPHINE Ay, but, noble ladies, do not confess in your countenance or outward bearing to 'em any discovery of their follies, that we may see how they will bear up again, with what assurance, and erection.

HAUGHTY We will not, Sir Dauphine.

CENTAURE *and* MAVIS Upon our honours, Sir Dauphine. 91

TRUEWIT Sir Amorous, Sir Amorous! The ladies are here.

LA FOOLE (*Within*) Are they?

TRUEWIT Yes, but slip out by and by, as their backs are turned, and meet Sir John here, as by chance, when I call you.—Jack Daw!

DAW (*Within*) What say you, sir?

TRUEWIT Whip out behind me suddenly; and no anger i' your looks to your adversary. Now, now! 100

LA FOOLE *and* DAW *come out of their studies and salute each other*

LA FOOLE Noble Sir John Daw! Where ha' you been?

DAW To seek you, Sir Amorous.

LA FOOLE Me! I honour you.

DAW I prevent you, sir.

CLERIMONT They have forgot their rapiers!

TRUEWIT Oh, they meet in peace, man.

DAUPHINE Where's your sword, Sir John?

CLERIMONT And yours, Sir Amorous?

DAW Mine? My boy had it forth to mend the handle, e'en now. 110

LA FOOLE And my gold handle was broke too, and my boy had it forth.

DAUPHINE Indeed, sir? How their excuses meet!

CLERIMONT What a consent there is, i' the handles!

TRUEWIT Nay, there is so i' the points too, I warrant you.

MISTRESS OTTER Oh me! Madam, he comes again, the madman; away!

*Exeunt* LADIES, DAW *and* LA FOOLE

# Act IV, scene vii

*Enter* MOROSE: *he had found the two swords drawn within*

MOROSE What make these naked weapons here, gentlemen?

TRUEWIT Oh, sir! Here hath like to been murder since you went! A couple of knights fallen out about the

---

44 lock: see III.v.75n
51 unbraced: exposed
53 engine: contrivance, device
57 suspicion: doubt
82 Pylades and Orestes: another type of loyal friendship. Pylades helped Orestes avenge the killing of his father, Agamemnon

88 erection: 'high spirits. The sexual pun is appropriate after the ritual castration' (Beaurline)
104 prevent: anticipate
109 handle: with pun on 'handle' meaning 'excuse'
115 points: a) sword-points, which both have been afraid to use; b) various points of their excuses (Holdsworth)

bride's favours: we were fain to take away their weapons; your house had been begged by this time else—

MOROSE  For what?

CLERIMONT  For manslaughter, sir, as being accessary.

MOROSE  And for her favours?  10

TRUEWIT  Ay, sir, heretofore, not present. Clerimont, carry 'em their swords now. They have done all the hurt they will do.    *Exit* CLERIMONT *with the swords*

DAUPHINE  Ha' you spoke with a lawyer, sir?

MOROSE  Oh no! There is such a noise i' the court, that they have frighted me home with more violence than I went! Such speaking, and counter-speaking, with their several voices of citations, appellations, allegations, certificates, attachments, intergatories, references, convictions, and afflictions indeed, among the doctors and proctors, that the noise here is silence to't! A kind of calm midnight!  22

TRUEWIT  Why, sir, if you would be resolved indeed, I can bring you hither a very sufficient lawyer and a learned divine, that shall enquire into every least scruple for you.

MOROSE  Can you, Master Truewit?

TRUEWIT  Yes, and are very sober grave persons, that will dispatch it in a chamber, with a whisper or two.

MOROSE  Good sir, shall I hope this benefit from you, and trust myself into your hands?  31

TRUEWIT  Alas, sir! Your nephew and I have been ashamed, and oft-times mad, since you went, to think how you are abused. Go in, good sir, and lock yourself up till we call you; we'll tell you more anon, sir.

MOROSE  Do your pleasure with me, gentlemen; I believe in you, and that deserves no delusion—    *Exit*

TRUEWIT  You shall find none, sir—but heaped, heaped plenty of vexation.  40

DAUPHINE  What wilt thou do now, Wit?

TRUEWIT  Recover me hither Otter, and the barber, if you can by any means, presently.

DAUPHINE  Why? To what purpose?

TRUEWIT  Oh, I'll make the deepest divine, and gravest lawyer, out o' them two for him—

DAUPHINE  Thou canst not, man, these are waking dreams.  48

TRUEWIT  Do not fear me. Clap but a civil gown with a

welt o' the one, and a canonical cloak with sleeves o' the other, and give 'em a few terms i' their mouths; if there come not forth as able a doctor and complete a parson for this turn as may be wished, trust not my election. And, I hope, without wronging the dignity of either profession, since they are but persons put on, and for mirth's sake, to torment him. The barber smatters Latin, I remember.  57

DAUPHINE  Yes, and Otter too.

TRUEWIT  Well then, if I make 'em not wrangle out this case, to his no comfort, let me be thought a Jack Daw, or La Foole, or anything worse. Go you to your ladies, but first send for them.  62

DAUPHINE  I will.

*Exeunt*

# Act V, scene i

*Enter* LA FOOLE, CLERIMONT, DAW

LA FOOLE  Where had you our swords, Master Clerimont?

CLERIMONT  Why, Dauphine took 'em from the madman.

LA FOOLE  And he took 'em from our boys, I warrant you?

CLERIMONT  Very like, sir.

LA FOOLE  Thank you, good Master Clerimont. Sir John Daw and I are both beholden to you.

CLERIMONT  Would I knew how to make you so, gentlemen.  11

DAW  Sir Amorous and I are your servants, sir.

*Enter* MAVIS

MAVIS  Gentlemen, have any of you a pen and ink? I would fain write out a riddle in Italian, for Sir Dauphine to translate.

CLERIMONT  Not I, in troth, lady, I am no scrivener.

DAW  I can furnish you, I think, lady.

*Exeunt* DAW *and* MAVIS

CLERIMONT  He has it in the haft of a knife, I believe!

LA FOOLE  No, he has his box of instruments.

CLERIMONT  Like a surgeon!  20

LA FOOLE  For the mathematics: his squire, his compasses, his brass pens, and black lead, to draw maps of every place and person where he comes.

---

  5  fain: obliged
  6  begged: begged for in anticipation of the confiscation of Morose's property as that of a criminal (eds)
15–22  derived from Libanius, Declamation XXVI, sections 3–6
 19  attachments: writs of arrest
     intergatories: interrogatories
 21  doctors . . . proctors: barristers . . . attorneys
 26  scruple: uncertainty
 49  fear: doubt

 50  welt: border (here, of fur)
 54  election: judgement, ability to make choices
54–6  without . . . him: Jonson had offended the legal profession with some of his earlier writings; Truewit's disclaimer is thus a precaution against further trouble
 16  scrivener: professional scribe
 18  haft: handle
 21  squire: square

CLERIMONT  How, maps of persons!

LA FOOLE  Yes, sir, of Nomentack, when he was here, and of the Prince of Moldavia, and of his mistress, Mistress Epicoene.

CLERIMONT  Away! He has not found out her latitude, I hope.

LA FOOLE  You are a pleasant gentleman, sir.                30

*Enter* DAW

CLERIMONT  Faith, now we are in private, let's wanton it a little, and talk waggishly. Sir John, I am telling Sir Amorous here that you two govern the ladies; where'er you come, you carry the feminine gender afore you.

DAW  They shall rather carry us afore them, if they will, sir.

CLERIMONT  Nay, I believe that they do, withal; but that you are the prime men in their affections, and direct all their actions—                40

DAW  Not I; Sir Amorous is.

LA FOOLE  I protest, Sir John is.

DAW  As I hope to rise i' the state, Sir Amorous, you ha' the person.

LA FOOLE  Sir John, you ha' the person, and the discourse too.

DAW  Not I, sir. I have no discourse—and then you have activity beside.

LA FOOLE  I protest, Sir John, you come as high from Tripoli as I do every whit, and lift as many joined stools and leap over 'em, if you would use it—                51

CLERIMONT  Well, agree on't together, knights; for between you, you divide the kingdom, or commonwealth of ladies' affections: I see it, and can perceive a little how they observe you, and fear you, indeed. You could tell strange stories, my masters, if you would, I know.

DAW  Faith, we have seen somewhat, sir.

LA FOOLE  That we have—velvet petticoats, and wrought smocks, or so.                60

DAW  Ay, and—

CLERIMONT  Nay, out with it, Sir John; do not envy your friend the pleasure of hearing, when you have had the delight of tasting.

DAW  Why—a—do you speak, Sir Amorous.

LA FOOLE  No, do you, Sir John Daw.

DAW  I' faith, you shall.

LA FOOLE  I' faith, you shall.

DAW  Why, we have been—

LA FOOLE  In the Great Bed at Ware together in our time. On, Sir John.                71

DAW  Nay, do you, Sir Amorous.

CLERIMONT  And these ladies with you, knights?

LA FOOLE  No, excuse us, sir.

DAW  We must not wound reputation.

LA FOOLE  No matter—they were these, or others. Our bath cost us fifteen pound, when we came home.

CLERIMONT  Do you hear, Sir John, you shall tell me but one thing truly, as you love me.

DAW  If I can, I will, sir.                80

CLERIMONT  You lay in the same house with the bride here?

DAW  Yes, and conversed with her hourly, sir.

CLERIMONT  And what humour is she of? Is she coming, and open, free?

DAW  Oh, exceeding open, sir. I was her servant, and Sir Amorous was to be.

CLERIMONT  Come, you have both had favours from her? I know and have heard so much.

DAW  Oh no, sir.                90

LA FOOLE  You shall excuse us, sir: we must not wound reputation.

CLERIMONT  Tut, she is married now, and you cannot hurt her with any report, and therefore speak plainly: how many times, i' faith? Which of you led first? Ha?

LA FOOLE  Sir John had her maidenhead, indeed.

DAW  Oh, it pleases him to say so, sir, but Sir Amorous knows what's what as well.

CLERIMONT  Dost thou i' faith, Amorous?

LA FOOLE  In a manner, sir.                100

CLERIMONT  Why, I commend you, lads. Little knows Don Bridegroom of this. Nor shall he, for me.

---

25  Nomentack: native American from Virginia, brought to England in 1608 as a hostage, and sent back in 1609; he was murdered in Bermuda on the return voyage

26  Prince of Moldavia . . . his mistress: see Dedicatory Epistle, l. 16n. Lady Arbella Stuart, James VI/I's cousin, took this to be a reference to her supposed engagement to Stephen Janiculo, the (bogus) Prince of Moldavia. As a result of her objection, the play was closed in February 1610. La Foole is, of course, referring to Daw's mistress, 'Mistress Epicoene', but his confused syntax results, deliberately or otherwise, in this ambiguity

28  latitude: locality; with pun on 'laxity of conduct'

30  pleasant: witty, humorous

34–5  you . . . afore you: a jibe at their own effeminacy

44  person: attractiveness

49–50  come . . . Tripoli: vault and tumble

50  use: practise

54  commonwealth: 'implying that Daw and La Foole's women are shared by everyone' (Holdsworth)

59–60  velvet . . . smocks: worn by courtly ladies and high-class prostitutes

70  Great Bed at Ware: famous bed, eleven feet square and capable of sleeping twelve people, originally at the Saracen's Head in Ware, now in the Victoria and Albert Museum, London

77  bath: probably medicinal, to treat venereal disease

84  humour: temperament, disposition

85  coming . . . free: eager, compliant (with sexual connotations)

DAW Hang him, mad ox.

CLERIMONT Speak softly: here comes his nephew, with the Lady Haughty. He'll get the ladies from you, sirs, if you look not to him in time.

LA FOOLE Why, if he do, we'll fetch 'em home again, I warrant you.

*Exeunt*

## Act V, scene ii

*Enter* HAUGHTY, DAUPHINE

HAUGHTY I assure you, Sir Dauphine, it is the price and estimation of your virtue only that hath embarked me to this adventure, and I could not but make out to tell you so; nor can I repent me of the act, since it is always an argument of some virtue in ourselves, that we love and affect it so in others.

DAUPHINE Your ladyship sets too high a price on my weakness.

HAUGHTY Sir, I can distinguish gems from pebbles—

DAUPHINE (*Aside*) Are you so skilful in stones?                10

HAUGHTY And howsoever I may suffer in such a judgement as yours, by admitting equality of rank, or society, with Centaure, or Mavis—

DAUPHINE You do not, madam; I perceive they are your mere foils.

HAUGHTY Then are you a friend to truth, sir. It makes me love you the more. It is not the outward, but the inward man that I affect. They are not apprehensive of an eminent perfection, but love flat and dully.    19

CENTAURE (*Within*) Where are you, my Lady Haughty?

HAUGHTY I come presently, Centaure.—My chamber, sir, my page shall show you; and Trusty, my woman, shall be ever awake for you; you need not fear to communicate anything with her, for she is a Fidelia. I pray you wear this jewel for my sake, Sir Dauphine. (*Enter* CENTAURE) Where's Mavis, Centaure?

CENTAURE Within, madam, a-writing. I'll follow you presently. I'll but speak a word with Sir Dauphine.

*Exit* HAUGHTY

DAUPHINE With me, madam?                29

CENTAURE Good Sir Dauphine, do not trust Haughty, nor make any credit to her, whatever you do besides.

Sir Dauphine, I give you this caution, she is a perfect courtier, and loves nobody but for her uses; and for her uses, she loves all. Besides, her physicians give her out to be none o' the clearest; whether she pay 'em or no, heaven knows; and she's above fifty too, and pargets! See her in a forenoon. Here comes Mavis, a worse face than she! You would not like this by candlelight. If you'll come to my chamber one o' these mornings early, or late in an evening, I'll tell you more. (*Enter* MAVIS) Where's Haughty, Mavis?

MAVIS Within, Centaure.                42

CENTAURE What ha' you there?

MAVIS An Italian riddle for Sir Dauphine (you shall not see it i' faith, Centaure). Good Sir Dauphine, solve it for me. I'll call for it anon.

*Exeunt* MAVIS *and* CENTAURE

*Enter* CLERIMONT

CLERIMONT How now, Dauphine? How dost thou quit thyself of these females?

DAUPHINE 'Slight, they haunt me like fairies, and give me jewels here; I cannot be rid of 'em.                50

CLERIMONT Oh, you must not tell, though.

DAUPHINE Mass, I forgot that; I was never so assaulted. One loves for virtue, and bribes me for this. Another loves me with caution, and so would possess me. A third brings me a riddle here; and all are jealous, and rail each at other.

CLERIMONT A riddle? Pray le'me see't? (*He reads the paper*) 'Sir Dauphine, I chose this way of intimation for privacy. The ladies here, I know, have both hope, and purpose, to make a collegiate and servant of you. If I might be so honoured as to appear at any end of so noble a work, I would enter into a fame of taking physic tomorrow, and continue it four or five days, or longer, for your visitation. Mavis.'—By my faith, a subtle one! Call you this a riddle? What's their plain dealing, trow?                66

DAUPHINE We lack Truewit to tell us that.

CLERIMONT We lack him for somewhat else too: his knights *reformados* are wound up as high, and insolent, as ever they were.

DAUPHINE You jest.

---

103  ox: fool; also suggests 'cuckold' because of its horns

1  price: worth

4  make out: contrive, manage

6  affect: seek

10  stones: a) gems; b) testicles

15  foils: a) settings for jewels; b) contrasts, which show one off to advantage

19  eminent: distinguished, prominent (with sexual pun)

24  Fidelia: Latin for 'trusty'; also a common name for the heroines of popular romances

31  make . . . to: put any faith in

35  clearest: a) most innocent; b) most free from disease

37  pargets: plasters (herself with make-up)

39  by candlelight: i.e. even by candlelight (the most flattering kind of light)

51  you . . . tell: revelation of a fairy's gift rendered it void and brought bad luck (eds)

54  this: i.e. this jewel
    caution: warnings

62  enter . . . fame: begin a rumour

63  physic: medical treatment (as an excuse for staying in)

69  *reformados*: disbanded soldiers who kept their rank; with pun on 'reformed'

CLERIMONT  No drunkards, either with wine or vanity, ever confessed such stories of themselves. I would not give a fly's leg in balance against all the women's reputations here, if they could be but thought to speak truth; and for the bride, they have made their affidavit against her directly—

DAUPHINE  What, that they have lien with her?

CLERIMONT  Yes, and tell times, and circumstances, with the cause why, and the place where. I had almost brought 'em to affirm that they had done it today.  **82**

DAUPHINE  Not both of 'em.

CLERIMONT  Yes, faith; with a sooth or two more I had effected it. They would ha' set it down under their hands.

DAUPHINE  Why, they will be our sport, I see, still! Whether we will or no.

## Act V, scene iii

*Enter* TRUEWIT

TRUEWIT  Oh, are you here? Come, Dauphine. Go, call your uncle presently. I have fitted my divine and my canonist, dyed their beards and all; the knaves do not know themselves, they are so exalted and altered. Preferment changes any man. Thou shalt keep one door, and I another, and then Clerimont in the midst, that he may have no means of escape from their cavilling, when they grow hot once. And then the women (as I have given the bride her instructions) to break in upon him, i' the *l'envoy*. Oh, 'twill be full and twanging! Away, fetch him. (*Exit* DAUPHINE) (*Enter* CUTBEARD *disguised as a canon lawyer,* OTTER *as a divine*) Come, master doctor, and master parson, look to your parts now, and discharge 'em bravely; you are well set forth, perform it as well. If you chance to be out, do not confess it with standing still, or humming, or gaping one at another; but go on, and talk aloud and eagerly, use vehement action, and only remember your terms, and you are safe. Let the matter go where it will: you have many will do so. But at first, be very solemn and grave like your garments, though you loose yourselves after, and skip out like a brace of jugglers on a table. Here he comes! Set your faces, and look superciliously while I present you.  **24**

*Enter* DAUPHINE *and* MOROSE

---

78  lien: lain
84  sooth: exclamation (e.g. 'really!', 'indeed!')
5  keep: guard
10  *l'envoy*: conclusion
11  twanging: exceptionally fine (with pun on 'noisy')
16  be out: forget your words
18  action: gestures

MOROSE  Are these the two learned men?

TRUEWIT  Yes, sir; please you salute 'em?

MOROSE  Salute 'em? I had rather do anything than wear out time so unfruitfully, sir. I wonder how these common forms, as 'God save you' and 'You are welcome', are come to be a habit in our lives! Or 'I am glad to see you!' when I cannot see what the profit can be of these words, so long as it is no whit better with him whose affairs are sad and grievous, that he hears this salutation.  **34**

TRUEWIT  'Tis true, sir; we'll go to the matter then. Gentlemen, master doctor and master parson, I have acquainted you sufficiently with the business for which you are come hither. And you are not now to inform yourselves in the state of the question, I know. This is the gentleman who expects your resolution, and therefore, when you please, begin.

OTTER  Please you, master doctor.  **42**

CUTBEARD  Please you, good master parson.

OTTER  I would hear the canon law speak first.

CUTBEARD  It must give place to positive divinity, sir.

MOROSE  Nay, good gentlemen, do not throw me into circumstances. Let your comforts arrive quickly at me, those that are. Be swift in affording me my peace, if so I shall hope any. I love not your disputations, or your court tumults. And that it be not strange to you, I will tell you. My father, in my education, was wont to advise me that I should always collect and contain my mind, not suff'ring it to flow loosely; that I should look to what things were necessary to the carriage of my life, and what not; embracing the one and eschewing the other. In short, that I should endear myself to rest, and avoid turmoil; which now is grown to be another nature to me. So that I come not to your public pleadings, or your places of noise; not that I neglect those things that make for the dignity of the commonwealth, but for the mere avoiding of clamours and impertinencies of orators, that know not how to be silent. And for the cause of noise am I now a suitor to you. You do not know in what a misery I have been exercised this day, what a torrent of evil! My very house turns round with the tumult! I dwell in a windmill! The perpetual motion is here, and not at Eltham.  **68**

---

27–34  derived from Libanius, Declamation XXVI, section 7
38  are not now: do not need now
45  positive: practical (as opposed to theoretical or speculative)
47  circumstances: circumstantialities
51–63  derived from Libanius, Declamation XXVI, section 6
60  neglect: do not care about
62  impertinencies: irrelevances
68  perpetual . . . Eltham: a Dutch scientist, Cornelius Drebbel, demonstrated his perpetual motion machine at Eltham Palace in 1609–10; it was much visited

TRUEWIT Well, good master doctor, will you break the ice? Master parson will wade after.

CUTBEARD Sir, though unworthy, and the weaker, I will presume.

OTTER 'Tis no presumption, *domine* doctor.

MOROSE Yet again!

CUTBEARD Your question is, for how many causes a man may have *divortium legitimum*, a lawful divorce. First, you must understand the nature of the word divorce, *a divertendo*—

MOROSE No excursions upon words, good doctor; to the question briefly. 80

CUTBEARD I answer then, the canon law affords divorce but in few cases, and the principal is in the common case, the adulterous case. But there are *duodecim impedimenta*, twelve impediments (as we call 'em) all which do not *dirimire contractum*, but *irritum reddere matrimonium*, as we say in the canon law, not take away the bond, but cause a nullity therein.

MOROSE I understood you before; good sir, avoid your impertinency of translation.

OTTER He cannot open this too much, sir, by your favour. 91

MOROSE Yet more!

TRUEWIT Oh, you must give the learned men leave, sir. To your impediments, master doctor.

CUTBEARD The first is *impedimentum erroris*.

OTTER Of which there are several species.

CUTBEARD Ay, as *error personae*.

OTTER If you contract yourself to one person, thinking her another.

CUTBEARD Then, *error fortunae*. 100

OTTER If she be a beggar, and you thought her rich.

CUTBEARD Then, *error qualitatis*.

OTTER If she prove stubborn, or headstrong, that you thought obedient.

MOROSE How? Is that, sir, a lawful impediment? One at once, I pray you, gentlemen.

OTTER Ay, *ante copulam*, but not *post copulam*, sir.

CUTBEARD Master parson says right. *Nec post nuptiarum benedictionem*. It doth indeed but *irrita*

*reddere sponsalia*, annul the contract; after marriage it is of no obstancy. 110

TRUEWIT Alas, sir, what a hope are we fall'n from, by this time!

CUTBEARD The next is *conditio*: if you thought her freeborn, and she prove a bondwoman, there is impediment of estate and condition.

OTTER Ay, but master doctor, those servitudes are *sublatae* now, among us Christians.

CUTBEARD By your favour, master parson—

OTTER You shall give me leave, master doctor. 120

MOROSE Nay, gentlemen, quarrel not in that question; it concerns not my case: pass to the third.

CUTBEARD Well then, the third is *votum*. If either party have made a vow of chastity. But that practice, as master parson said of the other, is taken away among us, thanks be to discipline. The fourth is *cognatio*: if the persons be of kin, within the degrees.

OTTER Ay: do you know what the degrees are, sir?

MOROSE No, nor I care not, sir: they offer me no comfort in the question, I am sure. 131

CUTBEARD But there is a branch of this impediment may, which is *cognatio spiritualis*. If you were her godfather, sir, then the marriage is incestuous.

OTTER That comment is absurd, and superstitious, master doctor. I cannot endure it. Are we not all brothers and sisters, and as much akin in that, as godfathers, and goddaughters?

MOROSE Oh me! To end the controversy, I never was a godfather, I never was a godfather in my life, sir. Pass to the next. 141

CUTBEARD The fifth is *crimen adulterii*: the known case. The sixth *cultus disparitas*, difference of religion: have you ever examined her what religion she is of?

MOROSE No, I would rather she were of none, than be put to the trouble of it!

OTTER You may have it done for you, sir.

MOROSE By no means, good sir; on, to the rest. Shall you ever come to an end, think you?

TRUEWIT Yes, he has done half, sir. (On, to the rest.) Be patient and expect, sir. 151

---

73 *domine*: master
78 *a divertendo*: derived from 'separating'
84 twelve impediments: the twelve impediments are taken from St Thomas Aquinas's *Summa Theologiae*
90 open: expound
95 *impedimentum erroris*: impediment arising from error
97 *error personae*: mistaken identity
100 *error fortunae*: error as to fortune
102 *error qualitatis*: mistake as to disposition
105–6 One at once: one at a time
107 *ante copulam . . . post copulam*: before the union . . . after the union
108–9 *Nec . . . benedictionem*: not after the sacrament of marriage

110 contract: betrothal
111 obstancy: judicial opposition
113 time: i.e. timing (Holdsworth)
114 *conditio*: social rank
118 *sublatae*: abolished
123 *votum*: vow
126 discipline: the church system (under Protestantism)
127 *cognatio*: (blood) relationship
128 degrees: i.e. of kinship within which marriage is forbidden
142 *crimen adulterii*: the crime of adultery
143 case: a) instance; b) vagina (a common pun) (Holdsworth)

CUTBEARD The seventh is *vis*: if it were upon compulsion, or force.

MOROSE Oh no, it was too voluntary, mine; too voluntary.

CUTBEARD The eighth is *ordo*: if ever she have taken holy orders.

OTTER That's superstitious too.

MOROSE No matter, master parson: would she would go into a nunnery yet. 160

CUTBEARD The ninth is *ligamen*: if you were bound, sir, to any other before.

MOROSE I thrust myself too soon into these fetters.

CUTBEARD The tenth is *publica honestas*, which is *inchoata quaedam affinitas*.

OTTER Ay, or *affinitas orta ex sponsalibus*, and is but *leve impedimentum*.

MOROSE I feel no air of comfort blowing to me, in all this.

CUTBEARD The eleventh is *affinitas ex fornicatione*. 170

OTTER Which is no less *vera affinitas* than the other, master doctor.

CUTBEARD True, *quae oritur ex legitimo matrimonio*.

OTTER You say right, venerable doctor. And *nascitur ex eo, quod per conjugium duae personae efficiuntur una caro*—

MOROSE Heyday, now they begin!

CUTBEARD I conceive you, master parson. *Ita per fornicationem aeque est verus pater, qui sic generat*—

OTTER *Et vere filius qui sic generatur*— 180

MOROSE What's all this to me?

CLERIMONT (*Aside*) Now it grows warm.

CUTBEARD The twelfth and last is *si forte coire nequibis*.

OTTER Ay, that is *impedimentum gravissimum*. It doth utterly annul and annihilate, that. If you have *manifestam frigiditatem*, you are well, sir.

TRUEWIT Why, there is comfort come at length, sir.

Confess yourself but a man unable, and she will sue to be divorced first.

OTTER Ay, or if there be *morbus perpetuus et insanabilis*, as paralysis, elephantiasis, or so— 191

DAUPHINE Oh, but *frigiditas* is the fairer way, gentlemen.

OTTER You say troth, sir, and as it is in the canon, master doctor.

CUTBEARD I conceive you, sir.

CLERIMONT (*Aside*) Before he speaks.

OTTER That 'a boy or child under years is not fit for marriage because he cannot *reddere debitum*'. So your *omnipotentes*—

TRUEWIT (*Aside to* OTTER) Your *impotente*s, you whoreson lobster. 201

OTTER Your *impotentes*, I should say, are *minime apti ad contrahenda matrimonium*.

TRUEWIT (*Aside to* OTTER) *Matrimonium*? We shall have most unmatrimonial Latin with you: *matrimonia*, and be hanged.

DAUPHINE (*Aside to* TRUEWIT) You put 'em out, man.

CUTBEARD But then there will arise a doubt, master parson, in our case, *post matrimonium*: that *frigiditate praeditus*—do you conceive me, sir? 210

OTTER Very well, sir.

CUTBEARD Who cannot *uti uxore pro uxore*, may *habere eam pro sorore*.

OTTER Absurd, absurd, absurd, and merely apostatical.

CUTBEARD You shall pardon me, master parson, I can prove it.

OTTER You can prove a will, master doctor, you can prove nothing else. Does not the verse of your own canon say, *Haec socianda vetant conubia, facta retractant*— 221

CUTBEARD I grant you, but how do they *retractare*, master parson?

MOROSE (Oh, this was it I feared.)

OTTER *In aeternum*, sir.

---

161 *ligamen*: bond
164 *publica honestas*: public reputation
165 *inchoata . . . affinitas*: (previous) unconsummated marriage
166 *affinitas . . . sponsalibus*: relationship arising from a betrothal
 *leve*: slight
170 *affinitas ex fornicatione*: relationship arising from fornication
171 *vera affinitas*: true relationship
173 *quae . . . matrimonio*: (than that) which comes from legal marriage
174–6 *nascitur . . . caro*: it follows from this, that through physical union two people are made one flesh
178–9 *Ita . . . generat*: thus that he is equally a true father who begets through fornication
180 *Et . . . generatur*: and he truly a son who is thus begotten
183 *si . . . nequibis*: if by chance you are unable to copulate
184 *gravissimum*: very weighty
186 *manifestam frigiditatem*: evident frigidity

190 *morbus . . . insanabilis*: a chronic and incurable disease
198 *reddere debitum*: render his obligation
199 *omnipotentes*: omnipotent men
200 *impotentes*: impotent men
202–3 *minime . . . matrimonium*: least suited to contracting marriages
205 unmatrimonial Latin: because Otter's errors disrupt the grammatical agreement or 'marriage' of words
207 put 'em out: make them forget their words
209 *post matrimonium*: after marriage
209–10 *frigiditate praeditus*: one who is frigid
212–13 *uti . . . sorore*: use a wife as a wife, may keep her as a sister
214–15 merely apostatical: absolutely heretical
220–1 *Haec . . . retractant*: these things forbid uniting in marriage, and after marriages have been made to annul them
225 *In aeternum*: forever

CUTBEARD That's false in divinity, by your favour.

OTTER 'Tis false in humanity to say so. Is he not *prorsus inutilis ad thorum*? Can he *praestare fidem datam*? I would fain know.

CUTBEARD Yes: how if he do *convalere*? 230

OTTER He cannot *convalere*, it is impossible.

TRUEWIT (*To* MOROSE) Nay, good sir, attend the learned men, they'll think you neglect 'em else.

CUTBEARD Or if he do *simulare* himself *frigidum, odio uxoris*, or so?

OTTER I say he is *adulter manifestus* then.

DAUPHINE (They dispute it very learnedly, i' faith.)

OTTER And *prostitutor uxoris*, and this is positive.

MOROSE Good sir, let me escape.

TRUEWIT You will not do me that wrong, sir? 240

OTTER And therefore, if he be *manifeste frigidus*, sir—

CUTBEARD Ay, if he be *manifeste frigidus*, I grant you—

OTTER Why, that was my conclusion.

CUTBEARD And mine too.

TRUEWIT Nay, hear the conclusion, sir.

OTTER Then *frigiditatis causa*—

CUTBEARD Yes, *causa frigiditatis*—

MOROSE Oh, mine ears!

OTTER She may have *libellum divortii* against you.

CUTBEARD Ay, *divortii libellum* she will sure have. 250

MOROSE Good echoes, forbear.

OTTER If you confess it.

CUTBEARD Which I would do, sir—

MOROSE I will do anything—

OTTER And clear myself *in foro conscientiae*—

CUTBEARD Because you want indeed—

MOROSE Yet more?

OTTER *Exercendi potestate.*

# Act V, scene iv

*Enter* EPICOENE, HAUGHTY, CENTAURE, MAVIS, MISTRESS OTTER, DAW, LA FOOLE

EPICOENE I will not endure it any longer. Ladies, I beseech you help me. This is such a wrong as never was offered to poor bride before. Upon her marriage-day, to have her husband conspire against her, and a couple of mercenary companions to be brought in for form's sake, to persuade a separation! If you had blood or virtue in you, gentlemen, you would not suffer such earwigs about a husband, or scorpions to creep between man and wife—

MOROSE Oh the variety and changes of my torment! 10

HAUGHTY Let 'em be cudgelled out of doors by our grooms.

CENTAURE I'll lend you my footman.

MAVIS We'll have our men blanket 'em i' the hall.

MISTRESS OTTER As there was one at our house, madam, for peeping in at the door.

DAW Content, i' faith.

TRUEWIT Stay, ladies and gentlemen, you'll hear before you proceed?

MAVIS I'd ha' the bridegroom blanketed too. 20

CENTAURE Begin with him first.

HAUGHTY Yes, by my troth.

MOROSE Oh mankind generation!

DAUPHINE Ladies, for my sake forbear.

HAUGHTY Yes, for Sir Dauphine's sake.

CENTAURE He shall command us.

LA FOOLE He is as fine a gentleman of his inches, madam, as any is about the town, and wears as good colours when he list. 29

TRUEWIT (*Aside to* MOROSE) Be brief, sir, and confess your infirmity, she'll be afire to be quit of you; if she but hear that named once, you shall not entreat her to stay. She'll fly you like one that had the marks upon him.

MOROSE Ladies, I must crave all your pardons—

TRUEWIT Silence, ladies.

MOROSE For a wrong I have done to your whole sex, in marrying this fair and virtuous gentlewoman—

CLERIMONT Hear him, good ladies. 39

MOROSE Being guilty of an infirmity which, before I conferred with these learned men, I thought I might have concealed—

TRUEWIT But now being better informed in his conscience by them, he is to declare it, and give satisfaction, by asking your public forgiveness.

---

227 humanity: secular learning
227–8 *prorsus . . . thorum*: utterly useless in bed. 'Otter's mistake of thorum for torum (Latin *torus* = bed) gives a pun on *thoros* (Greek θορος = semen)' (Procter)
228 *praestare . . . datam*: fulfil the promise given
231 *convalere*: recover
234–5 *simulare . . . uxoris*: pretend to be frigid, out of hatred for his wife
236 *adulter manifestus*: a manifest adulterer
238 *prostitutor uxoris*: the prostitutor of his wife
241 *manifeste*: manifestly
246 *frigiditatis causa*: on the ground of frigidity
249 *libellum divortii*: a petition for divorce
255 *in foro conscientiae*: at the bar of conscience (a legal proverb)
256 want: lack
258 *Exercendi potestate*: the power of putting to use (i.e. of consummation)

---

5 companions: fellows (contemptuous)
8 earwigs: ear whisperers, parasites
14 blanket: toss in a blanket
23 mankind: masculine, virago-like; also furious, savage (related to 'mankeen'; used of animals inclined to attack people)
27 of his inches: brave (with sexual pun)
29 colours: a knight's heraldic colours
   list: wishes
33 marks: of the plague

MOROSE I am no man, ladies.

ALL How!

MOROSE Utterly unabled in nature, by reason of frigidity, to perform the duties, or any the least office of a husband. 50

MAVIS Now, out upon him, prodigious creature!

CENTAURE Bridegroom uncarnate.

HAUGHTY And would you offer it, to a young gentlewoman?

MISTRESS OTTER A lady of her longings?

EPICOENE Tut, a device, a device, this, it smells rankly, ladies. A mere comment of his own.

TRUEWIT Why, if you suspect that, ladies, you may have him searched.

DAW As the custom is, by a jury of physicians. 60

LA FOOLE Yes, faith, 'twill be brave.

MOROSE Oh me, must I undergo that!

MISTRESS OTTER No, let women search him, madam: we can do it ourselves.

MOROSE Out on me, worse!

EPICOENE No, ladies, you shall not need, I'll take him with all his faults.

MOROSE Worst of all!

CLERIMONT Why, then 'tis no divorce, doctor, if she consent not? 70

CUTBEARD No, if the man be *frigidus*, it is *de parte uxoris* that we grant *libellum divortii*, in the law.

OTTER Ay, it is the same in theology.

MOROSE Worse, worse than worst!

TRUEWIT Nay, sir, be not utterly disheartened, we have yet a small relic of hope left, as near as our comfort is blown out. Clerimont, produce your brace of knights. What was that, master parson, you told me *in errore qualitatis*, e'en now? (*Aside to* DAUPHINE) Dauphine, whisper the bride that she carry it as if she were guilty and ashamed. 81

OTTER Marry, sir, *in errore qualitatis* (which master doctor did forbear to urge) if she be found *corrupta*, that is, vitiated or broken up, that was *pro virgine desponsa*, espoused for a maid—

MOROSE What then, sir?

OTTER It doth *dirimere contractum* and *irritum reddere* too.

---

51 prodigious: monstrous
52 uncarnate: not of flesh and blood (Centaure's coinage, from 'incarnate')
53 offer it: attempt to do such a thing
55 longings: a) wealth, belongings; b) sexual longings
57 comment: invention
59 searched: examined
71–2 *de . . . uxoris*: on the wife's behalf
80 carry it: behave
84 vitiated: deflowered
86 *dirimere . . . reddere*: cancel the contract and render it null and void

TRUEWIT If this be true, we are happy again, sir, once more. Here are an honourable brace of knights that shall affirm so much. 91

DAW Pardon us, good Master Clerimont.

LA FOOLE You shall excuse us, Master Clerimont.

CLERIMONT Nay, you must make it good now, knights, there is no remedy; I'll eat no words for you, nor no men: you know you spoke it to me?

DAW Is this gentleman-like, sir?

TRUEWIT (*Aside to* DAW) Jack Daw, he's worse than Sir Amorous: fiercer a great deal. (*Aside to* LA FOOLE) Sir Amorous, beware, there be ten Daws in this Clerimont. 101

LA FOOLE I'll confess it, sir.

DAW Will you, Sir Amorous? Will you wound reputation?

LA FOOLE I am resolved.

TRUEWIT So should you be too, Jack Daw: what should keep you off? She is but a woman, and in disgrace. He'll be glad on't.

DAW Will he? I thought he would ha' been angry.

CLERIMONT You will dispatch, knights; it must be done, i' faith. 111

TRUEWIT Why, an' it must, it shall, sir, they say. They'll ne'er go back. (*Aside to* DAW *and* LA FOOLE) Do not tempt his patience.

DAW It is true indeed, sir.

LA FOOLE Yes, I assure you, sir.

MOROSE What is true, gentlemen? What do you assure me?

DAW That we have known your bride, sir—

LA FOOLE In good fashion. She was our mistress, or so—

CLERIMONT Nay, you must be plain, knights, as you were to me. 122

OTTER Ay, the question is, if you have *carnaliter* or no.

LA FOOLE *Carnaliter*? What else, sir?

OTTER It is enough: a plain nullity.

EPICOENE I am undone, I am undone!

MOROSE Oh, let me worship and adore you, gentlemen!

EPICOENE I am undone!

MOROSE Yes, to my hand, I thank these knights; master parson, let me thank you otherwise. 130

*Gives* OTTER *money*

CENTAURE And ha' they confessed?

MAVIS Now out upon 'em, informers!

TRUEWIT You see what creatures you may bestow your favours on, madams.

HAUGHTY I would except against 'em as beaten knights, wench, and not good witnesses in law.

---

123 *carnaliter*: carnally
129 to my hand: see IV.v.18–19n
135 except against: object to
135–6 beaten knights: cowardly, and therefore not admissible as witnesses or jurymen

MISTRESS OTTER  Poor gentlewoman, how she takes it!

HAUGHTY  Be comforted, Morose, I love you the better for't.

CENTAURE  So do I, I protest.　　　　　　　　　140

CUTBEARD  But, gentlemen, you have not known her since *matrimonium*?

DAW  Not today, master doctor.

LA FOOLE  No, sir, not today.

CUTBEARD  Why, then I say, for any act before, the *matrimonium* is good and perfect, unless the worshipful bridegroom did precisely, before witness, demand if she were *virgo ante nuptias*.

EPICOENE  No, that he did not, I assure you, master doctor.　　　　　　　　　150

CUTBEARD  If he cannot prove that, it is *ratum conjugium*, notwithstanding the premises. And they do no way *impedire*. And this is my sentence, this I pronounce.

OTTER  I am of master doctor's resolution too, sir; if you made not that demand, *ante nuptias*.

MOROSE  Oh my heart! Wilt thou break? Wilt thou break? This is worst of all worst worsts, that hell could have devised! Marry a whore! And so much noise!　　　　　　　　　160

DAUPHINE  Come, I see now plain confederacy in this doctor and this parson, to abuse a gentleman. You study his affliction. I pray be gone, companions. And gentlemen, I begin to suspect you for having parts with 'em. Sir, will it please you hear me?

MOROSE  Oh, do not talk to me, take not from me the pleasure of dying in silence, nephew.

DAUPHINE  Sir, I must speak to you. I have been long your poor despised kinsman, and many a hard thought has strengthened you against me; but now it shall appear if either I love you or your peace, and prefer them to all the world beside. I will not be long or grievous to you, sir. If I free you of this unhappy match absolutely and instantly after all this trouble, and almost in your despair, now—　　　175

MOROSE  (It cannot be.)

DAUPHINE  Sir, that you be never troubled with a murmur of it more, what shall I hope for, or deserve of you?

MOROSE  Oh, what thou wilt, nephew! Thou shalt deserve me and have me.　　　　　　180

DAUPHINE  Shall I have your favour perfect to me, and love hereafter?

MOROSE  That and anything beside. Make thine own conditions. My whole estate is thine. Manage it, I will become thy ward.

DAUPHINE  Nay, sir, I will not be so unreasonable.

EPICOENE  Will Sir Dauphine be mine enemy too?

DAUPHINE  You know I have been long a suitor to you, uncle, that out of your estate, which is fifteen hundred a year, you would allow me but five hundred during life, and assure the rest upon me after: to which I have often by myself and friends tendered you a writing to sign, which you would never consent, or incline to. If you please but to effect it now—　　195

MOROSE  Thou shalt have it, nephew. I will do it, and more.

DAUPHINE  If I quit you not presently and forever of this cumber, you shall have power instantly, afore all these, to revoke your act, and I will become whose slave you will give me to, forever.　　　201

MOROSE  Where is the writing? I will seal to it, that, or to a blank, and write thine own conditions.

EPICOENE  Oh me, most unfortunate wretched gentlewoman!

HAUGHTY  Will Sir Dauphine do this?

EPICOENE  Good sir, have some compassion on me.

MOROSE  Oh, my nephew knows you belike; away, crocodile!　　　　　　　　　209

CENTAURE  He does it not, sure, without good ground.

DAUPHINE  Here, sir.　　　　　　*Gives him papers*

MOROSE  Come, nephew; give me the pen. I will subscribe to anything, and seal to what thou wilt, for my deliverance. Thou art my restorer. Here, I deliver it thee as my deed. If there be a word in it lacking, or writ with false orthography, I protest before—I will not take the advantage.　　　*Returns papers*

DAUPHINE  Then here is your release, sir: (*he takes off* EPICOENE's *peruke*) you have married a boy: a gentleman's son that I have brought up this half year, at my great charges, and for this composition which I have now made with you. What say you, master doctor? This is *justum impedimentum*, I hope, *error personae*?　　　　　　　　　224

---

147  precisely: expressly
148  *virgo . . . nuptias*: a virgin before marriage
151–2  *ratum conjugium*: a valid marriage
152  premises: previous events
161  confederacy: conspiracy
163  study: seek, aim at
182  perfect to me: entirely for myself

199  cumber: encumbrance
208  belike: very likely
209  crocodile: believed to weep as it took its prey; hence, one who weeps false tears
216  protest before: most eds take the dash to indicate an omitted oath ('God', or 'heaven'); however, Holdsworth argues (persuasively) that there are many instances of oaths in the text, and that the phrase is complete as it stands, and means 'declare in advance'
219  you have married a boy: the source for this trick of disguising a boy as a bride is principally Pietro Aretino's *Il Marescalco* (1533), but also Machiavelli's *Clizia* (1525) and Plautus' *Casina*
221  composition: settlement
223  *justum impedimentum*: just impediment

OTTER Yes, sir, *in primo gradu.*

CUTBEARD *In primo gradu.*

DAUPHINE I thank you, good Doctor Cutbeard, and Parson Otter. (*He pulls off their beards and disguise*) You are beholden to 'em, sir, that have taken this pains for you; and my friend, Master Truewit, who enabled 'em for the business. Now you may go in and rest, be as private as you will, sir. I'll not trouble you, till you trouble me with your funeral, which I care not how soon it come. (*Exit* MOROSE) Cutbeard, I'll make your lease good. Thank me not, but with your leg, Cutbeard. And Tom Otter, your princess shall be reconciled to you. How now, gentlemen! Do you look at me? 238

CLERIMONT A boy.

DAUPHINE Yes, Mistress Epicoene.

TRUEWIT Well, Dauphine, you have lurched your friends of the better half of the garland, by concealing this part of the plot! But much good do it thee, thou deserv'st it, lad. And Clerimont, for thy unexpected bringing in these two to confession, wear my part of it freely. Nay, Sir Daw and Sir La Foole, you see the gentlewoman that has done you the favours! We are all thankful to you, and so should the womankind here, specially for lying on her, though not with her! You meant so, I am sure? But that we have stuck it upon you today, in your own imagined persons, and so lately, this Amazon, the champion of the sex, should beat you now thriftily for the common slanders which ladies receive from such cuckoos as you are. You are they that, when no merit or fortune can make you hope to enjoy their bodies, will yet lie with their reputations, and make their fame suffer. Away, you common moths of these and all ladies' honours. Go, travail to make legs and faces, and come home with some new matter to be laughed at: you deserve to live in an air as corrupted as that wherewith you feed rumour. (*Exeunt* DAW *and* LA FOOLE) Madams, you are mute upon this new metamorphosis! But here stands she that has vindicated your fames. Take heed of such *insectae* hereafter. And let it not trouble you that you have discovered any mysteries to this young gentleman. He is (a'most) of years, and will make a good visitant within this twelvemonth. In the meantime we'll all undertake for his secrecy, that can speak so well of his silence. (*Coming forward*) Spectators, if you like this comedy, rise cheerfully, and now Morose is gone in, clap your hands. It may be that noise will cure him, at least please him. 274

*Exeunt*

THE END

EPICOENE

This comedy was first acted in the year 1609

By the Children of her Majesty's Revels

The principal comedians were

| | |
|---|---|
| Nathan Field | William Barksted |
| Giles Carey | William Penn |
| Hugh Attawell | Richard Allin |
| John Smith | John Blaney |

With the allowance of the Master of Revels

---

225 *in . . . gradu*: in the first degree
235 make . . . good: see Morose's promise, II.v.93–4
241 lurched: cheated
242 garland: wreath, given to mark a triumph; hence, 'glory'. Possibly an allusion to *Coriolanus*, II.ii.97
249 on: about
251–2 stuck it upon: cheated
252 this Amazon: Mistress Otter
253 thriftily: soundly
259 travail: travel and labour
   make legs and faces: bow and smirk
265 *insectae*: insects; the incorrect feminine form (in place of the correct neuter) highlights the knights' effeminacy

267 discovered: revealed
268 of years: adult
273 noise: i.e. of clapping
   Master of Revels: who licensed plays for performance; at this time, Sir George Buc

# The Roaring Girle.

## OR

### Moll Cut-Purse.

As it hath lately beene Acted on the Fortune-stage by
the Prince his Players.

Written by *T. Middleton* and *T. Dekkar*.

My case is alter'd, I must worke for my liuing.

Printed at *London* for *Thomas Archer*, and are to be sold at his
shop in Popes head-pallace, neere the Royall
Exchange. 1611.

Title page woodcut of the first edition of *The Roaring Girl* (1611) reproduced with
permission of the Bodleian Library, University of Oxford. Shelfmark Mal 246 (1)

# Thomas Middleton and Thomas Dekker,
## *The Roaring Girl*

First performed 1611
First published 1611

'My case is alter'd, I must worke for my living': so runs the punningly ambiguous caption to the woodcut of Moll Cutpurse on the title page of the first edition of *The Roaring Girl*. 'Case' meant 'clothing' (and in the print Moll is, characteristically, cross-dressed), but it was also slang for 'vagina', the fantasised alteration to which is perhaps emblematised here by Moll's strategically positioned phallic sword. The merging of these two meanings in one word suggests their inseparability in this play: Moll's adoption of male dress – an adoption that is not a disguise, for (unlike Shakespeare's cross-dressed heroines) everyone knows she is a woman – quite explicitly calls into question her body and its meanings, both sexual and social. Other characters in the play are all too eager to draw conclusions about the significance of her dress: for Sir Alexander, for example, Moll's refusal of a 'proper' mode of femininity suggests to him that she must also be a thief, whilst for Laxton, it marks her out as a whore. Both assume that other forms of disorderliness will accompany her sartorial choices, and both seek, unsuccessfully, to exploit their (mis)readings of her. Moll thus serves as a touchstone for testing the accuracy, validity and rectitude of the other characters' interpretations and values.

Moll herself explains her cross-dressing in terms that are at once quite distinct from these mistaken ones, and yet help to make sense of them. She argues that it sets her outside the conventional desires and ambitions associated with femininity, specifically with regard to marriage, saying, 'I have no humour to marry . . . I have the head now of myself, and am man enough for a woman; marriage is but a chopping and changing, where a maiden loses one head, and has a worse i'th'place' (II.ii.38–9, 45–8). Furthermore, cross-dressing frees her into an untrammelled and fluid social space, where she is equally at home with and respected by Lord Noland, at one social extreme, and the vagrant rogues Trapdoor and Tearcat, at the other. Here, Moll administers a rough but equitable judicial system, one markedly fairer than the corrupt and manipulable one in the pay of Sir Alexander and Sir Davy (see III.iii and IV.i). Moll also enjoys a carnivalesque allegiance to 'mirth' – an allegiance that, again, Moll says is all too often misread: 'I'm given to sport, I'm often merry,

jest:/Had mirth no kindred in the world but lust?' (III.i.107–8). So whilst her cross-dressing is *mis*recognised in the play as indicative of dishonesty, both sexual and with regard to property, it is *correctly* seen as a comment on the sexual and social mores that position women as subordinate to men, and property as superior to morality.

The figure of Moll thus condenses many of the play's thematic concerns. She is either trigger to, or comment on, the play's various interrogations of the circulation between appearance, gender, sexuality and power, just as she is a structural linchpin, the common element in the various strands of the plot, holding or bringing together those concerning the gentry, the gallants, the citizens and the underworld characters. Moll is without doubt the play's focal point, an object of fascination for the other characters just as the contemporary figure on whom Moll was based, the notorious Mary Frith (c. 1584–1659), was the object of popular fascination for readers and audiences at this time. Like Moll, Frith could be cast as a 'roaring girl': someone who, like her masculine counterparts, the swaggering, brawling 'roaring boys', lived on the margins of civil society, eschewing its conventions and regulations. Whilst the play seeks to capitalise on the contemporary predilection for figures such as Frith, it also seeks to rescue Moll from the social opprobrium that went along with it. As the Prologus makes clear, Moll is not of the common run of roaring girls: 'she flies/With wings more lofty' (lines 25–6); and in part this rescue is effected through her desexualisation. Whilst she exposes the hypocrisy of others' sexual machinations, and smoothes the course of the romance between Sebastian and Mary, she herself remains immune not only to marriage, but also to sexual desire. Moll's status as moral touchstone, it seems, is tenable only through her separation from the appetites that drive, threaten and compromise the other characters. Just as she has no stake in the acquisitiveness that we see in Sir Alexander and Sir Davy, so she has no personal investment in the sexual manoeuvrings of the citizens, their wives and the gallants. It is worth noting, however, that although Moll is at least allowed the pleasure of a moment of 'innocent' acquisitiveness—we see her being fitted for a new outfit in II.ii—there does not seem to be a way in which to conceptualise a parallel 'innocent' appetite for sexual pleasure in her. It is this immunity to appetite that distinguishes her from the other characters in the play, and which allows her to resolve the dilemmas in which they find themselves.

However, the singularity of Moll as a character should not be allowed to obscure what this play has in common with other city comedies. The generationally based conflict of money versus love, the sub-plots testing and, on the whole, endorsing the citizens' sexual constancy, and the fascination with the underworld can all be found in many other plays of the genre. In this sense, *The Roaring Girl* typifies and extends a generic preoccupation with analysing the fate of conventional meanings of gender and sexuality in the context of fast-changing social circumstances, thereby constituting a series of intriguingly open-ended questions regarding their origins in, and implications for, wider networks of social power relations. It is thus symptomatic of a more general and widespread contemporary anxiety about the instability of traditional values and certainties, which were increasingly under pressure from an emergent capitalism, and the profound social changes which were a part of it.

## Textual note

The text is based on the first edition of the play (in quarto), published in London in 1611. Q in the footnotes here signals a reference to this edition. Elizabeth Cook includes in her edition substantial extracts from the following texts, referred to here in the footnotes:

Awdeley, John (1561) *The Fraternity of Vagabonds*, London.
Dekker, Thomas (1608) *The Bellman of London*, London.
Dekker, Thomas (1608) *Lanthorn and Candlelight*, London.
Harman, Thomas, (1566) *A Caveat for Common Cursitors*, London.

# Further reading

## Editions

Bowers, Fredson (ed.) (1958) *The Dramatic Works of Thomas Dekker*, vol. III, Cambridge: Cambridge University Press.
Bullen, A. H. (ed.) (1885) *The Works of Thomas Middleton*, vol. IV, London: John C. Nimmo.
Cook, Elizabeth (ed.) (1997) *The Roaring Girl*, The New Mermaids (revised from Gomme's 1976 edition), London: A. & C. Black.
Ellis, Havelock (ed.) (1890) *Thomas Middleton*, vol. II, The Mermaid Series, London: T. Fisher Unwin.
Farmer, J. S. (ed.) (1914) *The Roaring Girle*, facsimile of 1611 edition, Amersham: Tudor Facsimile Texts.
Gomme, Andor (ed.) (1976) *The Roaring Girl*, The New Mermaids, London: Ernest Benn Limited.
Mulholland, Paul (ed.) (1987) *The Roaring Girl*, The Revels Plays, Manchester: Manchester University Press.

# Critical and contextual commentaries

Baston, Jane (1997) 'Rehabilitating Moll's Subversion in *The Roaring Girl*', *Studies in English Literature 1500–1900*, 37, 2: 317–35.
Chakravorty, Swapan (1996) *Society and Politics in the Plays of Thomas Middleton*, Oxford: Clarendon Press.
Cheney, Patrick (1983) 'Moll Cutpurse as Hermaphrodite in Dekker and Middleton's *The Roaring Girl*', *Renaissance and Reformation*, 7, 2: 120–34.
Comensoli, Viviana (1987) 'Play-making, Domestic Conduct, and the Multiple Plot in *The Roaring Girl*', *Studies in English Literature 1500–1900*, 27, 2: 249–66.
Dawson, Anthony B. (1993) 'Mistris Hic & Haec: Representations of Moll Frith', *Studies in English Literature 1500–1900*, 33, 2: 385–404.
Dekker, Rudolf M. and van de Pol, Lotte C. (1989) *The Tradition of Female Transvestism in Early Modern Europe*, Basingstoke: Macmillan.
Garber, Marjorie (1991) 'The Logic of the Transvestite: *The Roaring Girl*', in David Scott Kastan and Peter Stallybrass (eds) *Staging the Renaissance: Reinterpretations of Elizabethan and Jacobean Drama*, London: Routledge.
Gibbons, Brian (1980) *Jacobean City Comedy: A Study of Satiric Plays by Jonson, Marston and Middleton*, 2nd edition, London: Methuen.
Heinemann, Margot (1980) *Puritanism and Theatre: Thomas Middleton and Opposition Drama under the Early Stuarts*, Cambridge: Cambridge University Press.
Howard, Jean E. (1992) 'Sex and Social Conflict: The Erotics of *The Roaring Girl*', in Susan Zimmerman (ed.) *Erotic Politics: Desire on the Renaissance Stage*, London and New York: Routledge.
—— (1993) 'Cross-dressing, the Theater, and Gender Struggle in Early Modern England', in Lesley Ferris (ed.) *Crossing the Stage: Controversies on Cross-dressing*, London: Routledge.
Jardine, Lisa (1989) *Still Harping on Daughters: Women and Drama in the Age of Shakespeare*, 2nd edition, Hemel Hempstead: Harvester Wheatsheaf.
Kermode, Lloyd E. (1997) 'Destination Doomsday: Desires for Change and Changeable Desire in *The Roaring Girl*', *English Literary Renaissance*, 27, 3: 421–42.
Krantz, Susan E. 'The Sexual Identities of Moll Cutpurse in Dekker and Middleton's *The Roaring Girl* and in London', *Renaissance and Reformation*, 19, 1: 5–20.
McLuskie, Kathleen (1994) *Dekker and Heywood*, Basingstoke: Macmillan.
Miller, Jo E. (1990) 'Women and the Market in *The Roaring Girl*', *Renaissance and Reformation*, 14, 1: 11–23.
Mulholland, Paul (1977) 'The Date of *The Roaring Girl*', *Review of English Studies*, new series, 28: 18–31.
Orgel, Stephen (1992) 'The Subtexts of *The Roaring Girl*', in Susan Zimmerman (ed.) *Erotic Politics: Desire on the Renaissance Stage*, London and New York, NY: Routledge.
Rose, Mary Beth (1984) 'Women in Men's Clothing: Apparel and Social Stability in *The Roaring Girl*', *English Literary Renaissance*, 14, 3: 367–91.
Rustici, Craig (1999) 'The Smoking Girl: Tobacco and the Representation of Mary Frith', *Studies in Philology*, 96, 2: 159–79.

Shepherd, Simon (1981) *Amazons and Warrior Women*, Brighton: Harvester Wheatsheaf.

Wells, Susan (1981) 'Jacobean City Comedy and the Ideology of the City', *English Literary History*, 48: 37–60.

White, Martin (1992) *Middleton and Tourneur*, Basingstoke: Macmillan.

## Works of related interest

Ben Jonson, *Every Man in His Humour* (1598)

William Shakespeare, *As You Like It* (1599)

William Shakespeare, *Twelfth Night* (1601)

John Marston, *The Dutch Courtesan* (1604)

Thomas Middleton, *A Trick to Catch the Old One* (1605)

Francis Beaumont, *The Knight of the Burning Pestle* (1607)

Ben Jonson, *Epicoene, or The Silent Woman* (1609)

Ben Jonson, *The Alchemist* (1610)

Thomas Middleton, *A Chaste Maid in Cheapside* (1613)

Ben Jonson, *Bartholomew Fair* (1614)

Philip Massinger, *The City Madam* (1632)

Anon., *The Life and Death of Mrs. Mary Frith, Commonly Called Moll Cutpurse* (1662; republished 1993, Randall S. Nakayama (ed.) *The Life and Death of Mrs. Mary Frith*, New York, London: Garland)

# *The Roaring Girl* (1611)

## To the Comic Play-Readers, Venery and Laughter

The fashion of play-making I can properly compare to nothing so naturally as the alteration in apparel: for in the time of the great crop-doublet, your huge bombasted plays, quilted with mighty words to lean purpose, was only then in fashion. And as the doublet fell, neater inventions began to set up. Now in the time of spruceness, our plays follow the niceness of our garments, single plots, quaint conceits, lecherous jests, dressed up in hanging sleeves, and those are fit for the times and the termers: such a kind of light-colour summer stuff, mingled with diverse colours, you shall find this published comedy, good to keep you in an afternoon from dice, at home in your chambers; and for venery you shall find enough for sixpence, but well couched and you mark it. For Venus being a woman passes through the play in doublet and breeches, a brave disguise and a safe one, if the statute untie not her codpiece point. The book I make no question but is fit

for many of your companies, as well as the person itself, and may be allowed both gallery room at the playhouse, and chamber room at your lodging. Worse things I must needs confess the world has taxed her for, than has been written of her; but 'tis the excellency of a writer to leave things better than he finds 'em; though some obscene fellow (that cares not what he writes against others, yet keeps a mystical bawdy-house himself, and entertains drunkards to make use of their pockets and vent his private bottle-ale at midnight)— though such a one would have ripped up the most nasty vice that ever hell belched forth, and presented it to a modest assembly, yet we rather wish in such discoveries, where reputation lies bleeding, a slackness of truth, than fullness of slander.           **33**

THOMAS MIDDLETON

## Dramatis personae

SIR ALEXANDER WENGRAVE, *and* NEATFOOT, *his man*

SIR ADAM APPLETON

SIR DAVY DAPPER

SIR BEAUTEOUS GANYMEDE

SIR THOMAS LONG

---

Venery: good hunting, but also the pursuit of sexual pleasure; see III.i.45

3  crop-doublet: a short, very padded doublet, which went out of fashion about 1580

4  bombasted: bombast was cotton stuffing, but the word was also used figuratively

5  only then: i.e. the only thing then

5–6  the doublet fell: i.e. it became longer

7  niceness: elegance

8  single: Mulholland suggests 'simple', since otherwise the description does not fit this or other plays of the time; Cook suggests it may be meant ironically
quaint conceits: fanciful expressions

9  hanging sleeves: long, open-cuffed sleeves

10  termers: those who came to London for the terms of the Inns of Court, whether for amusement or business

14  sixpence: the usual price of a printed play
well couched: a) well hidden; b) richly embroidered

15  and: if

17  statute: Moll could have been prosecuted for cross-dressing 'in an ecclesiastical court for indecency or uncleanness' (cited by Mulholland)

18  codpiece point: lace holding up the breeches

25  obscene: offensive, loathsome

26  mystical: secret

28  vent . . . bottle-ale: seems to be an obscure sexual joke; 'bottle ale' meant, as well as beer, 'windy rhetoric'; 'vent' meant 'sniff out' as well as 'discharge', and 'bottle' was one of many words for the female genitals (see *Measure for Measure*, III.i.405) (Cook)

29  ripped up: exposed
Dramatis personae: this list follows the Prologus in Q

1  WENGRAVE: spelt thus in the text, but 'Went-grave' in the Dramatis Personae, suggesting he 'went grave' in response to the dowry to be brought by Mary Fitzallard if she married his son; see I.i.83–96
NEATFOOT: spelt thus in the text, but Neats-foot in the Dramatis Personae. A neats-foot was an ox-foot used for food

4  SIR BEAUTEOUS GANYMEDE: Ganymede was cup-bearer to the gods. The name had homosexual connotations ('catamite' is derived from it)

LORD NOLAND

*Young* SEBASTIAN WENGRAVE

JACK DAPPER, *and* GULL, *his page*

GOSHAWK

GREENWIT                                                                    10

LAXTON

TILTYARD, *a feather-seller* ⎫

OPENWORK, *a sempster*    ⎬  *Cives & Uxores*

GALLIPOT, *an apothecary*  ⎭

MOLL, *the Roaring Girl*

TRAPDOOR

TEARCAT

SIR GUY FITZALLARD

MARY FITZALLARD, *his daughter*

CURTILAX, *a Sergeant, and*                                                  20

HANGER, *his Yeoman*

*Ministri*

*Coachman, Porter, Tailor, Gentlemen, Cutpurses, Fellow*

---

8  JACK DAPPER: Mulholland notes that the term 'dapper
   jack' was commonly used scornfully or mockingly; see
   *Edward II*, I.iv.413

11 LAXTON: play on 'lack-stone': he has sold his land
   (III.i.51) and he is impotent ('stones' meant testicles); see
   I.ii.55–8

12 TILTYARD: a tiltyard was a jousting ground; the
   character is 'so named for the abundant use of feathers by
   tiltyard combatants' (Mulholland). 'Yard' also meant
   penis

13 OPENWORK: work featuring a pattern of holes, such
   as lace or crochet; the openness extends to his
   character
   *Cives et Uxores*: citizens and their wives

14 GALLIPOT: a gallipot was a small glazed pot used for
   medicines

15 MOLL: a general name for whores; a diminutive of 'Mary',
   a name signifying chastity. For 'roaring girl', see
   headnote, p. 327

16 TRAPDOOR: so called because of the danger he presents to
   others: see I.ii.246–7. Cook suggests that he might
   initially have appeared and disappeared through the
   trapdoor in the stage, to accentuate 'the infernal
   atmosphere he carries with him' (p. xxiv)

17 TEARCAT: a bully or swaggerer

20 CURTILAX: a cutlass

21 HANGER: a loop on a belt on which a sword was hung, or
   the sword itself

22 *Ministri*: servants

# Prologus

A play expected long makes the audience look
For wonders: that each scene should be a book,
Composed to all perfection; each one comes
And brings a play in's head with him: up he sums
What he would of a roaring girl have writ;
If that he finds not here, he mews at it.
Only we entreat you think our scene
Cannot speak high (the subject being but mean);
A roaring girl, whose notes till now never were,
Shall fill with laughter our vast theatre,                                  10
That's all which I dare promise: tragic passion,
And such grave stuff, is this day out of fashion.
I see attention sets wide ope her gates
Of hearing, and with covetous listening waits,
To know what girl this roaring girl should be,
For of that tribe are many. One is she
That roars at midnight in deep tavern bowls,
That beats the watch, and constables controls;
Another roars i'th'daytime, swears, stabs, gives
     braves,
Yet sells her soul to the lust of fools and slaves.                         20
Both these are suburb-roarers. Then there's
     besides
A civil city-roaring girl, whose pride,
Feasting, and riding, shakes her husband's state,
And leaves him roaring through an iron grate.
None of these roaring girls is ours: she flies
With wings more lofty. Thus her character lies,
Yet what need characters, when to give a guess
Is better than the person to express?
But would you know who 'tis? Would you hear her
     name?
She is called Mad Moll; her life our acts proclaim.                         30

---

6  mews: jeers by mewing

10 vast theatre: the Fortune was large (about 1,842 sq. ft.,
   capable of holding over 3,000 playgoers), but not
   excessively so: the Globe, for example, was 2,500 sq. ft.,
   and could take over 3,500 playgoers; see Gurr 1996:
   18–21

17 bowls: broad drinking cups

18 watch: street patrol which acted as police; they were in
   the charge of a constable

19 gives braves: makes a show of defiance
   (Mulholland)

21 suburb-roarers: the suburbs lay outside the city walls,
   beyond the jurisdiction of the city authorities; they were
   thus identified with those wary of the law, such as
   prostitutes and thieves

24 iron grate: i.e. of a prison

# Act I, scene i

*Enter* MARY FITZALLARD *disguised like a sempster with a case for bands, and* NEATFOOT *a serving-man with her, with a napkin on his shoulder and a trencher in his hand, as from table*

NEATFOOT  The young gentleman, our young master, Sir Alexander's son, is it into his ears, sweet damsel, emblem of fragility, you desire to have a message transported, or to be transcendent?

MARY  A private word or two, sir, nothing else.

NEATFOOT  You shall fructify in that which you come for: your pleasure shall be satisfied to your full contentation: I will, fairest tree of generation, watch when our young master is erected, that is to say, up, and deliver him to this your most white hand.  **10**

MARY  Thanks, sir.

NEATFOOT  And withal certify him, that I have culled out for him, now his belly is replenished, a daintier bit or modicum than any lay upon his trencher at dinner. Hath he notion of your name, I beseech your chastity?

MARY  One, sir, of whom he bespake falling bands.

NEATFOOT  Falling bands, it shall so be given him.—If you please to venture your modesty in the hall, amongst a curl-pated company of rude serving-men, and take such as they can set before you, you shall be most seriously, and ingeniously welcome.  **22**

MARY  I have dined indeed already, sir.

NEATFOOT  Or will you vouchsafe to kiss the lip of a cup of rich Orleans in the buttery amongst our waiting-women?

MARY  Not now in truth, sir.

NEATFOOT  Our young master shall then have a feeling of your being here: presently it shall so be given him.  *Exit* NEATFOOT

MARY  I humbly thank you, sir. But that my bosom  **30**

Is full of bitter sorrows, I could smile
To see this formal ape play antic tricks:
But in my breast a poisoned arrow sticks,
And smiles cannot become me. Love woven slightly
(Such as thy false heart makes) wears out as lightly,
But love being truly bred i'th'soul (like mine)
Bleeds even to death, at the least wound it takes:
The more we quench this fire, the less it slakes.
Oh me!

*Enter* SEBASTIAN WENGRAVE *with* NEATFOOT

SEBASTIAN  A sempster speak with me, sayest thou?  **40**

NEATFOOT  Yes sir, she's there, *viva voce*, to deliver her auricular confession.

SEBASTIAN  With me, sweetheart? What is't?

MARY  I have brought home your bands, sir.

SEBASTIAN  Bands?—Neatfoot.

NEATFOOT  Sir.

SEBASTIAN  Prithee look in, for all the gentlemen are upon rising.

NEATFOOT  Yes sir, a most methodical attendance shall be given.

SEBASTIAN  And dost hear? If my father call for me, say I am busy with a sempster.  **51**

NEATFOOT  Yes sir, he shall know it that you are busied with a needlewoman.

SEBASTIAN  In's ear, good Neatfoot.

NEATFOOT  It shall be so given him.  *Exit* NEATFOOT

SEBASTIAN  Bands? You'are mistaken, sweetheart, I bespake none. When, where, I prithee? What bands? Let me see them.

MARY  Yes sir, a bond fast sealed, with solemn oaths, Subscribed unto (as I thought) with your soul,  **60**
Delivered as your deed in sight of heaven.
Is this bond cancelled, have you forgot me?

SEBASTIAN  Ha! Life of my life, Sir Guy Fitzallard's daughter,
What has transformed my love to this strange shape?
Stay: make all sure. (*Shuts door*)—So: now speak and be brief,
Because the wolf's at door that lies in wait
To prey upon us both. Albeit mine eyes
Are blessed by thine, yet this so strange disguise
Holds me with fear and wonder.

MARY                              Mine's a loathed sight,

---

Act I, scene i: the only scene heading in Q. We follow divisions introduced by other eds here

SD  *sempster*: this form of the word was applicable to both men and women at this time
  *case for bands*: a box for collar-bands
  *trencher*: wooden plate or dish, used before pewter was commonplace

4  transcendent: affected language typical of Neatfoot; the exact meaning is unclear, but he uses it to imply a private meeting beween Mary and Sebastian

6  fructify . . . come for: sexual quibbles such as these continue through Neatfoot's speeches in this scene

17  falling bands: collars worn falling flat round the neck

22  ingeniously: ingenuously (the two words were often confused)

23  dined: eds (dyed Q)

25  Orleans: wine from the Loire area

29  presently: immediately

---

34  slightly: loosely

38  fire: eds (Q omits)

41  *viva voce*: by word of mouth

42  auricular confession: a term usually used of confession to a priest; the insinuation is the confession of sexual misdemeanours

53  needlewoman: 'needle' had sense of 'penis' at this time (Mulholland); hence sexual pun on 'prostitute'

59  bond: 'bond' and 'band' were used interchangeably

66  the wolf's at door: proverbial

Why from it are you banished else so long? 70

SEBASTIAN  I must cut short my speech: in broken language,
Thus much, sweet Moll: I must thy company shun,
I court another Moll, my thoughts must run
As a horse runs that's blind, round in a mill,
Out every step, yet keeping one path still.

MARY  Hm! Must you shun my company? In one knot
Have both our hands by th'hands of heaven been tied,
Now to be broke? I thought me once your bride:
Our fathers did agree on the time when;
And must another bedfellow fill my room? 80

SEBASTIAN  Sweet maid, let's lose no time: 'tis in heaven's book
Set down, that I must have thee: an oath we took
To keep our vows; but when the knight your father
Was from mine parted, storms began to sit
Upon my covetous father's brows, which fell
From them on me: he reckoned up what gold
This marriage would draw from him, at which he swore,
To lose so much blood could not grieve him more.
He then dissuades me from thee, called thee not fair,
And asked what is she but a beggar's heir? 90
He scorned thy dowry of five thousand marks.
If such a sum of money could be found,
And I would match with that, he'd not undo it,
Provided his bags might add nothing to it,
But vowed, if I took thee, nay more, did swear it,
Save birth, from him I nothing should inherit.

MARY  What follows then—my shipwreck?

SEBASTIAN                                  Dearest, no:
Though wildly in a labyrinth I go,
My end is to meet thee: with a side wind
Must I now sail, else I no haven can find, 100
But both must sink forever. There's a wench
Called Moll, mad Moll, or merry Moll, a creature
So strange in quality, a whole city takes
Note of her name and person: all that affection
I owe to thee, on her in counterfeit passion
I spend to mad my father: he believes

I doat upon this roaring girl, and grieves
As it becomes a father for a son
That could be so bewitched; yet I'll go on
This crooked way, sigh still for her, feign dreams 110
In which I'll talk only of her: these streams
Shall, I hope, force my father to consent
That here I anchor, rather than be rent
Upon a rock so dangerous. Art thou pleased,
Because thou seest we are waylaid, that I take
A path that's safe, though it be far about?

MARY  My prayers with heaven guide thee!

SEBASTIAN                                  Then I will on.
My father is at hand, kiss and begone;
Hours shall be watched for meetings; I must now,
As men for fear, to a strange idol bow. 120

MARY  Farewell.

SEBASTIAN      I'll guide thee forth: when next we meet,
A story of Moll shall make our mirth more sweet.

*Exeunt*

# Act I, scene ii

*Enter* SIR ALEXANDER WENGRAVE, SIR DAVY DAPPER,
SIR ADAM APPLETON, GOSHAWK, LAXTON, *and*
GENTLEMEN

OMNES  Thanks, good Sir Alexander, for our bounteous cheer.

SIR ALEXANDER  Fie, fie, in giving thanks you pay too dear.

SIR DAVY  When bounty spreads the table, faith 'twere sin,
At going off, if thanks should not step in.

SIR ALEXANDER  No more of thanks, no more. Ay, marry sir,
Th'inner room was too close; how do you like
This parlour, gentlemen?

OMNES                    Oh passing well.

SIR ADAM  What a sweet breath the air casts here, so cool!

GOSHAWK  I like the prospect best.

LAXTON                        See how 'tis furnished.

SIR DAVY  A very fair sweet room.

SIR ALEXANDER                    Sir Davy Dapper, 10
The furniture that doth adorn this room
Cost many a fair grey groat ere it came here,
But good things are most cheap, when they're most dear.

---

74  horse . . . mill: proverbial. A horse that turned a millstone walked in constant circles round the stone

76–83  one knot . . . our vows: these lines suggest that Sebastian and Mary have already taken vows that bind them legally: they 'have apparently entered into a precontract known as "spousals *de futuro*" . . . If *bedfellow* [l. 80] implies "carnal Copulation" . . . their spousals have become the equivalent of matrimony' (Mulholland)

91  five thousand marks: a mark (which was an amount, not a coin) was worth two-thirds of a pound sterling. This, then, was the equivalent of £3,333, a considerable sum of money, and well above the usual marriage settlement amongst the gentry; see Mulholland, p. 58, n. 65

106  mad: madden

11–32  these lines have been taken to describe the Fortune theatre, with its socially diverse audience

12  grey groat: a groat was a coin worth about 4d (about 1.5 pence); Sir Alexander is here boasting of his lavish spending on his house and furnishings

13  good things . . . dear: version of a proverb: 'the best is best cheap', Tilley, B319

Nay when you look into my galleries,
How bravely they are trimmed up, you all shall swear
You're highly pleased to see what's set down there:
Stories of men and women, mixed together
Fair ones with foul, like sunshine in wet weather;
Within one square a thousand heads are laid
So close that all of heads the room seems made;      20
As many faces there, filled with blithe looks,
Show like the promising titles of new books
Writ merrily, the readers being their own eyes,
Which seem to move and to give plaudities;
And here and there, whilst with obsequious ears
Thronged heaps do listen, a cutpurse thrusts and leers
With hawk's eyes for his prey; I need not show him:
By a hanging villainous look yourselves may know
      him,
The face is drawn so rarely. Then sir, below,
The very floor, as 'twere, waves to and fro,      30
And like a floating island seems to move,
Upon a sea bound in with shores above.

*Enter* SEBASTIAN *and* MASTER GREENWIT

OMNES These sights are excellent.
SIR ALEXANDER                    I'll show you all:
   Since we are met, make our parting comical.
SEBASTIAN This gentleman, my friend, will take his
   leave, sir.
SIR ALEXANDER  Ha, take his leave, Sebastian? Who?
SEBASTIAN                    This gentleman.
SIR ALEXANDER  Your love, sir, has already given me
   some time,
   And if you please to trust my age with more,
   It shall pay double interest: good sir, stay.
GREENWIT  I have been too bold.
SIR ALEXANDER                    Not so, sir. A merry day
   'Mongst friends being spent, is better than gold
      saved.      41

---

14–20 Nay . . . made: 'Sir Alexander's collection suggests a
      parody of the great collections which began to be made
      in Elizabeth's reign . . . Pictures were sometimes fixed to
      the wall so close together as to make a mosaic covering
      the wall entirely' (Cook)
      galleries: a) for the exhibition of art works; b) the
      balconies of the Fortune theatre
15  bravely . . . trimmed up: finely they are decorated
19  one square: the Fortune theatre was, unlike the other
      'public' theatres, built on a square plan
      a thousand heads: Elizabethan theatres could easily hold
      around 3,000 spectators; see Prologus, l. 10n
24  plaudities: rounds of applause
26  a cutpurse: a thief or pickpocket who cut his victims'
      purses from their belts. Cutpurses were one of the
      hazards of playgoing
30–1 The very floor . . . island: i.e. the stage is floating on a
      sea of seething spectators
34  comical: happy

Some wine, some wine. Where be these knaves I
   keep?

*Enter three or four* SERVING-MEN, *and* NEATFOOT

NEATFOOT  At your worshipful elbow, sir.
SIR ALEXANDER  You are kissing my maids, drinking, or
   fast asleep.
NEATFOOT  Your worship has given it us right.
SIR ALEXANDER  You varlets, stir:
   Chairs, stools, and cushions: prithee Sir Davy Dapper,
   Make that chair thine.
SIR DAVY                    'Tis but an easy gift,
   And yet I thank you for it, sir, I'll take it.
SIR ALEXANDER  A chair for old Sir Adam Appleton.  49
NEATFOOT  A back friend to your worship.
SIR ADAM                    Marry, good Neatfoot,
   I thank thee for it: back friends sometimes are good.
SIR ALEXANDER  Pray make that stool your perch, good
   Master Goshawk.
GOSHAWK  I stoop to your lure, sir.
SIR ALEXANDER                    Son Sebastian,
   Take Master Greenwit to you.
SEBASTIAN                    Sit, dear friend.
SIR ALEXANDER  Nay Master Laxton—furnish Master
   Laxton
   With what he wants, a stone—a stool I would say,
   A stool.
LAXTON  I had rather stand, sir.
SIR ALEXANDER                    I know you had,
   Good Master Laxton. So, so.
                    *Exeunt* NEATFOOT *and* SERVANTS
   Now here's a mess of friends; and, gentlemen,
   Because time's glass shall not be running long,      60
   I'll quicken it with a pretty tale.
SIR DAVY                    Good tales do well
   In these bad days, where vice does so excel.
SIR ADAM  Begin, Sir Alexander.
SIR ALEXANDER                    Last day I met
   An aged man upon whose head was scored
   A debt of just so many years as these
   Which I owe to my grave; the man you all know.

---

45  varlets: a) servants; b) knaves
50  back friend: a backer or supporter, with allusion to a
      variant meaning: a false friend
52–3 perch . . . stoop to your lure: playing on Goshawk's
      name: 'stoop' meant 'submit'; a 'lure' was a falconer's
      apparatus for recalling a hawk (eds)
56–8 eds' lineation (With what . . . stoole/I had . . . stand,
      sir/I know . . . Q)
56  what . . . stone: a play on Laxton's name (i.e. lack-stone);
      'stone' meant testicle; see 'Dramatis Personae' l. 11n
57  stand: with pun ('stand' meant to have an erection)
59  mess: company
60  Because . . . long: 'so that time should not hang heavy on
      us' (Cook)

OMNES  His name I pray you, sir.

SIR ALEXANDER                Nay, you shall pardon me.
　But when he saw me (with a sigh that brake,
　Or seemed to break, his heart-strings) thus he spake:
　Oh my good knight, says he (and then his eyes      70
　Were richer even by that which made them poor,
　They had spent so many tears they had no more),
　Oh sir, says he, you know it, for you ha' seen
　Blessings to rain upon mine house and me:
　Fortune, who slaves men, was my slave; her wheel
　Hath spun me golden threads, for, I thank heaven,
　I ne'er had but one cause to curse my stars.
　I asked him then what that one cause might be.

OMNES  So, sir.

SIR ALEXANDER  He paused; and as we often see
　A sea so much becalmed there can be found      80
　No wrinkle on his brow, his waves being drowned
　In their own rage; but when th'imperious winds
　Use strange invisible tyranny to shake
　Both heaven's and earth's foundation at their noise,
　The seas, swelling with wrath to part that fray,
　Rise up, and are more wild, more mad than they—
　Even so, this good old man was by my question
　Stirred up to roughness, you might see his gall
　Flow even in's eyes; then grew he fantastical.

SIR DAVY  Fantastical? Ha, ha.

SIR ALEXANDER                Yes, and talked oddly.  90

SIR ADAM  Pray sir, proceed,
　How did this old man end?

SIR ALEXANDER                Marry sir, thus.
　He left his wild fit to read o'er his cards;
　Yet then (though age cast snow on all his hairs)
　He joyed because, says he, the god of gold
　Has been to me no niggard; that disease
　Of which all old men sicken, avarice,
　Never infected me—

LAXTON  (Aside) He means not himself, I'm sure.

SIR ALEXANDER          For like a lamp
　Fed with continual oil, I spend and throw      100
　My light to all that need it, yet have still
　Enough to serve myself; oh but, quoth he,
　Though heaven's dew fall thus on this aged tree,
　I have a son that's like a wedge doth cleave
　My very heart-root.

SIR DAVY            Had he such a son?

SEBASTIAN  (Aside) Now I do smell a fox strongly.

SIR ALEXANDER  Let's see: no, Master Greenwit is not
　yet
　So mellow in years as he; but as like Sebastian,

Just like my son Sebastian—such another.      109

SEBASTIAN  (Aside) How finely, like a fencer, my father
　fetches his by-blows to hit me, but if I beat you not
　at your own weapon of subtlety—

SIR ALEXANDER  This son, saith he, that should be
　The column and main arch unto my house,
　The crutch unto my age, becomes a whirlwind
　Shaking the firm foundation—

SIR ADAM                'Tis some prodigal.

SEBASTIAN  (Aside) Well shot, old Adam Bell.

SIR ALEXANDER  No city monster neither, no prodigal,
　But sparing, wary, civil, and (though wifeless)
　An excellent husband, and such a traveller,      120
　He has more tongues in his head than some have
　teeth.

SIR DAVY  I have but two in mine.

GOSHAWK  So sparing and so wary:
　What then could vex his father so?

SIR ALEXANDER                Oh, a woman.

SEBASTIAN  A flesh-fly, that can vex any man.

SIR ALEXANDER                A scurvy woman,
　On whom the passionate old man swore he doated;
　A creature, saith he, nature hath brought forth
　To mock the sex of woman. It is a thing
　One knows not how to name: her birth began
　Ere she was all made: 'tis woman more than man,  130
　Man more than woman, and (which to none can hap)
　The sun gives her two shadows to one shape;
　Nay more, let this strange thing walk, stand or sit,
　No blazing star draws more eyes after it.

SIR DAVY  A monster, 'tis some monster.

SIR ALEXANDER                She's a varlet.

SEBASTIAN  (Aside) Now is my cue to bristle.

SIR ALEXANDER  A naughty pack.

SEBASTIAN                'Tis false.

SIR ALEXANDER                Ha, boy?

SEBASTIAN                'Tis false.

SIR ALEXANDER  What's false? I say she's naught.

SEBASTIAN                I say that tongue
　That dares speak so, but yours, sticks in the throat
　Of a rank villain. Set yourself aside—      140

SIR ALEXANDER  So sir, what then?

SEBASTIAN                Any here else had lied.

---

111  by-blows: side-strokes from a sword
117  Adam Bell: famous archer and outlaw who figures in a
　　number of ballads
125  flesh-fly: a fly which lives on, and lays its eggs on, dead
　　flesh
126  he: i.e. his son
134  blazing star: i.e. a meteor, taken as an ill omen
137  naughty pack: person of bad or worthless character
138  naught: wicked, perhaps with play on 'nothing'. The play
　　is picked up by Laxton in l. 157; see A Woman Killed with
　　Kindness, xvi.91 for similar wordplay
139  but: except

85  part that fray: 'i.e. end the disturbance begun by the
　　wind' (Mulholland)
86  they: i.e the winds
99  He . . . sure: the aside interrupts Sir Alexander's
　　complete blank verse line

(*Aside*) I think I shall fit you.

SIR ALEXANDER   Lie?

SEBASTIAN                Yes.

SIR DAVY                        Doth this concern him?

SIR ALEXANDER                        Ah sirrah boy,
Is your blood heated? Boils it? Are you stung?
I'll pierce you deeper yet.—Oh my dear friends,
I am that wretched father, this that son,
That sees his ruin, yet headlong on doth run.

SIR ADAM   Will you love such a poison?

SIR DAVY                        Fie, fie.

SEBASTIAN                        Y'are all mad.

SIR ALEXANDER   Th'art sick at heart, yet feel'st it not.
     Of all these,
What gentleman but thou, knowing his disease     150
Mortal, would shun the cure? Oh Master Greenwit,
Would you to such an idol bow?

GREENWIT                        Not I, sir.

SIR ALEXANDER   Here's Master Laxton, has he mind to
     a woman
As thou hast?

LAXTON           No, not I, sir.

SIR ALEXANDER                        Sir, I know it.

LAXTON   Their good parts are so rare, their bad so
     common,
I will have nought to do with any woman.

SIR DAVY   'Tis well done, Master Laxton.

SIR ALEXANDER                        Oh thou cruel boy,
Thou would'st with lust an old man's life destroy;
Because thou see'st I'm half-way in my grave,
Thou shovel'st dust upon me: would thou might'st have
Thy wish, most wicked, most unnatural!     161

SIR DAVY   Why sir, 'tis thought Sir Guy Fitzallard's
     daughter
Shall wed your son Sebastian.

SIR ALEXANDER                        Sir Davy Dapper,
I have upon my knees wooed this fond boy
To take that virtuous maiden.

SEBASTIAN                        Hark you a word, sir.
You on your knees have cursed that virtuous maiden,
And me for loving her, yet do you now
Thus baffle me to my face? Wear not your knees
In such entreats, give me Fitzallard's daughter.

SIR ALEXANDER   I'll give thee rats-bane rather.

SEBASTIAN                        Well then you know
What dish I mean to feed upon.     171

SIR ALEXANDER   Hark gentlemen, he swears
To have this cutpurse drab, to spite my gall.

OMNES   Master Sebastian—

SEBASTIAN                        I am deaf to you all.

---

142   fit you: a) provide you with what is necessary; b) punish
     you
164   fond: foolish
168   baffle: a) hoodwink, cheat; b) disgrace

I'm so bewitched, so bound to my desires,
Tears, prayers, threats, nothing can quench out those
     fires
That burn within me.                        *Exit*

SIR ALEXANDER   (*Aside*) Her blood shall quench it then.
     —Lose him not, oh dissuade him, gentlemen.

SIR DAVY   He shall be weaned, I warrant you.

SIR ALEXANDER                        Before his eyes
Lay down his shame, my grief, his miseries.     180

OMNES   No more, no more, away.

                        *Exeunt all but* SIR ALEXANDER

SIR ALEXANDER                        I wash a negro,
Losing both pains and cost: but take thy flight,
I'll be most near thee when I'm least in sight.
Wild buck, I'll hunt thee breathless, thou shalt run
     on,
But I will turn thee when I'm not thought upon.

*Enter* RALPH TRAPDOOR

Now sirrah, what are you? Leave your ape's tricks and
     speak.

TRAPDOOR   A letter from my captain to your worship.

SIR ALEXANDER   Oh, oh, now I remember, 'tis to prefer
     thee into my service.     190

TRAPDOOR   To be a shifter under your worship's nose of
     a clean trencher, when there's a good bit upon't.

SIR ALEXANDER   Troth, honest fellow—(*Aside*) Hm—
     ha—let me see,
This knave shall be the axe to hew that down
At which I stumble, 'has a face that promiseth
Much of a villain; I will grind his wit,
And if the edge prove fine make use of it.
     —Come hither sirrah, canst thou be secret, ha?

TRAPDOOR   As two crafty attorneys plotting the
     undoing of their clients.     200

SIR ALEXANDER   Didst never, as thou has walked about
     this town,
Hear of a wench called Moll, mad merry Moll?

TRAPDOOR   Moll Cutpurse, sir?

SIR ALEXANDER   The same; dost thou know her then?

TRAPDOOR   As well as I know 'twill rain upon Simon
     and Jude's day next. I will sift all the taverns i'th'city,
     and drink half-pots with all the watermen

---

181–2   I wash . . . cost: proverbial
185     turn: check, deflect (hunting term)
188     captain: Trapdoor is a discharged soldier. Mulholland
        notes that there were numerous statutes in the reigns of
        Elizabeth and James dealing with the problems
        associated with discharged soldiers turned beggars and
        vagrants
189     prefer: advance
205–6   Simon and Jude's day: 28 October, a day associated
        with the Lord Mayor's pageants put on by the City livery
        companies (held on the following day), and frequently
        stormy

o'th'Bankside, but if you will, sir, I'll find her out.

SIR ALEXANDER That task is easy, do't then. Hold thy
 hand up:
 What's this? Is't burnt? 210

TRAPDOOR No sir, no, a little singed with making
 fireworks.

SIR ALEXANDER There's money, spend it; that being
 spent, fetch more.

TRAPDOOR Oh sir, that all the poor soldiers in England
 had such a leader! For fetching, no water-spaniel is
 like me.

SIR ALEXANDER This wench we speak of strays so from
 her kind,
 Nature repents she made her. 'Tis a mermaid
 Has tolled my son to shipwreck.

TRAPDOOR I'll cut her comb for you. 220

SIR ALEXANDER I'll tell out gold for thee then; hunt her
 forth,
 Cast out a line hung full of silver hooks
 To catch her to thy company: deep spendings
 May draw her that's most chaste to a man's bosom.

TRAPDOOR The jingling of golden bells, and a good
 fool with a hobby-horse, will draw all the whores
 i'th'town to dance in a morris.

SIR ALEXANDER Or rather (for that's best—they say
 sometimes
 She goes in breeches) follow her as her man.

TRAPDOOR And when her breeches are off, she shall
 follow me. 231

SIR ALEXANDER Beat all thy brains to serve her.

TRAPDOOR Zounds sir, as country wenches beat cream,
 till butter comes.

SIR ALEXANDER Play thou the subtle spider, weave fine
 nets
 To ensnare her very life.

TRAPDOOR Her life?

SIR ALEXANDER Yes, suck

Her heart-blood if thou canst; twist thou but cords
 To catch her, I'll find law to hang her up.

TRAPDOOR Spoke like a worshipful bencher.

SIR ALEXANDER Trace all her steps: at this she-fox's
 den 240
 Watch what lambs enter; let me play the shepherd
 To save their throats from bleeding, and cut hers.

TRAPDOOR This is the goll shall do't.

SIR ALEXANDER Be firm, and gain me
 Ever thine own. This done, I entertain thee:
 How is thy name?

TRAPDOOR My name, sir, is Ralph Trapdoor, honest
 Ralph.

SIR ALEXANDER Trapdoor, be like thy name, a
 dangerous step
 For her to venture on, but unto me—

TRAPDOOR As fast as your sole to your boot or shoe,
 sir.

SIR ALEXANDER Hence then, be little seen here as thou
 canst, 250
 I'll still be at thine elbow.

TRAPDOOR The trapdoor's set.
 Moll, if you budge y'are gone. This me shall crown:
 A roaring boy the roaring girl puts down.

SIR ALEXANDER God-a-mercy, lose no time.

*Exeunt*

# Act II, scene i

*The three shops open in a rank: the first a pothecary's shop,
the next a feathershop, the third a sempster's shop:*
MISTRESS GALLIPOT *in the first,* MISTRESS TILTYARD *in
the next,* MASTER OPENWORK *and his* WIFE *in the third.
To them enters* LAXTON, GOSHAWK, *and* GREENWIT

MISTRESS OPENWORK Gentlemen, what is't you lack?
 What is't you buy? See fine bands and ruffs, fine
 lawns, fine cambrics. What is't you lack, gentlemen,
 what is't you buy?

LAXTON Yonder's the shop.

GOSHAWK Is that she?

LAXTON Peace.

GREENWIT She that minces tobacco?

LAXTON Ay: she's a gentlewoman born, I can tell you,

---

207–8 watermen o'th'Bankside: boatmen offering their boats
 for hire; it was estimated by a contemporary that there
 were 40,000 of them working between Gravesend and
 Windsor. The Bankside, Southwark, south of the
 Thames, was the location of several theatres and many
 brothels
210 burnt: i.e. branded, as a felon's would be
218 mermaid: regarded as sinister, and often associated with
 the Sirens (fabulous female creatures who lured sailors to
 shipwreck with their song)
220 cut her comb: humiliate; proverbial (cutting a cock's
 comb was a usual accompaniment of gelding)
221 tell out: count out
226 hobby-horse: part of a fool's equipment, but also a
 pantomine horse which had a part in the Morris dance;
 'hobby-horse' could also mean 'whore'
229 man: i.e. manservant
232 serve: 'not just as a servant but as a stallion serves a mare'
 (Cook)

239 bencher: magistrate
243 goll: cant word for 'hand'. Cant was the specialist slang
 associated with beggars and thieves
244 entertain: take into service
246 Ralph: pronounced Rafe; a common name for servants in
 contemporary plays
SD rank: row
1–2 what . . . buy: standard street cry of pedlars and
 shopkeepers
3 lawns . . . cambrics: both were kinds of fine linen
8 minces: shreds. Apothecaries commonly sold tobacco

though it be her hard fortune now to shred Indian pot-herbs. 11

GOSHAWK Oh sir, 'tis many a good woman's fortune, when her husband turns bankrupt, to begin with pipes and set up again.

LAXTON And indeed the raising of the woman is the lifting up of the man's head at all times: if one flourish, t'other will bud as fast, I warrant ye.

GOSHAWK Come, thou'rt familiarly acquainted there, I grope that.

LAXTON And you grope no better i'th'dark, you may chance lie i'th'ditch when you're drunk. 21

GOSHAWK Go, thou'rt a mystical lecher.

LAXTON I will not deny but my credit may take up an ounce of pure smoke.

GOSHAWK May take up an ell of pure smock. Away, go. (*Aside*) 'Tis the closest striker. Life, I think he commits venery forty foot deep, no man's aware on't. I, like a palpable smockster, go to work so openly with the tricks of art, that I'm as apparently seen as a naked boy in a vial, and were it not for a gift of treachery that I have in me to betray my friend when he puts most trust in me—mass, yonder he is, too— and by his injury to make good my access to her, I should appear as defective in courting as a farmer's son the first day of his feather, that doth nothing at court but woo the hangings and glass windows for a month together, and some broken waiting-woman for ever after. I find those imperfections in my venery that, were't not for flattery and falsehood, I should want discourse and impudence, and he that wants impudence among women is worthy to be kicked out at bed's feet. He shall not see me yet. 42

GREENWIT Troth this is finely shred.

LAXTON Oh, women are the best mincers.

---

11 pot-herbs: any herbs grown for boiling in a pot; here, presumably tobacco

14 pipes: tobacco, a new commodity, was good business; but 'pipe' here also has sexual quibble ('penis'); see l. 52 below, and *Romeo and Juliet*, IV.iv.123

15–16 raising . . . head: with sexual innuendo

19 grope: understand, but with sexual innuendo

20 And: if

22 mystical: secret

25 take up . . . smock: lift up a woman's underskirt; see *The Taming of the Shrew*, IV.iii.153–4. An 'ell' was 45 inches

26 closest striker: most secret fornicator

28 smockster: bawd

29–30 naked . . . vial: obscure, but Cook suggests that 'the point is presumably the visibility of nakedness seen through clear glass'

31 my friend: i.e. Openwork

35 first day . . . feather: 'the feather has been acquired to gentrify his appearance' (Cook)

37 broken: violated, defiled

44 mincers: i.e. of tobacco, and of words

---

MISTRESS GALLIPOT 'T had been a good phrase for a cook's wife, sir.

LAXTON But 'twill serve generally, like the front of a new almanac, as thus: calculated for the meridian of cook's wives, but generally for all Englishwomen. 49

MISTRESS GALLIPOT Nay, you shall ha't, sir, I have filled it for you. *She puts it to the fire*

LAXTON The pipe's in a good hand, and I wish mine always so.

GREENWIT But not to be used o'that fashion.

LAXTON Oh pardon me, sir, I understand no French. I pray be covered. Jack, a pipe of rich smoke.

GOSHAWK Rich smoke? That's sixpence a pipe, is't?

GREENWIT To me, sweet lady.

MISTRESS GALLIPOT (*Aside to* LAXTON) Be not forgetful; respect my credit; seem strange: art and wit makes a fool of suspicion; pray be wary. 61

LAXTON Push, I warrant you:—Come, how is't, gallants?

GREENWIT Pure and excellent.

LAXTON I thought 'twas good, you were grown so silent; you are like those that love not to talk at victuals, though they make a worse noise i'the nose than a common fiddler's prentice, and discourse a whole supper with snuffling.—I must speak a word with you anon. 70

MISTRESS GALLIPOT Make your way wisely then.

GOSHAWK Oh what else, sir? He's perfection itself, full of manners, but not an acre of ground belonging to 'em.

GREENWIT Ay and full of form, h'as ne'er a good stool in's chamber.

GOSHAWK But above all religious: he preyeth daily upon elder brothers.

GREENWIT And valiant above measure: h'as run three streets from a sergeant. 80

LAXTON Puh, puh. *He blows tobacco in their faces*

GREENWIT *and* GOSHAWK Oh, puh, ho, ho.

LAXTON So, so.

---

48 almanac: 'almanacs giving astrological and other predictions were sold cheaply to the gullible' (Mulholland)

55 French: i.e. bawdy language

56 be covered: put on your hat (to Goshawk)

60 credit: reputation
   seem strange: i.e. do not be too familiar with me

62 Push: an interjection

67–9 noise . . . snuffling: Mulholland points out that 'fiddle' carried sexual implications, so that a 'fiddler's prentice' may be 'assistant to a bawd'; the 'noise i'th'nose' and 'snuffling' may refer to the effects of venereal disease

72 He's: i.e. Laxton is
   manners: punning on 'manors'; see *A Woman Killed with Kindness*, xvi.9

75 form: propriety, etiquette, with pun on 'bench'

MISTRESS GALLIPOT What's the matter now, sir?

LAXTON I protest I'm in extreme want of money. If you can supply me now with any means, you do me the greatest pleasure, next to the bounty of your love, as ever poor gentleman tasted.

MISTRESS GALLIPOT What's the sum would pleasure ye, sir? Though you deserve nothing less at my hands. **90**

LAXTON Why, 'tis but for want of opportunity thou know'st. (*Aside*) I put her off with opportunity still. By this light I hate her, but for means to keep me in fashion with gallants; for what I take from her, I spend upon other wenches, bear her in hand still; she has wit enough to rob her husband, and I ways enough to consume the money.—Why, how now? What? The chincough?

GOSHAWK Thou hast the cowardliest trick to come before a man's face and strangle him ere he be aware: I could find in my heart to make a quarrel in earnest. **101**

LAXTON Pox, and thou dost—thou know'st I never use to fight with my friends—thou'lt but lose thy labour in't.—Jack Dapper!

*Enter* JACK DAPPER, *and his man* GULL

GREENWIT Monsieur Dapper, I dive down to your ankles.

JACK DAPPER Save ye, gentlemen, all three in a peculiar salute.

GOSHAWK He were ill to make a lawyer, he dispatches three at once. **110**

LAXTON So, well said.—(MISTRESS GALLIPOT *gives him money secretly*) But is this of the same tobacco, Mistress Gallipot?

MISTRESS GALLIPOT The same you had at first, sir.

LAXTON I wish it no better: this will serve to drink at my chamber.

GOSHAWK Shall we taste a pipe on't?

LAXTON Not of this by my troth, gentlemen; I have sworn before you.

GOSHAWK What, not Jack Dapper? **120**

LAXTON Pardon me, sweet Jack, I'm sorry I made such a rash oath, but foolish oaths must stand. Where art going, Jack?

JACK DAPPER Faith, to buy one feather.

LAXTON (*Aside*) One feather? The fool's peculiar still.

JACK DAPPER Gull.

GULL Master?

JACK DAPPER Here's three halfpence for your ordinary, boy, meet me an hour hence in Paul's. **129**

GULL (*Aside*) How? Three single halfpence? Life, this will scarce serve a man in sauce, a ha'p'orth of mustard, a ha'p'orth of oil, and a ha'p'orth of vinegar—what's left then for the pickle herring? This shows like small beer i'th'morning after a great surfeit of wine o'er night: he could spend his three pound last night in a supper amongst girls and brave bawdy-house boys: I thought his pockets cackled not for nothing: these are the eggs of three pound, I'll go sup 'em up presently. *Exit*

LAXTON (*Aside*) Eight, nine, ten angels: good wench i'faith, and one that loves darkness well, she puts out a candle with the best tricks of any drugster's wife in England; but that which mads her, I rail upon opportunity still, and take no notice on't. The other night she would needs lead me into a room with a candle in her hand to show me a naked picture, where no sooner entered but the candle was sent of an errand; now I not intending to understand her, but like a puny at the inns of venery, called for another light innocently: thus reward I all her cunning with simple mistaking. I know she cozens her husband to keep me, and I'll keep her honest as long as I can, to make the poor man some part of amends: an honest mind of a whoremaster!—How think you amongst you? What, a fresh pipe? Draw in a third man. **155**

GOSHAWK No, you're a hoarder, you engross by th'ounces.

*At the feathershop now*

JACK DAPPER Puh, I like it not.

---

90 Though . . . hands: Mulholland reads this as an aside, with 'nothing less' meaning 'anything but that', and signalling Mistress Gallipot's growing dissatisfaction with Laxton. Both this and the more literal (though perhaps ironic) reading make good sense

95 bear her in hand: lead her on, deceive her

98 chincough: whooping cough (as a result of Laxton's smoke)

105–6 dive . . . ankles: i.e. in a bow

107 peculiar: a) single; b) particular, special

112 is this . . . tobacco: he receives money, but pretends to be receiving only tobacco

115 drink: smoke

124 feather: Mulholland notes the proverbial association of fools with feathers

128 ordinary: an eating house serving meals for a fixed price

129 Paul's: i.e. St Paul's, a common meeting place for all social ranks; see *Arden of Faversham*, iii.8

130 ha'p'orth: halfpennyworth

134 small beer: weak beer

136 brave: handsome

137 cackled: 'playing on the normal cackling of a hen after laying an egg, and referring to the chinking of coins in Jack's pockets or purse—the residue of small change from his three pounds' (Mulholland)

140 angels: gold coins, worth about ten shillings (50 pence)

43–4 rail . . . still: 'i.e. always find excuses' (Mulholland)

148 understand: 'with a bawdy entendre on "under-stand"' (Mulholland)
puny: freshman

154 whoremaster: lecher, womaniser

156 engross: a) monopolise; b) grow fat

MISTRESS TILTYARD  What feather is't you'd have, sir?
These are most worn and most in fashion          160
Amongst the beaver gallants, the stone riders,
The private stage's audience, the twelvepenny-stool
gentlemen:
I can inform you 'tis the general feather.
JACK DAPPER  And therefore I mislike it—tell me of
general!
Now a continual Simon and Jude's rain
Beat all your feathers as flat down as pancakes.
Show me—a—spangled feather.
MISTRESS TILTYARD          Oh, to go a-feasting with?
You'd have it for a hench-boy? You shall.

*At the sempster's shop now*

MASTER OPENWORK  Mass, I had quite forgot.
His honour's footman was here last night, wife,          170
Ha' you done with my lord's shirt?
MISTRESS OPENWORK          What's that to you, sir?
I was this morning at his honour's lodging,
Ere such a snail as you crept out of your shell.
MASTER OPENWORK  Oh, 'twas well done, good wife.
MISTRESS OPENWORK          I hold it better, sir,
Than if you had done't yourself.
MASTER OPENWORK          Nay, so say I:
But is the countess's smock almost done, mouse?
MISTRESS OPENWORK  Here lies the cambric, sir, but
wants, I fear me.
MASTER OPENWORK  I'll resolve you of that presently.
MISTRESS OPENWORK  Heyday! Oh audacious groom,
Dare you presume to noblewomen's linen?          180
Keep you your yard to measure shepherd's holland,
I must confine you, I see that.

*At the tobacco shop now*

GOSHAWK  What say you to this gear?

LAXTON  I dare the arrantest critic in tobacco
To lay one fault upon't.

*Enter* MOLL *in a frieze jerkin and a black saveguard*

GOSHAWK          Life, yonder's Moll.
LAXTON  Moll, which Moll?
GOSHAWK  Honest Moll.
LAXTON  Prithee let's call her.—Moll.
ALL GALLANTS  Moll, Moll, pist, Moll.
MOLL  How now, what's the matter?          190
GOSHAWK  A pipe of good tobacco, Moll.
MOLL  I cannot stay.
GOSHAWK  Nay Moll, puh, prithee hark, but one word
i'faith.
MOLL  Well, what is't?
GREENWIT  Prithee come hither, sirrah.
LAXTON  (*Aside*) Heart, I would give but too much
money to be nibbling with that wench. Life, sh'as the
spirit of four great parishes, and a voice that will
drown all the city; methinks a brave captain might
get all his soldiers upon her, and ne'er be beholding
to a company of Mile End milksops, if he could
come on, and come off quick enough. Such a Moll
were a marrow-bone before an Italian, he would cry
bona roba till his ribs were nothing but bone. I'll lay
hard siege to her, money is that aquafortis that eats
into many a maidenhead: where the walls are flesh
and blood, I'll ever pierce through with a golden
auger.          209
GOSHAWK  Now thy judgment, Moll, is't not good?
MOLL  Yes faith 'tis very good tobacco; how do you sell
an ounce? Farewell. God b'i'you, Mistress Gallipot.
GOSHAWK  Why Moll, Moll.
MOLL  I cannot stay now i'faith, I am going to buy a
shag ruff, the shop will be shut in presently.

---

161  beaver gallants: those who wore the fashionable and
expensive beaver hats
stone riders: riders of stallions, with sexual entendre:
'stone' meant lascivious; 'to ride' meant to have sexual
intercourse. Since 'stone' also meant testicle, Cook
suggests 'stone riders' could be homosexuals
162  The private stage: the private theatres were more
expensive, and thus more select, than public ones such as
the Fortune
twelvepenny-stool gentlemen: the usual cost of the use of
a stool at the theatre was sixpence
165  Simon and Jude's rain: see I.ii.205–6n
168  hench-boy: page
173  snail: eds (snake Q)
176  mouse: term of endearment
177  wants: 'i.e. wants finishing, or perhaps there isn't enough
material' (Cook)
181  yard: measuring stick, with play on 'yard' meaning
penis
183  gear: stuff (referring to the tobacco)

SD  *frieze jerkin . . . saveguard*: a frieze jerkin was a short
jacket of coarse woollen cloth (usually worn by men); a
saveguard was an outer petticoat worn by women to
protect their clothes when riding. 'Moll's dress is
hermaphroditic in combining elements of the dress of
both sexes' (Mulholland)
196  sirrah: often used to address women as well as men
201  get: beget
202  Mile End: the green (now Stepney Green) was used as a
training ground for the city militia; their exercises were a
common object of mockery
202–3  come on . . . come off: 'battle terms meaning "advance" and
"retire" . . . [with] a secondary bawdy sense' (Mulholland)
204  marrow-bone: supposed to be an aphrodisiac
Italian: Italians had a reputation for lust and perverse
sexual proclivities
205  bona roba: wench, prostitute
206–7  money . . . maidenhead: see I.ii.223–4
206  aquafortis: nitric acid; used in dilute form as a solvent
215  shag: a cloth with a velvet nap on one side, usually of
worsted, sometimes of silk

GOSHAWK 'Tis the maddest fantasticallest girl—I never knew so much flesh and so much nimbleness put together.

LAXTON She slips from one company to another like a fat eel between a Dutchman's fingers. (*Aside*) I'll watch my time for her. 221

MISTRESS GALLIPOT Some will not stick to say she's a man
And some both man and woman.

LAXTON That were excellent: she might first cuckold the husband and then make him do as much for the wife.

*The feathershop again*

MOLL Save you; how does Mistress Tiltyard?
JACK DAPPER Moll.
MOLL Jack Dapper.
JACK DAPPER How dost Moll? 230
MOLL I'll tell thee by and by, I go but to th'next shop.
JACK DAPPER Thou shalt find me here this hour about a feather.
MOLL Nay and a feather hold you in play a whole hour, a goose will last you all the days of your life.

*The sempster shop*

Let me see a good shag ruff.
MASTER OPENWORK Mistress Mary, that shalt thou i'faith, and the best in the shop. 238
MISTRESS OPENWORK How now? Greetings! Love-terms, with a pox between you! Have I found out one of your haunts? I send you for hollands, and you're i'th'low countries with a mischief. I'm served with good ware by th'shift, that makes it lie dead so long upon my hands, I were as good shut up shop, for when I open it I take nothing.
MASTER OPENWORK Nay and you fall a-ringing once,

the devil cannot stop you; I'll out of the belfry as fast as I can.—Moll.
MISTRESS OPENWORK Get you from my shop.
MOLL I come to buy. 250
MISTRESS OPENWORK I'll sell ye nothing, I warn ye my house and shop.
MOLL You goody Openwork, you that prick out a poor living
And sews many a bawdy skin-coat together,
Thou private pandress between shirt and smock,
I wish thee for a minute but a man:
Thou should'st never use more shapes; but as th'art,
I pity my revenge. Now my spleen's up
I would not mock it willingly.

*Enter a* FELLOW *with a long rapier by his side*

—Ha, be thankful,
Now I forgive thee. 260
MISTRESS OPENWORK Marry hang thee, I never asked forgiveness in my life.
MOLL You, goodman swine's-face.
FELLOW What, will you murder me?
MOLL You remember, slave, how you abused me t'other night in a tavern?
FELLOW Not I, by this light.
MOLL No, but by candlelight you did: you have tricks to save your oaths, reservations have you? And I have reserved somewhat for you. (*Strikes him*) As you like that, call for more; you know the sign again. 271
FELLOW Pox on't, had I brought any company along with me to have borne witness on't, 'twould ne'er have grieved me; but to be struck and nobody by, 'tis my ill fortune still. Why, tread upon a worm, they say 'twill turn tail, but indeed a gentleman should have more manners. *Exit*
LAXTON Gallantly performed i'faith Moll, and manfully! I love thee forever for't. Base rogue, had he offered but the least counter-buff, by this hand I was prepared for him. 281
MOLL You prepared for him? Why should you be prepared for him, was he any more than a man?
LAXTON No, nor so much by a yard and a handful London measure.

---

241–5 I send . . . nothing: a passage that turns on a number of linked double entendres. 'Holland' was a linen cloth, hence the pun on 'low countries' as a) the Netherlands; b) low haunts, brothels; c) lower parts of the body, sexual organs (with, Cook suggests, play on 'cunt' in 'countries', as in *Hamlet*, III.ii.105). This wordplay echoes *2 Henry IV*, II.ii.19–20. 'Ware' meant a) goods; b) genitals (especially women's). 'Shift' meant a) trick; b) under-clothing. Mistress Openwork is thus making two complaints at once: a) that Master Openwork uses their business as a device to attract (female) customers, with the result that her goods remain unsold and she might as well shut up shop; b) because of his sexual activities elsewhere, her own 'good ware' (next to her 'shift') is ignored, and she is left to 'shift' for herself with her own 'hands' (i.e. through the 'dead' (unsatisfactory) activity of masturbation), so that she might as well give up sexual activity altogether, since when she offers herself, nothing comes of it

246 and: if
a-ringing: scolding

251 warn: deny
253 goody: goodwife
254 skin-coat: coat made of skins, but also a person's skin
255 shirt and smock: man and woman
258 spleen: temper
259 willingly: intentionally; i.e. 'if you can avoid it'
275–6 tread . . . tail: proverbial: even the humblest person will resent ill treatment
280 counter-buff: blow in return
284 yard and a handful: this was the 'London measure' (a little over a yard) used by London drapers; for sexual pun on yard, see l. 181 above and II.ii.90

MOLL Why do you speak this then? Do you think I
cannot ride a stone horse unless one lead him by
th'snaffle? 288

LAXTON Yes and sit him bravely, I know thou canst
Moll, 'twas but an honest mistake through love, and
I'll make amends for't any way; prithee sweet plump
Moll, when shall thou and I go out o'town together?

MOLL Whither? To Tyburn, prithee?

LAXTON Mass that's out o'town indeed; thou hang'st so
many jests upon thy friends still. I mean honestly to
Brainford, Staines, or Ware.

MOLL What to do there?

LAXTON Nothing but be merry and lie together; I'll
hire a coach with four horses. 299

MOLL I thought 'twould be a beastly journey: you may
leave out one well, three horses will serve if I play the
jade myself.

LAXTON Nay push, thou'rt such another kicking
wench, prithee be kind and let's meet.

MOLL 'Tis hard but we shall meet, sir.

LAXTON Nay but appoint the place then, there's ten
angels in fair gold, Moll, you see I do not trifle with
you; do but say thou wilt meet me, and I'll have a
coach ready for thee.

MOLL Why, here's my hand I'll meet you sir. 310

LAXTON (Aside) Oh good gold.—The place, sweet Moll?

MOLL It shall be your appointment.

LAXTON Somewhat near Holborn, Moll.

MOLL In Gray's Inn Fields then.

LAXTON A match.

MOLL I'll meet you there.

LAXTON The hour?

MOLL Three. 318

LAXTON That will be time enough to sup at Brainford.

*Fall from them to the other*

MASTER OPENWORK I am of such a nature, sir, I cannot
endure the house when she scolds, sh'has a tongue
will be heard further in a still morning than Saint
Antling's bell. She rails upon me for foreign

wenching, that I being a freeman must needs keep a
whore i'th'suburbs, and seek to impoverish the
liberties. When we fall out, I trouble you still to make
all whole with my wife.

GOSHAWK No trouble at all, 'tis a pleasure to me to join
things together.

MASTER OPENWORK (Aside) Go thy ways, I do this but
to try thy honesty, Goshawk. 331

*The feathershop*

JACK DAPPER How lik'st thou this, Moll?

MOLL Oh singularly; you're fitted now for a bunch.
(Aside) He looks for all the world with those spangled
feathers like a nobleman's bedpost. The purity of
your wench would I fain try, she seems, like Kent,
unconquered, and I believe as many wiles are in
her—oh, the gallants of these times are shallow
lechers, they put not their courtship home enough to
a wench; 'tis impossible to know what woman is
throughly honest, because she's ne'er thoroughly
tried. I am of that certain belief there are more
queans in this town of their own making than of any
man's provoking: where lies the slackness then?
Many a poor soul would down, and there's nobody
will push 'em: 346
Women are courted but ne'er soundly tried,
As many walk in spurs that never ride.

*The sempster's shop*

MISTRESS OPENWORK Oh abominable.

GOSHAWK Nay more, I tell you in private, he keeps a
whore i'th' suburbs. 351

MISTRESS OPENWORK Oh spital dealing! I came to him
a gentlewoman born. I'll show you mine arms when
you please, sir.

GOSHAWK (Aside) I had rather see your legs, and begin
that way.

MISTRESS OPENWORK 'Tis well known he took me from
a lady's service, where I was well beloved of the

---

287 stone horse: a stallion, and therefore likely to be spirited;
see l. 161 above; also, figuratively, meant 'man'
293 Tyburn: a place of execution
296 Brainford: a common spelling of Brentford. Brentford,
Staines and Ware were villages outside London, popular
for excursions and assignations; see *Epicoene*, III.ii.81
302 jade: a) worn-out horse; b) whore
313 Holborn: one of London's main thoroughfares
314 Gray's Inn Fields: open fields to the north of Gray's Inn,
frequented by footpads (highwaymen who robbed on
foot)
SD *Fall . . . other*: i.e. the focus shifts to the other group
323 Saint Antling's: St Antholin's church stood in Watling
Street, east of St Paul's. It was frequented by Puritans
who rang a bell for the morning lecture at 5 a.m., causing
a great nuisance in the neighbourhood (Sugden)

325 suburbs: these lay outside the control of the City, and
were notorious for their brothels. The 'liberties' were
outside the City's bounds but within, to some extent, its
control; as a freeman, Openwork's privileges would have
extended there
335 nobleman's bedpost: these were frequently festooned
with feathers and other hangings
purity: chastity, sexual honour
your wench: i.e. Mistress Tiltyard. This plot is never
developed
336–7 like Kent, unconquered: a common Kentish boast
341 throughly: often interchangeable with thoroughly, but
with additional sense of 'through the whole substance,
thickness, or extent', 'from beginning to end' (OED)
343 queans: whores
352 spital: hospital, originally for lepers, but later used for
whores suffering from venereal diseases

steward, I had my Latin tongue, and a spice of the French before I came to him, and now doth he keep a suburban whore under my nostrils.          **361**

GOSHAWK There's ways enough to cry quit with him: hark in thine ear.

MISTRESS OPENWORK There's a friend worth a million.

MOLL (*Aside*) I'll try one spear against your chastity, Mistress Tiltyard, though it prove too short by the burr.

*Enter* RALPH TRAPDOOR

TRAPDOOR (*Aside*) Mass, here she is. I'm bound already to serve her, though it be but a sluttish trick.—Bless my hopeful young mistress with long life and great limbs, send her the upper hand of all bailiffs and their hungry adherents.          **372**

MOLL How now, what art thou?

TRAPDOOR A poor ebbing gentleman, that would gladly wait for the young flood of your service.

MOLL My service! What should move you to offer your service to me, sir?

TRAPDOOR The love I bear to your heroic spirit and masculine womanhood.

MOLL So sir, put case we should retain you to us, what parts are there in you for a gentlewoman's service? **381**

TRAPDOOR Of two kinds, right worshipful: movable and immovable: movable to run of errands, and immovable to stand when you have occasion to use me.

MOLL What strength have you?

TRAPDOOR Strength, Mistress Moll? I have gone up into a steeple, and stayed the great bell as't has been ringing; stopped a windmill going.

MOLL And never struck down yourself?          **390**

TRAPDOOR Stood as upright as I do at this present.

MOLL *trips up his heels, he falls*

MOLL Come, I pardon you for this, it shall be no disgrace to you: I have struck up the heels of the high German's size ere now. What, not stand?

---

360 French: Mistress Openwork's attempts to impress by referring to her superior background misfire through a series of double entendres: the French were associated with perverse sexuality (as were the Italians: (see 'Latin tongue' and l. 204 above); 'French' also suggests syphilis

361 suburbian: obsolete spelling, often used to refer to licentiousness of suburbs

362 cry quit with: get even with

367 burr: a broad iron ring behind the handle of a tilting lance

375 young flood: the flow of tide up-river

376–85 What . . . use: sexual quibbles throughout on 'parts', 'service', 'stand' and 'use'

380 put case: suppose

392–3 the high German: apparently a reference to a German fencer of great size and strength currently in London; see Mulholland and Cook for other references

TRAPDOOR I am of that nature where I love, I'll be at my mistress' foot to do her service.

MOLL Why, well said; but say your mistress should receive injury, have you the spirit of fighting in you, durst you second her?

TRAPDOOR Life, I have kept a bridge myself, and drove seven at a time before me.          **401**

MOLL Ay?

TRAPDOOR (*Aside*) But they were all Lincolnshire bullocks by my troth.

MOLL Well, meet me in Gray's Inn Fields, between three and four this afternoon, and upon better consideration we'll retain you.

TRAPDOOR I humbly thank your good mistress-ship. (*Aside*) I'll crack your neck for this kindness.          *Exit*

MOLL *meets* LAXTON

LAXTON Remember three.          **410**

MOLL Nay if I fail you, hang me.

LAXTON Good wench i'faith.

*then* OPENWORK

MOLL Who's this?

MASTER OPENWORK 'Tis I, Moll.

MOLL Prithee tend thy shop and prevent bastards.

MASTER OPENWORK We'll have a pint of the same wine i'faith, Moll.

*Exeunt* MOLL *and* MASTER OPENWORK

*The bell rings*

GOSHAWK Hark the bell rings, come gentlemen. Jack Dapper, where shall's all munch?

JACK DAPPER I am for Parker's ordinary.          **420**

LAXTON He's a good guest to'm, he deserves his board, he draws all the gentlemen in a term-time thither. We'll be your followers, Jack, lead the way.— Look you by my faith the fool has feathered his nest well.

*Exeunt* GALLANTS

*Enter* MASTER GALLIPOT, MASTER TILTYARD, *and* SERVANTS *with water-spaniels and a duck*

MASTER TILTYARD Come shut up your shops. Where's Master Openwork?

MISTRESS GALLIPOT Nay ask not me, Master Tiltyard.

MASTER TILTYARD Where's his water-dog? Puh— pist—hur—hur—pist.

MASTER GALLIPOT Come wenches come, we're going all to Hogsden.          **431**

---

415 same wine: pun on 'bastard', a sweet Spanish wine

421 to'm: i.e. to him

SD water-spaniels and a duck: they are going duck-hunting

428–9 Puh . . . pist: presumably Tiltyard is calling and whistling for his dog

431 Hogsden: i.e. Hoxton, a popular place for excursions

MISTRESS GALLIPOT  To Hogsden, husband?

MASTER GALLIPOT  Ay, to Hogsden, pigsney.

MISTRESS GALLIPOT  I'm not ready, husband.

MASTER GALLIPOT  Faith that's well—hum—pist—pist. (*Spits in the dog's mouth*) Come Mistress Openwork, you are so long.

MISTRESS OPENWORK  I have no joy of my life, Master Gallipot.  **439**

MASTER GALLIPOT  Push, let your boy lead his water-spaniel along, and we'll show you the bravest sport at Parlous Pond. Hey Trug, hey Trug, hey Trug, here's the best duck in England, except my wife. Hey, hey, hey! Fetch, fetch, fetch!

Come let's away:

Of all the year this is the sportful'st day.

Exeunt

# Act II, scene ii

*Enter* SEBASTIAN *solus*

SEBASTIAN  If a man have a free will, where should the use

More perfect shine than in his will to love?

All creatures have their liberty in that,

*Enter* SIR ALEXANDER *and listens to him*

Though else kept under servile yoke and fear,

The very bondslave has his freedom there.

Amongst a world of creatures voiced and silent

Must my desires wear fetters?—(*Aside*) Yea, are you

So near? Then I must break with my heart's truth,

Meet grief at a back way.—(*Aloud*) Well: why, suppose

The two-leaved tongues of slander or of truth  **10**

Pronounce Moll loathsome: if before my love

She appear fair, what injury have I?

I have the thing I like: in all things else

Mine own eye guides me, and I find 'em prosper;

Life, what should ail it now? I know that man

Ne'er truly loves—if he gainsay't he lies—

That winks and marries with his father's eyes.

I'll keep mine own wide open.

*Enter* MOLL *and a* PORTER *with a viol on his back*

SIR ALEXANDER  (*Aside*)  Here's brave wilfulness;

A made match, here she comes, they met o'purpose.

PORTER  Must I carry this great fiddle to your chamber, Mistress Mary?  **21**

MOLL  Fiddle, goodman hog-rubber? Some of these porters bear so much for others, they have no time to carry wit for themselves.

PORTER  To your own chamber, Mistress Mary?

MOLL  Who'll hear an ass speak? Whither else, goodman pageant-bearer? They're people of the worst memories.  *Exit* PORTER

SEBASTIAN  Why, 'twere too great a burthen, love, to have them carry things in their minds and o'their backs together.  **31**

MOLL  Pardon me sir, I thought not you so near.

SIR ALEXANDER  (*Aside*) So, so, so.

SEBASTIAN  I would be nearer to thee, and in that fashion That makes the best part of all creatures honest. No otherwise I wish it.  **36**

MOLL  Sir, I am so poor to requite you, you must look for nothing but thanks of me: I have no humour to marry, I love to lie o'both sides o'th'bed myself; and again, o'th'other side, a wife you know ought to be obedient, but I fear me I am too headstrong to obey, therefore I'll ne'er go about it. I love you so well, sir, for your good will I'd be loath you should repent your bargain after, and therefore we'll ne'er come together at first. I have the head now of myself, and am man enough for a woman; marriage is but a chopping and changing, where a maiden loses one head, and has a worse i'th'place.

SIR ALEXANDER  (*Aside*) The most comfortablest answer from a roaring girl

That ever mine ears drunk in.

SEBASTIAN  This were enough  **50**

---

17  winks: i.e. shuts his eyes, is complaisant

19  made match: arranged meeting

22  Fiddle: perhaps with sexual quibble; see II.i.68
hog-rubber: term of abuse

22–4  Some of ... themselves: Mulholland notes a tradition that porters were considered weak-witted

27  pageant-bearer: a pageant was originally a portable stage, set up in the street for the acting of plays or municipal shows

34–5  fashion ... honest: i.e. in marriage

35  best part: most

38  humour: disposition

40  again ... side: besides, on the other hand

45  at first: in the first place

47–8  loses ... place: 'i.e. exchanges a maidenhead for a head of household' (Mulholland)

---

433  pigsney: darling, pet (from 'pig's eye'); Mulholland suggests a play on Hogsden

SD  *Spits ... mouth*: apparently an expression of affection for, and means of befriending, a dog (Mulholland)

442  Parlous Pond: a pool behind St Luke's Hospital, on the edge of Hoxton, used for bathing and duck-hunting. 'Parlous' is a corruption of 'perilous', so called because of the many drownings there
Trug: perhaps the name of the spaniel (eds)

SD  *solus*: alone

10  two-leaved: eds (two leaud Q). Most eds take this to be a comparison between the tongue and the two hinged parts of a door or gate, each of which can move independently and thus speak either slander or truth (as in 'double-tongued')

Now to affright a fool forever from thee,
When 'tis the music that I love thee for.

SIR ALEXANDER (*Aside*) There's a boy spoils all again.

MOLL Believe it, sir, I am not of that disdainful temper,
but I could love you faithfully.

SIR ALEXANDER (*Aside*) A pox on you for that word. I
like you not now;
Y'are a cunning roarer, I see that already.                    57

MOLL But sleep upon this once more, sir, you may
chance shift a mind tomorrow: be not too hasty to
wrong yourself. Never while you live, sir, take a wife
running, many have run out at heels that have done't.
You see, sir, I speak against myself, and if every
woman would deal with their suitor so honestly, poor
younger brothers would not be so often gulled with
old cozening widows, that turn o'er all their wealth in
trust to some kinsman, and make the poor gentleman
work hard for a pension. Fare you well sir.            67

SEBASTIAN Nay prithee one word more.

SIR ALEXANDER (*Aside*) How do I wrong this girl, she
puts him off still.

MOLL Think upon this in cold blood, sir; you make as
much haste as if you were a-going upon a sturgeon
voyage; take deliberation, sir, never choose a wife as if
you were going to Virginia.                               73

SEBASTIAN And so we parted, my too cursed fate.

SIR ALEXANDER (*Aside*) She is but cunning, gives him
longer time in't.

*Enter a* TAILOR

TAILOR Mistress Moll, Mistress Moll: so ho ho, so ho.

MOLL There boy, there boy. What, dost thou go a-
hawking after me with a red clout on thy finger?

TAILOR I forgot to take measure on you for your new
breeches.                                                 80

SIR ALEXANDER (*Aside*) Heyday, breeches? What, will
he marry a monster with two trinkets? What age is
this? If the wife go in breeches, the man must wear
long coats like a fool.

MOLL What fiddling's here? Would not the old pattern
have served your turn?

TAILOR You change the fashion, you say you'll have the
great Dutch slop, Mistress Mary.

MOLL Why sir, I say so still.

TAILOR Your breeches then will take up a yard more. **90**

MOLL Well, pray look it be put in then.

TAILOR It shall stand round and full, I warrant you.

MOLL Pray make 'em easy enough.

TAILOR I know my fault now, t'other was somewhat
stiff between the legs; I'll make these open enough, I
warrant you.

SIR ALEXANDER (*Aside*) Here's good gear towards! I
have brought up my son to marry a Dutch slop and a
French doublet, a codpiece-daughter.

TAILOR So, I have gone as far as I can go.        **100**

MOLL Why then, farewell.

TAILOR If you go presently to your chamber, Mistress
Mary, pray send me the measure of your thigh by
some honest body.

MOLL Well, sir, I'll send it by a porter presently.    *Exit*

TAILOR So you had need, it is a lusty one, both of them
would make any porter's back ache in England.    *Exit*

SEBASTIAN I have examined the best part of man,
Reason and judgment, and in love, they tell me,
They leave me uncontrolled: he that is swayed    **110**
By an unfeeling blood past heat of love,
His springtime must needs err: his watch ne'er goes
right
That sets his dial by a rusty clock.

SIR ALEXANDER So, and which is that rusty clock, sir,
you?

SEBASTIAN The clock at Ludgate, sir, it ne'er goes true.

SIR ALEXANDER But thou goest falser: not thy father's
cares
Can keep thee right, when that insensible work
Obeys the workman's art, lets off the hour
And stops again when time is satisfied;

---

64  younger brothers: i.e. with little or no inheritance

65–6  widows . . . kinsman: because a widow's wealth passed to
her husband if she remarried, cautious ones sometimes
placed it in the hands of a relative in order to prevent this
happening; see *Epicoene*, II.ii.153–6

71–2  sturgeon voyage: obscure; OED suggests a fishing voyage for sturgeon. 'The point here, and in what follows,
seems to be: don't choose a wife as if you were going to
be away from home and would never have to live with
her, or as if you were going to a barbaric country [Virgi-
nia] where any female will do' (quoted in Mulholland)

76  so . . . ho: a falconer's cry, hence Moll's reference in the
next speech

78  clout: strip of cloth, used for measuring or as a pin-cushion

82  two trinkets: given the preceding reference to 'monster',
'possibly signifying the sexual organs of both sexes'
(Mulholland)

85  fiddling: fidgeting, with sexual innuendo; see II.i.68

88  great Dutch slop: wide, baggy breeches, newly
fashionable; see *Epicoene*, IV.v.120n

90  yard: this, and the tailor's speeches that follow, turn on a
pun on 'yard' meaning penis

97  gear: a) business; b) clothing; c) genitals
towards: at hand (Bullen)

106  a lusty one: 'thighs are an obvious incitement to sexual
adventure' (Cook); see *Romeo and Juliet*, II.i.19–20, and
*Duchess of Malfi*, II.v.42

112  springtime: allusion to both youth and timekeeping (of
the watch/clock). The speech is a warning that the young
should not be controlled by the old or by those of
'unfeeling blood', or else they 'must needs err'

117  insensible work: i.e. the clock (which obeys the
'workman's art', unlike Sebastian, whose 'father's cares'
cannot keep him 'right')

But thou run'st on, and judgment, thy main wheel,
Beats by all stops, as if the work would break,          121
Begun with long pains for a minute's ruin:
Much like a suffering man brought up with care,
At last bequeathed to shame and a short prayer.

SEBASTIAN I taste you bitterer than I can deserve, sir.

SIR ALEXANDER Who has bewitched thee, son? What
    devil or drug
Hath wrought upon the weakness of thy blood,
And betrayed all her hopes to ruinous folly?
Oh wake from drowsy and enchanted shame,
Wherein thy soul sits with a golden dream          130
Flattered and poisoned. I am old, my son,
Oh let me prevail quickly,
For I have weightier business of mine own
Than to chide thee: I must not to my grave
As a drunkard to his bed, whereon he lies
Only to sleep, and never cares to rise.
Let me dispatch in time; come no more near her.

SEBASTIAN Not honestly? Not in the way of marriage?

SIR ALEXANDER What sayst thou? Marriage? In what
    place? The sessions house? And who shall give the
    bride, prithee? An indictment?          141

SEBASTIAN Sir, now ye take part with the world to
    wrong her.

SIR ALEXANDER Why, wouldst thou fain marry to be
    pointed at?
Alas the number's great, do not o'erburden't:
Why, as good marry a beacon on a hill,
Which all the country fix their eyes upon,
As her thy folly doats on. If thou long'st
To have the story of thy infamous fortunes
Serve for discourse in ordinaries and taverns,
Thou'rt in the way; or to confound thy name,          150
Keep on, thou canst not miss it; or to strike
Thy wretched father to untimely coldness,
Keep the left hand still, it will bring thee to't.
Yet if no tears wrung from thy father's eyes,
Nor sighs that fly in sparkles from his sorrows,
Had power to alter what is wilful in thee,
Methinks her very name should fright thee from her,
And never trouble me.

SEBASTIAN Why is the name of Moll so fatal, sir?

SIR ALEXANDER Many one, sir, where suspect is
    entered,          160

Forseek all London from one end to t'other
More whores of that name than of any ten other.

SEBASTIAN What's that to her? Let those blush for
    themselves.
Can any guilt in others condemn her?
I've vowed to love her: let all storms oppose me
That ever beat against the breast of man,
Nothing but death's black tempest shall divide us.

SIR ALEXANDER Oh folly that can doat on nought but
    shame!

SEBASTIAN Put case a wanton itch runs through one
    name
More than another: is that name the worse,          170
Where honesty sits possessed in't? It should rather
Appear more excellent, and deserve more praise,
When through foul mists a brightness it can raise.
Why, there are of the devil's, honest gentlemen,
And well descended, keep an open house,
And some o'th'good man's that are arrant knaves.
He hates unworthily that by rote contemns,
For the name neither saves, nor yet condemns;
And for her honesty, I have made such proof on't,
In several forms, so nearly watched her ways,          180
I will maintain that strict against an army,
Excepting you my father. Here's her worst,
Sh'has a bold spirit that mingles with mankind,
But nothing else comes near it: and oftentimes
Through her apparel somewhat shames her birth;
But she is loose in nothing but in mirth:
Would all Molls were no worse.

SIR ALEXANDER (Aside) This way I toil in vain and give
    but aim
To infamy and ruin: he will fall,
My blessing cannot stay him: all my joys          190
Stand at the brink of a devouring flood
And will be wilfully swallowed, wilfully.
But why so vain let all these tears be lost?
I'll pursue her to shame, and so all's crossed.          Exit

SEBASTIAN He is gone with some strange purpose,
    whose effect
Will hurt me little if he shoot so wide,
To think I love so blindly: I but feed
His heart to this match, to draw on th'other,
Wherein my joy sits with a full wish crowned,

---

120  judgment: see l. 109; his judgment is here misled by love
121–2  Beats by . . . ruin: 'threatens to wreck speedily the whole
    work . . . Begun (i.e. created or made) "with long pains"
    by "the workman's art" (i.e. "thy father's cares", l. 116)'
    (Mulholland)
131  Flattered: encouraged with false hopes
140  sessions house: court house
153  Keep . . . still: keep to the sinister way always
160  Many one: many a one (presumably constables)
    suspect: suspicion

161  Forseek: seek thoroughly
169  Put case: suppose
174  of the devil's: 'among those who appear to be of the
    devil's party' (Cook)
176  o'th'good man's: i.e. those apparently of God's party
    (from proverb 'God is a good man')
179  for: as for
184  But . . . it: 'but nothing besides her spirit comes near
    mankind' (Mulholland)
188  give but aim: an archery term: 'give one's aim by signalling
    the result of a previous shot' (quoted in Mulholland)

Only his mood excepted, which must change  200
By opposite policies, courses indirect:
Plain dealing in this world takes no effect.
This mad girl I'll acquaint with my intent,
Get her assistance, make my fortunes known:
'Twixt lovers' hearts she's a fit instrument,
And has the art to help them to their own:
By her advice, for in that craft she's wise,
My love and I may meet, spite of all spies.

*Exit*

## Act III, scene i

*Enter* LAXTON *in Gray's Inn Fields with the* COACHMAN

LAXTON  Coachman.

COACHMAN  Here sir.

LAXTON  There's a tester more; prithee drive thy coach
to the hither end of Marybone Park, a fit place for
Moll to get in.

COACHMAN  Marybone Park, sir.

LAXTON  Ay, it's in our way, thou knowest.

COACHMAN  It shall be done, sir.

LAXTON  Coachman.

COACHMAN  Anon, sir.  10

LAXTON  Are we fitted with good frampold jades?

COACHMAN  The best in Smithfield, I warrant you, sir.

LAXTON  May we safely take the upper hand of any
coached velvet cap or tufftaffety jacket? For they keep
a vild swaggering in coaches nowadays, the highways
are stopped with them.

COACHMAN  My life for yours, and baffle 'em too sir:
why, they are the same jades, believe it, sir, that have
drawn all your famous whores to Ware.

LAXTON  Nay, then they know their business; they need
no more instructions.  21

COACHMAN  They're so used to such journeys, sir, I
never use whip to 'em; for if they catch but the scent
of a wench once, they run like devils.

*Exit* COACHMAN *with his whip*

LAXTON  Fine Cerberus! That rogue will have the start
of a thousand ones, for whilst others trot afoot, he'll
ride prancing to hell upon a coach-horse.—Stay, 'tis
now about the hour of her appointment, but yet I see
her not. (*The clock strikes three*) Hark what's this?
One, two, three, three by the clock at Savoy: this is
the hour, and Gray's Inn Fields the place, she swore
she'd meet me. Ha, yonder's two Inns o' Court men
with one wench, but that's not she, they walk toward
Islington out of my way. I see none yet dressed like
her; I must look for a shag ruff, a frieze jerkin, a short
sword, and a saveguard, or I get none. Why, Moll,
prithee make haste, or the coachman will curse us
anon.  38

*Enter* MOLL *like a man*

MOLL  (*Aside*) Oh here's my gentleman: if they would
keep their days as well with their mercers as their
hours with their harlots, no bankrupt would give
seven score pound for a sergeant's place; for would
you know a catchpole rightly derived, the corruption
of a citizen is the generation of a sergeant. How his
eye hawks for venery!—Come, you are ready sir?

LAXTON  Ready? For what, sir?

MOLL  Do you ask that now, sir? Why was this meeting
'pointed?

LAXTON  I thought you mistook me sir.
You seem to be some young barrister;  50
I have no suit in law—all my land's sold,
I praise heaven for't; 't has rid me of much trouble.

MOLL  Then I must wake you, sir; where stands the
coach?

LAXTON  Who's this? Moll, honest Moll?

MOLL  So young, and purblind? You're an old wanton
in your eyes, I see that.

---

3  tester: sixpence (from the teston of Henry VIII, a small
coin originally worth a shilling)

4  Marybone Park: i.e. Marylebone Park, now part of
Regent's Park, at this time a centre for prostitution.
'Marybone' is punning on 'marrow-bone' (see II.i.204n).
Cook suggests an additional pun on 'park' as 'the female
body as a domain where the lover may freely roam'

11  frampold: spirited
jades: horses (contemptuous term), nags; see II.i.302

12  Smithfield: a horse and cattle market with a bad
reputation

14  coached: couched, embroidered with gold thread
tufftaffety: taffeta with a tufted nap or pile

15  vild: vile
nowadays: 'since the repeal of sumptuary law in 1603
which allowed the newly-wealthy middle classes to dress
more finely than before. These people also need coaches
– hitherto luxury items – creating traffic jams' (Cook)

17  baffle: disgrace; see I.ii.168

19  Ware: see II.i.296n

25  Cerberus: three-headed dog, guardian of the entrance to
the underworld

30  Savoy: a hospital, located between the Strand and the
river, built by Henry VII on the site of the Savoy Palace

34  Islington: suburb to the north of London; a popular place
for excursions and rendez-vous

36  saveguard: see II.i.185 SDn

SD  *like a man*: i.e. dressed as a man

40  mercers: dealers in fine fabrics

41-2  bankrupt . . . sergeant: Mulholland identifies this as
proverbial: 'A sergeant is the spawn of some decayed
shop-keeper'

43  catchpole: sheriff's officer; sergeant who arrests for debt
corruption: degeneration

51  all . . . sold: another instance of Laxton's 'lack'

56  purblind: totally blind

LAXTON  Th'art admirably suited for the Three Pigeons
at Brainford. I'll swear I knew thee not.

MOLL  I'll swear you did not: but you shall know me
now.  61

LAXTON  No, not here, we shall be spied i'faith; the
coach is better, come.

MOLL  Stay.

LAXTON  What, wilt thou untruss a point, Moll?

*She puts off her cloak and draws her sword*

MOLL                    Yes, here's the point
That I untruss: 't has but one tag, 'twill serve, though,
To tie up a rogue's tongue.

LAXTON                    How?

MOLL                         There's the gold
With which you hired your hackney, here's her pace,
She racks hard, and perhaps your bones will feel it:
Ten angels of mine own I've put to thine:  70
Win 'em and wear 'em.

LAXTON                    Hold Moll, Mistress Mary.

MOLL  Draw, or I'll serve an execution on thee
Shall lay thee up till doomsday.

LAXTON  Draw upon a woman? Why, what dost mean,
Moll?

MOLL  To teach thy base thoughts manners: thou'rt one
of those
That thinks each woman thy fond flexible whore;
If she but cast a liberal eye upon thee,
Turn back her head, she's thine; or, amongst
company,
By chance drink first to thee, then she's quite gone,
There's no means to help her: nay for a need,  80
Wilt swear unto thy credulous fellow lechers
That thou'rt more in favour with a lady
At first sight than her monkey all her lifetime.
How many of our sex by such as thou

Have their good thoughts paid with a blasted name
That never deserved loosely or did trip
In path of whoredom beyond cup and lip?
But for the stain of conscience and of soul,
Better had women fall into the hands
Of an act silent than a bragging nothing;  90
There's no mercy in't.—What durst move you, sir,
To think me whorish?—A name which I'd tear out
From the high German's throat if it lay ledger there
To dispatch privy slanders against me.
In thee I defy all men, their worst hates,
And their best flatteries, all their golden witchcrafts,
With which they entangle the poor spirits of fools.
Distressed needlewomen and trade-fallen wives,
Fish that must needs bite or themselves be bitten,
Such hungry things as these may soon be took  100
With a worm fastened on a golden hook:
Those are the lecher's food, his prey; he watches
For quarrelling wedlocks, and poor shifting sisters,
'Tis the best fish he takes. But why, good fisherman,
Am I thought meat for you, that never yet
Had angling rod cast towards me? 'Cause, you'll say,
I'm given to sport, I'm often merry, jest:
Had mirth no kindred in the world but lust?
Oh shame take all her friends then: but howe'er
Thou and the baser world censure my life,  110
I'll send 'em word by thee, and write so much
Upon thy breast, 'cause thou shalt bear't in mind:
Tell them 'twere base to yield, where I have conquered.
I scorn to prostitute myself to a man,
I that can prostitute a man to me;
And so I greet thee.

LAXTON                    Hear me.

MOLL                         Would the spirits
Of all my slanderers were clasped in thine,
That I might vex an army at one time.

LAXTON  I do repent me, hold.                    *They fight*

MOLL  You'll die the better Christian then.  120

LAXTON  I do confess I have wronged thee, Moll.

MOLL  Confession is but poor amends for wrong,
Unless a rope would follow.

LAXTON                         I ask thee pardon.

---

58  Three Pigeons: a famous inn at Brentford

62  No, not here: Laxton takes Moll's words to be the
prelude to a sexual encounter

65  point: lace that attached hose to doublet. Moll uses the
word to refer to the point of her sword

68  hackney: a) horse for hire; b) prostitute
pace: a) rate, speed; b) gait (of horse)

69  racks: moves with gait known as a 'rack', whereby the
fore and hind legs move together on one side and then
the other; at speed, a very rough pace

71  Win . . . wear 'em: proverbial

72  Draw . . . execution: to serve an execution is make formal
delivery of a process or writ. Cook also notes that 'draw'
meant to expose the penis ('as a sword from a scabbard'),
and an 'execution' was the performance of a sexual act;
'her threat therefore is that she will geld him'

76  fond: foolish
flexible: impressionable, tractable

77  liberal: a) generous; b) licentious

80  for a need: in an emergency, at a pinch

83  monkey: monkeys were popular as pets

87  beyond cup and lip: 'the allusion is to a betrothal'
(Mulholland)

88  But for: were it not for

90  act: i.e. a sexual act

93  high German's throat: see II.i.392–3n
lay ledger: resided

98  needlewomen: see I.i.53n

99  Fish: commonly meant 'prostitute' (eds)

101  worm . . . hook: proverbial

103  wedlocks: wives; or, perhaps, 'marriages'
shifting: deceitful

112  'cause: so that

116  greet: assail

MOLL I'm your hired whore, sir.

LAXTON I yield both purse and body.

MOLL                                        Both are mine,
And now at my disposing.

LAXTON                            Spare my life.

MOLL I scorn to strike thee basely.                      127

LAXTON Spoke like a noble girl, i'faith. (*Aside*) Heart, I
think I fight with a familiar, or the ghost of a fencer.
Sh'has wounded me gallantly. Call you this a
lecherous voyage? Here's blood would have served me
this seven year in broken heads and cut fingers, and it
now runs all out together. Pox o'the Three Pigeons, I
would the coach were here now to carry me to the
chirurgeons.                                    *Exit*

MOLL If I could meet my enemies one by one thus,
I might make pretty shift with 'em in time,
And make 'em know, she that has wit and spirit
May scorn to live beholding to her body for meat,
Or for apparel, like your common dame              140
That makes shame get her clothes to cover shame.
Base is that mind that kneels unto her body,
As if a husband stood in awe on's wife;
My spirit shall be mistress of this house,
As long as I have time in't.—Oh,

*Enter* TRAPDOOR

Here comes my man that would be: 'tis his hour.
Faith, a good well-set fellow, if his spirit
Be answerable to his umbles; he walks stiff,
But whether he will stand to't stiffly, there's the
    point;
Has a good calf for't, and ye shall have many a
    woman                                      150
Choose him she means to make her head by his calf;
I do not know their tricks in't. Faith, he seems
A man without; I'll try what he is within.

TRAPDOOR She told me Gray's Inn Fields 'twixt three
and four.
I'll fit her mistress-ship with a piece of service:
I'm hired to rid the town of one mad girl. *She jostles him*
What a pox ails you, sir?

MOLL He begins like a gentleman.

TRAPDOOR Heart, is the field so narrow, or your
eyesight?
Life, he comes back again.             *She comes towards him*

MOLL Was this spoke to me, sir?                        161

TRAPDOOR I cannot tell, sir.

MOLL Go, y'are a coxcomb.

TRAPDOOR Coxcomb?

MOLL Y'are a slave.

TRAPDOOR I hope there's law for you, sir.

MOLL Yea, do you see, sir?                    *Turns his hat*

TRAPDOOR Heart, this is no good dealing; pray let me
know what house you're of.

MOLL One of the Temple, sir.                   *Fillips him*

TRAPDOOR Mass, so methinks.                            171

MOLL And yet sometime I lie about Chick Lane.

TRAPDOOR I like you the worse because you shift your
lodging so often; I'll not meddle with you for that
trick, sir.

MOLL A good shift, but it shall not serve your turn.

TRAPDOOR You'll give me leave to pass about my
business, sir.

MOLL Your business? I'll make you wait on me before I
ha' done, and glad to serve me too.                    180

TRAPDOOR How sir? Serve you? Not if there were no
more men in England.

MOLL But if there were no more women in England, I
hope you'd wait upon your mistress then.

TRAPDOOR Mistress!

MOLL Oh you're a tried spirit at a push, sir.

TRAPDOOR What would your worship have me do?

MOLL You a fighter?

TRAPDOOR No, I praise heaven, I had better grace and
more manners.                                       190

MOLL As how, I pray, sir?

TRAPDOOR Life, 't had been a beastly part of me to
have drawn my weapons upon my mistress; all the
world would'a' cried shame of me for that.

MOLL Why, but you knew me not.

TRAPDOOR Do not say so, mistress. I knew you by your
wide straddle, as well as if I had been in your belly.

MOLL Well, we shall try you further, i'th'meantime we
give you entertainment.

TRAPDOOR Thank your good mistress-ship.               200

MOLL How many suits have you?

TRAPDOOR No more suits than backs, mistress.

MOLL Well, if you deserve, I cast off this next week,
And you may creep into't.

---

129 familiar: spirit
131 voyage: eds (viage Q); 'sexual adventure' (Mulholland)
135 chirurgeons: surgeons
140 common dame: whore
146 man: servant
148 answerable . . . umbles: consistent with his insides
    ('umbles' meant the edible inward parts of an animal,
    usually a deer)
    stiff: resolutely (with innuendo)
152 tricks: skills

170 One . . . Temple: i.e. a lawyer (the Middle and Inner
    Temples are Inns of Court)
SD *Fillips*: flicks with her finger
172 Chick Lane: in the district of Smithfield, and notorious
    for its thieves
175 trick: habit, practice
186 at a push: in an emergency; Mulholland speculates on
    bawdy innuendo ('push' meant copulate)
193 drawn my weapons: with innuendo; see l. 72n
199 give you entertainment: engage you
203 this: i.e. this suit

TRAPDOOR                    Thank your good worship.

MOLL  Come follow me to St Thomas Apostle's,
    I'll put a livery cloak upon your back
    The first thing I do.

TRAPDOOR                    I follow my dear mistress.

*Exeunt*

## Act III, scene ii

*Enter* MISTRESS GALLIPIOT *as from supper, her husband
after her*

MASTER GALLIPOT  What Pru, nay sweet Prudence.

MISTRESS GALLIPOT  What a pruing keep you! I think
    the baby would have a teat it kyes so. Pray be not so
    fond of me, leave your city humours; I'm vexed at you
    to see how like a calf you come bleating after me.

MASTER GALLIPOT  Nay, honey Pru: how does your
    rising up before all the table show? And flinging from
    my friends so uncivilly? Fie Pru, fie, come.

MISTRESS GALLIPOT  Then up and ride, i'faith.          9

MASTER GALLIPOT  Up and ride? Nay, my pretty Pru,
    that's far from my thought, duck: why, mouse, thy
    mind is nibbling at something; what is't? What lies
    upon thy stomach?

MISTRESS GALLIPOT  Such an ass as you: heyday, y'are
    best turn midwife, or physician: y'are a pothecary
    already, but I'm none of your drugs.

MASTER GALLIPOT  Thou art a sweet drug, sweetest
    Pru, and the more thou art pounded, the more
    precious.                                            19

MISTRESS GALLIPOT  Must you be prying into a
    woman's secrets: say ye?

MASTER GALLIPOT  Woman's secrets?

MISTRESS GALLIPOT  What? I cannot have a qualm
    come upon me but your teeth waters till your nose
    hang over it.

MASTER GALLIPOT  It is my love, dear wife.

MISTRESS GALLIPOT  Your love? Your love is all words;
    give me deeds! I cannot abide a man that's too fond
    over me, so cookish; thou dost not know how to
    handle a woman in her kind.                          30

MASTER GALLIPOT  No, Pru? Why, I hope I have
    handled—

MISTRESS GALLIPOT  Handle a fool's head of your
    own—fie—fie.

MASTER GALLIPOT  Ha, ha, 'tis such a wasp; it does me
    good now to have her sting me, little rogue.

MISTRESS GALLIPOT  Now fie how you vex me! I cannot
    abide these apron husbands: such cotqueans! You
    overdo your things, they become you scurvily.        39

MASTER GALLIPOT  (*Aside*) Upon my life she breeds.
    Heaven knows how I have strained myself to please
    her, night and day. I wonder why we citizens should
    get children so fretful and untoward in the breeding,
    their fathers being for the most part as gentle as
    milch kine.—Shall I leave thee, my Pru?

MISTRESS GALLIPOT  Fie, fie, fie.                       46

MASTER GALLIPOT  Thou shalt not be vexed no more,
    pretty kind rogue, take no cold, sweet Pru.      *Exit*

MISTRESS GALLIPOT  As your wit has done. Now
    Master Laxton, show your head; what news from
    you? Would any husband suspect that a woman
    crying 'Buy any scurvy-grass' should bring love letters
    amongst her herbs to his wife? Pretty trick, fine
    conveyance: had jealousy a thousand eyes, a silly
    woman with scurvy-grass blinds them all;
    Laxton, with bays
    Crown I thy wit for this, it deserves praise.
    This makes me affect thee more, this proves thee wise,
    'Lack, what poor shift is love forced to devise!—     59
    To th' point.                    *She reads the letter*
    'Oh sweet creature—' (a sweet beginning) 'pardon my
    long absence, for thou shalt shortly be possessed with
    my presence; though Demophon was false to Phyllis,
    I will be to thee as Pan-da-rus was to Cres-sida:
    though Aeneas made an ass of Dido, I will die to

---

205  St Thomas Apostle's: a church east of St Paul's and Bow
        Lane, near Garlick Hill and what is now Queen Street.
        There were clothiers' shops in the neighbourhood
  2  pruing: a nonce-word, from 'Prudence'
  3  kyes: i.e. cries (baby-talk)
  4  humours: moods
  9  up and ride: obscene riposte; 'ride' meant sexual
        intercourse
 16  drugs: with play on 'drudges'
 24  teeth waters: variant of 'mouth waters'
 29  cookish: like a cook
 30  in her kind: as she deserves

 36  sting: eds (sing Q); arouse sexually (Cook)
 38  apron husbands: husbands who follow their wives as if
        tied to their apron strings (eds)
        cotqueans: used of men who act the housewife and
        meddle with female affairs (eds)
        things: a) attentions; b) sexual organs (Mulholland)
 39  scurvily: meanly
 43  get: beget
        untoward: unruly
 52  scurvy-grass: spoonwort (*cochlearia officinalis*), used in
        anti-scorbutic preparations
 63  Demophon . . . Phyllis: Demophon, son of Theseus,
        failed to return to Phyllis, princess of Thrace, at the time
        appointed; she hanged herself, and was turned into an
        almond tree, which burst into flower when Demophon
        returned and embraced it
 64  Pan-da-rus . . . Cres-sida: thus in Q₂ 'to mark the
        difficulty with which such hard names were read by
        Mistress Gallipot' (eds). Pandarus was the go-between in
        the relationship of Troilus and Cressida
 65  Aeneas . . . Dido: when Aeneas left Carthage by order of
        the gods, Dido, whose love for him was unrequited,
        killed herself

thee ere I do so. Oh sweetest creature, make much of
me, for no man beneath the silver moon shall make
more of a woman than I do of thee: furnish me
therefore with thirty pounds; you must do it of
necessity for me; I languish till I see some comfort
come from thee. Protesting not to die in thy debt,
but rather to live so, as hitherto I have and will,    72
                  Thy true Laxton ever'.
Alas poor gentleman, troth I pity him.
How shall I raise this money? Thirty pound?
'Tis thirty sure, a 3 before an o,
I know his threes too well. My childbed linen?
Shall I pawn that for him? Then if my mark
Be known I am undone; it may be thought
My husband's bankrupt. Which way shall I turn?    80
Laxton, what with my own fears, and thy wants,
I'm like a needle 'twixt two adamants.

*Enter* MASTER GALLIPOT *hastily*

MASTER GALLIPOT  Nay, nay, wife, the women are all
  up. (*Aside*) Ha, how, reading o' letters? I smell a
  goose, a couple of capons, and a gammon of bacon
  from her mother out of the country, I hold my life.—
  Steal, steal—
MISTRESS GALLLIPOT  Oh beshrew your heart.
MASTER GALLIPOT             What letter's that?
  I'll see't.                    *She tears the letter*
MISTRESS GALLIPOT  Oh would thou hadst no eyes to
  see
  The downfall of me and thyself: I'm forever,
  Forever I'm undone.
MASTER GALLIPOT       What ails my Pru?    90
  What paper's that thou tear'st?
MISTRESS GALLIPOT           Would I could tear
  My very heart in pieces: for my soul
  Lies on the rack of shame, that tortures me
  Beyond a woman's suffering.
MASTER GALLIPOT          What means this?
MISTRESS GALLIPOT  Had you no other vengeance to
  throw down,
  But even in height of all my joys—
MASTER GALLIPOT            Dear woman—
MISTRESS GALLIPOT  When the full sea of pleasure and
  content
  Seemed to flow over me?
MASTER GALLIPOT       As thou desirest
  To keep me out of bedlam, tell what troubles thee,

Is not thy child at nurse fallen sick, or dead?    100
MISTRESS GALLIPOT  Oh no.
MASTER GALLIPOT           Heavens bless me, are my
  barns and houses
  Yonder at Hockley Hole consumed with fire?
  I can build more, sweet Pru.
MISTRESS GALLIPOT          'Tis worse, 'tis worse.
MASTER GALLIPOT  My factor broke? Or is the Jonas sunk?
MISTRESS GALLIPOT  Would all we had were swallowed
  in the waves,
  Rather than both should be the scorn of slaves.
MASTER GALLIPOT  I'm at my wit's end.
MISTRESS GALLIPOT           Oh my dear husband,
  Where once I thought myself a fixed star,
  Placed only in the heaven of thine arms,
  I fear now I shall prove a wanderer.    110
  Oh Laxton, Laxton, is it then my fate
  To be by thee o'erthrown?
MASTER GALLIPOT          Defend me, wisdom,
  From falling into frenzy. On my knees,
  Sweet Pru, speak what's that Laxton who so heavy
  Lies on thy bosom?
MISTRESS GALLIPOT     I shall sure run mad.
MASTER GALLIPOT  I shall run mad for company then.
  Speak to me,
  I'm Gallipot thy husband—Pru,—why Pru,
  Art sick in conscience for some villainous deed
  Thou wert about to act? Didst mean to rob me?
  Tush, I forgive thee; hast thou on my bed    120
  Thrust my soft pillow under another's head?
  I'll wink at all faults, Pru; 'las, that's no more
  Than what some neighbours near thee have done
  before.
  Sweet honey Pru, what's that Laxton?
MISTRESS GALLIPOT            Oh.
MASTER GALLIPOT  Out with him.
MISTRESS GALLIPOT          Oh he's born to be
  my undoer.
  This hand which thou call'st thine, to him was given,
  To him was I made sure i'th'sight of heaven.
MASTER GALLIPOT  I never heard this thunder.
MISTRESS GALLIPOT          Yes, yes, before
  I was to thee contracted, to him I swore:    129
  Since last I saw him, twelve months three times told
  The moon hath drawn through her light silver bow;

---

65–5 die to thee: with pun on sense of 'have an orgasm'
 76 a 3 before an o: eds suggest a sexual entendre: 'o' meant
    vagina; 3 may allude to 're' (Latin for 'thing', meaning
    penis), or to penis and testicles (i.e. 'three' parts)
 78 mark: laundry mark, for identification
 82 adamants: loadstones or magnets
 87 Steal, steal: Gallipot is stealing up behind his wife
 99 bedlam: Bethlehem hospital for the insane

100 at nurse: lodged with wet-nurse away from home
102 Hockley Hole: Hockley-in-the-Hole, near Clerkenwell
    Green
104 My factor broke: my agent absconded (or bankrupt)
108 fixed star: star which always appears in the same place in
    the sky, as opposed to a 'wanderer' (l. 110)
127 made sure: contracted, betrothed; see I.i.76–7
130–1 twelve . . . bow: similar to phrasing in others of
    Dekker's plays; see *The Whore of Babylon*, I.i.47, IV.ii.2–4;
    and *The Honest Whore*, part 2, V.ii.25–6 (eds)

For o'er the seas he went, and it was said
(But rumour lies) that he in France was dead.
But he's alive, oh he's alive, he sent
That letter to me, which in rage I rent,
Swearing with oaths most damnably to have me,
Or tear me from this bosom: oh heavens save me.

MASTER GALLIPOT My heart will break—shamed and
    undone forever.

MISTRESS GALLIPOT So black a day, poor wretch, went
    o'er thee never.

MASTER GALLIPOT If thou should'st wrestle with him
    at the law,                                                     140
    Th'art sure to fall; no odd sleight, no prevention.
    I'll tell him th'art with child.

MISTRESS GALLIPOT           Hm.

MASTER GALLIPOT            Or give out
    One of my men was ta'en abed with thee.

MISTRESS GALLIPOT Hm, hm.

MASTER GALLIPOT           Before I lose thee, my
    dear Pru,
    I'll drive it to that push.

MISTRESS GALLIPOT      Worse, and worse still,
    You embrace a mischief, to prevent an ill.

MASTER GALLIPOT I'll buy thee of him, stop his mouth
    with gold,
    Think'st thou 'twill do?

MISTRESS GALLIPOT Oh me, heavens grant it would!
    Yet now my senses are set more in tune,
    He writ, as I remember in his letter,                     150
    That he in riding up and down had spent,
    Ere he could find me, thirty pounds. Send that,
    Stand not on thirty with him.

MASTER GALLIPOT         Forty, Pru,
    Say thou the word, 'tis done: we venture lives
    For wealth, but must do more to keep our wives:
    Thirty or forty, Pru?

MISTRESS GALLIPOT     Thirty, good sweet;
    Of an ill bargain let's save what we can;
    I'll pay it him with my tears; he was a man
    When first I knew him of a meek spirit:
    All goodness is not yet dried up, I hope.            160

MASTER GALLIPOT He shall have thirty pound, let that
    stop all:
    Love's sweets taste best, when we have drunk down
    gall.

*Enter* MASTER TILTYARD *and his* WIFE, MASTER
GOSHAWK, *and* MISTRESS OPENWORK

God-so, our friends; come, come, smooth your
    cheek;
    After a storm the face of heaven looks sleek.

MASTER TILTYARD Did I not tell you these turtles were
    together?

MISTRESS TILTYARD How dost thou, sirrah? Why,
    sister Gallipot!

MISTRESS OPENWORK Lord, how she's changed!

GOSHAWK Is your wife ill, sir?                                        170

MASTER GALLIPOT Yes indeed, la sir, very ill, very ill,
    never worse.

MISTRESS TILTYARD How her head burns; feel how her
    pulses work.

MISTRESS OPENWORK Sister, lie down a little, that
    always does me good.

MASTER TILTYARD In good sadness, I find best ease
    in that too; has she laid some hot thing to her
    stomach?                                                        179

MISTRESS GALLIPOT No, but I will lay something anon.

MASTER TILTYARD Come, come fools, you trouble her.
    Shall's go, Master Goshawk?

GOSHAWK Yes, sweet Master Tiltyard.—Sirrah
    Rosamond, I hold my life Gallipot hath vexed his
    wife.

MISTRESS OPENWORK She has a horrible high colour
    indeed.

GOSHAWK We shall have your face painted with the
    same red soon at night, when your husband comes
    from his rubbers in a false alley; thou wilt not believe
    me that his bowls run with a wrong bias.           191

MISTRESS OPENWORK It cannot sink into me, that he
    feeds upon stale mutton abroad, having better and
    fresher at home.

GOSHAWK What if I bring thee where thou shalt see
    him stand at rack and manger?

MISTRESS OPENWORK I'll saddle him in's kind, and spur
    him till he kick again.

GOSHAWK Shall thou and I ride our journey then?

MISTRESS OPENWORK Here's my hand.                         200

---

163  God-so: an exclamation. Either a corruption of 'catso'
    (from Italian; meaning penis), or a variant of 'Uds-so', a
    corruption of 'By God's soul'
167, 183  sirrah: see II.i.196
177  In good sadness: in all seriousness
178–9  hot thing . . . stomach: as a medication; with sexual
    entendre
190  rubbers . . . false alley: from game of bowls: 'rubbers'
    meant set of three games, with sexual innuendo from
    'rub'
193  stale: with pun on 'stale' meaning prostitute
196  at rack and manger: in the midst of abundance
    (proverbial)
197  in's kind: in the same manner
199  ride our journey: with sexual innuendo; see 'ride' II.i.161,
    'voyage' III.i.131

---

141  odd sleight: cunning device (to outwit Laxton)
145  to that push: a) to that extremity; b) sexual sense (see
    III.i.186n)
153  Stand not on: do not scruple at
154–5  we venture . . . wives: proverbial

GOSHAWK  No more. Come, Master Tiltyard, shall we
  leap into the stirrups with our women, and amble
  home?
MASTER TILTYARD  Yes, yes, come wife.
MISTRESS TILTYARD  In troth sister, I hope you will do
  well for all this.
MISTRESS GALLIPOT  I hope I shall. Farewell good
  sister: sweet Master Goshawk.
MASTER GALLIPOT  Welcome brother, most kindly
  welcome sir.      **210**
OMNES  Thanks, sir, for our good cheer.
              *Exeunt all but* GALLIPOT *and his wife*
MASTER GALLIPOT  It shall be so; because a crafty knave
  Shall not outreach me, nor walk by my door
  With my wife arm in arm, as 'twere his whore,
  I'll give him a golden coxcomb; thirty pound,
  Tush Pru, what's thirty pound? Sweet duck, look
  cheerly.
MISTRESS GALLIPOT  Thou art worthy of my heart, thou
  buy'st it dearly.

*Enter* LAXTON *muffled*

LAXTON  (*Aside*) Uds light, the tide's against me; a pox
  of your pothecary-ship! Oh for some glister to set
  him going! 'Tis one of Hercules' labours to tread one
  of these city hens, because their cocks are still
  crowing over them. There's no turning tail here, I
  must on.      **223**
MISTRESS GALLIPOT  Oh husband see, he comes.
MASTER GALLIPOT  Let me deal with him.
LAXTON  Bless you, sir.
MASTER GALLIPOT  Be you blest too, sir, if you come in
  peace.
LAXTON  Have you any good pudding tobacco, sir?
MISTRESS GALLIPOT  Oh pick no quarrels, gentle sir; my
  husband      **230**
  Is not a man of weapon, as you are;
  He knows all, I have opened all before him
  Concerning you.
LAXTON  (*Aside*)    Zounds, has she shown my letters?
MISTRESS GALLIPOT  Suppose my case were yours, what
  would you do?

At such a pinch, such batteries, such assaults,
Of father, mother, kindred, to dissolve
The knot you tied, and to be bound to him?
How could you shift this storm off?
LAXTON            If I know, hang me.
MISTRESS GALLIPOT  Besides, a story of your death was
  read
  Each minute to me.      **239**
LAXTON  (*Aside*)    What a pox means this riddling?
MASTER GALLIPOT  Be wise, sir, let not you and I be
  tossed
  On lawyers' pens; they have sharp nibs and draw
  Men's very heart-blood from them; what need you,
    sir,
  To beat the drum of my wife's infamy,
  And call your friends together, sir, to prove
  Your precontract, when sh'has confessed it?
LAXTON            Hm sir,
  Has she confessed it?
MASTER GALLIPOT    Sh'has, faith, to me, sir,
  Upon your letter sending.
MISTRESS GALLIPOT    I have, I have.
LAXTON  (*Aside*) If I let this iron cool, call me slave.
  —Do you hear, you dame Prudence? Think'st thou,
    vile woman,      **250**
  I'll take these blows and wink?
MISTRESS GALLIPOT    Upon my knees—
LAXTON  Out, impudence.
MASTER GALLIPOT    Good sir—
LAXTON           You goatish slaves,
  No wild fowl to cut up but mine?
MASTER GALLIPOT    Alas sir,
  You make her flesh to tremble: fright her not,
  She shall do reason, and what's fit.
LAXTON           I'll have thee,
  Wert thou more common than an hospital,
  And more diseased.
MASTER GALLIPOT    But one word, good sir.
LAXTON           So sir.
MASTER GALLIPOT  I married her, have lien with her,
  and got
  Two children on her body, think but on that;
  Have you so beggarly an appetite    **260**
  When I upon a dainty dish have fed
  To dine upon my scraps, my leavings? Ha, sir?
  Do I come near you now, sir?
LAXTON           Be-lady, you touch me.
MASTER GALLIPOT  Would not you scorn to wear my
  clothes, sir?
LAXTON           Right, sir.

---

202  amble: originally used only of horses: a slower version of
    the 'gait'; see III.i.69n
212  because: so that
 SD  *muffled*: Mulholland suggests three reasons why Laxton
    might appear 'muffled' at all of his entrances from now
    on: a) shame (or wounds), after his drubbing from Moll;
    b) fear of his creditors (he has lost ten angels to Moll);
    c) in order to move incognito, like a lover or a patron of a
    brothel
219  glister: suppository, enema ('clyster')
220  tread: copulate with (of a male bird with a hen)
229  pudding tobacco: compressed tobacco, made into rolls
    resembling a pudding or sausage

246  precontract: of marriage; see l. 127
252  goatish: lustful
253  wild fowl: prostitute (eds)
263  Be-lady: corruption of 'By our Lady'

MASTER GALLIPOT  Then pray, sir, wear not her, for
   she's a garment
  So fitting for my body, I'm loath
  Another should put it on: you will undo both.
  Your letter (as she said) complained you had spent
  In quest of her some thirty pound, I'll pay it;
  Shall that, sir, stop this gap up 'twixt you two?   **270**

LAXTON  Well, if I swallow this wrong, let her thank
  you:
  The money being paid, sir, I am gone;
  Farewell. Oh women! Happy's he trusts none.

MISTRESS GALLIPOT  Dispatch him hence, sweet
  husband.

MASTER GALLIPOT                Yes, dear wife.
  Pray sir, come in: ere Master Laxton part
  Thou shalt in wine drink to him.

MISTRESS GALLIPOT          With all my heart.
                    *Exit* MASTER GALLIPOT
  How dost thou like my wit?

LAXTON              Rarely: that wile
  By which the serpent did the first woman beguile
  Did ever since all women's bosoms fill;
  Y'are apple-eaters all, deceivers still.     **280**
                         *Exeunt*

# Act III, scene iii

*Enter* SIR ALEXANDER WENGRAVE, SIR DAVY DAPPER, SIR
ADAM APPLETON *at one door, and* TRAPDOOR *at another
door*

SIR ALEXANDER  Out with your tale, Sir Davy, to Sir
  Adam:
  A knave is in mine eye deep in my debt.

SIR DAVY  Nay, if he be a knave, sir, hold him fast.

SIR DAVY *and* SIR ADAM *talk apart*

SIR ALEXANDER  Speak softly, what egg is there
  hatching now?

TRAPDOOR  A duck's egg, sir, a duck that has eaten a
  frog. I have cracked the shell, and some villainy or
  other will peep out presently; the duck that sits is the
  bouncing ramp, that roaring girl my mistress; the
  drake that must tread is your son Sebastian.

SIR ALEXANDER  Be quick.              **10**

TRAPDOOR  As the tongue of an oyster-wench.

SIR ALEXANDER  And see thy news be true.

TRAPDOOR  As a barber's every Saturday night. Mad
  Moll—

SIR ALEXANDER  Ah.

TRAPDOOR  Must be let in without knocking at your
  back gate.

SIR ALEXANDER  So.

TRAPDOOR  Your chamber will be made bawdy.

SIR ALEXANDER  Good.           **20**

TRAPDOOR  She comes in a shirt of mail.

SIR ALEXANDER  How, shirt of mail?

TRAPDOOR  Yes sir, or a male shirt, that's to say in
  man's apparel.

SIR ALEXANDER  To my son?

TRAPDOOR  Close to your son: your son and her moon
  will be in conjunction, if all almanacs lie not; her
  black saveguard is turned into a deep slop, the holes
  of her upper body to button-holes, her waistcoat to a
  doublet, her placket to the ancient seat of a codpiece,
  and you shall take 'em both with standing collars.  **31**

SIR ALEXANDER  Art sure of this?

TRAPDOOR  As every throng is sure of a pickpocket, as
  sure as a whore is of the clients all Michaelmas Term,
  and of the pox after the term.

SIR ALEXANDER  The time of their tilting?

TRAPDOOR  Three.

SIR ALEXANDER  The day?

TRAPDOOR  This.

SIR ALEXANDER  Away, ply it, watch her.     **40**

TRAPDOOR  As the devil doth for the death of a bawd,
  I'll watch her; do you catch her.

SIR ALEXANDER  She's fast: here, weave thou the nets,
  hark.

TRAPDOOR  They are made.

SIR ALEXANDER  I told them thou didst owe me money:
  hold it up, maintain't.

TRAPDOOR  Stiffly, as a puritan does contention;—
  (*Angrily, as in a quarrel*) Fox, I owe thee not the value
  of a halfpenny halter.          **50**

---

SD  Q indicates that Master and Mistress Gallipot exit
  together (after 'him', l. 276), leaving only Laxton on
  stage. We follow other eds in the arrangement given
  here, so that Mistress Gallipot hears his final words.
  However, she could just as well exit after Laxton's
  'Rarely'

2  A knave . . . eye: i.e. I can see a knave (who is)

8  bouncing ramp: swaggering bold woman

13  As a barber's: barbers had a reputation as news-mongers;
   see *Epicoene*, I.ii.39

27  in conjunction: i.e. like planets (when in the same sign of
   the zodiac); with innuendo: 'conjunction' meant
   copulation

28  saveguard: see II.i.185 SDn
   slop: see II.ii.88n

29  upper body: bodice, which was laced through a series of
   'holes'
   waistcoat: a waist-length undergarment

30  placket: the opening at the top of a skirt or petticoat; like
   'codpiece', the word usually has sexual associations

31  standing collars: high collars were fashionable for men at
   this time

34  Michaelmas Term: 'the first term of the legal year, when
   the termers will have plenty of money' (Cook)

36  tilting: encounter

46  them: i.e. Sir Davy and Sir Adam

SIR ALEXANDER  Thou shalt be hanged in't ere thou
　'scape so. Varlet, I'll make thee look through a grate.
TRAPDOOR  I'll do't presently, through a tavern grate.
　Drawer! Pish.　　　　　　　　　　　　　*Exit*
SIR ADAM  Has the knave vexed you, sir?
SIR ALEXANDER　　　　　　Asked him my money,
　He swears my son received it: oh that boy
　Will ne'er leave heaping sorrows on my heart,
　Till he has broke it quite.
SIR ADAM　　　　　　Is he still wild?
SIR ALEXANDER  As is a Russian bear.
SIR ADAM　　　　　　　　But he has left
　His old haunt with that baggage?
SIR ALEXANDER　　　　　　　　Worse still and worse,
　He lays on me his shame, I on him my curse.　　**61**
SIR DAVY  My son Jack Dapper then shall run with him,
　All in one pasture.
SIR ADAM　　　　　Proves your son bad too, sir?
SIR DAVY  As villainy can make him: your Sebastian
　Doats but on one drab, mine on a thousand;
　A noise of fiddlers, tobacco, wine, and a whore,
　A mercer that will let him take up more,
　Dice, and a water-spaniel with a duck: oh,
　Bring him abed with these; when his purse jingles,
　Roaring boys follow at's tail, fencers and ningles　**70**
　(Beasts Adam ne'er gave name to), these horse-
　　leeches suck
　My son; he being drawn dry, they all live on smoke.
SIR ALEXANDER  Tobacco?
SIR DAVY　　　　　　Right; but I have in my brain
　A windmill going that shall grind to dust
　The follies of my son, and make him wise,
　Or a stark fool. Pray lend me your advice.
BOTH  That shall you, good Sir Davy.
SIR DAVY　　　　　　　　Here's the springe
　I ha' set to catch this woodcock in: an action
　In a false name (unknown to him) is entered
　I'th'Counter to arrest Jack Dapper.
BOTH　　　　　　　　Ha, ha, he.　**80**

SIR DAVY  Think you the Counter cannot break him?
SIR ADAM　　　　　　　　Break him?
　Yes and break's heart too if he lie there long.
SIR DAVY  I'll make him sing a counter-tenor sure.
SIR ADAM  No way to tame him like it; there he shall
　learn
　What money is indeed, and how to spend it.
SIR DAVY  He's bridled there.
SIR ALEXANDER　　　　Ay, yet knows not how to mend it:
　Bedlam cures not more madmen in a year
　Than one of the counters does: men pay more dear
　There for their wit than anywhere; a counter,
　Why 'tis an university, who not sees?　　　　**90**
　As scholars there, so here men take degrees,
　And follow the same studies all alike.
　Scholars learn first logic and rhetoric,
　So does a prisoner; with fine honey'd speech
　At's first coming in he doth persuade, beseech
　He may be lodged with one that is not itchy,
　To lie in a clean chamber, in sheets not lousy;
　But when he has no money, then does he try
　By subtle logic and quaint sophistry
　To make the keeper trust him.
SIR ADAM　　　　　　　　Say they do?　**100**
SIR ALEXANDER  Then he's a graduate.
SIR DAVY　　　　　　Say they trust him not?
SIR ALEXANDER  Then is he held a freshman and a sot,
　And never shall commence, but, being still barred,
　Be expulsed from the master's side, to th' twopenny
　　ward,
　Or else i'th'Hole be placed.
SIR ADAM　　　　　　　When then, I pray,
　Proceeds a prisoner?
SIR ALEXANDER　　　When, money being the theme,
　He can dispute with his hard creditors' hearts,
　And get out clear, he's then a Master of Arts.
　Sir Davy, send your son to Wood Street College,
　A gentleman can nowhere get more knowledge.　**110**
SIR DAVY  There gallants study hard.
SIR ALEXANDER　　　　　　　True: to get money.

---

52　grate: prison grating
53　tavern grate: taverns were identifiable by the latticework
　　on their windows; see *Arden of Faversham*, xiv.30
　　Drawer: tapster (calling offstage)
59　Russian bear: imported for baiting, and proverbially
　　fierce
60　baggage: strumpet
66　noise: band
67　take up more: i.e. on credit
70　ningles: ingles: boy-favourites, catamites; see *Epicoene*,
　　I.i.27
71　horse-leeches: a) extortioners; b) whores (Mulholland)
77　springe . . . woodcock: proverbial; see *Hamlet*, I.iii.115. A
　　springe is a trap to catch small birds
80　the Counter: debtor's prison; there were two of this name
　　in London at this time

89–90　counter . . . university: Middleton makes the same
　　analogy elsewhere: see *The Phoenix*, IV.iii.19, and
　　*Michaelmas Term*, III.iv.82–5. Others too make the
　　comparison; see Mulholland
93　logic and rhetoric: principal subjects in the university
　　curriculum at this time
99　quaint: ingenious
103　commence: be admitted to a degree
104　the master's side . . . th' twopenny ward: rooms in the
　　Counter for which prisoners paid, in order to obtain
　　better conditions
105　th'Hole: the name of the worst dungeon in Wood Street
　　Counter, in which destitute prisoners were held
106　Proceeds: advances from BA to a higher degree
109　Wood Street College: i.e. Wood Street Counter; see l. 80n

SIR DAVY 'Lies by th' heels i'faith: thanks, thanks; I ha' sent
For a couple of bears shall paw him.

*Enter* SERGEANT CURTILAX *and* YEOMAN HANGER

SIR ADAM                    Who comes yonder?
SIR DAVY They look like puttocks; these should be they.
SIR ALEXANDER                    I know 'em,
They are officers; sir, we'll leave you.
SIR DAVY                    My good knights,
Leave me, you see I'm haunted now with sprites.
BOTH Fare you well, sir.
                    *Exeunt* SIR ALEXANDER *and* SIR ADAM
CURTILAX This old muzzle-chops should be he by the fellow's description.—Save you, sir.
SIR DAVY Come hither, you mad varlets; did not my man tell you I watched here for you?                    121
CURTILAX One in a blue coat, sir, told us that in this place an old gentleman would watch for us, a thing contrary to our oath, for we are to watch for every wicked member in a city.
SIR DAVY You'll watch then for ten thousand. What's thy name, honesty?
CURTILAX Sergeant Curtilax I, sir.
SIR DAVY An excellent name for a sergeant, Curtilax. Sergeants indeed are weapons of the law:                    130
When prodigal ruffians far in debt are grown,
Should not you cut them, citizens were o'erthrown.
Thou dwell'st hereby in Holborn, Curtilax?
CURTILAX That's my circuit, sir; I conjure most in that circle.
SIR DAVY And what young toward whelp is this?
HANGER Of the same litter: his yeoman; sir, my name's Hanger.
SIR DAVY Yeoman Hanger:
One pair of shears sure cut out both your coats;                    140
You have two names most dangerous to men's throats.
You two are villainous loads on gentlemen's backs;
Dear ware, this Hanger and this Curtilax.
CURTILAX We are as other men are, sir; I cannot see but he who makes a show of honesty and religion, if his claws can fasten to his liking, he draws blood; all that live in the world are but great fish and little fish, and feed upon one another: some eat up whole men; a sergeant cares but for the shoulder of a man. They call us knaves and curs, but many times he that sets us on worries more lambs one year than we do in seven.                    152
SIR DAVY Spoke like a noble Cerberus! Is the action entered?
HANGER His name is entered in the book of unbelievers.
SIR DAVY What book's that?
CURTILAX The book where all prisoners' names stand, and not one amongst forty, when he comes in, believes to come out in haste.                    160
SIR DAVY Be as dogged to him as your office allows you to be.
BOTH Oh sir.
SIR DAVY You know the unthrift Jack Dapper?
CURTILAX Ay, ay, sir, that gull? As well as I know my yeoman.
SIR DAVY And you know his father too, Sir Davy Dapper?
CURTILAX As damned a usurer as ever was among Jews: if he were sure his father's skin would yield him any money, he would when he dies flay it off, and sell it to cover drums for children at Barthol'mew Fair.                    172
SIR DAVY (*Aside*) What toads are these to spit poison on a man to his face!—Do you see, my honest rascals? Yonder Greyhound is the dog he hunts with; out of that tavern Jack Dapper will sally: sa, sa; give the counter; on, set upon him.
BOTH We'll charge him upo'th'back, sir.
SIR DAVY Take no bail; put mace enough into his caudle; double your files, traverse your ground.                    180
BOTH Brave, sir.
SIR DAVY Cry arm, arm, arm.
BOTH Thus, sir.
SIR DAVY There boy, there boy, away: look to your prey, my true English wolves, and—and so I vanish.
                    *Exit*
CURTILAX Some warden of the sergeants begat this old fellow, upon my life. Stand close.

---

112 'Lies by th' heels: i.e. 'he lies, shall lie'; 'by th' heels' meant in jail (the reference is to irons)
SD CURTILAX . . . HANGER: see notes to 'Dramatis Personae'
114 puttocks: kites; also used for catchpoles, sergeants
122 One in a blue coat: i.e. a servant
127 honesty: honourable fellow
136 toward: promising, willing, obliging
140 One pair . . . coats: i.e. you are two of a kind (proverbial)

153 Cerberus: see III.i.25n; 'dogged' (l. 161) plays on this
172 Barthol'mew Fair: held in Smithfield on St Bartholomew's Day (24 August); originally a cloth-fair, it expanded to become the largest annual London carnival. It was not abolished until 1855
175 Greyhound: probably the name of a tavern
176 sa, sa: either a term from hunting: 'a call to attention' (Cook); or from fencing: 'an exclamation made when delivering a thrust' (Mulholland)
176-7 give the counter: either (from hunting) 'to run a false scent', to turn him back; or (from fencing) to make a circular parry
179-80 mace . . . caudle: pun on 'mace': a) staff carried by sergeants; b) spice. 'Caudle' was gruel mixed with spiced ale
180 double . . . ground: military terms, used randomly here

HANGER Shall the ambuscado lie in one place?

CURTILAX No, nook thou yonder.

*Enter* MOLL *and* TRAPDOOR

MOLL Ralph. 190

TRAPDOOR What says my brave captain male and
female?

MOLL This Holborn is such a wrangling street.

TRAPDOOR That's because lawyers walks to and fro in't.

MOLL Here's such jostling, as if everyone we met were
drunk and reeled.

TRAPDOOR Stand, mistress, do you not smell carrion?

MOLL Carrion? No, yet I spy ravens.

TRAPDOOR Some poor wind-shaken gallant will anon
fall into sore labour, and these men-midwives must
bring him to bed i'the Counter: there all those that
are great with child with debts lie in. 202

MOLL Stand up.

TRAPDOOR Like your new maypole.

HANGER Whist, whew.

CURTILAX Hump, no.

MOLL Peeping? It shall go hard, huntsmen, but I'll
spoil your game. They look for all the world like two
infected maltmen coming muffled up in their cloaks
in a frosty morning to London. 210

TRAPDOOR A course, captain; a bear comes to the
stake.

*Enter* JACK DAPPER *and* GULL

MOLL It should be so, for the dogs struggle to be let
loose.

HANGER Whew.

CURTILAX Hemp.

MOLL Hark Trapdoor, follow your leader.

JACK DAPPER Gull.

GULL Master. 219

JACK DAPPER Didst ever see such an ass as I am, boy?

GULL No by my troth, sir, to lose all your money, yet
have false dice of your own, why 'tis as I saw a great
fellow used t'other day: he had a fair sword and

buckler, and yet a butcher dry-beat him with a cudgel.

MOLL AND TRAPDOOR Honest sergeant! Fly, fly,
Master Dapper, you'll be arrested else.

JACK DAPPER Run, Gull, and draw.

GULL Run, master, Gull follows you.

*Exeunt* JACK DAPPER *and* GULL

CURTILAX I know you well enough, you're but a whore
to hang upon any man. 230

MOLL Whores then are like sergeants, so now hang
you.—Draw, rogue, but strike not: for a broken pate
they'll keep their beds, and recover twenty marks
damages.

CURTILAX You shall pay for this rescue;—run down
Shoe Lane and meet him.

TRAPDOOR Shoo, is this a rescue, gentlemen, or no?

MOLL Rescue? A pox on 'em, Trapdoor, let's away;
I'm glad I have done perfect one good work today.
If any gentleman be in scrivener's bands, 240
Send but for Moll, she'll bail him by these hands.

*Exeunt*

# Act IV, scene i

*Enter* SIR ALEXANDER WENGRAVE *solus*

SIR ALEXANDER Unhappy in the follies of a son
Led against judgment, sense, obedience,
And all the powers of nobleness and wit;

*Enter* TRAPDOOR

Oh wretched father.—Now Trapdoor, will she come?

TRAPDOOR In man's apparel, sir; I am in her heart now,
And share in all her secrets.

SIR ALEXANDER                    Peace, peace, peace.
Here, take my German watch, hang't up in sight,

---

188 ambuscado: ambush, especially the force used therein

189 nook: hide in that nook

193 wrangling: a) noisy; b) disputatious

194 lawyers: several Inns of Court stood in Holborn

199 wind-shaken: flawed at heart, like timber by high winds

205–6 Whist . . . Hump: Hanger is trying to attract Curtilax's
attention by whistling; 'hump' is probably a signal in
response

208–9 two infected maltmen: Mulholland cites a practice of
those who carried malt into the city of carrying rags back
home 'for manuring of the soiling of the ground'. This
practice would have made them particularly susceptible
to infection by the plague

211 course: the animal pursued (whilst 'coursing' or pursuing
game with hounds)

224 dry-beat: beat him with blows that bruised but did not
draw blood

225 Honest sergeant!: we follow Mulholland in retaining the
Q reading here, on the grounds that 'stage business . . .
could clear up the apparent difficulty'. Other eds emend
to 'servant'

231 Whores . . . sergeants: playing on method of arrest; see
ll. 149

232 rogue: i.e. Trapdoor

233 twenty marks: a mark was worth two-thirds of a pound;
see I.i.91n

235 rescue: 'the forcible taking of a person or goods out of
custody—a very serious offence' (Cook)

236 Shoe Lane: ran from Holborn to Fleet Street

240 in scrivener's bands: 'i.e. in debt' (Mulholland); a
'scrivener' was a notary

5 heart: confidence

7 German watch: German clocks and watches are frequently
referred to in Jacobean drama; they had a reputation either
for ingenuity (as here), or for unreliabity (see *Epicoene*,
IV.ii.107–8n, *Love's Labours Lost*, III.i.175–8)

That I may see her hang in English for't.

TRAPDOOR I warrant you for that now, next sessions
rids her, sir. This watch will bring her in better than
a hundred constables.                                                   11

SIR ALEXANDER Good Trapdoor, sayst thou so? Thou
cheer'st my heart
After a storm of sorrow. My gold chain too;
Here, take a hundred marks in yellow links.

TRAPDOOR That will do well to bring the watch to
light, sir:
And worth a thousand of your headborough's
lanthorns.

SIR ALEXANDER Place that o'the court cupboard, let it lie
Full in the view of her thief-whorish eye.

TRAPDOOR She cannot miss it, sir; I see't so plain
That I could steal't myself.

SIR ALEXANDER                    Perhaps thou shalt too, 20
That or something as weighty; what she leaves,
Thou shalt come closely in, and filch away,
And all the weight upon her back I'll lay.

TRAPDOOR You cannot assure that, sir.

SIR ALEXANDER                    No? What lets it?

TRAPDOOR Being a stout girl, perhaps she'll desire
pressing,
Then all the weight must lie upon her belly.

SIR ALEXANDER Belly or back I care not so I've one.

TRAPDOOR You're of my mind for that, sir.

SIR ALEXANDER Hang up my ruff-band with the
diamond at it,
It may be she'll like that best.                              30

TRAPDOOR (Aside) It's well for her that she must have
her choice, he thinks nothing too good for her.—If
you hold on this mind a little longer, it shall be the
first work I do to turn thief myself; would do a man
good to be hanged when he is so well provided for.

SIR ALEXANDER So, well said; all hangs well; would she
hung so too,
The sight would please me more than all their
glisterings:
Oh that my mysteries to such straits should run,
That I must rob myself to bless my son.         Exeunt

*Enter* SEBASTIAN, *with* MARY FITZALLARD *like a page,
and* MOLL *in man's clothes*

SEBASTIAN Thou hast done me a kind office, without
touch                                                                        40
Either of sin or shame; our loves are honest.

MOLL I'd scorn to make such shift to bring you
together else.

SEBASTIAN Now have I time and opportunity
Without all fear to bid thee welcome, love.      *Kiss*

MARY Never with more desire and harder venture.

MOLL How strange this shows, one man to kiss
another.

SEBASTIAN I'd kiss such men to choose, Moll,
Methinks a woman's lip tastes well in a doublet.   49

MOLL Many an old madam has the better fortune then,
Whose breaths grew stale before the fashion came:
If that will help 'em, as you think 'twill do,
They'll learn in time to pluck on the hose too.

SEBASTIAN The older they wax, Moll—troth I speak
seriously,
As some have a conceit their drink tastes better
In an outlandish cup than in our own,
So methinks every kiss she gives me now
In this strange form is worth a pair of two.
Here we are safe, and furthest from the eye
Of all suspicion; this is my father's chamber,    60
Upon which floor he never steps till night.
Here he mistrusts me not, nor I his coming;
At mine own chamber he still pries unto me,
My freedom is not there at mine own finding,
Still checked and curbed; here he shall miss his
purpose.

MOLL And what's your business, now you have your
mind, sir?
At your great suit I promised you to come:
I pitied her for name's sake, that a Moll
Should be so crossed in love when there's so many
That owes nine lays apiece, and not so little:     70
My tailor fitted her, how like you his work?

SEBASTIAN So well, no art can mend it for this purpose;
But to thy wit and help we're chief in debt,
And must live still beholding.

MOLL                              Any honest pity
I'm willing to bestow upon poor ring-doves.

SEBASTIAN I'll offer no worse play.

MOLL                              Nay, and you should, sir,
I should draw first and prove the quicker man.

---

9  sessions: of the court
16  headborough: constable
17  court cupboard: a movable sideboard or cabinet used to
    display plate etc.
22  closely: secretly
24  lets: hinders
25  pressing: Mulholland identifies a double entendre on a)
    the *peine forte et dure* which involved the loading of
    weights upon accused persons to induce them to answer a
    charge, and b) a reference to coitus
38  mysteries: skills, craft

42  shift: effort
48  to choose: from choice
50  madam: bawd, whore
52  that: i.e. male dress
58  a pair: a set
70  lays: meaning uncertain; perhaps 'wagers' (Bullen); or
    'lodgings', especially those used for prostitution
    (Mulholland)
74  still: always
75  ring-doves: wood pigeons (i.e. lovers)

SEBASTIAN Hold, there shall need no weapon at this meeting,
But 'cause thou shalt not loose thy fury idle,
Here take this viol, run upon the guts,        80
And end thy quarrel singing.
MOLL                          Like a swan above bridge:
For look you here's the bridge, and here am I.
SEBASTIAN Hold on, sweet Moll.
MARY I've heard her much commended, sir, for one that was ne'er taught.
MOLL I'm much beholding to 'em. Well, since you'll needs put us together, sir, I'll play my part as well as I can: it shall ne'er be said I came into a gentleman's chamber and let his instrument hang by the walls.   89
SEBASTIAN Why well said, Moll, i'faith; it had been a shame for that gentleman then, that would have let it hung still and ne'er offered thee it.
MOLL There it should have been still then for Moll, for though the world judge impudently of me, I ne'er came into that chamber yet where I took down the instrument myself.
SEBASTIAN Pish, let 'em prate abroad; th'art here where thou art known and loved: there be a thousand close dames that will call the viol an unmannerly instrument for a woman, and therefore talk broadly of thee, when you shall have them sit wider to a worse quality.        102
MOLL Push, I ever fall asleep and think not of 'em, sir; and thus I dream.
SEBASTIAN Prithee let's hear thy dream, Moll.
MOLL

THE SONG
*I dream there is a mistress,*
*And she lays out the money,*
*She goes unto her sisters,*
*She never comes at any.*

*Enter* SIR ALEXANDER *behind them*

*She says she went to the Burse for patterns,*        110
*You shall find her at Saint Kathern's,*
*And comes home with never a penny.*
SEBASTIAN That's a free mistress, faith.
SIR ALEXANDER (*Aside*) Ay, ay, ay, like her that sings it; one of thine own choosing.
MOLL But shall I dream again?

*Here comes a wench will brave ye,*
*Her courage was so great,*
*She lay with one o' the navy,*
*Her husband lying i'the Fleet.*        120
*Yet oft with him she cavilled,*
*I wonder what she ails:*
*Her husband's ship lay gravelled,*
*When hers could hoise up sails;*
*Yet she began like all my foes*
*To call whore first: for so do those—*
*A pox of all false tails.*
SEBASTIAN Marry, amen say I.
SIR ALEXANDER (*Aside*) So say I too.        129
MOLL Hang up the viol now, sir; all this while I was in a dream, one shall lie rudely then; but being awake, I keep my legs together. A watch: what's o'clock here?
SIR ALEXANDER (*Aside*) Now, now she's trapped.
MOLL Between one and two; nay then I care not. A watch and a musician are cousin-germans in one thing, they must both keep time well, or there's no goodness in 'em; the one else deserves to be dashed against a wall, and t'other to have his brains knocked out with a fiddle case.        140
What, a loose chain and a dangling diamond?
Here were a brave booty for an evening-thief now;

There's many a younger brother would be glad
To look twice in at a window for't,
And wriggle in and out like an eel in a sandbag.
Oh, if men's secret youthful faults should judge 'em,
'Twould be the general'st execution
That ere was seen in England!     **148**
There would be but few left to sing the ballets, there
would be so much work: most of our brokers would
be chosen for hangmen, a good day for them: they
might renew their wardrobes of free cost then.

SEBASTIAN This is the roaring wench must do us good.

MARY No poison, sir, but serves us for some use,
Which is confirmed in her.

SEBASTIAN            Peace, peace.
Foot, I did hear him sure, where'er he be.

MOLL Who did you hear?

SEBASTIAN       My father.
'Twas like a sight of his; I must be wary.

SIR ALEXANDER (*Aside*) No? Wilt not be? Am I alone
so wretched     **159**
That nothing takes? I'll put him to his plunge for't.

SEBASTIAN Life, here he comes.—Sir, I beseech you
take it.
Your way of teaching does so much content me,
I'll make it four pound; here's forty shillings, sir:
I think I name it right (help me, good Moll),
Forty in hand.

MOLL       Sir, you shall pardon me,
I have more of the meanest scholar I can teach;
This pays me more than you have offered yet.

SEBASTIAN At the next quarter
When I receive the means my father 'lows me,
You shall have t'other forty.

SIR ALEXANDER (*Aside*)     This were well now,   **170**
Were't to a man whose sorrows had blind eyes,
But mine behold his follies and untruths
With two clear glasses.—How now?    *Comes forward*

SEBASTIAN       Sir.

SIR ALEXANDER       What's he there?

SEBASTIAN You're come in good time, sir, I've a suit to
you,
I'd crave your present kindness.

SIR ALEXANDER       What is he there?

---

SEBASTIAN A gentleman, a musician, sir, one of
excellent fingering.

SIR ALEXANDER Ay, I think so.— (*Aside*) I wonder how
they 'scaped her.

SEBASTIAN Has the most delicate stroke, sir.

SIR ALEXANDER A stroke indeed.— (*Aside*) I feel it at
my heart.     **180**

SEBASTIAN Puts down all your famous musicians.

SIR ALEXANDER Ay.—(*Aside*) A whore may put down a
hundred of 'em.

SEBASTIAN Forty shillings is the agreement, sir,
between us:
Now sir, my present means mounts but to half on't.

SIR ALEXANDER And he stands upon the whole.

SEBASTIAN       Ay indeed does he, sir.

SIR ALEXANDER And will do still, he'll ne'er be in other
tale.

SEBASTIAN Therefore I'd stop his mouth, sir, and I
could.

SIR ALEXANDER Hum, true, there is no other way
indeed;—
(*Aside*) His folly hardens, shame must needs succeed.
—Now sir, I understand you profess music.   **190**

MOLL I am a poor servant to that liberal science, sir.

SIR ALEXANDER Where is it you teach?

MOLL       Right against Clifford's Inn.

SIR ALEXANDER Hum, that's a fit place for it; you have
many scholars?

MOLL And some of worth, whom I may call my masters.

SIR ALEXANDER (*Aside*) Ay true, a company of
whoremasters.
—You teach to sing too?

MOLL       Marry do I, sir.

SIR ALEXANDER I think you'll find an apt scholar of my
son, especially for prick-song.

MOLL I have much hope of him.     **200**

SIR ALEXANDER (*Aside*) I am sorry for't, I have the less
for that.—You can play any lesson?

MOLL At first sight, sir.

---

145  eel . . . sandbag: proverbial
149  ballets: i.e. ballads, commemorating the last words of the
condemned
150  brokers: pawnbrokers
152  renew . . . cost: 'hangmen traditionally received their
victims' clothing' (Mulholland)
156  Foot: contraction of 'God's foot'
158  sight: sigh
160  takes: takes effect, succeeds
     plunge: dilemma
163  forty shillings: there were twenty shillings to a pound
167  This: i.e. the meanest scholar

177  fingering: a) of instrument; b) pilfering; c) with sexual
innuendo
178  how they . . . her: i.e. how they escaped her pilfering
fingers
181  Puts down: surpasses; Sir Alexander puns on a) a sexual
sense, and b) 'kills', through venereal disease
183  Forty shillings . . . agreement: this does not tally with the
previously agreed amount; see l. 163
186  he'll . . . tale: i.e. he'll never tell a different story; with
pun on 'tale' meaning reckoning, account: 'he'll never
reckon the account differently'
187  and: if
197  sing: with pun on 'sing' meaning copulate (see *Troilus
and Cressida*, V.ii.9–10)
199  prick-song: music written or 'pricked' down, as distinct
from that sung from memory or by ear; the obvious
sexual pun was common

SIR ALEXANDER  There's a thing called the witch, can
    you play that?
MOLL  I would be sorry anyone should mend me in't.
SIR ALEXANDER  (*Aside*) Ay, I believe thee, thou hast so
    bewitched my son,
No care will mend the work that thou hast done.
I have bethought myself, since my art fails,
I'll make her policy the art to trap her.
Here are four angels marked with holes in them   210
Fit for his cracked companions, gold he will give her;
These will I make induction to her ruin,
And rid shame from my house, grief from my heart.
—Here, son, in what you take content and pleasure,
Want shall not curb you; pay the gentleman
His latter half in gold.
SEBASTIAN         I thank you, sir.
SIR ALEXANDER  (*Aside*) Oh may the operation on't end
    three:
In her, life; shame in him; and grief in me.     *Exit*
SEBASTIAN  Faith thou shalt have 'em, 'tis my father's
    gift,
Never was man beguiled with better shift.   220
MOLL  He that can take me for a male musician,
    I cannot choose but make him my instrument
    And play upon him.
                      *Exeunt omnes*

# Act IV, scene ii

*Enter* MISTRESS GALLIPOT *and* MISTRESS OPENWORK

MISTRESS GALLIPOT  Is then that bird of yours, Master
    Goshawk, so wild?
MISTRESS OPENWORK  A goshawk, a puttock: all for
    prey. He angles for fish, but he loves flesh better.
MISTRESS GALLIPOT  Is't possible his smooth face
    should have wrinkles in't, and we not see them?
MISTRESS OPENWORK  Possible? Why, have not many
    handsome legs in silk stockings villainous splay feet
    for all their great roses?
MISTRESS GALLIPOT  Troth sirrah, thou sayst true.    10
MISTRESS OPENWORK  Didst never see an archer, as
    thou'st walked by Bunhill, look asquint when he
    drew his bow?

MISTRESS GALLIPOT  Yes, when his arrows have fline
    toward Islington, his eyes have shot clean contrary
    towards Pimlico.
MISTRESS OPENWORK  For all the world, so does Master
    Goshawk double with me.
MISTRESS GALLIPOT  Oh fie upon him, if he double
    once he's not for me.    20
MISTRESS OPENWORK  Because Goshawk goes in a
    shag-ruff band, with a face sticking up in't which
    shows like an agate set in a cramp-ring, he thinks I'm
    in love with him.
MISTRESS GALLIPOT  'Las, I think he takes his mark
    amiss in thee.
MISTRESS OPENWORK  He has by often beating into me
    made me believe that my husband kept a whore.
MISTRESS GALLIPOT  Very good.    29
MISTRESS OPENWORK  Swore to me that my husband
    this very morning went in a boat with a tilt over it to
    the Three Pigeons at Brainford, and his punk with
    him under his tilt.
MISTRESS GALLIPOT  That were wholesome.
MISTRESS OPENWORK  I believed it, fell a-swearing at
    him, cursing of harlots, made me ready to hoise up
    sail and be there as soon as he.
MISTRESS GALLIPOT  So, so.    38
MISTRESS OPENWORK  And for that voyage Goshawk
    comes hither incontinently: but sirrah, this water-
    spaniel dives after no duck but me; his hope is having
    me at Brainford to make me cry quack.
MISTRESS GALLIPOT  Art sure of it?
MISTRESS OPENWORK  Sure of it? My poor innocent
    Openwork came in as I was poking my ruff, presently
    hit I him i'the teeth with the Three Pigeons: he
    forswore all, I up and opened all, and now stands he
    in a shop hard by, like a musket on a rest, to hit
    Goshawk i'the eye when he comes to fetch me to the
    boat.    50
MISTRESS GALLIPOT  Such another lame gelding offered
    to carry me through thick and thin—Laxton,

---

204  the witch: the name of several popular songs
206  mend: surpass
210  angels: see II.i.140n
  3  puttock: kite
  4  fish: 'cant for loose women or female genitals' (Cook);
     see III.i.99n
  8  silk stockings: fashionable amongst gallants
  9  roses: ornamental rosettes decorating the shoe; see
     woodcut on page 326
 12  Bunhill: archery practice and matches were regularly held
     in this old artillery ground

---

14  fline: flown
16  Pimlico: part of London; a popular resort for excursions.
    It was in a different direction from Islington
19  double: act deceitfully
23  cramp-ring: worn as a protection againt illness. 'The
    image is of a small head in the centre of an enormous
    ruff' (Mulholland)
27  beating into me: i.e. repeating to me
31  tilt: awning over a boat
32  punk: whore
40  incontinently: immediately
41  duck: see 'wild fowl', III.ii.253
45  poking my ruff: crimping the pleats of the ruff; with
    quibble on 'ruff' (female genitals)
48  musket . . . rest: early muskets were so heavy that they
    needed a support for the barrel

sirrah—but I am rid of him now.

MISTRESS OPENWORK  Happy is the woman can be rid of 'em all; 'las, what are your whisking gallants to our husbands, weigh 'em rightly man for man?

MISTRESS GALLIPOT  Troth, mere shallow things.

MISTRESS OPENWORK  Idle simple things, running heads; and yet let 'em run over us never so fast, we shopkeepers, when all's done, are sure to have 'em in our purse-nets at length, and when they are in, Lord, what simple animals they are! Then they hang the head.                                                                63

MISTRESS GALLIPOT  Then they droop.

MISTRESS OPENWORK  Then they write letters.

MISTRESS GALLIPOT  Then they cog.

MISTRESS OPENWORK  Then deal they underhand with us, and we must ingle with our husbands abed; and we must swear they are our cousins, and able to do us a pleasure at court.                                                70

MISTRESS GALLIPOT  And yet when we have done our best, all's but put into a riven dish; we are but frumped at and libelled upon.

MISTRESS OPENWORK  Oh if it were the good Lord's will, there were a law made no citizen should trust any of 'em all.

*Enter GOSHAWK*

MISTRESS GALLIPOT  Hush sirrah, Goshawk flutters.

GOSHAWK  How now, are you ready?

MISTRESS OPENWORK  Nay are you ready? A little thing you see makes us ready.                                          80

GOSHAWK  Us? Why, must she make one i'the voyage?

MISTRESS OPENWORK  Oh by any means: do I know how my husband will handle me?

GOSHAWK  *(Aside)* Foot, how shall I find water to keep these two mills going?—Well, since you'll needs be clapped under hatches, if I sail not with you both till all split, hang me up at the mainyard and duck me.—It's but liquoring them both soundly, and then you shall see their cork heels fly up high, like two swans when their tails are above water, and their long necks under water, diving to catch gudgeons.—Come, come, oars stand ready, the tide's with us, on with those false faces; blow winds, and thou shalt take thy husband casting out his net to catch fresh salmon at Brainford.

MISTRESS GALLIPOT  I believe you'll eat of a cod's head of your own dressing before you reach half way thither.                                          *They mask themselves*

GOSHAWK  So, so, follow close; pin as you go.

*Enter LAXTON muffled*

LAXTON  Do you hear?                                          100

MISTRESS GALLIPOT  Yes, I thank my ears.

LAXTON  I must have a bout with your pothecaryship.

MISTRESS GALLIPOT  At what weapon?

LAXTON  I must speak with you.

MISTRESS GALLIPOT  No.

LAXTON  No? You shall.

MISTRESS GALLIPOT  Shall? Away, soused sturgeon, half fish, half flesh.

LAXTON  'Faith, gib, are you spitting? I'll cut your tail, puss-cat, for this.                                          110

MISTRESS GALLIPOT  'Las poor Laxton, I think thy tail's cut already. Your worst.

LAXTON  If I do not—                                          *Exit*

GOSHAWK  Come, ha' you done?

*Enter MASTER OPENWORK*

                                          'Sfoot, Rosamond, your husband.

MASTER OPENWORK  How now? Sweet Master Goshawk, none more welcome,

---

55  whisking: smart, lively
58  running: flighty
61  purse-nets: bag-shaped net with draw-string opening, used for catching rabbits. 'Rabbit' or 'cony' was thieves' cant for a dupe
62  . . . they are! Then they . . .: the duplication of a speech prefix between '. . . they are' and 'Then . . . ' leads some eds to conclude that a fault was introduced into Q here during type resetting, probably the omission of a speech from Mistress Gallipot; see Cook. Following Mulholland, however, we conclude that the sense is clear enough to justify running the two on
62–3  hang the head . . . droop: with double entendres
66  cog: a) wheedle; b) cheat
68  ingle: a) fondle; b) coax
72  all's put . . . dish: i.e. it's all in vain; 'riven' meant split, broken
73  frumped at: mocked
84  water: with sexual innuendo ('water' meaning semen: see *Epicoene*, IV.iii.36)

86  clapped under hatches: with sexual entendre: 'clapped' 'used catachrestically for "clip" (= embrace)' (Cook)
87  all split: all go to pieces
88  liquoring them: plying them with liquor
89  cork heels: fashionable at the time
91  gudgeons: small fish used for bait; with play on 'to swallow or gape for a gudgeon', meaning to be easily deceived
96–7  you'll eat . . . dressing: i.e. you'll be caught out by your own plans. A 'cod's head' was a blockhead; with sexual innuendo
99  pin: fasten (the masks)
102  bout: usually implies a sexual encounter; Laxton plays on this, as does Mistress Gallipot
109  gib: a term of reproach, especially for an old woman; literally, a male cat
112  Your worst: i.e. do your worst. Cook emends to 'you're worsed' (meant 'you're worsted'), but this does not lead well into Laxton's next line

I have wanted your embracements: when friends
  meet,
The music of the spheres sounds not more sweet
Than does their conference. Who is this? Rosamond?
Wife? How now, sister?
GOSHAWK            Silence if you love me.
MASTER OPENWORK  Why masked?
MISTRESS OPENWORK  Does a mask grieve you, sir?
MASTER OPENWORK            It does.
MISTRESS OPENWORK  Then y'are best get you a-
  mumming.                           **121**
GOSHAWK          'Sfoot, you'll spoil all.
MISTRESS GALLIPOT  May not we cover our bare faces
  with masks
As well as you cover your bald heads with hats?
MASTER OPENWORK  No masks; why, th'are thieves to
  beauty, that rob eyes
Of admiration in which true love lies.
Why are masks worn? Why good? Or why desired?
Unless by their gay covers wits are fired
To read the vildest looks; many bad faces
(Because rich gems are treasured up in cases)
Pass by their privilege current; but as caves   **130**
Damn misers' gold, so masks are beauties' graves.
Men ne'er meet women with such muffled eyes,
But they curse her that first did masks devise,
And swear it was some beldam. Come, off with't.
MISTRESS OPENWORK  I will not.
MASTER OPENWORK  Good faces masked are jewels kept
  by sprites:
Hide none but bad ones, for they poison men's
  sights;
Show them as shopkeepers do their broidered stuff,
By owl-light; fine wares cannot be open enough.
Prithee, sweet Rose, come strike this sail.
MISTRESS OPENWORK            Sail?
MASTER OPENWORK                Ha!
Yes, wife, strike sail, for storms are in thine eyes.  **141**
MISTRESS OPENWORK  They're here, sir, in my brows if
  any rise.

MASTER OPENWORK  Ha, brows? What says she, friend?
  Pray tell me why
Your two flags were advanced; the comedy,
Come, what's the comedy?
MISTRESS GALLIPOT          *Westward Ho.*
MASTER OPENWORK               How?
MISTRESS OPENWORK  'Tis *Westward Ho* she says.
GOSHAWK           Are you both mad?
MISTRESS OPENWORK  Is't market day at Brainford, and
  your ware
Not sent up yet?
MASTER OPENWORK  What market day? What ware?
MISTRESS OPENWORK  A pie with three pigeons in't, 'tis
  drawn and stays your cutting up.        **150**
GOSHAWK  As you regard my credit—
MASTER OPENWORK  Art mad?
MISTRESS OPENWORK  Yes, lecherous goat; baboon.
MASTER OPENWORK  Baboon? Then toss me in a
  blanket.
MISTRESS OPENWORK  (*To* MISTRESS GALLIPOT) Do I it
  well?
MISTRESS GALLIPOT  (*To* MISTRESS OPENWORK) Rarely.
GOSHAWK  Belike, sir, she's not well; best leave her.
MASTER OPENWORK              No,
I'll stand the storm now, how fierce so e'er it blow.
MISTRESS OPENWORK  Did I for this lose all my friends?
  Refuse                               **161**
Rich hopes and golden fortunes, to be made
A stale to a common whore?
MASTER OPENWORK        This does amaze me.
MISTRESS OPENWORK  Oh God, oh God, feed at
  reversion now?
A strumpet's leaving?
MASTER OPENWORK       Rosamond.

---

116 wanted: missed
117 music of the spheres: in the Ptolemaic system, the
    heavenly spheres were believed to make music as they
    moved
121 a-mumming: mummers' plays were mimed, without
    dialogue. She seems to be telling her husband to keep
    silent
130 Pass . . . current: 'i.e. are received as genuine or honest,
    because of the privilege conferred by masks' (Cook)
134 beldam: hag, witch
139 owl-light: twilight. There were frequent complaints that
    shopkeepers made use of bad light to obscure the poor
    quality of their goods
142 in my brows: Cook suggests a possible allusion to the
    female cuckold's horns

144 Your two flags: flags were hoisted on the tops of theatres
    shortly before a performance started. Mulholland
    suggests that the specific reference is to the masks
145 *Westward Ho*: play by Dekker and Webster (1604–5), in
    which citizens' wives and their gallants travel west to
    Brentford. 'Westward ho!' was the cry of watermen going
    west
147 ware: with sexual entendre; see II.i.241–5
149 three pigeons: referring to the Three Pigeons Inn, with
    possible reference to 'wild fowl' (prostitutes); this is
    supported by 'cutting up' (see III.ii.253)
153 baboon: traditionally viewed as a lustful animal
154–5 toss . . . blanket: a rough, irregular form of punishment;
    see *Epicoene*, V.iv.14. Cook suggests a play on 'blanket-
    love' (illicit amours)
163 stale: a) a lover or mistress ridiculed for the amusement
    of a rival; b) decoy
163–203 Q prints this as a mixture of prose and verse;
    however, there are some rhymes and clear pentameters
    that suggest it should all be set as verse, albeit rough
164 reversion: left-overs of a meal

GOSHAWK (*Aside*) I sweat; would I lay in Cold Harbour.

MISTRESS OPENWORK Thou hast struck ten thousand
    daggers through my heart.

MASTER OPENWORK Not I, by heaven, sweet wife.

MISTRESS OPENWORK                  Go, devil, go;
    That which thou swear'st by damns thee.

GOSHAWK (*To* MISTRESS OPENWORK) 'S heart, will you
    undo me?                                **170**

MISTRESS OPENWORK Why stay you here? The star by
    which you sail
    Shines yonder above Chelsea; you lose your shore;
    If this moon light you, seek out your light whore.

MASTER OPENWORK Ha?

MISTRESS GALLIPOT         Push, you western pug!

GOSHAWK (*Aside*)            Zounds, now hell roars.

MISTRESS OPENWORK With whom you tilted in a pair
    of oars,
    This very morning.

MASTER OPENWORK      Oars?

MISTRESS OPENWORK            At Brainford, sir.

MASTER OPENWORK Rack not my patience. Master
    Goshawk,
    Some slave has buzzed this into her, has he not?
    I run a tilt in Brainford with a woman?
    'Tis a lie:                                 **180**
    What old bawd tells thee this? 'Sdeath, 'tis a lie.

MISTRESS OPENWORK 'Tis one to thy face shall justify
    All that I speak.

MASTER OPENWORK Ud'soul, do but name that rascal.

MISTRESS OPENWORK No sir, I will not.

GOSHAWK (*Aside*)        Keep thee there, girl. (*To them*)
    Then!

MASTER OPENWORK Sister, know you this varlet?

MISTRESS GALLIPOT              Yes.

MASTER OPENWORK                 Swear true;
    Is there a rogue so low damned? A second Judas?
    A common hangman? Cutting a man's throat?
    Does it to his face? Bite me behind my back?
    A cur dog? Swear if you know this hell-hound.

MISTRESS GALLIPOT In truth I do.

MASTER OPENWORK            His name?

MISTRESS GALLIPOT                 Not for the world,
    To have you to stab him.

GOSHAWK (*Aside*)       Oh brave girls, worth gold. **191**

MASTER OPENWORK A word, honest Master Goshawk.
                             *Draws out his sword*

GOSHAWK           What do you mean, sir?

MASTER OPENWORK Keep off, and if the devil can give
    a name
    To this new fury, holla it through my ear,
    Or wrap it up in some hid character:
    I'll ride to Oxford and watch out mine eyes
    But I'll hear the brazen head speak; or else
    Show me but one hair of his head or beard,
    That I may sample it. If the fiend I meet
    In mine own house, I'll kill him—the street,    **200**
    Or at the church door:—there ('cause he seeks to untie
    The knot God fastens) he deserves most to die.

MISTRESS OPENWORK My husband titles him.

MASTER OPENWORK           Master Goshawk, pray sir,
    Swear to me that you know him or know him not,
    Who makes me at Brainford to take up a petticoat
    Besides my wife's.

GOSHAWK           By heaven that man I know not.

MISTRESS OPENWORK Come, come, you lie.

GOSHAWK             Will you not have all out?
    By heaven, I know no man beneath the moon
    Should do you wrong, but if I had his name,
    I'd print it in text letters.

MISTRESS OPENWORK         Print thine own then,    **210**
    Didst not thou swear to me he kept his whore?

MISTRESS GALLIPOT And that in sinful Brainford they
    would commit
    That which our lips did water at, sir,—ha?

MISTRESS OPENWORK Thou spider, that hast woven thy
    cunning web
    In mine own house t'insnare me: hast not thou
    Sucked nourishment even underneath this roof,
    And turned it all to poison, spitting it
    On thy friend's face (my husband), he as 'twere
    sleeping?

---

166 Cold Harbour: a seedy area of tenements on Upper
    Thames Street that had become a sanctuary for debtors,
    vagrants and malefactors; see *Epicoene*, II.v.118. Goshawk
    puns on the name
171–2 star . . . Chelsea: Chelsea is to the west of London, on
    the way to Brentford. 'Star' alludes to the whore, and
    Mulholland suggests a possible reference too to Venus
    (suggestive of wantonness), the morning or evening star
172 lose your shore: i.e. lose your way
173 light whore: wanton whore
174 western pug: a) whore (from Brentford in the west); b)
    bargemen who navigated down the Thames to London
175 tilted: jousted, with play on the boat with a tilt (see
    above, l. 31)
182 one to: i.e. one who to
183 Ud'soul: God's soul

191 worth gold: proverbial
195 hid character: code
197 brazen head: Friar Bacon and Friar Bungay spent seven
    years making a brass head, in order to ask it whether it
    were possible to build a wall of brass round England.
    However, owing to the ineptitude of a servant, they
    failed to hear it speak; see Robert Greene, *Friar Bacon
    and Friar Bungay* (1589), for which Middleton wrote a
    new prologue and epilogue in 1602
203 titles: addresses (Mulholland)
209 Should: i.e. who should
210 text letters: large or capital letters
217 poison: spiders were reputed to be poisonous

Only to leave him ugly to mine eyes, 219
That they might glance on thee?

MISTRESS GALLIPOT           Speak, are these lies?

GOSHAWK Mine own shame me confounds.

MASTER OPENWORK          No more, he's stung;
Who'd think that in one body there could dwell
Deformity and beauty, heaven and hell?
Goodness I see is but outside: we all set,
In rings of gold, stones that be counterfeit:
I thought you none.

GOSHAWK          Pardon me.

MASTER OPENWORK          Truth, I do.
This blemish grows in nature, not in you,
For man's creation stick even moles in scorn
On fairest cheeks. Wife, nothing is perfect born.

MISTRESS OPENWORK I thought you had been born
    perfect. 230

MASTER OPENWORK What's this whole world but a gilt
    rotten pill?
For at the heart lies the old core still.
I'll tell you, Master Goshawk,—ay, in your eye
I have seen wanton fire; and then to try
The soundness of my judgment, I told you
I kept a whore, made you believe 'twas true,
Only to feel how your pulse beat, but find
The world can hardly yield a perfect friend.
Come, come, a trick of youth, and 'tis forgiven;
This rub put by, our love shall run more even. 240

MISTRESS OPENWORK You'll deal upon men's wives no
    more?

GOSHAWK          No: you teach me
A trick for that.

MISTRESS OPENWORK Troth, do not; they'll o'erreach
    thee.

MASTER OPENWORK Make my house yours, sir, still.

GOSHAWK          No.

MASTER OPENWORK          I say you shall:
Seeing, thus besieged, it holds out, 'twill never fall.

*Enter* MASTER GALLIPOT, *and* GREENWIT *like a sumner,*
LAXTON *muffled, aloof off*

OMNES How now?

MASTER GALLIPOT With me, sir?

GREENWIT You, sir. I have gone snaffling up and down
by your door this hour to watch for you.

---

MISTRESS GALLIPOT What's the matter, husband? 249

GREENWIT I have caught a cold in my head, sir, by
sitting up late in the Rose tavern, but I hope you
understand my speech.

MASTER GALLIPOT So, sir.

GREENWIT I cite you by the name of Hippocrates
Gallipot, and you by the name of Prudence Gallipot,
to appear upon Crastino, do you see, Crastino sancti
Dunstani, this Easter term, in Bow Church.

MASTER GALLIPOT Where, sir? What says he? 258

GREENWIT Bow: Bow Church, to answer to a libel of
precontract on the part and behalf of the said
Prudence and another: you're best, sir, take a copy of
the citation; 'tis but twelvepence.

OMNES A citation?

MASTER GALLIPOT You pocky-nosed rascal, what slave
fees you to this?

LAXTON (*Coming forward*) Slave? (*Aside to Goshawk*) I
ha' nothing to do with you, do you hear, sir?

GOSHAWK (*Aside to Laxton*) Laxton, is't not? What
vagary is this?

MASTER GALLIPOT Trust me, I thought, sir, this storm
    long ago 270
Had been full laid, when (if you be remembered)
I paid you the last fifteen pound, besides
The thirty you had first; for then you swore—

LAXTON Tush, tush sir, oaths;
Truth, yet I'm loath to vex you—tell you what:
Make up the money I had an hundred pound,
And take your bellyful of her.

MASTER GALLIPOT          An hundred pound?

MISTRESS GALLIPOT What, a hundred pound? He gets
none: what, a hundred pound?

MASTER GALLIPOT Sweet Pru, be calm; the gentleman
    offers thus: 280
If I will make the moneys that are past
A hundred pound, he will discharge all courts,
And give his bond never to vex us more.

MISTRESS GALLIPOT A hundred pound? 'Las, take, sir,
    but threescore,
Do you seek my undoing?

LAXTON          I'll not bate one sixpence.—

---

228  moles: Mulholland identifies these as patches: beauty
    spots stuck on the face to hide a blemish or highlight a
    beautiful feature
232  core: i.e. of Adam and Eve's apple
240  rub: obstacle (from game of bowls)
241  deal upon: set to work upon
 SD  *sumner*: summoner, who summoned people to appear in
    court
248  snaffling: snuffling. Summoners were frequently
    represented as snuffling as a symptom of syphilis

251  Rose: a common name for taverns; perhaps the one at
    Temple Bar, frequented by lawyers
254  Hippocrates: the apothecary is, ironically, named after
    the famous Greek physician
256–7 Crastino sancti Dunstani: on the morrow of St
    Dunstan's Day: i.e. 20 May
259  Bow Church: the famous church on the south side of
    Cheapside, in which sat the Ecclesiastical Court of
    Arches
    libel: in ecclesiastical law, the plaintiff's written
    declaration of charges
264  pocky-nosed: i.e. from syphilis; see above l. 248n
285  bate: reduce (by)

(*Aside to Mistress Gallipot*) I'll maul you, puss, for
    spitting.
MISTRESS GALLIPOT (*Aside to Laxton*)   Do thy worst—
    Will fourscore stop thy mouth?
LAXTON                  No.
MISTRESS GALLIPOT          Y'are a slave,
    Thou cheat; I'll now tear money from thy throat.
    Husband, lay hold on yonder tawny-coat.
GREENWIT  Nay, gentlemen, seeing your women are so
    hot, I must lose my hair in their company, I see.   **291**
                              *Takes off his wig*
MISTRESS OPENWORK  His hair sheds off, and yet he
    speaks not so much in the nose as he did before.
GOSHAWK  He has had the better chirurgeon.—Master
    Greenwit, is your wit so raw as to play no better a
    part than a sumner's?
MASTER GALLIPOT  I pray, who plays *A Knack to Know*
    *an Honest Man* in this company?
MISTRESS GALLIPOT  Dear husband, pardon me, I did
    dissemble,
    Told thee I was his precontracted wife,          **300**
    When letters came from him for thirty pound,
    I had no shift but that.
MASTER GALLIPOT      A very clean shift:
    But able to make me lousy. On.
MISTRESS GALLIPOT        Husband, I plucked—
    When he had tempted me to think well of him—
    Gelt feathers from thy wings, to make him fly
    More lofty.
MASTER GALLIPOT  A' the top of you, wife: on.
MISTRESS GALLIPOT  He having wasted them, comes
    now for more,
    Using me as a ruffian doth his whore,
    Whose sin keeps him in breath. By heaven I vow
    Thy bed he never wronged more than he does now.
MASTER GALLIPOT  My bed? Ha, ha, like enough; a
    shop-board will serve                  **311**
    To have a cuckold's coat cut out upon:
    Of that we'll talk hereafter.—You're a villain.
LAXTON  Hear me but speak, sir, you shall find me
    none.

---

289  tawny-coat: i.e. Greenwit, who is wearing the tawny-
     coloured livery of the summoner
291  hot . . . hair: more allusions to syphilis; 'hot' meant
     sexually eager (with possible reference to burning effects
     of syphilis); hair loss was another symptom of the disease
294  chirurgeon: surgeon
297–8  *A Knack . . . Man*: the title of an early anonymous
     comedy of 1594
302  shift: strategem. Her husband then puns on the sense of
     'underclothing'
305  Gelt: eds (Get Q): golden. Most eds somewhat uneasily
     conclude that this is the most plausible emendation
308  ruffian: pimp
311  shop-board: shop counter

OMNES  Pray sir, be patient and hear him.
MASTER GALLIPOT  I am muzzled for biting, sir; use me
    how you will.
LAXTON  The first hour that your wife was in my eye,
    Myself with other gentlemen sitting by
    In your shop tasting smoke, and speech being used
    That men who have fairest wives are most abused  **320**
    And hardly 'scaped the horn, your wife maintained
    That only such spots in city dames were stained
    Justly but by men's slanders: for her own part,
    She vowed that you had so much of her heart,
    No man by all his wit, by any wile
    Never so fine spun, should yourself beguile
    Of what in her was yours.
MASTER GALLIPOT          Yet, Pru, tis well;
    Play out your game at Irish, sir: who wins?
MISTRESS OPENWORK  The trial is when she comes to
    bearing.
LAXTON  I scorned one woman thus should brave all
    men,                                 **330**
    And (which more vexed me) a she-citizen.
    Therefore I laid siege to her: out she held,
    Gave many a brave repulse, and me compelled
    With shame to sound retreat to my hot lust;
    Then seeing all base desires raked up in dust,
    And that to tempt her modest ears I swore
    Ne'er to presume again, she said her eye
    Would ever give me welcome honestly;
    And, since I was a gentleman, if it run low,
    She would my state relieve, not to o'erthrow    **340**
    Your own and hers; did so; then seeing I wrought
    Upon her meekness, me she set at nought;
    And yet to try if I could turn that tide,
    You see what stream I strove with; but, sir, I swear
    By heaven, and by those hopes men lay up there,
    I neither have nor had a base intent
    To wrong your bed. What's done is merriment;
    Your gold I pay back with this interest:
    When I had most power to do't, I wronged you least.
MASTER GALLIPOT  If this no gullery be, sir—
OMNES                No, no, on my life.
MASTER GALLIPOT  Then, sir, I am beholden—not to
    you, wife—                         **351**
    But Master Laxton, to your want of doing ill,
    Which it seems you have not. Gentlemen,
    Tarry and dine here all.
MASTER OPENWORK        Brother, we have a jest

---

322–3  only . . . slanders: Mulholland suggests this becomes
     clearer if 'but' means 'if not': 'the stains on women's
     characters are just only if not the result of men's slanders'
328  Irish: a game similar to backgammon
329  bearing: in Irish and backgammon, a term for the
     removal of a piece at the end of a game; with a quibble
     on 'child-bearing'
341  did so: i.e. she did so

As good as yours to furnish out a feast.

MASTER GALLIPOT We'll crown our table with it. Wife, brag no more
Of holding out: who most brags is most whore.

*Exeunt*

# Act V, scene i

*Enter* JACK DAPPER, MOLL, SIR BEAUTEOUS GANYMEDE, *and* SIR THOMAS LONG

JACK DAPPER But prithee Master Captain Jack, be plain and perspicuous with me: was it your Meg of Westminster's courage that rescued me from the Poultry puttocks indeed?

MOLL The valour of my wit, I ensure you, sir, fetched you off bravely, when you were i'the forlorn hope among those desperates. Sir Beauteous Ganymede here and Sir Thomas Long heard that cuckoo, my man Trapdoor, sing the note of your ransom from captivity.

SIR BEAUTEOUS Uds so, Moll, where's that Trapdoor? 10

MOLL Hanged I think by this time; a justice in this town, that speaks nothing but 'Make a mittimus, away with him to Newgate', used that rogue like a firework to run upon a line betwixt him and me.

OMNES How, how?

MOLL Marry, to lay trains of villainy to blow up my life; I smelt the powder, spied what linstock gave fire to shoot against the poor captain of the galley-foist, and

away slid I my man like a shovel-board shilling. He struts up and down the suburbs I think, and eats up whores, feeds upon a bawd's garbage. 21

SIR THOMAS Sirrah Jack Dapper.

JACK DAPPER What sayst, Tom Long?

SIR THOMAS Thou hadst a sweet-faced boy, hail-fellow with thee, to your little Gull: how is he spent?

JACK DAPPER Troth I whistled the poor little buzzard off o' my fist, because when he waited upon me at the ordinaries, the gallants hit me i'the teeth still, and said I looked like a painted alderman's tomb, and the boy at my elbow like a death's head.—Sirrah Jack, Moll. 31

MOLL What says my little Dapper?

SIR BEAUTEOUS Come, come, walk and talk, walk and talk.

JACK DAPPER Moll and I'll be i'the midst.

MOLL These knights shall have squires' places, belike then: well Dapper, what say you?

JACK DAPPER Sirrah Captain Mad Mary, the gull my own father, Dapper Sir Davy, laid these London boot-halers, the catchpoles, in ambush to set upon me. 40

OMNES Your father? Away, Jack.

JACK DAPPER By the tassels of this handkercher 'tis true; and what was his warlike stratagem, think you? He thought because a wicker cage tames a nightingale, a lousy prison could make an ass of me.

OMNES A nasty plot.

JACK DAPPER Ay: as though a counter, which is a park in which all the wild beasts of the city run head by head, could tame me.

*Enter the* LORD NOLAND

MOLL Yonder comes my Lord Noland. 50

OMNES Save you, my lord.

LORD NOLAND Well met, gentlemen all: good Sir

---

355 furnish out: complete
1 Jack: a generic name for a man (here, Moll in men's clothing)
2–3 Meg of Westminster: a cross-dressing heroine rather similar to Moll, whose exploits are recounted in *The Life and Pranks of Long Meg of Westminster* (1582); a play about her (now lost) was acted in 1594–5, which may still have been in the repertory at the time of *The Roaring Girl*, and she appears in the anti-masque of Jonson's *The Fortunate Isles* (1625)
4 Poultry puttocks: i.e. officers of the Poultry Counter; see III.iii.114
6 the forlorn hope: originally a picked body of men, detached to the front to lead the attack; used figuratively of any group in a desperate condition
10 Uds so: see III.ii.163n
12 mittimus: a warrant from a Justice of the Peace ordering the person named to be kept in custody until delivered to a court of law; from Latin: 'we send'
14 line: a train (see l. 15) or fuse of gunpowder which burns from one end to the other; used to detonate a bomb, mine etc.
17 linstock: a staff, similar to a musket rest, for holding a gunner's match
18 captain of the galley-foist: Mulholland identifies this as 'a term of contempt'. A 'galley-foist' was a state barge, especially that of the Lord Mayor of London used on state occasions

19 shovel-board shilling: 'shovel-board' (or shuffleboard) was a game resembling shove-halfpenny, in which coins were knocked along a highly polished board into compartments at the end; the coins most commonly used were shillings
21 garbage: a) refuse (with play on 'Ralph'/raff, meaning refuse); b) cant term for takings from theft
24 hail-fellow: intimate
to: in
26 whistled . . . off: dismissed, sent off (from falconry)
28 hit . . . teeth: mock me
29–30 painted . . . head: aldermen frequently had ostentatious tombs with painted effigies. A death's head was often placed on the tomb as a *memento mori*
36 knights . . . places: a reversal of squires' usual ceremonial positions on the outside of the knights whom they served
39–40 boot-halers: highwaymen, freebooter
catchpoles: see III.i.43n
42 handkercher: common form of 'handkerchief; these were often highly decorated
43 counter: see III.iii.80n

Beauteous Ganymede, Sir Thomas Long. And how
does Master Dapper?

JACK DAPPER  Thanks, my lord.

MOLL  No tobacco, my lord?

LORD NOLAND  No, 'faith, Jack.

JACK DAPPER  My Lord Noland, will you go to Pimlico
with us? We are making a boon voyage to that nappy
land of spice-cakes.                                        60

LORD NOLAND  Here's such a merry ging, I could find in
my heart to sail to the world's end with such
company; come, gentlemen, let's on.

JACK DAPPER  Here's most amorous weather, my lord.

OMNES  Amorous weather?                    *They walk*

JACK DAPPER  Is not amorous a good word?

*Enter* TRAPDOOR *like a poor soldier with a patch o'er one
eye, and* TEARCAT *with him, all tatters*

TRAPDOOR  Shall we set upon the infantry, these troops
of foot? Zounds, yonder comes Moll, my whorish
master and mistress; would I had her kidneys
between my teeth.                                          70

TEARCAT  I had rather have a cow-heel.

TRAPDOOR  Zounds, I am so patched up, she cannot
discover me: we'll on.

TEARCAT  Alla corago then.

TRAPDOOR  Good your honours and worships, enlarge
the ears of commiseration, and let the sound of a
hoarse military organ-pipe penetrate your pitiful
bowels to extract out of them so many small drops of
silver as may give a hard straw-bed lodging to a
couple of maimed soldiers.                                 80

JACK DAPPER  Where are you maimed?

TEARCAT  In both our nether limbs.

MOLL  Come, come, Dapper, let's give 'em something:
'las poor men, what money have you? By my troth, I
love a soldier with my soul.

SIR BEAUTEOUS  Stay, stay, where have you served?

SIR THOMAS  In any part of the Low Countries?

TRAPDOOR  Not in the Low Countries, if it please your
manhood, but in Hungary against the Turk at the
siege of Belgrade.                                         90

LORD NOLAND  Who served there with you, sirrah?

TRAPDOOR  Many Hungarians, Moldavians,
Valachians, and Transylvanians, with some
Sclavonians; and retiring home, sir, the Venetian
galleys took us prisoners, yet freed us, and suffered us
to beg up and down the country.

JACK DAPPER  You have ambled all over Italy then?

TRAPDOOR  Oh sir, from Venice to Roma, Vecchio,
Bononia, Romania, Bolonia, Modena, Piacenza, and
Tuscana with all her cities, as Pistoia, Valteria,
Mountepulchena, Arezzo, with the Siennois, and
diverse others.                                           102

MOLL  Mere rogues, put spurs to 'em once more.

JACK DAPPER  Thou look'st like a strange creature, a fat
butter-box, yet speak'st English. What art thou?

TEARCAT  *Ick, mine Here? Ick bin den ruffling Tearcat,
den brave Soldado, ick bin dorick all Dutchlant gueresen:
der Shellum das meere ine Beasa ine Woert gaeb. Ick
slaag um stroakes on tom Cop: dastick den hundred
touzun Divell halle, frollick mine Here.*              110

SIR BEAUTEOUS  Here, here, let's be rid of their
jobbering.

MOLL  Not a cross, Sir Beauteous. You base rogues, I have
taken measure of you better than a tailor can, and I'll fit
you as you, monster with one eye, have fitted me.

TRAPDOOR  Your worship will not abuse a soldier.

MOLL  Soldier? Thou deservest to be hanged up by that
tongue which dishonours so noble a profession:
soldier, you skeldering varlet? Hold, stand, there
should be a trapdoor hereabouts.     *Pulls off his patch*

TRAPDOOR  The balls of these glaziers of mine, mine
eyes, shall be shot up and down in any hot piece of
service for my invincible mistress.                    123

JACK DAPPER  I did not think there had been such

---

58  Pimlico: see IV.ii.16n

59  boon voyage: anglicisation of 'bon voyage': happy journey
nappy: heady, strong (usually of liquor)

61  ging: company

62  the world's end: several taverns at some distance from
London were so named

71  cow-heel: the foot of a cow stewed to form a jelly

74  Alla corago: corruption of Italian *coraggio* (courage)

78  bowels: taken to be the seat of compassion or pity

87  Low Countries: with possible quibble; see II.i.241–5n

89–90  Hungary . . . Belgrade: an impossibility: Belgrade, 'the
capital of Serbia . . . was held by the Hungarians from
1086 to 1522, when it was taken by the Turkish Sultan
Solyman' (quoted in Mulholland)

92–4  Moldavians . . . Sclavonians: i.e. soldiers from the
regions under Hungarian rule

98–101  Vecchio . . . Siennois: Vecchio was Civitavecchia (the
port of Rome); Bononia and Bolonia were the same
place, Bologna; Romania was Romagna; Valteria was
Volterra; Mountepulchena was Montepulciano. 'Moll
recognises that this is no proper journey but a string of
names picked up at hearsay' (Cook)

105  butter-box: contemptuous term for a Dutchman

106–10  Ick . . . Here: spelt as in Q, this is a phonetically
rendered piece of bastard Dutch, whose meaning is
roughly as follows: 'I, my lord? I am the ruffling Tearcat,
the brave soldier, I have travelled through all Dutchland:
[he is] the greater scoundrel who gives an angry word. I
beat him directly on the head, that you take out a
hundred thousand devils, [be] merry, sir' (Mulholland's
translation). For 'ruffling', see l. 162 below

112  jobbering: jabbering

113  cross: a coin

115  monster . . . eye: a reference to Trapdoor's eyepatch

119  skeldering: begging, sponging, swindling

121  glaziers: cant term for eyes

knavery in black patches as now I see.

MOLL Oh sir, he hath been brought up in the Isle of Dogs, and can both fawn like a spaniel and bite like a mastiff, as he finds occasion.

LORD NOLAND What are you, sirrah? A bird of this feather too? 130

TEARCAT A man beaten from the wars, sir.

SIR THOMAS I think so, for you never stood to fight.

JACK DAPPER What's thy name, fellow soldier?

TEARCAT I am called by those that have seen my valour, Tearcat.

OMNES Tearcat?

MOLL A mere whip-jack, and that is, in the commonwealth of rogues, a slave that can talk of sea-fight, name all your chief pirates, discover more countries to you than either the Dutch, Spanish, French, or English ever found out, yet indeed all his service is by land, and that is to rob a fair, or some such venturous exploit. Tearcat—foot sirrah, I have your name, now I remember me, in my book of horners: horns for the thumb, you know how. 145

TEARCAT No indeed, Captain Moll (for I know you by sight), I am no such nipping Christian, but a maunderer upon the pad, I confess; and meeting with honest Trapdoor here, whom you had cashiered from bearing arms, out at elbows under your colours, I instructed him in the rudiments of roguery, and by my map made him sail over any country you can name, so that now he can maunder better than myself. 153

JACK DAPPER So then, Trapdoor, thou art turned soldier now.

TRAPDOOR Alas sir, now there's no wars, 'tis the safest course of life I could take.

MOLL I hope then you can cant, for by your cudgels, you, sirrah, are an upright man.

TRAPDOOR As any walks the highway, I assure you. 160

MOLL And Tearcat, what are you? A wild rogue, an angler, or a ruffler?

TEARCAT Brother to this upright man, flesh and blood, ruffling Tearcat is my name, and a ruffler is my style, my title, my profession.

MOLL Sirrah, where's your doxy? Halt not with me.

OMNES Doxy, Moll, what's that?

MOLL His wench. 168

TRAPDOOR My doxy? I have, by the solomon, a doxy, that carries a kinchin mort in her slate at her back, besides my dell and my dainty wild dell, with all whom I'll tumble this next darkmans in the strommel, and drink ben booze, and eat a fat gruntling cheat, a cackling cheat, and a quacking cheat.

JACK DAPPER Here's old cheating.

TRAPDOOR My doxy stays for me in a boozing ken, brave captain.

---

126–7 the Isle of Dogs: the peninsula on the north bank of the Thames opposite Greenwich; by this time, a refuge for debtors and criminals

137 whip-jack: a vagabond who pretends to be a distressed sailor

145 horns . . . thumb: a horn thimble was used by cutpurses to protect the thumb from the blade of the knife when cutting purse-strings; hence cutpurses were known as 'horn-thumbs'

147 nipping: thieving

148 maunderer . . . pad: beggar on the highway

153 maunder: beg

158 cant: speak in the specialist slang of vagabonds and thieves

143 upright man: Dekker ranks the 'upright man' first in the hierarchy of rogues: he 'is a sturdy big-boned knave, that never walks but (like a commander) with a short truncheon in his hand, which he calls his filchman. At markets, fairs, and other meetings his voice among beggars is of the same sound that a constable's is of, it is not to be controlled' (Dekker, *The Bellman of London*, 1608); see too 'ruffler', l. 162 below

161 wild rogue: 'one that is born a rogue . . . begotten in barn or bushes, and from his infancy traded up in treachery . . . neither so stout or hardy as an upright man' (Thomas Harman, *A Caveat for Common Cursitors*, 1566)

162 angler: 'a limb of an upright man . . . in the day time, they beg from house to house, not so much for relief, as to spy what lies fit for their nets, which in the night following they fish for. The rod they angle with is a staff of five or six foot in length . . . into which . . . they put an iron hook . . . they angle at windows about midnight' (Dekker, *Bellman*)
ruffler: ranked second by Dekker in his hierarchy of rogues: 'the ruffler and the upright-man are so like in conditions, that you would swear them brothers: they walk with cudgels alike; they profess arms alike . . . and will swear they lost their limbs in their country's quarrel, when either they are lame by diseases, or have been mangled in some drunken quarrel. These commonly are fellows that have stood aloof in the wars, and whilst others fought, they took their heels and ran away' (Dekker, *Bellman*)

166 doxy: whore
Halt not: don't vacillate, play false (playing on Trapdoor's limp)

169 solomon: cant equivalent to 'the mass'

170 kinchin mort . . . slate: 'girls of a year or two old, which the 'morts' (their mothers) carry at their backs in their slates (which in the canting-tongue are sheets)' (Dekker, *Bellman*)
dell: 'a young wench, ripe for the act of generation, but as yet not spoiled of her maidenhead. These dells are reserved as dishes for the upright-men, for none but they must have the first taste of them' (Dekker, *Bellman*)

171 wild dell: a dell born to the position: 'those such as are born or begotten under a hedge' (Dekker, *Bellman*)

172–5 I'll tumble . . . cheat: i.e. I'll tumble this next night in the straw, and drink good booze, and eat a fat pig, a capon, and a duck. 'Cheat' was cant for 'thing'

176 old: fine, rare

MOLL  He says his wench stays for him in an alehouse. You are no pure rogues.  180

TEARCAT  Pure rogues? No, we scorn to be pure rogues, but if you come to our lib ken, or our stalling ken, you shall find neither him nor me a queer cuffin.

MOLL  So sir, no churl of you.

TEARCAT  No, but a ben cove, a brave cove, a gentry cuffin.

LORD NOLAND  Call you this canting?

JACK DAPPER  Zounds, I'll give a schoolmaster half a crown a week and teach me this pedlar's French.

TRAPDOOR  Do but stroll, sir, half a harvest with us, sir, and you shall gabble your bellyfull.  191

MOLL  Come you rogue, cant with me.

SIR THOMAS  Well said, Moll; cant with her, sirrah, and you shall have money, else not a penny.

TRAPDOOR  I'll have a bout if she please.

MOLL  Come on sirrah.

TRAPDOOR  Ben mort, shall you and I heave a booth, mill a ken, or nip a bung? And then we'll couch a hogshead under the ruffmans, and there you shall wap with me, and I'll niggle with you.  200

MOLL  Out, you damned impudent rascal.

TRAPDOOR  Cut benar whids, and hold your fambles and your stamps.

LORD NOLAND  Nay, nay, Moll, why art thou angry? What was his gibberish?

MOLL  Marry, this, my Lord, says he: Ben mort (good wench), shall you and I heave a booth, mill a ken, or nip a bung? Shall you and I rob a house, or cut a purse?

OMNES  Very good.  210

MOLL  And then we'll couch a hogshead under the ruffmans: and then we'll lie under a hedge.

TRAPDOOR  That was my desire, captain, as 'tis fit a soldier should lie.

MOLL  And there you shall wap with me, and I'll niggle with you,— and that's all.

SIR BEAUTEOUS  Nay, nay, Moll, what's that wap?

JACK DAPPER  Nay teach me what niggling is, I'd fain be niggling.

MOLL  Wapping and niggling is all one, the rogue my man can tell you.  221

TRAPDOOR  'Tis fadoodling, if it please you.

SIR BEAUTEOUS  This is excellent; one fit more, good Moll.

MOLL  Come you rogue, sing with me.

THE SONG

*A gage of ben rom-booze*
*In a boozing ken of Rom-ville*

TEARCAT  *Is benar than a caster,*
*Peck, pennam, lap or popler,*
*Which we mill in deuse a vill.*  230

BOTH  *Oh I would lib all the lightmans,*
*Oh I would lib all the darkmans,*
*By the solomon, under the ruffmans,*
*By the solomon, in the hartmans.*

TEARCAT  *And scour the queer cramp-ring,*
*And couch till a palliard docked my dell,*
*So my boozy nab might skew rom-booze well.*

BOTH  *Avast to the pad, let us bing,*
*Avast to the pad, let us bing.*

OMNES  Fine knaves, i'faith.  240

JACK DAPPER  The grating of ten new cartwheels, and the gruntling of five hundred hogs coming from Romford market, cannot make a worse noise than this canting language does in my ears; pray, my Lord Noland, let's give these soldiers their pay.

SIR BEAUTEOUS  Agreed, and let them march.

LORD NOLAND  Here, Moll.

MOLL  Now I see that you are stalled to the rogue, and are not ashamed of your professions, look you: my

---

180 pure rogues: Bullen reads this as ironical, Cook reads 'pure' as 'sexually pure or chaste', and Mulholland as 'thorough' (because so far they have confessed only to begging)

182 lib ken: place to sleep
stalling ken: house for receiving stolen goods

183 queer cuffin: 'a churl or a naughty man' (Dekker, *Lanthorn and Candlelight*, 1608)

184 of: in the person of

185 ben cove: 'a good fellow' (Dekker, *Lanthorn*)
gentry cuffin: 'a gentleman' (Dekker, *Lanthorn*)

189 pedlar's French: cant

197 heave a booth: rob a booth (i.e. at a fair)

198 mill a ken: rob a house

202–3 Cut . . . stamps: speak better words, and hold your hands and your legs

215 wap . . . niggle: cant terms for 'copulate'

222 fadoodling: euphemism for 'copulating'

223 fit: bout, strain

SP Tearcat's speech prefixes are in Q; others attributed by eds

226–39 The song: 'A quart of good wine in an ale-house of London is better than a cloak, meat, bread, butter-milk (or whey), or porridge, which we steal in the country. O I would lie all the day, O I would lie all the night, by the mass, under the woods (or bushes), by the mass, in the stocks, and wear bolts (or fetters), and lie till a palliard lay with my wench, so my drunken head might quaff wine well. Avast to the highway, let us hence, &c.' (Dyce, quoted in Mulholland); see Moll's paraphrase at ll. 269–79

235 *cramp-ring*: handcuffs

236 *palliard*: a tramp or beggar: 'he that goeth in a patched coat' (John Awdeley, *The Fraternity of Vagabonds*, 1561); 'to draw pity from men . . . will they in one night poison their leg, be it never so sound, and raise a blister, which at their pleasure they can take off again' (Dekker, *Bellman*)

243 Romford market: a famous hog-market was held in Romford in Essex every Tuesday

Lord Noland here and these gentlemen bestows upon
you two, two bordes and a half, that's two shillings
sixpence.                                                    252

TRAPDOOR  Thanks to your lordship.

TEARCAT  Thanks, heroical captain.

MOLL  Away.

TRAPDOOR  We shall cut ben whids of your masters and
mistress-ship, wheresoever we come.

MOLL  You'll maintain, sirrah, the old justice's plot to
his face?

TRAPDOOR  Else trine me on the cheats: hang me.    260

MOLL  Be sure you meet me there.

TRAPDOOR  Without any more maundering I'll do't:
follow, brave Tearcat.

TEARCAT  *I prae, sequor*, let us go, mouse.

*Exeunt they two, manet the rest*

LORD NOLAND  Moll, what was in that canting song?

MOLL  Troth my Lord, only a praise of good drink, the
only milk which these wild beasts love to suck, and
thus it was:

> *A rich cup of wine,*
> *Oh it is juice divine,*                                  270
> *More wholesome for the head*
> *Than meat, drink, or bread;*
> *To fill my drunken pate*
> *With that, I'd sit up late,*
> *By the heels would I lie,*
> *Under a lousy hedge die,*
> *Let a slave have a pull*
> *At my whore, so I be full*
> *Of that precious liquor*

—and a parcel of such stuff, my Lord, not worth the
opening.                                                    281

*Enter a* CUTPURSE *very gallant, with four or five men after
him, one with a wand*

LORD NOLAND  What gallant comes yonder?

SIR THOMAS  Mass, I think I know him; 'tis one of
Cumberland.

1 CUTPURSE  Shall we venture to shuffle in amongst yon
heap of gallants, and strike?

2 CUTPURSE  'Tis a question whether there be any silver
shells amongst them, for all their satin outsides.

OMNES (CUTPURSES)  Let's try.

MOLL  Pox on him, a gallant? Shadow me, I know him:
'tis one that cumbers the land indeed; if he swim near
to the shore of any of your pockets, look to your
purses.                                                     293

OMNES  Is't possible?

MOLL  This brave fellow is no better than a foist.

OMNES  Foist, what's that?

MOLL  A diver with two fingers, a pickpocket; all his
train study the figging-law, that's to say cutting of
purses and foisting. One of them is a nip; I took him
once i'the twopenny gallery at the Fortune; then
there's a cloyer, or snap, that dogs any new brother in
that trade, and snaps will have half in any booty. He
with the wand is both a stale, whose office is to face a
man i'the streets, whilst shells are drawn by another,
and then with his black conjuring rod in his hand, he,
by the nimbleness of his eye and juggling stick, will,
in cheaping a piece of plate at a goldsmith's stall,
make four or five rings mount from the top of his
caduceus, and as if it were at leap-frog, they skip into
his hand presently.                                         310

2 CUTPURSE  Zounds, we are smoked.

OMNES (CUTPURSES)  Ha?

2 CUTPURSE  We are boiled, pox on her; see Moll, the
roaring drab.

1 CUTPURSE  All the diseases of sixteen hospitals boil
her! Away.

MOLL  Bless you, sir.

1 CUTPURSE  And you, good sir.

MOLL  Dost not ken me, man?

1 CUTPURSE  No, trust me, sir.                              320

MOLL  Heart, there's a knight to whom I'm bound for
many favours lost his purse at the last new play i'the
Swan, seven angels in't: make it good, you're best; do
you see? No more.

1 CUTPURSE  A synagogue shall be called, Mistress
Mary; disgrace me not; *pacus palabros*, I will conjure
for you; farewell.                        *Exeunt* CUTPURSES

MOLL  Did not I tell you, my lord?

LORD NOLAND  I wonder how thou camest to the
knowledge of these nasty villains.                          330

---

251  bordes: shillings
256  cut ben whids: speak good words
260  trine . . . cheats: hang me on the gallows
262  maundering: talking; perhaps with reference to cant sense
     of 'begging'
264  *I prae, sequor*: go before, I follow
 SD  *manet*: remains
 SD  *gallant*: finely dressed
     *wand*: a light walking stick
286  strike: pick a pocket or cut a purse
288  shells: money

299  nip: cutpurse
303  stale: a decoy
307  cheaping: bargaining for
309  caduceus: either the cutpurse's wand, used to hook the
     rings, or the baton on which the goldsmith displayed the
     rings
311, 313  smoked . . . boiled: 'the spying of this villainy is called
     smoking or boiling' (Dekker, *Bellman*)
314  drab: whore
323  Swan: theatre on the south bank of the Thames near the
     Globe
325  synagogue: an assembly of thieves
326  pacus palabros: approximation of Spanish *pocas palabras*
     meaning 'few words'

SIR THOMAS  And why do the foul mouths of the world
  call thee Moll Cutpurse? A name, methinks, damned
  and odious.
MOLL  Dare any step forth to my face and say,
  'I have ta'en thee doing so, Moll'? I must confess,
  In younger days, when I was apt to stray,
  I have sat amongst such adders; seen their stings,
  As any here might, and in full playhouses
  Watched their quick-diving hands, to bring to shame
  Such rogues, and in that stream met an ill name.  340
  When next, my lord, you spy any one of those,
  So he be in his art a scholar, question him,
  Tempt him with gold to open the large book
  Of his close villainies; and you yourself shall cant
  Better than poor Moll can, and know more laws
  Of cheaters, lifters, nips, foists, puggards, curbers,
  With all the devil's black guard, than it is fit
  Should be discovered to a noble wit.
  I know they have their orders, offices,
  Circuits and circles, unto which they are bound,  350
  To raise their own damnation in.
JACK DAPPER                          How dost thou know it?
MOLL  As you do: I show it you, they to me show it.
  Suppose, my lord, you were in Venice.
LORD NOLAND                          Well.
MOLL  If some Italian pander there would tell
  All the close tricks of courtesans, would not you
  Hearken to such a fellow?
LORD NOLAND                          Yes.
MOLL                          And here,
  Being come from Venice, to a friend most dear
  That were to travel thither, you would proclaim
  Your knowledge in those villainies, to save
  Your friend from their quick danger: must you have
  A black ill name, because ill things you know?  361
  Good troth my lord, I am made Moll Cutpurse so.
  How many are whores in small ruffs and still looks!
  How many chaste, whose names fill slander's books!
  Were all men cuckolds, whom gallants in their scorns
  Call so, we should not walk for goring horns.
  Perhaps for my mad going some reprove me;
  I please myself, and care not else who loves me.
OMNES  A brave mind, Moll, i'faith.
SIR THOMAS  Come my Lord, shall's to the ordinary?
LORD NOLAND  Ay, 'tis noon sure.  371
MOLL  Good my lord, let not my name condemn me to

you or to the world; a fencer I hope may be called a
coward: is he so for that? If all that have ill names in
London were to be whipped, and to pay but
twelvepence apiece to the beadle, I would rather have
his office than a constable's.
JACK DAPPER  So would I, Captain Moll: 'twere a sweet
tickling office, i'faith.

                                                    *Exeunt*

# Act V, scene ii

*Enter* SIR ALEXANDER WENGRAVE, GOSHAWK *and*
GREENWIT, *and others*

SIR ALEXANDER  My son marry a thief, that impudent
  girl,
  Whom all the world stick their worst eyes upon?
GREENWIT  How will your care prevent it?
GOSHAWK                          'Tis impossible.
  They marry close, they're gone, but none knows
  whither.
SIR ALEXANDER  Oh gentlemen, when has a father's
  heart-strings
  Held out so long from breaking?

*Enter a* SERVANT

                                        Now what news, sir?
SERVANT  They were met upo'th'water an hour since,
  sir,
  Putting in towards the Sluice.
SIR ALEXANDER          The Sluice? Come gentlemen,
  'Tis Lambeth works against us.  *Exit* SERVANT
GREENWIT                          And that Lambeth
  Joins more mad matches than your six wet towns  10
  'Twixt that and Windsor Bridge, where fares lie
  soaking.
SIR ALEXANDER  Delay no time, sweet gentlemen: to
  Blackfriars,
  We'll take a pair of oars and make after 'em.

*Enter* TRAPDOOR

TRAPDOOR  Your son, and that bold masculine ramp

---

346  cheaters: or fingerers, who won money by false dice
    lifters: thieves
    nips, foists: see above, ll. 297, 299n
    puggards: probably 'thieves'; this is the only recorded
    usage
    curbers: thieves who hook goods out of windows
347  black guard: a guard of attendants, black in person, dress,
    or character
355  close: secret

359  tickling: diverting
  4  close: secretly
  8  the Sluice: an embankment on the Thames built to
    protect Lambeth from flooding; it was used as a landing
    place. Perhaps with pun on 'sluice' meaning copulate
  9  Lambeth: district on the south side of the Thames, and
    notorious for its thieves and prostitutes
 10  six wet towns: i.e. riverside towns; perhaps Fulham,
    Richmond, Kingston, Hampton, Chertsey and Staines
 11  where . . . soaking: 'the whole phrase suggests the use of
    the riverside towns for sexual excursions' (Cook)
 12  Blackfriars: Blackfriars Stairs was a landing stage on the
    north side of the Thames
 14  ramp: see III.iii.8n

My mistress, are landed now at Tower.

SIR ALEXANDER                    Heyday, at Tower?

TRAPDOOR  I heard it now reported.                    *Exit*

SIR ALEXANDER                    Which way, gentlemen,
Shall I bestow my care? I'm drawn in pieces
Betwixt deceit and shame.

*Enter* SIR GUY FITZALLARD

SIR GUY                    Sir Alexander,
You're well met, and most rightly served;
My daughter was a scorn to you.

SIR ALEXANDER                    Say not so, sir.    20

SIR GUY  A very abject she, poor gentlewoman.
Your house has been dishonoured. Give you joy, sir,
Of your son's gaskin-bride; you'll be a grandfather
    shortly
To a fine crew of roaring sons and daughters:
'Twill help to stock the suburbs passing well, sir.

SIR ALEXANDER  Oh play not with the miseries of my
    heart.
Wounds should be dressed and healed, not vexed, or
    left
Wide open, to the anguish of the patient,
And scornful air let in: rather let pity
And advice charitably help to refresh 'em.    30

SIR GUY  Who'd place his charity so unworthily,
Like one that gives alms to a cursing beggar?
Had I but found one spark of goodness in you
Toward my deserving child, which then grew fond
Of your son's virtues, I had eased you now.
But I perceive both fire of youth and goodness
Are raked up in the ashes of your age,
Else no such shame should have come near your
    house,
Nor such ignoble sorrow touch your heart.

SIR ALEXANDER  If not for worth, for pity's sake assist
    me.                    40

GREENWIT  You urge a thing past sense; how can he
    help you?
All his assistance is as frail as ours,
Full as uncertain where's the place that holds 'em.
One brings us water-news; then comes another
With a full-charged mouth, like a culverin's voice,
And he reports the Tower: whose sounds are truest?

GOSHAWK  In vain you flatter him. Sir Alexander—

SIR GUY  I flatter him? Gentlemen, you wrong me
    grossly.

GREENWIT  He does it well i'faith.

SIR GUY                    Both news are false,
Of Tower or water: they took no such way yet.    50

SIR ALEXANDER  Oh strange: hear you this, gentlemen,
    yet more plunges?

SIR GUY  They're nearer than you think for, yet more
    close
Than if they were further off.

SIR ALEXANDER                    How am I lost
In these distractions?

SIR GUY                    For your speeches, gentlemen,
In taxing me for rashness, 'fore you all
I will engage my state to half his wealth,
Nay to his son's revenues, which are less,
And yet nothing at all till they come from him,
That I could (if my will stuck to my power)
Prevent this marriage yet, nay banish her    60
Forever from his thoughts, much more his arms.

SIR ALEXANDER  Slack not this goodness, though you
    heap upon me
Mountains of malice and revenge hereafter:
I'd willingly resign up half my state to him,
So he would marry the meanest drudge I hire.

GREENWIT  He talks impossibilities, and you believe
    'em.

SIR GUY  I talk no more than I know how to finish,
My fortunes else are his that dares stake with me.
The poor young gentleman I love and pity,
And to keep shame from him (because the spring    70
Of his affection was my daughter's first,
Till his frown blasted all), do but estate him
In those possessions which your love and care
Once pointed out for him, that he may have room
To entertain fortunes of noble birth,
Where now his desperate wants casts him upon her;
And if I do not, for his own sake chiefly,
Rid him of this disease that now grows on him,
I'll forfeit my whole state, before these gentlemen.

GREENWIT  Troth but you shall not undertake such
    matches;                    80
We'll persuade so much with you.

SIR ALEXANDER                    Here's my ring,
He will believe this token: 'fore these gentlemen

---

23  gaskin-bride: i.e. a bride wearing gaskins or loose
    breeches
37  raked up: smothered
45  culverin: a large cannon
47  In vain . . . Alexander—: we follow Bullen and
    Mulholland's punctuation here (in Q₂ there is no
    punctuation after 'him'), in which Greenwit addresses
    first Sir Guy, and then Sir Alexander, at which point Sir
    Guy interrupts
    flatter: give hope to, on insufficient grounds

49  He . . . i'faith: here and at l. 92, Greenwit comments on
    the impact of Sir Guy's words
51  plunges: dilemmas
52  think for: suppose
56  I will . . . wealth: I will pledge my estate to the value of
    half of Sir Alexander's
59  if . . . power: 'if I would do what I could' (Cook)
72  his: i.e. Sir Alexander's
76  her: i.e. Moll
81  persuade: plead

I will confirm it fully: all those lands
My first love 'lotted him, he shall straight possess
In that refusal.
SIR GUY              If I change it not,
Change me into a beggar.
GREENWIT                          Are you mad, sir?
SIR GUY 'Tis done.
GOSHAWK           Will you undo yourself by doing,
And show a prodigal trick in your old days?
SIR ALEXANDER 'Tis a match, gentlemen.
SIR GUY                                   Ay, ay, sir, ay.
I ask no favour, trust to you for none;                90
My hope rests in the goodness of your son.       *Exit*
GREENWIT He holds it up well yet.
GOSHAWK                          Of an old knight, i'faith.
SIR ALEXANDER Cursed be the time I laid his first love
barren,
Wilfully barren, that before this hour
Had sprung forth fruits of comfort and of honour;
He loved a virtuous gentlewoman.

*Enter* MOLL *in male dress*

GOSHAWK Life, here's Moll.
GREENWIT Jack?
GOSHAWK           How dost thou, Jack?
MOLL                          How dost thou, gallant?
SIR ALEXANDER Impudence, where's my son?
MOLL                          Weakness, go look him.
SIR ALEXANDER Is this your wedding gown?
MOLL                          The man talks monthly:
Hot broth and a dark chamber for the knight;       101
I see he'll be stark mad at our next meeting.       *Exit*
GOSHAWK Why sir, take comfort now, there's no such
matter.
No priest will marry her, sir, for a woman
Whiles that shape's on, and it was never known
Two men were married and conjoined in one:
Your son hath made some shift to love another.
SIR ALEXANDER Whate'er she be, she has my blessing
with her,
May they be rich and fruitful, and receive
Like comfort to their issue as I take       110
In them. Has pleased me now: marrying not this,
Through a whole world he could not choose amiss.
GREENWIT Glad you're so penitent for your former sin,
sir.
GOSHAWK Say he should take a wench with her smock-
dowry,

No portion with her but her lips and arms?
SIR ALEXANDER Why, who thrive better, sir? They
have most blessing,
Though other have more wealth, and least repent:
Many that want most know the most content.
GREENWIT Say he should marry a kind youthful sinner?
SIR ALEXANDER Age will quench that; any offence but
theft       120
And drunkenness, nothing but death can wipe away;
Their sins are green even when their heads are grey.
Nay, I despair not now, my heart's cheered,
gentlemen,
No face can come unfortunately to me.

*Enter a* SERVANT

Now, sir, your news?
SERVANT                          Your son with his fair bride
Is near at hand.
SIR ALEXANDER Fair may their fortunes be.
GREENWIT Now you're resolved, sir, it was never she?
SIR ALEXANDER I find it in the music of my heart.

*Enter* MOLL *in female dress, masked, in* SEBASTIAN's *hand,
and* FITZALLARD

See where they come.
GOSHAWK                          A proper lusty presence, sir.
SIR ALEXANDER Now has he pleased me right. I always
counselled him       130
To choose a goodly personable creature:
Just of her pitch was my first wife his mother.
SEBASTIAN Before I dare discover my offence,
I kneel for pardon.
SIR ALEXANDER           My heart gave it thee
Before thy tongue could ask it:
Rise; thou hast raised my joy to greater height
Than to that seat where grief dejected it.
Both welcome to my love and care for ever.
Hide not my happiness too long: all's pardoned;
Here are our friends.—Salute her, gentlemen.       140
                                        *They unmask her*
OMNES Heart, who's this? Moll!
SIR ALEXANDER Oh my reviving shame! Is't I must live
To be struck blind? Be it the work of sorrow,
Before age take't in hand.
SIR GUY                          Darkness and death.
Have you deceived me thus? Did I engage
My whole estate for this?
SIR ALEXANDER                          You asked no favour,
And you shall find as little; since my comforts
Play false with me, I'll be as cruel to thee
As grief to fathers' hearts.

---

84  my first love: i.e. my love originally
85  refusal: i.e. of Moll
92  Of: characteristic of
100  monthly: madly, as if under the influence of the moon
101  Hot . . . chamber: traditional treatments for insanity
114  smock-dowry: i.e. no dowry but her smock

---

119  sinner: i.e. unchaste woman
127  resolved: convinced, persuaded
132  pitch: height

MOLL               Why, what's the matter with you,
'Less too much joy should make your age forgetful?
Are you too well, too happy?
SIR ALEXANDER           With a vengeance.   **151**
MOLL  Methinks you should be proud of such a daughter,
As good a man as your son.
SIR ALEXANDER          Oh monstrous impudence.
MOLL  You had no note before, an unmarked knight;
Now all the town will take regard on you,
And all your enemies fear you for my sake:
You may pass where you list, through crowds most
     thick,
And come off bravely with your purse unpicked.
You do not know the benefits I bring with me:
No cheat dares work upon you with thumb or knife,
While you've a roaring girl to your son's wife.   **161**
SIR ALEXANDER  A devil rampant.
SIR GUY               Have you so much charity
Yet to release me of my last rash bargain,
And I'll give in your pledge?
SIR ALEXANDER          No sir, I stand to't;
I'll work upon advantage, as all mischiefs
Do upon me.
SIR GUY           Content: bear witness all then,
His are the lands, and so contention ends.
Here comes your son's bride, 'twixt two noble friends.

*Enter the* LORD NOLAND *and* SIR BEAUTEOUS GANYMEDE
*with* MARY FITZALLARD *between them, the* CITIZENS *and
their* WIVES *with them*

MOLL  Now are you gulled as you would be: thank me
     for't,
I'd a forefinger in't.
SEBASTIAN         Forgive me, father:   **170**
Though there before your eyes my sorrow feigned,
This still was she for whom true love complained.
SIR ALEXANDER  Blessings eternal and the joys of angels
Begin your peace here, to be signed in heaven!
How short my sleep of sorrow seems now to me,
To this eternity of boundless comforts,
That finds no want but utterance and expression.
My lord, your office here appears so honourably,
So full of ancient goodness, grace, and worthiness,
I never took more joy in sight of man   **180**
Than in your comfortable presence now.
LORD NOLAND  Nor I more delight in doing grace to
     virtue,

---

150  'Less: unless
154  unmarked: unremarked, unnoticed
157  list: please
160  cheat: thief
      thumb: see V.i.145n
164  And: if
165  work . . . advantage: take advantage of the situation
169  would be: would wish to be

Than in this worthy gentlewoman, your son's bride,
Noble Fitzallard's daughter, to whose honour
And modest fame I am a servant vowed;
So is this knight.
SIR ALEXANDER       Your loves make my joys proud.
—Bring forth those deeds of land my care laid ready,
        *Exit* SERVANT, *who then re-enters with deeds*
And which, old knight, thy nobleness may challenge,
Joined with thy daughter's virtues, whom I prize now
As dearly as that flesh I call mine own.   **190**
Forgive me, worthy gentlewoman, 'twas my
     blindness:
When I rejected thee, I saw thee not;
Sorrow and wilful rashness grew like films
Over the eyes of judgment, now so clear
I see the brightness of thy worth appear.
MARY  Duty and love may I deserve in those,
And all my wishes have a perfect close.
SIR ALEXANDER  That tongue can never err, the sound's
     so sweet.
Here, honest son, receive into thy hands
The keys of wealth, possession of those lands   **200**
Which my first care provided, they're thine own;
Heaven give thee a blessing with 'em; the best joys
That can in worldly shapes to man betide
Are fertile lands and a fair fruitful bride,
Of which I hope thou'rt sped.
SEBASTIAN             I hope so too sir.
MOLL  Father and son, I ha' done you simple service
     here.
SEBASTIAN  For which thou shalt not part, Moll,
     unrequited.
SIR ALEXANDER  Thou art a mad girl, and yet I cannot
     now
Condemn thee.
MOLL              Condemn me? Troth and you
     should, sir,
I'd make you seek out one to hang in my room,   **210**
I'd give you the slip at gallows, and cozen the people.
Heard you this jest, my lord?
LORD NOLAND        What is it, Jack?
MOLL  He was in fear his son would marry me,
But never dreamt that I would ne'er agree.
LORD NOLAND  Why? Thou hadst a suitor once, Jack;
     when wilt marry?
MOLL  Who, I, my lord? I'll tell you when, i'faith:
When you shall hear
Gallants void from sergeants' fear,
Honesty and truth unslandered,
Woman manned but never pandered,   **220**

---

188  challenge: claim
196  those: i.e. the eyes of judgement
205  sped: provided
209  and: if

Cheats booted but not coached,
Vessels older ere they're broached.
If my mind be then not varied,
Next day following I'll be married.

LORD NOLAND  This sounds like doomsday.

MOLL                                Then were marriage best,
For if I should repent, I were soon at rest.

SIR ALEXANDER  In troth thou'rt a good wench; I'm
  sorry now
The opinion was so hard I conceived of thee.
Some wrongs I've done thee.

*Enter* TRAPDOOR

TRAPDOOR                          Is the wind there now?
'Tis time for me to kneel and confess first,        230
For fear it come too late and my brains feel it.
Upon my paws I ask you pardon, mistress.

MOLL  Pardon? For what, sir? What has your rogueship
  done now?

TRAPDOOR  I have been from time to time hired to
  confound you
By this old gentleman.

MOLL                          How?

TRAPDOOR                          Pray forgive him,
But may I counsel you, you should never do't.
Many a snare to entrap your worship's life
Have I laid privily, chains, watches, jewels,
And when he saw nothing could mount you up,    240
Four hollow-hearted angels he then gave you,
By which he meant to trap you, I to save you.

SIR ALEXANDER  To all which, shame and grief in me
  cry guilty.
Forgive me; now I cast the world's eyes from me,
And look upon thee freely with mine own,
I see the most of many wrongs before thee
Cast from the jaws of envy and her people,
And nothing foul but that. I'll never more
Condemn by common voice, for that's the whore
That deceives man's opinion, mocks his trust,    250
Cozens his love, and makes his heart unjust.

MOLL  Here be the angels, gentlemen; they were given
  me
As a musician. I pursue no pity:
Follow the law: and you can cuck me, spare not:

Hang up my viol by me, and I care not.

SIR ALEXANDER  So far I'm sorry, I'll thrice double 'em
  To make thy wrongs amends.
Come, worthy friends, my honourable lord,
Sir Beauteous Ganymede, and noble Fitzallard,
And you kind gentlewomen, whose sparkling
  presence                                                260
Are glories set in marriage, beams of society,
For all your loves give lustre to my joys:
The happiness of this day shall be remembered
At the return of every smiling spring:
In my time now 'tis born, and may no sadness
Sit on the brows of men upon that day,
But as I am, so all go pleased away.

                                              *Exeunt*

# Epilogus

A painter having drawn with curious art
The picture of a woman (every part
Limned to the life) hung out the piece to sell.
People who passed along, viewing it well,
Gave several verdicts on it: some dispraised
The hair, some said the brows too high were raised,
Some hit her o'er the lips, misliked their colour,
Some wished her nose were shorter, some the eyes
  fuller;
Others said roses on her cheeks should grow,
Swearing they looked too pale, others cried no.    10
The workman, still as fault was found, did mend it
In hope to please all; but, this work being ended
And hung open at stall, it was so vile,
So monstrous and so ugly, all men did smile
At the poor painter's folly. Such we doubt
Is this our comedy: some perhaps do flout
The plot, saying 'tis too thin, too weak, too mean;
Some for the person will revile the scene,
And wonder that a creature of her being
Should be the subject of a poet, seeing            20
In the world's eye none weighs so light: others look
For all those base tricks published in a book

---

221  Cheats . . . coached: 'Moll apparently awaits the time
     when *cheaters* are allowed the expense of a horse (or
     simply footwear), but not the extravagence of a coach'
     (Mulholland)
222  Vessels: i.e. women's bodies
229  Is the wind . . . now?: referring to Sir Alexander's
     changed attitude to Moll
240  mount you up: i.e. on the gallows
246  before thee: done to thee
254  and . . . cuck me: if you can get me in a cucking stool
     (punishment given to women seen as disorderly)

260  gentlewomen: eds (gentlewoman Q); i.e. the citizens'
     wives
261  beams: sunbeams
     Epilogus: probably spoken by Moll
1–15  compare the Epilogue to *A Woman Killed with Kindness*
  1  curious: skilful
  7  hit her o'er: criticised
 15  doubt: suspect
 18  person: character (i.e. Moll)
 22  a book: apparently a reference to Samuel Rid who wrote
     *Martin Mark-All, Beadle of Bridewell; His Defence and
     Answer to the Bellman of London* (1610) in which he
     criticised Dekker's work and his knowledge of thieves'
     cant; see Mulholland 1977: 19–20

(Foul as his brains they flowed from) of cutpurses,
Of nips and foists, nasty, obscene discourses,
As full of lies, as empty of worth or wit,
For any honest ear, or eye, unfit.
And thus,
If we to every brain that's humorous
Should fashion scenes, we (with the painter) shall
In striving to please all, please none at all.
Yet for such faults, as either the writers' wit

Or negligence of the actors do commit,
Both crave your pardons: if what both have done
Cannot full pay your expectation,
The Roaring Girl herself, some few days hence,
Shall on this stage give larger recompense.
Which mirth that you may share in, herself does woo
   you,
30   And craves this sign, your hands to beckon her to you.

FINIS

---

28   humorous: fanciful, whimsical

35–6   The Roaring Girl . . . recompense: generally taken to be
   a reference to an appearance by Mary Frith (the 'real'
   Moll Cutpurse) herself; see Mulholland 1977: 21–2

# Thomas Middleton and William Rowley, *The Changeling*

First performed 1622
First published 1653

There is a profound sense of claustrophobia in *The Changeling*, a play that treats space as a metaphor for the relations between reality and appearance, truth and deception, sanity and madness. Indeed, it may be that the resources of the private theatres (The Phoenix in the case of *The Changeling*) may have encouraged the dramatists who wrote for them to experiment with the increasing complexity of the theatre's facilities (doors, artificial lighting and galleries) as symbolic reference points in their unfolding narratives. Certainly, from the outset, there is an ominous sense that the grandeur of Vermandero's castle (a symbol of rank, familial continuity and moral certainty) may actually constitute an 'outward view' for those on its inside, as well as for those viewing it from a distance. As Vermandero remarks:

> We use not to give survey
> Of our chief strengths to strangers: our citadels
> Are placed conspicuous to outward view
> On promonts' tops, but within are secrets.
> (I.i.166–9)

This sense of airiness, backed by the forceful symbol of the nearby sea, gives way to passages, dungeons, madhouses, chambers and closets. It is as if the castle, with its 'chief strengths', is turned inside out and upside down by the destructive agents of change and transformation that inhabit it.

A 'changeling' was a child left by fairies as a replacement for one they had stolen (or sometimes the stolen child itself) but, by the time of this play, it had become a broad term for those exhibiting mental anxiety or 'abnormality': thus most critics regard the sub-plot's Antonio (who pretends to be a 'natural fool') as the changeling of the title. However, whilst the madhouse scenes show the comic potential of pretence and disguise, they contextualise the sense of psychological change, either pretended or real, in the main plot. As cruel as it is, the madhouse has a rationale for its regime and a taxonomy of its patients (between idiots and lunatics). Those who work there, or enter disguised, proceed to at least some sense of self-awareness and moral resolution at the end of the play.

Nothing is as clear in the society Vermandero presides over, a world of the sudden change-of-heart and its consequences: the sudden desire of Alsemero for Beatrice; her sudden change of attitude to De Flores (a role which she initially only plays but later cannot discard); and the sudden, almost instinctive, recognition by Vermandero that in order to preserve his authority and name, he must turn from paternalism to pragmatism. Thus the play contains a host of 'changeling' figures, and, as Richard Dutton has remarked, 'the essential attribute of "the changeling" is not that of changing, but that of revealing its true nature, in spite of efforts – conscious or otherwise – to conceal them' (Dutton 1999: xxix).

*The Changeling* can be seen as part of the tradition of revenge plays that includes Kyd's *The Spanish Tragedy* (1585) and Shakespeare's *Hamlet* (1600) yet, by the 1620s, the genre itself had undergone a considerable amount of change, so that the frustrated revenger is no longer necessarily the protagonist. Indeed Tomazo's search for justice for his murdered brother, whilst recognisable as a vehicle for showing the narrowness of Vermandero's judgement (IV.ii.23–32), makes less of an impact upon the audience than the central preoccupation with sexual transgression. The complexity of the system of obscene double-meanings in the madhouse scenes alerts us to a no less complex (and only slightly more decorous) code of language at work between Beatrice and De Flores. Here we observe the plurality of language itself; there is precision in these exchanges, yet the precision is in the choice of vocabulary that signifies in a number of areas of meaning simultaneously. A good example of this is with the words 'serve' and 'service' which continually slide between the realms of sexual desire and servitude, realms that mesh in their fateful pact.

Central to this is a reversal of the codes of conduct that early modern ideological mores set out for women and for servants. Beatrice's transgression is compelling because it is so total: she refuses the authority of her father to inflict an unwelcome but 'suitable' husband upon her; she resigns herself to the fate that will be hers for transgressing the law of God (another father); and she chooses De Flores as accomplice and, ultimately, lover. Her clever manipulation of Alsemero's virginity test is perhaps the most novel of her transgressions, since it throws into relief both his self-righteous discourse of 'romantic' love and his contemporary sounding belief in chemistry.

As White (1992) has pointed out, the play dramatises a contemporary preoccupation with the power of passion to overwhelm reason. Francis Bacon wrote in *De Dignitate et Augmentis Scientiarum* (1623) that:

Tigers likewise are kept in the stables of the passions, and at times yoked to their chariot; for when passion ceases to go on foot and comes to ride in its chariot, as in celebration of its victory and triumph over reason, then it is cruel, savage and pitiless towards all that withstand or oppose it.

In a play like *The Changeling*, the cultural institutions which attempted to contain these passions (the family, religion and justice) are exposed and severely questioned. Its Catholic Spanish setting might usefully have distanced Middleton and Rowley from censure over its religious scepticism (only Catholic doctrine drives people towards the random fate of the 'barley-break' game). Its ending secures the dominant culture of male authority and new kinships for old, however unsatisfactory this, and the hollow-sounding Epilogue, may seem to a twenty-first-century audience. What we experience in order to reach that conclusion remains eloquent and disturbing to us, and must surely have invited radical disquiet among seventeenth-century audiences. In this, the play is far removed from the smug moralising of its principal source, John Reynolds's *The Triumphs of God's Revenge against the Crying and Execrable Sin of Wilful and Premeditated Murder* (1621).

## Textual note

The copytext for this edition is the quarto of 1653 (referred to in the footnotes to the text as Q). Copies of the quarto are held in the Bodleian Library in Oxford and the British Library in London and these vary slightly as some of the sheets were corrected during printing. The play was reissued in 1668 with a new title page (by the widow of the original publisher, Humphrey Moseley) but in effect there is only one seventeenth-century edition of the play. The quarto had act divisions but not scene divisions; we have followed the scene structure established by Dyce.

# Further reading

## Editions

Bawcutt, N. W. (ed.) (1958) *The Changeling*, The Revels Plays Series, London: Methuen.

—— (ed.) (1998) *The Changeling*, The Revels Student Editions, Manchester and New York, NY: Manchester University Press.

Black, M. W. (ed.) (1966) *The Changeling*, Philadelphia, PA: University of Pennsylvania.

Daalder, Joost, (ed.) (1990) *The Changeling*, The New Mermaids, London: A. & C. Black.

Dutton, Richard (ed.) (1999) *Thomas Middleton: Women Beware Women and Other Plays*, Oxford World's Classics Series, Oxford: Oxford University Press.

Dyce, Alexander (ed.) (1840) *The Works of Thomas Middleton*, vol. 4, London: Lumley.

Frost, David L. (ed.) (1978) *The Selected Plays of Thomas Middleton*, Cambridge: Cambridge University Press.

Kinney, Arthur F. (ed.) (1999) *Renaissance Drama: An Anthology of Plays and Entertainments*, Oxford: Blackwell.

Loughrey, Brian and Taylor, Neil (eds) (1988) *Thomas Middleton: Five Plays*, Harmondsworth: Penguin.

Sampson, Martin W. (ed.) (1915) *Thomas Middleton*, New York, NY: American Book Company.

Williams, G. W. (ed.) (1966) *The Changeling*, Regents Renaissance Drama Series, Lincoln, NE: University of Nebraska Press.

Wine, M. L. (ed.) (1969) *Drama of the English Renaissance*, Modern Library College Editions, New York, NY: Random House.

## Critical and contextual commentaries

Bromham, A. A. and Bruzzi, Zara (1990) *'The Changeling' and the Years of Crisis, 1619–1624: A Hieroglyph of Britain*, London: Pinter Publishers.

Bueler, Lois E. (1984) 'The Rhetoric of Change in *The Changeling*', *English Literary Renaissance*, 14, 3: 95–113.

Burks, Deborah G. (1995) 'I'll Want My Will Else': *The Changeling* and Women's Complicity with their Rapists', *English Literary History*, 62, 4: 759–90.

Chakravorty, Swapan (1996) *Society and Politics in the Plays of Thomas Middleton*, Oxford: Clarendon Press.

Cherry, Charlotte L. (1973) *The Most Unvaluedst Purchase: Women in the Plays of Thomas Middleton*, Salzburg: Institut für englische Sprache und Literatur, Universität Salzburg.

Craig, T. W. (1977 and 1980), Emendations to *The Changeling, Notes and Queries*, March–April 1977, 120–2; August 1980, 324–7.

Daalder, Joost (1988) 'Folly and Madness in *The Changeling*', *Essays in Criticism*, 38, 1: 1–21.

—— (1992) 'The Role of Isabella in *The Changeling*', *English Studies*, 73, 1: 22–9.

Doob, Penelope B. R. (1973) 'A Reading of *The Changeling*', *English Literary Renaissance*, 3, 1: 183–206.

Heinemann, Margot (1980) *Puritanism and Theatre: Thomas Middleton and Opposition Drama under the Early Stuarts*, Cambridge: Cambridge University Press.

Jackson, K. (1995) 'Bedlam, *The Changeling, The Pilgrim* and

the Protestant Critique of Catholic Good Works',
*Philological Quarterly*, 74, 4: 373–93.

Kowsar, Mohammad (1986) 'Middleton and Rowley's *The
Changeling*: The Besieged Temple', *Criticism*, 28, 2: 145–64.

Malcolmson, Cristina (1990) '"As Tame as the Ladies":
Politics and Gender in *The Changeling*', *English Literary
Renaissance*, 20, 2: 320–39.

Morrison, Peter (1983) 'A Cangoun in Zombieland:
Middleton's Teratological *Changeling*', in Kenneth
Friedenreich (ed.) *'Accompaninge the Players': Essays
Celebrating Thomas Middleton 1580–1980*, New York, NY:
AMS Press.

Randall, D. B. (1984) 'Some Observations on the Theme of
Chastity in *The Changeling*', *English Literary Renaissance*,
14, 3: 347–66.

Simmons, J. L. (1980) 'Diabolical Realism in Middleton and
Rowley's *The Changeling*', *Renaissance Drama*, 11: 135–70.

Slater, A. P. (1983) 'Hypallage, Barley-break, and *The
Changeling*', *The Review of English Studies*, 34: 429–40.

Tricomi, A. H. (1989) *Anticourt Drama in England 1603–1642*,
Charlottesville, VA: University of Virginia Press.

White, Martin (1992) *Middleton and Tourneur*, Basingstoke:
Macmillan.

Wiggins, Martin (1991) *Journeyman in Murder: The Assassin in
English Renaissance Drama*, Oxford: Clarendon Press.

## Works of related interest

Thomas Kyd, *The Spanish Tragedy* (1585)
William Shakespeare, *Titus Andronicus* (1593)
William Shakespeare, *Richard III* (1593)
William Shakespeare, *Romeo and Juliet* (1595)
William Shakespeare, *Hamlet* (1600)
Thomas Middleton or Cyril Tourneur, *The Revenger's Tragedy*
(1606)
George Chapman, *The Revenge of Bussy D'Ambois* (1610)
Cyril Tourneur, *The Atheist's Tragedy* (1611)
John Webster, *The White Devil* (1612)
John Webster, *The Duchess of Malfi* (1614)
Thomas Middleton, *Women Beware Women* (1625)
John Ford, *'Tis Pity She's a Whore* (1633)

# The Changeling (1622)

## Dramatis personae

VERMANDERO, *father to Beatrice*

TOMAZO DE PIRACQUO, *a noble lord*

ALONZO DE PIRACQUO, *his brother, suitor to Beatrice*

ALSEMERO, *a nobleman, afterwards married to Beatrice*

JASPERINO, *his friend*

ALIBIUS, *a jealous doctor*

LOLLIO, *his man*

PEDRO, *friend to Antonio*

ANTONIO, *the changeling*

FRANCISCUS, *the counterfeit madman*

DE FLORES, *servant to Vermandero*

MADMEN

SERVANTS

GENTLEMEN

BEATRICE JOANNA, *daughter to Vermandero*

DIAPHANTA, *her waiting-woman*

ISABELLA, *wife to Alibius*

GENTLEWOMEN

---

Dramatis personae: the names of all the characters except Lollio, Pedro, Antonio and Franciscus can be traced to John Reynolds's *The Triumphs of God's Revenge against the Crying and Execrable Sin of Wilful and Premeditated Murder* (1621)
TOMAZO: possibly derived from the 'doubting Thomas' of the Bible (see John 20.25)
ALIBIUS: (Latin) translates as 'he who is elsewhere'
FRANCISCUS: Frenchman (and therefore, in Elizabethan thinking, licentious)
DE FLORES: a) 'deflower'; b) (ironically) 'of the flowers' (Deflores in Q)
BEATRICE JOANNA: Beatrice means 'she who makes happy' and Joanna means 'the Lord's grace' (both ironic)
DIAPHANTA: a) transparent; b) 'the red-hot one' (with sexual overtones)
ISABELLA: 'God has sworn'

*The scene*

ALICANT

## Act I, scene i

*Enter* ALSEMERO

ALSEMERO 'Twas in the temple where I first beheld her,
　And now again the same. What omen yet
　Follows of that? None but imaginary:
　Why should my hopes of fate be timorous?
　The place is holy, so is my intent:
　I love her beauties to the holy purpose,
　And that, methinks, admits comparison
　With man's first creation, the place blest,
　And is his right home back, if he achieve it.
　The church hath first begun our interview,　　**10**
　And that's the place must join us into one
　So there's beginning, and perfection too.

*Enter* JASPERINO

JASPERINO O sir, are you here? Come, the wind's fair
　　with you;
　Y'are like to have a swift and pleasant passage.
ALSEMERO Sure y'are deceived, friend; 'tis contrary
　In my best judgement.
JASPERINO　　　　　　What, for Malta?
　If you could buy a gale amongst the witches
　They could not serve you such a lucky pennyworth
　As comes a' God's name.

---

ALICANT: Alicante, a seaport on the east coast of Spain
6　the holy purpose: i.e. marriage
8　the place blest: Eden (the place man lost through disobedience to God but that can be regained through marriage)
10　interview: meeting
12　perfection: wedlock (as the completion of a circle)
14　like: likely
17　If you . . . the witches: referring to the belief that witches could sell winds
18　pennyworth: bargain
19　a' God's name: in God's name, and naturally (as opposed to a bargain struck with witches)

ALSEMERO             Even now I observed
The temple's vane to turn full in my face;      **20**
I know it is against me.
JASPERINO           Against you?
Then you know not where you are.
ALSEMERO            Not well, indeed.
JASPERINO   Are you not well, sir?
ALSEMERO           Yes, Jasperino;
Unless there be some hidden malady
Within me that I understand not.
JASPERINO          And that
I begin to doubt, sir. I never knew
Your inclinations to travels at a pause,
With any cause to hinder it, till now.
Ashore you were wont to call your servants up,
And help to trap your horses for the speed;     **30**
At sea I have seen you weigh the anchor with 'em,
Hoist sails for fear to lose the foremost breath,
Be in continual prayers for fair winds:
And have you changed your orisons?
ALSEMERO          No, friend,
I keep the same church, same devotion.
JASPERINO   Lover I'm sure y'are none, the stoic was
Found in you long ago; your mother nor
Best friends, who have set snares of beauty (ay,
And choice ones, too), could never trap you that way.
What might be the cause?
ALSEMERO         Lord, how violent    **40**
Thou art! I was but meditating of
Somewhat I heard within the temple.
JASPERINO           Is this
Violence? 'Tis but idleness compared
With your haste yesterday.
ALSEMERO   I'm all this while a-going, man.

*Enter* SERVANTS

JASPERINO   Backwards, I think, sir. Look, your servants.
1 SERVANT   The seamen call; shall we board your
trunks?
ALSEMERO   No, not today.

JASPERINO           'Tis the critical day,
It seems, and the sign in Aquarius.        **50**
2 SERVANT   (*Aside*) We must not to sea today; this
smoke will bring forth fire!
ALSEMERO   Keep all on shore; I do not know the end,
Which needs I must do, of an affair in hand
Ere I can go to sea.
1 SERVANT   Well, your pleasure.
2 SERVANT   (*Aside*) Let him e'en take his leisure too; we
are safer on land.        *Exeunt* SERVANTS

*Enter* BEATRICE, DIAPHANTA, *and* SERVANTS. ALSEMERO
*greets* BEATRICE *and kisses her*

JASPERINO   (*Aside*) How now! The laws of the Medes
are changed, sure! Salute a woman? He kisses too.
Wonderful! Where learnt he this? And does it
perfectly too; in my conscience, he ne'er rehearsed it
before. Nay, go on; this will be stranger and better
news at Valencia than if he had ransomed half
Greece from the Turk.        **65**
BEATRICE   You are a scholar, sir?
ALSEMERO           A weak one, lady.
BEATRICE   Which of the sciences is this love you speak
of?
ALSEMERO   From your tongue I take it to be music.
BEATRICE   You are skilful in't, can sing at first sight.
ALSEMERO   And I have showed you all my skill at once.
I want more words to express me further,     **71**
And must be forced to repetition:
I love you dearly.
BEATRICE        Be better advised, sir.
Our eyes are sentinels unto our judgements,
And should give certain judgement what they see;
But they are rash sometimes, and tell us wonders

---

20   The temple's . . . my face: the weather vane ironically and
ominously turns against Alsemero, despite the 'fair
weather' reported by Jasperino
26   doubt: fear, suspect
30   to trap . . . the speed: 'to put harnesses on your horses to
increase their speed'
31   'em: servants (or crew)
34   orisons: prayers
35   church, same devotion: manner, outlook (possibly with
Beatrice in mind rather than the prayers)
36   stoic: a person undisturbed by emotion
38   snares: traps (for animals)
40   violent: obsessively concerned
42   Somewhat: something
47   board: put on board

49   critical: crucial (in astrology)
50   Aquarius: the water-carrier; the sun has entered the sign
of the zodiac thought to favour sea voyages
51–2   this smoke . . . forth fire!: from the proverbial expression
'there's no smoke without fire' (fire in this case being
Alsemero's sexual passion)
56   your pleasure: as you please
59   the laws . . . the Medes: laws that were supposed to be
unalterable (see Daniel 6.8)
60   Salute: greet with a kiss
62   in my conscience: truthfully, upon my word (colloquial)
64   Valencia: Alsemero's home, another Spanish port
64–5   if he . . . the Turk: Greece had been under Turkish rule
since 1460
57   sciences: branches of learning, including the arts
69   sing at first sight: sight-read music (but also, perhaps,
referring to love at first sight)
71   want: lack
74–8   Our eyes . . . them blind: Beatrice warns against the
irrationality (or 'blindness') that can be caused by 'our
eyes' (sexual arousal)

Of common things, which when our judgements find,
They can then check the eyes, and call them blind.
ALSEMERO But I am further, lady: yesterday
 Was mine eyes' employment, and hither now  **80**
 They brought my judgement, where are both agreed.
 Both houses then consenting, 'tis agreed;
 Only there wants the confirmation
 By the hand royal—that is your part, lady.
BEATRICE O there's one above me, sir. (*Aside*) For five
 days past
 To be recalled! Sure, mine eyes were mistaken:
 This was the man was meant me. That he should come
 So near his time and miss it!  **88**
JASPERINO (*Aside*) We might have come by the carriers
 from Valencia, I see, and saved all our sea-provision;
 we are at farthest, sure. Methinks I should do
 something too—I meant to be a venturer in this
 voyage. Yonder's another vessel; I'll board her. If she
 be lawful prize, down goes her top-sail.
       *Greets* DIAPHANTA

*Enter* DE FLORES

DE FLORES Lady, your father—
BEATRICE       Is in health, I hope.
DE FLORES Your eye shall instantly instruct you, lady.
 He's coming hitherward.
BEATRICE      What needed then
 Your duteous preface? I had rather
 He had come unexpected: you must stall
 A good presence with unnecessary blabbing,  **100**

And how welcome for your part you are
I'm sure you know.
DE FLORES (*Aside*)  Will't never mend, this scorn,
 One side nor other? Must I be enjoined
 To follow still whilst she flies from me? Well,
 Fates, do your worst; I'll please myself with sight
 Of her, at all opportunities,
 If but to spite her anger. I know she had
 Rather see me dead than living—and yet
 She knows no cause for't but a peevish will.
ALSEMERO You seemed displeased, lady, on the
 sudden.  **110**
BEATRICE Your pardon, sir; 'tis my infirmity.
 Nor can I other reason render you
 Than his or hers, of some particular thing
 They must abandon as a deadly poison
 Which to a thousand other tastes were wholesome.
 Such to mine eyes is that same fellow there,
 The same that report speaks of, the basilisk.
ALSEMERO This is a frequent frailty in our nature.
 There's scarce a man amongst a thousand found
 But hath his imperfection: one distastes  **120**
 The scent of roses, which to infinites
 Most pleasing is, and odoriferous;
 One oil, the enemy of poison;
 Another wine, the cheerer of the heart
 And lively refresher of the countenance.
 Indeed this fault, if so it be, is general:
 There's scarce a thing but is both loved and loathed.
 Myself, I must confess, have the same frailty.
BEATRICE And what may be your poison, sir? I am
 bold with you.
ALSEMERO What might be your desire perhaps: a cherry.
BEATRICE I am no enemy to any creature  **131**
 My memory has but yon gentleman.
ALSEMERO He does ill to tempt your sight, if he knew it.
BEATRICE He cannot be ignorant of that, sir:

---

77 Of: about
78 check: restrain
78–81 But I . . . both agreed: Alesmero says that he is further
 advanced than the state Beatrice described, having used
 his eyes yesterday and his judgement today, and finding
 that the two agree
82–4 Both houses . . . hand royal: 'The metaphor is legislative;
 both house of parliament (the sense and the intellect)
 have approved the bill; it now needs only the queen's
 signature to make it law' (Williams)
85 one above me: her father Vermandero (but also implying
 that he is god-like in his authority)
85–6 For five . . . be recalled: she wishes the five days of her
 engagement to Alonzo could be rescinded
89 the carriers: land transport
91 at farthest: a) most distant from our destination;
 b) neglectful of our purpose
92 venturer: one who shares business risks and profits
93–4 Yonder's another . . . top-sail: Diaphanta is seen as a
 ship that can be 'boarded' (with sexual symbolism); if she
 is 'lawful prize' (single) she will lower her topsail in
 surrender, as must a vessel at sea that no regulation
 prohibits from capturing
99 stall: forestall
100 A good presence: i.e. Vermandero
 blabbing: babbling

103 One side nor other?: whatever I do
104 still: all the time
107 to spite her anger: in compensation for frustrated desire
109 peevish: perverse
112 render: give
113 his or hers: 'that which anyone could give'
114 abandon: reject
117 report: rumour
 basilisk: a fabulous reptile whose breath and glance were
 deadly
120 distastes: has a distaste for
121 infinites: an infinite number of people (i.e. the vast
 majority)
122 odoriferous: fragrant
123 oil: a laxative (to flush out poison)
125 countenance: face, demeanour, but here 'outlook' or spirits
130 a cherry: Alsemero chooses something considered trivial
132 yon gentleman: De Flores
133 tempt: makes trial of

I have not spared to tell him so; and I want
To help myself, since he's a gentleman
In good respect with my father, and follows him.

ALSEMERO  He's out of his place then now.

*They talk apart*

JASPERINO  I am a mad wag, wench.    **139**

DIAPHANTA  So methinks; but for your comfort I can
tell you we have a doctor in the city that undertakes
the cure of such.

JASPERINO  Tush, I know what physic is best for the
state of mine own body.

DIAPHANTA  'Tis scarce a well-governed state, I believe.

JASPERINO  I could show thee such a thing with an
ingredient that we two would compound together,
and if it did not tame the maddest blood i'th'town for
two hours after, I'll ne'er profess physic again.    **149**

DIAPHANTA  A little poppy, sir, were good to cause you
sleep.

JASPERINO  Poppy? I'll give thee a pop i'th'lips for that
first, and begin there (*Kisses her*): poppy is one simple
indeed, and cuckoo what-you-call't another. I'll
discover no more now; another time I'll show thee all.

BEATRICE  My father, sir.

*Enter* VERMANDERO *and* SERVANTS

VERMANDERO             O Joanna, I came to meet thee.
Your devotion's ended?

BEATRICE                        For this time, sir.
(*Aside*) I shall change my saint, I fear me; I find

A giddy turning in me. (*To* VERMANDERO) Sir, this
while
I am beholding to this gentleman             **160**
Who left his own way to keep me company,
And in discourse I find him much desirous
To see your castle. He hath deserved it, sir,
If ye please to grant it.

VERMANDERO             With all my heart, sir.
Yet there's an article between: I must know
Your country. We use not to give survy
Of our chief strengths to strangers: our citadels
Are placed conspicuous to outward view
On promonts' tops, but within are secrets.

ALSEMERO  A Valencian, sir.

VERMANDERO             A Valencian?             **170**
That's native, sir. Of what name, I beseech you?

ALSEMERO  Alsemero, sir.

VERMANDERO             Alsemero? Not the son
Of John de Alsemero?

ALSEMERO             The same, sir.

VERMANDERO  My best love bids you welcome.

BEATRICE  (*Aside*)                        He was wont
To call me so, and then he speaks a most
Unfeignèd truth.

VERMANDERO             O sir, I knew your father;
We two were in acquaintance long ago
Before our chins were worth Iulan down,
And so continued till the stamp of time
Had coined us into silver. Well, he's gone;             **180**
A good soldier went with him.

ALSEMERO  You went together in that, sir.

VERMANDERO  No, by Saint Jaques; I came behind him.
Yet I have done somewhat too. An unhappy day
Swallowed him at last at Gibraltar
In fight with those rebellious Hollanders,

---

135  want: have need
137  respect: repute
      follows him: is one of his retainers
138  out of his place: a) not acting according to his social
      station; b) 'he should not be here'
139  mad wag: '"uncontrolled by reason", and specifically
      "sexually infatuated"' (Daalder)
      wench: young woman
141  a doctor: i.e. Alibius
143  physic: medicine (but with sexual overtones)
144  state: condition
145  state: a) condition; b) body politic (which should be
      governed more rationally)
146  thing: a) the remedy for the poorly governed state;
      b) copulation (slang)
147  ingredient: mixture of semen and ovaries
      compound: mix (with pestle and mortar, a sexual image)
148  blood: (sexual) passion
150  poppy: opium (made from poppy seeds)
      sleep: could also mean copulate
152  pop i'th'lips: thrust in the lips (with play on the 'lips' of
      the vagina)
154  cuckoo what-you-call't: cuckoo-pintle (wild flower
      shaped like a penis) with play on 'cuckoo' as madness
      discover: reveal
157  devotion: act of worship
158  change my saint: pray to a new 'saint' i.e. Alsemero

159  giddy turning: a) feeling of dizziness; b) a sensation of
      madness
160  beholding: indebted
165  article between: stipulation, condition
166  use not: are unaccustomed
167  strengths: fortifications
169  promonts: promontories
      secrets: ironic in view of Alsemero's real interest (in
      Beatrice) and what is to unfold later in the play
171  native: i.e. Valencia is in the same region as Alicant (and
      thus no potential enemy)
174–6  He was . . . Unfeignèd truth: Vermandero used to call
      Beatrice 'best love'
178  Iulan: adjective denoting youth (from Iulus Ascanius, the
      son of Aeneas in Virgil's *Aeneid*)
180  coined us into silver: turned us grey
182  went together: were his equal
183  Saint Jacques: St James of Compostela, the patron saint
      of Spain
185  Gibraltar: the Spanish were defeated by the Dutch at the
      Battle of Gibraltar on 25 April 1607

Was it not so?

ALSEMERO       Whose death I had revenged,
Or followed him in fate, had not the late league
Prevented me.

VERMANDERO     Ay, ay, 'twas time to breathe.—
O Joanna, I should ha' told thee news:     **190**
I saw Piracquo lately.

BEATRICE (*Aside*)     That's ill news.

VERMANDERO He's hot preparing for his day of triumph:
Thou must be a bride within this sevennight.

ALSEMERO (*Aside*)     Ha!

BEATRICE Nay, good sir, be not so violent; with speed
I cannot render satisfaction
Unto the dear companion of my soul,
Virginity, whom I thus long have lived with,
And part with it so rude and suddenly.
Can such friends divide, never to meet again,
Without a solemn farewell?

VERMANDERO     Tush, tush, there's a toy.

ALSEMERO (*Aside*) I must now part, and never meet
again     **201**
With any joy on earth. (*To* VERMANDERO) Sir, your
pardon;
My affairs call on me.

VERMANDERO     How, sir? By no means;
Not changed so soon, I hope. You must see my castle,
And her best entertainment, ere we part;
I shall think myself unkindly us'd else.
Come, come, let's on. I had good hope your stay
Had been a while with us in Alicant:
I might have bid you to my daughter's wedding.

ALSEMERO (*Aside*) He means to feast me, and poisons
me beforehand.     **210**
(*To* VERMANDERO) I should be dearly glad to be
there, sir,
Did my occasions suit as I could wish.

BEATRICE I shall be sorry if you be not there
When it is done, sir;—but not so suddenly.

VERMANDERO I tell you, sir, the gentleman's complete,
A courier and a gallant, enriched
With many fair and noble ornaments.

I would not change him, for a son-in-law,
For any he in Spain, the proudest he;
And we have great ones, that you know.

ALSEMERO     He's much
Bound to you, sir.

VERMANDERO     He shall be bound to me   **221**
As fast as this tie can hold him; I'll want
My will else.

BEATRICE (*Aside*) I shall want mine if you do it.

VERMANDERO But come, by the way I'll tell you more
of him.

ALSEMERO (*Aside*) How shall I dare to venture in his
castle,
When he discharges murderers at the gate?
But I must on, for back I cannot go.

BEATRICE (*Aside*) Not this serpent gone yet?

          *Drops a glove*

VERMANDERO     Look, girl, thy glove's fall'n.
Stay, stay.—De Flores, help a little.

    *Exeunt* VERMANDERO, ALSEMERO, JASPERINO, *and*
                 SERVANTS

DE FLORES     Here lady. *Offers the glove*

BEATRICE Mischief on your officious forwardness!   **230**
Who bade you stoop? They touch my hand no more:
There, for t'other's sake I part with this—

    *Takes off and throws down the other glove*

Take 'em and draw thine own skin off with 'em.

    *Exeunt* BEATRICE, DIAPHANTA, *and* SERVANTS

DE FLORES Here's a favour come, with a mischief! Now
I know
She had rather wear my pelt tanned in a pair
Of dancing pumps than I should thrust my fingers
Into her sockets here. I know she hates me,

---

187 had: would have

188 late league: a truce was signed in 1609

189 'twas time to breathe: 'the truce put a pause to hostilities;
an English audience would have wished Spain defeated'
(Kinney)

192 hot: ardent (with sexual overtone)
day of triumph: wedding day

200 toy: trifle

210 He means . . . me beforehand: Vermandero invites
Alsemero to a feast, but has poisoned him already with
the news of the wedding

214 suddenly: soon

215 complete: perfect

216 gallant: accomplished lover

219 he: man

221 Bound: a) indebted; b) tied

222 want: not have

223 want mine: lack my desire

226 murderers: small cannon (metaphor for the idea that
Alsemero is 'killed' by talking further about Alonzo)

228 this serpent: i.e. De Flores, as either a venomous reptile
(as in the basilisk mentioned at I.i.117) or as the serpent
in the Garden of Eden, the tempter of Eve.
glove's fall'n: a) as a love token for Alsemero; b) acci-
dentally; c) unconsciously (for De Flores) 'prompted by
her response to De Flores at a deep sexual level' (Daalder)

229 Stay, stay: spoken to Beatrice

233 draw thine own skin off: a) a reference to De Flores's
ugly skin; b) another reference to his serpent-like
qualities (as snakes shed their old skins for new ones)

234 favour: love token
mischief: sign of disfavour

235 pelt: skin

236 pumps: shoes
fingers: metaphorically, his penis

237 sockets: the finger-holes of the gloves (but
metaphorically her vagina)

Yet cannot choose but love her.
No matter: if but to vex her I'll haunt her still;
Though I get nothing else, I'll have my will.          240

*Exit*

# Act I, scene ii

*Enter* ALIBIUS *and* LOLLIO

ALIBIUS  Lollio, I must trust thee with a secret,
   But thou must keep it.
LOLLIO  I was ever close to a secret, sir.
ALIBIUS  The diligence that I have found in thee,
   The care and industry already past,
   Assures me of thy good continuance.
   Lollio, I have a wife.
LOLLIO  Fie, sir, 'tis too late to keep her secret; she's
   known to be married all the town and country over.
ALIBIUS  Thou goest too fast, my Lollio. That
      knowledge          10
   I allow no man can be barred it;
   But there is a knowledge which is nearer,
   Deeper and sweeter, Lollio.
LOLLIO  Well, sir, let us handle that between you and I.
ALIBIUS  'Tis that I go about, man. Lollio,
   My wife is young.
LOLLIO  So much the worse to be kept secret, sir.
ALIBIUS  Why, now thou meet'st the substance of the
      point:
   I am old, Lollio.
LOLLIO  No, sir, 'tis I am old Lollio.          20
ALIBIUS  Yet why may not this concord and
      sympathize?
   Old trees and young plants often grow together,
   Well enough agreeing.
LOLLIO  Ay, sir, but the old trees raise themselves
   higher and broader than the young plants.
ALIBIUS  Shrewd application! There's the fear, man.

I would wear my ring on my own finger;
   Whilst it is borrowed it is none of mine,
   But his that useth it.
LOLLIO  You must keep it on still then; if it but lie by,
   one or other will be thrusting into't.          31
ALIBIUS  Thou conceiv'st me, Lollio; here thy watchful
      eye
   Must have employment. I cannot always be
   At home.
LOLLIO  I dare swear you cannot.
ALIBIUS  I must look out.
LOLLIO  I know't, you must look out; 'tis every man's
   case.
ALIBIUS  Here I do say must thy employment be:
   To watch her treadings, and in my absence
   Supply my place.          40
LOLLIO  I'll do my best, sir; yet surely I cannot see who
   you should have cause to be jealous of.
ALIBIUS  Thy reason for that, Lollio? 'Tis a comfortable
   question.
LOLLIO  We have but two sorts of people in the house,
   and both under the whip: that's fools and madmen.
   The one has not wit enough to be knaves, and the
   other not knavery enough to be fools.
ALIBIUS  Ay, those are all my patients, Lollio.
   I do profess the cure of either sort;
   My trade, my living 'tis, I thrive by it.          50
   But here's the care that mixes with my thrift:
   The daily visitants, that come to see
   My brainsick patients, I would not have
   To see my wife. Gallants I do observe
   Of quick enticing eyes, rich in habits,

---

239  if but to vex her: even if sexually frustrated, he intends to
   find satisfaction in harassing her
3  close to a secret: a) able to conceal a secret; b) close to a
   private part (i.e. lustful)
8  keep her secret: a) keep her status as a wife secret;
   b) preserve her private part
11  allow: admit
12  knowledge: carnal knowledge
14  handle: manage (with sexual overtones)
15  'Tis that I go about: that is exactly my point
18  now thou . . . the point: Alibius thinks Lollio means that
   it is difficult to keep a young wife concealed; Lollio has
   actually implied that she should not be
21  this: i.e this kind of marriage
24–5  Ay, sir . . . young plants: the tree might rise higher by
   having the horns of a cuckold (i.e. one betrayed by
   unfaithfulness)
26  Shrewd: accurate, if painful

27  ring: a) wedding ring; b) vagina (slang)
   finger: could also represent the penis (slang)
32  conceiv'st: understand
33  employment: could also mean copulation (slang)
34  At home: could also mean 'in my wife's vagina'
   (slang)
36  look out: a) be vigilant; b) go away (on business, although
   the term could also refer to brief sexual adventures, as
   Lollio implies)
37  case: a) plight; b) vagina; c) brothel
39  treadings: a) movements; b) sexual acts
40  Supply my place: a) act as supervisor b) (as Lollio sees it)
   have intercourse with her on Alibius's behalf
42  jealous: suspicious
43  comfortable: comforting
45  fools: imbeciles
51  care: responsibility
   thrift: profit
52  daily visitants: those who come to view the inmates for
   entertainment, as at Bethlehem Hospital (Bedlam) in
   London
   see: 'often used with innuendo – "for sexual purposes"'
   (Daalder)
55  habits: clothes

Of stature and proportion very comely:
These are most shrewd temptations, Lollio.

LOLLIO They may be easily answered, sir. If they come
to see the fools and madmen, you and I may serve the
turn, and let my mistress alone; she's of neither sort.

ALIBIUS 'Tis a good ward; indeed, come they to see    61
Our madmen or our fools, let 'em see no more
Than what they come for. By that consequent
They must not see her: I'm sure she's no fool.

LOLLIO And I'm sure she's no madman.

ALIBIUS Hold that buckler fast, Lollio; my trust
Is on thee, and I account it firm and strong.
What hour is't, Lollio?

LOLLIO Towards belly-hour, sir.

ALIBIUS Dinner time? Thou mean'st twelve o'clock?    70

LOLLIO Yes, sir, for every part has his hour. We wake
at six and look about us, that's eye-hour; at seven we
should pray, that's knee-hour; at eight walk, that's
leg-hour; at nine gather flowers and pluck a rose,
that's nose-hour; at ten we drink, that's mouth-hour;
at eleven lay about us for victuals, that's hand-hour;
at twelve go to dinner, that's belly-hour.

ALIBIUS Profoundly, Lollio! It will be long
Ere all thy scholars learn this lesson, and
I did look to have a new one ent'red;—stay,    80
I think my expectation is come home.

*Enter* PEDRO, *and* ANTONIO *like an idiot*

PEDRO Save you, sir. My business speaks itself:
This sight takes off the labour of my tongue.

ALIBIUS Ay, ay, sir,
'Tis plain enough; you mean him for my patient.

PEDRO And if your pains prove but commodious, to
give but some little strength to the sick and weak part
of nature in him, these are (*Gives money*) but patterns
to show you of the whole pieces that will follow to

you, beside the charge of diet, washing, and other
necessaries fully defrayed.    **91**

ALIBIUS Believe it, sir, there shall no care be wanting.

LOLLIO Sir, an officer in this place may deserve
something: the trouble will pass through my hands.

PEDRO 'Tis fit something should come to your hands
then, sir.                              *Gives him money*

LOLLIO Yes, sir, 'tis I must keep him sweet and read to
him. What is his name?

PEDRO His name is Antonio. Marry, we use but half to
him, only Tony.    **100**

LOLLIO Tony, Tony; 'tis enough, and a very good name
for a fool.—What's your name, Tony?

ANTONIO He, he, he! Well, I thank you, cousin! He,
he, he!

LOLLIO Good boy! Hold up your head.—He can laugh:
I perceive by that he is no beast.

PEDRO Well, sir,
If you can raise him but to any height,
Any degree of wit—might he attain
(As I might say) to creep but on all four    **110**
Towards the chair of wit, or walk on crutches,
'Twould add an honour to your worthy pains,
And a great family might pray for you,
To which he should be heir, had he discretion
To claim and guide his own; assure you, sir,
He is a gentleman.

LOLLIO Nay, there's nobody doubted that; at first sight
I knew him for a gentleman—he looks no other yet.

PEDRO Let him have good attendance and sweet
lodging.    **120**

LOLLIO As good as my mistress lies in, sir; and, as you
allow us time and means, we can raise him to the
higher degree of discretion.

PEDRO Nay, there shall no cost want, sir.

LOLLIO He will hardly be stretched up to the wit of a
magnifico.

PEDRO O no, that's not to be expected—far shorter will
be enough.

---

57  shrewd: subtle, hard to resist
59–60  serve the turn: 'be adequate' (said as a joke)
61  ward: guard (from fencing)
63  consequent: logic
64  I'm sure she's no fool: Alibius is in charge of lunatics and
     Lollio of fools; each knows only his own kind of inmate
66  buckler: shield
71  his: its
74  pluck a rose: a) urinate (most eds); b) euphemism for
     defecate (Wine)
76  lay about us for victuals: look around for provisions
SD  *like an idiot*: presumably dressed in a long coat and
     pointed cap. Directors of the play need to establish
     whether or not the audience should be aware from the
     start of Antonio's delusion
82  Save you: God save you (a common greeting)
83  takes off: removes
86  commodious: beneficial
88  patterns: samples (small coins)
89  whole pieces: substantial coins

97  sweet: clean
100  Tony: common name for a 'fool'
106  no beast: it was believed that the ability to laugh
      distinguished humans from animals
107–16  Pedro hopes that Lollio will help raise Antonio's 'wit'
      (understanding) to the point where he would be of
      financial benefit since he would be able to 'claim and
      guide' his own estate using his own 'discretion'
      (judgement)
118  he looks no other yet: a) his disguise can be seen through;
      b) he is not yet a true fool
124  there shall no cost want: all necessary payment will be
      made
125  hardly: with difficulty
      stretched up: advanced to
126  magnifico: magistrate (one with judgement)

LOLLIO I warrant you I'll make him fit to bear office in five weeks; I'll undertake to wind him up to the wit of constable. **131**

PEDRO If it be lower than that it might serve turn.

LOLLIO No, fie, to level him with a headborough, beadle, or watchman were but little better than he is; constable I'll able him. If he do come to be a justice afterwards, let him thank the keeper. Or I'll go further with you—say I do bring him up to my own pitch, say I make him as wise as myself.

PEDRO Why, there I would have it.

LOLLIO Well, go to; either I'll be as arrant a fool as he, or he shall be as wise as I, and then I think 'twill serve his turn. **142**

PEDRO Nay, I do like thy wit passing well.

LOLLIO Yes, you may. Yet if I had not been a fool, I had had more wit than I have too: remember what state you find me in.

PEDRO I will, and so leave you. Your best cares, I beseech you. *Exit* PEDRO

ALIBIUS Take you none with you; leave 'em all with us.

ANTONIO O my cousin's gone! Cousin, cousin, O! **150**

LOLLIO Peace, peace, Tony! You must not cry, child— you must be whipped if you do. Your cousin is here still: I am your cousin, Tony.

ANTONIO He, he! Then I'll not cry, if thou be'st my cousin! He, he, he!

LOLLIO I were best try his wit a little, that I may know what form to place him in.

ALIBIUS Ay, do, Lollio, do.

LOLLIO I must ask him easy questions at first.—Tony, how many true fingers has a tailor on his right hand?

ANTONIO As many as on his left, cousin. **161**

LOLLIO Good. And how many on both?

ANTONIO Two less than a deuce, cousin.

LOLLIO Very well answered. I come to you again, cousin Tony. How many fools goes to a wise man?

ANTONIO Forty in a day sometimes, cousin.

LOLLIO Forty in a day? How prove you that?

ANTONIO All that fall out amongst themselves, and go to a lawyer to be made friends. **169**

LOLLIO A parlous fool! He must sit in the fourth form at least, I perceive that.—I come again, Tony. How many knaves make an honest man?

ANTONIO I know not that, cousin.

LOLLIO No, the question is too hard for you. I'll tell you, cousin: there's three knaves may make an honest man—a sergeant, a jailor, and a beadle. The sergeant catches him, the jailor holds him. and the beadle lashes him. And if he be not honest then, the hangman must cure him.

ANTONIO Ha, ha, ha! That's fine sport, cousin! **180**

ALIBIUS This was too deep a question for the fool, Lollio.

LOLLIO Yes, this might have served yourself, though I say't. Once more, and you shall go play, Tony.

ANTONIO Ay, play at push-pin, cousin, ha, he!

LOLLIO So thou shalt. Say how many fools are here.

ANTONIO Two, cousin: thou and I.

LOLLIO Nay, y'are too forward there, Tony. Mark my question: how many fools and knaves are here? A fool before a knave, a fool behind a knave, between every two fools a knave: how many fools, how many knaves?

ANTONIO I never learnt so far, cousin. **192**

ALIBIUS Thou putt'st too hard questions to him, Lollio.

LOLLIO I'll make him understand it easily.—Cousin, stand there.

ANTONIO Ay, cousin.

LOLLIO Master, stand you next the fool.

ALIBIUS Well, Lollio?

LOLLIO Here's my place. Mark now, Tony, there's a fool before a knave. **200**

ANTONIO That's I, cousin.

LOLLIO Here's a fool behind a knave, that's I; and

---

131 constable: constables were proverbially stupid
133 headborough: petty constable
134 beadle: parish constable
  watchman: constable of the watch
135 able him: make him fit for
  justice: also seen as stupid
138 pitch: level
140 go to: common expression of astonishment
  arrant: unmitigated, wandering
142 serve his turn: be sufficient
143 passing: extremely
146 state: a) condition; b) position (as keeper of fools) that erodes one's wits, and would only have been chosen by a fool in the first place
150 cousin: term for any close relative or friend
156 try: test
157 form: class in school
160 true: honest (tailors were considered dishonest)
163 Two less than a deuce: i.e. none

165 goes to: a) make up; b) visit
168–9 All that . . . made friends: only fools think that lawyers would help since, in fact, they prolong litigation in the pursuit of profit
170 parlous: perilous, dangerously cunning
172 make: a) make up; b) create
180 sport: entertainment (both the description of the knave's plight and Lollio's rendering of it)
183 served yourself: 'been appropriate for you'
185 push-pin: a children's game (but here with sexual connotations)
188 forward: eager
189–91 A fool . . . many knaves: the actors must stand in order with Alibius in the middle
201 That's I: Antonio is supposed to be a fool and the configuration turns Alibius into a knave

between us two fools there is a knave, that's my
master. 'Tis but we three, that's all.

ANTONIO We three, we three, cousin! MADMEN *within*

1 MADMAN (*within*) Put's head i'th'pillory, the bread's
too little.

2 MADMAN (*within*) Fly, fly, and he catches the swallow.

3 MADMAN (*within*) Give her more onion, or the devil
put the rope about her crag.                               210

LOLLIO You may hear what time of day it is: the
chimes of Bedlam goes.

ALIBIUS Peace, peace, or the wire comes!

3 MADMAN (*within*) Cat-whore, cat-whore, her
permasant, her permasant.

ALIBIUS Peace, I say!—Their hour's come; they must
be fed, Lollio.

LOLLIO There's no hope of recovery of that Welsh
madman was undone by a mouse that spoiled him a
permasant; lost his wits for't.                             220

ALIBIUS Go you to your charge, Lollio; I'll to mine.

LOLLIO Go you to your madmen's ward; let me alone
with your fools.

ALIBIUS And remember my last charge, Lollio.    *Exit*

LOLLIO Of which your patients do you think I am?—
Come, Tony, you must amongst your school-fellows
now. There's pretty scholars amongs'em, I can tell
you; there's some of 'em at *stultus, stulta, stultum.*

ANTONIO I would see the madmen, cousin, if they
would not bite me.                                         230

LOLLIO No, they shall not bite thee, Tony.

---

204  we three: 'a common joke on a picture of two fools called
"we three" to include the spectator' (Kinney)
206  pillory: wooden frame with holes for hands and feet used
as a public punishment
bread's too little: provisions are short
208  Fly, fly . . . the swallow: something seems possible that is
not (proverbial)
209  Give her more onion: Give me more onion (an urgent
demand for food from the proverb: 'if thou hast not a
capon feed on an onion')
rope: noose. The 'her' for 'me' is stage Welsh
210  crag: neck
212  chimes of Bedlam: the inmates' cries for food
213  the wire: whips (made of wire)
214  Cat-whore . . . permasant: the cat behaves like a whore
because it allows a mouse to eat his ('her') cheese
215  permasant: Parmesan cheese
218–19  Welsh madman: a seventeenth-century audience would
have associated the Welsh with a fondness for cheese
221  charge: duty
224  my last charge: 'my last instruction' (i.e. to spy on
Isabella)
225  Of which: of which kind (i.e. fool or madman)
227  pretty: clever
228  Some of . . . *stulta, stultum*: some of the patients can
decline the Latin word for stupid
230  bite: could also mean 'steal from'

ANTONIO They bite when they are at dinner, do they
not, coz?

LOLLIO They bite at dinner indeed, Tony. Well, I hope
to get credit by thee; I like thee the best of all the
scholars that ever I brought up, and thou shalt prove
a wise man, or I'll prove a fool myself.

*Exeunt*

# Act II, scene i

*Enter* BEATRICE *and* JASPERINO *severally*

BEATRICE O sir, I am ready now for that fair service
Which makes the name of friend sit glorious on you!
Good angels and this conduct be your guide.
*Gives a paper*
Fitness of time and place is there set down, sir.

JASPERINO The joy I shall return rewards my service.
*Exit*

BEATRICE How wise is Alsemero in his friend!
It is a sign he makes his choice with judgement.
Then I appear in nothing more approved
Than making choice of him;
For 'tis a principle, he that can choose            10
That bosom well who of his thoughts partakes,
Proves most discreet in every choice he makes.
Methinks I love now with the eyes of judgement,
And see the way to merit, clearly see it.
A true deserver like a diamond sparkles;
In darkness you may see him, that's in absence,
Which is the greatest darkness falls on love:
Yet is he best discerned then,
With intellectual eyesight. What's Piracquo
My father spends his breath for? And his blessing  20
Is only mine as I regard his name;
Else it goes from me, and turns head against me,
Transformed into a curse. Some speedy way
Must be rememb'red—he's so forward too,
So urgent that way, scarce allows me breath
To speak to my new comforts.

---

232  coz: cousin
3  conduct: sheet of paper with directions
5  return: take back to Alsemero
8  approved: justified
11  bosom: intimate friend
14  to: to recognize
15  diamond: diamonds were thought to be luminous
17  falls: that falls
20–1  And his . . . his name: Vermandero's blessing will only
be given to a marriage that maintains the family's name
and reputation
22  turns head: directs its power
24  rememb'red: brought to mind
he's so forward: Vermandero is so eager, impatient
26  speak to . . . new comforts: address the new joys that
Alsemero's love has brought

*Enter* DE FLORES

DE FLORES (*Aside*)                                     Yonder's she.
  Whatever ails me, now a-late especially
  I can as well be hanged as refrain seeing her.
  Some twenty times a day, nay not so little,
  Do I force errands, frame ways and excuses          30
  To come into her sight—and I have small reason
    for't,
  And less encouragement: for she baits me still
  Every time worse than other, does profess herself
  The cruellest enemy to my face in town,
  At no hand can abide the sight of me,
  As if danger or ill luck hung in my looks.
  I must confess my face is bad enough,
  But I know far worse has better fortune,
  And not endured alone, but doted on:
  And yet such pick-haired faces, chins like witches', 40
  Here and there five hairs, whispering in a corner
  As if they grew in fear one of another,
  Wrinkles like troughs, where swine-deformity swills
  The tears of perjury that lie there like wash
  Fallen from the slimy and dishonest eye—
  Yet such a one plucks sweets without restraint,
  And has the grace of beauty to his sweet.
  Though my hard fate has thrust me out to servitude,
  I tumbled into th' world a gentleman.
  She turns her blessed eye upon me now,              50
  And I'll endure all storms before I part with't.
BEATRICE (*Aside*) Again!
  This ominous, ill-faced fellow more disturbs me
  Than all my other passions.
DE FLORES (*Aside*)                     Now't begins again;
  I'll stand this storm of hail though the stones pelt me.
BEATRICE Thy business? What's thy business?
DE FLORES (*Aside*)                          Soft and fair;
  I cannot part so soon now.
BEATRICE (*Aside*)                        The villain's fixed.—

(*To* DE FLORES) Thou standing toad-pool!
DE FLORES (*Aside*)                             The shower
  falls amain now.
BEATRICE Who sent thee? What's thy errand? Leave
  my sight!
DE FLORES My Lord your father charged me to deliver
  A message to you.
BEATRICE               What, another since?           61
  Do't and be hanged then; let me be rid of thee.
DE FLORES True service merits mercy.
BEATRICE                          What's thy message?
DE FLORES Let beauty settle but in patience,
  You shall hear all.
BEATRICE              A dallying, trifling torment!
DE FLORES Signor Alonzo de Piracquo, lady,
  Sole brother to Tomazo de Piracquo—
BEATRICE Slave, when wilt make an end?
DE FLORES (*Aside*)                      Too soon I shall.
BEATRICE What all this while of him?
DE FLORES                          The said Alonzo,
  With the foresaid Tomazo—
BEATRICE                     Yet again?                70
DE FLORES Is new alighted.
BEATRICE                    Vengeance strike the news!
  Thou thing most loathed, what cause was there in
    this
  To bring thee to my sight?
DE FLORES                    My lord your father
  Charged me to seek you out.
BEATRICE                       Is there no other
  To send his errand by?
DE FLORES                 It seems 'tis my luck
  To be i'th'way still.
BEATRICE               Get thee from me!
DE FLORES (*Aside*)                      So!—
  Why, am not I an ass to devise ways
  Thus to be railed at? I must see her still;
  I shall have a mad qualm within this hour again,
  I know't, and, like a common Garden-bull,           80
  I do but take breath to be lugged again.
  What this may bode I know not. I'll despair the less
  Because there's daily precedents of bad faces

---

27  a-late: of late
30  force: invent
32  baits: a) tempts (as in fishing and hunting); b) taunts
      (as in bull-baiting)
34  in town: publicly
35  At no hand: on no account
40  pick-haired: beard made up of a few hairs
43  swine-deformity: pig-like resemblance
44  perjury: hypocrisy
      wash: discharge
46  plucks sweets: enjoys sexual favours
47  to his sweet: in the eyes of his sweetheart
49  tumbled: was born
54  passions: a) sufferings; b) strong emotions; c) sexual
      desires
56  soft and fair: speak calmly and well; from the expression
      'fair and softly goes far' (proverbial)

---

58  standing toad pool: stagnant water harbouring only the
      ugliest of creatures
      shower: shower of abuse
      amain: forcefully
61  since: yet
65  dallying: time-wasting
68  Slave: wretch
78  railed at: insulted
79  mad qualm: attack of a) illness; b) sexual desire
80  like a . . . Garden-bull: 'like one of the bulls baited in the
      Paris Garden in Southwark' (Wine)
81  lugged: pulled by the 'lugs' (ears) as the dogs would do in
      bear-baiting

Beloved beyond all reason. These foul chops
May come into favour one day 'mongst his fellows.
Wrangling has proved the mistress of good pastime;
As children cry themselves asleep, I ha' seen
Women have chid themselves a-bed to men.

*Exit* DE FLORES

BEATRICE  I never see this fellow but I think
Of some harm towards me: danger's in my mind still,
I scarce leave trembling of an hour after.          91
The next good mood I find my father in,
I'll get him quite discarded.—O, I was
Lost in this small disturbance and forgot
Affliction's fiercer torrent that now comes
To bear down all my comforts!

*Enter* VERMANDERO, ALONZO, TOMAZO

VERMANDERO                    Y'are both welcome,
But an especial one belongs to you, sir,
To whose most noble name our love presents
The addition of a son, our son Alonzo.

ALONZO  The treasury of honour cannot bring forth  100
A title I should more rejoice in, sir.

VERMANDERO  You have improved it well.—Daughter,
  prepare:
The day will steal upon thee suddenly.

BEATRICE  (*Aside*) Howe'er, I will be sure to keep the
  night,
If it should come so near me.

BEATRICE *and* VERMANDERO *talk apart*

TOMAZO                    Alonzo.
ALONZO                         Brother?
TOMAZO  In troth I see small welcome in her eye.
ALONZO  Fie, you are too severe a censurer
Of love in all points; there's no bringing on you.
If lovers should mark everything a fault
Affection would be like an ill-set book          110
Whose faults might prove as big as half the volume.

BEATRICE  That's all I do entreat.

VERMANDERO                    It is but reasonable.
I'll see what my son says to 't.—Son Alonzo,
Here's a motion made but to reprieve
A maidenhead three days longer. The request
Is not far out of reason, for indeed
The former time is pinching.

ALONZO                    Though my joys
Be set back so much time as I could wish
They had been forward, yet, since she desires it,
The time is set as pleasing as before;          120
I find no gladness wanting.

VERMANDERO                    May I ever
Meet it in that point still. Y'are nobly welcome, sirs.

*Exeunt* VERMANDERO *and* BEATRICE

TOMAZO  So. Did you mark the dullness of her parting
  now?
ALONZO  What dullness? Thou art so exceptious still!
TOMAZO  Why, let it go then. I am but a fool
To mark your harms so heedfully.
ALONZO                    Where's the oversight?
TOMAZO  Come, your faith's cozened in her, strongly
  cozened:
Unsettle your affection with all speed
Wisdom can bring it to; your peace is ruined else.
Think what a torment 'tis to marry one          130
Whose heart is leapt into another's bosom:
If ever pleasure she receive from thee,
It comes not in thy name, or of thy gift—
She lies but with another in thine arms,
He the half father unto all thy children
In the conception; if he get 'em not,
She helps to get 'em for him, in his passions;
And how dangerous
And shameful her restraint may go in time to
It is not to be thought on without sufferings.          140
ALONZO  You speak as if she loved some other then.
TOMAZO  Do you apprehend so slowly?
ALONZO                    Nay, and that

---

84  chops: jaws (metonymy for the face)
85  his: theirs (the 'chops')
88  chid: chided
91  of: for
93  discarded: sacked, dismissed
99  addition: i.e. additional title
100  treasury of honour: 'the whole compendium of honorific
  titles' (Frost)
102  improved: enhanced
104  keep the night: unclear. Beatrice possibly means 'avoid the
  day by keeping hold of the night before' or 'keep control
  during the wedding night' (denying herself to Alonzo)
107  severe a censurer: strict a critic
108  points: a) respects; b) punctuation marks (or details, as
  from a strict critic)
  bringing on you: 'bringing you around to see that'
110  ill-set: badly typeset
111  faults: list of misprints (errata)

114  motion: proposal
117  pinching: a) admittedly short; b) inadequate
  joys: with sexual overtones
121–2  May I . . . point still: Vermandero hopes that he will
  always be able to reach such accords with Alonzo
123  dullness: indifference
124  exceptious: given to making objections
126  heedfully: sensitively
  the: my
127  cozened: deceived
128  Unsettle: detach
132  pleasure: sexual enjoyment
134  She lies . . . thine arms: she imagines that she is sleeping
  with someone else while she is in your arms
136  get: beget
139  her restraint . . . in time: her behaviour may become if so
  restrained
142  and: if

Be your fear only, I am safe enough.
Preserve your friendship and your counsel, brother,
For times of more distress; I should depart
An enemy, a dangerous, deadly one
To any but thyself that should but think
She knew the meaning of inconstancy,
Much less the use and practice. Yet w'are friends: 150
Pray let no more be urged; I can endure
Much, till I meet an injury to her,
Then I am not myself. Farewell, sweet brother;
How much w'are bound to heaven to depart lovingly!
*Exit*

TOMAZO  Why, here is love's tame madness: thus a man
Quickly steals into his vexation.
*Exit*

# Act II, scene ii

*Enter* DIAPHANTA *and* ALSEMERO

DIAPHANTA  The place is my charge; you have kept
    your hour,
And the reward of a just meeting bless you!
I hear my lady coming. Complete gentleman,
I dare not be too busy with my praises;
Th'are dangerous things to deal with.  *Exit*

ALSEMERO                    This goes well.
These women are the ladies' cabinets;
Things of most precious trust are locked into 'em.

*Enter* BEATRICE

BEATRICE  I have within mine eye all my desires;
Requests that holy prayers ascend heaven for,
And brings 'em down to furnish our defects,  10
Come not more sweet to our necessities
Than thou unto my wishes.

ALSEMERO                    We are so like
In our expressions, lady, that unless I borrow
The same words, I shall never find their equals.
*Kisses her*

BEATRICE  How happy were this meeting, this embrace,
If it were free from envy! This poor kiss,
It has an enemy, a hateful one,
That wishes poison to't. How well were I now

If there were none such name known as Piracquo,
Nor no such tie as the command of parents!  20
I should be but too much blessed.

ALSEMERO                    One good service
Would strike off both your fears, and I'll go near it
    too,
Since you are so distressed. Remove the cause,
The command ceases; so there's two fears blown out
With one and the same blast.

BEATRICE                    Pray let me find you, sir;
What might that service be, so strangely happy?

ALSEMERO  The honourablest piece about man, valour.
I'll send a challenge to Piracquo instantly.

BEATRICE  How? Call you that extinguishing of fear
When 'tis the only way to keep it flaming?  30
Are not you ventured in the action,
That's all my joys and comforts? Pray, no more, sir.
Say you prevailed, you're danger's and not mine then:
The law would claim you from me, or obscurity
Be made the grave to bury you alive.
I'm glad these thoughts come forth; O keep not one
Of this condition, sir! Here was a course
Found to bring sorrow on her way to death:
The tears would ne'er ha' dried till dust had
    choked'em.
Blood-guiltiness becomes a fouler visage;  40
*(Aside)*—And now I think on one: I was to blame
I ha' marred so good a market with my scorn.
'T had been done questionless: the ugliest creature

---

20  command: i.e. Vermandero's 'command' that Beatrice
    should marry Alonzo
22  strike off: as with a) fetters; b) items on a list of debts
    go near it: be more explicit
23  the cause: i.e. Alonzo
24–5  two fears . . . same blast: either two 'enemies' eliminated
    with one blast of gunpowder (Kinney) or two lights
    blown out with one puff of air (Sampson)
25  find: understand, follow
26  happy: fortunate
27  piece about: attribute of
31  ventured: risked
33  you're danger's: you belong to danger
34  the law: i.e. against duelling
    obscurity: the need to hide (from the law)
37  condition: kind
38  on her way: i.e. all the way
40  becomes: makes, suits
41  one: i.e. a fouler face in reality, De Flores
42  I ha' . . . a good market: spoiled a profitable opportunity
    (proverbial)
43  'T had been done questionless: a) the scorn had been
    instinctive (and therefore the opportunity lost); b) De
    Flores would have acted (on the idea of the elimination
    of Alonzo) without hesitation
43–4  the ugliest . . . some use: refers to the notion that
    everyone is created for some purpose

---

149  yet: still
151  injury: insult
155  steals: proceeds with ignorance
    vexation: suffering
1  my charge: my responsibility
3  Complete: perfect
4  busy: open
5  dangerous: since Beatrice might hear them
6  cabinets: metaphor for confidants
10  defects: what we lack
16  envy: enmity
17  enemy: i.e. Alonzo

Creation framed for some use! Yet to see
I could not mark so much where it should be!

ALSEMERO Lady—

BEATRICE (*Aside*) Why, men of art make much of
    poison,
Keep one to expel another. Where was my art?

ALSEMERO Lady, you hear not me.

BEATRICE                    I do especially, sir.
The present times are not so sure of our side
As those hereafter may be; we must use 'em then   50
As thrifty folks their wealth, sparingly now,
Till the time opens.

ALSEMERO           You teach wisdom, lady.

BEATRICE Within there! Diaphanta!

*Enter* DIAPHANTA

DIAPHANTA              Do you call, madam?

BEATRICE Perfect your service, and conduct this
    gentleman
The private way you brought him.

DIAPHANTA            I shall, madam.

ALSEMERO My love's as firm as love e'er built upon.
                 *Exeunt* DIAPHANTA *and* ALSEMERO

*Enter* DE FLORES

DE FLORES (*Aside*) I have watched this meeting, and do
    wonder much
What shall become of t'other; I'm sure both
Cannot be served unless she transgress. Happily
Then I'll put in for one; for if a woman   60
Fly from one point, from him she makes a husband,
She spreads and mounts then, like arithmetic,
One, ten, a hundred, a thousand, ten thousand—
Proves in time sutler to an army royal.
Now do I look to be most richly railed at,
Yet I must see her.

BEATRICE (*Aside*) Why, put case I loathed him
As much as youth and beauty hates a sepulchre,
Must I needs show it? Cannot I keep that secret,

And serve my turn upon him? See, he's here.
(*To him*) De Flores.

DE FLORES (*Aside*)       Ha, I shall run mad with joy!   70
She called me fairly by my name, De Flores,
And neither rogue nor rascal.

BEATRICE                What ha' you done
To your face a-late? Y'have met with some good
    physician;
Y'have pruned yourself methinks: you were not wont
To look so amorously.

DE FLORES (*Aside*)        Not I;—
'Tis the same physnomy, to a hair and pimple,
Which she called scurvy scarce an hour ago.
How is this?

BEATRICE      Come hither, nearer, man!

DE FLORES (*Aside*) I'm up to the chin in heaven.

BEATRICE                 Turn, let me see.
Faugh, 'tis but the heat of the liver, I perceive't;   80
I thought it had been worse.

DE FLORES (*Aside*)         Her fingers touched me!
She smells all amber.

BEATRICE I'll make a water for you shall cleanse this
Within a fortnight.

DE FLORES           With your own hands, lady?

BEATRICE Yes, mine own, sir; in a work of cure
I'll trust no other.

DE FLORES (*Aside*) 'Tis half an act of pleasure
To hear her talk thus to me.

BEATRICE              When w'are used
To a hard face, it is not so unpleasing;
It mends still in opinion, hourly mends,
I see it by experience.

DE FLORES (*Aside*)       I was blest   90
To light upon this minute; I'll make use on't.

BEATRICE Hardness becomes the visage of a man well:
It argues service, resolution, manhood,
If cause were of employment.

DE FLORES            'Twould be soon seen,
If e'er your ladyship had cause to use it.
I would but wish the honour of a service
So happy as that mounts to.

---

45  mark so . . . should be!: i.e. perceive the usefulness of De
    Flores
46  art: a) science, knowledge; b) cunning (artfulness)
47  expel: neutralise
49  sure of: securely on
52  opens: becomes more favourable
54  Perfect: complete
58  t'other: Alonzo
59  Happily: puns on 'haply', perhaps
60  put in for one: offer my services (implying a bid for
    Beatrice's sexual favour)
61  point: a) situation: b) penis
62  spreads and mounts: as with birds (but with sexual
    connotation)
64  sutler: a) provisioner to an army; b) prostitute
66  put case: suppose

69  serve my . . . upon him?: make use of him for myself
74  pruned: preened (as with a bird and its feathers)
75  amorously: a) lovely; b) lusty
76  physnomy: physiognomy, face
77  scurvy: scabby
80  heat of the liver: inflammation of the organ thought in the
    seventeenth century to be responsible for violent passions
82  amber: i.e. ambergris, used in perfume
83  water: lotion
86  pleasure: copulation
88  hard: ugly
94  If cause: were there cause
    employment: a) work; b) copulation
97  mounts: amounts

BEATRICE  We shall try you.—O my De Flores!
DE FLORES  (*Aside*)                              How's that?
  She calls me hers already, 'my' De Flores!
  (*To Beatrice*) You were about to sigh out somewhat,
    madam?                                                    100
BEATRICE  No, was I? I forgot.—O!
DE FLORES                              There 'tis again,
  The very fellow on't.
BEATRICE                    You are too quick, sir.
DE FLORES  There's no excuse for't now; I heard it
  twice, madam.
  That sigh would fain have utterance; take pity on't,
  And lend it a free word. 'Las, how it labours
  For liberty! I hear the murmur yet
  Beat at your bosom.
BEATRICE                    Would creation—
DE FLORES  Ay, well said, that's it.
BEATRICE                              Had formed me man.
DE FLORES  Nay, that's not it.
BEATRICE                    O 'tis the soul of freedom!
  I should not then be forced to marry one          110
  I hate beyond all depths; I should have power
  Then to oppose my loathings, nay, remove 'em
  For ever from my sight.
DE FLORES                    O blest occasion!—
  Without change to your sex you have your wishes.
  Claim so much man in me.
BEATRICE                    In thee, De Flores?
  There's small cause for that.
DE FLORES                    Put it not from me,
  It's a service that I kneel for to you.          *He kneels*
BEATRICE  You are too violent to mean faithfully.
  There's horror in my service, blood and danger;
  Can those be things to sue for?
DE FLORES                    If you knew          120
  How sweet it were to me to be employed
  In any act of yours, you would say then
  I failed, and used not reverence enough
  When I received the charge on't.
BEATRICE  (*Aside*)          This is much,
  methinks;
  Belike his wants are greedy, and to such
  Gold tastes like angels' food. (*To* DE FLORES) Rise.
DE FLORES  I'll have the work first.
BEATRICE  (*Aside*)                    Possible his need

Is strong upon him. (*Gives him money*)—There's to
  encourage thee;
  As thou art forward and thy service dangerous,
  Thy reward shall be precious.
DE FLORES                    That I have thought on.
  I have assured myself of that beforehand,          131
  And know it will be precious; the thought ravishes!
BEATRICE  Then take him to thy fury.
DE FLORES                    I thirst for him.
BEATRICE  Alonzo de Piracquo.
DE FLORES                    His end's upon him,
  He shall be seen no more.                    *Rises*
BEATRICE                    How lovely now
  Dost thou appear to me! Never was man
  Dearlier rewarded.
DE FLORES          I do think of that.
BEATRICE  Be wondrous careful in the execution.
DE FLORES  Why, are not both our lives upon the cast?
BEATRICE  Then I throw all my fears upon thy service.
DE FLORES  They ne'er shall rise to hurt you.          141
BEATRICE                    When the deed's done,
  I'll furnish thee with all things for thy flight;
  Thou may'st live bravely in another country.
DE FLORES  Ay, ay, we'll talk of that hereafter.
BEATRICE  (*Aside*)                    I shall rid myself
  Of two inveterate loathings at one time,
  Piracquo, and his dog-face.                    *Exit*
DE FLORES                    O my blood!
  Methinks I feel her in mine arms already,
  Her wanton fingers combing out this beard,
  And, being pleased, praising this bad face.
  Hunger and pleasure, they'll commend sometimes 150
  Slovenly dishes, and feed heartily on 'em,
  Nay, which is stranger, refuse daintier for 'em.
  Some women are odd feeders.—I'm too loud:
  Here comes the man goes supperless to bed,
  Yet shall not rise tomorrow to his dinner.

*Enter* ALONZO

ALONZO  De Flores.
DE FLORES          My kind, honourable lord?

---

98 try: can mean 'take the sexual measure of'
102 quick a) hasty; b) sexually vigorous
104 fain: truly
107 creation: De Flores hears this as 'procreation'
113 occasion: opportunity
118 to mean faithfully: to intend to do what you claim
125 Belike his wants are greedy: perhaps his needs are like
    hunger
126 angels' food: manna from heaven (see Psalm 78.25)
127 Possible: possibly

130 precious: Beatrice means financially; De Flores
    understands the reward as the 'deflowering' of
    Beatrice
135 lovely: worthy of love
139 cast: i.e. of dice (as in gambling)
143 bravely: splendidly
150 pleasure: sexual desire
    commend: command
151 slovenly: base, lewd
    feed: devour sexually
154–5 Here comes . . . his dinner: Alonzo will be killed before
    supper that day and before sexual consummation
    (continuing the association in this speech between
    appetite for food and sexual appetite)

ALONZO  I am glad I ha' met with thee.
DE FLORES                              Sir.
ALONZO                         Thou canst show me
  The full strength of the castle?
DE FLORES                        That I can, sir.
ALONZO  I much desire it.
DE FLORES                        And if the ways and straits
  Of some of the passages be not too tedious for you, **160**
  I will assure you, worth your time and sight, my lord.
ALONZO  Puh, that shall be no hindrance.
DE FLORES                        I'm your servant, then.
  'Tis now near dinner-time; 'gainst your lordship's
    rising
  I'll have the keys about me.
ALONZO                        Thanks, kind De Flores.
DE FLORES  (*Aside*) He's safely thrust upon me beyond
    hopes.

*Exeunt*

# Act III, scene i

*Enter* ALONZO *and* DE FLORES. *In the act-time* DE FLORES
*hides a naked rapier*

DE FLORES  Yes, here are all the keys. I was afraid, my
    lord,
  I'd wanted for the postern; this is it.
  I've all, I've all, my lord; this for the sconce.
ALONZO  'Tis a most spacious and impregnable fort.
DE FLORES  You'll tell me more, my lord. This descent
  Is somewhat narrow, we shall never pass
  Well with our weapons, they'll but trouble us.

*Takes off his sword*

ALONZO  Thou sayest true.
DE FLORES                    Pray let me help your lordship.

*Takes Alonzo's sword*

ALONZO  'Tis done. Thanks, kind De Flores.
DE FLORES                        Here are hooks, my lord,
  To hang such things on purpose. *Hangs up the swords*
ALONZO  Lead, I'll follow thee.                          **11**

*Exeunt at one door and enter at the other*

# Act III, scene ii

DE FLORES  All this is nothing; you shall see anon
  A place you little dream on.
ALONZO                              I am glad
  I have this leisure; all your master's house
  Imagine I ha' taken a gondola.
DE FLORES  All but myself, sir,—(*Aside*) which makes
    up my safety.
  (*To* ALONZO) My lord, I'll place you at a casement
    here
  Will show you the full strength of all the castle.
  Look, spend your eye a while upon that object.
ALONZO  Here's rich variety, De Flores.
DE FLORES                        Yes, sir.
ALONZO  Goodly munition.
DE FLORES                        Ay, there's ordnance, sir—
  No bastard metal—will ring you a peal like bells    **11**
  At great men's funerals. Keep your eye straight, my
    lord,
  Take special notice of that sconce before you:
  There you may dwell awhile.

*Takes up the hidden rapier*

ALONZO                              I am upon't.
DE FLORES  And so am I.                        *Stabs him*
ALONZO                        De Flores! O, De Flores!
  Whose malice hast thou put on?
DE FLORES                        Do you question
  A work of secrecy? I must silence you.    *Stabs him*
ALONZO  O, O, O!
DE FLORES          I must silence you. *Stabs him and he dies*
  So, here's an undertaking well accomplished.
  This vault serves to good use now.—Ha! What's that
  Threw sparkles in my eye?—O, 'tis a diamond    **21**
  He wears upon his finger. It was well found:
  This will approve the work. What, so fast on?
  Not part in death? I'll take a speedy course then:

---

159  straits: narrow parts (as at sea), implying danger
160  tedious: troublesome
163  'gainst: before
     rising: getting up from dinner
165  safely: 'in that the murder and the body can be kept from
     view; otherwise ironic' (Daalder)
SD   *act-time*: between the acts. De Flores hides a rapier with
     which to kill Alonzo while openly wearing a sword
2    wanted: had not got the key
     postern: back door
3    sconce: small, separate fortification

---

2   place: both an inner part of the castle and, ironically, the
    grave
4   gondola: small boat (to leave Alicant temporarily)
5   All but myself, sir: i.e. everyone but De Flores thinks that
    Alonzo has taken a boat trip (hence De Flores' 'safety' in
    the plot)
6   casement: an aperture or window, serving as a viewing
    point for the fortifications
7   Will: which will
10  munition: general weaponry
    ordnance: large artillery
11  bastard: impure, low quality
    peal: discharge
14  dwell: a) pause; b) stay (once dead)
16  malice: hatred
23  approve the work: confirm that the deed has been done
    (to Beatrice)
    fast: tightly

Finger and all shall off. (*Cuts off the finger*) So, now
I'll clear
The passages from all suspect or fear.

*Exit with body*

# Act III, scene iii

*Enter* ISABELLA *and* LOLLIO

ISABELLA Why, sirrah? Whence have you commission
To fetter the doors against me? If you
Keep me in a cage, pray whistle to me,
Let me be doing something.

LOLLIO You shall be doing, if it please you; I'll whistle
to you if you'll pipe after.

ISABELLA Is it your master's pleasure or your own
To keep me in this pinfold?

LOLLIO 'Tis for my master's pleasure; lest, being taken
in another man's corn, you might be pounded in
another place. 11

ISABELLA 'Tis very well, and he'll prove very wise.

LOLLIO He says you have company enough in the
house, if you please to be sociable, of all sorts of
people.

ISABELLA Of all sorts? Why, here's none but fools and
madmen.

LOLLIO Very well: and where will you find any other, if
you should go abroad? There's my master and I to
boot too.

ISABELLA Of either sort one, a madman and a fool. 20

LOLLIO I would ev'n participate of both then, if I were as
you: I know y'are half mad already, be half foolish too.

ISABELLA Y'are a brave, saucy rascal. Come on, sir,
Afford me then the pleasure of your bedlam;
You were commending once today to me
Your last-come lunatic: what a proper
Body there was without brains to guide it,
And what a pitiful delight appeared
In that defect, as if your wisdom had found
A mirth in madness. Pray sir, let me partake, 30

If there be such a pleasure.

LOLLIO If I do not show you the handsomest,
discreetest madman, one that I may call the
understanding madman, then say I am a fool.

ISABELLA Well, a match: I will say so.

LOLLIO When you have had a taste of the madman,
you shall, if you please, see Fools' College, o' th'other
side. I seldom lock there; 'tis but shooting a bolt or
two, and you are amongst 'em. (*Exit. Enter presently*)
—Come on, sir, let me see how handsomely you'll
behave yourself now. 41

*Enter* FRANCISCUS

FRANCISCUS How sweetly she looks! O, but there's a
wrinkle in her brow as deep as philosophy.—
Anacreon, drink to my mistress' health, I'll pledge it.
Stay, stay, there's a spider in the cup! No, 'tis but a
grape-stone; swallow it, fear nothing, poet. So, so; lift
higher.

ISABELLA Alack, alack, it is too full of pity
To be laughed at. How fell he mad? Canst thou tell?

LOLLIO For love, mistress. He was a pretty poet too,
and that set him forwards first. The Muses then
forsook him; he ran mad for a chambermaid, yet she
was but a dwarf neither. 53

FRANCISCUS Hail, bright Titania!
Why stand'st thou idle on these flow'ry banks?
Oberon is dancing with his Dryades;
I'll gather daisies, primrose, violets,
And bind them in a verse of poesy.

*Approaches* ISABELLA

LOLLIO Not too near! You see your danger.

*Holds up a whip*

FRANCISCUS O hold thy hand, great Diomed! 60
Thou feed'st thy horses well, they shall obey thee.
Get up, Bucephalus kneels. *Kneels*

---

26 suspect: suspicion
1 sirrah: a form of 'sir' (used for inferiors)
5 doing: i.e. copulating
5–6 I'll whistle . . . pipe after: Lollio alludes to the saying 'to
dance after a person's pipe', with a sexual sense of 'dance'
(copulate) and 'pipe' (penis)
8 pinfold: pound for animals
10 pounded: a) placed in a pound; b) pounded with a pestle
(with sexual connotation)
11 another place: her vagina
18 abroad: beyond the madhouse
21 participate: i.e. sexually
22 be half foolish too: i.e. have a relationship with us both
23 brave: bold
saucy: impudent
26 proper: handsome, well-endowed

33 discreetest: i.e. showing the qualities described
35 a match: agreed
38 shooting: pulling back
44 Anacreon: a Greek poet said to have choked to death on
a grape pip while drinking wine
48 full of pity: pitiful
53 but a dwarf neither: only a dwarf
54 Titania: Queen of the Fairies (in Shakespeare's
*A Midsummer Night's Dream* (1595))
56 Oberon: King of the Fairies, unfaithful to Titania with
Dryades (wood-nymphs). 'Franciscus suggests that
Isabella may be too inactive while Alibius (Oberon) is
copulating ("dancing") with other women' (Daalder)
57 daisies, primroses, violets: symbols of praise
58 poesy: a) poetry; b) bunch of flowers
60 Diomed: Diamedes, King of the Bistonians, who fed his
horses with human flesh
62 Bucephalus: Alexander the Great's horse, which only he
could mount. Franciscus urges Lollio to mount ('get up')
as he pretends to be the horse

LOLLIO  You see how I awe my flock. A shepherd has
not his dog at more obedience.

ISABELLA  His conscience is unquiet; sure that was
The cause of this. A proper gentleman.

FRANCISCUS  Come hither, Aesculapius. Hide the poison.

LOLLIO  Well, 'tis hid.                          *Hides the whip*

FRANCISCUS  (*Rising*) Didst thou never hear of one
Tiresias,
A famous poet?                                      **70**

LOLLIO  Yes, that kept tame wild-geese.

FRANCISCUS  That's he; I am the man.

LOLLIO  No!

FRANCISCUS  Yes. But make no words on't: I was a man
Seven years ago—

LOLLIO  A stripling, I think, you might—

FRANCISCUS  Now I'm a woman, all feminine.

LOLLIO  I would I might see that.

FRANCISCUS  Juno struck me blind.

LOLLIO  I'll ne'er believe that; for a woman, they say,
has an eye more than a man.                          **81**

FRANCISCUS  I say she struck me blind.

LOLLIO  And Luna made you mad: you have two trades
to beg with.

FRANCISCUS  Luna is now big-bellied, and there's room
For both of us to ride with Hecate;
I'll drag thee up into her silver sphere,
And there we'll kick the dog—and beat the bush—
That barks against the witches of the night;
The swift lycanthropi that walks the round,          **90**
We'll tear their wolvish skins, and save the sheep.
                                    *Tries to seize* LOLLIO

LOLLIO  Is't come to this? Nay, then my poison comes
forth again (*Shows the whip*): mad slave indeed—
abuse your keeper!

ISABELLA  I prithee, hence with him, now he grows
dangerous.

---

67  Aesculapius: the Greek god of medicine
69  Tiresias: the blind prophet of Thebes who changed from
man to woman and back to man again after seven years.
Juno blinded him for revealing that woman derived more
pleasure from sex than men did
71  wild-geese: prostitutes
74  make no words on't: 'don't get alarmed by this'
81  an eye: a) perception; b) vagina
83  Luna: the moon, a source of madness (hence the term
'lunatics')
two trades: i.e. madness and blindness
85  big-bellied: a) full; b) pregnant
86  ride: a) move; b) copulate with
Hecate: the Greek goddess of witchcraft, associated in
classical mythology with the moon
88  the dog . . . the bush: the Man in the Moon was said to
own a dog and a bush
90  lycanthropi: those suffering from lycanthropia saw
themselves as wolves (see Ferdinand in John Webster's
*The Duchess of Malfi* (1614))

FRANCISCUS
(*Sings*)          *Sweet love, pity me;*
                   *Give me leave to lie with thee.*

LOLLIO  No, I'll see you wiser first. To your own kennel!

FRANCISCUS  No noise, she sleeps; draw all the curtains
round,
Let no soft sound molest the pretty soul            **100**
But love, and love creeps in at a mouse-hole.

LOLLIO  I would you would get into your hole!
(*Exit* FRANCISCUS) Now, mistress, I will bring you
another sort: you shall be fooled another while.—
Tony, come hither, Tony! Look who's yonder, Tony.

*Enter* ANTONIO

ANTONIO  Cousin, is it not my aunt?

LOLLIO  Yes, 'tis one of 'em, Tony.

ANTONIO  He, he! How do you, uncle?

LOLLIO  Fear him not, mistress, 'tis a gentle nigget; you
may play with him, as safely with him as with his
bauble.                                             **111**

ISABELLA  How long hast thou been a fool?

ANTONIO  Ever since I came hither, cousin.

ISABELLA  Cousin? I'm none of thy cousins, fool.

LOLLIO  O mistress, fools have always so much wit as to
claim their kindred.

MADMAN  (*within*) Bounce, bounce! He falls, he falls!

ISABELLA  Hark you, your scholars in the upper room
Are out of order.                                   **119**

LOLLIO  Must I come amongst you there?—Keep you
the fool, mistress; I'll go up and play left-handed
Orlando amongst the madmen.                       *Exit*

ISABELLA  Well, sir.

ANTONIO  'Tis opportuneful now, sweet lady! Nay,
Cast no amazing eye upon this change.

ISABELLA  Ha!

ANTONIO  This shape of folly shrouds your dearest love,
The truest servant to your powerful beauties,

---

97  *lie*: copulate
101  love creeps . . . mouse-hole: 'creeps' is an innuendo for
sexual entry, 'mouse' can mean a beloved woman and
'hole' is an obscene word for vagina
102  hole: cell (but also an obscene image)
106  aunt: can also mean prostitute
108  uncle: can also mean pander, pimp
109  nigget: contraction of 'an idiot'
111  bauble: a) a jester's baton; b) penis
114  cousins: Isabella takes Antonio's 'cousin' to mean
'strumpet' or 'lover'
121  left-handed Orlando: meaning unclear. Orlando was the
love-mad, violent protagonist in Ariosto's *Orlando
Furioso*, and 'left-handed' implies ineptitude
124  opportuneful: seasonal
125  amazing: amazed
change: of attitude
127  shape: guise
shrouds: a) conceals; b) disguises

Whose magic had this force thus to transform me.

ISABELLA You are a fine fool indeed.

ANTONIO                                    O 'tis not strange!
Love has an intellect that runs through all
The scrutinous sciences, and, like a cunning poet,
Catches a quantity of every knowledge,
Yet brings all home into one mystery,
Into one secret, that he proceeds in.

ISABELLA Y'are a parlous fool.

ANTONIO No danger in me; I bring nought but love
And his soft-wounding shafts to strike you with.
Try but one arrow; if it hurt you, I
Will stand you twenty back in recompense.            **140**

*Kisses her*

ISABELLA A forward fool too!

ANTONIO                          This was love's teaching:
A thousand ways he fashioned out my way,
And this I found the safest and the nearest
To tread the Galaxia to my star.

ISABELLA Profound withal! Certain you dreamed of this;
Love never taught it waking.

ANTONIO                          Take no acquaintance
Of these outward follies. There is within
A gentleman that loves you.

ISABELLA                          When I see him
I'll speak with him; so in the meantime keep
Your habit, it becomes you well enough.            **150**
As you are a gentleman, I'll not discover you;
That's all the favour that you must expect.
When you are weary, you may leave the school,
For all this while you have but played the fool.

*Enter* LOLLIO

ANTONIO And must again.—He, he! I thank you,
cousin;
I'll be your valentine tomorrow morning.

LOLLIO How do you like the fool, mistress?

ISABELLA Passing well, sir.

LOLLIO Is he not witty, pretty well, for a fool?

ISABELLA If he hold on as he begins, he is like
To come to something.            **160**

LOLLIO Ay, thank a good tutor. You may put him to't;
he begins to answer pretty hard questions.—Tony,
how many is five times six?

ANTONIO Five times six is six times five.

LOLLIO What arithmetician could have answered
better? How many is one hundred and seven?

ANTONIO One hundred and seven is seven hundred
and one, cousin.

LOLLIO This is no wit to speak on!—Will you be rid of
the fool now?            **171**

ISABELLA By no means; let him stay a little.

MADMAN (*within*) Catch there, catch the last couple in
hell!

LOLLIO Again! Must I come amongst you? Would my
master were come home! I am not able to govern
both these wards together.            *Exit*

ANTONIO Why should a minute of love's hour be lost?

ISABELLA Fie, out again! I had rather you kept
Your other posture; you become not your tongue   **180**
When you speak from your clothes.

ANTONIO                          How can he freeze
Lives near such a warmth? Shall I alone
Walk through the orchard of the Hesperides
And cowardly not dare to pull an apple?
This with the red cheeks I must venture for.

*Kisses her*

*Enter* LOLLIO *above*

ISABELLA Take heed, there's giants keep 'em.

LOLLIO (*Aside*) How now, fool, are you good at that?
Have you read Lipsius? He's past *Ars Amandi*; I
believe I must put harder questions to him, I perceive
that—            **190**

---

132 scrutinous: searching
     cunning: clever and artful
134 mystery: skill known to masters and apprentices (as with
     the guilds of craftsmen responsible for the Mystery plays)
135 secret: can also mean 'secret part'
     proceeds: a) mentally; b) sexually
138 soft-wounding shafts: of Cupid
     strike: with an innuendo of copulate
140 stand: give (as payment)
141 forward: a) impudent; b) lustful
142 fashioned out: contrived
     my way: my approach (towards Isabella)
144 Galaxia: Milky Way
145 Profound withal!: ingenious, as well!
150 habit: dress (of a fool)
151 discover: reveal, uncover
152 all the favour: i.e. rather than a sexual favour
156 valentine tomorrow morning: probably a reference to
     Ophelia's song in Shakespeare's *Hamlet* (IV.v.47–54)

158 passing: exceedingly
160–1 If he . . . to something: a) he may achieve some level of
     learning if he persists; b) he may achieve orgasm
173–4 Catch there . . . in hell!: reference to 'barley-break', a
     traditional game in which couples attempt to run past
     other players (representing hell) without being caught
179 out: i.e. out of role
181 from: out of keeping with
182 Lives: who lives
183 the Hesperides: the dragon Ladon (offspring of a giant)
     guarded the tree on which the golden apples of the
     Hesperides grew; it was one of the tasks of Hercules to
     slay it
184 pull: pick
186 giants: i.e. guardians (meaning Lollio and Alibius)
188 Lipsius: Julius Lipsius (1547–1606), a scholar famous for
     his inconstancy (changing religious affiliation a number
     of times throughout his life); also a play on 'lips'
     *Ars Amandi*: *The Art of Loving*, a treatise by Ovid

ISABELLA You are bold without fear too.

ANTONIO What should I
    fear,
  Having all joys about me? Do you smile,
  And love shall play the wanton on your lip,
  Meet and retire, retire and meet again;
  Look you but cheerfully, and in your eyes
  I shall behold mine own deformity,
  And dress myself up fairer. I know this shape
  Becomes me no, but in those bright mirrors
  I shall array me handsomely.                    199

LOLLIO (*Aside*) Cuckoo, cuckoo—              *Exit*

*Enter* MADMEN *above, some as birds, others as beasts.*

ANTONIO What are these?

ISABELLA Of fear enough to part us,
  Yet are they but our schools of lunatics
  That act their fantasies in any shapes
  Suiting their present thoughts: if sad, they cry;
  If mirth be their conceit they laugh again;
  Sometimes they imitate the beasts and birds,
  Singing or howling, braying, barking—all
  As their wild fancies prompt 'em.
                        *Exeunt* MADMEN *above*

*Enter* LOLLIO

ANTONIO These are no fears.

ISABELLA But here's a large one—my man.

ANTONIO Ha, he! That's fine sport indeed, cousin!  210

LOLLIO I would my master were come home! 'Tis too
  much for one shepherd to govern two of these flocks.
  Nor can I believe that one churchman can instruct
  two benefices at once: there will be some incurable
  mad of the one side, and very fools on the other.—
  Come, Tony.

ANTONIO Prithee, cousin, let me stay here still.

LOLLIO No, you must to your book now; you have
  played sufficiently.

ISABELLA Your fool is grown wondrous witty.       220

LOLLIO Well, I'll say nothing, but I do not think but he

will put you down one of these days.
                        *Exeunt* LOLLIO *and* ANTONIO

ISABELLA Here the restrained current might make
    breach,
  Spite of the watchful bankers. Would a woman stray,
  She need not gad abroad to seek her sin,
  It would be brought home one ways or other:
  The needle's point will to the fixed north,
  Such drawing arctics women's beauties are.

*Enter* LOLLIO

LOLLIO How dost thou, sweet rogue?

ISABELLA How now?                                 230

LOLLIO Come, there are degrees: one fool may be
  better than another.

ISABELLA What's the matter?

LOLLIO Nay, if thou giv'st thy mind to fool's flesh, have
  at thee!                            *Tries to kiss her*

ISABELLA You bold slave, you!

LOLLIO I could follow now as t'other fool did:
  'What should I fear,
  Having all joys about me? Do you but smile,
  And love shall play the wanton on your lip,     240
  Meet and retire, retire and meet again;
  Look you but cheerfully, and in your eyes
  I shall behold my own deformity,
  And dress myself up fairer. I know this shape
  Becomes me not—'
  And so as it follows; but is not this the more foolish
  way? Come, sweet rogue, kiss me, my little
  Lacedaemonian. Let me feel how thy pulses beat.
  Thou hast a thing about thee would do a man
  pleasure—I'll lay my hand on't.                 250

ISABELLA Sirrah, no more! I see you have discovered
  This love's knight-errant, who hath made adventure
  For purchase of my love. Be silent, mute,
  Mute as a statue, or his injunction
  For me enjoying shall be to cut thy throat:

---

192 Do you smile: do but smile
193 the wanton: lasciviously
197 shape: guise (of a fool)
198 bright mirrors: Isabella's eyes
200 Cuckoo: the cry suggests 'cuckold' (i.e Alibius)
201 of fear: frightening
203 fantasies: a) delusions; b) imagined things
205 conceit: fancy
209 my man: Lollio (her servant)
213–14 one churchman . . . two benefices: referring to the
    practice of clergy who derived their income from two or
    more churches (considered disreputable in the
    seventeenth century)
215 of: on

222 put you down: a) outwit in argument; b) copulate with
224 bankers: builders of dikes, levees
226 brought home: delivered
227 needle's point: of the compass, but with phallic
    implications
    will: will move
228 drawing artics: magnetic poles
237 I could . . . fool did: 'having overheard you, I can play
    your part' (Kinney)
246 this: Lollio's own way (more straightforward)
248 Lacedaemonian: a) someone given to understatement;
    b) prostitute (implying that prostitutes do not talk much).
    Let me . . . pulses beat: sexual innuendo
249 thing: vagina
250 lay: a) place; b) bet
253 purchase: reward

I'll do it, though for no other purpose, and
Be sure he'll not refuse it.
LOLLIO My share, that's all! I'll have my fool's part with
you.
ISABELLA No more! Your master. 259

*Enter* ALIBIUS

ALIBIUS                    Sweet, how dost thou?
ISABELLA Your bounden servant, sir.
ALIBIUS                        Fie, fie, sweetheart,
No more of that.
ISABELLA            You were best lock me up.
ALIBIUS In my arms and bosom, my sweet Isabella,
I'll lock thee up most nearly!—Lollio,
We have employment, we have task in hand.
At noble Vermandero's, our castle-captain,
There is a nuptial to be solemnized—
Beatrice Joanna, his fair daughter, bride—
For which the gentleman hath bespoke our pains;
A mixture of our madmen and our fools, 270
To finish, as it were, and make the fag
Of all the revels, the third night from the first.
Only an unexpected passage over,
To make a frightful pleasure, that is all—
But not the all I aim at. Could we so act it
To teach it in a wild, distracted measure,
Though out of form and figure, breaking time's head,
It were no matter ('twould be healed again
In one age or other, if not in this):
This, this Lollio, there's a good reward begun, 280
And will beget a bounty, be it known.
LOLLIO This is easy, sir, I'll warrant you. You have
about you fools and madmen that can dance very
well; and 'tis no wonder: your best dancers are not the
wisest men—the reason is, with often jumping they
jolt their brains down into their feet, that their wits
lie more in their heels than in their heads.

256 no other purpose: i.e. to have Alibius rid me of you
261 bounden: a) duty-bound; b) confined (sarcastically)
262 lock me up: in a chastity belt (although Alibius does not
    catch this allusion)
264 most nearly: a) intimately; b) more securely
269 bespoke our pains: commissioned our help
271 fag: last part
273–4 Only an . . . is all: the madmen and fools are to rush
    across in front of the revellers, giving them a pleasant
    fright
275–81 Could we . . . it known: 'If only we could so perform it
    as to teach them to do it by means of a wild, crazy dance,
    then that, though not according to proper form and
    pattern, making a cuckold of the musical rhythm, would
    not be objected to (for it would be remedied at some
    future stage if not now) . . . such a thing, Lollio, would
    be the beginning of a good reward and generate bountiful
    commissions for the future, if it became widely known'
    (Daalder)

ALIBIUS Honest Lollio, thou giv'st me a good reason,
And a comfort in it.
ISABELLA              Y'have a fine trade on't;
Madmen and fools are a staple commodity. 290
ALIBIUS O wife, we must eat, wear clothes, and live;
Just at the lawyer's haven we arrive,
By madmen and by fools we both do thrive.
*Exeunt*

# Act III, scene iv

*Enter* VERMANDERO, ALSEMERO, JASPERINO, *and*
BEATRICE

VERMANDERO Valencia speaks so nobly of you, sir,
I wish I had a daughter now for you.
ALSEMERO The fellow of this creature were a partner
For a king's love.
VERMANDERO        I had her fellow once, sir,
But heaven has married her to joys eternal;
'Twere sin to wish her in this vale again.
Come, sir, your friend and you shall see the pleasures
Which my health chiefly joys in.
ALSEMERO I hear the beauty of this seat largely.
VERMANDERO It falls much short of that.
*Exeunt. Manet* BEATRICE
BEATRICE                              So here's one step
Into my father's favour; time will fix him. 11
I have got him now the liberty of the house.
So wisdom by degrees works out her freedom;
And if that eye be dark'ned that offends me
(I wait but that eclipse), this gentleman
Shall soon shine glorious in my father's liking
Through the refulgent virtue of my love.

*Enter* DE FLORES

DE FLORES (*Aside*) My thoughts are at a banquet for the
deed;
I feel no weight in't, 'tis but light and cheap

288 a good reason: i.e. for going ahead with the plan
292 lawyer's haven: a) referring to the idea that fools and
    madmen often sought the services of lawyers (see
    I.ii.168–9); b) lawyers are fools and madmen
3 fellow: match
4 fellow: i.e. Vermandero's late wife
6 vale: of tears, earthly life
8 health: well-being
9 seat: estate, property
    largely: extensively reported upon
11 fix: establish (Alsemero)
14 if that . . . offends me: refers to the biblical idea that 'if
    thine eye offend thee, pluck it out' (Matthew 18.9) with
    Alonzo as the 'eye'
17 refulgent: radiant
18 banquet: celebration
    the deed: the killing of Alonzo

For the sweet recompense that I set down for't.   **20**
BEATRICE  De Flores?
DE FLORES           Lady?
BEATRICE              Thy looks promise cheerfully.
DE FLORES  All things are answerable: time,
    circumstance,
  Your wishes, and my service.
BEATRICE              Is it done then?
DE FLORES  Piracquo is no more.
BEATRICE  My joys start at mine eyes; our sweet'st
    delights
  Are evermore born weeping.
DE FLORES              I've a token for you.
BEATRICE  For me?
DE FLORES  But it was sent somewhat unwillingly;
  I could not get the ring without the finger.

*Shows her the finger*

BEATRICE  Bless me! What hast thou done?
DE FLORES              Why, is that more
  Than killing the whole man? I cut his heart-strings. **30**
  A greedy hand thrust in a dish at court
  In a mistake hath had as much as this.
BEATRICE  'Tis the first token my father made me send
    him.
DE FLORES  And I have made him send it back again
  For his last token. I was loath to leave it,
  And I'm sure dead men have no use of jewels.
  He was as loath to part with't, for it stuck
  As if the flesh and it were both one substance.
BEATRICE  At the stag's fall, the keeper has his fees;
  'Tis soon applied: all dead men's fees are yours, sir. **40**
  I pray, bury the finger; but the stone
  You may make use on shortly—the true value,
  Take't of my truth, is near three hundred ducats.
DE FLORES  'Twill hardly buy a capcase for one's
    conscience, though,
  To keep it from the worm, as fine as 'tis.
  Well, being my fees, I'll take it;

Great men have taught me that, or else my merit
  Would scorn the way on't.
BEATRICE              It might justly, sir.
  Why, thou mistak'st, De Flores: 'tis not given
  In state of recompense.
DE FLORES              No, I hope so, lady;   **50**
  You should soon witness my contempt to't then.
BEATRICE  Prithee, thou look'st as if thou wert
    offended.
DE FLORES  That were strange, lady; 'tis not possible
  My service should draw such a cause from you.
  Offended? Could you think so? That were much
  For one of my performance, and so warm
  Yet in my service.
BEATRICE  'Twere misery in me to give you cause, sir.
DE FLORES  I know so much, it were so: misery
  In her most sharp condition.
BEATRICE              'Tis resolved then;   **60**
  Look you, sir, here's three thousand golden florins:
  I have not meanly thought upon thy merit.
DE FLORES  What? Salary? Now you move me.
BEATRICE              How, De Flores?
DE FLORES  Do you place me in the rank of verminous
    fellows,
  To destroy things for wages? Offer gold
  For the life blood of man! Is anything
  Valued too precious for my recompense?
BEATRICE  I understand thee not.
DE FLORES              I could ha' hired
  A journeyman in murder at this rate,
  And mine own conscience might have had, and have
    had   **70**
  The work brought home.

---

47–8  Great men . . . way on't: great men have taught De
    Flores to accept a material reward for his service,
    although he claims his true merit is above such exchanges
  50  In state of: by way of
  54  cause: reproach
55–7  That were . . . my service: De Flores notes the gravity of
    his 'performance' (the killing) and how recent it was
    (against the notion of Beatrice's apparent reproach)
  58  misery: ingratitude
  59  misery: suffering
  60  'tis resolved then: the misunderstanding is resolved
  61  three thousand golden florins: gold coins (or a
    promissory note, since this large sum would have
    weighed a great deal)
  62  meanly: ungenerously
  63  Salary: financial reward
    move: offend
  66  Is anything: can anything be
68–71  I could . . . brought home: De Flores says that he could
    have hired someone (a journeyman) to undertake the
    murder so that he could have stayed at home and had the
    'work' delivered, thus sparing his conscience direct
    contact with the deed

---

  20  sweet recompense: in exchange for
    set down: specified (as in an account)
  22  answerable: fitting
  26  token: a) of love; b) of the murder
31–2  A greedy . . . as this: De Flores notes that it is easy
    enough to lose a finger in an accident, so it is nothing by
    comparison to the killing of a whole man which is what
    the finger and the ring are evidence of
  36  jewels: can also mean a) signs of virginity; b) genitalia
  38  one substance: in the biblical sense, like the union of
    marriage which the ring had come to signify (see
    Matthew 19.5)
  39  keeper: gamekeeper, entitled to a share of a slaughtered
    deer
  44  capcase: travelling bag, wallet
  45  worm: the gnawings of conscience

BEATRICE (*Aside*)          I'm in a labyrinth;
  What will content him? I would fain be rid of him.
  (*To* DE FLORES) I'll double the sum, sir.
DE FLORES                            You take a course
  To double my vexation, that's the good you do.
BEATRICE (*Aside*) Bless me! I am now in worse plight
    than I was:
  I know not what will please him. (*To* DE FLORES)—
    For my fears' sake,
  I prithee make away with all speed possible.
  And if thou be'st so modest not to name
  The sum that will content thee, paper blushes not;
  Send thy demand in writing, it shall follow thee    80
  But prithee take thy flight.
DE FLORES                        You must fly too then.
BEATRICE  I?
DE FLORES   I'll not stir a foot else.
BEATRICE                          What's your meaning?
DE FLORES  Why, are not you as guilty, in, I'm sure,
  As deep as I? And we should stick together.
  Come, your fears counsel you but ill: my absence
  Would draw suspect upon you instantly;
  There were no rescue for you.
BEATRICE (*Aside*)              He speaks home.
DE FLORES  Nor is it fit we two, engaged so jointly,
  Should part and live asunder.        *Tries to kiss her*
BEATRICE                      How now, sir?
  This shows not well.
DE FLORES            What makes your lip so strange? 90
  This must not be 'twixt us.
BEATRICE (*Aside*)          The man talks wildly.
DE FLORES  Come, kiss me with a zeal now.
BEATRICE (*Aside*)              Heaven, I doubt him!
DE FLORES  I will not stand so long to beg 'em shortly.
BEATRICE  Take heed, De Flores, of forgetfulness,
  'Twill soon betray us.
DE FLORES            Take you heed first;
  Faith, y'are grown much forgetful, y'are to blame
    in't.
BEATRICE (*Aside*) He's bold, and I am blamed for't!
DE FLORES                          I have eased you

Of your trouble; think on't. I'm in pain
  And must be eased of you; 'tis a charity.
  Justice invites your blood to understand me.    100
BEATRICE  I dare not.
DE FLORES        Quickly!
BEATRICE                O, I never shall!
  Speak it yet further off, that I may lose
  What has been spoken, and no sound remain on't.
  I would not hear so much offence again
  For such another deed.
DE FLORES            Soft, lady, soft!
  The last is not yet paid for. O, this act
  Has put me into spirit: I was as greedy on't
  As the parched earth of moisture, when the clouds
    weep.
  Did you not mark, I wrought myself into't,
  Nay, sued and kneeled for't? Why was all that pains
    took?                                          110
  You see I have thrown contempt upon your gold:
  Not that I want it not, for I do piteously—
  In order I will come unto't, and make use on't—
  But 'twas not held so precious to begin with,
  For I place wealth after the heels of pleasure;
  And were I not resolved in my belief
  That thy virginity were perfect in thee,
  I should but take my recompense with grudging,
  As if I had but half my hopes I agreed for.
BEATRICE  Why, 'tis impossible thou canst be so
    wicked,                                        120
  Or shelter such a cunning cruelty,
  To make his death the murderer of my honour!
  Thy language is so bold and vicious,
  I cannot see which way I can forgive it
  With any modesty.
DE FLORES        Push, you forget yourself!
  A woman dipped in blood, and talk of modesty?
BEATRICE  O misery of sin! Would I had been bound
  Perpetually unto my living hate

---

77  make away: flee
84  stick together: a) as partners in crime; b) as the finger and
    the ring
86  suspect: suspicion
87  home: a) directly; b) truthfully
88  engaged so jointly: bound together in the crime (but with
    play on the sense of betrothal)
90  strange: unfriendly, distant
92  doubt: fear, distrust
93  I will . . . 'em shortly: soon I shall refuse to wait for so
    long, begging for your kisses
94  forgetfulness: of her superior social rank
    forgetful: of her complicity and her obligation to him

98   in pain: caused by sexual desire
99   eased: sexually relieved
     charity: gift to someone sexually deprived
100  blood: sexuality, passions
     understand: satisfy
102  lose: forget
104  offence: offensive suggestions
105  such another: any such
     Soft: 'slow down' or 'wait a moment'
106  act: of blood
109  wrought: forced
113  In order: in due course
115  pleasure: sexual pleasure
122  his death: i.e. that of Alonzo
     honour: chastity
126  modesty: De Flores weighs her complicity in murder
     against her concern for her female 'modesty' (implying
     also her virginity)

In that Piracquo, than to hear these words!
Think but upon the distance that creation          **130**
Set 'twixt thy blood and mine, and keep thee there.
DE FLORES  Look but into your conscience, read me
       there;
'Tis a true book, you'll find me there your equal.
Push, fly not to your birth, but settle you
In what the act has made you; y'are no more now.
You must forget your parentage to me:
Y'are the deed's creature; by that name you lost
Your first condition; and I challenge you
As peace and innocency has turned you out
And made you one with me.
BEATRICE                        With thee, foul villain?
DE FLORES  Yes, my fair murd'ress. Do you urge me,  **141**
Though thou writ'st 'maid', thou whore in thy
       affection?
'Twas changed from thy first love, and that's a kind
Of whoredom in thy heart; and he's changed now
To bring thy second on, thy Alsemero,
Whom (by all sweets that ever darkness tasted)
If I enjoy thee not, thou ne'er enjoy'st:
I'll blast the hopes and joys of marriage—
I'll confess all; my life I rate at nothing.
BEATRICE  De Flores!
DE FLORES  I shall rest from all lovers' plagues then;  **150**
I live in pain now: that shooting eye
Will burn my heart to cinders.
BEATRICE                        O sir, hear me!
DE FLORES  She that in life and love refuses me,
In death and shame my partner she shall be.
BEATRICE  Stay, hear me once for all. (*Kneels*) —I make
       thee master
Of all the wealth I have in gold and jewels;
Let me go poor unto my bed with honour,
And I am rich in all things.

---

129  than: rather than
131  blood: social rank
133  equal: in terms of sin, which supersedes other forms of
       rank
136  to: in favour of
137  the deed's creature: a) shaped or recreated by the deed;
       b) enslaved to the deed
138  first condition: a) innocence; b) original state (in terms of
       family and rank)
139  turned you out: expelled you from that state (with play
       on the dismissal of Eve from Paradise)
141  urge: provoke me
142  writ'st 'maid': call yourself virgin
       affection: passion
143  changed from thy first love: transferred (from Alonzo)
144  changed: from life to death (with emphasis on 'change' as
       in the title of the play)
146  sweets: sexual pleasures
150  plagues: torments
151  shooting eye: direct, provocative look

DE FLORES                        Let this silence thee:
The wealth of all Valencia shall not buy
My pleasure from me.                        **160**
Can you weep fate from its determined purpose?
So soon may you weep me.
BEATRICE                        Vengeance begins;
Murder I see is followed by more sins.
Was my creation in the womb so curst
It must engender with a viper first?
DE FLORES  Come, rise, and shroud your blushes in my
       bosom.                        *Raises her*
Silence is one of pleasure's best receipts:
Thy peace is wrought for ever in this yielding.
'Las, how the turtle pants! Thou'lt love anon
What thou so fear'st and faint'st to venture on.  **170**
                        *Exeunt*

# Act IV, scene i

*Dumb show.* Enter GENTLEMEN, VERMANDERO *meeting
them with action of wonderment at the flight of* PIRACQUO.
*Enter* ALSEMERO, *with* JASPERINO *and* GALLANTS;
VERMANDERO *points to him, the* GENTLEMEN *seeming to
applaud the choice. Exeunt in procession* VERMANDERO,
ALSEMERO, JASPERINO *and* GENTLEMEN. *Enter*
BEATRICE, *the bride, following in great state, accompanied
with* DIAPHANTA, ISABELLA, *and other* GENTLEWOMEN.
*Enter* DE FLORES *after all, smiling at the accident.*
ALONZO's *ghost appears to* DE FLORES *in the midst of his
smile; startles him, showing him the hand whose finger he
had cut off. They pass over in great solemnity*

*Enter* BEATRICE

BEATRICE  This fellow has undone me endlessly:
Never was bride so fearfully distressed.
The more I think upon th'ensuing night,
And whom I am to cope with in embraces—
One who's ennobled both in blood and mind,
So clear in understanding (that's my plague now),
Before whose judgement will my fault appear
Like malefactors' crimes before tribunals
(There is no hiding on't)—the more I dive
Into my own distress. How a wise man          **10**

---

162  Vengeance: the consequences of sin
164–5  Was my . . . viper first?: i.e. was my birth so cursed that
       I should copulate with a viper first? (before a man)
167  receipts: recipes
169  turtle: turtle dove (known to protect its mate)
       anon: at once
1  fellow: someone of lower rank
       undone me: a) ruined; b) ravished
2  distressed: a) anxious; b) deprived (sexually, as a bride)
4  cope: contend (but with play on 'copulate')
5  One: i.e. Alsemero

Stands for a great calamity! There's no venturing
Into his bed, what course soe'er I light upon,
Without my shame, which may grow up to danger.
He cannot but in justice strangle me
As I lie by him, as a cheater use me;
'Tis a precious craft to play with a false die
Before a cunning gamester. Here's his closet,
The key left in't, and he abroad i'th'park;
Sure 'twas forgot, I'll be so bold as look in't.

*Opens closet*

Bless me! A right physician's closet 'tis, 20
Set round with vials, every one her mark too.
Sure he does practise physic for his own use,
Which may be safely called your great man's wisdom.
What manuscript lies here? 'The Book of
  Experiment,
Called *Secrets in Nature*'; so 'tis, 'tis so
'How to know whether a woman be with child or no.'
I hope I am not yet; if he should try though!
Let me see: 'folio forty-five.' Here 'tis;
The leaf tucked down upon't, the place suspicious.
'If you would know whether a woman be with child
or not, give her two spoonfuls of the white water in
glass C—' Where's that glass C? O, yonder, I see't
now—'and if she be with child, she sleeps full twelve
hours after; if not, not.' 34
None of that water comes into my belly:
I'll know you from a hundred. I could break you now,
Or turn you into milk, and so beguile
The master of the mystery, but I'll look to you.
Ha! That which is next is ten times worse:
'How to know whether a woman be a maid or not.' 40
If that should be applied, what would become of me?

---

11 Stands for: represents (because he will be hard to deceive)
13 grow up to danger: increase to produce danger
15 use: copulate with
16 precious: risky (because obtainable only at great cost)
17 closet: small private room
20 right: true, veritable
21 vials: small bottles for medicines or chemicals
   her mark: its label
22–3 for his . . . man's wisdom: the medicine is to protect Alsemero against poison
25 *Secrets in Nature*: or *De Arcanis Naturae* by Antonius Mizaldus (1520–78). Although this text does not include the virginity tests used in this play such tests could be found in similar works. The title usefully represents the secretive and suspicious nature of Alsemero's interests (which correspond to those of Alibius in the sub-plot)
31 water: medicinal liquid
32 glass: a vial or other container
36 you: i.e. glass C
37 Or turn you into milk: by changing the contents or the label
38 mystery: secret
   look to: watch out for

Belike he has a strong faith of my purity,
That never yet made proof; but this he calls
'A merry sleight, but true experiment, the author
Antonius Mizaldus. Give the party you suspect the
quantity of a spoonful of the water in the glass M,
which upon her that is a maid makes three several
effects: 'twill make her incontinently gape, then fall
into a sudden sneezing, last into a violent laughing;
else dull, heavy, and lumpish.' 50
Where had I been?
I fear it, yet 'tis seven hours to bedtime.

*Enter* DIAPHANTA

DIAPHANTA Cuds, madam, are you here?
BEATRICE (*Aside*) Seeing that wench now
  A trick comes in my mind; 'tis a nice piece
  Gold cannot purchase. (*To* DIAPHANTA) I come
    hither, wench,
  To look my lord.
DIAPHANTA (*Aside*) Would I had such a cause
  To look him too! (*To* BEATRICE) Why, he's i'th'park,
    madam.
BEATRICE There let him be.
DIAPHANTA Ay, madam, let him compass
  Whole parks and forests, as great rangers do;
  At roosting time a little lodge can hold 'em. 60
  Earth-conquering Alexander, that thought the world
  Too narrow for him, in the end had but his pit-hole.
BEATRICE I fear thou art not modest, Diaphanta.
DIAPHANTA Your thoughts are so unwilling to be
    known, madam;
  'Tis ever the bride's fashion towards bed-time
  To set light by her joys, as if she owed 'em not.
BEATRICE Her joys? Her fears, thou would'st say.
DIAPHANTA Fear of what?
BEATRICE Art thou a maid, and talk'st so to a maid?

---

42–3 Belike he . . . made proof: 'perhaps, not having tested my purity, he has strong faith in it and will therefore not proceed to do so (ironic in several ways)' (Daalder)
44 sleight: trick
48 incontinently gape: yawn immediately and uncontrollably
51 Where had I been?: i.e. where would I have been had I not discovered all this?
53 Cuds: God's (mild oath)
54 a nice piece: i.e. an exceptionally principled girl that
57 look: look for
58 compass: ride around
59 parks: colloquial for female bodies
   rangers: a) keepers of parks; b) penises
60 lodge: can also mean vagina
61 Alexander: Alexander the Great (356–323 BC)
62 pit-hole: a) grave; b) vagina
64 Your thoughts . . . be known: Diaphanta implies that Beatrice's secret thoughts may well be similarly unchaste
66 owed: owned
68 maid: virgin

You leave a blushing business behind,
Beshrew your heart for't!
DIAPHANTA       Do you mean good sooth, madam? **70**
BEATRICE   Well, if I'd thought upon the fear at first,
Man should have been unknown.
DIAPHANTA       Is't possible?
BEATRICE   I will give a thousand ducats to that woman
Would try what my fear were, and tell me true
Tomorrow, when she gets from't; as she likes
I might perhaps be drawn to't.
DIAPHANTA       Are you in earnest?
BEATRICE   Do you get the woman, then challenge me,
And see if I'll fly from't. But I must tell you
This by the way: she must be a true maid,
Else there's no trial, my fears are not hers else.    **80**
DIAPHANTA   Nay, she that I would put into your hands,
   madam,
Shall be a maid.
BEATRICE       You know I should be shamed else,
Because she lies for me.
DIAPHANTA       'Tis a strange humour!
But are you serious still? Would you resign
Your first night's pleasure, and give money too?
BEATRICE   As willingly as live. (*Aside*)—Alas, the gold
Is but a by-bet to wedge in the honour.
DIAPHANTA   (*Aside*) I do not know how the world goes
   abroad
For faith or honesty; there's both required in this.—
Madam, what say you to me, and stray no further? **90**
I've a good mind, in troth, to earn your money.
BEATRICE   Y'are too quick, I fear, to be a maid.
DIAPHANTA   How? Not a maid? Nay, then you urge
   me, madam!
Your honourable self is not a truer,
With all your fears upon you—
BEATRICE   (*Aside*)       Bad enough then.
DIAPHANTA   Than I with all my lightsome joys about
   me.

---

69   You leave . . . business behind: Diaphanta's words make
    Beatrice blush
70   good sooth: truth (i.e. are you serious?)
72   Man should have been unknown: a) she would have
    wished men did not exist; b) she would never know a
    man
74   try: experience
75   when she gets from't: when she removes herself from
    intercourse
77   challenge me: demand the money from me
83   lies: a) tells lies; b) substitutes; lies down (to make love)
87   by-bet: extra incentive (literally, a side-bet)
88–9   I do . . . or honesty: 'I do not know how much faith or
    honesty can be found in the world nowadays'
    (Bawcutt)
92   quick: lively (sexually)
93   urge: provoke
96   lightsome: lighthearted

BEATRICE   I'm glad to hear't. Then you dare put your
   honesty
Upon an easy trial?
DIAPHANTA       Easy?—Anything.
BEATRICE   I'll come to you straight.      *Goes to the closet*
DIAPHANTA   (*Aside*)       She will not search
   me, will she,
Like the forewoman of a female jury?       **100**
BEATRICE   (*Aside*) Glass M: ay, this is it.—Look,
   Diaphanta,
You take no worse than I do.       *Drinks*
DIAPHANTA       And in so doing,
I will not question what it is, but take it.      *Drinks*
BEATRICE   (*Aside*) Now if the experiment be true, 'twill
   praise itself,
And give me noble ease.—Begins already:
                    DIAPHANTA *gapes*
There's the first symptom. And what haste it makes
To fall into the second, there by this time!
                 DIAPHANTA *sneezes*
Most admirable secret!—On the contrary,
It stirs not me a whit, which most concerns it.
DIAPHANTA   Ha, ha, ha!
BEATRICE   (*Aside*)       Just in all things, and in order
As if 'twere circumscribed; one accident       **III**
Gives way unto another.
DIAPHANTA       Ha, ha, ha!
BEATRICE   How now, wench?
DIAPHANTA       Ha, ha, ha! I am so—so light
At heart! Ha, ha, ha!—So pleasurable!
But one swig more, sweet madam.
BEATRICE       Ay, tomorrow;
We shall have time to sit by't.
DIAPHANTA       Now I'm sad again.
BEATRICE   (*Aside*) It lays itself so gently too! (*To*
   DIAPHANTA) Come, wench;
Most honest Diaphanta I dare call thee now.
DIAPHANTA   Pray tell me, madam, what trick call you
   this?
BEATRICE   I'll tell thee all hereafter; we must study    **120**
The carriage of this business.
DIAPHANTA       I shall carry't well,
Because I love the burden.
BEATRICE       About midnight

---

99–100   She will . . . female jury: 1613 saw the case of the
      Countess of Essex who sued for divorce on the grounds
      of non-consummation and was examined by a group of
      women
104   praise itself: show its worth
III   circumscribed: as if written in a circle (as on a coin) and
    therefore in a neat sequence
    accident: symptom, effect
116   by't: and enjoy it
117   lays itself: subsides
121   carriage: management

You must not fail to steal forth gently,
That I may use the place.
DIAPHANTA                  O fear not, madam;
I shall be cool by that time. (*Aside*) The bride's place,
And with a thousand ducats! I'm for a justice now:
I bring a portion with me; I scorn small fools.
                                *Exeunt*

# Act IV, scene ii

*Enter* VERMANDERO *and* SERVANT

VERMANDERO  I tell thee, knave, mine honour is in
    question,
A thing till now free from suspicion,
Nor ever was there cause. Who of my gentlemen
Are absent? Tell me, and truly, how many and who.
SERVANT  Antonio, sir, and Franciscus.
VERMANDERO  When did they leave the castle?
SERVANT  Some ten days since, sir, the one intending to
Briamata, th'other for Valencia.
VERMANDERO  The time accuses 'em. A charge of
    murder
Is brought within my castle gate, Piracquo's murder;
I dare not answer faithfully their absence.      11
A strict command of apprehension
Shall pursue 'em suddenly, and either wipe
The stain off clear, or openly discover it.
Provide me winged warrants for the purpose.
                          *Exit* SERVANT
See, I am set on again.

*Enter* TOMAZO

TOMAZO  I claim a brother of you.
VERMANDERO                Y'are too hot;
Seek him not here.
TOMAZO         Yes, 'mongst your dearest bloods,
If my peace find no fairer satisfaction.
This is the place must yield account for him,    20
For here I left him; and the hasty tie
Of this snatched marriage gives strong testimony
Of his most certain ruin.
VERMANDERO           Certain falsehood!
This is the place indeed: his breach of faith
Has too much marred both my abused love—

The honourable love I reserved for him—
And mocked my daughter's joy. The prepared
    morning
Blushed at his infidelity; he left
Contempt and scorn to throw upon those friends
Whose belief hurt 'em. O, 'twas most ignoble    30
To take his flight so unexpectedly,
And throw such public wrongs on those that loved
    him!
TOMAZO  Then this is all your answer?
VERMANDERO             'Tis too fair
For one of his alliance, and I warn you
That this place no more see you.         *Exit*

*Enter* DE FLORES

TOMAZO                The best is,
There is more ground to meet a man's revenge on.—
Honest De Flores?
DE FLORES          That's my name indeed.
Saw you the bride? Good sweet sir, which way took
    she?
TOMAZO  I have blest mine eyes from seeing such a false
    one.
DE FLORES  (*Aside*) I'd fain get off, this man's not for
    my company:    40
I smell his brother's blood when I come near him.
TOMAZO  Come hither, kind and true one; I remember
My brother loved thee well.
DE FLORES           O purely, dear sir!
(*Aside*)—Methinks I am now again a-killing on him,
He brings it so fresh to me.
TOMAZO          Thou canst guess, sirrah—
One honest friend has an instinct of jealousy—
At some foul guilty person?
DE FLORES  'Las, sir, I am so charitable, I think none
Worse than myself.—You did not see the bride then?
TOMAZO  I prithee, name her not. Is she not wicked?  50
DE FLORES  No, no: a pretty, easy, round-packed sinner,
As your most ladies are (else you might think
I flattered her), but, sir, at no hand wicked,
Till th'are so old their chins and noses meet,
And they salute witches.—I am called, I think, sir.

---

125  cool: sexually satisfied
126–7  I'm for . . . small fools: a justice is seen as a desirable
    'big fool' now that she has a dowry (portion)
8  Briamata: Vermandero's country estate
11  answer faithfully: explain in good faith
12  apprehension: arrest
14  discover: reveal
16  set on: harassed (seeing Tomazo arrive)
18  bloods: kin
25  marred: tainted

30  belief: mistaken confidence
33  fair: kind
34  alliance: lineage
36  There is . . . revenge on: 'there are other ways to pursue
    revenge'
46  instinct of jealousy: intuitive suspicion
51  easy: of easy virtue
    round-packed: full-figured, shapely
53  at no hand: by no means
54  chins and noses: Q has 'sins and noses'. We follow the
    usual emendation
55  salute: a) are called; b) greet (as they look like witches
    themselves)

(*Aside*)—His company ev'n o'erlays my conscience.

*Exit*

TOMAZO  That De Flores has a wondrous honest heart;
He'll bring it out in time, I'm assured on't.
O, here's the glorious master of the day's joy.
'Twill not be long till he and I do reckon.　　　60

*Enter* ALSEMERO

Sir!

ALSEMERO  You are most welcome.

TOMAZO　　　　　　　You may call that word back:
I do not think I am, nor wish to be.

ALSEMERO  'Tis strange you found the way to this house
then.

TOMAZO  Would I'd ne'er known the cause! I'm none of
those, sir,
That come to give you joy, and swill your wine;
'Tis a more precious liquor that must lay
The fiery thirst I bring.

ALSEMERO　　　　　Your words and you
Appear to me great strangers.

TOMAZO　　　　　　　Time and our swords
May make us more acquainted. This the business:—
I should have had a brother in your place;　　　70
How treachery and malice have disposed of him
I'm bound to enquire of him which holds his right,
Which never could come fairly.

ALSEMERO　　　　　　You must look
To answer for that word, sir.

TOMAZO　　　　　　　Fear you not;
I'll have it ready drawn at our next meeting.
Keep your day solemn. Farewell, I disturb it not;
I'll bear the smart with patience for a time.　　*Exit*

ALSEMERO  'Tis somewhat ominous, this: a quarrel
ent'red
Upon this day. My innocence relieves me;

*Enter* JASPERINO

I should be wondrous sad else.—Jasperino,　　80
I have news to tell thee, strange news.

JASPERINO　　　　　　I ha' some too,
I think as strange as yours. Would I might keep

Mine, so my faith and friendship might be kept in't!
Faith, sir, dispense a little with my zeal,
And let it cool in this.

ALSEMERO　　　　　This puts me on,
And blames thee for thy slowness.

JASPERINO　　　　　All may prove nothing,
Only a friendly fear that leapt from me, sir.

ALSEMERO  No question it may prove nothing; let's
partake it though.

JASPERINO  'Twas Diaphanta's chance—for to that
wench
I pretend honest love, and she deserves it—　　90
To leave me in a back part of the house,
A place we chose for private conference;
She was no sooner gone but instantly
I heard your bride's voice in the next room to me,
And, lending more attention, found De Flores
Louder than she.

ALSEMERO　　　　　De Flores? Thou art out now.

JASPERINO  You'll tell me more anon.

ALSEMERO　　　　　　Still I'll prevent thee;
The very sight of him is poison to her.

JASPERINO  That made me stagger too, but Diaphanta
At her return confirmed it.

ALSEMERO　　　　　　Diaphanta!　　100

JASPERINO  Then fell we both to listen, and words
passed
Like those that challenge interest in a woman—

ALSEMERO  Peace, quench thy zeal; 'tis dangerous to thy
bosom.

JASPERINO  Then truth is full of peril.

ALSEMERO　　　　　　Such truths are.—
O, were she the sole glory of the earth,
Had eyes that could shoot fire into kings' breasts,
And touched, she sleeps not here! Yet I have time,
Though night be near, to be resolved hereof;
And prithee do not weigh me by my passions.

JASPERINO  I never weighed friend so.

ALSEMERO　　　　　　Done charitably.

---

56　o'erlays my conscience: oppresses my mind
58　bring it out: a) reveal his 'honest heart'; b) reveal the
　　identity of the killer
59　glorious: a scornful term, as in vainglorious, proud
60　reckon: settle (our account)
66　liquor: i.e. blood
　　lay: allay, quench
72　his right: as husband to Beatrice (in place of Alonzo)
74　that word: the accusation
75　it: a sword (as answer)
76　Keep your day solemn: i.e. observe the rituals of your
　　wedding day
77　smart: pain

83　so: provided that
84–5　dispense a . . . in this: allow my zealous service to 'cool' a
　　little (so that I should not have to relay this news)
　　puts me on: provokes me
88　partake: share
90　pretend: offer
　　honest: a) genuine; b) chaste (Diaphanta is still a virgin)
92　private conference: as in a lovers' meeting
96　out: mistaken
97　tell me more: speak differently (when more of the story is
　　revealed)
97　prevent: forestall
102　challenge: claim
107　touched: unchaste
108　resolved: satisfied
109　weigh: judge

That key will lead thee to a pretty secret,    *Gives key*
By a Chaldean taught me, and I've made    **112**
My study upon some. Bring from my closet
A glass inscribed there with the letter M,
And question not my purpose.
JASPERINO              It shall be done, sir.    *Exit*
ALSEMERO  How can this hang together? Not an hour since,
    Her woman came pleading her lady's fears,
    Delivered her for the most timorous virgin
    That ever shrunk at man's name, and so modest,
    She charged her weep out her request to me,    **120**
    That she might come obscurely to my bosom.

*Enter* BEATRICE

BEATRICE  (*Aside*) All things go well. My woman's preparing yonder
    For her sweet voyage, which grieves me to lose;
    Necessity compels it, I lose all else.
ALSEMERO  (*Aside*) Push, modesty's shrine is set in yonder forehead.
    I cannot be too sure, though. (*To her*)—My Joanna!
BEATRICE  Sir, I was bold to weep a message to you;
    Pardon my modest fears.
ALSEMERO  (*Aside*)        The dove's not meeker;
    She's abused, questionless.

*Enter* JASPERINO *with glass*

                —O, are you come, sir?
BEATRICE  (*Aside*) The glass, upon my life! I see the letter.    **130**
JASPERINO  Sir, this is M.
ALSEMERO           'Tis it.
BEATRICE  (*Aside*)        I am suspected.
ALSEMERO  How fitly our bride comes to partake with us!
BEATRICE  What is't, my lord?
ALSEMERO           No hurt.
BEATRICE              Sir, pardon me,
    I seldom taste of any composition.
ALSEMERO  But this, upon my warrant, you shall venture on.    *Gives her the glass*
BEATRICE  I fear 'twill make me ill.
ALSEMERO           Heaven forbid that.
    *Talks apart to* JASPERINO

BEATRICE  (*Aside*) I'm put now to my cunning.
    Th'effects I know—
    If I can now but feign 'em handsomely.    *Drinks*
ALSEMERO  It has that secret virtue it ne'er missed, sir,
    Upon a virgin.
JASPERINO        Treble-qualited?    **140**
                BEATRICE *gapes, then sneezes*
ALSEMERO  By all that's virtuous, it takes there, proceeds!
JASPERINO  This is the strangest trick to know a maid by.
BEATRICE  Ha, ha, ha!
    You have given me joy of heart to drink, my lord.
ALSEMERO  (*To her*) No, thou hast given me such joy of heart
    That never can be blasted.
BEATRICE             What's the matter, sir?
ALSEMERO  (*To* JASPERINO) See, now 'tis settled in a melancholy
    Keeps both the time and method.— (*To her*) My Joanna,    **148**
    Chaste as the breath of heaven, or morning's womb
    That brings the day forth, thus my love encloses thee!
    *Embraces her. Exeunt*

# Act IV, scene iii

*Enter* ISABELLA *and* LOLLIO

ISABELLA  O heaven! Is this the waxing moon?
    Does love turn fool, run mad, and all at once?
    Sirrah, here's a madman, akin to the fool too,
    A lunatic lover.
LOLLIO  No, no!—Not he I brought the letter from?
ISABELLA  Compare his inside with his out, and tell me.
    *Gives him the letter*
LOLLIO  The out's mad, I'm sure of that; I had a taste on't. (*Reads*) 'To the bright Andromeda, chief

---

111  pretty: ingenious
112  Chaldean: a seer or soothsayer (see Daniel 2.2)
113  some: i.e. secrets
118  Delivered her for: described her as
121  obscurely: a) in the dark; b) unseen
123  sweet voyage: her sexual encounter
129  She's abused, questionless: she's undoubtedly maligned
134  composition: medicine (of more than one ingredient)
135  warrant: guarantee

138  handsomely: convincingly
139  that secret virtue: i.e. such rare quality
140  Treble-qualited: producing three effects (Alsemero has clearly briefed Jasperino on the effects of the potion)
141  takes: takes effect
146  blasted: destroyed
148  time: sequence
      method: effect
1  waxing: Q has 'waiting' but we follow other eds in this emendation. A waxing moon (one growing bigger) was thought to increase lunacy
3  madman: i.e. Franciscus, 'related' to the fool Antonio
6  inside with his out: a) compare Franciscus and his disguise; b) compare what is written on the outside of the letter with its contents
7–8  The out's . . . taste on't: Lollio thinks that Franciscus is mad when he is disguised and recalls his earlier violence

chambermaid to the Knight of the Sun, at the sign of Scorpio, in the middle region, sent by the bellows-mender of Aeolus. Pay the post.' This is stark madness. 12

ISABELLA Now mark the inside. (*Takes the letter and reads*) 'Sweet lady, having now cast off this counterfeit cover of a madman, I appear to your best judgement a true and faithful lover of your beauty.'

LOLLIO He is mad still.

ISABELLA 'If any fault you find, chide those perfections in you which have made me imperfect: 'tis the same sun that causeth to grow and enforceth to wither, —'

LOLLIO O rogue! 21

ISABELLA '—Shapes and transshapes, destroys and builds again. I come in winter to you, dismantled of my proper ornaments: by the sweet splendour of your cheerful smiles I spring and live a lover.'

LOLLIO Mad rascal still!

ISABELLA 'Tread him not under foot, that shall appear an honour to your bounties. I remain—mad till I speak with you, from whom I expect my cure, yours all, or one beside himself, Franciscus.' 30

LOLLIO You are like to have a fine time on't. My master and I may give over our professions; I do not think but you can cure fools and madmen faster than we, with little pains too.

ISABELLA Very likely.

LOLLIO One thing I must tell you, mistress. You perceive that I am privy to your skill: if I find you minister once and set up the trade, I put in for my thirds; I shall be mad or fool else.

ISABELLA The first place is thine, believe it, Lollio, If I do fall— 41

LOLLIO I fall upon you.

ISABELLA So.

LOLLIO Well, I stand to my venture.

ISABELLA But thy counsel now, how shall I deal with 'em?

LOLLIO Why, do you mean to deal with 'em?

ISABELLA Nay, the fair understanding—how to use 'em.

LOLLIO Abuse 'em! That's the way to mad the fool and make a fool of the madman, and then you use 'em kindly. 52

ISABELLA 'Tis easy; I'll practise. Do thou observe it. The key of thy wardrobe.

LOLLIO There; fit yourself for 'em, and I'll fit 'em both for you. *Gives her the key*

ISABELLA Take thou no further notice than the outside. *Exit*

LOLLIO Not an inch: I'll put you to the inside.

*Enter* ALIBIUS

ALIBIUS Lollio, art there? Will all be perfect, think'st thou?
Tomorrow night, as if to close up the solemnity, 60
Vermandero expects us.

LOLLIO I mistrust the madmen most. The fools will do well enough; I have taken pains with them.

ALIBIUS Tush, they cannot miss. The more absurdity, The more commends it, so no rough behaviours Affright the ladies. They are nice things, thou know'st.

LOLLIO You need not fear, sir; so long as we are there with our commanding pizzles, they'll be as tame as the ladies themselves.

ALIBIUS I will see them once more rehearse before they go. 70

LOLLIO I was about it, sir. Look you to the madmen's

---

8–12 'To the . . . stark madness: Andromeda (Isabella) was rescued from the dragon by Perseus (Franciscus). Chambermaids were thought to be lascivious and typical of the readers of such romances as *The Mirror of Knighthood* (nine parts, printed in England 1578–1601), in which the Knight of the Sun is the hero. The zodiacal sign Scorpio was thought to govern the sexual organs ('the middle region') and Aeolus, the bellows-mender, is significant as the ruler of the winds who would create (sexual) activity, 'bellow' being a term for the phallus. 'Pay the post' (courier) is humorously matter-of-fact in the context of this 'stark madness'

23–4 dismantled of my proper ornaments: not in my proper clothes

27–8 appear an honour: be honourable

30 beside himself: distracted by love

32–3 I do not think but: I am sure that

37 privy to your skill: aware of your profession
minister: a) provide medical treatment; b) respond to the letter

38 trade: a) our trade (as keepers); b) the trade of prostitute.
my thirds: a) a one-third share of the medical business; b) a one-third share of what she offers sexually (along with Alibius and her lover)

40–1 The first . . . do fall: she says that Lollio would indeed be the first recipient of her favour but she is interrupted as she qualifies this with 'If I fall'

43 So: yes, but it will not happen

44 I stand to my venture: I shall keep to my plan (with sexual connotation)

47 deal with: a) treat: b) copulate with

48 fair understanding: i.e the decent meaning of 'deal with'

50 Abuse: deceive

52 kindly: appropriately (according to their natures)

53 practise: scheme

55 fit: a) dress; b) prepare; c) arouse (sexually)

57 Take thou . . . the outside: treat me as a madwomen

58 I'll put . . . the inside: I'll make you have sexual intercourse

60 solemnity: celebration

65 so: provided that

66 nice: delicate

68 pizzles: whips made from the penises of bulls

morris, and let me alone with the other; there is one
or two that I mistrust their fooling. I'll instruct them,
and then they shall rehearse the whole measure.

ALIBIUS  Do so; I'll see the music prepared. But, Lollio,
By the way, how does my wife brook her restraint?
Does she not grudge at it?

LOLLIO  So, so. She takes some pleasure in the house,
she would abroad else. You must allow her a little
more length, she's kept too short.                      80

ALIBIUS  She shall along to Vermandero's with us:
That will serve her for a month's liberty.

LOLLIO  What's that on your face, sir?

ALIBIUS  Where, Lollio? I see nothing.

LOLLIO  Cry you mercy, sir, 'tis your nose: it showed
like the trunk of a young elephant.

ALIBIUS  Away, rascal! I'll prepare the music, Lollio.
                                        *Exit* ALIBIUS

LOLLIO  Do, sir, and I'll dance the whilst.—Tony,
where art thou, Tony?

*Enter* ANTONIO

ANTONIO  Here, cousin. Where art thou?            90

LOLLIO  Come, Tony, the footmanship I taught you.

ANTONIO  I had rather ride, cousin.

LOLLIO  Ay, a whip take you! But I'll keep you out.
Vault in—look you, Tony: fa, la, la, la, la.    *Dances*

ANTONIO  Fa, la, la, la, la.                      *Dances*

LOLLIO  There, an honour.                           *Bows*

ANTONIO  Is this an honour, coz?                    *Bows*

LOLLIO  Yes, and it please your worship.

ANTONIO  Does honour bend in the hams, coz?

LOLLIO  Marry does it, as low as worship, squireship,
nay, yeomanry itself sometimes, from whence it first
stiffened. There, rise, a caper.                  102

ANTONIO  Caper after an honour, coz?

LOLLIO  Very proper: for honour is but a caper—rises as
fast and high, has a knee or two, and falls to th'
ground again. You can remember your figure, Tony?
                                                    *Exit*

ANTONIO  Yes, cousin; when I see thy figure I can
remember mine.

*Enter* ISABELLA *like a madwoman*

ISABELLA  Hey, how he treads the air!
Shough, shough, t'other way—he burns his wings
else!                                              110
Here's wax enough below, Icarus—more
Than will be cancelled these eighteen moons.
                                        ANTONIO *falls*
He's down, he's down! What a terrible fall he had!
Stand up, thou son of Cretan Daedalus,
And let us tread the lower labyrinth;
I'll bring thee to the clue.               *Seizes him*

ANTONIO  Prithee, coz, let me alone.

ISABELLA  Art thou not drowned?
About thy head I saw a heap of clouds
Wrapped like a Turkish turban; on thy back    120
A crookt chameleon-coloured rainbow hung
Like a tiara down unto thy hams.
Let me suck out those billows in thy belly:
                                    *Kneels and listens*
Hark how they roar and rumble in the straits!
Bless thee from the pirates.

ANTONIO  Pox upon you, let me alone!

ISABELLA  Why shouldst thou mount so high as
Mercury,
Unless thou hadst reversion of his place?

---

72  morris: Morris dance
72–3  one or two: i.e. Franciscus (and Antonio)
74  measure: dance
76  brook: tolerate
77  grudge: complain
78  She takes . . . the house: i.e. Isabella can find sexual
pleasure here
79–80  You must . . . too short: a) she must be allowed more
latitude and not be confined: b) she requires a longer penis
85  Cry you mercy: I beg your pardon
85–6  'tis your . . . young elephant: a) analogous to the horns of
a cuckold; b) enlarged because Lollio leads him by it; c)
play on size of penis
92  ride: copulate
94  Vault in: jump into the dance (with sexual connotation in
the sense of 'riding' a horse)
96  honour: bow
98  and: if
99  hams: hips
100  Marry: by Mary
102  stiffened: became formal; became an erection
caper: leap (in dancing)

104–6  rises as . . . ground again: 'quick ascent presages quick
descent' (Kinney)
107  figure: dance steps
110  Shough: 'shoo' (an exclamation to drive him away (used
for birds)
111  Icarus: in classical mythology the son of the Cretan
Daedalus, who made wings of wax in order to fly but fell
when the wings were melted by the sun
112  cancelled: refers to the process of sealing documents with
wax
116  the clue: the thread which Ariadne gave to Theseus to
unwind as he entered the labyrinth (the madhouse) to kill
the Minotaur (Alibius) so that he could return. Here
Isabella supposes that Icarus had ended up in the
labyrinth, thus conflating two myths
121  chameleon-coloured: of ever-changing colour
122  tiara: head-dress
123  billows: sea water (into which Icarus fell)
124  the straits: the sea between Crete and Greece where
Icarus fell
125  Bless thee: may God preserve thee
127  Mercury: the winged messenger of the gods
128  reversion: the right of succession

Stay in the moon with me, Endymion,
And we will rule these wild rebellious waves          130
That would have drowned my love.
ANTONIO I'll kick thee if again thou touch me,
Thou wild unshapen antic; I am no fool,
You bedlam!
ISABELLA          But you are, as sure as I am, mad.
Have I put on this habit of a frantic,
With love as full of fury, to beguile
The nimble eye of watchful jealousy,
And am I thus rewarded?          *Reveals herself*
ANTONIO Ha, dearest beauty!
ISABELLA          No, I have no beauty now,
Nor never had, but what was in my garments.          140
You a quick-sighted lover? Come not near me!
Keep your caparisons, y'are aptly clad;
I came a feigner, to return stark mad.          *Exit*

*Enter* LOLLIO

ANTONIO Stay, or I shall change condition,
And become as you are.
LOLLIO Why, Tony, whither now? Why, fool?
ANTONIO Whose fool, usher of idiots? You coxcomb!
I have fooled too much.
LOLLIO You were best be mad another while then.
ANTONIO So I am, stark mad: I have cause enough,          150
And I could throw the full effects on thee,
And beat thee like a fury!
LOLLIO Do not, do not. I shall not forbear the
gentleman under the fool if you do—alas, I saw
through your fox-skin before now! Come, I can give
you comfort. My mistress loves you, and there is as
arrant a madman i'th'house as you are a fool, your
rival, whom she loves not. If after the masque we can
rid her of him, you earn her love, she says, and the
fool shall ride her.          160
ANTONIO May I believe thee?
LOLLIO Yes, or you may choose whether you will or no.
ANTONIO She's eased of him; I have a good quarrel
on't.

LOLLIO Well, keep your old station yet, and be quiet.
ANTONIO Tell her I will deserve her love.          *Exit*
LOLLIO And you are like to have your desire.

*Enter* FRANCISCUS

FRANCISCUS (*Sings*) 'Down, down, down a-down a-
down'; and then with a horse-trick          167
To kick Latona's forehead, and break her bowstring.
LOLLIO (*Aside*) This is t'other counterfeit; I'll put him
out of his humour. (*Takes out letter and reads*) 'Sweet
lady, having now cast off this counterfeit cover of a
madman, I appear to your best judgement a true and
faithful lover of your beauty.' This is pretty well for a
madman.
FRANCISCUS Ha! What's that?
LOLLIO 'Chide those perfections in you which have
made me imperfect.'
FRANCISCUS I am discovered to the fool.
LOLLIO I hope to discover the fool in you, ere I have
done with you. 'Yours all, or one beside himself,
Franciscus.' This madman will mend sure.          181
FRANCISCUS What do you read, sirrah?
LOLLIO Your destiny, sir. You'll be hanged for this
trick, and another that I know.
FRANCISCUS Art thou of counsel with thy mistress?
LOLLIO Next her apron-strings.
FRANCISCUS Give me thy hand.
LOLLIO Stay, let me put yours in my pocket first (*Puts
away the letter*). Your hand is true is it not? It will not
pick? I partly fear it, because I think it does lie.          190
FRANCISCUS Not in a syllable.
LOLLIO So; if you love my mistress so well as you have
handled the matter here, you are like to be cured of
your madness.
FRANCISCUS And none but she can cure it.
LOLLIO Well, I'll give you over then, and she shall cast
your water next.
FRANCISCUS Take for thy pains past.          *Gives him money*
LOLLIO I shall deserve more, sir, I hope. My mistress

---

129 Endymion: a youth beloved by Luna (the moon) who
  controlled the seas
133 unshapen antic: deformed grotesque figure
134 bedlam: lunatic
135 frantic: lunatic
142 caparisons: grotesque clothes
143 feigner: pretender
147 usher: a) doorkeeper; b) assistant school master
153–4 forbear the . . . the fool: tolerate this behaviour, even if
  it comes from a disguised gentleman
155 fox-skin: cunning disguise
157 arrant: wandering
159 rid her of: set her free from
160 ride her: copulate with

164 station: position (as a fool)
167 horse-trick: a) horse-play; b) copulation
168 Latona's: in classical mythology Latona was the mother
  of Diana (or Artemis) who hunted with a bow and arrow.
  Here Lollio means Diana herself (represented by
  Isabella)
178 discovered to: found out by
179 discover: expose
183–4 this trick: fraud
184 another: i.e. the horse-trick, l. 167
185 of counsel in: confidence
188 yours: referring to a) hand; b) handwriting
189 true: honest
190 pick: i.e. pick his pocket
197 cast your water: make a diagnosis through examining
  urine

loves you, but must have some proof of your love to her. 201

FRANCISCUS There I meet my wishes.

LOLLIO That will not serve: you must meet her enemy and yours.

FRANCISCUS He's dead already!

LOLLIO Will you tell me that, and I parted but now with him?

FRANCISCUS Show me the man.

LOLLIO Ay, that's a right course now: see him before you kill him in any case. And yet it needs not go so far neither. 'Tis but a fool that haunts the house and my mistress in the shape of an idiot. Bang but his fool's coat well-favouredly, and 'tis well. 213

FRANCISCUS Soundly, soundly!

LOLLIO Only reserve him till the masque be past, and if you find him not now in the dance yourself, I'll show you. In, in! My master! *Dances*

FRANCISCUS He handles him like a feather. Hey!
*Exit dancing*

*Enter* ALIBIUS

ALIBIUS Well said. In a readiness, Lollio?

LOLLIO Yes, sir. 220

ALIBIUS Away then, and guide them in, Lollio;
Entreat your mistress to see this sight. *Exit* LOLLIO
Hark, is there not one incurable fool
That might be begged? I have friends.

LOLLIO (*Within*) I have him for you: one that shall deserve it too.

ALIBIUS Good boy, Lollio.

*Enter* ISABELLA, *then* LOLLIO *with* MADMEN *and* FOOLS.
*The* MADMEN *and* FOOLS *dance*

ALIBIUS 'Tis perfect. Well, fit but once these strains,
We shall have coin and credit for our pains.
*Exeunt*

# Act V, scene i

*Enter* BEATRICE. *A clock strikes one*

BEATRICE One struck, and yet she lies by't!—O my fears!
This strumpet serves her own ends, 'tis apparent now,
Devours the pleasure with a greedy appetite,
And never minds my honour or my peace,
Makes havoc of my right. But she pays dearly for't:
No trusting of her life with such a secret,
That cannot rule her blood to keep her promise.
Beside, I have some suspicion of her faith to me,
Because I was suspected of my lord, 9
And it must come from her.—Hark, by my horrors,
Another clock strikes two. *Strikes two*

*Enter* DE FLORES

DE FLORES Pist, where are you?

BEATRICE De Flores!

DE FLORES Ay. Is she not come from him yet?

BEATRICE As I am a living soul, not.

DE FLORES Sure the devil
Hath sowed his itch within her. Who would trust
A waiting-woman?

BEATRICE I must trust somebody.

DE FLORES Push, they are termagants,
Especially when they fall upon their masters
And have their ladies' first-fruits; th'are mad whelps,
You cannot stave 'em off from game royal. Then,
You are so harsh and hardy, ask no counsel; 20
And I could have helped you to an apothecary's daughter
Would have fall'n off before eleven, and thanked you too.

BEATRICE O me, not yet? This whore forgets herself.

DE FLORES The rascal fares so well. Look, y'are undone:
The day-star, by this hand! See Phosphorus plain yonder.

---

205 He's dead: He's as good as dead
213 well-favouredly: soundly
215 reserve: spare
217 In, in! . . . My master: Lollio sees Alibius as he guides Franciscus to another part of the stage
218 him: himself
219 said: done
223–4 there not . . . be begged: to 'beg a fool' was to apply to the Court of Wards and Liveries for the supervision of a person who was proved to be a congenital 'idiot'. A successful applicant would have powers of attorney over that person's wealth and property
225 him: Antonio
228 fit but . . . these strains: apply efforts that will match the music

---

1 and yet she lies by't: and still she (Diaphanta) is having intercourse
2 ends: with possible pun on pudendum
4 peace: peace of mind
5 right: rights
6 secret: i.e. the bed-trick
7 blood: sexual passion
9 of: by
14 itch: a) inclination to evil; b) sexual impulse
16 termagants: fierce, violent women
17 fall upon: have sex with
19 stave 'em . . . game royal: 'divert them from hunting game which are a royal preserve' (Frost)
20 harsh and hardy: rough and rash
25 Phosphorus: Venus, the morning star

BEATRICE Advise me now to fall upon some ruin;
  There is no counsel safe else.
DE FLORES             Peace! I ha't now,
  For we must force a rising; there's no remedy.
BEATRICE How? Take heed of that.
DE FLORES Tush, be you quiet, or else give over all.   **30**
BEATRICE Prithee, I ha' done then.
DE FLORES             This is my reach: I'll set
  Some part a-fire of Diaphanta's chamber.
BEATRICE How? Fire, sir? That may endanger the
  whole house.
DE FLORES You talk of danger when your fame's on
  fire?
BEATRICE That's true; do what thou wilt now.
DE FLORES             Push, I aim
  At a most rich success, strikes all dead sure:
  The chimney being a-fire, and some light parcels
  Of the least danger in her chamber only,
  If Diaphanta should be met by chance then
  Far from her lodging (which is now suspicious),   **40**
  It would be thought her fears and affrights then
  Drove her to seek for succour; if not seen
  Or met at all, as that's the likeliest,
  For her own shame she'll hasten towards her lodging.
  I will be ready with a piece high-charged,
  As 'twere to cleanse the chimney; there 'tis proper,
  But she shall be the mark.
BEATRICE            I'm forced to love thee now,
  'Cause thou provid'st so carefully for my honour.
DE FLORES 'Slid, it concerns the safety of us both,
  Our pleasure and continuance.
BEATRICE            One word now,   **50**
  Prithee. How for the servants?
DE FLORES            I'll despatch them
  Some one way, some another in the hurry,

For buckets, hooks, ladders. Fear not you;
  The deed shall find its time.—And I've thought since
  Upon a safe conveyance for the body too.
  How this fire purifies wit! Watch you your minute.
BEATRICE Fear keeps my soul upon't; I cannot stray
  from't.

*Enter* ALONZO's *ghost*

DE FLORES Ha! What art thou, that tak'st away the light
  'Twixt that star and me? I dread thee not;
  'Twas but a mist of conscience.—All's clear again.   **60**
                             *Exit*
BEATRICE Who's that, De Flores? Bless me! It slides
  by!                           *Exit ghost*
  Some ill thing haunts the house; 't has left behind it
  A shivering sweat upon me. I'm afraid now.
  This night hath been so tedious! O, this strumpet!
  Had she a thousand lives, he should not leave her
  Till he had destroyed the last. List! O my terrors!
                      *Struck three o'clock*
  Three struck, by Saint Sebastian's!
VOICES (*within*) Fire, fire, fire!
BEATRICE Already! How rare is that man's speed!
  How heartily he serves me! His face loathes one,   **70**
  But look upon his care, who would not love him?
  The east is not more beauteous than his service.
VOICES (*within*) Fire, fire, fire!

*Enter* DE FLORES; SERVANTS *pass over, ring a bell*

DE FLORES Away, despatch! Hooks, buckets, ladders!
  That's well said!—
  The fire-bell rings, the chimney works; my charge,
  The piece is ready.              *Exit*
BEATRICE         Here's a man worth loving!—

*Enter* DIAPHANTA

  O, y'are a jewel!
DIAPHANTA         Pardon frailty, madam;
  In troth I was so well I ev'n forgot myself.
BEATRICE Y'have made trim work.
DIAPHANTA         What?
BEATRICE             Hie quickly to your chamber;

---

26 fall upon some ruin: devise some destruction (of
    Diaphanta)
27 counsel safe else: safe alternative plan
28 force a rising: make everyone (including Diaphanta and
    Alsemero) rise from their beds
30 give over all: surrender all hope
31 reach: plan
34 fame: reputation
36 success: outcome
    strikes all dead sure: solves all the problems
37 parcel: items
40 lodging: bedroom
45 piece high-charged: heavily load gun
46 proper: Q has 'proper now' but the 'now' seems
    superfluous. De Flores means that it would be
    appropriate in the circumstances (now) to have a gun
    nearby to put out a chimney fire
47 mark: target
49 'Slid: by God's eyelid
50 Our pleasure and continuance: sexual pleasure and its
    continuance, and their continued existence

---

54 The deed . . . its time: the killing of Diaphanta will be
    timed appropriately
55 conveyance: removal
56 minute: your timing (she is to return to Alsemero's bed)
64 tedious: painful and long
70 loathes one: is loathsome to one
72 The east: sunrise
75–6 the chimney . . . is ready: Q has 'the chimney works, my
    charge;/The piece is ready', but since the gun has yet to
    be fired, 'the chimney works' presumably means 'the
    chimney is on fire' or 'the chimney trick is working'
77 jewel: a) a gem; b) chastity itself (ironically)
79 trim work: a good job of it (sarcastically)

Your reward follows you.

DIAPHANTA                    I never made                    80
So sweet a bargain.                              *Exit*

*Enter* ALSEMERO

ALSEMERO                    O my dear Joanna!
Alas, art thou risen too? I was coming,
My absolute treasure.

BEATRICE                    When I missed you
I could not choose but follow.

ALSEMERO                              Th'art all sweetness!
The fire is not so dangerous.

BEATRICE                              Think you so, sir?

ALSEMERO  I prithee, tremble not; believe me, 'tis not.

*Enter* VERMANDERO, JASPERINO

VERMANDERO  O, bless my house and me!

ALSEMERO                              My lord your father.

*Enter* DE FLORES *with a piece*

VERMANDERO  Knave, whither goes that piece?

DE FLORES                    To scour the chimney.    *Exit*

VERMANDERO  O, well said, well said!
That fellow's good on all occasions.              90

BEATRICE  A wondrous necessary man, my lord.

VERMANDERO  He hath a ready wit; he's worth 'em all,
sir.
Dog at a house on fire—I ha' seen him singed ere
now.                              *The piece goes off*
Ha, there he goes.

BEATRICE  (*Aside*)          'Tis done.

ALSEMERO                    Come, sweet, to bed now;
Alas, thou wilt get cold.

BEATRICE                    Alas, the fear keeps that out!
My heart will find no quiet till I hear
How Diaphanta, my poor woman, fares;
It is her chamber, sir, her lodging chamber.

VERMANDERO  How should the fire come there?

BEATRICE  As good a soul as ever lady countenanced,
But in her chamber negligent and heavy.          101
She 'scaped a ruin twice.

VERMANDERO                    Twice?

BEATRICE                              Strangely, twice, sir.

VERMANDERO  Those sleepy sluts are dangerous in a
house,
And they be ne'er so good.

*Enter* DE FLORES

DE FLORES                    O poor virginity!
Thou hast paid dearly for't.

VERMANDERO                    Bless us! What's that?

DE FLORES  A thing you all knew once—Diaphanta's
burnt.

BEATRICE  My woman! O my woman!

DE FLORES                              Now the flames
Are greedy of her: burnt, burnt, burnt to death, sir.

BEATRICE  O my presaging soul!

ALSEMERO                    Not a tear more!
I charge you by the last embrace I gave you        110
In bed, before this raised us.

BEATRICE                              Now you tie me:
Were it my sister, now she gets no more.

*Enter* SERVANT

VERMANDERO  How now?

SERVANT                    All danger's past; you may now take
Your rests, my lords. The fire is throughly quenched.
Ah, poor gentlewoman, how soon was she stifled!

BEATRICE  De Flores, what is left of her inter,
And we as mourners all will follow her.
I will entreat that honour to my servant
Ev'n of my lord himself.

ALSEMERO                    Command it, sweetness.   119

BEATRICE  Which of you spied the fire first?

DE FLORES                    'Twas I, madam.

BEATRICE  And took such pains in't too? A double
goodness!
'Twere well he were rewarded.

VERMANDERO                    He shall be.
De Flores, call upon me.

ALSEMERO                    And upon me, sir.
                              *Exeunt all except* DE FLORES

DE FLORES  Rewarded? Precious! Here's a trick beyond
me!
I see in all bouts, both of sport and wit,
Always a woman strives for the last hit.
                                                *Exit*

# Act V, scene ii

*Enter* TOMAZO

TOMAZO  I cannot taste the benefits of life
With the same relish I was wont to do.
Man I grow weary of, and hold his fellowship
A treacherous bloody friendship; and because

---

80  your reward: a) payment; b) your death
93  Dog at: skilled in
100  countenanced: favoured, employed
101  heavy: sluggish
102  ruin: Q has 'mine' which makes sense (as a 'blast') but we
follow Craik's emendation
104  And they . . . so good: no matter how good as servants

104  O poor virginity!: i.e perhaps if Diaphanta had had a
husband she might have survived. De Flores may enter
carrying Diaphanta's body
111  tie: constrain
114  throughly: thoroughly
124  Precious: by God's precious body
125  sport: a) games; b) sexual play

I am ignorant in whom my wrath should settle,
I must think all men villains, and the next
I meet, whoe'er he be, the murderer
Of my most worthy brother.—Ha! What's he?

*Enter* DE FLORES, *passes over the stage*

O, the fellow that some call honest De Flores.
But methinks honesty was hard bested          10
To come there for a lodging—as if a queen
Should make her palace of a pest-house.
I find a contrariety in nature
Betwixt that face and me; the least occasion
Would give me game upon him. Yet he's so foul,
One would scarce touch him with a sword he loved
And made account of; so most deadly venomous,
He would go near to poison any weapon
That should draw blood on him. One must resolve
Never to use that sword again in fight,          20
In way of honest manhood, that strikes him.
Some river must devour it; 'twere not fit
That any man should find it.—What, again?

*Enter* DE FLORES

He walks a' purpose by, sure, to choke me up,
To infect my blood.
DE FLORES                    My worthy noble lord!
TOMAZO Dost offer to come near and breathe upon
     me?                              *Strikes him*
DE FLORES A blow!                *Draws his sword*
TOMAZO                  Yea, are you so prepared?
I'll rather like a soldier die by th' sword
Than like a politician by thy poison.          *Draws*
DE FLORES Hold, my lord, as you are honourable.   30
TOMAZO All slaves that kill by poison are still cowards.
DE FLORES (*Aside*) I cannot strike: I see his brother's
     wounds
Fresh bleeding in his eye, as in a crystal.
(*To* TOMAZO) I will not question this: I know y'are
     noble                    *Sheathes his sword*
I take my injury with thanks given, sir,
Like a wise lawyer, and as a favour
Will wear it for the worthy hand that gave it.
(*Aside*) Why this from him, that yesterday appeared
So strangely loving to me?
O, but instinct is of a subtler strain!          40

Guilt must not walk so near his lodge again—
He came near me now.                    *Exit*
TOMAZO All league with mankind I renounce for ever
Till I find this murderer. Not so much
As common courtesy but I'll lock up,
For in the state of ignorance I live in
A brother may salute his brother's murderer,
And wish good speed to th'villain in a greeting.

*Enter* VERMANDERO, ALIBIUS *and* ISABELLA

VERMANDERO Noble Piracquo!
TOMAZO                    Pray keep on your way, sir;
I've nothing to say to you.
VERMANDERO                  Comforts bless you, sir.  50
TOMAZO I have forsworn compliment; in troth I have,
     sir.
As you are merely man, I have not left
A good wish for you, nor any here.
VERMANDERO Unless you be so far in love with grief
You will not part from't upon any terms,
We bring that news will make a welcome for us.
TOMAZO What news can that be?
VERMANDERO                  Throw no scornful smile
Upon the zeal I bring you; 'tis worth more, sir.
Two of the chiefest men I kept about me
I hide not from the law, or your just vengeance.   60
TOMAZO Ha!
VERMANDERO To give your peace more ample
     satisfaction,
Thank these discoverers.
TOMAZO                  If you bring that calm,
Name but the manner I shall ask forgiveness in
For that contemptuous smile upon you:
I'll perfect it with reverence that belongs
Unto a sacred altar.                    *Kneels*
VERMANDERO                  Good sir, rise.
Why, now you overdo as much a' this hand,
As you fell short a't'other.—Speak, Alibius.
ALIBIUS 'Twas my wife's fortune—as she is most lucky
At a discovery—to find out lately          71
Within our hospital of fools and madmen

---

10  hard bested: hard pressed
12  pest-house: hospital for plague victims
15  game upon: a reason to fight
24  choke me up: suffocate by his mere proximity
29  politician: schemer (a word derived from
     Machiavelli)
31  still: always
33  crystal: crystal ball
36–7  Like a . . . gave it: lawyers were thought to tolerate
     humiliation so as to press charges later

42  came near me: seemed (instinctively) to sense something
     of my guilt
43  league: alliance, connection
44–5  Not so . . . lock up: 'I'll display no more than something
     less than common courtesy' (Daalder)
48  speed: success
51  compliment: formal courtesy
58  zeal: good will
59  Two of the chiefest men: i.e Franciscus and Antonio
60  or your just vengeance: private revenge, seen by some as a
     proper substitute for legal process (which Vermandero
     also offers)
63  these discoverers: Alibius and Isabella

Two counterfeits slipped into these disguises;
Their names, Franciscus and Antonio.
VERMANDERO Both mine, sir, and I ask no favour for
'em.
ALIBIUS Now that which draws suspicion to their habits:
The time of their disguisings agrees justly
With the day of the murder.
TOMAZO                            O blest revelation!
VERMANDERO Nay more, nay more, sir—I'll not spare
mine own
In way of justice—they both feigned a journey      80
To Briamata, and so wrought out their leaves;
My love was so abused in't.
TOMAZO                            Time's too precious
To run in waste now. You have brought a peace
The riches of five kingdoms could not purchase.
Be my most happy conduct. I thirst for 'em:
Like subtle lightning will I wind about 'em,
And melt their marrow in 'em.
                                            *Exeunt*

# Act V, scene iii

*Enter* ALSEMERO *and* JASPERINO

JASPERINO Your confidence, I'm sure, is now of proof.
The prospect from the garden has showed
Enough for deep suspicion.
ALSEMERO                            The black mask
That so continually was worn upon't
Condemns the face for ugly ere't be seen—
Her despite to him, and so seeming bottomless.
JASPERINO Touch it home then. 'Tis not a shallow
probe

---

73 these disguises: either the guises of 'fools and madmen'
   or, as Daalder suggests, Alibius has the actual disguises
   with him
75 mine: 'my men'
   favour: lenient treatment
76 habits: clothes
77 justly: exactly
81 wrought out their leaves: worked out their requests for
   leave of absence
85 conduct: guide
86–7 subtle lightening . . . in 'em: lightning was believed to
   melt the marrow of the bones without disfiguring the
   body and was thus an image of sudden and unusual death
1 confidence: distrust in Beatrice
   of proof: confirmed and strong
2 prospect from the garden: Jasperino and Alsemero have
   seen an exchange between Beatrice and De Flores which
   has supported their suspicion
3 black mask: Beatrice's deceitful outward show
5 ugly ere't be seen: her face is morally tainted even before
   it is revealed
6 despite to: scorn of
7 Touch it home: investigate it to the end

Can search this ulcer soundly: I fear you'll find it
Full of corruption.—'Tis fit I leave you.
She meets you opportunely from that walk;      10
She took the back door at his parting with her.
                                            *Exit* JASPERINO
ALSEMERO Did my fate wait for this unhappy stroke
At my first sight of woman?—She's here.

*Enter* BEATRICE

BEATRICE Alsemero!
ALSEMERO                            How do you?
BEATRICE                                                How do I?
Alas! How do you? You look not well.
ALSEMERO You read me well enough. I am not well.
BEATRICE Not well, sir? Is't in my power to better you?
ALSEMERO Yes.
BEATRICE            Nay, then y'are cured again.
ALSEMERO Pray resolve me one question, lady.
BEATRICE                                                If I can.
ALSEMERO None can so sure. Are you honest?      20
BEATRICE Ha, ha, ha! That's a broad question, my lord.
ALSEMERO But that's not a modest answer, my lady.
Do you laugh? My doubts are strong upon me.
BEATRICE 'Tis innocence that smiles, and no rough
brow
Can take away the dimple in her cheek.
Say I should strain a tear to fill the vault,
Which would you give the better faith to?
ALSEMERO 'Twere but hypocrisy of a sadder colour,
But the same stuff. Neither your smiles not tears
Shall move or flatter me from my belief:      30
You are a whore.
BEATRICE                    What a horrid sound it hath!
It blasts a beauty to deformity;
Upon what face soever that breath falls,
It strikes it ugly. O, you have ruined
What you can ne'er repair again!
ALSEMERO I'll all demolish, and seek out truth within
you,
If there be any left. Let your sweet tongue

---

12–13 Did my . . . of woman?: Beatrice was Alsemero's first
   love (see I.i.1–12) and he wonders whether it was his
   destiny to receive this 'unhappy stroke' of fortune
19 resolve: answer
20 honest: a) truthful; b) chaste (as in faithful)
21 broad: a) unfocused; b) vulgar
22 modest: chaste
25 her: i.e. innocence (Beatrice personifies innocence and
   remains truthful)
26 strain: force
   the vault: the arch of the sky
27 Which: i.e. a smile or tears
28 sadder: more solemn, graver
29 the same stuff: cut from the same cloth

Prevent your heart's rifling; there I'll ransack
And tear out my suspicion.

BEATRICE                              You may, sir,
'Tis an easy passage. Yet, if you please,                    **40**
Show me the ground whereon you lost your love.
My spotless virtue may but tread on that
Before I perish.

ALSEMERO              Unanswerable!
A ground you cannot stand on: you fall down
Beneath all grace and goodness when you set
Your ticklish heel on it. There was a visor
O'er that cunning face, and that became you;
Now impudence in triumph rides upon't.
How comes this tender reconcilement else
'Twixt you and your despite, your rancorous loathing,
De Flores? He that your eye was sore at sight of,     **51**
He's now become your arms' supporter, your
Lips' saint!

BEATRICE      Is there the cause?

ALSEMERO                              Worse; your lust's devil,
Your adultery!

BEATRICE              Would any but yourself say that,
'Twould turn him to a villain.

ALSEMERO                              It was witnessed
By the counsel of your bosom, Diaphanta.

BEATRICE  Is your witness dead then?

ALSEMERO                              'Tis to be feared
It was the wages of her knowledge. Poor soul,
She lived not long after the discovery.

BEATRICE  Then hear a story of not much less horror **60**
Than this your false suspicion is beguiled with.
To your bed's scandal, I stand up innocence,
Which even the guilt of one black other deed

---

38    your heart's rifling: the tearing open of her heart to see
      into it
41    ground: basis
42    may but tread on that: can only crush it
43    Unanswerable: the basis (ground) is so strong that it is
      beyond any denial or argument
46    ticklish: a) unsteady: b) easily aroused (sexually)
      visor: the mask mentioned at the beginning of the scene
47    became: a) flattered; b) was appropriately false
48    impudence: shamelessness
50    despite: object of scorn
52    arms' supporter: some eds emend to 'arm's'; we follow Q
      and note the suggestion by Williams that this may refer
      to the men or beasts that support a shield of arms in
      heraldry; the elevated, martial tone of the passage would
      justify such a reading
53    Lips' saint: a) lover (colloquial); b) object of prayer and
      spiritual appeal
      there: that
54    adultery: partner in adultery
56    counsel of your bosom: confidante
62    To: in response to the accusation of

Will stand for proof of. Your love has made me
A cruel murd'ress.

ALSEMERO              Ha!

BEATRICE              A bloody one;
I have kissed poison for it, stroked a serpent:
That thing of hate—worthy in my esteem
Of no better employment, and him most worthy
To be so employed—I caused to murder
That innocent Piracquo, having no                    **70**
Better means than that worst, to assure
Yourself to me.

ALSEMERO              O, the place itself e'er since
Has crying been for vengeance: the temple
Where blood and beauty first unlawfully
Fired their devotion, and quenched the right one;
'Twas in my fears at first, 'twill have it now:
O, thou art all deformed!

BEATRICE              Forget not, sir,
It for your sake was done. Shall greater dangers
Make the less welcome?

ALSEMERO              O, thou shouldst have gone
A thousand leagues about to have avoided                **80**
This dangerous bridge of blood! Here we are lost.

BEATRICE  Remember I am true unto your bed.

ALSEMERO  The bed itself's a charnel, the sheets shrouds
For murdered carcasses. It must ask pause
What I must do in this. Meantime you shall
Be my prisoner only. Enter my closet;
                              *Exit* BEATRICE *into closet*
I'll be your keeper yet.—O, in what part
Of this sad story shall I first begin?—Ha!

*Enter* DE FLORES

This same fellow has put me in.—De Flores?

DE FLORES  Noble Alsemero!

ALSEMERO                              I can tell you     **90**
News, sir. My wife has her commended to you.

DE FLORES  That's news indeed, my lord; I think she
      would

---

64    Your love: my love for you
66    stroked: possibly with the sense 'copulated with'
72    the place: the temple
74    blood: sexual desire
75    right one: i.e. religious devotion
76    'twill have it now: unclear, but possibly: a) the temple will
      have vengeance; b) Alsemero will now take vengeance
78–9  Shall greater . . . less welcome?: 'shall the greater
      dangers I have dared for you make my welcome the less?'
      (Black)
80    about: out of your way
83    charnel: charnel-house (repository for the dead)
84    pause: i.e. for consideration of
87    yet: for the time being
89    put me in: put me in mind (i.e. shown me where to
      begin)
91    her commended to you: asked to be remembered

Commend me to the gallows if she could,
She ever loved me so well. I thank her.

ALSEMERO What's this blood upon your band, De
    Flores?

DE FLORES Blood? No, sure; 'twas washed since.

ALSEMERO              Since when, man?

DE FLORES Since t'other day I got a knock
In a sword-and-dagger school; I think 'tis out.

ALSEMERO Yes, 'tis almost out, but 'tis perceived
    though.—
  I had forgot my message. This it is:        **100**
  What price goes murder?

DE FLORES          How, sir?

ALSEMERO            I ask you, sir.
  My wife's behindhand with you, she tells me,
  For a brave bloody blow you gave for her sake
  Upon Piracquo.

DE FLORES     Upon? 'Twas quite through him, sure.
  Has she confessed it?

ALSEMERO         As sure as death to both of you,
  And much more than that.

DE FLORES         It could not be much more:
  'Twas but one thing, and that—she's a whore.

ALSEMERO It could not choose but follow. O cunning
    devils!
  How should blind men know you from fair-faced
    saints?         **109**

BEATRICE (*within*) He lies, the villain does belie me!

DE FLORES Let me go to her, sir.

ALSEMERO         Nay, you shall to her.—
  Peace, crying crocodile, your sounds are heard!
  Take your prey to you.—Get you in to her, sir.

                  *Exit* DE FLORES *into closet*
  I'll be your pander now: rehearse again
  Your scene of lust, that you may be perfect
  When you shall come to act it to the black audience
  Where howls and gnashings shall be music to you.
  Clip your adult'ress freely—'tis the pilot
  Will guide you to the Mare Mortuum,
  Where you shall sink to fathoms bottomless.   **120**

*Enter* VERMANDERO, ALIBIUS, ISABELLA, TOMAZO,
FRANCISCUS, *and* ANTONIO

VERMANDERO O Alsemero, I have a wonder for you.

ALSEMERO No sir, 'tis I, I have a wonder for you.

VERMANDERO I have suspicion near as proof itself
  For Piracquo's murder.

ALSEMERO           Sir, I have proof
  Beyond suspicion for Piracquo's murder.

VERMANDERO Beseech you, hear me. These two have
    been disguised
  E'er since the deed was done.

ALSEMERO          I have two other
  That were more close disguised than your two could
    be,
  E'er since the deed was done.

VERMANDERO You'll hear me—these mine own
    servants—         **130**

ALSEMERO Hear me—those nearer than your servants,
  That shall acquit them, and prove them guiltless.

FRANCISCUS That may be done with easy truth, sir.

TOMAZO How is my cause bandied through your
    delays!
  'Tis urgent in my blood, and calls for haste:
  Give me a brother alive or dead—
  Alive, a wife with him; if dead, for both
  A recompense, for murder and adultery.

BEATRICE (*within*) O, O, O!

ALSEMERO         Hark, 'tis coming to you.

DE FLORES (*within*) Nay, I'll along for company.

BEATRICE (*within*)             O, O!

VERMANDERO What horrid sounds are these?   **141**

ALSEMERO Come forth, you twins of mischief!

*Enter* DE FLORES *bringing in* BEATRICE *wounded*

DE FLORES Here we are. If you have any more
  To say to us, speak quickly; I shall not
  Give you the hearing else. I am so stout yet,
  And so, I think, that broken rib of mankind.

VERMANDERO An host of enemies ent'red my citadel
  Could not amaze like this. Joanna! Beatrice! Joanna!

BEATRICE O come not near me, sir; I shall defile you.
  I am that of your blood was taken from you   **150**

---

95 band: cuff
102 behindhand with: indebted to
103 brave: a) courageous; b) splendid
112 crying crocodile: crocodiles were believed to shed false
    tears over their prey
113 in to: Q has 'into' (with possible sexual connotation)
114 pander: pimp
116 black audience: devils of hell
118 clip: embrace
    pilot: i.e. Beatrice, who will guide De Flores to hell
119 Mare Mortuum: the Dead Sea, here pictured as hell

126 these two: i.e. Antonio and Franciscus
128 close: covertly
131 nearer: a) in rank and kin; b) to the truth of the crime
134 bandied: tossed about (thus neglected)
138 adultery: Tomazo regards Beatrice's marriage to
    Alsemero as adulterous as she was engaged to Alonzo
139 'tis: i.e. revenge
140 I'll along for company: De Flores 'accompanies' Beatrice
    by wounding himself
145 stout: strong enough still (to talk, despite the wounds)
146 that broken rib of mankind: Beatrice is described as though
    she is Eve, created from Adam's rib (see Genesis, 2.21–3)
148 amaze: perplex, confound (make a labyrinth of
    Vermandero's citadel)
149 defile: infect
150–1 I am . . . better health: Beatrice refers to phlebotomy
    (the removal of bad blood in order to cure illness)

For your better health. Look no more upon't,
But cast it to the ground regardlessly;
Let the common sewer take it from distinction.
Beneath the stars, upon yon meteor

*pointing to* DE FLORES

Ever hung my fate, 'mongst things corruptible;
I ne'er could pluck it from him. My loathing
Was prophet to the rest, but ne'er believed;
Mine honour fell with him, and now my life.—
Alsemero, I am a stranger to your bed:
Your bed was coz'ned on the nuptial night,     **160**
For which your false bride died.

ALSEMERO                  Diaphanta!

DE FLORES Yes; and the while I coupled with your mate
At barley-break. Now we are left in hell.

VERMANDERO We are all there; it circumscribes us here.

DE FLORES I loved this woman in spite of her heart;
Her love I earned out of Piracquo's murder.

TOMAZO Ha! My brother's murderer!

DE FLORES               Yes, and her honour's prize
Was my reward, I thank life for nothing
But that pleasure; it was so sweet to me
That I have drunk up all, left none behind     **170**
For any man to pledge me.

VERMANDERO             Horrid villain!
Keep life in him for further tortures.

DE FLORES                      No:—
I can prevent you, here's my penknife still.
It is but one thread more, (*Stabs himself*)—and now
'tis cut.
Make haste, Joanna, by that token to thee
Canst not forget, so lately put in mind;
I would not go to leave thee far behind.     *Dies*

BEATRICE Forgive me, Alsemero, all forgive!
'Tis time to die, when 'tis a shame to live.     *Dies*

VERMANDERO O, my name is ent'red now in that record     **180**

Where till this fatal hour 'twas never read.

ALSEMERO Let it be blotted out; let your heart lose it,
And it can never look you in the face,
Nor tell a tale behind the back of life
To your dishonour. Justice hath so right
The guilty hit, that innocence is quit
By proclamation, and may joy again.
Sir, you are sensible of what truth hath done;
'Tis the best comfort that your grief can find.

TOMAZO (*To* VERMANDERO) Sir, I am satisfied; my injuries     **190**
Lie dead before me. I can exact no more,
Unless my soul were loose, and could o'ertake
Those black fugitives, that are fled from thence,
To take a second vengeance. But there are wraths
Deeper than mine, 'tis to be feared, about 'em.

ALSEMERO What an opacous body had that moon
That last changed on us! Here is beauty changed
To ugly whoredom; here, servant-obedience
To a master-sin, imperious murder;
I, a supposed husband, changed embraces     **200**
With wantonness, but that was paid before;
(*To* TOMAZO) Your change is come too, from an ignorant wrath
To knowing friendship. Are there any more on's?

ANTONIO Yes, sir, I was changed too, from a little ass
as I was to a great fool as I am; and had like to ha'
been changed to the gallows but that you know my
innocence always excuses me.

FRANCISCUS I was changed from a little wit to be stark mad,
Almost for the same purpose.

ISABELLA (*To* ALIBIUS)     Your change is still behind,
But deserve best your transformation:     **210**
You are a jealous coxcomb, keep schools of folly,
And teach your scholars how to break your own head.

ALIBIUS I see all apparent, wife, and will change now
Into a better husband, and never keep

---

153 from distinction: anything identifying it as separate (from the filth of the common sewer)
154 stars: fixed symbols of purity
     meteor: symbol of sublunary transience (and thus impurity)
156–7 My loathing . . . ne'er believed: Beatrice's original loathing for De Flores predicted the present outcome, yet she ignored the warning
163 barley-break: reference to the game (mentioned at III.iii.173–4) where some players end up in 'hell'
165 heart: disposition, attitude (i.e. her original loathing)
167 honour's prize: her maidenhead
171 pledge: toast
175 that token: probably the first wound (made in the closet) now recalled ('put in mind') by the second wound
180 record: the record kept in heaven of earthly misdeeds

---

182 lose: forget
186 quit: acquitted
188 sensible: aware
     done: shown
190 injuries: injustices (accounted for, or 'dead', now that the culprits are dead)
193 black fugitives: the damned souls of Beatrice and De Flores now flying towards hell
194 wraths: the punishments of hell
196 opacous: clouded, ominous
201 wantonness: of Diaphanta
     paid before: punished by her earlier death
207 innocence: a) lack of guilt; b) foolishness
209 behind: to come
212 break your own head: make you a cuckold

Scholars that shall be wiser than myself.
ALSEMERO (*To* VERMANDERO) Sir, you have yet a son's
duty living;
Please you, accept it. Let that your sorrow,
As it goes from your eye, go from your heart.
Man and his sorrow at the grave must part.

# Epilogue

ALSEMERO All we can do, to comfort one another,  **220**
To stay a brother's sorrow for a brother,
To dry a child from the kind father's eyes,
Is to no purpose; it rather multiplies.
Your only smiles have power to cause re-live
The dead again, or in their rooms to give
Brother a new brother, father a child;
If these appear, all griefs are reconciled.

*Exeunt omnes*

FINIS

---

215  wiser: more clever, sane
216  son's duty: Alsemero will still give Vermandero the duty
of the son
218  from your eye: by weeping

221  stay: bring to a close
223  multiplies: increases the grief
224  Your only smiles: your smiles only
225  in their rooms: in their place (instead of the dead)
226  Brother a . . . a child: Alsemero will be a new brother to
Tomazo and a new child to Vermandero
227  these appear: a) the smiles (of the audience); and
therefore b) the new relationships

# John Ford, *'Tis Pity She's a Whore*

First performed 1629–33
First published 1633

John Ford's preoccupation with melancholy, madness and obsessive sexuality has intrigued and sometimes appalled readers across the centuries. The consistent level of grim irony in his plays (his characters tend 'unwittingly' to predict later events) and his compelling verse invite speculation over the kind of intelligence that could have created *'Tis Pity She's a Whore*. During the early twentieth century it was not unusual to find the play dismissed by critics for its unwholesome decadence, the implication being that, by the time Ford was writing, the theatre had succumbed to mere sensationalism and spectacle, and that the days of thoughtful, philosophical drama, epitomised by Shakespeare, were now over. However, as Marion Lomax has remarked, Ford 'tantalises with apparent echoes of, or allusions to, other Renaissance drama (including some of Shakespeare's best-known plays), which is not a sign of slavish dependence but a way of stressing the different contexts and perspectives of his own work – and those contexts and perspectives often owe their fascination to their very perverseness' (Lomax 1995: viii).

This is important when we consider the fairly obvious similarities between this play and *Romeo and Juliet* (1595). The Italian setting recalls Shakespeare's Verona and there are clear parallels between the two sets of lovers, as well as between Shakespeare's Nurse and Ford's Putana, and between Friar Lawrence and Friar Bonaventura, Capulet and Florio. The plays also share an interest in matters of spectacle and occasion: banquets or balls, swordplay, disguise, poisonings and other, more sudden, deaths. Yet in *Romeo and Juliet* audiences are at least invited to sympathise with the lovers' dilemma and to condemn their parents' feuding. While Shakespeare's play could be rewritten to end happily, Giovanni and Annabella's incestuous love posits an extreme and insoluble problem, allowing displays of sexuality and foregrounding the politics of gender at a consistently high level of tension and debate. In Ford's Parma, almost everyone is preoccupied with their sexuality. The play shows how infidelity can lead to revenge, how the potentially creative act of sexual intercourse can lead to death, and how sexual desire affects human relationships more fundamentally than the institutions (marriage, family and religion) which attempt to keep it in check.

Historians have noted the establishment in the seventeenth century of a regime of sexual repression which was central to the doctrines of social and familial uniformity associated with Puritanism. A relative tolerance of sexual transgression in earlier times gave way to a new policing of the boundaries of sexual experience. However, in order to contain and classify what was considered 'normal', such doctrines had to locate what was considered 'deviant'. *'Tis Pity She's a Whore* can be seen in relation to a process through which an evolution of sexual mores into the modern institutions of marriage and the family had paradoxically opened to view a potentially subversive, alternative realm of transgression. In short, to repress sexuality in terms of the religious and social codes which were to become important during the seventeenth century (and since), it was necessary to re-press them (in the sense of re-presenting or re-printing them) in a diverse set of contemporary books, pamphlets, sermons and plays. Indeed, *'Tis Pity She's a Whore* may have reminded its audiences of the real case of Sir Giles Allington, who was put on trial in 1631 for marrying the daughter of his half-sister. Incest may have interested contemporary society because it tested the authority and the boundaries of society's sexual codes.

Just as the play repeatedly connects female sexuality with disease and dysfunction, rather than with fertility and reproduction, and food and drink bring death rather than sustenance, the religious doctrine of Bonaventura is seen as unable to contain the lovers' desire. Parma's judicial system, and especially as represented by the Cardinal, seems to serve only its own agents. Some of the moral relativism Ford dramatises has an echo or parallel in the twenty-first century, and this is perhaps why the play still fascinates modern readers and audiences, yet it is important to read the play in terms of a seventeenth-century shift in consciousness with regard to gender and sexuality which itself has to be viewed in relation to the ever-changing religious and moral circumstances which helped define the intellectual environment in which Ford worked. Although critics and historians have noted the strength of contemporary orthodox teaching in favour of a regulated sexuality, they have also accepted that Ford's was a period of considerable and growing religious scepticism.

That incest was against God's will was clear from biblical sources (Leviticus 20.17 and Deuteronomy 27.22), but a comment in Thomas Beard's totally orthodox treatise, *The Theatre of God's Judgement* (1597), is revealing in that he feels compelled to extend the argument against incest into a secular and non-Christian realm, remarking that 'incest is a wicked and abominable sin, and forbidden both by the law of God and man, in so much that the very heathen held it in detestation' (p. 356). The implication is that incest offends not only against Christian teaching but also against a uniformly natural law recognised by 'man' in general and thus even by non-Christians. Although it was presumably not Beard's intention to undermine Christian doctrine, there is a slight hesitation in this remark over the universality of Christian authority in the material shaping of human behaviour. Much exercised as to how to celebrate classical civilisations whilst acknowledging their pre-Christianity, and intrigued by alluring colonial encounters with the inhabitants of overseas lands, early Stuart intellectuals were compelled to test the authority of Christianity against alternative authorities such as nature, fate and human wit (or intelligence). Against the corrupt moral world of his Parma, Ford manages to invite an audience's sympathy, if only for a moment, on behalf of actors playing out one of the great religious and secular taboos of the period. And even if the audience observes the restoration of a kind of order at the end of the play, and the inevitable deaths of those who have transgressed, it has still glimpsed *en route* to this closure a suggested 'other world' which, finally contained as it may be, still exists as an experiment only possible in the complex set of aesthetic co-ordinates that go into making theatre. Form against form, the theatre powerfully and publicly interrogates for its audience the set positions prescribed more narrowly in the private act of reading a treatise or listening to a sermon. *'Tis Pity She's a Whore* remains a powerful and compelling demonstration of this kind of experiment.

*'Tis Pity She's a Whore* was first staged between 1629 and 1633 at the Phoenix Theatre in Drury Lane, a private theatre. Samuel Pepys witnessed a revival of the play in 1661 at the Salisbury Court, but it was only in the twentieth century that it began to be performed regularly. It is likely that twenty-first century audiences and readers will continue to take an interest in Ford's disturbing, yet compelling, work.

## Textual note

The copytext for this edition is the quarto of 1633 (referred to in the footnotes as Q). Copies of this edition are held in the Bodleian Library in Oxford and the British Library in London. Since the quarto includes his

dedication to John Mordaunt it is generally thought that Ford authorised its publication. The quarto divided the play into five acts; the scene divisions in this version are those established by modern editors.

# Further reading

## Editions

Barker, Simon (ed.) (1997) *'Tis Pity She's a Whore*, Routledge English Texts Series, London and New York, NY: Routledge.

Bawcutt, N. W. (ed.) (1966) *'Tis Pity She's a Whore*, Nebraska, NE: University of Nebraska Press.

Gifford, W. and Dyce, A. (eds) (1869) *The Works of John Ford*, London: J. Toovey.

Morris, Brian (ed.) (1988) *'Tis Pity She's a Whore*, The New Mermaids, London: A. & C. Black.

Kinney, Arthur F. (ed.) (1999) *Renaissance Drama: An Anthology of Plays and Entertainments*, Oxford: Blackwell.

Lomax, Marion (ed.) (1995) *'Tis Pity She's a Whore and Other Plays*, World's Classics Series, Oxford: Oxford University Press.

Roper, Derek (ed.) (1997) *'Tis Pity She's a Whore*, The Revels Plays Series, Manchester: Manchester University Press.

Weber, W. (ed.) (1811) *The Dramatic Works of John Ford*, Edinburgh: A. Constable.

## Critical and contextual commentaries

Amtower, L. (1998) '"This idol thou ador'st": The Iconography of *'Tis Pity She's a Whore*', *Papers on Language and Literature*, 34, 2: 179–206.

Anderson, Donald (ed.) (1986) *'Concord in Discord': The Plays of John Ford, 1586–1986*, New York, NY: AMS Press.

Boehrer, Bruce (1984) '"Nice Philosophy": *'Tis Pity She's a Whore* and *The Two Books of God*', *Studies in English Literature 1500–1900*, 14: 355–71.

Boling, Ronald, J. (1991) 'Prayer, Mirrors, and Self-Deification in John Ford's *'Tis Pity She's a Whore*', *Publications of the Arkansas Philological Association*, 17: 1–12.

Bowers, Rick (1986) 'John Ford and the Sleep of Death', *Texas Studies in Language and Literature*, 28: 358–87.

Bueler, L. (1984) 'The Structural Uses of Incest in English Renaissance Drama', *Renaissance Drama*, 15: 115–46.

Clerico, Terri (1992) 'The Politics of Blood: John Ford's *'Tis Pity She's a Whore*', *English Literary Renaissance*, 22, 3: 404–34.

Defaye, Claudine (1979) 'Annabella's Unborn Baby: The Heart in the Womb in *'Tis Pity She's a Whore*', *Cahiers Elisabéthains*, 15: 35–42.

Farr, Dorothy M. (1979) *John Ford and the Caroline Theatre*, London: Macmillan.

Forker, Charles R. (1990) *Fancy's Images*, Carbondale and Edwardsville, IL: University of Illinois Press.

Gauer, Denis (1987) 'Heart and Blood: Nature and Culture in *'Tis Pity She's a Whore*', *Cahiers Elisabéthains*, 23: 43–57.

Hogan, A. (1977) '*'Tis Pity She's a Whore*: The Overall Design', *Studies in English Literature 1500–1900*, 17: 303–16.

Hopkins, Lisa (1994) *John Ford's Political Theatre*, Manchester: Manchester University Press.

—— (1994) 'A Source for John Ford's *'Tis Pity She's a Whore*', *Notes & Queries*, 41: 520–1.

—— (1998) 'Knowing their Loves: Knowledge, Ignorance and Blindness in *'Tis Pity She's a Whore*', *Renaissance Forum*, 3:1 (electronic journal).

Jephson, Valerie L. and Boehrer, Bruce (1994) 'Mythologizing the Middle Class: *'Tis Pity She's a Whore* and the Urban Bourgeoisie', *Renaissance and Reformation*, 18, 3: 5–28.

Leech, Clifford (1957) *John Ford and the Drama of His Time*, London: Chatto and Windus.

Lomax, Marion (1987) *Stage Images and Traditions: Shakespeare to Ford*, Cambridge: Cambridge University Press.

Marienstras, Richard (1985) *New Perspectives on the Shakespearean World* (trans. Janet Lloyd), Cambridge: Cambridge University Press.

McCabe, Richard A. (1993) *Incest, Drama and Nature's Law 1550–1700*, Cambridge: Cambridge University Press.

Monserrat, G. D. (1980) 'The Unity of John Ford: *'Tis Pity She's a Whore* and *Christ's Bloody Sweat*', *Studies in Philology*, 77: 247–70.

Mousley, Andy (2000) *Renaissance Drama and Contemporary Literary Theory*, Basingstoke: Macmillan.

Neil, Michael (ed.) (1988) *John Ford: Critical Re-visions*, Cambridge: Cambridge University Press.

Oliver, H. J. (1955) *The Problem of John Ford*, Melbourne, Australia: Melbourne University Press.

Ornstein, Robert (1960) *The Moral Vision of Jacobean Tragedy*, Madison, WI: University of Wisconsin Press.

Requa, Kenneth A. (1971) 'Music in the Ear: Giovanni as Tragic Hero in Ford's *'Tis Pity She's a Whore*', *Papers on Language and Literature*, 7: 13–25.

Rose, Mary Beth (1991) *The Expense of Spirit: Love and Sexuality in English Renaissance Drama*, Ithaca, NY: Cornell University Press.

Rosen, Carol C. (1974) 'The Language of Cruelty in Ford's *'Tis Pity She's a Whore*', *Comparative Drama*, 8: 356–68.

Sargeaunt, Joan M. (1935) *John Ford*, Oxford: Basil Blackwell.

Sensabaugh, G. F. (1944) *The Tragic Muse of John Ford*, Stanford, CA: Stanford University Press.

Smallwood, R. L. (1981) '*'Tis Pity She's a Whore* and *Romeo and Juliet*', *Cahiers Elisabéthains*, 7: 49–70.

Smith, Molly (1998) *Breaking Boundaries: Politics and Play in the Drama of Shakespeare and His Contemporaries*, Aldershot: Ashgate.

Stavig, Mark (1968) *John Ford and the Traditional Moral Order*, Madison, WI: University of Wisconsin Press.

Stout, Nathaniel (1990) 'The Tragedy of Annabella in *'Tis Pity She's a Whore*', in David G. Allen (ed.) *Traditions and Innovations*, Newark, DE: University of Delaware Press.

Wilks, John S. (1990) *The Idea of Conscience in Renaissance Tragedy*, London: Routledge.

Wiseman, Susan (1990) '*'Tis Pity She's a Whore*: Representing the Incestuous Body', in Lucy Gent and Nigel Llewellyn (eds), *Renaissance Bodies*, London: Reaktion.

Wymer, Rowland (1995) *Webster and Ford*, Basingstoke: Macmillan.

## Works of related interest

Thomas Kyd, *The Spanish Tragedy* (1585)
William Shakespeare, *Titus Andronicus* (1593)
William Shakespeare, *Richard III* (1593)
William Shakespeare, *Romeo and Juliet* (1595)
William Shakespeare, *Hamlet* (1600)
Thomas Middleton or Cyril Tourneur, *The Revenger's Tragedy* (1606)
George Chapman, *The Revenge of Bussy D'Ambois* (1610)
Cyril Tourneur, *The Atheist's Tragedy* (1611)
John Webster, *The White Devil* (1612)
John Webster, *The Duchess of Malfi* (1614)
Thomas Middleton, *The Changeling* (1622)
Thomas Middleton, *Women Beware Women* (1625)
John Ford, *The Broken Heart* (1631)

# 'Tis Pity She's a Whore (1633)

## To My Friend the Author

With admiration I beheld this Whore
Adorned with beauty such as might restore
(If ever being as thy muse hath famed)
Her Giovanni, in his love unblamed:
The ready Graces lent their willing aid,
Pallas herself now played the chambermaid,
And helped to put her dressings on. Secure
Rest thou that thy name herein shall endure
To th' end of age; and Annabella be
Gloriously fair, even in her infamy.

THOMAS ELLICE

## To the Truly Noble John, Earl of Peterborough, Lord Mordaunt, Baron of Turvey

MY LORD,
Where a truth of merit hath a general warrant, there
love is but a debt, acknowledgment a justice. Greatness
cannot often claim virtue by inheritance; yet in this,
yours appears most eminent, for that you are not more
rightly heir to your fortunes than glory shall be to your
memory. Sweetness of disposition ennobles a freedom
of birth; in both, your lawful interest adds honour to
your own name and mercy to my presumption. Your
noble allowance of these first fruits of my leisure in the
action emboldens my confidence of your as noble
construction in this presentment; especially since my
service must ever owe particular duty to your favours by
a particular engagement. The gravity of the subject may
easily excuse the lightness of the title, otherwise I had
been a severe judge against mine own guilt. Princes
have vouchsafed grace to trifles offered from a purity of
devotion; your lordship may likewise please to admit
into your good opinion, with these weak endeavours,
the constancy of affection from the sincere lover of your
deserts in honour,                                        **20**

JOHN FORD

## The Actors' Names

BONAVENTURA, *a friar*

A CARDINAL, *nuncio to the Pope*

SORANZO, *a nobleman*

FLORIO, *a citizen of Parma*

DONADO, *another citizen*

---

9  allowance: approval
9–10  in the action: on the stage
11  construction: interpretation
   in this presentment: in print
   The Actors' Names: Ford's characters derive their names
   from a rich variety of literary and scholastic sources.
   Robert Burton's *The Anatomy of Melancholy* (1621), which
   influenced much of Ford's work, mentions Bonaventura
   and Poggio as well-known Italian writers. Florio was
   probably suggested by John Florio's Italian dictionary *A
   World of Words* (1598) which translates *putana* as 'whore'.
   George Whetstone's 1582 *Heptameron of Civil Discourses*
   provided the names Soranzo and Bergetto, while
   Hippolita is drawn from Hippolyta, the Amazon Queen,
   although an allusion to Hippolyte, the lustful wife of
   Acastus, would not have been lost on the better-educated
   members of Ford's audience. Philotis is from the Greek
   for 'love', and so on. The whole scheme of the actors'
   names provides clues about Ford's reading and its
   influence

---

To My Friend the Author: the poem by Thomas Ellice
appears in only a few copies of the Quarto. Ellice was
probably the brother of Robert Ellice of Gray's Inn, to
whom Ford dedicated another play, *The Lover's
Melancholy*. Thomas entered Gray's Inn in 1626 and was
responsible for a commendatory poem for Sir William
Davenant's 1629 play *Albovine*
To the Truly Noble . . . Turvey: although Ford's patron
came from an old Catholic family, he had been converted
to Anglicanism by the time of his marriage to the
wealthy Elizabeth Howard. Despite holding a favoured
position in the court of James I and being created first
Earl of Peterborough by Charles I, he raised a regiment
for Parliament against the King in 1642, the year of his
death. Little is known of his relationship with Ford

GRIMALDI, *a Roman gentleman*

GIOVANNI, *son to Florio*

BERGETTO, *nephew to Donado*

RICHARDETTO, *a supposed physician*

VASQUES, *servant to Soranzo*

POGGIO, *servant to Bergetto*

BANDITTI, *Officers, Servants, etc.*

### Women

ANNABELLA, *daughter to Florio*

HIPPOLITA, *wife to Richardetto*

PHILOTIS, *his niece*

PUTANA, *tut'ress to Annabella*

### *The scene*

PARMA

# Act I, scene i

*Enter* FRIAR *and* GIOVANNI

FRIAR Dispute no more in this, for know, young man,
  These are no school-points; nice philosophy
  May tolerate unlikely arguments,
  But Heaven admits no jest: wits that presumed
  On wit too much, by striving how to prove
  There was no God, with foolish grounds of art,
  Discovered first the nearest way to hell,
  And filled the world with devilish atheism.
  Such questions, youth, are fond; for better 'tis
  To bless the sun than reason why it shines;    10
  Yet He thou talk'st of is above the sun.
  No more; I may not hear it.
GIOVANNI                Gentle father,
  To you I have unclasped my burdened soul,
  Emptied the storehouse of my thoughts and I

Made myself poor of secrets; have not left
Another word untold, which hath not spoke
All what I ever durst, or think, or know;
And yet is here the comfort I shall have,
Must I not do what all men else may, love?
FRIAR Yes, you may love, fair son.
GIOVANNI                 Must I not praise
  That beauty which, if framed anew, the gods    21
  Would make a god of, if they had it there,
  And kneel to it, as I do kneel to them?
FRIAR Why, foolish madman!
GIOVANNI              Shall a peevish sound,
  A customary form, from man to man,
  Of brother and of sister, be a bar
  'Twixt my perpetual happiness and me?
  Say that we had one father, say one womb
  (Curse to my joys) gave both us life and birth;
  Are we not therefore each to other bound    30
  So much the more by nature? By the links
  Of blood, of reason? Nay, if you will have't,
  Even of religion, to be ever one,
  One soul, one flesh, one love, one heart, one all?
FRIAR Have done, unhappy youth, for thou art lost.
GIOVANNI Shall then, for that I am her brother born,
  My joys be ever banished from her bed?
  No, father; in your eyes I see the change
  Of pity and compassion; from your age,
  As from a sacred oracle, distils    40
  The life of counsel: tell me, holy man,
  What cure shall give me ease in these extremes?
FRIAR Repentance, son, and sorrow for this sin:
  For, thou hast moved a Majesty above
  With thy unranged (almost) blasphemy.
GIOVANNI O do not speak of that, dear confessor.
FRIAR Art thou, my son, that miracle of wit
  Who once, within these three months, wert esteemed
  A wonder of thine age, throughout Bononia?
  How did the university applaud    50
  Thy government, behaviour, learning, speech,
  Sweetness, and all that could make up a man!
  I was proud of my tutelage, and chose
  Rather to leave my books than part with thee.
  I did so: but the fruits of all my hopes
  Are lost in thee, as thou art in thyself.
  O, Giovanni, hast thou left the schools

---

PARMA: the northern Italian city is famous for its ancient university and for an elegance and sophistication characteristic of neighbouring cities such as Verona, Mantua and Venice, which figure prominently in the plays of Shakespeare and his contemporaries as places of romance, double-dealing and intrigue
2 school-points: topics for scholarly debate
4 admits: allows
6 art: learning
9 fond: foolish

24 peevish: trifling, petty
25 customary form: convention
32 Of blood: of kinship, family
45 unranged: deranged, crazy
49 Bononia: Bologna, not far from Parma, famous for its university
51 government: general conduct and possibly, here, self-discipline
57 Giovanni: pronounced with four syllables rather than the three of modern Italian

Of knowledge to converse with lust and death?
For death waits on thy lust. Look through the world,
And thou shalt see a thousand faces shine          60
More glorious than this idol thou ador'st:
Leave her, and take thy choice, 'tis much less sin,
Though in such games as those they lose that win.

GIOVANNI  It were more ease to stop the ocean
From floats and ebbs than to dissuade my vows.

FRIAR  Then I have done, and in thy wilful flames
Already see thy ruin; Heaven is just.
Yet hear my counsel.

GIOVANNI                    As a voice of life.

FRIAR  Hie to thy father's house, there lock thee fast
Alone within thy chamber, then fall down          70
On both thy knees, and grovel on the ground:
Cry to thy heart, wash every word thou utter'st
In tears (and if't be possible) of blood:
Beg Heaven to cleanse the leprosy of lust
That rots thy soul, acknowledge what thou art,
A wretch, a worm, a nothing: weep, sigh, pray
Three times a day, and three times every night.
For seven days' space do this, then if thou find'st
No change in thy desires, return to me:
I'll think on remedy. Pray for thyself          80
At home, whilst I pray for thee here.—Away,
My blessing with thee, we have need to pray.

GIOVANNI  All this I'll do, to free me from the rod
Of vengeance; else I'll swear my fate's my god.

                                        *Exeunt*

# Act I, scene ii

*Enter* GRIMALDI *and* VASQUES *ready to fight*

VASQUES  Come sir, stand to your tackling; if you prove
craven, I'll make you run quickly.

GRIMALDI  Thou art no equal match for me.

VASQUES  Indeed I never went to the wars to bring

---

62  'tis much less sin: Brian Morris has pointed out that the
view that fornication was a lesser sin than incest was
probably based on the argument exemplified by Michel
Montaigne in *Essais* which Ford may have read in John
Florio's translation of 1603: 'The love we beare to women
is very lawful; yet both Divinite bridle and restraine the
same. I remember to have read in Saint Thomas, in a
place where he condemneth marriages of kinsfolkes in
forbidden degrees, this one reason amongst others; that
the love a man beareth to such a woman may be
immoderate; for, if the wedlocke, or husband-like
affection be sound and perfect, as it ought to be, and also
surcharged with that a man oweth to alliance and
kindred; there is no doubt but that surcease may easily
transport a husband beyond the bounds of reason'
65  floats: tides, pronounced with three syllables
    vows: prayers, as in the Latin *vota*
1  tackling: weaponry

home news, nor cannot play the mountebank for a
meal's meat, and swear I got my wounds in the field.
See you these grey hairs? They'll not flinch for a
bloody nose. Wilt thou to this gear?

GRIMALDI  Why, slave, think'st thou I'll balance my
reputation with a cast-suit? Call thy master, he shall
know that I dare—                                11

VASQUES  Scold like a cot-quean, that's your profession.
Thou poor shadow of a soldier, I will make thee
know my master keeps servants thy betters in quality
and performance. Com'st thou to fight or prate?

GRIMALDI  Neither, with thee. I am a Roman and a
gentleman; one that have got mine honour with
expense of blood.

VASQUES  You are a lying coward and a fool. Fight, or by
these hilts I'll kill thee—brave my lord!—you'll fight?

GRIMALDI  Provoke me not, for if thou dost—          21

VASQUES  Have at you!

                    *They fight;* GRIMALDI *hath the worst*

*Enter* FLORIO, DONADO, *and* SORANZO

FLORIO  What mean these sudden broils so near my
doors?
Have you not other places but my house
To vent the spleen of your disordered bloods?
Must I be haunted still with such unrest
As not to eat or sleep in peace at home?
Is this your love, Grimaldi? Fie, 'tis naught.

DONADO  And Vasques, I may tell thee 'tis not well
To broach these quarrels; you are ever forward          30
In seconding contentions.

*Enter above* ANNABELLA *and* PUTANA

FLORIO                    What's the ground?

SORANZO  That, with your patience, signors, I'll resolve:
This gentleman, whom fame reports a soldier,
(For else I know not) rivals me in love
To Signor Florio's daughter, to whose ears
He still prefers his suit, to my disgrace,
Thinking the way to recommend himself
Is to disparage me in his report.
But know, Grimaldi, though, may be, thou art
My equal in thy blood, yet this bewrays          40

---

8  gear: the business to hand, the fight
10  cast-suit: a servant, one who might wear his master's
    cast-off clothing
12  cot-quean: a 'cottage-wife', a shrill woman or, in this
    case, an effeminate man
14  quality: birth, rank
23  sudden: violent
SD  *Enter above*: on the upper stage, allowing them to witness
    unobserved the action below. They descend to the main
    stage during Giovanni's soliloquy (ll. 150–69)
32  resolve: answer
40  bewrays: reveals

A lowness in thy mind which, wert thou noble,
Thou wouldst as much disdain as I do thee
For this unworthiness; and on this ground
I willed my servant to correct his tongue,
Holding a man so base no match for me.

VASQUES  And had not your sudden coming prevented
us, I had let my gentleman blood under the gills; I
should have wormed you, sir, for running mad.

GRIMALDI  I'll be revenged, Soranzo.                    49

VASQUES  On a dish of warm broth to stay your
stomach—do, honest innocence, do; spoon-meat is a
wholesomer diet than a Spanish blade.

GRIMALDI  Remember this.

SORANZO  I fear thee not, Grimaldi.          *Exit* GRIMALDI

FLORIO  My Lord Soranzo, this is strange to me,
Why you should storm, having my word engaged:
Owing her heart, what need you doubt her ear?
Losers may talk by law of any game.

VASQUES  Yet the villainy of words, Signor Florio, may
be such as would make any unspleened dove choleric.
Blame not my lord in this.                              61

FLORIO  Be you more silent.
I would not for my wealth my daughter's love
Should cause the spilling of one drop of blood.
Vasques, put up, let's end this fray in wine.

     *Exeunt* FLORIO, DONADO, SORANZO *and* VASQUES

PUTANA  How like you this, child? Here's threatening,
challenging, quarrelling, and fighting, on every side,
and all is for your sake; you had need look to yourself,
charge, you'll be stolen away sleeping else shortly.

ANNABELLA  But, tut'ress, such a life gives no content
To me, my thoughts are fixed on other ends;         71
Would you would leave me.

PUTANA  Leave you? No marvel else. Leave me no
leaving, charge; this is love outright. Indeed I blame
you not, you have choice fit for the best lady in Italy.

ANNABELLA  Pray do not talk so much.

PUTANA  Take the worst with the best, there's Grimaldi
the soldier, a very well-timbered fellow. They say he
is a Roman, nephew to the Duke Montferrato, they
say he did good service in the wars against the
Milanese, but 'faith, charge, I do not like him, an't be
for nothing but for being a soldier; not one amongst
twenty of your skirmishing captains but have some
privy maim or other that mars their standing upright.
I like him the worse, he crinkles so much in the
hams; though he might serve if there were no more
men, yet he's not the man I would choose.           **87**

ANNABELLA  Fie, how thou prat'st.

PUTANA  As I am a very woman, I like Signor Soranzo
well; he is wise, and what is more, rich; and what is
more than that, kind, and what is more than all this,
a nobleman; such a one, were I the fair Annabella
myself, I would wish and pray for. Then he is
bountiful; besides, he is handsome, and by my troth,
I think wholesome (and that's news in a gallant of
three and twenty); liberal, that I know; loving, that
you know; and a man sure, else he could never ha'
purchased such a good name with Hippolita, the
lusty widow, in her husband's lifetime: and 'twere but
for that report, sweet-heart, would 'a were thine.
Commend a man for his qualities, but take a husband
as he is a plain-sufficient, naked man: such a one is
for your bed, and such a one is Signor Soranzo, my
life for't.                                           **104**

ANNABELLA  Sure the woman took her morning's
draught too soon.

*Enter* BERGETTO *and* POGGIO

PUTANA  But look, sweetheart, look what thing comes
now: here's another of your ciphers to fill up the
number. O brave old ape in a silken coat. Observe.

BERGETTO  Didst thou think, Poggio, that I would spoil
my new clothes, and leave my dinner, to fight?    **111**

POGGIO  No, sir, I did not take you for so arrant a baby.

BERGETTO  I am wiser than so: for I hope, Poggio, thou
never heardst of an elder brother that was a coxcomb.
Didst, Poggio?

POGGIO  Never indeed, sir, as long as they had either
land or money left them to inherit.

---

48  wormed: refers to the contemporary practice of cutting
    out a small ligament beneath a dog's tongue which was
    supposed to prevent rabies
51  innocence: fool
    spoon-meat: baby food
57  Owing: possessing
60  unspleened: it was thought that birds had no spleen and
    were therefore incapable of becoming angry or 'choleric'
65  put up: sheathe your sword
71  ends: matters
78  well-timbered: well-built
79  Duke Montferrato: Montferrat became a duchy in 1575
    having for a long time been controlled by the Gonzaga
    family of the Mantua area near Parma

84  mars . . . upright: the implication is of sexual impotence;
    'privy' or 'private' meaning both secret and referring to
    the genitals
86  he might serve: he 'might do' but also that he might give
    sexual satisfaction
89  very: true, real
95  wholesome: free from disease, particularly that of a sexual
    nature
96  liberal: generous
98  such a good name: a favourable reputation. This is the
    first reference to Soranzo's affair with Hippolita
105–6  morning's draught: alcoholic drinks taken in the morning
108  ciphers: nonentities
109  O brave old ape: refers to an old proverb: 'An ape is an
    ape though dressed in scarlet'
114  coxcomb: simpleton

BERGETTO Is it possible, Poggio? O monstrous. Why, I'll undertake with a handful of silver to buy a headful of wit at any time; but sirrah, I have another purchase in hand, I shall have the wench, mine uncle says. I will but wash my face, and shift socks, and then have at her i'faith. Mark my pace, Poggio. 123

POGGIO Sir—(*Aside*) I have seen an ass and a mule trot the Spanish pavin with a better grace, I know not how often.

*Exeunt* BERGETTO *and* POGGIO

ANNABELLA This idiot haunts me too.

PUTANA Ay, ay, he needs no description; the rich magnifico that is below with your father, charge, Signor Donado his uncle, for that he means to make this his cousin a golden calf, thinks that you will be a right Israelite and fall down to him presently: but I hope I have tutored you better. They say a fool's bauble is a lady's playfellow, yet you having wealth enough, you need not cast upon the dearth of flesh at any rate: hang him, innocent. 136

*Enter* GIOVANNI

ANNABELLA But see, Putana, see: what blessèd shape
Of some celestial creature now appears?
What man is he, that with such sad aspect
Walks careless of himself?

PUTANA                    Where?

ANNABELLA                    Look below. 140

PUTANA O, 'tis your brother, sweet.

ANNABELLA                    Ha!

PUTANA                    'Tis your brother.

ANNABELLA Sure 'tis not he; this is some woeful thing
Wrapped up in grief, some shadow of a man.
Alas, he beats his breast, and wipes his eyes
Drowned all in tears: methinks I hear him sigh.
Let's down, Putana, and partake the cause;

I know my brother, in the love he bears me,
Will not deny me partage in his sadness.
My soul is full of heaviness and fear.

*Exit with* PUTANA

GIOVANNI Lost. I am lost. My fates have doomed my death. 150
The more I strive, I love; the more I love
The less I hope: I see my ruin, certain.
What judgement or endeavours could apply
To my incurable and restless wounds
I throughly have examined, but in vain.
O that it were not in religion sin
To make our love a god, and worship it.
I have even wearied Heaven with prayers, dried up
The spring of my continual tears, even starved
My veins with daily fasts: what wit or art 160
Could counsel, I have practised; but alas,
I find all these but dreams and old men's tales
To fright unsteady youth; I'm still the same.
Or I must speak, or burst. 'Tis not, I know,
My lust, but 'tis my fate that leads me on.
Keep fear and low faint-hearted shame with slaves;
I'll tell her that I love her, though my heart
Were rated at the price of that attempt.
O me! She comes.

*Enter* ANNABELLA *and* PUTANA

ANNABELLA                    Brother.

GIOVANNI (*Aside*)                    If such a thing
As courage dwell in men, ye heavenly powers, 170
Now double all that virtue in my tongue.

ANNABELLA Why, brother, will you not speak to me?

GIOVANNI Yes; how d'ee, sister?

ANNABELLA Howsoever I am, methinks you are not well.

PUTANA Bless us, why are you so sad, sir?

GIOVANNI Let me entreat you, leave us a while, Putana. Sister, I would be private with you.

ANNABELLA Withdraw, Putana.

PUTANA I will. (*Aside*) If this were any other company for her, I should think my absence an office of some credit; but I will leave them together. *Exit* PUTANA

GIOVANNI Come, sister, lend your hand, let's walk together. 182
I hope you need not blush to walk with me;
Here's none but you and I.

ANNABELLA How's this?

GIOVANNI Faith, I mean no harm.

ANNABELLA Harm?

GIOVANNI No, good faith; how is't with 'ee?

---

125 pavin: pavan, a courtly dance
129 magnifico: noble
131 cousin: generally a kinsman but here specifically a nephew
131–2 a golden calf . . . Israelite: biblical reference (see Exodus 32. 6–7) in which Aaron persuades the people to worship a golden calf he made from their earnings: 'And they rose up early on the morrow, and offered burnt offerings, and brought peace offerings; and the people sat down to eat and to drink, and rose up to play. And the Lord said unto Moses, Go, get thee down; for thy people, which thou broughtest out of the land of Eygpt, have corrupted themselves'
134 bauble: baton or stick, but with an indecent implication. The origin of the word is 'baubel' meaning a 'play thing'
134–6 yet you . . . rate: you are rich and do not need to gamble on Bergetto for fear of a shortage of alternative suitors
SD *Enter* GIOVANNI: on the stage below
146 partake: be informed of

155 throughly: thoroughly
160 what wit or art: intelligence or medical knowledge
180–1 of some credit: deserving payment

ANNABELLA (*Aside*) I trust he be not frantic.—I am
  very well, brother.
GIOVANNI Trust me, but I am sick, I fear so sick   **190**
  'Twill cost my life.
ANNABELLA Mercy forbid it. 'Tis not so, I hope.
GIOVANNI I think you love me, sister.
ANNABELLA Yes, you know I do.
GIOVANNI I know't indeed.—Y'are very fair.
ANNABELLA Nay then, I see you have a merry sickness.
GIOVANNI That's as it proves. The poets feign, I read,
  That Juno for her forehead did exceed
  All other goddesses: but I durst swear
  Your forehead exceeds hers, as hers did theirs.   **200**
ANNABELLA Troth, this is pretty.
GIOVANNI                Such a pair of stars
  As are thine eyes would, like Promethean fire,
  If gently glanced, give life to senseless stones.
ANNABELLA Fie upon 'ee.
GIOVANNI The lily and the rose, most sweetly strange,
  Upon your dimpled cheeks do strive for change.
  Such lips would tempt a saint; such hands as those
  Would make an anchorite lascivious.
ANNABELLA D'ee mock me, or flatter me?
GIOVANNI If you would see a beauty more exact   **210**
  Than art can counterfeit or nature frame,
  Look in your glass and there behold your own.
ANNABELLA O you are a trim youth.
GIOVANNI               Here.
                  *Offers his dagger to her*
ANNABELLA              What to do?
GIOVANNI And here's my breast, strike home.
  Rip up my bosom, there thou shalt behold
  A heart in which is writ the truth I speak.
  Why stand 'ee?
ANNABELLA         Are you earnest?
GIOVANNI                Yes, most earnest.
  You cannot love?
ANNABELLA         Whom?
GIOVANNI             Me. My tortured soul
  Hath felt affliction in the heat of death.
  O Annabella, I am quite undone.   **220**
  The love of thee, my sister, and the view
  Of thy immortal beauty hath untuned
  All harmony both of my rest and life.
  Why d'ee not strike?
ANNABELLA         Forbid it, my just fears.

---

189  frantic: insane
198  That Juno . . . did exceed: Juno, the significantly
    beautiful wife, but also the sister, of the god Jupiter
202  Promethean fire: Prometheus stole fire from heaven to
    give life to the man and woman he had created from clay
205  strange: opposed
206  change: interchange
208  anchorite: hermit

If this be true, 'twere fitter I were dead.
GIOVANNI True, Annabella; 'tis no time to jest.
  I have too long suppressed the hidden flames
  That almost have consumed me; I have spent
  Many a silent night in sighs and groans,
  Ran over all my thoughts, despised my fate,   **230**
  Reasoned against the reasons of my love,
  Done all that smoothed-cheek virtue could advise,
  But found all bootless: 'tis my destiny
  That you must either love, or I must die.
ANNABELLA Comes this in sadness from you?
GIOVANNI               Let some mischief
  Befall me soon, if I dissemble aught.
ANNABELLA You are my brother Giovanni.
GIOVANNI                You
  My sister Annabella; I know this:
  And could afford you instance why to love
  So much the more for this; to which intent   **240**
  Wise nature first in your creation meant
  To make you mine; else't had been sin and foul
  To share one beauty to a double soul.
  Nearness in birth or blood doth but persuade
  A nearer nearness in affection.
  I have asked counsel of the holy church,
  Who tells me I may love you, and 'tis just
  That since I may, I should; and will, yes, will.
  Must I now live, or die?
ANNABELLA           Live. Thou hast won
  The field, and never fought; what thou hast urged
  My captive heart had long ago resolved.   **251**
  I blush to tell thee—but I'll tell thee now—
  For every sigh that thou hast spent for me
  I have sighed ten; for every tear shed twenty:
  And not so much for that I loved, as that
  I durst not say I loved, nor scarcely think it.
GIOVANNI Let not this music be a dream, ye gods,
  For pity's sake, I beg 'ee.
ANNABELLA          On my knees,   *She kneels*
  Brother, even by our mother's dust, I charge you,
  Do not betray me to your mirth or hate,   **260**
  Love me, or kill me, brother.
GIOVANNI           On my knees,   *He kneels*
  Sister, even by my mother's dust, I charge you,
  Do not betray me to your mirth or hate,
  Love me, or kill me, sister.
ANNABELLA You mean good sooth then?
GIOVANNI            In good troth I do,
  And so do you, I hope: say, I'm in earnest.
ANNABELLA I'll swear't, I.
GIOVANNI        And I, and by this kiss,   *Kisses her*

---

233  bootless: useless
235  sadness: seriousness
255  for that: because
265  sooth: truth

(Once more, yet once more; now let's rise by this)

*They rise*

I would not change this minute for Elysium.
What must we now do?

ANNABELLA            What you will.

GIOVANNI                 Come then,   **270**
  After so many tears as we have wept,
  Let's learn to court in smiles, to kiss, and sleep.

*Exeunt*

# Act I, scene iii

*Enter* FLORIO *and* DONADO

FLORIO  Signor Donado, you have said enough,
  I understand you; but would have you know
  I will not force my daughter 'gainst her will.
  You see I have but two, a son and her;
  And he is so devoted to his book,
  As I must tell you true, I doubt his health:
  Should he miscarry, all my hopes rely
  Upon my girl; as for worldly fortune,
  I am, I thank my stars, blest with enough.
  My care is how to match her to her liking:   **10**
  I would not have her marry wealth, but love,
  And if she like your nephew, let him have her.
  Here's all that I can say.

DONADO              Sir, you say well,
  Like a true father, and for my part I,
  If the young folks can like ('twixt you and me),
  Will promise to assure my nephew presently
  Three thousand florins yearly during life,
  And after I am dead, my whole estate.

FLORIO  'Tis a fair proffer, sir; meantime your nephew
  Shall have free passage to commence his suit.   **20**
  If he can thrive, he shall have my consent.
  So for this time I'll leave you, signor.     *Exit*

DONADO                 Well,
  Here's hope yet, if my nephew would have wit;
  But he is such another dunce, I fear
  He'll never win the wench. When I was young
  I could have done't, i'faith, and so shall he
  If he will learn of me; and in good time
  He comes himself.

*Enter* BERGETTO *and* POGGIO

---

268  let's rise by this: they rise, but also a sense of spiritual
     elevation
  6  doubt: fear for
  7  miscarry: come to harm
  8  girl: pronounced as two syllables
 16  presently: at once
 23  wit: some intelligence
 27  in good time: at an appropriate moment

How now, Bergetto, whither away so fast?   **29**

BERGETTO  O uncle, I have heard the strangest news
  that ever came out of the mint, have I not, Poggio?

POGGIO  Yes indeed, sir.

DONADO  What news, Bergetto?

BERGETTO  Why, look ye, uncle, my barber told me just
  now that there is a fellow come to town who
  undertakes to make a mill go without the mortal help
  of any water or wind, only with sand-bags: and this
  fellow hath a strange horse, a most excellent beast, I'll
  assure you, uncle (my barber says), whose head, to
  the wonder of all Christian people, stands just behind
  where his tail is. Is't not true, Poggio?   **41**

POGGIO  So the barber swore, forsooth.

DONADO  And you are running thither?

BERGETTO  Ay forsooth, uncle.

DONADO  Wilt thou be a fool still? Come sir, you shall
  not go: you have more mind of a puppet-play than on
  the business I told ye; why, thou great baby, wilt
  never have wit, wilt make thyself a may-game to all
  the world?

POGGIO  Answer for yourself, master.   **50**

BERGETTO  Why, uncle, should I sit at home still, and
  not go abroad to see fashions like other gallants?

DONADO  To see hobby-horses. What wise talk, I pray,
  had you with Annabella, when you were at Signor
  Florio's house?

BERGETTO  O, the wench! Uds sa' me, uncle, I tickled
  her with a rare speech, that I made her almost burst
  her belly with laughing.

DONADO  Nay, I think so; and what speech was't?

BERGETTO  What did I say, Poggio?   **60**

POGGIO  Forsooth, my master said that he loved her almost
  as well as he loved parmasent, and swore (I'll be sworn
  for him) that she wanted but such a nose as his was to
  be as pretty a young woman as any was in Parma.

DONADO  O gross!

BERGETTO  Nay, uncle, then she asked me whether my
  father had any more children than myself: and I said

---

29  How . . . fast: line given to Poggio in Q but to Donado
    in all editions since William Weber's *The Dramatic Works
    of John Ford* (1811)
 31  that . . . mint: new or fresh, as in a newly minted coin
36–7  undertakes . . . sandbags: a machine displaying perpetual
    motion
38–41  a strange horse . . . his tail is: a trick seen at
    contemporary fairs
 46  have more mind of: are more interested in
 48  a may-game: laughing-stock, a butt for ridicule in the
    festivities associated with the first of May
 53  hobby-horses: performers dressed as horses
 56  Uds sa' me: God save me
    tickled: amused
 62  parmasent: parmesan, the local cheese
 63  wanted: lacked

'No, 'twere better he should have had his brains
knocked out first.'
DONADO  This is intolerable.                              70
BERGETTO  Then said she 'Will Signor Donado your
uncle leave you all his wealth?'
DONADO  Ha! That was good; did she harp upon that
string?
BERGETTO  Did she harp upon that string? Ay, that she
did. I answered 'Leave me all his wealth? Why,
woman, he hath no other wit; if he had, he should
hear on't to his everlasting glory and confusion: I
know,' quoth I, 'I am his white boy, and will not be
gulled'; and with that she fell into a great smile and
went away. Nay, I did fit her.                            81
DONADO  Ah, sirrah, then I see there is no changing of
nature. Well, Bergetto, I fear thou wilt be a very ass
still.
BERGETTO  I should be sorry for that, uncle.
DONADO  Come, come you home with me. Since you
are no better a speaker, I'll have you write to her after
some courtly manner, and enclose some rich jewel in
the letter.
BERGETTO  Ay marry, that will be excellent.               90
DONADO  Peace, innocent.
    Once in my time I'll set my wits to school,
    If all fail, 'tis but the fortune of a fool.
BERGETTO  Poggio, 'twill do, Poggio.
                                              Exeunt

# Act II, scene i

*Enter* GIOVANNI *and* ANNABELLA, *as from their chamber*

GIOVANNI  Come Annabella: no more sister now,
    But love, a name more gracious; do not blush,
    Beauty's sweet wonder, but be proud to know
    That yielding thou hast conquered, and inflamed
    A heart whose tribute is thy brother's life.
ANNABELLA  And mine is his. O, how these stol'n
        contents
    Would print a modest crimson on my cheeks,
    Had any but my heart's delight prevailed.
GIOVANNI  I marvel why the chaster of your sex
    Should think this pretty toy called maidenhead      10
    So strange a loss, when, being lost, 'tis nothing,
    And you are still the same.
ANNABELLA                      'Tis well for you;
    Now you can talk.

---

77  wit: thought
78  glory: a malapropism by Bergetto for 'shame'
79  white boy: a pet or favourite
80  gulled: made a fool of
81  fit her: answer appropriately
10  toy: trifle
11  strange: extraordinary

GIOVANNI                  Music as well consists
    In th' ear as in the playing.
ANNABELLA                      O, y'are wanton.
    Tell on't, y'are best: do.
GIOVANNI                      Thou wilt chide me then.
    Kiss me:—so. Thus hung Jove on Leda's neck,
    And sucked divine ambrosia from her lips.
    I envy not the mightiest man alive,
    But hold myself in being king of thee
    More great than were I king of all the world.       20
    But I shall lose you, sweetheart.
ANNABELLA                      But you shall not.
GIOVANNI  You must be married, mistress.
ANNABELLA                      Yes? To whom?
GIOVANNI  Someone must have you.
ANNABELLA                  You must.
GIOVANNI                      Nay, some other.
ANNABELLA  Now prithee do not speak so: without
        jesting,
    You'll make me weep in earnest.
GIOVANNI                      What, you will not?
    But tell me, sweet, canst thou be dared to swear
    That thou wilt live to me, and to no other?
ANNABELLA  By both our loves I dare, for didst thou
        know,
    My Giovanni, how all suitors seem
    To my eyes hateful, thou wouldst trust me then.      30
GIOVANNI  Enough, I take thy word. Sweet, we must
        part.
    Remember what thou vowst; keep well my heart.
ANNABELLA  Will you be gone?
GIOVANNI                      I must.
ANNABELLA                      When to return?
GIOVANNI  Soon.
ANNABELLA      Look you do.
GIOVANNI                      Farewell.          *Exit*
ANNABELLA  Go where thou wilt, in mind I'll keep thee
        here,
    And where thou art, I know I shall be there.
    Guardian!

---

13–14  Music . . . playing: music is as much the art of listening
    as of playing, but also a sexual connotation since music is
    a metaphor of love-making and the ear refers to the
    female genitalia
16  thus hung Jove . . . neck: Giovanni pictures himself as
    Jove who, in a similarly unnatural act, seduced Leda
17  ambrosia: the food of the gods which gave them
    everlasting life
22  Yes? To whom?: Q reads 'Yes, to whom?' but modern
    editors prefer to suggest that Annabella is being more
    playful in the early speeches of this scene, unaware of
    Giovanni's seriousness
23  Someone must have you: in terms of marriage but also in
    the cruder sense of carnal possession
26  dared to: so daring as to

*Enter* PUTANA

PUTANA  Child, how is't, child? Well, thank Heaven,
ha?

ANNABELLA  O guardian, what a paradise of joy
Have I passed over!                                          40

PUTANA  Nay, what a paradise of joy have you passed
under! Why, now I commend thee, charge; fear
nothing, sweetheart; what though he be your
brother? Your brother's a man, I hope, and I say still,
if a young wench feel the fit upon her, let her take
anybody, father or brother, all is one.

ANNABELLA  I would not have it known for all the
world.

PUTANA  Nor I, indeed, for the speech of the people;
else 'twere nothing.

FLORIO  (*within*) Daughter Annabella.                      50

ANNABELLA  O me, my father!—Here, sir!—Reach my
work.

FLORIO  (*within*) What are you doing?

ANNABELLA                          So: let him come now.

*Enter* FLORIO, RICHARDETTO *like a doctor of physic, and*
PHILOTIS *with a lute in her hand*

FLORIO  So hard at work? That's well; you lose no time.
Look, I have brought you company; here's one,
A learned doctor lately come from Padua,
Much skilled in physic, and for that I see
You have of late been sickly, I entreated
This reverend man to visit you some time.

ANNABELLA  Y'are very welcome, sir.

RICHARDETTO                          I thank you, mistress.
Loud fame in large report hath spoke your praise   60
As well for virtue as perfection:
For which I have been bold to bring with me
A kinswoman of mine, a maid, for song
And music, one perhaps will give content;
Please you to know her.

ANNABELLA                          They are parts I love,
And she for them most welcome.

PHILOTIS                          Thank you, lady.

FLORIO  Sir, now you know my house, pray make not
strange
And if you find my daughter need your art,
I'll be your paymaster.

RICHARDETTO                          Sir, what I am
She shall command.

FLORIO                          You shall bind me to you.   70
Daughter, I must have conference with you
About some matters that concerns us both.
Good master doctor, please you but walk in,
We'll crave a little of your cousin's cunning.
I think my girl hath not quite forgot
To touch an instrument: she could have done't.
We'll hear them both.

RICHARDETTO                          I'll wait upon you, sir.

*Exeunt*

# Act II, scene ii

*Enter* SORANZO *in his study reading a book*

SORANZO  'Love's measure is extreme, the comfort,
pain:
The life unrest, and the reward disdain.'
What's here? Look't o'er again: 'tis so, so writes
This smooth licentious poet in his rhymes.
But Sannazar, thou lie'st, for had thy bosom
Felt such oppression as is laid on mine,
Thou would'st have kissed the rod that made thee
smart.
To work then, happy muse, and contradict
What Sannazar hath in his envy writ.
'Love's measure is the mean, sweet his annoys,   10
His pleasure's life, and his reward all joys.'
Had Annabella lived when Sannazar
Did in his brief encomium celebrate
Venice, that queen of cities, he had left
That verse which gained him such a sum of gold,
And for one only look from Annabel
Had writ of her and her diviner cheeks.
O how my thoughts are—

VASQUES  (*within*) Pray forbear; in rules of civility, let
me give notice on't: I shall be taxed of my neglect of
duty and service.                                          21

SORANZO  What rude intrusion interrupts my peace?

---

40  over: through
45  fit: sexual desire
48  for the speech of the people: i.e. to avoid a public scandal
51  Reach my work: pass me my needlework
55  Padua: an Italian city famous for its university medical
    school
56  physic: medicine
    for that: because
65  parts: abilities or qualities
67  pray make not strange: please do not be too formal

74  your cousin's cunning: your niece's musical skills
76  To touch: to play
5  Sannazar: Jacopa Sannazaro (c. 1455–1530) was a
   Neopolitan love poet whose romance *Arcadia* was known
   in England
9  envy: ill will
10  mean: moderation
13  encomium: a short Latin poem
12–15  Had Annabella . . . sum of gold: Sannazaro had written
    a Latin poem in praise of Venice which was mentioned
    in Thomas Coryat's *Crudities* (1611) and, in translation, in
    a letter written from Venice to Robert Brown dated
    12 August 1621. Brown received the letter at the Middle
    Temple to which John Ford belonged
20  taxed of: blamed for

Can I be nowhere private?

VASQUES (*within*) Troth you wrong your modesty.

SORANZO What's the matter, Vasques? Who is't?

*Enter* HIPPOLITA *and* VASQUES

HIPPOLITA                                        'Tis I:
Do you know me now? Look, perjured man, on her
Whom thou and thy distracted lust have wronged.
Thy sensual rage of blood hath made my youth
A scorn to men and angels, and shall I
Be now a foil to thy unsated change?                30
Thou knowst, false wanton, when my modest fame
Stood free from stain or scandal, all the charms
Of hell or sorcery could not prevail
Against the honour of my chaster bosom.
Thine eyes did plead in tears, thy tongue in oaths
Such and so many, that a heart of steel
Would have been wrought to pity, as was mine:
And shall the conquest of my lawful bed,
My husband's death urged on by his disgrace,
My loss of womanhood, be ill rewarded               40
With hatred and contempt? No; know, Soranzo,
I have a spirit doth as much distaste
The slavery of fearing thee, as thou
Dost loathe the memory of what hath passed.

SORANZO Nay, dear Hippolita—

HIPPOLITA                          Call me not dear,
Nor think with supple words to smooth the grossness
Of my abuses; 'tis not your new mistress,
Your goodly Madam Merchant, shall triumph
On my dejection: tell her thus from me,
My birth was nobler and by much more free.          50

SORANZO You are too violent.

HIPPOLITA                      You are too double
In your dissimulation. Seest thou this,
This habit, these black mourning weeds of care?
'Tis thou art cause of this, and hast divorced
My husband from his life and me from him,
And made me widow in my widowhood.

SORANZO Will you yet hear?

HIPPOLITA                   More of thy perjuries?
Thy soul is drowned too deeply in those sins;
Thou need'st not add to th' number.

SORANZO                           Then I'll leave you;
You are past all rules of sense.

HIPPOLITA                        And thou of grace.   60

VASQUES Fie, mistress, you are not near the limits of

reason: if my lord had a resolution as noble as virtue
itself, you take the course to unedge it all. Sir, I
beseech you, do not perplex her; griefs, alas, will have
a vent. I dare undertake Madam Hippolita will now
freely hear you.

SORANZO Talk to a woman frantic! Are these the fruits
of your love?

HIPPOLITA They are the fruits of thy untruth, false man.
Didst thou not swear, whilst yet my husband lived, 70
That thou wouldst wish no happiness on earth
More than to call me wife? Didst thou not vow,
When he should die, to marry me? For which,
The devil in my blood, and thy protests,
Caused me to counsel him to undertake
A voyage to Ligorn, for that we heard
His brother there was dead, and left a daughter
Young and unfriended, who, with much ado,
I wished him to bring hither: he did so,
And went; and as thou know'st died on the way.    80
Unhappy man, to buy his death so dear
With my advice. Yet thou for whom I did it
Forget'st thy vows, and leav'st me to my shame.

SORANZO Who could help this?

HIPPOLITA                  Who? Perjured man, thou couldst,
If thou hadst faith or love.

SORANZO                       You are deceived.
The vows I made, if you remember well,
Were wicked and unlawful: 'twere more sin
To keep them than to break them. As for me,
I cannot mask my penitence. Think thou
How much thou hast digressed from honest shame
In bringing of a gentleman to death                91
Who was thy husband; such a one as he,
So noble in his quality, condition,
Learning, behaviour, entertainment, love,
As Parma could not show a braver man.

VASQUES You do not well; this was not your promise.

SORANZO I care not. Let her know her monstrous life.
Ere I'll be servile to so black a sin,
I'll be accursed. Woman, come here no more.
Learn to repent and die, for by my honour         100

---

27  distracted: changeable
28  blood: sexual passion
30  change: promiscuity
31  modest fame: reputation
48  Madam Merchant: a sneer at Annabella's lineage
48–9  triumph/On my dejection: gloat over my humiliation
50  free: high-born
61  not near: beyond

---

63  unedge: blunt
64  perplex her: drive her towards madness
66  freely: without interruption
76  Ligorn: Livorno (or Leghorn), about a hundred miles
     from Parma, is reached through mountains which were
     noted for the danger to travellers from bandits
86–8  The vows . . . break them: refers to the doctrine of
     St Augustine which stated (in *De Bono Coniugali*) that it
     was no sin to break a contract made in sin
93  quality, condition: class, social position
94  entertainment: hospitality
95  braver: finer
99  accursed: the uncorrected Q has 'a curse' and the corrected
     Q 'a Coarse.' Modern eds follow Bawcutt's emendation

I hate thee and thy lust: you have been too foul.  *Exit*

VASQUES (*Aside*) This part has been scurvily played.

HIPPOLITA  How foolishly this beast contemns his fate,
 And shuns the use of that which I more scorn
 Than I once loved, his love. But let him go;
 My vengeance shall give comfort to this woe.

*She offers to go away*

VASQUES  Mistress, mistress, Madam Hippolita, pray, a
 word or two!

HIPPOLITA  With me, sir?

VASQUES  With you, if you please.                    110

HIPPOLITA  What is't?

VASQUES  I know you are infinitely moved now, and you
 think you have cause; some I confess you have, but
 sure not so much as you imagine.

HIPPOLITA  Indeed.

VASQUES  O, you were miserably bitter, which you
 followed even to the last syllable. Faith, you were
 somewhat too shrewd; by my life you could not have
 took my lord in a worse time, since I first knew him:
 tomorrow you shall find him a new man.          120

HIPPOLITA  Well, I shall wait his leisure.

VASQUES  Fie, this is not a hearty patience, it comes
 sourly from you; troth, let me persuade you for once.

HIPPOLITA  (*Aside*) I have it, and it shall be so; thanks,
 opportunity!—Persuade me to what?

VASQUES  Visit him in some milder temper. O if you
 could but master a little your female spleen, how
 might you win him.

HIPPOLITA  He will never love me. Vasques, thou hast
 been a too trusty servant to such a master, and I
 believe thy reward in the end will fall out like mine.

VASQUES  So perhaps too.                              132

HIPPOLITA  Resolve thyself it will. Had I one so true, so
 truly honest, so secret to my counsels, as thou hast
 been to him and his, I should think it a slight
 acquittance, not only to make him master of all I
 have, but even of myself.

VASQUES  O you are a noble gentlewoman.

HIPPOLITA  Wilt thou feed always upon hopes? Well, I
 know thou art wise, and seest the reward of an old
 servant daily, what it is.                          141

VASQUES  Beggary and neglect.

HIPPOLITA  True: but Vasques, wert thou mine, and
 wouldst be private to me and my designs, I here
 protest myself and all what I can else call mine should
 be at thy dispose.

VASQUES (*Aside*) Work you that way, old mole? Then I
 have the wind of you.—I were not worthy of it by any
 desert that could lie within my compass; if I could—

HIPPOLITA  What then?                                150

VASQUES  I should then hope to live in these my old
 years with rest and security.

HIPPOLITA  Give me thy hand: now promise but thy
 silence,
 And help to bring to pass a plot I have,
 And here in sight of Heaven, that being done,
 I make thee lord of me and mine estate.

VASQUES  Come, you are merry; this is such a happiness
 that I can neither think or believe.

HIPPOLITA  Promise thy secrecy, and 'tis confirmed. 159

VASQUES  Then here I call our good genii for witnesses,
 whatsoever your designs are, or against whomsoever,
 I will not only be a special actor therein, but never
 disclose it till it be effected.

HIPPOLITA  I take thy word, and with that, thee for
 mine;
 Come then, let's more confer of this anon.
 On this delicious bane my thoughts shall banquet:
 Revenge shall sweeten what my griefs have tasted.

*Exeunt*

# Act II, scene iii

*Enter* RICHARDETTO *and* PHILOTIS

RICHARDETTO  Thou seest, my lovely niece, these
 strange mishaps,
 How all my fortunes turn to my disgrace,
 Wherein I am but as a looker-on,
 Whiles others act my shame, and I am silent.

PHILOTUS  But uncle, wherein can this borrowed shape
 Give you content?

RICHARDETTO         I'll tell thee, gentle niece:
 Thy wanton aunt in her lascivious riots
 Lives now secure, thinks I am surely dead
 In my late journey to Ligorn for you
 (As I have caused it to be rumoured out).          10
 Now would I see with what an impudence
 She gives scope to her loose adultery,
 And how the common voice allows hereof:
 Thus far I have prevailed.

PHILOTIS                   Alas, I fear

---

102  scurvily played: badly acted
103  contemns: scorns
106  this woe: Q has 'his woe'
118  shrewd: outspoken
122  hearty: genuine
133  Resolve: assure
136  acquittance: discharge of a debt
144  be private to: be privy to

147–8  I have the wind of you: as a hunter scents the hunted, I
   have knowledge of your intention
157  merry: joking
160  good genii: guardian spirits
   for witnesses: Q reads 'foe-witnesses'
166  bane: poison
  5  borrowed shape: a disguise, a term taken from actors'
   costumes
 13  how the . . . allows hereof: how people judge her

You mean some strange revenge.

RICHARDETTO O be not troubled;
Your ignorance shall plead for you in all.
But to our business: what, you learned for certain
How Signor Florio means to give his daughter
In marriage to Soranzo?

PHILOTIS Yes, for certain.

RICHARDETTO But how find you young Annabella's
love                                                          20
Inclined to him?

PHILOTIS For aught I could perceive,
She neither fancies him or any else.

RICHARDETTO There's mystery in that which time
must show.
She used you kindly?

PHILOTIS Yes.

RICHARDETTO And craved your company?

PHILOTIS Often.

RICHARDETTO 'Tis well; it goes as I could wish.
I am the doctor now, and as for you,
None knows you; if all fail not, we shall thrive.
But who comes here?

*Enter* GRIMALDI

I know him: 'tis Grimaldi,
A Roman and a soldier, near allied
Unto the duke of Montferrato, one                            30
Attending on the nuncio of the Pope
That now resides in Parma, by which means
He hopes to get the love of Annabella.

GRIMALDI Save you, sir.

RICHARDETTO And you, sir.

GRIMALDI I have heard
Of your approvèd skill, which through the city
Is freely talked of, and would crave your aid.

RICHARDETTO For what, sir?

GRIMALDI Marry, sir, for this—
But I would speak in private.

RICHARDETTO Leave us, cousin.
*Exit* PHILOTIS

GRIMALDI I love fair Annabella, and would know
Whether in art there may not be receipts           40
To move affection.

RICHARDETTO Sir, perhaps there may,
But these will nothing profit you.

GRIMALDI Not me?

RICHARDETTO Unless I be mistook, you are a man
Greatly in favour with the cardinal.

GRIMALDI What of that?

RICHARDETTO In duty to his grace,
I will be bold to tell you, if you seek
To marry Florio's daughter, you must first
Remove a bar 'twixt you and her.

GRIMALDI Who's that?

RICHARDETTO Soranzo is the man that hath her heart;
And while he lives, be sure you cannot speed.        50

GRIMALDI Soranzo! What, mine enemy! Is't he?

RICHARDETTO Is he your enemy?

GRIMALDI The man I hate
Worse than confusion;
I'll kill him straight.

RICHARDETTO Nay then, take mine advice
(Even for his grace's sake, the cardinal):
I'll find a time when he and she do meet,
Of which I'll give you notice, and to be sure
He shall not 'scape you, I'll provide a poison
To dip your rapier's point in; if he had
As many heads as Hydra had, he dies.                 60

GRIMALDI But shall I trust thee, doctor?

RICHARDETTO As yourself;
Doubt not in aught. (*Aside*) Thus shall the fates
decree:
By me Soranzo falls, that ruined me.

*Exeunt*

# Act II, scene iv

*Enter* DONADO, BERGETTO *and* POGGIO

DONADO Well, sir, I must be content to be both your
secretary and your messenger myself. I cannot tell
what this letter may work, but as sure as I am alive, if
thou come once to talk with her, I fear thou wilt mar
whatsoever I make.

BERGETTO You make, uncle? Why, am not I big
enough to carry mine own letter, I pray?

DONADO Ay, ay, carry a fool's head o' thy own. Why,
thou dunce, wouldst thou write a letter and carry it
thyself?                                                     10

BERGETTO Yes, that I would, and read it to her with
my own mouth; for you must think, if she will not
believe me myself when she hears me speak, she will
not believe another's hand-writing. O, you think I
am a blockhead, uncle. No, sir, Poggio knows I have
indited a letter myself, so I have.

POGGIO Yes truly, sir; I have it in my pocket.

DONADO A sweet one, no doubt; pray let's see't.

BERGETTO I cannot read my own hand very well,

16 Your ignorance . . . in all: since you know nothing of my
plans you will not risk being held responsible for them
31 nuncio of the pope: the pope's official representative
34 Save you, sir: God save you, sir; a common greeting but
with an ironic sense in this encounter
40 art: Q has 'arts', the art of medicine
receipts: recipes for love potions

50 speed: succeed
53 confusion: ruin
60 Hydra: a many-headed beast which grew two more heads
for each that was cut off
16 indited: written

Poggio; read it, Poggio. 20

DONADO Begin.

POGGIO (*reads*) 'Most dainty and honey-sweet mistress, I could call you fair, and lie as fast as any that loves you, but my uncle being the elder man I leave it to him, as more fit for his age and the colour of his beard. I am wise enough to tell you I can bourd where I see occasion; or if you like my uncle's wit better than mine, you shall marry me; if you like mine better than his, I will marry you in spite of your teeth. So commending my best parts to you, I rest— Yours upwards and downwards, or you may choose, Bergetto.' 32

BERGETTO Aha, here's stuff, uncle.

DONADO Here's stuff indeed to shame us all. Pray whose advice did you take in this learned letter?

POGGIO None, upon my word, but mine own.

BERGETTO And mine, uncle, believe it, nobody's else; 'twas mine own brain, I thank a good wit for't.

DONADO Get you home, sir, and look you keep within doors till I return. 40

BERGETTO How! That were a jest indeed; I scorn it i'faith.

DONADO What! You do not?

BERGETTO Judge me, but I do now.

POGGIO Indeed, sir, 'tis very unhealthy.

DONADO Well, sir, if I hear any of your apish running to motions and fopperies, till I come back, you were as good no; look to't. *Exit* DONADO

BERGETTO Poggio, shall's steal to see this horse with the head in's tail? 50

POGGIO Ay, but you must take heed of whipping.

BERGETTO Dost take me for a child, Poggio? Come, honest Poggio.

*Exeunt*

# Act II, scene v

*Enter* FRIAR *and* GIOVANNI

FRIAR Peace. Thou hast told a tale, whose every word
Threatens eternal slaughter to the soul.
I'm sorry I have heard it; would mine ears
Had been one minute deaf, before the hour
That thou cam'st to me. O young man cast away,
By the religious number of mine order,
I day and night have waked my aged eyes,

---

Above my strength, to weep on thy behalf:
But Heaven is angry, and be thou resolved,
Thou art a man remarked to taste a mischief. 10
Look for't; though it come late, it will come sure.

GIOVANNI Father, in this you are uncharitable;
What I have done I'll prove both fit and good.
It is a principle (which you have taught
When I was yet your scholar), that the frame
And composition of the mind doth follow
The frame and composition of the body:
So where the body's furniture is beauty,
The mind's must needs be virtue; which allowed,
Virtue itself is reason but refined, 20
And love the quintessence of that. This proves
My sister's beauty being rarely fair
Is rarely virtuous; chiefly in her love,
And chiefly in that love, her love to me.
If hers to me, then so is mine to her;
Since in like causes are effects alike.

FRIAR O ignorance in knowledge. Long ago,
How often have I warned thee this before?
Indeed, if we were sure there were no deity,
Nor Heaven nor hell, then to be led alone 30
By nature's light (as were philosophers
Of elder times) might instance some defence.
But 'tis not so; then, madman, thou wilt find
That nature is in Heaven's positions blind.

GIOVANNI Your age o'errules you; had you youth like mine,
You'd make her love your Heaven, and her divine.

FRIAR Nay then, I see th'art too far sold to hell,
It lies not in the compass of my prayers
To call thee back; yet let me counsel thee:
Persuade thy sister to some marriage. 40

GIOVANNI Marriage? Why, that's to damn her. That's to prove
Her greedy of variety of lust.

FRIAR O fearful! If thou wilt not, give me leave
To shrive her, lest she should die unabsolved.

GIOVANNI At your best leisure, father; then she'll tell you

---

26  bourd: jest
29–30  in spite of your teeth: despite your opposition
30  parts: see II.i.65n
47  motions: puppet-shows
   fopperies: follies
49–50  this horse . . . in's tail?: a reference to the fair exhibit mentioned in I.iii.38–41
5  cast away: considered damned

9  resolved: see II.ii.133n
10  remarked: marked out
   mischief: ruin
14–21  It is a principle . . . of that: Morris compares this to Edmund Spenser's *An Hymne in Honour of Beautie*:
   For of the soule the bodie forme doth take:
   For soule is forme, and doth the bodie make.
   Giovanni is making vague reference to the Neoplatonic notion of the relationship between beauty and truth
31–2  (as were . . . elder times): the idea that pre-Christian philosophers would be brought to a state of grace by nature's light
34  That nature . . . positions blind: implies that studying nature teaches us nothing of the truly divine
44  shrive: administer the act of confession

How dearly she doth prize my matchless love.
Then you will know what pity 'twere we two
Should have been sundered from each other's arms.
View well her face, and in that little round
You may observe a world of variety:                50
For colour, lips; for sweet perfumes, her breath;
For jewels, eyes; for threads of purest gold,
Hair; for delicious choice of flowers, cheeks;
Wonder in every portion of that throne.
Hear her but speak, and you will swear the spheres
Make music to the citizens in Heaven.
But, father, what is else for pleasure framed,
Lest I offend your ears, shall go unnamed.
FRIAR   The more I hear, I pity thee the more,
  That one so excellent should give those parts    60
  All to a second death; what I can do
  Is but to pray: and yet I could advise thee,
  Wouldst thou be ruled.
GIOVANNI               In what?
FRIAR                             Why, leave her yet;
  The throne of mercy is above your trespass;
  Yet time is left you both—
GIOVANNI                  To embrace each other,
  Else let all time be struck quite out of number.
  She is like me, and I like her, resolved.
FRIAR   No more! I'll visit her. This grieves me most,
  Things being thus, a pair of souls are lost.
                                        *Exeunt*

# Act II, scene vi

*Enter* FLORIO, DONADO, ANNABELLA, PUTANA

FLORIO   Where's Giovanni?
ANNABELLA                Newly walked abroad,
  And, as I heard him say, gone to the friar,
  His reverend tutor.
FLORIO              That's a blessèd man,
  A man made up of holiness; I hope
  He'll teach him how to gain another world.
DONADO   Fair gentlewoman, here's a letter sent
  To you from my young cousin; I dare swear
  He loves you in his soul: would you could hear
  Sometimes what I see daily, sighs and tears,
  As if his breast were prison to his heart.       10
FLORIO   Receive it, Annabella.
ANNABELLA   Alas, good man.
DONADO   What's that she said?
PUTANA   And please you, sir, she said, 'Alas, good
  man.' Truly I do commend him to her every night
  before her first sleep, because I would have her dream
  of him, and she hearkens to that most religiously.

DONADO   Say'st so? God-a-mercy, Putana, there's
  something for thee, and prithee do what thou canst
  on his behalf; sha' not be lost labour, take my word
  for't.                                           21
PUTANA   Thank you most heartily, sir; now I have a
  feeling of your mind, let me alone to work.
ANNABELLA   Guardian!
PUTANA   Did you call?
ANNABELLA   Keep this letter.
DONADO   Signor Florio, in any case bid her read it
  instantly.
FLORIO   Keep it for what? Pray read it me hereright.
ANNABELLA   I shall, sir.                    *She reads*
DONADO   How d'ee find her inclined, signor?       31
FLORIO   Troth, sir, I know not how; not all so well
  As I could wish.
ANNABELLA   Sir, I am bound to rest your cousin's
    debtor.
  The jewel I'll return; for if he love,
  I'll count that love a jewel.
DONADO                    Mark you that?
  Nay, keep them both, sweet maid.
ANNABELLA                        You must excuse me,
  Indeed I will not keep it.
FLORIO                   Where's the ring,
  That which your mother in her will bequeathed,
  And charged you on her blessing not to give't    40
  To any but your husband? Send back that.
ANNABELLA   I have it not.
FLORIO                   Ha, have it not! Where is't?
ANNABELLA   My brother in the morning took it from
    me,
  Said he would wear't today.
FLORIO                     Well, what do you say
  To young Bergetto's love? Are you content
  To match with him? Speak.
DONADO                      There's the point indeed.
ANNABELLA   (*Aside*) What shall I do? I must say
    something now.
FLORIO   What say? Why d'ee not speak?
ANNABELLA                        Sir, with your leave,
  Please you to give me freedom?
FLORIO                       Yes, you have it.
ANNABELLA   Signor Donado, if your nephew mean   50
  To raise his better fortunes in his match,
  The hope of me will hinder such a hope;
  Sir, if you love him, as I know you do,
  Find one more worthy of his choice than me.
  In short, I'm sure I sha' not be his wife.

---

54   throne: i.e. Annabella's face
60   parts: see II.i.65n
61   second death: damnation

23   a feeling: an understanding
29   hereright: immediately
49   freedom: a free choice of a husband
51   To raise his better fortunes: to improve his social
     position

DONADO Why, here's plain dealing; I commend thee
    for't,
  And all the worst I wish thee is, Heaven bless thee!
  Your father yet and I will still be friends,
  Shall we not, Signor Florio?
FLORIO                Yes, why not?
  Look, here your cousin comes.        60

*Enter* BERGETTO *and* POGGIO

DONADO (*Aside*) O, coxcomb, what doth he make here?
BERGETTO Where's my uncle, sirs?
DONADO What's the news now?
BERGETTO Save you, uncle, save you. You must not
  think I come for nothing, masters; and how, and how
  is't? What, you have read my letter? Ah, there I—
  tickled you i'faith.
POGGIO But 'twere better you had tickled her in
  another place.
BERGETTO Sirrah sweetheart, I'll tell thee a good jest;
  and riddle what 'tis.             71
ANNABELLA You say you'd tell me.
BERGETTO As I was walking just now in the street, I met
  a swaggering fellow would needs take the wall of me,
  and because he did thrust me, I very valiantly called
  him rogue. He hereupon bade me draw; I told him I
  had more wit than so, but when he saw that I would
  not, he did so maul me with the hilts of his rapier that
  my head sung whilst my feet capered in the kennel.
DONADO (*Aside*) Was ever the like ass seen?    80
ANNABELLA And what did you all this while?
BERGETTO Laugh at him for a gull, till I see the blood
  run about mine ears, and then I could not choose but
  find in my heart to cry; till a fellow with a broad
  beard (they say he is a new-come doctor) called me
  into his house, and gave me a plaster—look you, here
  'tis—and, sir, there was a young wench washed my
  face and hands most excellently, i'faith, I shall love
  her as long as I live for't, did she not, Poggio?
POGGIO Yes, and kissed him too.         90
BERGETTO Why, la now, you think I tell a lie, uncle, I
  warrant.
DONADO Would he that beat thy blood out of thy head
  had beaten some wit into it; for I fear thou never wilt
  have any.
BERGETTO O, uncle, but there was a wench would have
  done a man's heart good to have looked on her—by
  this light she had a face methinks worth twenty of
  you, Mistress Annabella.

DONADO Was ever such a fool born?      100
ANNABELLA I am glad she liked you, sir.
BERGETTO Are you so? By my troth I thank you,
  forsooth.
FLORIO Sure 'twas the doctor's niece, that was last day
  with us here.
BERGETTO 'Twas she, 'twas she.
DONADO How do you know that, simplicity?
BERGETTO Why, does not he say so? If I should have
  said no, I should have given him the lie, uncle, and so
  have deserved a dry beating again; I'll none of that.
FLORIO A very modest well-behaved young maid   111
  As I have seen.
DONADO          Is she indeed?
FLORIO                  Indeed
  She is, if I have any judgment.
DONADO Well, sir, now you are free, you need not care
  for sending letters: now you are dismissed, your
  mistress here will none of you.
BERGETTO No. Why, what care I for that? I can have
  wenches enough in Parma for half-a-crown apiece,
  cannot I, Poggio?
POGGIO I'll warrant you, sir.         120
DONADO Signor Florio,
  I thank you for your free recourse you gave
  For my admittance; and to you, fair maid,
  That jewel I will give you 'gainst your marriage.
  Come, will you go, sir?
BERGETTO Ay, marry will I. Mistress, farewell,
  mistress. I'll come again tomorrow. Farewell,
  mistress.       *Exit* DONADO, BERGETTO, *and* POGGIO

*Enter* GIOVANNI

FLORIO Son, where have you been? What, alone, alone
  still?
  I would not have it so, you must forsake    130
  This over-bookish humour. Well, your sister
  Hath shook the fool off.
GIOVANNI          'Twas no match for her.
FLORIO 'Twas not indeed, I meant it nothing less;
  Soranzo is the man I only like—
  Look on him, Annabella. Come, 'tis supper-time.
  And it grows late.          *Exit* FLORIO
GIOVANNI Whose jewel's that?
ANNABELLA          Some sweetheart's.
GIOVANNI               So I think.
ANNABELLA A lusty youth,
  Signor Donado, gave it me to wear

---

67 tickled: pleased
71 riddle: guess
74 take the wall of me: take the cleanest and safest place on
   the pavement, closest to the wall
79 kennel: gutter
82 gull: dupe

101 liked: pleased
109 given him the lie: accused him of lying
   dry: bloodless
118 half-a-crown: the price charged by English prostitutes
124 'gainst: in anticipation of
134 only: specially

Against my marriage.

GIOVANNI          But you shall not wear it.   **140**
  Send it him back again.

ANNABELLA          What, you are jealous?

GIOVANNI  That you shall know anon, at better leisure.
  Welcome, sweet night, the evening crowns the day.

                           *Exeunt*

## Act III, scene i

*Enter* BERGETTO *and* POGGIO

BERGETTO  Does my uncle think to make me a baby
  still? No, Poggio, he shall know I have a sconce now.

POGGIO  Ay, let him not bob you off like an ape with an
  apple.

BERGETTO  'Sfoot, I will have the wench if he were ten
  uncles, in despite of his nose, Poggio.

POGGIO  Hold him to the grindstone and give not a jot of
  ground. She hath in a manner promised you already.

BERGETTO  True, Poggio, and her uncle the doctor
  swore I should marry her.               **10**

POGGIO  He swore, I remember.

BERGETTO  And I will have her, that's more; didst see
  the codpiece-point she gave me and the box of
  marmalade?

POGGIO  Very well; and kissed you, that my chops
  watered at the sight on't. There's no way but to clap
  up a marriage in hugger-mugger.

BERGETTO  I will do't; for I tell thee, Poggio, I begin to
  grow valiant methinks, and my courage begins to rise.

POGGIO  Should you be afraid of your uncle?     **20**

BERGETTO  Hang him, old doting rascal. No, I say I
  will have her.

POGGIO  Lose no time then.

BERGETTO  I will beget a race of wise men and
  constables, that shall cart whores at their own
  charges, and break the duke's peace ere I have done
  myself.—Come away.

                           *Exeunt*

---

  2  sconce: head, brain

  3  bob: fob

  5  'Sfoot: 'by God's foot'

13  codpiece-point: a lace fastening for a codpiece, the
    decorative garment which covered but also drew
    attention to the male gentitalia. Elaborate codpieces had
    become unfashionable by the time the play was first
    performed

16–17  to clap up . . . in hugger-mugger: to arrange a quick and
    secret marriage. There is an echo here of the speech
    made by Claudius in *Hamlet* concerning the death of
    Polonius (IV.v.80)

19  courage: bravery, but also sexual desire

25  cart whores: prostitutes were paraded in the streets in
    carts as a punishment
    charges: expense

## Act III, scene ii

*Enter* FLORIO, GIOVANNI, SORANZO, ANNABELLA,
PUTANA *and* VASQUES

FLORIO  My Lord Soranzo, though I must confess
  The proffers that are made me have been great
  In marriage of my daughter, yet the hope
  Of your still rising honours have prevailed
  Above all other jointures. Here she is;
  She knows my mind, speak for yourself to her,
  And hear you, daughter, see you use him nobly;
  For any private speech I'll give you time.
  Come, son, and you the rest, let them alone:
  Agree they as they may.

SORANZO              I thank you, sir.     **10**

GIOVANNI  (*Aside*) Sister, be not all woman, think on
  me.

SORANZO  Vasques.

VASQUES  My lord?

SORANZO  Attend me without.

      *Exeunt omnes, manet* SORANZO *and* ANNABELLA

ANNABELLA  Sir, what's your will with me?

SORANZO             Do you not know
  What I should tell you?

ANNABELLA         Yes, you'll say you love me.

SORANZO  And I'll swear it too; will you believe it?

ANNABELLA  'Tis not a point of faith.

*Enter* GIOVANNI *above*

SORANZO            Have you not will to love?

ANNABELLA  Not you.

SORANZO        Whom then?

ANNABELLA          That's as the fates infer.

GIOVANNI  (*Aside*) Of those I'm regent now.

SORANZO            What mean you, sweet?

ANNABELLA  To live and die a maid.

SORANZO            O, that's unfit.   **21**

GIOVANNI  (*Aside*) Here's one can say that's but a
  woman's note.

SORANZO  Did you but see my heart, then would you
  swear—

ANNABELLA  That you were dead.

GIOVANNI  (*Aside*)          That's true, or
  somewhat near it.

SORANZO  See you these true love's tears?

ANNABELLA           No.

---

  5  jointures: proposals of marriage

10  Q has 'agree as they may'

11  be not all woman: Giovanni refers to a stereotype of
    women as inconstant

SD  *manet*: he stays, though in fact both Soranzo and
    Annabella remain on stage

18  point of faith: an article of faith necessary for salvation.
    Q has ''Tis not point of faith'

GIOVANNI (*Aside*)                    Now she winks.
SORANZO  They plead to you for grace.
ANNABELLA                    Yet nothing speak.
SORANZO  O grant my suit.
ANNABELLA                    What is't?
SORANZO                    To let me live—
ANNABELLA  Take it.
SORANZO          —still yours.
ANNABELLA                    That is not mine to give.
GIOVANNI (*Aside*) One such another word would kill
    his hopes.
SORANZO  Mistress, to leave those fruitless strifes of wit,
    Know I have loved you long and loved you truly;    **31**
    Not hope of what you have, but what you are,
    Have drawn me on; then let me not in vain
    Still feel the rigour of your chaste disdain.
    I'm sick, and sick to th' heart.
ANNABELLA                    Help, *aqua-vitae*.
SORANZO  What mean you?
ANNABELLA          Why, I thought you had been sick.
SORANZO  Do you mock my love?
GIOVANNI (*Aside*)                    There, sir, she was too
    nimble.
SORANZO (*Aside*) 'Tis plain, she laughs at me.—These
    scornful taunts
    Neither become your modesty or years.
ANNABELLA  You are no looking glass; or if you were,
    I'd dress my language by you.                        **41**
GIOVANNI (*Aside*)          I'm confirmed.
ANNABELLA  To put you out of doubt, my lord,
    methinks
    Your common sense should make you understand
    That if I loved you, or desired your love,
    Some way I should have given you better taste:
    But since you are a nobleman, and one
    I would not wish should spend his youth in hopes,
    Let me advise you here to forbear your suit,
    And think I wish you well, I tell you this.
SORANZO  Is't you speak this?
ANNABELLA                    Yes, I myself; yet know—
    Thus far I give you comfort—if mine eyes            **51**
    Could have picked out a man (amongst all those
    That sued to me) to make a husband of,
    You should have been that man. Let this suffice;
    Be noble in your secrecy and wise.
GIOVANNI (*Aside*) Why, now I see she loves me.
ANNABELLA                    One word more:
    As ever virtue lived within your mind,
    As ever noble courses were your guide,
    As ever you would have me know you loved me,
    Let not my father know hereof by you;              **60**
    If I hereafter find that I must marry,

It shall be you or none.
SORANZO                    I take that promise.
ANNABELLA  O, O, my head.
SORANZO                    What's the matter? Not well?
ANNABELLA  O, I begin to sicken.
GIOVANNI (*Aside*)                    Heaven forbid.
                                        *Exit from above*
SORANZO  Help, help within there, ho!

*Enter* FLORIO, GIOVANNI *and* PUTANA

    Look to your daughter, Signor Florio.
FLORIO  Hold her up, she swoons.
GIOVANNI  Sister, how d'ee?
ANNABELLA  Sick—brother, are you there?              **70**
FLORIO  Convey her to her bed instantly, whilst I send
    for a physician; quickly, I say.
PUTANA  Alas, poor child!        *Exeunt, manet* SORANZO

*Enter* VASQUES

VASQUES  My lord.
SORANZO  O Vasques, now I doubly am undone
    Both in my present and my future hopes.
    She plainly told me that she could not love,
    And thereupon soon sickened, and I fear
    Her life's in danger.                               **79**
VASQUES (*Aside*) By'r lady, sir, and so is yours, if you
    knew all.—'Las, sir, I am sorry for that; may be 'tis
    but the maid's sickness, an overflux of youth, and
    then, sir, there is no such present remedy as present
    marriage. But hath she given you an absolute denial?
SORANZO  She hath and she hath not; I'm full of grief,
    But what she said I'll tell thee as we go.
                                            *Exeunt*

# Act III, scene iii

*Enter* GIOVANNI *and* PUTANA

PUTANA  O sir, we are all undone, quite undone, utterly
    undone, and shamed forever; your sister, O your
    sister.
GIOVANNI  What of her? For Heaven's sake, speak; how
    does she?
PUTANA  O that ever I was born to see this day.
GIOVANNI  She is not dead, ha? Is she?
PUTANA  Dead? No, she is quick; 'tis worse, she is with
    child. You know what you have done; Heaven forgive
    'ee. 'Tis too late to repent now, Heaven help us.
GIOVANNI  With child? How dost thou know't?          **10**
PUTANA  How do I know't? Am I at these years
    ignorant what the meanings of qualms and water-

---

25  winks: turns a blind eye
35  *aqua-vitae*: a reviving spirit, usually brandy

82  maid's sickness: greensickness, chlorosis, a form of
    anaemia associated with female puberty
    overflux: overflow, surplus
8  quick: alive, but also pregnant

pangs be? Of changing of colours, queasiness of stomachs, pukings, and another thing that I could name? Do not, for her and your credit's sake, spend the time in asking how, and which way, 'tis so; she is quick, upon my word: if you let a physician see her water y'are undone.

GIOVANNI But in what case is she?  19

PUTANA Prettily amended; 'twas but a fit which I soon espied, and she must look for often henceforward.

GIOVANNI Commend me to her, bid her take no care;
Let not the doctor visit her, I charge you,
Make some excuse, till I return. O me!
I have a world of business in my head.
Do not discomfort her.—
How does this news perplex me! If my father
Come to her, tell him she's recovered well,
Say 'twas but some ill diet; d'ee hear, woman?
Look you to't.  30

PUTANA I will, sir.

*Exeunt*

# Act III, scene iv

*Enter* FLORIO *and* RICHARDETTO

FLORIO And how d'ee find her, sir?

RICHARDETTO                Indifferent well;
I see no danger, scarce perceive she's sick,
But that she told me she had lately eaten
Melons, and, as she thought, those disagreed
With her young stomach.

FLORIO                Did you give her aught?

RICHARDETTO An easy surfeit-water, nothing else.
You need not doubt her health; I rather think
Her sickness is a fulness of her blood—
You understand me?

FLORIO                I do; you counsel well,
And once, within these few days, will so order't  10
She shall be married ere she know the time.

RICHARDETTO Yet let not haste, sir, make unworthy choice;
That were dishonour.

FLORIO                Master Doctor, no;
I will not do so neither; in plain words,
My Lord Soranzo is the man I mean.

RICHARDETTO A noble and a virtuous gentleman.

FLORIO As any is in Parma. Not far hence
Dwells Father Bonaventure, a grave friar,
Once tutor to my son; now at his cell
I'll have 'em married.

RICHARDETTO                You have plotted wisely.  20

FLORIO I'll send one straight to speak with him tonight.

RICHARDETTO Soranzo's wise, he will delay no time.

FLORIO It shall be so.

*Enter* FRIAR *and* GIOVANNI

FRIAR                Good peace be here and love.

FLORIO Welcome, religious friar; you are one
That still brings blessing to the place you come to.

GIOVANNI Sir, with what speed I could, I did my best
To draw this holy man from forth his cell
To visit my sick sister, that with words
Of ghostly comfort, in this time of need,
He might absolve her, whether she live or die.  30

FLORIO 'Twas well done, Giovanni; thou herein
Hast showed a Christian's care, a brother's love.
Come, father, I'll conduct you to her chamber,
And one thing would entreat you.

FRIAR                Say on, sir.

FLORIO I have a father's dear impression,
And wish, before I fall into my grave,
That I might see her married, as 'tis fit;
A word from you, grave man, will win her more
Than all our best persuasions.

FRIAR                Gentle sir,
All this I'll say, that Heaven may prosper her.  40

*Exeunt*

# Act III, scene v

*Enter* GRIMALDI

GRIMALDI Now if the doctor keep his word, Soranzo,
Twenty to one you miss your bride; I know
'Tis an unnoble act, and not becomes
A soldier's valour, but in terms of love,
Where merit cannot sway, policy must.
I am resolved; if this physician
Play not on both hands, then Soranzo falls.

*Enter* RICHARDETTO

---

12–13 water-pangs: compulsion to urinate
13–14 and another . . . could name: cessation of menstruation
  14 credit's: good name's
  19 case: state
  20 Prettily amended: recovered
  22 take no care: not worry
   1 Indifferent: fairly
   6 surfeit-water: a cure for indigestion
   8 a fulness of her blood: a case of sexual frustration
  10 once: at some time

---

25 still: always
29 ghostly: spiritual
35 dear impression: the meaning is not clear although some modern editors note that Florio means to suggest his loving feelings as a father
 4 terms: circumstances
 5 policy: cunning
 7 Play not . . . both hands: is not working for both sides

RICHARDETTO You are come as I could wish; this very
    night
    Soranzo, 'tis ordained, must be affied
    To Annabella, and, for aught I know,                    10
    Married.
GRIMALDI How!
RICHARDETTO     Yet your patience:
    The place, 'tis Friar Bonaventure's cell.
    Now I would wish you to bestow this night
    In watching thereabouts; 'tis but a night:
    If you miss now, tomorrow I'll know all.
GRIMALDI Have you the poison?
RICHARDETTO                     Here 'tis in this box.
    Doubt nothing, this will do't; in any case,
    As you respect your life, be quick and sure.
GRIMALDI I'll speed him.
RICHARDETTO              Do. Away; for 'tis not safe
    You should be seen much here — Ever my love.    20
GRIMALDI And mine to you.              Exit GRIMALDI
RICHARDETTO So. If this hit, I'll laugh and hug revenge;
    And they that now dream of a wedding-feast
    May chance to mourn the lusty bridegroom's ruin.
    But to my other business.—Niece Philotis!

*Enter* PHILOTIS

PHILOTIS Uncle?
RICHARDETTO My lovely niece,
    You have bethought 'ee?
PHILOTIS                    Yes, and, as you counselled
    Fashioned my heart to love him; but he swears
    He will tonight be married, for he fears          30
    His uncle else, if he should know the drift,
    Will hinder all, and call his coz to shrift.
RICHARDETTO Tonight? Why, best of all; but let me see,
    Ay—ha—yes—so it shall be; in disguise
    We'll early to the friar's, I have thought on't.

*Enter* BERGETTO *and* POGGIO

PHILOTIS Uncle, he comes.
RICHARDETTO              Welcome, my worthy coz.
BERGETTO Lass, pretty lass, come buss, lass! Aha,
    Poggio!                              *Kisses her*
POGGIO There's hope of this yet.
RICHARDETTO You shall have time enough; withdraw a
    little,
    We must confer at large.                          40
BERGETTO Have you not sweetmeats or dainty devices
    for me?

PHILOTIS You shall have enough, sweetheart.
BERGETTO Sweetheart! Mark that, Poggio. By my troth,
    I cannot choose but kiss thee once more for that word
    'sweetheart'. Poggio, I have a monstrous swelling
    about my stomach, whatsoever the matter be.
POGGIO You shall have physic for't, sir.
RICHARDETTO Time runs apace.
BERGETTO Time's a blockhead.
RICHARDETTO Be ruled; when we have done what's fit
    to do,                                            50
    Then you may kiss your fill, and bed her too.
                                            *Exeunt*

# Act III, scene vi

*Enter the* FRIAR *in his study sitting in a chair,* ANNABELLA
*kneeling and whispering to him; a table before them and
wax-lights; she weeps and wrings her hands*

FRIAR I am glad to see this penance; for, believe me,
    You have unripped a soul so foul and guilty
    As I must tell you true, I marvel how
    The earth hath borne you up; but weep, weep on,
    These tears may do you good; weep faster yet,
    Whiles I do read a lecture.
ANNABELLA                      Wretched creature!
FRIAR Ay, you are wretched, miserably wretched,
    Almost condemned alive. There is a place—
    List, daughter—in a black and hollow vault,
    Where day is never seen; there shines no sun,    10
    But flaming horror of consuming fires,
    A lightless sulphur, choked with smoky fogs
    Of an infected darkness; in this place
    Dwell many thousand thousand sundry sorts
    Of never-dying deaths—there damnèd souls
    Roar without pity; there are gluttons fed
    With toads and adders; there is burning oil
    Poured down the drunkard's throat, the usurer
    Is forced to sup whole draughts of molten gold;
    There is the murderer forever stabbed,            20
    Yet can he never die; there lies the wanton
    On racks of burning steel, whiles in his soul
    He feels the torment of his raging lust.

---

47 physic: see II.i.56n
SD *in his study*: critics have disagreed over the location of the
    scene since the Friar has previously been directed to
    Annabella's 'chamber' but Richardetto and Grimaldi
    have discussed a betrothal in the Friar's cell. It is certainly
    thought that the stage direction is Ford's. An alternative
    interpretation is that the phrase 'in his study' refers to the
    way that the Friar is observed wrapped up in his
    contemplation of damnation
2 unripped: exposed
6 I do read a lecture: deliver a cautionary reprimand
9 List: listen

---

 9 affied: betrothed
19 speed: dispatch, kill
22 hit: succeed
31 drift: plan
32 his coz to shrift: summon his nephew (cousin) to confession
37 buss: kiss
40 at large: at length

ANNABELLA  Mercy, O mercy!

FRIAR  There stands these
   wretched things
  Who have dreamed out whole years in lawless sheets
  And secret incests, cursing one another.
  Then you will wish each kiss your brother gave
  Had been a dagger's point; then you shall hear
  How he will cry, 'O would my wicked sister
  Had first been damned, when she did yield to lust!'—
  But soft, methinks I see repentance work     31
  New motions in your heart; say, how is't with you?

ANNABELLA  Is there no way left to redeem my miseries?

FRIAR  There is, despair not; Heaven is merciful,
  And offers grace even now. 'Tis thus agreed,
  First, for your honour's safety, that you marry
  The Lord Soranzo; next, to save your soul,
  Leave off this life, and henceforth live to him.

ANNABELLA  Ay me.

FRIAR  Sigh not; I know the baits of sin
  Are hard to leave. O, 'tis a death to do't.     40
  Remember what must come. Are you content?

ANNABELLA  I am.

FRIAR  I like it well; we'll take the time.
  Who's near us there?

*Enter* FLORIO *and* GIOVANNI

FLORIO  Did you call, father?

FRIAR  Is Lord Soranzo come?

FLORIO  He stays below.

FRIAR  Have you acquainted him at full?

FLORIO  I have,
  And he is overjoyed.

FRIAR  And so are we.
  Bid him come near.

GIOVANNI  (*Aside*) My sister weeping, ha?
  I fear this friar's falsehood.—I will call him.    *Exit*

FLORIO  Daughter, are you resolved?

ANNABELLA  Father, I am.    50

*Enter* GIOVANNI, SORANZO, *and* VASQUES

FLORIO  My Lord Soranzo, here
  Give me your hand; for that I give you this.

SORANZO  Lady, say you so too?

ANNABELLA  I do, and vow
  To live with you and yours.

FRIAR  Timely resolved:
  My blessing rest on both; more to be done,
  You may perform it on the morning sun.

                     *Exeunt*

---

42  we'll take the time: take the opportunity
44  stays: waits
51–6  My Lord . . . morning sun: the Friar joins Annabella and
    Soranzo in a betrothal which would be followed by the
    formal act of marriage at a later date

# Act III, scene vii

*Enter* GRIMALDI *with his rapier drawn and a dark lantern*

GRIMALDI  'Tis early night as yet, and yet too soon
  To finish such a work; here I will lie
  To listen who comes next.    *He lies down*

*Enter* BERGETTO *and* PHILOTIS *disguised, and after* RICHARDETTO *and* POGGIO

BERGETTO  We are almost at the place, I hope,
  sweetheart.

GRIMALDI  (*Aside*) I hear them near, and heard one say
  'sweetheart'.
  'Tis he; now guide my hand, some angry justice,
  Home to his bosom. Now have at you, sir!
           *Strikes* BERGETTO *and exit*

BERGETTO  O help, help! Here's a stitch fallen in my
  guts. O for a flesh-tailor quickly!—Poggio!

PHILOTIS  What ails my love?    10

BERGETTO  I am sure I cannot piss forward and
  backward, and yet I am wet before and behind.—
  Lights, lights! Ho, lights!

PHILOTIS  Alas, some villain here has slain my love.

RICHARDETTO  O Heaven forbid it.—Raise up the next
  neighbours
  Instantly, Poggio, and bring lights.    *Exit* POGGIO
  How is't, Bergetto? Slain? It cannot be;
  Are you sure y'are hurt?

BERGETTO  O my belly seethes like a porridge-pot;
  some cold water, I shall boil over else; my whole body
  is in a sweat, that you may wring my shirt; feel
  here—Why, Poggio!    22

*Enter* POGGIO *with* OFFICERS *and lights and halberts*

POGGIO  Here. Alas, how do you?

RICHARDETTO  Give me a light. What's here? All
  blood! O sirs,
  Signor Donado's nephew now is slain.
  Follow the murderer with all thy haste
  Up to the city, he cannot be far hence;
  Follow, I beseech you.

OFFICERS  Follow, follow, follow.    *Exeunt* OFFICERS

RICHARDETTO  Tear off thy linen, coz, to stop his
  wounds.    30
  Be of good comfort, man.

BERGETTO  Is all this mine own blood? Nay then, good
  night with me. Poggio, commend me to my uncle,
  dost hear? Bid him for my sake make much of this

---

SD  *dark lantern*: a lantern with a sliding shutter which could
    conceal the light
9  flesh-tailor: surgeon
SD  *halberts*: spears with axe handles
26  with all thy haste: Q has 'with all the haste'

wench. O!—I am going the wrong way sure, my belly
aches so.—O, farewell, Poggio! O! — O!        *Dies*
PHILOTIS  O, he is dead.
POGGIO                How! Dead!
RICHARDETTO              He's dead indeed.
'Tis now too late to weep; let's have him home,
And with what speed we may, find out the murderer.
POGGIO  O my master, my master, my master!        **40**
                                        *Exeunt*

# Act III, scene viii

*Entr* VASQUES *and* HIPPOLITA

HIPPOLITA  Betrothed?
VASQUES  I saw it.
HIPPOLITA  And when's the marriage-day?
VASQUES  Some two days hence.
HIPPOLITA  Two days? Why, man, I would but wish
    two hours
    To send him to his last, and lasting sleep.
    And, Vasques, thou shalt see I'll do it bravely.
VASQUES  I do not doubt your wisdom, nor, I trust, you
    my secrecy;
    I am infinitely yours.
HIPPOLITA  I will be thine in spite of my disgrace.        **10**
    So soon? O, wicked man, I durst be sworn,
    He'd laugh to see me weep.
VASQUES  And that's a villainous fault in him.
HIPPOLITA  No, let him laugh, I'm armed in my resolves;
    Be thou still true.
VASQUES  I should get little by treachery against so
    hopeful a preferment as I am like to climb to.
HIPPOLITA  Even to my bosom, Vasques. Let my youth
    Revel in these new pleasures; if we thrive,
    He now hath but a pair of days to live.        **20**
                                        *Exeunt*

# Act III, scene ix

*Enter* FLORIO, DONADO, RICHARDETTO, POGGIO *and
Officers*

FLORIO  'Tis bootless now to show yourself a child,
    Signor Donado; what is done, is done.
    Spend not the time in tears, but seek for justice.
RICHARDETTO  I must confess, somewhat I was in fault
    That had not first acquainted you what love
    Passed 'twixt him and my niece; but, as I live,
    His fortune grieves me as it were mine own.
DONADO  Alas, poor creature, he meant no man harm,

That I am sure of.
FLORIO            I believe that too.
    But stay, my masters, are you sure you saw        **10**
    The murderer pass here?
OFFICER  And it please you, sir, we are sure we saw a
    ruffian, with a naked weapon in his hand all bloody,
    get into my lord Cardinal's grace's gate, that we are
    sure of; but for fear of his grace, bless us, we durst go
    no further.
DONADO  Know you what manner of man he was?
OFFICER  Yes, sure, I know the man; they say 'a is a
    soldier; he that loved your daughter, sir, an't please
    ye; 'twas he for certain.        **20**
FLORIO  Grimaldi, on my life.
OFFICER                Ay, ay, the same.
RICHARDETTO  The Cardinal is noble; he no doubt
    Will give true justice.
DONADO  Knock someone at the gate.
POGGIO  I'll knock, sir.        POGGIO *knocks*
SERVANT  (*within*) What would 'ee?
FLORIO  We require speech with the lord Cardinal
    About some present business; pray inform
    His grace that we are here.

*Enter* CARDINAL *and* GRIMALDI

CARDINAL  Why, how now, friends! What saucy mates
    are you        **30**
    That know nor duty nor civility?
    Are we a person fit to be your host,
    Or is our house become your common inn,
    To beat our doors at pleasure? What such haste
    Is yours as that it cannot wait fit times?
    Are you the masters of this commonwealth,
    And know no more discretion? O, your news
    Is here before you; you have lost a nephew,
    Donado, last night by Grimaldi slain:
    Is that your business? Well, sir, we have knowledge
    on't.        **40**
    Let that suffice.
GRIMALDI            In presence of your grace,
    In thought I never meant Bergetto harm.
    But Florio, you can tell, with how much scorn
    Soranzo, backed with his confederates,
    Hath often wronged me; I, to be revenged,
    For that I could not win him else to fight,
    Had thought by way of ambush to have killed him,
    But was unluckily therein mistook;
    Else he had felt what late Bergetto did:
    And though my fault to him were merely chance,        **50**
    Yet humbly I submit me to your grace,

---

7   bravely: handsomely
16  against so hopeful: in exchange for so promising
18  my youth: Soranzo
1   bootless: pointless

12  And: if
18  'a: he
28  present: urgent
50  chance: by accident

To do with me as you please.

CARDINAL                                    Rise up, Grimaldi.
  You citizens of Parma, if you seek
  For justice, know, as nuncio from the Pope,
  For this offence I here receive Grimaldi
  Into his holiness's protection.
  He is no common man, but nobly born;
  Of princes' blood, though you, Sir Florio,
  Thought him too mean a husband for your daughter.
  If more you seek for, you must go to Rome,          60
  For he shall thither; learn more wit, for shame.
  Bury your dead.—Away, Grimaldi; leave 'em.
                        *Exeunt* CARDINAL *and* GRIMALDI
DONADO  Is this a churchman's voice? Dwells justice
      here?
FLORIO  Justice is fled to Heaven and comes no nearer.
  Soranzo. Was't for him? O impudence.
  Had he the face to speak it, and not blush?
  Come, come, Donado, there's no help in this,
  When cardinals think murder's not amiss.
  Great men may do their wills, we must obey;
  But Heaven will judge them for't another day.       70
                                          *Exeunt*

# Act IV, scene i

*A Banquet. Hautboys. Enter the* FRIAR, GIOVANNI,
ANNABELLA, PHILOTIS, SORANZO, DONADO, FLORIO,
RICHARDETTO, PUTANA, *and* VASQUES

FRIAR  These holy rites performed, now take your times
  To spend the remnant of the day in feast;
  Such fit repasts are pleasing to the saints,
  Who are your guests, though not with mortal eyes
  To be beheld.—Long prosper in this day,
  You happy couple, to each other's joy.
SORANZO  Father, your prayer is heard; the hand of
      goodness
  Hath been a shield for me against my death;
  And, more to bless me, hath enriched my life
  With this most precious jewel; such a prize          10
  As earth hath not another like to this.
  Cheer up, my love, and gentlemen, my friends,
  Rejoice with me in mirth; this day we'll crown
  With lusty cups to Annabella's health.
GIOVANNI  (*Aside*) O torture. Were the marriage yet
      undone,
  Ere I'd endure this sight, to see my love

---

  Clipped by another, I would dare confusion,
  And stand the horror of ten thousand deaths.
VASQUES  Are you not well, sir?
GIOVANNI                        Prithee, fellow, wait;
  I need not thy officious diligence.                  20
FLORIO  Signor Donado, come, you must forget
  Your late mishaps, and drown your cares in wine.
SORANZO  Vasques.
VASQUES              My lord?
SORANZO                        Reach me that weighty bowl.
  Here, brother Giovanni, here's to you;
  Your turn comes next, though now a bachelor.
  Here's to your sister's happiness and mine.
GIOVANNI  I cannot drink.
SORANZO                    What?
GIOVANNI                          'Twill indeed offend me.
ANNABELLA  Pray do not urge him, if he be not willing.
                                          *Hautboys*
FLORIO  How now, what noise is this?                   29
VASQUES  O, sir, I had forgot to tell you; certain young
      maidens of Parma, in honour to Madam Annabella's
      marriage, have sent their loves to her in a masque, for
      which they humbly crave your patience and silence.
SORANZO  We are much bound to them, so much the
      more
  As it comes unexpected; guide them in.

*Enter* HIPPOLITA *and* LADIES *in masks and white robes,
with garlands of willows. Music and a dance*

SORANZO  Thanks, lovely virgins; now might we but know
  To whom we have been beholding for this love,
  We shall acknowledge it.
HIPPOLITA                    Yes, you shall know; (*Unmasks*)
  What think you now?
OMNES                  Hippolita!
HIPPOLITA                          'Tis she,
  Be not amazed; nor blush, young lovely bride,        40
  I come not to defraud you of your man.
  'Tis now no time to reckon up the talk
  What Parma long hath rumoured of us both:
  Let rash report run on; the breath that vents it
  Will, like a bubble, break itself at last.
  But now to you, sweet creature: lend's your hand;
  Perhaps it hath been said that I would claim

---

59  mean: lowly
61  wit: sense
64  Justice is . . . no nearer: when the Golden Age came to
    an end the goddess of justice, Astraea, fled to the heavens
    and became the constellation Virgo
SD  *Hautboys*: oboes

17  Clipped: embraced
19  wait: wait on the guests
24  brother: as in brother-in-law
27  offend: displease, but also, cause illness
SD  *Hautboys*: after l. 35 in Q
29  noise: music
34  bound: obliged
SD  *willows*: a traditional symbol of disappointed love
37  love: act of kindness
44  rash report: gossip

Some interest in Soranzo, now your lord.
What I have right to do, his soul knows best;
But in my duty to your noble worth,                    50
Sweet Annabella, and my care of you,
Here take, Soranzo, take this hand from me:
I'll once more join what by the holy church
Is finished and allowed. Have I done well?
SORANZO You have too much engaged us.
HIPPOLITA                                One thing more.
That you may know my single charity,
Freely I here remit all interest
I e'er could claim, and give you back your vows;
And to confirm't, reach me a cup of wine.
My Lord Soranzo, in this draught I drink            60
Long rest t'ee.—Look to it, Vasques.
VASQUES Fear nothing.
                        *He gives her a poisoned cup: she drinks*
SORANZO Hippolita, I thank you, and will pledge
This happy union as another life;
Wine, there!
VASQUES You shall have none, neither shall you pledge
her.
HIPPOLITA How!
VASQUES Know now, Mistress She-Devil, your own
mischievous treachery hath killed you; I must not
marry you.                                            70
HIPPOLITA Villain.
OMNES What's the matter?
VASQUES Foolish woman, thou art now like a firebrand
that hath kindled others and burnt thyself; *troppo
sperar, inganna*, thy vain hope hath deceived thee,
thou art but dead; if thou hast any grace, pray.
HIPPOLITA Monster.                                     77
VASQUES Die in charity, for shame. This thing of
malice, this woman, had privately corrupted me with
promise of marriage, under this politic reconciliation,
to poison my lord, whiles she might laugh at his
confusion on his marriage day. I promised her fair,
but I knew what my reward should have been, and
would willingly have spared her life, but that I was
acquainted with the danger of her disposition, and
now have fitted her a just payment in her own coin.
There she is, she hath yet—and end thy days in

---

54  allowed: approved
55  engaged: placed under obligation
56  single charity: sincere love
74–5  *troppo sperar, inganna*: too much hope deceives. Q has
      *niganna* but this is a compositor's error
78  charity: Christian love, ironically recalling Hippolita's
      remark at l. 56
80  this politic reconciliation: this clever arrangement
87  yet—and: there is a gap in the line here possibly owing to
      the illegibility of the manuscript from which the
      compositor worked. Morris suggests a phrase such as 'a
      moment to live. Pray then'

peace, vile woman; as for life there's no hope, think
not on't.                                              89
OMNES Wonderful justice!
RICHARDETTO                      Heaven, thou art righteous.
HIPPOLITA O, 'tis true,
I feel my minute coming. Had that slave
Kept promise (O, my torment) thou this hour
Had'st died, Soranzo—heat above hell fire—
Yet ere I pass away—cruel, cruel flames -
Take here my curse amongst you: may thy bed
Of marriage be a rack unto thy heart,
Burn blood and boil in vengeance—O, my heart,
My flame's intolerable—May'st thou live
To father bastards, may her womb bring forth    100
Monsters, and die together in your sins,
Hated, scorned, and unpitied—O!—O!—        *Dies*
FLORIO Was e'er so vile a creature?
RICHARDETTO                          Here's the end
Of lust and pride.
ANNABELLA            It is a fearful sight.
SORANZO Vasques, I know thee now a trusty servant,
And never will forget thee.—Come, my love,
We'll home, and thank the Heavens for this escape.
Father and friends, we must break up this mirth;
It is too sad a feast.
DONADO                  Bear hence the body.
FRIAR Here's an ominous change;                    110
Mark this, my Giovanni, and take heed.
I fear the event; that marriage seldom's good,
Where the bride-banquet so begins in blood.
                                                *Exeunt*

# Act IV, scene ii

*Enter* RICHARDETTO *and* PHILOTIS

RICHARDETTO My wretched wife, more wretched in
her shame
Than in her wrongs to me, hath paid too soon
The forfeit of her modesty and life;
And I am sure, my niece, though vengeance hover,
Keeping aloof yet from Soranzo's fall,
Yet he will fall, and sink with his own weight.
I need not now—my heart persuades me so—
To further his confusion; there is One
Above begins to work, for, as I hear,
Debates already 'twixt his wife and him          10
Thicken and run to head; she, as 'tis said,
Slightens his love, and he abandons hers.

---

92   my minute: my death
112  event: outcome
10   Debates: arguments
11   Thicken and run to head: come to a head ready to burst,
     like a boil
12   Slightens: disdains

Much talk I hear. Since things go thus, my niece,
In tender love and pity of your youth,
My counsel is, that you should free your years
From hazard of these woes by flying hence
To fair Cremona, there to vow your soul
In holiness a holy votaress:
Leave me to see the end of these extremes.
All human worldly courses are uneven;          20
No life is blessed but the way to Heaven.
PHILOTIS  Uncle, shall I resolve to be a nun?
RICHARDETTO  Ay, gentle niece, and in your hourly
    prayers
Remember me, your poor unhappy uncle.
Hie to Cremona now, as fortune leads,
Your home your cloister, your best friends your
    beads.
Your chaste and single life shall crown your birth;
Who dies a virgin lives a saint on earth.
PHILOTIS  Then farewell, world, and worldly thoughts,
    adieu.
Welcome, chaste vows; myself I yield to you.     30
                                    *Exeunt*

# Act IV, scene iii

*Enter* SORANZO *unbraced, and* ANNABELLA *dragged in*

SORANZO  Come, strumpet, famous whore! Were every
    drop
Of blood that runs in thy adulterous veins
A life, this sword, dost see't, should in one blow
Confound them all. Harlot, rare, notable harlot,
That with thy brazen face maintain'st thy sin,
Was there no man in Parma to be bawd
To your loose cunning whoredom else but I?
Must your hot itch and pleurisy of lust,
The heyday of your luxury, be fed
Up to a surfeit, and could none but I            10
Be picked out to be cloak to your close tricks,
Your belly-sports? Now I must be the dad
To all that gallimaufry that's stuffed
In thy corrupted bastard-bearing womb,
Say, must I?
ANNABELLA  Beastly man! Why, 'tis thy fate.

---

17 Cremona: a city known for its cathedral. Parma and
   Cremona are traditionally 'rival' cities
18 votaress: a nun
26 beads: a rosary
SD *unbraced*: with part of his clothing undone
 1 famous: notorious
 4 Confound: destroy
 5 maintains't: persist in or defend
 8 pleurisy: excess
 9 heyday of your luxury: height of your lust
11 close: secret
13 gallimaufry: mixture

I sued not to thee; for, but that I thought
Your over-loving lordship would have run
Mad on denial, had ye lent me time,
I would have told 'ee in what case I was.
But you would needs be doing.
SORANZO                  Whore of whores!     20
Dar'st thou tell me this?
ANNABELLA                  O yes, why not?
You were deceived in me; 'twas not for love
I chose you, but for honour; yet know this,
Would you be patient yet, and hide your shame,
I'd see whether I could love you.
SORANZO                  Excellent quean!
Why, art thou not with child?
ANNABELLA                  What needs all this
When 'tis superfluous? I confess I am.
SORANZO  Tell me by whom.
ANNABELLA          Soft, sir, 'twas not in my bargain.
Yet somewhat, sir, to stay your longing stomach,
I am content t'acquaint you with; the man,        30
The more than man, that got this sprightly boy.
For 'tis a boy, and that for glory, sir,
Your heir shall be a son.
SORANZO                  Damnable monster!
ANNABELLA  Nay, and you will not hear. I'll speak no
    more.
SORANZO  Yes, speak, and speak thy last.
ANNABELLA                  A match, a match!
This noble creature was in every part
So angel-like, so glorious, that a woman
Who had not been but human, as was I,
Would have kneeled to him, and have begged for
    love.
You! Why, you are not worthy once to name       40
His name without true worship, or, indeed,
Unless you kneeled, to hear another name him.
SORANZO  What was he called?
ANNABELLA                  We are not come to that.
Let it suffice that you shall have the glory
To father what so brave a father got.
In brief, had not this chance fallen out as't doth,
I never had been troubled with a thought
That you had been a creature; but for marriage,
I scarce dream yet of that.
SORANZO  Tell me his name.
ANNABELLA                  Alas, alas, there's all.   50

---

20 doing: sexually active
25 quean: prostitute
29 stay: satisfy
32 and that for glory: Q has 'that for' and some editors
   prefer 'for your glory' as a substitute for what is clearly an
   inadequate line
35 A match, a match!: agreed, a bargain!
45 brave: splendid
48 had been a creature: had existed

Will you believe?

SORANZO                What?

ANNABELLA                        You shall never know.

SORANZO  How!

ANNABELLA         Never; if you do, let me be cursed.

SORANZO  Not know it, strumpet? I'll rip up thy heart,
  And find it there.

ANNABELLA            Do, do.

SORANZO                        And with my teeth
  Tear the prodigious lecher joint by joint.

ANNABELLA  Ha, ha, ha, the man's merry!

SORANZO                        Dost thou laugh?
  Come, whore, tell me your lover, or, by truth,
  I'll hew thy flesh to shreds; who is't?

ANNABELLA  (sings)
  *Che morte più dolce che morire per amore?*

SORANZO  Thus will I pull thy hair, and thus I'll drag **60**
  Thy lust-belepered body through the dust.
  Yet tell his name.

ANNABELLA  (sings)
  *Morendo in gratia Dei, morirei senza dolore.*

SORANZO  Dost thou triumph? The treasure of the earth
  Shall not redeem thee; were there kneeling kings
  Did beg thy life, or angels did come down
  To plead in tears, yet should not all prevail
  Against my rage. Dost thou not tremble yet?

ANNABELLA  At what? To die? No, be a gallant
    hangman.
  I dare thee to the worst: strike, and strike home; **70**
  I leave revenge behind, and thou shalt feel't.

SORANZO  Yet tell me ere thou diest, and tell me truly,
  Knows thy old father this?

ANNABELLA                        No, by my life.

SORANZO  Wilt thou confess, and I will spare thy life?

ANNABELLA  My life? I will not buy my life so dear.

SORANZO  I will not slack my vengeance.

*Enter* VASQUES

VASQUES  What d'ee mean, sir?

SORANZO  Forbear, Vasques; such a damned whore
  Deserves no pity.                        **79**

VASQUES  Now the gods forfend! And would you be her
  executioner, and kill her in your rage too? O, 'twere

---

55  prodigious: monstrous
59  *Che morte . . . per amore?*: what death is sweeter than to
    die for love?
63  *Morendo in . . . senza dolore*: dying in the grace of God, I
    should die without sorrow. Although apparently
    quotations, no editor has indentified Annabella's Italian
    lines which have been amended in the light of Q's
    numerous errors. The lines sound like proverbs
69  hangman: a generic term for an executioner
74  confess: admit your lover's name
76  slack: reduce
80  forfend: forbid

---

most unmanlike. She is your wife: what faults hath
been done by her before she married you, were not
against you; alas, poor lady, what hath she committed
which any lady in Italy in the like case would not?
Sir, you must be ruled by your reason and not by your
fury; that were unhuman and beastly.

SORANZO  She shall not live.                        **88**

VASQUES  Come, she must. You would have her confess
  the author of her present misfortunes, I warrant 'ee;
  'tis an unconscionable demand, and she should lose
  the estimation that I, for my part, hold of her worth,
  if she had done it. Why, sir, you ought not of all men
  living to know it. Good sir, be reconciled; alas, good
  gentlewoman.

ANNABELLA  Pish, do not beg for me; I prize my life
  As nothing; if the man will needs be mad
  Why, let him take it.

SORANZO                        Vasques, hear'st thou this?  **98**

VASQUES  Yes, and commend her for it; in this she
  shows the nobleness of a gallant spirit, and beshrew
  my heart, but it becomes her rarely. (*Aside*) Sir, in any
  case smother your revenge; leave the scenting-out
  your wrongs to me; be ruled, as you respect your
  honour, or you mar all. (*Aloud*) Sir, if ever my service
  were of any credit with you, be not so violent in your
  distractions. You are married now; what a triumph
  might the report of this give to other neglected
  suitors. 'Tis as manlike to bear extremities as godlike
  to forgive.                        **109**

SORANZO  O Vasques, Vasques, in this piece of flesh,
  This faithless face of hers, had I laid up
  The treasure of my heart. Hadst thou been virtuous,
  Fair, wicked woman, not the matchless joys
  Of life itself had made me wish to live
  With any saint but thee; deceitful creature
  How hast thou mocked my hopes, and in the shame
  Of thy lewd womb even buried me alive.
  I did too dearly love thee.

VASQUES  (*Aside*) This is well; follow this temper with
  some passion. Be brief and moving; 'tis for the
  purpose.                        **121**

SORANZO  Be witness to my words thy soul and
    thoughts,
  And tell me, didst not think that in my heart
  I did too superstitiously adore thee?

ANNABELLA  I must confess I know you loved me well.

SORANZO  And wouldst thou use me thus? O,
    Annabella

---

90   author: Q has 'authors'
100  beshrew: curse
101–2  in any case: by any means
105  credit: esteem
108  extremities: hardships
119  temper: attitude
124  superstitiously: idolatrously

Be thou assured, whatsoe'er the villain was
That thus hath tempted thee to this disgrace,
Well he might lust, but never loved like me.
He doted on the picture that hung out    **130**
Upon thy cheeks, to please his humorous eye;
Not on the part I loved, which was thy heart,
And, as I thought, thy virtues.
ANNABELLA                  O my lord!
These words wound deeper than your sword could
   do.
VASQUES  Let me not ever take comfort, but I begin to
weep myself, so much I pity him; why, madam, I
knew when his rage was over-past, what it would
come to.
SORANZO  Forgive me, Annabella. Though thy youth
Hath tempted thee above thy strength to folly,   **140**
Yet will not I forget what I should be,
And what I am, a husband; in that name
Is hid divinity; if I do find
That thou wilt yet be true, here I remit
All former faults, and take thee to my bosom.
VASQUES  By my troth, and that's a point of noble charity.
ANNABELLA  Sir, on my knees—
SORANZO               Rise up, you shall not kneel.
Get you to your chamber, see you make no show
Of alteration; I'll be with you straight.
My reason tells me now that 'tis as common    **150**
To err in frailty as to be a woman.
Go to your chamber.          *Exit* ANNABELLA
VASQUES  So, this was somewhat to the matter; what do
you think of your heaven of happiness now, sir?
SORANZO  I carry hell about me; all my blood
Is fired in swift revenge.
VASQUES  That may be, but know you how, or on
whom? Alas, to marry a great woman, being made
great in the stock to your hand, is a usual sport in
these days; but to know what ferret it was that
haunted your cony-berry, there's the cunning.   **161**
SORANZO  I'll make her tell herself, or—
VASQUES  Or what? You must not do so. Let me yet
persuade your sufferance a little while; go to her, use
her mildly, win her if it be possible to a voluntary, to

---

131  humorous: capricious
151  in frailty: through human weakness
158  great woman: pregnant, but also a reference to
     Annabella's social rank
159  stock: body, but also referring to family
     to your hand: ready for you
160  ferret: Q reads 'secret' but the line is usually amended to
     fit with Vasques' metaphor
161  haunted your cony-berry: resided in your rabbit burrow,
     an obscene image for the female genitalia
     cunning: the hunter's skill
165  voluntary: refers to an improvised piece of music as well
     as a spontaneous confession

a weeping tune; for the rest, if all hit, I will not miss
my mark. Pray, sir, go in; the next news I tell you
shall be wonders.
SORANZO  Delay in vengeance gives a heavier blow.  **169**
                                                  *Exit*
VASQUES  Ah, sirrah, here's work for the nonce. I had a
suspicion of a bad matter in my head a pretty whiles
ago; but after my madam's scurvy looks here at home,
her waspish perverseness and loud fault-finding, then
I remembered the proverb, that where hens crow and
cocks hold their peace there are sorry houses. 'Sfoot,
if the lower parts of a she-tailor's cunning can cover
such a swelling in the stomach, I'll never blame a
false stitch in a shoe whiles I live again. Up and up so
quick? And so quickly too? 'Twere a fine policy to
learn by whom; this must be known; and I have
thought on't—(*Enter* PUTANA) Here's the way, or
none—what, crying, old mistress! Alas, alas, I cannot
blame 'ee, we have a lord, Heaven help us, is so mad
as the devil himself, the more shame for him.   **184**
PUTANA  O Vasques, that ever I was born to see this
day. Doth he use thee so too, sometimes, Vasques?
VASQUES  Me? Why, he makes a dog of me. But if some
were of my mind, I know what we would do; as sure
as I am an honest man, he will go near to kill my lady
with unkindness. Say she be with child, is that such a
matter for a young woman of her years to be blamed
for?                                                          **192**
PUTANA  Alas, good heart, it is against her will full
sore.
VASQUES  I durst be sworn, all his madness is for that
she will not confess whose 'tis, which he will know,
and when he doth know it, I am so well acquainted
with his humour, that he will forget all straight.
Well, I could wish she would in plain terms tell all,
for that's the way indeed.                   **200**
PUTANA  Do you think so?
VASQUES  Foh, I know't; provided that he did not win
her to't by force. He was once in a mind that you
could tell, and meant to have wrung it out of you, but
I somewhat pacified him for that; yet sure you know
a great deal.
PUTANA  Heaven forgive us all! I know a little, Vasques.
VASQUES  Why should you not? Who else should?
Upon my conscience, she loves you dearly, and you
would not betray her to any affliction for the world.
PUTANA  Not for all the world, by my faith and troth,
Vasques.                                                   **212**

---

166  all hit: goes well, as in archery
170  nonce: the present
174–5  where hens . . . sorry houses: a contemporary
       proverb
175–8  'Sfoot . . . whiles I live again: an indecent pun
198  humour: obsession

VASQUES 'Twere pity of your life if you should; but in this you should both receive her present discomforts, pacify my lord, and gain yourself everlasting love and preferment.

PUTANA Dost think so, Vasques?

VASQUES Nay, I know't; sure 'twas some near and entire friend.

PUTANA 'Twas a dear friend indeed; but— 220

VASQUES But what? Fear not to name him; my life between you and danger. Faith, I think 'twas no base fellow.

PUTANA Thou wilt stand between me and harm?

VASQUES 'Ud's pity, what else? You shall be rewarded too, trust me.

PUTANA 'Twas even no worse than her own brother.

VASQUES Her brother Giovanni, I warrant 'ee!

PUTANA Even he, Vasques; as brave a gentleman as ever kissed fair lady. O, they love most perpetually. 230

VASQUES A brave gentleman indeed; why, therein I commend her choice.—Better and better!—You are sure 'twas he?

PUTANA Sure; and you shall see he will not be long from her too.

VASQUES He were to blame if he would: but may I believe thee?

PUTANA Believe me! Why, dost think I am a Turk or a Jew? No, Vasques, I have known their dealings too long to belie them now. 240

VASQUES Where are you? There within, sirs.

*Enter* BANDITTI

PUTANA How now, what are these?

VASQUES You shall know presently. Come, sirs, take me this old damnable hag, gag her instantly, and put out her eyes. Quickly, quickly!

PUTANA Vasques, Vasques! 246

VASQUES Gag her, I say. 'Sfoot, d'ee suffer her to prate? What d'ee fumble about? Let me come to her; I'll help your old gums, you toad-bellied bitch. Sirs, carry her closely into the coalhouse, and put out her eyes instantly; if she roars, slit her nose: d'ee hear, be speedy and sure. Why, this is excellent and above expectation. (*Exeunt* BANDITTI *with* PUTANA) Her own brother! O horrible! To what a height of liberty in damnation hath the devil trained our age. Her brother! Well, there's yet but a beginning: I must to my lord, and tutor him better in his points of vengeance; now I see how a smooth tale goes beyond

a smooth tail. But soft—What thing comes next? (*Enter* GIOVANNI) Giovanni! As I would wish; my belief is strengthened, 'tis as firm as winter and summer. 262

GIOVANNI Where's my sister?

VASQUES Troubled with a new sickness, my lord; she's somewhat ill.

GIOVANNI Took too much of the flesh, I believe.

VASQUES Troth, sir, and you, I think, have e'en hit it. But my virtuous lady—

GIOVANNI Where's she? 269

VASQUES In her chamber; please you visit her; she is alone. (GIOVANNI *gives him money*) Your liberality hath doubly made me your servant, and ever shall, ever. (*Exit* GIOVANNI. *Enter* SORANZO) Sir, I am made a man, I have plied my cue with cunning and success; I beseech you let's be private.

SORANZO My lady's brother's come; now he'll know all.

VASQUES Let him know't; I have made some of them fast enough.

How have you dealt with my lady? 279

SORANZO Gently, as thou hast counselled. O, my soul Runs circular in sorrow for revenge.
But, Vasques, thou shalt know—

VASQUES Nay, I will know no more, for now comes your turn to know; I would not talk so openly with you. Let my young master take time enough, and go at pleasure; he is sold to death, and the devil shall not ransom him. Sir, I beseech you, your privacy.

SORANZO No conquest can gain glory of my fear.
*Exeunt*

# Act V, scene i

*Enter* ANNABELLA *above*

ANNABELLA Pleasures, farewell, and all ye thriftless minutes
Wherein false joys have spun a weary life.
To these my fortunes now I take my leave.
Thou, precious Time, that swiftly rid'st in post
Over the world, to finish up the race
Of my last fate, here stay thy restless course,
And bear to ages that are yet unborn
A wretched, woeful woman's tragedy.
My conscience now stands up against my lust

---

220 dear friend: a friend, but also 'expensive'
243 presently: see I.iii.16n
251 slit her nose: a common punishment for sexual transgression
254 liberty: licence
255 trained: lured

259 smooth: deceitful
266 Took too . . . the flesh: a) overeating; b) sexual indulgence
271 liberality: a) generosity; b) sexual licence
273–4 made a man: a made man
274 plied my cue: played my part
SD *Exeunt*: Q has *Exit*
1 thriftless: without profit
4 rid'st in post: at great speed, as with post horses
9 against: as witness against

With depositions charactered in guilt,                    10

*Enter* FRIAR *below*

And tells me I am lost: now I confess
Beauty that clothes the outside of the face
Is cursed if it be not clothed with grace.
Here like a turtle (mewed up in a cage)
Unmated, I converse with air and walls,
And descant on my vile unhappiness.
O Giovanni, that hast had the spoil
Of thine own virtues and my modest fame,
Would thou had'st been less subject to those stars
That luckless reigned at my nativity:                     20
O would the scourge due to my black offence
Might pass from thee, that I alone might feel
The torment of an uncontrollèd flame.

FRIAR (*Aside*) What's this I hear?

ANNABELLA                    That man, that blessed friar,
Who joined in ceremonial knot my hand
To him whose wife I now am, told me oft
I trod the path to death, and showed me how.
But they who sleep in lethargies of lust
Hug their confusion, making Heaven unjust,
And so did I.

FRIAR (*Aside*)  Here's music to the soul.                30

ANNABELLA Forgive me, my good genius, and this once
Be helpful to my ends. Let some good man
Pass this way, to whose trust I may commit
This paper double-lined with tears and blood:
Which being granted, here I sadly vow
Repentance, and a leaving of that life
I long have died in.

FRIAR                    Lady, Heaven hath heard you,
And hath by providence ordained that I
Should be his minister for your behoof.

ANNABELLA Ha, what are you?

FRIAR                    Your brother's friend, the friar;
Glad in my soul that I have lived to hear                  41
This free confession 'twixt your peace and you.
What would you, or to whom? Fear not to speak.

ANNABELLA Is Heaven so bountiful? Then I have found
More favour than I hoped. Here, holy man—

                                        *Throws a letter*

---

10  depositions charactered in guilt: a pun involving the idea
    of a legal document (lettered in gold) and Annabella's
    guilt
14  turtle: turtle-dove
    mewed up: imprisoned
15  Unmated: without its mate
16  descant: sing
17  spoil: booty, but also despoliation
31  good genius: see II.ii.160n
35  sadly: seriously
37  died: in the sense of the spirit
39  behoof: advantage

Commend me to my brother; give him that,
That letter; bid him read it and repent.
Tell him that I (imprisoned in my chamber,
Barred of all company, even of my guardian,
Who gives me cause of much suspect) have time   50
To blush at what hath passed; bid him be wise,
And not believe the friendship of my lord.
I fear much more than I can speak: good father,
The place is dangerous, and spies are busy;
I must break off—you'll do't?

FRIAR                    Be sure I will;
And fly with speed—my blessing ever rest
With thee, my daughter; live, to die more blessed.

                                        *Exit* FRIAR

ANNABELLA Thanks to the Heavens, who have
    prolonged my breath
To this good use: now I can welcome death.

                                        *Exit*

# Act V, scene ii

*Enter* SORANZO *and* VASQUES

VASQUES Am I to be believed now? First marry a
    strumpet that cast herself away upon you but to laugh
    at your horns, to feast on your disgrace, riot in your
    vexations, cuckold you in your bride-bed, waste your
    estate upon panders and bawds!

SORANZO No more, I say, no more.

VASQUES A cuckold is a goodly tame beast, my lord.

SORANZO I am resolved; urge not another word.
    My thoughts are great, and all as resolute
    As thunder; in mean time I'll cause our lady   10
    To deck herself in all her bridal robes,
    Kiss her, and fold her gently in my arms.
    Begone—yet hear you, are the banditti ready
    To wait in ambush?

VASQUES Good sir, trouble not yourself about other
    business than your own resolution; remember that
    time lost cannot be recalled.

SORANZO With all the cunning words thou canst, invite
    The states of Parma to my birthday's feast;
    Haste to my brother-rival and his father,   20
    Entreat them gently, bid them not to fail.
    Be speedy, and return.

VASQUES Let not your pity betray you till my coming
    back; think upon incest and cuckoldry.

SORANZO Revenge is all the ambition I aspire:
    To that I'll climb or fall; my blood's on fire.

                                        *Exeunt*

---

50  suspect: suspicion
3  horns: the traditional sign of the deceived husband
   riot: revel
19  states: nobles

# Act V, scene iii

*Enter* GIOVANNI

GIOVANNI Busy opinion is an idle fool,
  That, as a school-rod keeps a child in awe,
  Frights the unexperienced temper of the mind:
  So did it me; who, ere my precious sister
  Was married, thought all taste of love would die
  In such a contract; but I find no change
  Of pleasure in this formal law of sports.
  She is still one to me, and every kiss
  As sweet and as delicious as the first
  I reaped, when yet the privilege of youth         10
  Entitled her a virgin. O the glory
  Of two united hearts like hers and mine!
  Let poring book-men dream of other worlds,
  My world, and all of happiness, is here,
  And I'd not change it for the best to come:
  A life of pleasure is Elysium.

*Enter* FRIAR

  Father, you enter on the jubilee
  Of my retired delights; now I can tell you,
  The hell you oft have prompted is nought else
  But slavish and fond superstitious fear;          20
  And I could prove it too—
FRIAR                      Thy blindness slays thee.
  Look there, 'tis writ to thee.         *Gives the letter*
GIOVANNI  From whom?
FRIAR  Unrip the seals and see;
  The blood's yet seething hot, that will anon
  Be frozen harder than congealèd coral.
  Why d'ee change colour, son?
GIOVANNI                      'Fore Heaven, you make
  Some petty devil factor 'twixt my love
  And your religion-masked sorceries.
  Where had you this?
FRIAR              Thy conscience, youth, is seared,  30
  Else thou wouldst stoop to warning.
GIOVANNI                          'Tis her hand,
  I know't; and 'tis all written in her blood.
  She writes I know not what. Death? I'll not fear

An armèd thunderbolt aimed at my heart.
She writes we are discovered—pox on dreams
Of low faint-hearted cowardice! Discovered?
The devil we are; which way is't possible?
Are we grown traitors to our own delights?
Confusion take such dotage, 'tis but forged;
This is your peevish chattering, weak old man.      40

*Enter* VASQUES

  Now, sir, what news bring you?
VASQUES  My lord, according to his yearly custom
  keeping this day a feast in honour of his birthday, by
  me invites you thither. Your worthy father, with the
  Pope's reverend nuncio, and other magnificoes of
  Parma, have promised their presence; will't please
  you to be of the number?
GIOVANNI  Yes, tell him I dare come.
VASQUES  'Dare come'?
GIOVANNI  So I said; and tell him more, I will come.   50
VASQUES  These words are strange to me.
GIOVANNI  Say I will come.
VASQUES  You will not miss?
GIOVANNI  Yet more? I'll come! Sir, are you answered?
VASQUES  So I'll say.— My service to you.
                                    *Exit* VASQUES
FRIAR  You will not go, I trust.
GIOVANNI                    Not go? For what?
FRIAR  O, do not go. This feast, I'll gage my life,
  Is but a plot to train you to your ruin.
  Be ruled, you sha' not go.
GIOVANNI              Not go? Stood Death
  Threatening his armies of confounding plagues,     60
  With hosts of dangers hot as blazing stars,
  I would be there. Not go? Yes, and resolve
  To strike as deep in slaughter as they all.
  For I will go.
FRIAR        Go where thou wilt; I see
  The wildness of thy fate draws to an end,
  To a bad fearful end. I must not stay
  To know thy fall; back to Bononia I
  With speed will haste, and shun this coming blow.
  Parma, farewell; would I had never known thee,
  Or aught of thine. Well, young man, since no prayer
  Can make thee safe, I leave thee to despair.        71
                                    *Exit* FRIAR

---

  1  Busy opinion: commonly held views
  7  formal law of sports: legal sanctions against sexual
     activity
  8  one: joined
 16  Elysium: the paradise of the classical world
 17  jubilee: a time of celebration
 18  retired: hidden
 19  prompted: put forward as part of an argument
 20  fond: foolish
 28  factor: a legal agent or intermediary
 30  seared: dried up
 31  stoop: give in, yield

---

 34  armèd: ready for release
 SD  Vasques's entrance is after l. 41 in Q
 45  nuncio: see II.iii.31n
     magnificoes: see I.ii.129n
 53  miss: fail
 57  gage: wager, bet, pledge
 58  train: lure
 60  confounding: destroying
 61  blazing stars: comets taken as signs of disaster and
     apocalypse

GIOVANNI Despair, or tortures of a thousand hells,
　All's one to me; I have set up my rest.
　Now, now, work serious thoughts on baneful plots,
　Be all a man, my soul; let not the curse
　Of old prescription rend from me the gall
　Of courage, which enrols a glorious death.
　If I must totter like a well-grown oak,
　Some under-shrubs shall in my weighty fall
　Be crushed to splits: with me they all shall perish. **80**
　　　　　　　　　　　　　　　　　　　　*Exit*

# Act V, scene iv

*Enter* SORANZO, VASQUES, *and* BANDITTI

SORANZO You will not fail, or shrink in the attempt?
VASQUES I will undertake for their parts. Be sure, my
　masters, to be bloody enough, and as unmerciful as if
　you were preying upon a rich booty on the very
　mountains of Liguria; for your pardons, trust to my
　lord, but for reward you shall trust none but your
　own pockets.
BANDITTI OMNES We'll make a murder.
SORANZO Here's gold, here's more; want nothing; what
　you do
　Is noble, and an act of brave revenge. **10**
　I'll make ye rich banditti, and all free.
OMNES Liberty, liberty!
VASQUES Hold, take every man a vizard; when ye are
　withdrawn, keep as much silence as you can possibly.
　You know the watchword; till which be spoken, move
　not, but when you hear that, rush in like a stormy
　flood; I need not instruct ye in your own profession.
OMNES No, no, no.
VASQUES In, then; your ends are profit and
　preferment.—Away! **20**
　　　　　　　　　　　　　　　*Exeunt* BANDITTI

---

73　set up my rest: a metaphor deriving from Primero, a
　　contemporary card-game. Players who 'set their rest' have
　　decided to play their hand. Here Giovanni means that he
　　plans to risk all on the decisions he has made
75–6　the curse . . . prescription: the biblical curse on incest:
　　'And if a man shall take his sister, his father's daughter,
　　or his mother's daughter, and see her nakedness, and she
　　see his nakedness; it is a wicked thing; and they shall be
　　cut off in the sight of their people; he hath uncovered his
　　sister's nakedness; he shall bear his iniquity' (Leviticus
　　20.17); 'Cursed be he that lieth with his sister, the
　　daughter of his father, or the daughter of his mother and
　　all the people shall say, Amen' (Deuteronomy 27.22)
80　splits: splinters
2　undertake: give an assurance
5　Liguria: the mountain region between Parma and the
　　west coast of Italy
11　free: from the threat of the law
13　vizard: mask

SORANZO The guests will all come, Vasques?
VASQUES Yes, sir. And now let me a little edge your
　resolution. You see nothing is unready to this great
　work, but a great mind in you: call to your
　remembrance your disgraces, your loss of honour,
　Hippolita's blood, and arm your courage in your own
　wrongs; so shall you best right those wrongs in
　vengeance, which you may truly call your own.
SORANZO 'Tis well; the less I speak, the more I burn,
　And blood shall quench that flame. **30**
VASQUES Now you begin to turn Italian. This beside—
　when my young incest-monger comes, he will be
　sharp set on his old bit: give him time enough, let
　him have your chamber and bed at liberty; let my hot
　hare have law ere he be hunted to his death, that if it
　be possible, he may post to hell in the very act of his
　damnation.

*Enter* GIOVANNI

SORANZO It shall be so; and see, as we would wish,
　He comes himself first. Welcome, my much-loved
　　brother,
　Now I perceive you honour me; y'are welcome. **40**
　But where's my father?
GIOVANNI　　　　　　　With the other states,
　Attending on the nuncio of the Pope,
　To wait upon him hither. How's my sister?
SORANZO Like a good housewife, scarcely ready yet;
　Y'are best walk to her chamber.
GIOVANNI　　　　　　　　　　If you will.
SORANZO I must expect my honourable friends;
　Good brother, get her forth.
GIOVANNI　　　　　　　You are busy, sir. *Exit* GIOVANNI
VASQUES Even as the great devil himself would have it;
　let him go and glut himself in his own destruction.

*Flourish. Enter* CARDINAL, FLORIO, DONADO,
RICHARDETTO, *and* ATTENDANTS

SORANZO Most reverend lord, this grace hath made me
　proud, **50**
　That you vouchsafe my house; I ever rest
　Your humble servant for this noble favour.

---

22　edge: sharpen
31　turn Italian: in the understanding of a seventeenth-
　　century English audience, to become Italian was to
　　become expert in the art of revenge; see Introduction
33　sharp set on his old bit: hungry for his old food, in the
　　sense of sexual appetite
34–5　hot hare: hares were seen as excessively lustful creatures
　　law: the advantage or 'start' given to a hare before the
　　chase begins
36–7　he may . . . his damnation: refers to the notion that if
　　Giovanni dies in the very act of sinning his soul will go
　　straight to hell
51　vouchsafe: deign to visit

CARDINAL You are our friend, my lord; his holiness
Shall understand how zealously you honour
Saint Peter's vicar in his substitute:
Our special love to you.

SORANZO                    Signors, to you
My welcome, and my ever best of thanks
For this so memorable courtesy.
Pleaseth your grace to walk near?

CARDINAL                         My lord, we come
To celebrate your feast with civil mirth,          60
As ancient custom teacheth: we will go.

SORANZO Attend his grace there!—Signors, keep your
way.

                                        *Exeunt*

# Act V, scene v

*Enter* GIOVANNI *and* ANNABELLA *lying on a bed*

GIOVANNI What, changed so soon? Hath your new
    sprightly lord
Found out a trick in night-games more than we
Could know in our simplicity? Ha! Is't so?
Or does the fit come on you, to prove treacherous
To your past vows and oaths?

ANNABELLA                         Why should you jest
At my calamity, without all sense
Of the approaching dangers you are in?

GIOVANNI What danger's half so great as thy revolt?
Thou art a faithless sister, else thou know'st
Malice, or any treachery beside,                    10
Would stoop to my bent brows; why, I hold fate
Clasped in my fist, and could command the course
Of time's eternal motion, hadst thou been
One thought more steady than an ebbing sea.
And what? You'll now be honest, that's resolved?

ANNABELLA Brother, dear brother, know what I have
    been,
And know that now there's but a dining-time
'Twixt us and our confusion: let's not waste
These precious hours in vain and useless speech.

---

55 Saint Peter's vicar: the pope
62 keep: continue on
SD *lying on a bed*: the bed may have been revealed to the
    audience by drawing back a curtain to show it on the
    inner stage, or it may have been pushed on to the main
    playing area
4 fit: caprice
11 stoop: yield
11–12 I hold . . . my fist: a comparison is often made between
    this phrase and that of the protagonist in Christopher
    Marlowe's *Tamburlaine*, Part I.369–70:
        I hold the Fates bound fast in iron chains,
        And with my hand turn Fortune's wheel about . . .
17 dining-time: the period of the midday meal, corrected
    from 'dying' in Q

Alas, these gay attires were not put on              20
But to some end; this sudden solemn feast
Was not ordained to riot in expense;
I, that have now been chambered here alone,
Barred of my guardian, or of any else,
Am not for nothing at an instant freed
To fresh access. Be not deceived, my brother,
This banquet is an harbinger of death
To you and me; resolve yourself it is,
And be prepared to welcome it.

GIOVANNI                         Well, then;
The schoolmen teach that all this globe of earth    30
Shall be consumed to ashes in a minute.

ANNABELLA So I have read too.

GIOVANNI                    But 'twere somewhat strange
To see the waters burn; could I believe
This might be true, I could believe as well
There might be hell or Heaven.

ANNABELLA                         That's most certain.

GIOVANNI A dream, a dream! Else in this other world
We should know one another.

ANNABELLA                    So we shall.

GIOVANNI Have you heard so?

ANNABELLA                    For certain.

GIOVANNI                         But d'ee think
That I shall see you there?—You look on me?
May we kiss one another, prate or laugh,            40
Or do as we do here?

ANNABELLA                    I know not that.
But good, for the present, what d'ee mean
To free yourself from danger? Some way think
How to escape; I'm sure the guests are come.

GIOVANNI Look up, look here; what see you in my
    face?

ANNABELLA Distraction and a troubled countenance.

GIOVANNI Death, and a swift repining wrath—yet look,
What see you in mine eyes?

ANNABELLA                    Methinks you weep.

GIOVANNI I do indeed; these are the funeral tears
Shed on your grave; these furrowed up my cheeks    50
When first I loved and knew not how to woo.
Fair Annabella, should I here repeat
The story of my life, we might lose time.
Be record all the spirits of the air
And all things else that are, that day and night,
Early and late, the tribute which my heart
Hath paid to Annabella's sacred love
Hath been these tears, which are her mourners now.
Never till now did Nature do her best

---

30 schoolmen: medieval theologians
40 prate: casual talk or gossip
42 good: good brother
47 repining: discontented
51 woo: corrected from Q which reads 'woe'

To show a matchless beauty to the world,     60
Which in an instant, ere it scarce was seen,
The jealous Destinies required again.
Pray, Annabella, pray; since we must part,
Go thou, white in thy soul, to fill a throne
Of innocence and sanctity in Heaven.
Pray, pray, my sister.
ANNABELLA          Then I see your drift.
   Ye blessed angels, guard me.
GIOVANNI             So say I.
   Kiss me. If ever after-times should hear
Of our fast-knit affections, though perhaps
The laws of conscience and of civil use     70
May justly blame us, yet when they but know
Our loves, that love will wipe away that rigour
Which would in other incests be abhorred.
Give me your hand; how sweetly life doth run
In these well-coloured veins. How constantly
These palms do promise health. But I could chide
With Nature for this cunning flattery.
Kiss me again—forgive me.
ANNABELLA           With my heart.
GIOVANNI   Farewell.
ANNABELLA       Will you be gone?
GIOVANNI           Be dark, bright sun,
   And make this midday night, that thy gilt rays    80
May not behold a deed will turn their splendour
More sooty than the poets feign their Styx.
One other kiss, my sister.
ANNABELLA         What means this?
GIOVANNI   To save thy fame, and kill thee in a kiss.
*Stabs her*
   Thus die, and die by me, and by my hand.
Revenge is mine; honour doth love command.
ANNABELLA   O brother, by your hand?
GIOVANNI          When thou art dead
   I'll give my reasons for't; for to dispute
With thy (even in thy death) most lovely beauty,
Would make me stagger to perform this act,    90
Which I most glory in.
ANNABELLA   Forgive him, Heaven, and me my sins;
     farewell.
Brother unkind, unkind!—Mercy, great Heaven—
O!—O!                           *Dies*
GIOVANNI   She's dead, alas, good soul. The hapless fruit
That in her womb received its life from me
Hath had from me a cradle and a grave.
I must not dally. This sad marriage-bed,

---

70   civil use: civilised behaviour
72   rigour: violence
82   More sooty . . . their Styx: the classical underworld was
     reached across the black waters of the river Styx
84   fame: good name, reputation
93   unkind: cruel and unnatural
94   hapless: luckless

In all her best, bore her alive and dead.
Soranzo, thou hast missed thy aim in this;
I have prevented now thy reaching plots,     100
And killed a love, for whose each drop of blood
I would have pawned my heart. Fair Annabella,
How over-glorious art thou in thy wounds,
Triumphing over infamy and hate!
Shrink not, courageous hand, stand up, my heart,
And boldly act my last and greater part.
*Exit with the body*

## Act V, scene vi

*A Banquet. Enter* CARDINAL, FLORIO, DONADO,
SORANZO, RICHARDETTO, VASQUES, *and* ATTENDANTS;
*they take their places*

VASQUES   Remember, sir, what you have to do; be wise
   and resolute.
SORANZO   Enough; my heart is fixed.—Pleaseth your
   grace
To taste these coarse confections; though the use
Of such set entertainments more consists
In custom than in cause, yet, reverend sir,
I am still made your servant by your presence.
CARDINAL   And we your friend.
SORANZO   But where's my brother Giovanni?

*Enter* GIOVANNI *with a heart upon his dagger*

GIOVANNI   Here, here, Soranzo; trimmed in reeking
   blood,                                  10
That triumphs over death; proud in the spoil
Of love and vengeance! Fate or all the powers
That guide the motions of immortal souls
Could not prevent me.
CARDINAL   What means this?
FLORIO   Son Giovanni!
SORANZO   Shall I be forestalled?
GIOVANNI   Be not amazed; if your misgiving hearts
Shrink at an idle sight, what bloodless fear
Of coward passion would have seized your senses,    20
Had you beheld the rape of life and beauty
Which I have acted? My sister, O my sister.
FLORIO   Ha! What of her?
GIOVANNI          The glory of my deed
Darkened the midday sun, made noon as night.
You came to feast, my lords, with dainty fare;
I came to feast too, but I digged for food
In a much richer mine than gold or stone

---

100   prevented: forestalled
      reaching: cunning
4   coarse confections: modest dishes
10   trimmed: adorned
11   spoil: plunder
19   idle sight: a sight of little consequence

Of any value balanced; 'tis a heart,
A heart, my lords, in which is mine entombed:
Look well upon't; d'ee know't? 30

VASQUES What strange riddle's this?

GIOVANNI 'Tis Annabella's heart, 'tis; why d'ee startle?
I vow 'tis hers: this dagger's point ploughed up
Her fruitful womb, and left to me the fame
Of a most glorious executioner.

FLORIO Why, madman, art thyself?

GIOVANNI Yes, father; and that times to come may
know
How as my fate I honoured my revenge,
List, father, to your ears I will yield up
How much I have deserved to be your son. 40

FLORIO What is't thou say'st?

GIOVANNI Nine moons have had their changes
Since I first throughly viewed and truly loved
Your daughter and my sister.

FLORIO How!—Alas
My lords, he's a frantic madman!

GIOVANNI Father, no.
For nine months' space in secret I enjoyed
Sweet Annabella's sheets; nine months I lived
A happy monarch of her heart and her.
Soranzo, thou know'st this; thy paler cheek
Bears the confounding print of thy disgrace,
For her too fruitful womb too soon bewrayed 50
The happy passage of our stol'n delights,
And made her mother to a child unborn.

CARDINAL Incestuous villain!

FLORIO O, his rage belies him.

GIOVANNI It does not, 'tis the oracle of truth;
I vow it is so.

SORANZO I shall burst with fury.
Bring the strumpet forth.

VASQUES I shall, sir. *Exit* VASQUES

GIOVANNI Do, sir.—Have you all no faith
To credit yet my triumphs? Here I swear
By all that you call sacred, by the love
I bore my Annabella whilst she lived. 60
These hands have from her bosom ripped this heart.

*Enter* VASQUES

Is't true or no, sir?

VASQUES 'Tis most strangely true.

FLORIO Cursed man!—Have I lived to— *Dies*

CARDINAL Hold up, Florio.—
Monster of children, see what thou hast done,
Broke thy old father's heart. Is none of you

Dares venture on him?

GIOVANNI Let 'em.—O, my father,
How well his death becomes him in his griefs!
Why, this was done with courage; now survives
None of our house but I, gilt in the blood
Of a fair sister and a hapless father. 70

SORANZO Inhuman scorn of men, hast thou a thought
T'outlive thy murders?

GIOVANNI Yes, I tell thee, yes;
For in my fists I bear the twists of life.
Soranzo, see this heart, which was thy wife's;
Thus I exchange it royally for thine, *Stabs him*
And thus and thus. Now brave revenge is mine.

VASQUES I cannot hold any longer.—You, sir, are you
grown insolent in your butcheries? Have at you!
*They fight*

GIOVANNI Come, I am armed to meet thee.

VASQUES No, will it not be yet? If this will not, another
shall. Not yet? I shall fit you anon.—Vengeance! 81

*Enter* BANDITTI *and fight* GIOVANNI

GIOVANNI Welcome, come more of you whate'er you
be,
I dare your worst—
O, I can stand no longer! Feeble arms,
Have you so soon lost strength?

VASQUES Now you are welcome, sir!—Away, my
masters, all is done, shift for yourselves. Your reward
is your own; shift for yourselves.

BANDITTI Away, away! *Exeunt* BANDITTI

VASQUES How d'ee, my lord; see you this? How is't? 90

SORANZO Dead; but in death well pleased that I have
lived
To see my wrongs revenged on that black devil.
O Vasques, to thy bosom let me give
My last of breath; let not that lecher live—O! *Dies*

VASQUES The reward of peace and rest be with him, my
ever dearest lord and master.

GIOVANNI Whose hand gave me this wound?

VASQUES Mine, sir, I was your first man; have you
enough?

GIOVANNI I thank thee; thou hast done for me but
what 100
I would have else done on myself. Art sure
Thy lord is dead?

VASQUES O impudent slave! As sure as I am sure to see
thee die.

---

28 balanced: tested by weight
42 throughly: thoroughly
50 bewrayed: revealed
51 passage: course
53 rage belies him: his madness has made him lie

69 gilt: a) the adornment of the blood; b) guilty of the deed
73 twists of life: Giovanni refers to himself as one of the
Parcae, the Greek mythological figures who spun the
thread of each human life before cutting it to signal
death
81 fit you anon: deal with you shortly
Vengeance!: the signal previously agreed with the
Banditti

CARDINAL Think on thy life and end, and call for mercy.

GIOVANNI Mercy? Why, I have found it in this justice.

CARDINAL Strive yet to cry to Heaven.

GIOVANNI                              O, I bleed fast.
Death, thou art a guest long looked for; I embrace
Thee and thy wounds; O, my last minute comes.
Where'er I go, let me enjoy this grace,             110
Freely to view my Annabella's face.            *Dies*

DONADO Strange miracle of justice!

CARDINAL Raise up the city; we shall be murdered all.

VASQUES You need not fear, you shall not; this strange task being ended, I have paid the duty to the son which I have vowed to the father.

CARDINAL Speak, wretched villain, what incarnate fiend
Hath led thee on to this?                          118

VASQUES Honesty, and pity of my master's wrongs; for know, my lord, I am by birth a Spaniard, brought forth my country in my youth by Lord Soranzo's father, whom whilst he lived I served faithfully; since whose death I have been to this man as I was to him. What I have done was duty, and I repent nothing but that the loss of my life had not ransomed his.

CARDINAL Say, fellow, know'st thou any yet unnamed
Of counsel in this incest?

VASQUES Yes, an old woman, sometimes guardian to this murdered lady.

CARDINAL And what's become of her?                130

VASQUES Within this room she is; whose eyes, after her confession, I caused to be put out, but kept alive, to confirm what from Giovanni's own mouth you have heard. Now, my lord, what I have done you may judge of, and let your own wisdom be a judge in your own reason.

CARDINAL Peace!—First this woman, chief in these effects:
My sentence is, that forthwith she be ta'en
Out of the city, for example's sake,
There to be burnt to ashes.

DONADO                              'Tis most just.    140

CARDINAL Be it your charge, Donado, see it done.

DONADO I shall.

VASQUES What for me? If death, 'tis welcome; I have been honest to the son as I was to the father.

CARDINAL Fellow, for thee, since what thou didst was done
Not for thyself, being no Italian,
We banish thee forever, to depart

Within three days; in this we do dispense
With grounds of reason, not of thine offence.

VASQUES 'Tis well; this conquest is mine, and I rejoice that a Spaniard outwent an Italian in revenge.    151
                                      *Exit* VASQUES

CARDINAL Take up these slaughtered bodies, see them buried;
And all the gold and jewels, or whatsoever,
Confiscate by the canons of the church,
We seize upon to the Pope's proper use.

RICHARDETTO (*reveals himself*) Your grace's pardon: thus long I lived disguised
To see the effect of pride and lust at once
Brought both to shameful ends.

CARDINAL What, Richardetto whom we thought for dead?

DONADO Sir, was it you—

RICHARDETTO                  Your friend.

CARDINAL                              We shall have time
To talk at large of all; but never yet            161
Incest and murder have so strangely met.
Of one so young, so rich in nature's store,
Who could not say, 'tis pity she's a whore?
                                         *Exeunt*

FINIS

*The Printer's Apology*
The general commendation deserved by the actors in their presentment of this tragedy may easily excuse such few faults as are escaped in the printing. A common charity may allow him the ability of spelling whom a secure confidence assures that he cannot ignorantly err in the application of sense.

---

127 Of counsel: involved
128 sometimes: formerly
137 this woman: some scholars have pointed to the ambiguity of this reference, remarking that the body referred to could be that of either Putana or Annabella

148–9 dispense with . . . reason: offer a dispensation in the light of Vasques' motives
151 Spaniard: Spaniards were considered second only to the Italians in the art of revenge
155 proper: personal
157 at once: together
161 at large: at length